World directory of

AIRLINER CRASHES

As part of our ongoing market research, we are always pleased to receive comments about our books, suggestions for new titles, or requests for catalogues. Please write to: The Editorial Director, Patrick Stephens Limited, Sparkford, Near Yeovil, Somerset BA22 7JJ

World directory of AIRLINER CRASHES

A comprehensive record of more than 10,000 passenger aircraft accidents

Terry Denham

Patrick Stephens Limited

This book is dedicated to Liz
for all her encouragement
and to Andrew with apologies
for all the hours he spent without his Dad

First published in 1996

British Library Cataloguing-in-Publication Data:
A catalogue record for this book is
available from the British Library

ISBN: 1 85260 554 5

Library of Congress catalog card No. 96-075173

Patrick Stephens Limited is an imprint of Haynes Publishing,
Sparkford, Nr Yeovil, Somerset BA22 7JJ

Contents

Introduction

This book attempts to bring together details of all the world's airliner accidents. The following pages contain entries for almost 11,000 accidents, from the well-known to the obscure. Most of the information contained in this book is already available to the public from thousands of documents and publications, both official and commercial, but it is not believed to exist anywhere in one volume. *World Directory of Airliner Crashes* seeks to rectify this situation and to provide an authoritative reference work for both the aviation enthusiast and the professional researcher.

The gathering of data for the book began in 1968, firstly as a hobby and later as a serious attempt to build a valuable work of reference. This has continued right up to the present day. Initially, only accidents to the larger airliners were included but gradually the coverage expanded as interest in the project grew.

To make the Directory as complete as possible the criteria for inclusion in the listings have been stretched a little further than the title would suggest. All accidents to transport category aircraft capable of carrying approximately eight passengers or more are included, no matter whether operated by an airline, a corporate body or a private individual. Additionally, smaller aircraft used by commercial operators are included, giving greater coverage to the pre-1940s era and to the thousands of smaller companies in existence today. Aircraft losses are also listed where the cause was not a crash – ground accidents, sabotage, hijacking and military action all feature.

Again, to give as comprehensive a picture as possible, you will also find entries for military 'airlines' running scheduled flights (such as Satena in Colombia) and civil examples of large military aircraft preserved in flying condition for display purposes. To avoid confusion the Directory also contains details of military transport accidents where the machine was flying with a civil style serial – a common practice in many African countries. However, accidents to regular military transports are excluded due to the limitations of space.

The one common factor relating to all the entries in this book is that the accident concerned led to the write-off of the aircraft involved. You will see that the entries range from the tragic disasters of Tenerife and Lockerbie to more minor incidents that have finished an aircraft's flying career. The older an airliner gets, the more likely it is to be withdrawn after only a small incident due to the cost of repairs.

No attempt has been made to give in-depth details of the actual causes of each accident but the general circumstances surrounding the events are included. There are often several unrelated factors leading to a crash and on many occasions the cause is either unknown or is disputed. Detailed reports of the more serious accidents are usually available from official sources.

World Directory of Airliner Crashes is designed to make the checking of a specific accident as easy as possible. The main body of the work consists of accident entries listed in date order. Following this, you will find two large appendices giving a cross reference by aircraft type and by operator.

In compiling this Directory, many tens of thousands of pieces of information have been collated. During this process, some conflicting details were found. In these instances, the information most likely to be correct has been included with an appropriate note if necessary.

This Directory does not claim to be 100 per cent complete as that would be an impossibility. Many details have been lost over the years and information has not always been readily available from some countries. Also, more research remains to be done, particularly relating to smaller aircraft. Therefore, any additions or amendments which can be provided by users of the Directory will be gratefully received for inclusion in future editions.

Terry Denham (November 1995)

About this Directory

The layout of the information in this book is generally self-explanatory but a few notes are included here to make the use of the Directory even easier. The main data section of the work is presented in a standard column format but the following should answer any queries.

Date: Dates are presented in the British style (Day/Month/Year). When the exact day or month of an accident is unknown, it is replaced by 'oo' and the listing appears at the end of the appropriate month or year. An appendix of accidents occurring on unknown dates will be found at the back of the Directory. The main listings are in date order but no attempt has been made to place accidents occurring on the same day in any time order.

Aircraft type: As detailed a description of the exact type and model of each aircraft is included where possible. Exceptions to this are the ubiquitous ex-military DC-3s, which are referred to as such instead of by their former military designations. Where the name of an aircraft's manufacturer has changed during its lifetime, the designation in use at the time of the accident is given, a good example of this being the builders of the 125 corporate jet (de Havilland, Hawker Siddeley, British Aerospace and Corporate Jets).

Registration: This column gives the nationality mark and registration as allocated to each aircraft. Where this is not known it is replaced by '*'. A few machines have flown without a registration and these are signified by 'n/a'. In these cases, where a name was carried on the aircraft it is shown in the Accident Details column. A list of current and defunct nationality marks is given in an appendix.

C/n: The details listed here consist of the manufacturer's construction numbers. These are the serial numbers allocated by most aircraft builders to identify each machine and which stay with it throughout its life no matter what registration mark is carried. If the number is unknown, it is replaced by '*' and by '–' if no number is believed to have been assigned.

Operator: The operator of an aircraft is listed rather than the actual owner. Nowadays, the owner is often a leasing company or financial institution rather than the operating airline. Although this is a directory of civil accidents, a few military crashes are included where they involve airline operations run by air forces or where a military aircraft carries a civil style serial. Military transports in civilian hands (usually the manufacturers) are also included, as are larger aircraft operated by some quasi-military units (Police, Coast Guards etc.).

Accident details: The brief circumstances surrounding an accident are given. Longer notes are given where the incident has some unusual aspects (hijacking, military action etc.). When the term 'Written-off' is used, it means that details are lacking. More detailed explanations of accident causes are beyond the scope of this Directory.

Location: All towns and countries are listed using the names in force at the time of an accident.

Fatalities and Survivors: The final two columns (headed 'F' and 'S') give details of all known casualties. The figure given in the 'F' column is the number of fatalities on board the aircraft concerned. Fatalities in any other aircraft involved are shown in brackets '( )'. Any casualties incurred amongst bystanders on the ground are shown in wavy brackets '{ }'. Again the use of '*' means that the casualties are unknown.

Acknowledgements: It would be impossible to list all the individuals, publications, organizations, and companies which have been consulted in compiling the Directory over the past 27 years but the following have been particularly helpful: *Aeroplane Monthly*, Air Britain, *Air Pictorial*, Airclaims, *Aviation Letter*, *Aviation News*, Airlife, *Flight International*, HMSO, *JP Airline Fleets*, LAASI, *Lloyds List*, PSL, *Propliner*, Public Record Office, Putnam Aeronautical Books, TAHS, and many, many more. The assistance of all involved is gratefully acknowledged.

1906–1939

Before the First World War there was no commercial aviation worth speaking of anywhere in the world, with the notable exception of early airship operations in Germany. A few of these machines were destroyed by various means but with no fatalities. The pioneering of airline travel with dirigibles was pursued after the war and only came to an end with the *Hindenburg* tragedy of 1937 – the worst accident of the period to a machine in regular airline service.

Following the outbreak of peace in 1918 most European countries rapidly began to build up airline services, at first with war-surplus machines but changing to new commercial types as they appeared. France and Britain led the way but the rest of Europe soon caught up. However, airline operations got off to an inauspicious start in Britain when the first commercial flight permitted since the war ended in a crash in Hampshire.

In this early period of operations, there were many accidents and 7 April 1922 saw the first mid-air collision between airliners over France. As most of the aircraft in use had a small passenger capacity, the consequences of accidents in the 'twenties were usually modest except, very occasionally, when airships were involved.

Larger aircraft were being developed and the new generation of monoplane airliners were making their debuts. The Boeing 247, Douglas DC-2, and, most importantly, the DC-3 all appeared and suffered their first accidents. European manufacturers also were producing new designs and held their own against the Americans until the outbreak of the Second World War.

This increase in activity led to an inevitable rise in accidents with larger casualty rates. Britain suffered the shock of losing the prestigious airship R101 in 1930 with 48 fatalities, thus ending lighter-than-air development for many years. The worst accident of the 'thirties, however, was caused when a Soviet ANT-20 suffered a mid-air collision in 1935 during an air display, killing 51 people.

Air travel in the 'twenties and 'thirties was the preserve of the wealthy and the important, inevitably leading to a number of prominent people dying in accidents. These included American football coach Knute Rockne, actors Carlos Gardel and Will Rogers, and aviation pioneers Wiley Post and Juan de la Cierva.

The 1930s ended with the outbreak of the

The disaster that heralded the end of passenger carrying airships. Approaching its mooring mast at Lakehurst, New Jersey on 6 May 1937, Hindenburg *(D-LZ219) burst into flames killing 35 on board.* (Topham)

Second World War, which was to change life in so many ways including the shape and fortunes of commercial aviation. By the end of 1939 the first losses of the war had been suffered by LOT Polish Airlines. Many more would follow.

First write-offs 1906–1939

(* military example crashed earlier)

Zeppelin Airship	17.01.06
Vickers Vimy Commercial	27.02.20
Farman Goliath	26.08.21
Breguet 14	25.05.25
Lockheed Vega	16.08.27
Fokker VIII	22.08.27
Rohrbach Roland	19.04.28
Ford Tri-Motor	12.05.28*
Fokker F.VIIb/3m	31.07.28
DH.66 Hercules	06.09.29
Fokker F.32	27.11.29
Armstrong Whitworth Argosy	22.04.31
Lockheed Orion	05.11.31
Boeing 80	10.07.32
Junkers Ju.32/3m	29.07.32
Curtiss Condor	14.02.33
Boeing 247	12.05.33
DH.84 Dragon	23.07.33
Dewoitine D.332	14.01.34
Stinson SM-6000	30.01.34
Wibault 282	09.05.34
Lockheed 10 Electra	07.08.34
DH.89 Dragon Rapide	02.10.34
DH.86	19.10.34
Douglas DC-2	20.12.34
Consolidated Commodore	16.04.35
Potez 62	10.12.35
Sikorsky S-42	20.12.35
Armstrong Whitworth Atalanta	29.09.36
Douglas DC-3	09.02.37
Short S.23	24.03.37
Handley Page HP.42	31.05.37
Junkers Ju.90	06.02.38
Lockheed 14	16.05.38
Martin M.130	28.07.38
Fokker F.XVIII	13.01.39
Boeing Stratoliner	18.03.39

On 17 June 1929 Handley Page W.10 (G-EBMT) of Imperial Airways crashed into the English Channel with the loss of four lives. The Belgian trawler Gaby *is seen here salvaging the wreckage.* (Topham)

Date	Type	Reg'n	C/n	Operator	Accident	Location	F	S
17.01.06	Zeppelin Type B	LZ2	LZ2	Forderung-der Motorluft-Schiffahrt	Destroyed in storm	Kisslegg, Germany	0	0
05.08.08	Zeppelin Type C	LZ4	LZ4	Forderung-der Motorluft-Schiffahrt	Crash landed & caught fire	Echterdingen, Germany	0	3
28.06.10	Zeppelin Type E	LZ7	LZ7	Delag	Crashed after engine failure	Teutoburger Wald, Germany	0	*
14.09.10	Zeppelin Type D	LZ6A	LZ6A	Delag	Destroyed in hangar fire	Oos, Germany	0	0
16.05.11	Zeppelin Type E	LZ8	LZ8	Delag	Dbr when blown into hangar	Dusseldorf, Germany	0	*
24.09.11	HM Airship No.1	n/a	–	Vickers	Broke in half on leaving shed [Mayfly]	Barrow-in-Furness, UK	0	*
28.06.12	Zeppelin Type F	LZ10	LZ10	Delag	Destroyed by fire during storm	Baden-Baden, Germany	0	*
17.07.13	Schutte-Lanz S.L.1	S.L.1	S.L.1	Luftschiffbau Schutte-Lanz	Force-landed	nr Berlin, Germany	*	*
26.09.13	R-BVZ Russkiy Vityaz	n/a	–	Russko-Baltiski Vagoni Zavrod	Struck by falling engine from another aircraft while parked	Korpusnoi, Russia	0	0
12.10.15	Zeppelin Type G	LZ11	LZ11	Delag	Damaged leaving hangar	Liegnitz, Germany	0	*
01.05.19	de Havilland DH.9	C6054	–	Aircraft Transport & Travel	Crashed into hill on first commercial flight in UK	Portsdown Hill, Hants, UK	*	*
31.05.19	Blackburn Kangaroo	G-EADF	–	Grahame-White Aviation	Crashed on take-off	Hendon, Middx, UK	*	*
29.06.19	Blackburn Kangaroo	G-EADE	–	Grahame-White Aviation	Damaged beyond repair	Hendon, Middx, UK	*	*
oo.08.19	Armstrong Whitworth F.K.8	G-EAET	–	London & Provincial Aviation	Crashed	Great Yarmouth, Suffolk, UK	*	*
29.10.19	de Havilland DH.4A	G-EAHG	–	Aircraft Transport & Travel	Crashed	English Channel	*	*
08.12.19	Blackburn Kangaroo	G-EAOW	–	Blackburn Aeroplane & Motor Co	Damaged on landing	Suda Bay, Crete, Greece	0	*
11.12.19	de Havilland DH.4A	G-EAHF	–	Aircraft Transport & Travel	Crashed	Caterham, Surrey, UK	*	*
23.02.20	Handley Page O/7	G-EANV	HP.7	Handley Page S.A. Transport Co	Crashed	Acacia Siding, South Africa	0	9
25.02.20	Handley Page HP.12	G-EAMC	HP.27	Handley Page Transport	Crashed	nr El Shereik, Sudan	*	*
27.02.20	Vickers Vimy Commercial	G-EAAV	–	Vickers	Crashed on take-off	Tabora, Tanganyika	*	*
oo.03.20	de Havilland DH.16	G-EACT	1	Aircraft Transport & Travel	Crashed	Location Unknown	*	*
30.06.20	Handley Page HP.12	G-EAKE	HP.22	Handley Page Transport	Crashed	nr Stockholm, Sweden	*	*
oo.07.20	Avro 504K	G-EAGW	–	North Sea Aerial Navigation Co	Crashed	Scarborough, Yorks, UK	*	*
16.08.20	de Havilland DH.18	G-EARI	1	Aircraft Transport & Travel	Crashed	Wallington, Surrey, UK	*	*
16.08.20	Armstrong Whitworth F.K.8	G-EALW	–	By Air	Crashed	nr Bedford, UK	1	0
31.08.20	Savoia FBA	CH-18	*	Ad Astra Aero	Crashed	Zurichhorn, Switzerland	*	*
oo.08.20	de Havilland DH.9B	G-EAGX	–	Aircraft Transport & Travel	Crashed	Location Unknown	*	*
oo.09.20	Avro 504K	G-EAGV	–	North Sea Aerial Navigation Co	Crashed	Location Unknown	*	*
oo.09.20	de Havilland DH.9	G-EAOP	–	Aircraft Transport & Travel	Written off	Location Unknown	*	*
oo.09.20	de Havilland DH.9B	G-EAPO	P.34E	Aircraft Transport & Travel	Written off	Location Unknown	*	*
oo.10.20	Handley Page O/7	G-IAAC	HP.11	Indo-Burmese Transport	Damaged in gale	India	*	*
oo.11.20	de Havilland DH.9B	G-EAPU	P.35E	Aircraft Transport & Travel	Written off	Location Unknown	*	*
14.12.20	Handley Page HP.12	G-EAMA	HP.25	Handley Page Transport	Crashed after striking tree on take-off in fog	Golders Green, London, UK	4	0
28.12.20	Zeppelin-Staaken E.4/20	n/a	*	Zeppelin-Staaken	Damaged in heavy landing after engine failure	Germany	*	*
oo.oo.20	Handley Page O/7	*	*	Chinese Government	Caught fire & crashed	China	*	*
oo.oo.20	Avro 504K	G-EANN	–	Adastral Air Lines	Crashed	France	*	*
25.01.21	de Havilland DH.4	O-BAIN	–	SNETA	Crashed	Folkestone, Kent, UK	*	*
oo.01.21	de Havilland DH.9B	G-EAQA	P.36E	Aircraft Transport & Travel	Crashed	Location Unknown	*	*
oo.03.21	Caproni CA-60	n/a	–	Caproni	Crashed into sea on first flight	Lake Maggiore, Italy	0	1
00.04.21	de Havilland DH.4A	G-EAVL	–	Handley Page Transport	Crashed	Location Unknown	*	*
oo.04.21	Handley Page O/10	G-EATL	HP.41	Handley Page Transport	Written off	UK	*	*
13.05.21	de Havilland DH.18	G-EAUF	3	Instone Air Line	Crashed	Location Unknown	*	*
21.06.21	Vickers R.36	G-FAAF	R.36	Air Council	Damaged while mooring	Pulham, Norfolk, UK	0	*
24.08.21	Royal Airship Works ZR-2	R38	R.38	Royal Airship Works	Crashed due to structural failure	River Humber, UK	44	5
26.08.21	Farman F.60 Goliath	O-BLAN	7248/17	SNETA	Crashed	English Channel	*	*
02.09.21	de Havilland DH.9B	H-NABP	–	KLM Royal Dutch Airlines	Crashed	Waalhaven, Netherlands	*	*
18.09.21	Wild WT-S	CH-71	*	Ad Astra Aero	Crashed	Switzerland	*	*
27.09.21	Farman F.60 Goliath	O-BRUN	6840	SNETA	Destroyed in hangar fire	Evere, Belgium	*	*
27.09.21	Farman F.60 Goliath	O-BLEU	6837	SNETA	Destroyed in hangar fire	Evere, Belgium	*	*
27.09.21	de Havilland DH.4	O-BADO	–	SNETA	Destroyed in hangar fire	Evere, Belgium	*	*
27.09.21	de Havilland DH.4A	O-BATO	–	SNETA	Destroyed in hangar fire	Evere, Belgium	*	*
27.09.21	de Havilland DH.4A	O-BARI	–	SNETA	Destroyed in hangar fire	Evere, Belgium	*	*
27.09.21	Bleriot Spad 33	O-BAHE	3065	SNETA	Destroyed in hangar fire	Evere, Belgium	*	*
17.10.21	de Havilland DH.9	T-DOBC	–	DDL	Crashed	Solbjerg, Denmark	*	*

Date	Type	Reg'n	C/n	Operator	Accident	Location	F	S
10.11.21	Fokker F.III	H-NABL	1534	KLM Royal Dutch Airlines	Crashed	Waalhaven, Netherlands	*	*
26.11.21	Avro 504K	G-EAFQ	–	Stallard Airways	Crashed	Hildenborough, Kent, UK	*	*
30.12.21	Handley Page O/10	G-EATM	HP.42	Handley Page Transport	Crashed	Senlis, France	*	*
14.01.22	Handley Page O/10	G-EATN	HP.43	Handley Page Transport	Crashed	France	*	*
29.03.22	Hanriot HD.1	CH-77	*	Ad Astra Aero	Crashed	Switzerland	*	*
07.04.22	Farman F.60 Goliath	F-GEAD	*	Grands Express Aeriens	Collision with Daimler DH.18 G-EAWO [1st commercial mid-air]	Grandvilliers, France	5(2)	0
07.04.22	de Havilland DH.18	G-EAWO	4	Daimler Hire	Collision with GEA Goliath F-GEAD [1st commercial mid-air]	Grandvilliers, France	2(5)	0
17.05.22	Fokker F.III	H-NABT	1532	KLM Royal Dutch Airlines	Crashed	Hythe, Kent, UK	*	*
30.05.22	de Havilland DH.9B	H-NABE	P.33E	KLM Royal Dutch Airlines	Written off	Location Unknown	*	*
31.07.22	BAT F.K.26	G-EAPK	32	S.Instone & Co	Crashed	Location Unknown	*	*
03.11.22	de Havilland DH.34	G-EBBU	31	Daimler Hire	Crashed	Berck, France	*	*
17.11.22	de Havilland DH.9C	H-NABO	–	KLM Royal Dutch Airlines	Written off	Location Unknown	*	*
oo.11.22	Caudron C.74	F-ESAB	*	Avions Caudron	Crashed	France	*	*
oo.oo.22	Vickers 61 Vulcan	G-EBDH	2	Instone Air Line	Crashed	Oxted, Surrey, UK	*	*
25.02.23	Armstrong Whitworth F.K.8	G-AUCF	–	Queensland & N.T. Aerial Transport	Crashed on take-off	Jericho, Qld, Australia	*	*
04.05.23	Caudron C.61	F-AFCP	10	CFRA	Crashed	nr Calye-Souilly, France	*	*
10.07.23	Handley Page W.8	G-EAPJ	W8-1	Handley Page Transport	Crash landed	Poix, France	*	*
oo.07.23	Fokker F.III	H-NABM	1509	KLM Royal Dutch Airlines	Crashed	Croydon, Surrey, UK	*	*
oo.08.23	de Havilland DH.34	G-EBBQ	27	Daimler Hire	Crashed	Location Unknown	*	*
oo.08.23	Caudron C.61	F-AEHQ	01	CANA	Destroyed by tornado on ground	Kaffrine, French West Africa	0	*
13.09.23	Armstrong Whitworth F.K.8	G-AUDE	–	Queensland & N.T. Aerial Transport	Crashed	Blackall, Qld, Australia	*	*
14.09.23	de Havilland DH.34	G-EBBS	29	Daimler Hire	Crashed	Ivinghoe Beacon, Berks, UK	6	0
19.10.23	Fokker F.III	H-NABH	1504	KLM Royal Dutch Airlines	Crashed	Goodwin Sands, North Sea	*	*
oo.oo.23	Junkers F.13	J1	*	SCADTA	Crashed	Colombia	*	*
oo.oo.23	Junkers F.13	A2	*	SCADTA	Crashed	Colombia	1	*
24.04.24	Fokker F.III	H-NABS	1535	KLM Royal Dutch Airlines	Crashed	English Channel	*	*
02.05.24	de Havilland DH.18	G-EAWW	5	Air Ministry	Ditched on purpose in flotation test	Off Felixstowe, Suffolk, UK	0	1
05.05.24	de Havilland DH.4	O-BALO	–	SNETA	Crashed	Strasbourg, France	*	*
21.05.24	Supermarine Sea Eagle	G-EBFK	1163	British Marine Air Navigation Co	Crashed	Location Unknown	*	*
27.05.24	de Havilland DH.34	G-EBBR	28	Imperial Airways	Crashed on take-off	Ostend, Belgium	*	*
08.06.24	Junkers F.13	A16	*	SCADTA	Crashed	Barranquilla, Colombia	3	*
31.07.24	Bleriot Spad 46	F-AEGS	30	CIDNA	Crashed	Location Unknown	*	*
21.08.24	CMASA Wal	I-DEOR	012	Dep Marina di Pisa	Force-landed & sunk by gunfire from USS *Richmond*	off Cape Farewell, Greenland	0	*
23.09.24	de Havilland DH.34	G-EBCX	40	Imperial Airways	Damaged beyond repair	Croydon, Surrey, UK	*	*
oo.10.24	LVG C.VI	RR14	4590	Deruluft	Crashed	USSR	*	*
24.12.24	de Havilland DH.34B	G-EBBX	36	Imperial Airways	Crashed	Purley, Surrey, UK	8	0
27.01.25	Bristol Tourer 28	G-AUDF	6108	West Australian Airways	Crashed	Onslow, WA, Australia	*	*
10.02.25	Liore et Olivier 13	F-AGFY	33	CGEA	Crashed	Location Unknown	*	*
22.03.25	Junkers F.13	R-RECA	590	Zakavia	Crashed	nr Tiflis, Georgia, USSR	5	0
11.04.25	Liore et Olivier 13	F-AFGP	18	CGEA	Crashed	Location Unknown	*	*
05.05.25	Blackburn Kangaroo	G-EAIT	–	North Sea Aerial & General Transport	Crashed	Brough, Lancs, UK	*	*
18.05.25	Khioni Konek-Gorbutnok	RRODE	02	Aviakhim	Crashed	USSR	*	*
25.05.25	Breguet 14A.2	F-AFBB	*	Lignes Aeriennes Latecoere	Crashed	Location Unknown	*	*
25.05.25	Farman F.30	*	240	ODVF	Crashed	USSR	*	*
30.05.25	Caudron C.81	F-AGFU	04	CIDNA	Destroyed by fire	Innsbruck, Austria	*	*
21.06.25	Breguet 14A.2	F-AGCD	*	Lignes Aeriennes Latecoere	Written off	North Africa	*	*
25.06.25	Fokker F.III	H-NABM	2	KLM Royal Dutch Airlines	Crashed	Landrecies, France	*	*
26.06.25	Bleriot Spad 33	F-FREM	0029	CIDNA	Crashed	Location Unknown	*	*
20.07.25	Breguet 14A.2	F-AFBI	*	Lignes Aeriennes Latecoere	Crashed	Location Unknown	*	*
23.07.25	Sablatnig P.III	D-730	*	Lloyd-Luftverkehr Sablatnig	Crashed	Germany	*	*
14.08.25	Liore et Olivier 13	F-AFDH	07	CGEA	Crashed	Location Unknown	*	*
20.08.25	Kalinin AK-1	R-RDAX	*	Dobrolet	Crashed	USSR	*	*
24.08.25	Bleriot Spad 33	F-FREJ	0026	CIDNA	Crashed	Location Unknown	*	*

Date	Type	Reg'n	C/n	Operator	Accident	Location	F	S
01.09.25	Breguet 14A.2	F-AFBG	*	Lignes Aeriennes Latecoere	Crashed	Location Unknown	*	*
25.09.25	Khioni Konek-Gorbutnok	RRUOA	14	Aviakhim	Crashed	USSR	*	*
29.09.25	Breguet 14Tbis	F-ADBM	1912	Air Union	Crashed	Location Unknown	*	*
17.10.25	Breguet 14A.2	F-AEGZ	*	Lignes Aeriennes Latecoere	Crashed	Location Unknown	*	*
01.11.25	Fokker F.III	T-DOFB	1562	DDL	Crashed	Kastrup, Denmark	*	*
04.11.25	Fokker F.III	H-NABI	1505	KLM Royal Dutch Airlines	Crashed	Hamburg, Germany	*	*
11.12.25	Breguet 14A.2	F-AEEN	*	Lignes Aeriennes Latecoere	Crashed	Location Unknown	*	*
19.12.25	Liore et Olivier 13-3	F-AHBF	03	CGEA	Crashed	Location Unknown	*	*
25.12.25	Breguet 14A.2	F-AEHD	*	Lignes Aeriennes Latecoere	Crashed	Location Unknown	*	*
00.00.25	Fokker F.VIIa	H-NACZ	4899	Fokker	Damaged in forced landing	USA	*	*
00.00.25	CMASA Wal	N-24	019	Norsk Luftseiladsforenings	Abandoned on ice during Amundsen expedition	Antarctica	0	0
00.00.25	Breguet 14A.2	F-AEIS	*	Lignes Aeriennes Latecoere	Destroyed by tribesmen	Africa	*	*
00.00.25	Breguet 14A.2	F-AGBY	*	Lignes Aeriennes Latecoere	Written off	Sahara Desert	*	*
00.00.25	Junkers F.13	D-409	739	Deutsche Lufthansa	Crashed	Location Unknown	*	*
13.01.26	Liore et Olivier 13	F-AHEU	36	CGEA	Crashed	Location Unknown	*	*
00.01.26	Junkers F.13	n/a	711	SCADTA	Crashed [BENI]	Colombia	*	*
05.02.26	Breguet 14A.2	F-AFEF	*	Lignes Aeriennes Latecoere	Crashed	Location Unknown	*	*
00.02.26	de Havilland DH.9B	H-NABF	P.32E	KLM Royal Dutch Airlines	Written off	Location Unknown	*	*
13.03.26	Breguet 14	F-FYMS	1827	Lignes Aeriennes Latecoere	Crashed	Location Unknown	*	*
13.04.26	Fokker F.III	H-NABU	1662	KLM Royal Dutch Airlines	Written off	Amsterdam, Netherlands	*	*
07.05.26	Vickers 61 Vulcan	G-EBEM	5	L.Hamilton	Crashed	Off Italy	*	*
22.05.26	Breguet 14A.2	F-AHEM	*	Lignes Aeriennes Latecoere	Written off	Rio de Oro	*	*
05.06.26	Khioni Konek-Gorbutnok	n/a	30	Dobrolet	Crashed [Nizhegorodets]	USSR	*	*
21.06.26	Fokker F.VII	H-NACL	4841	KLM Royal Dutch Airlines	Crashed at sea	Hythe, Kent, UK	*	*
30.06.26	Fokker F.III	D-516	1557	Deutsche Lufthansa	Crashed	Berlin, Germany	1	*
30.06.26	Fokker F.III	D-533	1559	Deutsche Lufthansa	Written off	Location Unknown	*	*
03.07.26	Caudron C.61	F-AFBT	05	CIDNA	Crashed	Czechoslovakia	7	0
09.07.26	Fokker F.VII	H-NACC	4759	KLM Royal Dutch Airlines	Written off	Wolverthem, Belgium	*	*
00.07.26	Polikarpov PM-1	RRUSS	*	Aviakhim	Crashed	USSR	*	*
02.08.26	CMASA Wal	G-CAJI	057	E.Hosmer	Crash landed & caught fire	Atlantic Ocean	0	4
07.08.26	Sablatnig P.III	D-727	269	Lloyd-Luftverkehr Sablatnig	Crashed	Germany	*	*
18.08.26	Bleriot 155	F-AIEB	2	Air Union	Crashed after engine failure in bad weather	Hurst, Kent, UK	4	*
03.09.26	Junkers F.13	A10	615	SCADTA	Crashed	La Victoria, Colombia	*	*
08.10.26	Fokker F.III	D-468	1554	Deutsche Lufthansa	Written off	Location Unknown	*	*
17.10.26	Breguet 14A.2	F-AFBE	*	Lignes Aeriennes Latecoere	Destroyed by tribesmen	Africa	*	*
17.10.26	Sablatnig P.III	D-50	258	Lloyd-Luftverkehr Sablatnig	Crashed	Germany	*	*
21.10.26	Handley Page W.10	G-EBMS	W10/3	Imperial Airways	Crashed after engine failure	English Channel	0	12
11.11.26	Breguet 14A.2	F-AFAX	*	Lignes Aeriennes Latecoere	Destroyed by tribesmen	Africa	*	*
11.11.26	Breguet 14A.2	F-AGBS	*	Lignes Aeriennes Latecoere	Destroyed by tribesmen	Africa	*	*
08.12.26	Douglas M-2	*	246	Western Air Express	Crashed	Salt Lake City, UT, USA	*	*
30.12.26	de Havilland DH.50	G-EBOP	281	North Sea Aerial & General Transport	Crashed	Kisumu, Kenya	*	*
00.12.26	Fokker-Grulich V.1	D-902	1653	Deruluft	Crashed	USSR	*	*
00.00.26	Bleriot 155	F-AICQ	1	Air Union	Destroyed	Location Unknown	*	*
00.00.26	CMASA Wal	A20	018	SCADTA	Crashed on forced landing	nr Paraguana Peninsula, Venezuela	*	*
00.00.26	Fokker F.III	CH-156	1529	Balair	Crashed	Borex, Switzerland	*	*
00.00.26	Junkers G.24	D-944	907	Deutsche Lufthansa	Written off	Location Unknown	*	*
00.00.26	Udet U.8	D-670	*	Deutsche Lufthansa	Written off	Location Unknown	*	*
00.00.26	Breguet 14A.2	F-AGBT	*	Lignes Aeriennes Latecoere	Written off	Sahara Desert	*	*
00.00.26	Breguet 14A.2	F-AHEP	*	Lignes Aeriennes Latecoere	Crashed	Location Unknown	*	*
00.00.26	Junkers F.13	D-272	660	Deutsche Lufthansa	Crashed	Location Unknown	*	*
00.00.26	Junkers F.13	D-290	665	Deutsche Lufthansa	Crashed	Location Unknown	*	*
00.00.26	Sopwith 1 1/2 Strutter	*	*	Aviakhim	Crashed	USSR	*	*
10.01.27	Supermarine Sea Eagle	G-EBGS	1165	Imperial Airways	Sunk when struck by ship	Guernsey, Channel Islands	*	*

Date	Type	Reg'n	C/n	Operator	Accident	Location	F	S
12.01.27	Fokker F.VIIa	H-NADH	4938	Fokker	Crashed	Estaires, France	*	*
01.02.27	de Havilland DH.54 Highclere	G-EBKI	151	Imperial Airways	Destroyed when hangar collapsed	Croydon, Surrey, UK	*	*
25.02.27	Fokker F.VIIa	*	4909	G.H.Wilkins	Abandoned in damaged condition	Arctic	0	*
13.03.27	Fairey IIID	G-EBPZ	F.814	North Sea Aerial & General Transport	U/c collapsed on water landing	Lake Victoria, Kisumu, Kenya	*	*
24.03.27	de Havilland DH.9C	G-AUED	86	Qantas	Crashed on approach	Tambo, Qld, Australia	3	0
06.04.27	CMASA Wal	*	051	Portuguese Air Ministry	Crash landed	Off Belem, Brazil	0	*
20.04.27	Farman F.121 Jabiru	T-DOXD	45	DDL	Crashed	Karise, Denmark	*	*
21.04.27	Sablatnig P.III	D-171	262	Lloyd-Luftverkehr Sablatnig	Crashed	Germany	*	*
22.04.27	Fokker F.III	D-729	1567	Deutsche Lufthansa	Written off	Location Unknown	*	*
28.05.27	Junkers F.13	K-SALA	700	Aero O/Y	Crashed	Tallinn, Estonia	0	5
31.05.27	Sablatnig P.III	D-453	275	Lloyd-Luftverkehr Sablatnig	Crashed	Germany	*	*
oo.05.27	Farman F.60 Goliath	F-ADFN	22	Farman Line	Crashed	Atlantic Ocean	*	0
05.06.27	Junkers F.13	A9	618	SCADTA	Crashed	Barranquilla, Colombia	*	*
18.06.27	Atlantic F.VII/3m	NC55	1/701	Colonial Air Transport	Crashed on landing	Hasbrouck Heights, NJ, USA	*	*
30.06.27	Atlantic F.VII/3m	NX206	3/703	R.E.Byrd	Crashed	Off Ver-sur-Mer, France	*	*
oo.06.27	Fokker F.III	RR7	1657	Deruluft	Crashed	USSR	*	*
09.07.27	Caudron C.61	F-AFAO	03	CIDNA	Crashed	Pforzheim, Germany	*	*
12.07.27	Fokker F.VIIa	H-NADQ	4991	KLM Royal Dutch Airlines	Written off	St Omer, France	*	*
27.07.27	Junkers F.13	D-206	591	Deutsche Lufthansa	Crashed	Amoneburg, Germany	5	0
28.07.27	Dornier Komet III	RRUAH	68	Ukrvozdukhput	Crashed	USSR	*	*
30.07.27	Sablatnig P.III	D-984	*	Lloyd-Luftverkehr Sablatnig	Crashed	Germany	*	*
03.08.27	Fokker-Grulich F.II	D-784	1592	Deutsche Lufthansa	Crashed	Germany	*	*
16.08.27	Lockheed Vega 1	NX913	001	G.Hearst	Crashed during air race	Pacific Ocean	2	0
22.08.27	Fokker F.VIII	H-NADU	4993	KLM Royal Dutch Airlines	Crashed	nr Sevenoaks, Kent, UK	1	1
31.08.27	Fokker F.VIIa	G-EBTQ	5023	L.Minchin	Crashed	Atlantic Ocean	*	*
06.09.27	Fokker F.VIIa	NX703	0501	W.R.Hearst	Crashed	Off Newfoundland	*	*
17.09.27	Fokker F.VII	NC776	4840	Reynolds Airways	Crashed after engine failure	Hadley, NJ, USA	7	5
19.09.27	Fokker F.III	T-DOFD	1560	DDL	Crashed on take-off	Kastrup, Denmark	*	*
23.09.27	Dornier Merkur	D-585	075	Deutsche Lufthansa	Crashed	Schleiz, Germany	6	0
23.09.27	Sablatnig P.III	D-962	*	Lloyd-Luftverkehr Sablatnig	Crashed	Germany	*	*
03.10.27	Fokker F.III	D-447	1553	Deutsche Lufthansa	Crashed	nr Reutlingen, Germany	*	*
16.11.27	Junkers F.13	K-SALD	798	Aero O/Y	Crashed	Gulf of Finland	*	*
25.11.27	Atlantic F.VII/3m	NC3085	610/5007	Reynolds Airways	Written off	Hadley, NJ, USA	*	*
10.12.27	Douglas M-2	NC1476	*	Western Air Express	Crashed	Denver, CO, USA	*	*
12.12.27	Liore et Olivier 196	F-AIGM	*	Air Union	Damaged in forced landing	Ustica Is, Sicily, Italy	*	*
oo.oo.27	Fokker F.III	CH-153	1506	Balair	Crashed	Lausanne, Switzerland	*	*
oo.oo.27	Bleriot Spad 46	F-AEBL	10/3143	CIDNA	Written off	Location Unknown	*	*
oo.oo.27	Breguet 14A.2	F-AGBN	*	Lignes Aeriennes Latecoere	Crashed	Location Unknown	*	*
oo.oo.27	Breguet 14A.2	F-ALKU	6365	Lignes Aeriennes Latecoere	Crashed	Location Unknown	*	*
oo.oo.27	Breguet 14A.2	F-ALSE	7334	Lignes Aeriennes Latecoere	Crashed	Location Unknown	*	*
oo.oo.27	Junkers F.13	D-560	756	Deutsche Lufthansa	Crashed	Location Unknown	*	*
oo.oo.27	Junkers F.13	D-ONIQ	790	Deutsche Lufthansa	Crashed	Location Unknown	*	*
oo.oo.27	Junkers F.13	A4	554	SCADTA	Crashed	Colombia	*	*
oo.oo.27	Grigorovich L-1	RRUOC	*	Aviakhim	Crashed	USSR	*	*
oo.oo.27	B.E.2c	RRODD	3800	Aviakhim	Crashed	USSR	*	*
02.01.28	Liore et Olivier 13-3	F-AHBI	4	CGEA	Crashed	Off Almeira, Spain	*	*
05.01.28	Fokker Universal	G-CAGE	407	Operator Unknown	Crashed on landing	Pas, MN, Canada	*	*
06.01.28	Junkers G.24ge	D-1088	941	Deutsche Lufthansa	Crashed	Ain, France	*	*
20.01.28	Farman F.170 Jabiru	F-AIBX	3	SGTA	Crashed	nr Tecklenburg, Germany	*	*
22.01.28	Breguet 14	F-AHEQ	*	Aeropostale	Crashed	Tarragona, Spain	2	0
27.01.28	Breguet 14	F-AFHN	*	Aeropostale	Crashed	Morgonera, Spain	*	*
04.02.28	Ford 2-AT	NC2431	2-AT-04	Stout Air Services	Crashed	Wayne, MI, USA	*	*
11.02.28	CMASA Wal	P-BADA	062	Syndicato Condor	Destroyed by fire during refuelling	Santos Dumont, Brazil	0	*
15.02.28	Handley Page W.8b	G-EBBG	W8-2	Imperial Airways	Crash landed	Abbeville, France	*	*

Date	Type	Reg'n	C/n	Operator	Accident	Location	F	S
17.02.28	Fokker Universal	G-CAHG	410	Operator Unknown	Abandoned after forced landing	Off Labrador, Newfoundland	*	*
26.02.28	Messerschmitt M.20b	n/a	*	Messerschmitt	Crashed on first flight	Augsburg, Germany	1	0
06.03.28	Fokker Universal	G-CAIY	428	Operator Unknown	Destroyed by fire	Reindeer Lake, Canada	*	*
11.03.28	Farman 60	F-AEFC	6943	Air Union	Crashed at sea in snowstorm	Off Cap Gris Nez, France	2	0
19.04.28	Rohrbach Roland	M-CCCC	*	Iberia	Crashed in fog	Minuesa, Spain	0	9
oo.04.28	Fokker F.VIII	H-NAEE	5042	KLM Royal Dutch Airlines	Crashed	Nigtevecht, Netherlands	*	*
oo.04.28	Ford 2-AT	NC2432	2-AT-05	Stout Air Services	Crashed	Cleveland, OH, USA	*	*
12.05.28	Ford 4-AT-A Tri-Motor	NC1492	4-AT-01	Ford Air Freight Lines	Crashed on take-off	Dearborn, MI, USA	2	0
16.05.28	Fokker F.III	D-200	1658	Deruluft	Crashed	USSR	*	*
22.05.28	Pitcairn PA-5 Mailwing	4231	13	Pitcairn Aviation	Crashed in fog	nr Richmond, VA, USA	1	0
23.05.28	Farman F.63bis Goliath	F-AEIE	7248/17	Farman Line	Crashed	nr Cologne, Germany	3	*
26.05.28	Junkers F.13	D-583	742	Deutsche Lufthansa	Crash landed in fog & struck cow	Dortmund, Germany	*	*
26.05.28	Pitcairn PA-5 Mailwing	5564	23	Pitcairn Aviation	Crashed in bad weather	Ellerson, VA, USA	1	0
14.06.28	AEG K	D-74	439	Deutsche Lufthansa	Crashed [Also reported as Junkers]	Frankfurt, Germany	0	5
22.06.28	de Havilland DH.9	DL-10	5580	Dobrolet	Crashed	USSR	*	*
29.06.28	Latecoere 26.2R	F-AINF	680	CGEA	Crashed in emergency landing	Cape Juby, Morocco	*	*
oo.06.28	Albatros L58	D-576	10006	Deutsche Lufthansa	Crashed	Germany	*	*
oo.06.28	de Havilland DH.9	6	5778	Dobrolet	Crashed	USSR	*	*
10.07.28	Junkers F.13	K-SALB	760	Aero O/Y	Crashed	Gulf of Finland	*	*
13.07.28	Vickers 74 Vulcan	G-EBLB	9	Imperial Airways	Crashed after take-off	Purley, Surrey, UK	*	*
24.07.28	Fokker F.III	H-NABR	1533	KLM Royal Dutch Airlines	Crashed	Waalhaven, Netherlands	1	*
31.07.28	Fokker F.VIIb/3m	P-PAAA	5057	LOT Polish Airlines	Crashed	Baghdad, Iraq	*	*
oo.07.28	CMASA Wal	I-DAER	029	SANA	Written off	Location Unknown	*	*
08.08.28	Couzinet 27	F-AMBI	*	S.A. Rene Couzinet	Crashed after wings failed	Paris, France	2	1
14.08.28	Fokker Universal	G-CAJH	403	Operator Unknown	Damaged in storm	Goldpines, Canada	*	*
15.08.28	Fokker F.VIIa/3m	NC53	703	Pan American Airways	Force-landed	Gulf of Mexico	*	*
15.08.28	Atlantic F.VII/3m	NC55	704	Pan American Airways	Crashed	Off Egmont Key, FL, USA	*	*
17.08.28	Fokker F.III	D-1028	1539	Deutsche Lufthansa	Written off	Location Unknown	*	*
23.08.28	Sablatnig P.III	D-395	265	Lloyd-Luftverkehr Sablatnig	Crashed	Germany	*	*
23.08.28	Bleriot Spad 56/4	F-AIMO	4382	Air Union	Crashed	La Fare-les-Oliviers, France	*	*
25.08.28	Ford 4-AT-B Tri-Motor	G-CATX	4-AT-26	British Columbia Airways	Crashed in fog	nr Port Townsend, BC, Canada	6	0
29.08.28	Fokker Universal	G-CAHH	411	Operator Unknown	Damaged beyond repair	Eric Cove, Canada	*	*
04.09.28	Fokker Super Universal	NC7242	809	National Parks Airways	Crashed	Pocatello, ID, USA	*	*
06.09.28	Fokker F.III	D-180	1531	Aero Lloyd	Crashed	nr Heroldsbach, Germany	3	0
13.09.28	Lockheed Vega	NX7430	019	Macfadden Publications	Crashed at night during air race	nr Decateur, IN, USA	0	2
25.09.28	Junkers G.31	D-1427	3004	Deutsche Lufthansa	Crashed & caught fire	Arnberg, Germany	0	*
25.09.28	Blackburn Kangaroo	G-EBOM	–	North Sea Aerial & General Transport	Crashed on landing	Brough, Lancs, UK	*	*
oo.09.28	Junkers G.24	D-946	916	Deutsche Lufthansa	Written off	Location Unknown	*	*
oo.09.28	CMASA Wal	I-AYZZ	050	SANA	Destroyed by fire	Location Unknown	*	*
03.10.28	Breguet 14	F-AEEJ	*	Aeropostale	Crashed	Gerona, Spain	*	*
11.10.28	Fokker F.III	RRUAW	1659	Ukrvozdukhput	Crashed	USSR	*	*
13.10.28	Ford 4-AT-A Tri-Motor	NC880	4-AT-08	Stout Air Services	Crashed	Detroit, MI, USA	0	3
23.10.28	de Havilland DH.61 Giant Moth	G-CAJT	323	Western Canada Airways	Destroyed by fire	High River, AB, Canada	*	*
23.10.28	de Havilland DH.50	G-EBKZ	133	Imperial Airways	Crashed on take-off	Plymouth, Devon, UK	*	*
29.10.28	Loening C-W Air Yacht	NC8042	210	Pan American Airways	Crashed	San Juan, Puerto Rico	*	*
31.10.28	Bleriot Spad 56/4	F-AIMN	4381	Air Union	Crashed	Secheras, Spain	1	1
03.11.28	Lockheed Vega 5	NX4769	007	H.J.Tucker	Crashed on record attempt	Palace Station, AZ, USA	2	0
15.11.28	Latecoere 32	F-AISN	80	Aeropostale	Crashed	Palma, Majorca, Spain	*	*
18.11.28	Rohrbach Romar	D-1693	29	Deutsche Lufthansa	Broke adrift & damaged beyond repair	Travemunde, Germany	*	*
oo.11.28	Fokker F.III	D-489	1555	Deutsche Lufthansa	Written off	Location Unknown	*	*
oo.11.28	de Havilland DH.9	3	1285	Dobrolet	Crashed	USSR	*	*
01.12.28	Ford 4-AT-C Tri-Motor	NC7862	4-AT-47	Sunbeam Air Transport Co	Crashed	Spur, TX, USA	5	0
03.12.28	CMASA Wal	P-BACA	063	Syndicato Condor	Crashed	Brazil	*	*
09.12.28	SPCA Meteore 63	F-AIPA	3	Air Union	Crashed	Off Corsica, France	*	*

Date	Type	Reg'n	C/n	Operator	Accident	Location	F	S
10.12.28	Ford 4-AT-B Tri-Motor	NC7687	4-AT-45	S.J.Wilson	Crashed in fog	Spokane, WA, USA	3	2
11.12.28	Junkers G.31fi	D-1473	3005	Deutsche Lufthansa	Crashed	Letzlingen, Germany	3	*
29.12.28	Ford 4-AT-A Tri-Motor	NC3443	4-AT-14	Texaco	Crashed on take-off	Floresville, TX, USA	0	4
31.12.28	Bleriot Spad 66	F-AEHX	40	CIDNA	Crashed into high ground in fog	Givry-les-Noisy, France	0	1
oo.12.28	Junkers G.31	D-1137	3001	Deutsche Lufthansa	Crashed	Location Unknown	*	*
oo.oo.28	Sikorsky S.29A	n/a	–	R.Turner	Crashed during filming of 'Hell's Angels'	Pacoima, CA, USA	1	1
oo.oo.28	Dornier Merkur	D-1101	085	Deutsche Lufthansa	Written off	Location Unknown	*	*
oo.oo.28	Junkers A 20	D-443	464	Deutsche Lufthansa	Crashed	Location Unknown	*	*
oo.oo.28	Dornier Komet II	RRUAA	7/35	Ukrvozdukhput	Crashed	USSR	*	*
01.01.29	Loening C2-C Air Yacht	NC9713	214	Pan American Airways	Crashed	San Jose, Costa Rica	*	*
09.01.29	Fairchild FC.2W	G-CAIQ	049	Operator Unknown	Damaged beyond repair	Chibougamau, Canada	*	*
16.01.29	Ford 4-AT-A Tri-Motor	NC1076	4-AT-09	Stout Air Services	Crashed after in-flight fire	Toledo, OH, USA	0	2
25.01.29	CMASA Wal	I-AZDA	053	Aeroespresso	Crashed	nr Corfu, Greece	2	7
oo.01.29	de Havilland DH.9	G-EBIX	–	Air Taxis	Crashed	Location Unknown	*	*
01.02.29	Latecoere 26	F-AIMU	674	Aeropostale	Crashed on beach	nr Sidi Moussa, Morocco	2	0
18.02.29	Atlantic F.VII/3m	NC3080	603/4956	Reynolds Airways	Damaged beyond repair	Cincinnati, OH, USA	*	*
19.02.29	Breguet 284T	F-AIYB	1	Breguet	Crashed	nr Bondy, France	0	3
oo.02.29	Junkers G.24	D-899	904	Deutsche Lufthansa	Written off	Location Unknown	*	*
05.03.29	Lockheed Vega 1	NC198E	039	Lockheed Aircraft Company	Destroyed by fire at Los Angeles Auto Show	Los Angeles, CA, USA	0	0
05.03.29	Lockheed Vega 5	NC196E	027	Lockheed Aircraft Company	Destroyed by fire at Los Angeles Auto Show	Los Angeles, CA, USA	0	0
17.03.29	Ford 4-AT-B Tri-Motor	NC7683	4-AT-41	Colonial Western Airways	Crashed after double engine failure	Newark, NJ, USA	14	1
19.03.29	Ford 5-AT-B Tri-Motor	NC9674	5-AT-032	Ford Motor Co	Crashed after wing struck ground on landing	Dearborn, MI, USA	4	0
29.03.29	Atlantic F.VII/3m	C7888	617	Standard Airlines	Crashed	Beaumont, CA, USA	*	*
29.03.29	Lockheed Vega 1	NX3625	003	B.Macfadden	Crashed on take-off	Belle, MO, USA	*	*
12.04.29	Dornier Superwal	I-RIDE	142	SANA	Destroyed by fire	Naples, Italy	*	*
21.04.29	Ford 5-AT-B Tri-Motor	NC9636	5-AT-010	Maddux Airlines	Mid-air collision with USAAF Boeing PW-9D 28-37	San Diego, CA, USA	5(1)	0
oo.04.29	Fokker C.IV	SSSR-166	2303	Dobrolet	Crashed	USSR	*	*
07.05.29	Stearman C3B	NC3709	105	Western Air Express	Crashed	Denver, CO, USA	*	*
09.05.29	Avia B.H.25	L-BABD	4	Ceskoslovenska Letecka Spolecnost	Crashed	Attenhagen, Germany	3	*
15.05.29	Dornier Komet II	SSSR-201	4/29	Ukrvozdukhput	Crashed	USSR	*	*
16.05.29	Vickers 103 Vanguard	G-EBCP	1	Air Ministry	Crashed	Shepperton, Middx, UK	2	*
18.05.29	Fokker F.III	H-MABC	1604	Malert	Crashed after wing failed	River Danube, Hungary	2	*
19.05.29	Lockheed Vega 5	NC5885	008	Air Associates	Crashed	Garden City, NY, USA	*	*
19.05.29	Farman 63	F-GEAI	24	Operator Unknown	Crashed & caught fire	Paddock Wood, Kent, UK	0	*
22.05.29	CAMS 53	F-AISX	06	Aeropostale	Overturned on take-off & sank	Algiers, Algeria	4	1
24.05.29	Heinkel HD.24	D-1165	263	DVS	Crashed at sea	nr Bremen, Germany	*	*
oo.05.29	Fairchild FC.2	G-CARI	120	Operator Unknown	Damaged beyond repair	Hudsons Bay, Canada	*	*
02.06.29	Fokker F-10A	NC393E	1013	Western Air Express	Destroyed in storm	Wichita, KS, USA	*	*
05.06.29	Sikorsky S-38A	NC8021	14-05	Western Air Express	Written off	Avalon, CA, USA	*	*
10.06.29	Fokker F.VIIb/3m	G-AADZ	5105	Van Lear Black Ltd	Crashed	Dum Dum, India	*	*
13.06.29	Fokker F-10A	NC9700	1010	Pan American Airways	Crashed	Santiago, Cuba	*	*
17.06.29	Handley Page W.10	G-EBMT	W10/4	Imperial Airways	Crashed due to engine failure	English Channel	4	9
24.06.29	Ford 5-AT-A Tri-Motor	NC7416	5-AT-002	Northwest Airways	Crashed after triple engine failure on take-off	St Paul, MN, USA	1	7
25.06.29	Kalinin K-4	SSSR-219	110	Ukrvozdukhput	Crashed in sea after take-off	Off Sukhumi, Georgia, USSR	2	*
29.06.29	Dornier Delphin III	D-1620	151	Aero Lloyd	Crashed on landing	Lake Constance, Switzerland	5	*
oo.06.29	Fairchild 71	NC9726	602	Panagra	Crashed	Panama	*	*
13.07.29	Fokker Super Universal	G-CASJ	805	Operator Unknown	Sank in forced landing	Canada	*	*
22.07.29	Fokker-Grulich F.II	D-780	1572	Deutsche Lufthansa	Crashed	Germany	*	*
25.07.29	Lockheed Vega 5	NX7441	021	Schlee-Brock Aircraft Corporation	Crashed	Chicago, IL, USA	*	*
oo.07.29	Fokker F.VIIb/3m	G-EBYI	5063	G.Kidston	Crashed	Tomba, Sudan	*	*
oo.07.29	Khioni Konek-Gorbutnok	SSSR-107	24	Dobrolet	Crashed	USSR	*	*
oo.07.29	Junkers Ju.21	SSSR-124	385	Dobrolet	Crashed	USSR	*	*
04.08.29	Lockheed Vega 5	NR393H	085	General Tire & Rubber Co	Crashed on delivery flight	Randsburg, CA, USA	1	*
04.08.29	Lockheed Vega 1	NX34E	035	Lockheed Aircraft Corporation	Crashed	Flint, MI, USA	*	*

Date	Type	Reg'n	C/n	Operator	Accident	Location	F	S
09.08.29	Fairchild FC.2	G-CARJ	130	Operator Unknown	Damaged beyond repair	Canada	*	*
09.08.29	Tupolev ANT-4	URSS-300	601	Dobrolet	Crashed	USSR	*	*
11.08.29	Lockheed Vega 5	NC870E	070	Middle States Airlines	Crashed on delivery flight	Clovis, NM, USA	4	0
12.08.29	Lockheed Vega 5	NC513E	052	Middle States Airlines	Crashed	Pittsburgh, PA, USA	1	*
24.08.29	Fokker-Grulich F.II	D-757	1501	Deutsche Lufthansa	Crashed in fog	Kassel, Germany	*	*
24.08.29	Kalinin K-4	SSSR-217	108	Ukrvozdukhput	Crashed on take-off	Sochi, Georgia, USSR	1	*
26.08.29	Fokker Super Universal	G-CASP	823	Operator Unknown	Damaged in storm	Churchill, Canada	*	*
02.09.29	Lockheed Vega 5B	NR859E	067	Associated Aviators	Crashed in storm	nr Needles, CA, USA	1	1
03.09.29	Ford 5-AT-B Tri-Motor	NC9649	5-AT-020	Transcontinental Air Transport	Crashed in thunderstorm	Mt Taylor, NM, USA	8	0
04.09.29	Fokker F.VIIb/3m	G-EBZJ	5087	A.P.Holt	Crashed	Location Unknown	*	*
06.09.29	de Havilland DH.66 Hercules	G-EBMZ	239	Imperial Airways	Caught fire after crash landing	Jask, Iraq	3	2
10.09.29	Rohrbach Romar	D-1734	30	Deutsche Lufthansa	Crashed & sank after engine failure	Baltic Sea	0	*
11.09.29	Fokker F.III	G-AALC	1558	British Air Lines	Crashed	Croydon, Surrey, UK	*	*
19.09.29	Sikorsky S-38B	NC197H	214-01	Pan American Airways	Crashed on take-off	Miami, FL, USA	*	*
20.09.29	Atlantic F.VII/3m	C3908	602/4955	Continental Air Express	Damaged beyond repair	Saugus, CA, USA	*	*
12.10.29	Savoia-Marchetti S.55R	I-AASZ	10521	Ministry of Aviation	Crashed	Off Ibiza, Balearic Is, Spain	*	*
17.10.29	Junkers G.24	M-CAFF	915	CLASSA	Crashed on landing	Madrid, Spain	0	3
19.10.29	Sabca W.8b	OO-AHK	*	Sabena	Crashed after engine fire	Edegen, Belgium	0	12
19.10.29	Fokker F.VIIb	PH-AGB	5179	KLM Royal Dutch Airlines	Crashed into hill in fog	Istanbul, Turkey	*	*
26.10.29	Short Calcutta	G-AADN	5748	Imperial Airways	Force-landed & sank in tow	Off Spezia, Italy	7	0
04.11.29	Lockheed Vega 5	NC46M	097	Corp Aeronautica de Transportes	Crashed	Cerro del Carbon, Mexico	4	*
06.11.29	Junkers G.24	D-903	911	Deutsche Lufthansa	Crashed	nr Godstone, Surrey, UK	7	1
16.11.29	Fokker Super Universal	G-CASO	822	Operator Unknown	Damaged beyond repair	Aylmer Lake, Canada	*	*
20.11.29	Savoia-Marchetti S.55P	I-TACO	10519	Societa Aerea Mediterranea	Crashed on landing	Cagliari, Sardinia, Italy	*	*
27.11.29	Fokker F.32	NX124M	1201	Fokker	Crashed into houses due to engine failure	Long Island, NY, USA	*	*
30.11.29	Latecoere 26.6	F-AJCN	694	Aeropostale	Crashed after stalling	nr Malaga, Spain	2	0
07.12.29	Fairchild 71	NC9145	632	Braniff Airways	Destroyed in hangar fire	Dallas, TX, USA	*	*
19.12.29	Arado V 1	D-1594	47	Deutsche Lufthansa	Crashed	Neuruppin, Germany	2	1
23.12.29	Fokker Universal	G-CASD	431	Operator Unknown	Destroyed by fire	Winnipeg, Canada	*	*
24.12.29	CMASA Wal	I-AZDB	059	Aeroespresso	Crashed	Aegean Sea	*	*
26.12.29	Fokker F-10	NC5358	1002	Western Air Express	Crashed	Oakland, CA, USA	*	*
30.12.29	Sikorsky S-38B	NC8020	14-04	Pan American Airways	Damaged beyond repair	Location Unknown	*	*
oo.oo.29	Junkers F.13	C-30	*	SCADTA	Crashed	Colombia	*	*
oo.oo.29	Junkers F.13	C-31	*	SCADTA	Crashed	Colombia	*	*
oo.oo.29	Junkers F.13	C-41	*	SCADTA	Crashed	Girardot, Colombia	*	*
oo.oo.29	Polikarpov U-1	SSSR-110	59/339	Dobrolet	Crashed	USSR	*	*
oo.oo.29	Junkers Ju.21	SSSR-122	*	Dobrolet	Crashed	USSR	*	*
06.01.30	Stearman C3B	NC8820	235	Western Air Express	Crashed	Denver, CO, USA	*	*
17.01.30	Lockheed Air Express 3	NC7955	EX-2	The Texas Co	Crashed	West Palm Beach, FL, USA	0	3
18.01.30	Kalinin K-4	*	*	Ukrvozdukhput	Crashed after striking mast	Baku, Azerbaijan, USSR	3	*
19.01.30	de Havilland DH.61 Giant Moth	G-AAEV	335	Imperial Airways	Crashed	Broken Hill, Northern Rhodesia	*	*
19.01.30	Ford 5-AT-C Tri-Motor	NC9689	5-AT-046	Maddux Airlines	Crashed in bad weather	Oceanside, CA, USA	16	0
21.01.30	Boeing 95	NC420E	1064	Western Air Express	Crashed	Cedar City, UT, USA	*	*
08.02.30	Ford 4-AT-A Tri-Motor	NC2492	4-AT-06	D.Seitz	Crashed on landing when u/c failed	San Marcos, TX, USA	0	7
10.02.30	Farman F.63bis Goliath	F-FHMY	6844/21	Air Union	Crash landed & caught fire	Marden, Kent, UK	2	*
10.02.30	Lockheed Vega 1	NC7896	031	Wolverine Flying Service	Crashed	Lansing, MI, USA	*	*
14.02.30	de Havilland DH.66 Hercules	G-EBNA	240	Imperial Airways	Damaged on landing	Gaza, Egypt	*	*
23.02.30	Fokker F-10A	NC279E	1011	Western Air Express	Crashed	Lake Arrowhead, CA, USA	*	*
24.02.30	Boeing 95	NC419E	1063	Western Air Express	Crashed	St George, UT, USA	*	*
01.03.30	Lockheed Vega 2	NC574E	057	C.J.Conner & A.C.Chesher	Damaged beyond repair	Littlefield, TX, USA	*	*
02.03.30	Ford 4-AT-A Tri-Motor	R-131	4-AT-11	New York, Rio & Buenos Aires Airlines	Crashed	Cordoba, Argentina	*	*
04.03.30	Lockheed Vega 5B	NC536M	105	A.Candler	Destroyed in hangar fire	USA	*	*
22.03.30	Lockheed Vega 5A	NC396H	089	Lockheed Aircraft Corporation	Crashed	Seattle, WA, USA	0	*
26.03.30	Lockheed Vega 5	NC102N	113	Alaska-Washington Airways	Damaged beyond repair	Inglewood, CA, USA	*	*

Date	Type	Reg'n	C/n	Operator	Accident	Location	F	S
07.04.30	Junkers W.33	D-1649	2544	Deutsche Lufthansa	Crashed	Limpsfield, Surrey, UK	*	*
08.04.30	Ford 5-AT-C Tri-Motor	R-148	5-AT-063	New York, Rio & Buenos Aires Airlines	Crashed	Buenos Aires, Argentina	*	*
27.04.30	Lockheed Vega 5	NC194E	025	Texas Worth Tool Co	Crashed	Alvord, TX, USA	3	*
29.04.30	Fairchild FC.2	G-CANC	026	Operator Unknown	Damaged beyond repair	St Sylvere, Canada	*	*
30.04.30	Lockheed Vega 1	NC7894	029	Schlee-Brock Aircraft Corporation	Crashed	St Paul, WI, USA	*	*
10.05.30	Latecoere 28	F-AJPD	918	Aeroposta Argentina	Crashed	Off Buenos Aires, Argentina	4	1
14.05.30	Lockheed Vega 5B	NC892E	074	Schlee-Brock Aircraft Corporation	Crashed	Hamilton, ON, Canada	*	*
20.05.30	Junkers Ju.21	SSSR-197	*	Dobrolet	Crashed	USSR	*	*
27.05.30	Lockheed Vega 5B	NC504K	090	Corp Aeronautica de Transportes	Damaged beyond repair	nr Monterrey, Mexico	0	*
30.05.30	Bleriot Spad 66	F-AEAY	4/3137	CIDNA	Crashed on take-off	Yesilkoy, Bulgaria	0	*
31.05.30	Handley Page W.9 Hampstead	VH-ULK	W9/1	Ellyou Goldfields Development Corp	Crashed	Kuper Range, New Guinea	0	*
oo.05.30	Latecoere 28.3	F-AJNQ	919	Aeropostale	Forced landed at sea and abandoned	Atlantic Ocean	0	3
02.06.30	Fokker Universal	G-CASF	433	Operator Unknown	Damaged beyond repair	Allanwater Lake, Canada	*	*
05.06.30	Ford 5-AT-B Tri-Motor	NC9675	5-AT-033	Colonial Air Transport	Crashed into sea after engine failure on take-off	Boston, MA, USA	1	14
10.06.30	CMASA Wal	I-AZDH	065	Aeroespresso	Destroyed by fire	Off Mitylene, Greece	*	*
25.06.30	Lockheed Vega 5	NC31M	098	Beardsley & Piper	Destroyed by fire	Chicago, IL, USA	*	*
25.06.30	Ford 5-AT-A Tri-Motor	NC7739	5-AT-003	Northwest Airways	Destroyed in hangar fire	Chicago, IL, USA	0	*
07.07.30	Dornier Do J Wal	D-864	044	Deutsche Lufthansa	Force-landed & sank in tow	nr Bornholm, Sweden	*	*
10.07.30	Lockheed Vega 5	NC394H	087	Cross Airways	Crashed	Aransas Pass, TX, USA	5	0
21.07.30	Junkers F.13ge	G-AAZK	2052	Walcot Airlines	Crashed after structural failure	Meopham, Kent, UK	*	*
26.07.30	Fokker-Grulich F.II	D-758	1586	Deutsche Lufthansa	Crashed	Germany	*	*
29.07.30	Fokker C.IV	SSSR-155	2323	Dobrolet	Crashed	USSR	*	*
oo.07.30	Fokker F.VIIb/3m	X-ABCP	614/5024	Mexicana	Crashed	Location Unknown	*	*
01.08.30	Lockheed Vega 5B	NC160W	126	Bowen Air Lines	Destroyed by tornado	Houston, TX, USA	*	*
03.08.30	Lockheed Vega 5B	NR500V	112	J.H.Mears	Crashed	Harbour Grace, Newfoundland	0	2
04.08.30	Fairchild FC.2W2	G-CAVL	515	Operator Unknown	Destroyed by fire	Newark, NJ, USA	*	*
04.08.30	Lockheed Vega 5B	NC102W	119	Alaska-Washington Airways	Caught fire after forced landing	Kingston, WA, USA	0	*
10.08.30	Stearman C3B	NC3863	106	Western Air Express	Crashed	Denver, CO, USA	*	*
12.08.30	Fairchild FC.2	G-CAGC	004	Operator Unknown	Damaged beyond repair	Senneterre, PQ, Canada	*	*
14.08.30	Fairchild 71	NC9737	606	Panagra	Written off	Location Unknown	*	*
22.08.30	Ford 5-AT-C Tri-Motor	OK-FOR	5-AT-050	Ceskoslovenske Aerolinie	Crashed in storm	Iglau, Czechoslovakia	12	0
02.09.30	Junkers F.13	A12	573	SCADTA	Destroyed by fire while refuelling	El Banco, Colombia	*	*
03.09.30	Junkers F.13	A-3	575	Operator Unknown	Crashed	Krotten Klein, Austria	*	*
11.09.30	Sabca F.VIIb/3m	OO-AIN	*	Sabena	Crashed	Croydon, Surrey, UK	*	*
05.10.30	Royal Airship Works R.101	G-FAAW	R.101	Air Council	Crashed & caught fire [Lord Thomson, S of S for Air, killed]	nr Beauvais, France	48	6
06.10.30	Messerschmitt M.20b	D-1930	443	Deutsche Lufthansa	Crashed when blown into hill on approach	Dresden, Germany	8	0
12.10.30	Latecoere 28	F-AJUU	*	Aeropostale	Crashed	Larache, France	4	*
28.10.30	Lockheed Vega 5B	NC103W	120	Alaska-Washington Airways	Crashed	nr Prince Rupert, BC, Canada	3	0
30.10.30	Handley Page W.8g	G-EBIX	W8-7	Imperial Airways	Crashed in fog	nr Boulogne, France	4	2
30.10.30	Fokker F.VIIb/3m	CH-161	5207	Balair	Crashed in fog	nr Essen, Germany	*	*
10.11.30	Junkers G.24	PP-CAH	921	Syndicato Condor	Sank	Iguape, Brazil	1	*
21.11.30	Dornier Superwal	I-RONY	170	SANA	Crashed at sea	En route Marseilles-Barcelona	*	*
21.11.30	Ford 4-AT-B Tri-Motor	NC7118	4-AT-32	Curtiss-Wright Flying Service	Damaged by strong winds	Burbank, CA, USA	0	*
22.11.30	Lockheed Vega 5	NC435E	051	Texas Pipe Line Co	Crashed	Houston, TX, USA	1	*
24.11.30	Ford 5-AT-C Tri-Motor	NX419H	5-AT-079	Ford Motor Co	Crashed on landing	Dearborn, MI, USA	2	0
oo.11.30	Fokker F-10A	NC810H	1049	Pan American Airways	Destroyed in hurricane	Santo Domingo, Dominican Rep.	*	*
20.12.30	Ford 4-AT-E Tri-Motor	NC9611	4-AT-54	Pittsburgh Airways	Crashed	Jennerstown, PA, USA	*	*
22.12.30	Ford Tri-Motor	*	*	LAN-Chile	Crashed	Chile	*	*
22.12.30	Fokker F-10A	NC591E	1021	Western Air Express	Crashed	Alhambra, CA, USA	*	*
oo.oo.30	Fokker F.VIIb	OO-AID	4992	Sabena	Crashed	Location Unknown	*	*
oo.oo.30	Junkers W.33	D-1826	2557	Deutsche Lufthansa	Written off	Location Unknown	*	*
oo.oo.30	Focke-Wulf A.29 Mowe	D-1922	063	Deutsche Lufthansa	Destroyed	Location Unknown	*	*
oo.oo.30	Junkers F.13	D-422	699	Deutsche Lufthansa	Crashed	Location Unknown	*	*
oo.oo.30	Kalinin K-4	SSSR-225	113	Ukrvozdukhput	Crashed	USSR	*	*

Date	Type	Reg'n	C/n	Operator	Accident	Location	F	S
07.01.31	Lockheed Vega 5B	NC537M	106	Wedell-Williams Air Service	Crashed	Marshall, TX, USA	*	*
19.01.31	Kalinin K-4	SSSR-202	156	Dobrolet	Crashed	USSR	*	*
26.01.31	Fokker F-10	NC5170	1001	Western Air Express	Written off	Alhambra, CA, USA	*	*
27.01.31	Ford 5-AT-B Tri-Motor	NC9647	5-AT-021	Transcontinental & Western Air	Crashed	Harrisburg, PA, USA	*	*
30.01.31	Dornier Merkur	SSSR-210	70	VO-GVF	Crashed	USSR	*	*
03.02.31	Fairchild FC.2	NC8023	168	Panagra	Crashed	Off Buenos Aires, Argentina	*	*
07.02.31	Sikorsky S-38B	NC306N	414-04	Panagra	Crashed	nr France Field, Panama Canal Zone	*	*
08.02.31	Desoutter II	ZK-ACA	D.36	Dominion Airlines	Crashed	Wairoa, New Zealand	1	0
24.02.31	Latecoere 32	F-AITX	84	Aeropostale	Crashed	Off Cap Creus, France	1	*
oo.02.31	Fairchild FC.2W2	NC8026	519	Panagra	Crashed	Chile	*	*
oo.02.31	Fokker C.IV	SSSR-173	2313	Dobrolet	Crashed	USSR	*	*
04.03.31	Fokker F.VIIb/3m	G-CASC	5104	Canadian Airways	Destroyed in hangar fire	Winnipeg, AB, Canada	*	*
04.03.31	Fokker Super Universal	G-CASM	810	Operator Unknown	Destroyed in hangar fire	Winnipeg, AB, Canada	*	*
04.03.31	Fokker Super Universal	G-CASN	821	Operator Unknown	Destroyed in hangar fire	Winnipeg, AB, Canada	*	*
07.03.31	Rohrbach Ro.VIII Roland Ia	D-1338	40	Deutsche Lufthansa	Crashed & caught fire	Netherlands	*	*
12.03.31	Fokker Universal	G-CAIX	427	Operator Unknown	Damaged beyond repair	Elk Lake, Canada	*	*
21.03.31	Avro Ten	VH-UMF	241	Australian National Airways	Crashed [Wreck found 26.10.58]	Strathbozie Mts, NSW, Australia	*	*
31.03.31	Fokker F-10A	NC999E	*	Transcontinental & Western Air	Crashed in storm [Football coach Knute Rockne killed]	Bazaar, KS, USA	7	*
01.04.31	Ford 5-AT-C Tri-Motor	NC8418	5-AT-056	Panagra	Crashed on landing	Ovalle, Chile	0	7
14.04.31	Messerschmitt M.20b	D-1928	442	Deutsche Lufthansa	Crashed	Reitschin, Germany	2	8
17.04.31	Ford 5-AT-C Tri-Motor	CV-FAI	5-AT-088	Prince Bilbesco	Crashed after striking vulture	Benares, India	0	4
19.04.31	de Havilland DH.66 Hercules	G-EBMW	236	Imperial Airways	Crash landed out of fuel	Kupang, Timor, Dutch East Indies	*	*
22.04.31	Armstrong Whitworth Argosy II	G-AACH	AW.326	Imperial Airways	Crashed & caught fire	Croydon, Surrey, UK	0	*
25.04.31	Junkers A.50	P-BAAE	3534	Varig	Damaged in forced landing	Mosquito Island, Brazil	*	*
29.04.31	Ford 5-AT-C Tri-Motor	NC421H	5-AT-081	National Air Transport	Crash landed after engine failure	Elyria, OH, USA	0	10
oo.04.31	Sikorsky S-38B	NC309N	414-07	SCADTA	Written off	Location Unknown	*	*
11.05.31	Lockheed Vega 2	NC857E	064	Rubner Flying Service	Crashed	Toledo, NM, USA	2	1
16.05.31	Lockheed Vega 5A	NX308H	079	B.F.Goodrich Company	Crashed	Vineland, ON, Canada	*	*
22.05.31	Junkers W.34d	VH-UNR	2611	Guinea Airways	Crashed	Wampit, Papua & New Guinea	*	*
07.06.31	Fokker F.VIIb/3m	PH-AEO	5096	Air Orient	Crashed	Sandoway, Burma	*	*
16.06.31	Armstrong Whitworth Argosy I	G-EBLO	AW.155	Imperial Airways	Crashed	Aswan, Egypt	0	*
16.06.31	Fokker-Grulich F.II	D-175	1503	Deutsche Lufthansa	Crashed	Germany	*	*
12.07.31	Lockheed Vega DL-1B	NC8497	154	Braniff Airways	Crashed	Chicago, IL, USA	2	*
14.07.31	Lasco Lascowl	VH-UGF	3	Australian Aerial Services	Crashed & caught fire	Temora, NSW, Australia	2	*
oo.07.31	Breguet 391T	*	*	Breguet	Crashed after propeller broke away	France	1	0
01.08.31	Avro 504K	G-AASS	–	South Wales Airways	Damaged when submerged by tide on beach	Swansea, Glamorgan, UK	0	0
04.08.31	Fokker F.IX	PH-AFK	5241	KLM Royal Dutch Airlines	Crashed	Waalhaven, Netherlands	*	*
07.08.31	Fokker F-10A	X-ABCR	1050	Mexicana	Crashed	Miami, FL, USA	*	*
09.08.31	Ford 5-AT-B Tri-Motor	NC9662	5-AT-029	American Airways	Crashed after engine failure on take-off	Cincinnati, OH, USA	6	0
12.08.31	Sikorsky S-38A	NC5933	14-A	Pan American Airways	Struck submerged object	San Juan, Puerto Rico	*	*
19.08.31	Ford 5-AT-B Tri-Motor	NC9665	5-AT-024	Transcontinental & Western Air	Crashed on landing in storm	Pittsburgh, PA, USA	0	*
oo.08.31	Focke-Wulf A.29 Mowe	D-1775	062	Deutsche Lufthansa	Destroyed	Location Unknown	*	*
oo.08.31	Polikarpov AP	SSSR-A14	2672	Selkhozaviatsiya	Crashed	USSR	*	*
oo.08.31	Polikarpov AP	SSSR-A27	2685	Selkhozaviatsiya	Crashed	USSR	*	*
12.09.31	CMASA Wal	PP-CAL	107	Syndicato Condor	Struck wreck on take-off & crashed	Brazil	1	*
13.09.31	Junkers W.33b	D-2072	2516	Deutsche Lufthansa	Crashed	Atlantic Ocean	*	*
14.09.31	Lockheed Vega 5	NC606	056	Chicago-Detroit Airways	Crashed	Chicago, IL, USA	1	*
15.09.31	Fokker F.VIIb/3m	F-AIGT	*	CIDNA	Crashed	Balacita, Romania	*	*
22.09.31	Fokker F.VIIb/3m	F-AJBH	5133	CIDNA	Damaged beyond repair	La Ferte-Gaucher, France	*	*
22.09.31	Lockheed Vega 1	NC35E	037	Navin Air Transport	Crashed	nr Lansing, KS, USA	2	*
06.10.31	CMASA Wal	D-861	024	German Ministry of Transport	Sank	Location Unknown	*	*
06.10.31	Heinkel He.12	D-1717	334	Deutsche Lufthansa	Crashed	Location Unknown	*	*
10.10.31	Kalinin K-4	SSSR-L5	*	VO-GVF	Crashed	USSR	*	*

Date	Type	Reg'n	C/n	Operator	Accident	Location	F	S
25.10.31	Latecoere 26.2	F-AIXU	684	Aeropostale	Crashed	nr Skirat, French Morocco	*	*
27.10.31	Ford 5-AT-C Tri-Motor	NC427H	5-AT-087	National Air Transport	Crashed	Ashley, IN, USA	*	*
oo.10.31	Polikarpov AP	SSSR-A15	2673	Selkhozaviatsiya	Crashed	USSR	*	*
oo.10.31	Polikarpov AP	SSSR-A26	2684	Selkhozaviatsiya	Destroyed by fire	USSR	*	*
05.11.31	Lockheed Orion 9	NC12221	178	New York, Philadelphia & Washington AW	Crashed	Camden, NJ, USA	5	0
23.11.31	Fokker-Grulich F.II	D-766	1588	Deutsche Lufthansa	Crashed	Germany	*	*
26.11.31	Avro Ten	VH-UNA	388	Australian National Airways	Crashed	Alor Star, Malaya	*	*
05.12.31	Lockheed Vega 5	NC433E	049	Braniff Airways	Crashed	Kewanee, IL, USA	2	4
06.12.31	Fokker F.VIIb	PH-AFO	5236	KLM Royal Dutch Airlines	Crashed	Bangkok, Thailand	*	*
09.12.31	CAMS 56	F-AIOX	03	Aeropostale	Crashed	Mediterranean Sea	2	*
10.12.31	Fokker Universal	G-CAJD	430	Operator Unknown	Damaged beyond repair	Charron Lake, Canada	*	*
15.12.31	Fokker Universal	G-CAIV	425	Operator Unknown	Damaged on take-off	Peace River, Canada	*	*
17.12.31	Latecoere 300	F-AKCU	01	Latecoere	Stalled and crashed on first flight	Etang de Berre, France	*	*
19.12.31	Ford 4-AT-E Tri-Motor	NC7119	4-AT-33	Transcontinental & Western Air	Crashed on take-off	Oklahoma City, OK, USA	1	1
31.12.31	Fokker Super Universal	ZS-ABR	854	Union Airways	Crashed	nr Kaysers Beach, South Africa	*	*
oo.oo.31	Fokker F.VIIb/3m	CH-193	5136	Swissair	Destroyed by fire	Paris, France	*	*
oo.oo.31	American Aeronautics S.55P	NC379N	1	Transportes Aereos Mexico-Cuba	Written off	Location Unknown	*	*
05.01.32	Lockheed Vega 1	NR7973	032	R.Stewart	Crashed	nr Newville, PA, USA	2	0
07.01.32	Blackburn Dart	G-EBKF	8312/1	North Sea Aerial & General Transport	Crashed	nr Digby, Lincs, UK	*	*
05.02.32	Lockheed Orion 9	NC991Y	175	Continental Airways	Destroyed in hangar fire	Chicago, IL, USA	*	*
05.02.32	Lockheed Vega 1	NC7162	012	T.R.Navin	Crashed	Chicago, IL, USA	*	*
07.02.32	Boeing 40B	NC273	884	United Air Lines	Crashed	USA	*	*
09.02.32	Boeing 40B-4	NC742K	1149	Western Air Express	Crashed	USA	*	*
16.02.32	CMASA Wal	I-AZEA	092	SANA	Damaged in forced landing	nr Malta	0	*
22.02.32	Junkers K.30	SSSR-L718	901	Dobrolet	Crashed	USSR	*	*
27.02.32	Latecoere 28-0	F-AJOX	917	Aeropostale	Crashed	nr Montevideo, Uruguay	*	*
01.03.32	de Havilland DH.50	VH-UMC	074	West Australian Airways	Crashed	Mia Mia, WA, Australia	*	*
07.03.32	Kalinin K-4	SSSR-L47	141	VO-GVF	Crashed	USSR	*	*
12.03.32	Junkers W.33	CF-ASI	2591	Canadian Airways	Crashed in snowstorm	Kagianagami Lake, ON, Canada	*	*
15.03.32	Ford 4-AT-B Tri-Motor	NC4805	4-AT-17	Skyway	Destroyed in hangar fire	Blackwell, OK, USA	*	*
18.03.32	Farman F.303	F-AJIG	1	Air Orient	Crashed	Syria	*	*
29.03.32	Farman F.190	F-AJDP	20	Air Orient	Crashed	Syria	3	*
03.04.32	Loening C2-C Air Yacht	NC9717	215	Pan American Airways	Crashed	Montevideo, Uruguay	*	*
19.04.32	Kalinin K-4	SSSR-L52	128	VO-GVF	Destroyed by fire	USSR	*	*
oo.04.32	Polikarpov U-2	SSSR-N5	*	Polyarnaya Aviatsiya	Crashed	USSR	*	*
02.05.32	Fokker-Grulich F.II	D-765	1587	Deutsche Lufthansa	Crashed	Germany	*	*
16.05.32	Boeing 40B-4	NC5589	1042	Pacific Air Transport	Crashed	Burbank, CA, USA	3	*
30.05.32	Fokker Universal	NR1776	421	Operator Unknown	Crashed	Puget Sound, WA, USA	0	2
30.05.32	Boeing 40B-4	NC830M	1155	Varney Air Transport	Crashed in river	Portland, OR, USA	1	1
02.06.32	Boeing 40B-4	NC10348	1429	Pacific Air Transport	Caught fire after forced landing	nr Fresno, CA, USA	0	1
14.06.32	Sikorsky S-38B	NC944M	314-02	New York Airways	Crashed	Location Unknown	*	*
29.06.32	Fokker Super Universal	G-CASL	806	Operator Unknown	Crashed	nr Mazenod Lake, Canada	*	*
06.07.32	Lockheed Vega 5	NR869E	069	J.J.Mattern	Crashed on landing after cockpit front brcke away	nr Borisov, Bylorussia, USSR	0	2
10.07.32	Boeing 80A	*	*	Boeing Air Transport	Crashed on landing in bad weather	Stirling, IL, USA	0	8
16.07.32	Ford 5-AT-C Tri-Motor	NC403H	5-AT-062	Panagra	Crashed into mountain [Found 20 months later]	Vitacura, Chile	9	0
29.07.32	Junkers Ju.52/3m	D-2201	4013	Deutsche Lufthansa	Mid-air collision with Udet Flamingo D-1296 of DVS	nr Munich, Germany	*(*)	*
31.07.32	Fairchild FC.2	G-CARH	110	Operator Unknown	Damaged beyond repair	Canada	*	*
12.08.32	CAMS 53-1	F-AIQY	07	Air Orient	Crashed on landing	Beirut, Lebanon	2	*
15.08.32	Polikarpov P-5	SSSR-N6	*	Polyarnaya Aviatsiya	Crashed	USSR	*	*
16.08.32	Fokker F.VIIb/3m	PK-AFE	5123	KNILM	Written off	Tabanan, Bali, Dutch East Indies	*	*
26.08.32	Junkers W.33	I	2545	Eurasia	Crashed	nr Lanchow, China	*	*
31.08.32	Junkers G.23	SE-AAE	863	AB Aerotransport	Crash landed after engine failure	Tubbergen, Germany	2	*
01.09.32	Junkers W.33	VI	2563	Eurasia	Crashed	Lanchow, China	*	*

Date	Type	Reg'n	C/n	Operator	Accident	Location	F	S
08.09.32	Fokker F-10A	NC9716	1009	American Airlines	Crashed into mountain in fog	El Paso, TX, USA	3	0
08.09.32	Dornier Wal	SSSR-N3	123	Polyarnaya Aviatsiya	Crashed	USSR	*	*
17.09.32	Liore et Olivier 213	F-AIFE	2	Air Union	Crashed in fog	Selsdon Park, Surrey, UK	1	1
17.09.32	Farman F.303	F-AJVS	7217/4	Air Orient	Crashed	nr Rutbah, Iraq	*	*
18.09.32	de Havilland DH.80A Puss Moth	VH-UPM	2052	New England Airways	Crashed	Bryom Bay, NSW, Australia	3	0
25.09.32	Sikorsky S-38B	NC113M	214-09	Pan American Airways	Stolen by Brazilian rebels & crashed	Merity, Brazil	*	*
oo.09.32	Kalinin K-4	SSSR-L60	*	Transaviatsiya	Crashed	USSR	*	*
02.10.32	Ford 5-AT-B Tri-Motor	NC9664	5-AT-023	Pan American Airways	Crashed in bad weather	El Accituno, Honduras	0	*
12.10.32	Latecoere 28-1	F-AJJM	908	Aeropostale	Crashed	Port Etienne, Algeria	*	*
21.10.32	Standard D-27	NC9124	118	Pennsylvania Air Lines	Crashed after in-flight fire	nr Somerset, PA, USA	0	1
26.10.32	Ford 5-AT-D Tri-Motor	n/a	5-AT-113	Lloyd Aereo Boliviano	Crashed [Cruz Del Sur]	Villa Montes, Bolivia	2	0
29.10.32	Junkers W.33f	D-2017	2583	Deutsche Lufthansa	Crashed	Off Ramsgate, Kent, UK	2	0
30.10.32	Latecoere 26.6	F-AJOM	*	Aeropostale	Crashed	French West Africa	*	*
02.11.32	Junkers F.13	D-724	596	Deutsche Lufthansa	Crashed in mountains	Echterpfuhl, Germany	5	0
03.11.32	CMASA Wal	I-AZDL	082	SANA	Crashed	Off Sicily, Italy	*	*
04.11.32	Schlee-Brock/Lockheed Vega 5	NR496M	619	Crosley Radio Corporation	Crashed on take-off	Floyd Bennett Field, NY, USA	0	*
17.11.32	Lockheed Orion 9A Special	NC12229	187	Hal Roach Studios	Crashed	Victoria Falls, Northern Rhodesia	1	2
30.11.32	Fokker Universal	G-CAGD	406	Operator Unknown	Crashed	Edmonton, Canada	*	*
oo.11.32	Dornier Merkur	D-1079	[illegible]27	Deruluft	Crashed	Location Unknown	*	*
10.12.32	Latecoere 25	F-AIUT	712	Aeropostale	Crashed	nr Ste Marie de la Mer, France	2	0
11.12.32	Fokker F-10A	NC39N	1028	Western Air Express	Crashed	Lynndyl, UT, USA	*	*
13.12.32	Boeing 40B-4	NC842M	1168	Boeing Air Transport	Caught fire after crash landing	nr McClelland, IA, USA	*	*
14.12.32	Ford 5-AT-B Tri-Motor	NC9650	5-AT-037	Transcontinental & Western Air	Crashed on landing in snowstorm	Amarillo, TX, USA	2	0
15.12.32	Fokker Super Universal	C-44	828	SCADTA	Crashed	La Mesa, Colombia	*	*
15.12.32	Junkers F.13	III	*	Eurasia	Crashed	nr Shanghai, China	*	*
28.12.32	Fokker Super Universal	NC9127	845	American Airways	Crashed	New Orleans, LA, USA	*	*
oo.oo.32	Sikorsky S-38B	C-45	*	SCADTA	Crashed	Location Unknown	*	*
10.01.33	Northrop Alpha 4	NC992Y	12	Transcontinental & Western Air	Crashed on take-off	Pittsburgh, PA, USA	0	1
11.01.33	CAMS 53	F-AISV	05	Aeropostale	Crashed on take-off	Algiers, Algeria	*	*
13.01.33	Liore et Olivier 213	F-AJNS	7	Air Union	Caught fire & crashed	Poix, France	*	*
13.01.33	Junkers W.33f	D-2018	2584	Deutsche Lufthansa	Crashed	Tanagra	*	*
14.01.33	Curtiss Condor 18	NC185H	1168	Eastern Air Transport	Crashed	Newark, NJ, USA	2	*
20.01.33	Stearman 4CM1	NC490W	4038	American Airways	Crashed into mountain	Marietta, GA, USA	1	0
20.01.33	Stearman 4CM1	NC11721	4039	American Airways	Crashed into hill	Bourne, TX, USA	1	0
24.01.33	Ford 5-AT-D Tri-Motor	NC431H	5-AT-098	Pacific Air Transport	Crashed on take-off	Eugene, OR, USA	2	1
25.01.33	Supermarine Air Yacht	G-AASE	1285	J.J.James	Crashed	Off Positano, Italy	0	*
08.02.33	Stinson Model U	NX12132	9013	Stinson	Crashed on test flight	Wayne County, CA, USA	3	0
09.02.33	Fairchild FC.2	G-CATR	CV.88	Operator Unknown	Damaged in storm	Canada	*	*
10.02.33	Ford 5-AT-B Tri-Motor	NC9666	5-AT-025	Transcontinental & Western Air	Crash landed after in-flight fire	Bakersfield, CA, USA	0	9
25.02.33	Boeing 95	NC425E	1069	National Air Transport	Crashed	Toledo, USA	*	*
oo.02.33	Focke-Wulf A.17 Mowe	D-1380	045	Deutsche Lufthansa	Destroyed	Location Unknown	*	*
11.03.33	Fairchild FC.2W	NC9723	527	Panagra	Crashed	nr Mendoza, Mexico	*	*
16.03.33	Loening Lo-8	G-CARS	204	Canadian Airways	Crashed on take-off	Quesnel, BC, Canada	*	*
16.03.33	Fairchild Pilgrim 100A	NC732N	66[illegible]2	American Airways	Crashed on take-off	Fort Worth, TX, USA	0	1
25.03.33	Lockheed Orion 9	NC12226	184	Varney Speed Lines	Crashed	Hayward, CA, USA	3{11}	0
28.03.33	Armstrong Whitworth Argosy II	G-AACI	AW.363	Imperial Airways	Crashed after fire in mid-air – possibly due to sabotage	nr Dixmunde, Belgium	15	0
31.03.33	Fokker Super Universal	G-CASK	803	Operator Unknown	Destroyed by fire	Fort McMurray, Canada	*	*
31.03.33	Ford 4-AT-B Tri-Motor	NC7686	4-AT-44	J.H.O'Brien	Crashed on landing	Neodesha, KS, USA	7	6
18.04.33	Lockheed Vega 5	NR7429	018	W.N.Gregory	Crashed	Valmeyer, IL, USA	5	0
22.04.33	Lockheed Vega 5	NC195E	026	Braniff Airways	Destroyed	St Louis, MO, USA	*	*
23.04.33	CAMS 53	F-ALCE	29	Air Orient	Crashed into mountain	Mont Terrione, Italy	6	0
27.04.33	Lockheed Vega 5	NC657E	054	Shell Aviation	Crashed	Seattle, WA, USA	*	*
29.04.33	Junkers W.34	D-4	2737	Deutsche Lufthansa	Crashed before delivery to Eurasia	Germany	*	*
02.05.33	Fokker F.VIIa	OY-DAC	5058	DDL	Crashed in fog	Hanover, Germany	1	*

Date	Type	Reg'n	C/n	Operator	Accident	Location	F	S
07.05.33	de Havilland DH.80A Puss Moth	G-ABSB	2213	Hillman's Airways	Written off	Clacton, Essex, UK	*	*
09.05.33	Latecoere 28-1	F-AJIX	904	Aeropostale	Crashed on landing in fog	Viladrau, Spain	6	*
12.05.33	Boeing 247	NC13320	1701	National Air Transport	Crashed into mountain in fog	nr Provo, UT, USA	0	2
24.05.33	Fairchild FC.2	*	*	LAN-Chile	Crashed	Location Unknown	*	*
25.05.33	CMASA Wal	I-CITO	126	SANA	Crashed on take-off	Marseilles, France	2	*
26.05.33	Sikorsky S-38A	NC8044	14-10	Pan American Airways	Damaged beyond repair	Location Unknown	*	*
26.05.33	Koolhoven FK.43	PH-AIL	4302	KLM Royal Dutch Airlines	Crashed	Eelde, Netherlands	*	*
27.05.33	Junkers Ju.52cai	D-2356	4005	Deutsche Lufthansa	Crashed	Location Unknown	*	*
02.06.33	Lockheed Orion 9	NC960Y	168	Bowen Air Lines	Crashed	Tulsa, OK, USA	0	4
02.06.33	Ford 4-AT-E Tri-Motor	NR9614	4-AT-57	Plane Speaking Corporation	Destroyed in hangar fire	Roosevelt Field, NY, USA	0	*
03.06.33	Fokker F.III	D-743	1568	Deutsche Lufthansa	Written off	Location Unknown	*	*
04.06.33	Pitcairn PA-6	*	*	Eastern Air Transport	Crashed after engine failure	Bowling Green, VA, USA	1	0
10.06.33	Fokker Universal	G-CASE	432	Operator Unknown	Damaged beyond repair	Gull Lake, Canada	*	*
11.06.33	Sikorsky S-38B	NC141M	214-12	A.L.Caperton	Crashed	Chicago, IL, USA	*	*
22.06.33	de Havilland DH.80A Puss Moth	HS-PAA	2171	Aerial Transport Co	Crashed	Bangkok, Siam	*	*
29.06.33	Latecoere 28-0	F-AJVK	927	Aeropostale	Damaged beyond repair	St Louis, Senegal	*	*
oo.06.33	Lockheed Vega 5B	NR869E	118	J.J.Mattern	Crashed on emergency landing on second record attempt	Anadyr River, USSR	0	1
01.07.33	Savoia Marchetti S.55X	I-DINI	*	Italian Air Force	Crashed on landing during record breaking flight	Amsterdam, Netherlands	1	*
11.07.33	Lockheed Vega 1	NR7805	028	Cardiff & Peacock	Crashed	Dos Palos, CA, USA	*	*
18.07.33	CMASA Wal	I-AZEE	127	Aeroespresso	Crashed	Off Greece	*	*
23.07.33	de Havilland Dragon 1	G-ACCV	6014	A.Mollison	Crashed on landing after transatlantic flight	Bridgeport, CN, USA	0	2
28.07.33	Lockheed Orion 9A Special	NC12277	192	Transcontinental & Western Air	Crashed into river on take-off	nr Kansas City, MO, USA	1	*
oo.07.33	Sikorsky S-38B	PP-PAL	214-16	Panair do Brasil	Written off	Location Unknown	*	*
11.08.33	Dornier Superwal	I-RATA	145	SANA	Crashed at sea	Off Valencia, Spain	*	*
15.08.33	Fairchild 71	CF-AJP	651	Wells Air Transport	Crashed	Anderson Lake, Canada	*	*
19.08.33	Lockheed Vega 5	NC658E	055	Skyloft	Crashed	nr Leipsic, DL, USA	1	*
29.08.33	Ford 5-AT-B Tri-Motor	NC9607	5-AT-005	Transcontinental & Western Air	Crashed in storm	Quay, NM, USA	5	0
12.09.33	Farman F.306	YU-SAH	*	Aeroput	Crashed on take-off	Ljubljana, Yugoslavia	8	*
16.09.33	Boeing 95A	NC415E	1061	United Air Lines	Crashed in storm	nr Leoni, MI, USA	1	0
20.09.33	Fairchild 71	NC9765	*	Pacific Alaska Airways	Crashed	Livengood, Alaska	*	*
21.09.33	Curtiss Condor	NC12373	34	Eastern Air Transport	Damaged beyond repair	Newark, NJ, USA	*	*
26.09.33	de Havilland Dragon 1	ZS-AEF	6026	Aircraft Operating Co	Crashed	Baragwanath, South Africa	*	*
26.09.33	Ford 5-AT-D Tri-Motor	NS-1	*	US Commerce Department	Crashed	nr Lakeland, CA, USA	*	*
10.10.33	Boeing 247	NC13304	1685	National Air Transport	Crashed when cargo exploded	nr Chesterton, IN, USA	6	0
11.10.33	Vickers Viastra II	VH-UOM	2	West Australian Airways	Damaged on landing	Redcliffe, WA, Australia	0	*
12.10.33	Type Unknown	*	*	Johnson Airways	Crashed	Belle Chaise, LA, USA	*	*
18.10.33	Ford 4-AT-B Tri-Motor	NC4806	4-AT-18	F.Free	Crashed	Managua, Nicaragua	3	0
21.10.33	Boulton & Paul P.64 Mailplane	G-ABYK	P.64	Boulton & Paul	Crashed on test flight	Mousehold, Norfolk, UK	1	*
25.10.33	Polikarpov AP	SSSR-A11	2481	Selkhozaviatsiya	Crashed	USSR	*	*
31.10.33	Farman F.301	F-AJMI	4	Air France	Crashed	nr Etobon, France	2	0
02.11.33	Douglas Dolphin	NC12212	1002	Wilmington-Catalina Airways	Crashed on take-off	Catalina Is, CA, USA	*	*
09.11.33	Boeing 247	NC13345	1727	Pacific Air Transport	Crashed in fog	nr Portland, OR, USA	4	6
10.11.33	Northrop Delta 1A	NC12292	03	Transcontinental & Western Air	Crashed after engine fire	Moriarty, NM, USA	0	1
16.11.33	Liore et Olivier 213	F-AIFD	2	Air France	Crashed	Beauvais, France	0	2
21.11.33	Kalinin K-7	n/a	–	Kalinin	Crashed after tail boom failure	nr Kharkov, Ukraine, USSR	15	5
21.11.33	Lockheed Orion 9D	NC229Y	200	American Airways	Crashed after fire in flight	nr El Paso, TX, USA	0	1
24.11.33	Boeing 247	NC13324	1705	National Air Transport	Crashed	nr Wedron, IL, USA	2	0
24.11.33	Sikorsky S-38B	NC16V	314-20	CNAC	Crashed in fog	Hangchow Bay, China	0	*
24.11.33	Fokker F-10A	X-ABEA	1014	Aerovias Centrales	Crashed	Leon, Mexico	*	*
28.11.33	Fokker Super Universal	NC326N	866	National Parks Airways	Crashed	Pauline, ID, USA	*	*
oo.11.33	Fairchild 71	NC9172	644	Pacific Alaska Airways	Crashed	Alaska	*	*
02.12.33	Fokker Super Universal	NC122M	863	Western Air Express	Crashed	Colorado Springs, CO, USA	*	*
03.12.33	Fokker Super Universal	NC8011	812	Western Air Express	Crashed	nr Watrous, NM, USA	*	*
08.12.33	de Havilland Dragon 1	VP-KAW	6047	Wilson Airways	Crashed	Kilindini, Kenya	*	*

Date	Type	Reg'n	C/n	Operator	Accident	Location	F	S
08.12.33	Polikarpov AP	SSSR-A16	2674	Selkhozaviatsiya	Crashed	USSR	*	*
11.12.33	Northrop Alpha	NC947Y	7	Transcontinental & Western Air	Crashed in storm	Roaring Springs, PA, USA	0	1
11.12.33	Northrop Alpha	NC127W	2	Transcontinental & Western Air	Crashed in storm	Portage, PA, USA	0	1
14.12.33	Junkers W.34f	ZS-AEB	2735	Union Airways	Crashed	Eshowe, South Africa	4	2
17.12.33	CAMS 53-1	F-ALCH	32	Air France	Crashed at sea	Off Marseilles, France	*	*
22.12.33	Fokker F.VIIb/3m	OO-AIE	*	Sabena	Crashed	Dortmund, Germany	*	*
30.12.33	Avro Ten	G-ABLU	528	Imperial Airways	Crashed into radio mast in fog	nr Ruysselade, Belgium	*	*
31.12.33	Fokker Super Universal	NC9789	830	Western Air Express	Crashed	Las Vegas, NV, USA	*	*
oo.12.33	Focke-Wulf A.17 Mowe	D-1388	046	Deutsche Lufthansa	Destroyed	Location Unknown	*	*
oo.oo.33	Atlantic F.VII/3m	NR1661	609/5094	Plane Speaking Corporation	Damaged beyond repair	Garden City, NY, USA	*	*
oo.oo.33	Ford 4-AT-B Tri-Motor	NC7120	4-AT-34	Morgan Air Lines	Crashed	Honduras	*	*
oo.oo.33	Junkers F.13	D-232	644	Deutsche Lufthansa	Crashed	Location Unknown	*	*
oo.oo.33	Junkers F.13	D-534	694	Deutsche Lufthansa	Crashed	Location Unknown	*	*
oo.oo.33	Consolidated Fleetster 17A	N704Y	*	Pan American Airways	Crashed	Alaska	*	*
oo.oo.33	Junkers F.13	C-36	*	SCADTA	Crashed	Colombia	*	*
oo.oo.33	Dornier Merkur	URSS-D306	126	Deruluft	Crashed	USSR	*	*
06.01.34	Fairchild 71	NC9170	642	Pacific Alaska Airways	Crashed	Eagle, Alaska	*	*
14.01.34	Dewoitine D.332	F-AMMY	01	Air France	Crashed in bad weather	Corbigny, France	10	0
30.01.34	Stinson SM-6000B	CF-ATE	5017	Canadian Colonial Airways	Destroyed by fire	Albany, NY, USA	0	0
31.01.34	Lockheed Vega DL-1	NC497H	135	Transcontinental & Western Air	Crashed	St James, MO, USA	*	*
09.02.34	CAMS 53-1	F-ALFF	34	Air France	Damaged beyond repair in forced landing	nr Korbus, Tunisia	*	*
12.02.34	Fairchild Pilgrim 100A	NC982M	6611	American Airways	Crashed on take-off	USA	0	3
23.02.34	Boeing 247	NC13357	1739	Boeing Air Transport	Crashed in blizzard	nr Salt Lake City, UT, USA	8	0
26.02.34	Latecoere 28-0	F-AJPA	925	Air France	Crashed	Rio de Oro	1	*
oo.02.34	Fairchild 71	NC153H	666	Pacific Alaska Airways	Crashed	Alaska	*	*
06.03.34	Fairchild Pilgrim 100A	NC710Y	6606	American Airways	Crashed due to icing	Petersburg, IL, USA	4	0
10.03.34	Sikorsky S-38B	C-46	14-06	SCADTA	Crashed	Colombia	3	*
20.03.34	Latecoere 25-3R	F-AISB	650	Air France	Crashed	Berre, Spain	*	*
22.03.34	Ford 5-AT-C Tri-Motor	NC407H	5-AT-066	Panagra	Crashed on take-off due to engine failure	nr Lima, Peru	3	12
10.04.34	Sikorsky S-38B	NC17V	414-08	CNAC	Crashed	Hangchow Bay, China	*	*
27.04.34	Lockheed Air Express 3	NC522K	092	Swiflight Aircraft Corporation	Crashed	nr Palmetto, GA, USA	0	2
oo.04.34	Junkers F.24	D-1019	843	Deutsche Lufthansa	Written off	Location Unknown	*	*
05.05.34	Northrop Delta 1B	X-ABED	04	Aerovias Centrales	Exploded on delivery flight	Location Unknown	*	*
09.05.34	Wibault 282T.12	F-AMHP	8	Air France	Crashed in fog	English Channel	6	0
18.05.34	Clark GA-43	M-701	*	Manchurian Air Lines	Crashed on approach	Haneda, Japan	*	*
24.05.34	Fokker AF-14A	CF-AUD	1421	Mackenzie Air Services	Crashed & caught fire on take-off	Edmonton, AB, Canada	*	*
31.05.34	Liore et Olivier 213	F-AIVG	3	Air France	Crashed into radio mast on take-off	Croydon, Surrey, UK	2	0
oo.05.34	Savoia-Marchetti S.55P	NC105H	10514	Operator Unknown	Destroyed by fire	Lake Mohawk, NY, USA	*	*
01.06.34	Lockheed Vega 5C	NC934Y	138	Central Airlines	Crashed	Pittsburgh, PA, USA	*	*
07.06.34	Boeing 247	NC13302	1683	United Air Lines	Crashed in bad weather	nr Selleck, WA, USA	0	*
09.06.34	Curtiss Condor T-32	NC12354	22	American Airways	Crashed	Mongaup Mt, NY, USA	7	0
11.06.34	Ford 5-AT-C Tri-Motor	NC8417	5-AT-055	Panagra	Crashed in heavy rain	Junin, Argentina	6	4
11.06.34	Latecoere 26.2R	F-AILG	658	Air France	Crashed	Recife, Brazil	0	*
22.06.34	Ford 4-AT-B Tri-Motor	NC7685	4-AT-43	Mulzer Flying Service	Destroyed by tornado	Columbus, OH, USA	*	*
23.06.34	Lockheed Orion 9	XA-BEJ	173	Aerovias Centrales	Crashed	Burbank, CA, USA	1	*
24.06.34	Ford 5-AT-D Tri-Motor	C-31	5-AT-112	SCADTA	Struck by Trimotor F31 of SACO	Medellin, Colombia	9(8)	0
24.06.34	Ford 5-AT-B Tri-Motor	F-31	5-AT-006	Servicio Aereo Colombiano	Struck Trimotor of SCADTA [Actor Carlos Gardel killed]	Medellin, Colombia	8(9)	0
24.06.34	Lockheed Vega 1	NC4097	006	P.F.Jones & J.B.McJunkin	Crashed	Youngstown, OH, USA	*	*
oo.06.34	Letov S-32	OK-ADB	S.32.2	Ceskoslovenske Aerolinie	Crashed	Location Unknown	*	*
01.07.34	Ford 4-AT-B Tri-Motor	NC7586	4-AT-40	R.Loomis	Crashed	Lima, OH, USA	*	*
06.07.34	Northrop Delta 1E	SE-ADW	29	AB Aerotransport	Crashed	Almhut, Sweden	0	2
09.07.34	Lockheed Vega 1	NC32E	033	United Air Services	Crashed	San Bernadino, CA, USA	3	1
13.07.34	de Havilland Dragon 2	G-ACRH	6078	Aberdeen Airways	Crashed on take-off	Aberdeen, UK	*	*
24.07.34	Fokker-Grulich F.II	D-OGOT	1594	Deutsche Lufthansa	Crashed	Germany	*	*

Date	Type	Reg'n	C/n	Operator	Accident	Location	F	S
27.07.34	Curtiss Condor	CH-170	53	Swissair	Crashed	nr Tuttlingen, Germany	12	*
07.08.34	Lockheed 10A Electra	NC14243	1002	Northwest Airlines	Crashed	Location Unknown	*	*
12.08.34	de Havilland Dragon 1	G-ACJM	6049	J.R.Ayling	Damaged on landing	Hamble, Hants, UK	*	*
16.08.34	V4 Airship	SSSR-V4	–	TsAGI	Destroyed by fire	USSR	*	*
29.08.34	de Havilland Dragon 1	G-ACCE	6010	Highland Airways	Crashed on take-off	Kirkwall, Orkneys, UK	*	*
31.08.34	Stinson SM-6000B	NC1118	5004	Rapid Air Transport	Crashed in heavy rain	Oregon, MS, USA	5	*
01.09.34	Fokker Super Universal	NC9129	847	Atlantic Coast Airways	Crashed	Bluefields, Nicaragua	*	*
02.09.34	Ford 5-AT-D Tri-Motor	NC9655	5-AT-110	Hanfords Tri-State Airlines	Crashed	Cochrane, WI, USA	*	*
08.09.34	Polikarpov P-5	SSSR-N45	7472	Polyarnaya Aviatsiya	Crashed	USSR	*	*
12.09.34	Lockheed Vega 5A	NC904Y	132	Central Airlines	Crashed	nr Everett, PA, USA	1	0
22.09.34	Handley Page W.10	G-EBMR	W10/2	National Aviation Day Displays	Damaged beyond repair	Hal Far, Malta	*	*
24.09.34	Handley Page W.10	G-EBMM	W10/1	National Aviation Day Displays	Crashed	Aston Clinton, Bucks, UK	2	0
27.09.34	Fokker F-10A	X-ABCS	1053	Mexicana	Crashed	Irapuato, Mexico	*	*
29.09.34	Airspeed Courier	G-ACSY	16	London Scottish & Provincial Airways	Crashed	Sevenoaks, Kent, UK	4	0
02.10.34	de Havilland DH.89 Dragon Rapide	G-ACPM	6251	Hillman's Airways	Crashed in bad weather	Off Folkestone, Kent, UK	7	*
03.10.34	de Havilland DH.50A	VH-UHE	4	Qantas	Crashed in dust storm	nr Winton, Qld, Australia	3	0
03.10.34	GVF PS-4	SSSR-L417	*	Aeroflot	Crashed	USSR	*	*
10.10.34	Lockheed Vega 5	NC974H	094	Alaska Southern Airways	Crashed	Pinta Bay, Alaska	*	*
17.10.34	Lockheed Vega 5C	NC306H	076	Hanford Airlines	Damaged beyond repair	Albany, MN, USA	*	*
17.10.34	Airspeed Courier	G-ACLS	13	Air Taxis	Crashed	Genoble, France	*	*
19.10.34	de Havilland DH.86	VH-URN	2301	Holyman Airways	Crashed	Bass Strait, Australia	11	0
22.10.34	Tupolev ANT-9	D-2831	145	Deruluft	Crashed	USSR	*	*
26.10.34	Ford 4-AT-E Tri-Motor	NC8403	4-AT-65	Ptarmigan Airlines	Damaged beyond repair in ground loop	Flat, Alaska	0	*
29.10.34	Ford 4-AT Tri-Motor	*	*	TACA	Destroyed	La Ceiba, Honduras	*	*
31.10.34	Fokker Super Universal	C-48	880	SCADTA	Crashed	Location Unknown	*	*
02.11.34	de Havilland DH.61 Giant Moth	G-AUHW	330	Holden Air Transport	Crashed into building	Rabaul, New Guinea	*	*
03.11.34	Heinkel He.70	D-AHUX	403	Deutsche Lufthansa	Crashed	nr Carcassonne, France	*	*
06.11.34	Junkers Ju.52/3m	D-AVAN	*	Deutsche Reichbahngesellschaft	Crashed	Gross-Rackitt, Germany	5	0
15.11.34	de Havilland DH.86	VH-USG	2311	Qantas	Crashed	nr Longreach, NSW, Australia	4	0
15.11.34	Lockheed Orion 9D	NC12285	197	American Airlines	Crashed	Memphis, TN, USA	*	*
15.11.34	Northrop Alpha	NC999Y	4	Transcontinental & Western Air	Crashed after force-landing in bad weather	nr Newhall, CA, USA	0	1
25.11.34	PZL F.VIIb/3m	SP-ABG	7	LOT Polish Airlines	Written off	Poland	*	*
04.12.34	Airspeed Envoy I	VH-UXY	31	C.T.P.Ulm	Crashed	Pacific Ocean	*	*
07.12.34	Fokker F.VIIb/3m	OO-AII	*	Sabena	Destroyed by fire after Fairey Fox O-47 crashed into hangar	Evere, Belgium	*(*)	*
08.12.34	Lockheed Vega 5B	NC106W	123	Braniff Airways	Crashed due to icing	Columbia, MO, USA	1	*
10.12.34	Ford 4-AT-E Tri-Motor	NM-7	4-AT-63	Cubana	Crashed into mountain	Palma Soriano, Cuba	4	4
19.12.34	Curtiss Condor AT-32B	NC12395	47	American Airways	Destroyed by fire after landing	Buffalo, NY, USA	*	*
20.12.34	Douglas DC-2-115A	PH-AJU	1317	KLM Royal Dutch Airlines	Crashed	Rutbah Wells, Iraq	7	*
22.12.34	Wibault 280T	F-AMHO	5	Air France	Crashed on landing	Croydon, Surrey, UK	0	*
22.12.34	Lockheed Orion 9D	NC12286	198	American Airlines	Crashed	nr Sunbright, TN, USA	1	*
24.12.34	Ford 5-AT-D Tri-Motor	NC433H	5-AT-100	Panagra	Crashed into house on approach	nr Lima, Peru	0(2)	2
00.00.34	Junkers F.13	D-207	592	Deutsche Lufthansa	Crashed	Location Unknown	*	*
00.00.34	Junkers A 20	D-404	459	Deutsche Lufthansa	Crashed	Location Unknown	*	*
00.00.34	Junkers F.13	A32	*	SCADTA	Crashed	Colombia	*	*
00.00.34	Dornier Wal	SSSR-N9	*	Polyarnaya Aviatsiya	Crashed	USSR	*	*
00.00.34	Polikarpov U-2	SSSR-N18	4940	Polyarnaya Aviatsiya	Crashed	USSR	*	*
08.01.35	de Havilland Dragon 1	G-ACGK	6033	Highland Airways	Crashed	Off Inverness, UK	0	3
10.01.35	Lockheed Orion 9D	NC12287	199	American Airlines	Crashed	Pittsburgh Landing, TN, USA	0	1
20.01.35	CAMS 53	F-ALCF	30	Air France	Crash landed & sank	Cape Santa Maria de Leuca, Italy	0	*
25.01.35	Type Unknown	*	*	CGT	Crashed after encountering tornado	Parakou, French West Africa	0	1
26.01.35	Consolidated Fleetster 20A	NC13212	5	Transcontinental & Western Air	Crashed due to icing	Pittsburgh, PA, USA	1	0
31.01.35	Junkers Ju.52/3m	D-AREN	4051	Deruluft	Crashed	Location Unknown	*	*
31.01.35	Northrop Alpha	NC994Y	17	Transcontinental & Western Air	Crashed after engine failure	Glendale, CA, USA	0	1
05.02.35	Fairchild FC.2	G-CAJJ	060	Operator Unknown	Damaged by fire	Amos, PQ, Canada	*	*

Date	Type	Reg'n	C/n	Operator	Accident	Location	F	S
11.02.35	Stinson SM-6000B	NC11155	5022	Chicago & Southern Airlines	Crashed	Yorkville, IL, USA	*	*
07.03.35	Rohrbach Roland II	D-AJYP	45	Deruluft	Crashed	Schievelbein, Germany	*	*
15.03.35	de Havilland Dragon 1	SU-ABI	6031	Misrair	Crashed	nr El Arish, Egypt	*	*
oo.03.35	Rohrbach Ro.VIII Roland II	D-1712	45	Deutsche Lufthansa	Destroyed by fire	Location Unknown	*	*
oo.03.35	Junkers W.34	n/a	2790	Aero Survey	Crashed	China	*	*
01.04.35	Farman F.306	F-ALHO	2/7243	Air France	Damaged in forced landing	Bremontiers, France	1	2
06.04.35	Fokker F.XII	PH-AFL	5242	KLM Royal Dutch Airlines	Crashed	Brilon, Germany	*	*
16.04.35	Consolidated Commodore 16	NC660M	04	Pan American Airways	Destroyed in hangar fire	Miami, FL, USA	*	*
21.04.35	Sabca F.VIIb/3m	OO-AGK	*	Sabena	Crashed	Senlis, France	*	*
21.04.35	Lockheed Vega 1	NC7425	012B	R.E.Morrison	Damaged in forced landing in mountains	nr Fishtrap, MT, USA	*	*
25.04.35	Heinkel He.70	*	*	Deutsche Lufthansa	Crashed	nr Wiesbaden, Germany	1	*
28.04.35	Ford 4-AT-B Tri-Motor	NC7863	4-AT-48	V.N.Johns	Crashed	Gasden, AL, USA	*	*
30.04.35	Junkers W.34	D-OMYI	*	Deutsche Lufthansa	Crashed	Schneeburg, Germany	*	*
01.05.35	Lockheed Vega 5C	NC891E	073	Varney Air Transport	Crashed	Rattlesnake Butte, CO, USA	3	0
06.05.35	Douglas DC-2-112	NC13785	1295	Transcontinental & Western Air	Crashed on landing in bad weather	Macon, MO, USA	4	*
07.05.35	Ford Tri-Motor	*	*	Operator Unknown	Crashed	Lake Izabel, Guatemala	1	1
08.05.35	Lockheed Vega 5	NC9424	078	Panagra	Crashed	Lima, Peru	*	*
11.05.35	Spartan Cruiser I	G-ABTY	24M	Commercial Air Hire	Crashed	English Channel	0	2
11.05.35	Junkers W.34	III	2763	Eurasia	Crashed	nr Canton, China	*	*
18.05.35	Tupolev ANT-20	SSSR-I20	*	Gor'ky Eskadril'ya	Mid-air collision with I-15 during aerobatics	nr Moscow, RSFSR, USSR	48(2)(1)	0
18.05.35	Ford 4-AT-E Tri-Motor	NC7864	4-AT-49	Knowles Flying Service	Crashed	Flint, MI, USA	3	9
24.05.35	Boeing 247	D-AGAR	1945	Deutsche Lufthansa	Destroyed when struck by taxiing Air France aircraft	Nuremburg, Germany	*	*
28.05.35	Stinson SM-6000B	NC10894	5050	Chicago & Southern Airlines	Crashed	Maywood, IL, USA	2	*
29.05.35	Boeing 221A Monomail	NC725W	1153	Inland Airlines	Crashed	North of Cheyenne, WY, USA	*	*
oo.06.35	Polikarpov P-5	SSSR-F48	*	Aerogeodeziya	Crashed	USSR	*	*
01.07.35	de Havilland Dragon 2	G-ADED	6098	Railway Air Services	Crashed on take-off	Ronaldsway, Isle of Man	*	*
03.07.35	Westland Wessex	G-ADEW	WA.1899	Cobham Air Routes	Crashed	English Channel	*	*
04.07.35	Junkers W.34	I	2738	Eurasia	Crashed	Lanchow, China	*	*
14.07.35	Fokker F.XXII	PH-AJQ	5358	KLM Royal Dutch Airlines	Crashed after engine fire	Amsterdam, Netherlands	6	13
16.07.35	de Havilland Dragon 1	G-ACGU	6034	Blackpool & West Coast Air Services	Crashed on take-off	Heston, Middx, UK	*	*
17.07.35	Douglas DC-2-115E	PH-AKM	1359	KLM Royal Dutch Airlines	Crashed	Bushire, Persia	*	*
18.07.35	de Havilland DH.89A Dragon Rapide	CF-AEO	6279	Canadian Airways	Crashed on take-off	Moncton, NB, Canada	*	*
20.07.35	Douglas DC-2-115E	PH-AKG	1335	KLM Royal Dutch Airlines	Crashed	Pian San Giacomo, Switzerland	*	*
23.07.35	de Havilland Dragon 2	G-ACMP	6063	Western Airways	Crashed on mudflats	Splott, Cardiff, UK	*	*
27.07.35	Curtiss Condor AT-32B	NC12393	45	American Airways	Overshot on landing in fog	Nashville, TN, USA	0	13
30.07.35	Boeing-Canada C204 Thunderbird	CF-ALD	4	Pioneer Airways	Crashed	Alta Lake, BC, Canada	*	*
oo.07.35	Fokker F.III	D-353	1551	Deutsche Lufthansa	Written off	Location Unknown	*	*
oo.07.35	Fokker F.III	D-378	1552	Deutsche Lufthansa	Written off	Location Unknown	*	*
oo.07.35	Fokker F.III	D-575	1563	Deutsche Lufthansa	Written off	Location Unknown	*	*
oo.07.35	Fokker F.III	D-OTIK	1564	Deutsche Lufthansa	Written off	Location Unknown	*	*
oo.07.35	Fokker F.III	D-701	1565	Deutsche Lufthansa	Written off	Location Unknown	*	*
02.08.35	de Havilland DH.60M Moth	LN-ABU	141	Wideroe	Crashed	Sandnes, Norway	0	2
03.08.35	Douglas DC-2-112	NC13722	1248	Transcontinental & Western Air	Crashed	Albuquerque, NM, USA	*	*
04.08.35	de Havilland DH.60X Moth	VP-KAC	1004	Wilson Airways	Crashed on landing	Nairobi, Kenya	0	2
13.08.35	Sikorsky S-38B	NC40V	514-4	CNAC	Destroyed by storm	Hankow, China	*	*
14.08.35	Stinson Model A	NC14599	9103	Delta Air Lines	Crashed after engine fell off	Gilmer, TX, USA	4	0
15.08.35	Lockheed Orion-Explorer	NR12283	195	W.Post	Crashed on take-off [Wiley Post & actor Will Rogers killed]	Walakpi, Alaska	2	0
25.08.35	de Havilland DH.83 Fox Moth	VO-ABC	4093	Imperial Airways	Destroyed in gale	St Johns, Newfoundland	*	*
oo.08.35	CMASA Wal	D-ARIP	088	DVS	Damaged in forced landing	Travemunde, Germany	*	*
oo.08.35	Douglas RD-4 Dolphin	V130	1273	United States Coast Guard	Crashed	USA	*	*
01.09.35	Boeing 247D	NC13314	1695	Western Air Express	Crashed into high tension cables after take-off	Los Angeles, CA, USA	3	0
06.09.35	GAL ST-12 Monospar	VH-UTZ	42	Australian Transcontinental Airways	Crashed	Australia	*	*
08.09.35	Ford 5-AT-C Tri-Motor	NC430H	5-AT-C90	Cia Nacional de Aviacion Guatemala	Crashed on take-off	Solola, Guatemala	*	*
27.09.35	Sikorsky S-38B	n/a	*	Lloyd Aereo Boliviano	Crashed [Marihui]	Location Unknown	*	*

Date	Type	Reg'n	C/n	Operator	Accident	Location	F	S
oo.09.35	Savoia-Marchetti S.55	SSSR-L840	*	Aeroflot	Crashed	USSR	*	*
01.10.35	de Havilland Dragon 1	VH-URO	6068	W.R.Carpenter Ltd	Crashed	Wau, New Guinea	*	*
02.10.35	de Havilland DH.86	VH-URT	2312	Holyman Airways	Crashed	Off Flinders Island, Vic, Australia	5	0
06.10.35	Douglas DC-2A-127	NC14285	1328	Standard Oil of California	Crashed	Great Salt Lake, UT, USA	*	*
07.10.35	Boeing 247	NC13317	1698	United Air Lines	Crashed into mountain	nr Cheyenne, WY, USA	10	0
09.10.35	Spartan Cruiser II	G-ACDX	004	British Airways	Damaged in forced landing	Gosport, Hants, UK	*	*
09.10.35	Junkers F.13	OH-ALI	2033	Aero O/Y	Crashed into sea in fog	Gulf of Finland	6	0
22.10.35	de Havilland DH.86	G-ADCM	2317	Imperial Airways	Crashed	Zwettl, Austria	0	*
23.10.35	de Havilland DH.61 Giant Moth	G-AUJC	333	W.R.Carpenter Ltd	Crashed	Salamaua, New Guinea	*	*
24.10.35	Stearman 4CM1	NC487W	4035	American Airlines	Crashed on emergency landing	Franconia, VA, USA	0	1
25.10.35	Boulton & Paul P.71A	G-ACOY	P.71A/2	Imperial Airways	Crashed	Brussels, Belgium	*	*
26.10.35	de Havilland Dragon 2	G-ADEE	6099	Railway Air Services	Crashed	Fairsnape Fell, Lancs, UK	*	*
30.10.35	Boeing 247	NC13323	1704	United Air Lines	Crashed into hill in bad weather	nr Cheyenne, WY, USA	4	0
02.11.35	Latecoere 28-1	F-AJIQ	906	Air France	Crashed	Off Nhambupe, Brazil	4	*
07.11.35	Savoia-Marchetti SM.73	OO-AGM	30002	Sabena	Crashed	Croydon, Surrey, UK	*	*
09.11.35	Short Kent	G-ABFB	S.759	Imperial Airways	Destroyed by fire	Brindisi, Italy	12	1
09.11.35	Ford Tri-Motor	*	*	TACA	Crashed	nr Juticalpa, Honduras	14	0
09.11.35	Lockheed Vega 5C	NC980Y	191	Braniff Airways	Crashed	Fort Worth, TX, USA	1	0
11.11.35	Latecoere 28-1	F-AJPB	926	Air France	Crashed in storm	Istres, France	3	0
23.11.35	de Havilland DH.66 Hercules	G-ABCP	347	Imperial Airways	Crashed in swamp	Entebbe, Uganda	0	*
23.11.35	Avia F.VIIb/3m	F-ALGT	18	CIDNA	Crashed	Vienna, Austria	*	*
27.11.35	Junkers W.34	V	2746	Eurasia	Crashed	nr Sian, China	*	*
29.11.35	Laville ZIG-1	n/a	–	Laville	Crashed after tail broke off	nr Moscow, RSFSR, USSR	5	*
04.12.35	Caudron 630 Simoun	F-ANRK	7013	Air Bleu	Crashed in poor weather	Parcay Meslay, France	1	1
08.12.35	de Havilland DH.50A	VH-UER	116	Rockhampton Aerial Services	Crashed	Off Bribie Island, Qld, Australia	*	*
10.12.35	Savoia-Marchetti SM.73	OO-AGN	30004	Sabena	Crashed	nr Tatsfield, Kent, UK	*	*
10.12.35	Potez 62	F-ANPH	3845/2	Air France	Crash landed in bad weather & caught fire	Auxerre, France	0	*
13.12.35	de Havilland DH.86	VH-USW	2315	Holyman Airways	Crash landed	Hunter Island, Vic, Australia	*	*
18.12.35	Koolhoven FK.43	PH-AJJ	4304	KLM Royal Dutch Airlines	Crashed	Amsterdam, Netherlands	*	*
20.12.35	Sikorsky S-42	NC824M	4202	Pan American Airways	Damaged on landing & sank	Port of Spain, Trinidad	3	22
24.12.35	Lockheed 8A Sirius	NC167W	167	Delta Air Lines	Crashed	Birmingham, AL, USA	*	*
25.12.35	Junkers Ju.160	XVI	4215	Eurasia	Crashed	nr Shanghai, China	*	*
31.12.35	Short Calcutta	G-AASJ	S752	Imperial Airways	Crashed out of fuel	Off Alexandria, Egypt	12	1
oo.12.35	CAMS 53	F-AJZX	26	Air France	Crashed on take-off	Ajaccio, Corsica, France	*	*
oo.oo.35	Avia F.VIIb/3m	OK-ABT	20	Ceskoslovenska Letecka Spolecnost	Written off	Czechoslovakia	*	*
oo.oo.35	Junkers F.24	D-USAH	840	Deutsche Lufthansa	Written off	Location Unknown	*	*
oo.oo.35	Junkers F.24	D-ULET	834	Deutsche Lufthansa	Written off	Location Unknown	*	*
oo.oo.35	Junkers F.24	D-UQAN	845	Deutsche Lufthansa	Written off	Location Unknown	*	*
oo.oo.35	Messerschmitt M.28	D-2059	527	Deutsche Lufthansa	Crashed	Germany	*	*
oo.oo.35	Boeing 221A Monomail	NC10225	1154	Inland Airlines	Crashed	Pueblo, CO, USA	*	*
oo.oo.35	Junkers F.13	D-OHIL	723	Deutsche Lufthansa	Crashed	Location Unknown	*	*
oo.oo.35	Putilov Stal'-2	SSSR-L1196	196	Aeroflot	Crashed	USSR	*	*
oo.oo.35	Junkers F.13	SSSR-L19	*	Transaviatsiya	Crashed	USSR	*	*
oo.oo.35	Junkers W.33	SSSR-L20	*	Transaviatsiya	Crashed	USSR	*	*
oo.oo.35	Junkers W.33	SSSR-L21	*	Transaviatsiya	Crashed	USSR	*	*
oo.oo.35	Junkers G-1	SSSR-L43	945	Transaviatsiya	Crashed	USSR	*	*
oo.oo.35	Polikarpov U-2	SSSR-L78	*	Transaviatsiya	Crashed	USSR	*	*
oo.oo.35	Junkers F.13	SSSR-L92	*	Transaviatsiya	Crashed	USSR	*	*
14.01.36	Douglas DC-2-120	NC14274	1307	American Airlines	Crashed	Goodwin, AR, USA	17	0
17.01.36	Junkers Ju.52/3mce	n/a	4018	Lloyd Aereo Boliviano	Crashed [Chorolque]	nr Cochabamba, Bolivia	13	*
21.01.36	CAMS 53-1	F-AJIR	19	Air France	Crashed	Off Ajaccio, Corsica, France	6	0
22.01.36	de Havilland Dragon 1	G-ACCR	6011	Commercial Air Hire	Crashed	English Channel	*	*
29.01.36	Vultee V-1A	NC13767	05	American Airlines	Crash landed in snowstorm	nr Denton, TX, USA	1	5
05.02.36	Junkers Ju.52/3mge	PP-CAU	2720	Cruzeiro	Crashed	Rio de Janeiro, Brazil	*	*

Date	Type	Reg'n	C/n	Operator	Accident	Location	F	S
06.02.36	Stinson Model U	NC12119	9007	American Airlines	Crashed on take-off	Albany, NY, USA	0	*
10.02.36	Latecoere 301	F-AOIK	01/1016	Air France	Crashed	Atlantic Ocean	*	*
14.02.36	Sikorsky S-41	n/a	*	SCADTA	Crashed [Alfonso Lopez]	Barranquilla, Colombia	*	*
15.02.36	Dornier Do J-IIf Bos Wal	D-ADYS	299	Deutsche Lufthansa	Crashed	South Atlantic	4	*
17.02.36	Lockheed Vega 1	NC7428	016	United Air Services	Crashed	Nogales, Mexico	*	*
28.02.36	Douglas DC-2-115B	HB-ITI	1321	Swissair	Crashed	Dubendorf, Switzerland	*	*
05.03.36	Ford 5-AT-D Tri-Motor	n/a	5-AT-115	CNAC	Crashed in snow	Yunnan, China	0	6
07.03.36	de Havilland DH.89 Dragon Rapide	PK-AKW	6294	KNILM	Written off	New Guinea	*	*
14.03.36	Fairchild FC.2	*	*	LAN-Chile	Crashed	Location Unknown	*	*
16.03.36	Junkers Ju.52/3m	OE-LAL	5289	Olag	Crashed	Location Unknown	*	*
17.03.36	Fokker F.VIIa	n/a	*	International Red Cross	Destroyed by bombing [Red Cross Fokker]	Korem, Abyssinia	*	*
17.03.36	Fokker F.VIIa	n/a	*	Abyssinian Government	Destroyed by bombing [Government Fokker]	Korem, Abyssinia	*	*
23.03.36	Spartan Cruiser II	G-ACVT	011	British Airways	Crashed	Ronaldsway, Isle of Man	*	*
26.03.36	Ford 5-AT-B Tri-Motor	X-ABCO	5-AT-012	Mexicana	Caught fire & crashed	Amemeca, Mexico	14	0
26.03.36	de Havilland Dragon 1	G-ACAP	6002	Commercial Air Hire	Crashed	Lyndhurst, Hants, UK	*	*
oo.03.36	Ford 5-AT Tri-Motor	*	*	CNAC	Caught fire & destroyed after landing	Nanking, China	0	*
01.04.36	Stinson Model A	NC15152	9112	American Airlines	Crashed in flames	Pavilion, NY, USA	2	0
07.04.36	Douglas DC-2-112	NC13721	1247	Transcontinental & Western Air	Crashed	Uniontown, PA, USA	13	2
07.04.36	Waco RNF	LN-BAN	3434	Wideroe	Crashed on take-off	Nystuen, Norway	*	*
08.04.36	Stinson SM-6000B	NC976W	5007	Central Vermont Airways	Crashed	Burlington, VT, USA	*	*
15.04.36	OFM F.VII/3m	I-AAXZ	359	Avio Linee Italiane	Crashed	nr Turin, Italy	7	*
21.04.36	Douglas DC-2-115K	OK-AIA	1581	Ceskoslovenska Letecka Spolecnost	Crashed	Elburg, Netherlands	*	*
21.04.36	Fokker F.VIIb/3m	OO-AIF	*	Sabena	Crashed	Senlis, France	2	*
24.04.36	Junkers Ju.52/3m	D-ASOR	5044	Deutsche Lufthansa	Written off	Lechfeld, Germany	*	*
28.04.36	Fokker F.VIIa	OO-ADO	4983	Societe Aera	Destroyed	Location Unknown	*	*
30.04.36	Clark GA-43	HB-ITU	2204	Swissair	Crashed on overshoot in bad weather	Basle, Switzerland	2	0
03.05.36	Polikarpov P-5	SSSR-N43	*	Polyarnaya Aviatsiya	Crashed	USSR	*	*
14.05.36	Saro Windhover	VH-UPB	A.21/1	Matthews Aviation	Washed onto rocks after forced landing previous day	Off King Island, Tas, Australia	*	*
16.05.36	de Havilland DH.89 Dragon Rapide	G-ADBX	6289	British Airways	Crashed into hangar on landing	Ronaldsway, Isle of Man	*	*
16.05.36	GAL ST-4 Monospar II	G-ADLM	30	Commercial Air Hire	Crashed on take-off	Croydon, Surrey, UK	*	*
16.05.36	Dornier Merkur	D-OKES	752	Deruluft	Crashed	USSR	*	*
23.05.36	de Havilland Canada Giant Moth	CF-OAK	DHC.141	Ontario Provincial Govt Air Service	Sank after striking submerged rock on landing	Gander Lake, ON, Canada	*	*
26.05.36	Stinson Model A	NC14141	9100	American Airlines	Caught fire & force-landed	Chicago, IL, USA	0	3
30.05.36	Westland Wessex	G-ABVB	WA.2156	Portsmouth, Southsea & IOW Aviation	Damaged beyond repair	Ryde, IOW, Hants, UK	*	*
31.05.36	Douglas DC-2-172	NC14979	1409	Transcontinental & Western Air	Crashed	Chicago, IL, USA	*	*
oo.05.36	Airspeed Envoy I	G-ACVH	28	Airspeed	Force-landed	Langstone Harbour, Hants, UK	*	*
oo.05.36	Fokker F.VIIb/3m	n/a	5225	Abyssinian Royal Flight	Destroyed by fire [The Emperor's Fokker]	nr Addis Ababa, Abyssinia	*	*
oo.05.36	GAL ST-4 Monospar II	G-ADIK	27	Inner Circle Air Line	Crashed	United Kingdom	*	*
06.06.36	PZL F.VIIb/3m	SP-AOF	8/6	LOT Polish Airlines	Written off	Location Unknown	*	*
09.06.36	Fokker F.XXII	SE-ABA	5359	AB Aerotransport	Crashed on take-off	Malmo, Sweden	1	12
10.06.36	Fokker-Grulich F.II	D-OVYF	1582	Deutsche Lufthansa	Crashed	Germany	*	*
12.06.36	Vultee V-1AD	NC14249	12A	United Gas Public Service	Crashed	Ferris, TX, USA	*	*
16.06.36	Junkers Ju.52/3m	LN-DAE	4077	DNL	Crashed into mountain	Lihesten Mt, Norway	7	0
23.06.36	Latecoere 28.0	R293	929	Aeroposta Argentina	Crashed	nr Comodoro Rivadavia, Argentina	*	*
24.06.36	Fokker-Grulich F.II	D-OJIP	1593	Deutsche Lufthansa	Crashed	Germany	*	*
09.07.36	Curtiss Condor	NC728K	66	Chamberlin Flying Services	Destroyed by fire	Terre Haute, IN, USA	0	*
15.07.36	Fokker F.VIIb	PH-AEZ	5122	KLM Royal Dutch Airlines	Damaged beyond repair by gale	Haamstede, Netherlands	*	*
26.07.36	Short Scion 2	G-ADDT	S.790	Pobjoy Airmotors & Aircraft	Crashed	Porthcawl, Glam, UK	*	*
29.07.36	Curtiss Condor	*	38	LAN-Chile	Crashed	Location Unknown	*	*
31.07.36	Saro Cloud	G-ABXW	A.19/4	Guernsey Airways	Crashed	Off Jersey, Channel Islands	10	0
oo.07.36	GVF PS-4	SSSR-L416	*	Aeroflot	Crashed	USSR	*	*
02.08.36	Wibault 280T	F-ANBL	*	Air France	Crashed	nr Mazamet, France	3	*
03.08.36	Lockheed Orion 9	XA-BAY	169	Mexicana	Crashed	Pico de Orizaba, Mexico	1	*
05.08.36	Lockheed 10B Electra	NC16022	1057	Chicago & Southern Airlines	Crashed	St Louis, MI, USA	*	*

Date	Type	Reg'n	C/n	Operator	Accident	Location	F	S
06.08.36	Sikorsky S-38B	C-52	*	SCADTA	Crashed	Location Unknown	*	*
06.08.36	Junkers F.13	C-40	*	SCADTA	Crashed	Choco, Colombia	2	*
08.08.36	Ford 4-AT-B Tri-Motor	NC5811	4-AT-27	E.Saltzgaber	Crashed	Hundred, WV, USA	*	*
10.08.36	Vickers Vellox	G-ABKY	1	Imperial Airways	Crashed on take-off at night	Croydon, Surrey, UK	*	*
12.08.36	de Havilland DH.86	G-ADEB	2324	British Airways	Crashed	Altenkirchen, Germany	2	*
15.08.36	Fokker F.XII	G-ADZI	5285	British Airways	Crash landed	Biarritz, France	*	*
16.08.36	Fokker F.XII	G-ADZK	5301	British Airways	Damaged on landing in fog	La Rochelle, France	*	*
22.08.36	Short Kent	G-ABFA	S.758	Imperial Airways	Sank on landing	Mirabella, Crete, Greece	2	9
27.08.36	Stinson Model A	NC15134	9111	Delta Air Lines	Crashed	Atlanta, GA, USA	*	*
28.08.36	Airspeed Envoy I	*	36	L'Office General de l'Air	Shot down by Spanish forces	Ales, France	*	*
oo.08.36	de Havilland DH.89 Dragon Rapide	G-ADNG	6297	Iraq Petroleum Transport Co	Crashed	Location Unknown	*	*
15.09.36	de Havilland DH.86A	G-ADYF	2347	British Airways	Crashed on take-off at night	Croydon, Surrey, UK	*	*
18.09.36	Type Unknown	*	*	Air France	Crashed in storm	Spain	*	*
25.09.36	Boulton & Paul P.71A	G-ACOX	P.71/1	Imperial Airways	Crashed at sea	English Channel	2	0
27.09.36	Cant Z.506	I-RODI	*	Ala Littoria	Damaged by fire & sank	Off Benghazi, Libya	*	*
28.09.36	Lockheed Vega 5B	NC176W	129	Varney Air Transport	Crashed in snowstorm	nr Walsenberg, CO, USA	3	0
29.09.36	Armstrong Whitworth Atalanta	G-ABTK	AW.744	Imperial Airways	Destroyed in hangar fire	Delhi, India	0	*
29.09.36	Lockheed Vega 5C	NC959Y	170	Blue Bird Air Service	Crashed	Napierville, IL, USA	4	0
01.10.36	Airspeed Ferry	VT-AFO	5	Himalayan Airways	Set on fire by rioters	Hardwar, India	0	0
01.10.36	Airspeed Envoy III	G-AENA	60	M.H.Findlay & K.H.F.Waller	Crashed	Abercorn, Northern Rhodesia	*	*
06.10.36	Lockheed Orion 9	XA-BDH	174	Mexicana	Crashed	Poblado Francisco Rueda, Mexico	1	*
07.10.36	GAL Monospar ST-18 Croydon	G-AECB	501	C.R.Anson	Crashed when off course	Seringapatam Reef, Australia	*	*
09.10.36	Blackburn B.2	G-ABWI	4700/1	North Sea Aerial & General Transport	Crashed	nr Selby, Yorks, UK	1	0
11.10.36	Douglas DC-2-118B	NC14273	1306	Panagra	Crashed	Guatemala City, Guatemala	*	*
24.10.36	Lockheed Orion 9D	NC13749	207	Wyoming Air Service	Crashed	Buffalo, WY, USA	*	*
oo.10.36	Fokker F.VIIb/3m	I-UGRI	5209	Ala Littoria	Destroyed by fire	Italy	*	*
oo.10.36	Fokker F.III	D-ORIP	1556	Deutsche Lufthansa	Written off	Location Unknown	*	*
oo.10.36	Fokker F.III	D-OLYK	1566	Deutsche Lufthansa	Written off	Location Unknown	*	*
01.11.36	Junkers Ju.52/3m	D-APOO	5506	Deutsche Lufthansa	Crashed	nr Tabarz, Germany	11	4
06.11.36	Tupolev ANT-9	URSS-D311	160	Deruluft	Crashed	nr Moscow, RSFSR, USSR	9	5
17.11.36	Junkers Ju.52/3m	D-ASU	5498	Deutsche Lufthansa	Crashed	Halle, Germany	*	*
19.11.36	Fokker F.XII	G-AEOT	5300	British Airways	Crashed	Tilgate, Surrey, UK	2	2
20.11.36	Spartan Cruiser III	G-ADEM	103	Northern & Scottish Airways	Crashed	Blackpool, Lancs, UK	*	*
21.11.36	Avro Ten	VH-UMG	230	Transcontinental Airways	Crashed in high winds	Mascot, NSW, Australia	0	7
23.11.36	Boeing 247D	NC13319	1700	United Air Lines	Crashed	nr Newark, NJ, USA	*	*
28.11.36	Junkers Ju.52/3m	D-ATAK	5169	Deutsche Lufthansa	Crashed	nr Hanover, Germany	*	*
oo.11.36	de Havilland DH.89 Dragon Rapide	G-ADBU	6280	Northern & Scottish Airways	Damaged beyond repair	Location Unknown	*	*
01.12.36	Lockheed 10A Electra	SP-AYB	1046	LOT Polish Airlines	Crashed	Athens, Greece	*	*
04.12.36	Junkers Ju.52/3m	D-ASIH	5078	Deutsche Lufthansa	Crashed into mountain during gale	Grand Bornaud, France	6	*
05.12.36	Douglas RD-2 Dolphin	V111	1122	United States Coast Guard	Crashed	Virginia, USA	1	*
07.12.36	Latecoere 300	F-AKGF	1	Air France	Crashed [Aviator Jean Mermoz killed]	Off Dakar, French West Africa	5	0
08.12.36	Lockheed Orion 9E	NC12278	193	R.Blair	Damaged beyond repair	Jackson, OH, USA	*	*
09.12.36	Douglas DC-2-115E	PH-AKL	1358	KLM Royal Dutch Airlines	Crashed into houses on t/o in fog [Juan de la Cierva killed]	Croydon, Surrey, UK	14	2
15.12.36	Boeing 247	NC13370	1957	Western Air Express	Crashed into mountain	Lone Peak, UT, USA	10	0
18.12.36	Lockheed 10A Electra	NC14935	1024	Northwest Airlines	Crashed into mountain	Kellogg, ID, USA	2	0
19.12.36	Douglas DC-2-112	NC13732	1258	Eastern Air Lines	Crashed due to icing	Fort Jervis, NY, USA	14	0
23.12.36	Lockheed 10A Electra	NC14905	1018	Braniff Airways	Crashed	nr Dallas, TX, USA	6	0
25.12.36	Douglas DC-2-118B	NC14269	1302	CNAC	Crashed	Nanking, China	*	*
27.12.36	Boeing 247D	NC13355	1737	United Air Lines	Crashed on approach	Newhall, CA, USA	12	0
28.12.36	Short Calcutta	G-EBVG	S712	Imperial Airways	Destroyed by storm	Mirabella, Crete, Greece	0	*
28.12.36	Lockheed 10A Electra	SP-AYA	1045	LOT Polish Airlines	Crashed due to icing	Susiec, Poland	*	*
30.12.36	de Havilland DH.89 Dragon Rapide	G-AEGS	6335	Iraq Petroleum Transport Co	Crashed	Location Unknown	*	*
oo.oo.36	Junkers G.38	D-AZUR	3301	Deutsche Lufthansa	Crashed on take-off	Dessau, Germany	*	*
oo.oo.36	Liore et Olivier H.242	F-ANQG	10	Air France	Crashed at sea	Off Algeria	*	*

Date	Type	Reg'n	C/n	Operator	Accident	Location	F	S
00.00.36	Westland Wessex	G-ABEG	WA.1901	Imperial Airways	Damaged beyond repair	Chirindu, Northern Rhodesia	*	*
00.00.36	Messerschmitt M.20b	D-UNAH	540	Deutsche Lufthansa	Crashed	Germany	*	*
00.00.36	Focke-Wulf A.17 Mowe	D-1430	049	Deutsche Lufthansa	Destroyed	Location Unknown	*	*
00.00.36	Junkers F.13	D-OBAZ	738	Deutsche Lufthansa	Crashed	Location Unknown	*	*
00.00.36	Fairchild Pilgrim 100A	NC737N	6701	Pan American Airways	Written off	Location Unknown	*	*
00.00.36	Fairchild Pilgrim 100A	NC742N	6706	Pan American Airways	Written off	Location Unknown	*	*
12.01.37	Boeing 247	NC13315	1696	Western Air Express	Crashed into mountain	nr Newhall, CA, USA	5	8
15.01.37	Lockheed Vega 5B	NR105N	117	J.Costa	Crashed	Conceicao do Serro, Brazil	0	*
20.01.37	Lockheed Vega 5	NC624E	053	Hanford Airlines	Destroyed in hangar fire	Sioux City, IA, USA	*	*
20.01.37	Ford 5-AT-C Tri-Motor	NC422H	5-AT-096	DePonti Aviation	Destroyed in hangar fire	Sioux City, IA, USA	*	*
22.01.37	Airspeed Envoy I	G-ADBZ	35	Air Dispatch	Crashed	Titsey Hill, Surrey, UK	2	0
02.02.37	de Havilland DH.90 Dragonfly	G-AEHC	7514	London Express Newspapers	Crashed	Newton Stewart, Wigtown, UK	*	*
08.02.37	Sikorsky S-43	PP-PAR	4307	Panair do Brasil	Crashed	Vitoria, Brazil	*	*
09.02.37	Douglas DC-3	NC16073	1913	United Air Lines	Crashed in bay	San Francisco, CA, USA	11	0
12.02.37	Simmonds Spartan	ZK-AAY	4	New Zealand Airways	Crashed	Staveley, New Zealand	*	*
18.02.37	Douglas DC-2-112	NC13734	1260	Eastern Air Lines	Crashed	Atlanta, GA, USA	*	*
19.02.37	Stinson Model A	VH-UHH	9126	Airlines of Australia	Crashed in gale [Found 01.03.37]	McPherson Ranges, Qld, Australia	5	2
20.02.37	Sabca S.73	OO-AGR	*	Sabena	Crashed	Oran, Algeria	*	*
27.02.37	Fairchild FC.2	*	*	LAN-Chile	Crashed	Location Unknown	*	*
12.03.37	Heinkel He.111V2	D-ALIX	715	Deutsche Lufthansa	Crashed in swamp	nr Bathurst, Gambia	4	0
13.03.37	Junkers W.33	CB-20	*	Lloyd Aereo Boliviano	Crashed	Cuybaja, Bolivia	*	*
15.03.37	de Havilland DH.86	G-ACVZ	2303	Railway Air Services	Crashed	nr Elsdorf, Germany	*	*
21.03.37	Fokker Super Universal	G-CAWB	815	Operator Unknown	Damaged on landing	Takla, Canada	*	*
24.03.37	Short S.23	G-ADVA	S.818	Imperial Airways	Crashed in snowstorm	nr Ouroux, France	5	*
25.03.37	Douglas DC-2-112	NC13730	1256	Transcontinental & Western Air	Crashed due to icing	Clifton, PA, USA	13	0
27.03.37	Potez 56	5	*	LAN-Chile	Crashed	Palca, Peru	*	*
28.03.37	Stinson Model A	VH-UGG	9122	Airlines of Australia	Crashed into tree on take-off	Archerfield, Qld, Australia	2	0
03.04.37	Douglas DC-3	PH-ALP	1938	KLM Royal Dutch Airlines	Crashed before delivery	McCary, AZ, USA	*	*
14.04.37	de Havilland Dragon 1	VP-KBG	6079	Wilson Airways	Crashed on take-off	Nairobi, Kenya	*	*
23.04.37	Fairchild 82B	*	*	Linea Aeropostal Venezolana	Crashed	Cuyuni River, Venezuela	*	*
27.04.37	Lockheed Vega DL-1B	NC483M	136	Varney Air Transport	Crashed	El Paso, TX, USA	0	*
00.04.37	Douglas DC-2-115M	EC-BFF	1527	LAPE	Destroyed in air raid	Santander, Spain	*	*
06.05.37	Zeppelin LZ.129	D-LZ219	LZ129	Deutsche Zeppelin-Reederei	Caught fire & crashed while mooring	Lakehurst, NJ, USA	35	62
12.05.37	de Havilland DH.89 Dragon Rapide	VH-UVS	6265	Airlines of Australia	Caught fire on ground	Sydney, NSW, Australia	0	1
15.05.37	Lockheed Vega 1	NR7426	014	F.O.Y.Fetterman	Crashed	Roosevelt Field, NY, USA	*	*
15.05.37	Lockheed Vega 1	XA-BHG	009	VAT Inc	Crashed	El Paso, TX, USA	0	*
19.05.37	Liore et Olivier H.47	n/a	*	Liore et Olivier	Crashed due to structural failure on take-off	Off Antibes, France	5	5
20.05.37	Heinkel He.70	D-UXUV	*	Deutsche Lufthansa	Crashed on take-off	Stuttgart, Germany	4	0
26.05.37	Lockheed Vega 1	NC7427	015	J.Lewis	Crashed	Santa Maria, CA, USA	*	*
29.05.37	Ford 4-AT-B Tri-Motor	NC8404	4-AT-66	O.K.Southwick	Crashed	Belleville, IL, USA	*	*
29.05.37	Airspeed Courier	G-ACSZ	19	North Eastern Airways	Crashed	Doncaster, UK	*	*
31.05.37	Handley Page HP.42E	G-AAXE	HP.42/7	Imperial Airways	Destroyed in hangar fire	Karachi, India	0	*
02.06.37	Sikorsky S-43	*	4319	LAN-Chile	Crashed	Location Unknown	*	*
16.06.37	Junkers Ju.52/3m	ZS-AKY	*	South African Airways	Crashed	Rand Airport, South Africa	*	*
19.06.37	Fairchild FC.2	G-CARA	093	Operator Unknown	Crashed	Lac La Ronge, Canada	*	*
01.07.37	Lockheed 10E Electra	NR16020	1055	Purdue Research Foundation	Crashed [Amelia Earhart killed]	Off Lae, New Guinea	2	0
02.07.37	Fokker F.VIIb/3m	F-AJBJ	5135	Air France	Crashed	Cannes, France	*	*
03.07.37	de Havilland Dragon 2	G-ADFI	6100	Aberdeen Airways	Crashed	Thurso, Caithness, UK	*	*
23.07.37	Type Unknown	*	*	Cape Cod Airlines	Crashed into ferry on landing	Egartown, MA, USA	0	5
27.07.37	Fokker F.VIIa	PH-EHE	4984	C.E.Jacobs	Destroyed by fire	Toulon, France	*	*
28.07.37	Douglas DC-2-115L	PH-ALF	1585	KLM Royal Dutch Airlines	Crashed after in-flight fire	Hal, Belgium	15	0
29.07.37	Junkers Ju.52/3m	ZS-AJE	*	South African Airways	Crashed on delivery flight	Juha, South Africa	*	*
01.08.37	Junkers Ju.52/3m	XVIII	5294	Eurasia	Crashed	Kunming, China	*	*

Date	Type	Reg'n	C/n	Operator	Accident	Location	F	S
02.08.37	Sikorsky S-43	NC15065	4305	Panagra	Crashed	Coco Solo, Panama Canal Zone	*	*
02.08.37	Savoia-Marchetti SM.73	I-SUSA	30014	Ala Littoria	Crashed	Wadi Halfa, Egypt	9	0
05.08.37	Type Unknown	*	*	Japan Air Transport	Crashed into building on take-off	Haneda, Japan	1	*
06.08.37	Douglas DC-2-152	URSS-M25	1413	Aeroflot	Crashed	nr Bistrita, Romania	*	*
08.08.37	Type Unknown	*	*	Air Commerciale	Crashed after in-flight fire [Farman ?]	Santa Cruz Bay, Portugal	5	0
10.08.37	Douglas DC-2-112	NC13739	1289	Eastern Air Lines	Crashed after striking pylon on landing at night	Daytona Beach, FL, USA	3	*
12.08.37	Tupolev DB-A	URSS-N209	*	GU-SMA	Crashed on trans-polar flight	Siberia, RSFSR, USSR	6	0
13.08.37	Boeing 247	D-AKIN	1944	Deutsche Lufthansa	Crashed	Hanover, Germany	*	*
15.08.37	Vultee V-1A	*	*	Operator Unknown	Crashed on take-off on delivery flight to Spain	Le Bourget, France	*	*
17.08.37	de Havilland DH.90 Dragonfly	G-AEEK	7518	Sir William Firth	Crashed	Beeding, Sussex, UK	0	1
21.08.37	Ford 5-AT-C Tri-Motor	NR9648	5-AT-057	Republic Oil Co	Overturned in forced landing	Anchorage, Alaska	0	3
23.08.37	Douglas DC-2-118A	NC14298	1370	Panagra	Crashed	nr San Luis, Argentina	3	*
oo.08.37	Savoia Marchetti S.66	I-NAVE	15014	Ala Littoria	Damaged on landing at night	Malta	*	*
oo.08.37	Junkers W.33	VIII	2543	Eurasia	Destroyed in Japanese air-raid	Shanghai, China	*	*
oo.08.37	Junkers F.13	IV	*	Eurasia	Bombed by Japanese forces	Shanghai, China	*	*
oo.08.37	Dornier Wal	SSSR-N2	122	Polyarnaya Aviatsiya	Destroyed	USSR	*	*
15.09.37	Faucett F.19	OA-BBR	09	Faucett	Crashed	nr Atocongo, Peru	*	*
20.09.37	Koolhoven FK.50	HB-AMO	5002	Alpar	Crashed on take-off in fog	nr Basle, Switzerland	3	*
28.09.37	Ford 5-AT-B Tri-Motor	LG-AAE	5-AT-028	TACA	Crashed	nr Puerto Cabezas, Nicaragua	*	*
30.09.37	Savoia-Marchetti S.55P	NC20K	10517	Alaska Airways	Damaged beyond repair while moored	Juneau, Alaska	0	*
oo.09.37	Vultee V-1A	*	*	Operator Unknown	Damaged in belly landing	Beauvistille, France	*	*
01.10.37	Short S.23	G-ADVC	S.820	Imperial Airways	Crashed on landing	Athens, Greece	3	*
03.10.37	Ford Tri-Motor	*	*	TACA	Crashed	nr Puerto Cabezas, Nicaragua	*	*
06.10.37	Douglas DC-3	PH-ALS	1940	KLM Royal Dutch Airlines	Crashed	Palembang, Dutch East Indies	*	*
13.10.37	Potez 56	*	*	LAN-Chile	Crashed	Chile	*	*
16.10.37	Junkers W.34f	ZS-AEC	2736	South African Airways	Crashed	George, South Africa	*	*
17.10.37	Douglas DC-3	NC16074	1914	United Air Lines	Crashed in bad weather	Haydens Peak, WY, USA	19	0
27.10.37	Dewoitine D.333	F-ANCA	01	Air France	Crashed	nr Mogador, Morocco	7	*
27.10.37	Mitsubishi Hina-Zuru	*	*	Mitsubishi Nainenki Seizo	Crashed on take-off	Kagamigahara, Japan	*	*
11.11.37	Lockheed 10A Electra	SP-AYD	1048	LOT Polish Airlines	Crashed	Piaseczno, Poland	*	*
16.11.37	Junkers Ju.52/3m	OO-AUB	5827	Sabena	Crashed [Grand Duke & Duchess of Hess killed]	Ostende, Belgium	11	0
16.11.37	Junkers Ju.52/3m	OO-AGW	5672	Sabena	Crashed	Location Unknown	*	*
23.11.37	Douglas DC-2-115D	SP-ASJ	1318	LOT Polish Airlines	Crashed	Rhodope Mts, Bulgaria	*	*
25.11.37	de Havilland DH.90 Dragonfly	R326	7537	Shell Mex Argentina	Destroyed in hangar fire	San Fernando, Argentina	*	*
26.11.37	Junkers Ju.52/3m	D-AGAV	4023	Deutsche Lufthansa	Crashed into hangar on take-off	Croydon, Surrey, UK	3	0
01.12.37	Junkers W.34ho	SE-AEF	2828	Aero O/Y	Crash landed on frozen lake	Lake Fjaturen, Sweden	2	0
05.12.37	Short S.23	G-ADUZ	S.817	Imperial Airways	Crashed on take-off	Brindisi, Italy	2	*
08.12.37	Potez 621	F-AOTZ	4213	Air France	Crashed in bad weather	nr Saillans, France	2	5
13.12.37	Lockheed 10A Electra	G-AEPP	1082	British Airways	Crashed into petrol pump on landing	Croydon, Surrey, UK	0	*
15.12.37	Junkers Ju.52/3mce	CB-18	4009	Lloyd Aereo Boliviano	Crashed	Bolivia	*	*
17.12.37	Short Scion 2	G-AEOY	S.789	Arabian Airways	Crashed	Location Unknown	*	*
17.12.37	Koolhoven FK.43	PH-AKC	4308	KLM Royal Dutch Airlines	Crashed	Eelde, Netherlands	*	*
20.12.37	Fairchild FC.2	G-CANB	062	Operator Unknown	Damaged beyond repair	Fish Lake, Canada	*	*
24.12.37	Wibault 280T	F-AMYD	*	Air France	Crashed	Kasperske Hory, Czechoslovakia	3	*
oo.oo.37	Airspeed Envoy III	F-APPQ	69	Air Pyrenees	Damaged in forced landing after attack by Spanish fighters	Location Unknown	0	*
oo.oo.37	Messerschmitt M.20b	D-UXYN	545	Deutsche Lufthansa	Crashed	Germany	*	*
oo.oo.37	Junkers A 20	D-IBUX	353	Deutsche Lufthansa	Crashed	Location Unknown	*	*
01.01.38	Northrop Delta 1D-3	NC14265	40	W.H.Danforth	Destroyed in hangar fire	Miami, FL, USA	*	*
04.01.38	Junkers Ju.52/3m	D-ABUR	5777	Deutsche Lufthansa	Crashed in snowstorm on approach	Frankfurt, Germany	*	*
08.01.38	Lockheed Vega 5B	XA-BHJ	061	M.Hanratty	Crashed	Chicago, IL, USA	*	*
11.01.38	Sikorsky S-42	NC16734	4207	Pan American Airways	Crashed due to fuel explosion	Pago Pago, US Samoa	*	*
12.01.38	PZL F.VIIb/3m	SP-AOE	6/5	LOT Polish Airlines	Damaged beyond repair	Helsinki, Finland	*	*
12.01.38	Stinson SR-9EM Reliant	CF-BEI	5212-S	General Airways	Crashed after wing failure	North Pine, ON, Canada	1	0
14.01.38	Spartan Cruiser III	G-ACYK	101	Northern & Scottish Airways	Crash landed	Largs, Ayrshire, UK	*	*

Date	Type	Reg'n	C/n	Operator	Accident	Location	F	S
22.01.38	Caudron 630 Simoun	F-ANRI	7011/2	Air Bleu	Overturned on landing in fog	Le Bourget, France	0	3
04.02.38	Fokker F.VIIb/3m	PK-AFB	5070	KNILM	Written off	Location Unknown	*	*
05.02.38	V6 Airship	SSSR-V6	–	TsAGI	Crashed	Kandalaksha, RSFSR, USSR	13	6
06.02.38	Junkers Ju.90V1	D-AALU	4913	Junkers Flugzeug und Motorenwerke	Crashed on test flight	Germany	*	*
09.02.38	Liore et Olivier H.242	F-ANPB	05	Air France	Crashed on take-off	Etang de Berre, France	*	*
09.02.38	Lockheed 10E Electra	XA-BAS	1043	Mexicana	Crashed on test flight	Guadalupe, Mexico	2	0
11.02.38	Fokker Super Universal	*	831	Nippon Air Transport	Crashed on landing	Kochi, Japan	*	*
22.02.38	Junkers Ju.52/3m	D-APAR	4040	Deutsche Lufthansa	Crashed	nr Pontoise, France	*	*
24.02.38	Vultee V-1	NC14250	14	Examiner Printing Co	Crashed	San Simeon, CA, USA	*	*
26.02.38	de Havilland Dragon 2	VH-UZX	6084	Operator Unknown	Crashed	Beddington, Surrey, UK	*	*
oo.02.38	Fokker F.XX	EC-45-E	5347	LAPE	Crashed	Prat de Llobregat, Spain	*	*
01.03.38	Douglas DC-2-112	NC13789	1299	Transcontinental & Western Air	Crashed into mountain [found 12.06.38]	nr Wawona, CA, USA	9	0
04.03.38	Junkers W.34	D-OJIL	489	SEDTA	Crashed	Location Unknown	*	*
07.03.38	Potez 62	F-ANQR	4031/12	Air France	Crashed	Datia, India	7	0
23.03.38	Dewoitine D.338	F-AQBB	02	Air France	Crashed into mountain	Corsavy, France	7	0
28.03.38	Type Unknown	*	*	Japan Air Transport	Crashed in forced landing	Sammai-Cho, Japan	0	1
01.04.38	Renard R35	OO-ARM	*	Constructions Aeronautiques Renard	Crashed on first flight	Belgium	*	*
14.04.38	Douglas DC-3	PH-ARY	2021	KLM Royal Dutch Airlines	Crashed	Amsterdam, Netherlands	*	*
25.04.38	Sikorsky S-43	PP-PBL	4322	Panair do Brasil	Crashed	Morant Point, Jamaica	*	*
25.04.38	de Havilland Dragon 1	G-ACHX	6036	Wrightways	Crashed	Purley, Surrey, UK	*	*
30.04.38	Junkers G.24	I-BAUS	924	Ala Littoria	Crashed into mountain	nr Formia, Italy	19	0
oo.04.38	Grumman G-21A Goose	NC16917	1012	G.A.Wood	Destroyed by fire	Miami, FL, USA	*	*
05.05.38	Lockheed Vega 5B	XA-BFR	124	Lineas Aereas Mineras	Crashed	Mexico City, Mexico	1	5
09.05.38	de Havilland DH.61 Giant Moth	G-AUJB	334	Stephens Aviation	Crashed	Mubo, New Guinea	*	*
10.05.38	Lockheed 10A Electra	ZK-AFC	1092	Union Airways of New Zealand	Crashed on take-off due to engine failure	Mangere, New Zealand	2	0
10.05.38	Ford Tri-Motor	*	*	LAN-Chile	Crashed	Location Unknown	*	*
16.05.38	Lockheed 14-H2 Super Electra	NC17394	1439	Northwest Airlines	Crashed on landing	nr Saugus, CA, USA	*	*
22.05.38	Junkers Ju.52/3mge	PP-CBC	5453	Cruzeiro	Crashed	Sao Paulo, Brazil	6	11
24.05.38	Douglas DST	NC18108	1956	United Air Lines	Crash landed after engine fire	Cleveland, OH, USA	10	0
27.05.38	Heinkel He.116V2	D-ATIO	*	Deutsche Lufthansa	Crashed	nr Langeoog	3	*
27.05.38	Fairchild 51A	CF-AUX	769	Ginger Coote Airways	Crashed into hill [Found 09.03.39]	Alberno Canal, BC, Canada	1	0
02.06.38	Sabca F.VIIb/3m	OO-AIL	*	Sabena	Crashed	Lympne, Kent, UK	*	*
08.06.38	de Havilland DH.85 Leopard Moth	VP-KBE	7055	Wilson Airways	Crashed	nr Singida, Tanganyika	3	0
13.06.38	de Havilland Dragon 2	F-AMUZ	6064	Air Afrique	Crashed in fog	El Aria, Algeria	0	6
22.06.38	de Havilland Dragon 1	SU-ABJ	6051	Misrair	Destroyed by fire	Almaza, Egypt	*	*
22.06.38	Gasuden TR-2	*	*	Gasuden	Crashed on landing	Japan	*	*
25.06.38	de Havilland Dragon 2	G-ADCR	6094	Blackpool & West Coast Air Services	Crashed	Location Unknown	*	*
26.06.38	Junkers Ju.52/3m	OA-HHB	5043	Deutsche Lufthansa Sucursal	Crashed	Chillingua, Peru	0	*
01.07.38	GAL ST-12 Monospar	VH-UTK	38	Airlines of Australia	Caught fire on ground	Mackay, Qld, Australia	0	*
03.07.38	de Havilland DH.89 Dragon Rapide	G-AEBX	6328	Railway Air Services	Crashed	Location Unknown	*	*
08.07.38	Lockheed 14H Super Electra	NC17383	1402	Northwest Airlines	Crashed on take-off	Billings, MT, USA	1	9
10.07.38	Caudron Goeland	F-AOMT	4/7269	Aeromaritime	Crashed on landing after engine fire	Mikki, French West Africa	2	1
14.07.38	Savoia Marchetti S.66	I-VOLO	15013	Ala Littoria	Crashed	Off Sardinia, Italy	20	*
15.07.38	Douglas DC-3	NC18114	1990	Pan American Airways	Crashed into hospital on take-off	Moron, Argentina	0{1}	13
16.07.38	Junkers Ju.52/3m	XXI	5087	Eurasia	Crashed	Hankow, China	*	*
19.07.38	Douglas DC-2-118A	NC14272	1305	Panagra	Crashed [Found 02.41]	Mt Mercedario, Chile	4	0
22.07.38	Lockheed 14H Super Electra	SP-BNG	1432	LOT Polish Airlines	Crashed after being struck by lightning	Stulpica, Romania	14	*
27.07.38	Armstrong Whitworth Atalanta	G-ABTG	AW.735	Imperial Airways	Crashed	Kisumu, Kenya	*	*
28.07.38	Martin M.130	NC14714	556	Pan American Airways	Crashed	Between Manila & Guam	14	0
10.08.38	Douglas DF	J-ANES	*	Dai Nippon Airlines	Crash landed & sank	Off Chichijima, Japan	6	0
11.08.38	Ford 5-AT-C Tri-Motor	NC8413	5-AT-051	Transcontinental & Western Air	Destroyed by fire on ground	Mankato, MN, USA	*	*
12.08.38	Type Unknown	*	*	Pan American Airways	Crashed into mountain in rain	San Andres Tuxtla, Mexico	*	*
15.08.38	Junkers Ju.52/3mge	PP-CAT	4024	Cruzeiro	Crashed	Rio de Janeiro, Brazil	*	*
16.08.38	de Havilland DH.89A Dragon Rapide	PK-AKU	6296	KNILM	Written off	Ketapangdaja, Dutch East Indies	*	*

Date	Type	Reg'n	C/n	Operator	Accident	Location	F	S
18.08.38	Lockheed 14H Super-Electra	SP-BNJ	1424	LOT Polish Airlines	Damaged by fire after ground loop	Bucharest, Romania	*	*
18.08.38	Macchi C.94	I-NILO	94001	Macchi	Crashed	Motnago, Italy	15	0
23.08.38	Savoia-Marchetti SM.73	OK-BAG	30040	Ceskoslovenske Aerolinie	Crashed	Oberkirsch, Germany	*	1
29.08.38	de Havilland Dragon 1	VH-UXK	6053	Operator Unknown	Crashed	Mundoo, Qld, Australia	*	*
oo.08.38	Fleet 50K Freighter	CF-BDX	200	United Air Transport	Crashed	British Columbia, Canada	*	*
03.09.38	Stinson Model U	NC12121	9009	Mayflower Airlines	Destroyed in ground accident	Nantucket, MA, USA	*	*
03.09.38	Ford 5-AT-D Tri-Motor	NC435H	5-AT-102	Johnson Flying Service	Crashed on landing	Big Prairie, MT, USA	0	*
07.09.38	Cant Z.506	I-DENO	*	Ala Littoria	Destroyed by fire	Melilla, Spanish Morocco	*	*
17.09.38	Bellanca Skyrocket	RX-15	*	Transportes Aereos Gelabert	Crashed on take-off	Panama City, Panama	*	*
01.10.38	Junkers Ju.52/3m	D-AVFB	*	Deutsche Lufthansa	Crashed	Grisons, Switzerland	13	0
01.10.38	Dornier Do.18E	D-AROZ	255	Deutsche Lufthansa	Crashed	Off Bathurst, Gambia	5	0
10.10.38	Sabca S.73	OO-AGT	*	Sabena	Crashed	Soest, Germany	19	0
19.10.38	Douglas DC-2-112	NC13735	1261	Eastern Air Lines	Crashed	Montgomery, AL, USA	*	*
20.10.38	Ford 4-AT-B Tri-Motor	NC7865	4-AT-50	H.W.Musleh	Crashed	Powellsville, NC, USA	1	*
25.10.38	Douglas DC-2-210	VH-UYC	1566	Australian National Airways	Crashed	Mt Dandenong, Vic, Australia	18	0
04.11.38	de Havilland DH.86	G-ACZN	2316	Jersey Airways	Crashed	Jersey, Channel Islands	14	0
10.11.38	Douglas DC-3	*	*	Great Northern Airways	Crashed	Fukoka, Japan	*	*
16.11.38	Bloch 120	F-ANJX	1	Air Afrique	Forced landed & turned over	nr Coquilhatville, Belgian Congo	0	3
17.11.38	Fokker Super Universal	G-CASQ	824	Operator Unknown	Crashed	Disappointment Inlet, BC, Canada	*	*
20.11.38	de Havilland DH.89A Dragon Rapide	VT-AJA	6379	Tata & Sons	Written off	Juhu, India	*	*
21.11.38	Lockheed 14H2 Super Electra	CF-TCL	1475	Trans Canada Airlines	Crashed on take-off	Regina, SK, Canada	2	0
22.11.38	Lockheed 14-WF62 Super Electra	G-AFGO	1468	British Airways	Crashed	Walton Bay, Somerset, UK	2	0
26.11.38	Junkers Ju.90V2	D-AIVI	4914	Deutsche Lufthansa	Crashed on take-off	Bathurst, Gambia	16	0
27.11.38	Short S.23	G-AETW	S.839	Imperial Airways	Crashed in sandstorm	Lake Habbaniyah, Iraq	4	*
29.11.38	Douglas DC-3	NC16066	1906	United Air Lines	Crashed out of fuel	Off Point Reyes, CA, USA	*	*
02.12.38	Junkers Ju.52/3m	D-ANOY	5663	Deutsche Lufthansa	Crashed & caught fire	nr Vienna, Austria	0	8
03.12.38	de Havilland DH.86	G-ADCN	2319	Imperial Airways	Destroyed by fire	Bangkok, Thailand	*	*
06.12.38	Focke-Wulf Fw.200 Condor	D-ACON	2000	Deutsche Lufthansa	Crashed due to fuel mismanagement	Off Manila, Philippines	*	*
08.12.38	Nakajima DC-2	*	*	Japan Aviation Corporation	Crashed after engine failure	Off Kubashima, Japan	10	2
09.12.38	Lockheed 14-WF62 Super Electra	PH-APE	1413	KLM Royal Dutch Airlines	Crashed	Amsterdam, Netherlands	4	0
10.12.38	Junkers Ju.52/3m	HC-SAB	5915	SEDTA	Crashed into mountain	Mt Chimborazo, Ecuador	*	*
13.12.38	Lockheed Vega 5C	NC48M	100	United Air Services	Crashed during filming of 'Only Angels Have Wings' as F-LTM	St George, UT, USA	0	1
20.12.38	de Havilland DH.90 Dragonfly	VP-YAX	7512	Rhodesia & Nyasaland Airways	Crashed	nr Gwelo, Southern Rhodesia	*	*
20.12.38	Fokker F.VIIb/3m	PK-AFD	5072	KNILM	Written off	Location Unknown	*	*
oo.oo.38	Ford 5-AT-D Tri-Motor	C-60	5-AT-114	SCADTA	Crashed	Quibdo, Colombia	*	*
oo.oo.38	Douglas DC-2-115B	EC-AGK	1334	LAPE	Written off	Spain	*	*
oo.oo.38	Sikorsky S-38B	PP-PAM	214-06	Panair do Brasil	Crashed	Rio Branco, Brazil	*	*
oo.oo.38	Junkers G.24	PP-CAB	944	Syndicato Condor	Crashed	Location Unknown	*	*
oo.oo.38	Junkers G.24	D-896	850	Deutsche Lufthansa	Written off	Location Unknown	*	*
01.01.39	de Havilland DH.90 Dragonfly	VP-YBR	7503	Rhodesia & Nyasaland Airways	Crashed	nr Kasama, Southern Rhodesia	*	*
07.01.39	Douglas DC-2-115B	HB-ITA	1329	Swissair	Crashed	Senlis, France	*	*
13.01.39	Junkers Ju.52/3mge	PP-CAY	4042	Syndicato Condor	Crashed	Rio de Janeiro, Brazil	10	0
13.01.39	Fokker F.XVIII	VQ-PAF	5310	Operator Unknown	Crashed	Lydda, Palestine	*	*
13.01.39	Lockheed 14-H Super Electra	NC17389	1408	Northwest Airlines	Crashed on take-off	Miles City, MT, USA	*	*
18.01.39	Lockheed 14-H Super Electra	VH-ABI	1418	Guinea Airways	Crashed	Katherine River, NT, Australia	*	*
21.01.39	Short S.23	G-ADUU	S.812	Imperial Airways	Sank	Between New York & Bermuda	3	*
27.01.39	Potez 62	F-ANPJ	3926/4	Air France	Crashed	Tourbe, Germany	*	*
23.02.39	Beechcraft E17B	VT-AKJ	232	Indian National Airways	Crashed – possibly collided with Gull Six VT-AJD	nr Karachi, India	*	*
23.02.39	Percival Gull Six	VT-AJD	K.72	Indian National Airways	Crashed – possibly collided with Beechcraft E17B VT-AKJ	nr Karachi, India	*	*
24.02.39	Junkers Ju.52/3m	D-ALUS	*	Deutsche Lufthansa	Crashed	Roubion, France	10	0
oo.02.39	Fleet 50K Freighter	CF-BJT	201	United Air Transport	Destroyed by fire	Chicago, IL, USA	*	*
02.03.39	Ford 6-AT-A Tri-Motor	CF-BEP	6-AT-1	Royal Canadian Air Force	Struck by RCAF Hurricane taking off	Vancouver, BC, Canada	*	*

Date	Type	Reg'n	C/n	Operator	Accident	Location	F	S
06.03.39	Fokker F.VIIb/3m	I-AFRO	5208	Ala Littoria	Written off	Bologna, Italy	*	*
09.03.39	Fairchild FC.2	*	*	LAN-Chile	Crashed	Location Unknown	*	*
12.03.39	Short S.23	G-ADUY	S.816	Imperial Airways	Destroyed	Batavia, Dutch East Indies	0	*
12.03.39	Junkers Ju.52/3m	XXIII	4074	Eurasia	Crashed	nr Weining, China	*	*
14.03.39	Junkers Ju.52/3m	OO-AUA	5815	Sabena	Crashed	Haren, Belgium	3	0
14.03.39	Junkers Ju.86	*	*	LAN-Chile	Crashed	Location Unknown	*	*
14.03.39	Ford 5-AT Tri-Motor	n/a	*	SCADTA	Crashed [Leticia]	Location Unknown	*	*
15.03.39	Boeing 247D	C-149	*	SCADTA	Crashed	Location Unknown	*	*
16.03.39	Junkers Ju.86	*	*	Deutsche Lufthansa	Crashed	nr Manzanares, Colombia	8	*
18.03.39	Boeing Stratoliner	NX19901	1994	Boeing Airplane Company	Crashed after tail broke off	nr Alder, WA, USA	13	0
26.03.39	Douglas DC-2-112	NC13727	1253	Braniff Airways	Crashed	Oklahoma City, OK, USA	8	4
oo.03.39	Ford 5-AT-B Tri-Motor	LG-AAH	5-AT-014	TACA	Destroyed by fire	Tegucigalpa, Honduras	*	*
03.04.39	Caudron 635 Simoun	F-AOOT	7372	Air France	Crashed into mountain	nr Marrakesh, Morocco	9	0
12.04.39	Junkers W.34	n/a	2607	Lloyd Aereo Boliviano	Crashed [Vanguardia]	Bolivia	*	*
15.04.39	Ford 5-AT-C Tri-Motor	NC8411	5-AT-049	South American Gulf Oil Co	Crashed into mountain	nr El Carmen, Colombia	2	0
oo.04.39	Fokker F.VIIa	*	5041	Operator Unknown	Written off	Venezuela	*	*
01.05.39	Short S.23	G-ADVD	S.821	Imperial Airways	Crashed	Mozambique Harbour, Mozambique	2	*
03.05.39	Dewoitine D.338	F-ARIC	25	Air France	Crashed due to icing	nr Marrakesh, Morocco	9	0
06.05.39	Junkers Ju.52/3m	XVII	5104	Eurasia	Shot down by Japanese aircraft	Hanchung, China	*	*
17.05.39	de Havilland DH.89A Dragon Rapide	CF-AVJ	6295	Quebec Airways	Destroyed by fire on engine start-up	St John, NB, Canada	0	*
18.05.39	de Havilland DH.89 Dragon Rapide	G-AEAK	6324	Isle of Man Air Services	Crashed	Speke, Lancs, UK	*	*
10.06.39	Koolhoven FK.43	PH-AJK	4305	KLM Royal Dutch Airlines	Crashed	Vlissingen, Netherlands	3	0
12.06.39	Short S.23	G-ADVE	S.822	Imperial Airways	Capsized & sank on landing	Calcutta, India	0	*
15.06.39	Fairchild FC.2W2	G-CARM	132	Operator Unknown	Destroyed by fire after striking buoy	Canada	*	*
19.06.39	Short S.30	G-AFCW	S.882	Imperial Airways	Destroyed when refuelling barge caught fire	Hythe, Kent, UK	0	*
20.06.39	de Havilland DH.89A Dragon Rapide	G-AERE	6355	L.H.Falk	Crashed	Forest-in-Teesdale, Durham, UK	*	*
oo.06.39	Armstrong Whitworth Atalanta	G-ABTH	AW.741	Imperial Airways	Damaged beyond repair	Cairo, Egypt	0	*
02.07.39	de Havilland DH.85 Leopard Moth	VP-YAY	7101	Rhodesia & Nyasaland Airways	Crashed	Novo Lusitania, Mozambique	*	*
20.07.39	Junkers Ju.86z-2	HB-IXA	086/0951	Swissair	Crashed after engine fire	Konstanz, Switzerland	6	*
21.07.39	de Havilland DH.90 Dragonfly	G-AEXN	7559	Mutual Finance	Crashed	Hampden, Bucks, UK	*	*
03.08.39	Junkers Ju.52/3m	D-ANJH	5747	Deutsche Lufthansa	Crashed	Mingaladon, Burma	*	*
04.08.39	Type Unknown	*	*	Deutsche Lufthansa	Crashed & caught fire	Hospitales, Spain	7	0
06.08.39	Fokker Super Universal	VH-UJT	436	Catholic Mission of the Holy Ghost	Crashed	Alexishaven, New Guinea	5	*
11.08.39	Lockheed 14-WF62 Super Electra	G-AFGN	1467	British Airways	Destroyed by fire after forced landing	Luxeuil, France	0	12
12.08.39	Sikorsky S-38B	F-AOUC	314-19	Cie des Chargeurs Reunis	Crashed	Calibar, French West Africa	*	*
13.08.39	Sikorsky S-43B	PP-PBM	4316	Panair do Brasil	Crashed	Rio de Janeiro, Brazil	*	*
15.08.39	Lockheed 10A Electra	G-AESY	1102	British Airways	Crashed in sea after fire	Off Denmark	5	1
28.08.39	de Havilland Dragon 1	VT-AEL	6048	Indian National Airways	Crashed	nr Lahore, India	2	0
30.08.39	Junkers Ju.52/3mte	D-AFOP	5800	Deutsche Lufthansa	Crashed after take-off	Hanover, Germany	7	0
oo.08.39	Short Scion Senior	G-AENX	S.835	Elders Colonial Airways	Sank at moorings	Bathurst, Gambia	*	*
03.09.39	Airspeed Oxford	G-AFVS	83	Airspeed	Sunk in *Athenia* when torpedoed	Atlantic Ocean	*	*
12.09.39	Lockheed 10A Electra	SP-BGJ	1089	LOT Polish Airlines	Destroyed by enemy action	Horodenka, Poland	*	*
oo.09.39	Fokker F.VIIa	SP-AAP	5091	LOT Polish Airlines	Destroyed by enemy action	Warsaw, Poland	*	*
oo.09.39	PZL F.VIIb/3m	SP-AOC	9/4	LOT Polish Airlines	Destroyed by enemy action	Warsaw, Poland	*	*
13.10.39	Caproni Ca.133	I-DIRE	*	Ala Littoria	Crashed on approach after engine failure	Gabode, Djibouti	0	6
oo.10.39	Fokker F.VIIb/3m	PK-AFF	5188	KNILM	Written off	Kiunga, New Guinea	*	*
07.11.39	Handley Page HP.42W	G-AAXD	HP.42/6	Imperial Airways	Crash landed	Tiverton, Devon, UK	0	*
20.11.39	Airspeed Oxford	G-AFFM	75	British Airways	Struck balloon cable & crashed	Gosport, Hants, UK	2	0
17.12.39	Fokker Universal	G-CAFU	404	Operator Unknown	Crashed	Fort St John, BC, Canada	*	*
20.12.39	de Havilland Dragon 1	G-ACJT	6043	Western Airways	Crashed	Weston-super-Mare, Somerset, UK	*	*
21.12.39	Lockheed 14-WF62 Super Electra	G-AFYU	1444	British Airways	Crashed	Off Malta	5	*
24.12.39	Savoia-Marchetti SM.83	I-ARPA	34017	LATI	Crashed in storm	Dar Caid Allal, Morocco	7	0

Date	Type	Reg'n	C/n	Operator	Accident	Location	F	S
oo.oo.39	Noorduyn Norseman	CF-MPE	016	RCMP Air Services	Damaged beyond repair	Sioux Lookout, Canada	*	*
oo.oo.39	Junkers G.24	D-ALAB	*	Deutsche Lufthansa	Written off	Location Unknown	*	*

1940–1949

The first half of this decade was obviously totally dominated by the Second World War. This conflict brought air services in Europe and most of Asia to an end in any normal sense. Airlines of both sides nevertheless struggled to maintain air links no matter how dangerous or tortuous the routes became. Only in the Americas was commercial air traffic unaffected by hostilities.

Britain struggled on using pre-war transports and aircraft borrowed from the RAF, managing to keep open its links with the Empire at all times. The newly formed BOAC even kept a route open to Scandinavia using civilianized Mosquito aircraft, and in Germany Lufthansa maintained a network of services with its reliable Ju.52/3m fleet.

There were many losses to hostile action either during air raids or from being shot down – one notorious such case resulting in the death of the British actor Leslie Howard. Many such losses have never been recorded, particularly those from Japan, China and the USSR.

The USA became the transport aircraft factory for Europe, paving the way for its dominance of the industry after the war. Airlines prospered in the USA using the Douglas family of airliners – the same types that were to serve the rest of the world's airline operators in the second half of the decade and the 'fifties.

After the defeat of Germany and Japan in 1945, airlines sprang up throughout Europe using the vast numbers of ex-military transports available. A plethora of new, inexperienced operators flying in difficult conditions led to many accidents.

Accidents continued and numbers of casualties began to rise, with several crashes exceeding 50 fatalities for the first time. Serious crashes struck

The remains of DC-3 OK-WDB of CSA after it had been struck by another DC-3 of Spencer Airways on take-off at Croydon on 25 January 1947. There were 16 fatalities. (Popperfoto)

United Air Lines, Air France and Avianca amongst others. The worst of these came in 1949 when an Eastern Air Lines DC-4 collided with a military aircraft, killing all 55 on board.

For many years the threat of hijacking has blighted air travel. The first such action involving a civil airliner occurred in 1948, when a Cathay Pacific aircraft was taken over in mid-air resulting in the deaths of 26 people. In the years to follow many aircraft would be lost to this new crime.

The Cold War accounted for several civilian aircraft crashes when the West successfully kept supplies flowing during the Berlin Air Lift. The pressures of round the clock flying took their toll of both aircraft and crews. Several civilian airliners were written off in this operation.

The first losses resulting from the Arab-Israeli conflicts occurred in 1948. Hostile action during local conflicts would increase and affect air operations in many parts of the globe after the Second World War.

First write-offs 1940–1949

(* military example crashed earlier)

Armstrong Whitworth Ensign	23.05.40
de Havilland Albatross	06.10.40
Douglas DC-1	00.12.40
Lockheed Lodestar	28.03.41
Vought-Sikorsky VS-44	03.10.42
Douglas DC-4	15.01.43
Boeing 314	22.02.43
SNCASO Bordeaux	02.04.43
Short Sunderland	28.07.43*
AAC.1 Toucan	10.09.45
Handley Page Hermes	03.12.45
Avro Lancastrian	24.03.46
Vickers Viking	23.04.46
Budd Conestoga	15.05.46
Bristol 170	04.07.46
Lockheed Constellation	11.07.46*
Curtiss C-46	13.07.46*
SNCASO Corse	23.07.46
de Havilland Dove	14.08.46
Avro York	06.09.46*
Short Sandringham	18.01.47
Savoia-Marchetti SM.95	15.02.47
Avro Tudor	23.08.47
SNCASE Languedoc	07.10.47
Douglas DC-6	24.10.47
Latecoere 631	21.02.48
Miles Marathon	28.05.48
Fiat G.212	01.07.48
Canadair C-4	12.08.48
Martin 202	29.08.48
Handley Page Halton	01.04.49
Convair 240	22.06.49

This Constellation of TWA (NC86507) crashed on landing at Newcastle, Delaware, on 18 November 1947, killing all five on board. (Popperfoto)

ƒDate	Type	Reg'n	C/n	Operator	Accident	Location	F	S
10.01.40	GAL Monospar ST-25 Jubilee	G-AEDY	72	Utility Airways	Crashed	nr Hanworth, Middx, UK	*	*
15.01.40	Lockheed 14-WF62 Super Electra	G-AFMO	1490	British Airways	Crashed on landing	Heston, Middx, UK	0	9
22.01.40	Lockheed 14-WF62 Super Electra	PK-AFO	1415	KNILM	Crashed	Off Bali, Dutch East Indies	8	1
30.01.40	Ford 4-AT-E Tri-Motor	NC5092	4-AT-19	White Pass Airways	Crashed into hangar on landing	Carcross, Yukon, Canada	0	*
12.02.40	Douglas DC-2-123	J-BBOI	1323	Dai Nippon Airlines	Written off	Japan	*	*
13.02.40	Short Scion 2	G-AETT	PA.1005	Lundy & Atlantic Coast Air Lines	Crashed	Barnstaple, Devon, UK	*	*
13.02.40	Heston Phoenix I	G-AEHJ	1/3	British American Air Services	Crashed	River Mersey, Lancs, UK	*	*
14.02.40	de Havilland Dragon 2	G-ADCT	6095	Scottish Airways	Crashed	Longman, Inverness, UK	*	*
19.02.40	de Havilland DH.89 Dragon Rapide	G-ACPR	6255	Great Western & Southern Air Lines	Damaged beyond repair	Burford, Salop, UK	*	*
20.02.40	Ford Tri-Motor	*	*	TACA	Crashed	nr Prinzpolka, Nicaragua	0	2
25.02.40	Ford 5-AT-C Tri-Motor	TI-33	5-AT-070	TACA	Crashed	San Isidro, Costa Rica	*	*
29.02.40	Boeing 247D	C-79	*	SCADTA	Crashed	Location Unknown	*	*
01.03.40	Handley Page HP.42E	G-AAGX	HP.42/1	Imperial Airways	Crashed	Gulf of Oman	*	*
03.03.40	Bloch 220	F-AOHA	01	Air France	Crashed into mountain	nr Orange, France	3	0
05.03.40	Ford 5-AT-B Tri-Motor	XA-BCW	5-AT-045	Mexicana	Crashed in forest	San Martin Volcano, Mexico	0	*
13.03.40	Lockheed Vega 2	XA-BKG	058	CAFSSA	Crashed	Ixtepec, Mexico	*	*
15.03.40	de Havilland DH.86B	VH-UYW	2361	W.R.Carpenter Ltd	Crashed	New Guinea	*	*
18.03.40	de Havilland DH.89A Dragon Rapide	G-AFEY	6402	Scottish Airways	Crashed	Kirkwall, Orkneys, UK	*	*
19.03.40	Handley Page HP.42W	G-AAUD	HP.42/3	Imperial Airways	Damaged by gale	Whitchurch, Somerset, UK	0	*
19.03.40	Handley Page HP.42W	G-AAXC	HP.42/5	Imperial Airways	Damaged by gale	Whitchurch, Somerset, UK	0	*
03.04.40	Douglas DC-2-112	NC13786	1296	Transcontinental & Western Air	Damaged in ground loop on landing in storm	Pittsburgh, PA, USA	0	*
03.04.40	Avro Ten	G-AASP	384	British Overseas Airways Corporation	Destroyed	Location Unknown	*	*
19.04.40	de Havilland Dragon 2	G-ACNG	6069	Scottish Airways	Crashed	Kirkwall, Orkneys, UK	*	*
22.04.40	Lockheed 14-WF62 Super Electra	G-AFKD	1484	British Overseas Airways Corporation	Crashed	nr Loch Lomond, Dunbarton, UK	5	0
22.04.40	Focke-Wulf Fw.200 Condor	D-ABOD	3324	Deutsche Lufthansa	Crashed during invasion	Norway	*	*
25.04.40	Short Scion 2	G-AEIL	PA.1003	Arabian Airways	Crashed	Mukerius, Aden	*	*
oo.04.40	Fairchild 71C	VO-AFG	14	Imperial Airways	Crashed	Canada Bay, Newfoundland	*	*
02.05.40	de Havilland DH.86B	OH-IPA	2353	Finnish Government	Mid-air collision with Finnish AF Brewster 239 BW-394	Malmi, Finland	*(*)	*
03.05.40	de Havilland DH.89 Dragon Rapide	G-AEMM	6339	Anglo Iranian Oil Co	Crashed	Middle East	*	*
05.05.40	Type Unknown	*	*	Air France	Crashed & caught fire on landing	Marseilles, France	0	*
10.05.40	Douglas DC-3	PH-ALU	1942	KLM Royal Dutch Airlines	Destroyed by German bombing	Amsterdam, Netherlands	*	*
10.05.40	Douglas DC-3	PH-ARX	2020	KLM Royal Dutch Airlines	Destroyed by German bombing	Amsterdam, Netherlands	*	*
10.05.40	Douglas DC-3	PH-ASP	2109	KLM Royal Dutch Airlines	Destroyed by German bombing	Amsterdam, Netherlands	*	*
10.05.40	Douglas DC-3	PH-AST	2111	KLM Royal Dutch Airlines	Destroyed by German bombing	Amsterdam, Netherlands	*	*
10.05.40	Fokker F.VIII	PH-OTO	5045	KLM Royal Dutch Airlines	Destroyed by German bombing	Waalhaven, Netherlands	*	*
10.05.40	Douglas DC-2-115E	PH-AKK	1357	KLM Royal Dutch Airlines	Destroyed during German air raid	Amsterdam, Netherlands	*	*
10.05.40	Douglas DC-2-115E	PH-AKN	1360	KLM Royal Dutch Airlines	Destroyed during German air raid	Amsterdam, Netherlands	*	*
10.05.40	Douglas DC-2-115E	PH-AKO	1361	KLM Royal Dutch Airlines	Destroyed during German air raid	Amsterdam, Netherlands	*	*
10.05.40	Douglas DC-2-115E	PH-AKP	1362	KLM Royal Dutch Airlines	Destroyed during German air raid	Amsterdam, Netherlands	*	*
10.05.40	Douglas DC-2-115L	PH-ALD	1583	KLM Royal Dutch Airlines	Destroyed during German air raid	Amsterdam, Netherlands	*	*
10.05.40	Fokker F.VIIa	PH-ACT	4901	KLM Royal Dutch Airlines	Destroyed by German bombing	Amsterdam, Netherlands	*	*
10.05.40	Fokker F.VIIa	PH-AEB	0003	KLM Royal Dutch Airlines	Destroyed by German bombing	Amsterdam, Netherlands	*	*
10.05.40	Airspeed Envoy III	PH-ARK	55	D.V.Reinders	Destroyed by German bombing	Ypenburg, Netherlands	*	*
10.05.40	Airspeed Envoy III	PH-ARL	56	D.V.Reinders	Destroyed by German bombing	Ypenburg, Netherlands	*	*
10.05.40	Fokker F.VIIb/3m	OO-ADO	4983	AERA	Destroyed by German bombing	Belgium	*	*
10.05.40	Fokker F.VII	PH-ACJ	4839	KLM Royal Dutch Airlines	Destroyed by enemy action	Amsterdam, Netherlands	*	*
10.05.40	Carley Werkspoor	PH-AFI	1	KLM Royal Dutch Airlines	Destroyed by German bombing	Amsterdam, Netherlands	*	*
10.05.40	Koolhoven FK.43	PH-AKB	4307	KLM Royal Dutch Airlines	Destroyed by German bombing	Amsterdam, Netherlands	*	*
10.05.40	Koolhoven FK.48	PH-AJX	4801	KLM Royal Dutch Airlines	Damaged by German bombing	Amsterdam, Netherlands	*	*
10.05.40	Koolhoven FK.43	PH-AKD	4309	KLM Royal Dutch Airlines	Destroyed by German bombing	Amsterdam, Netherlands	*	*
10.05.40	Koolhoven FK.43	PH-AJL	4306	KLM Royal Dutch Airlines	Destroyed by German bombing	Amsterdam, Netherlands	*	*
23.05.40	Armstrong Whitworth Ensign I	G-ADSZ	AW.1164	British Overseas Airways Corporation	Shot down by German fighters	Merville, France	*	*
23.05.40	Armstrong Whitworth Ensign I	G-ADTA	AW.1165	British Overseas Airways Corporation	Damaged on landing	Lympne, Kent, UK	0	*
23.05.40	Sabca S.73	OO-AGS	*	Royal Air Force	Shot down by ground fire	nr Calais, France	*	*

Date	Type	Reg'n	C/n	Operator	Accident	Location	F	S
23.05.40	Douglas DC-3	OO-AUI	2094	Royal Air Force	Shot down	nr Calais, France	*	*
30.05.40	Lockheed Vega 5B	NR625E	063	H.G.Fales	Destroyed by fire	Hermosillo, Mexico	*	*
oo.05.40	Savoia-Marchetti SM.73	OO-AGP	30003	Sabena	Destroyed to avoid capture by German forces	Brussels, Belgium	*	*
oo.05.40	Atlantic F.VIIb/3m	PH-TOL	612/5022	De Zevende Bouw Mij	Destroyed by enemy action	Netherlands	*	*
14.06.40	Junkers Ju.52/3mge	OH-ALL	5494	Aero O/Y	Shot down by Soviet Air Force SB-2	Kar, Estonia	9	0
18.06.40	de Havilland DH.89 Dragon Rapide	G-AEBW	6327	Isle of Man Air Services	Lost in evacuation	Bordeaux, France	*	*
18.06.40	de Havilland DH.89A Dragon Rapide	G-AEPF	6353	Air Commerce	Lost in evacuation	France	*	*
20.06.40	Dewoitine D.338	F-ARTD	22	Air France	Shot down in error by French anti-aircraft fire	Ouistreham, France	1	0
oo.06.40	Lockheed 14 Super Electra	SP-BPM	1494	LOT Polish Airlines	Shot down	nr Paris, France	*	*
oo.06.40	de Havilland DH.86B	G-AEFH	2350	Railway Air Services	Destroyed by enemy action	France	*	*
oo.06.40	de Havilland DH.86B	G-AEWR	2354	Railway Air Services	Destroyed by enemy action	France	*	*
07.07.40	Dewoitine D.338	F-AQBA	01	Air France	Shot down by Japanese fighter	Gulf of Tonkin	*	*
08.07.40	de Havilland DH.83 Fox Moth	G-ACEY	4057	Crilly Airways	Destroyed by fire	Hooton, Essex, UK	*	*
24.07.40	Lockheed 14-H Super Electra	G-AFZZ	1493	British Overseas Airways Corporation	Crashed	Bucharest, Romania	*	*
24.07.40	Lockheed 14-H Super Electra	G-AGAA	1492	British Overseas Airways Corporation	Crashed on purpose	Bucharest, Romania	*	*
24.07.40	Lockheed 14-H Super Electra	SP-BNE	1420	LOT Polish Airlines	Destroyed [Possibly was SP-BPK cn 1492]	Bucharest, Romania	*	*
oo.07.40	Ford 4-AT-E Tri-Motor	CF-AZB	4-AT-03	British Yukon Navigation Co	Damaged when towed into hangar wall	Whitehorse, BC, Canada	0	*
18.08.40	Armstrong Whitworth AW.23	G-AFRX	–	Flight Refuelling	Destroyed by German bombing	Ford, Sussex, UK	*	*
18.08.40	Handley Page Harrow I	G-AFRL	–	Flight Refuelling	Destroyed by German bombing	Ford, Sussex, UK	*	*
23.08.40	Douglas DC-3	*	*	Lares	Crashed [either YR-PAF cn 1986 or YR-PIF cn 1985]	Cluj, Romania	21	*
31.08.40	Douglas DC-3	NC21789	2188	Pennsylvania Central Airlines	Crashed in storm	nr Lovettsville, VA, USA	23	0
oo.08.40	Douglas DC-2-115D	EC-AAD	1330	Iberia	Crashed	Spain	*	*
14.09.40	Short L.17	G-ACJJ	S.768	British Overseas Airways Corporation	Damaged by gale	Drem, Lothian, UK	*	*
21.09.40	Douglas DC-3	G-AGBC	1939	British Overseas Airways Corporation	Crashed	Heston, Middx, UK	*	*
03.10.40	Fairchild Super 71	CF-AUJ	50	Canadian Airways	Struck log on take-off & sank	Sioux Lookout, ON, Canada	*	*
06.10.40	de Havilland Albatross	G-AFDL	6805	British Overseas Airways Corporation	Crash landed	Pucklechurch, Glos, UK	0	*
11.10.40	Dewoitine D.338	F-AQBJ	10	Air France	Crashed	nr Cotonu, French West Africa	*	*
26.10.40	Junkers Ju.52/3m	XXV	6014	Eurasia	Shot down by Japanese aircraft	China	*	*
29.10.40	Douglas DC-3	D-AAIH	1973	Deutsche Lufthansa	Crashed	Templehof, Berlin, Germany	*	*
29.10.40	Douglas DC-2	*	1369	CNAC	Force-landed & strafed by Japanese fighters	nr Changyi, China	9	5
03.11.40	Junkers Ju.52/3mce	CB-17	4008	Lloyd Aereo Boliviano	Crashed	Location Unknown	*	*
04.11.40	Douglas DC-3	NC16086	1925	United Air Lines	Crashed into mountain	nr Centerville, UT, USA	10	0
24.11.40	Douglas DC-3	G-AGBI	2019	British Overseas Airways Corporation	Destroyed by German bombing	Whitchurch, Somerset, UK	*	*
24.11.40	Armstrong Whitworth Ensign I	G-ADTC	AW.1167	British Overseas Airways Corporation	Destroyed by German bombing	Whitchurch, Somerset, UK	*	*
27.11.40	Farman F.2234	F-AROA	2	Air France	Shot down by Italian aircraft	Mediterranean Sea	*	*
oo.11.40	Fiat G.18	I-ELIO	1	Nucleo Comunicazioni Avio Linee	Crashed and burned on landing	Italy	*	*
04.12.40	Douglas DC-3	NC25678	2175	United Air Lines	Crashed due to icing	Chicago, IL, USA	10	6
04.12.40	Ford 5-AT-B Tri-Motor	TI-51	5-AT-019	TACA	Crashed	Puntarenas, Costa Rica	*	*
20.12.40	de Havilland Albatross	G-AFDI	6802	British Overseas Airways Corporation	Destroyed by German bombing	Whitchurch, Somerset, UK	*	*
20.12.40	Savoia-Marchetti SM.83	I-ASTA	34018	LATI	Destroyed on ground by bombing	Abyssinia	*	*
24.12.40	Junkers Ju.52/3m	CX-ABB	5886	CAUSA	Sunk in gale	Buenos Aires, Argentina	*	*
30.12.40	Junkers Ju.52/3m	XX	5502	Eurasia	Destroyed by Japanese bombing	Chengtu, China	*	*
oo.12.40	Douglas DC-1-109	EC-AAE	1137	Iberia	Crashed	Malaga, Spain	*	*
oo.12.40	Fiat G.18	I-ETRA	2	Nucleo Comunicazioni Avio Linee	Collided on ground with Italian AF Fiat CR.42	Italy	*(*)	*
oo.oo.40	Dewoitine D.338	F-AQBH	08	Air France	Crashed	French Indo-China	*	*
oo.oo.40	Junkers Ju.52/3m	D-ACBO	4049	Deutsche Lufthansa	Written off	Location Unknown	*	*
oo.oo.40	Sikorsky S-38B	C-49	*	SCADTA	Destroyed	Location Unknown	*	*
07.01.41	Beechcraft S18A	CF-BGY	0172	Starratt Airways & Transportation	Crashed	Canada	*	*
10.01.41	Savoia-Marchetti SM.83	I-AREM	34019	LATI	Crashed	Mediterranean Sea	*	*
12.01.41	Douglas DC-3	NC16072	1912	Eastern Air Lines	Destroyed in hangar fire	Salt Lake City, UT, USA	*	*
12.01.41	Boeing 247D	NC13339	1721	Western Air Express	Destroyed in hangar fire	Salt Lake City, UT, USA	*	*
15.01.41	Savoia-Marchetti SM.75	I-BAYR	32013	LATI	Crashed	Off South Africa	10	0
18.01.41	Junkers Ju.52/3m	HA-JUA	5523	Malert	Crashed	nr Nagy-Varad, Hungary	12	*
19.01.41	Lockheed 14-WF62 Super Electra	G-AFGR	1470	British Overseas Airways Corporation	Crashed	El Fasher, Sudan	*	*

Date	Type	Reg'n	C/n	Operator	Accident	Location	F	S
20.01.41	Ford 5-AT Tri-Motor	*	*	CNAC	Crashed in mountains	nr Kian, China	*	*
23.01.41	Douglas DC-3	NC17315	1930	Transcontinental & Western Air	Crashed on overshoot	St Louis, MO, USA	2	12
06.02.41	de Havilland DH.66 Hercules	VH-UJO	344	Stephens Aviation	Crashed	Wau, New Guinea	*	0
06.02.41	Lockheed 14-H2 Super Electra	CF-TCP	1501	Trans Canada Airlines	Crashed into trees on approach	Armstrong, ON, Canada	12	0
15.02.41	Short S.30	G-AFCX	S.883	British Overseas Airways Corporation	Sunk during hurricane	River Tagus, Lisbon, Portugal	*	*
26.02.41	Douglas DC-3	NC28394	3250	Eastern Air Lines	Crashed	Atlanta, GA, USA	8	*
oo.02.41	Savoia-Marchetti SM.83	I-AMER	34010	LATI	Written off	Location Unknown	*	*
oo.02.41	Savoia-Marchetti SM.82	I-BAIA	23	LATI	Crashed	Location Unknown	*	*
10.03.41	Sikorsky S-42	NC15376	4206	Pan American Airways	Sank	San Juan, Puerto Rico	2	25
28.03.41	Lockheed 18 Lodestar	ZS-AST	2034	South African Airways	Crashed into mountain	Elands Bay, South Africa	10	0
oo.03.41	Lockheed Vega 5A	XA-BFP	108	Cia Aeronautica Francisco Sarabia	Crashed	Merida, Mexico	0	*
03.04.41	Douglas DC-3	NC21727	2143	Eastern Air Lines	Crashed during storm	Vero Beach, FL, USA	0	16
04.04.41	Ford Tri-Motor	*	*	TACA	Crashed	Nicaragua	2	0
16.04.41	Boeing 247D	NC13359	1741	Pennsylvania Central Airlines	Crashed on take-off	Charleston, WV, USA	0	9
25.04.41	Douglas DC-3	URSS-C	*	Aeroflot	Crashed on take-off in snowstorm	Moscow, RSFSR, USSR	0	3
11.05.41	Short S.21	G-ADHK	S.797	British Overseas Airways Corporation	Destroyed by German bombing	Poole Harbour, Dorset, UK	1	0
21.05.41	de Havilland Dragon 1	G-ACAN	6000	Aberdeen Airways	Crashed	nr Dunbeath, UK	*	*
29.05.41	Lockheed 414 Hudson I	G-AGAR	1761	F.S.Cotton	Destroyed by enemy action	Le Luc, France	*	*
03.06.41	de Havilland Dragon 2	G-ACPY	6076	Olley Air Services	Shot down by German aircraft	Off Scilly Is, UK	*	*
14.06.41	Ford 4-AT-B Tri-Motor	NC5809	4-AT-25	Hangar Six	Crashed on landing	Yoakum, TX, USA	0	*
17.06.41	de Havilland DH.86	G-ACWC	2304	British Overseas Airways Corporation	Crashed	Minaa, Nigeria	*	*
19.06.41	Douglas DC-3	*	*	Lares	Crashed on take-off [YR-PAF cn 1986 or YR-PIF cn 1985]	Bucharest, Romania	15	*
21.06.41	Mitsubishi MC-20	M-604	*	Manchurian Air Lines	Crashed	Sea of Japan	18	0
26.06.41	Sikorsky S-43	NC16928	4317	Panagra	Crashed on landing	Rio de Janeiro, Brazil	0	4
oo.06.41	Saro Cloud	G-ABHG	A.19/2	British Overseas Airways Corporation	Damaged beyond repair	Ibsley, UK	*	*
30.07.41	Macchi C.100	I-PACE	4153	Ala Littoria	Crashed after take-off	Rome, Italy	*	*
02.08.41	Douglas DC-2-120	NC14279	1312	US Treasury	Crashed on delivery flight to RAF	Bathurst, Gambia	*	*
04.08.41	Lockheed 14-WF62 Super Electra	G-AFGP	1469	British Overseas Airways Corporation	Crashed	Khartoum, Sudan	*	*
04.08.41	Caudron Goeland	F-AOMR	7267/3	Air France	Crashed into high ground in bad weather	Salvezines, France	3	0
05.08.41	Douglas RD-4 Dolphin	V126	1269	United States Coast Guard	Crashed	Farallons, CA, USA	3	*
11.08.41	Lockheed Vega 5	NR7954	024	L.Ingalls	Crashed	Albuquerque, NY, USA	0	1
18.08.41	Lockheed 18 Lodestar	PP-PBD	2083	Panair do Brasil	Crashed	nr Sao Paulo, Brazil	8	*
01.09.41	Bloch 220	F-AQNL	12	Air France	Crashed into lake after engine failure on take-off	Bollemont, France	15	2
03.09.41	Caudron Goeland	F-BAAE	8710/155	SCLAM	Crashed into high ground	Panosas, France	4	0
05.09.41	Beechcraft S18D	CF-BMI	0224	Hudson Bay Company	Sank & written off	Canada	*	*
11.09.41	Beechcraft 18D	CF-BVC	0265	British Yukon Navigation Co	Crashed	Canada	*	*
26.09.41	Ford 5-AT-C Tri-Motor	CB-CAM-2	5-AT-080	Cia Aramayo de Mines	Crashed after engine failure	Challhuani Mts, Bolivia	5	*
30.09.41	Lockheed Orion 9D	NC13748	206	Aircraft Export Corporation	Belly landed & caught fire	Pine Bluffs, WY, USA	*	*
09.10.41	de Havilland DH.89A Dragon Rapide	SU-ABQ	6299	Misrair	Written off	Port Said, Egypt	*	*
10.10.41	Sikorsky S-38B	n/a	414-05	Lloyd Aereo Boliviano	Crashed [Nicolas Suarez]	Guayaramerin, Bolivia	*	*
14.10.41	Lockheed 10A Electra	YV-ADE	1132	Linea Aeropostal Venezolana	Damaged beyond repair	Venezuela	*	*
20.10.41	Douglas DC-3	NC21712	2124	Northwest Airlines	Crashed due to icing	Moorhead, MN, USA	14	1
23.10.41	Ford 5-AT-C Tri-Motor	VH-UTB	5-AT-068	Guinea Airways	Ran off runway into river	Wau, New Guinea	0	1
30.10.41	Douglas DC-3	NC25663	2207	American Airlines	Crashed	New London, ON, Canada	20	*
06.11.41	Lockheed Vega DL-1	NC239M	156	C.H.Babb	Crashed	Dallas, TX, USA	*	*
14.11.41	Lockheed 14-H2 Super Electra	CR-AAX	1508	DETA	Written off	Inhambane, Mozambique	*	*
15.11.41	Ford 4-AT-B Tri-Motor	NC6894	4-AT-30	B.F.Gregory	Crashed on take-off	Old Staley, TX, USA	*	*
25.11.41	de Havilland DH.89A Dragon Rapide	G-AGDH	6548	Scottish Airways	Damaged by gale	Stornoway, Shetlands, UK	*	*
01.12.41	Lockheed 10A Electra	YV-ACE	1078	Linea Aeropostal Venezolana	Written off	Location Unknown	*	*
07.12.41	Sikorsky S-42	NC16735	4208	Pan American Airways	Destroyed by Japanese bombing	Manila, Philippines	*	*
08.12.41	Junkers W.33	VII	2564	Eurasia	Destroyed by Japanese bombing	Shanghai, China	*	*
08.12.41	Junkers W.34	VI	2830	Eurasia	Destroyed by Japanese bombing	Shanghai, China	*	*
08.12.41	Junkers Ju.52/3m	XXII	4068	Eurasia	Destroyed by Japanese bombing	China	*	*
08.12.41	Junkers Ju.52/3m	XXIV	4072	Eurasia	Destroyed by Japanese bombing	China	*	*

Date	Type	Reg'n	C/n	Operator	Accident	Location	F	S
11.12.41	Sikorsky S-38B	NC21V	414-12	Pan American Airways	Crashed	Biscayne Bay, FL, USA	3	0
11.12.41	Junkers Ju.52/3m	XV	5329	Eurasia	Destroyed by Japanese bombing	China	*	*
18.12.41	de Havilland DH.89A Dragon Rapide	VR-SAV	6360	Malayan Volunteer Air Force	Destroyed in air raid	Ipoh, Malaya	*	*
21.12.41	Lockheed 18 Lodestar	G-AGCZ	2023	British Overseas Airways Corporation	Crashed	Egypt	*	*
25.12.41	Sikorsky S-38	PK-AKT	314-12	Ned. Nieuw Guinea Petroleum	Destroyed by enemy action	Buitengorg, Dutch East Indies	*	*
26.12.41	Grumman G-21 Goose	PK-AER	1009	NV Mijnbouw	Destroyed by enemy action	Lake Tondano, Dutch East Indies	*	*
26.12.41	Sikorsky S-43B	PK-AFT	4352	KNILM	Destroyed by enemy action	Lake Tondano, Dutch East Indies	*	*
29.12.41	Douglas DC-3	PK-ALN	1936	KNILM	Destroyed by Japanese bombing	Polonia, Dutch East Indies	*	*
29.12.41	Short S.23	G-ADUX	S.815	British Overseas Airways Corporation	Crashed	Sabang, Dutch East Indies	*	*
oo.12.41	Douglas DC-2-115G	PK-AFJ	1374	KNILM	Crashed	Darmo, Dutch East Indies	*	*
oo.oo.41	Dewoitine D.338	F-AQBF	06	Air France	Destroyed	Syria	*	*
oo.oo.41	Dewoitine D.338	F-AQBO	15	Air France	Destroyed	Syria	*	*
oo.oo.41	Dewoitine D.338	F-AQBS	17	Air France	Destroyed	Syria	*	*
oo.oo.41	Dewoitine D.338	F-ARIA	23	Air France	Destroyed	Syria	*	*
oo.oo.41	Junkers Ju.52/3m	D-AFYS	4020	Deutsche Lufthansa	Crashed	Location Unknown	*	*
oo.oo.41	Junkers Ju.52/3m	D-AHUT	4021	Deutsche Lufthansa	Written off	Location Unknown	*	*
oo.oo.41	Junkers Ju.52/3m	D-AHIH	4025	Deutsche Lufthansa	Written off	Location Unknown	*	*
oo.oo.41	Junkers Ju.52/3m	D-AJAN	4026	Deutsche Lufthansa	Written off	Location Unknown	*	*
oo.oo.41	Junkers Ju.52/3m	D-ALUN	4036	Deutsche Lufthansa	Written off	Location Unknown	*	*
oo.oo.41	Junkers Ju.52/3m	D-ANAL	4039	Deutsche Lufthansa	Written off	Location Unknown	*	*
oo.oo.41	Junkers Ju.52/3m	D-AGIS	4048	Deutsche Lufthansa	Written off	Location Unknown	*	*
oo.oo.41	Junkers Ju.52/3m	D-AXES	4052	Deutsche Lufthansa	Written off	Location Unknown	*	*
oo.oo.41	Junkers Ju.52/3m	D-ANYF	4071	Deutsche Lufthansa	Written off	Location Unknown	*	*
oo.oo.41	Junkers Ju.52/3m	D-ANOL	5014	Deutsche Lufthansa	Written off	Location Unknown	*	*
oo.oo.41	Junkers Ju.52/3m	D-AKUO	5484	Deutsche Lufthansa	Written off	Location Unknown	*	*
oo.oo.41	Junkers Ju.52/3m	D-AFCD	5938	Deutsche Lufthansa	Written off	Location Unknown	*	*
oo.oo.41	Junkers Ju.52/3m	D-ANXG	5979	Deutsche Lufthansa	Written off	Location Unknown	*	*
oo.oo.41	Junkers Ju.52/3m	D-AHMS	6042	Deutsche Lufthansa	Written off	Location Unknown	*	*
oo.oo.41	Junkers Ju.52/3m	D-ARIW	6180	Deutsche Lufthansa	Written off	Location Unknown	*	*
oo.oo.41	Junkers Ju.52/3m	D-AVAJ	6370	Deutsche Lufthansa	Written off	Location Unknown	*	*
oo.oo.41	Junkers Ju.52/3m	D-AEAO	6670	Deutsche Lufthansa	Written off	Location Unknown	*	*
oo.oo.41	Junkers Ju.52/3m	D-AUXZ	7172	Deutsche Lufthansa	Written off	Location Unknown	*	*
oo.oo.41	Savoia Marchetti S.79	I-ALAN	19052	LATI	Damaged beyond repair	Abyssinia	*	*
oo.oo.41	Messerschmitt M.20b	D-UHEN	549	Deutsche Lufthansa	Crashed	Germany	*	*
oo.oo.41	Messerschmitt M.20a	D-UFON	392	Deutsche Lufthansa	Crashed	Germany	*	*
oo.oo.41	Focke-Wulf Fw.200 Condor	D-ADHR	2893	Deutsche Lufthansa	Written off	Location Unknown	*	*
oo.oo.41	Lockheed 10A Electra	*	*	Aeroflot	Crashed [Either cn 1090 or cn 1089]	USSR	*	*
07.01.42	de Havilland Dragon 2	VH-UVN	6106	Operator Unknown	Crashed	Broome, WA, Australia	*	*
17.01.42	Douglas DC-3	NC1946	3295	Transcontinental & Western Air	Crashed into mountain [Actress Carole Lombard killed]	nr Las Vegas, NV, USA	20	0
20.01.42	de Havilland DH.90 Dragonfly	VR-SAX	7511	Malayan Volunteer Air Force	Destroyed in air raid	Kallang, Malaya	*	*
23.01.42	Beechcraft 18D	CF-BVM	0169	Hudson Bay Company	Destroyed by fire	Canada	*	*
24.01.42	Douglas DC-3	PK-AFW	1982	KNILM	Shot down by Japanese	Samarinda, Dutch East Indies	*	*
26.01.42	Grumman G-21 Goose	PK-AES	1008	NV Mijnbouw	Written off	Koepang, Dutch East Indies	*	*
26.01.42	Grumman G-21A Goose	PK-AFS	1081	KNILM	Shot down by Japanese aircraft	Kupang, Dutch East Indies	*	*
30.01.42	Short S.23	G-AEUH	S.850	British Overseas Airways Corporation	Shot down by Japanese aircraft	Off Timor, Dutch East Indies	*	*
oo.01.42	Ford 4-AT-E Tri-Motor	VH-USX	4-AT-68	Guinea Airways	Destroyed by Japanese Forces	Papua & New Guinea	*	*
02.02.42	Douglas DC-3	NC21788	2187	Pennsylvania Central Airlines	Crashed	nr Lorettsville, VA, USA	*	*
02.02.42	Grumman G-21A Goose	PK-AKB	1057	Ned. Nieuw Guinea Petroleum	Destroyed by enemy action	Dobu, Dutch East Indies	*	*
06.02.42	Macchi C.100	I-PLUS	4159	Ala Littoria	Destroyed by fire	Cagliari, Sardinia, Italy	*	*
09.02.42	Fokker F.VIIb/3m	PK-AFG	5189	KNILM	Destroyed by enemy action	Kemayoran, Dutch East Indies	*	*
10.02.42	de Havilland DH.89A Dragon Rapide	VR-SAW	6364	Malayan Volunteer Air Force	Struck by RAF Hurricane	Palembang, Dutch East Indies	*	*
15.02.42	Consolidated 32-2 Liberator I	G-AGDR	9	British Overseas Airways Corporation	Shot down in error	Off Eddystone, UK	*	*
19.02.42	Sikorsky S-43B	PK-AFU	4353	KNILM	Destroyed by enemy action	Semplak, Dutch East Indies	*	*
19.02.42	Sikorsky S-43B	PK-AFX	4351	KNILM	Destroyed by enemy action	Semplak, Dutch East Indies	*	*

Date	Type	Reg'n	C/n	Operator	Accident	Location	F	S
19.02.42	Sikorsky S-38	PK-AKS	414-14	Ned. Nieuw Guinea Petroleum	Destroyed by enemy action	Buitengorg, Dutch East Indies	*	*
19.02.42	Fokker F.XII/3m	PK-AFI	5247	KNILM	Written off by enemy action	Semplak, Dutch East Indies	*	*
20.02.42	de Havilland DH.86	VH-USE	2309	Qantas	Crashed	Mt Pirie, Qld, Australia	*	*
22.02.42	Noorduyn Norseman IV	CF-BDG	014	Canadian Airways	Damaged by fire	Dumas Lake, NWT, Canada	*	*
24.02.42	Junkers Ju.52/3m	D-AGDA	4080	Deutsche Lufthansa	Written off	Location Unknown	*	*
26.02.42	Douglas DC-3	PK-AFZ	1981	KNILM	Crashed on landing	Djamni, Dutch East Indies	*	*
28.02.42	Short S.23	G-AETZ	S.842	British Overseas Airways Corporation	Shot down by Japanese aircraft	Between Java & Broome, Australia	*	*
28.02.42	Junkers Ju.52/3m	PP-VAL	4058	Varig	Crashed	Porto Alegre, Brazil	*	*
03.03.42	Douglas DC-3	PK-ALO	1937	KNILM	Destroyed on landing during Japanese air raid	Broome, WA, Australia	*	*
03.03.42	Douglas DC-3	PK-AFV	1965	KNILM	Shot down by Japanese Zeros	nr Wyndham, WA, Australia	4	8
03.03.42	Short S.23	G-AEUC	S.845	British Overseas Airways Corporation	Destroyed by Japanese bombing	Broome, WA, Australia	*	*
08.03.42	Ford 4-AT-E Tri-Motor	NC9613	4-AT-56	Aircraft Export Corporation	Destroyed by strong winds	Corpus Christi, TX, USA	0	*
10.03.42	Douglas C-49H	42-38257	2126	Pan American Airways	Destroyed by fire	Khartoum, Sudan	*	*
22.03.42	Short S.23	G-AEUF	S.848	British Overseas Airways Corporation	Crashed on landing	Port Darwin, NT, Australia	*	*
22.03.42	Airspeed Envoy III	VT-AHR	57	Indian National Airways	Crashed	India	*	*
25.03.42	Savoia-Marchetti SM.82	I-BENI	*	LATI	Written off	Location Unknown	*	*
26.03.42	Lockheed 14-WF62 Super Electra	PK-AFM	1411	KNILM	Crashed	Australia	*	*
28.03.42	Savoia-Marchetti SM.75	I-BURA	32040	LATI	Shot down	nr Sicily, Italy	*	*
oo.03.42	Avro 642	VH-UXD	642	Mandated Airlines	Destroyed by Japanese	New Guinea	*	*
02.05.42	Douglas DST	NC18146	1978	United Air Lines	Crashed into mountain	Salt Lake City, UT, USA	17	0
07.05.42	Lockheed 10A Electra	ZK-AFE	1103	Union Airways of New Zealand	Crashed	Mount Richmond, New Zealand	5	0
12.05.42	Douglas DC-3	NC21714	2129	Northwest Airlines	Crashed	Miles City, MT, USA	3	11
13.05.42	Lockheed 18 Lodestar	G-AGCR	2072	British Overseas Airways Corporation	Damaged on take-off	Malta	*	*
09.06.42	Savoia-Marchetti SM.82	I-BRAZ	41	LATI	Written off	Location Unknown	*	*
10.06.42	Ford 4-AT-B Tri-Motor	NC5493	4-AT-22	Atlantic Airmotive	Crashed	West Orange, NJ, USA	1	0
18.06.42	Savoia-Marchetti SM.83	I-ARGE	34016	LATI	Written off	Location Unknown	*	*
23.06.42	Lockheed 414 Hudson I	G-AGDF	3772	British Overseas Airways Corporation	Crashed	Off Skredewick, Sweden	*	*
02.07.42	Lockheed 18-07 Lodestar	F-ARTL	2011	Air France	Crashed after take-off	Port Etienne, French West Africa	0	3
04.08.42	de Havilland DH.80A Puss Moth	VP-YAR	2195	Rhodesia & Nyasaland Airways	Crashed	Location Unknown	*	*
12.08.42	Armstrong Whitworth Whitley VIII	G-AGDU	AW.1126	British Overseas Airways Corporation	Damaged beyond repair	Whitchurch, Somerset, UK	0	*
13.08.42	Liore et Olivier H.246	F-AREJ	403	Air France	Damaged by RAF Hurricanes & sank on landing	Algiers, Algeria	4	*
16.08.42	Savoia-Marchetti SM.83	I-ANDE	34011	LATI	Crashed on take-off	Athens, Greece	2	*
20.08.42	de Havilland DH.89A Dragon Rapide	G-AFIA	6419	Anglo Iranian Oil Co	Destroyed by fire	Abadan, Iran	*	*
22.08.42	Lockheed 14 Super Electra	PJ-AIP	*	KLM Royal Dutch Airlines	Crashed	Trinidad	*	*
13.09.42	de Havilland Flamingo	G-AFYI	95012	British Overseas Airways Corporation	Damaged on landing	Adana, Turkey	*	*
24.09.42	Short S.30	G-AFCZ	S.885	British Overseas Airways Corporation	Crashed	Off West Africa	*	*
26.09.42	Armstrong Whitworth Whitley V	G-AGCI	AW.2716	British Overseas Airways Corporation	Crashed	Off Gibraltar	*	*
27.09.42	Dewoitine D.342	F-ARIZ	01	Air France	Crashed on take-off	Ameur el Ain, Algeria	25	0
03.10.42	Vought-Sikorsky VS-44A	NC41880	4401	American Export Airlines	Crashed on take-off	Botwood, Newfoundland	11	26
23.10.42	Douglas DC-3	NC16017	1555	American Airlines	Mid-air collision with USAAF B-34	Palm Springs, CA, USA	12(*)	0
24.10.42	Boeing 247D	C-144	*	SCADTA	Crashed	Location Unknown	*	*
04.11.42	Douglas DC-3	NC18951	2015	Transcontinental & Western Air	Mid-air collision with USAAF C-53 41-20116	nr Kansas City, MO, USA	0(*)	3
09.11.42	Fiat G.12	I-FELI	18	LATI	Crashed	Mediterranean Sea	0	*
15.11.42	Savoia-Marchetti SM.75	I-TELO	32047	LATI	Shot down	Location Unknown	*	0
16.11.42	Lockheed Vega 5B	XA-BLZ	109	Lineas Aereas Mineras	Crashed	Parral, Mexico	*	*
17.11.42	Boeing C-73	42-68367	1707	Transcontinental & Western Air	Damaged on landing	Allegheny City, PA, USA	0	*
18.11.42	de Havilland Flamingo	G-AFYG	95010	British Overseas Airways Corporation	Damaged on take-off	Addis Ababa, Abyssinia	*	*
18.11.42	Douglas DC-3	NC16064	1904	United Air Lines	Crashed	Dayton, OH, USA	*	*
21.11.42	Ford 4-AT-B Tri-Motor	NC6892	4-AT-28	Atlantic Airmotive	Crashed due to icing	Billings, MT, USA	2	0
26.11.42	Lockheed Vega 5	XA-BAW	059	Cia Aeronautica Francisco Sarabia	Crashed	Mexico City, Mexico	*	*
oo.11.42	Dewoitine D.338	FL-ARI	27	Lignes Aeriennes Militaire	Force-landed after engine failure	Bangui, French Equatorial Africa	*	*
oo.11.42	Savoia-Marchetti SM.73	I-DOUL	*	LATI	Written off	Location Unknown	*	*
01.12.42	Short S.23	G-AETX	S.840	British Overseas Airways Corporation	Exploded at moorings	Durban, South Africa	0	*

Date	Type	Reg'n	C/n	Operator	Accident	Location	F	S
09.12.42	Douglas DC-3	D-ABBF	2110	Deutsche Lufthansa	Crashed	Madrid, Spain	*	*
12.12.42	Tupolev PS-124	SSSR-L760	*	Aeroflot	Crashed on landing	Uzbekistan, USSR	*	*
15.12.42	Douglas DC-3	NC16060	1900	Western Air Lines	Crashed after violent manoeuvre	Fairfield, UT, USA	17	2
21.12.42	de Havilland DH.90 Dragonfly	ZK-AGP	7566	Air Travel	Crashed	Off Westport, New Zealand	4	*
oo.12.42	Barkley-Grow T8P-1	CF-BMV	05	Maritime Central Airways	Destroyed in attempted rescue of B-17 crew	Greenland	*	*
oo.oo.42	Junkers G.31	VH-UOW	3010	Guinea Airways	Destroyed by Japanese	New Guinea	*	*
oo.oo.42	Junkers G.31	VH-UOU	3011	Bulolo Gold Dredging	Destroyed by Japanese	New Guinea	*	*
oo.oo.42	Junkers G.31	VH-UOV	3012	Bulolo Gold Dredging	Destroyed by Japanese	New Guinea	*	*
oo.oo.42	Junkers G.31	VH-URQ	3000	Bulolo Gold Dredging	Destroyed by Japanese	New Guinea	*	*
oo.oo.42	Junkers Ju.52/3m	D-AGUK	4022	Deutsche Lufthansa	Written off	Location Unknown	*	*
oo.oo.42	Junkers Ju.52/3m	D-AKEP	4029	Deutsche Lufthansa	Written off	Location Unknown	*	*
oo.oo.42	Junkers Ju.52/3m	D-AKOK	4030	Deutsche Lufthansa	Written off	Location Unknown	*	*
oo.oo.42	Junkers Ju.52/3m	D-AFES	4047	Deutsche Lufthansa	Written off	Location Unknown	*	*
oo.oo.42	Junkers Ju.52/3m	D-ATON	4054	Deutsche Lufthansa	Written off	Location Unknown	*	*
oo.oo.42	Junkers Ju.52/3m	D-ALAN	5010	Deutsche Lufthansa	Written off	Location Unknown	*	*
oo.oo.42	Junkers Ju.52/3m	D-ANEN	5072	Deutsche Lufthansa	Written off	Location Unknown	*	*
oo.oo.42	Junkers Ju.52/3m	D-ARDS	5919	Deutsche Lufthansa	Written off	Location Unknown	*	*
oo.oo.42	Junkers Ju.52/3m	D-ABVF	5954	Deutsche Lufthansa	Written off	Location Unknown	*	*
oo.oo.42	Junkers Ju.52/3m	D-AHFN	6047	Deutsche Lufthansa	Written off	Location Unknown	*	*
oo.oo.42	Junkers Ju.52/3m	D-ASLG	6369	Deutsche Lufthansa	Written off	Location Unknown	*	*
oo.oo.42	Junkers Ju.52/3m	D-AXFH	6372	Deutsche Lufthansa	Written off	Location Unknown	*	*
oo.oo.42	Junkers Ju.52/3m	D-AGEP	6386	Deutsche Lufthansa	Written off	Location Unknown	*	*
oo.oo.42	Junkers Ju.52/3m	D-AGBI	6659	Deutsche Lufthansa	Written off	Location Unknown	*	*
oo.oo.42	Junkers Ju.52/3m	D-AYGX	7208	Deutsche Lufthansa	Written off	Location Unknown	*	*
oo.oo.42	Douglas DC-2-118A	NC14292	1352	Panagra	Crashed	Between Arequipa & Lima, Peru	0	5
oo.oo.42	de Havilland DH.66 Hercules	VH-UJP	345	Stephens Aviation	Destroyed by Japanese forces	New Guinea	*	*
oo.oo.42	Douglas DC-5	VH-CXA	428	Royal Australian Air Force	Crashed on landing	Parrafield, Australia	*	*
oo.oo.42	de Havilland DH.89 Dragon Rapide	PK-AKV	6292	KNILM	Destroyed to avoid capture by Japanese	Dutch East Indies	*	*
oo.oo.42	Messerschmitt M.20b	D-UKUM	542	Deutsche Lufthansa	Destroyed	Germany	*	*
oo.oo.42	Messerschmitt M.20b	D-UREK	543	Deutsche Lufthansa	Destroyed	Germany	*	*
oo.oo.42	Messerschmitt M.20b	D-UVOK	544	Deutsche Lufthansa	Destroyed	Germany	*	*
oo.oo.42	Messerschmitt M.20b	D-UMOK	547	Deutsche Lufthansa	Destroyed	Germany	*	*
oo.oo.42	Lockheed Air Express Special	NC974Y	130	Pacific Airmotive Corporation	Destroyed on ground by windstorm	nr Reno, NV, USA	0	0
oo.oo.42	Ford 4-AT-B Tri-Motor	NC5093	4-AT-20	H.W.Robinson	Crashed on landing	Metz, MO, USA	0	*
01.01.43	Junkers Ju.52/3m	OO-AUG	6036	Sabena	Crashed	nr Bangui, Fr Equatorial Africa	*	*
09.01.43	Short S.26	G-AFCK	S.873	British Overseas Airways Corporation	Crashed	River Tagus, Lisbon, Portugal	13	*
11.01.43	Douglas DC-3	NC16090	1929	United Air Lines	Crashed	Oakland, CA, USA	*	*
15.01.43	Douglas C-54 Skymaster	41-32939	3114	Transcontinental & Western Air	Crashed	nr Paramaribo, Surinam	*	*
21.01.43	Martin M.130	NC14715	557	Pan American Airways	Crashed into mountain	Boonville, CA, USA	19	0
22.01.43	Douglas DC-3	NC33645	4124	Panagra	Crashed	Mt Chaparra, Peru	14	1
02.02.43	de Havilland DH.89A Dragon Rapide	G-AGED	6621	Scottish Airways	Crashed	Renfrew, UK	*	*
15.02.43	de Havilland Flamingo	G-AFYE	95007	British Overseas Airways Corporation	Crashed	Asmara, Eritrea	*	*
18.02.43	Potez 56	*	*	LAN-Chile	Crashed	Chile	*	*
22.02.43	Boeing 314	NC18603	1990	Pan American Airways	Crashed on landing [Novelist Ben Robertson killed]	River Tagus, Lisbon, Portugal	24	15
19.03.43	Douglas DC-3	VH-ACB	2030	Australian National Airways	Crashed	nr Essendon, Vic, Australia	*	*
23.03.43	Consolidated Catalina	G-AGDA	*	British Overseas Airways Corporation	Crashed	Poole Harbour, Dorset, UK	*	*
29.03.43	Potez 56	*	*	LAN-Chile	Crashed	Chile	*	*
04.04.43	Lockheed 18 Lodestar	G-AGEJ	2085	British Overseas Airways Corporation	Crashed	North Sea	*	*
10.04.43	Savoia-Marchetti SM.75	I-BONI	32071	LATI	Shot down	Location Unknown	*	*
22.04.43	Short S.23	VH-ADU	S.844	Qantas	Crashed	Off Port Moresby, New Guinea	*	*
03.05.43	Liore et Olivier 45	*	*	Air France	Crashed on approach	Venissieux, France	5	0
07.05.43	Savoia-Marchetti SM.75	I-BELO	32072	LATI	Destroyed on ground in air raid	Tunis, Tunisia	*	*
31.05.43	Sabca F.VIIb/3m	OO-AIP	*	Sabena	Crashed	Belgian Congo	*	*
01.06.43	Douglas DC-3	G-AGBB	1590	British Overseas Airways Corporation	Shot down by German aircraft [Actor Leslie Howard killed]	Bay of Biscay	*	0

Date	Type	Reg'n	C/n	Operator	Accident	Location	F	S
16.06.43	Lockheed Hudson VI	FK459	*	British Overseas Airways Corporation	Crashed	Khartoum, Sudan	17	0
23.06.43	Lockheed Vega 5C	XA-DAI	102	Lineas Aereas Mineras	Destroyed by fire	Parral, Mexico	*	*
30.06.43	Lockheed Hudson VI	FK618	*	British Overseas Airways Corporation	Crashed	Khartoum, Sudan	16	0
06.07.43	de Havilland Albatross	G-AFDK	6804	British Overseas Airways Corporation	Crash landed	nr Shannon, Eire	0	*
07.07.43	Savoia-Marchetti SM.83	I-ARMA	34020	LATI	Destroyed	Tunis, Tunisia	*	*
27.07.43	Sikorsky S-42	NC16736	4209	Pan American Airways	Crashed	Manaus, Brazil	*	*
28.07.43	Short Sunderland 3	G-AGES	–	British Overseas Airways Corporation	Crashed	Brandon Head, Eire	10	15
28.07.43	Douglas DC-3	NC16014	1552	American Airlines	Crashed in storm	Tramniel, KY, USA	19	2
04.08.43	Stinson Model A	VT-ACW	9113	Tata & Sons	Crashed	India	6	*
17.08.43	de Havilland Mosquito 6	G-AGGF	–	British Overseas Airways Corporation	Crashed on approach	Invermairk, Fifeshire, UK	*	*
18.08.43	Savoia-Marchetti SM.75	I-BETA	001	LATI	Written off	Location Unknown	*	*
26.08.43	Lockheed 14H Super Electra	VP-TAH	1406	British West Indian Airways	Destroyed by fire while refuelling	Piarco, Trinidad	*	*
26.08.43	Lockheed Vega 5C High-Speed Special	NC965Y	171	F.M.Matthews	Destroyed in ground fire	Memphis, TN, USA	*	*
27.08.43	Junkers Ju.52/3m	PP-SPD	5459	VASP	Struck building & crashed	Rio de Janeiro, Brazil	18	3
28.08.43	Douglas DC-3	SE-BAF	2133	AB Aerotransport	Shot down by German aircraft	North Sea	7	0
00.08.43	Ford 5-AT-B Tri-Motor	NC9651	5-AT-034	Star Air Lines	Crashed on take-off	Fairbanks, Alaska	0	*
15.09.43	Douglas DC-3	NC33657	4803	American Airlines	Crashed	Dallas, TX, USA	*	*
24.09.43	Consolidated Commodore	NC668M	12	Pan American Airways	Crashed on test flight	Miami, FL, USA	1	2
10.10.43	Lockheed Vega 5C	NC972Y	160	US Engineers Office	Destroyed in hangar fire	Van Nuys, CA, USA	*	*
15.10.43	Douglas DC-3	NC16008	1588	American Airlines	Crashed due to icing	nr Centerville, TN, USA	*	*
22.10.43	Douglas DC-3	SE-BAG	2132	AB Aerotransport	Shot down by German aircraft	Hallo, Sweden	13	2
25.10.43	de Havilland Mosquito 6	G-AGGG	–	British Overseas Airways Corporation	Crashed on approach	nr Leuchars, Fifeshire, UK	*	*
06.11.43	Short Sunderland 3	G-AGIB	–	British Overseas Airways Corporation	Crashed	Sollum, Libya	*	*
19.11.43	Lockheed 10A Electra	G-AFCS	1025	British Overseas Airways Corporation	Crashed	Almaza, Egypt	*	*
17.12.43	Lockheed 18 Lodestar	G-AGDE	2086	British Overseas Airways Corporation	Crashed	Off Leuchars, Fifeshire, UK	*	*
00.00.43	Focke-Wulf Fw.200 Condor	D-AMHC	2895	Deutsche Lufthansa	Written off	Location Unknown	*	*
00.00.43	Douglas DC-3	D-AAIF	2024	Deutsche Lufthansa	Destroyed by bombing	Location Unknown	*	*
00.00.43	Junkers Ju.52/3m	D-ANAZ	5128	Deutsche Lufthansa	Written off	Location Unknown	*	*
00.00.43	Junkers Ju.52/3m	D-AXAT	5693	Deutsche Lufthansa	Written off	Location Unknown	*	*
00.00.43	Junkers Ju.52/3m	D-ALAM	5740	Deutsche Lufthansa	Written off	Location Unknown	*	*
00.00.43	Junkers Ju.52/3m	D-ADHF	6066	Deutsche Lufthansa	Written off	Location Unknown	*	*
00.00.43	Junkers Ju.52/3m	D-APXD	6149	Deutsche Lufthansa	Written off	Location Unknown	*	*
00.00.43	Junkers Ju.52/3m	D-ABEW	6432	Deutsche Lufthansa	Written off	Location Unknown	*	*
00.00.43	Junkers Ju.52/3m	D-ACBE	6550	Deutsche Lufthansa	Written off	Location Unknown	*	*
00.00.43	Boeing 247D	C-138	*	SCADTA	Destroyed by fire	Location Unknown	*	*
00.00.43	Grumman G-21A Goose	*	*	United States Coast Guard	Crashed [Not found until 26.08.87]	240km west of Kodiak, Alaska	*	*
00.00.43	Messerschmitt M.20a	D-UDAL	421	Deutsche Lufthansa	Destroyed	Germany	*	*
00.00.43	Messerschmitt M.20b	D-UJAR	548	Deutsche Lufthansa	Crashed	Germany	*	*
03.01.44	Noorduyn Norseman IV	CF-BAW	009	Arrow Airways	Destroyed by fire	Yellowknife, NWT, Canada	*	*
03.01.44	de Havilland Mosquito 6	G-AGGD	–	British Overseas Airways Corporation	Crashed on emergency landing	Sarenas, Sweden	*	*
26.01.44	de Havilland DH.89A Dragon Rapide	VH-ADE	6341	Australian National Airways	Crashed	Cape Sidmouth, Qld, Australia	*	*
03.02.44	Douglas DC-2-115J	EC-AAC	1521	Iberia	Crashed	Prat de Uobregat, Spain	*	*
10.02.44	Douglas DC-3	NC21767	2165	American Airlines	Crashed in heavy snow	nr Memphis, TN, USA	24	0
13.02.44	Lockheed 14-WF62 Super Electra	PK-AFN	1414	KNILM	Written off	Location Unknown	*	*
23.02.44	Lockheed 14-H2 Super Electra	CR-AAV	1507	DETA	Crashed on take-off	Quelimane, Mozambique	*	*
27.02.44	Boeing 247	C-146	1708	Avianca	Crashed after engine failure	nr Medellin, Colombia	0	*
25.03.44	Junkers Ju.52/3m	OO-AGU	5510	Sabena	Crashed	Costermansville, Belgian Congo	*	*
03.04.44	Junkers Ju.52/3m	OO-AUF	5852	Sabena	Crashed	Mongana, Belgian Congo	*	*
05.04.44	Dewoitine D.338	F-AOZA	001	Air France	Destroyed in Allied air raid	Toulouse, France	*	*
05.04.44	Dewoitine D.338	F-AQBL	12	Air France	Destroyed in Allied air raid	Toulouse, France	*	*
14.04.44	Lockheed 10A Electra	G-AEPR	1083	British Overseas Airways Corporation	Destroyed	Egypt	*	*
21.04.44	Douglas DC-3	D-AAIG	2095	Deutsche Lufthansa	Crashed	Off Frederikstad, Norway	*	*
21.04.44	Douglas DC-3	G-AGFZ	6225	British Overseas Airways Corporation	Crashed on landing	Bromma, Sweden	*	*
11.05.44	Lockheed Vega 5B	XA-DAH	125	Lineas Aereas Mineras	Crashed	San Luis Potosi, Mexico	*	*

Date	Type	Reg'n	C/n	Operator	Accident	Location	F	S
27.05.44	Type Unknown	*	*	CNAC	Crashed at sea in bad weather [? DC-3 or DC-2]	Off Calcutta, India	14	0
20.06.44	Lockheed 10C Electra	PP-VAQ	1008	Varig	Crashed into river	Porto Alegre, Brazil	10	0
30.06.44	de Havilland Dragon 2	ZK-AHT	6090	Air Travel	Crashed into mountain	Mount Hope, New Zealand	*	*
03.07.44	Ford Tri-Motor	*	*	TACA	Crashed into mountain	nr Matagalpa, Nicaragua	1	0
20.07.44	de Havilland DH.89A Dragon Rapide	VH-UBN	6253	Operator Unknown	Crashed	Mt Kitchener, SA, Australia	*	*
25.07.44	Lockheed 14 Super Electra	YV-ADI	1509	Linea Aeropostal Venezolana	Crashed	Barcelona, Venezuela	*	*
02.08.44	Lockheed Vega 5B	NC162W	128	Alaska Airlines	Crashed	Kuskokwin River, Alaska	0	5
08.08.44	Sikorsky S-42	NC823M	4201	Pan American Airways	Crashed on take-off & sank	Antilla, Cuba	17	14
09.08.44	Douglas DC-2-115D	HB-ISI	1331	Swissair	Destroyed by US bombing	Stuttgart, Germany	*	*
14.08.44	Douglas DC-3	D-AAIE	2023	Deutsche Lufthansa	Destroyed by US bombing	Stuttgart, Germany	*	*
19.08.44	de Havilland Mosquito 6	G-AGKP	–	British Overseas Airways Corporation	Crashed	North Sea	*	*
21.08.44	Lockheed 18 Lodestar	CB-25	2088	Lloyd Aereo Boliviano	Destroyed by fire	La Paz, Bolivia	0	*
28.08.44	Douglas DC-3	G-AGIR	11932	British Overseas Airways Corporation	Crashed	Morocco	*	*
29.08.44	Lockheed 18 Lodestar	G-AGIH	2491	British Overseas Airways Corporation	Crashed	Kinnekulle, Sweden	4	4
29.08.44	de Havilland Mosquito 6	G-AGKR	–	British Overseas Airways Corporation	Crashed at sea	North Sea	*	*
30.08.44	Lockheed 18 Lodestar	PP-PBI	2114	Panair do Brasil	Crashed in fog	Sao Paulo, Brazil	16	0
oo.08.44	Latecoere 522	F-ARAP	01	Air France	Destroyed when German forces blew up hangar	Etang de Berre, France	*	*
oo.08.44	Latecoere 521	F-NORD	*	French Navy	Destroyed when Germans blew up hangar	Etang de Berre, France	*	*
18.09.44	Faucett F.19	OA-BBJ-261	01	Faucett	Crashed	Cerro Chao, Peru	6	0
21.09.44	Lockheed 18 Lodestar	PP-PBH	2113	Panair do Brasil	Crashed	Rio Doce, Brazil	17	0
oo.09.44	Junkers Ju.90V3	D-AURE	4915	Deutsche Lufthansa	Destroyed by Allied bombing	Stuttgart, Germany	*	*
09.10.44	de Havilland DH.86	VH-USC	2307	Qantas	Written off	Darwin, NT, Australia	*	*
11.10.44	Lockheed 18 Lodestar	PP-NAF	2150	Navegacao Aerea Brasiliera	Crashed	Pirapora, Brazil	*	*
16.10.44	Junkers Ju.52/3mg8e	D-ADQV	640608	Deutsche Lufthansa	Crashed into mountain in bad weather	Telemark, Norway	15	0
04.11.44	Douglas DC-3	NC28310	2251	Transcontinental & Western Air	Crashed after wing broke off in storm	Hartford, CA, USA	24	0
10.11.44	Lockheed Hudson	*	*	Central Air Transport	Crashed	Kunming, China	*	*
18.11.44	Short S.33	VH-ACD	S.1025	Qantas	Crashed	Rose Bay, Sydney, NSW, Australia	*	*
29.11.44	Focke-Wulf Fw.200 Condor	D-ARHW	2994	Deutsche Lufthansa	Crashed	Baltic Sea	*	*
29.11.44	Lockheed 18 Lodestar	G-AGBW	2094	British Overseas Airways Corporation	Crashed	Kinangop Peak, Kenya	*	*
29.11.44	Ford 5-AT-B Tri-Motor	XH-TAN	*	TACA	Crashed	Tegucigalpa, Honduras	*	*
01.12.44	Douglas DC-3	NC17322	1968	Transcontinental & Western Air	Crashed in fog	Van Nuys, CA, USA	8	15
30.12.44	Avro Lancaster X	CF-CMU	–	Trans Canada Airlines	Crashed	Atlantic Ocean	5	0
oo.oo.44	Fleet 50K Freighter	CF-BJU	202	Labrador Mining & Exploration Co	Crashed	Labrador, Canada	*	*
oo.oo.44	Liore et Olivier H.246	F-AREK	404	French Navy	Destroyed in allied attack	Lyon, France	*	*
04.01.45	Douglas DC-3	NC19470	11680	Panagra	Crashed after being stolen from Limatambo, Peru	Off Chorillos, Peru	*	*
07.01.45	Douglas DC-3	*	*	CNAC	Crashed	Talifu, China	*	*
08.01.45	Martin M.130	NC14716	558	Pan American Airways	Crashed on landing	Port of Spain, Trinidad	23	7
10.01.45	Douglas DC-3	NC25684	2215	American Airlines	Crashed	Burbank, CA, USA	24	0
06.02.45	de Havilland DH.89A Dragon Rapide	SU-ABP	6298	Misrair	Written off	Mairuit, Egypt	*	*
15.02.45	Lockheed 18 Lodestar	PP-NAE	2149	Navegacao Aerea Brasiliera	Crashed	Lagoa Santa, Brazil	11	0
19.02.45	Lockheed Vega 5B	AN-ABL	066	J.Angel & J.Baker	Crashed	Boaco, Nicaragua	*	*
22.02.45	Lockheed Vega 5	XA-BFT	050	Lineas Aereas Mexicanas	Crashed	Monclova, Mexico	*	*
23.02.45	Douglas DC-3	NC18142	2138	American Airlines	Crashed into mountain	Marion, VA, USA	16	5
08.04.45	Douglas DC-3	G-AGKM	14986/26431	British Overseas Airways Corporation	Damaged beyond repair	El Adem, Libya	*	*
14.04.45	Douglas DC-3	NC25692	2262	Pennsylvania Central Airlines	Crashed into mountain	Morgantown, WV, USA	20	0
21.04.45	Focke-Wulf Fw.200 Condor	D-ASHH	0009	Deutsche Lufthansa	Shot down by Allied forces	Piesenkofen, Germany	*	*
21.04.45	Douglas C-54A Skymaster	41-107452	7471	American Export Airlines	Damaged beyond repair	Location Unknown	*	*
01.05.45	Douglas DC-3	G-AGNA	14967/26412	British Overseas Airways Corporation	Crashed	Basra, Iraq	*	*
02.05.45	Lockheed 18 Lodestar	G-AGLI	2620	British Overseas Airways Corporation	Crashed	Gulf of Bothnia	*	*
13.05.45	Lockheed 18 Lodestar	ZK-AHU	2490	Union Airways of New Zealand	Crashed on take-off while being stolen	Auckland, New Zealand	*	*
03.06.45	Douglas DC-3	YS-22	11724	Aerovias Brasil	Crashed	Ipiabas, Brazil	*	*
04.06.45	Douglas DC-3	NC33611	4102	Pan American Airways	Crashed on take-off	Port of Spain, Trinidad	0	12
09.06.45	Lockheed Vega 5C	NC48610	210	R.B.Boardman	Crashed	El Paso, TX, USA	1	3
12.06.45	Ford 5-AT-B Tri-Motor	AN-AAR	5-AT-013	TACA	Crashed on take-off	Puerto Cabezas, Nicaragua	*	*

Date	Type	Reg'n	C/n	Operator	Accident	Location	F	S
24.06.45	de Havilland DH.86	VH-USF	2310	MacRobertson-Miller Airlines	Crashed	Geraldton, WA, Australia	*	*
24.06.45	Faucett F.19	OB-BBP-279	16	Faucett	Crashed	nr Motupe, Peru	3	0
09.07.45	Beechcraft 18D	TF-ISL	0176	Icelandair	Destroyed by fire	Stori-Kroppur, Iceland	*	*
12.07.45	Douglas DC-3	NC25647	2235	Eastern Air Lines	Mid-air collision with USAAF A-26	Florence, SC, USA	1(2)	*
01.08.45	Boeing 247D	XA-DUY	1723	Lineas Aereas Mineras	Crashed into mountains	nr San Luis Potosi, Mexico	12	0
03.08.45	Sikorsky S-43	NC15066	4306	Pan American Airways	Sank on landing	Fort de France, Martinique	4	10
11.08.45	Douglas DC-2-243	XA-DOT	2075	Mexicana	Crashed in bad weather	Ixtaccihuatl, Mexico	16	0
27.08.45	Lockheed 18 Lodestar	NC25636	2028	Continental Airlines	Crashed	Albuquerque, NM, USA	*	*
07.09.45	Douglas DC-3	NC33631	4137	Eastern Air Lines	Crashed after in-flight fire	Florence, SC, USA	1	*
10.09.45	AAC.1 Toucan	F-BAJP	019	Air France	Written off	Le Bourget, France	*	*
10.09.45	Faucett F.19	OB-PAF-133	19	Faucett	Crashed	Tablabambe, Peru	6	*
13.09.45	Lockheed 18 Lodestar	NC33349	2370	National Airlines	Crashed on overshoot	Tampa, FL, USA	*	*
29.09.45	Boeing 247D	C-140	*	Avianca	Damaged in forced landing	Corozal, Colombia	0	*
05.10.45	Lockheed 18 Lodestar	NC18199	2265	National Airlines	Crashed into lake	Lakeland, FL, USA	2	13
11.10.45	Lockheed 18 Lodestar	NC15555	2207	National Airlines	Crashed on landing	Banana River, FL, USA	0	16
24.10.45	Douglas DC-3	G-AGHR	10097	British Overseas Airways Corporation	Crashed on take-off	Luqa, Malta	*	*
24.10.45	Faucett F.19	OB-PAG-139	24	Faucett	Crashed on take-off	Tarapoto, Peru	5	0
26.10.45	Avro Anson I	SU-ACX	–	Misrair	Collided with RAF Stirling PJ947	Lydda, Palestine	1(*)	3
31.10.45	Junkers Ju.52/3mce	OH-LAK	4014	Aero O/Y	Crashed on approach	Hyvinkaa, Finland	0	14
oo.10.45	Douglas DC-2-115J	EC-AAB	1417	Iberia	Crashed	Spain	*	*
04.11.45	Boeing 314	NC18601	1988	Pan American Airways	Ditched after engine failure & sunk by gunfire from US ship	Pacific Ocean	*	*
05.11.45	Avro Anson II	PP-ATD	BAC 11809	L.A. Transcontinental Brasiliera	Crashed	Tupa, Brazil	*	*
10.11.45	AAC.1 Toucan	F-BANO	149	Air France	Written off	Le Bourget, France	*	*
13.11.45	Douglas DC-3	VH-CDC	3232	Australian National Airways	Crashed on take-off	Tacloban, Philippines	*	*
23.11.45	AAC.1 Toucan	F-BAKL	102	Air France	Written off	Toulouse, France	*	*
oo.11.45	Barkley-Grow T8P-1	CF-BTX	11	Canadian Pacific Airlines	Damaged in forced landing	Katawa Lake, Canada	*	*
03.12.45	Handley Page Hermes 1	G-AGSS	HP.68/1	Handley Page	Crashed on first flight	Radlett, Herts, UK	2	0
04.12.45	Boeing B-17	SE-BAM	*	AB Aerotransport	Crashed	Strangas, Sweden	6	0
14.12.45	Lockheed 18 Lodestar	OO-CAK	2340	Sabena	Force landed & caught fire	Kouande, French Equatorial Africa	0	*
17.12.45	Fokker F.XII	OY-DIG	75	DDL	Crashed	Kastrup, Denmark	*	*
19.12.45	Avro Anson II	PP-MTA	3085	Companhia Meridional de Transportes	Crashed into mountain after take-off	nr Itaipu, Brazil	*	*
25.12.45	Lockheed 18 Lodestar	F-BALV	2380	Air France	Crashed	nr Bangui, French Equatorial Africa	8	0
28.12.45	Avro Anson I	SU-ADB	–	Misrair	Crashed	nr Baghdad, Iraq	*	*
29.12.45	Noorduyn Norseman IV	CF-BDD	011	Canadian Airways	Damaged on landing	Tofino, BC, Canada	*	*
30.12.45	Douglas DC-3	NC18123	1999	Eastern Air Lines	Crashed in bay	La Guardia, NY, USA	1	13
30.12.45	de Havilland DH.89A Dragon Rapide	VT-AHB	6308	Air Services of India	Crashed	Kanpur, India	*	*
oo.oo.45	Lockheed Vega 5B	XA-DEB	133	Lineas Aereas Mexicanas	Damaged beyond repair	Tayoltita, Mexico	*	*
oo.oo.45	Junkers W.34	II	2739	Civil Air Transport	Written off	China	*	*
06.01.46	Douglas DC-3	NC21786	4131	Pennsylvania Central Airlines	Overshot on landing	Birmingham, AL, USA	2	17
12.01.46	Noorduyn Norseman	TF-RVE	113	Loftleidir	Destroyed	Patreksfjordur, Iceland	*	*
13.01.46	AAC.1 Toucan	F-BANP	150	Air France	Crashed into church steeple	Le Bouscat, France	*	0
18.01.46	Douglas DC-3	NC19970	3254	Eastern Air Lines	Crashed due to wing fire	Cheshire, CT, USA	17	0
18.01.46	Douglas DC-2-124	CX-AEG	1324	Pluna	Damaged by storm	Uruguay	*	*
23.01.46	Douglas DC-3	G-AGIY	12102	British Overseas Airways Corporation	Crash landed	El Adem, Libya	*	*
30.01.46	Boeing B-17G	OY-DFE	*	DDL	Collided with another aircraft on landing	Kastrup, Denmark	*	*
31.01.46	Douglas DC-3	NC25675	2147	United Air Lines	Crashed	Mt Elk, WY, USA	20	0
02.02.46	AAC.1 Toucan	F-BALK	096	Air France	Written off	Belo, Madagascar	*	*
02.02.46	Avro Anson V	XA-DUU	–	Aerotransportes del Sureste	Crashed	Mexico	*	*
04.02.46	AAC.1 Toucan	F-BAKO	057	Air France	Damaged beyond repair	Mahon, Balearic Is, Spain	*	*
05.02.46	Douglas DC-3	PP-CBS	4963	Cruzeiro	Destroyed by fire	Ilheos, Brazil	*	*
09.02.46	Lockheed 10A Electra	YV-ADA	1126	Linea Aeropostal Venezolana	Written off	Location Unknown	*	*
12.02.46	Lockheed 18 Lodestar	YV-AFI	2166	Linea Aeropostal Venezolana	Written off	Location Unknown	*	*
15.02.46	Short Sunderland 3	G-AGET	–	British Overseas Airways Corporation	Destroyed by fire during refuelling	Calcutta, India	*	*
18.02.46	Lockheed 414-56 Hudson 3	VP-TAL	7560	British West Indian Airways	Crashed on take-off	Ciudad Trujillo, Dominican Republic	0	9

Date	Type	Reg'n	C/n	Operator	Accident	Location	F	S
21.02.46	Consolidated Liberator II	G-AGEM	26	British Overseas Airways Corporation	Crashed	Charlottetown, PEI, Canada	1	*
25.02.46	Douglas DC-3	NC14941	4468	Operator Unknown	Crashed	Location Unknown	*	*
01.03.46	Douglas DC-2-243	C-157	2086	TACA	Crashed	Medellin, Colombia	*	*
03.03.46	Douglas DC-3	NC21799	2203	American Airlines	Crashed into mountain	San Diego, CA, USA	25	0
04.03.46	Short Sunderland 3	G-AGEV	–	British Overseas Airways Corporation	Damaged on landing	Poole, Dorset, UK	*	*
05.03.46	Junkers Ju.52/3m	*	*	Ceskoslovenske Aerolinie	Crashed on approach	Prague, Czechoslovakia	10	4
06.03.46	Avro Anson II	PP-MTB	F356	Companhia Meridional de Transportes	Damaged beyond repair	Volta Redonda, Brazil	*	*
08.03.46	Douglas DC-3	NC39188	19636	Air Cargo Transport	Damaged by fire	Newark, NJ, USA	*	*
08.03.46	Douglas DC-3	NC41798	4208	Air Cargo Transport	Destroyed by fire	Newark, NJ, USA	*	*
08.03.46	Avro Anson II	PP-MTC	735	Companhia Meridional de Transportes	Damaged in ground loop on landing	Rio de Janeiro, Brazil	*	*
09.03.46	de Havilland DH.89A Dragon Rapide	CF-BNG	6472	Ginger Coote Airways	Damaged by fire	Great Lakes, PQ, Canada	*	*
10.03.46	Douglas DC-3	VH-AET	6013	Australian National Airways	Crashed	Off Hobart, Tasmania, Australia	24	0
10.03.46	Short Sunderland 3	G-AGHV	–	British Overseas Airways Corporation	Broke from moorings & sank	Rod-el-Farag, Egypt	*	*
24.03.46	Avro Lancastrian 1	G-AGLX	1178	British Overseas Airways Corporation	Crashed	North of Cocos Islands	10	0
29.03.46	Lockheed 049 Constellation	NC86510	2034	Transcontinental & Western Air	Crashed	Washington, DC, USA	0	*
01.04.46	de Havilland DH.89A Dragon Rapide	G-AERZ	6356	Railway Air Services	Crashed	Craigavad, Co Down, UK	6	*
05.04.46	Ford 4-AT-B Tri-Motor	HC-SBC	4-AT-24	Shell Co of Ecuador	Crashed	Ayuy, Ecuador	*	*
08.04.46	de Havilland DH.89A Dragon Rapide	VT-ART	6656	Indian National Airways	Crashed & caught fire	Pastabgath, India	2	0
17.04.46	Douglas DC-3	G-AGHK	9406	British Overseas Airways Corporation	Crashed	Oviedo, Spain	*	*
21.04.46	Douglas DC-3	PP-CCA	15732/27177	Cruzeiro	Crashed	Corumba, Brazil	*	*
21.04.46	Avro Anson II	PP-ATC	BA46704	L.A. Transcontinental Brasiliera	Crashed	Sao Paulo, Brazil	*	*
22.04.46	Lockheed 14 Super Electra	AN-ACC	*	Operator Unknown	Written off	Location Unknown	*	*
23.04.46	Vickers Viking 1A	G-AGOK	1/101	Vickers Armstrong	Damaged in forced landing	Effingham, Surrey, UK	0	*
24.04.46	Douglas DC-3	NC33621	3286	Western Air Lines	Crashed due to engine failure	Hollywood, CA, USA	3	0
28.04.46	Douglas DC-3	PP-CCD	15811/32559	Cruzeiro	Crashed & sank	Rio Negro, Brazil	*	*
oo.04.46	Douglas DC-2-115D	EC-AAA	1320	Iberia	Crashed	Spain	*	*
02.05.46	Avro Lancastrian 1	G-AGMC	1183	British Overseas Airways Corporation	Crashed	Sydney, NSW, Australia	*	*
15.05.46	Budd Conestoga	HC-SBE	006	Shell Co of Ecuador	Written off	Location Unknown	*	*
16.05.46	Douglas DC-3	NC53218	19626	Viking Air Transport	Crashed	nr Richmond, VA, USA	25	0
17.05.46	Avro Lancastrian 1	G-AGMH	1188	British Overseas Airways Corporation	Crashed	Karachi, India	*	*
22.05.46	Junkers Ju.52/3m2e	LN-LAB	6048	DNL	Crashed on take-off	Oslo, Norway	12	1
29.05.46	Douglas C-54A	NX30065	10388	United Air Lines	Crashed during practice landing	Chicago, IL, USA	0	4
12.06.46	Douglas DC-3	EC-ABO	4832	Iberia	Crashed on take-off	Madrid, Spain	0	*
13.06.46	Ford 5-AT-B Tri-Motor	XA-FOH	5-AT-031	Servicios Aereos Nacionales	Crash landed after engine failure	El Arenal, Mexico	0	*
18.06.46	Douglas DC-3	EI-ACA	2178	Aer Lingus	Crash landed & caught fire	Shannon, Eire	0	19
25.06.46	Douglas DC-4	XA-FOW	10493	Mexicana	Crashed on take-off	Mexico City, Mexico	*	*
26.06.46	Noorduyn Norseman	TF-RVD	126	Loftleidir	Destroyed	Valnagardar, Iceland	*	*
28.06.46	de Havilland DH.89A Dragon Rapide	VP-KCU	6848	East African Airways	Damaged in forced landing	Garsen, Kenya	*	*
29.06.46	AAC.1 Toucan	F-BAJS	020	Air France	Crashed into HT cables	nr Pau, France	2	1
02.07.46	Douglas DC-3	NC28383	4091	Transcontinental & Western Air	Crashed	Chicago, IL, USA	0	21
04.07.46	Bristol 170 Freighter IIA	G-AHJB	12734	Bristol Aeroplane Co	Crashed out of fuel	Off Natal, Brazil	0	*
08.07.46	Handley Page Halifax C.VIII	PP325	–	British Overseas Airways Corporation	Crashed on landing	Aldermaston, UK	*	*
11.07.46	Lockheed 049 Constellation	NC86513	2040	Transcontinental & Western Air	Crashed due to electrical fire	Reading, PA, USA	5	1
13.07.46	Curtiss C-46	*	*	Central Air Transport	Crashed on take-off	Tsinan, China	13	36
22.07.46	SNCAC Martinet	F-BBFA	0124	Air France	Crashed	Pontarme, France	*	*
23.07.46	Budd Conestoga	HC-SBF	008	Shell Co of Ecuador	Written off	Location Unknown	*	*
23.07.46	SNCASO SO-93 Corse I	F-BBAP	001	SNCASO	Crashed	Mangininhos, Argentina	*	*
25.07.46	Fokker F.XVIII	PJ-AIO	5308	KLM Royal Dutch Airlines	Written off	Location Unknown	*	*
28.07.46	Douglas DC-3	XA-DEE	2196	Mexicana	Crashed	nr Mexico City, Mexico	*	*
07.08.46	Douglas DC-3	G-AHCS	12348	British Overseas Airways Corporation	Crashed	nr Oslo, Norway	3	2
08.08.46	AAC.1 Toucan	F-BAJT	044	Air France	Written off	Le Bourget, France	*	*
08.08.46	Douglas DC-3	NC50040	19980	Trans Caribbean Air Cargo Line	Crashed	Lumberton, NC, USA	*	*
09.08.46	Lockheed 18 Lodestar	*	*	Atlantic Central Airlines	Crashed on landing	Lakehurst, NJ, USA	3	3

Date	Type	Reg'n	C/n	Operator	Accident	Location	F	S
14.08.46	Douglas DC-3	G-AGHT	10103	British Overseas Airways Corporation	Crashed & caught fire	Luqa, Malta	*	*
14.08.46	de Havilland Dove 1	G-AGUC	04000/P/2	British Overseas Airways Corporation	Crashed on take-off	West Howe, Hants, UK	*	*
15.08.46	Avro Lancastrian 1	G-AGLU	1175	British Overseas Airways Corporation	Damaged beyond repair	Hurn, Hants, UK	0	*
16.08.46	Avro Nineteen I	G-AGUE	1276	Railway Air Services	Crashed & caught fire	Speke, Liverpool, UK	*	*
20.08.46	Avro Lancastrian 1	G-AGMF	1186	British Overseas Airways Corporation	Crashed	Broglie, France	8	*
21.08.46	Douglas DC-3	NC51878	4542	Trans-Luxury Airlines	Crashed due to engine failure	Moline, IL, USA	2	24
24.08.46	Avro Anson XII	SU-ADJ	1272	Misrair	Crashed & caught fire	nr Almaza, Egypt	6	3
25.08.46	Douglas DC-3	NC88826	19776	American Airlines	Crashed	Holly Springs, MI, USA	*	*
26.08.46	Budd Conestoga	HC-SBG	*	Shell Co of Ecuador	Written off	Location Unknown	*	*
30.08.46	Avro Lancastrian 3	G-AGWJ	1282	British South American Airways	Crashed	Bathurst, Gambia	*	*
31.08.46	Canadian Vickers Stranraer	CF-BYL	CV186	Spilsbury & Hepburn	Crashed	Bet. Pr.Rupert & Stewart,BC, Canada	7	*
03.09.46	Douglas DC-3	F-BAOB	11714	Air France	Crashed	nr Kjoje, Sweden	22	0
04.09.46	Focke-Wulf Fw.200 Condor	OY-DEM	2993	DDL	Damaged beyond repair in crosswind landing	Northolt, Middx, UK	0	*
04.09.46	Douglas DC-3	F-BAXD	42975	Air France	Crashed	Le Bourget, France	20{1}	7
05.09.46	Douglas DC-3	NC57850	9214	Trans-Luxury Airlines	Crashed	nr Elko, NV, USA	21	1
06.09.46	Avro York	G-AHEW	1300	British South American Airways	Crashed on take-off	Bathurst, Gambia	24	0
07.09.46	Douglas DC-3	VH-ANM	9071	Australian National Airways	Destroyed in hangar fire	Sydney, NSW, Australia	*	*
07.09.46	Ford 4-AT Tri-Motor	*	*	Expresso Aero Inter-Americano	Crashed out of fuel in bad weather	La Esperanza, Cuba	7	0
10.09.46	Ford 5-AT Tri-Motor	HC-SBI	*	Shell Co of Ecuador	Crashed on take-off	Tiputini, Ecuador	*	*
12.09.46	Douglas C-54A	NC91068	10342	Pennsylvania Central Airlines	Engine caught fire & fell off – Landed safely	Washington, DC, USA	0	4
16.09.46	Handley Page Halifax C.8	G-AHZM	1333	London Aero & Motor Services	U/c collapsed on landing	Elstree, Herts, UK	0	*
17.09.46	Douglas DC-3	OO-AUR	4549	Sabena	Crashed on take-off	Brussels, Belgium	1	6
18.09.46	Douglas DC-4-1009	OO-CBG	42986	Sabena	Crashed	nr Gander, Newfoundland	32	17
20.09.46	Type Unknown	*	*	CNAC	Crashed [32 passengers held by Lolo natives]	nr Sichang, China	*	*
24.09.46	Lockheed 049 Constellation	NC88831	2031	Pan American Airways	U/c collapsed on landing	Limerick, Eire	0	*
26.09.46	Handley Page Halifax C.8	G-AHZN	1328	London Aero & Motor Services	Crashed	Off Knocke, Belgium	*	*
26.09.46	Lisunov Li-2	SP-LBC	18419010	LOT Polish Airlines	Crashed	nr Popowie, Poland	*	*
27.09.46	Douglas DC-3	PP-PCH	4087	Panair do Brasil	Crashed	Rio Doce, Brazil	25	0
27.09.46	de Havilland DH.89A Dragon Rapide	G-AFFF	6386	Railway Air Services	Crashed	Milngavie, UK	7	*
03.10.46	Douglas C-54E	NC90904	27290	American Overseas Airlines	Crashed into hill	Stephenville, Newfoundland	39	0
03.10.46	Douglas DC-2-115L	G-AGBH	1584	Southampton Air Service	Crashed on take-off	Luqa, Malta	0	23
08.10.46	Douglas DC-4	NC30051	10471	United Air Lines	Crashed on approach	Cheyenne, WY, USA	2	44
10.10.46	AAC.1 Toucan	F-BCAA	281	Air Ocean	Written off	Sefrou, Morocco	*	*
11.10.46	Douglas C-54B	NC88729	18396	Eastern Air Lines	Crashed into pole in fog	Alexandria, VA, USA	0	27
11.10.46	SNCAC Martinet	F-BBFX	0123	SNCAC	Written off	Sete, France	*	*
12.10.46	Lockheed 049 Constellation	NC86512	2039	Transcontinental & Western Air	Overran on landing in storm	Newcastle, PA, USA	0	7
13.10.46	SNCAC Martinet	F-BAOP	0068	Institute Geographique Nationale	Crashed	Vichy, France	*	*
16.10.46	Douglas DC-3	PI-C92	*	Philippine Air Lines	Crashed	Location Unknown	*	*
16.10.46	Airspeed Consul	G-AHYW	3923	Portsmouth Aviation	Damaged in forced landing	nr Salisbury, Southern Rhodesia	*	*
17.10.46	Douglas DC-3	NC38942	12971	National Air Transport Services	Crashed in snowstorm	Laramie, WY, USA	13	0
17.10.46	Lockheed 10E Electra	XH-TAB	1133	TACA	Crashed on take-off	Yoro, Honduras	*	*
22.10.46	Lockheed 18 Lodestar	PP-PBQ	2115	Panair do Brasil	Crashed on take-off after repair following crash on 18.10.46	Catanduvas, Brazil	*	*
23.10.46	AAC.1 Toucan	F-BCHD	311	SOCOTRA	Written off	Baherya, Egypt	*	*
26.10.46	AAC.1 Toucan	F-BBYL	232	TAI	Written off	Marignane, France	*	*
29.10.46	Miles Aerovan 3	G-AIHL	6385	Air Contractors	Destroyed in forced landing	Dragor, Denmark	*	*
31.10.46	de Havilland DH.89A Dragon Rapide	ZS-AYG	6759	Operator Unknown	Written off	El Adem, Libya	*	*
31.10.46	Avro Nineteen I	G-AHYO	1360	Westminster Airways	Crashed	nr Lubushi, Northern Rhodesia	*	*
oo.10.46	Fleet 50K Freighter	CF-BJW	203	Austin Airways	Destroyed by engine fire	Canada	*	*
01.11.46	AAC.1 Toucan	F-BCAD	284	CTA Languedoc Roussillon	Crashed	St Leger-la-Montagne, France	24	0
05.11.46	Douglas C-54A	PH-TAE	3066	KLM Royal Dutch Airlines	Destroyed by fire	Location Unknown	*	*
06.11.46	Douglas DC-3	PH-TBO	13638	KLM Royal Dutch Airlines	Crash landed	Shere, Surrey, UK	0	20
10.11.46	Douglas DC-3	NC20750	4993	Delta Air Lines	Destroyed	Meridian, MS, USA	*	*
11.11.46	Douglas DC-3	NC19947	4873	United Air Lines	Undershot on landing & hit trees	Cleveland, OH, USA	*	*

Date	Type	Reg'n	C/n	Operator	Accident	Location	F	S
11.11.46	Douglas DC-3	XA-FOZ	*	Comm. Aereas de Veracruz	Crashed	nr Jalapa, Mexico	9	0
13.11.46	Douglas DC-3	NC18645	11662	Western Air Lines	Crashed	White Mt, CA, USA	11	0
13.11.46	Avro Anson I	G-AIIC	–	Tanganyika Government	Damaged in forced landing	Tanganyika	*	*
14.11.46	Douglas DC-3	PH-TBW	20122	KLM Royal Dutch Airlines	Crashed on landing in bad weather	Amsterdam, Netherlands	26	0
15.11.46	Ford 4-AT-B Tri-Motor	HC-SBD	4-AT-29	Shell Co of Ecuador	Crashed when tyre burst on landing	Ayuy, Ecuador	*	*
15.11.46	Ford 5-AT Tri-Motor	HC-SBJ	*	Shell Co of Ecuador	Damaged on landing	Ecuador	*	*
18.11.46	Douglas DC-3	G-AGBE	2022	Skyways	Crashed	Lons-le-Saulnier, France	*	*
22.11.46	Avro Anson I	VH-AVZ	–	Interstate Air Services	Crashed	Port Moresby, Papua New Guinea	*	*
26.11.46	Douglas DC-3	RX-76	20590	LACSA	Crashed	San Jose, Costa Rica	22	0
29.11.46	Boeing 247D	AN-ACB	1731	Lanica	Written off	Nicaragua	*	*
oo.11.46	Douglas DC-3	F-BAIF	16371/33119	Air France	Damaged beyond repair	Location Unknown	*	*
02.12.46	Douglas C-54B	NC56743	18343	Willis Air Service	Damaged in heavy landing	San Juan, Puerto Rico	*	*
03.12.46	Grumman G-21A Goose	HC-SBL	1106	Shell Co of Ecuador	Written off	Location Unknown	*	*
04.12.46	Lisunov Li-2	*	*	Aeroflot	Crashed	Meshed, Iran	24	0
06.12.46	Ford 5-AT-B Tri-Motor	XA-FUP	5-AT-018	NAAM	Damaged beyond repair	Mexico	*	*
08.12.46	Avro Lancastrian 3	G-AHCA	1295	Skyways	Destroyed in hangar fire	Dunsfold, Surrey, UK	*	*
09.12.46	Noorduyn Norseman IV	CF-BXL	456	Canadian Pacific Airlines	Damaged beyond repair	Lake Indin, BC, Canada	*	*
10.12.46	Beechcraft D-18S	SU-AEA	A-0302	Misrair	Written off	Haifa, Palestine	*	*
11.12.46	Douglas DC-3	NC12919	4121	Pennsylvania Central Airlines	Damaged beyond repair	Location Unknown	*	*
11.12.46	de Havilland DH.89A Dragon Rapide	ZS-ATW	6915	Operator Unknown	Written off	Beit Bridge, South Africa	*	*
14.12.46	Douglas DC-3	PI-C1	13991/25436	Far Eastern Air Transport	Crashed	Mt Banahaur, Philippines	*	*
15.12.46	de Havilland DH.89A Dragon Rapide	G-AGLN	6795	Operator Unknown	Crashed	Abadan, Iran	*	*
15.12.46	Douglas DC-3	*	*	Central Air Transport	Crashed	nr Changsing, China	5	0
17.12.46	Douglas DC-3	NC88876	9249	Winged Cargo	Crashed in mountains [Found 29.11.47]	Tilaran, Costa Rica	7	0
19.12.46	Douglas DC-3	G-AGZA	12455	Railway Air Services	Crashed	South Ruislip, Middx, UK	0	*
20.12.46	Consolidated PBY-5A Catalina	C-406	*	Operator Unknown	Written off	Location Unknown	*	*
23.12.46	Douglas DC-3	G-AGKD	14150/25595	British Overseas Airways Corporation	Crashed	Malta	*	*
23.12.46	Avro York	LV-XIG	1365	FAMA	Crashed into mountain	nr Rio de Janeiro, Brazil	21	1
23.12.46	Airspeed Consul	G-AHMA	3428	Atlas Aviation	Crashed	Villemoireau, France	*	*
24.12.46	Douglas DC-4	NC30050	10450	United Air Lines	Overshot & crashed	Los Angeles, CA, USA	*	*
24.12.46	Douglas DC-3	NC45395	11642	Western Air Lines	Crashed	Mt Cuyapaipe, CA, USA	12	0
25.12.46	Curtiss C-46	*	*	CNAC	Crashed out of fuel in fog [No.115]	Shanghai, China	29	7
25.12.46	Douglas DC-3	*	*	Central Air Transport	Crashed in fog [No.48]	Shanghai, China	10{1}	0
25.12.46	Douglas DC-3	*	*	CNAC	Crashed in fog [No.140]	Shanghai, China	10	12
26.12.46	Lockheed 049 Constellation	NC86505	2026	Transcontinental & Western Air	Crashed	nr Shannon, Eire	13	10
28.12.46	Douglas DC-3	NC15577	4805	American Airlines	Crashed due to engine failure	Michigan City, IN, USA	*	*
28.12.46	Douglas DC-3	NC58024	9378	Kansas City Southern	Crashed	Walshville, IL, USA	*	*
31.12.46	Douglas DC-3	NC88873	13640	Intercontinental Air Transport	Crashed on approach	Charleston, SC, USA	5	0
oo.oo.46	Curtiss C-46	CB-42	*	Corporacion Boliviano de Fomento	Crashed	Saavedra, Bolivia	*	*
oo.oo.46	Fokker F.XII	SE-ACZ	5303	Svensk Flygtjanst	Destroyed in hangar fire	Sweden	*	*
oo.oo.46	Fleet 50K Freighter	XA-DOE	204	Operator Unknown	Written off	Mexico	*	*
oo.oo.46	Lockheed Vega DL-1	XA-DAY	157	Lineas Aereas Mexicanas	Crashed	Parral, Mexico	*	*
oo.oo.46	Ford 5-AT Tri-Motor	*	*	TACA	Crashed on approach	nr Puerto Cabezas, Nicaragua	0	3
01.01.47	Douglas DC-2-112	NC13715	1241	E.M.Calvert	Crashed	Nashville, TN, USA	0	16
03.01.47	Douglas DC-3	G-AGJU	12169	British Overseas Airways Corporation	Crashed on landing	Whitchurch, Glos, UK	0	*
03.01.47	Sikorsky S-43B	PP-PBN	4315	Panair do Brasil	Crashed	Sao Paulo, Brazil	11	3
05.01.47	Douglas DC-3	NC21746	2104	American Airlines	Crashed	Jones Beach, NY, USA	*	*
05.01.47	Douglas DC-4	*	*	CNAC	Crashed into mountain [Possibly C-46]	Tsingtao, China	38	0
06.01.47	AAC.1 Toucan	F-BBYK	231	TAI	Written off	Mont Ventoux, France	*	*
06.01.47	Douglas C-54B	NC95412	18330	Northwest Airlines	U/c collapsed on landing	Chicago, IL, USA	0	41
06.01.47	Airspeed Consul	OO-GVP	4312	Air Transport	Crashed	Tambur, Sudan	*	*
07.01.47	Douglas DC-3	OO-CBO	12454	Sabena	Crashed	Costermansville, Belgium	*	*
08.01.47	Lockheed 18 Lodestar	NC25687	*	Caribbean Atlantic Airlines	Overshot on landing	Jacksonville, FL, USA	*	*
10.01.47	Douglas DC-3	VT-AUF	13712	Air India	Crashed	India	*	*

Date	Type	Reg'n	C/n	Operator	Accident	Location	F	S
11.01.47	Douglas DC-3	G-AGJX	12014	British Overseas Airways Corporation	Crashed	Stowting, Kent, UK	8	*
11.01.47	Douglas C-54A	PI-C100	3106	Far Eastern Air Transport	Crashed	West of Lasag, Philippines	*	*
12.01.47	Douglas DC-3	NC88872	3274	Eastern Air Lines	Crashed off course	Galax, VA, USA	18	1
12.01.47	Miles Aerovan 4	G-AIKV	6389	Air Contractors	Force-landed on beach & washed out to sea	nr Cherbourg, France	*	*
16.01.47	Beechcraft D18S	PH-UBV	A-0106	Rijksluchtvaartschool	Written off	Twente, Netherlands	*	*
18.01.47	Short Sandringham 5	G-AHYZ	SH.35C	British Overseas Airways Corporation	Destroyed by fire during conversion	Belfast, Northern Ireland, UK	*	*
22.01.47	Douglas DC-3	C-108	4829	Avianca	Crashed	Puerto Arujo, Colombia	*	*
22.01.47	Douglas DC-3	C-204	19725	TACA	Crashed	Guayas, Ecuador	*	*
22.01.47	Lockheed 14H2 Super Electra	VH-ADT	1409	Qantas	Crashed on take-off	Scholfield, NSW, Australia	0	4
25.01.47	Douglas DC-3	PI-C12	13508	Philippine Air Lines	Crashed	Mt Parker, Hong Kong	*	*
25.01.47	Douglas DC-3	*	*	CNAC	Crashed	Chungking, China	*	*
25.01.47	Douglas DC-3	VP-YFD	19979	Spencer Airways	Crashed on take-off & struck CSA DC-3 OK-WDB	Croydon, Surrey, UK	16(0)	2
25.01.47	Douglas DC-3	OK-WDB	9503	Ceskoslovenske Aerolinie	Destroyed by crashing Spencer Airways DC-3 VP-YFD	Croydon, Surrey, UK	0(16)	0
26.01.47	Douglas DC-3	PH-TCR	14034/25479	KLM Royal Dutch Airlines	Crashed on take-off [Singer Grace Moore killed]	Copenhagen, Denmark	22	0
26.01.47	Junkers Ju.52/3mg8e	G-AHOK	2998	British European Airways	Damaged beyond repair	Renfrew, Fifeshire, UK	*	*
28.01.47	Curtiss C-46	*	*	CNAC	Crashed	nr Hankow, China	26	*
oo.01.47	Lockheed Y1C-37 Electra	*	*	Operator Unknown	Crashed	Honduras	*	*
01.02.47	Douglas DC-3	F-BAXQ	13806/25251	Air France	Crashed	nr Lisbon, Portugal	14	1
01.02.47	Barkley-Grow T8P-1	CF-BMG	04	Canadian Pacific Airlines	Damaged beyond repair after sinking	Port Alberini, YK, Canada	0	*
01.02.47	Fokker F.VIIa/3m	SE-APR	5086	Skaneflyg	Sank through ice	Bromolla, Sweden	*	*
05.02.47	Douglas DC-3	NC54451	*	International Air Freight	Crashed into trees	Harrington, DL, USA	1	2
05.02.47	Douglas DC-2-112	PP-AVG	1245	Aerovias SA	Crashed	Lagoa Santa, Brazil	*	*
06.02.47	Douglas C-54B	NC44567	18386	Aerovias Cubanas Internacionales	Crashed	Pedro Bernados, Spain	*	*
12.02.47	Avro Anson I	G-AHKJ	–	CL Air Surveys	Crashed	Croydon, Surrey, UK	*	*
13.02.47	Douglas DC-3	*	*	Ceskoslovenske Aerolinie	Crashed after take-off	nr Klavno, Czechoslovakia	3	0
14.02.47	Curtiss C-46	NC59486	2944	Slick Airways	Crashed	Denver, CO, USA	2	0
14.02.47	Douglas DC-3	NC59398	9965	Atlantic & Pacific Airlines	Crashed & caught fire	League City, TX, USA	0	1
15.02.47	Douglas DC-4	C-114	10439	Avianca	Crashed into mountains	nr Bogota, Colombia	53	0
17.02.47	Douglas DC-3	OY-AEB	12473	DDL	Crashed	Off Malmo, Sweden	*	*
24.02.47	Douglas DC-3	NC33646	4125	United Air Lines	Crashed	Philadelphia, PA, USA	*	*
01.03.47	Avro Anson I	VH-AKH	–	Guinea Air Traders	Crashed	nr Bullolo, Papua & New Guinea	4	*
05.03.47	AAC.1 Toucan	F-BAKP	058	Air France	Written off	Le Bourget, France	*	*
08.03.47	Focke-Wulf Fw.200 Condor	PP-CBI	2996	Cruzeiro	Damaged beyond repair by DC-3 on ground	Rio de Janeiro, Brazil	*(*)	*
09.03.47	Douglas DC-3	C-400	4792	Vias Aereas Colombianas	Crashed	nr Villa Vincento, Colombia	9	0
13.03.47	de Havilland Dove 1	G-AHRA	04003	British Overseas Airways Corporation	Crashed into tree in poor visibility	Chewton Common, Hants, UK	3	*
13.03.47	Grumman G-21A Goose	TF-RVI	1139	Loftleidir	Crashed	Budardalur, Iceland	*	*
14.03.47	Douglas DC-3	F-BAXO	20488	Air France	Crashed	Mt Moucherolles, France	23	0
14.03.47	Douglas DC-3	NC88804	9921	US Airlines	Crashed	Charleston, SC, USA	2	0
16.03.47	Grumman G-21A Goose	VP-BAE	1002	Bahamas Airways	Crashed on take-off	Nassau South Shore, Bahamas	0	2
17.03.47	Lockheed 18 Lodestar	YS-28	2450	Operator Unknown	Written off	Location Unknown	*	*
19.03.47	Lockheed 18 Lodestar	C-202	*	Operator Unknown	Written off	Location Unknown	*	*
19.03.47	de Havilland DH.89A Dragon Rapide	CF-BBH	6370	Canadian Airways	Damaged on take-off	Pentecost, PQ, Canada	*	*
20.03.47	Douglas DC-3	YV-C-AMU	9512	Linea Aeropostal Venezolana	Crashed	nr Caracas, Venezuela	*	*
20.03.47	AAC.1 Toucan	F-BAKM	055	Air France	Written off	Freetown, Sierra Leone	*	*
20.03.47	Avro Nineteen Srs 1	OO-APN	1357	John Mahieu Aviation	Crashed	Location Unknown	*	*
24.03.47	Beechcraft D-18S	SU-AED	A-0368	Misrair	Written off on delivery	St Marin, Azores, Portugal	*	*
25.03.47	Budd Conestoga	HC-SBH	*	Shell Co of Ecuador	Written off	Location Unknown	*	*
04.04.47	Douglas DC-3	NC52710	19095	International Air Freight	Crashed in lake	Lantana, USA	*	*
10.04.47	Noorduyn Norseman 6	VT-AZF	787	Indian Overseas Airlines	Crashed	Tirupur, India	*	*
13.04.47	Avro York	G-AHEZ	1303	British South American Airways	Crashed on landing	Dakar, French West Africa	7	*
15.04.47	de Havilland DH.89A Dragon Rapide	G-AHKR	6824	British European Airways	Crashed into hill	nr Greeba, Isle of Man	0	7
19.04.47	Douglas DC-3	ZS-BNB	4098	Mercury Aviation	Crashed	Malakal, South Africa	*	*
22.04.47	Douglas DC-3	NC49657	9066	Delta Air Lines	Mid-air collision on approach with BT-13 NC55312	Columbus, CA, USA	8(1)	0
23.04.47	Beechcraft D-18S	SU-AEC	A-0304	Misrair	Written off	Almaza, Egypt	*	*

Date	Type	Reg'n	C/n	Operator	Accident	Location	F	S
24.04.47	Avro Anson I	VH-AVQ	–	Guinea Air Traders	Crashed	nr Port Moresby, Papua & New Guinea	*	*
25.04.47	Type Unknown	*	*	CNAC	Crashed after take-off	Lungwa, China	*{3}	*
29.04.47	de Havilland DH.89A Dragon Rapide	G-AHTS	6962	Operator Unknown	Crashed	Location Unknown	*	*
30.04.47	Douglas DC-3	YS-30	4461	Aerovias Latinas Americanas	Crashed into train on landing	San Salvador, El Salvador	*	*
30.04.47	AAC.1 Toucan	F-BBYG	227	Air France	Crashed	Niamey, French West Africa	*	*
oo.04.47	Avro Anson IV	TI-16	–	TAN	Destroyed by fire	San Jose, Costa Rica	*	*
04.05.47	Lockheed 18 Lodestar	TI-84	2374	TACA	Crashed	nr Nicoya, Costa Rica	*	*
10.05.47	Lockheed 18 Lodestar	C-801	*	Operator Unknown	Written off	Location Unknown	*	*
11.05.47	Lockheed 049 Constellation	NC86508	2029	Transcontinental & Western Air	Crashed	Off Cape May, NJ, USA	*	*
11.05.47	Avro Lancastrian 1	G-AGLF	1172	Skyways	Crashed	Landing Ground H3, Iraq	*	*
11.05.47	Caudron Goeland	F-BAQJ	10076/1190	Institute Geographique Nationale	Written off	Chatillon-sous-Colmont, France	*	*
12.05.47	Noorduyn Norseman 6	VT-AZK	803	Indian Overseas Airlines	Crashed	Birkaner, India	*	*
12.05.47	Ford 4-AT-A Tri-Motor	XA-DOL	4-AT-05	Mexicana	Crashed	Ometepec, Mexico	*	*
14.05.47	Percival Proctor 1	G-AHMS	K.248	Bond Air Services	Crashed	Off Tonnere, France	*	*
17.05.47	Percival Proctor 5	G-AGSX	As.2	Hunting Air Travel	Crashed	Off Haven, Belgium	*	*
22.05.47	Douglas DC-3	PP-AVM	15998/32746	Aerovias Brasil	Crashed	Rio de Janeiro, Brazil	*	*
22.05.47	Caudron Goeland	F-BAPJ	10028/1142	Air France	Written off	Persan-Beaumont, France	*	*
24.05.47	Avro Anson I	VH-AYD	–	Guinea Air Traders	Crashed	nr Bullolo, Papua & New Guinea	*	*
28.05.47	Douglas DC-3	CB-32	19445	Lloyd Aereo Boliviano	Crashed	Mamore, Bolivia	*	*
29.05.47	Douglas DC-4	NC30046	18324	United Air Lines	Overran & caught fire	La Guardia, NY, USA	43	*
29.05.47	Douglas DC-3	TF-ISI	13389	Flugfelag Islands	Crashed	Hedinsfjordur, Iceland	*	*
30.05.47	Douglas C-54B	NC88814	18380	Eastern Air Lines	Crashed	Point Deposit, MD, USA	53	*
30.05.47	AAC.1 Toucan	F-BBYH	228	Ser de Telecom. et de Signalisation	Crashed	Aoulef, Algeria	*	*
30.05.47	Handley Page Halifax C.8	G-AICH	1324	Bond Air Services	Crash landed	Barcelona, Spain	*	*
31.05.47	Grumman G-21A Goose	*	*	Ellis Airlines	Crashed on landing in water with u/c lowered	Ketchikan, Alaska	*	*
03.06.47	Douglas DC-3	VH-AOH	13603	Butler Air Transport	Crashed	Schofields, NSW, Australia	*	*
05.06.47	Handley Page Halifax C.8	G-AIHW	1357	Lancashire Aircraft Corporation	Crashed on landing	Heathrow, London, UK	*	*
05.06.47	AAC.1 Toucan	F-BANB	136	Air France	Crashed	Gemenos, France	2	1
07.06.47	AAC.1 Toucan	F-BAKV	074	Air France	Written off	Dakar-Yoff, French West Africa	*	*
13.06.47	Douglas C-54	NC88842	3112	Pennsylvania Central Airlines	Crashed into mountain	Lookout Rock, WV, USA	0	*
14.06.47	Miles Aerovan 4	G-AISG	6405	North Sea Air Transport	Crashed on take-off	Croydon, Surrey, UK	*	*
16.06.47	Douglas DC-3	PI-C11	19181	Philippine Air Lines	Crashed on beach	Cebu, Philippines	*	*
19.06.47	Lockheed 049 Constellation	NC88845	2045	Pan American Airways	Crash landed	nr Meyadin, Syria	15	*
20.06.47	Noorduyn UC-64A Norseman	VO-ABL	571	Buchans Mining Co	Crashed	Hall's Bay, Newfoundland	*	*
21.06.47	Douglas DC-3	VT-AZC	4331	Mistry Airways	Crashed	Location Unknown	*	*
26.06.47	SNCAC Martinet	F-BBFO	0140	SATI	Crashed	Calcutta, India	*	*
27.06.47	Miles Aerovan 4	G-AJOB	6409	Ulster Aviation	Crashed	Irish Sea	*	*
01.07.47	Douglas DC-3	TI-107	4444	TAN	Disappeared & presumed crashed	Location Unknown	*	*
01.07.47	AAC.1 Toucan	F-BALF	091	Air France	Crashed into hill	Eseka, French Cameroons	*	*
02.07.47	Miles Aerovan 2	G-AGWO	6432	Marquess of Londonderry	Crashed	Newtownards, UK	*	*
03.07.47	Avro Anson I	G-AHFV	–	Air Transport Association	Crashed on approach	Off Eastleigh, Hants, UK	2	0
08.07.47	Caudron Goeland	F-BAQT	10057/1171	Air Azur	Crashed at sea	Between Tunis & Bizerte, Tunisia	*	*
13.07.47	Douglas DC-3	NC79024	9887	Burke Air Transport	Crashed	Melbourne, FL, USA	22	13
14.07.47	AAC.1 Toucan	F-BCHH	323	Aerocargo	Written off	Vichy, France	*	*
15.07.47	Miles Aerovan 5	G-AISJ	6404	Miles Aircraft	Damaged during braking trials	Woodley, Berks, UK	*	*
16.07.47	Avro York	G-AGNR	1219	British Overseas Airways Corporation	Crashed	Az-Zubair, Iraq	6	*
16.07.47	Ford 5-AT-C Tri-Motor	HC-SBK	5-AT-067	Shell Co of Ecuador	Crashed	Ecuador	*	*
18.07.47	Avro Anson I	G-AIXT	–	Southern Aerowork	Crashed	Croydon, Surrey, UK	*	*
23.07.47	Douglas C-54D	NC91086	22162	Seaboard & Western Airlines	Destroyed by fire	St Joseph, PA, USA	*	*
23.07.47	Douglas C-54D	NC91077	22157	Seaboard & Western Airlines	Destroyed by fire	St Joseph, PA, USA	*	*
25.07.47	Avro York	G-AIUP	1374	Skyways	Crashed on landing	Heathrow, London, UK	*	*
25.07.47	Avro York	LV-XIH	1366	FAMA	Crashed	Moron, Argentina	*	*
30.07.47	Douglas DC-3	LV-ADD	19545	ZONDA	Written off	Location Unknown	*	*

Date	Type	Reg'n	C/n	Operator	Accident	Location	F	S
31.07.47	Handley Page Halifax C.8	G-AHZJ	1331	London Aero & Motor Services	Damaged beyond repair	Milan, Italy	*	*
02.08.47	Avro Lancastrian 3	G-AGWH	1280	British South American Airways	Crashed in mountains	Andes, Argentina	11	*
04.08.47	Lockheed 10A Electra	CC-CLE	1141	LAN-Chile	Crashed	Location Unknown	*	*
06.08.47	Douglas DC-3	NC65350	4736	Indamer	Destroyed by fire on delivery	Miami, FL, USA	*	*
06.08.47	de Havilland DH.89A Dragon Rapide	G-AGJF	6499	British European Airways	Crashed	Barra, Hebrides, UK	*	*
08.08.47	Douglas DC-3	NX88787	9639	American Airlines	Crashed after engine failure on approach	New York, NY, USA	3	2
08.08.47	Avro Anson I	VH-BCH	–	New England Airways	Damaged on landing	Kempsey, NSW, Australia	*	*
09.08.47	Douglas DC-3	SE-BAY	19559	AB Aerotransport	Crashed	Malmo, Sweden	*	*
12.08.47	Douglas C-54A	LV-ABL	3080	FAMA	Crashed in forced landing	Itapemeririm, Argentina	*	*
13.08.47	Caudron Goeland	F-BCCK	10109/1223	STARO	Written off	Pau, France	*	*
13.08.47	Lisunov Li-2	YR-TAV	18423801	TARS	Crashed	Bucharest, Romania	*	*
15.08.47	Vought-Sikorsky VS-44A	CX-AIR	4403	TACI	Crashed on ldg after smuggling flight to Paraguayan rebels	River Plate, Uruguay	*	*
15.08.47	Airspeed Consul	G-AIOZ	4335	Milburnair	Crashed	Tatsfield, Surrey, UK	*	*
21.08.47	Curtiss C-46	NC59488	2935	Slick Airways	Crashed	Hanksville, UT, USA	3	*
22.08.47	Short Sandringham 5	G-AHZB	SH.38C	British Overseas Airways Corporation	Crashed	Bahrain	10	*
23.08.47	Avro Tudor 2	G-AGSU	1235	Ministry of Supply	Crashed	Woodford, Cheshire, UK	*	*
28.08.47	Short Sandringham 6	LN-IAV	SH.48C	DNL	Crashed	Tjelesund, Norway	*	*
30.08.47	AAC.1 Toucan	F-BCHQ	322	Air Atlas	Written off	El Ajeb	*	*
30.08.47	Avro Anson V	OB-QAH-202	–	Transportes Aereos Peruanas	Crashed	nr Sapasoa, Peru	*	*
03.09.47	Douglas DC-3	SX-BAB	18981	Tech. & Aeronautical Exploitation	Crashed	Athens, Greece	3	0
05.09.47	Avro Lancastrian 3	G-AGWK	1283	British South American Airways	Crashed into mast on landing	Bermuda	*	*
05.09.47	Handley Page Halifax C.8	G-AIWT	1338	London Aero & Motor Services	Damaged beyond repair	Bovingdon, Herts, UK	*	*
09.09.47	Boeing 247	XA-DUA	1719	Servicios Aereos Panini	Crashed	Obregon, Mexico	*	*
13.09.47	Douglas DC-3	PI-C59	*	Philippine Air Lines	Crashed	Zamboanga, Philippines	*	*
17.09.47	Curtiss C-46	NC59495	2937	Slick Airways	Crash landed out of fuel	Burbank, CA, USA	0	*
18.09.47	Douglas DC-3	VT-CFL	20248	Tata Airlines	Crashed	Junagarh, India	*	*
18.09.47	de Havilland DH.89A Dragon Rapide	G-AJSJ	6826	Operator Unknown	Crashed	Tunisia	*	*
20.09.47	Douglas DC-4	NC88911	27229	Pan American Airways	Belly landed & caught fire after engine failure	Floyd Bennet Field, NY, USA	0	*
21.09.47	de Havilland DH.89A Dragon Rapide	VP-UAW	6631	Uganda Co Ltd	Written off	Zanzibar	*	*
03.10.47	Avro Lancastrian 3	G-AHBU	1289	Skyways	Crashed	Belfast, Northern Ireland, UK	*	*
04.10.47	AAC.1 Toucan	F-BAJB	002	Air France	Written off	Pau, France	*	*
07.10.47	SNCASE Languedoc	F-BATY	25	Air France	Crashed	Bone, France	*	*
14.10.47	Boeing 314A	NC18612	2086	American International Airlines	Force-landed out of fuel & sunk by gunfire	Atlantic Ocean	0	69
14.10.47	Douglas DC-3	PI-C648	*	Aguinaldo Development Co	Written off	Location Unknown	*	*
16.10.47	Bristol 170 Freighter I	F-BCJN	12788	Societe Aerienne du Littoral	Crashed	Off Cartagena, Spain	42	2
16.10.47	Douglas DC-3	*	*	Strato Freight	Crashed into mountain	Location Unknown	3	0
17.10.47	Douglas DC-3	*	*	Civil Air Transport	Crashed	nr Hopeh, China	3	0
21.10.47	Douglas DC-3	VT-CLA	15471/26916	Orissa State Government	Shot down by Indonesian Air Force P-40	Over Java, Indonesia	*	*
23.10.47	Avro Lancaster B.3	G-AGUL	–	British South American Airways	Crashed	Heathrow, London, UK	0	*
24.10.47	Douglas DC-6	NC37510	42875	United Air Lines	Crashed following fire	Bryce Canyon, UT, USA	52	0
25.10.47	SNCAC Martinet	F-BAOQ	0069	Institute Geographique Nationale	Crashed	St Etienne, France	*	*
26.10.47	Douglas DC-4-1009	SE-BBG	42930	AB Aerotransport	Crashed during storm	nr Mt Hymettus, Greece	44	0
26.10.47	Douglas DC-4	NC88920	10317	Pan American Airways	Crashed	nr Juneau, Alaska	18	0
27.10.47	Douglas DC-3	*	*	CNAC	Shot down	Yulin, China	2	1
oo.10.47	Vickers PBY-5A Canso	YV-C-AQA	CV413	Transporte Aereo Transandino	Written off	Location Unknown	*	*
02.11.47	Percival Q.6	G-AHTB	Q.39	S.E.Norman	Damaged beyond repair	Almaza, Egypt	*	*
02.11.47	Douglas DC-3	*	*	Philippine Air Express	Crashed at sea	Off Barrio Rizal, Philippines	4	*
13.11.47	Douglas DC-3	VT-ATI	4922	Air India	Crashed	Jammu, India	*	*
13.11.47	Avro Lancastrian 3	G-AGWG	1279	British South American Airways	Crashed on landing	Bermuda	*	*
13.11.47	AAC.1 Toucan	F-BDYH	401	SANA	Written off	St Claude, France	*	*
13.11.47	Beechcraft D18S	PH-UBS	A-0103	Rijksluchtvaartschool	Written off	Soesterberg, Netherlands	*	*
13.11.47	Airspeed Consul	G-AJGC	5119	D.L.Steiner	Damaged in forced landing	nr La Rochelle, France	*	*
14.11.47	Airspeed Consul	G-AJGI	5125	Airspan	Crashed in forced landing	nr Chalons, France	*	*
18.11.47	Lockheed 049 Constellation	NC86507	2023	Transcontinental & Western Air	Crashed on approach	Newcastle, DE, USA	5	0

Date	Type	Reg'n	C/n	Operator	Accident	Location	F	S
18.11.47	Bristol 170 Freighter XI	SE-BNG	12792	Trafik-Turist-Transportflyg	Crashed into mountain	Ravello, Italy	20	*
19.11.47	Short Sunderland 3	G-AGHW	–	British Overseas Airways Corporation	Crashed into high ground	Brightstone Down, IoW, UK	*	*
19.11.47	Douglas DC-3	*	*	Transair Sweden	Crashed	Santa Maria del Monte Scala, Italy	20	*
20.11.47	Avro Anson I	G-AIWW	–	British Air Transport	Crashed	St Boniface Down, IoW, UK	2	*
20.11.47	Percival Proctor 5	G-AIAB	Ae.43	International Airways	Crashed	Luton, Beds, UK	*	*
21.11.47	Lisunov Li-2	YR-TAI	18423509	TARS	Crashed	Phouznicie, Romania	*	*
23.11.47	Bristol 170 Freighter IA	G-AIMC	12793	Bristol Aeroplane Co	Damaged when parking brake failed	Wau, Papua & New Guinea	0	0
25.11.47	Handley Page Halifax C.8	ZS-BUL	1329	LAMS (South Africa) Ltd	Crash landed	Port Sudan, Sudan	*	*
27.11.47	Douglas DC-3	NC95486	6065	Columbia Air Cargo	Crashed into trees	Yakutat, Alaska	13	0
27.11.47	Douglas DC-3	YU-ABC	*	JAT Yugoslav Airlines	Crashed	Montenegrin Mts, Yugoslavia	22	0
27.11.47	Airspeed Consul	G-AIOO	4357	Payloads	Crashed	Perpignan, France	*	*
30.11.47	Douglas C-54A	NC91009	7453	Alaska Airlines	Overran in fog & struck car	Seattle, WA, USA	6{1}	23
oo.11.47	Lockheed Orion 9D2	NC799W	208	F.H.Steward & T.M.Gibson	Crashed	Los Angeles, CA, USA	*	*
04.12.47	de Havilland DH.89A Dragon Rapide	G-AJFN	6520	Operator Unknown	Destroyed by fire	Kosti, Sudan	*	*
04.12.47	de Havilland DH.89A Dragon Rapide	G-AJFO	6726	Operator Unknown	Destroyed by fire	Kosti, Sudan	*	*
05.12.47	Handley Page Halifax C.8	G-AIHU	1306	Lancashire Aircraft Corporation	Crashed into hill	Rhyl, Flintshire, UK	*	*
10.12.47	Curtiss C-46	*	*	Slick Airways	Stalled on take-off & struck 4 National Guard aircraft	Chicago, IL, USA	*(*)	*
12.12.47	Douglas DC-3	F-BCYF	13807/25252	Air Algerie	Written off	Orly, Paris, France	*	*
22.12.47	Short Stirling V	OO-XAC	–	Air Transport	Crashed	Kunming, China	1	*
22.12.47	Douglas DC-3	EC-ACG	19553	Iberia	Crashed	Barajas, Spain	*	*
23.12.47	Douglas DC-3	*	*	Coastal Airlines	Crashed out of fuel	Miami, FL, USA	2	0
24.12.47	Lockheed 18 Lodestar	OO-CAR	2419	Sabena	Crashed	Mitwaba, Belgian Congo	*	*
26.12.47	Douglas DC-3	PI-C53	*	Philippine Air Lines	Destroyed by typhoon	Philippines	*	*
27.12.47	Douglas DC-3	PH-TCV	12309	KLM Royal Dutch Airlines	Crashed	Leeuwarden, Netherlands	*	*
27.12.47	Douglas DC-3	VT-AUG	4175	Air India	Crashed	Korangi Creek, India	*	*
28.12.47	Douglas DC-2	XA-GEE	*	Servicio Aereo Panini	Crashed	nr Leon, Mexico	6{5}	0
29.12.47	Vickers Viking 1B	OY-DLI	197	DDL	Crashed	Off Copenhagen, Denmark	*	*
oo.12.47	Handley Page Halifax C.8	G-AIWK	1368	London Aero & Motor Services	Destroyed by vandals	Sydney, NSW, Australia	0	0
oo.12.47	Handley Page Halifax C.8	F-BCJZ	1337	Aero Cargo	Damaged beyond repair	France	*	*
oo.12.47	Avro Anson I	VH-BEP	–	A.R.Wegener	Crashed	nr Calcutta, India	*	*
oo.oo.47	SNCAC Martinet	F-BAIP	0001	SNCAC	Destroyed	Location Unknown	*	*
oo.oo.47	Vickers-Supermarine Walrus I	G-AIIB	–	A.C.Brown & L.C.S.Odstone	Wrecked by gale	Weston-super-Mare, Somerset, UK	*	*
oo.oo.47	Avro Nineteen 2	VT-CJZ	1384	Bharat Airways	Crashed	Srinagar, India	*	*
oo.oo.47	Lockheed 18 Lodestar	*	*	Trans Canada Airlines	Crashed into woods [Found 1994]	nr Vancouver, BC, Canada	*	0
02.01.48	AAC.1 Toucan	F-BBZC	248	SOCOTRA	Written off	Casablanca, Morocco	*	*
05.01.48	Lockheed 18 Lodestar	ZS-ASW	2037	South African Airways	Damaged beyond repair	Palmietfontein, South Africa	*	*
06.01.48	Vickers Viking 1B	G-AHPK	148	British European Airways	Crashed into trees on approach	Ruislip, Middx, UK	1	17
06.01.48	Douglas DC-3	F-BAXC	42972	Air France	Crashed	Le Bourget, France	*	*
06.01.48	Percival Proctor 5	G-AHWP	Ae.69	London Aero & Motor Services	Crashed	Margate, Kent, UK	*	*
07.01.48	Douglas DC-3	NC60331	12968	Coastal Airlines	Crashed	Savannah River, GA, USA	*	*
07.01.48	Avro Nineteen 2	G-AIXE	1376	Sivewright Airways	Damaged in forced landing	nr Knutsford, Cheshire, UK	*	*
08.01.48	SNCAC Martinet	F-BDLG	0275	CATA	Crashed	Palestro, Algeria	*	*
11.01.48	Douglas DC-3	HI-6	4735	Dominicana	Crashed	Ciudad Havajillo, Dominican Rep.	*	*
13.01.48	Douglas C-54A	LV-AFG	7479	FAMA	Crashed after engine fire	Ponta Galeria, Italy	*	*
13.01.48	Douglas DC-3	NC28384	4092	Eastern Air Lines	Crashed in poor weather	Oxon Hill, MD, USA	5	4
13.01.48	Douglas DC-3	XA-GOC	4101	Operator Unknown	Crashed	Cuaymas, Mexico	*	*
17.01.48	de Havilland Dove 1	VT-CQA	04077	Airways (India) Ltd	Crashed	Mt Urbanu, Italy	*	*
20.01.48	Curtiss C-46	*	*	CNAC	Crashed on take-off in snowstorm	Mukden, China	2	*
20.01.48	Avro Anson I	VP-KDJ	–	African Air Cars	Damaged in forced landing	nr El Duen, Sudan	*	*
21.01.48	Lockheed 649A Constellation	NC111A	2532	Eastern Air Lines	U/c collapsed on landing & caught fire	Boston, MA, USA	0	*
21.01.48	Douglas DC-3	NC206	4776	US Civil Aeronautics Authority	Crashed	Navaso Peak, CO, USA	*	*
21.01.48	Douglas DC-3	PI-C145	*	Philippine Air Lines	Crashed	Iloilo, Philippines	*	*
24.01.48	Airspeed Consul	G-AIOM	4347	Chartair	Forced landed & destroyed by flood water	nr Lyons, France	*	*

Date	Type	Reg'n	C/n	Operator	Accident	Location	F	S
24.01.48	Avro Anson I	VH-BAK	–	Townsville & Country Airways	Damaged when u/c collapsed on landing	Julia Creek, Qld, Australia	*	*
25.01.48	Bristol 170 Wayfarer IIA	F-BCJA	12802	Soc Indochinoise de Transports Aer.	Crashed	Off Cyprus	5	*
26.01.48	SNCASE Languedoc	F-BCUC	29	Air France	Written off	Romainville, France	*	*
27.01.48	Douglas DC-3	CS-TDB	10033	Transportes Aereos Portugueses	Crashed	Off Sagnes, Portugal	*	*
28.01.48	Douglas DC-3	NC36480	16850/33598	Airline Transport Carriers	Crashed after wing detached due to fire	Diablo Mts, CA, USA	32	0
30.01.48	Avro Tudor 4B	G-AHNP	1349	British South American Airways	Crashed	North east of Bermuda	31	0
30.01.48	Douglas DC-3	LR-AAA	13192	Middle East Airlines	Collided on ground with Ju.52/3m of CGT	Beirut, Lebanon	*(*)	*
01.02.48	Fokker F.VIIa	SE-APR	5086	DDL	Written off	Location Unknown	*	*
04.02.48	SNCASE Languedoc	F-BATK	11	Air France	Written off	Marignane, France	*	*
06.02.48	Vickers Viking 1B	VT-CLY	205	Air India	Damaged beyond repair	Bombay, India	*	*
09.02.48	de Havilland Dove 2	G-AJHL	04043	British Overseas Airways Corporation	Crashed	Off Lochri, Greece	*	*
09.02.48	Avro Anson I	VR-HDX	–	Cathay Pacific Airways	Crashed	Sandoway, Burma	*	*
10.02.48	SNCASE Languedoc	F-BATH	08	Air France	Damaged beyond repair	Paris, France	*	*
10.02.48	Douglas DC-3	PK-REA	16380/33128	KLM Royal Dutch Airlines	Crashed	Padalarang, Indonesia	*	*
11.02.48	Lockheed 10A Electra	VH-AEC	1034	Qantas	Crashed in forced landing after engine failure	Condamine, Qld, Australia	*	*
12.02.48	Douglas DC-3	OY-DCI	7330	DDL	Crashed	Ubrichstein, Germany	*	*
13.02.48	Handley Page Halifax C.8	PP285	*	Handley Page	Damaged beyond repair	Location Unknown	*	*
20.02.48	Douglas DC-3	I-REGI	4312	Aero Teseo	Crashed	Florence, Italy	*	*
21.02.48	Latecoere 631	F-BDRD	07	Latecoere	Crashed on delivery flight	St Marcouf, France	19	0
23.02.48	Douglas DC-3	YV-AGU	4205	Linea Aeropostal Venezolana	Crashed	Las Cumbres, Venezuela	*	*
25.02.48	Douglas DC-3	NC36498	12527	Bruning Aviation	Crashed into trees on night approach	Columbus, OH, USA	1	1
27.02.48	Airspeed Consul	G-AJGE	5121	Pullman Airways	Crashed	Off Libya	*	*
oo.02.48	Northrop Pioneer	NX8500H	2501	Northrop Aircraft	Crashed on test flight	USA	1	*
02.03.48	Douglas DC-3	OO-AWH	43154	Sabena	Crashed [Last DC-3 built]	Heathrow, London, UK	20	2
03.03.48	AAC.1 Toucan	F-BBYC	223	Air France	Crashed	Off Oran, Algeria	*	*
04.03.48	Airspeed Consul	VR-TAR	5139	United Air Services	Damaged beyond repair	Mombasa, Kenya	*	*
07.03.48	Lockheed 10A Electra	PP-VAS	1028	Varig	Damaged beyond repair	Porto Alegre, Brazil	*	*
07.03.48	Avro Anson V	TF-RVL	4135	Loftleidir	Crashed into mountains	nr Skalafell, Iceland	5	0
08.03.48	Douglas DC-3	NC64722	10052	Eagle Air Freight	Crashed into mountain	nr San Jose, CA, USA	2	0
08.03.48	Consolidated PBY-5A Catalina	PK-CTA	22025	KLM Royal Dutch Airlines	Written off	Poso, Indonesia	*	*
10.03.48	Douglas DC-4	NC37478	18390	Delta Air Lines	Crashed on take-off	Chicago, IL, USA	12	*
12.03.48	Douglas C-54G	NC95422	35966	Northwest Airlines	Crashed	Mt Sanford, Alaska	30	*
13.03.48	Douglas DC-3	PP-CBX	11658	Cruzeiro	Crashed on approach	Juqueiri Range, Brazil	3	*
15.03.48	Douglas DC-3	C-1002	6252	Agencia Interamericana de Aviada	Crashed	Villa Pinzon, Colombia	14	1
20.03.48	Vultee V-1	NC22077	16	G.H.Armitage	Crashed	Somerset, PA, USA	*	*
25.03.48	Miles Aerovan 4	G-AJKJ	6406	Ulster Aviation	Crashed	Off Southport, Lancs, UK	*	*
27.03.48	Vickers Viking 1B	VT-CEL	166	Indian National Airlines	Crashed	Monte Cardo, Corsica, France	19	*
05.04.48	Vickers Viking 1B	G-AIVP	229	British European Airways	Mid-air collision with Soviet Air Force YAK-3	Gatow, Berlin, Germany	14(1)	*
07.04.48	Avro Nineteen Srs 2	OO-CFB	1362	Air Congo	Crashed	Kindu, Belgian Congo	*	*
10.04.48	Bristol 170 Freighter 21E	F-BENG	12812	Cie Air Transport	Crashed on take-off	nr Algeciras, Spain	5	*
10.04.48	Douglas DC-4-1009	F-BBDC	42935	Air France	Crashed into building	Kano, Nigeria	1	*
15.04.48	Lockheed 049 Constellation	NC88858	2058	Pan American Airways	Crashed on approach	Shannon, Eire	30	1
19.04.48	Lockheed 10A Electra	ZK-AGJ	1127	New Zealand National Airways	Crashed on approach	Tauranga, New Zealand	*	*
20.04.48	Douglas DC-3	PI-C14	13193	Philippine Air Lines	Crashed	Jolo, Philippines	*	*
20.04.48	Douglas DC-3	YV-AVN	19984	Avensa	Crashed	Off La Guaira, Venezuela	*	*
21.04.48	Vickers Viking 1B	G-AIVE	218	British European Airways	Crashed into mountain	Largs, Ayrshire, UK	0	20
24.04.48	Douglas DC-3	TI-161	*	TAN	Destroyed by fire	El General, Costa Rica	*	*
oo.04.48	Avro Anson V	CF-GFP	MDF-342	Central Northern Airways	Sank through ice	Favorable Lake, MN, Canada	*	*
01.05.48	Douglas DC-6	PH-TKW	43112	KLM Royal Dutch Airlines	Crashed on landing	Amsterdam, Netherlands	0	5
05.05.48	Castel-Mauboussin CM-10	n/a	CM-10-01	Castel-Mauboussin	Crashed	Bretigny, France	0	1
05.05.48	Douglas DC-3	NC17645	13978/25423	Superior Oil Corporation	Written off	Location Unknown	*	*
09.05.48	Handley Page Halifax C.8	AP-ABZ	1374	Pakistan Airways	Crashed out of fuel	nr Basra, Iraq	*	*
09.05.48	Douglas DC-2-112	VH-AEN	1259	New Holland Airways	Crashed	Darwin, NT, Australia	*	*
13.05.48	Handley Page Halifax C.8	F-BCJX	1347	CTAI	Damaged beyond repair	Bovingdon, Herts, UK	*	*

Date	Type	Reg'n	C/n	Operator	Accident	Location	F	S
13.05.48	Douglas DC-4-1009	OO-CBE	42932	Sabena	Crashed in thunderstorm	nr Magazini, Belgian Congo	31	1
13.05.48	de Havilland Dove 1	G-AJOU	04058	Skyways	Crashed during storm	Mount Coron, France	10	0
14.05.48	Vickers Viking 1B	LV-AFL	192	FAMA	Crashed on landing	Moron, Argentina	*	*
15.05.48	Douglas DC-3	ZS-BWY	6341	Mercury Aviation	Crashed	Vrede, South Africa	13	0
16.05.48	Curtiss C-46	NC59489	2938	Slick Airways	Crashed when fuselage failed in storm	Columbus, OH, USA	2	0
17.05.48	Handley Page Halifax C.8	G-AKAD	1356	British American Air Services	Damaged in belly landing	Rennes, France	*	*
17.05.48	Douglas DC-3	PI-C143	*	Philippine Air Lines	Crashed	nr Cebu, Philippines	*	*
20.05.48	Douglas DC-3	G-AJBG	14003/25448	Air Transport Charter	Crashed	nr Bovingdon, Hants, UK	3	1
20.05.48	Noorduyn Norseman	NC79822	*	Operator Unknown	Crashed on take-off after bomb explosion	Rome, Italy	2	0
23.05.48	Handley Page Halifax C.8	G-AIZO	1366	Bond Air Services	Crashed after cargo shifted	Berkhamsted, Herts, UK	0	5
24.05.48	Airspeed Consul	G-AIOU	4355	Morton Air Services	Crashed	nr Cairo, Egypt	*	*
25.05.48	Handley Page Halifax C.8	G-AKBA	1303	Alpha Airways	Crashed on take-off	Albacete, Spain	*	*
28.05.48	Miles Marathon	G-AGPD	6265	Miles Aircraft	Overstressed & crashed	nr Amesbury, Wilts, UK	2	0
05.06.48	Avro Anson I	VH-BES	–	C.R.Rudd & W.R.Murphy	Destroyed in hangar fire	Nhill, Vic, Australia	*	*
05.06.48	Avro Anson I	VH-BET	–	C.R.Rudd & W.R.Murphy	Destroyed in hangar fire	Nhill, Vic, Australia	*	*
05.06.48	Avro Anson I	VH-BGO	–	Adastra Airways	Destroyed in hangar fire	Nhill, Vic, Australia	*	*
08.06.48	Douglas DC-3	CS-TDF	18998	Transportes Aereos Portugueses	Crashed	nr Lisbon, Portugal	*	*
10.06.48	de Havilland DH.89A Dragon Rapide	G-AIUI	6675	Hargreaves Airways	Crashed	Isle of Man	6	2
11.06.48	Avro Nineteen I	G-AGNI	1214	Universal Flying Services	Crashed at sea	Off Bradda Head, Isle of Man	*	*
12.06.48	Douglas DC-3	NC79042	9394	Eagle Air Freight	Crashed	Elroy, AZ, USA	*	*
14.06.48	SNCASE Languedoc	F-BATG	07	Air France	Crashed	Coulommiers, France	*	*
14.06.48	Airspeed Consul	G-AIDY	3094	British Air Transport	Damaged in emergency landing	Berck, France	*	*
16.06.48	Douglas DC-4-1009	PH-TCF	42996	KLM Royal Dutch Airlines	Damaged beyond repair	Amsterdam, Netherlands	0	*
17.06.48	Douglas DC-6	NC37506	42871	United Air Lines	Crashed after crew poisoned by fumes from fire in hold	Mt Carmel, PA, USA	43	0
19.06.48	Curtiss C-46	XT-44	*	Civil Air Transport	Damaged on landing	Peking, China	*	*
21.06.48	Douglas DC-3	YV-C-AQC	19126	Transporte Aereo Transandino	Destroyed by fire	Location Unknown	*	*
25.06.48	de Havilland DH.89A Dragon Rapide	G-AGOP	6873	Operator Unknown	Crashed	Syria	*	*
26.06.48	Douglas DC-3	YV-C-AHI	16992/34254	Linea Aeropostal Venezolana	Crashed	Maiquetia, Venezuela	*	*
26.06.48	Avro Anson V	CF-FYI	BRU-14	Spartan Air Services	Damaged in belly landing	Mount Joli, PQ, Canada	*	*
29.06.48	Avro Anson I	VH-BIU	–	Airlines (WA) Ltd	Crashed into trees after engine failure on take-off	Cue, WA, USA	*	*
oo.06.48	Avro Nineteen I	SU-ADN	1285	Misrair	Damaged in ground collision with Lodestar G-AGBR	Cairo, Egypt	*(*)	*
oo.06.48	Avro Anson I	VP-KEM	–	Clairways	Damaged in forced landing	Merka, Italian Somaliland	*	*
01.07.48	Avro Anson I	VP-KDW	–	Clairways	Damaged in forced landing	nr Merka, Italian Somaliland	*	*
01.07.48	Fiat G.212	I-ELSA	04	Avio Linee Italiane	Crashed in heavy rain	Keerbergen, Belgium	8	3
04.07.48	Douglas DC-6	SE-BDA	43119	Scandinavian Airlines System	Mid-air collision on approach with RAF York MW248	Northolt, Middx, UK	32(7)	0
07.07.48	Douglas DC-3	F-BCYP	9158	Aigle Azur	Crashed in mountains	Djiring, French Indo-China	20	0
10.07.48	Curtiss C-46	CU-P198	33534	Expreso Aereo Inter-Americano	Crashed on approach	Maiquetia, Venezuela	*	*
12.07.48	Douglas DC-4-1009	F-BBDL	42989	Air France	Crashed	Paris, France	*	*
14.07.48	Douglas DC-3	PP-AVO	19113	Aerovias Brasil	Crashed	Belem, Brazil	*	*
14.07.48	Douglas DC-3	G-AGKN	14984/26429	British Overseas Airways Corporation	Crashed	nr Toulon, France	6	*
15.07.48	Consolidated PBY-5A Catalina	YV-P-APJ	*	Operator Unknown	Written off	Puerto la Bello, Venezuela	*	*
16.07.48	Consolidated OA-10 Catalina	VR-HDT	*	Cathay Pacific Airways	Crashed after being hijacked [1st airliner to be hijacked]	Between Hong Kong & Macao	26	1
17.07.48	Airspeed Consul	G-AIIO	4349	Extractors (Hull) Ltd	Crashed	nr Lumbreras, Spain	3	0
20.07.48	Handley Page Halifax C.8	G-AJPJ	1336	Mayflower Air Services	Crashed on landing after unauthorised flight from UK	Lydda, Israel	*	*
20.07.48	SNCAC Cormoran	n/a	NC-211-01	SNCAC	Crashed	Villacoublay, France	5	0
22.07.48	Douglas DC-3	ET-T-5	19416	Ethiopian Airlines	Written off	Gore, Ethiopia	*	*
24.07.48	Douglas DC-3	CF-FKY	6246	Rimouski Airlines	Crashed	Grande Greve, PQ, Canada	28	0
27.07.48	de Havilland DH.89A Dragon Rapide	SU-ACS	6544	Misrair	Damaged beyond repair	Zaarfarane, Egypt	*	*
27.07.48	Lockheed 18 Lodestar	OO-GVP	2320	Air Transport	Crashed	Wadi Halfa, Sudan	*	*
28.07.48	SNCAC Martinet	F-BDLR	0281	SNECMA	Crashed	Reau-Villaroche, France	*	*
29.07.48	Curtiss C-46	XT-822	22355	Civil Air Transport	Crashed	Tsingtao, China	19	*
29.07.48	Short Sandringham 2	LV-AAP	SH.02C	ALFA	Sank after forced landing in fog	Buenos Aires, Argentina	18	5
30.07.48	Douglas DC-3	G-AGIX	12053	British European Airways	Force-landed after striking cables	nr Sywell, Northants, UK	0	18
01.08.48	Avro Lancaster XPP	AP-ACM	–	Onzeair	Crashed when cargo broke loose	Manipur, Pakistan	4	0

Date	Type	Reg'n	C/n	Operator	Accident	Location	F	S
01.08.48	Latecoere 631	F-BDRC	06	Air France	Crashed	Atlantic Ocean	52	0
08.08.48	de Havilland DH.89A Dragon Rapide	VP-KFW	6545	Operator Unknown	Written off	Mauritius	*	*
09.08.48	Douglas DC-3	ZK-AOE	16383/33131	New Zealand National Airways	Crashed	Port Underwood, New Zealand	*	*
11.08.48	Lockheed 18 Lodestar	PJ-AKA	2540	Operator Unknown	Written off	Location Unknown	*	*
11.08.48	Lockheed 18 Lodestar	PJ-AKB	2541	Operator Unknown	Written off	Location Unknown	*	*
12.08.48	Canadair DC-4M-1	CF-TEL	103	Trans Canada Airlines	Crashed into earth mound on landing	Sydney, NS, Canada	0	17
13.08.48	Lockheed 14F-62 Super Electra	PJ-AIK	1440	Operator Unknown	Written off	Location Unknown	*	*
13.08.48	Lockheed 14F-62 Super Electra	PJ-AIT	1412	Operator Unknown	Written off	Location Unknown	*	*
24.08.48	Caudron Goeland	OO-CCJ	10041/1155	Congo Motor	Written off	Belgian Congo	*	*
24.08.48	Caudron Goeland	OO-CCR	10116/1230	Operator Unknown	Written off	Location Unknown	*	*
26.08.48	Beechcraft D18S	SU-ADZ	*	Misrair	Written off	Amman, Jordan	*	*
27.08.48	Avro Lancastrian 1	G-AGMB	1182	British Overseas Airways Corporation	Crashed	Singapore	0	*
27.08.48	Douglas DC-3	AN-ACZ	4662	Lanica	Damaged beyond repair	Location Unknown	*	*
27.08.48	Douglas DC-3	*	*	Aerovias Cubanas Internacionales	Crashed	Location Unknown	*	*
29.08.48	Martin 202	NC93044	9165	Northwest Airlines	Crashed after loss of wing in storm	Winona, MN, USA	37	0
29.08.48	SNCASE Languedoc	F-BATO	32	Air France	Written off	Le Bourget, France	*	*
31.08.48	Douglas DC-3	OO-UBL	12420	Sabena	Crashed	Elizabethville, Belgian Congo	*	*
02.09.48	Douglas DC-3	VH-ANK	9939	Australian National Airways	Crashed into mountain	nr Quirindi, NSW, Australia	*	*
02.09.48	Airspeed Consul	G-AIUZ	5105	Transair	Crashed	nr Berne, Switzerland	*	*
03.09.48	Handley Page Halifax C.8	G-AIHX	1367	Lancashire Aircraft Corporation	Crashed on landing	Squires Gate, Lancs, UK	*	*
05.09.48	Short Sunderland 3	G-AGEW	–	British Overseas Airways Corporation	Damaged on take-off & sank	Sourabaya, Indonesia	*	*
07.09.48	Douglas DC-3	NC75402	4523	Superior Oil Corporation	Crashed	Rome, Italy	*	*
09.09.48	Percival Proctor 5	G-AHWY	Ae.81	Somerton Airways	Crashed	Off Bembridge, IoW, UK	*	*
20.09.48	Douglas DC-3	NC17335	1921	Colonial Airlines	Overshot on landing & hit trees	Burlington, VT, USA	0	17
22.09.48	Douglas C-54A	XA-GUU	10390	Aerovias Guest	Crashed	Santa Maria, Azores, Portugal	0	*
28.09.48	Douglas DC-4	NC45345	27346	Transcontinental & Western Air	Destroyed by fire	La Guardia, NY, USA	*	*
28.09.48	Handley Page Halifax C.8	G-AJNZ	1385	World Air Freight	Crashed into mountain	Port St Mary, Isle of Man	4	0
02.10.48	Short Sandringham 6	LN-IAW	SH.52C	DNL	Crashed on landing in rough weather	nr Trondheim, Norway	19	26
04.10.48	Douglas DC-3	NC58121	17086/34353	New England Air Express	Forced landed on beach out of fuel & damaged by tide	Haines Bay, Bahamas	0	23
07.10.48	Douglas DC-3	PP-LPB	12723	Linhas Aereas Paulistas	Crashed	Campina Grande, Brazil	*	*
08.10.48	Handley Page Halifax C.8	G-AKGZ	1400	World Air Freight	Crashed on take-off	Gatow, Berlin, Germany	*	*
08.10.48	Vickers Viking 1B	VT-CEJ	143	Indian National Airlines	Crashed on take-off	New Delhi, India	*	*
12.10.48	Douglas DC-3	ZS-BWZ	9145	Mercury Aviation	Damaged in forced landing after in-flight fire	Wadi Halfa, Sudan	0	*
13.10.48	Consolidated Liberator II	G-AHZP	14	Scottish Airlines	Crashed on landing	Speke, Lancs, UK	0	*
15.10.48	Avro Anson V	CF-DTO	–	Department of Transport	Damaged beyond repair	Ottawa, ON, Canada	*	*
20.10.48	Lockheed 049 Constellation	PH-TEN	2083	KLM Royal Dutch Airlines	Crashed into power lines after abandoned landing	nr Prestwick, Ayrshire, UK	39	1
23.10.48	Lockheed 10A Electra	ZK-AGK	1128	New Zealand National Airways	Crashed into mountain	Mt Ruapehu, New Zealand	13	0
27.10.48	Douglas C-54A	NC88785	10406	Northwest Airlines	Crashed after take-off	nr Edmonton, AB, Canada	2	*
29.10.48	Lockheed 14-08 Super Electra	G-AKPD	1429	R.A.Brand & Co Ltd	Crashed	Off Elba, Italy	*	*
03.11.48	Miles Aerovan 4	G-AJTD	6415	Ulster Aviation	Blown over while taxiing	Newtownards, N Ireland, UK	*	*
04.11.48	Douglas DC-3	NC66637	11800	Pacific Alaska Air Express	Crashed	nr Cape Spencer, Alaska	*	*
08.11.48	Douglas DC-3	VH-UZK	2003	Australian National Airways	Crashed into mountain	Mt Macedon, Vic, Australia	2	20
10.11.48	Douglas DC-3	C-119	6217	Avianca	Crashed	Bogota, Colombia	*	*
10.11.48	Beechcraft D-18S	SU-AEE	A-0373	Misrair	Written off	Landing Ground H2, Iraq	*	*
11.11.48	de Havilland DH.89A Dragon Rapide	G-AKOF	6533	Mannin Airways	Crashed out of fuel	River Mersey, UK	7	1
13.11.48	Consolidated Liberator II	G-AHYC	5	British Overseas Airways Corporation	Damaged on landing	Prestwick, Ayrshire, UK	*	*
15.11.48	Douglas DC-6	PI-C291	43060	Philippine Air Lines	Overshot runway	Wake Island	*	*
20.11.48	Douglas DC-3	ZS-BWX	4254	Mercury Aviation	Crashed	Orly, Paris, France	*	*
21.11.48	Noorduyn Norseman 6	VT-AYF	762	Ambica Air Lines	Written off	Juhu, India	*	*
21.11.48	Noorduyn Norseman 6	VT-AZE	722	Indian Overseas Airlines	Written off	India	*	*
21.11.48	Noorduyn Norseman 6	VT-CBW	792	Ambica Air Lines	Written off	Juhu, India	*	*
21.11.48	Stinson L-5 Sentinel	VT-CAG	76-1631	Ambica Air Lines	Written off	Juhu, India	*	*
22.11.48	Avro Lancaster 3	G-AHJW	–	Flight Refuelling	Crashed	nr Andover, Hants, UK	7	1
22.11.48	Miles Aerovan 4	G-AIDJ	6387	Arab Contracting & Trading Co	Crashed on take-off	Rutbah Wells, Iraq	*	*

Date	Type	Reg'n	C/n	Operator	Accident	Location	F	S
23.11.48	SNCASE Languedoc	F-BATM	13	Air France	Written off	Toulouse, France	*	*
25.11.48	Lockheed 049 Constellation	NC90824	2086	Transcontinental & Western Air	Caught fire after hard landing	Los Angeles, CA, USA	0	*
26.11.48	Douglas DC-3	AP-ACE	12775	Pak Air	Crashed	Verhari, Pakistan	*	*
01.12.48	Handley Page Halifax C.8	F-BCJS	1360	Aero Cargo	Crashed	Lyons, France	*	*
05.12.48	Curtiss C-46	XT-538	*	Central Air Transport	Overshot & destroyed by fire	Kiangwan, China	9	*
06.12.48	Douglas DC-3	I-ETNA	4396	ALI	Crashed	Milan, Italy	*	*
07.12.48	Douglas DC-3	NC57667	6030	R.W.Duff	Damaged beyond repair	Maracaibo, Venezuela	*	*
07.12.48	Douglas DC-3	HK-306	12977	Lansa	Written off	Bogota, Colombia	*	*
12.12.48	Douglas C-54A	OB-SAF-175	10286	Peruvian International Airways	Crash landed	Cerro Morimo, Chile	0	6
12.12.48	Douglas DC-3	*	*	CNAC	Crashed	Taipei, China	2	8
15.12.48	Douglas DC-3	OB-PAY-226	14374/25819	Faucett	Damaged in forced landing	Playa Viru, Peru	*	*
15.12.48	Douglas DC-3	C-310	13807	Lansa	Written off	Location Unknown	*	*
21.12.48	Douglas C-54B	N8342C	18348	Civil Air Transport	Crashed	Basalt Is, China	*	*
23.12.48	Douglas DC-3	EC-ABK	4256	Iberia	Crashed	nr Madrid, Spain	*	*
24.12.48	Canadian Vickers Stranraer	CF-BYJ	CV205	Queen Charlotte Airlines	Crashed & sank	Belize Inlet, BC, Canada	2	*
26.12.48	Douglas DC-3	EP-ACI	15670/27115	Iranian Airways	Destroyed by fire	Birjande, Iran	*	*
27.12.48	de Havilland DH.89A Dragon Rapide	G-AHXY	6808	British European Airways	Crashed	Renfrew, UK	*	*
28.12.48	Douglas DC-3	NC16002	1496	Airborne Transport	Crashed	Off San Juan, Puerto Rico	*	*
29.12.48	Douglas DC-3	VH-UZJ	2002	Australian National Airways	Crashed	Mangalore, Vic, Australia	*	*
29.12.48	Douglas DC-3	C-110	4181	Avianca	Destroyed by fire	Villavicencio, Colombia	*	*
31.12.48	Douglas DC-3	ZS-BYX	12587	Pan African Air Charter	Crashed	Mt Argentarie, Italy	*	*
oo.12.48	de Havilland Dove 1	LV-YAZ	04226	Civil Aeronautics Board	Crashed on delivery flight	Location Unknown	*	*
oo.oo.48	Handley Page Halifax	VH-BDT	–	Air Carriers	Destroyed by vandals	Sydney, NSW, Australia	0	0
oo.oo.48	Douglas DC-3	PI-C3	*	Philippine Air Lines	Written off	Location Unknown	*	*
oo.oo.48	Douglas DC-3	PI-C10	*	Philippine Air Lines	Written off	Location Unknown	*	*
oo.oo.48	Douglas DC-3	PI-C36	9816	Philippine Air Lines	Written off	Location Unknown	*	*
oo.oo.48	Canadian Vickers Stranraer	CF-BYI	CV184	Queen Charlotte Airlines	Damaged on landing	Rock Bay, BC, Canada	0	*
oo.oo.48	AAC.1 Toucan	F-BBYA	221	STA	Written off	Location Unknown	*	*
oo.oo.48	Ford 4-AT Tri-Motor	HC-SBQ	*	Shell Co of Ecuador	Written off	Location Unknown	*	*
oo.oo.48	Avro Anson I	G-AIEZ	–	Cookers & Geysers Ltd	Force-landed on illegal flight to Israel	Rhodes, Greece	*	*
oo.oo.48	Douglas C-54A	N54083	10422	Trans Caribbean Airways	Written off	Location Unknown	*	*
oo.oo.48	Douglas C-54B	N90426	10433	American Airlines	Written off	Location Unknown	*	*
oo.oo.48	Douglas DC-4	CS-TSB	3059	Transportes Aereos Portugueses	Written off	Location Unknown	*	*
oo.oo.48	Lockheed Vega 1	R-48	004	Argentine Government	Crashed	Buenos Aires, Argentina	*	*
oo.oo.48	Ford 4-AT-F Tri-Motor	EC-BAB	4-AT-71	Iberia	Crashed	Spain	*	*
oo.oo.48	Ford 5-AT-C Tri-Motor	C-207	5-AT-086	Operator Unknown	Crashed	Villavicencio, Colombia	*	*
02.01.49	Douglas C-54B	4X-ACA	18395	Israeli Air Force	Crashed	nr Tel Aviv, Israel	*	*
02.01.49	Douglas DC-3	NC79025	10181	Seattle Air Charter	Crashed into hangar on take-off in fog	Seattle, WA, USA	14	16
05.01.49	Avro York	G-AHEX	1301	British South American Airways	Crashed on take-off	Caravellas, Brazil	*	*
05.01.49	Curtiss C-46	*	30247	L.A.Piedra	Crashed after take-off	Zacatecas, Mexico	*	*
06.01.49	Douglas DC-3	NC53210	13777	Coastal Cargo	Crashed	Brandywine, IN, USA	*	*
08.01.49	Douglas DC-3	F-BCYO	12101	Air Algerie	Crashed	Lyon-Bron, France	*	*
12.01.49	Douglas DC-3	ZS-AYB	19584	Pan African Air Charter	Crashed	Ras-el-Tin	*	*
15.01.49	de Havilland DH.89A Dragon Rapide	G-AHXV	6747	British European Airways	Crashed	Ronaldsway, Isle of Man	*	*
16.01.49	Douglas DC-3	VT-CDZ	14145/25590	Dalmia Jain Airways	Crashed	Banihal Pass, India	*	*
17.01.49	Curtiss C-46	OB-OAD-233	267	ANDES	Crashed out of fuel	Rio Yavari, Peru	*	*
17.01.49	Avro Tudor 1	G-AGRE	1253	British South American Airways	Crashed	Between Jamaica & Bermuda	40	0
17.01.49	Beechcraft 34 Twin Quad	NX90521	*	Beech Aircraft Corporation	Crashed after take-off	USA	2	0
20.01.49	Douglas DC-3	NC91006	20208	Alaska Airlines	Crashed	Homer, Alaska	5	*
22.01.49	Douglas DC-3	SE-BBN	12896	Scandinavian Airlines System	Destroyed by fire	Lulea, Sweden	*	*
26.01.49	Curtiss C-46	NC1241N	22474	Alaska Airlines	Crashed on take-off after engine failure [Also was 4X-AQD]	Asmara, Ethiopia	*	*
26.01.49	Avro Anson I	VP-KDI	–	African Air Cars	Damaged when tyre burst on landing	Tanga, Tanganyika	*	*
27.01.49	Douglas DC-3	NC17713	4582	United Air Lines	Crashed	Oakland, CA, USA	*	*
29.01.49	Douglas DC-3	*	*	CNAC	Crashed	Location Unknown	*	*

Date	Type	Reg'n	C/n	Operator	Accident	Location	F	S
01.02.49	Avro York	G-AGJD	1210	British Overseas Airways Corporation	Crashed on take-off	Castel Benito, Libya	*	*
02.02.49	Avro Anson V	CF-FEO	3708	St Lawrence Airways	Crashed	Trinity Bay, Newfoundland	6	0
04.02.49	Douglas C-54A	G-AJPL	7464	Skyways	Crashed	Castel Benito, Libya	*	*
06.02.49	Douglas DC-3	NC54335	20217	Flamingo Air Services	Crashed	nr Quito, Ecuador	*	*
08.02.49	Vickers Viking 1B	OY-DLU	199	Scandinavian Airlines System	Crashed	Off Copenhagen, Denmark	28	*
10.02.49	Douglas DC-3	OB-PAV-223	15374/26819	Faucett	Crashed	Cerro Carpish, Peru	*	*
10.02.49	Douglas DC-3	XT-T72	*	Lutheran Mission	Crash landed & abandoned	Paiyangho, China	0	*
11.02.49	Handley Page Halifax C.8	G-AKBB	1321	British American Air Services	Damaged on landing	Schleswigland, West Germany	*	*
11.02.49	Airspeed Consul	G-AGVY	3204	Air Enterprises	Crashed	Lebanon	*	*
11.02.49	Avro Anson IV	XA-FUG	96349	Aeronaves de Mexico	Crashed	Cacahuatepec, Mexico	*	*
14.02.49	Avro Anson V	VO-ABP	MDF-258	Newfoundland Airways	Damaged beyond repair	Corner Brook, Newfoundland	*	*
15.02.49	Handley Page Halifax C.8	G-AIOI	1327	Bond Air Services	Damaged while taxiing	Tegel, Berlin, West Germany	0	*
17.02.49	Grumman G-21A Goose	HC-SBB	1005	Shell Co of Ecuador	Damaged beyond repair	Location Unknown	*	*
19.02.49	Douglas DC-3	G-AHCW	13308	British European Airways	Mid-air collision with RAF Anson	nr Coventry, Warks, UK	14(*)	*
21.02.49	Short Sunderland 3	G-AGJO	–	British Overseas Airways Corporation	Struck by ship & sank	Hythe, Kent, UK	0	0
22.02.49	Curtiss C-46	*	*	Golden North Airlines	Crash landed	Annette Is, Alaska	*	*
24.02.49	Douglas DC-3	VR-HDG	20576	Cathay Pacific Airways	Crashed	Braemar Reservoir, Hong Kong	*	*
oo.02.49	Douglas DC-3	VT-AZZ	4267	Indian Overseas Airlines	Damaged beyond repair	Bombay, India	0	*
oo.02.49	Avro Anson V	XA-HEC	BFU-49C	Lineas Aereas Unidas	Damaged beyond repair	Mexico	*	*
08.03.49	Avro Anson I	G-ALFJ	–	K.J.Nalson	Crashed into hangar	Croydon, Surrey, UK	*	*
11.03.49	Boeing B-17G	F-BEEB	*	Institute Geographique Nationale	Crashed	Yaounde, French Equatorial Africa	*	*
14.03.49	de Havilland Dove 1	XY-ABO	04176	Union of Burma Airways	Crashed	Gulf of Martaban, Burma	*	*
16.03.49	Avro York	G-AHFI	1316	Skyways	Crashed on approach	Gatow, Berlin, West Germany	3	*
16.03.49	Douglas DC-2-243	VH-ARC	2089	Guinea Air Traders	Crashed	Kerowagi, New Guinea	*	*
16.03.49	Airspeed Consul	F-BDPX	5161	SITA	Damaged beyond repair	Namdinh, French Indo-China	*	*
18.03.49	Lockheed 18 Lodestar	ZK-AKX	2382	New Zealand National Airways	Crashed	nr Waikanae, New Zealand	15	0
21.03.49	Handley Page Halifax C.8	G-AJZZ	1396	Lancashire Aircraft Corporation	Crashed on landing	Schleswigland, West Germany	3	*
26.03.49	Curtiss C-46	NC1664M	22549	Freight Air	Crashed out of fuel	Campeche, Mexico	*	*
29.03.49	Douglas DC-2-243	PP-MGA	2058	Aerovias SA	Crashed	Belo Horizonte, Brazil	*	*
01.04.49	Handley Page Halton	G-AHDL	1308/SH.23C	Westminster Airways	Crashed	Gatow, Berlin, West Germany	*	*
07.04.49	Avro Lancastrian 1	VH-EAS	1184	Qantas	Destroyed by fire	Dubbo, NSW, Australia	*	*
07.04.49	Vickers Viking 1B	VT-CIZ	202	Air India	Belly landed on beach	nr Bombay, India	0	*
09.04.49	Handley Page Halton	G-AHDP	1341/SH.25C	Aviation Traders	U/c collapsed	Schleswigland, West Germany	0	*
09.04.49	SNCASE Languedoc	F-BATU	23	Air France	Crashed	Nice, France	*	*
20.04.49	Douglas DC-3	PP-ASB	20467	Transportes Carga Aerea	Crashed	Porto Nacional, Brazil	*	*
21.04.49	Avro Nineteen 2	G-AIKM	1364	British South American Airways	Crashed	nr Luton, Beds, UK	*	*
23.04.49	Douglas DC-3	SX-BAF	12322	Tech. & Aeronautical Exploitation	Damaged beyond repair	Location Unknown	*	*
23.04.49	de Havilland Dove 1	XY-ABP	04183	Union of Burma Airways	Crashed	nr Myaungmya, Burma	*	*
26.04.49	Beechcraft D18S	PH-UDI	A-0426	Rijksluchtvaartschool	Written off	Amsterdam, Netherlands	*	*
28.04.49	Grumman G-21A Goose	HC-SBV	1018	Shell Co of Ecuador	Written off	Location Unknown	*	*
29.04.49	Handley Page Halifax C.8	G-AKAC	1340	World Air Freight	Crashed	nr Berlin, West Germany	4	*
29.04.49	Lockheed Vega 5A	XB-KAQ	096	A.Brito	Crashed	Cutzamala de Pinzon, Mexico	2	*
02.05.49	de Havilland Dove 1	VR-NAG	04049	West African Airways	Crashed	Benin, Nigeria	*	*
03.05.49	Miles Aerovan 4	G-AJKM	6402	East Anglian Flying Services	Blown over by gale while refuelling	Lympne, Kent, UK	*	*
04.05.49	Curtiss C-46	*	*	Continental Charters	Struck hangar on take-off	St Thomas, US Virgin Is	0	3
05.05.49	Douglas DC-3	PI-C98	16743/33491	Philippine Air Lines	Crashed after bomb explosion	Between Daet & Manila, Philippines	*	*
06.05.49	Bristol 170 Freighter 21	G-AIFF	12766	Bristol Aeroplane Co	Crashed attempting one engine climb	English Channel	7	0
06.05.49	Percival Q.6	G-AFIX	Q.31	Starways	Crashed	Broomhall, UK	*	*
10.05.49	Handley Page Halifax C.8	G-ALBZ	1348	Lancashire Aircraft Corporation	Collided on landing with LAC Halifax G-AHWN	Schleswigland, West Germany	*(*)	*
10.05.49	Avro Lancaster XPP	G-AKDP	–	Flight Refuelling	Damaged in forced landing	East Germany	0	*
11.05.49	Avro Anson I	VH-BBZ	–	Qantas	Crashed on take-off	Kerowagi, Papua & New Guinea	*	*
13.05.49	Curtiss C-46	HC-SIB	33480	Transandina Ecuador	Crashed	Quito, Ecuador	*	*
18.05.49	Airspeed Consul	F-BDPY	5150	SITA	Damaged beyond repair	Tonkin, French Indo-China	*	*

Date	Type	Reg'n	C/n	Operator	Accident	Location	F	S
24.05.49	Sikorsky S-51	G-AKCU	5128	BEA Helicopters	Crashed due to turbulence	nr Croesor Dam, Wales, UK	0	*
27.05.49	Curtiss C-46F	N5615V	22368	Trans-Air Hawaii	Crashed after engine fire	Maui, Hawaii	2	0
01.06.49	Handley Page Halifax C.8	G-AKBJ	1317	Lancashire Aircraft Corporation	Crash landed	Tegel, Berlin, West Germany	0	*
02.06.49	Curtiss C-46	XT-520	*	Central Air Transport	Crashed	North of Chungking, China	3	*
03.06.49	Curtiss C-46	YV-C-ARE	33483	Southern Air Transport	Crashed on take-off	Miami, FL, USA	*	*
03.06.49	Auster V	PH-FCB	1976	KLM Royal Dutch Airlines	Crashed	nr Liemde, Netherlands	*	*
06.06.49	Douglas DC-3	SX-BAI	12162	Tech. & Aeronautical Exploitation	Crashed	Malahasa Attica, Greece	22	0
07.06.49	Curtiss C-46D	N92857	30506	Strato Freight	Crashed after take-off due to engine failure	Off San Juan, Puerto Rico	53	28
10.06.49	Avro York	G-ALBX	PC4494	Skyways	Crashed	Neustadt, West Germany	*	*
13.06.49	Vickers Viking 1B	YI-ABR	232	Iraqi Airways	Belly landed	Baghdad, Iraq	0	*
13.06.49	Douglas DC-3	*	*	El Al Israel Airlines	Damaged beyond repair on landing	Jerusalem, Israel	*	*
15.06.49	Avro Anson IV	XA-FOU	52450	Aerovias Reformas	Damaged on landing	Puerto Mexico, Mexico	*	*
16.06.49	de Havilland DH.89A Dragon Rapide	G-AGPI	6885	Somerton Airways	Crashed	Cowes, IOW, Hants, UK	*	*
19.06.49	Consolidated PBY-5A Catalina	N1096M	56	La Legion Caribe	Sunk by Dominican Rep Air Force fighters during invasion	Off Luperon, Dominican Republic	*	*
22.06.49	Convair 240-0	N94266	139	American Airlines	Crashed on take-off	Memphis, TN, USA	0	44
23.06.49	Lockheed 749 Constellation	PH-TER	2541	KLM Royal Dutch Airlines	Crashed	Off Bari, Italy	33	0
26.06.49	Avro Lancastrian 2	G-AKFH	–	Skyways	Caught fire on landing	Gatow, Berlin, West Germany	*	*
26.06.49	Curtiss C-46	4X-ACG	30575	El Al Israel Airlines	Crashed on take-off & cargo of mines exploded	Avraham, Israel	0	13
28.06.49	Airspeed Consul	F-BDPV	5157	SITA	Damaged beyond repair	Haiphong, French Indo-China	*	*
02.07.49	Douglas DC-3	VH-MME	9350	MacRobertson-Miller Airlines	Crashed	Guildford, WA, Australia	*	*
06.07.49	Handley Page Halifax C.8	G-AHWN	1314	Lancashire Aircraft Corporation	U/c collapsed on landing	Schleswigland, West Germany	0	*
11.07.49	Douglas DC-3	VR-HDQ	9863	Hong Kong Airways	Crashed	Kai Tak, Hong Kong	*	*
12.07.49	Lockheed 749 Constellation	PH-TDF	2558	KLM Royal Dutch Airlines	Crashed in heavy rain	nr Bombay, India	*	*
12.07.49	Curtiss C-46E	N79978	2936	Standard Airlines	Crashed into mountain	Chatsworth, CA, USA	35	13
15.07.49	Airspeed Consul	G-AJGD	5120	Olley Air Services	Damaged in forced landing	Chiswick, London, UK	*	*
16.07.49	de Havilland DH.89A Dragon Rapide	G-AJGZ	6883	Operator Unknown	Destroyed by fire	Agha Jari, Iran	*	*
19.07.49	Curtiss C-46F	N5075N	22463	Air Transport Associates	Crashed on take-off due to engine failure	Boeing Field, WA, USA	6{4}	27
23.07.49	de Havilland DH.89A Dragon Rapide	G-AKSF	6490	Scottish Airlines	Destroyed by fire	Prestwick, Ayrshire, UK	*	*
26.07.49	Beechcraft D-18S	SU-ADK	A-0054	Misrair	Written off	Alexandria, Egypt	*	*
30.07.49	Douglas DC-3	N19963	2260	Eastern Air Lines	Mid-air collision with USN F-6F Bu72887	Chesterfield, NJ, USA	16(1)	0
30.07.49	de Havilland DH.89A Dragon Rapide	G-AIWZ	6867	North Sea Air Transport	Crashed	Brough, UK	*	*
03.08.49	Douglas DC-3	PP-AJB	9971	Lineas Aereas Brasil	Crashed	Sao Francisco, Brazil	*	*
06.08.49	Bristol 170 Freighter 21	HC-SBU	12739	Shell Co of Ecuador	Crashed	Salasaca, Ecuador	35	*
10.08.49	Curtiss C-46	CB-37	433	Lloyd Aereo Boliviano	Crashed	Rurrenabaque, Bolivia	*	*
11.08.49	Convair 240-13	N91241	161	Northeast Airlines	Crashed on landing	Portland, ME, USA	0	27
13.08.49	Douglas DC-3	HK-1200	*	S.A. Tolima	Crashed	Bogota, Colombia	*	*
14.08.49	Avro Anson I	OO-SRA	–	Belgian Air Service	Crashed on landing due to fuel shortage	Amsterdam, Netherlands	*	*
15.08.49	Douglas C-54A	N79998	3076	Transocean Airlines	Crashed out of fuel	Off Lurga Point, Eire	8	50
16.08.49	Ford 5-AT-C Tri-Motor	XA-GIJ	5-AT-075	Lineas Aereas Guerrero Oaxaca	Crashed on take-off when u/c failed	Putla, Mexico	0	2
19.08.49	Douglas DC-3	G-AHCY	12355	British European Airways	Crashed	Oldham, Lancs, UK	24	*
21.08.49	AAC.1 Toucan	F-BANQ	151	CATI	Written off	Red River, Laos	*	*
22.08.49	Douglas DC-3	F-BEFK	19471	Alpes Provence	Crashed due to engine failure	Laghouat, Algeria	1	3
24.08.49	Beechcraft C18S Expeditor	G-AIYI	–	Prince Aly Khan	Crashed	Sherburn-in-Elmet, Yorks, UK	*	*
27.08.49	Douglas DC-3	OO-CBK	14600/26045	Sabena	Crashed after take-off	Leopoldville, Belgian Congo	5	14
29.08.49	Douglas DC-3	CB-33	*	Lloyd Aereo Boliviano	Destroyed during civil war	Bolivia	*	*
31.08.49	Vickers-Supermarine Walrus I	LN-TAK	*	Vestlandske Luftfartselskap	Sank	Soerfjorten, Norway	*	*
oo.08.49	Lockheed 14F-62 Super Electra	PJ-AIM	1441	Operator Unknown	Written off	Location Unknown	*	*
04.09.49	de Havilland DH.89A Dragon Rapide	EI-AEA	6433	Weston Ltd	Written off	Hutton Cranswick, Yorks, UK	*	*
09.09.49	Douglas DC-3	CF-CUA	4518	Canadian Pacific Airlines	Destroyed by bomb	St Joachim, PQ, Canada	*	*
12.09.49	Douglas DC-3	XA-GAM	4350	Mexicana	Crashed on take-off	Mexico	*	*
13.09.49	Douglas DC-3	VR-HDW	13985/25430	Cathay Pacific Airways	Crashed on take-off	Aru Sakau, Burma	*	*
19.09.49	Lisunov Li-2P	HA-LIK	18427501	Maszovlet	Written off	Pecs, Hungary	*	*
24.09.49	de Havilland Dove 1	G-AHYX	04018	Anglo Iranian Oil Co	Crashed after engine failure on take-off	Isfahan, Iran	*	*
25.09.49	Curtiss C-46	PP-VBI	33100	Varig	Crash landed & caught fire	Jaquiraro, Brazil	5	*

Date	Type	Reg'n	C/n	Operator	Accident	Location	F	S
26.09.49	Douglas DC-3	XA-DUH	11725	Mexicana	Crashed	Mt Popocatapetl, Mexico	*	*
27.09.49	Douglas C-54A	LV-ABI	7445	FAMA	Crashed after in-flight fire	Buenos Aires, Argentina	*	*
oo.09.49	Lockheed 18 Lodestar	CB-26	2098	Lloyd Aereo Boliviano	Crashed	Sucre, Bolivia	*	*
01.10.49	SNCASE SE.1010	F-WEEE	01	SNCASE	Crashed	Carces, France	*	*
02.10.49	Miles Aerovan 3	G-AIHK	6384	Arab Contracting & Trading Co	Damaged on landing after losing propeller	Landing Ground K1, Iraq	*	*
07.10.49	Waco ZQC-6	CF-BDZ	147	Northern Airways	Destroyed by fire	Carcross, Yukon, Canada	*	*
09.10.49	Curtiss C-46	N59485	2939	Slick Airways	Crashed due to icing	Cheyenne, WY, USA	4	0
10.10.49	Douglas DC-3-277B	XA-HOU	2208	Aerovias Coahuila	Crashed	Sierra de Ovallos, Mexico	8	0
12.10.49	Avro Anson I	VH-BDO	–	East-West Airlines	Crashed on take-off after engine failure	Tamworth, NSW, Australia	*	*
13.10.49	Avro Anson V	XA-HIM	BRU-15C	C.C.Cordonez	Crashed	Mexico	*	*
14.10.49	Avro Anson I	VH-BMS	–	Charter Flite Aviation Service	Damaged in hangar fire	Bankstown, NSW, Australia	*	*
15.10.49	Short Sealand 1	G-AKLM	SH.1562	Short Brothers & Harland	Crashed into mountain	Lindesnes, Norway	*	*
17.10.49	Fiat G.212	SU-AFX	07	SAIDE	Damaged on take-off when runway collapsed	Alexandria, Egypt	*	*
18.10.49	SNCASE SE.200	F-BAIY	3	SNCASE	Damaged beyond repair after porpoising	Berre Lake, France	*	*
20.10.49	Douglas C-54A	F-BBDS	10423	Air France	Crashed	Karachi, Pakistan	*	*
22.10.49	Douglas DC-3	F-BFGH	19561	Societe Transatlantique Aerienne	Written off	Malakal, Sudan	*	*
28.10.49	Douglas C-54A	PI-C107	10396	Philippine Air Lines	Damaged on landing	Tokyo, Japan	*	*
28.10.49	Lockheed 749 Constellation	F-BAZN	2546	Air France	Crashed into mountain	San Miguel Is, Azores, Portugal	48	0
01.11.49	Douglas C-54B	N88727	18365	Eastern Air Lines	Mid-air collision with Bolivian Air Force P-38 NX26927	Washington, DC, USA	55(0)	0
01.11.49	Airspeed Consul	G-AIIS	4398	International Airways	Damaged beyond repair	Normanton, Yorks, UK	*	*
04.11.49	Douglas DC-3	N29086	4304	Harrington's Inc	Crashed into trees	Akron, OH, USA	*	*
04.11.49	Lockheed 18 Lodestar	CF-TCU	2060	Pacific Petroleum	Crashed & caught fire after tyre burst on take-off	Calgary, AL, Canada	0	8
07.11.49	Avro Lancastrian 1	G-AGMM	1192	British Overseas Airways Corporation	Destroyed	Castel Benito, Libya	*	*
13.11.49	Douglas DC-3	XY-ACC	13512	Union of Burma Airways	Damaged beyond repair	Lanywa, Burma	*	*
17.11.49	Douglas DC-3	HS-TA-180	*	Trans Asiatic Airlines	Crashed	Cap d'Aguilar, Hong Kong	*	*
20.11.49	Douglas DC-3	PH-TFA	13462	Aero Holland	Crashed	nr Oslo, Norway	*	*
24.11.49	Bristol 170 Freighter 21E	EC-ADK	12777	Aviaco	Overshot on landing	Mahon, Minorca, Spain	*	*
27.11.49	Douglas DC-3	F-OABJ	14429/25874	Aigle Azur	Written off	Dong Khe, French Indo-China	*	*
28.11.49	Douglas C-54A	F-BELO	10391	Air France	Crashed	St Just Chalignin, France	*	*
29.11.49	Douglas DC-6	N90728	42895	American Airlines	Stalled & crashed on take-off	Dallas, TX, USA	28	27
29.11.49	de Havilland DH.89A Dragon Rapide	VP-KFV	6406	E.M.Noon	Destroyed by fire	Masindi, Kenya	*	*
oo.11.49	Avro Anson I	VH-BMC	–	Aircraft Disposals	Damaged in forced landing	Agra, India	*	*
oo.11.49	Savoia Marchetti SM.95	I-LATI	17	LATI	Damaged beyond repair	Villa Cisneros, Rio de Oro	*	*
01.12.49	Douglas DC-3	PP-YPM	4241	REAL	Crashed	Ribeiro Claro, Brazil	*	*
02.12.49	Consolidated PBY-5A Catalina	PK-AKC	*	Battafsche Petroleum	Written off	Muntok Bay, Indonesia	*	*
04.12.49	Curtiss C-46	*	*	Civil Air Transport	Crashed out of fuel with cargo of petrol	French Indo-China	5	0
07.12.49	Douglas DC-3	N60256	9201	Arrow Airways	Crashed	nr Pacheco, CA, USA	*	*
09.12.49	Curtiss C-46	*	*	Civil Air Transport	Crashed [Possibly XT-820 cn 22354 or XT-814 cn 22347]	nr Lanchow, China	36	0
10.12.49	Curtiss C-46	*	*	Civil Air Transport	Crashed [Possibly XT-814 cn 22347 or XT-820 cn 22354]	Nr Hoikow, China	17	23
12.12.49	Douglas DC-3	AP-ADI	4841	Pak Air	Crashed	Karachi, Pakistan	*	*
12.12.49	Douglas DC-3	N25691	2256	Capitol Airlines	Crashed on landing	Washington, DC, USA	*	*
16.12.49	Douglas DC-3	XA-DUK	11721	Mexicana	Crashed	Orizaba, Mexico	*	*
18.12.49	Douglas DC-3	OO-AUQ	10241	Sabena	Crashed on take-off due to wing failure	Aulnay-sous-Blois, France	8	0
18.12.49	Avro Anson I	G-AKFL	–	Air Jordan	Crashed on beach	nr Beirut, Lebanon	*	*
19.12.49	Douglas DC-3	PP-AXG	13850/25295	Aerovias Brasil	Crashed	Viteria, Brazil	*	*
21.12.49	Douglas DC-3	VP-CAT	11927	Air Ceylon	Crashed on landing	Trichinopoli, Ceylon	*	*
23.12.49	Avro Lancastrian 3	I-AHBX	1292	Alitalia	Destroyed by fire	Dakar, French West Africa	*	*
28.12.49	Handley Page Halifax C.8	G-AIHY	1325	Lancashire Aircraft Corporation	Damaged while taxiing	Le Bourget, France	0	*
30.12.49	Douglas C-54A	VT-CYK	3089	Bharat Airways	Crashed after cargo fire	Comillah, Pakistan	*	*
31.12.49	Miles Aerovan 4	VP-KEN	6408	Airwork (East Africa) Ltd	Crashed	Rift Valley, Tanganyika	*	*
31.12.49	Avro Anson I	VP-KEO	–	Caspar Air Charters	Crashed	Nairobi, Kenya	*	*
oo.oo.49	Consolidated Commodore	VP-BAA	11	Bahamas Airways	Damaged beyond repair in hurricane	Location Unknown	*	*

1950 – 1959

The first post-war decade saw the air transport industry rapidly expand after the enforced restrictions of the 1940s.

The ready supply of ex-military transports enabled the major airlines to resume services quickly. They also provided inexpensive equipment for the many smaller operators appearing in the early 'fifties. Demobbed DC-3s saw service in all parts of the globe and were the mainstay of air transport for most of the decade. The ubiquitous DC-3 appears many times in this volume (1,297 to be exact!) but that is no reflection on the type's safety record, being instead an indication of its universal popularity.

However, the expansion of air travel and the increase in aircraft capacity inevitably led to a rise in the number of accidents involving higher casualty rates. The worst civil aviation disaster of the period occurred in 1956 when a Super Constellation and a DC-7 collided over the Grand Canyon killing all 128 on board — the first crash to claim more than a hundred lives. In all, 31 flights ended in crashes with 50 or more fatalities. In the previous ten years there had only been six!

The dawn of the jet age in air transport was unfortunately marred by the well documented series of Comet crashes. Seven of the early models were written off although not always due to the structural fatigue problem later identified as the cause of the worst crashes. Unfamiliarity with jet operations also played its part.

Even though the Comet's problems were solved by the end of the decade, the damaging delay robbed Britain of its lead in jet airliner development and handed the initiative to Boeing and Douglas. These two manufacturers forged ahead

KLM lost one of their Super Constellations (PH-LKY) when it crashed on take-off from Shannon, Ireland, on 5 September 1954, killing 28. (Popperfoto)

in airliner design and production, building up a dominance which has only recently been challenged by Airbus Industrie.

In British minds, probably the most tragic accident took place in 1958. An Ambassador crashed after failing to take-off from a slush covered runway at Munich. It was certainly not the worst accident of the time but it robbed English football of seven Manchester United players. The blame was initially put on the pilot's shoulders but he was later exonerated by a British enquiry.

Since the Second World War many airlines have had to cope with flying in or near danger zones caused by the many colonial, nationalist and civil wars which continue to erupt. In the 1950s this problem was only just rearing its head, but conflicts in French Indo-China, Cyprus and Suez amongst others all claimed civil airliners. The worst such loss to hostile action occurred in 1955 when an Israeli Constellation was shot down by Bulgarian aircraft with the loss of 58 lives. This was only the first of several Cold War incidents to claim civilian fatalities.

First write-offs 1950–1959

(* military example crashed earlier)

Short Solent	01.02.50
Cierva Air Horse	13.06.50
SNCASE Armagnac	30.06.50
de Havilland Drover	16.07.51
Boeing Stratocruiser	12.09.51
SNCASO Bretagne	30.10.51
Hunting Percival Prince	09.03.52
Nord Noratlas	06.07.52
Ilyushin IL-12	18.07.52
Vickers Viscount	27.08.52
de Havilland Comet	26.10.52
de Havilland Heron	27.03.53
Bristol Britannia	04.02.54
Convair 340	16.03.54
Airspeed Ambassador	08.04.55
Martin 404	17.02.56
Douglas DC-7	30.06.56
Convair 440	17.07.56
Bristol 173	16.09.56
Hurel-Dubois HD-321	30.10.56
Ilyushin IL-14	14.06.57*
Scottish Avn Twin Pioneer	30.08.57
Tupolev TU-114	18.02.58
Tupolev TU-104	19.02.58
Fairchild F-27	09.05.58
Handley Page Herald	30.08.58
Saab Scandia	30.12.58
Lockheed 188 Electra	03.02.59
de Havilland Canada Caribou	24.02.59
VEB 152	04.03.59
Boeing 707	15.08.59
Antonov AN-10	16.11.59
Ilyushin IL-18	13.12.59

This was the result of a SAGETA Armagnac (F-BAVG) overturning on landing at Paris-Orly on 29 January 1957. Luckily only one person died out of the 67 on board. (Popperfoto)

Date	Type	Reg'n	C/n	Operator	Accident	Location	F	S
03.01.50	Avro Anson I	VR-TAT	–	United Air Services	Crashed	Dar-es-Salaam, Tanganyika	*	*
07.01.50	Boeing 247	XA-CAB	1684	Lineas Aereas Guerrero Oaxaca	Crashed	nr Los Parajitos, Mexico	*	*
10.01.50	Douglas DC-3	F-BEFQ	14362/25807	Air Nolis	Crashed	Niger, French West Africa	*	*
15.01.50	de Havilland DH.89A Dragon Rapide	ZK-ALC	6664	New Zealand National Airways	Destroyed by fire after exhaust ignited dry grass	Rotorua, New Zealand	*	*
18.01.50	Douglas DC-3	PI-C184	*	Trans Asiatic Airlines	Crashed	Rangoon, Burma	*	*
20.01.50	Handley Page Halifax C.8	G-AITC	1382	World Air Freight	Damaged on landing	Brindisi, Italy	*	*
22.01.50	Douglas DC-4-1009	F-BBDB	42912	Air France	Crashed	Paris, France	*	*
22.01.50	de Havilland Dove 1	VP-YER	04007	Central African Airways	Crashed	Livingstone, Southern Rhodesia	*	*
24.01.50	Douglas DC-3	PI-C22	*	Philippine Air Lines	Crashed	nr Iliolo, Philippines	4	0
24.01.50	Douglas DC-3	F-BFGD	10046	Societe Transatlantique Aerienne	Crashed into mountain	Tamatave, Madagascar	14	0
25.01.50	Douglas DC-3	VT-CPQ	13558	Air Services of India	Crashed	Gauhati, India	*	*
30.01.50	Douglas DC-3	F-BEIH	15412/26857	Air Nolis	Crashed	Le Treport, France	*	*
01.02.50	Short Solent 2	G-AHIX	S.1310	British Overseas Airways Corporation	Crashed on landing	Southampton, Hants, UK	*	*
02.02.50	Douglas DC-3	PH-TEU	13396	KLM Royal Dutch Airlines	Crashed	North Sea	7	0
05.02.50	Douglas C-54A	4X-ACD	10339	El Al Israel Airlines	Crashed on take-off	Lydda, Israel	*	*
05.02.50	Curtiss C-46	*	*	Transporte Aereo Transandino	Crashed into houses	Maracaibo, Venezuela	*	*
06.02.50	Avro Anson I	VH-BDX	–	G.A.Michaelov	Damaged in forced landing	Horsmonden, Kent, UK	*	*
09.02.50	Canadair C-4-1	CF-CPR	148	Canadian Pacific Airlines	Crashed on landing in bad weather	Tokyo, Japan	*	*
10.02.50	Avro Anson I	G-AJBA	–	Transair	Destroyed by fire	Montge, France	*	*
16.02.50	Douglas DC-3	F-BAOD	11720	Air France	Destroyed	Cotonou, French West Africa	*	*
20.02.50	Avro Anson 18C	VT-CXX	1481	Indian Department of Civil Aviation	Crashed	nr Rahimabad, India	1	*
27.02.50	Douglas DC-3	*	*	Ceskoslovenske Aerolinie	Crashed	nr Prague, Czechoslovakia	5	*
01.03.50	Douglas DC-3	HK-507	4725	Servicios Aereos Medellin	Crashed	Medellin, Colombia	*	*
02.03.50	Beechcraft D-18S	SU-ADM	A-0056	Misrair	Written off	Ras Matarma, Egypt	*	*
02.03.50	Avro Nineteen 2	G-AKDV	1424	Secretary of State for the Colonies	Crashed	Sombula, Southern Rhodesia	*	*
07.03.50	Martin 202	N93050	9134	Northwest Airlines	Crashed into flag pole at night	Minneapolis, MN, USA	13{2}	0
10.03.50	Bristol 170 Freighter 21	F-BECR	12782	Soc Indochinoise de Transports Aer.	Crashed into hill in bad weather	nr Hue, French Indo-China	4	0
11.03.50	Douglas DC-3	HK-123	6160	Avianca	Crashed	Ipiates, Colombia	*	*
12.03.50	Avro Tudor 5	G-AKBY	1417	Airflight	Crashed on approach with incorrect centre of gravity	Llandow, Glam, UK	81	3
21.03.50	Bristol 170 Freighter 21	G-AHJJ	12742	Bristol Aeroplane Co	Crashed after take-off	nr Cowbridge, Glam, UK	4	0
25.03.50	Douglas DC-3	TC-BAL	19423	Devlet Hava Yollari	Caught fire on landing	Ankara, Turkey	16	*
28.03.50	Latecoere 631	F-BANU	03	SEMAF	Crashed	Off Cap Ferret, France	12	0
28.03.50	Douglas DC-3	SP-LCC	9903	LOT Polish Airlines	Damaged beyond repair	Location Unknown	*	*
29.03.50	Lisunov Li-2T	SP-LBA	18422000	LOT Polish Airlines	Damaged beyond repair	Location Unknown	*	*
05.04.50	Douglas DC-3	VT-CJD	12826	Deccan Airways	Crashed	Hatiara, India	*	*
05.04.50	Avro Anson V	CF-GHI	MDF-333	Central Northern Airways	Destroyed	Bissett, MN, Canada	*	*
09.04.50	Consolidated PBY-5A Catalina	VP-BAO	118	Caribbean International Airways	Written off	Location Unknown	*	*
15.04.50	Douglas DC-3	HK-309	*	Lansa	Crashed	Santa Ana, Colombia	25	*
16.04.50	Handley Page Halton	G-AHDX	1378/SH.28C	Worldair Carriers	Crashed	Switzerland	6	*
18.04.50	Douglas DC-3	VT-CGM	9320	Bharat Airways	Damaged by fire in hangar	Calcutta, India	*	*
24.04.50	Curtiss C-46	CB-51	26369	Lloyd Aereo Boliviano	Crashed	Cochabamba, Bolivia	*	*
26.04.50	Avro Anson I	G-AIXW	–	Dennis Aviation	Crashed into house	Mons, France	*	*
01.05.50	Douglas DC-3	F-OAFP	20000	Fr High Commissioner to Cameroons	Crashed	Tenkodogo, French West Africa	*	*
02.05.50	Douglas DC-3	HK-120	4314	Avianca	Crashed	Chimborcza, Ecuador	15	*
05.05.50	Noorduyn Norseman VI	ET-P-5	*	D.Rundstrom	Damaged in ground loop	Lidetta, Ethiopia	*	*
12.05.50	de Havilland DH.89A Dragon Rapide	VP-KEC	6893	East African Airways	Crashed	Mafia Island, Tanganyika	*	*
12.05.50	Airspeed Consul	G-AHJX	541	Morton Air Services	Crashed	Guernsey, Channel Islands	*	*
14.05.50	Douglas DC-4-1009	F-BBDM	42990	Air France	Crashed on approach	Bahrain	13	38
15.05.50	Short Sandringham 6	LN-IAU	SH.51C	DNL	Crashed	nr Harstad, Norway	*	*
17.05.50	Douglas DC-3	VT-CHB	13023	Airways (India) Ltd	Crashed	Balurghat, India	*	*
24.05.50	Douglas DC-3	C-307	10194	Lansa	Crashed into mountain	nr Pasto, Colombia	26	1
26.05.50	Douglas DC-3	PP-SPV	14540/25985	VASP	Crashed	Sao Paulo, Brazil	*	*
27.05.50	Boeing 247D	NR13352	1734	Operator Unknown	Crashed while cropspraying	Walla Walla, WA, USA	*	*
30.05.50	Douglas DC-3	PP-AVZ	9156	Aerolineas Brasil	Crashed	nr Ilheus, Brazil	13	*

Date	Type	Reg'n	C/n	Operator	Accident	Location	F	S
05.06.50	Curtiss C-46	N1248N	22496	Westair	Crashed due to engine failure	Off Florida, USA	28	37
09.06.50	Douglas DC-3	N16030	1546	New Tribes Mission	Crashed	nr Barranco, Colombia	15	*
11.06.50	Noorduyn UC-64A Norseman	ET-T-30	*	Sinclair Petroleum Company	Damaged in forced landing	Belet Uen, Italian Somaliland	0	*
12.06.50	Douglas DC-4-1009	F-BBDE	42937	Air France	Crashed on approach	Off Bahrain	46	4
12.06.50	Douglas DC-3	LV-ACL	12020	Aerolineas Argentinas	Crashed	Pistarini, Argentina	*	*
13.06.50	Cierva Air Horse	G-ALCV	W.11/1	Cierva Autogyro Co	Crashed after rotor failure	Eastleigh, Hants, UK	3	0
15.06.50	Curtiss C-46	N74170	22477	Pan American World Airways	Belly landed	Merida, Mexico	0	*
23.06.50	Douglas DC-4	N95425	10270	Northwest Airlines	Crashed during storm	Benton Harbor, MI, USA	58	0
26.06.50	Douglas DC-4-1009	VH-ANA	42910	Australian National Airways	Crashed	York, WA, Australia	28	*
26.06.50	Curtiss C-46	HK-391	30196	Lloyd Aereo Colombiano	Damaged in forced landing	Puerto, Colombia	0	*
30.06.50	Douglas DC-3	YV-C-ARG	4522	RANSA	Crashed	El Lorza, Venezuela	*	*
30.06.50	SNCASE Armagnac	F-WAVA	01	SNCASE	Crashed	nr Toulouse, France	*	*
30.06.50	de Havilland DH.89A Dragon Rapide	G-AKME	6767	Wolverhampton Aviation	Destroyed by fire	Lympne, Kent, UK	*	*
09.07.50	Douglas DC-3	F-BFGL	13824	Aigle Azur	Crashed	Casablanca, Morocco	22	*
09.07.50	Avro Anson II	PP-ETD	–	Territorio de Acre	Crashed	Seringal Riozinho, Brazil	*	*
10.07.50	de Havilland DH.89A Dragon Rapide	G-AHTR	6964	Operator Unknown	Destroyed by fire	Abadan, Iran	*	*
17.07.50	Douglas DC-3	VT-ATS	20359	Indian National Airlines	Crashed when wing failed in turbulence	Patharkot, India	22	0
18.07.50	Douglas DC-3	CR-LBK	13769	Departamento de Transporte Aereo	Crashed	nr Bocoio, Angola	9	*
24.07.50	Douglas DC-3	*	*	Air Liban	Shot down by Israeli forces	Northern Israel	3	*
27.07.50	Curtiss C-46	N9406H	22582	Regina Cargo Airlines	Crashed on take-off	Teterboro, NJ, USA	1	*
28.07.50	Lockheed 049 Constellation	PP-PCG	2062	Panair do Brasil	Crashed into power lines on landing	Porte Alegre, Brazil	50	0
29.07.50	Bristol 170 Freighter 21	F-BENF	12738	Cie Air Transport	Crashed after wing failure	Tunbukta, Algeria	26	0
30.07.50	Curtiss C-46	N67960	22511	Flying Tiger Line	Crashed into power cables on take-off	Denver, CO, USA	0	2
30.07.50	SNCASE Languedoc	F-BCUI	39	Air France	Written off	Marignane, France	*	*
30.07.50	Avro Nineteen 2	G-AKDU	1423	Secretary of State for the Colonies	Forced landing after engine failure	nr Heany, UK	*	*
01.08.50	Auster J/1 Autocrat	G-AIGY	2168	Cambrian Airways	Crashed	Off Pwllheli, UK	*	*
18.08.50	Noorduyn Norseman VI	CF-GPG	*	Newfoundland Airways	Stalled & crashed on take-off from lake	Gander Lake, NF, Canada	2	0
20.08.50	Miles Aerovan 4	G-AILF	6400	Pickfords Ltd	Damaged on landing	Guernsey, Channel Islands	*	*
26.08.50	Boeing 247D	XA-DEZ	1724	Servicios Aereos Nacionales	Crashed & caught fire	Vera Cruz, Mexico	3	0
28.08.50	Consolidated PBY-5A Catalina	PK-AKR	*	Operator Unknown	Written off	Hong Kong	*	*
29.08.50	Douglas DC-3	HK-116	4786	Avianca	Crashed	Barranquilla, Colombia	*	*
30.08.50	Noorduyn Norseman V	CF-OBH	N29-2	Operator Unknown	Crashed after engine failure	Milne Lake, ON, Canada	6	0
31.08.50	Lockheed 749A Constellation	N6004C	2636	Trans World Airlines	Caught fire after forced landing	nr Wadi Natrun, Egypt	55	0
04.09.50	Douglas DC-3	N18936	2011	Robinson Airlines	Crashed into trees after engine failure	Utica, NY, USA	16	7
08.09.50	Curtiss C-46	PP-LDB	30204	Transportes Aereas Bandeirantes	Crashed	Guanabara Bay, Brazil	*	*
12.09.50	Douglas DC-3	F-OACA	6241	Air Outremer	Crashed	Nanen Sonla, French Indo-China	*	*
14.09.50	Douglas C-54B	TF-RVC	27240	Loftleidir	Crashed	Vatnajokull, Iceland	*	*
14.09.50	Douglas DC-3	EP-AAG	9813	Iran Air	Crashed	Tehran, Iran	8	*
21.09.50	Douglas DC-3	*	*	JAT Yugoslav Airlines	Crashed on landing	nr Zagreb, Yugoslavia	10	*
22.09.50	Avro Nineteen I	G-AGPB	1271	Ministry of Civil Aviation	Overshot on landing	Bovingdon, Herts, UK	*	*
23.09.50	Avro Nineteen I	SE-BRS	1321	Svenska Aero	Crashed on take-off	Karlstad, Sweden	10	0
26.09.50	Douglas DC-3	VT-DAT	13168	Air India	Crashed	Barrackpore, India	*	*
09.10.50	Curtiss C-46	CB-38	*	Lloyd Aereo Boliviano	Crashed	Beni, Bolivia	*	*
12.10.50	Douglas DC-3	VH-SMH	13157	John Fairfax & Sons	Crashed	Bungulla, NSW, Australia	*	*
13.10.50	Douglas DC-3	F-BAXM	20245	Air Atlas	Crashed	Casablanca, Morocco	4	*
13.10.50	Martin 202	N93037	9158	Northwest Airlines	Crashed after prop failure	Almelund, MN, USA	6	0
17.10.50	Douglas DC-3	G-AGIW	12186	British European Airways	Crashed	Mill Hill, London, UK	28	1
25.10.50	Airspeed Consul	G-AJLJ	5128	Air Enterprises	Damaged beyond repair	Beirut, Lebanon	*	*
25.10.50	Airspeed Consul	G-AJLH	5126	Lancashire Aircraft Corporation	Damaged beyond repair	Seaton, UK	*	*
26.10.50	Airspeed Consul	F-BEDP	5162	SITA	Destroyed by fire	Saigon, French Indo-China	*	*
31.10.50	Vickers Viking 1B	G-AHPN	155	British European Airways	Crashed in fog	Heathrow, London, UK	28	2
31.10.50	Airspeed Consul	TJ-ABA	5175	Air Jordan	Crashed	Jerusalem, Transjordan	*	*
03.11.50	Lockheed 749 Constellation	VT-CQP	2506	Air India	Crashed	Mont Blanc, France	48	0
04.11.50	Douglas DC-3	PP-IBC	4360	Central Aerea	Crashed	Vitoria da Conquista, Brazil	*	*

Date	Type	Reg'n	C/n	Operator	Accident	Location	F	S
07.11.50	Martin 202	N93040	9161	Northwest Airlines	Crashed into mountain	Butte, MT, USA	21	0
08.11.50	Curtiss C-46	CB-47	33245	Frigorificos Ballivian	Crashed	La Paz, Bolivia	*	*
13.11.50	Douglas C-54B	CF-EDN	10518	Curtiss Reid Flying Services	Crashed into mountain	Mt de l'Obiou, France	58	0
14.11.50	de Havilland Dove 1	VR-NEW	04101	West African Airways	Crashed	nr Kaduna, Nigeria	*	*
17.11.50	Douglas DC-3	PK-DPB	19005	KNILM	Crashed	Souraba, Malaya	*	*
22.11.50	de Havilland Dove 1	XY-ABR	04195	Union of Burma Airways	Crashed on take-off	Mingaladon, Burma	0	*
23.11.50	Douglas DC-3	OB-PAU-201	15992/32740	Faucett	Crashed	Cuzco, Peru	9	*
24.11.50	Curtiss C-46	HK-330	33470	LIDCA	Crashed	Medellin, Colombia	*	*
25.11.50	Handley Page Halifax C.8	G-AIAP	1354	Eagle Aviation	Crashed on take-off	Calcutta, India	*	*
25.11.50	Douglas DC-3	VT-COI	14037/25482	Indamer	Crashed	Khitka, Bhutan	*	*
25.11.50	Douglas DC-3	CU-T7	11646	Cubana	Crashed	Holguin, Cuba	*	*
01.12.50	Douglas DC-3	EP-AAJ	13572	Iran Air	Crashed	nr Qom, Iran	8	*
03.12.50	Miles Aerovan 4	G-AJXK	HPR.144	Handley Page	Crashed on landing	Woodley, Berks, UK	*	*
04.12.50	Avro Nineteen I	SE-BRP	1352	Aero Scandia	Fell through ice on landing	Langsjon, Sweden	*	*
05.12.50	Avro Anson I	VH-BKL	–	East-West Airlines	Damaged in forced landing	Orchard Stanthorpe, Qld, Australia	*	*
07.12.50	Miles Aerovan 4	G-AJOI	6411	Patrick Motors	Destroyed by gale	Birmingham, UK	*	*
08.12.50	Douglas C-54A	F-BELB	3084	T.A. Intercontinentaux	Crashed into hill after take-off	Bangui, French Equatorial Africa	46	10
08.12.50	Douglas DC-3	F-BAXY	16100/32848	Air Atlas	Crashed	Ruig Piner, France	5	*
09.12.50	Avro Anson I	VH-AYE	–	T.M.S.Hall	Crashed after engine failure	Tuggerah Lakes, NSW, Australia	*	*
12.12.50	Boeing B-17G	F-BDAT	*	Institute Geographique Nationale	Crashed	Niamey, French West Africa	*	*
13.12.50	Douglas DC-4-1009	HB-ILE	43093	Swissair	Struck pylon on landing & caught fire	Sydney, NS, Canada	0	31
13.12.50	Douglas DC-3	VT-CFK	14604/26049	Air India	Crashed	Katagiri, India	20	*
13.12.50	Douglas DC-3	PP-SPT	20543	VASP	Crashed	Londrina, Brazil	*	*
14.12.50	Douglas DC-3	PP-SPW	17097/34364	VASP	Crashed into houses	Ribeirao, Brazil	1{3}	*
15.12.50	Douglas DC-3	YV-C-AVU	4432	Avensa	Crashed on take-off	Valera, Venezuela	31	*
17.12.50	Curtiss C-46	PP-LDD	30346	Loide Aereo Nacional	Crashed	Caminho Grande, Brazil	*	*
22.12.50	Douglas DC-3	CF-CUF	12855	Canadian Pacific Airlines	Crashed	Okanagan Park, BC, Canada	2	15
25.12.50	Avro Anson I	SX-BDA	–	Aeroporikai Metaphorai Ellados	Damaged by gale	Athens, Greece	*	*
30.12.50	Douglas DC-3	LV-ACH	13027	Aerolineas Argentinas	Crashed	Santiago del Estado, Argentina	*	*
oo.oo.50	Miles Aerovan 4	G-AJWI	6418	Mayfair Air Services	Damaged beyond repair	Location Unknown	*	*
oo.oo.50	Beechcraft D-18S	VT-CIS	A-0365	Operator Unknown	Written off	Location Unknown	*	*
oo.oo.50	Boeing 247	XA-BFK	1738	Lineas Aereas Guerrero Oaxaca	Crashed	Mexico	*	*
01.01.51	Douglas DC-3	CB-31	13837	Lloyd Aereo Boliviano	Crashed	La Paz, Bolivia	*	*
02.01.51	Douglas DC-3	CF-ECN	4702	McInnes Products Corp	Crashed on take-off	Great Slave Lake, NWT, Canada	*	*
04.01.51	Curtiss C-46	N79982	33564	Monarch Air Services	Swung off runway & struck Vultee SNV-1 & BT-13	Chicago, IL, USA	0(*)	47
12.01.51	de Havilland Dove 1	ZS-DDW	04017	United Airways	Crashed after breaking up in turbulence	Ixopo, South Africa	12	0
13.01.51	Douglas DC-3	VR-HEP	15782/32530	Air Carriers	Crashed into mountain	Thailand	10	*
14.01.51	Douglas DC-4-1009	N74685	43102	National Airlines	Overshot into ditch & caught fire	Philadelphia, PA, USA	7	21
16.01.51	Martin 202	N93054	9144	Northwest Airlines	Crashed	Reardon, WA, USA	10	*
17.01.51	Savoia Marchetti SM.95	I-DALO	10	Alitalia	Crashed on approach after being struck by lightning	nr Civitavecchia, Italy	14	3
27.01.51	Grumman G-73 Mallard	PK-AKE	J-41	Battafsche Petroleum	Destroyed by fire	Kemajoran, Indonesia	*	*
28.01.51	Short Solent 3	VH-TOA	S.1294	Trans Oceanic Airways	Sank on take-off	Malta	1	*
31.01.51	Douglas DC-3	TF-ISG	12482	Icelandair	Crashed	Off Hafnarfjorour, Iceland	20	*
31.01.51	Douglas DC-3	HK-311	20183	Lansa	Crashed	Madrid, Colombia	*	*
03.02.51	Douglas DC-4-1009	F-BBDO	42992	Air France	Crashed	nr Buea, Nigeria	29	0
05.02.51	Avro Anson I	G-AIXZ	–	Dennis Aviation	Crashed	Jersey, Channel Islands	*	*
06.02.51	Avro Anson V	CF-EKJ	MDF-287	Yellowknife Airways	Crashed on take-off due to icing & being overloaded	Yellowknife, NWT, Canada	2	0
10.02.51	Avro Anson I	VH-AJP	–	South Coast Airways	Crashed on take-off	Jervis Bay, NSW, Australia	*	*
12.02.51	Douglas DC-3	F-OABK	19592	Aigle Azur	Written off	Luang Prabang, Laos	*	*
14.02.51	Curtiss C-46	HK-333	49	Lansa	Crashed	Yali, Colombia	*	*
15.02.51	Avro Anson V	YV-P-APY	MDF-414	Gamez Calcan y Cia	Crashed in sea	Off Puerto Cumarebo, Venezuela	3	0
21.02.51	Curtiss C-46	PP-ITF	382/2925	ITAU	Crashed	Rio de Janeiro, Brazil	*	*
23.02.51	Curtiss C-46	N59490	2942	Slick Airways	Damaged in forced landing	Newhall, CA, USA	*	*

Date	Type	Reg'n	C/n	Operator	Accident	Location	F	S
25.02.51	de Havilland DH.89A Dragon Rapide	SU-ACT	6551	Misrair	Destroyed by fire	Almaza, Egypt	*	*
27.02.51	Convair 240-2	N90664	059	Mid Continent Airlines	Crashed on take-off	Tulsa, OK, USA	0	33
02.03.51	Douglas DC-3	N19928	7400	Mid Continent Airlines	Crashed on approach & caught fire	Sioux City, IA, USA	16	9
05.03.51	de Havilland DH.89A Dragon Rapide	G-AHIA	6948	Skyways	Damaged beyond repair	Maritse, Rhodes, Greece	*	*
08.03.51	Handley Page Halifax C.8	G-AJZY	1322	Lancashire Aircraft Corporation	Crashed due to icing	Great Missenden, Herts, UK	4	0
11.03.51	Douglas DC-4	HS-PCS	*	Pacific Overseas Airways	Crashed after take-off	Mt Butler, Hong Kong	26	*
21.03.51	Douglas DC-3	HK-315	9073	Lansa	Crashed	Corozal, Colombia	*	*
22.03.51	Douglas DC-3	PP-CCX	7341	Cruzeiro	Crashed	Florianopolis, Brazil	3	*
26.03.51	Douglas DC-3	LV-ACY	12291	Aerolineas Argentinas	Crashed on take-off	Rio Grande, Argentina	11{2}	*
27.03.51	Douglas DC-3	G-AJVZ	19361	Air Tansport Charter	Crashed after take-off in snow	Manchester, UK	2	0
27.03.51	Douglas DC-3	VH-CAQ	12285	Australian Dept. of Civil Aviation	Crashed	Camden, NSW, Australia	*	*
30.03.51	Douglas C-54B	N74644	10540	Seaboard & Western Airlines	Crashed on landing	Keflavik, Iceland	*	*
01.04.51	Douglas DC-3	SE-BBM	20128	Scandinavian Airlines System	Crashed	Stockholm, Sweden	*	*
02.04.51	Douglas DC-3	HK-142	1957	Avianca	Crashed	Bogota, Colombia	*	*
06.04.51	Douglas DC-3	N63439	20229	Southwest Airlines	Crashed into high ground	Refugio Pass, CA, USA	22	0
07.04.51	Avro Anson V	CF-GSA	4178	Eastern Provincial Airways	Sank through ice	Millertown Junction, NF, Canada	*	*
09.04.51	Douglas DC-3	HS-SAE	*	Siamese Airways	Crashed on approach	Hong Kong	16	*
10.04.51	Handley Page Hermes 5	G-ALEU	HP.82/1	Ministry of Supply	Belly landed	Chilbolton, Hants, UK	0	*
12.04.51	Airspeed Consul	TF-RPM	2647	Operator Unknown	Crashed	Deepcar, UK	*	*
13.04.51	Avro Anson V	CF-GJV	MDF-288	Central Northern Airways	Damaged after u/c collapsed	Lynn Lake, MN, Canada	*	*
15.04.51	Curtiss C-46	PP-LDC	30443	Loide Aereo Nacional	Crashed	Guanabara Bay, Brazil	*	*
25.04.51	Douglas DC-4	CU-T188	10368	Cubana	Mid-air collision with USN Beech SNB	Key West, FL, USA	39(5)	0
28.04.51	Douglas DC-3A	N16038	1927	United Air Lines	Crashed on approach in heavy rain	Fort Wayne, IN, USA	11	0
28.04.51	Curtiss C-46	CC-CYA-0141	26445	Lyon Air	Crashed	nr Los Antigues, Argentina	*	*
08.05.51	Vickers Viking 1	G-AHPD	134	Hunting Air Travel	Belly landed due to engine failure	Bordeaux, France	0	31
08.05.51	de Havilland Dove 2	VT-CTX	04134	Civil Air Training Centre	Crashed	Allahabad, India	*	*
12.05.51	AAC.1 Toucan	F-BDYE	404	Air Fret Transimax	Written off	Rouigo, Algeria	*	*
15.05.51	Douglas DC-3	PP-LPC	19120	Linhas Aereas Paulistas	Crashed	Location Unknown	*	*
18.05.51	Douglas DC-3	PP-SPL	17011/34274	VASP	Damaged beyond repair	Rancharia, Brazil	6	*
22.05.51	Auster J/1 Autocrat	G-AIBS	2154	Somerton Airways	Crashed	Peterborough, UK	*	*
03.06.51	Douglas DC-3	LV-AGE	20083	Aerolineas Argentinas	Crashed	Jujuy, Argentina	*	*
05.06.51	de Havilland DH.89A Dragon Rapide	ZS-ATV	6914	Operator Unknown	Written off	Thysville, Belgian Congo	*	*
06.06.51	Douglas DC-3	PP-NAL	42979	L.A. Transcontinental Brasileira	Crashed on landing	Rio de Janeiro, Brazil	2	*
08.06.51	Douglas DC-3	YU-ABE	*	JAT Yugoslav Airlines	Crashed	Munich, West Germany	*	*
09.06.51	de Havilland Dove 2	G-AJZT	04059	Prince Aly Khan	Crashed into tree during air display	Banstead, Surrey, UK	4	*
15.06.51	Douglas DC-3	HK-504	10062	Servicios Aereos Medellin	Crashed	Medellin, Colombia	*	*
22.06.51	Lockheed 049 Constellation	N88846	2046	Pan American World Airways	Crashed into hill at night	nr Sanoyea, Liberia	40	0
29.06.51	AAC.1 Toucan	YU-ACE	316	JAT Yugoslav Airlines	Crashed	nr Rijeka, Yugoslavia	14	*
30.06.51	Douglas DC-6	N37543	43144	United Air Lines	Crashed into mountain	nr Fort Collins, CO, USA	50	0
oo.06.51	de Havilland DH.86B	G-ADUH	2336	Gulf Aviation	Damaged in ground collision with Auster J-1 G-AIBO	Bahrein	*(*)	*
09.07.51	Douglas DC-3	HK-126	4290	Avianca	Crashed	Barranquilla, Colombia	*	*
10.07.51	de Havilland DH.89A Dragon Rapide	G-ALGO	6830	Operator Unknown	Crashed	Abadan, Iran	*	*
10.07.51	de Havilland DH.89A Dragon Rapide	G-ALXJ	6863	Air Navigation & Trading	Crashed	Off Laxey Head, Isle of Man	*	*
10.07.51	Avro Anson I	G-AJFX	–	Trans Arabia Air Services	Force-landed & collided with donkey	Gizeh, Egypt	*	*
11.07.51	Lockheed 18-08 Lodestar	CF-ETC	2219	T.Eaton Co	Destroyed by fire after emegency landing	Montreal, PQ, Canada	0	2
12.07.51	Douglas DC-3	PP-LPG	14822/26267	Loide Aereo Nacional	Crashed on landing	Aracaju, Brazil	33	*
12.07.51	Douglas DC-3	VT-CHT	20662	Indamer	Crashed	Tezpur, India	*	*
13.07.51	Douglas C-54B	HS-POA	18368	Siamese Airways	Damaged when u/c collapsed on landing	Don Muang, Thailand	*	*
14.07.51	Avro Anson I	VH-BAB	–	Butler Air Transport	Crashed at sea	Off Swansea, NSW, Australia	0	11
14.07.51	Lockheed 14H Super Electra	SE-BTN	1421	Airtaco	Crashed on take-off	Stockholm, Sweden	4	2
16.07.51	de Havilland Drover 1	VH-EBQ	5003	Qantas	Crashed	Huon Gulf, New Guinea	*	*
18.07.51	Douglas C-54A	F-BDRI	3079	TAI	Crashed on take-off	Tananarive, Madagascar	*	*
20.07.51	Douglas DC-3	F-OABX	19634	Air Outremer	Written off	Saigon, Vietnam	*	*
21.07.51	Douglas DC-4	CF-CPC	10327	Canadian Pacific Airlines	Crashed	nr Sitka, Alaska	37	0

Date	Type	Reg'n	C/n	Operator	Accident	Location	F	S
24.07.51	Douglas DC-3	OO-CBA	6327	Sabena	Crashed	Gao, French Sudan	*	*
26.07.51	Douglas DC-3	PP-CCK	4750	Cruzeiro	Crash landed	Trinidad, Bolivia	*	*
26.07.51	AAC.1 Toucan	F-BBYF	226	Autrex	Written off	Lao Kay, French Indo-China	*	*
27.07.51	Bristol 170 Freighter 21	VR-NAX	12784	West African Airways	Crashed out of fuel in fog	Kaduna, Nigeria	*	*
27.07.51	Avro Anson V	TF-RVF	4263	Loftleidir	Damaged when u/c collapsed on landing	Vestmannaeyjar, Iceland	*	*
29.07.51	Curtiss C-46	CB-39	26488	Lloyd Aereo Boliviano	Crashed on take-off	Cochabamba, Bolivia	7	*
01.08.51	Avro Anson I	VP-KHT	–	Airwork (East Africa) Ltd	Force-landed in storm & struck tree	nr Arusha, Tanganyika	*	*
08.08.51	Curtiss C-46	N74176	22592	Pan American World Airways	Overran embankment	Sao Paulo, Brazil	*	*
08.08.51	Douglas DC-3	VH-TAT	13083	Trans Australia Airlines	Crashed	Barilla Bay, Tas, Australia	*	*
11.08.51	Curtiss C-46	N3908B	22516	All American Airways	Crashed on take-off	Newark, NJ, USA	0	*
11.08.51	Douglas DC-3	F-BAXB	42971	Air France	Crashed	Moisville, France	5	0
17.08.51	Douglas DC-3	PP-YPX	9154	REAL	Crashed	Ubatuba, Brazil	10	*
20.08.51	Douglas DC-3	HS-SAF	12150	Siamese Airways	Crashed	Bah Fai, Thailand	*	*
21.08.51	Consolidated Canso A	VP-JAT	*	Caribbean International Airways	Destroyed in gale	Palisadoes, Jamaica	*	*
24.08.51	Douglas DC-6B	N37550	43260	United Air Lines	Crashed into hill	nr Union City, CA, USA	50	0
28.08.51	de Havilland DH.89A Dragon Rapide	G-AHXZ	6825	British European Airways	Destroyed by fire	Renfrew, UK	*	*
31.08.51	Avro Anson I	VH-BFC	–	Aerial Surveys	U/c collapsed on landing	Wallaroo, SA, Australia	*	*
oo.08.51	Avro Anson I	VH-ARL	–	Overland Air Services	Damaged by flooding	Geelong, Vic, Australia	*	*
oo.08.51	Avro Anson I	VH-BAX	–	Corio Air Engineers	Damaged by flooding	Geelong, Vic, Australia	*	*
oo.08.51	Avro York C.1	G-AGSN	1238	Lancashire Aircraft Corporation	Damaged beyond repair	Fayid, Egypt	*	*
01.09.51	Douglas DC-6	XA-JOR	43211	Mexicana	Crashed	Lake Texcoco, Mexico	0	*
02.09.51	Convair 240-2	N90662	049	Pan American World Airways	Crashed in sea on approach	Kingston, Jamaica	0	34
08.09.51	Douglas DC-3	PP-SPQ	15591/27036	VASP	Crashed into house on take-off	Sao Paulo, Brazil	13(3)	*
12.09.51	Boeing Stratocruiser	N31230	15970	United Air Lines	Crashed	San Francisco Bay, CA, USA	3	0
12.09.51	Douglas DC-3	F-BEIZ	15985/32733	Alpes Provence	Crashed	Off Balearic Is, Spain	39	0
15.09.51	Douglas DC-3	VT-CCA	13853/25298	Air India	Crashed	Bangalore, India	*	*
19.09.51	CCF Norseman V	CF-GPB	N29-39	Operator Unknown	Crashed	Newfoundland, Canada	*	*
29.09.51	Curtiss C-46	CB-43	33346	Frigorificos Co-operativo Los Andes	Crashed	La Paz, Bolivia	*	*
08.10.51	Douglas DC-3	XA-GOR	14007/25452	Aero Transportes	Crashed	Blanco, Mexico	8	*
15.10.51	Douglas DC-3	ZS-AVJ	12016	South African Airways	Crashed	East Griqualand, South Africa	17	*
15.10.51	de Havilland Dove 1	VH-AQO	04002	Airlines (WA) Ltd	Damaged in belly landing	Kurawang, WA, Australia	0	*
15.10.51	de Havilland DH.89A Dragon Rapide	VP-KEB	6891	East African Airways	Crashed	Kasese, Kenya	*	*
17.10.51	Consolidated PBY-5A Catalina	CF-FOQ	400	Queen Charlotte Airlines	Crashed	Mt Benson, BC, Canada	23	0
18.10.51	Douglas DC-3	CF-DXR	13376	Hollinger Ungava Transport	Crashed	Sept Isles, PQ, Canada	*	*
22.10.51	Douglas DC-3	YU-ACC	13014	JAT Yugoslav Airlines	Crashed	Skopje, Yugoslavia	12	*
26.10.51	Avro Tudor 5	G-AKCC	1421	William Dempster Ltd	Damaged when overshot on landing	Bovingdon, Herts, UK	0	*
28.10.51	Curtiss C-46	*	*	Operator Unknown	Crashed on take-off	Cuidad Flores, Guatemala	27	*
30.10.51	SNCASO Bretagne	F-OAIY	12	Air Algerie	Written off	Paris, France	*	*
02.11.51	Miles Aerovan 4	ZK-AWV	6428	Airwork	Destroyed in gale	Rongotai, New Zealand	*	*
05.11.51	Martin 202	N93039	9160	Transocean Airlines	Crashed in snow	Tucumcari, NM, USA	1	22
05.11.51	Douglas DC-3	F-BCYL	6112	C.A. de Transports Indochinois	Crashed	Hanoi, Vietnam	*	*
05.11.51	Avro Nineteen I	G-AHXM	1353	Sperry Gyroscope Co	U/c collapsed on landing	Blackbushe, Hants, UK	*	*
07.11.51	Douglas DC-3	F-BEIV	19870	Ste des Tran. Aer. Camerounais	Crashed	Fort Lamy, French West Africa	*	*
09.11.51	Miles Aerovan 3	G-AHTX	6380	Arab Contracting & Trading Co	Damaged on landing	Baalbeck, Lebanon	*	*
14.11.51	Douglas DC-3	SP-LCG	9165	LOT Polish Airlines	Crashed on take-off	Lotz, Poland	16	*
14.11.51	Douglas DC-3	VT-CKU	13857/25302	Airways (India) Ltd	Crashed	Gauhati, India	*	*
17.11.51	Douglas C-54D	N79992	10832	Overseas National Airlines	Mid-air collision with California Eastern DC-4 N4002B	San Francisco, CA, USA	3(0)	0
17.11.51	Avro Lancastrian 3	VH-EAV	1291	Qantas	Damaged on take-off	Sydney, NSW, Australia	*	*
19.11.51	Douglas DC-3	TC-ACA	7352	Devlet Hava Yollari	Crashed on landing	Cairo, Egypt	5	*
21.11.51	Douglas DC-3	VT-AUO	13265	Deccan Airways	Crashed on landing	Calcutta, India	16	*
24.11.51	Douglas DC-4	4X-ADN	10512	El Al Israel Airlines	Crashed on approach	Zurich, Switzerland	6	1
27.11.51	Douglas DC-2-243	XA-DOQ	2077	Lineas Aereas Unidas	Crashed	Luis-Acatlan, Mexico	*	*
28.11.51	Douglas DC-3	I-LETR	4686	Linee Aeree Italiane	Crashed	Milan, Italy	*	*
oo.11.51	Beechcraft C-45	VP-RCA	6116	Operator Unknown	Written off	Choma, Northern Rhodesia	*	*

Date	Type	Reg'n	C/n	Operator	Accident	Location	F	S
04.12.51	Douglas DC-3	N17109	4999	United Air Lines	Crashed	Denver, CO, USA	3	0
06.12.51	de Havilland DH.89A Dragon Rapide	G-AGPH	6889	British European Airways	Damaged beyond repair	Barra, Hebrides, UK	*	*
14.12.51	Douglas DC-4-1009	HB-ILO	43098	Swissair	Crashed in fog	Amsterdam, Netherlands	0	*
16.12.51	Curtiss C-46F	N1678M	22572	Miami Airlines	Crashed after engine fire	Elizabeth, NJ, USA	56	0
23.12.51	Douglas DC-6	I-LUCK	43215	Linee Aeree Italiane	Crashed on landing	Milan, Italy	*	*
23.12.51	SNCASE Languedoc	SU-AHH	41	Misrair	Crashed on landing	Tehran, Iran	22	*
29.12.51	Curtiss C-46A	N3944C	30466	Continental Charters	Crashed into hill	nr Little Valley, NY, USA	25	14
30.12.51	Curtiss C-46	N68963	22485	Transocean Airlines	Crashed into mountain	Fairbanks, Alaska	4	*
30.12.51	Beechcraft D-18S	SU-AEB	A-0303	Misrair	Written off	Almaza, Egypt	*	*
31.12.51	Douglas DC-3	VT-COA	13859/25304	Kalinga Airlines	Crashed	Calcutta, India	*	*
00.00.51	Boeing 314A	N18611	2085	Operator Unknown	Destroyed	Baltimore, MA, USA	*	*
00.00.51	de Havilland Dove 2A	N4952N	04293	Andrau Air Park	Written off	Location Unknown	*	*
00.00.51	Noorduyn Norseman VI	HS-SGF	698	Siamese Airways	Written off	Tak, Thailand	*	*
00.00.51	de Havilland DH.89A Dragon Rapide	VT-ARZ	6717	Bihar State Government	Damaged beyond repair	India	*	*
00.00.51	Lisunov Li-2	YR-TAA	18423501	TARS	Crashed	Fagaras Mts, Romania	*	*
01.01.52	AAC.1 Toucan	F-BAMQ	106	Air France	Crashed	nr Andapa, Madagascar	6	*
02.01.52	Consolidated PBY-5A Catalina	VP-JAW	187	Caribbean International Airways	Crashed in sea	Off Grand Cayman, Cayman Is	*	*
04.01.52	Avro Nineteen I	G-AGZS	1330	Ministry of Civil Aviation	Crashed at night	nr Petersfield, Hants, UK	*	*
09.01.52	de Havilland Dove 1	ZS-BTM	04087	Central Mining Corporation	Crashed after engine failure	Baragwanath, South Africa	*	*
10.01.52	Douglas DC-3	EI-AFL	16699/33447	Aer Lingus	Crashed	Gwynynt Lake, Wales	*	*
12.01.52	Douglas DC-3	N41718	11827	General Airways	Crashed	Mt Crillon, Alaska	2	0
13.01.52	Avro Anson I	VH-BFI	–	Overland Air Services	Crashed after engine failure	Padstow, NSW, Australia	2	*
14.01.52	Convair 240-13	N91238	158	Northeast Airlines	Crashed in bay	New York, NY, USA	0	36
19.01.52	Douglas C-54E	N45342	27279	Northwest Airlines	Crashed in sea on overshoot	Sandspit, BC, Canada	36	7
22.01.52	Convair 240-0	N94229	054	American Airlines	Crashed on landing	Elizabeth, NJ, USA	23{7}	0
27.01.52	Douglas C-54A	TF-RVH	7435	Loftleidir	Destroyed by fire on landing	San Giusto, Italy	*	*
28.01.52	Lockheed 18 Lodestar	N94538	2095	Operator Unknown	Crashed	New Jersey, USA	*	*
28.01.52	Lockheed 18-56 Lodestar	N94537	2421	Operator Unknown	Crashed	New Jersey, USA	*	*
29.01.52	Beechcraft 18A	CF-BQG	0291	Gulf Aviation	Crashed	Canada	*	*
02.02.52	Avro Anson V	CF-EKL	MDF-30	Riverton Airways	Damaged in ground loop on take-off after forced landing	nr Riverton, MN, Canada	*	*
04.02.52	Douglas DC-3	OO-CBN	13450	Sabena	Crashed	Kikwit, Belgian Congo	15	0
08.02.52	Douglas DC-3	VT-COK	12095	Indian National Airlines	Crashed	Baghdogra, India	*	*
11.02.52	Douglas DC-6	N90891	43055	National Airlines	Crashed on take-off	Newark, NJ, USA	29{4}	34
16.02.52	Vickers Viking 1	G-AHPI	142	Hunting Air Travel	Crashed	nr Burgio, Italy	31	0
17.02.52	Avro Anson I	G-ALFD	–	Transair	Crashed into buildings on landing in fog	Brussels, Belgium	*	*
19.02.52	Consolidated Liberator	*	*	STAAP	Crashed	Yaounde, Cameroons	9	*
19.02.52	Douglas DC-3	VT-AXE	19160	Deccan Airways	Crashed	Sonegar, India	3	14
21.02.52	Curtiss C-46	PP-VCB	26641	Varig	Crashed	Guanabara Bay, Brazil	*	*
21.02.52	Miles Aerovan 4	G-AKHG	6424	Arab Contracting & Trading Co	Crashed	Hama, Syria	*	*
22.02.52	Avro Anson X	G-AIRN	–	Tradeastern Ltd	Forced landed out of fuel in fog	Piadena, Italy	*	*
23.02.52	Boeing 247D	XA-GUW	1693	J.Tilghman	Crashed	nr Mexico City, Mexico	*	*
28.02.52	Douglas DC-3	PP-PCN	3284	Panair do Brasil	Crashed	Uberlandia, Brazil	8	0
29.02.52	de Havilland Dove 2A	N4964N	04352	de Havilland Aircraft of Canada	Crashed on landing in bad weather	Goose, NF, Canada	2	*
03.03.52	SNCASE Languedoc	F-BCUM	43	Air France	Crashed on take-off	Nice, France	38	0
09.03.52	Hunting Percival Prince	PP-NBA	P.50/2	Aeronorte	Damaged beyond repair	Brazil	*	*
10.03.52	Douglas DC-3	PI-C5	9754	Philippine Air Lines	Crashed on take-off	Lahug, Cebu, Philippines	*	*
11.03.52	Avro York	G-AMGL	1354	Air Charter	Crashed	nr Hamburg, West Germany	*	*
22.03.52	Douglas DC-3	CF-BXZ	4695	Maritime Central Airways	Crashed due to icing [Found 27.08.53]	nr Gaspe, PQ, Canada	5	0
22.03.52	Douglas DC-6	PH-TPJ	43114	KLM Royal Dutch Airlines	Crashed on approach	Frankfurt, West Germany	44	5
23.03.52	Lockheed 749A Constellation	PH-TFF	2652	KLM Royal Dutch Airlines	Caught fire after forced landing	Bangkok, Thailand	0	44
24.03.52	Lockheed 18 Lodestar	F-ARTE	2005	S. Aerienne de Transports Tropicaux	Crashed after take-off	Gao, French West Africa	17	2
26.03.52	Douglas C-54A	N65143	10336	Braniff Airlines	Crash landed after engine fell off following fire	Hugoton, KS, USA	0	49
26.03.52	Type Unknown	*	*	Aeroflot	Overshot & collided with Soviet military aircraft	Moscow, RSFSR, USSR	70(*)	*
29.03.52	Douglas DC-3	YV-C-AZU	*	TACA	Crashed	Cerro Grande Mt, Venezuela	*	*

Date	Type	Reg'n	C/n	Operator	Accident	Location	F	S
30.03.52	Douglas DC-3	PI-C270	13808	Philippine Air Lines	Crashed	Baguio, Philippines	*	*
04.04.52	Douglas DC-3	LN-NAE	12372	Fred Olsen Air Transport	Crashed	nr Mimizan, Norway	*	*
05.04.52	Curtiss C-46F	N1911M	22464	US Airlines	Overshot & crashed	New York, NY, USA	3{3}	0
07.04.52	SNCASE Languedoc	F-BATB	02	Air France	Crashed	Le Bourget, France	*	*
09.04.52	Martin 202	N93043	9164	Japan Air Lines	Crashed	Mihara Volcano, Japan	37	0
10.04.52	Douglas DC-3	VT-DFN	13628	Kalinga Airlines	Crashed	Agartala, India	*	*
11.04.52	Douglas DC-4	N88899	10503	Pan American World Airways	Landed in sea after engine failure	Off San Juan, Puerto Rico	52	17
16.04.52	de Havilland Drover 1	VH-DHA	5001	Australian Dept. of Civil Aviation	Crashed	Coral Sea	*	*
18.04.52	Curtiss C-46F	N8404C	22466	North Continent Airlines	Crashed on landing	nr Whittier, CA, USA	29	0
19.04.52	de Havilland DH.89A Dragon Rapide	G-ALWY	6741	Air Enterprises	Damaged beyond repair	Isle of Islay, UK	*	*
29.04.52	Boeing Stratocruiser	N1039V	15939	Pan American World Airways	Crashed after engine failure	nr Carolina, Brazil	50	0
30.04.52	Douglas DC-3	VT-AUN	13405	Deccan Airways	Crashed	Safdarjung, India	*	*
04.05.52	Douglas DC-3	F-BEIB	15116/26561	Ste des Tran. Aer. d'Extreme Orient	Destroyed	Phan Thiet, Vietnam	*	*
05.05.52	Douglas DC-3	LN-NAD	12148	Fred Olsen Air Transport	Crashed	nr Skien, Norway	*	*
05.05.52	Boeing 247D	XA-JUV	1958	Taxis Aereos Nacionales	Crashed on take-off	Mexico City, Mexico	0	2
09.05.52	Douglas DC-3	PK-DPA	42954	Garuda Indonesian Airlines	Crashed	Ipoh, Malaya	*	*
09.05.52	Noorduyn Norseman	CF-PAA	32	Gold Belt Air Service	Crashed into building after emergency landing	Lake Mondor, PQ, Canada	0	6
13.05.52	Douglas DC-3	PP-SPM	16894/34151	VASP	Written off	Sao Paulo, Brazil	*	*
19.05.52	Lisunov Li-2	SP-LBD	18419804	LOT Polish Airlines	Crashed	nr Sowina, Poland	*	*
23.05.52	de Havilland DH.89 Dragon Rapide	VH-UUO	6259	Adelaide Airways	Crashed	Tooraweenah, NSW, Australia	*	*
24.05.52	Curtiss C-46	PP-LDE	446	Loide Aereo Nacional	Crashed	Manaus, Brazil	*	*
28.05.52	Handley Page Hermes 4	G-ALDN	HP.81/15	British Overseas Airways Corporation	Force landed out of fuel	nr Atar, Fr West Africa	1	16
04.06.52	de Havilland DH.89A Dragon Rapide	G-ALXA	6727	Operator Unknown	Destroyed by fire	Hanoi, French Indo-China	*	*
14.06.52	Airspeed Consul	G-AHFT	2593	Morton Air Services	Crashed after engine failure	English Channel	*	2
15.06.52	Lockheed 18 Lodestar	*	*	LAN-Chile	Crashed	nr Copiapo, Chile	7	*
06.07.52	Nord Noratlas	F-WFUN	002	Nord Aviation	Crashed [Aviatrix Maryse Bastie killed]	France	6	*
18.07.52	Ilyushin IL-12	SP-LHC	93013506	LOT Polish Airlines	Damaged on landing	Warsaw, Poland	*	*
18.07.52	Airspeed Oxford	G-AIRZ	2816	Hunting Aerosurveys	Crashed	nr Luxembourg	*	*
23.07.52	Handley Page Hermes 4A	G-ALDB	HP.81/3	Airwork	Crashed	Pithiviers, France	*	*
27.07.52	Vickers Viking 1A	G-AHON	116	Crewsair	Crashed on landing due to fuel starvation	Luqa, Malta	0	*
27.07.52	Douglas DC-3	ZS-DFB	12414	Tropic Airways	Crashed after engine failure	Off Benghazi, Libya	0	32
30.07.52	SNCASE Languedoc	SU-AHX	46	Misrair	Written off	Cairo, Egypt	*	*
01.08.52	de Havilland DH.89A Dragon Rapide	G-ALBB	6829	Island Air Services	Crashed on landing in wake turbulence from Stratocruiser	Heathrow, London, UK	0	9
04.08.52	Curtiss C-46	N79097	*	Resort Airlines	Crashed	Miami, FL, USA	4	*
12.08.52	Douglas DC-3	PP-ANH	20187	Transportes Aereos Nacionales	Crashed	Palmeira de Goias, Brazil	*	*
15.08.52	Douglas DC-3	PP-SDD	20435	Viacao Aereo Santos Dumont	Crashed	Guaira, Brazil	*	*
21.08.52	Handley Page Hermes 4A	G-ALDF	HP.81/7	Airwork	Crashed after double engine failure	Off Trapani, Italy	7	50
21.08.52	Beechcraft Bonanza	N8765A	D-2187	Lake Central Airlines	Crashed when caught in wake of Eastern A/L Constellation	Indianapolis, IN, USA	0	3
24.08.52	Avro York	G-AGNZ	1227	Eagle Aviation	Crashed after engine fire on take-off	nr Berlin, West Germany	*	*
27.08.52	Vickers Viscount 609	G-AHRF	001	Vickers Armstrong	Damaged on landing	Khartoum, Sudan	0	*
29.08.52	Douglas DC-2-115B	ZS-DFW	1322	Phoenix Airlines	Crashed short of fuel	Kosti, Sudan	2	2
04.09.52	Miles Aerovan 4	EC-ACQ	6394	Aerotechnica	Crashed	Santander, Spain	*	*
06.09.52	de Havilland DH.89A Dragon Rapide	ZS-BCI	6510	Operator Unknown	Written off	Welkom, South Africa	*	*
14.09.52	de Havilland DH.89A Dragon Rapide	G-AIZI	6861	Operator Unknown	Crashed	Wallington, Surrey, UK	*	*
15.09.52	Douglas DC-3	ZS-AVI	9630	South African Airways	Crashed	Carolina, South Africa	*	*
15.09.52	Douglas DC-3	VT-CGB	9945	Kalinga Airlines	Crashed	nr Wadi Halfa, Sudan	*	*
24.09.52	Avro Anson I	VP-RCJ	–	Lusaka Air Charter	Crashed on landing	Kumalo, Southern Rhodesia	*	*
02.10.52	Lisunov Li-2P	HA-LIL	18428003	Maszovlet	Crashed	Nyiregyhaza, Hungary	*	*
02.10.52	de Havilland Dove 2A	N1515V	04336	Campbell Chain Corporation	Crashed	USA	*	*
07.10.52	Lisunov Li-2P	SP-LAO	18424007	LOT Polish Airlines	Damaged beyond repair	Location Unknown	*	*
14.10.52	Douglas DC-3	PP-AXJ	6177	REAL	Crashed	San Francisco do Paula, Brazil	*	*
14.10.52	Avro Anson V	CF-GDZ	CCF-13	Northern Wings	Crashed on take-off	Havre St Pierre, PQ, Canada	*	*
16.10.52	Douglas DC-4-1009	VH-AND	42950	Australian National Airways	Crashed on landing	Sydney, NSW, Australia	*	*
18.10.52	Lockheed 10B Electra	PP-VAU	1036	Varig	Crashed	Lajes, Brazil	*	*

Date	Type	Reg'n	C/n	Operator	Accident	Location	F	S
22.10.52	Douglas DC-3	AP-AAZ	12670	Orient Airways	Crashed	Jamshedpur, India	*	*
26.10.52	de Havilland Comet 1	G-ALYZ	06012	British Overseas Airways Corporation	Damaged beyond repair overrunning runway	Rome, Italy	0	42
31.10.52	Short Sandringham 4	VH-BRD	SH.33C	Ansett Flying Boat Services	Wrecked by storm	Brisbane, Qd, Australia	0	*
oo.10.52	Ilyushin IL-12	SP-LHE	93013505	LOT Polish Airlines	Destroyed by fire	Poland	*	*
03.11.52	de Havilland DH.89A Dragon Rapide	LV-FEP	6550	Operator Unknown	Crashed on smuggling flight	Location Unknown	*	*
06.11.52	Douglas C-54B	F-BFVO	10498	UAT	Crashed	Lake Chad, French Equatorial Africa	5	*
07.11.52	Avro Anson I	VH-AVS	–	Aerial Surveys	Crashed	Carnamah, WA, Australia	*	*
10.11.52	Boeing B-17G	N5116N	*	Mark Hurd Mapping Co	Crashed	Nevada, USA	*	*
12.11.52	Douglas DC-3	VT-CLE	4653	Bharat Airways	Crashed	Agartala, India	*	*
14.11.52	Lockheed Vega 5B	NC49M	101	Alaska Coastal Airlines	Destroyed by fire	Sitka, Alaska	*	*
27.11.52	Avro York	G-AMGM	1355	Air Charter	Crashed on landing	Lyneham, Wilts, UK	0	5
oo.11.52	Short Sandringham 6	LN-LAI	SH.62C	France Hydro	Sank	Bangui, French Equatorial Africa	*	*
05.12.52	AAC.1 Toucan	F-BANK	145	Air France	Damaged beyond repair	Antalaha, Madagascar	*	*
05.12.52	Avro Anson V	CF-FGM	MDF-248	Queen Charlotte Airlines	Crashed into mountain	nr Vancouver, BC, Canada	1	0
06.12.52	Lisunov Li-2	*	*	Tabso	Crashed	nr Sofia, Bulgaria	18	*
06.12.52	Douglas DC-4	CU-T397	10319	Cubana	Crashed on take-off	Findley Field, Bermuda	37	*
09.12.52	de Havilland Dove 2A	N4277C	04359	Pacific Airmotive Corporation	Crashed	Staten Island, NY, USA	*	*
17.12.52	Handley Page Halifax C.8	G-AKGN	1395	Chartair	Damaged by gale	Thame, Oxon, UK	0	*
17.12.52	Handley Page Halifax C.8	G-AKEC	1355	Lancashire Aircraft Corporation	Blown into LAC Halton G-AHDV by gale	Squires Gate, Lancs, UK	0(0)	*
17.12.52	Handley Page Halton	G-AHDV	1376/SH.21C	Lancashire Aircraft Corporation	Blown into LAC Halifax G-AKEC by gale	Squires Gate, Lancs, UK	0(0)	*
21.12.52	Curtiss C-46	YV-C-ARC	33486	RANSA	Crashed	Location Unknown	*	*
25.12.52	Douglas DC-3	EP-ACJ	9692	Iran Air	Crashed	Tehran, Iran	*	*
25.12.52	Douglas DC-3	YV-C-AVX	7391	Avensa	Crashed	Off La Guacos, Venezuela	*	*
30.12.52	Douglas DC-3	PI-C38	*	Philippine Air Lines	Crashed	Off Taiwan	*	*
oo.oo.52	SNCASO Bretagne	F-BEHA	23	Air Maroc	Damaged beyond repair	Location Unknown	*	*
oo.oo.52	Yakovlev YAK-24	*	*	Yakovlev Design Bureau	Damaged on ground due to rotor vibration	USSR	0	*
oo.oo.52	Avro Anson V	CF-EJX	BFC-1134C	Austin Airways	Crashed after engine failure	Ross Lake, MN, Canada	*	*
oo.oo.52	Boeing 247D	N41813	1725	Lineas Aereas del Pacifico	Crashed	Off Long Beach, CA, USA	*	*
01.01.53	Douglas DC-3	EI-ACF	42957	Aer Lingus	Crashed after double engine failure	Spernall, Warks, UK	0	26
05.01.53	Vickers Viking 1B	G-AJDL	262	British European Airways	Crashed after hitting beacon	Belfast, UK	27	8
07.01.53	Curtiss C-46	N1648M	22395	Associated Air Transport	Crashed into mountain [Found 12.01.53]	Fish Haven, ID, USA	40	0
07.01.53	Douglas C-54B	N86574	18350	Flying Tiger Line	Crashed on approach	Issaquah, WA, USA	7	0
10.01.53	Douglas DC-3	XY-ACL	14373/25818	Union of Burma Airways	Crashed into tree on landing & caught fire	Mergui, Burma	0	18
11.01.53	Lockheed 18-56 Lodestar	SE-BUX	2071	Dagens Nyheter	Crashed after stalling	Jonkoping, Sweden	2	0
17.01.53	Avro Anson I	VH-BKZ	–	Adastra Airways	Crashed	Moorabbin, Vic, Australia	*	*
19.01.53	Bristol 170 Freighter IA	G-AICM	12756	Silver City Airways	Crashed in fog due to fuel starvation	Berlin, West Germany	*	*
21.01.53	Short Sunderland 3	G-AGJN	–	Aquila Airways	Damaged beyond repair	Madeira, Portugal	*	*
22.01.53	Lockheed C-69 Constellation	N38936	1962	Intercontinent Airways	Landed with u/c retracted in error & caught fire	Burbank, CA, USA	0	10
26.01.53	Douglas DC-3	I-LAIL	4308	Linee Aeree Italiane	Crashed after wing failure	Sinnai, Sardinia, Italy	19	0
27.01.53	Grumman G-21 Goose	CF-BHL	1003	Central BC Airways	Written off	Location Unknown	*	*
28.01.53	Short Sunderland 3	G-AGKY	–	Aquila Airways	Sank	Off Calshot, Isle of Wight, UK	*	*
29.01.53	Curtiss C-46	HK-605	30362	Linea Interamericana Aerea	Damaged beyond repair	Bogota, Colombia	*	*
02.02.53	Avro York	G-AHFA	1304	Lancashire Aircraft Corporation	Crashed	North Atlantic	39	0
03.02.53	Douglas DC-3	F-OAFR	15283/26728	Air Outremer	Crashed due to bomb explosion	Lai Chau, French Indo-China	*	*
04.02.53	Avro Anson I	VH-BDD	–	Goilala Air Service	Damaged in forced landing	Embassa, Papua & New Guinea	0	12
07.02.53	Douglas C-54A	F-BFGR	10290	Autrex	Crashed after engine failure	Eysines, France	7	15
13.02.53	Douglas DC-3	F-OAHY	12793	Air Outremer	Destroyed by shelling	Muong Sai, Laos	*	*
13.02.53	de Havilland DH.89A Dragon Rapide	F-BGPM	6476	Aigle Azur	Destroyed after engine caught fire on starting	Siemreap, Cambodia	0	5
14.02.53	Douglas DC-6	N90893	43057	National Airlines	Crashed due to wing failure in turbulence	Off Mobile, AL, USA	46	0
20.02.53	Avro Anson I	VH-BKT	–	Brain & Brown Airfreighters	Damaged on landing	Moorabbin, Vic, Australia	*	*
03.03.53	de Havilland Comet 1A	CF-CUN	06014	Canadian Pacific Airlines	Crashed on take-off during delivery flight	Karachi, Pakistan	11	0
04.03.53	Curtiss C-46F	N4717N	22400	Slick Airways	Crashed short of runway in rain	Windsor Locks, CT, USA	2	0
13.03.53	Douglas DC-3	SP-LCH	9106	LOT Polish Airlines	Crashed	Katowice, Poland	*	*

Date	Type	Reg'n	C/n	Operator	Accident	Location	F	S
14.03.53	Convair 240-7	AP-AEG	082	Orient Airways	Crashed into mountain	Kalasahar, India	16	0
15.03.53	Douglas DC-3	PP-AJA	11844	Transportes Aereos Catarinense	Crashed	nr Salvador, Brazil	*	*
17.03.53	Douglas DC-3	F-BEFG	19105	Aigle Azur	Crashed & caught fire	Da Nang, Vietnam	8	0
20.03.53	Curtiss C-46	N66559	30504	Aerovias Sud Americana	Overshot on landing	St Petersberg, FL, USA	0	*
20.03.53	Douglas C-54G	N88942	36076	Transocean Airlines	Crashed on approach due to icing	Alvarado, CA, USA	35	0
27.03.53	de Havilland Heron 1B	PP-SLG	14004	Transportes Aereos Salvador	Crashed	Itapebi, El Salvador	*	*
27.03.53	Curtiss C-46	HC-SJA	*	AREA	Crashed	Panama City, Panama	*	*
27.03.53	Douglas R5D-1	N229A	10322	California Eastern Airlines	Ditched at sea after engine failure	Off San Francisco, CA, USA	0	4
29.03.53	Vickers Viking 1B	VP-YEY	168	Central African Airways	Crashed after wing failure	Mtara, Tanganyika	13	0
03.04.53	Avro Anson I	VH-BNS	–	Adastra Airways	Crashed on take-off	Moorabbin, Vic, Australia	*	*
06.04.53	Avro Anson V	CF-FZE	BRC-1196C	Salmita Consolidated Mines	Crashed	MacKay Lake, NWT, Canada	*	*
10.04.53	Lockheed 18-56 Lodestar	VP-JBC	2568	Caribbean International Airways	Crashed on take-off	Kingston, Jamaica	13	*
10.04.53	AAC.1 Toucan	F-BALE	090	Air France	Crashed on take-off	Miandrivazo, Madagascar	4	0
10.04.53	Avro Anson I	VR-SDL	–	Nanyang Airways	Crashed into tree on landing	Kuala Lumpur, Malaya	2	*
12.04.53	Beechcraft 18S	CF-BQQ	0290	Northern Wings	Crashed	Canada	*	*
14.04.53	Douglas DC-3	VT-AUJ	19149	Airways (India) Ltd	Crashed into hills	Khasi Hills, India	3	0
16.04.53	Douglas DC-3	F-BESS	19498	Aigle Azur	Crashed on take-off after wing failure	North west of Hanoi, Vietnam	30	0
20.04.53	Douglas DC-6B	N91303	43823	Western Air Lines	Crashed into bay after take-off	Oakland, CA, USA	8	2
23.04.53	Curtiss C-46	N1693M	22498	American Air Transport	Crashed into mountain	Cedar Mt, WA, USA	2	2
02.05.53	de Havilland Comet 1	G-ALYV	06008	British Overseas Airways Corporation	Crashed due to wing failure	Calcutta, India	43	0
06.05.53	Ford 5-AT-B Tri-Motor	N9606	5-AT-004	Northwest Agricultural Aviation	Crashed on take-off	Choteau, MO, USA	0	2
09.05.53	Douglas DC-3	VT-AXD	13294	Air Services of India	Crashed	Bombay, India	*	*
09.05.53	Douglas DC-3	VT-AUD	13716	Air India	Crashed after take-off	New Delhi, India	18	0
11.05.53	AAC.1 Toucan	F-BBZL	230	Autrex	Written off	Hanoi, Vietnam	*	*
11.05.53	Consolidated PBY-5A Catalina	CF-CRV	21984	Canadian Pacific Airlines	Crashed on landing	Prince Rupert, BC, Canada	2	17
17.05.53	Douglas DC-3	N28345	2224	Delta Air Lines	Crashed on approach in thunderstorm	Waskom, TX, USA	19	1
22.05.53	Curtiss C-46F	N1669M	22536	Resort Airlines	Crashed after wing failed during storm	Des Moines, IA, USA	2	0
25.05.53	Convair 240-4	PH-TEI	125	KLM Royal Dutch Airlines	Crashed on take-off	Amsterdam, Netherlands	0{2}	34
15.06.53	Douglas DC-3	TI-1002	14633/26078	Lacsa	Crashed into hill	nr San Ramon, Costa Rica	9	5
15.06.53	Lockheed 18 Lodestar	CC-CLD-0100	2617	LAN-Chile	Crashed after engine fire	Copiapo, Chile	7	0
16.06.53	Douglas DC-3	F-BEST	19100	Aigle Azur	Crashed after fire – possibly shot down [Found 29.06.53]	Phou-Lassy, French Indo-China	34	0
17.06.53	Douglas C-54A	LV-ABQ	7468	Aerolineas Argentinas	Crashed short of runway	Cordova, Argentina	0	41
17.06.53	Lockheed 049 Constellation	PP-PDA	2066	Panair do Brasil	Crashed on landing	Sao Paulo, Brazil	17	*
24.06.53	Douglas DC-3	HK-167	4272	Avianca	Crashed	Pereira, Colombia	*	*
25.06.53	de Havilland Comet 1A	F-BGSC	06019	UAT	Skidded off runway & damaged beyond repair	Dakar, French West Africa	0	*
29.06.53	Douglas DC-3	N15569	4887	Western Air Lines	Crashed on take-off	Los Angeles, CA, USA	1	2
30.06.53	Douglas DC-3	EP-ACV	12919	Iran Air	Crashed making emergency landing	Tehran, Iran	0	6
05.07.53	de Havilland DH.89A Dragon Rapide	G-AIYP	6456	Dragon Airways	Force-landed & caught fire	Pwllheli, UK	*	*
06.07.53	Avro Anson I	OO-CCA	–	Ins. Geographique du Congo Belge	Crashed	Kindu, Belgian Congo	4	0
12.07.53	Douglas DC-6	N90806	42901	Transocean Airlines	Crashed	East of Wake Island	57	0
14.07.53	Ford 4-AT-E Tri-Motor	N8400	4-AT-62	Johnson Flying Service	Crashed into cable	Boulder, MT, USA	2	0
19.07.53	Curtiss C-46	N1697M	22573	Southern Air Transport	Overturned on landing	Dallas, TX, USA	*	*
25.07.53	de Havilland Comet 1	G-ALYR	06004	British Overseas Airways Corporation	Skidded off runway & damaged beyond repair	Calcutta, India	0	*
30.07.53	Douglas DC-3	F-VNAD	9339	Vietnamese Government	Destroyed	Hanoi, Vietnam	*	*
02.08.53	Douglas DC-3	AP-AAD	9143	Orient Airways	Crashed	Sharjah, Trucial States	1	22
03.08.53	Lockheed 749A Constellation	F-BAZS	2628	Air France	Force landed after engine detached	Off Kastellorizo, Turkey	4	38
04.08.53	Handley Page Marathon	XY-ACX	138	Union of Burma Airways	Overran on landing	Myaungmya, Burma	0	*
04.08.53	de Havilland Dove 2A	N4272C	04351	Ellis Airlines	Crashed	Ketchikan, Alaska	*	*
12.08.53	Vickers Viking 1B	G-AIVG	220	British European Airways	Damaged after tyre burst on take-off	Le Bourget, France	0	*
17.08.53	Ford 5-AT-B Tri-Motor	N69905	5-AT-040	Johnson Flying Service	Crashed after engine failure	Flathead Forest, MT, USA	0	*
23.08.53	Douglas DC-3	PP-YQK	4732	REAL	Crashed	Campo Grande, Brazil	*	*
23.08.53	Noorduyn Norseman I	CF-AYO	001	Operator Unknown	Crashed	Round Island Lake, ON, Canada	*	*
30.08.53	de Havilland DH.89A Dragon Rapide	VP-RCP	6659	Northern Rhodesia Government	Written off	Nyasaland border	*	*
01.09.53	Douglas DC-3	N19941	6333	Regina Cargo Airlines	Crashed into mountain	nr Vail, WA, USA	21	0

Date	Type	Reg'n	C/n	Operator	Accident	Location	F	S
01.09.53	Lockheed 749A Constellation	F-BAZZ	2674	Air France	Crashed in mountains	nr Barcelonnette, France	42	*
03.09.53	de Havilland DH.89A Dragon Rapide	ET-P-16	6950	Meat Export & Supply Co	Written off	Dire Dawa, Ethiopia	*	*
06.09.53	Lockheed 1049 Super Constellation	N6214C	4014	Northwest Airlines	Crashed on landing	Tacoma, WA, USA	0	32
08.09.53	Douglas DC-3	XH-TAR	*	TACA	Crashed	nr San Andres, Honduras	3	0
14.09.53	Curtiss C-46	PP-LDM	26397	Loide Aereo Nacional	Crashed	Congonhas, Brazil	*	*
14.09.53	Douglas DC-3	XA-GIC	13113	TAMSA	Crashed after striking tower in fog	Chablekal, Mexico	1	*
16.09.53	Convair 240-0	N94255	116	American Airlines	Crashed on landing	Albany, NY, USA	28	*
19.09.53	Douglas DC-3	HK-143	10088	Avianca	Crashed	San Luis de Pelenque, Colombia	*	*
25.09.53	Douglas DC-3	TC-EGE	9694	Devlet Hava Yollari	Crashed on take-off	nr Ankara, Turkey	6	*
28.09.53	Curtiss C-46	N66534	22384	Seminole Aircraft	Crashed on landing	Louisville, KY, USA	25	*
10.10.53	SNCASO Bretagne	F-DABD	34	Air Maroc	Crashed	Tangier, Morocco	*	*
14.10.53	Convair 240-12	OO-AWQ	154	Sabena	Crashed on take-off	Frankfurt, West Germany	44	0
15.10.53	Douglas DC-3	PI-C142	13397	Philippine Air Lines	Crashed	nr Tuguegarao, Philippines	*	*
17.10.53	Douglas DC-3	F-VNAE	14146/25591	Compagnie Sila	Crashed	nr Laichau, French Indo-China	*	*
19.10.53	Lockheed 749A Constellation	N119A	2616	Eastern Air Lines	Crashed on take-off	New York, NY, USA	2	*
29.10.53	Douglas DC-6	VH-BPE	43125	British Commonwealth Pacific Airlines	Crashed on approach	San Francisco, CA, USA	19	0
03.11.53	Douglas DC-3	CP-600	2181	Lloyd Aereo Boliviano	Crashed on landing	Potosi, Bolivia	28	*
04.12.53	Bristol 170 Freighter 21	EC-AEG	12797	Aviaco	Crashed in bad weather	Guadarrama Mts, Spain	23	0
06.12.53	Avro Anson V	CF-ESB	MDF-382	Mannix Ltd	Crashed in snowstorm	Lake Manuan, PQ, Canada	*	*
12.12.53	Douglas DC-3	VT-CHF	11810	Indian Airlines	Crashed in take-off	Nagpur, India	13	*
15.12.53	Vickers Viking 1B	SU-AFK	213	Misrair	Crashed	Almaza, Egypt	6	*
15.12.53	Curtiss C-46	TG-AQA	33589	Aviateca	Crashed in bad weather	Tecpan Mt, Guatemala	2	*
19.12.53	Convair 240-12	OO-AWO	128	Sabena	Crashed on landing	Zurich, Switzerland	1	44
20.12.53	Vickers Viking 1B	G-AHPO	157	Eagle Aviation	Ran off runway & damaged beyond repair	Nuremburg, West Germany	*	*
20.12.53	de Havilland Dove 1	OO-CBM	04014	Ins. Geographique du Congo Belge	Crashed	Yalinga, Belgian Congo	*	*
21.12.53	Douglas DC-3	YK-AAF	*	Syrian Airways	Crashed	Dah-el-Kadeeb, Syria	*	*
oo.oo.53	Curtiss C-46	XA-GOT	26403	Aerovias Contreras	Damaged beyond repair	Mexico	*	*
oo.oo.53	Yakovlev YAK-24	*	*	Yakovlev Design Bureau	Damaged during tethered test flight	USSR	0	1
oo.oo.53	de Havilland Dove 2A	N4962N	04326	Montgomery Construction Co	Written off	Location Unknown	*	*
oo.oo.53	Douglas DC-3	LV-ABX	13435	Aerolineas Argentinas	Written off	Location Unknown	*	*
oo.oo.53	Short Sealand 1C	PK-CMA	SH.1568	Christian & Missionary Alliance	Forced landed during thunderstorm	Java, Indonesia	*	*
05.01.54	Douglas DC-3	TC-BAG	19616	Devlet Hava Yollari	Crashed into hill	Lapeiki, Turkey	4	6
06.01.54	SNCASE Languedoc	OD-ABU	14	Air Liban	Crashed	Beirut, Lebanon	*	*
10.01.54	de Havilland Comet 1	G-ALYP	06003	British Overseas Airways Corporation	Crashed due to structural failure	Off Elba, Italy	35	0
10.01.54	Avro Anson I	VP-YKT	–	A.G.Mechin & Co	Crashed out of fuel	nr Ndola, Northern Rhodesia	*	*
10.01.54	Douglas A-26B Invader	N65Y	7240	Grand Central Aircraft	Crashed into power cables after take-off	Glendale, CA, USA	0{1}	2
11.01.54	Douglas DC-3	HK-160	19540	Avianca	Crashed into mountain	Manizales, Colombia	23	0
14.01.54	Douglas DC-6	PI-C294	42902	Philippine Air Lines	Crashed on landing after engine fire	Rome, Italy	18	*
14.01.54	Douglas DC-3	*	*	Ceskoslovenske Aerolinie	Crashed on take-off [Possibly was Li-2]	Prague, Czechoslovakia	15	*
20.01.54	Convair 240-0	N94244	088	American Airlines	Crash landed due to engine failure	Buffalo, NY, USA	0	25
20.01.54	Douglas DC-3	N49551	4940	Zantop Air Transport	Destroyed	Kansas City, MO, USA	*	*
24.01.54	Douglas DC-3	F-BEFS	12416	Autrex	Crashed	nr Hanoi, Vietnam	*	*
24.01.54	de Havilland DH.89A Dragon Rapide	VP-KEA	6890	East African Airways	Crashed	Butaiba, Kenya	*	*
31.01.54	Curtiss C-46	HK-603	33273	Linea Interamericana Aerea	Crashed	Techo Airport, Colombia	*	*
31.01.54	Douglas DC-3	F-BGXD	13312	Aigle Azur	Crashed after u/c retracted on take-off	Dien Bien Phu, French Indo-China	0	*
04.02.54	Bristol Britannia 101	G-ALRX	12874	Bristol Aeroplane Co	Force-landed on river bank & damaged by tide	Severn Estuary, UK	0	13
19.02.54	de Havilland DH.89A Dragon Rapide	G-AFMF	6432	Oldstead Airlines	Crashed due to icing	Hexham, Northumberland, UK	0	8
25.02.54	Douglas DC-3	VT-ATU	20358	Indian Airlines	Crashed	nr New Delhi, India	3	0
26.02.54	Convair 240-1	N8407H	037	Western Air Lines	Crashed in bad weather	Wright, WY, USA	9	0
26.02.54	Miles Aerovan 4	ZK-AWW	6427	Southland Aerial Fertilisers	Crashed on landing at night	Ranfurly, New Zealand	*	*
04.03.54	Douglas DC-3	F-OANH	6172	Cie de Trans. Aer. et de Commerce	Destroyed by rebels	Giam Lam, Vietnam	*	*
04.03.54	Curtiss C-46	PP-LPH	33283	Linhas Aereas Paulistas	Crashed	Guanabara Bay, Brazil	*	*
04.03.54	Douglas DC-3	F-OAPC	4969	Aigle Azur	Destroyed by rebels	Giam Lam, Vietnam	*	*
04.03.54	Airspeed Consul	F-BCJE	5130	Aigle Azur	Destroyed by rebels	Giam Lam, Vietnam	*	*

Date	Type	Reg'n	C/n	Operator	Accident	Location	F	S
04.03.54	de Havilland Canada Beaver	F-OAMH	420	Aigle Azur	Destroyed by rebels	Giam Lam, French Indo-China	*	*
04.03.54	de Havilland Canada Beaver	F-OAMI	440	Aigle Azur	Destroyed by rebels	Giam Lam, French Indo-China	*	*
11.03.54	Fairchild C-119 Flying Boxcar	*	*	Civil Air Transport	Crashed	nr Hanoi, Vietnam	*	*
13.03.54	Lockheed 749A Constellation	G-ALAM	2554	British Overseas Airways Corporation	Crashed short of runway	Singapore	33	0
13.03.54	Douglas DC-3	F-BCYI	4502	Autrex	Shot down by rebels	Xieng Khouang, Laos	*	*
13.03.54	Curtiss C-46	F-DAAR	2943	Aigle Azur	Shot down by Communist aircraft	Dien Bien Phu, Vietnam	*	*
14.03.54	Douglas DC-3	VH-BBV	12360	Queensland Airlines	Crashed	Off Mackey, Qld, Australia	*	*
16.03.54	Convair 340-35	N90853	044	Continental Airlines	Crashed	Midland, TX, USA	0	*
19.03.54	Lisunov Li-2P	SP-LAH	18423201	LOT Polish Airlines	Crashed	Limanova, Poland	*	*
25.03.54	Douglas DC-3	XA-GUN	7358	Aeronaves de Mexico	Crashed on approach	Monterrey, Mexico	18	*
03.04.54	Douglas DC-3	TC-ARK	19509	Devlet Hava Yollari	Crashed after take-off	Adana, Turkey	25	*
04.04.54	Douglas C-54A	F-BFGQ	10341	Autrex	Crashed on approach	Giam Lam, Vietnam	4	*
08.04.54	de Havilland Comet 1	G-ALYY	06011	British Overseas Airways Corporation	Crashed due to structural failure	Off Stromboli, Italy	21	0
08.04.54	Canadair C-4-1	CF-TFW	150	Trans Canada Airlines	Mid-air collision with RCAF Harvard	Moose Jaw, SK, Canada	35(2)	0
10.04.54	Douglas DC-3	I-LENT	4548	Linee Aeree Italiane	Crashed	Rome, Italy	*	*
13.04.54	Avro York	G-AMUM	–	Scottish Airlines	Damaged on landing	Luqa, Malta	*	*
19.04.54	de Havilland Dragon 2	VH-UXG	6077	Operator Unknown	Crashed	Archerfield, Australia	*	*
23.04.54	Douglas DC-3	LV-ACX	12387	Aerolineas Argentinas	Crashed	Sierra del Vilgo, Argentina	24	0
24.04.54	SNCASE Languedoc	SU-AHZ	19	Misrair	Crashed	Damascus, Syria	*	*
24.04.54	Avro Anson V	XA-KED	–	S.A. de Chiapas	Crashed	San Gabriel, Mexico	*	*
25.04.54	Douglas DC-3	F-BCYJ	4572	Autrex	Crashed on landing	Nam Bac, Laos	*	*
26.04.54	de Havilland DH.89A Dragon Rapide	G-AGUV	6912	British European Airways	Crashed & destroyed by fire	Taif, Bahrain	*	*
26.04.54	de Havilland DH.89A Dragon Rapide	VQ-FAL	6707	Fiji Airways	Crashed	Labasa, Fiji	*	*
30.04.54	SNCASO Bretagne	F-OAMA	14	Air Laos	Crashed after engine fire	Saigon, Vietnam	*	*
30.04.54	Douglas DC-3	VT-DEM	13792	Darbhanga Aviation	Crashed	nr Calcutta, India	5	*
01.05.54	de Havilland Dove 1	OO-CFD	04083	Sabena	Crashed on approach when windscreen wipers failed in rain	Kamembe, Belgian Congo	*	*
01.05.54	Avro Anson I	OO-CED	–	Comituri	Crashed	Kamembe, Belgian Congo	*	*
03.05.54	Short S.26	G-AFCI	S.871	F.C.Bettison	Damaged during gale	Harty Ferry, Kent, UK	0	0
06.05.54	Fairchild C-119 Flying Boxcar	*	*	Civil Air Transport	Shot down	SE of Dien Bien Phu, Vietnam	2	0
15.05.54	Douglas DC-3	VT-DGO	16186/32914	Indian Airlines	Crashed on landing	Bengal, India	*	*
17.05.54	Curtiss C-46	CU-C556	264	Cubana	Damaged beyond repair	Rando Boyeros, Cuba	*	*
21.05.54	Douglas DC-3	F-BEIP	4517	Autrex	Crashed	Hanoi, Vietnam	3	0
22.05.54	Douglas DC-3	ZK-AQT	15948/32696	New Zealand National Airways	Crashed	Paraparaumu, New Zealand	2	*
29.05.54	Douglas DC-3	CC-CLH-0184	11883	LAN-Chile	Crashed on landing & caught fire	El Porvenir, Chile	*	*
31.05.54	Douglas DC-3	PP-ANO	19830	Transportes Aereos Nacionales	Crashed	Cipo Mt, Brazil	19	*
04.06.54	Curtiss C-46	PP-VBZ	30400	Varig	Crashed on take-off	Sao Paulo, Brazil	*	*
08.06.54	Douglas DC-3	F-BCCL	4464	Ste des Tran. Aer. d'Extreme Orient	Crashed	nr Tourane, French Indo-China	4	*
11.06.54	Avro Anson V	HC-SJN-014	MDF-182	AREA	Crashed	Hacienda La Rinconada, Ecuador	1	*
15.06.54	Douglas C-54G	N30070	35931	United Air Lines	Destroyed by fire after engine fire in flight	Gage, OK, USA	*	*
15.06.54	Douglas DC-3	N51359	13759	Delta Air Lines	Crashed	nr Atlanta, GA, USA	*	*
15.06.54	de Havilland DH.89A Dragon Rapide	G-AKLA	6764	Operator Unknown	Damaged beyond repair	nr Jodhpur, India	*	*
17.06.54	Curtiss C-46	HK-489	*	Lineas Aereas del Caribe	Crashed	Barranquilla, Colombia	*	*
18.06.54	Avro Anson V	OB-ABO-341	MDF-98	J.P.Miguel	Crashed	nr San Borja, Bolivia	*	*
19.06.54	Convair 240-4	HB-IRW	061	Swissair	Crashed	Off Folkestone, Kent, UK	3	*
26.06.54	Avro York	G-AGNY	1226	Skyways	Crashed after engine failure	Kyritz, East Germany	3	*
03.07.54	Ford 4-AT-B Tri-Motor	N9610	4-AT-53	Travelair Taxi	Crashed on take-off	Kellys Island, OH, USA	*	*
09.07.54	Avro Anson I	VP-KHS	–	Airwork (East Africa) Ltd	Damaged on take-off	Kitale, Kenya	*	*
23.07.54	Douglas C-54A	VR-HEU	10310	Cathay Pacific Airways	Shot down by Chinese aircraft	Off Hainan, China	10	*
23.07.54	de Havilland Dove 2A	N4278C	04366	Gordon Air Services	Crashed	Waldens Ridge, TN, USA	*	*
25.07.54	Avro Anson I	VP-YKF	–	A.G.Mechin & Co	Crashed after engine fell off	nr Salisbury, Southern Rhodesia	*	*
29.07.54	Fiat G.212	G-ANOE	10	Arabian Desert Airlines	Damaged beyond repair	Kuwait	*	*
02.08.54	de Havilland DH.89A Dragon Rapide	G-AGUR	6910	British European Airways	Crashed on landing	Frankfurt, West Germany	*	*
03.08.54	Lockheed 1049C Super Constellation	F-BGNA	4510	Air France	Crashed	Preston City, CT, USA	0	*
05.08.54	Vickers Viking 1B	SU-AGO	195	Misrair	Damaged on landing	Luxor, Egypt	*	*

Date	Type	Reg'n	C/n	Operator	Accident	Location	F	S
08.08.54	Douglas DC-3	N91008	13977/25422	Alaska Airlines	Crashed	nr McGrath, Alaska	*	*
09.08.54	Lockheed 749A Constellation	HK-163	2664	Avianca	Crashed into mountain	Terceira Is, Azores, Portugal	30	0
15.08.54	Vickers Viking 1B	G-AIXS	234	Airwork	Crashed on landing	Blackbushe, Hants, UK	0	37
16.08.54	Bristol 170 Freighter 21E	F-VNAI	12809	Air Vietnam	Crashed into river	nr Pakse, Laos	*	*
22.08.54	Douglas DC-3	N61451	4630	Braniff Airlines	Crashed	Mason City, IA, USA	12	*
23.08.54	Douglas DC-6B	PH-DFO	43556	KLM Royal Dutch Airlines	Crashed	North Sea	21	0
24.08.54	Beechcraft D-18S	JA5012	A-0975	Operator Unknown	Crashed	Tokyo Bay, Japan	*	*
25.08.54	Lockheed 749 Constellation	F-BAZI	2513	Air France	Damaged beyond repair	Gander, NF, Canada	0	*
28.08.54	Beechcraft D-18S	CR-LCJ	A-0568	DTA	Written off	Luanda, Angola	*	*
30.08.54	SNCASO Bretagne	F-BEHS	41	Aigle Azur	Crashed	Hanoi, Vietnam	*	*
oo.08.54	de Havilland Drover 2	VQ-FAO	5005	Fiji Airways	Crashed on reef	Telau Is, Fiji	*	*
04.09.54	Douglas DC-3	F-BEIO	14815/26260	Air Outremer	Destroyed	Hanoi, Vietnam	*	*
05.09.54	Lockheed 1049C Super Constellation	PH-LKY	4509	KLM Royal Dutch Airlines	Crashed after take-off	River Shannon, Eire	28	28
10.09.54	de Havilland DH.89A Dragon Rapide	ZS-BZU	6761	Operator Unknown	Written off	Mokhotlong, Basutoland	*	*
12.09.54	Douglas DC-3	PP-CDJ	19278	Cruzeiro	Crashed	Off Rio de Janeiro, Brazil	6	*
15.09.54	Vickers Viking 1B	SU-AFO	212	Misrair	Crashed	Almaza, Egypt	*	*
22.09.54	Avro York	G-ANRC	–	Scottish Airlines	Destroyed by fire on take-off	Stansted, Essex, UK	*	*
25.09.54	Beechcraft C18S	JA5002	6176	Operator Unknown	Written off	Minami Aizu-gun, Japan	*	*
08.10.54	Douglas DC-3	TG-AJA	11874	Aviateca	Destroyed	Guatamala City, Guatamala	*	*
13.10.54	Douglas DC-3	AP-AAF	4562	Orient Airways	Crashed on take-off due to engine failure	nr Skardu, Pakistan	0	*
16.10.54	Convair 240-6	LV-ADQ	077	Aerolineas Argentinas	Crashed in bad weather	nr Buenos Aires, Argentina	*	*
20.10.54	Douglas DC-3	B-811	18947	Air America	Crashed [Possibly c/n 19932]	Gulf of Siam	*	*
21.10.54	Douglas DC-3	PP-CCP	4226	Cruzeiro	Crashed into bay	Rio de Janeiro, Brazil	*	*
31.10.54	Vickers Viscount 720	VH-TVA	044	Trans Australia Airlines	Crashed on take-off	Magalore, Vic, Australia	3	5
15.11.54	Lisunov Li-2	SP-LKA	18438505	LOT Polish Airlines	Crashed	nr Lotz, Poland	*	*
24.11.54	Airspeed Consul	SE-BTU	2942	Aero Propaganda	Crashed	Sundsvall, Sweden	*	*
25.11.54	Douglas DC-3	PK-DPD	19279	Garuda Indonesian Airlines	Crashed	Djambia, Indonesia	*	*
27.11.54	Short Sunderland 5	G-ANAK	–	Aquila Airways	Damaged by gale	Hamble, IoW, Hants, UK	0	*
30.11.54	Douglas DC-3	N17891	11745	Northeast Airlines	Crashed	Mt Success, USA	*	*
01.12.54	de Havilland Dove 2B	VH-DHD	04400	de Havilland Aircraft	Crashed	Camden, NSW, Australia	*	*
02.12.54	Douglas DC-2-118B	LV-AHI	1351	F.Coloma	Crashed	Harding Green, Argentina	*	*
04.12.54	Douglas DC-3	F-BEIA	19211	Air Laos	Crashed	nr Luang Prabang, Laos	28	*
06.12.54	Douglas DC-3	N85B	2233	Oklahoma Pipe Line Construction	Destroyed in hangar fire	Calgary, AB, Canada	*	*
06.12.54	de Havilland Dove 2A	CF-EYM	04390	Shell Aviation	Destroyed in hangar fire	Calgary, AB, Canada	*	*
06.12.54	Avro Anson V	CF-EIG	MDF-257	K.K.Paget	Destroyed by fire	Calgary, AB, Canada	*	*
10.12.54	Douglas DC-3	YV-C-AGI	10111	Linea Aeropostal Venezolana	Crashed	Guasualito, Venezuela	*	*
10.12.54	Avro Anson V	CF-ESA	MDF-431	Central Northern Airways	Sank through ice	God's River, MN, Canada	*	*
17.12.54	Lockheed 1049E Super Constellation	CF-TGG	4564	Trans Canada Airlines	Crashed on approach	Brampton, ON, Canada	0	*
18.12.54	Douglas DC-6B	I-LINE	44418	Linee Aeree Italiane	Crashed on approach	New York, NY, USA	26	6
18.12.54	Douglas DC-3	YV-C-AMP	19292	Linea Aeropostal Venezolana	Crashed	nr Cuidad Bolivar, Venezuela	*	*
18.12.54	Avro Anson I	VH-BMD	–	Papuan Air Transport	Crashed on landing	Embi, Papua & New Guinea	0	15
22.12.54	Avro Anson I	VH-BMN	–	Papuan Air Transport	Crashed on landing	Bereina, Papua & New Guinea	*	*
23.12.54	Lisunov Li-2P	HA-LIF	18425604	Malev	Belly landed in storm	Polna, Czechoslovakia	*	*
23.12.54	Lisunov Li-2P	HA-LII	18427006	Malev	Belly landed in storm	Brno, Czechoslovakia	*	*
25.12.54	Boeing Stratocruiser	G-ALSA	15943	British Overseas Airways Corporation	Crashed on approach	Prestwick, Ayrshire, UK	28	*
26.12.54	Lockheed 18 Lodestar	CF-FYR	2049	Operator Unknown	Destroyed in hangar fire	St Eugene, ON, Canada	*	*
29.12.54	Curtiss C-46	HK-459	*	Lineas Aereas del Caribe	Crashed	Barranquilla, Colombia	*	*
29.12.54	Type Unknown	*	*	Aeroflot	Crashed	nr Moscow, RSFSR, USSR	45	*
31.12.54	Type Unknown	*	*	Aeroflot	Crashed on take-off	Irkutsk, RSFSR, USSR	17	*
oo.oo.54	Lockheed Vega 5C Special	NR12282	194	D.J.Murphy	Broken in two by heavy snowfall	Anchorage, Alaska	0	0
04.01.55	Bell 47B-3	G-AKFA	69	BEA Helicopters	Blown over by high winds on landing	Gatwick, Surrey, UK	0	2
06.01.55	de Havilland DH.89A Dragon Rapide	VP-YEZ	6680	Central African Airways	Damaged in hangar collapse	Victoria Falls, Southern Rhodesia	*	*
06.01.55	de Havilland DH.89A Dragon Rapide	VP-YLV	6660	Zambesi Airways	Damaged in hangar collapse	Victoria Falls, Southern Rhodesia	*	*
06.01.55	Avro Anson V	CF-FVZ	MDF-297	Saskatchewan Government Airways	Crashed on landing	Buffalo Narrows, SK, Canada	8	0

Date	Type	Reg'n	C/n	Operator	Accident	Location	F	S
12.01.55	Martin 202A	N93211	14081	Trans World Airlines	Mid-air collision with Castleton Inc DC-3 N999B	Covington, KY, USA	10{2}(3)*	
12.01.55	Douglas DC-3	N999B	4255	Castleton Inc	Mid-air collision with TWA Martin 202 N93211	Covington, KY, USA	3{2}(10)*	
21.01.55	Douglas DC-3	VT-COZ	13569	Indian Airlines	Crashed	Gauhati, India	*	*
22.01.55	Curtiss C-46	*	*	Resort Airlines	Crashed into trees	Chattanooga, TN, USA	*	*
23.01.55	de Havilland DH.89A Dragon Rapide	VP-KHF	6627	Caspair	Written off	Garissa, Kenya	*	*
31.01.55	Consolidated PBY-5A Catalina	HK-1000E	*	AIDA	Crashed on landing	Caqueta River, Colombia	5	*
01.02.55	Douglas DC-3	VT-CVB	13037	Indian Airlines	Crashed	Nagpur, India	10	*
04.02.55	de Havilland Dove 1	YI-ABJ	04072	Iraqi Airways	Crash landed after engine fire	nr Al Mansour, Iraq	*	*
05.02.55	Bristol 170 Freighter 21E	VR-NAD	12779	West African Airways	Crashed due to wing failure	nr Calabar, Nigeria	13	0
13.02.55	Douglas DC-6	OO-SDB	43063	Sabena	Crashed on approach	nr Rome, Italy	29	0
21.02.55	Consolidated B-24 Liberator	CC-CAN	–	ALA	Damaged beyond repair	Location Unknown	*	*
21.02.55	Consolidated Liberator	CC-CAH	33544	Air Chile	Damaged beyond repair	Chile	*	*
22.02.55	de Havilland DH.89A Dragon Rapide	ZS-BEA	6626	Operator Unknown	Written off	Otjimarongo, South West Africa	*	*
23.02.55	Douglas DC-3	VP-YKO	15109/26554	Central African Airways	Crashed	Salisbury, Southern Rhodesia	*	*
06.03.55	Douglas DC-3	PP-YPZ	11699	REAL	Crashed	Vitoria de Conquista, Brazil	*	*
07.03.55	Lockheed 18 Lodestar	*	*	Operator Unknown	Crashed	nr Ciudad de Valles, Mexico	7	*
08.03.55	Douglas DC-3	XA-DIK	3292	Mexicana	Crashed	Mascota, Mexico	26	*
09.03.55	Douglas DC-3	HK-328	20224	Avianca	Crashed	nr Trujillo, Colombia	8	*
13.03.55	Avro Anson XII	VH-GVB	–	Southern Airlines	Damaged in ground loop on landing	Corowa, NSW, Australia	*	*
14.03.55	Douglas DC-3	F-BFGN	9785	Air Laos	Destroyed	Phong Savanh, French Indo-China	*	*
15.03.55	de Havilland DH.89A Dragon Rapide	CR-ADM	6840	DETA	Written off	Praia Zulala, Mozambique	*	*
17.03.55	Vickers Viking 1B	VP-YEX	159	Central African Airways	Crashed on landing	Salisbury, Southern Rhodesia	*	*
17.03.55	AAC.1 Toucan	F-BBOF	007	French Police	Damaged on take-off	Gonesse, France	*	*
18.03.55	Douglas DC-3	F-BAXL	20047	Air France	Written off	Beauvais, France	*	*
18.03.55	de Havilland DH.89A Dragon Rapide	VP-KND	6640	Caspair	Written off	Kisumu, Kenya	*	*
20.03.55	Convair 240-0	N94234	066	American Airlines	Crashed on landing	Springfield, MS, USA	13	*
26.03.55	Boeing Stratocruiser	N1032V	15932	Pan American World Airways	Crashed	Off Seattle, WA, USA	4	*
26.03.55	Short Sealand 1	AP-AGB	SH.1572	East Pakistan Government	Destroyed in storm	Dacca, Pakistan	*	*
26.03.55	Short Sealand 1	AP-AGC	SH.1573	East Pakistan Government	Destroyed in storm	Dacca, Pakistan	*	*
26.03.55	Avro Nineteen I	AP-AGA	1325	East Pakistan Government	Damaged beyond repair in storm	Dacca, Pakistan	*	*
29.03.55	Douglas DC-3	VT-CUZ	13029	Airways (India) Ltd	Crashed	Khowai, India	*	*
02.04.55	Curtiss C-46	N51424	30430	Aaxico Airlines	Crashed during storm	Gulf of Mexico	2	*
04.04.55	Douglas DC-6	N37512	43001	United Air Lines	Crashed	Ronkonkoma, NY, USA	*	*
08.04.55	Airspeed Ambassador 2	G-AMAB	5224	British European Airways	Forced landing after engine failure	Dusseldorf, West Germany	*	*
11.04.55	Lockheed 749A Constellation	VT-DEP	2666	Air India	Crashed after bomb explosion	Off Great Natuna Is, Sarawak	15	3
11.04.55	Avro York	CF-HMZ	–	Associated Airways	Crashed on take-off	Yellowknife, NWT, Canada	0	*
14.04.55	Lisunov Li-2P	SP-LAE	18424001	LOT Polish Airlines	Crashed	nr Katowice, Poland	*	*
18.04.55	de Havilland Heron 1B	F-BGOI	14010	UAT	Crashed [Found 19.02.56]	Kupe Mts, Cameroons	12	0
28.04.55	Short Sealand 1	JZ-PTA	SH.1769	Christian & Missionary Alliance	Crashed	En route Eidenburg-Baliem, N Guinea	*	*
01.05.55	Avro Anson I	OH-ANA	–	Tampereen Lentoliikenne	Damaged when taxiied into hole	Tampere, Finland	*	*
12.05.55	Avro York	CF-HMX	–	Arctic Wings	Crashed on landing	Hall Lake, NWT, Canada	0	*
18.05.55	Douglas DC-3	VP-KKH	16820/33568	East African Airways	Crashed	Mt Kilimanjaro, Kenya	20	*
20.05.55	Douglas DC-3	LV-ACQ	13159	Aerolineas Argentinas	Crashed	Rio Chaco, Argentina	*	*
21.05.55	Douglas DC-3	YV-C-ALU	4791	Linea Aeropostal Venezolana	Crashed	Off Barcelona, Spain	4	*
26.05.55	Avro York	CF-HMY	–	Associated Airways	Crashed on take-off	Edmonton, MN, Canada	2	0
03.06.55	Douglas C-54A	F-BFVT	10292	UAT	Crashed on landing	Fort Lamy, Chad	*	*
13.06.55	Noorduyn Norseman IV	ZS-DMB	733	Maluti Air Services	Crashed	Leribe, Basutoland	*	*
16.06.55	Lockheed 049 Constellation	PP-PDJ	2032	Panair do Brasil	Crashed	nr Asuncion, Paraguay	14	*
18.06.55	Curtiss C-46	CF-HVJ	30222	World Wide Airways	Crashed	Northern Canada	*	*
18.06.55	Curtiss C-46	XA-LID	*	Tigres Voladores	Crashed	Leon, Mexico	*	*
22.06.55	de Havilland Dove 2	G-ALTM	04236	British Overseas Airways Corporation	Crashed after engine failure	Heathrow, London, UK	*	*
03.07.55	Vickers-Supermarine Walrus I	G-AHFN	6S/35698	C.Fulford	Blown ashore & wrecked	Stranraer, UK	*	*
03.07.55	Ford 5-AT-D Tri-Motor	XA-FON	5-AT-103	Servicios Aereos de Chiapas	Crashed	Sierra de San Andreas, Mexico	0	4

Date	Type	Reg'n	C/n	Operator	Accident	Location	F	S
14.07.55	Douglas DC-2-243	XA-DOB	2088	Lineas Aereas Unidas	Crashed	nr Oaxaca, Mexico	*	*
17.07.55	Convair 340-32	N3422	071	Braniff Airlines	Crashed on landing	Chicago, IL, USA	22	*
23.07.55	de Havilland Dove 1B	G-AKSK	04116	Cambrian Air Service	Crashed when pilot shut down wrong engine	nr Fritham, Hants, UK	1	6
27.07.55	Lockheed C-69 Constellation	4X-AKC	1968	El Al Israel Airlines	Shot down by Bulgarian aircraft	nr Petrich, Bulgaria	58	0
04.08.55	Convair 240-0	N94221	040	American Airlines	Crashed	Fort Leonard Wood, MO, USA	30	*
06.08.55	Type Unknown	*	*	Aeroflot	Crashed	nr Voronezh, RSFSR, USSR	25	*
06.08.55	Avro Nineteen I	G-AHIG	1322	Fairways (Jersey) Ltd	Crashed out of fuel	Off Calshot, IoW, Hants, UK	*	*
26.08.55	Douglas DC-3	PP-CBY	11692	Cruzeiro	Crashed	Caparao Mt, Brazil	13	*
30.08.55	Douglas DC-3	VT-AZX	13285	Kalinga Airlines	Crashed	Simra, Nepal	*	*
02.09.55	Douglas DC-3	XY-ACQ	12579	Union of Burma Airways	Crashed	Meikitila, Burma	9	*
05.09.55	Curtiss C-46	YV-C-EVL	*	Avensa	Crashed	Off Maracaibo, Venezuela	*	*
05.09.55	Boeing B-17G	CP-597	*	Lloyd Aereo Boliviano	Crashed	Trinidad, Bolivia	*	*
08.09.55	Douglas DC-3	N74663	6257	Currey Air Transport	Crashed	Burbank, CA, USA	*	*
10.09.55	Latecoere 631	F-BDRE	08	France Hydro	Crashed	nr Banzo, French Equatorial Africa	16	*
14.09.55	Avro York	EP-ADA	–	Persian Air Services	Force landed	nr Basra, Iraq	0	*
17.09.55	Bristol 170 Freighter 31	CF-GBT	12831	Pacific Western Airlines	Crashed after engine failure	Abee, AB, Canada	2	4
20.09.55	Curtiss C-46	CP-549	47	Corporacion Boliviano de Fomento	Crashed	nr La Paz, Bolivia	*	*
21.09.55	Douglas DC-3	F-BCYU	10151	Air France	Crashed on landing	Bordeaux, France	*	*
21.09.55	Canadair C-4	G-ALHL	158	British Overseas Airways Corporation	Crashed on landing in sandstorm	Idris, Libya	15	*
21.09.55	Boeing B-17F-DL	CP-570	8296	Lloyd Aereo Boliviano	Crashed	El Alto, Bolivia	*	*
23.09.55	Miles Aerovan 4	G-AJTC	6414	Air Ads	Crashed	Dachau, West Germany	*	*
24.09.55	Douglas C-54A	N90433	10410	Flying Tiger Line	Crashed	West of Hawaii	3	*
25.09.55	de Havilland Canada Otter	PK-PHA	306	Operator Unknown	Written off	Location Unknown	*	*
29.09.55	Avro York	CF-HMV	–	Associated Airways	Crashed in lake	nr Yellowknife, NWT, Canada	1	1
02.10.55	Douglas C-54A	OB-PAZ-228	10277	Faucett	Crashed	Pico Oiriruma-Vinac, Peru	19	*
06.10.55	Douglas DC-4	N30062	18389	United Air Lines	Crashed	nr Laramie, WY, USA	66	0
10.10.55	Vickers Viking 1B	YI-ABQ	231	Iraqi Airways	Crashed on take-off	Baghdad, Iraq	0	*
10.10.55	Convair 340-58	YU-ADC	178	JAT Yugoslav Airlines	Crashed on landing	Vienna, Austria	7	*
22.10.55	Short Sandringham 7	CX-ANA	SH.59C	CAUSA	Written off	Location Unknown	*	*
25.10.55	Douglas DC-3	CF-HTP	19140	Maritime Central Airways	Crashed	Northern Canada	*	*
01.11.55	Douglas DC-6B	N37559	43538	United Air Lines	Crashed after bomb explosion	Long Mount, CO, USA	44	0
08.11.55	Piper PA-22-150 Tri-Pacer	VQ-ZBA	22-3131	Basutair	Crashed	Semakong, Basutoland	*	*
17.11.55	Douglas C-54	N88852	3123	Kerkorian, R.R.	Crashed on take-off	Seattle, WA, USA	28	*
01.12.55	Douglas DC-3	PP-CCC	15845/32593	Cruzeiro	Crashed on take-off	Belem, Brazil	6	*
15.12.55	Douglas DC-3	VH-AOG	10083	Butler Air Transport	Crashed	Bourke, NSW, Australia	*	*
17.12.55	Lockheed 749A Constellation	F-BAZG	2626	Air Algerie	Caught fire on take-off	Algiers, Algeria	*	*
17.12.55	Curtiss C-46	N9904F	30262	Riddle Airlines	Crashed after take-off with engine failure	Hollywood, SC, USA	2	*
17.12.55	Douglas DC-3	XH-SAG	13800/25245	Sahsa	Crashed	Nuevo Octotepeque, Honduras	*	*
18.12.55	Avro Shackleton MR.2	WL799	–	Avro	Destroyed in ground fire	Langar, UK	0	*
19.12.55	Douglas DC-3	*	*	Operator Unknown	Crashed	Sao Paulo, Brazil	26	*
21.12.55	Lockheed 749A Constellation	N112A	2533	Eastern Air Lines	Crashed on approach in bad weather	Jacksonville, FL, USA	17	0
22.12.55	Douglas DC-3	G-AMZC	16522/33270	Manx Airlines	Crashed on approach in bad weather	Dusseldorf, West Germany	3	*
25.12.55	Beechcraft AT-11 Kansan	PP-CCG	3304	Cruzeiro	Written off	Piloes, Brazil	*	*
30.12.55	Martin 202	N93061	9150	Southwest Airlines	Damaged in hangar fire	San Francisco, CA, USA	0	*
30.12.55	de Havilland Drover 2	VQ-FAQ	5008	Fiji Airways	Crashed	Wainivatumboso Gorge, Fiji	*	*
00.00.55	Convair 340-42	N8420H	096	Union Producing Co	Damaged by fire	Shreveport, LA, USA	*	*
00.00.55	Ford 5-AT-B Tri-Motor	XB-NET	5-AT-008	F.Oergel	Written off	Mexico	*	*
12.01.56	Douglas DC-3	VH-BZA	4651	Ansett-ANA	Crashed	Frederick Henry Bay, Tas, Australia	*	*
17.01.56	Douglas DC-3	CF-GVZ	15552/26997	Quebecair	Crashed attempting forced landing	Creway, NF, Canada	4	*
18.01.56	Douglas DC-3	*	*	Ceskoslovenske Aerolinie	Crashed	Torysa, Czechoslovakia	22	*
21.01.56	Vickers Viscount 701	G-AMOM	026	British European Airways	Crashed on take-off	Blackbushe, Hants, UK	0	*
22.01.56	Douglas DC-3	HK-303	10032	Avianca	Written off	Location Unknown	*	*
24.01.56	Douglas DC-3	F-BAXT	9274	Air France	Crashed	nr Nantes, France	*	*
24.01.56	Avro York	CF-HMU	–	Maritime Central Airways	U/c failed on landing	Fort Chimo, PQ, Canada	0	4

Date	Type	Reg'n	C/n	Operator	Accident	Location	F	S
28.01.56	Douglas DC-3	F-BCYK	4509	Air France	Crashed	nr Lyons, France	*	*
04.02.56	Avro Anson I	VH-AYN	–	Commercial Aviation	Crashed	nr Derby, WA, Australia	5	0
04.02.56	Avro Anson I	VH-ICA	–	West Darling Air Service	Damaged beyond repair	Wanaaring, NSW, Australia	*	*
13.02.56	Bristol 170 Freighter 31	CF-FZU	13136	Maritime Central Airways	Crashed when cargo shifted	Baffin Is, Canada	*	*
14.02.56	Douglas DC-3	CF-BZH	6079	Aerovias Inc	Crashed	nr Fort Chino, PQ, Canada	*	*
16.02.56	Douglas DC-3	HZ-AAO	*	Saudi Arabian Airlines	Crashed	Neiran, Saudi Arabia	*	*
16.02.56	Avro Anson I	OY-DYY	–	CATS	Crashed	Tirstrup, Denmark	*	*
16.02.56	Avro Anson I	OY-DYC	–	CATS	Crashed after engine failure	nr Grenca, Denmark	*	*
17.02.56	Martin 404	N445A	14122	Eastern Air Lines	Stalled on approach & crashed	Owensboro, KY, USA	*	*
18.02.56	Avro York C.1	XG929	–	Scottish Airlines	Crashed on take-off	Luqa, Malta	50	0
18.02.56	Douglas DC-3	G-AMSL	14966/26411	Kuwait National Airways	Damaged beyond repair	Durkham, Saudi Arabia	*	*
19.02.56	Martin 404	N40416	14120	Trans World Airlines	Crashed on take-off	Albuquerque, NM, USA	16	*
20.02.56	Douglas DC-6B	F-BGOD	43835	Transport Aerien Intercontinentaux	Crashed on approach	nr Cairo, Egypt	52	12
20.02.56	Vickers Viscount 744	N7404	090	Capital Airlines	Damaged in heavy landing	Chicago, IL, USA	0	*
24.02.56	Douglas DC-3	YK-AAE	14918/26362	Syrian Airways	Crashed	nr Aleppo, Syria	19	*
25.02.56	Douglas DC-3	AP-ACZ	16813/33561	Pakistan International Airlines	Crashed	Lash Golath Mt, Pakistan	*	*
04.03.56	Handley Page Hermes 4	G-ALDW	HP.81/23	Skyways	Blown up by terrorists on ground	Nicosia, Cyprus	0	0
18.03.56	Curtiss C-46	N9995F	22409	Flying Tiger Line	Crashed into hill	Keewatin, ON, Canada	*	*
21.03.56	Douglas DC-3	VT-CGN	12989	Indian Airlines	Crashed	Tezpur, India	2	*
28.03.56	Douglas DC-3	G-AMRB	16670/33418	Starways	Crashed	Largs, Ayrshire, UK	1	*
31.03.56	Douglas DC-3	VT-DCM	10230	National Air Operators	Crashed	Indarpur, India	*	*
01.04.56	Martin 404	N40403	14103	Trans World Airlines	Crashed on take-off	Pittsburgh, PA, USA	22	*
02.04.56	Boeing Stratocruiser	N74608	15954	Northwest Airlines	Crashed on take-off	Off Seattle, WA, USA	5	*
18.04.56	Consolidated Catalina	*	*	PAB	Crashed	nr Parcentius, Brazil	3	*
22.04.56	Avro York	G-AGNS	1220	British Overseas Airways Corporation	Crashed on take-off	Idris, Libya	*	*
30.04.56	Avro York	G-AMUL	–	Scottish Airlines	Crashed on take-off	Stansted, Essex, UK	2	*
07.05.56	Douglas DC-3	PP-SPX	12257	VASP	Damaged beyond repair	Sao Paulo, Brazil	*	*
15.05.56	Douglas DC-3	VT-DBA	13165	Indian Airlines	Crashed	Kathmandu, Nepal	14{1}	*
18.05.56	Douglas DC-3	VT-CCD	14023/25468	Indian Airlines	Damaged on landing	Ahmedabad, India	*	*
24.05.56	Douglas DC-3	TG-AHA	6052	Aviateca	Crashed	North of Guatemala City, Guatemala	30	*
30.05.56	Bristol 170 Freighter 31	CF-TFZ	13139	Pacific Western Airlines	Crashed through ice on landing	Beaver Lodge Lake, NWT, Canada	0	*
18.06.56	Bristol 170 Freighter 31	CF-TFY	13138	Transair	Sank through ice after landing	Hudson Bay, Canada	*	*
19.06.56	Ford 4-AT-E Tri-Motor	N9642	4-AT-58	Johnson Flying Service	Crashed	nr Townsend, MT, USA	*	*
20.06.56	Lockheed 1049E Super Constellation	YV-C-AMS	4561	Linea Aeropostal Venezolana	Crashed due to fire while dumping fuel	Off New York, NY, USA	74	0
22.06.56	Avro Anson I	OY-FAD	–	CATS	Damaged when u/c collapsed	Ronne, Denmark	*	*
24.06.56	Canadair C-4	G-ALHE	151	British Overseas Airways Corporation	Crashed on take-off	Kano, Nigeria	32	*
30.06.56	Douglas DC-7	N6324C	44288	United Air Lines	Mid-air collision with TWA Super Constellation N6902C	Grand Canyon, AZ, USA	58(70)	0
30.06.56	Lockheed 1049 Super Constellation	N6902C	4016	Trans World Airlines	Mid-air collision with United A/L DC-7 N6324C	Grand Canyon, AZ, USA	70(58)	0
oo.06.56	Caudron Goeland	F-BAPE	8906/1102	Air France	Damaged beyond repair	Cormeilles, France	*	*
02.07.56	de Havilland Dove 2A	N26W	04352	Munz Airways	Crashed	nr Moses Point, Alaska	*	*
08.07.56	de Havilland DH.89A Dragon Rapide	OO-CMS	6902	Air Brousse	Written off	Kikwit, Belgian Congo	*	*
16.07.56	Douglas DC-3	LV-ACD	13328	Aerolineas Argentinas	Crashed	Rio Cuarto, Argentina	18	*
17.07.56	Convair 440-11	HB-IMD	335	Swissair	Crashed on landing	Shannon, Eire	*	*
29.07.56	Avro Nineteen Srs 1	OO-APG	1363	L.Lekeu	Crashed	Baardegem, Belgium	*	*
05.08.56	Handley Page Hermes 4A	G-ALDK	HP.81/12	Britavia	Crash landed	Karachi, Pakistan	*	*
08.08.56	Douglas DC-3	XY-ADC	14348/25793	Union of Burma Airways	Crashed	Thazi, Burma	12	*
09.08.56	Douglas DC-3	HK-308	19758	Avianca	Crashed	Location Unknown	*	*
18.08.56	de Havilland Dove 1	ZS-AVZ	04021	Stewart & Lloyds Ltd	Crashed	Johannesburg, South Africa	*	*
25.08.56	Douglas DC-3	CP-605	15794/32542	Lloyd Aereo Boliviano	Crashed on landing	La Paz, Bolivia	2	*
26.08.56	Miles Aerovan 4	G-AJWD	6412	Air Ads	Crashed	nr Dunkirk, France	*	*
26.08.56	Avro Anson V	TG-CES-40	MDF-330	Aeroservicios de Emergencia	Written off	Coban, Guatemala	*	*
29.08.56	Douglas DC-6B	CF-CUP	43843	Canadian Pacific Airlines	Crashed	Cold Bay, Alaska	15	7
06.09.56	Douglas DC-3	PP-ANK	13773	Loide Aereo Nacional	Crashed	Pampulha, Brazil	*	*

Date	Type	Reg'n	C/n	Operator	Accident	Location	F	S
09.09.56	Curtiss C-46	JY-ABV	27069	Jordan International Airlines	Crashed on take-off	Amman, Jordan	1	*
09.09.56	Curtiss C-46	*	*	Westair	Struck parked DC-3 on take-off & crashed into sea	Off Kotzebue, Alaska	*(*)	*
11.09.56	Short Sunderland 3	CX-AFA	SH.05C	CAUSA	Crashed	Location Unknown	*	*
13.09.56	Avro York	CF-HFQ	–	TransAir	Damaged on take-off	Fox, NWT, Canada	0	*
14.09.56	de Havilland DH.89A Dragon Rapide	G-ALEJ	6484	Lancashire Aircraft Corporation	Crashed	nr Eccleshall, Staffs, UK	*	*
16.09.56	Bristol 173	G-AMJI	12872	Bristol Aeroplane Co	Damaged beyond repair during air display	Filton, Glos, UK	0	*
17.09.56	Avro York	EP-ADB	1224	Persian Air Services	Exploded on ground	Stansted, Essex, UK	1	*
22.09.56	de Havilland DH.89A Dragon Rapide	G-AESR	6363	Air Kruise	Written off	Gerdes el Adol, Libya	*	*
23.09.56	Curtiss C-46	CF-IHR	32866	World Wide Airways	Crashed	North West Territories, Canada	*	*
26.09.56	Short Solent 3	G-ANAJ	S.1293	Aquila Airways	Destroyed by gale	Santa Margherita, Italy	0	*
26.09.56	Avro York	CF-HMW	–	Maritime Central Airways	Force-landed due to engine fire	nr Fort Chimo, PQ, Canada	2	1
29.09.56	SNCASE Languedoc	EC-AKV	26	Aviaco	Crashed	Tenerife, Canary Is, Spain	*	*
oo.09.56	Curtiss C-46	HI-36	432	Dominicana	Written off	Location Unknown	*	*
oo.09.56	de Havilland DH.89A Dragon Rapide	F-OAVZ	6453	Operator Unknown	Written off	Location Unknown	*	*
01.10.56	Vickers Viscount 739	SU-AIC	085	Misrair	Destroyed on ground during British air raid	Almaza, Egypt	*	*
01.10.56	Avro Anson I	VP-KJK	–	Airwork (East Africa) Ltd	Crashed when wing broke off after take-off	Kitale, Kenya	3	*
05.10.56	Vickers Viking 1B	VP-YMO	227	Central African Airways	Crashed	Salisbury, Southern Rhodesia	2	*
05.10.56	Avro Anson V	OY-DZI	3732	Zone-Redningskorpset Flyvetjenesten	Crashed into mountain	Mt Grammont, Switzerland	2	0
07.10.56	de Havilland DH.89A Dragon Rapide	G-AGLR	6781	Don Everall Aviation	Crashed	Berkswell, Warks, UK	*	*
11.10.56	Beechcraft AT-11 Kansan	PP-CCF	3070	Cruzeiro	Written off	Itacuru, Brazil	*	*
16.10.56	Boeing Stratocruiser	N90943	15959	Pan American World Airways	Crashed after engine failure	Pacific Ocean	*	*
19.10.56	Douglas DC-3	VT-DGK	*	Kalinga Airlines	Crashed	Agartala, India	*	*
23.10.56	Curtiss C-46	CB-45	26977	Frigorificos Co-operativo Los Andes	Crashed	La Paz, Bolivia	*	*
30.10.56	Hurel-Dubois HD-321	F-BHHA	02	SGACC	Crashed	Rio de Janeiro, Brazil	*	*
02.11.56	Fiat G.212	SU-AFF	09	SAIDE	Destroyed by enemy action	Suez, Egypt	*	*
03.11.56	Curtiss C-46	CC-CAH-0331*		Lyon Air	Crashed on beach	San Miguel Bay, Panama	*	*
05.11.56	Handley Page Hermes 4A	G-ALDJ	HP.81/11	Britavia	Crashed on landing	Blackbushe, Hants, UK	7	*
07.11.56	de Havilland Heron 2B	LN-SUR	14093	Braathens SAFE	Crashed	Hommelfjell, Norway	2	*
14.11.56	de Havilland DH.89A Dragon Rapide	F-OAUH	6612	Operator Unknown	Written off	Location Unknown	*	*
15.11.56	Martin 404	N40404	14104	Trans World Airlines	Damaged in belly landing	Las Vegas, NV, USA	*	*
15.11.56	Douglas C-54A	XA-HEG	10324	Aerovias Guest	Crashed after fire	Puerto Somoza, Nicaragua	25	*
17.11.56	Douglas DC-3	HK-385	1971	Empresa Aviacion del Pacifico	Crashed	El Rucio Mt, Colombia	36	*
24.11.56	Douglas DC-6B	I-LEAD	45075	Linee Aeree Italiane	Crashed on take-off	Paris, France	33	0
24.11.56	Ilyushin IL-12	OK-DBP	93013517	Ceskoslovenske Aerolinie	Crashed on take-off	nr Eglisau, Switzerland	23	*
27.11.56	Lockheed 749 Constellation	YV-C-AMA	2560	Linea Aeropostal Venezolana	Crashed on approach	Cevilla, Venezuela	25	*
oo.11.56	Bristol 170 Freighter 31E	F-OAOU	13165	Air Laos	Crashed on approach	Vientiane, Laos	*	*
08.12.56	Consolidated PBY-5A Catalina	HK-133	*	AIDA	Crashed into mountains	Caqueta, Colombia	14	*
09.12.56	Canadair C-54GM North Star	CF-TFD	128	Trans Canada Airlines	Crashed into mountain	Mt Slesse, BC, Canada	62	0
12.12.56	Vickers Viscount 708	F-BGNK	008	Air France	Crashed after engine fire	Milly-le-Foret, France	5	*
12.12.56	Curtiss C-46	N1662M	22545	Aerovias Sud Americana	Crashed on take-off	Gulf of Panama	*	*
16.12.56	Curtiss C-46	N2028A	30380	Zantop Air Transport	Crashed on landing	Long Beach, CA, USA	*	*
22.12.56	Convair 340-58	YU-ADA	132	JAT Yugoslav Airlines	Crashed on landing	Grub, Austria	3	*
22.12.56	Douglas DC-3	I-LINC	9101	Linee Aeree Italiane	Crashed	Mt Oiner, Italy	21	*
oo.oo.56	Curtiss C-46	CF-HZI	22387	Transair	Crashed	Location Unknown	*	*
oo.oo.56	Curtiss C-46	CF-HZL	22394	Transair	Crashed	Location Unknown	*	*
oo.oo.56	Barkley-Grow T8P-1	CF-BMW	06	Northland Airlines	Damaged in forced landing	Nettley, MN, Canada	*	*
02.01.57	Douglas DC-3	I-LEDA	4411	Alitalia	Crashed	Reggio Calabria Airport, Italy	*	*
03.01.57	Avro Nineteen I	G-AGZT	1331	Fairways (Jersey) Ltd	Damaged in belly landing	Croydon, Surrey, UK	0	*
06.01.57	Convair 240-0	N94247	104	American Airlines	Crashed on approach	Owasso, OK, USA	1	*
08.01.57	Avro York	CF-HIQ	–	TransAir	Crashed after engine failure	Rankin Inlet, NWT, Canada	0	*
23.01.57	Douglas DC-3	AN-AEC	12312	Lanica	Crashed	Ometepe Is, Nicaragua	16	*
29.01.57	SNCASE Armagnac	F-BAVG	06	SAGETA	Crashed on landing	Paris, France	1	66
31.01.57	Douglas DC-7B	N8210H	45192	Douglas Aircraft	Mid-air collision on first flight with USAF F-89 52-1870	nr Sunland, CA, USA	4{3}(*)	0
01.02.57	Douglas DC-6A	N34954	44678	Northeast Airlines	Crashed after take-off in storm	Rickers Is, NY, USA	21	*

Date	Type	Reg'n	C/n	Operator	Accident	Location	F	S
18.02.57	Boeing B-17G-VE	CP-622	8726	Aerovias Los Andes	Crashed	Laja, Bolivia	*	*
23.02.57	Junkers Ju.52/3m	*	*	Operator Unknown	Crashed	Sao Paulo, Brazil	6	*
02.03.57	Douglas C-54B	N90449	27239	Alaska Airlines	Crashed	Blyn, WA, USA	5	*
09.03.57	Douglas DC-3	HK-155	4338	Avianca	Crashed	El Soldado, Colombia	15	*
10.03.57	Martin 404	N453A	14144	Eastern Air Lines	Damaged in heavy landing	Louisville, KY, USA	*	*
14.03.57	Vickers Viscount 701	G-ALWE	004	British European Airways	Crashed into houses on approach	Wythenshawe, Cheshire, UK	20{2}	0
18.03.57	Douglas DC-3	CP-535	4867	Lloyd Aereo Boliviano	Crashed	nr Sayari, Bolivia	19	*
19.03.57	Douglas DC-3	CF-ILY	4410	Northern Wings	Crashed	Seven Is, PQ, Canada	*	*
19.03.57	Douglas DC-3	XY-ADB	16769/33517	Union of Burma Airways	Caught fire on take-off & crashed	Loikaw, Burma	*	*
07.04.57	Curtiss C-46	PP-VCF	30283	Varig	Crashed due to engine fire	Bage, Brazil	40	*
08.04.57	Douglas DC-3	F-BEIK	14411/25856	Air France	Crashed on take-off	Algiers, Algeria	32	*
10.04.57	Douglas DC-3	PP-ANX	13048	REAL	Crashed into mountain	Anchieta Is, Brazil	26	*
11.04.57	Curtiss C-46	CC-CNC-0466	443	Transa Chile	Crashed	nr Arica, Chile	*	*
12.04.57	Douglas DC-3	YV-C-AFA	4525	Linea Aeropostal Venezolana	Written off	Calabozo, Venezuela	*	*
14.04.57	Consolidated Liberator	*	*	TAMSA	Struck obstruction on take-off	Merida, Mexico	3	*
18.04.57	Douglas DC-4	N88839	3060	Capital Airlines	Crashed	Pittsburgh, PA, USA	*	*
29.04.57	Douglas DC-3	EC-ABC	19334	Iberia	Crashed	Valdemeca, Spain	*	*
29.04.57	Miles Aerovan 4	G-AISF	6396	Meridian Air Maps	Crashed on take-off	Manchester, UK	*	*
oo.04.57	Avro Anson V	CF-ICQ	BRC-1309C	Spartan Air Services	Damaged in belly landing	Lac Parent, PQ, Canada	*	*
01.05.57	Vickers Viking 1B	G-AJBO	241	Eagle Aviation	Crashed on landing	Blackbushe, Hants, UK	34	1
05.05.57	Douglas DC-3	VT-AUV	20318	Indian Airlines	Crashed	Cechar, India	1	*
09.05.57	Bristol 170 Freighter 21	EC-ADI	12757	Aviaco	Crashed on approach	Madrid, Spain	37	*
10.05.57	de Havilland DH.89A Dragon Rapide	CR-LBH	6846	DTA	Written off	Ambriz, Angola	*	*
13.05.57	Douglas C-54A	N68736	7449	US Overseas Airlines	Crashed	Narsarrssuak, Greenland	2	0
13.05.57	Douglas DC-3	VT-CFB	13626	Indian Airlines	Crashed	Kingsway Camp, India	*	*
21.05.57	de Havilland Canada Otter	PI-56	178	Operator Unknown	Damaged beyond repair	Location Unknown	*	*
23.05.57	Douglas DC-3	HK-503	10171	Aerovias Condor de Colombia	Crashed	Barranquilla, Colombia	*	*
27.05.57	de Havilland DH.89A Dragon Rapide	G-AKTZ	6482	Operator Unknown	Damaged beyond repair	nr Benghazi, Libya	*	*
04.06.57	Airspeed Consul	G-ALTZ	5134	L.M.Berner & Co	Crashed	Leopoldville, Belgian Congo	*	*
09.06.57	Lisunov Li-2P	HA-LIM	23442803	Malev	Damaged on take-off	Budapest, Hungary	*	*
14.06.57	Ilyushin IL-14	SP-LNF	6341607	LOT Polish Airlines	Crashed in storm	nr Moscow, RSFSR, USSR	9	*
14.06.57	de Havilland Dove 1	CR-CAC	04000/P/1	Aero Club of Cabo Verde	Damaged in belly landing	Achada Grande, Cape Verde Is	0	*
14.06.57	Avro Anson V	CF-GRU	BRU-1476C	Austin Airways	Crashed on landing in snowstorm	Desolation Lake, NWT, Canada	*	*
18.06.57	Douglas DC-3	HB-IRK	20737	Swissair	Crashed	nr Arbon, Switzerland	9	*
19.06.57	Curtiss C-46	N8013E	192	Indian Government	Damaged in hangar collapse	Panagarh, India	*	*
19.06.57	Curtiss C-46	*	30347	Western Hemisphere Import Export Co	Destroyed in hangar collapse	Panagarh, India	*	*
21.06.57	de Havilland Canada Otter	PI-52	070	Operator Unknown	Written off	Location Unknown	*	*
23.06.57	Douglas DC-3	CF-EPI	7408	Queen Charlotte Airlines	Crashed on take-off	Port Hardy, BC, Canada	14	*
25.06.57	Avro York	CF-HFP	–	Pacific Western Airlines	Damaged after brake failure on landing	Cape Perry, NWT, Canada	0	*
28.06.57	Douglas DC-7B	N808D	44859	Eastern Air Lines	Ran into Eastern Constellation N6212C after brakes failed	Miami, FL, USA	0(0)	*
28.06.57	Lockheed 1049 Super Constellation	N6212C	4012	Eastern Air Lines	Struck by Eastern DC-7 N808D when brakes failed	Miami, FL, USA	0(0)	*
29.06.57	de Havilland DH.89A Dragon Rapide	G-AGUF	6855	Operator Unknown	Crashed	Ramsgate, Kent, UK	*	*
01.07.57	Douglas DC-3	AP-AJS	12501	Pakistan International Airlines	Crashed during storm	Bay of Bengal	24	*
10.07.57	Lockheed C-121A Constellation	ET-T-35	2608	Ethiopian Airlines	Caught fire & force-landed	nr Khartoum, Sudan	0	*
15.07.57	Lockheed 1049C Super Constellation	PH-LKT	4504	KLM Royal Dutch Airlines	Crashed	Off Biak, Indonesia	58	10
25.07.57	Curtiss C-46	HK-513	33210	Sociedad Aeronautica Medellin	Crashed	Planeta Rico, Colombia	2	*
11.08.57	Douglas DC-4	CF-MCF	18374	Maritime Central Airways	Crashed on approach	Issoudun, PQ, Canada	79	0
15.08.57	Ilyushin IL-14P	SSSR-L1874	146000607	Aeroflot	Crashed into harbour after striking chimney	Copenhagen, Denmark	23	*
16.08.57	Lockheed 1049G Super Constellation	PP-VDA	4610	Varig	Crashed after engine failure	Off Puerta Plata, Dominican Rep.	1	*
20.08.57	Douglas DC-3	VT-ARH	4851	Indamer	Crashed	Assam, India	8	*
29.08.57	Douglas DC-3	XH-SAF	17139/34406	Sahsa	Crashed on take-off	nr Juticalpa, Honduras	12	*
30.08.57	Scottish Aviation Twin Pioneer 3	JZ-PPX	509	de Kroonduif	Crashed	Japen Straits, New Guinea	2	0
01.09.57	Handley Page Hermes 4A	XD632	HP.81/1	Airwork	Collided with Indian A/L DC-3 VT-AUA	Calcutta, India	0(3)	*
01.09.57	Douglas DC-3	VT-AUA	13245	Indian Airlines	Collided with Airwork Hermes XD632	Calcutta, India	3(0)	*

Date	Type	Reg'n	C/n	Operator	Accident	Location	F	S
03.09.57	Douglas DC-3	YV-C-AVG	4764	Avensa	Crashed in storm	Niquito Trujillo, Venezuela	9	*
11.09.57	Bristol 170 Freighter 21E	EC-AEH	12786	Aviaco	Crashed on landing	Tetuan, Morocco	*	*
15.09.57	Douglas DC-3	N34417	7337	Northeast Airlines	Crashed into trees on approach	New Bedford, MA, USA	10	*
18.09.57	Convair 440-62	PP-AQE	456	REAL	Crashed in fog	Montevideo, Uruguay	1	*
20.09.57	Curtiss C-46	*	27080	Western Hemisphere Import Export Co	Crashed	nr Panagarh, India	*	*
26.09.57	Vickers Viking 1B	D-ADEL	226	Karl Herfurtner	Crashed on landing	Palma, Majorca, Spain	0	*
28.09.57	de Havilland Heron 1B	G-AOFY	14099	British European Airways	Crashed	Port Ellen, Islay, Hebrides, UK	3	*
30.09.57	Douglas DC-4-1009	JA6011	42982	Japan Air Lines	Crashed	Itami, Japan	*	*
01.10.57	Canadian Vickers Stranraer	CF-BYM	*	Pacific Western Airlines	Crashed on take-off	Sovereign Lake, BC, Canada	4	*
03.10.57	Curtiss C-46	OD-ACK	30249	Lebanese International Airways	Crashed on take-off	Beirut, Lebanon	27	*
08.10.57	Bristol 170 Freighter 21E	HZ-AAC	12772	Saudi Arabian Airlines	Damaged beyond repair on landing	Taraif, Saudi Arabia	*	*
18.10.57	Douglas DC-3	PP-VCS	19757	Varig	Crashed	Porto Alegre, Brazil	*	*
20.10.57	Vickers Viscount 806A	G-AOYF	255	Vickers Armstrong	Damaged on landing	Johannesburg, South Africa	0	*
23.10.57	Vickers Viscount 802	G-AOJA	150	British European Airways	Crashed on approach in bad weather	Belfast, Northern Ireland, UK	7	*
26.10.57	de Havilland Heron 2D	EC-AOA	14120	Aviaco	Crashed	San Sebastian, Spain	*	*
26.10.57	Avro Anson V	CF-DTS	–	Northern Wings	Crashed	Natashquan River, PQ, Canada	*	*
28.10.57	Douglas DC-3	EC-ACH	19332	Iberia	Crashed	Madrid, Spain	21	*
29.10.57	Fairchild C-82 Packet	*	*	TAMSA	Crashed	nr Campeche, Argentina	3	*
oo.10.57	Consolidated Canso	CF-HFL	*	Eastern Provincial Airways	Crash landed	nr Goose Bay, NF, Canada	0	3
oo.10.57	Avro Anson V	HC-SJO	MDF-117	AREA	Crashed	nr Tulcan, Ecuador	*	*
02.11.57	Vickers Viking 1B	CR-IAD	215	T.A. da Indias Portugueses	Crashed	Karachi, Pakistan	*	*
02.11.57	Douglas C-54A	F-BHKY	3055	Air France	Destroyed by fire	Toulouse, France	0	*
03.11.57	Douglas C-54A	D-ALAF	7459	Karl Herfurtner	Crashed on take-off	Dusseldorf, West Germany	8	*
04.11.57	Douglas C-54A	PP-AXS	7467	REAL	Crashed in sea	Off Sao Sebastiao, Brazil	*	*
04.11.57	Ilyushin IL-14	YR-PCC	146001010	Romanian Government	Crashed on landing	Moscow, RSFSR, USSR	4	*
06.11.57	Bristol Britannia 301	G-ANCA	12917	Bristol Aeroplane Co	Crashed	nr Bristol, UK	15	*
09.11.57	Boeing Stratocruiser	N90944	15960	Pan American World Airways	Crashed	Pacific Ocean	44	0
14.11.57	Martin 404	N492A	14240	Eastern Air Lines	Damaged in heavy landing	Massena, NY, USA	*	*
15.11.57	de Havilland Heron 2D	EC-ANZ	14117	Aviaco	Crashed	nr Palma, Spain	4	*
15.11.57	Short Solent 3	G-AKNU	S.1299	Aquila Airways	Crashed	Chessell Down, IoW, Hants, UK	46	0
16.11.57	de Havilland Canada Beaver	JZ-PAB	*	KLM Royal Dutch Airlines	Crashed	nr Morauke, Indonesia	*	*
17.11.57	Vickers Viscount 802	G-AOHP	165	British European Airways	Damaged in forced landing	nr Copenhagen, Denmark	0	2
21.11.57	Bristol 170 Freighter 31	ZK-AYH	12828	Straights Air Freight Express	Crashed after wing failed	Christchurch, New Zealand	4	*
25.11.57	de Havilland DH.89A Dragon Rapide	VP-YOY	6678	Gibb Coyne & Sager (Kariba) Ltd	Written off	Kariba, Southern Rhodesia	*	*
28.11.57	Douglas DC-6B	SE-BDP	43747	Scandinavian Airlines System	Belly landed	Norrkoping, Sweden	*	*
03.12.57	Ilyushin IL-14P	SSSR-L1657	*	Aeroflot	Overran on landing	Helsinki, Finland	0	*
04.12.57	Douglas DC-3	CF-DGJ	14009/25454	Eldorado Aviation	Crashed	Fort McMurray, Canada	*	*
06.12.57	Lockheed 1049G Super Constellation	F-BHMK	4670	Air France	Crashed on landing	Paris, France	0	*
07.12.57	Scottish Aviation Twin Pioneer 3	G-AOEO	503	Scottish Airlines	Crashed	Tripoli, Libya	*	*
08.12.57	Douglas DC-4	LV-AHZ	27227	Aerolineas Argentinas	Crashed in storm	Bolivar, Argentina	61	0
10.12.57	Douglas DC-3	CF-GKV	13837/25282	Northern Wings	Crashed	Jeannine Lake, PQ, Canada	3	*
11.12.57	de Havilland Dragon 1	VH-URE	6029	Adelaide Airways	Crashed	Katherine, NT, Australia	*	*
16.12.57	de Havilland Dove 5	OE-FAC	04500	Aero Transport	Undershot on landing prior to delivery	Leavesden, Herts, UK	*	*
17.12.57	Miles Aerovan 4	G-AJKP	6401	Meridian Air Maps	Crashed	Oldbury, Warks, UK	*	*
21.12.57	Caudron Goeland	F-BAPI	8910/1106	Air France	Damaged beyond repair	Cormeilles, France	*	*
22.12.57	Curtiss C-46	ZP-CBM	30554	Paraguay Air Services	Crashed	Off Ara Cruz, Brazil	*	*
23.12.57	Avro York	G-AMUN	–	Scottish Airlines	Crashed on approach	Stansted, Essex, UK	4	*
oo.oo.57	Budd Conestoga	HK-344X	*	Aero Llanos	Crashed after wing fire	Colombia	*	*
oo.oo.57	Boeing 247D	XA-GUV	1690	Servicios Aereos Nacionales	Crashed	Mexico	*	*
03.01.58	Douglas DC-3	PP-VDL	4115	Varig	Crashed	Porto Alegre, Brazil	*	*
08.01.58	Douglas DC-3	F-BAOA	11708	Air France	Written off	Poitiers, France	*	*
11.01.58	Fairchild C-82 Packet	PP-CEH	10115	Cruzeiro	Crashed in bay	Rio de Janeiro, Brazil	*	*
15.01.58	de Havilland Dove 1	G-AOCE	04044	East Anglian Flying Services	Damaged in forced landing on beach	Dungeness Point, Kent, UK	0	*
15.01.58	Lockheed Vega 5	NC47M	099	Alaska Coastal Airlines	Crashed	nr Tenakee, Alaska	1	*

Date	Type	Reg'n	C/n	Operator	Accident	Location	F	S
16.01.58	Fairchild C-82 Packet	PP-CEF	10200	Cruzeiro	Crashed	Belem, Brazil	*	*
16.01.58	Douglas DC-3	N75391	14921/26366	Interior Enterprises	Crashed	Aklavik, YK, Canada	*	*
17.01.58	Avro Anson V	CF-ETG	MDF-276	Riverton Airways	Crashed	Grass River, MN, Canada	*	*
21.01.58	Douglas DC-3	TAM-04	*	Transporte Aereo Militar	Crashed	nr La Paz, Bolivia	11	*
22.01.58	Piper PA-22-150 Tri-Pacer	VQ-ZBF	22-5196	Basutair	Crashed	Mokhotlong, Basutoland	*	*
27.01.58	Avro Anson V	CF-EFZ	MDF-220	Pacific Western Airlines	Crashed	nr Point Radium, Canada	*	*
01.02.58	Douglas DC-4	PP-LEM	18336	Loide Aereo Nacional	Crashed on take-off	Rio de Janeiro, Brazil	5	*
06.02.58	Airspeed Ambassador 2	G-ALZU	5217	British European Airways	Crashed on take-off in snow [8 of Manchester United killed]	Munich, West Germany	23	21
13.02.58	Convair 240-1	N8405H	022	Western Air Lines	Crashed on take-off	Palm Springs, CA, USA	*	*
18.02.58	Tupolev TU-114A	SSSR-L5612	7270102	Aeroflot	Crashed on test flight after engine fire	Kuybishev, RSFSR, USSR	1	*
19.02.58	de Havilland Heron 1B	G-APJS	14001	Gulf Aviation	Crashed into mountain [Found 10.05.58]	Mt Saraceno, Italy	3	0
19.02.58	Tupolev TU-104	SSSR-L5414	1681304	Aeroflot	Crashed on approach out of fuel	Savosteevka, RSFSR, USSR	*	*
26.02.58	Vickers Viking 1	G-AGRT	111	Eagle Aviation	Destroyed by fire on ground	El Adem, Libya	0	*
27.02.58	Bristol 170 Freighter 21	G-AICS	12762	Silver City Airways	Crashed into hill on approach	Horwich, Lancs, UK	35	7
oo.02.58	Douglas DC-4	N37474	27238	California Eastern Airlines	Written off	Location Unknown	*	*
01.03.58	Convair 240-0	N94213	023	American Airlines	Crashed when u/c retracted on take-off	New Haven, CT, USA	*	*
02.03.58	Bell 47J	ET-H-2	1579	Ethiopian Airlines	Crashed	Saio, Ethiopia	*	*
07.03.58	Vickers Viking 1B	SU-AGN	196	Misrair	Crashed	nr Port Said, Egypt	8	*
10.03.58	Douglas DC-7B	N846D	45452	Douglas Aircraft	Crashed before delivery	USA	*	*
17.03.58	Martin 404	N496A	14244	Eastern Air Lines	Destroyed by fire on landing	Melbourne, FL, USA	*	*
22.03.58	Douglas DC-3	PI-C262	*	Fleming Airways System Transport	Written off	Location Unknown	*	*
24.03.58	Douglas DC-3	VT-CYN	19988	Indian Airlines	Crashed	Kathmandu, Nepal	20	*
25.03.58	Douglas DC-7C	N5904	45072	Braniff Airlines	Crashed after engine fire on take-off	Miami, FL, USA	9	*
25.03.58	Bristol 170 Freighter 21E	HZ-AAB	12783	Saudi Arabian Airlines	Crashed on landing	Guriat, Saudi Arabia	*	*
26.03.58	Avro Anson I	F-BGOG	–	Societe General Photo-Topographie	Written off	Bilbao, Spain	*	*
30.03.58	Curtiss C-46	TI-1019	120	Aerolineas Nacionales	Forced down by rebels & set on fire	Havana, Cuba	*	*
01.04.58	Handley Page Hermes 4A	G-ALDV	HP.81/22	Skyways	Crashed due to jammed elevators	Meesden Green, Herts, UK	3	*
02.04.58	Junkers Ju.52/3m	HC-SND	5109	Transportes Aereos Orientales	Crashed	Quito, Ecuador	3	*
04.04.58	Beechcraft E-18S	4R-AAR	BA-343	Department of Survey	Written off	Location Unknown	*	*
06.04.58	Vickers Viscount 745D	N7437	135	Capital Airlines	Crashed following stall	Midland, MI, USA	47	0
07.04.58	Douglas DC-3	HC-ACL	19779	AREA	Crashed	Mt Illiniza, Ecuador	32	*
10.04.58	Douglas DC-3	EC-ABN	7346	Iberia	Damaged beyond repair	Palma, Balearic Is, Spain	*	*
11.04.58	Convair 240-12	SP-LPB	155	LOT Polish Airlines	Crashed	Warsaw, Poland	*	*
14.04.58	de Havilland Heron 2D	EC-ANJ	14113	Aviaco	Crashed	Off Castell de Fels, Spain	16	*
16.04.58	Beechcraft C18S	JA5036	5944	Operator Unknown	Written off	Chofu, Japan	*	*
20.04.58	Douglas C-54A	F-BELK	7451	Air France	Forced landing	In-Salah, Algeria	*	*
21.04.58	Douglas DC-7	N6328C	45142	United Air Lines	Mid-air collision with USAF F-100F 56-3755	Arden, NV, USA	47(2)	0
28.04.58	Vickers Viscount 802	G-AORC	254	British European Airways	Crashed	Craigie, Ayrshire, UK	0	5
02.05.58	de Havilland DH.89A Dragon Rapide	F-LAAF	6935	Cie Veha-Akat	Written off	Laos	*	*
09.05.58	Fairchild F-27	N1027	0001	Fairchild Aircraft	Damaged when u/c retracted during static tests	Hagerstown, MO, USA	0	0
10.05.58	Boeing Stratoliner	N75385	2002	Quaker City Airways	Crashed on test flight	nr Madras, OR, USA	*	*
15.05.58	Convair 240-7	AP-AEH	052	Pakistan International Airlines	Crashed on take-off	New Delhi, India	21{2}	*
16.05.58	Douglas DC-3	G-AGHP	9408	British European Airways	Crashed during storm	Chatenoy, France	3	*
18.05.58	Douglas DC-7C	OO-SFA	45157	Sabena	Crashed on overshoot	Casablanca, Morocco	65	4
20.05.58	Vickers Viscount 745D	N7410	108	Capital Airlines	Mid-air collision with USAF T-33	Brunswick, MD, USA	11(1)	0
20.05.58	Avro York	G-AMUT	–	Dan-Air	Damaged after overrunning on landing	Luqa, Malta	0	3
25.05.58	Avro York	G-AMUV	–	Dan-Air	Forced landing after engine fire	Gurgaon, India	4	*
31.05.58	Douglas DC-3	F-BHKV	20001	Air France	Crashed	South west of Algiers, Algeria	14	*
31.05.58	Curtiss C-46	N1302N	22479	Reeve Aleutian Airlines	Crashed after take-off due to shifting cargo	Driftwood Bay, Alaska	*	*
31.05.58	Curtiss C-46	PP-BTB	33304	Paraense Transportes Aereos	Crashed on take-off	Rio de Janeiro, Brazil	4	*
02.06.58	Lockheed 749A Constellation	XA-MEV	2665	Aeronaves de Mexico	Crashed in mountains	nr Guadalajara, Mexico	45	0
02.06.58	Boeing Stratocruiser	N1023V	15923	Pan American World Airways	Damaged in belly landing	Manila, Philippines	*	*
04.06.58	Douglas DC-3	N49553	4820	Capital Airlines	Destroyed	Martinsburg, VA, USA	1	*
06.06.58	Hunting Percival Prince 4D	G-AMOT	P.50/47	Hunting Aerosurveys	Damaged in belly landing	Mackinnon Road Airfield, Kenya	*	*

Date	Type	Reg'n	C/n	Operator	Accident	Location	F	S
07.06.58	Consolidated PBY-5A Catalina	HK-811	*	TALA	Written off	Location Unknown	*	*
10.06.58	Douglas DC-6	LV-ADV	43034	Aerolineas Argentinas	Forced landing	Off Ilha Grande, Brazil	*	*
16.06.58	Convair 440-59	PP-CEP	493	Cruzeiro	Crashed on approach	Curitiba, Brazil	21	*
19.06.58	Curtiss C-46	LX-LAA	22422	Luxair	U/c collapsed on landing	Stuttgart, West Germany	*	*
25.06.58	Douglas DC-3	VT-COJ	10051	Indian Airlines	Crashed on take-off	Mahanbari, India	4	*
28.06.58	Hurel Dubois/Miles HDM.105	G-AHDM	105/1009	Miles Aircraft	Damaged beyond repair	Shoreham, Sussex, UK	*	*
08.07.58	Avro Nineteen 2	G-ANWW	–	Fairey Air Surveys	Crashed	Maidenhead Thicket, Berks, UK	*	*
09.07.58	Douglas DC-3	VT-CYM	19317	Indian Airlines	Crashed	Dacca, Pakistan	3	*
13.07.58	Douglas DC-3	CF-QBG	13337	Quebecair	Destroyed in hangar fire	Rimouski, PQ, Canada	*	*
13.07.58	Douglas DC-3	CF-QBF	12092	Quebecair	Destroyed in hangar fire	Rimouski, PQ, Canada	*	*
13.07.58	Douglas DC-3	CF-QBE	9649	Quebecair	Destroyed in hangar fire	Rimouski, PQ, Canada	*	*
13.07.58	Douglas DC-3	CF-QBD	3256	Quebecair	Destroyed in hangar fire	Rimouski, PQ, Canada	*	*
13.07.58	Douglas DC-3	CF-QBH	20219	Quebecair	Destroyed in hangar fire	Rimouski, PQ, Canada	*	*
17.07.58	Curtiss C-46	HI-16	442	Dominicana	Crashed on take-off	Cuidad Trujillo, Dominican Republic	2	*
28.07.58	Boeing B-17G-DL	CP-623	32391	Lloyd Aereo Boliviano	Crashed	El Alto, Bolivia	*	*
oo.07.58	Beechcraft C-45G	HC-ACR	AF-072	Operator Unknown	Written off	Location Unknown	*	*
09.08.58	Vickers Viscount 748D	VP-YNE	102	Central African Airways	Crashed on approach	Benghazi, Libya	36	18
11.08.58	Avro York	OD-ACJ	1306	Trans Mediterranean Airways	Damaged beyond repair	Dharan, Saudi Arabia	0	*
12.08.58	Douglas DC-4	PP-LEQ	10544	Loide Aereo Nacional	Crashed on approach	Maraso Bay, Brazil	10	*
12.08.58	Douglas DC-3	JA5045	7336	All Nippon Airways	Crashed	Sakiya Saugye, Japan	33	*
14.08.58	Lockheed 1049H Super Constellation	PH-LKM	4841	KLM Royal Dutch Airlines	Crashed	Off Shannon, Eire	99	0
15.08.58	de Havilland Heron 1B	G-AMYU	14017	Jersey Airlines	Crash landed	Guernsey	*	*
15.08.58	Convair 240-2	N90670	090	Northeast Airlines	Crashed on approach in bad weather	Nantucket, MA, USA	25	*
15.08.58	Tupolev TU-104A	SSSR-L5442	*	Aeroflot	Crashed	nr Chita, RSFSR, USSR	64	0
19.08.58	Douglas DC-3	PP-CDI	4684	Cruzeiro	Crashed	Itajai, Brazil	*	*
20.08.58	Avro Anson V	CF-FOF	MDF-89	Pacific Western Airlines	Damaged beyond repair	Cambridge Bay, NWT, Canada	*	*
25.08.58	Beechcraft E-18S	4R-AAS	BA-376	Department of Survey	Written off	Location Unknown	*	*
28.08.58	Douglas DC-6B	N575	45200	Northwest Airlines	Struck fence on take-off & caught fire	Minneapolis, MN, USA	0	*
30.08.58	Handley Page Herald 100	G-AODE	147	Handley Page	Crashed	Godalming, Surrey, UK	0	8
02.09.58	Vickers Viking 1	G-AIJE	127	Independent Air Travel	Crashed due to pilot fatigue	Southall, Middx, UK	3{2}	*
05.09.58	Curtiss C-46	PP-LDX	30288	Loide Aereo Nacional	Crashed on approach	Campina Grande, Brazil	13	*
08.09.58	Douglas C-54A	VT-DIA	3094	Indian Airlines	Damaged on landing	Madras, India	*	*
09.09.58	Lockheed 1049H Super Constellation	N6920C	4822	Flying Tiger Line	Crashed	Atsugi, Japan	8	*
16.09.58	Curtiss C-46	HK-514	30363	Sociedad Aeronautica Medellin	Crashed	nr Medellin, Colombia	0	*
21.09.58	de Havilland DH.86	G-ACZP	2321	V.H.Bellamy	Damaged on landing	Madrid, Spain	0	*
22.09.58	Convair 240-2	PP-VCK	039	Varig	Crashed on approach	Brasilia, Brazil	*	*
22.09.58	Douglas DC-3	PP-NAR	14574/26019	Navegacao Aerea Brasiliera	Crashed	Barrairas, Brazil	*	*
24.09.58	de Havilland Dove 1	EP-ACF	04060	Iran Air	Crashed into mound after aborting take-off	Khaneh, Iran	*	*
25.09.58	Douglas DC-3	CF-TET	13393	Transair	Crashed	Coal Harbour, NWT, Canada	*	*
26.09.58	de Havilland Dove 1	VR-NAY	04096	West African Airways	Crashed	Port Harcourt, Nigeria	*	*
29.09.58	Avro York	OD-ADB	1307	Middle East Airlines	Crashed	Mediterranean Sea	5	0
08.10.58	Avro York	OD-ACP	1231	Trans Mediterranean Airways	Destroyed by fire on ground	Beirut, Lebanon	0	*
08.10.58	Avro Anson V	CF-FJL	BRC-1559	Pacific Western Airlines	Crashed	DEW Site 'CAM C', NWT, Canada	*	*
14.10.58	Lockheed 1049E Super Constellation	YV-C-ANC	4575	Linea Aeropostal Venezolana	Crashed	Mt Alto del Cedro, Venezuela	24	0
15.10.58	Douglas C-47A	TAM-03	13839	Transporte Aereo Militar	Crashed	Villa Montes, Bolivia	20	*
17.10.58	Tupolev TU-104A	SSSR-42362	*	Aeroflot	Crashed	nr Kanash, RSFSR, USSR	80	0
17.10.58	Vickers Viking 1B	D-BELA	250	Deutsche Flugdienst	Forced landing after fire	Zele, Belgium	0	*
22.10.58	Vickers Viscount 701C	G-ANHC	063	British European Airways	Mid-air collision with Italian Air Force F-86	Anzio, Italy	31(0)	0
22.10.58	Douglas DC-3	G-AMVB	14637/26082	Hunting Aerosurveys	Destroyed during refuelling	Masjid-i-Sulaiman, Iran	*	*
01.11.58	Vickers Viscount 755D	CU-T603	091	Cubana	Crashed out of fuel	Nipe Bay, Cuba	17	3
03.11.58	Douglas DC-3	YE-AAB	4345	Yemen Airlines	Crashed	nr Rome, Italy	8	*
04.11.58	Bristol 170 Freighter 21	G-AGVB	12731	Silver City Airways	Crashed into beacon on landing	Le Touquet, France	*	*
08.11.58	Douglas DC-3	TAM-05	*	Transporte Aereo Militar	Crashed	Location Unknown	*	*

Date	Type	Reg'n	C/n	Operator	Accident	Location	F	S
09.11.58	Martin Mariner	*	*	Aerolineas Topografica	Crashed	North Atlantic	42	*
10.11.58	Vickers Viscount 724	CF-TGL	043	Trans Canada Airlines	Struck by crashing SWA Constellation N6503C	New York, NY, USA	0(0)	*
10.11.58	Lockheed 1049D Super Constellation	N6503C	4165	Seaboard & Western Airlines	Crashed on take-off & struck TCA Viscount CF-TGL	New York, NY, USA	0(0)	*
11.11.58	Curtiss C-46	LV-FTP	30356	Transcontinental Airlines	Crashed	Buenos Aires, Argentina	*	*
14.11.58	Douglas DC-3	CN-CCJ	13805/25250	Royal Air Maroc	Damaged beyond repair	Tangiers, Morocco	*	*
16.11.58	Curtiss C-46	N1301N	22480	Capitol Airlines	Crashed into mountains	Fort Collins, CO, USA	2	*
25.11.58	Caudron Goeland	F-BAPQ	8918/1114	Air France	Damaged beyond repair	Cormeilles, France	*	*
27.11.58	Caudron Goeland	OO-CCK	10067/1181	Congo Motor	Written off	Belgian Congo	*	*
02.12.58	Vickers Viscount 732	G-ANRR	074	Clanair	Crashed	Frimley, Surrey, UK	6	0
03.12.58	Lockheed PV-2 Harpoon	CP-648	151218	J.Villaroel	Written off	Laja, Bolivia	*	*
04.12.58	SNCASE Languedoc	EC-ANR	28	Aviaco	Crashed	Guadarrama Mts, Spain	21	*
10.12.58	de Havilland Heron 1B	PK-GHP	14032	Garuda Indonesian Airlines	Damaged beyond repair	Djakarta, Indonesia	*	*
24.12.58	Bristol Britannia 312	G-AOVD	13235	British Overseas Airways Corporation	Crashed	nr Hurn, Hants, UK	9	3
24.12.58	Lockheed 749A Constellation	F-BAZX	2527	Air France	Crashed on approach	Vienna, Austria	0	*
26.12.58	Douglas DC-6B	F-BGTZ	43827	UAT	Crashed in heavy rain on take-off	Salisbury, Southern Rhodesia	3	*
29.12.58	Boeing B-17F-BO	CP-579	3119	Frigorificos Grigota	Crashed	Uncio, Bolivia	*	*
30.12.58	Saab Scandia	PP-SQE	103	VASP	Crashed on take-off	Rio de Janeiro, Brazil	21	*
oo.oo.58	Vickers Viscount 663	VX217	002	Ministry of Supply	Damaged by fire	Seighford, Staffs, UK	0	*
oo.oo.58	de Havilland DH.89A Dragon Rapide	F-LAAC	6729	Cie Veha-Akat	Written off	Laos	*	*
oo.oo.58	de Havilland DH.89A Dragon Rapide	F-LAAE	6845	Cie Veha-Akat	Written off	Laos	*	*
oo.oo.58	Boeing B-17G	N5845N	*	Aero Service Corporation	Crashed	Location Unknown	*	*
04.01.59	Curtiss C-46	OB-QAL-487	26655	TAPSA	Damaged on landing	Moyabamba, Peru	0	*
05.01.59	Avro York	OD-ACE	–	Trans Mediterranean Airways	Damaged beyond repair	Brindisi, Italy	0	*
06.01.59	Curtiss C-46	PP-LDH	30350	Paraense Transportes Aereos	Crashed on take-off	Rio de Janeiro, Brazil	0	*
06.01.59	Douglas DC-3	XH-SAA	19667	Servicios Aereos de Honduras	Crashed	Pena Blanca Mt, Guatemala	5	*
08.01.59	Douglas DC-3	N18941	2007	Southeast Airlines	Crashed	Mt Holston, TN, USA	10	*
11.01.59	Lockheed 1049G Super Constellation	D-ALAK	4602	Lufthansa	Crashed on landing	Rio de Janeiro, Brazil	36	3
14.01.59	Curtiss C-46	N1240N	22404	California Air Freight	Crashed	Sequoia National Park, CA, USA	2	*
16.01.59	Curtiss C-46	LV-GED	30514	Austral	Crashed on landing	Mar del Plata, Argentina	51	*
22.01.59	Convair 240-2	JY-ACB	055	Air Jordan	Crashed	Dabouk, Jordan	10	*
27.01.59	Avro Super Trader 4	G-AGRG	1255	Air Charter	Destroyed by fire on take-off	Brindisi, Italy	2	*
01.02.59	Lockheed 18 Lodestar	ZS-ASV	2036	South African Airways	Crashed	Durban, South Africa	*	*
01.02.59	Douglas DC-3	N17314	1924	General Airways	Crashed	Kerville, TX, USA	3	*
03.02.59	Lockheed Electra 188A	N6101A	1015	American Airlines	Crashed short of runway	La Guardia, NY, USA	65	8
03.02.59	Beechcraft Bonanza	*	*	Dwyers Flying Service	Crashed in storm [Buddy Holly,Richie Valens,Big Bopper died]	nr Mason City, IA, USA	4	0
09.02.59	de Havilland DH.89A Dragon Rapide	VT-ARY	6681	Jokai (Assam) Tea Co	Crashed	nr Mohanbari, India	*	*
17.02.59	Vickers Viscount 794D	TC-SEV	429	Turk Hava Yollari	Crashed on approach [Turkish PM survived]	Gatwick, Surrey, UK	15	10
18.02.59	Curtiss C-46	N68823	26818	Southern Cross Airways	Crashed after engine failure	Belem, Chile	5	*
18.02.59	Lockheed 10E Electra	ZK-BUT	1138	Trans-Island Airways	Damaged in ground loop	Christchurch, New Zealand	0	*
20.02.59	Douglas DC-7C	N740PA	44882	Pan American World Airways	Crashed on landing	San Francisco, CA, USA	*	*
24.02.59	de Havilland Canada Caribou	CF-LKI-X	003	de Havilland Aircraft of Canada	Crashed after tail broke up	Canada	0	2
04.03.59	VEB 152	DM-ZYA	1	VEB-Dresden	Crashed	Dresden, East Germany	4	0
05.03.59	Vickers Viscount 763	YS-09C	082	TACA International Airlines	Crashed after take-off	Managua, Nicaragua	15	*
12.03.59	Douglas DC-3	VT-CYH	12493	Indian Airlines	Crashed	nr Tobu, India	*	*
12.03.59	Curtiss C-46	CP-552	51	Corporacion Boliviano de Fomento	Crashed	Charagua, Bolivia	*	*
13.03.59	Bristol 170 Freighter 21	EC-ADH	12776	Aviaco	Crashed on landing	Mahon, Minorca, Spain	0	18
15.03.59	Convair 240-0	N94273	150	American Airlines	Crashed	Chicago, IL, USA	*	*
29.03.59	Douglas DC-3	VT-CGI	20176	Indian Airlines	Crashed	nr Silchar, India	24	*
29.03.59	Nord Noratlas	F-BGZB	002	UAT	Crashed	nr Boda, Central African Republic	*	*
30.03.59	Curtiss C-46	N7840B	30242	Riddle Airlines	Crashed	Alma, GA, USA	2	*
01.04.59	Bell 47G-2	ET-H-1	1415	Ethiopian Airlines	Crashed	Dessie, Ethiopia	*	*
10.04.59	Boeing Stratocruiser	N1033V	15933	Pan American World Airways	Crashed short of runway	Juneau, AK, USA	*	*
17.04.59	Curtiss C-46	XA-MIS	22586	Tigres Voladores	Crashed	Puerto Kino, Mexico	26	*
23.04.59	Avro Super Trader 4B	G-AGRH	1256	Air Charter	Crashed	Mt Suphan Dag, Turkey	*	*

Date	Type	Reg'n	C/n	Operator	Accident	Location	F	S
25.04.59	Douglas DC-3	EP-ACL	9308	Iran Air	Crashed	Kerman, Iran	*	*
30.04.59	Douglas DC-3	F-BAII	14105/25550	Air France	Crashed	Poitiers, France	*	*
02.05.59	Douglas DC-3	OE-FDA	12210	Austrian Airlines	Crashed	Alfabia Peak, Majorca, Spain	5	*
06.05.59	Curtiss C-46	PP-BTA	26901	Paraense Transportes Aereos	Crashed after explosion	Pedro Afonso, Brazil	*	*
06.05.59	de Havilland Dove 2A	G-ALEC	04402	Lec Refrigeration	Crashed during air display	Cardiff, UK	4	*
08.05.59	Curtiss C-46	OB-QAM-488	26709	Transportes Aereos Peruanas	Crashed on take-off	Cuzco, Peru	0	*
12.05.59	Vickers Viscount 745D	N7463	287	Capital Airlines	Broke up in turbulence	Chase, MD, USA	31	0
12.05.59	Lockheed C-69 Constellation	N2735A	1978	Capital Airlines	Crashed on landing	Charleston, WV, USA	2	*
13.05.59	Curtiss C-46	OB-WBP-507	26829	Transportes Aereos Peruanas	Crashed	nr Tournavista, Peru	12	*
15.05.59	Douglas DC-3	LV-AFW	19790	Aerolineas Argentinas	Crashed on take-off	Mar del Plata, Argentina	10	*
18.05.59	Vickers Viscount 815	AP-AJC	335	Pakistan International Airlines	Overran on landing	Rawalpindi, Pakistan	0	*
21.05.59	Curtiss C-46	CC-CIA-0497	30482	Lineas Aereas Interpolar	Crashed into mountain	Chimbote, Peru	8	*
21.05.59	de Havilland DH.89A Dragon Rapide	G-AHLL	6576	Operator Unknown	Crashed	St Just, Cornwall, UK	*	*
16.06.59	Beechcraft C18S	YV-C-LBL	6825	Lebca	Written off	Location Unknown	*	*
19.06.59	de Havilland Dove 1	OO-DAL	04011	Satroma	Crashed into pylon	Cugny, France	2	*
19.06.59	Noorduyn UC-64 Norseman	HK-454	*	Operator Unknown	Written off	Location Unknown	*	*
22.06.59	Douglas DC-6B	N5026K	44426	Pan American World Airways	Crashed on take-off	Shannon, Eire	*	*
23.06.59	Douglas DC-4	HK-135	10418	Avianca	Crashed	Cerro Baco, Peru	14	*
26.06.59	Lockheed 1649A Starliner	N7313C	1015	Trans World Airlines	Crashed after lightning strike	Milan, Italy	68	0
oo.06.59	Avro Anson I	ZK-BCL	–	Southland Scenic Air Services	Destroyed by fire	Queenstown, New Zealand	*	*
05.07.59	Avro York	EP-ADE	–	Persian Air Services	Crashed	nr Kuwait	0	*
07.07.59	de Havilland DH.89A Dragon Rapide	G-AHPT	6478	Don Everall Aviation	Crashed	nr Leverstock, Herts, UK	*	*
09.07.59	Boeing Stratocruiser	N90941	15957	Pan American World Airways	Damaged in belly landing	Tokyo, Japan	*	*
10.07.59	Curtiss C-46	TI-1022	*	Aeronaves Nacionales	Shot down by Nicaraguan fighters	Nicaragua	60	*
14.07.59	Douglas DC-3	LV-ACM	9490	Aerolineas Argentinas	Crashed	Santiago del Estado, Argentina	*	*
15.07.59	Curtiss C-46	PT-BEE	27051	Paraense Transportes Aereos	Crashed after engine fire	Babaculandia, Brazil	*	*
19.07.59	Lockheed 1049G Super Constellation	VT-DIN	4667	Air India	Crashed on landing	Bombay, India	0	*
28.07.59	Vickers Viking 1	G-AHPH	141	East Anglian Flying Services	U/c collapsed	Southend, Essex, UK	0	*
29.07.59	Northrop C-125 Raider	CP-631	2508	Corporacion Minera de Bolivia	Damaged on landing	Achocalla, Bolivia	*	*
02.08.59	Douglas DC-3	N28324	2254	Capital Airlines	Damaged when struck on ground by Northwest Stratocruiser	Pittsburgh, PA, USA	*(*)	*
03.08.59	Douglas DC-3	VT-DGP	9549	Kalinga Airlines	Crashed	Sagone, India	6	*
04.08.59	Ford 5-AT-C Tri-Motor	N8419	5-AT-058	Johnson Flying Service	Crashed	Moose Creek, ID, USA	4	2
05.08.59	Beechcraft C18S Expeditor	G-APBX	0269	Falcon Airways	Damaged in ground fire	Hurn, Hants, UK	*	*
14.08.59	Vickers Viscount 815	AP-AJE	337	Pakistan International Airlines	Crashed	Karachi, Pakistan	2	*
14.08.59	Boeing Stratocruiser	N74607	15953	Northwest Airlines	Damaged by fire	Minneapolis, MN, USA	*	*
15.08.59	Boeing 707-123	N7514A	17641	American Airlines	Crashed after simulated engine failure	Calverton, NY, USA	5	*
15.08.59	Douglas DC-3	TI-1005C	4959	Lacsa	Crashed	San Isidro del General, Costa Rica	*	*
19.08.59	Douglas DC-3	G-AMZD	16112/32860	Transair	Crashed	nr Barcelona, Spain	32	*
21.08.59	Martin 202A	N93202	14072	Pacific Air Lines	Damaged in ground collision with C-46 N111E	Burbank, CA, USA	*	*
23.08.59	de Havilland Heron 2B	VP-BAO	14052	Leeward Islands Air Transport	Crashed	St Kitts	0	*
27.08.59	de Havilland Comet 4	LV-AHP	06411	Aerolineas Argentinas	Crashed on approach	Asuncion, Paraguay	2	*
27.08.59	Douglas DC-3	PP-AVY	13632	REAL	Damaged beyond repair	Maringa, Brazil	*	*
02.09.59	Curtiss C-46	N5140B	26809	Aaxico Airlines	Crashed on landing	Dyess AFB, TX, USA	2	*
05.09.59	Vickers Viking 1B	F-BFDN	248	Air Nautic	Crashed	Off Trani Setto, Corsica, France	*	*
08.09.59	Douglas DC-3	*	*	Mexicana	Crashed after bomb explosion	Mexico	2	*
12.09.59	Douglas DC-4	N88900	10504	Pan American World Airways	Crashed	Tegucigalpa, Honduras	3	*
23.09.59	Curtiss C-46	PP-ITI	30498	R.de Paoli	Crashed	Rondonepolis, Brazil	*	*
23.09.59	Saab Scandia	PP-SQV	106	VASP	Crashed on take-off	Sao Paulo, Brazil	20	*
24.09.59	Douglas DC-7C	F-BIAP	45366	T.A. Intercontinentaux	Crashed on take-off	Bordeaux, France	53	*
24.09.59	Douglas C-54B	N63396	10486	Reeve Aleutian Airlines	Crashed	Great Sitkin Is, AK, USA	16	*
25.09.59	Douglas C-54A	HZ-AAF	7474	Saudi Arabian Airlines	Damaged on take-off	Jeddah, Saudi Arabia	*	*
29.09.59	Lockheed Electra 188A	N9705C	1090	Braniff Airlines	Crashed	Buffalo, TX, USA	34	*
03.10.59	Vickers Viscount 757	CF-TGY	143	Trans Canada Airlines	Struck water tower on landing	Toronto, ON, Canada	0	*
10.10.59	Curtiss C-46	LV-FTO	193	Transcontinental Airlines	Crashed due to u/c failure	Cordoba, Argentina	24	*

Date	Type	Reg'n	C/n	Operator	Accident	Location	F	S
19.10.59	Boeing 707-227	N7071	17691	Boeing Airplane Company	Crashed after Dutch roll	Arlington, WA, USA	4	0
25.10.59	Boeing B-17G-DL	CP-626	32450	Corporacion Boliviano de Fomento	Crashed	Caranavi, Bolivia	*	*
29.10.59	Douglas DC-3	SX-BAD	9491	Olympic Airways	Crashed	Athens, Greece	21	0
30.10.59	Douglas DC-3	N55V	20447	Piedmont Airlines	Crashed	Waynesborough, VA, USA	26	*
02.11.59	Douglas DC-3	YA-AAD	18910	Ariana Afghan Airlines	Written off	Location Unknown	*	*
04.11.59	Douglas C-54A	CF-ILI	10360	Wheeler Airlines	Crashed	St Cleophas, PQ, Canada	*	*
05.11.59	Douglas DC-3	N38G	4759	National Aero Sales Corp	Crashed	Burke Lakefront Airport, CO, USA	*	*
15.11.59	Douglas DC-7B	N4891C	45355	Delta Air Lines	Crashed	Gulf of Mexico	40	*
16.11.59	Antonov AN-10	SSSR-11167	*	Aeroflot	Crashed on approach	Lvov, Ukraine, USSR	40	0
17.11.59	Boeing B-17G-BO	CP-625	10285	Lloyd Aereo Boliviano	Crashed	San Lorenzo, Bolivia	*	*
21.11.59	Douglas DC-4	YA-BAG	18367	Ariana Afghan Airlines	Crashed after take-off	Beirut, Lebanon	24	*
21.11.59	Airspeed Consul	G-AJXE	5164	T.D.Keegan	Damaged beyond repair	Elstree, Herts, UK	*	*
22.11.59	Douglas DC-3	PP-NAZ	7387	Navegacao Aerea Brasiliera	Crashed	Rio de Janeiro, Brazil	*	*
24.11.59	Lockheed 1049H Super Constellation	N102R	4824	Trans World Airlines	Crashed on approach	Chicago, IL, USA	*	*
28.11.59	de Havilland Dove 6A	LV-GIT	04487	Sargo S.A.	Crashed	Mount Cachi, Argentina	2	*
01.12.59	Douglas DC-3	YV-C-AKU	4581	Linea Aeropostal Venezolana	Crashed	Caracas, Venezuela	*	*
01.12.59	Martin 202	N174A	9159	Allegheny Airlines	Crashed on approach	Williamsport, PA, USA	25	*
08.12.59	Curtiss C-46	HK-515	26941	Sociedad Aeronautica Medellin	Crashed	Off Cartagena, Colombia	45	*
12.12.59	Scottish Aviation Twin Pioneer 3	G-AOEN	502	Scottish Airlines	Damaged beyond repair on landing	River Zambesi, Mozambique	*	*
12.12.59	Convair 240-6	LV-ADM	035	Aerolineas Argentinas	Crashed on landing	Mendoza, Argentina	*	*
13.12.59	Ilyushin IL-18	*	*	Aeroflot	Crashed into hill	nr Tashkent, Uzbekistan, USSR	29	*
21.12.59	Vickers Viscount 785D	I-LIZT	378	Alitalia	Crashed	Rome, Italy	2	*
22.12.59	Vickers Viscount 827	PP-SRG	401	VASP	Mid-air collision with Brazilian Air Force AT-6	Rio de Janeiro, Brazil	31{10} (1)	0
22.12.59	Vickers Viking 1B	G-AMGG	290	Eagle Aviation	Crashed	Agadir, Morocco	0	36
24.12.59	Douglas DC-3	PK-GDV	13535	Garuda Indonesian Airlines	Crashed	Talang Suak, Indonesia	*	*
28.12.59	Bell 47J	ET-H-6	1751	Ethiopian Airlines	Crashed on landing	Ismala Ghiorgies, Ethiopia	*	*
31.12.59	Douglas DC-3	CP-584	19226	Lloyd Aereo Boliviano	Crashed	nr San Jose de Chiquitos, Bolivia	11	*
00.00.59	Martin B-26 Marauder	N1502	8904	Continental Can Co	Crashed	Location Unknown	*	*
00.00.59	Avro Anson I	VH-BLG	–	E.H.Loneragan	Damaged in forced landing	nr Mudgee, NSW, Australia	*	*

1960–1969

This was the decade in which the jet airliner took over from its piston predecessor. The turbine-powered products of Boeing and Douglas, together with those of BAC, Hawker Siddeley, and Aerospatiale in Europe, had relegated older machines to second and third rank operators by 1969.

A massive increase in air transport followed the advent of the jet. Flying became a regular activity for ordinary people, either to take foreign holidays or for business travel. Visiting a relative on the other side of the world became a real possibility.

The new aircraft and the increase in air services were bound to lead to an upsurge in accidents. However, the jet was to prove itself both reliable and economic, and crashes became less frequent compared with the number of flights undertaken. It did not take long for the jet to become associated with safety and for an aircraft with propellers to be regarded with suspicion by the public at large.

Unfortunately, tragedies did occur. During these ten years there were 19 crashes involving over a hundred fatalities each. Amongst these were a number of incidents which involved aircraft crashing into occupied buildings and inflicting heavy ground casualties.

The worst disaster was the mid-air collision between a TWA Super Constellation and a United DC-8 over New York City in 1960. This resulted in 128 fatalities in the two aircraft plus six more on the ground. The collision of two heavily laden airliners over a major city has been one of the industry's worst nightmares ever since.

The 1960s saw a number of serious and savage wars break out, leading to civil airliner losses.

The aftermath of a BKS Ambassador (G-AMAD) crash at Heathrow on 3 July 1968 which killed six. Two BEA Tridents lost their tails, with G-ARPT being written off. The second aircraft (G-ARPI) was repaired but tragically crashed at Staines, 18 June 1972. (Popperfoto)

These included civil war in the Congo (claiming the life of Dag Hammerskjold, UN Secretary General, in a DC-6 crash), the Six Day War between the Arab nations and Israel, the Biafran War in Nigeria and the Vietnam War. Losses were due both to direct military action and to the unusual problems of flying in a war zone. The high attrition rate of transport aircraft in Biafra attested to this.

The most prominent hostile act took place on 28 December 1968 when Israeli commandos raided Beirut Airport, Lebanon, in retaliation for an earlier attack on an El Al aircraft. Fourteen airliners were destroyed in the attack although no fatalities resulted.

The British air transport industry suffered six major crashes in the 1960s. These involved both scheduled and charter carriers, including a DC-7 in the Cameroons, Britannias in Austria and Yugoslavia, and two crashes in two days involving a DC-4 in France and a Canadair Argonaut at Stockport. However, the worst was the breaking up in turbulence of a BOAC 707 over Mt Fuji, killing 124 people.

First write-offs 1960–1969

(* military example crashed earlier)

Sud Aviation Caravelle	19.01.60
Convair 880	23.05.60
Fokker F-27 Friendship	10.06.60
Douglas DC-8	16.12.60
Antonov AN-24	29.07.62
Aviation Traders Carvair	28.12.62
Antonov AN-12	02.04.63
Convair 990	30.05.63
Tupolev TU-124	21.08.63
BAC One-Eleven	22.10.63
Convair 580	21.12.63
Rockwell Sabreliner	28.01.64
Lear Jet	04.06.64
Ilyushin IL-62	00.00.64
Hawker Siddeley Argosy	04.07.65
Hawker Siddeley HS.748	11.07.65
Boeing 727	16.08.65
Vickers Vanguard	27.10.65
Hawker Siddeley HS.125	24.02.66
Canadair CL-44	21.03.66
Hawker Siddeley Trident	03.06.66
Rockwell Jet Commander	26.09.66
Douglas DC-9	01.10.66
Britten-Norman Islander	09.11.66
NAMC YS-11	13.11.66
Convair 640	23.01.67
Short Skyvan	06.03.67
DHC Twin Otter	11.03.67
Grumman Gulfstream I	11.07.67
Dassault Falcon	01.10.67
Lockheed Hercules	11.04.68*
Mitsubishi MU-2	21.12.68
BAC VC-10	28.12.68
Beechcraft 99	20.06.69
Handley Page Jetstream	29.09.69
Tupolev TU-134	19.11.69

A tragedy at Shannon. This charter DC-6 (N90773) of President Airlines crashed on take-off on 10 September 1961, killing all 84 passengers and crew. (Popperfoto)

Date	Type	Reg'n	C/n	Operator	Accident	Location	F	S
03.01.60	Lockheed 649 Constellation	N110A	2531	Eastern Air Lines	U/c collapsed on landing	Philadelphia, PA, USA	*	*
03.01.60	Douglas DC-3	VT-CGG	12821	Indian Airlines	Shot down by Chinese forces	Taksing, China	8	*
05.01.60	Vickers Viscount 701	G-AMNY	006	British European Airways	Crashed into control tower after brake failure	Luqa, Malta	0	*
06.01.60	Douglas DC-6B	N8225H	43742	National Airlines	Crashed due to bomb explosion	Bolivia, NC, USA	34	*
07.01.60	Vickers Viscount 802	G-AOHU	169	British European Airways	Damaged by fire after u/c collapsed on landing	Heathrow, London, UK	0	*
11.01.60	Bristol Sycamore 4	VH-INO	13403	Australian National Airways	Crashed	Nundle State Forest, NSW, Australia	*	*
12.01.60	Scottish Aviation Twin Pioneer 2	PI-C430	562	Philippine Air Lines	Crashed on landing	Bulacan, Philippines	*	*
18.01.60	Vickers Viscount 745D	N7462	217	Capital Airlines	Crashed due to icing & engine failure	Holdcroft, VA, USA	50	0
19.01.60	Sud Aviation Caravelle 1	OY-KRB	014	Scandinavian Airlines System	Crashed on approach	Ankara, Turkey	42	*
21.01.60	Lockheed 1049G Super Constellation	HK-177	4556	Avianca	Crashed on landing	Montego Bay, Jamaica	37	9
26.01.60	de Havilland Heron 2D	CR-TAI	14132	Transportes Aereos de Timor	Crashed	Off Port Darwin, NT, Australia	9	*
26.01.60	Fairchild C-82 Packet	PP-CEM	10180	Cruzeiro	Damaged beyond repair	Rio de Janeiro, Brazil	*	*
29.01.60	Curtiss C-46	CF-PWD	2940	Pacific Western Airlines	Crashed after engine failure	Port Hardy, BC, Canada	0	*
oo.01.60	Barkley-Grow T8P-1	CF-BLV	03	Pacific Western Airlines	Crashed on take-off	Peace River, AB, Canada	*	*
05.02.60	Douglas DC-4	CP-609	10510	Lloyd Aereo Boliviano	Crashed due to engine fire	Laguna de Huana-Costa, Bolivia	59	*
07.02.60	Auster V	G-AKTF	1443	Skyways Coach Air	Crashed	Beachy Head, Sussex, UK	*	*
10.02.60	Avro Anson I	VH-FIB	–	Flinders Island Airways	Crashed into hill	nr Loch, Vic, Australia	2	*
13.02.60	Curtiss C-46	N46Q	26684	Associated Air Transport	Crashed out of fuel	McGuire AFB, NJ, USA	0	*
19.02.60	de Havilland Dove 1B	G-AMKT	04291	Hunting Surveys	Crashed out of fuel	Walton, Malaya	*	*
20.02.60	de Havilland Comet 4	LV-AHO	06410	Aerolineas Argentinas	Damaged on landing	Buenos Aires, Argentina	0	*
22.02.60	Douglas C-118A Liftmaster	N11817	44653	Alaska Airlines	Struck high ground on approach	Elmendorf AFB, AK, USA	0	*
25.02.60	Douglas DC-3	PP-AXD	13326	REAL	Mid-air collision with USN R6D 131582	Rio de Janeiro, Brazil	30(35)	*
26.02.60	Douglas DC-7C	I-DUVO	45231	Alitalia	Crashed after take-off	Shannon, Eire	34	*
26.02.60	Antonov AN-10	SSSR-11180	*	Aeroflot	Crashed on approach	Lvov, Ukraine, USSR	32	0
29.02.60	Lockheed 1049G Super Constellation	N7101C	4582	Trans World Airlines	U/c collapsed	Chicago, IL, USA	0	*
oo.02.60	Douglas DC-3	AN-ADQ	9212	Lanica	Damaged beyond repair	Location Unknown	*	*
08.03.60	Handley Page Hermes 4A	G-ALDH	HP.81/9	Skyways	U/c collapsed	Heathrow, London, UK	0	*
10.03.60	Scottish Aviation Twin Pioneer 3	G-ANTP	501	Scottish Airlines	Crashed on take-off	Jorhat, India	*	*
16.03.60	Douglas DC-3	JA5018	6006	All Nippon Airways	Mid-air collision with JASDF F-86	Komaki, Japan	3(*)	*
17.03.60	Lockheed Electra 188C	N121US	1057	Northwest Airlines	Broke up in mid-air	Tell City, IN, USA	63	0
18.03.60	Hiller UH-12E	ET-AAD	2026	Ethiopian Airlines	Crashed	Dehanacos, Ethiopia	*	*
20.03.60	Curtiss C-46	HK-516	384/2927	SAMSA	Forced landing after engine failure	Cordoba, Colombia	25	*
20.03.60	Douglas DC-3	OB-PAM-146	16947/34206	Faucett	Crashed	Cerro Machete, Peru	*	*
20.03.60	Consolidated Canso	*	*	Colombian Aico Canso	Crashed on landing	Colombia	6	*
25.03.60	Curtiss C-46	CF-IHQ	448	Wheeler Airlines	Crashed	Quebec, Canada	0	*
05.04.60	Curtiss C-46	AN-AIN	26945	Lanica	Crashed	nr Suina, Nicaragua	2	*
06.04.60	de Havilland Dove 1	LQ-YAU	04192	Sec. de Aeronautica	Crashed	San Juan, Argentina	*	*
12.04.60	de Havilland Dove 1B	G-ALMR	04099	English Electric Co	Crashed landed	Lytham Marsh, Lancs, UK	*	*
12.04.60	Avro Anson I	VH-BAB	–	Brain & Brown Airfreighters	Damaged when u/c collapsed on landing	Moorabbin, Vic, Australia	*	*
14.04.60	Curtiss C-46	CU-C644	*	Avion S.A.	Crashed on take-off	Miami, FL, USA	*	*
15.04.60	Douglas DC-3	CU-T172	11671	Cubana	Destroyed by bombing during civil war	Havana, Cuba	*	*
22.04.60	Douglas C-54A	OO-SBL	3099	Sobelair	Crashed into mountain	Bunia, Belgian Congo	35	*
27.04.60	Ilyushin IL-18	*	*	Aeroflot	Crashed on approach	Sverdlovsk, RSFSR, USSR	*	*
28.04.60	Douglas DC-3	YV-C-AFE	15353/26798	Linea Aeropostal Venezolana	Crashed due to sabotage	Caracas, Venezuela	13	*
03.05.60	Curtiss C-46	PP-NMD	32924	Navegacao Aerea Brasiliera	Crashed on approach	Ramey AFB, Puerto Rico	5	*
12.05.60	Douglas DC-3	PP-CDS	4823	Varig	Struck another aircraft on take-off	Peatas, Brazil	5	*
15.05.60	Douglas DC-4-1009	HB-ILA	43072	Balair	Crashed into mountain	Jebel Marra, Sudan	12	*
17.05.60	Douglas DC-2-267	LV-GGT	2060	Transaer	Damaged beyond repair	El Sosneado, Argentina	*	*
18.05.60	Curtiss C-46	LV-GGJ	22554	Transamerican Air Transport	Crashed due to structural failure [Not found until 21.11.61]	El Sosneado, Argentina	10	0
19.05.60	Curtiss C-46	YV-C-LBG	262	Lebca	Forced landing	David, Panama	*	*
20.05.60	Aerospatiale SE.3130 Alouette II	VQ-ZBG	1090	Basutair	Crashed	Basutoland	*	*
21.05.60	Consolidated C-87 Liberator	CP-618	*	Boliviana de Aviacion	Crashed	El Alto, Bolivia	*	*
23.05.60	Convair 880-22-2	N8804E	16	Delta Air Lines	Crashed after take-off	Atlanta, GA, USA	4	*

Date	Type	Reg'n	C/n	Operator	Accident	Location	F	S
25.05.60	Douglas DC-3	TI-1023	*	Aerolineas Nacionales	Crashed	nr San Jose, Costa Rica	1	*
27.05.60	Avro York	OD-ACD	–	Trans Mediterranean Airways	Crashed on take-off	Tehran, Iran	0	*
29.05.60	Vickers Viking 1A	G-AHOR	118	Air Safaris	Belly landed	Tarbes, France	0	*
10.06.60	Fokker F-27 Friendship 100	VH-TFB	10112	Trans Australia Airlines	Crashed	Off Mackay, Qld, Australia	29	*
14.06.60	Lockheed 749A Constellation	N1554V	2555	Pacific Northern Airlines	Crashed	Mt Gilbert, AK, USA	14	0
20.06.60	de Havilland DH.89A Dragon Rapide	OO-ARN	6785	Air Brousse	Crashed	Luozi, Belgian Congo	*	*
24.06.60	Convair 340-62	PP-YRB	191	REAL	Crashed	Rio de Janeiro, Brazil	53	*
10.07.60	Douglas DC-3	VT-DGS	4273	Gulf Aviation	Crashed	Persian Gulf	16	*
14.07.60	Douglas DC-3	*	*	US Mission to Colombia	Crashed	Mt Pichincha, Ecuador	18	*
14.07.60	Douglas DC-7C	N292	45462	Northwest Airlines	Crashed after wing fire	Off Luzon, Philippines	1	*
14.07.60	Douglas DC-3	PI-C16	13908	Philippine Air Lines	Crashed out of fuel	Off Mindanao, Philippines	*	*
16.07.60	Douglas DC-3	ET-T-18	12926	Ethiopian Airlines	Crashed	nr Bulcha, Ethiopia	1	*
16.07.60	de Havilland DH.89A Dragon Rapide	OY-DZY	6956	Zone-Redningskorpset Flyvetjenesten	Crashed	Kastrup, Denmark	*	*
26.07.60	Beechcraft C18S	JA5037	6240	Operator Unknown	Written off	Miyazaki, Japan	*	*
27.07.60	Sikorsky S-58C	N879	*	Chicago Helicopter Airways	Crashed after losing rotor blade	Forest Park, IL, USA	13	0
31.07.60	Convair 240-4	D-BELU	078	Deutsche Flugdienst	Crashed on approach	Rimini, Italy	1	*
01.08.60	Douglas C-47	TAM-09	9030	Transporte Aereo Militar	Crashed	Tipuani, Bolivia	6	*
15.08.60	Lisunov Li-2P	SP-LAL	1842008	LOT Polish Airlines	Crashed	Off Gdansk, Poland	*	*
15.08.60	Northrop C-125A Raider	PZ-TAO	2505	Surinam Airways	Crashed	Oelemarie, Surinam	*	*
15.08.60	Saab Scandia	PP-SQS	113	VASP	Crashed	Campinas, Argentina	*	*
17.08.60	Ilyushin IL-18	SSSR-75705	189001702	Aeroflot	Crashed after in-flight fire	Kiev, Ukraine, USSR	35	*
24.08.60	Lockheed 1049G Super Constellation	VH-EAC	4606	Qantas	Crashed on take-off	Mauritius	0	*
24.08.60	Vickers Viking 1B	G-AMNK	210	Don Everall Aviation	Crashed	Off Heraklion, Crete, Greece	3	0
24.08.60	Curtiss C-46	PP-BTJ	27021	Paraense Transportes Aereos	Crashed	Rio Jari, Brazil	*	0
24.08.60	Fairchild C-82 Packet	CP-665	*	D.A.C.	Crashed	El Palmar, Bolivia	*	*
29.08.60	Lockheed 1049G Super Constellation	F-BHBC	4622	Air France	Crashed in turbulence	Off Dakar, Senegal	63	0
01.09.60	Douglas DC-4-1009	YK-AAR	43097	Syrian Airways	Crashed	River Congo, Congo	0	14
03.09.60	Douglas DC-4-1009	ZS-CIG	42913	Trek Airways	Damaged in forced landing	nr Assiout, Egypt	*	*
07.09.60	Douglas DC-6	LV-ADS	43031	Aerolineas Argentinas	Crashed in storm	nr Salto, Uruguay	31	*
14.09.60	Lockheed Electra 188A	N6127A	1117	American Airlines	Crashed	La Guardia, NY, USA	0	*
18.09.60	Douglas DC-6AB	N90779	44914	World Airways	Crashed on take-off	Agana, Guam	80	14
22.09.60	Curtiss C-46	PP-BTF	26944	Paraense Transportes Aereos	Crashed on take-off	Belem, Brazil	*	*
24.09.60	Avro Nineteen 2	EP-CAA	–	C.Agar	Damaged beyond repair	Location Unknown	*	*
26.09.60	Vickers Viscount 837	OE-LAF	437	Austrian Airlines	Crashed on approach	Moscow, RSFSR, USSR	30	*
28.09.60	Douglas DC-3	XA-HUS	7388	Mexicana	Crashed on landing	Jucitepec, Mexico	5	*
29.09.60	Vickers Viscount 739B	SU-AKW	427	United Arab Airlines	Crashed	Off Elba, Italy	23	*
04.10.60	Lockheed Electra 188A	N5533	1062	Eastern Air Lines	Crashed on take-off due to bird ingestion	Boston, MA, USA	62	10
06.10.60	de Havilland DH.89A Dragon Rapide	9O-CJT	6925	Air Brousse	Crashed out of fuel	Molegbe, Belgian Congo	*	*
08.10.60	Lisunov Li-2	YR-TAX	18423803	Tarom	Crashed	Mironeasa-Iassy, Romania	*	*
09.10.60	Handley Page Hermes 4	G-ALDC	HP.81/4	Falcon Airways	Crash landed	Southend, Essex, UK	0	*
11.10.60	Airspeed Oxford	G-AHGU	3277	Overseas Aviation	Damaged beyond repair	Fairoaks, Glos, UK	*	*
14.10.60	de Havilland Heron 2	I-AOMU	14090	Itavia	Crashed	Elba, Italy	11	*
15.10.60	Curtiss C-46	N1300N	22481	Capitol Airlines	Crashed after wing failure	Plain City, UT, USA	2	*
20.10.60	Tupolev TU-104A	SSSR-42452	*	Aeroflot	Crashed on approach in bad weather	Ust-Orda, RSFSR, USSR	3	0
22.10.60	Curtiss C-46	N1244N	22458	Arctic Pacific Airlines	Crashed on take-off	Toledo, OH, USA	22	*
28.10.60	Douglas C-54A	N48762	10320	Northwest Airlines	Crashed into mountain	nr Missoula, MT, USA	12	*
31.10.60	de Havilland Dove 1B	G-AKST	04125	Burmah Oil Co	Destroyed when hangar collapsed in cyclone	Chittagong, Pakistan	*	*
05.11.60	Douglas DC-3	9N-AAD	19792	Royal Nepal Airlines	Crashed on take-off	Bairihawa, Nepal	4	*
07.11.60	Fairchild F-27A	HC-ADV	0001A	AREA	Crashed into mountain	nr Quito, Ecuador	37	0
08.11.60	Lockheed 1049G Super Constellation	N7125C	4652	Iberia	Crashed on landing	Barcelona, Spain	0	*
11.11.60	Bristol Britannia 102	G-ANBC	12904	British Overseas Airways Corporation	Belly landed	Khartoum, Sudan	0	*
18.11.60	Curtiss C-46	TI-1024C	268	Lacsa	Swerved off runway avoiding light aircraft & hit trees	Palma Sur, Costa Rica	0	*
19.11.60	Douglas DC-3	PI-C15	13990/25435	Philippine Air Lines	Destroyed by typhoon	Manila, Philippines	*	*
21.11.60	Douglas DC-3	VP-BBN	16411/33159	Bahamas Airways	Destroyed by fire	Nassau, Bahamas	*	*

Date	Type	Reg'n	C/n	Operator	Accident	Location	F	S
23.11.60	Douglas DC-3	PI-C133	*	Philippine Air Lines	Crashed on take-off	Manila, Philippines	32	*
26.11.60	Fairchild C-82 Packet	CP-678	10128	Aerovias Condor	Crashed	Santa Cruz, Bolivia	*	*
04.12.60	Hunting Percival Prince 3C	ZK-BMQ	P50/38	Polynesian Airlines	Damaged when landing on flat tyre	Faleolo, Western Samoa	*	*
07.12.60	Curtiss C-46	PP-AKF	295	REAL	Crashed	Cochabamba, Brazil	5	*
11.12.60	Douglas DC-3	VH-INI	12252	Airlines of New South Wales	Crashed	Off Sydney, NSW, Australia	3	*
15.12.60	Douglas DC-3	*	15251/26696	Royal Air Lao	Damaged beyond repair	Location Unknown	*	*
16.12.60	Lockheed 1049 Super Constellation	N6907C	4021	Trans World Airlines	Mid-air collision with United DC-8 N8013U	New York, NY, USA	44{6} (84)	0
16.12.60	Douglas DC-8-11	N8013U	45290	United Air Lines	Mid-air collision with TWA Super Constellation N6907C	New York, NY, USA	84{6} (44)	0
18.12.60	Curtiss C-46	PP-VCT	260	Varig	Crashed	Sao Paulo, Brazil	0	*
21.12.60	Douglas DC-3	N17085	6084	Sinclair Somali Corp	Damaged by fire	Mogadishu, Somalia	*	*
21.12.60	de Havilland DH.89A Dragon Rapide	VR-OAC	6812	Borneo Airways	Crashed	Jesselton, North Borneo	*	*
22.12.60	Douglas DC-3	PI-C126	20593	Philippine Air Lines	Crashed on take-off	Cebu City, Philippines	28	*
23.12.60	Scottish Aviation Twin Pioneer 3	VH-BHJ	504	Australian Iron & Steel Pty Ltd	Destroyed in hurricane	Koolan Is, WA, Australia	*	*
28.12.60	Ilyushin IL-18	*	*	Aeroflot	Crashed on take-off	Ulyanovsk, RSFSR, USSR	*	*
30.12.60	Beechcraft D18S	PH-UBW	A-0107	Rijksluchtvaartschool	Written off	Eelde, Netherlands	*	*
oo.oo.60	de Havilland Dove 6BA	N4276C	04357	Rigsby Truck Lines	Crashed	USA	*	*
oo.oo.60	de Havilland DH.89A Dragon Rapide	F-BGOL	6559	Operator Unknown	Crashed	Atlantic Ocean	*	*
02.01.61	Avia 14	OK-MCZ	105807110	Ceskoslovenske Aerolinie	Crashed into power cables on take-off	Ruzyne, Czechoslovakia	10	*
03.01.61	Douglas DC-3	OH-LCC	14066/25511	Finnair	Crashed	Koivulahti, Finland	25	*
19.01.61	Douglas DC-8-21	XA-XAX	45432	Aeronaves de Mexico	Overshot after aborted take-off	New York, NY, USA	4	*
22.01.61	Curtiss C-46	N1308V	22583	Capitol Airlines	Crashed after engine fire	Katy, TX, USA	2	*
24.01.61	Douglas DC-3	PK-GDI	19672	Garuda Indonesian Airlines	Crashed	Mt Burangrang, Indonesia	21	*
26.01.61	Lockheed 049 Constellation	PP-PDC	2056	Panair do Brasil	Skidded off runway & damaged beyond repair	Belo Horizonte, Brazil	0	*
28.01.61	Boeing 707-123	N7502A	17629	American Airlines	Crashed	Off Long Island, NY, USA	6	*
01.02.61	Tupolev TU-104A	SSSR-42357	*	Aeroflot	Overran on landing	Vladivostok, RSFSR, USSR	0	*
04.02.61	Vickers Viking 1B	D-BALI	222	Luftransport Union	Struck building on take-off	Dusseldorf, West Germany	0	*
04.02.61	Convair 440	YU-ADL	112	JAT Yugoslav Airlines	Belly landed	Titograd, Yugoslavia	*	*
05.02.61	Douglas DC-3	PK-GDY	13052	Garuda Indonesian Airlines	Crashed	Off Surabaya, Indonesia	26	*
15.02.61	Boeing 707-329	OO-SJB	17624	Sabena	Crashed after overshoot	Brussels, Belgium	72{1}	0
18.02.61	Douglas DC-7CF	N745PA	44887	Pan American World Airways	Belly landed after engine & u/c failure	Nuremburg, West Germany	*	*
19.02.61	Convair 240-0	N94256	117	L.B.Johnson	Crashed	LBJ Ranch, Johnson City, TX, USA	*	*
03.03.61	de Havilland DH.90 Dragonfly	G-AEWZ	7555	V.H.Bellamy	Damaged beyond repair	Elmdon, Warks, UK	*	*
04.03.61	Douglas DC-3	PT-BJC	19214	C.E.de Campos	Crashed	Location Unknown	*	*
06.03.61	Lockheed 1049G Super Constellation	EC-AIP	4552	Iberia	Crashed on landing	Sao Paulo, Brazil	0	*
10.03.61	Douglas DC-3	YV-C-AZQ	19986	Linea Aeropostal Venezolana	Crashed into mountain	nr Caracas, Venezuela	12	*
15.03.61	Douglas DC-3	PP-YQS	4914	Aeronorte	Crashed	Ponta Grossa, Brazil	*	*
15.03.61	Consolidated PBY-5A Catalina	HK-1001E	*	AIDA	Written off	Location Unknown	*	*
16.03.61	Tupolev TU-104B	SSSR-42438	*	Aeroflot	Crash landed on lake after take-off	Sverdlovsk, RSFSR, USSR	5	*
22.03.61	Douglas C-54A	N5519V	10347	Seven Seas Airlines	Crash landed	Nagpur, India	*	*
22.03.61	Douglas DC-3	AP-AAC	9543	Pakistan International Airlines	Damaged beyond repair	Paksi, Pakistan	*	*
22.03.61	Avro Anson I	VH-BIX	–	Brain & Brown Airfreighters	Damaged in forced landing	nr Lancelin, WA, Australia	*	*
26.03.61	Douglas DC-6A	G-APOM	45519	Cunard Eagle Airways	Crashed during touch & go landing	Shannon, Eire	0	*
28.03.61	Ilyushin IL-18	OK-OAD	180002102	Ceskoslovenske Aerolinie	Crashed after mid-air explosion	Russelbach, East Germany	52	0
oo.03.61	Piaggio P.166	VH-PAU	*	Patair	Crashed at sea while lost	Off Port Moresby, Papua & New Guinea	1	0
03.04.61	Douglas DC-3	CC-C-LDP	9716	LAN-Chile	Crashed due to icing	Llico, Chile	24	*
04.04.61	Douglas DC-3	CF-JNR	4595	Eastern Provincial Airways	Crashed on take-off	St Pierre, St Pierre & Miquelon	*	*
08.04.61	Douglas DC-3	VH-PAT	16494/33242	Papuan Air Transport	Destroyed by fire	Bereina, Papua & New Guinea	*	*
08.04.61	Curtiss C-46	HK-489E	26778	Texaco	Destroyed	Calderon, Colombia	*	*
12.04.61	Douglas DC-3	CF-GXE	12159	Department of Transport	Crashed	St Johns, PQ, Canada	*	*
15.04.61	Douglas DC-3	CF-FKQ	4301	Maritime Central Airways	Crashed on landing	Moncton, NB, Canada	*	*

Date	Type	Reg'n	C/n	Operator	Accident	Location	F	S
19.04.61	Bell 47J-2	ET-AAF	1808	Ethiopian Airlines	Crashed after engine failure	Jiga, Ethiopia	3	0
21.04.61	Douglas DC-3	N200	20400	Federal Aviation Administration	Crashed	Mustang, OK, USA	*	*
01.05.61	de Havilland DH.89A Dragon Rapide	G-AGOJ	6850	Skyways Coach Air	Damaged beyond repair	Lympne, Kent, UK	*	*
05.05.61	Sikorsky S-58	OO-SHK	58-0363	Sabena	Crashed	Evere, Belgium	*	*
06.05.61	Douglas DC-3	SU-ALP	14662/26107	United Arab Airlines	Crashed	Kamishli, Syria	*	*
10.05.61	Lockheed 1649A Starliner	F-BHBM	1027	Air France	Crashed	nr In Amenas, Libya	78	0
12.05.61	Douglas DC-3	TI-1006C	4960	Lacsa	Crashed	Arenal Volcano, Costa Rica	2	*
19.05.61	Lockheed Vega 1	N161N	041	L.Mauldin	Crashed en route to air show	Brownsville, TX, USA	0	*
22.05.61	Boeing Stratoliner	F-BHHR	1995	Aigle Azur	Overshot on landing	Saigon, South Vietnam	0	*
24.05.61	Douglas DC-4-1009	VH-TAA	43065	Trans Australia Airlines	Crashed when pilot suffered heart attack	nr Brisbane, Qld, Australia	2	*
25.05.61	Avro York	OD-ACO	1222	Trans Mediterranean Airways	Damaged in emergency landing	Azaiba, Muscat & Oman	0	*
26.05.61	Cessna 310	OO-CUA	310-35526	Air Congo	Crashed	Usumbura, Ruanda-Urundi	*	*
30.05.61	Douglas DC-8-53	PH-DCL	45615	KLM Royal Dutch Airlines	Crashed into sea after take-off	Off Lisbon, Portugal	61	0
12.06.61	Lockheed Electra 188C	PH-LLM	2019	KLM Royal Dutch Airlines	Crashed into hill on approach	Cairo, UAR	19	*
12.06.61	Vickers Viscount 744	G-APKJ	088	All Nippon Airways	Damaged in heavy landing	Itami, Japan	0	*
13.06.61	Douglas DC-4	TJ-ABC	7473	Air Cameroun	Crashed on take-off	Douala, Cameroons	5	*
17.06.61	Douglas C-54B	D-ABEB	10530	Continentale Deutsche Luftreederei	Crashed on approach	Kano, Nigeria	1	*
19.06.61	Douglas DC-4	G-ARJY	10288	Starways	Overshot on landing	Dublin, Eire	0	*
19.06.61	Lockheed 1649A Starliner	LV-GLH	1006	Transatlantica Argentina	Damaged on landing	Rio de Janeiro, Brazil	0	*
20.06.61	Douglas DC-7	N312A	44133	Overseas National Airlines	Collided while on tow with Miami Constellation N5595A	Oakland, CA, USA	*(*)	*
20.06.61	Lockheed 749A Constellation	N5595A	2620	International Aircraft Services	Struck by Overseas National DC-7 N312A which was on tow	Oakland, CA, USA	*(*)	*
22.06.61	de Havilland DH.90 Dragonfly	G-ANYK	7529	Metropolitan Air Movements	Crashed on landing	La Baule, France	*	*
22.06.61	Cessna 310	OO-SEC	310-35597	Sabena	Crashed	Kasenga, Congo	*	*
23.06.61	Martin JRM-3 Mars	CF-LYJ	*	Forest Industries Flying Tankers	Crashed into trees	Canada	*	*
10.07.61	Tupolev TU-104B	SSSR-42447	*	Aeroflot	Crashed into lights on approach	Odessa, Ukraine, USSR	1	*
11.07.61	Douglas DC-8-12	N8040U	45307	United Air Lines	Veered off runway & crashed after landing	Denver, CO, USA	17{1}	*
11.07.61	Ilyushin IL-18B	OK-PAF	181002904	Ceskoslovenske Aerolinie	Crashed into power cables on approach	Casablanca, Morocco	73	*
16.07.61	de Havilland Heron 2	G-AMTS	14007	Metropolitan Air Movements	Crashed on take-off	Biggin Hill, Kent, UK	2	0
19.07.61	Douglas DC-6	LV-ADW	43136	Aerolineas Argentinas	Crashed after being struck by lightning	nr Azul, Brazil	67	*
21.07.61	Douglas DC-6A	N6118C	45243	Alaska Airlines	Crashed on approach	Shemya Island, AK, USA	6	*
27.07.61	Boeing 707-328	F-BHSA	17613	Air France	Swung on take-off & crashed	Hamburg, West Germany	0	*
03.08.61	Lockheed 1049C Super Constellation	N6220C	4528	Eastern Air Lines	Destroyed by fire after u/c collapsed	New York, NY, USA	0	*
04.08.61	Douglas DC-4	EP-ADK	10384	Iran Air	Forced landing out of fuel	Caspian Sea, Iran	*	*
06.08.61	Douglas DC-3	HA-TSA	20492	Malev	Crashed	Budapest, Hungary	27{3}	*
09.08.61	Curtiss C-46	CF-HEI	22419	Nordair	Crashed	Scapa Lake, NWT, Canada	*	*
09.08.61	Vickers Viking 1B	G-AHPM	152	Cunard Eagle Airways	Crashed into mountain	Stavanger, Norway	39	0
10.08.61	Curtiss C-46	CU-T607	*	Cubana	Forced down by rebels & crashed	nr Havana, Cuba	*	*
13.08.61	Curtiss C-46	*	*	Air America	Crashed	nr Vientiane, Laos	6	0
13.08.61	Ilyushin IL-18	*	*	Aeroflot	Crashed on landing	Riga, Latvia, USSR	*	*
14.08.61	Vickers Viking 1B	G-AJCE	256	Overseas Aviation	U/c collapsed on landing	Lyons, France	0	*
14.08.61	Airspeed Oxford	G-ALTR	–	T.H.Marshall	Crashed on take-off	Bordeaux, France	*	*
26.08.61	Douglas DC-3	VT-AXA	19874	Indian Airlines	Crashed	Calcutta, India	*	*
oo.08.61	de Havilland DH.89A Dragon Rapide	F-OBKH	6477	Operator Unknown	Written off	Gabon	*	*
01.09.61	Lockheed 049 Constellation	N86511	2035	Trans World Airlines	Crashed after take-off	Hinsdale, IL, USA	78	0
01.09.61	Douglas DC-3	CU-T138	2229	Cubana	Destroyed during rebel invasion	Cuba	*	*
04.09.61	Bristol Sycamore 3A	VH-INQ	13068	Ansett-ANA	Crashed	Glengyle, Qld, Australia	*	*
05.09.61	Douglas DC-3	ET-T-16	13305	Ethiopian Airlines	Crashed	Sendafar, Ethiopia	4	*
06.09.61	Douglas DC-3	PP-AVL	9886	REAL	Crashed	Videira, Brazil	*	*
07.09.61	de Havilland Dove 1	CR-CAD	04005	Aero Club of Cabo Verde	U/c collapsed on landing	San Pedro, Cape Verde Islands	0	*
10.09.61	Douglas DC-6B	N90773	44058	President Airlines	Crashed on take-off	Shannon, Eire	84	0
12.09.61	Sud Aviation Caravelle 3	F-BJTB	068	Air France	Crashed on approach	Rabat, Morocco	77	0
12.09.61	Curtiss C-46	CP-687	26585	CAMBA	Crashed	Cara Caro, Bolivia	*	*
14.09.61	Beechcraft C18S	JA5035	8233	Operator Unknown	Written off	Sendai, Japan	*	*
15.09.61	Douglas DC-4-1009	OO-ADN	43099	Air Katanga	Destroyed on ground by Katangan air raid	Elizabethville, Congo	*	*

Date	Type	Reg'n	C/n	Operator	Accident	Location	F	S
16.09.61	Lockheed Electra 188C	N137US	1142	Northwest Airlines	Crashed after take-off	Chicago, IL, USA	36	*
17.09.61	Douglas C-54D	G-APIN	10736	Starways	Destroyed on ground during Katangan air raid	Kamina, Congo	*	*
17.09.61	Consolidated C-87 Liberator	CP-589	*	Boliviana de Aviacion	Crashed	Santa Rosa de Yacuma, Bolivia	*	*
17.09.61	Tupolev TU-104A	SSSR-42388	8350703	Aeroflot	Damaged in hard landing	Tashkent, Uzbekistan, USSR	0	*
18.09.61	Douglas DC-6B	SE-BDY	43559	United Nations Organisation	Crashed [Dag Hammerskjold, UN Secretary General killed]	nr N'Dola, Northern Rhodesia	16	0
23.09.61	Fokker F-27 Friendship 100	TC-TAY	10182	Turk Hava Yollari	Crashed into hill on approach	Ankara, Turkey	28	*
26.09.61	Douglas DC-7	N317A	44138	Overseas National Airlines	Crashed into bank after u/c failed	Norfolk, VA, USA	*	*
27.09.61	Sud Aviation Caravelle 3	PP-VJD	015	Varig	Skidded on landing & caught fire	Brasilia, Brazil	0	*
29.09.61	Beechcraft 18A	CF-BQH	0318	Pacific Western Airlines	Crashed	Canada	*	*
oo.09.61	Douglas DC-3	*	14814/26259	Air Courier	Shot down by UN aircraft	Kolwezi, Congo	*	*
01.10.61	Bristol 170 Freighter 31E	EC-AHK	13130	Aviaco	Damaged on landing	Ibiza, Spain	*	*
07.10.61	Douglas DC-3	G-AMSW	16171/32919	Derby Aviation	Crashed	Mt Canigou, France	34	*
08.10.61	Douglas C-54A	G-ARLF	10278	Lloyd International Airways	Destroyed by fire on ground after fuel bowser exploded	Malaga, Spain	*	*
14.10.61	Douglas DC-7C	PP-PDL	45122	Panair do Brasil	Veered off runway & crashed	Belem, Brazil	*	*
17.10.61	Douglas DC-3	G-AMVC	16642/33390	BKS Air Transport	Crashed on approach	Kirkoswald, Cumberland, UK	4	0
30.10.61	Vickers Viscount 736	G-AODH	078	British United Airways	Damaged by heavy landing	Frankfurt, West Germany	0	*
01.11.61	Douglas DC-7C	PP-PDO	44872	Panair do Brasil	Crashed into hill on approach	Recife, Brazil	49	*
01.11.61	Bristol 170 Superfreighter 32	G-ANWL	13260	Silver City Airways	Crashed	Les Provosts, Guernsey	2	8
02.11.61	Tupolev TU-104B	SSSR-42504	021902	Aeroflot	Crashed into mast on approach & crash landed	Vladivostok, RSFSR, USSR	*	*
08.11.61	Lockheed C-69 Constellation	N2737A	1976	Imperial Airlines	Crashed on landing	Richmond, VA, USA	77	2
11.11.61	Lockheed 749A Constellation	HH-ABA	2615	Air Haiti International	Crashed	East of Puerto Rico	3	0
14.11.61	Douglas DC-4	N30061	10331	Zantop Air Transport	Crashed on landing	Covington, KY, USA	*	*
14.11.61	de Havilland Dove 1B	JA5008	04430	All Nippon Airways	Crash landed in river on approach	Tama River, Japan	*	*
15.11.61	Vickers Viscount 768D	VT-DIH	195	Indian Airlines	Skidded off runway	Colombo, Ceylon	0	*
15.11.61	Vickers Viscount 745D	N6592C	234	Northeast Airlines	Struck by landing National DC-6 N8228H	Boston, MA, USA	0(0)	*
15.11.61	Douglas DC-6B	N8228H	43821	National Airlines	Struck tail of Northeast Viscount N6592C on landing	Boston, MA, USA	0(0)	*
19.11.61	Douglas DC-7C	N5905	45073	Braniff International Airlines	Destroyed by fire on ground	Dallas, TX, USA	0	*
22.11.61	Douglas DC-3	VP-YRX	19351	Rhodesian Air Services	Destroyed by fire on take-off	Salisbury, Southern Rhodesia	*	*
23.11.61	de Havilland Comet 4	LV-AHR	06430	Aerolineas Argentinas	Crashed after take-off	Campinas, Argentina	52	*
30.11.61	Vickers Viscount 720	VH-TVC	046	Trans Australia Airlines	Crashed after take-off	Sydney, NSW, Australia	15	0
04.12.61	Boeing 720-030B	D-ABOK	18058	Lufthansa	Crashed	Ebersheim, West Germany	3	*
07.12.61	Douglas DC-3	VT-AZV	13253	Kalinga Airlines	Crashed	Amritsar, India	*	*
12.12.61	Curtiss C-46	PP-VBM	134	Varig	Crashed at sea	Location Unknown	*	*
12.12.61	de Havilland DH.89A Dragon Rapide	G-AKZB	6790	British European Airways	Crashed	Land's End, Cornwall, UK	*	*
15.12.61	Curtiss C-46	AN-AOE	*	Lanica	Crashed	Managua, Nicaragua	2	*
16.12.61	Douglas DC-7	N4871C	44251	Delta Air Lines	Damaged on landing	Chicago, IL, USA	*	*
17.12.61	Ilyushin IL-18	*	*	Aeroflot	Crashed	Millerovo, RSFSR, USSR	*	*
18.12.61	Bristol 170 Freighter 21	VH-AAH	12774	Pacific Aviation	Crashed after engine failure	Albion Park, NSW, Australia	*	*
21.12.61	de Havilland Comet 4B	G-ARJM	06456	British European Airways	Crashed after take-off	Ankara, Turkey	27	*
29.12.61	Douglas DC-3	PK-GDZ	12514	Garuda Indonesian Airlines	Crashed	Surabaya, Indonesia	*	*
31.12.61	Ilyushin IL-18	*	*	Aeroflot	Crashed on approach	Mineralnye Vodny, RSFSR, USSR	*	*
oo.12.61	Douglas DC-3	KA-DFN	12151	Air Courier	Destroyed by UN bombing	Kolwesi, Congo	*	*
oo.oo.61	Douglas DC-3	XW-PAD	*	Bird & Sons	Damaged by shellfire	Vientiane, Laos	*	*
oo.oo.61	Douglas DC-3	N541S	43192	US Steel Co	Crashed on landing	Location Unknown	*	*
oo.oo.61	Douglas DC-3	UN-203	*	United Nations Organisation	Damaged beyond repair in forced landing	Tschikapa, Congo	*	*
oo.oo.61	Douglas DC-2-243	XA-KIC	2069	Aerolineas Vega	Crashed	Oaxaca, Mexico	*	*
oo.oo.61	de Havilland Dove 1	ST-AAB	04010	Sudan Airways	Written off	Sudan	*	*
oo.oo.61	Avro Nineteen I	EC-ALF	1277	Spantax	Damaged when u/c collapsed while taxiing	Villa Cisneros, Rio de Oro	*	*
01.01.62	Airspeed Oxford	G-ALTP	–	T.H.Marshall	Damaged by engine fire	Christchurch, Hants, UK	*	*
02.01.62	Douglas DC-3	EP-ABB	6043	Iran Air	Crashed on take-off	Kabul, Afghanistan	*	*
11.01.62	Curtiss C-46	HP-312	33381	Aerovias Panama	Force-landed & destroyed by rebel gunfire	Maniamuna, Congo	*	*
13.01.62	Douglas DC-3	ET-T-1	10053	Ethiopian Airlines	Crashed after take-off	Tippi, Ethiopia	5	*
15.01.62	Douglas DC-3	CF-IQF	6101	Nordair	Crashed	Arctic Bay, NWT, Canada	*	*
16.01.62	Boeing B-17F-BO	CP-571	6035	Aerovias Moxos	Crashed	Viacha, Bolivia	*	*

Date	Type	Reg'n	C/n	Operator	Accident	Location	F	S
17.01.62	Curtiss C-46	ZP-CAI	30447	Aerocarga	Crash landed & set on fire after smuggling flight	Curuzu Cuatia, Argentina	*	*
22.01.62	Curtiss C-46	CP-541	33579	Lloyd Aereo Boliviano	Crashed on take-off	Caranavi, Bolivia	2	*
27.01.62	Antonov AN-10A	SSSR-11148	*	Aeroflot	Crashed on take-off	Batataevka, Ukraine, USSR	13	0
28.01.62	Curtiss C-46	CX-AYI	170	J.A.Nachez	Damaged beyond repair in forced landing	Location Unknown	*	*
28.01.62	Douglas C-54B	HK-130	10469	Avianca	Crashed	Oucuta, Colombia	*	*
02.02.62	Beechcraft Queen Air 65	PI-C835	LC-136	Operator Unknown	Written off	Location Unknown	*	*
04.02.62	Douglas DC-3	OB-PBH-530	7331	Faucett	Crashed	Tino Maria, Peru	18	*
04.02.62	Curtiss C-46	*	*	Air America	Shot down by Communist forces	Plain of Jars, Laos	6	*
12.02.62	de Havilland DH.90 Dragonfly	ZK-AFB	7560	Air Charter	Crashed	Off Christchurch, New Zealand	5	0
20.02.62	Douglas DC-3	EP-AEI	13552	Iran Air	Crashed	Ahvaz, Iran	*	*
23.02.62	de Havilland Heron 1B	JA6158	14028	Toa Airways	Crashed	Mt Ohira, Japan	*	*
25.02.62	Fairchild F-27	YV-C-EVH	0012	Avensa	Struck tree on approach	Margarita Island, Venezuela	23	*
25.02.62	Douglas DC-3	HK-502	19653	Avianca	Crashed into mountain	nr Bogota, Colombia	*	*
01.03.62	Boeing 707-123B	N7506A	17633	American Airlines	Crashed after take-off	Off New York, NY, USA	95	0
03.03.62	Lockheed 049 Constellation	PP-PCR	2060	Panair do Brasil	Damaged beyond repair on landing without nosewheel	Rio de Janeiro, Brazil	*	*
03.03.62	Douglas DC-3	PP-YQN	1919	Varig	Crashed	Nanuque, Brazil	*	*
04.03.62	Douglas DC-7C	G-ARUD	45160	Caledonian Airways	Crashed on take-off	Douala, Cameroons	111	0
05.03.62	Douglas DC-3	G-AMSF	14380/25825	Alares Developments	Crashed	Birmingham, UK	*	*
06.03.62	Douglas DC-3	ZS-DJC	16189/32937	South African Airways	Crashed	Mt Katberg, South Africa	2	*
08.03.62	Douglas DC-6B	I-DIMO	44254	Societa Aerea Mediterranea	Crashed	nr Avezzano, Italy	5	*
08.03.62	Fairchild F-27	TC-KOP	0083	Turk Hava Yollari	Crashed in bad weather	Mt Medetsiz, Turkey	11	*
15.03.62	Lockheed 1049H Super Constellation	N6921C	4817	Flying Tiger Line	Crashed after explosion	Between Guam & Philippines	107	0
15.03.62	Lockheed 1049H Super Constellation	N6911C	4804	Flying Tiger Line	Undershot runway	Adak, AK, USA	1	*
16.03.62	Vickers Viscount 739	SU-AID	086	United Arab Airlines	Damaged in belly landing	Wadi Halfa, Sudan	0	*
27.03.62	Ilyushin IL-14	CU-T819	*	Cubana	Crashed after take-off	Santiago de Cuba, Cuba	22	*
05.04.62	Douglas DC-3	PK-GDM	13731	Garuda Indonesian Airlines	Exploded in mid-air	Djakarta, Indonesia	*	*
05.04.62	Douglas DC-3	TG-APA	19454	Aviateca	Crashed	Guatemala City, Guatemala	*	*
06.04.62	Curtiss C-46	*	*	Air America	Crashed on take-off	Vientiane, Laos	4	*
06.04.62	Avro York	OD-ACN	–	Trans Mediterranean Airways	U/c collapsed on landing	Lahore, Pakistan	0	*
09.04.62	Antonov AN-2	YR-ANO	116911	Aviatia Utilitara	Crashed	Draganscu, Romania	*	*
10.04.62	Douglas C-54	JA6003	3115	Japan Air Lines	U/c collapsed while taxiing	Osaka, Japan	0	*
11.04.62	Canadair C-4	VP-KNY	161	East African Airways	Crashed on approach	Nairobi, Kenya	*	*
18.04.62	Douglas DC-3	N3588	20178	Purdue Aeron Corp	Crashed on take-off	Dallas, TX, USA	*	*
19.04.62	Bristol 170 Freighter 31E	EC-AHJ	13129	Aviaco	U/c collapsed	Valencia, Spain	*	*
19.04.62	Breguet Atlantic	02	02	Breguet	Written off	France	*	*
22.04.62	Douglas DC-3	HK-524	12075	Aerovias Pilotos Asociados Medellin	Crashed into mountain	nr Quibdo, Colombia	31	*
26.04.62	Lockheed 749A Constellation	F-BAZE	2624	Air Algerie	Blown up by OAS terrorists while in store	Algiers, Algeria	0	*
26.04.62	Lockheed 749A Constellation	N116	2611	Federal Aviation Administration	Crashed	Canton Island	5	*
03.05.62	Douglas C-54A	VT-CZT	10419	Indian Airlines	Destroyed in hangar fire	Calcutta, India	0	*
06.05.62	Douglas DC-3	G-AGZB	12180	Channel Airways	Crashed	St Boniface, IoW, Hants, UK	10	*
07.05.62	Convair 340-54	CC-C-LCA	136	LAN-Chile	Damaged beyond repair	Vallenar, Chile	*	*
07.05.62	Douglas C-54A	VT-DIC	10376	Indian Airlines	Crashed	Haveri, India	*	*
09.05.62	Convair 240-0	PP-CEZ	025	Cruzeiro	Crashed into trees	Vitoria, Brazil	24	*
12.05.62	Consolidated Catalina	*	*	Eastern Provincial Airways	Crashed on landing	Godthaab, Greenland	15	*
15.05.62	Douglas DC-3	SU-AJM	*	United Arab Airlines	Crashed on take-off	Cairo, UAR	3	*
21.05.62	Curtiss C-46	HR-196P	30533	Honduras International	Crashed	Barandillas, Honduras	2	*
22.05.62	Boeing 707-124	N70775	17611	Continental Airlines	Crashed after bomb explosion	Unionville, IA, USA	45	0
24.05.62	Douglas DC-3	VT-AYG	12848	Darbhanga Aviation	Crashed after fire	nr Rajshani, Pakistan	4	*
24.05.62	Avro Anson V	CF-BCA	MDF-305	Department of Public Works	Crashed	Victoria, BC, Canada	*	*
29.05.62	de Havilland Dove 6	G-ANDY	04441	Ferranti Ltd	Crashed into power cables	Edinburgh, UK	*	*
03.06.62	Boeing 707-328	F-BHSM	17920	Air France	Crashed after aborting take-off	Paris, France	130	2
04.06.62	Tupolev TU-104B	SSSR-42491	021604	Aeroflot	Crashed into mountain	nr Sofia, Bulgaria	5	0
07.06.62	Curtiss C-46	HR-SAL	248	Sahsa	U/c collapsed on landing	Tegucigalpa, Honduras	*	*
08.06.62	Curtiss C-46	SE-CFB	98	United Nations Organisation	Crashed	Albertville, Congo	*	*

Date	Type	Reg'n	C/n	Operator	Accident	Location	F	S
08.06.62	de Havilland DH.89A Dragon Rapide	F-OBRU	6748	Operator Unknown	Written off	Podor, Senegal	*	*
22.06.62	Boeing 707-328	F-BHST	18247	Air France	Crashed on approach	Guadeloupe	113	0
27.06.62	Curtiss C-46	PP-BTE	30260	Paraense Transportes Aereos	Crashed	Pedro Afonso, Brazil	*	*
28.06.62	Douglas DC-3	TC-EFE	9307	Turk Hava Yollari	Crashed	Bandirma, Turkey	*	*
28.06.62	Antonov AN-10A	SSSR-11185	*	Aeroflot	Crashed into hill on approach	nr Sochi, Ukraine, USSR	81	0
30.06.62	Bristol 170 Freighter 21	G-AGVC	12732	Manx Airlines	U/c collapsed on landing	Ronaldsway, Isle of Man	*	*
30.06.62	Tupolev TU-104A	SSSR-42370	*	Aeroflot	Crashed	nr Krasnoyarsk, RSFSR, USSR	84	0
06.07.62	Douglas DC-8-43	I-DIWD	45631	Alitalia	Crashed into hill on approach	Junnar, India	94	0
06.07.62	Ilyushin IL-14	*	*	Aeroflot	Crashed	nr Tashkent, Uzbekistan, USSR	14	*
06.07.62	Koolhoven FK.50	EL-ADV	5003	Maryland Flying Service	Crashed	Monrovia, Liberia	*	*
06.07.62	Canadair C-4-1	YV-C-LBV	147	Linea Expresa Bolivar	Crashed	Off Caracas, Venezuela	*	*
08.07.62	Vickers Viscount 812	N243V	354	Continental Airlines	Crashed after take-off	Amarillo, TX, USA	0	16
09.07.62	Douglas DC-4-1009	OD-AEC	42918	Trans Mediterranean Airways	Crashed after take-off	Off Brindisi, Italy	6	*
14.07.62	Lockheed 049 Constellation	PP-PCF	2049	Panair do Brasil	Belly landed	Rio de Janeiro, Brazil	*	*
16.07.62	Douglas DC-3	VT-DFZ	4647	Kalinga Airlines	Crashed after engine failure	Nagaland, India	9	*
19.07.62	de Havilland Comet 4C	SU-AMW	06464	United Arab Airlines	Crashed on approach	nr Bangkok, Thailand	26	*
22.07.62	Bristol Britannia 314	CF-CZB	13394	Canadian Pacific Airlines	Crashed on landing	Honolulu, HI, USA	27	*
29.07.62	Antonov AN-2	YR-AND	19711	Aviatia Utilitara	Crashed	Batanii Mici, Romania	*	*
29.07.62	Antonov AN-24	*	*	Aeroflot	Crashed on take-off	Ternopol, Ukraine, USSR	*	*
30.07.62	Douglas DC-3	F-BAOE	11769	Air France	Crashed	Coulommiers, France	*	*
01.08.62	Douglas DC-3	9N-AAH	6216	Royal Nepal Airlines	Crashed	nr Kathmandu, Nepal	10	*
06.08.62	Lockheed Electra 188A	N6102A	1019	American Airlines	Crashed	Knoxville, TN, USA	0	*
17.08.62	Convair 240-23	PK-GCE	175	Garuda Indonesian Airlines	Crashed	Ambon, Indonesia	*	*
20.08.62	Douglas DC-8-33	PP-PDT	45273	Panair do Brasil	Overran into sea	Rio de Janeiro, Brazil	15	*
21.08.62	Martin 404	N40401	14101	Piedmont Airlines	Crashed during single engine landing	Wilmington, NC, USA	*	*
21.08.62	Douglas DC-3	CP-536	20619	Lloyd Aereo Boliviano	Crashed	La Paz, Bolivia	*	*
23.08.62	Douglas DC-3	HK-794	4551	Taxader	Crashed into Hiller UH-12 HK-781E after tyre burst on t/o	Berranca Bermeja, Colombia	20(*)	*
25.08.62	Douglas DC-3	OB-PBN-659	14394/25839	Faucett	Crashed in storm	nr Cerropuena Paz, Peru	9	*
25.08.62	Douglas DC-3	YU-ABH	9488	JAT Yugoslav Airlines	Crashed	nr Mostar, Yugoslavia	*	*
02.09.62	Tupolev TU-104A	SSSR-42366	*	Aeroflot	Crashed	nr Khabarovsk, RSFSR, USSR	86	0
04.09.62	Lockheed 18 Lodestar	*	*	Ashland Oil & Refining Co	Crashed after mid-air explosion	Ravenna, OH, USA	13	*
09.09.62	Avro York	OD-ADA	1311	Middle East Airlines	Damaged in crash landing	Azaiba, Muscat & Oman	0	*
10.09.62	Douglas DC-3	CP-710	20230	Aerolineas Abaroa	Crashed	Alcoche, Bolivia	4	*
10.09.62	Avia 14	OK-MCT	90807103	Ceskoslovenske Aerolinie	Crashed on approach	Brno, Czechoslovakia	11	*
18.09.62	Curtiss C-46	N67937	22386	Puerto Rican American Airlines	Crashed	Off San Pedro Sula, Honduras	*	*
19.09.62	Douglas DC-3	EC-AGO	13057	Iberia	Damaged beyond repair	Location Unknown	*	*
20.09.62	Douglas DC-3	UN-202	*	United Nations Organisation	Shot down	Katanga, Congo	*	*
21.09.62	Douglas DC-3	VT-DGX	12142	Kalinga Airlines	Crashed	Sela, India	8	*
23.09.62	Lockheed 1049H Super Constellation	N6923C	4827	Flying Tiger Line	Crashed after engine failure	Atlantic Ocean	28	48
07.10.62	de Havilland DH.89A Dragon Rapide	VP-KCJ	6366	Caspair	Crashed	Entebbe, Uganda	*	*
09.10.62	Douglas DC-3	CX-AGE	12113	Pluna	Exploded on take-off	Montevideo, Uruguay	*	*
10.10.62	Fokker F-27 Friendship 200	EP-MRP	10126	Iranian Royal Flight	Crashed	nr Tehran, Iran	4	*
12.10.62	Fokker F-27 Friendship 100	PI-C503	10191	Philippine Air Lines	Crashed after take-off	Manila, Philippines	3	*
12.10.62	Martin JRM-3 Mars	CF-LYM	*	Forest Industries Flying Tankers	Sank during hurricane	Victoria, BC, Canada	*	*
13.10.62	Douglas DC-3	PI-C485	*	Philippine Air Lines	Crashed	Cagayan de Oro, Philippines	*	*
22.10.62	Douglas DC-7CF	N285	45204	Northwest Airlines	Crashed after engine fire	nr Biorka Is, AK, USA	0	*
25.10.62	Tupolev TU-104B	SSSR-42495	021703	Aeroflot	Crashed on take-off	nr Moscow, RSFSR, USSR	11	0
29.10.62	Douglas DC-7B	N51702	44702	Panagra	Damaged beyond repair	La Paz, Bolivia	*	*
oo.10.62	de Havilland DH.89A Dragon Rapide	ZP-TDH	6436	Operator Unknown	Written off	Location Unknown	*	*
02.11.62	Curtiss C-46	YV-C-LBH	441	Lebca	Ground looped & caught fire	Carora, Venezuela	*	*
10.11.62	Douglas DC-3	XV-NID	16074/32822	Air Vietnam	Crashed into mountain	nr Tourane, South Vietnam	26	*
12.11.62	Convair 440-62	EC-ATB	443	Iberia	Crashed	Carmona, Spain	18	*
19.11.62	Vickers Viscount 828	JA8202	444	All Nippon Airways	Crashed	nr Nagoya, Japan	4	*
23.11.62	Vickers Viscount 745D	N7430	128	United Air Lines	Crashed due to birdstrike on tail	nr Baltimore, MD, USA	18	0

Date	Type	Reg'n	C/n	Operator	Accident	Location	F	S
23.11.62	Ilyushin IL-18D	HA-MOD	180002002	Malev	Crashed on approach	Le Bourget, France	21	*
26.11.62	Saab Scandia	PP-SRA	107	VASP	Mid-air collision with Cessna	Paraibuna, Brazil	23(3)	*
26.11.62	Curtiss C-46	HK-354X	*	Lineas Aereas La Urraca	Crashed	nr Kingston, Jamaica	2	*
27.11.62	Boeing 707-441	PP-VJA	17906	Varig	Crashed on approach	Lima, Peru	97	0
30.11.62	Douglas DC-7B	N815D	45084	Eastern Air Lines	Crashed on landing in bad weather	New York, NY, USA	25	*
06.12.62	Douglas DC-3	HK-437E	4697	Taxader	Crashed	Barranca Bermeja, Colombia	24	*
06.12.62	Douglas DC-3	CP-695	19389	Aerolineas Abaroa	Crashed	Uncia, Bolivia	*	*
14.12.62	Lockheed 049 Constellation	PP-PDE	2047	Panair do Brasil	Crashed	nr Manaus, Brazil	50	0
14.12.62	Lockheed 1049H Super Constellation	N6913C	4810	Flying Tiger Line	Crashed on landing in fog	Burbank, CA, USA	5{3}	0
19.12.62	Vickers Viscount 804	SP-LVB	395	LOT Polish Airlines	Crashed after lightning strike	Warsaw, Poland	33	0
21.12.62	Convair 340-31	N73130	059	Frontier Airlines	Crashed short of runway	Grand Is, NE, USA	*	*
22.12.62	Convair 240-2	PP-VCQ	103	Varig	Crashed on approach	Brasilia, Brazil	*	*
28.12.62	Aviation Traders ATL.98 Carvair	G-ARSF	18339/3	Channel Air Bridge	Crashed short of runway	Rotterdam, Netherlands	0{1}	*
29.12.62	Boeing Stratoliner	F-BELZ	2001	Air Nautic	Crashed	Monte Renosa, Corsica, France	24	0
29.12.62	de Havilland DH.89A Dragon Rapide	OO-ITI	6913	V.Risseghem	Destroyed by UN Saab J23s in air attack	Kolwezi, Congo	*	*
oo.oo.62	Miles Aerovan 4	PH-EAB	6382	Nastra Luchtreclame Service	Damaged by gales	Netherlands	*	*
oo.oo.62	de Havilland DH.89A Dragon Rapide	9Q-CJE	6918	AMAMZ	Written off	Mweka, Zaire	*	*
11.01.63	Lockheed 749A Constellation	F-BAZM	2545	SGAC	Crashed into mountain	nr Perpignan, France	*	*
11.01.63	Curtiss C-46	CF-HTI	2932	Maritime Central Airways	Destroyed in hangar fire	Moncton, NB, Canada	*	*
16.01.63	Scottish Aviation Twin Pioneer 3	5N-ABR	526	Bristow Helicopters (Nigeria) Ltd	Crashed	Off Chepbica, Morocco	*	*
17.01.63	Fairchild F-27	N2703	0006	West Coast Airlines	Crashed after engine failure	Great Salt Lake, UT, USA	3	*
21.01.63	Douglas DC-4-1009	OD-ADO	42949	Trans Mediterranean Airways	Undershot on landing	Azaiba, Muscat & Oman	*	*
22.01.63	Convair 340-59	PP-CDY	166	Cruzeiro	Crashed on landing	Parnaiba, Brazil	*	*
28.01.63	Vickers Viscount 812	N242V	356	Continental Airlines	Swerved on landing & crashed	Kansas City, MO, USA	8	
01.02.63	Vickers Viscount 754D	OD-ADE	244	Middle East Airlines	Mid-air collision with Turkish Air Force DC-3 6028	Ankara, Turkey	14{87} (3)	0
03.02.63	Lockheed 1049H Super Constellation	N9740Z	4851	Slick Airways	Crash landed in fog	San Francisco, CA, USA	4	*
05.02.63	Beechcraft C18S	JA5034	8403	Operator Unknown	Written off	Chofu, Japan	*	*
08.02.63	Antonov AN-10	SSSR-11193	*	Aeroflot	Crashed	Syktyvkar, RSFSR, USSR	7	0
12.02.63	Boeing 720-051B	N724US	18354	Northwest Airlines	Broke up in turbulence	nr Miami, FL, USA	43	0
16.02.63	Curtiss C-46	N616Z	22590	Zantop Air Transport	Crashed	Puyallup, WA, USA	0	*
18.02.63	de Havilland Dove 1B	JA5003	04375	All Nippon Airways	Overshot & crashed on landing	Tanega Shima, Japan	*	*
23.02.63	Boeing B-17G-DL	CP-624	22779	Corporacion Boliviano de Fomento	Crashed	Reyes, Bolivia	*	*
26.02.63	Curtiss C-46	N67933	22380	Skyvan Airways	Crashed	Off Cape Lisburne, AK, USA	1	*
26.02.63	Ilyushin IL-18	*	*	Aeroflot	Sank after emergency landing on ice	En route Magadan, RSFSR, USSR	*	*
oo.02.63	Ilyushin IL-14	DM-SBL	6341206	Interflug	Forced landing	Konigsbruck, East Germany	*	*
02.03.63	Douglas DC-3	PI-C489	16115/32863	Philippine Air Lines	Crashed	nr Davao City, Philippines	27	*
04.03.63	Douglas DC-3	N16067	1907	Flugtransport	Overshot on landing & crashed into ditch	Herzogenaurach, West Germany	0	*
05.03.63	Ilyushin IL-18	*	*	Aeroflot	Crashed on landing	Ashkhabad, Turkmenistan, USSR	*	*
15.03.63	Avro York	OD-ACZ	1218	Middle East Airlines	Crashed	nr Karaj, Iran	4	0
15.03.63	Douglas DC-6B	CP-707	43547	Lloyd Aereo Boliviano	Crashed	nr Tacora Volcano, Peru	41	*
20.03.63	de Havilland Comet 4C	SA-R-7	06461	Saudi Arabian Royal Flight	Crashed into mountain	Monte Matto, Italy	18	*
25.03.63	Avro Anson V	CF-INT	BRC-1642	Northland Airlines	Damaged when u/c collapsed on landing on ice	Riverton, MN, Canada	*	*
27.03.63	Vickers Varsity T.1	G-APAZ	561	Smiths Aviation	Crashed into houses after take-off	Gloucester, Glos, UK	*	*
29.03.63	Douglas DC-3	9Q-CUS	13431/43092	Air Congo	Crashed	Kasongo, Congo	*	*
30.03.63	Douglas DC-3	I-TAVI	16477/33225	Itavia	Crashed in storm	Trenta Paggi, Italy	8	*
02.04.63	Antonov AN-12	*	*	Aeroflot	Crashed on take-off	Magadan, RSFSR, USSR	*	*
04.04.63	Ilyushin IL-18	*	*	Aeroflot	Crashed	Kazan, RSFSR, USSR	*	*
07.04.63	Douglas DC-6B	YK-AEB	43749	Syrian Arab Airlines	Caught fire on take-off	Hama, Syria	1	*
08.04.63	Douglas DC-7C	PP-PDM	45124	Panair do Brasil	Crashed	Rio de Janeiro, Brazil	*	*
09.04.63	Avro Nineteen 2	G-ALXH	–	BKS Air Survey	Crashed after engine failure	nr Guisley, Yorks, UK	*	*
13.04.63	Douglas DC-6B	OY-EAP	43750	Sterling Airways	Crashed on landing	Copenhagen, Denmark	0	*
14.04.63	Vickers Viscount 759D	TF-ISU	149	Icelandair	Crashed on approach	Oslo, Norway	12	0
16.04.63	Avro Anson V	CF-GOA	4134	Northland Airlines	Damaged on landing on frozen lake	nr Winnipeg, MN, Canada	*	*

Date	Type	Reg'n	C/n	Operator	Accident	Location	F	S
30.04.63	Douglas DC-3	JA5039	3253	All Nippon Airways	Crashed	Hochijojima, Japan	*	*
01.05.63	de Havilland Canada Otter	JA3115	233	Operator Unknown	Written off	Awaji-Shima, Japan	*	*
02.05.63	Boeing B-17G-DL	CP-588	22555	Aerovias Moxos	Crashed	Location Unknown	*	*
03.05.63	Douglas DC-6B	F-BIAO	45479	Air Afrique	Crashed into mountain	nr Buca, Cameroons	55	0
03.05.63	Convair 340-59	PP-CDW	159	Cruzeiro	Crashed due to engine failure	Sao Paulo, Brazil	35	*
05.05.63	Douglas DC-4	PP-BTR	27237	Paraense Transportes Aereos	Damaged beyond repair	Sao Paulo, Brazil	*	*
10.05.63	Douglas DC-3	JA5040	6349	All Nippon Airways	Crashed	Sendai, Japan	*	*
12.05.63	Douglas DC-3	SU-AJX	*	United Arab Airlines	Crashed	Ayayda, UAR	34	*
14.05.63	Scottish Aviation Twin Pioneer 3	PK-GTC	579	Garuda Indonesian Airlines	Damaged on take-off	Indonesia	*	*
18.05.63	Tupolev TU-104B	SSSR-42483	021501	Aeroflot	Crashed on approach	Leningrad, RSFSR, USSR	*	*
22.05.63	Douglas DC-3	F-OAVR	*	Air Algerie	Crashed	Hassi Messaoud, Algeria	*	*
29.05.63	Lockheed 1049G Super Constellation	N189S	4541	Standard Airways	Undershot runway	Manhattan, KS, USA	0	*
30.05.63	Convair 990-30-5	N5616	28	American Airlines	Caught fire on ground	Newark, NJ, USA	0	*
03.06.63	Douglas DC-7CF	N290	45209	Northwest Airlines	Crashed	nr Annette Is, AK, USA	101	0
03.06.63	Douglas DC-3	VT-AUL	20265	Indian Airlines	Crashed	Sarna, India	29	*
10.06.63	Douglas DC-3	XY-ACS	9877	Union of Burma Airways	Crashed on landing	Yunnan, Burma	21	*
16.06.63	VEB 14P	YR-ILL	14803072	Tarom	Crashed	Bekkessamson, Romania	31	*
01.07.63	Douglas DC-3	PP-VBV	15444/26889	Varig	Crashed	Passo Fundo, Brazil	15	*
02.07.63	Martin 404	N449A	14140	Mohawk Airlines	Crashed on take-off in bad weather	Rochester, NY, USA	7	*
03.07.63	Sud Aviation Caravelle 6N	LV-HGY	127	Aerolineas Argentinas	Crashed on approach	Cordoba, Argentina	0{3}	*
03.07.63	Douglas DC-3	ZK-AYZ	15204/26649	New Zealand National Airways	Crashed on landing	Tauranga, New Zealand	23	*
03.07.63	Short Sandringham 4	VH-BRE	SH.32C	Ansett Flying Boat Services	Destroyed by hurricane	Lord Howe Is, Australia	0	*
10.07.63	Douglas C-54A	HP-382	10387	Aeronaves de Panama	Crashed	Off Carcos Is, Bahamas	*	*
13.07.63	Tupolev TU-104B	SSSR-42492	021605	Aeroflot	Crashed on approach	nr Irkutsk, RSFSR, USSR	35	*
14.07.63	Lockheed R6V Constitution	N7673C	1002	Air Traders	Destroyed by arson	Opa Locka, FL, USA	0	*
16.07.63	Douglas DC-3	5R-MAJ	12813	Air Madagascar	Crashed on take-off	Farafangana, Malagasy Republic	6	*
17.07.63	Curtiss C-46F	B-148	22510	Air America	Crashed into mountain in fog	Pak Tha, Laos	6	0
20.07.63	de Havilland DH.89A Dragon Rapide	G-AHLM	6708	Mayflower Air Services	Crashed	St Mary's, Scilly Is, UK	0	8
28.07.63	de Havilland Comet 4C	SU-ALD	06441	United Arab Airlines	Crashed in sea on approach	Off Bombay, India	63	0
29.07.63	Douglas DC-7B	N843D	45449	Eastern Air Lines	U/c collapsed	Nashville, TN, USA	*	*
04.08.63	Douglas DC-3	PP-SLL	1500	Transportes Aereos Salvador	Crashed	Tangara, Brazil	*	*
04.08.63	Cessna 180C	ET-AAC	50861	Ethiopian Airlines	Crashed on landing	Awash, Ethiopia	*	*
12.08.63	Vickers Viscount 708	F-BGNV	039	Air Inter	Crashed after lightning strike	Lyon, France	15{1}	1
14.08.63	Curtiss C-46	N67941	22391	Aaxico Airlines	Crashed	Great Falls, MT, USA	1	*
16.08.63	Tupolev TU-104A	OK-LDB	76600601	Ceskoslovenska Aerolinie	Destroyed by fire while refuelling on ground	Bombay, India	0	*
17.08.63	de Havilland Heron 1B	JA6155	14026	Fujita Airlines	Crashed	Mt Mt Hachijo-Fuji, Japan	19	0
21.08.63	Tupolev TU-124	SSSR-45021	2350701	Aeroflot	Crash landed after u/c failure on take-off	River Neva, Leningrad, RSFSR, USSR	0	*
24.08.63	Fairchild F-27	N2707	0032	West Coast Airlines	Crashed short of runway	Calgary, AB, Canada	0	*
29.08.63	Douglas DC-3	VP-KJT	16530/33278	East African Airways	Destroyed by fire	Francistown, Kenya	*	*
04.09.63	Sud Aviation Caravelle 3	HB-ICV	147	Swissair	Crashed after take-off	Duerrenaesch, Switzerland	80	0
05.09.63	Curtiss C-46	*	*	Air America	Crashed	Laos	7	0
06.09.63	Sud Aviation Caravelle 6R	PP-PDU	118	Panair do Brasil	Damaged when overstressed avoiding mid-air collision	nr Recife, Brazil	0	*
07.09.63	Scottish Aviation Twin Pioneer 1	VR-OAE	517	Borneo Airways	Crashed	nr Sibu, North Borneo	*	*
11.09.63	Vickers Viscount 768D	VT-DIO	192	Indian Airlines	Crashed	Agra, India	18	0
12.09.63	Vickers Viking 1B	F-BJER	216	Air Nautic	Crashed	Perpignan, France	40	0
20.09.63	Scottish Aviation Twin Pioneer 3	PK-GTB	511	Garuda Indonesian Airlines	Crashed	Indonesia	*	*
21.09.63	Vickers Valetta C.1	G-APKR	363	Decca Navigator Co	U/c collapsed	Gatwick, Surrey, UK	0	*
24.09.63	Bristol 170 Superfreighter 32	G-AMWA	13073	British United Air Ferries	Crashed on take-off	Guernsey	0	4
26.09.63	Douglas DC-3	F-BHKU	14012/25457	Air France	Damaged beyond repair	Oran, Algeria	*	*
09.10.63	Douglas C-74 Globemaster I	HP-385	13915	Aeronaves de Panama	Crashed after take-off	nr Marseilles, France	6	*
11.10.63	de Havilland DH.89A Dragon Rapide	ZS-DJT	6498	Operator Unknown	Written off	Ladysmith, South Africa	*	*
14.10.63	Vertol 107	*	*	New York Airways	Crashed when rotor failed	Idlewild, NY, USA	6	0
22.10.63	BAC One-Eleven 200AB	G-ASHG	004	British Aircraft Corporation	Crashed after stalling on test flight	Chicklade, Wilts, UK	7	0

Date	Type	Reg'n	C/n	Operator	Accident	Location	F	S
23.10.63	Douglas C-54A	TF-IST	10313	Danish Government	Destroyed by fire on ground	Narsarssuak, Greenland	*	*
29.10.63	Douglas DC-3	JA5024	13194	All Nippon Airways	Crashed	Toyama, Japan	*	*
01.11.63	Douglas DC-3	N45335	4964	Lake Central Airlines	Destroyed in hangar fire	Indianapolis, IN, USA	*	*
02.11.63	Martin 202	N177A	9147	Allegheny Airlines	Destroyed in ground collision with TWA B.707 N752TW	Newark, NJ, USA	*(*)	*
08.11.63	Douglas DC-3	OH-LCA	9799	Finnair	Crashed in fog	Mariehamn, Aaland Is, Finland	22	*
29.11.63	Douglas DC-8-54	CF-TJN	45654	Air Canada	Crashed after take-off	Ste Therese de Blanville, Canada	118	0
29.11.63	Douglas DC-3	N386T	20411	Purdue Aeron Corp	Crashed	Morgantown, WV, USA	*	*
30.11.63	Douglas DC-3	ET-AAT	13483	Ethiopian Airlines	Crashed	Addis Ababa, Ethiopia	0	3
07.12.63	Curtiss C-46	N609Z	26571	Zantop Air Transport	Crashed in bad weather [Found 08.07.64]	nr Nederland, CO, USA	3	0
07.12.63	Antonov AN-12	*	*	Aeroflot	Crashed on take-off	Kirensk, RSFSR, USSR	*	*
08.12.63	Boeing 707-121	N709PA	17588	Pan American World Airways	Crashed after lightning strike	Elkton, ME, USA	81	0
09.12.63	Curtiss C-46	N5160V	26512	Carolina Aircraft Corporation	Crashed	Off Azores, Portugal	3	*
12.12.63	Douglas C-54A	OD-AEB	10424	Trans Mediterranean Airways	Crashed	nr Ghanzi, Afghanistan	3	0
18.12.63	Boeing B-17G	CP-694	8733	Servicios Aereos Cochabamba	Crashed	El Alto, Bolivia	*	*
21.12.63	Convair 580	N7601	452	Union Oil Co of California	Crashed	Midland, TX, USA	*	*
30.12.63	de Havilland DH.89A Dragon Rapide	G-ALBC	6572	Solair Flying Services	Crashed into hill	Edale, Derbs, UK	0	2
oo.oo.63	Douglas DC-3	YA-AAA	4242	Ariana Afghan Airlines	Crashed	Logarh Valley, Afghanistan	*	*
oo.oo.63	Curtiss C-46	ZP-CCE	22460	International Products Corp	Crashed	Asuncion, Paraguay	*	*
oo.oo.63	de Havilland Dove 1	N91827	04015	S.J.Phillips	Written off	Alaska, USA	*	*
oo.oo.63	Avro Anson IV	XA-NEI	1556	Cia Impulsora de Aviacion	Crashed	Mexico	*	*
oo.oo.63	Tupolev TU-114B	SSSR-76462	8270301	Aeroflot	Crashed	USSR	*	*
09.01.64	Douglas DC-3	LV-FYJ	14713/26158	Aerolineas Litoral Argentina	Crashed when pilot was overcome by fumes from engine fire	Zarate, Argentina	31	*
09.01.64	Douglas DC-3	CF-ILQ	12377	Austin Airways	Crashed	nr Rupert River, PQ, Canada	*	*
09.01.64	de Havilland Dove 6BA	N4267C	04337	National Executive Flight Service	Crashed	Stuart, FL, USA	*	*
13.01.64	Curtiss C-46	SE-CFF	53	Transair Congo	Crashed on take-off	Thysville, Congo	*	*
03.02.64	Douglas DC-3	TC-ETI	12319	Turk Hava Yollari	Crashed	nr Ankara, Turkey	3	*
04.02.64	Douglas DC-3	CP-568	19024	Lloyd Aereo Boliviano	Crashed after take-off	Yacuiba, Bolivia	2	*
06.02.64	Douglas DC-3	PT-ATP	2197	Perdigao SA Comercio y Industria	Crashed	Cacador, Brazil	*	*
08.02.64	Consolidated C-87 Liberator	CP-575	*	Boliviana de Aviacion	Crashed	El Alto, Bolivia	*	*
17.02.64	VEB 14P	HA-MAH	14803033	Malev	Destroyed in hangar fire	Budapest, Hungary	*	*
18.02.64	Grumman G-73 Mallard	JA5067	J-40	Nitto Airlines	Crashed after engine trouble	nr Osaka, Japan	2	*
21.02.64	Douglas DC-3	PI-C97	14944/26389	Philippine Air Lines	Crashed	Marawi City, Philippines	31	*
21.02.64	de Havilland Canada Otter	PI-55	168	Operator Unknown	Written off	Location Unknown	*	*
23.02.64	Vickers Viscount 732	SU-AKX	076	United Arab Airlines	Overran on landing	Beirut, Lebanon	0	*
25.02.64	Douglas DC-8-21	N8607	45428	Eastern Air Lines	Crashed in turbulence	Lake Pontchartrain, LA, USA	58	0
26.02.64	de Havilland Dove 2	G-ANGE	04167	Libyan Aviation Co	U/c collapsed on landing	Airfield No.12, Libya	*	*
27.02.64	Convair 240-0	JA5098	053	Fuji Airlines	Crashed into embankment	Oita, Japan	20	*
29.02.64	Bristol Britannia 312	G-AOVO	13423	British Eagle Airways	Crashed into mountain	nr Innsbruck, Austria	83	0
01.03.64	Lockheed 049 Constellation	N86504	2025	Paradise Airlines	Crashed on approach	Tahoe Valley, NV, USA	85	0
05.03.64	Douglas DC-3	LN-PAS	12181	Wideroe	Caught fire on take-off	Oslo, Norway	*	*
08.03.64	Douglas DC-3	HK-862	12374	Taxi Aereo de Santander	Crashed	Bogota, Colombia	28	*
08.03.64	Saab Scandia	PP-SQY	110	VASP	Crashed	Londrina, Brazil	*	*
09.03.64	Douglas DC-3	N410D	4970	Snow Valley Ski Lines	Crashed on approach due to icing	Chicago, IL, USA	1	29
10.03.64	Douglas DC-4	N384	18379	Slick Airways	Crashed due to tail icing	Boston, MA, USA	3	0
12.03.64	Douglas DC-3	N61442	9642	Frontier Airlines	Crashed in snowstorm	Miles City, MT, USA	5	*
16.03.64	Beechcraft C-18S	JA5028	8547	Operator Unknown	Written off	Kagoshima, Japan	*	*
18.03.64	BAC One-Eleven 201AC	G-ASJB	006	British Aircraft Corporation	Damaged in heavy landing	Wisley, Surrey, UK	0	*
21.03.64	Curtiss C-46	PP-LDL	33467	VASP	Crashed	Rio de Janeiro, Brazil	*	*
21.03.64	Piper PA-23-160 Apache	G-ASHC	23-1312	Westway Air Taxis	Crashed	Aintree, Lancs, UK	*	*
22.03.64	de Havilland Comet 4	G-APDH	06409	Malaysian Airlines	U/c failed on landing	Singapore, Malaysia	0	*
28.03.64	Vickers Viscount 785D	I-LAKE	328	Alitalia	Crashed on approach	Mt Vesuvius, Italy	45	0
28.03.64	Douglas C-54A	N4726V	10315	Facilities Management Corp	Crashed	Pacific Ocean	9	*
oo.03.64	Grumman G-21A Goose	N68174	1173	Operator Unknown	Destroyed in earthquake	Anchorage, AK, USA	*	*
02.04.64	Douglas DC-3	VT-COU	13570	Kalinga Airlines	Crashed	Calcutta, India	*	*

Date	Type	Reg'n	C/r	Operator	Accident	Location	F	S
04.04.64	Douglas DC-4	PP-BTQ	10506	Paraense Transportes Aereos	Crashed	Belem, Brazil	*	*
07.04.64	Boeing 707-139	N779PA	17904	Pan American World Airways	Overran into sea	New York, NY, USA	0	*
07.04.64	Douglas DC-3	VT-CMD	12491	Kalinga Airlines	Crashed	Along, India	*	*
07.04.64	Curtiss C-46	PT-BVG	30456	N.L.Clearo	Crashed on smuggling flight	Location Unknown	*	*
12.04.64	Douglas DC-3	VR-AAM	15530/26975	Aden Airways	Damaged beyond repair	Hargeisa, Somalia	*	*
17.04.64	Sud Aviation Caravelle 3	OD-AEM	023	Middle East Airlines	Crashed into sea on approach	Dahran, Saudi Arabia	49	*
21.04.64	Vickers Viscount 754D	OD-ACX	245	Middle East Airlines	Damaged when runway collapsed	El Arish, Morocco	0	*
22.04.64	de Havilland DH.89A Dragon Rapide	ZK-BAU	6654	Southern Scenic Air Services	Crashed	Milford Sound, New Zealand	*	*
24.04.64	Douglas DC-7	N68N	44275	Federal Aviation Administration	Controlled crash for test purposes	Deer Valley, AZ, USA	0	0
04.05.64	Douglas DC-3	EP-ADI	6350	Iran Air	Crashed	Isfahan, Iran	*	*
07.05.64	Fairchild F-27A	N2770R	0036	Pacific Air Lines	Crashed after both pilots shot by passenger	nr Concord, CA, USA	44	0
20.05.64	Douglas DC-3	PI-C568	13786/25231	Fleming Airways System Transport	Destroyed in hangar fire	Pasay City, Philippines	*	*
20.05.64	de Havilland Canada Otter	PI-51	068	Operator Unknown	Written off	Location Unknown	*	*
27.05.64	Douglas DC-3	PP-SPZ	4649	VASP	Crashed	Off Sao Paulo, Brazil	*	*
29.05.64	Douglas DC-4	CP-717	10274	Transportes Aereos Benianos	Crashed	S.E. of Trinidad, Bolivia	*	*
29.05.64	Douglas C-54A	CP-747	10294	Transportes Aereos Benianos	Crashed	Location Unknown	*	*
04.06.64	Lear Jet 23	N801L	23-001	Lear Jet Corporation	Crashed	Wichita, KS, USA	*	*
06.06.64	Douglas DC-3	CP-729	15798/32546	Aerolineas Abaroa	Crashed	La Paz, Bolivia	*	*
06.06.64	Douglas DC-3	PP-SPK	15958/32706	VASP	Crashed	Brasilia, Brazil	*	*
09.06.64	Tupolev TU-104B	SSSR-42476	021304	Aeroflot	Damaged after overrunning in rain on landing	Novosibirsk, RSFSR, USSR	*	*
13.06.64	Vickers Viscount 757	CF-THT	302	Air Canada	Undershot runway	Toronto, ON, Canada	0	*
13.06.64	Douglas DC-3	HZ-AAN	12899	Saudi Arabian Airlines	Crashed	Red Sea, off Saudi Arabia	*	*
13.06.64	Lisunov Li-2	YR-DAC	23441507	Tarom	Crashed	Paragina, Romania	*	*
20.06.64	Curtiss C-46	B-908	*	Civil Air Transport	Crashed after engine fire on take-off	Taichung, Taiwan	57	0
21.06.64	Douglas DC-3	EC-AQH	20072	TASSA	Crashed on take-off	Las Palmas, Spain	1	*
25.06.64	Fokker F-27 Friendship 200	AP-ALO	10165	Pakistan International Airlines	Crashed on landing	Dacca, Pakistan	0	*
28.06.64	Douglas DC-3	PP-BTU	13790/25235	Paraense Transportes Aereos	Crashed	Porto Velho, Brazil	*	*
30.06.64	Douglas C-54A	N188S	10297	Zantop Air Transport	Destroyed by fire	Location Unknown	*	*
09.07.64	Vickers Viscount 745D	N7405	103	United Air Lines	Caught fire & crashed	Parrotsville, TN, USA	39	*
15.07.64	Boeing 720-030B	D-ABOP	18249	Lufthansa	Overstressed & broke up	nr Petersdorf, West Germany	3	0
17.07.64	Douglas DC-7B	N809D	44860	Eastern Air Lines	Landed short & caught fire	Richmond, VA, USA	*	*
20.07.64	Douglas DC-7B	N831D	45340	Eastern Air Lines	U/c collapsed on landing	Charlotte, NC, USA	0	*
22.07.64	Curtiss C-46	AN-AKY	*	Lanica	Crashed	Managua, Nicaragua	*	*
24.07.64	Beechcraft C-45H	9Q-CXA	AF-778	AMAZ	Written off	Location Unknown	*	*
26.07.64	Antonov AN-2	DM-SKS	117047315	Interflug	Crashed	nr Magdenburg, East Germany	*	*
03.08.64	Ilyushin IL-18	SSSR-75824	182004903	Aeroflot	Crashed short of runway	Magadan, RSFSR, USSR	*	*
15.08.64	Bristol Sycamore 3A	G-AMWH	13069	British European Airways	Crashed on landing	Cowes, IoW, UK	*	*
16.08.64	Curtiss C-46	PP-NMF	26971	VASP	Crashed after propeller failure	Rio Capim Para, Brazil	3	*
19.08.64	Douglas DC-3	N61350	4535	Hawthorne Nevada Airlines	Crash landed after engine failure	nr Tonapah, NV, USA	*	*
22.08.64	Douglas DC-3	CP-680	13371	Servicios Aereos Cochabamba	Crashed	Huayna, Bolivia	4	*
24.08.64	Avro Anson V	CF-GML	MDF-304	Spartan Air Services	Crashed	nr Whitehorse, YT, Canada	1	0
27.08.64	Canadair DC-4M-2	YV-C-LBU	129	Linea Expresa Bolivar	Damaged by hurricane	Miami, FL, USA	*	*
27.08.64	Curtiss C-46	N9903F	30264	Airlift International	Blown half a mile by hurricane	Miami, FL, USA	0	0
27.08.64	Canadair DC-4M-2	CF-TFQ	141	Keegan Aviation	Damaged by hurricane	Miami, FL, USA	0	*
27.08.64	Canadair DC-4M-2	CF-TFJ	134	Linea Expresa Bolivar	Damaged by hurricane	Miami, FL, USA	0	*
27.08.64	Douglas DC-3	N34963	16891/34148	Boreas Corporation	Damaged by hurricane	Miami, FL, USA	*	*
27.08.64	Curtiss C-46	N1823M	22578	Airlift International	Blown into another aircraft during hurricane	Miami, FL, USA	*(*)	*
02.09.64	Ilyushin IL-18	*	*	Aeroflot	Crashed into hill	Yuzhno-Sakhalinsk, RSFSR, USSR	*	*
03.09.64	Lockheed 1649A Starliner	N7307C	1008	Federal Aviation Administration	Controlled crash for test purposes	Deer Valley, AZ, USA	0	0
03.09.64	Cessna 180A	ET-ABK	32146	Ethiopian Airlines	Crashed	Maghi Georgis, Ethiopia	*	*
04.09.64	Vickers Viscount 701C	PP-SRR	066	VASP	Crashed into mountain	Mt Nova, Brazil	39	0
13.09.64	Fokker F-27 Friendship 100	HB-AAI	10141	Balair	Damaged in forced landing	Malaga, Spain	0	*
15.09.64	Douglas DC-3	HK-319	19680	Avianca	Crashed	Mandinga, Colombia	*	*

Date	Type	Reg'n	C/n	Operator	Accident	Location	F	S
20.09.64	Scottish Aviation Twin Pioneer 3	XW-PBO	566	Bird & Sons	Damaged beyond repair	Saigon, South Vietnam	*	*
22.09.64	Douglas DC-3	N1549V	13480	Caribair	Damaged beyond repair	San Juan, Puerto Rico	*	*
28.09.64	Douglas DC-7C	G-ASID	45161	Caledonian Airways	Undershot runway	Istanbul, Turkey	*	*
02.10.64	Lockheed 749A Constellation	LX-IOK	2562	Interocean Airways	Ran off runway & damaged beyond repair	Addis Ababa, Ethiopia	1	*
02.10.64	Douglas DC-6B	F-BHMS	44062	UTA	Crashed into mountain	nr Trevelez, Spain	80	0
02.10.64	Douglas C-54A	YK-ADA	3101	Syrian Arab Airlines	Damaged beyond repair after overrunning runway	Damascus, Syria	*	*
09.10.64	Ilyushin IL-14	YR-ILB	146000926	Tarom	Crashed	nr Sibiu, Romania	32	*
10.10.64	Ilyushin IL-18B	YR-IMB	181003702	Tarom	Crashed into mountains	Carpathian Mts, Romania	*	*
19.10.64	Ilyushin IL-18	*	*	Aeroflot	Crashed into mountain	Mt Avala, Yugoslavia	33	*
30.10.64	Boeing B-17G	CP-741	32502	Co Boliviana de Rutas Aereas	Crashed	San Borja, Bolivia	*	*
15.11.64	Fairchild F-27A	N745L	0029	Bonanza Airlines	Crashed in snowstorm	nr Las Vegas, NV, USA	29	*
20.11.64	Convair 440	SE-CCK	195	Linjeflyg	Crashed into power cables	Angelholm, Sweden	31	*
20.11.64	Curtiss C-46	N3971B	22594	Zantop Air Transport	Crashed after take-off due to icing	Detroit, MI, USA	*	*
21.11.64	Douglas DC-3	CF-GOC	7362	Eastern Provincial Airways	Crashed	Lourdes du Blanc Sablon, PQ, Canada	*	*
23.11.64	Boeing 707-331	N769TW	17685	Trans World Airlines	Crashed after aborted take-off	Rome, Italy	50	*
24.11.64	Curtiss C-46	CC-CIB-0504	*	Lineas Aereas Interpolar	Damaged beyond repair	Los Cerillos, Chile	*	*
24.11.64	Curtiss C-46	N9885F	32878	Delta Air Lines	Crashed	Baton Rouge, LA, USA	*	*
26.11.64	Douglas DC-3	PP-SQP	1952	VASP	Destroyed in hangar fire	Sao Paulo, Brazil	*	*
29.11.64	Douglas DC-4	OO-DEP	18384	Belgian International Air Services	Crashed on take-off due to rebel gunfire	Leopoldville, Congo	7	*
08.12.64	Douglas DC-3	CP-639	7375	Aerolineas Abaroa	Crashed after explosion caused by passenger	nr Tipuani, Bolivia	5	*
16.12.64	Boeing B-17G	CP-762	8715	Bolivian Air System	Crashed	El Alto, Bolivia	*	*
21.12.64	Douglas DC-3	PI-C569	20396	Fleming Airways System Transport	Crashed	nr Kaliba, Philippines	1	*
24.12.64	Lockheed 1049H Super Constellation	N6915C	4812	Flying Tiger Line	Crashed	nr San Francisco, CA, USA	3	*
24.12.64	Douglas DC-3	OB-XAU-654	14541/25986	Satco	Crashed	Yurimaguas, Peru	*	*
28.12.64	de Havilland Canada Otter	VP-FAJ	377	British Antarctic Survey	Crashed on landing	Adelaide, British Antarctic Terr	0	1
29.12.64	Curtiss C-46	CC-CAN	*	Lineas Aereas Sud Americana	Crashed	nr Turrialba, Costa Rica	5	*
30.12.64	Curtiss C-46	N608Z	30328	Zantop Air Transport	Crashed on landing	Detroit, MI, USA	4	*
oo.oo.64	Ilyushin IL-62	SSSR-06300	40005	Ilyushin Design Bureau	Written off	USSR	*	*
oo.oo.64	Vickers Viking C.2	XB-FIP	179	B.Pasquelle	Destroyed by ground loop	Mexico	*	*
02.01.65	Aermacchi AL.60B-2	VQ-ZBM	5/6147	Basutair	Crashed	Maseru, Basutoland	*	*
03.01.65	Ilyushin IL-18	*	*	Aeroflot	Crashed	Alma-Ata, Kazakhstan, USSR	*	*
09.01.65	de Havilland Canada Otter	PK-PHB	309	Operator Unknown	Written off	Location Unknown	*	*
15.01.65	Douglas DC-3	PP-SPU	20729	VASP	Crashed	Santa Izabel do Morro, Brazil	*	*
15.01.65	Convair 240-0	PP-CEV	006	Cruzeiro	Crashed on approach	Sao Paulo, Brazil	8{7}	*
20.01.65	Douglas DC-3	PI-C945	4822	Fairways	Crashed	Mindoro Is, Philippines	*	*
20.01.65	de Havilland Dove 2	G-AKJG	04071	Shackleton Aviation	Crash landed after engine fire	nr Northampton, Northants, UK	0	*
22.01.65	Douglas DC-3	PP-PEE	7396	Panair do Brasil	Crashed	Porto Velho, Brazil	*	*
06.02.65	Douglas DC-6B	CC-CCG	45513	LAN-Chile	Crashed into mountain	San Jose Volcano, Chile	87	0
07.02.65	Boeing B-17G-BO	CP-580	9300	Lloyd Aereo Boliviano	Crashed	El Alto, Bolivia	*	*
08.02.65	Vickers Viking 1B	F-BJEQ	298	Air Nautic	Damaged on take-off	Calvi, Corsica, France	0	*
08.02.65	Douglas DC-7C	SE-CCC	45325	Scandinavian Airlines System	Destroyed by fire after aborted take-off	Tenerife, Canary Is, Spain	0	*
08.02.65	Douglas DC-7B	N849D	45455	Eastern Air Lines	Crashed after violent manoeuvre to avoid collision	Off New York, NY, USA	84	0
13.02.65	Curtiss C-46	YS-012C	127	Aerolineas El Salvador	Crashed after take-off	Miami, FL, USA	2	0
14.02.65	Douglas DC-3	JA5080	4436	Japan Domestic Airlines	Crashed	Mt Nakanoone, Japan	2	0
15.02.65	Vickers Viscount 782D	EP-AHC	299	Iran Air	Destroyed on landing	Isfahan, Iran	0	*
20.02.65	Douglas DC-3	YU-ACB	13367	JAT Yugoslav Airlines	Crashed	nr Belgrade, Yugoslavia	5	0
21.02.65	Boeing B-17G	CP-742	32499	Co Boliviana de Rutas Aereas	Crashed	Santa Ana, Bolivia	*	*
27.02.65	Convair 880-22M-22	JA8023	59	Japan Air Lines	Crashed after u/c struck obstruction	Nagasaki, Japan	0	*
02.03.65	Curtiss C-46	F-OAFI	26810	Air Cameroun	Crashed	Garoua, Cameroons	4	*
03.03.65	Vickers Viscount 701C	PP-SRQ	065	VASP	Veered off runway	Rio Galeao, Brazil	0	*
08.03.65	Douglas DC-3	PI-C948	4892	Fairways	Crashed	Libmanan, Philippines	10	2
08.03.65	Tupolev TU-124	SSSR-45028	2350803	Aeroflot	Crashed after take-off	Kuibyshev, RSFSR, USSR	25	0
11.03.65	Douglas DC-3	HK-153	4711	Avianca	Crashed on take-off	Bucaramanga, Colombia	*	*

Date	Type	Reg'n	C/n	Operator	Accident	Location	F	S
16.03.65	Douglas DC-3	CF-PQG	12055	Dept. of Transportation & Comm.	Crashed on take-off	Blanc Sablon, PQ, Canada	*	*
17.03.65	Fokker F-27 Friendship 200	VH-FNH	10180	Ansett-ANA	Wing touched ground on landing & caught fire	Launceston, Tas, Australia	0	*
17.03.65	Handley Page Dart Herald 211	CF-NAF	160	Eastern Provincial Airways	Crashed after take-off	nr Halifax, Canada	8	*
18.03.65	Douglas DC-3	N4997E	12191	Miami Aviation	Crashed	nr Clarenvillem, NF, Canada	2	0
18.03.65	Curtiss C-46	OB-R-577	33724	Satco	Crashed	Cerro Saguan, Peru	*	*
19.03.65	Vickers Viscount 773	YI-ACU	331	Iraqi Airways	Damaged on landing	Cairo, UAR	0	*
20.03.65	Antonov AN-24	*	*	Aeroflot	Crashed short of runway	Hanty-Mansiysk, RSFSR, USSR	*	*
22.03.65	Douglas DC-3	HK-109	4753	Avianca	Crashed	nr San Vicente, Colombia	29	0
22.03.65	Curtiss C-46	PP-VBJ	33481	Varig	Damaged beyond repair	Porto Nacional, Brazil	*	*
26.03.65	Douglas DC-3	VR-AAA	14141/25586	Aden Airways	Crashed	Hadibo, Aden	*	*
26.03.65	Douglas DC-3	AP-AAH	12089	Pakistan International Airlines	Crashed after take-off	Lowery Pass, Pakistan	22	2
27.03.65	Lockheed Electra 188C	ZK-TEC	2011	Tasman Empire Airways	Crashed	Whenuapai, New Zealand	0	*
31.03.65	Convair 440-62	EC-ATH	388	Iberia	Crashed	Off Tangiers, Morocco	50	3
01.04.65	Douglas DC-3	VH-ANJ	9105	Airlines of New South Wales	Crash landed	Warranambool, Vic, Australia	*	*
03.04.65	Douglas DC-3	CF-FAJ	12099	Eastern Provincial Airways	Crashed on landing	St Pierre, St Pierre & Miquelon	*	*
06.04.65	Douglas DC-3	N150A	6178	E.Marger	Crashed	Off Andros Is, Bahamas	*	*
10.04.65	Handley Page Dart Herald 207	JY-ACQ	170	Alia	Crashed after take-off	nr Damascus, Syria	45	0
14.04.65	Douglas DC-3	G-ANTB	15762/27207	British United (C.I.) Airways	Crashed	Jersey	26	1
16.04.65	Fairchild F-27A	N757L	0054	Bonanza Airlines	Damaged by ground loop on take-off	Las Vegas, NV, USA	0	*
23.04.65	Douglas DC-6A	N6541C	45369	Aaxico Airlines	Crashed into mountain	Mt Rainier, WA, USA	5	0
26.04.65	de Havilland Dove 2	G-AJLW	04033	Aircruise	Crashed in poor weather	nr Droitwich, Worcs, UK	*	*
27.04.65	de Havilland DH.89A Dragon Rapide	F-OBOD	6412	Operator Unknown	Written off	Libreville, Gabon	*	*
05.05.65	Lockheed 1049G Super Constellation	EC-AIN	4550	Iberia	Crashed on landing	Tenerife, Canary Is, Spain	32	18
12.05.65	MBB HFB.320 Hansa	D-CHFB	1001	Hamburger Flugzeugbau	Crashed	Torrejon, Spain	*	*
20.05.65	Boeing 720-040B	AP-AMH	18379	Pakistan International Airlines	Crashed on approach	Cairo, UAR	121	6
24.05.65	Westland Wessex HAS.1	XS118	097	Rolls Royce	Crashed after engine failure	M1 motorway, Notts, UK	*	*
29.05.65	Convair 240-1	JA5088	027	Japan Domestic Airlines	Crashed	Obihiro, Japan	*	*
29.05.65	Douglas DC-3	N91016	11853	Reeve Aleutian Airlines	Crashed	Nikolski, AK, USA	*	*
30.05.65	Aerospatiale 3210 Super Frelon	F-WMCU	03	Aerospatiale	Written off	France	*	*
06.06.65	Douglas DC-6B	PI-C950	43820	Filipinas Orient Airways	Crashed	Cebu City, Philippines	*	*
11.06.65	Douglas C-54A	7T-VAC	10421	Air Algerie	Damaged beyond repair	Dar-el-Beida, Algeria	*	*
15.06.65	de Havilland DH.89A Dragon Rapide	ZK-AKS	6647	Southern Scenic Air Services	Crashed into ridge	Mt Soho, New Zealand	*	*
18.06.65	Douglas DC-6A	N6579C	45480	Aaxico Airlines	Struck trees on approach	Knobnoster, MT, USA	0	*
23.06.65	Beechcraft G18S	PZ-TAR	BA-584	Operator Unknown	Written off	Kabelebo, Surinam	*	*
oo.06.65	Douglas DC-3	SU-AJW	*	United Arab Airlines	Written off	Cairo, UAR	*	*
01.07.65	Boeing 707-124	N70773	17609	Continental Airlines	Overran on wet runway	Kansas City, MO, USA	0	*
04.07.65	Hawker Siddeley Argosy 222	G-ASXL	6800	British European Airways	Forced landing	Piacenza, Italy	0	*
06.07.65	Douglas DC-3	6V-AAA	4351	Air Mauritanie	Damaged beyond repair	Nouackchott, Mauritania	*	*
07.07.65	Aermacchi AL.60B-1	G-ARZG	6219-39	Air Navigation & Trading	Crashed	Blackpool, Lancs, UK	*	*
08.07.65	Douglas DC-6B	CF-CUQ	43844	Canadian Pacific Airlines	Crashed after bomb explosion	North of Vancouver, BC, Canada	52	0
09.07.65	Bristol Britannia 302	XA-MEC	12918	Aeronaves de Mexico	U/c collapsed & veered off runway	Tijuana, Mexico	*	*
11.07.65	Hawker Siddeley HS.748 1	G-ARMV	1536	Skyways Coach Air	Crash landed	Lympne, Kent, UK	0	*
15.07.65	de Havilland Dove 2A	N6503D	04377	Virgin Islands Airways	Stalled on take-off & crashed	St Thomas, US Virgin Islands	8	4
20.07.65	Vickers Viscount 701	G-AMOL	025	Cambrian Airways	Crashed on approach in poor weather	Liverpool, UK	2{2}	0
23.07.65	Convair 440	N8415H	125	Allegheny Airlines	Crashed on take-off	Montoursville, PA, USA	*	*
02.08.65	Vickers Viking 1B	G-AHPL	149	Invicta Airways	Damaged in aborted take-off	Manston, Kent, UK	0	*
04.08.65	Douglas C-54D	OB-R-769	10826	Rutas Internacionales Peruanas	Caught fire on take-off	Panama City, Panama	7	0
08.08.65	Douglas DC-3	PP-AJE	3283	Transportes Aereos Catarinense	Crashed	Carauari, Brazil	*	*
12.08.65	Curtiss C-46	PP-BTH	30571	Paraense Transportes Aereos	Crashed	Cuiaba, Brazil	13	0
16.08.65	Boeing 727-22	N7036U	18328	United Air Lines	Crashed on approach	Lake Michigan, MI, USA	30	0
20.08.65	Vickers Viscount 804	SP-LVA	249	LOT Polish Airlines	Crashed after structural failure in turbulence	St Trond, Belgium	4	0
20.08.65	Convair 240-0	PP-CFD	142	Cruzeiro	Damaged in heavy landing	Rio de Janeiro, Brazil	*	*
04.09.65	Kawasaki-Vertol 107	JA9501	4010	Airlift Co	Written off	Motosu-gum, Japan	*	*
11.09.65	Douglas DC-3	PI-C942	1926	Fairways	Crashed	nr Cebu City, Philippines	*	*

Date	Type	Reg'n	C/n	Operator	Accident	Location	F	S
11.09.65	Antonov AN-12	*	*	Aeroflot	Crashed on approach	Ulan-Ude, RSFSR, USSR	*	*
13.09.65	Convair 880-22-1	N820TW	26	Trans World Airlines	Crash landed	Kansas City, MO, USA	0	*
13.09.65	Curtiss C-46	N5132B	32700	Airlift International	Crash landed	Dover AFB, DE, USA	*	*
14.09.65	Douglas DC-3	ET-ABI	12000	Ethiopian Airlines	Crashed	Gore, Ethiopia	*	*
16.09.65	Douglas DC-3	XV-NIC	20301	Air Vietnam	Shot down by Communist ground fire	Quang Ngai, South Vietnam	38	1
16.09.65	Douglas DC-3	HC-AFQ	17009/34272	Transportes Aereos Orientales	Crashed	Pastaza, Ecuador	9	2
17.09.65	Boeing 707-121B	N708PA	17586	Pan American World Airways	Crashed into high ground on approach	Montserrat	30	0
20.09.65	Lockheed 1049G Super Constellation	N9719C	4574	American Flyers Airline	Overran on landing	Ardmore, OK, USA	*	*
08.10.65	Fokker F-27 Friendship 200	AP-ATT	10279	Pakistan International Airlines	Crashed	nr Naran, Pakistan	4	*
14.10.65	Hawker Siddeley Argosy 101	N601Z	6659	Zantop Air Transport	Crash landed on road out of fuel	Pique, OH, USA	0	*
16.10.65	Douglas DC-7B	N824D	45333	Eastern Air Lines	U/c collapsed on landing	Charlotte, NC, USA	0	*
16.10.65	Beechcraft Queen Air 70	7T-VSD	LB-009	Air Algerie	Written off	Location Unknown	*	*
17.10.65	Douglas DC-3	HK-118	6182	Avianca	Mid-air collision with Piper PA-18 HK-922E	Bucaramanga, Colombia	19(*)	0
17.10.65	Douglas DC-3	VT-AUQ	19431	Kalinga Airlines	Crashed	Mohan Bari, India	8	0
17.10.65	Douglas DC-6	N37519	43008	United Air Lines	U/c collapsed on take-off	Huntsville, AL, USA	*	*
18.10.65	Boeing Stratoliner	F-BELV	1996	International Control Commission	Crashed – possibly shot down	nr Hanoi, North Vietnam	12	0
20.10.65	Douglas DC-3	PI-C144	13403	Philippine Air Lines	Crashed after take-off	Manila, Philippines	1	33
21.10.65	Lear Jet 23	N804LJ	23-015A	Robert J.Graf Inc	Crashed	Jackson, MI, USA	*	*
27.10.65	Vickers Vanguard 951	G-APEE	708	British European Airways	Crashed attempting overshoot	Heathrow, London, UK	36	0
29.10.65	Douglas DC-3	CP-645	20199	Transportes Aereos Acre	Crashed	San Ramon, Bolivia	*	*
04.11.65	Boeing B-17F-VE	CP-686	6369	Lloyd Aereo Boliviano	Crashed	Trinidad, Bolivia	*	*
08.11.65	Boeing 727-23	N1996	18901	American Airlines	Crashed on approach	Cincinnati, OH, USA	58	4
10.11.65	Tupolev TU-124	SSSR-45086	5351801	Aeroflot	Crashed on approach	Murmansk, RSFSR, USSR	32	*
11.11.65	Boeing 727-22	N7030U	18322	United Air Lines	Undershot on landing	Salt Lake City, UT, USA	43	54
14.11.65	Lear Jet 23	N234F	23-063	Paul Kelly Flying Service	Crashed	Palm Springs, CA, USA	*	*
23.11.65	Curtiss C-46	N1210W	33595	Associated Aviation Industries	Crashed on smuggling flight	Frontino, Colombia	*	*
24.11.65	McDonnell Douglas DC-8-54	N8784R	45769	Trans Caribbean Airlines	Destroyed by fire on ground	Miami, FL, USA	0	*
27.11.65	Douglas DC-3	N485	4848	Edde Airlines	Crashed	Salt Lake City, UT, USA	13	0
04.12.65	Lockheed 1049C Super Constellation	N6218C	4526	Eastern Air Lines	Mid-air collision with TWA B.707 N748TW & crash landed	North Salem, NY, USA	4(*)	46
07.12.65	Curtiss C-46	LV-HIJ	22346	Aerolineas Carreras	Crashed	nr Panama City, Panama	*	*
07.12.65	Curtiss C-46	LV-GGN	*	Aerolineas Carreras	Crashed	nr Panama City, Panama	*	*
07.12.65	Douglas DC-3	EC-ARZ	13474	Spantax	Crashed into hill	Tenerife, Canary Is, Spain	32	0
11.12.65	de Havilland Heron 1B	VQ-FAL	14033	Fiji Airways	Crashed	Taveuni, Fiji	*	*
12.12.65	Lear Jet 23	D-IHAQ	23-007	H.Quandt	Crashed	Zurich, Switzerland	*	*
15.12.65	Lockheed 1049H Super Constellation	N6914C	4811	Flying Tiger Line	Crashed	nr Alamosa, NM, USA	*	*
16.12.65	Douglas DC-3	PI-C856	*	Air Manila	Overshot on landing	Legaspi, Philippines	2	19
17.12.65	Douglas DC-3	G-AMWX	15846/32594	Skyways Coach Air	Crashed on beach & covered by tide	Le Treport, France	*	*
19.12.65	Curtiss C-46	PP-LDQ	30343	VASP	Crashed	San Salvador, Brazil	*	*
oo.oo.65	Ilyushin IL-62	SSSR-06156	30001	Ilyushin Design Bureau	Written off	USSR	*	*
oo.oo.65	Martin B-26 Marauder	XB-PEX	4590	Operator Unknown	Crashed	Location Unknown	*	*
01.01.66	Douglas DC-3	PK-GDU	13463	Garuda Indonesian Airlines	Mid-air collision with Garuda DC-3 PK-GDE	Sumatra, Indonesia	10(7)	*
01.01.66	Douglas DC-3	PK-GDE	19719	Garuda Indonesian Airlines	Mid-air collision with Garuda DC-3 PK-GDU	Sumatra, Indonesia	7(10)	*
02.01.66	Grumman G-21A Goose	*	*	BC Air Lines	Crashed on approach in snowstorm	Vancouver, BC, Canada	3	7
03.01.66	LTV XC-142	62-5923	3	LTV Aerospace	Damaged in hard landing	Edwards AFB, CA, USA	0	*
15.01.66	Douglas C-54B	HK-730	18325	Avianca	Crashed	Off Cartagena, Colombia	56	8
20.01.66	Douglas R4D-1	TL-KAA	9124	Central African Republic Air Force	Crashed	nr Yaounde, Cameroons	*	*
22.01.66	Douglas DC-3	*	*	COHATA	Crashed on take-off	Port-au-Prince, Haiti	30	5
24.01.66	Boeing 707-437	VT-DMN	18055	Air India	Crashed into mountain	Mont Blanc, France	117	0
26.01.66	Lockheed 1049G Super Constellation	N7115C	4596	Trans World Airlines	Damaged when nosewheel collapsed during towing	New York, NY, USA	0	*
27.01.66	Curtiss C-46	LV-GFW	26961	Aerovias Halcon	Damaged on landing	nr Rio Cuarto, Argentina	*	*
28.01.66	Convair 440-0	D-ACAT	464	Lufthansa	Crashed on approach in fog	Bremen, West Germany	46	0
oo.01.66	Beechcraft C-45H	TF-AIS	AF-731	Flugsyn	Crashed in bad weather	Off Neskaupstadu, Iceland	*	*
02.02.66	Sikorsky S-61N	AP-AOC	61-225	Pakistan International Airlines	Crashed after birdstrike on rotor	Faridpur, Pakistan	23	1
02.02.66	Antonov AN-24V	SU-AOB	57302101	Misrair	Crashed on take-off	Luxor, UAR	*	*

Date	Type	Reg'n	C/n	Operator	Accident	Location	F	S
02.02.66	Fokker F-27 Friendship 200	PH-SAB	10271	Indian Airlines	Crashed into high ground after navigation error	Srinagar, India	37	0
04.02.66	Boeing 727-81	JA8302	18822	All Nippon Airways	Crashed in bay on approach	Tokyo Bay, Japan	133	0
15.02.66	Sud Aviation Caravelle 6N	VT-DPP	130	Indian Airlines	Undershot & crashed	New Delhi, India	1	*
18.02.66	Douglas DC-6B	OO-ABG	43829	Belgian International Air Services	Crashed on approach	Milan, Italy	4	0
22.02.66	Curtiss C-46	XA-LOS	32693	Aerocarga	Crashed	Mexico	*	*
23.02.66	Curtiss C-46	OB-R-606	33477	Trans Peruana	Crashed	nr Rioja, Peru	*	*
24.02.66	Hawker Siddeley HS.125-1A	N1135K	25019	Pieter Kiewit & Son	Crashed	Des Moins, IA, USA	*	*
02.03.66	North American B-25 Mitchell	CP-718	*	F.Vasquez	Written off	Cobija, Bolivia	*	*
04.03.66	McDonnell Douglas DC-8-43	CF-CPK	45761	Canadian Pacific Airlines	Undershot on landing	Tokyo, Japan	64	8
04.03.66	Northrop C-125 Raider	CP-650	2516	South American Placers	Crashed	Caranavi, Bolivia	*	*
05.03.66	Boeing 707-436	G-APFE	17706	British Overseas Airways Corporation	Broke up in turbulence	Mt Fuji, Japan	124	0
06.03.66	Curtiss C-46	SE-CFG	26710	Transair Congo	Damaged in hard landing	Stanleyville, Congo	*	*
06.03.66	Lockheed 1049 Super Constellation	N6901C	4015	L.A. Patagonicas Argentinas	Crashed on smuggling flight	Off Callao, Peru	1	*
10.03.66	Douglas DC-6A	OD-AEL	45504	Trans Mediterranean Airways	Crashed	Mt Parnon, Greece	4	0
10.03.66	Grumman G-21A Goose	*	*	Pacific Western Airlines	Crashed in bad weather	nr Prince Rupert, BC, Canada	6	1
11.03.66	Beechcraft King Air 90	N529N	LJ-0112	Operator Unknown	Written off	Green Castle, MO, USA	*	*
12.03.66	Tupolev TU-124	SSSR-45017	2350602	Aeroflot	Crashed on landing	Minsk, Bylorussia, USSR	0	*
18.03.66	Antonov AN-24B	SU-AOA	57302009	United Arab Airlines	Crashed on approach during snowstorm	Cairo, UAR	30	0
19.03.66	Lear Jet 23	N316M	23-061	Mutual Benefit Health & Accident	Crashed	Lake Michigan, MI, USA	*	*
20.03.66	Curtiss C-46	N1245N	22473	Servicios Americanos	Crashed on smuggling flight	Asuncion, Paraguay	3	*
20.03.66	Beechcraft H-18	SU-ANH	BA-624	Eastern Petroleum	Written off	nr Cairo, Egypt	*	*
21.03.66	Canadair CL-44D4-2	N453T	022	Flying Tiger Line	Crash landed	Norfolk, VA, USA	0	*
oo.03.66	Douglas DC-7B	HC-AIP	45194	Ecuatoriana	Taxiied into ditch	Miami, FL, USA	0	*
01.04.66	Douglas DC-3	N91375	16432/33180	C.D.Stoltzfus & Associates	Crashed	Litchfield Park, AZ, USA	*	*
14.04.66	Airspeed Ambassador 2	G-ALZX	5220	Dan-Air	Damaged on landing	Beauvais, France	0	*
17.04.66	Douglas DC-3	N8744R	20156	Continental Air Services	Crashed	Sam Neua, Laos	*	*
20.04.66	Douglas DC-3	PP-VAY	17013/34276	Varig	Damaged beyond repair	Porto Nacional, Brazil	*	*
22.04.66	Lockheed Electra 188C	N185H	1136	American Flyers Airline	Crashed when pilot suffered heart attack	Ardmore, OK, USA	83	15
23.04.66	Lear Jet 23	N235R	23-032	Rexall Drug & Chemical Corporation	Crashed	Clarendon, TX, USA	*	*
25.04.66	Douglas DC-3	VT-DDR	12070	Indian Airlines	Written off	Nagpur, India	*	*
27.04.66	Lockheed 749A Constellation	OB-R-771	2521	Lansa	Crashed into mountain	Tomas, Peru	49	0
28.04.66	Curtiss C-46	B-1535	22367	Air America	Crashed on take-off	Kon Tum, South Vietnam	*	*
10.05.66	Sikorsky S-58	JA7067	58-0410	Aero Asahi	Crashed	Niigata, Japan	*	*
11.05.66	Douglas DC-3	5W-FAB	13996/25441	Polynesian Airlines	Crashed	Off Savai'i, Western Samoa	*	*
18.05.66	Douglas DC-7	N6339C	45153	United Air Lines	Damaged on landing	Denver, CO, USA	*	*
03.06.66	Hawker Siddeley Trident 1C	G-ARPY	2126	Hawker Siddeley Aviation	Crashed	Felthorpe, Norfolk, UK	4	0
05.06.66	Hawker Siddeley HS.125-1	F-BKMF	25007	Air Affaires	Crashed	Off Nice, France	*	*
06.06.66	Lockheed 749A Constellation	N86523	2659	Pacific Northern Airlines	Damaged in hard landing	Kenai, AK, USA	0	*
16.06.66	Curtiss C-46	N10415	341	Zantop Air Transport	Mid-air collision with Aztec N5628Y	Colombia City, IN, USA	2(*)	*
20.06.66	Curtiss C-46	CF-FBJ	2941	Sudair	Crashed in storm	Quebec, PQ, Canada	2	*
23.06.66	Douglas DC-3	PP-YPK	20181	Varig	Crashed	Porto Nacional, Brazil	*	*
25.06.66	Fokker F-27 Friendship 200	XY-ADL	10236	Union of Burma Airways	Overran and damaged	Moulmein, Burma	*	*
27.06.66	Douglas DC-3	N17337	1962	Aeronaut Air Services	Crashed	Long Beach, MS, USA	*	*
29.06.66	Douglas DC-3	PI-C17	20573	Philippine Air Lines	Crashed	Mindoro Islands, Philippines	26	2
30.06.66	Hawker Siddeley Trident 1E	9K-ACG	2113	Kuwait Airways	Crash landed	nr Kuwait, Kuwait	0	83
30.06.66	Douglas DC-6	HR-TNG	42887	TAN	Ran off runway & caught fire	Toncontin, Honduras	*	*
04.07.66	McDonnell Douglas DC-8-52	ZK-NZB	45751	Air New Zealand	Crashed after take-off	Auckland, New Zealand	2	3
04.07.66	Douglas DC-3	*	*	Transporte Aereo Militar	Crashed	Rio Orton, Bolivia	*	*
09.07.66	Martin 404	N40446	14238	Piedmont Airlines	U/c collapsed	Roanoke, VA, USA	*	*
10.07.66	Ilyushin IL-18	CU-T830	182004905	Cubana	Damaged in forced landing	Cienfuegos, Cuba	*	*
11.07.66	Curtiss C-46	HK-527	33215	Aeropesca	Crashed	Cerro el Planchon, Chile	*	*
15.07.66	Douglas DC-3	PP-YPT	13488	REAL	Damaged beyond repair	Sao Paulo, Brazil	*	*
24.07.66	Douglas DC-3	HS-000	3266	Thai Government	Crashed	Off California, USA	*	*
27.07.66	Douglas DC-3	N4994E	12442	Frontier Airlines	Crashed	Gallup, NM, USA	*	*

Date	Type	Reg'n	C/n	Operator	Accident	Location	F	S
28.07.66	Curtiss C-46	N9905F	30316	Zantop Air Transport	Crashed on take-off due to overweight cargo	Newark, NJ, USA	*	*
03.08.66	Curtiss C-46	CP-730	33457	Lloyd Aereo Boliviano	Crashed	nr Cochabamba, Bolivia	*	*
06.08.66	BAC One-Eleven 203AE	N1553	070	Braniff International Airlines	Broke up in turbulence	Falls City, NE, USA	42	0
11.08.66	Lisunov Li-2	YR-TAN	18428005	Tarom	Crashed	Lotrioara Valley, Romania	*	*
13.08.66	McDonnell Douglas DC-8-51	XA-PEI	45652	Aeronaves de Mexico	Crashed on approach	Acapulco, Mexico	6	0
15.08.66	Lockheed 749A Constellation	N65	2648	Federal Aviation Administration	Crashed on landing	Tachikawa AFB, Japan	0	*
17.08.66	Douglas DC-3	G-AOFZ	9131	Gulf Aviation	Crashed on take-off	Azaiba, Muscat & Oman	*	*
18.08.66	Curtiss C-46	LV-GLA	22534	Aerovias Halcon	Crash landed	Puertos Lobos, Argentina	*	*
21.08.66	Grumman G-21A Goose	*	*	Alaska Coastal Airlines	Crashed on glacier	nr Juneau, AK, USA	9	0
26.08.66	Convair 880-22M-3	JA8030	45	Japan Air Lines	Crashed on take-off	Tokyo, Japan	5	5
27.08.66	Ilyushin IL-18	*	*	Aeroflot	Crashed on take-off	Arkhangelsk, RSFSR, USSR	*	*
31.08.66	Bristol Britannia 102	G-ANBB	12903	Britannia Airways	Crashed on approach	Ljubljana, Yugoslavia	98	19
01.09.66	Piper PA-23-160 Apache	G-ATFZ	23-1314	Dan-Air	Crashed	nr Godalming, Surrey, UK	*	*
04.09.66	Sud Aviation Caravelle 6N	VT-DSB	134	Indian Airlines	Undershot & crashed	Bombay, India	4	*
12.09.66	Douglas DC-7CF	N2282	45128	Airlift International	Crashed on take-off	Tachikawa AFB, Japan	*	*
13.09.66	de Havilland DH.89A Dragon Rapide	5H-AAM	6492	Operator Unknown	Written off	Dar-es-Salaam, Tanzania	*	*
15.09.66	Curtiss C-46	CP-786	30224	R.Vasquez	Crashed	nr Santa Cruz, Bolivia	*	*
16.09.66	Douglas DC-3	EC-ACX	19410	Spantax	Crashed	Off Tenerife, Canary Is, Spain	1	26
19.09.66	Beechcraft C-45G	EL-AFO	AF-638	Major & White	Damaged beyond repair	Grand Coss, Liberia	*	*
22.09.66	Vickers Viscount 832	VH-RMI	416	Ansett-ANA	Crashed after engine fire	Winton, Qld, Australia	24	0
22.09.66	Douglas DC-4	*	*	Avianca	Crashed on take-off	Bogota, Colombia	2	0
23.09.66	Beechcraft C-45C	HP-319	7730	Aerovias Darientas	Written off	Darien, Panama	*	*
26.09.66	Rockwell 1121 Jet Commander	N500JR	065	Jim Robbins Airborne Division	Crashed	North Platte, SD, USA	*	*
27.09.66	Dornier Do.27Q-4	VQ-ZBL	2036	Basutair	Crashed	Basutoland	*	*
30.09.66	Antonov AN-24B	SU-AOM	*	Misrair	Struck camel on take-off & crashed	Cairo, UAR	*	*
01.10.66	Douglas DC-9-14	N9101	45794	West Coast Airlines	Crashed into high ground	Cascade Mts, OR, USA	18	0
11.10.66	Canadair DC-4M-2	I-ACOA	137	H.Wharton	Crashed on gun running flight [Illegal registration]	nr Garoua, Cameroons	*	*
15.10.66	Curtiss C-46F	CP-746	26417	Bolivian Air System	Crash landed	Apolo, Bolivia	0	3
18.10.66	Lockheed 1049C Super Constellation	N6219C	4527	Eastern Air Lines	Damaged beyond repair	Miami, FL, USA	*	*
31.10.66	Vickers Viscount 701	PP-SRM	019	VASP	Overran on landing	Santos Dumont, Brazil	0	*
04.11.66	Curtiss C-46	HK-512	26784	Aerocarga	Crashed	nr Funza, Colombia	*	*
05.11.66	Ilyushin IL-14	TZ-ABH	7342501	Air Mali	Crashed in mountains	Col de la Cayolle, France	7	0
09.11.66	de Havilland Heron 1B	VQ-FAX	14012	Fiji Airways	Damaged beyond repair on landing	Suva, Fiji	*	*
09.11.66	Britten-Norman BN-2 Islander	G-ATCT	0001	Britten-Norman	Crashed after structural failure in bad weather	Sneek, Netherlands	2	0
13.11.66	NAMC YS-11-111	JA8658	2023	All Nippon Airways	Crashed after overshoot	Off Matsuyama, Japan	50	0
15.11.66	Boeing 727-21	N317PA	18995	Pan American World Airways	Crashed on approach	Berlin, East Germany	3	0
19.11.66	Curtiss C-46	N68966	22492	Carolina Aircraft Corporation	Veered off runway	Keflavik, Iceland	*	*
20.11.66	Martin 404	N40406	14170	Piedmont Airlines	Crashed on approach	New Bern, NC, USA	3	0
21.11.66	Hawker Siddeley HS.125-1A	N235KC	25096	Kellogg Co	Crashed	Pinder Point, Bahamas	*	*
22.11.66	Ilyushin IL-18	*	*	Aeroflot	Crashed on take-off	Alma-Ata, Kazakhstan, USSR	*	*
23.11.66	Douglas DC-3	VR-AAN	4284	Aden Airways	Crashed after bomb explosion	Wadi Rabta, Aden	28	0
24.11.66	Ilyushin IL-18	LZ-BEN	184007101	Tabso	Crashed	nr Bratislava, Czechoslovakia	82	0
29.11.66	Convair 440	N3414	045	Allegheny Airlines	Damaged beyond repair	Harrisburg, PA, USA	*	*
30.11.66	Douglas DC-3	OB-R-568	15238/26683	Satco	Crashed	Chachapoyas, Peru	*	*
01.12.66	Vickers PBY-5A Catalina	PP-PCW	CV429	Cruzeiro	Crashed	nr Pedrera, Brazil	9	2
02.12.66	Tupolev TU-114B	SSSR-76457	8270201	Aeroflot	Crashed on take-off	Moscow, RSFSR, USSR	22	*
06.12.66	Curtiss C-46	ZP-CAP	26658	Germa Inc.	Crashed	Olavo Pato, Argentina	*	*
10.12.66	Sikorsky S-61N	AP-AOA	61-159	Pakistan International Airlines	Crashed	nr Dacca, Pakistan	1	1
18.12.66	Lockheed 1649A Starliner	N7301C	1002	Aerocondor	Crashed on landing	Bogota, Colombia	17	39
24.12.66	McDonnell Douglas DC-8-51	XA-NUS	45633	Aeronaves de Mexico	Crash landed	Texcoco, Mexico	0	*
24.12.66	Canadair CL-44D4-1	N228SW	031	Flying Tiger Line	Crashed into village	Da Nang, South Vietnam	4{107}	0
24.12.66	Douglas DC-3	HK-161	19630	Avianca	Crashed	nr Cascubel River, Colombia	29	*
28.12.66	LTV XC-142	62-5925	5	LTV Aerospace	Damaged when taxied into hangar	Edwards AFB, CA, USA	0	*
30.12.66	Douglas DC-7CF	N4059K	44926	Airlift International	U/c collapsed & caught fire	Saigon, South Vietnam	0	*

Date	Type	Reg'n	C/n	Operator	Accident	Location	F	S
30.12.66	Antonov AN-24	*	*	Aeroflot	Crashed	Liepaya, RSFSR, USSR	*	*
oo.oo.66	Antonov AN-2	YU-BBJ	IG49-30	Operator Unknown	Written off	Yugoslavia	*	*
14.01.67	Antonov AN-12	*	*	Aeroflot	Caught fire on take-off & crashed	Novosibirsk, RSFSR, USSR	*	*
17.01.67	Cessna 310	OO-SEA	310-35545	Sabena	Crashed	Zaventem, Belgium	*	*
18.01.67	Conrad 10200	N102S	*	Operator Unknown	Crashed	Ditchling Beacon, Sussex, UK	*	*
19.01.67	Vickers Viscount 745D	N7431	129	United Air Lines	Collided with snowplough on landing	Norfolk, VA, USA	0	*
21.01.67	Douglas C-54A	G-ASOG	10359	Air Ferry	Crashed on approach in rain	Frankfurt, West Germany	2	0
21.01.67	de Havilland Dove 1	TJ-ACC	04121	Cameroons Air Transport	Crashed	Tiko, Cameroons	*	*
23.01.67	Convair 640	N3408	021	Caribair	Undershot on landing	San Juan, Puerto Rico	0	*
24.01.67	Douglas DC-6	N74841	43056	Saturn Airways	U/c collapsed on landing	Oakland, CA, USA	0	*
24.01.67	Douglas DC-6B	SU-ANL	44104	United Arab Airlines	Damaged beyond repair	Hodeidah, Yemen Arab Republic	*	*
30.01.67	Douglas DC-6	XA-LAU	43059	Mexicana	Stalled on approach & crashed	Merida, Mexico	*	*
30.01.67	Douglas DC-3	9M-AMU	12006	Malaysia-Singapore Airlines	Crashed	Lutong, Sarawak, Malaysia	*	*
31.01.67	Douglas DC-6A	N640NA	45475	Saturn Airways	Undershot on landing	San Antonio, TX, USA	3	0
oo.01.67	Ilyushin IL-18V	DM-STF	181004105	Interflug	Destroyed by fire on ground during overhaul	Moscow, RSFSR, USSR	*	*
03.02.67	Curtiss C-46	*	*	Linea Aerea Ala de Chile	Crashed	La Yareta Pass, Chile	*	*
06.02.67	Douglas DC-3	YK-ACB	16811/33559	Syrian Arab Airlines	Crashed into building on landing	Aleppo, Syria	1	*
09.02.67	Antonov AN-12	CU-T827	401504	Cubana	Crashed due to possible bomb explosion	nr Mexico City, Mexico	10	0
10.02.67	Convair 440-11	HB-IMF	355	Swissair	Crashed on take-off	Hochwacht, Switzerland	4	0
12.02.67	Beechcraft D-18S	ZS-BVR	A-0393	Operator Unknown	Written off	Johannesburg, South Africa	*	*
16.02.67	Lockheed Electra 188C	PK-GLB	2021	Garuda Indonesian Airlines	Crashed on landing	Menado, Indonesia	20	43
16.02.67	Beechcraft King Air A90	D-ILNU	LJ-0178	Operator Unknown	Written off	Bremen, West Germany	*	*
18.02.67	North American B-25J Mitchell	CP-796	*	SANIA	Written off	Laja, Bolivia	*	*
20.02.67	Douglas DC-6	HR-SAG	42394	Sahsa	Overran runway	Toncontin, Honduras	4	49
21.02.67	Douglas DC-3	ST-AAM	15524/26969	Sudan Airways	Crashed into building on take-off	Khartoum, Sudan	1	1
23.02.67	Douglas DC-3	TF-ISA	12184	Flugfelag Islands	Damaged beyond repair	Danmarkshavn, Iceland	*	*
24.02.67	Douglas DC-6B	N8224H	43741	Northeast Airlines	Dbr when cabin section blew out – Landed safely	Holmdel, NJ, USA	0	*
26.02.67	Beechcraft Expeditor	CF-MPA	5848	RCMP Air Services	Destroyed in hangar fire	Edmonton, AB, Canada	*	*
28.02.67	Fokker F-27 Friendship 100	PI-C501	10147	Philippine Air Lines	Undershot runway	Mactan, Philippines	12	8
01.03.67	Douglas DC-3	PP-ASS	12985	Sadia	Damaged beyond repair	Caravelas, Brazil	*	*
01.03.67	Beechcraft D18S	ET-ABM	3333	Ethiopian Airlines	Damaged in ground loop	Gondar, Ethiopia	0	*
03.03.67	Scottish Aviation Twin Pioneer 1	9M-ANO	532	Malaysian Airlines	Damaged on landing	Limbang, Malaysia	*	*
03.03.67	Antonov AN-12	*	*	Aeroflot	Crashed on take-off	Salekhard, RSFSR, USSR	*	*
04.03.67	Curtiss C-46	HK-758	32815	Aerocondor	Damaged on take-off	Bogota, Colombia	*	*
04.03.67	Douglas DC-8-33	PP-PEA	45253	Varig	Crashed on approach	Monrovia, Liberia	51{5}	39
05.03.67	Convair 580	N73130	023	Lake Central Airlines	Crashed	nr Marseille, OH, USA	*	*
06.03.67	Short Skyvan 2	I-TORE	SH.1832	Aeralpi	Crashed	Venice, Italy	*	*
08.03.67	Aviation Traders ATL-98 Carvair	F-BMHU	10338/4	Cie Air Transport	Crashed on take-off	Karachi, Pakistan	4	2
09.03.67	McDonnell Douglas DC-9-15	N1063T	45777	Trans World Airlines	Mid-air collision with Baron	Urbana, OH, USA	25(1)	0
10.03.67	Fairchild F-27	N2712	0073	West Coast Airlines	Crashed due to ice formation	Klamath Falls, OR, USA	4	*
11.03.67	de Havilland Canada Twin Otter 100	I-CLAI	030	Aeralpi	Crashed	Mt Visenti, Italy	4	0
13.03.67	Vickers Viscount 818	ZS-CVA	317	South African Airways	Crashed into sea after pilot became incapacitated	Off East London, South Africa	25	0
17.03.67	Douglas DC-3	EP-AEF	19239	Iran Air	Crashed	Bandar Abbas, Iran	*	*
24.03.67	Douglas DC-3	N54370	19220	Amerine Turkey Breeding Farms	Crashed	Merced, CA, USA	*	*
30.03.67	McDonnell Douglas DC-8-51	N802E	45409	Delta Air Lines	Crashed into hotel on approach	New Orleans, LA, USA	6{13}	0
02.04.67	Lockheed 18 Lodestar	*	*	Caribbean Airlines	Crashed	Off Lima, Peru	5	*
04.04.67	Scottish Aviation Twin Pioneer 3	5N-ABQ	523	Bristow Helicopters (Nigeria) Ltd	Damaged beyond repair	Ugheli, Nigeria	*	*
06.04.67	Ilyushin IL-18	*	*	Aeroflot	Crashed after take-off due to engine failure	Moscow, RSFSR, USSR	*	*
08.04.67	Douglas DC-3	G-AMYW	16272/33020	Hunting Surveys	Crashed	nr Hail, Saudi Arabia	*	*
11.04.67	Douglas DC-4	7T-VAU	3065	Air Algerie	Crashed into mountain	Tamanrasset, Algeria	35	4
13.04.67	Boeing B-17G	CP-767	32500	Co Boliviana de Rutas Aereas	Crashed	El Alto, Bolivia	*	*
14.04.67	Beechcraft G18S	PZ-TAT	AF-333	Operator Unknown	Written off	Paramaribo, Surinam	*	*
15.04.67	de Havilland DH.89A Dragon Rapide	ZK-AKT	6673	Southern Scenic Air Services	Crashed	Shotover River, New Zealand	*	*
16.04.67	Beechcraft King Air A90	N129GP	LJ-0216	Operator Unknown	Written off	Endicott, NY, USA	*	*

Date	Type	Reg'n	C/n	Operator	Accident	Location	F	S
17.04.67	Lockheed 1049H Super Constellation	N7777C	4803	Alaska Airlines	Damaged on landing	Kotzebue, AK, USA	0	*
20.04.67	Bristol Britannia 313	HB-ITB	13232	Globe Air	Crashed after overshoot	Nicosia, Cyprus	126	4
20.04.67	Bristol Britannia 305	G-ANCG	12923	British Eagle Airways	Belly landed	Manston, Kent, UK	0	*
23.04.67	de Havilland Dragon 1	ZK-AXI	2057	Auckland Flying School	Damaged beyond repair	Ardmore, New Zealand	*	*
26.04.67	Douglas DC-3	HK-326	4631	Avianca	Crashed on take-off	Sogamoso, Colombia	17	1
27.04.67	Fokker F-27 Friendship 400	PK-PFB	10306	Fokker	Crashed after take-off on demonstration flight	Malaybalay, Indonesia	17	*
02.05.67	Curtiss C-46	CP-712	84	Aerovias Boliviana Transandina	Crashed	Incahuara, Bolivia	*	*
03.05.67	Vickers Viscount 812	G-AVJZ	360	Channel Airways	Crashed on take-off	Southend, Essex, UK	0{2}	3
03.05.67	Douglas DC-3	TF-AIO	16668/33416	Flugsyn	Crashed on landing	Vestmann Is, Finland	3	0
07.05.67	de Havilland DH.89A Dragon Rapide	G-AJKW	6539	Operator Unknown	Damaged beyond repair	Halfpenny Green, Salop, UK	*	*
10.05.67	LTV XC-142	62-5921	1	LTV Aerospace	Crashed	Mt Creek Lake, TX, USA	3	0
15.05.67	Curtiss C-46	CF-NAD	30200	Nordair	Crashed	Cape Dyer, Baffin Is, Canada	4	*
16.05.67	Rockwell Sabre 40	N739R	282-078	Container Corporation of America	Crashed	Ventura, CA, USA	*	*
17.05.67	Scottish Aviation Twin Pioneer 1	9M-ANC	519	Malaysian Airlines	Crashed on take-off	Limbang, Malaysia	*	*
17.05.67	Douglas DC-3	XC-BII	14836/26281	Petroleos Mexicanos	Written off	Location Unknown	*	*
19.05.67	McDonnell Douglas DC-8-54	CF-TJM	45653	Air Canada	Crashed on approach	Ottawa, ON, Canada	3	0
23.05.67	Douglas DC-3	PI-C854	13559	Air Manila	Damaged when ran into stream	Iligan, Philippines	*	*
26.05.67	Convair 240-6	ZP-CDP	072	Lineas Aereas Paraguayas	Crashed on landing	Buenos Aires, Argentina	0	*
03.06.67	Curtiss C-46	CP-769	22393	Rutas Aereas Uncia	Crashed	San Ramon, Bolivia	*	*
03.06.67	Douglas C-54A	G-APYK	10279	Air Ferry	Crashed into mountain	Mt Canigou, France	88	0
04.06.67	Canadair C-4	G-ALHG	153	British Midland Airways	Crashed after engine failure on approach	Stockport, Cheshire, UK	72	12
04.06.67	Antonov AN-12	*	*	Aeroflot	Overran on landing & crashed	Blagoveshinsk, RSFSR, USSR	*	*
05.06.67	Douglas DC-7	JY-ACO	44145	Alia	Destroyed during Israeli air raid	Damascus, Syria	*	*
05.06.67	Douglas DC-7	JY-ACP	44137	Alia	Destroyed by Israeli air raid	Beirut, Lebanon	*	*
05.06.67	Gates Learjet 23	5A-DAD	23-075	Libyan Arab Airlines	Destroyed in Israeli air raid	Damascus, Syria	*	*
11.06.67	Douglas DC-3	HZ-AAJ	15235/26680	Saudi Arabian Airlines	Crashed	Jeddah, Saudi Arabia	*	*
12.06.67	Bristol 170 Freighter 31E	EI-APM	13076	Aer Turas	Crashed into building on approach at night	Dublin, Eire	2	0
12.06.67	Douglas DC-3	XA-FUW	3260	Aerolineas Moxi	Crashed on take-off	La Paz, Mexico	3	*
22.06.67	Lockheed 1049H Super Constellation	N6936C	4849	Airlift International	Mid-air collision with USAF F-4 65-0861	Saigon, South Vietnam	7(*)	0
22.06.67	Vickers Viscount 803	EI-AOF	176	Aer Lingus	Crashed	Ashbourne, Eire	3	0
23.06.67	BAC One-Eleven 204AF	N1116J	098	Mohawk Airlines	Crashed after in-flight fire	Blossburg, PA, USA	34	0
24.06.67	Douglas DC-3	HZ-AAM	*	Saudi Arabian Airlines	Crashed	Khalif Nseir, Saudi Arabia	16	1
29.06.67	Douglas DC-6	XA-NAH	43133	Saesa	Crashed	Mazatlan, Mexico	*	*
29.06.67	Sud Aviation Caravelle 3	HS-TGI	025	Thai Airways International	Crashed in sea on approach	Hong Kong	27	59
30.06.67	Vickers Viscount 760D	VR-AAV	187	Aden Airways	Destroyed by terrorists on ground	Aden, South Arabian Federation	0	*
06.07.67	Fokker F-27 Friendship 100	PI-C527	10285	Philippine Air Lines	Crashed in bad weather	nr Baclod, Philippines	21	0
09.07.67	Ilyushin IL-18	3X-GAB	181003703	Air Guinee	Crashed	Casablanca, Morocco	0	*
11.07.67	Grumman Gulfstream I	N129GP	147	Honeywell Inc	Crashed	nr Le Center, MN, USA	*	*
11.07.67	Consolidated PBY-5A Catalina	HP-425	1596B	Cie Darienitas de Servicios	Written off	Location Unknown	*	*
19.07.67	Boeing 727-22	N68650	18295	Piedmont Airlines	Mid-air collision with Lanseair Cessna 310 N3121S	Hendersonville, NC, USA	79(3)	0
19.07.67	Douglas DC-4-1009	5R-MAD	42991	Air Madagascar	Crashed on take-off	Tananarive, Malagasy Republic	41	34
25.07.67	Grumman Gulfstream I	N205M	062	Mellon Bank	Crashed	New Cumberland, PA, USA	*	*
25.07.67	Douglas DC-3	B-112	*	Taiwan Aviation	Crashed	Luang Prabang, Laos	16	*
05.08.67	Kawasaki-Vertol 107	JA9503	4004	Airlift Co	Written off	Fukui, Japan	*	*
11.08.67	Douglas DC-3	*	*	Operator Unknown	Crashed	Marinilla, Colombia	6	*
13.08.67	Curtiss C-46	N9473Z	22293	Continental Air Services	Crashed on take-off	Phu Cum, Laos	*	*
17.08.67	Boeing B-17G	CP-640	32516	Boliviana de Aviacion	Crashed	El Alto, Bolivia	*	*
21.08.67	Douglas DC-3	B-1523	*	China Airlines	Crashed	Off South Vietnam	2	*
27.08.67	Lockheed 10E Electra	*	*	Provincetown-Boston Airlines	Crashed on beach	Massachusetts Bay, MA, USA	*	*
oo.08.67	Mil Mi-6	SSSR-06174	*	Aeroflot	Crashed fighting forest fire	USSR	*	*
oo.08.67	Douglas DC-3	9G-GAD	12199	Ghana Airways	Destroyed in air raid while impounded	Port Harcourt, Biafra, Nigeria	*	*
oo.08.67	Boeing Stratocruiser	N90942	15958	Aero Spacelines	Damaged in ground collision with Stratocruiser N402Q	Mojave, CA, USA	0(0)	*
05.09.67	Ilyushin IL-18	OK-WAI	187009705	Ceskoslovenske Aerolinie	Caught fire after take-off	Gander, Nfd, Canada	35	34
13.09.67	Curtiss C-46	N1309V	22599	Capitol Airlines	Crashed into sea after take-off	Oakland, CA, USA	*	*

Date	Type	Reg'n	C/n	Operator	Accident	Location	F	S
13.09.67	Curtiss C-46	*	*	Colonial Corporation	Crashed after take-off	Kingston Harbour, Jamaica	*	*
14.09.67	Airspeed Ambassador 2	G-ALZS	5215	Autair	Damaged beyond repair	Luton, Beds, UK	0	*
21.09.67	Vickers Viscount 808	EI-AKK	422	Aer Lingus	Crashed on landing in poor weather	Bristol, UK	0	*
21.09.67	Beechcraft King Air A90	D-ILNI	LJ-0116	Operator Unknown	Written off	nr Milan, Italy	*	*
30.09.67	Douglas DC-3	N91003	9708	Central Airlines	Damaged beyond repair	Location Unknown	*	*
01.10.67	Dassault Falcon 20C	HB-VAP	037	Operator Unknown	Written off	Goose Bay, Nfld, Canada	*	*
05.10.67	Beechcraft H-18	JA5137	BA-745	Operator Unknown	Written off	Murayama-shi, Japan	*	*
07.10.67	Fokker F-27 Friendship 200	5N-AAV	10216	Biafran Air Force	Crashed after home-made bomb exploded during bombing run	Ikoy, Nigeria	*	*
12.10.67	de Havilland Comet 4B	G-ARCO	06449	British European Airways	Crashed due to bomb explosion	Off Rhodes, Greece	66	0
14.10.67	Douglas DC-3	PP-VBH	17036/34301	Varig	Crashed	Brazil	*	*
16.10.67	Ilyushin IL-18	*	*	Aeroflot	Crashed after take-off	Sverdlovsk, RSFSR, USSR	130	0
17.10.67	Douglas DC-3	OY-DNP	11638	Fairline	Damaged by gale	Kastrup, Denmark	*	*
24.10.67	Douglas DC-3	*	*	China Airlines	Crashed	South Vietnam	16	*
25.10.67	Gates Learjet 23	N432EJ	23-028A	Executive Jet Sales Inc	Crashed	Muskegon, MI, USA	*	*
oo.10.67	LTV XC-142	62-5922	2	LTV Aerospace	Damaged in hard landing	Edwards AFB, CA, USA	0	*
03.11.67	Handley Page Dart Herald 214	PP-SDJ	190	Sadia	Crashed	Curitiba, Brazil	21	4
04.11.67	Sud Aviation Caravelle 10R	EC-BDD	202	Iberia	Crashed on approach	Fernhurst, Sussex, UK	37	0
04.11.67	Ilyushin IL-18	*	*	Aeroflot	Crash landed	Moscow, RSFSR, USSR	4	*
05.11.67	Convair 880-22M-3	VR-HFX	37	Cathay Pacific Airways	Overran into sea on take-off	Hong Kong	1	125
06.11.67	Boeing 707-131	N742TW	17669	Trans World Airlines	Overran on landing	Covington, KY, USA	1	*
06.11.67	Douglas C-47A	5N-AAK	13921/25366	Biafran Air Force	Destroyed by bombing	Biafra, Nigeria	*	*
20.11.67	Convair 880-22-1	N821TW	27	Trans World Airlines	Crashed on approach	nr Covington, KY, USA	70	12
21.11.67	Cessna 180A	ET-ABL	32901	Ethiopian Airlines	Crashed after tyre burst on take-off	Mount Megenez, Ethiopia	*	*
22.11.67	Douglas DC-3	CP-691	15976/32724	Aerolineas Abaroa	Crashed	Reyes, Bolivia	*	*
28.11.67	Vickers Viscount 745D	N7465	231	United Air Lines	U/c collapsed on landing	Raleigh-Durham, NC, USA	0	*
30.11.67	Gates Learjet 23	N690LJ	23-078	Jet International	Crashed	Orlando, FL, USA	*	*
oo.11.67	de Havilland Heron 1B	VP-WAM	14008	Air Trans Africa	Destroyed in air raid	Enugu, Biafra, Nigeria	*	*
04.12.67	Hawker Siddeley Argosy 222	G-ASXP	6804	British European Airways	Crashed on take-off	Stansted, Essex, UK	0	*
07.12.67	Douglas DC-3	XW-PFM	*	Lao Cathay Airlines	Crashed	Muong Soui, Laos	8	*
08.12.67	Douglas C-54A	OB-R-148	10284	Faucett	Crashed into mountain	Carpich Huanuco Mt, Peru	67	0
09.12.67	Gates Learjet 23	N822LJ	23-080	Jet International	Crashed	Detroit, MI, USA	*	*
11.12.67	Vickers Viscount 745D	N7429	127	United Air Lines	Overshot on landing	Akron, OH, USA	0	*
21.12.67	Douglas DC-3	N65276	19202	Frontier Airlines	Crashed	Denver, CO, USA	*	*
21.12.67	Douglas DC-3	N28360	2271	R.Werner	Destroyed by tornado	McBride, MS, USA	*	*
21.12.67	Rockwell Sabre 40	N30W	282-005	Korda Kentucky Leasing	Crashed	Perryville, MO, USA	*	*
23.12.67	Douglas DC-6B	OY-EAN	43275	Sterling Airways	Damaged in hard landing	Gothenburg, Sweden	*	*
23.12.67	Hawker Siddeley HS.125-3B	G-AVGW	25120	Beecham Group	Crashed	Luton, Beds, UK	*	*
27.12.67	Douglas DC-3	HS-TDH	*	Thai Airways	Crashed on approach	Chiengmai, Thailand	3	28
31.12.67	Antonov AN-24V	SSSR-46201	*	Aeroflot	Crashed short of runway in bad weather	Voronezh, RSFSR, USSR	*	*
oo.oo.67	Avro York	CF-HAS	–	Syrota Brothers	Destroyed when Indians lit fire in fuselage to keep warm	Pas, MN, Canada	0	*
01.01.68	Martin 404	N251S	14243	Southern Airlines	Destroyed by fire on landing	Oxford, MS, USA	*	*
06.01.68	Antonov AN-24	*	*	Aeroflot	Crashed	Olyominsk, RSFSR, USSR	*	*
07.01.68	Piper PA-18-150 Super Cub	ET-AAB	18-7159	Ethiopian Airlines	Crash landed in swamp after engine failure	Assaita, Ethiopia	*	*
08.01.68	Douglas DC-3	YU-ABK	16529/33277	JAT Yugoslav Airlines	Crashed	St Floriaan, Austria	*	*
09.01.68	Boeing 720-060B	ET-AAG	18454	Middle East Airlines	Caught fire after nosewheel collapsed on landing	Beirut, Lebanon	0	*
09.01.68	Ilyushin IL-18	*	*	Aeroflot	Crashed short of runway on approach	Karaganda, Kazakhstan, USSR	*	*
15.01.68	Douglas DC-3	SU-AJG	*	United Arab Airlines	Crashed after take-off	Zifta, UAR	4	0
17.01.68	Douglas C-47A	5N-AAL	13919/25364	Nigerian Air Force	Crashed on take-off	Lagos, Nigeria	*	*
20.01.68	Douglas DC-7B	SE-ERC	45088	Turk Hava Yollari	U/c collapsed on landing	Munich, West Germany	*	*
27.01.68	de Havilland Heron 1B	F-OECD	14040	Air Comores	Crashed into lights on landing	Moroni, Comoro Islands	16	0
29.01.68	Antonov AN-12	*	*	Aeroflot	Damaged in crash landing	Magadan, RSFSR, USSR	*	*
oo.01.68	Lockheed 1049G Super Constellation	5T-TAC	4645	North American Aircraft Trading	Crashed on approach	Port Harcourt, Biafra, Nigeria	*	*
07.02.68	Boeing 707-138B	N791SA	17698	Canadian Pacific Airlines	Ran into building after hard landing	Vancouver, BC, Canada	1{1}	60
09.02.68	Douglas DC-3	HZ-AAE	4501	Saudi Arabian Airlines	Crashed	Location Unknown	*	*

Date	Type	Reg'n	C/n	Operator	Accident	Location	F	S
16.02.68	Boeing 727-92C	B-1018	19175	Civil Air Transport	Crashed on approach	Linklow, Taiwan	21	42
19.02.68	Type Unknown	*	*	Aeroflot	Crashed into building on landing	Baghdad, Iraq	2	*
24.02.68	Douglas DC-3	XW-TAD	*	Royal Air Lao	Crashed	Ban Napa, Laos	37	0
24.02.68	Ilyushin IL-18	*	*	Aeroflot	Crashed on take-off	Donetsk, Ukraine, USSR	*	*
29.02.68	Douglas DC-3	N525W	20054	Millers Aviation	Damaged beyond repair	Statesville, NC, USA	*	*
29.02.68	Ilyushin IL-18	SSSR-74252	187010601	Aeroflot	Crashed	nr Bratsk, RSFSR, USSR	*	*
05.03.68	Boeing 707-328C	F-BLCJ	19724	Air France	Crashed on approach	nr Basse-Terre, Guadeloupe	63	0
07.03.68	Tupolev TU-124	SSSR-45019	2350604	Aeroflot	Crashed on take-off	Volgograd, RSFSR, USSR	1	*
08.03.68	Fairchild F-27	PI-C871	0019	Air Manila	Crashed	Off Panay Is, Philippines	14	0
08.03.68	de Havilland Riley Dove	N999NJ	04456	E.H.Litchfield	Crashed	Lake Michigan, MI, USA	6	0
13.03.68	Dassault Falcon 20C	N1846	047	Mair Inc	Crashed	Parkersburg, WV, USA	*	*
20.03.68	Convair 340-38	N4820C	152	Delta Air Lines	Crashed on landing	Evansville, IN, USA	*	*
21.03.68	Boeing 727-22QC	N7425U	19200	United Air Lines	Crashed & caught fire on take-off	Chicago, IL, USA	0	*
24.03.68	Vickers Viscount 803	EI-AOM	178	Aer Lingus	Broke up in mid-air	Irish Sea	61	0
26.03.68	Lockheed 18-56 Lodestar	ZK-CMX	2595	Airland (NZ) Ltd	Crashed	nr Pahiatua, New Zealand	*	*
27.03.68	Douglas DC-3	PP-BTX	9203	Paraense Transportes Aereos	Written off	Location Unknown	*	*
30.03.68	Lockheed 1049G Super Constellation	HP-467	4678	Rutas Aereas Panamenas	Crashed after take-off	Tocumen, Panama	3	0
08.04.68	Boeing 707-465	G-ARWE	18373	British Overseas Airways Corporation	Crash landed after engine fire	Heathrow, London, UK	5	121
08.04.68	Douglas DC-3	CC-CBM	6330	Ladeco	Crashed on approach	Coyhaique, Chile	36	0
10.04.68	Douglas DC-3	XA-GEV	7339	Aerovias Rojas	Crashed into mountain when lost	nr Mexico City, Mexico	18	0
10.04.68	Bristol 170 Freighter 31E	ZK-CPU	13125	Safe Air	Damaged beyond repair by hurricane	Blenheim, New Zealand	*	*
11.04.68	Lockheed L-100 Hercules	9J-RBX	4137	Zambia Air Cargoes	Collided on ground with ZAC Hercules 9J-RCY	Ndola, Zambia	0(0)	*
11.04.68	Lockheed L-100 Hercules	9J-RCY	4109	Zambia Air Cargoes	Collided on ground with ZAC Hercules 9J-RBX	Ndola, Zambia	0(0)	*
16.04.68	Kawasaki-Vertol 107	JA9502	4002	Airlift Co	Written off	Gifu, Japan	*	*
19.04.68	Douglas DC-3	CP-734	17045/34311	Lloyd Aereo Boliviano	Crashed	Trinidad, Bolivia	*	*
20.04.68	Boeing 707-344C	ZS-EUW	19705	South African Airways	Crashed after take-off	Windhoek, South West Africa	123	5
22.04.68	Ilyushin IL-18	*	*	Aeroflot	Crashed into cables	Moscow, RSFSR, USSR	*	*
24.04.68	Lisunov Li-2P	HA-LIO	18439505	Malev	Damaged while refuelling	Szolnok, Hungary	*	*
28.04.68	McDonnell Douglas DC-8-31	N1802	45277	Capitol International Airlines	Crashed on landing	Atlantic City, NJ, USA	0	*
03.05.68	Lockheed Electra 188A	N9707C	1099	Braniff International Airlines	Broke up in turbulence	Dawson, TX, USA	85	0
04.05.68	Fairchild F-27J	N27W	0123	Eastex	Stalled & crashed	nr Bruni, TX, USA	2	*
05.05.68	Vickers Viscount 812	G-APPU	364	Channel Airways	Overran on landing	Southend, Essex, UK	0	87
09.05.68	Fairchild F-27	PI-C873	0008	Air Manila	Landed short of runway	Davao, Philippines	0	*
16.05.68	Lockheed L-100 Hercules	N9267R	4146	AREA	Destroyed by fire on ground	Macuma, Ecuador	0	*
22.05.68	Sikorsky S-61L	N303Y	*	Los Angeles Airlines	Crashed after rotor failure	Paramount City, CA, USA	23	0
28.05.68	Convair 990-30-5	PK-GJA	03	Garuda Indonesian Airlines	Crashed	Nalla Sopora, India	29	0
03.06.68	Lockheed 1049D Super Constellation	5T-TAC	4166	North American Aircraft Trading	Destroyed by sabotage	Bissau, Portuguese Guinea	*	*
08.06.68	Douglas DC-3	N74139	4930	Aerodyne Engineering Corporation	Damaged beyond repair	Franton Isle, Mexico	*	*
12.06.68	Fairchild F-27J	CF-GND	0113	Great Northern Airways	Crashed out of fuel	Inuvik, NWT, Canada	0	*
13.06.68	Boeing 707-321C	N798PA	18790	Pan American World Airways	Crashed on approach	Calcutta, India	6	57
18.06.68	Piaggio PD-808VIP	I-PIAI	503	Rinaldo Piaggio	Crashed	San Sebastian, Spain	*	*
26.06.68	Piper PA-27-250 Aztec B	G-ATCM	27-2834	Aircruise	Crashed	Brest, France	*	*
28.06.68	Beechcraft King Air A90	LN-VIP	LJ-0271	Operator Unknown	Written off	Bodo, Norway	*	*
29.06.68	McDonnell Douglas DC-8-53	PH-DCH	45383	KLM Royal Dutch Airlines	Destroyed by explosion & fire in hangar	Amsterdam, Netherlands	0	*
01.07.68	Lockheed 1049G Super Constellation	5T-TAG	4642	North American Aircraft Trading	Crashed on approach	Uli, Biafra, Nigeria	4	0
01.07.68	Rockwell 1121 Jet Commander	N196KC	068	Kansas City Life Insurance Co	Crashed	Fayetteville, AR, USA	*	*
02.07.68	Douglas DC-7BF	N762Z	44922	Universal Airlines	U/c collapsed on landing	Philadelphia, PA, USA	*	*
03.07.68	Airspeed Ambassador 2	G-AMAD	5211	BKS Air Transport	Crashed due to metal fatigue & struck BEA Trident G-ARPT	Heathrow, London, UK	6(0)	2
03.07.68	Hawker Siddeley Trident 1C	G-ARPT	2121	British European Airways	Struck by crashing BKS Ambassador G-AMAD	Heathrow, London, UK	0(6)	*
08.07.68	Convair 340-68B	HZ-AAZ	219	Saudi Arabian Airlines	Crashed	nr Dharan, Saudi Arabia	11	0
09.07.68	de Havilland Dove 1	N4914V	04273	J.Fender & Partner	Crashed on overshoot	Colusa, CA, USA	*	*
11.07.68	Antonov AN-2	OK-MYC	1G193-14	Svazarm	Destroyed in gale	Kunovice, Czechoslovakia	*	*
13.07.68	Boeing 707-329C	OO-SJK	19211	Sabena	Crashed on approach	Lagos, Nigeria	7	0
18.07.68	Curtiss C-46	CC-CDI	33445	ALFA	Crashed	Straits of Magellan, Chile	5	0

Date	Type	Reg'n	C/n	Operator	Accident	Location	F	S
oo.07.68	Consolidated Privateer	N7974A	*	Avery Aviation	Crashed into mountain	nr McGrath, AL, USA	4	0
02.08.68	McDonnell Douglas DC-8-43	I-DIWF	45630	Alitalia	Crashed on approach	nr Milan, Italy	13	83
07.08.68	de Havilland DH.89A Dragon Rapide	5Y-KLB	6877	Operator Unknown	Written off	Bukoba, Kenya	*	*
08.08.68	Antonov AN-10	SSSR-11172	*	Aeroflot	Crashed into vehicle after u/c collapsed on landing	Mirny, RSFSR, USSR	*	*
09.08.68	Vickers Viscount 739A	G-ATFN	394	British Eagle Airways	Broke up in mid-air	Pfaffenhofen, West Germany	48	0
10.08.68	Fairchild-Hiller FH.227B	N712U	557	Piedmont Airlines	Crashed on approach	Charleston, WV, USA	34	3
14.08.68	Sikorsky S-61L	N300Y	*	Los Angeles Airlines	Crashed after rotor failure	Compton, CA, USA	21	0
18.08.68	Antonov AN-24V	SU-AOL	67302806	United Arab Airlines	Crashed	Off Port Said, UAR	40	0
18.08.68	Douglas DC-3	9Q-CUM	42973	Air Congo	Damaged by fire	N'Djili, Congo	*	*
20.08.68	Hawker Siddeley HS.748 2	YV-C-AMY	1580	Linea Aeropostal Venezolana	Crashed	Maturin, Venezuela	4	*
22.08.68	Convair 240-13	N91239	159	East Coast Leasing	Destroyed on ground by fire bombs	Martinsburg, WV, USA	*	*
22.08.68	Convair 600	N278E	032	East Coast Leasing	Damaged on ground by fire bombs	Martinsburg, WV, USA	*	*
23.08.68	Curtiss C-46	CP-760	22535	Transportes Aereos Benianos	Crashed after take-off	Nieuve, Bolivia	4	1
03.09.68	Avro Anson 19 Srs 2	G-AWMG	276926	Mercy Missions	Crashed	Uzuakoli, Biafra, Nigeria	*	*
04.09.68	de Havilland Heron 2D	LN-NPH	14127	Norflyselskap	Crashed	Off Bodo, Norway	*	*
04.09.68	Ilyushin IL-18	LZ-BEG	187009101	Tabso	Crashed on approach	Bourgas, Bulgaria	47	39+
06.09.68	Northrop F-15A Black Widow	N9768Z	*	Sis-Q Flying Service	Crashed	Hollister, CA, USA	*	*
07.09.68	Boeing 707-341C	PP-VJR	19320	Varig	Destroyed in hangar fire	Rio de Janeiro, Brazil	0	*
11.09.68	Sud Aviation Caravelle 3	F-BOHB	244	Air France	Crashed after fire	Off Cap d'Antibes, France	95	0
13.09.68	Rockwell 1121 Jet Commander	N148E	022	Eversharp Inc	Crashed	Burbank, CA, USA	*	*
15.09.68	Vickers Viscount 827	PP-SRE	399	VASP	Crashed	Sao Paulo, Brazil	2{1}	*
20.09.68	Curtiss C-46	HC-AMC	167	ANDES	Crashed	Managua, Nicaragua	1	*
21.09.68	de Havilland Dove 8	N6533D	04515	E.J.Benes & Co	Crashed after engine failure on take-off	Richmond, OH, USA	*	*
25.09.68	de Havilland Dove 5BA	N4957N	04309	W.J.Stack	Crashed after engine failed on landing	Charlotte, NC, USA	2	*
27.09.68	Douglas DC-7CF	N7466	45090	Universal Airlines	Crashed on approach	Cherry Point, NC, USA	0	*
28.09.68	Aviation Traders ATL.98 Carvair	CF-EPU	7480/6	Eastern Provincial Airways	Crashed	Twin Falls, NF, Canada	*	*
28.09.68	Douglas C-54B	N90427	10445	Pan African Airlines	Crashed into trees at night	Port Harcourt, Biafra, Nigeria	57	0
28.09.68	Lockheed 1649A Starliner	N8081H	1026	Willair International	U/c collapsed on landing	Stockton, CA, USA	0	*
29.09.68	Douglas DC-3	N64423	9251	Ford Motor Co	Crashed after cargo shifted	Teterboro, NJ, USA	*	*
30.09.68	Airspeed Ambassador 2	G-AMAG	5229	Dan-Air	Damaged in belly landing	Manston, Kent, UK	*	*
03.10.68	Douglas DC-7C	5T-TAR	45308	North American Aircraft Trading	Damaged in ground collision	Uli, Biafra, Nigeria	4	*
06.10.68	Antonov AN-24	*	*	Aeroflot	Crashed on take-off	Mary, Uzbekistan, USSR	*	*
08.10.68	de Havilland Dove 6BA	N4040B	04328	Catalina Vegas Airlines	Crashed after fire on take-off	Las Vegas, NV, USA	4	*
08.10.68	Britten-Norman BN-2 Islander	TI-1063C	0014	Aerovias del Valle	Written off	Puerto Cortes, Costa Rica	10	0
11.10.68	Avia 14-40	OK-MCJ	805120	Ceskoslovenske Aerolinie	Crashed after take-off	nr Prague, Czechoslovakia	11	29
11.10.68	Avia 14	OK-MCK	806104	Ceskoslovenske Aerolinie	Crashed	Ptic, Czechoslovakia	*	*
18.10.68	Beechcraft King Air A90	N703WC	LJ-0188	Operator Unknown	Written off	Location Unknown	*	*
20.10.68	Douglas DC-3	PP-SAD	13764	Cruzeiro	Crashed	Fejo Acre, Brazil	*	*
20.10.68	Ilyushin IL-18	*	*	Aeroflot	Caught fire after emergency landing	Krasnoyarsk, RSFSR, USSR	*	*
25.10.68	Fairchild-Hiller FH.227C	N380NE	517	Northeast Airlines	Crashed into mountain	Lebanon, NH, USA	32	10
26.10.68	Douglas DC-3	PH-DAA	11855	KLM Royal Dutch Airlines	Crashed	Table Mt, Surinam	*	*
oo.10.68	Curtiss C-46	HI-39	468	Dominicana	Damaged beyond repair	San Juan, Puerto Rico	*	*
02.11.68	Antonov AN-12	*	*	Aeroflot	Crashed short of runway on approach	Lensk, RSFSR, USSR	*	*
04.11.68	Convair 580	N73135	035	Tex Johnston Inc	Damaged in belly landing	USA	*	*
06.11.68	Douglas C-54A	PP-LEW	10348	VASP	Damaged beyond repair	Rio de Janeiro, Brazil	*	*
11.11.68	Curtiss C-46	CP-791	26515	Aerolineas Abaroa	Crashed	San Borja, Bolivia	*	*
17.11.68	de Havilland Dove 5	VH-CTS	04119	City Centre Air Taxies	Damaged in heavy landing	Lovely Banks, Vic, Australia	*	*
23.11.68	de Havilland Canada Twin Otter 200	N7666	148	Cable Commuter	Crashed in fog	Orange County Airport, CA, USA	9	0
25.11.68	Curtiss C-46	N1386N	22265	Air America	Crashed on take-off	nr Savannakhet, Laos	25	2
02.12.68	Fairchild F-27B	N4905	0049	Wien Consolidated Airlines	Broke up in turbulence	Fox Lake, AK, USA	39	0
07.12.68	Douglas DC-7C	VR-BCY	45545	North American Aircraft Trading	Crashed on approach	Uli, Biafra, Nigeria	4	0
09.12.68	Lockheed 1649A Starliner	N7314C	1016	Fly by Night Safaris	Crashed on take-off	Las Vegas, NV, USA	0	*
12.12.68	Boeing 707-321B	N494PA	19696	Pan American World Airways	Crashed	Off Caracas, Venezuela	51	0
21.12.68	Mitsubishi MU-2B	N3550X	018	Operator Unknown	Written off	Springfield, MO, USA	*	*

Date	Type	Reg'n	C/n	Operator	Accident	Location	F	S
24.12.68	Convair 580	N5802	410	Allegheny Airlines	Crashed into high ground during snowstorm	Bradford, PA, USA	20	27
24.12.68	Lockheed L-100 Hercules	N760AL	4229	Interior Airways	Crashed on landing	Anchorage, AK, USA	2	2
24.12.68	Douglas DC-3	5Y-ADI	13447	Kenya Police Air Wing	Crashed	Nairobi, Kenya	*	*
26.12.68	Boeing 707-321C	N799PA	18824	Pan American World Airways	Overran on take-off	Elmendorf, AK, USA	3	0
27.12.68	Convair 580	N2045	369	North Central Airlines	Struck hangar door during overshoot	Chicago, IL, USA	27	18
27.12.68	McDonnell Douglas DC-9-15	N974Z	47034	Ozark Air Lines	Crashed after aborting take-off	Sioux City, IA, USA	0	*
28.12.68	de Havilland Comet 4C	OD-ADR	06445	Middle East Airlines	Destroyed during Israeli commando raid	Beirut, Lebanon	0	*
28.12.68	de Havilland Comet 4C	OD-ADQ	06446	Middle East Airlines	Destroyed during Israeli commando raid	Beirut, Lebanon	0	*
28.12.68	de Havilland Comet 4C	OD-ADS	06448	Middle East Airlines	Destroyed during Israeli commando raid	Beirut, Lebanon	0	*
28.12.68	Convair 990-30-5	OD-AEX	10	Lebanese International Airways	Destroyed during Israeli commando raid	Beirut, Lebanon	0	*
28.12.68	Convair 990-30-5	OD-AEW	31	Lebanese International Airways	Destroyed during Israeli commando raid	Beirut, Lebanon	0	*
28.12.68	BAC VC-10 1102	9G-ABP	824	Middle East Airlines	Destroyed during Israeli commando raid	Beirut, Lebanon	0	*
28.12.68	Boeing 707-384C	OD-AFC	20225	Middle East Airlines	Destroyed during Israeli commando raid	Beirut, Lebanon	0	*
28.12.68	Sud Aviation Caravelle 6N	OD-AEE	153	Middle East Airlines	Destroyed during Israeli commando raid	Beirut, Lebanon	0	*
28.12.68	Sud Aviation Caravelle 6N	OD-AEF	157	Middle East Airlines	Destroyed during Israeli commando raid	Beirut, Lebanon	0	*
28.12.68	Vickers Viscount 754D	OD-ACT	239	Middle East Airlines	Destroyed during Israeli commando raid	Beirut, Lebanon	0	*
28.12.68	Douglas C-54B	OD-ADI	10534	Trans Mediterranean Airways	Destroyed during Israeli commando raid	Beirut, Lebanon	0	*
28.12.68	Douglas DC-6B	OD-AEY	44431	Trans Mediterranean Airways	Destroyed during Israeli commando raid	Beirut, Lebanon	0	*
28.12.68	Douglas DC-7	OD-AEI	44141	Lebanese International Airways	Destroyed during Israeli commando raid	Beirut, Lebanon	0	*
28.12.68	Douglas DC-7	OD-AEK	44146	Lebanese International Airways	Destroyed during Israeli commando raid	Beirut, Lebanon	0	*
31.12.68	Vickers Viscount 720	VH-RMQ	045	MacRobertson-Miller Airlines	Crashed after wing failure	Port Hedland, WA, Australia	30	0
31.12.68	Douglas DC-3	XA-SAE	20554	Saesa	Crashed into mountain	Ciudad Vitoria, Mexico	26	0
oo.12.68	Lisunov Li-2	SSSR-04214	*	Aeroflot	Damaged on landing & later destroyed by high winds	Mawson, Antarctica	0	*
oo.oo.68	Curtiss C-46	PP-NME	30418	VASP	Damaged beyond repair	Rio de Janeiro, Brazil	*	*
oo.oo.68	de Havilland DH.89A Dragon Rapide	5R-MAN	6591	Operator Unknown	Written off	Location Unknown	*	*
oo.oo.68	de Havilland DH.89A Dragon Rapide	G-AHJA	6486	Operator Unknown	Damaged beyond repair	Halfpenny Green, Salop, UK	*	*
oo.oo.68	Douglas R5D-1	VP-YTY	10397	Air Trans Africa	Destroyed	Biafra, Nigeria	*	*
02.01.69	Douglas DC-3	B-309	12541	China Airlines	Crashed into mountain	Mt Paku, Taiwan	24	0
03.01.69	Britten-Norman BN-2A Islander	N587JA	0040	General Airlines	Crashed on delivery flight	nr Narsassurc, Greenland	*	*
05.01.69	Boeing 727-13C	YA-FAR	19690	Ariana Afghan Airlines	Crashed into hill on approach	Gatwick, Sussex, UK	48{2}	14
06.01.69	Douglas DC-3	*	*	Continental Air Services	Crashed	North East Thailand	55	*
06.01.69	Convair 580	N5825	386	Allegheny Airlines	Crashed on approach	Bedford, PA, USA	11	17
11.01.69	Douglas DC-3	PP-SPR	20544	VASP	Damaged beyond repair	Loanda, Brazil	*	*
13.01.69	McDonnell Douglas DC-8-62	LN-MOO	45822	Scandinavian Airlines System	Crashed on approach	Off Los Angeles, CA, USA	15	25
13.01.69	Britten-Norman BN-2 Islander	N584JA	0005	Sud Aviacion	Written off	Argentina	*	*
14.01.69	BAC One-Eleven 201AC	G-ASJJ	014	British United Airways	Crashed on take-off	Milan, Italy	0	33
15.01.69	Sikorsky Sea King HAS.1	XV372	61-395	Westland Helicopters	Crashed after engine failure due to ice ingestion	West Harptree, Somerset, UK	*	*
15.01.69	Douglas DC-3	YA-AAB	4275	Ariana Afghan Airlines	Damaged in ground collision with Ariana DC-6 YA-DAN	Kabul, Afghanistan	*(*)	*
17.01.69	Douglas DC-3	VT-DTH	10139	Hindu Publications	Crashed	nr Calicut, India	*	*
18.01.69	Douglas DC-3	*	20415	Air America	Crashed	nr Da Nang, South Vietnam	9	*
18.01.69	Boeing 727-22QC	N7434U	19891	United Air Lines	Crashed after take-off	Off Los Angeles, CA, USA	38	0
24.01.69	Antonov AN-24V	SP-LTE	67302405	LOT Polish Airlines	Landed short of runway	Wroclaw, Poland	*	*
oo.01.69	Vought-Sikorsky VS-44A	N41881	*	Antilles Air Boats	Damaged by rocks while taxiing	Charlotte Amalie, US Virgin Is	*	*
01.02.69	Curtiss C-46	CP-745	42	Bolivian Air System	Crashed	Reyes, Bolivia	*	*
02.02.69	Vickers Viscount 794D	TC-SET	432	Turk Hava Yollari	Crashed after striking cables on approach	Ankara, Turkey	0	26
04.02.69	Curtiss C-46	N5133B	26988	Carolina Aircraft Corporation	Crashed	Brazil	*	*
05.02.69	Lockheed 18 Lodestar	*	*	Operator Unknown	Crashed	nr Albuquerque, NM, USA	11	*
08.02.69	Fairchild F-27F	CF-PAP	0125	Stanair	Crashed	Mikaa Lake, Canada	*	*
10.02.69	Beechcraft C-45H	F-OGCA	AF-040	Operator Unknown	Written off	Location Unknown	*	*
13.02.69	Curtiss C-46	HK-683	33367	Aeropesca	Crashed on take-off	Bogota, Colombia	0	2
15.02.69	Douglas DC-3	B-241	*	Far Eastern Air Transport	Crashed	Kaohsiung, Taiwan	*	*
18.02.69	Douglas DC-3	N15570	6320	Mineral County Airlines	Crashed	Sierra Nevada Mts, NV, USA	35	*
20.02.69	Vickers Viscount 736	G-AODG	077	British Midland Airways	U/c collapsed on landing	Castle Donington, Derbs, UK	0	53
20.02.69	Piper PA-27-250 Aztec C	G-ASTE	27-2557	Northair	Crashed	Leeds, UK	*	*

Date	Type	Reg'n	C/n	Operator	Accident	Location	F	S
23.02.69	de Havilland Riley Dove	N880JG	04491	Trans Isles Airways	Crashed after engine failure	140 miles off Long Beach, CA, USA	0	*
24.02.69	Handley Page Dart Herald 201	B-2009	157	Far Eastern Air Transport	Crashed after engine fire	Tainan, Taiwan	36	0
03.03.69	de Havilland Canada Otter	VP-FAM	395	British Antarctic Survey	Crash landed after engine failure	Stonington Is, Br Antarctic Terr	0	*
03.03.69	Avro Anson V	CF-DTW	MDF-282	Austin Airways	Damaged on landing	Severn Lake, Ont, Canada	*	*
07.03.69	Douglas DC-3	N65134	19025	Zamrud Airlines	Crashed after engine failure	Off Honolulu, HI, USA	*	*
07.03.69	Douglas DC-4	N3821	10356	United States Airways	Crashed without trace	Atlantic Ocean	3	0
16.03.69	McDonnell Douglas DC-9-32	YV-C-AVD	47243	Viasa	Collided with obstruction on take-off	Maracaibo, Venezuela	84{71}	0
19.03.69	Douglas DC-3	4W-AAS	*	Yemen Airlines	Crashed	Taiz, Yemen	4	0
20.03.69	Douglas DC-3	N142D	1946	Avion	Crashed on landing in fog	New Orleans, LA, USA	16	11
20.03.69	Ilyushin IL-18	SU-APC	*	United Arab Airlines	Crashed on approach	Aswan, UAR	100	5
20.03.69	Vickers Viscount 815	G-AVJA	336	British Midland Airways	Wing struck ground on take-off & overturned	Manchester, UK	3	1
24.03.69	Antonov AN-24	*	*	Aeroflot	Crashed on take-off	Alma Ata, Kazakhstan, USSR	*	*
26.03.69	Lockheed 1649A Starliner	N7311C	1013	Trans American Leasing	Crash landed on smuggling flight	Isluga, Chile	0	*
28.03.69	Douglas DC-3	OO-SBH	11979	Belgian International Air Services	Crashed	Libya	*	*
02.04.69	Curtiss C-46	N3914	22445	Islands of the Bahamas Inc	Crashed	Off New Providence Is, Bahamas	2	*
02.04.69	Douglas DC-6B	XV-NUC	44699	Air Vietnam	Destroyed on ground during Communist attack	Hue, South Vietnam	*	*
02.04.69	Antonov AN-24V	SP-LTF	67302406	LOT Polish Airlines	Crashed	Zawoja, Poland	51	0
02.04.69	Douglas DC-4	PP-LET	18393	VASP	Damaged beyond repair	Rio Galeao, Brazil	*	*
07.04.69	Vickers Viscount 757	CF-THK	271	Air Canada	Forced landing after engine fire on take-off	Seven Is, PQ, Canada	1	20
10.04.69	Douglas DC-3	ET-AAQ	20174	Ethiopian Airlines	Shot down while off course	Cairo, UAR	3	0
14.04.69	Douglas DC-3	PP-CBZ	11767	Cruzeiro	Crashed	Tapuruquara, Brazil	*	*
14.04.69	Fairchild F-27	PI-C870	0020	Air Manila	Damaged beyond repair	Roscas, Philippines	*	*
15.04.69	Douglas DC-3	N4296	42962	Aviation Enterprises	Destroyed by fire	Coventry, UK	*	*
15.04.69	Mitsubishi MU-2F	N758Q	134	Operator Unknown	Written off	Mercer, NJ, USA	*	*
17.04.69	Gates Learjet 25	N515VW	25-013	Volkswagen Pacific Inc	Crashed	Delemont, Switzerland	*	*
21.04.69	Fokker F-27 Friendship 100	VT-DOJ	10214	Indian Airlines	Crashed in bad weather	Doulatpoor, Pakistan	44	0
23.04.69	Douglas DC-3	PI-C947	1909	Fairways	Destroyed on landing	Manila, Philippines	*	*
24.04.69	Douglas DC-3	B-251	3587	Far Eastern Air Transport	Crashed	Phantiet, South Vietnam	*	*
24.04.69	Douglas DC-3	9G-AAF	9407	Ghana Airways	Crashed	Takoradi, Ghana	1	*
26.04.69	Bell 205A	PK-HBA	30003	Bristow Maseyu Helicopters	Crashed	Duri, Indonesia	*	*
28.04.69	Boeing 727-16	CC-CAQ	19812	LAN-Chile	Crash landed	nr Colina, Chile	0	*
28.04.69	Tupolev TU-104B	SSSR-42436	*	Aeroflot	Damaged after overrunning	Irkutsk, RSFSR, USSR	*	*
01.05.69	Canadair CL-44D4-2	N446T	015	Mobil Oil	Damaged in emergency landing	Anchorage, AK, USA	0	*
01.05.69	Douglas C-54B	F-BELL	10501	Air Vietnam	Destroyed in ground fire	Saigon, South Vietnam	*	*
05.05.69	Douglas DC-3	LQ-IPC	4280	Sec. de Aeronautica	Crashed on landing	Las Hiqueras, Argentina	*	*
05.05.69	Rockwell Turbo Commander 690	N9001N	11000	Operator Unknown	Written off	Location Unknown	*	*
07.05.69	Curtiss C-46	N1243N	22456	Flying W Airways	Crashed on take-off	Medford, NJ, USA	2	*
07.05.69	Douglas DC-6A/C	HB-IBT	45532	International Red Cross	Crashed on approach	Uli, Biafra, Nigeria	4	*
08.05.69	Boeing C-97 Stratofreighter	N52679	*	Nordchurchaid	Crashed	Biafra, Nigeria	*	*
18.05.69	Douglas DC-3	HI-159	*	Lansa	Written off	Location Unknown	*	*
23.05.69	Curtiss C-46	N1247N	22565	Kimex Inc	Crashed on landing	nr Barcelona, Venezuela	1	*
24.05.69	Douglas DC-3	XY-ACR	9629	Union of Burma Airways	Crashed after mid-air explosion	Lashio, Burma	6	*
24.05.69	Fokker F-27 Friendship 600	I-ATIT	10363	Aero Transporti Italiani	Undershot runway	Reggio di Calabria, Italy	1	*
24.05.69	Douglas DC-4	N9982H	10513	Pan African Airlines	Destroyed in rocket attack	Port Harcourt, Nigeria	*	*
28.05.69	Douglas C-54A	F-BFCP	10346	Air France	Veered off runway on take-off	Paris, France	0	3
02.06.69	Douglas DC-6	TF-AAE	43130	Aid by Air	Damaged during Nigerian rocket attack	Uli, Biafra, Nigeria	*	*
04.06.69	Boeing 727-64	XA-SEL	19256	Mexicana	Crashed on approach in storm	nr Monterrey, Mexico	79	0
05.06.69	Douglas DC-7B	SE-ERP	45401	Swedish Red Cross	Shot down by Nigerian aircraft	Eket, Biafra, Nigeria	4	0
11.06.69	Bristol 170 Superfreighter 32	F-BLHH	13212	Cie Air Transport	Damaged when struck by ground vehicle	Le Touquet, France	*	*
20.06.69	Beechcraft 99	N2550A	U106	Cascade Airways	Crashed	Pasco, WA, USA	*	*
20.06.69	Avro Anson 19 Srs 2	G-AWMH	33002	Mercy Missions	Crashed	Off River Cess, Liberia	*	*
23.06.69	Aviation Traders ATL.98 Carvair	HI-168	10485/16	Dominicana	Crashed after engine failure	Miami, FL, USA	3{4}	0
25.06.69	Convair 880-22M-3	JA8028	49	Japan Air Lines	Crashed after take-off	Moses Lake, WA, USA	3	2

Date	Type	Reg'n	C/n	Operator	Accident	Location	F	S
25.06.69	Antonov AN-12	*	*	Aeroflot	Crashed on landing	Myrniy, RSFSR, USSR	*	*
27.06.69	Vickers Viscount 754D	N7410	242	Aloha Airlines	Damaged in ground collision with DC-9	Hawaii, USA	0(*)	*
29.06.69	Douglas DC-7C	EC-BEO	45541	Transportes Aereos Espanoles	Destroyed by fire	Las Palmas, Spain	*	*
06.07.69	Beechcraft 99	N844NS	U016	Air South	Crashed	Monroe, GA, USA	*	*
09.07.69	Sud Aviation Caravelle 3	HS-TGK	034	Thai Airways International	U/c collapsed on landing	Bangkok, Thailand	0	*
10.07.69	Douglas DC-3	N139D	2027	J.H.Logsdon	Damaged beyond repair	Malcolm Is, SK, Canada	*	*
11.07.69	de Havilland Heron 1B	TN-ABA	14034	Cogeair	Crashed after engine fire	Ruddervoorde, Belgium	*	*
12.07.69	Douglas DC-3	9N-AAO	20135	Royal Nepal Airlines	Crashed	nr Nepalgunji, Nepal	*	*
12.07.69	Douglas DC-3	9N-AAP	42956	Royal Nepal Airlines	Crashed	Hitauda, Nepal	35	0
15.07.69	de Havilland Canada Twin Otter 200	N558MA	175	New York Airways	Crashed on take-off due to wake of B.707	New York, NY, USA	3	11
15.07.69	Hawker Siddeley HS.748 1	LV-IEV	1558	Aerolineas Argentinas	Undershot in bad visibility	Bahia Blanca, Argentina	0	35
16.07.69	Lockheed L-100 Hercules	CF-PWO	4197	Pacific Western Airlines	Crashed on landing	Cayaya, Peru	0	*
22.07.69	Pilatus PC-6/B1 Porter	SX-AFB	694	Synetairistikon Propsidevtikcn Eno.	Written off	Location Unknown	*	*
23.07.69	Douglas DC-3	F-OCKT	4495	Air Djibouti	Crashed	Off Djibouti, Fr Ter Afars & Issas	0	4
25.07.69	de Havilland Riley Dove	N88G	04360	Sky Tours Hawaii	Crashed after engine failure	Kekaha, HI, USA	1	12
26.07.69	Airspeed Ambassador 2	G-ALZR	5214	Dan-Air	Damaged when nosewheel collapsed	Gatwick, Sussex, UK	0	8
26.07.69	Sud Aviation Caravelle 6N	7T-VAK	073	Air Algerie	Forced landing after cabin fire	Biskra, Algeria	35	2
26.07.69	Boeing 707-331C	N787TW	18712	Trans World Airlines	Crashed on approach	Pomona, NJ, USA	5	0
29.07.69	Hawker Siddeley Trident 1C	G-ARPS	2120	British European Airways	Damaged by fire on ground	Heathrow, London, UK	0	0
31.07.69	Antonov AN-2	OK-KHD	1G162-16	Slovair	Written off	Drahomsyl, Czechoslovakia	*	*
oo.07.69	Douglas C-54A	F-OCNU	3073	Air Fret	Destroyed on ground	Uli, Biafra, Nigeria	*	*
02.08.69	Sud Aviation Caravelle 6N	I-DABF	179	Alitalia	Overran into sea	Marseilles, France	0	45
03.08.69	Lockheed 1049H Super Constellation	CF-NAJ	4828	Canairelief	Crashed on landing	Uli, Biafra, Nigeria	4	0
03.08.69	Antonov AN-24	*	*	Aeroflot	Crashed after take-off	Preobrazhenka, Ukraine, USSR	*	*
04.08.69	Lockheed 749A Constellation	N120A	2617	Trans Southern Corporation	Crashed on take-off from farm on smuggling flight	Aracatuba, Brazil	0	*
09.08.69	Lockheed 1049G Super Constellation	F-BGNC	4512	Catair	Crashed	nr Douala, Cameroons	*	*
12.08.69	Antonov AN-12	*	*	Aeroflot	Crash landed short of runway	Novosibirsk, RSFSR, USSR	*	*
13.08.69	Beechcraft King Air 90	D-ILMA	LJ-0048	Operator Unknown	Written off	nr Munster, West Germany	*	*
14.08.69	de Havilland Dove 6	I-TURI	04466	Harrys Moda	Crashed on take-off	Rome, Italy	2	*
20.08.69	Douglas DC-6	XA-MOO	42877	Mexicana	Damaged on landing	Tuxtla, Mexico	*	*
25.08.69	Douglas DC-3	HC-ALK	15777/27222	Transportes Aereos Orientales	Crashed on take-off	Location Unknown	*	*
26.08.69	Ilyushin IL-18	*	*	Aeroflot	Landed with u/c retracted	Moscow, RSFSR, USSR	16	96
30.08.69	Gates Learjet 23	PP-FMX	23-090	Inst. Brasileiro de Reforma Agraria	Crashed	Rio de Janeiro, Brazil	*	*
06.09.69	de Havilland Canada Twin Otter 100	N2711N	038	Interior Airways	Crashed	Sagwan, AK, USA	*	*
06.09.69	Curtiss C-46	CP-834	26902	SANIA	Crashed	Caranavi, Bolivia	*	*
08.09.69	Douglas DC-3	FAC.685	*	Satena	Crashed	Colombia	32	0
09.09.69	McDonnell Douglas DC-9-31	N988VJ	47211	Allegheny Airlines	Mid-air collision with Cherokee N73745	Indianapolis, IN, USA	82(1)	0
10.09.69	Ilyushin IL-18	*	*	Aeroflot	Crashed into vehicle on landing	Yakutsk, RSFSR, USSR	*	*
11.09.69	de Havilland Dove 2	N13114	04092	Eureka Aero Industries	Crashed on approach	San Francisco Bay, CA, USA	*	*
12.09.69	BAC One-Eleven 402AP	PI-C1131	092	Philippine Air Lines	Crashed into high ground on approach	nr Manila, Philippines	45	2
14.09.69	Douglas DC-3	PP-SPP	15618/27063	VASP	Crashed on take-off	Londrina, Brazil	20	1
17.09.69	Beechcraft Queen Air B80	HK-1095X	LD-313	Operator Unknown	Written off	Location Unknown	*	*
18.09.69	Convair 640	CF-PWR	440	Pacific Western Airlines	Crashed on approach	Vancouver Is, BC, Canada	4	12
20.09.69	Douglas C-54D	XV-NUG	10860	Air Vietnam	Mid-air collision with USAF F-4E 67-393	Da Nang, South Vietnam	75(2)(0)	2
21.09.69	Boeing 727-64	XA-SEJ	19255	Mexicana	Crashed on approach	Mexico City, Mexico	27	0
26.09.69	Douglas DC-6B	CP-698	43273	Lloyd Aereo Boliviano	Crashed into mountain	nr La Paz, Bolivia	74	0
26.09.69	Boeing C-97 Stratofreighter	N52676	*	Nordchurchaid	Crashed	Biafra, Nigeria	*	*
29.09.69	Handley Page Jetstream 1	G-AXEL	207	British Steel Corporation	Crashed	nr Hunstanton, Norfolk, UK	*	*
11.10.69	Britten-Norman BN-2A Islander	N852JA	0072	San Juan Air	Crashed on delivery	Off San Juan, Puerto Rico	*	*
12.10.69	Antonov AN-10	SSSR-11189	*	Aeroflot	Damaged in hard landing	Mirny, RSFSR, USSR	*	*
13.10.69	Antonov AN-24	SSSR-47772	*	Aeroflot	Crashed short of runway	Nizhne-Vartovsk, RSFSR, USSR	*	*
17.10.69	McDonnell Douglas DC-8-63CF	N8634	46021	Seaboard World Airlines	Ran off runway & caught fire	Stockton, CA, USA	0	*
20.10.69	NAMC YS-11A-213	JA8708	2085	All Nippon Airways	Overran on landing	Miyazaki, Japan	*	*
26.10.69	Vickers Viscount 833	4X-AVC	425	Arkia	Damaged on landing	Lod, Israel	0	*

Date	Type	Reg'n	C/n	Operator	Accident	Location	F	S
31.10.69	Rockwell 1121 Jet Commander	N236JP	116	Pittston Corporation	Crashed	Marion, VA, USA	*	*
01.11.69	Convair 440-75	SE-BSU	395	Linjeflyg	Damaged by ground loop	Stockholm, Sweden	0	*
02.11.69	Douglas DC-6A	LN-FOM	45375	Joint Church Aid	Destroyed by bomb blast after landing	Uli, Biafra, Nigeria	*	*
03.11.69	de Havilland Riley Dove	N669R	04388	Sky Tours Hawaii	Undershot on landing & crashed	Kalaupapa, HI, USA	0	*
06.11.69	Gates Learjet 23	N1021B	23-086	Mack Trucks Inc	Crashed	Racine, WI, USA	*	*
09.11.69	Douglas DC-3	CF-AAL	15383/26828	Austin Airways	Crashed	nr Timmins, ON, Canada	4	*
10.11.69	Douglas DC-4-1009	N480G	42920	Pan African Airlines	Destroyed during Biafran air raid	Port Harcourt, Nigeria	*	*
13.11.69	Antonov AN-12	*	*	Aeroflot	Crashed short of runway	Anderma, RSFSR, USSR	*	*
19.11.69	Fairchild-Hiller FH.227B	N7811M	531	Mohawk Airlines	Crashed during storm	Mt Pilot Knob, NY, USA	14	0
19.11.69	Tupolev TU-134	HA-LBA	8350604	Malev	Crashed	Istanbul, Turkey	*	*
20.11.69	BAC VC-10 1101	5N-ABD	804	Nigeria Airways	Crashed on approach	nr Lagos, Nigeria	87	0
20.11.69	Britten-Norman BN-2 Islander	VH-ATK	0029	Aerial Tours	Crashed	Bolovip, Papua New Guinea	*	*
25.11.69	Douglas DC-3	HR-ANA	13301	Sahsa	Crashed	Tegucigalpa, Honduras	*	*
26.11.69	Beechcraft King Air A90	N500X	LJ-0199	Operator Unknown	Written off	Location Unknown	*	*
27.11.69	Hawker Siddeley HS.748 1	LV-HHI	1547	Aerolineas Argentinas	Damaged on landing	Santa Rosa, Argentina	0	*
28.11.69	Lockheed 749A Constellation	5N-85H	2662	Air Interamerica	Crashed after three engines failed	Algeria	*	*
02.12.69	Fokker F-27 Friendship 400M	TC-77	10416	Lineas Aereas del Estado	Crashed	Maranbod, Argentina	*	*
03.12.69	Boeing 707-328B	F-BHSZ	18459	Air France	Crashed	Off Caracas, Venezuela	62	0
04.12.69	Rockwell 1121 Jet Commander	SE-DCY	136	Ehrenstrom Flyg	Crashed	Stockholm, Sweden	2	0
05.12.69	Douglas DC-3	CC-CBY	9783	LAN-Chile	Crashed	El Tepual, Chile	*	*
05.12.69	Britten-Norman BN-2A Islander	9M-APE	0063	Malaysia-Singapore Airlines	Crashed	Sarawak, Malaysia	*	*
06.12.69	Antonov AN-12	*	*	Aeroflot	Crashed on approach	Khatanga, RSFSR, USSR	*	*
08.12.69	Douglas DC-6B	SX-DAE	45540	Olympic Airways	Crashed	nr Keratea, Greece	90	0
11.12.69	NAMC YS-11-125	HL5208	2043	Korean Air Lines	Hijacked to North Korea & damaged on landing	Pyongyang, North Korea	*	*
12.12.69	Curtiss C-46	CP-800	30392	Transportes Aereos Litoral	Crashed on take-off	Corani, Bolivia	*	*
14.12.69	Hawker Siddeley HS.748 2	PP-VDQ	1628	Varig	Crash landed	Uberlandia, Brazil	0	*
16.12.69	Rockwell 1121 Jet Commander	N403M	132	Western Leasing Co	Crashed	Salt Lake City, UT, USA	*	*
17.12.69	Lockheed 1049H Super Constellation	CF-NAK	4829	Canairelief	Bombed by Nigerian aircraft	Uli, Biafra, Nigeria	0	*
17.12.69	Curtiss C-46	LV-GEB	30325	Austral	Crashed on take-off	Buenos Aires, Argentina	*	*
19.12.69	Beechcraft D-18S	JA5020	A-1020	Operator Unknown	Written off	Fukuoka, Japan	*	*
20.12.69	Fairchild F-27J	CF-GNG	0114	Great Northern Airways	Ran off runway	Inuvik, NWT, Canada	0	*
22.12.69	Douglas DC-6B	B-2005	44694	Air Vietnam	Overshot & crashed into school	Nha Trang, South Vietnam	25{100}	0
22.12.69	Vickers Viscount 815	LX-LGC	376	Luxair	U/c collapsed after striking snow-bank	Luxembourg	0	*
23.12.69	Douglas DC-3	XW-TDJ	13529	Laos Air Charter	Crashed	nr Luang Prabang, Laos	6	*
27.12.69	Fokker F-27 Friendship 500	OY-APB	10426	Maersk Air	Crashed in shallow water	Copenhagen, Denmark	0	4
00.00.69	Douglas DC-3	CF-UZA	19028	Keir Air Transport	Damaged beyond repair	Location Unknown	*	*
00.00.69	Mil V-12	*	*	Mil Design Bureau	Crashed	USSR	0	*
00.00.69	Curtiss C-46	HK-682	33226	Aeropesca	Crashed	San Andres Is, Colombia	*	*
00.00.69	Convair 240-1	N8410H	070	Hughes Tool Co	Crashed	Wyoming, USA	*	*
00.00.69	Lockheed 1649A Starliner	N7324C	1030	Six T Ranch	Damaged striking trees on take-off. Landed safely but dbr	Paramaribo, Surinam	0	*
00.00.69	Lockheed 749A Constellation	CX-BGP	2668	Bahamas Government	Set on fire by authorities after smuggling flight	Freeport, Bahamas	0	*
00.00.69	de Havilland Dove 6BA	N1542V	04364	Center Aviation	Crashed	Location Unknown	*	*
00.00.69	Douglas DC-6B	OB-R-920	45176	Faucett	Damaged beyond repair	Location Unknown	*	*

1970–1979

The 1970s were the years when the words 'jumbo jet' entered the English language. The Boeing 747 quickly became the standard long haul aircraft, closely followed by its rivals – the Tristar and the DC-10.

Obviously, these large capacity aircraft increased the chances of disasters on a huge scale but they also proved to be remarkably safe. There were few major accidents in the early 'seventies involving these types but, unfortunately, this was to change before the decade was out.

The 747 suffered six losses, although two were blown up by terrorists on the ground. The Tristar had only two losses but the DC-10 fared worse with eight. In the late 'seventies this aircraft was to be the subject of an unwarranted campaign to have it grounded after a number of highly publicized crashes. After a period of being grounded the DC-10 returned to service and has largely outlasted its rival, the Tristar, with the main airlines.

1977 saw the world's worst airline tragedy to date when a KLM 747 collided with a Pan American 747 on a foggy runway in Tenerife. A total of 583 were killed, with 77 survivors in the American aircraft. With the increase in passenger capacities it had been only a matter of time before a crash of this magnitude occurred.

Terrorism in the air was a major problem during this decade, with hijackings and bombings being all too common. (The two 747s that crashed at Tenerife had only been there after being diverted due to an earlier terrorist bomb at their destination airport.) The most spectacular such event occurred in 1970, when three airliners belonging to BOAC, Swissair and TWA were hijacked to Dawson's Field, Jordan, and blown up, thankfully without

A dramatic shot of a disaster in progress. A PSA Boeing 727 (N533PS) crashing on 25 September 1978 after a mid-air collision with a Cesssna 172 over San Diego, California. A total of 144 were killed in both aircraft and on the ground.

anyone being injured.

Wars continued to affect airline activity. There were aircraft losses in Vietnam and Cambodia, Cyprus, Ethiopia, Mozambique, and Chad. The Cold War claimed another victim when a Soviet aircraft shot down a South Korean 707 which had strayed off course. This proved to be an ominous rehearsal for a more serious incident involving these two nations in 1983.

Another growing cause of airliner losses was the increasing use of larger aircraft for smuggling purposes. Many machines were lost in South and Central America while undertaking illegal activities, either as a result of action by the authorities or botched, clandestine landings under difficult conditions.

The number of crashes with a hundred fatalities or more increased to 45. Apart from Tenerife, the worst single aircraft accident was that in 1974 to a THY DC-10 which suffered an explosive decompression after take-off from Paris, resulting in 346 fatalities.

Britain again suffered a number of major crashes with heavy loss of life. 176 were killed when a British Airways Trident collided with an Inex-Adria DC-9 over Zagreb in 1976. Four years previously another Trident belonging to BEA had crashed after take-off from Heathrow, killing 118, making it the most serious accident within the UK up to that time.

First write-offs 1970–1979

(* military example crashed earlier)

Swearingen Metro	29.01.70
Aero Spacelines Guppy	12.05.70
Canadair CL-215	04.07.70
Antonov AN-22	18.07.70
Boeing 737	19.07.70
Yakovlev YAK-40	03.09.70
Boeing 747	06.09.70
IAI Arava	19.11.70
Nord 262	31.12.70
Hindustan 748	09.12.71
VFW 614	01.02.72
Fokker F-28 Fellowship	18.09.72
Lockheed Jetstar	27.12.72*
Lockheed Tristar	29.12.72
Tupolev TU-154	19.02.73
Tupolev TU-144	03.06.73
McDonnell Douglas DC-10	17.12.73
Grumman Gulfstream II	24.06.74
Cessna Citation	22.11.74
Embraer Bandeirante	27.02.75
GAF Nomad	25.10.75
Antonov AN-26	23.05.76
CASA Aviocar	01.06.76
Britten-Norman Trislander	10.01.77
Cessna 421	27.01.77
LET 410	18.01.79

The fog that contributed to the crash of this TWA Boeing 707 (N18701) on 22 December 1975 at Milan's Malpensa Airport can be seen clearly in this picture. Miraculously, there were no fatalities. (Popperfoto)

Date	Type	Reg'n	C/n	Operator	Accident	Location	F	S
02.01.70	Douglas DC-3	XW-PGJ	*	Bird & Sons	Crashed	Long Cheng, Cambodia	*	*
03.01.70	Cessna 402A	CN-MBI	402A-0104	Operator Unknown	Written off	El Borduj, Morocco	*	*
05.01.70	Convair 990-30-5	EC-BNM	32	Spantax	Crashed after take-off	Stockholm, Sweden	5	5
05.01.70	Fokker F-27 Friendship 600	EC-BOD	10360	Iberia	Crashed	Santa Cruz, Canary Is, Spain	*	*
13.01.70	Douglas DC-3	5W-FAC	16964/34224	Polynesian Airlines	Crashed after take-off	Apia, Western Samoa	33	0
13.01.70	Antonov AN-24V	SU-AOK	67302805	United Arab Airlines	U/c collapsed on landing	Luxor, Egypt	*	*
14.01.70	de Havilland Comet 4C	SU-ANI	06475	United Arab Airlines	Crashed	Addis Ababa, Ethiopia	*	*
14.01.70	Douglas C-54D	OB-R-778	10591	Faucett	Crashed	Mt Pumacona, Peru	28	0
15.01.70	Beechcraft 99	F-BRUF	U121	Air Alpes	Crashed	France	*	*
16.01.70	Mitsubishi MU-2F	N764Q	141	Operator Unknown	Written off	Salisbury, MD, USA	*	*
17.01.70	Convair 240-12	N270L	157	Aspen Airways	Belly landed	Aspen, CO, USA	*	*
19.01.70	Vickers Viscount 701	G-AMOA	009	Cambrian Airways	Damaged in heavy landing	Bristol, UK	0	63
21.01.70	Rockwell 1121 Jet Commander	4X-COJ	029	Israel Aircraft Industries	Crashed	Tel Aviv, Israel	*	*
21.01.70	Douglas C-54E	HK-171	7461	Avianca	Damaged beyond repair	Location Unknown	*	*
22.01.70	Vickers Viscount 814	G-AWXI	339	British Midland Airways	Damaged by fire on take-off	Heathrow, London, UK	0	42
25.01.70	Fokker F-27 Friendship 200	9N-AAR	10290	Royal Nepal Airlines	Overshot in storm	New Delhi, India	1	22
25.01.70	Convair 240-2	XB-DOK	071	Federal Electricity Commission	Crashed	Poza Rica, Mexico	19	0
28.01.70	de Havilland Dove 6A	N2300H	04444	Tag Airlines	Crashed after wing failure	Lake Erie, MI, USA	9	0
28.01.70	Antonov AN-24	SSSR-47701	59900202	Aeroflot	Crashed into hill on approach	Batagay, RSFSR, USSR	34	0
29.01.70	Swearingen Merlin IIB	N239P	T26-147	Operator Unknown	Written off	Willoughby, OH, USA	*	*
29.01.70	Tupolev TU-124	SSSR-45083	5351706	Aeroflot	Crashed on approach	nr Murmansk, RSFSR, USSR	11	0
31.01.70	Curtiss C-46	CP-825	22541	Transportes Aereos Litoral	Crashed	nr Tacna, Peru	*	*
04.02.70	Antonov AN-24TV	YR-AMT	77303310	Tarom	Crashed	Apuseni Mts, Romania	21	0
04.02.70	Hawker Siddeley HS.748 1	LV-HGW	1539	Aerolineas Argentinas	Crashed during storm	Corrientes, Argentina	39	0
05.02.70	Lockheed Electra 188A	PP-VJP	1049	Varig	Landed short of runway	Porto Alegre, Brazil	*	*
06.02.70	Ilyushin IL-18	SSSR-75798	*	Aeroflot	Crashed into hill	Samarkand, Uzbekistan, USSR	92	0
09.02.70	de Havilland Comet 4C	SU-ALE	06444	United Arab Airlines	Forced landed	Munich, West Germany	0	23
09.02.70	de Havilland Canada Otter	OO-HAD	1757	Ex. Antartique Belgo-Neerlandaise	Crashed	Antarctica	*	*
10.02.70	de Havilland Canada Twin Otter 100	N124PM	041	Pilgrim Airlines	Crashed	Off New London, CN, USA	*	*
12.02.70	Douglas DC-3	TAM-11	*	Transporte Aereo Militar	Crashed	Laja, Bolivia	*	*
12.02.70	Douglas DC-3	CC-CBT	14727/26172	Aero Aysen	Crashed	Off Llaque Is, Chile	*	*
15.02.70	McDonnell Douglas DC-9-32	HI-177	47500	Dominicana	Crashed after take-off	Santo Domingo, Dominican Republic	102	0
15.02.70	Douglas DC-3	9Q-CUP	10063	Air Congo	Crashed	Location Unknown	*	*
17.02.70	Fokker F-27 Friendship 100	TC-TEZ	10123	Turk Hava Yollari	Overshot on landing	Samsun, Turkey	0	*
19.02.70	Douglas DC-3	9Q-CUD	9780	Air Congo	Crashed	Location Unknown	*	*
20.02.70	Convair 240-0	N741J	146	Jet International	Belly landed	Hampton, VA, USA	*	*
21.02.70	Douglas DC-3	B-243	*	Far Eastern Air Transport	Crashed	nr Taipeh, Taiwan	*	*
21.02.70	Convair 990-30-6	HB-ICD	15	Swissair	Crashed after bomb explosion	Zurich, Switzerland	47	*
21.02.70	Douglas DC-3	N163J	19402	S.Burnstein	Crashed	Location Unknown	*	*
25.02.70	Curtiss C-46	TI-1065	*	Servicios Aereos Curtiss	Damaged by fire on landing	Beni, Bolivia	*	*
26.02.70	Antonov AN-12	SSSR-12966	*	Aeroflot	Damaged in hard landing	Beryozovo, RSFSR, USSR	*	*
27.02.70	de Havilland Canada Twin Otter 100	9N-RF9	102	Nepalese Royal Flight	Crashed on take-off	Jomson, Nepal	*	*
oo.02.70	Lockheed C-130E Hercules	64-0506	3990	Air America	Believed written off	S.E. Asia	*	*
oo.02.70	Lockheed C-130E Hercules	64-0507	3991	Air America	Believed written off	S.E. Asia	*	*
06.03.70	Handley Page Jetstream 1	D-INAH	205	Bavaria Flug	Crashed	St Moritz, Switzerland	11	0
12.03.70	Douglas DC-3	HK-1270	4544	Lineas Aereas La Urraca	Crashed	Puerta Infrida, Colombia	12{2}	*
12.03.70	Douglas DC-6B	ET-AAY	45524	Ethiopian Airlines	Destroyed by fire on landing	Asmara, Ethiopia	0	*
14.03.70	Antonov AN-24B	SU-AOC	57302103	Misrair	Crash landed after explosion	Cairo, UAR	0	*
14.03.70	Fairchild-Hiller FH.227B	PP-BUF	556	Paraense Transportes Aereos	Crashed during storm	Belem Bay, Brazil	34	4
15.03.70	Fairchild C-82 Packet	CP-677	10117	Transportes Aereos Benianos	Crashed	Sasasama, Bolivia	*	*
22.03.70	Douglas DC-3	XC-CFE	1551	Federal Electricity Commission	Crashed	Aleman, Mexico	*	*
24.03.70	de Havilland Canada Caribou	*	*	Thai Police	Crashed into mountain	Nang Keo, Thailand	6	0
27.03.70	Fokker F-27 Friendship 200	CR-AIB	10205	DETA	Crashed into trees	nr Lourenco Marques, Mozambique	3{1}	*

Date	Type	Reg'n	C/n	Operator	Accident	Location	F	S
00.03.70	Curtiss C-46	HK-790	26480	Aeropesca	Crashed	San Carlos de Guabor, Colombia	*	*
00.03.70	Britten-Norman BN-2A Islander	F-OGDR	0037	Guyane Air Transport	Written off	Location Unknown	*	*
01.04.70	Aerospatiale Caravelle 3	CN-CCV	032	Royal Air Maroc	Crashed on approach	Casablanca, Morocco	61	22
01.04.70	Antonov AN-24	SSSR-47751	79901204	Aeroflot	Crashed after collision with balloon	Novosibirsk, RSFSR, USSR	45	0
07.04.70	Britten-Norman BN-2A Islander	G-AXRJ	0123	Britten-Norman	Crashed	Rawalpindi, Pakistan	*	*
09.04.70	de Havilland Dove 8	G-AVHV	04542	Dowty Group Services	Crashed on approach	Wolverhampton, Staffs, UK	2{1}	0
13.04.70	Douglas DC-3	EP-AGZ	15423/26868	Air Taxi Co	Crashed	Ahwaz, Iran	*	*
14.04.70	Douglas DC-4	*	*	California Eastern Airlines	Crashed on take-off	Miami, FL, USA	2	0
14.04.70	Douglas C-54D	HC-AON	10608	Ecuatoriana	Crashed	Miami, FL, USA	2	0
16.04.70	de Havilland Dove 6BA	N420D	04414	Mid Continent Airlines	Crashed making emergency landing after engine failure	Morris, IL, USA	*	*
19.04.70	McDonnell Douglas DC-8-62	SE-DBE	45823	Scandinavian Airlines System	Caught fire on take-off	Rome, Italy	0	*
22.04.70	Boeing 707-131	N743TW	17670	Trans World Airlines	Damaged by fire	Indianapolis, IN, USA	0	*
25.04.70	Douglas DC-3	B-308	12790	Winner Airways	Overran into sea	Tuy Hoa, South Vietnam	*	*
28.04.70	de Havilland Canada Twin Otter 100	VH-TGR	006	Trans Australia Airlines	Crashed	Kainatu, Papua & New Guinea	7	4
02.05.70	McDonnell Douglas DC-9-33CF	N935F	47407	ALM Antillean Airlines	Crashed	Off St Croix, US Virgin Is	22	38
03.05.70	Bristol 170 Freighter 31M	CF-WAG	13249	Wardair	Crashed through ice on lake	Great Slave Lake, NWT, Canada	*	*
05.05.70	Lockheed 1049G Super Constellation	N174W	4636	North Slope Supply Co	Collided with snowbank on landing	Barrow, AK, USA	0	*
06.05.70	Vickers Viscount 785D	6O-AAJ	379	Somali Airlines	Crashed	Mogadiscio, Somalia	5	25
06.05.70	Grumman G-73 Mallard	PK-AKH	J-17	Operator Unknown	Written off	Location Unknown	*	*
07.05.70	Curtiss C-46	HI-170	*	Domaire	Ran into trees	Santo Domingo, Dominican Republic	0	*
08.05.70	Douglas DC-3	OO-AUX	43088	Delta Air Transport	Damaged beyond repair	Amsterdam, Netherlands	*	*
09.05.70	Fokker F-27 Friendship 100	PI-C532	10311	Philippine Air Lines	Swerved on take-off	Iligan, Philippines	1	32
09.05.70	Gates Learjet 23	N434EJ	23-046	Executive Jet Sales Inc	Crashed	Peliston, MI, USA	*	*
12.05.70	Aero Spacelines Super Guppy 101	N111AS	0001	Aero Spacelines	Crashed after take-off	Mojave, CA, USA	4	0
15.05.70	Antonov AN-10	SSSR-11149	*	Aeroflot	Crashed	Kishiniev, Moldavia, USSR	11	0
21.05.70	Douglas DC-3	N75430	4490	D.Cavener	Crashed	Prudhoe Bay, AK, USA	*	*
22.05.70	Curtiss C-46	YV-C-AMK	254	Linea Aeropostal Venezolana	Crashed	Off Puntarenas, Costa Rica	5	*
26.05.70	de Havilland Heron 1B	HR-ASN	14009	Aeroservicios S. de R.L.	Crashed on approach	Tegucigalpa, Honduras	6	0
30.05.70	Martin 404	N40412	14116	Lehigh Acres Development Co	Crashed after take-off due to wrong fuel being supplied	Atlanta, GA, USA	*	*
01.06.70	Tupolev TU-104A	OK-NDD	96601803	Ceskoslovenske Aerolinie	Crashed on approach in fog	Tripoli, Libya	13	*
03.06.70	Vickers Viscount 745D	HC-ART	288	Saeta	Overran on landing	Cuenca, Ecuador	0	*
04.06.70	Douglas DC-3	PK-ZDF	19648	Zamrud Airlines	Crashed	Menado, Indonesia	*	*
05.06.70	Ilyushin IL-18V	SSSR-75533	*	Aeroflot	Crashed on take-off	Samarkand, Uzbekistan, USSR	*	*
06.06.70	Lockheed 1049G Super Constellation	N8021	4673	International Aerodyne	U/c collapsed on ldg & set on fire by crew of smugglers	La Rioja, Argentina	0	*
07.06.70	Fokker F-27 Friendship 200	VT-DVG	10309	Indian Airlines	Overshot on landing	Agartala, India	0	*
10.06.70	Fokker F-27 Friendship 400M	TC-75	10411	Lineas Aereas del Estado	Crashed	Peruvian Andes	*	*
12.06.70	Bell 206A JetRanger	PK-HBE	00338	Bristow Masayu Helicopters	Crashed	Medan, Indonesia	*	*
19.06.70	Douglas DC-3	CF-AAC	13924/25369	Austin Airways	Damaged beyond repair	Val d'Or, PQ, Canada	*	*
25.06.70	Douglas DC-3	EL-AAB	4284	Liberian National Airlines	Crashed	Tchien, Liberia	*	*
26.06.70	Rockwell Turbo Commander 690	N9202N	11002	Operator Unknown	Written off	Location Unknown	*	*
29.06.70	Douglas DC-3	XW-TDO	14561/26006	Lao Airlines	Written off	Location Unknown	*	*
01.07.70	Fokker F-27 Friendship 100	PI-C504	10209	Philippine Air Lines	Overran during single engine landing	Dumaquete, Philippines	0	29
02.07.70	Short Skyvan 200	N21CK	SH.1858	Jetco Aviation International	Crashed on approach	Potomac River, DC, USA	*	*
03.07.70	Douglas DC-3	N154R	6156	Reeder Flying Service	Crashed after take-off	McGrath, AK, USA	7	20
03.07.70	de Havilland Comet 4	G-APDN	06415	Dan-Air	Crashed on approach	Barcelona, Spain	112	0
04.07.70	Canadair CL-215-1	F-ZBAX	1022	Securite Civile	Crashed	France	*	*
05.07.70	McDonnell Douglas DC-8-63	CF-TIW	46114	Air Canada	Crashed on overshoot	Toronto, ON, Canada	109	0
12.07.70	Bristol Britannia 312	LV-JNL	13230	Aerotransportes Entre Rios	Struck radar while landing in fog	Buenos Aires, Argentina	0	12
12.07.70	Beechcraft Queen Air 80	OO-CHG	LD-010	Rentavia	Crashed	Liege, Belgium	*	*
14.07.70	Douglas DC-3	TAM-17	*	Transporte Aereo Militar	Damaged beyond repair	Location Unknown	*	*
15.07.70	Curtiss C-46	CP-914	249	Servicios Aereos Bolivianos	Crashed	Espiritu, Bolivia	*	*
15.07.70	Curtiss C-46	9T-PLK	30483	SODEMAC	Damaged on landing	Mbuji Mayi, Congo	*	*
18.07.70	Antonov AN-22	SSSR-09303	9340205	Aeroflot	Crashed	North Atlantic	23	0

Date	Type	Reg'n	C/n	Operator	Accident	Location	F	S
18.07.70	Consolidated PBY-6A Catalina	N6459C	*	Hemet Valley Flying Service	Crashed	Columbia, CA, USA	*	*
19.07.70	Antonov AN-24V	SU-ANZ	57302007	United Arab Airlines	Crash landed	Cairo, UAR	3	*
19.07.70	Boeing 737-222	N9005U	19043	United Air Lines	Aborted take-off & overran	Philadelphia, PA, USA	0	61
20.07.70	Hawker Siddeley HS.125-3B	G-AXPS	25135	Imperial Tobacco Group	Crashed	Edinburgh, UK	*	*
20.07.70	IRMA BN-2A Islander	9Q-CTS	0607	Tramaco Services	Crashed	Busira River, Zaire	*	*
23.07.70	Douglas DC-3	XW-TDC	16864/33612	Xiengkhouang Air	Damaged on landing	Long Cheng, Laos	*	*
26.07.70	Douglas DC-7CF	VR-BCT	44875	ARCO Bermuda	Belly landed	Abidjan, Ivory Coast	*	*
27.07.70	McDonnell Douglas DC-8-63AF	N785FT	46005	Flying Tiger Line	Crashed in sea on approach	Off Okinawa, Ryukyu Is	4	0
28.07.70	Grumman TBM3 Avenger	N9082Z	*	Hemet Valley Flying Service	Crashed	Bear Mountain, CA, USA	*	*
28.07.70	Grumman TBM3 Avenger	N3356G	*	Hemet Valley Flying Service	Crashed	California, USA	*	*
01.08.70	Bolkow Bo.208 Junior	G-ATRI	602	Loganair	Crashed	Loch Lomond, UK	*	*
06.08.70	Fokker F-27 Friendship 200	AP-ALM	10163	Pakistan International Airlines	Crashed into high ground after take-off	Islamabad, Pakistan	30	0
08.08.70	Convair 990-30-8	N5603	13	Modern Air	Crashed on landing	Acapulco, Mexico	0	8
08.08.70	Antonov AN-10A	SSSR-11188	*	Aeroflot	Damaged on landing after in-flight fire	Kishiniev, Moldavia, USSR	1	*
09.08.70	Lockheed Electra 188A	OB-R-939	1106	Lansa	Crashed after take-off	Cuzco, Peru	99	1
12.08.70	NAMC YS-11A-219	B-156	2110	China Airlines	Crashed on approach during storm	Taipei, Taiwan	14	17
18.08.70	Tupolev TU-124	OK-TEB	4351504	Ceskoslovenske Aerolinie	Belly landed & caught fire	Zurich, Switzerland	0	20
18.08.70	Boeing B-17F	N1340N	6402	Aero Flite	Crashed due to engine failure	Yellowstone, WY, USA	*	*
22.08.70	Douglas DC-3	PP-CCL	13802/25247	Cruzeiro	Crashed	Cruzeiro do Sol Acre, Brazil	*	*
23.08.70	Ilyushin IL-18V	SSSR-75823	182004902	Aeroflot	Crashed on landing in bad weather	Yuzhno-Sakhalinsk, RSFSR, USSR	*	*
24.08.70	Lockheed Electra 188CF	N855U	2012	Universal Airlines	Crashed	Hill AFB, UT, USA	0	*
25.08.70	Douglas DC-6	XA-SAR	43110	E.R.Andrade	Crashed	Bahia de Tortugas, Mexico	*	*
28.08.70	Hughes 269B	B-15103	*	Great China Airlines	Crashed	Taiwan	*	*
29.08.70	Fokker F-27 Friendship 400	VT-DWT	10336	Indian Airlines	Crashed	nr Silcher, India	39	0
30.08.70	Douglas DC-3	CF-JRY	4585	D.G.Harris Productions	Destroyed on ground by high winds	Toronto, ON, Canada	0	*
30.08.70	Britten-Norman BN-2A Islander	PH-NVA	0111	Dutch Continental Airlines	Crashed	nr Veer, Netherlands	*	*
02.09.70	Tupolev TU-124	SSSR-45012	*	Aeroflot	Crashed	nr Dnepropetrovsk, Ukraine, USSR	37	0
03.09.70	Yakovlev YAK-40	SSSR-87690	*	Aeroflot	Crashed into mountain	Leninabad, Tajikistan, USSR	21	0
06.09.70	Boeing 747-121	N752PA	19656	Pan American World Airways	Blown up by hijackers on ground	Cairo, UAR	0	0
08.09.70	McDonnell Douglas DC-8-63CF	N4863T	45951	Trans International Airlines	Crashed on take-off	New York, NY, USA	11	0
09.09.70	Britten-Norman BN-2A Islander	N855JA	0087	San Juan Air	Crashed	Orocicvis, Puerto Rico	*	*
13.09.70	Boeing 707-331B	N8715T	18917	Trans World Airlines	Blown up on ground by hijackers	El Khana, Jordan	0	0
13.09.70	McDonnell Douglas DC-8-53	HB-IDD	45656	Swissair	Blown up on ground by hijackers	El Khana, Jordan	0	0
13.09.70	BAC Super VC-10 1151	G-ASGN	864	British Overseas Airways Corporation	Blown up on ground by hijackers	El Khana, Jordan	0	0
15.09.70	McDonnell Douglas DC-8-62	I-DIWZ	46026	Alitalia	Broke in two when u/c collapsed on landing	New York, NY, USA	0	156
20.09.70	Cessna 402A	TS-DAA	402A-0009	Tunis Air	Written off	Zaghouan Mts, Tunisia	*	*
22.09.70	Vickers Viscount 776	G-APNF	225	BKS Air Transport	Damaged by fire on ground	Woolsington, UK	0	*
26.09.70	Fokker F-27 Friendship 300	TF-FIL	10356	Icelandair	Crashed on approach in fog	Mygganaes, Faroe Is	8	*
30.09.70	Douglas DC-3	B-305	3251	Air Vietnam	Crashed	North of Da Nang, South Vietnam	*	*
01.10.70	Douglas DC-3	N47	16407/33155	Federal Aviation Administration	Crashed	nr Anchorage, AK, USA	*	*
01.10.70	Antonov AN-12	SSSR-11031	7345003	Aeroflot	Crashed on take-off	Kamenniy Cape, RSFSR, USSR	8	*
02.10.70	Martin 404	N464M	14151	Golden Eagle Aviation	Crashed	nr Denver, CO, USA	32	11
02.10.70	Douglas DC-7C	EC-ATQ	45162	Spantax	Damaged beyond repair	Madrid, Spain	*	*
03.10.70	Rockwell Turbo Commander 680T	N541W	1554-13	Operator Unknown	Written off	Ponpano Beach, FL, USA	*	*
06.10.70	Douglas DC-3	ZS-DKR	16660/33408	National Airways	Crashed on take-off	Johannesburg, South Africa	2	9
07.10.70	de Havilland Comet 4	G-APDL	06413	Dan-Air	Belly landed	Newcastle, UK	0	11
07.10.70	Douglas DC-3	CF-TAR	4594	Trans Air	Crashed	Location Unknown	*	*
11.10.70	Lockheed L-100 Hercules	N9248R	4221	Saturn Airways	Crashed short of runway	McGuire AFB, NJ, USA	3	0
13.10.70	Mitsubishi MU-2B	N549LK	022	Operator Unknown	Written off	Northfield, OH, USA	*	*
14.10.70	Cessna 180	ET-ABO	32645	Ethiopian Airlines	Crashed after tyre burst on take-off	Addis Ababa, Ethiopia	*	*
16.10.70	Ilyushin IL-18V	SSSR-75578	185008103	Aeroflot	Crashed	Simferopol, Ukraine, USSR	*	*
22.10.70	Short Skyvan 200	N123PA	SH.1861	Pan Alaska Airways	Crashed	nr Fairbanks, AK, USA	*	*
28.10.70	Fairchild C-82 Packet	PT-DNZ	*	Amazonia	Crashed	Serra do Norte, Brazil	*	*
28.10.70	Curtiss C-46	HK-792	33060	Aerocosta	Crashed	Pointe-a-Pitre, Guadeloupe	2	*

Date	Type	Reg'n	C/n	Operator	Accident	Location	F	S
01.11.70	Curtiss C-46	B-1543	*	Air Vietnam	Forced landed on beach & destroyed by tide	Qui Nhon, South Vietnam	0	*
05.11.70	Douglas DC-6B	SX-DAI	45544	Olympic Airways	Damaged in hard landing	Corfu, Greece	0	*
06.11.70	Douglas DC-3	ZK-AXS	15995/32743	New Zealand Ministry of Transport	Damaged beyond repair	Paraparumu, New Zealand	*	*
09.11.70	de Havilland Canada Twin Otter 200	N956SM	203	Mississippi Valley Airlines	Crashed	La Crosse, WI, USA	*	*
14.11.70	McDonnell Douglas DC-9-31	N97S	47245	Southern Airlines	Crashed on approach	Huntingdon, WV, USA	75	0
14.11.70	Rockwell 1121 Jet Commander	N100RC	060	Royal Crown Cola Corporation	Crashed	Lexington, KY, USA	*	*
15.11.70	Sikorsky S-61N-II	G-ASNM	61-221	BEA Helicopters	Crashed due to rotor failure	Off Aberdeen, UK	0	3
16.11.70	Douglas DC-6B	N6113C	44113	Transportes Aereos Latin America	Forced landed & caught fire	La Antigua, Argentina	*	*
19.11.70	Douglas DC-3	PI-C9	12648	Philippine Air Lines	Damaged by typhoon	Manila, Philippines	*	*
19.11.70	Douglas DC-3	PI-C944	42967	Fairways	Damaged by typhoon	Manila, Philippines	*	*
19.11.70	IAI Arava 101	4X-IAI	002	Israel Aircraft Industries	Crashed	Judean Hills, Israel	*	*
25.11.70	Rockwell Turbo Commander 681	N9060N	6011	Operator Unknown	Written off	Altus, OK, USA	*	*
27.11.70	McDonnell Douglas DC-8-63CF	N4909C	46060	Capitol International Airlines	Overran on take-off	Anchorage, AK, USA	47	182
30.11.70	Boeing 707-373C	N790TW	18738	Trans World Airlines	Collided on t/o with IDFAF Stratofreighter 4X-FPS on tow	Tel Aviv, Israel	0(2)(0)	7
30.11.70	Boeing KC-97G Stratofreighter	4X-FPS/037	16658	Israeli Defence Force Air Force	Struck while being towed by TWA 707 N790TW on take-off	Tel Aviv, Israel	0(2)(0)	0
oo.11.70	Handley Page Dart Herald 204	PI-C869	163	Air Manila	Damaged when hangar collapsed	Manila, Philippines	0	*
02.12.70	Canadair CL-44J	TF-LLG	036	Cargolux	Crashed on approach	Dacca, Pakistan	4(4)	0
05.12.70	Douglas DC-3	VT-CZC	12103	Jamair	Crashed after take-off	New Delhi, India	4	12
06.12.70	Douglas DC-3	PP-CDH	11730	LASA	Written off	Location Unknown	*	*
07.12.70	BAC One-Eleven 424EU	YR-BCA	130	Tarom	Crashed on approach	nr Constanza, Romania	18	9
15.12.70	Beechcraft Queen Air B80	PK-LEB	LD-356	SAATAS-Eastindio	Written off	Location Unknown	*	*
15.12.70	Beechcraft C-45H	9Q-CXC	AF-765	AMAZ	Written off	Location Unknown	*	*
18.12.70	MBB HFB.320 Hansa	D-CIRO	1044	General Air	Crashed	Texel, Netherlands	0	*
19.12.70	Antonov AN-22	SSSR-09305	*	Aeroflot	Crashed on landing	Panagarh, India	25	0
20.12.70	Douglas DC-6B	OO-CTL	43832	Sobelair	Crashed	Malaga, Spain	*	*
28.12.70	Boeing 727-2A7	N8790R	20240	Trans Caribbean Airlines	Overran on landing	St Thomas, US Virgin Is	2	51
28.12.70	Hawker Siddeley HS.125-1A	N36MK	25073	Operator Unknown	Crashed	Boise, ID, USA	*	*
30.12.70	Fokker F-27 Friendship 200	AP-AUV	10330	Pakistan International Airlines	Crashed on landing	Shamshernagar, Pakistan	7	28
31.12.70	Ilyushin IL-18V	SSSR-75773	181003603	Aeroflot	Crashed on take-off	Leningrad, RSFSR, USSR	93	0
31.12.70	Nord 262E	F-BNGB	002	Rousseau Aviation	Crashed	Off Algeria	31	0
oo.oo.70	Convair 440-0	YU-ADO	470	JAT Yugoslav Airlines	Belly landed	Belgrade, Yugoslavia	*	*
oo.oo.70	Douglas DC-3	N28343	2267	Lauderdale Leasing Co	Crashed on smuggling flight	Yucatan, Mexico	*	*
oo.oo.70	Douglas DC-3	N12978	4983	Air Carrier	Damaged by fire	Opa Locka, FL, USA	*	*
oo.oo.70	Mil Mi-4	9G-OTP	15145	Operator Unknown	Written off	Location Unknown	*	*
02.01.71	de Havilland Comet 4C	SU-ALC	06439	United Arab Airlines	Crashed during sandstorm	Ben Gashir, Libya	16	0
04.01.71	Aerospatiale Caravelle 3	F-BNKI	214	Air Inter	Damaged by fire	Paris, France	0	*
04.01.71	Douglas DC-3	N7	20426	Federal Aviation Administration	Crashed	La Guardia, NY, USA	*	*
10.01.71	Scottish Aviation Twin Pioneer 3	G-ARBA	548	Iraq Petroleum Transport Co	Damaged beyond repair	nr Basra, Iraq	*	*
12.01.71	Beechcraft 99A	N12RA	U131	Rio Airways	Crashed	Location Unknown	*	*
18.01.71	Ilyushin IL-18	LZ-BED	186009002	Balkan Bulgarian Airlines	Crashed in fog	Zurich, Switzerland	45	2
21.01.71	Rockwell 1121 Jet Commander	N400CP	030	Cousin Properties	Crashed	Burlington, VT, USA	*	*
21.01.71	Beechcraft Queen Air 70	7T-VSI	LB-015	Air Algerie	Written off	Aures Mts, Algeria	*	*
22.01.71	Aerospatiale Caravelle 3	XU-JTA	145	Air Cambodge	Destroyed by enemy action	Phnom Penh, Khmer Republic	0	*
22.01.71	Hawker Siddeley HS.748 2A	9G-ABW	1685	Ghana Airways	Crashed	Accra, Ghana	0	3
22.01.71	Beechcraft King Air B90	D-ILTU	LJ-0359	Operator Unknown	Written off	Frankfurt, West Germany	*	*
22.01.71	Antonov AN-12	SSSR-11000	*	Aeroflot	Crashed on approach	Surgut, RSFSR, USSR	13	*
23.01.71	Boeing 707-437	VT-DJI	17722	Air India	Crashed on take-off after tyre burst	Bombay, India	0	5
23.01.71	Fokker F-27 Friendship 500	HL5212	10428	Korean Air Lines	Crash landed during hijack attempt	Kansong Port, South Korea	*	*
25.01.71	Vickers Viscount 749	YV-C-AMV	094	Linea Aeropostal Venezolana	Crashed into mountains	Merida, Spain	18	31
26.01.71	Britten Norman BN-2A Islander	A2-ZEV	0099	Botswana Airways	Crashed	nr Maun, Botswana	0	8
30.01.71	Fokker F-27 Friendship 100	VT-DMA	10171	Indian Airlines	Blown up by hijackers	Lahore, Pakistan	*	*
31.01.71	Antonov AN-12	SSSR-12996	*	Aeroflot	Crashed short of runway	USSR	7	*
10.02.71	Curtiss C-46	N10012	33271	Reeve Aleutian Airlines	Crashed & sank through ice	Nondalton, AK, USA	*	*
14.02.71	Beechcraft H-18	JA5164	BA-756	Operator Unknown	Written off	Nagoya, Japan	*	*

Date	Type	Reg'n	C/n	Operator	Accident	Location	F	S
14.02.71	Beechcraft H-18	JA5169	BA-761	Operator Unknown	Written off	Ohmura, Japan	*	*
17.02.71	Curtiss C-46	TAM-60	*	TAME	Crashed in bad weather	Mt Cunatineuta, Ecuador	12	0
19.02.71	Douglas C-54A	LV-JPG	10328	Aero Palas	Crashed	nr Cervo Huaycas, Peru	*	*
19.02.71	Douglas DC-3	N99H	15840/32588	E.W.Brown	Damaged beyond repair	Houston, TX, USA	*	*
25.02.71	Douglas DC-3	LV-JTC	2122	Automovil Club Argentino	Written off	Tocuman, Argentina	*	*
27.02.71	Boeing Stratoliner	XW-PGR	2000	Royal Air Lao	Written off	Luang Prabang, Laos	*	*
02.03.71	Curtiss C-46	CP-908	33494	Aerovias Las Minas	Crashed	Santiago, Bolivia	*	*
02.03.71	Douglas DC-3	HC-ALC	19871	Transportes Aereos Orientales	Damaged beyond repair	Location Unknown	*	*
18.03.71	Aviation Traders ATL.98 Carvair	G-APNH	18333/11	British Air Ferries	Damaged when nosewheel collapsed	Le Touquet, France	0	*
23.03.71	Aerospatiale Corvette	F-WRSN	01	Aerospatiale	Crashed	Istres, France	*	*
25.03.71	Fokker F-27 Friendship 200	VH-FNE	10145	Ansett Airlines of Australia	Destroyed in hangar fire	Melbourne, Vic, Australia	0	*
26.03.71	Douglas DC-3	VT-ATT	20363	Jamair	Crashed	Gauhati, India	15	0
26.03.71	Douglas DC-3	N49319	15231/26676	Vanderpool Flying Service	Ran into snowbank on landing	Red Devil, AK, USA	*	*
31.03.71	Boeing 720-047B	N3166	19439	Western Air Lines	Crashed	Ontario, Canada	5	0
31.03.71	Antonov AN-24V	SSSR-46747	*	Aeroflot	Crashed	Moscow, RSFSR, USSR	*	*
31.03.71	Antonov AN-10	SSSR-11145	*	Aeroflot	Crashed on approach	Voroshilovgrad, Ukraine, USSR	64	0
oo.03.71	Douglas DC-6	TG-ABA-C	42883	Aviateca	Damaged beyond repair	Location Unknown	*	*
01.04.71	NAMC YS-11-102	PK-MYN	2011	Merpati Nusantara Airlines	Damaged beyond repair	Djakarta, Indonesia	*	*
01.04.71	Aerospatiale 330C Puma	7T-WUD	1026	Algerian Air Force	Written off	Algeria	*	*
04.04.71	Fokker F-27 Friendship 200	5N-AAX	10218	Nigeria Airways	Veered off runway & crashed	Jos, Nigeria	*	*
05.04.71	Douglas DC-3	N57372	10136	Vinair	Damaged when u/c sheered off on landing	Beef Is, US Virgin Is	*	*
06.04.71	Douglas DC-3	5Y-DCA	15288/26733	Kenya Department of Civil Aviation	Damaged beyond repair	Nairobi, Kenya	*	*
10.04.71	Tupolev TU-134	*	*	Aeroflot	Overshot on landing	Moscow, RSFSR, USSR	0	*
17.04.71	Gates Learjet 24D	N123CB	24D-232	Operator Unknown	Crashed	Butte, MT, USA	*	*
20.04.71	Pilatus Porter	*	*	Air America	Crashed	Doi Suthep, Thailand	0	3
24.04.71	Lockheed 18-50 Lodestar	ZK-CGV	2051	Airland (NZ) Ltd	Crashed	Off Napier, New Zealand	*	*
28.04.71	Hughes 269B	B-15106	*	Great China Airlines	Crashed	Taiwan	*	*
oo.04.71	Handley Page Dart Herald 203	I-TIVE	168	Itavia	Written off	Rome, Italy	*	*
04.05.71	Douglas DC-3	TAM-22	*	Transporte Aereo Militar	Crashed on take-off	La Paz, Bolivia	*	*
06.05.71	Carstedt CJ600a	N4922V	04285	Apache Airlines	Crashed after wing broke off	Coolidge, AZ, USA	12	0
11.05.71	Curtiss C-46	TG-ACA-A	121	Aviateca	Crashed into mountain after take-off	Guatemala City, Guatemala	5	27
14.05.71	Convair 240-14	N1015G	127	Department of the Interior	Damaged in belly landing	Buhl, ID, USA	*	*
14.05.71	Douglas DC-3	N14273	7366	Patterson McCarthy Leasing	Crashed	nr Shawnee, OK, USA	*	*
23.05.71	Tupolev TU-134A	YU-AHZ	1351205	Aviogenex	Overturned on landing	Rijecke, Yugoslavia	78	5
25.05.71	Curtiss C-46	CC-CAZ	*	Austral	Crashed after engine failure	Santiago, Chile	4	0
25.05.71	Antonov AN-12	SSSR-11024	*	Aeroflot	Damaged on landing	Batagay, RSFSR, USSR	*	*
01.06.71	Antonov AN-24	SSSR-47729	*	Aeroflot	Crashed	Ulan-Ude, RSFSR, USSR	*	*
03.06.71	Douglas DC-3	PH-MOA	16605/33353	Moormanair	Damaged on landing	Southend, Essex, UK	0	*
06.06.71	McDonnell Douglas DC-9-31	N9345	47441	Hughes Air West	Mid-air collision with USMC F-4B 151458	Los Angeles, CA, USA	49(1)	0
07.06.71	Convair 580	N5832	384	Allegheny Airlines	Crashed on approach	New Haven, CN, USA	30	3
08.06.71	Westland Wessex 1	PK-HBR	696	Bristow Masayu Helicopters	Crashed	Off Kalimantan, Indonesia	*	*
13.06.71	Douglas DC-3	EP-ADG	10237	Air Taxi Co	Crashed	Shiraz, Iran	*	*
17.06.71	Douglas DC-6	CP-926	43043	Savco	Crashed	Arica, Bolivia	6	0
18.06.71	Rockwell Turbo Commander 681	CP-894	6015	Corporacion Minera de Bolivia	Crashed	nr Puerto Suarez, Bolivia	*	*
27.06.71	Douglas DC-3	N90627	4642	Lake Riverside Estates	Crashed on take-off	nr Eureka, CA, USA	16	4
30.06.71	Douglas DC-3	XW-TDI	15700/27145	Lao Airlines	Crashed	Ban Honeisai, Laos	*	*
oo.06.71	Curtiss C-46	CF-NAE	27063	Nordair	Destroyed in hangar fire	Hall Beach, NWT, Canada	*	*
oo.06.71	Dornier Do.28D-1 Skyservant	TR-LOS	4029	Ste Air Service	Written off	Location Unknown	*	*
01.07.71	de Havilland Dove 1	LV-XZT	04137	Aerotaxis Astro	Crashed on approach	River Plate, Argentina	*	*
03.07.71	NAMC YS-11A-227	JA8764	2134	Toa Domestic Airlines	Crashed	Hakodate, Japan	68	0
05.07.71	Dassault Falcon 20C	N805F	060	General Transportation Co	Crashed	Boca Raton, FL, USA	*	*
12.07.71	Boeing B-17G	N9324Z	32183	Aero Union	Crashed	USA	*	*
16.07.71	Douglas DC-3	N74844	15013/26458	New England Propeller Service	Written off	Windsor Locks, CN, USA	*	*
17.07.71	Kawasaki-Bell 47G-2	B-12105	108	Yung Shing Airlines	Crashed	Taiwan	*	*

Date	Type	Reg'n	C/n	Operator	Accident	Location	F	S
22.07.71	Tupolev TU-134	YI-AED	9350915	Iraqi Airways	Written off	Jeddah, Saudi Arabia	*	*
24.07.71	Douglas DC-3	6V-AAP	20505	Air Ivoire	Crashed into hill	Bamako, Mauritania	6	0
25.07.71	Boeing 707-321C	N461PA	19371	Pan American World Airways	Crashed on approach	Manila, Philippines	4	0
25.07.71	Tupolev TU-104B	SSSR-42405	*	Aeroflot	Crashed on landing	Irkutsk, RSFSR, USSR	97	0
28.07.71	Yakovlev YAK-40	SSSR-87719	*	Aeroflot	Crashed on landing	Moscow, RSFSR, USSR	*	*
29.07.71	Antonov AN-12B	SSSR-12993	00347307	Aeroflot	Crash landed after being struck by lightning	Calcutta, India	0	7
30.07.71	Boeing 727-2E2	JA8329	20436	All Nippon Airways	Mid-air collision with JASDF F-86F 92-7932	Morioko, Japan	162(0)	0
oo.07.71	Grumman G-21A Goose	N101LB	1136	Operator Unknown	Crashed	Location Unknown	*	*
06.08.71	Bell 47J	ET-ABB	742	Ethiopian Airlines	Crashed after rotor failure	Caday Mekael, Ethiopia	*	*
09.08.71	Vickers Viscount 768D	VT-DIX	292	Indian Airlines	Crashed	Jaipur, India	*	*
20.08.71	Convair 580	N5844	043	Allegheny Airlines	Damaged beyond repair on ground	Pittsburgh, PA, USA	*	*
22.08.71	Douglas DC-3	B-304	4808	Air Vietnam	Written off	Kampot, Khmer Republic	*	*
28.08.71	Ilyushin IL-18D	HA-MOC	181002903	Malev	Crashed	Off Copenhagen, Denmark	31	3
oo.08.71	Vickers Viscount 745D	N7415	113	Aloha Airlines	Destroyed by fire on ground	Hawaii, USA	0	*
03.09.71	Canadair CL-215-1	F-ZBBG	1025	Securite Civile	Crashed	France	*	*
04.09.71	Boeing 727-93	N2969G	19304	Alaska Airlines	Crashed into mountain	Juneau, AK, USA	111	0
04.09.71	Grumman TBM3 Avenger	N6825C	*	Hemet Valley Flying Service	Crashed	Columbia, CA, USA	*	*
06.09.71	BAC One-Eleven 515FB	D-ALAR	207	Paninternational	Crashed on motorway	Hamburg, West Germany	22	99
09.09.71	Douglas DC-3	8P-AAC	14917/26363	Carib West Airways	Crashed into mountain	Guadeloupe	2	0
12.09.71	Douglas C-47A	HC-AUX	20179	TAME	Crashed	Cerro de Hojas, Ecuador	*	*
16.09.71	Douglas DC-3	4W-ABI	9334	Yemen Airlines	Crashed	Presvo, Yugoslavia	4	0
16.09.71	Tupolev TU-134	HA-LBD	8350801	Malev	Crashed	Kiev, Ukraine, USSR	49	0
17.09.71	Boeing KC-97G Stratofreighter	4X-FPR/033	16714	Israeli Defence Force Air Force	Shot down by Egyptian missiles	Suez, Egypt	*	*
17.09.71	Canadair C-54GM North Star	CF-UXB	117	Air Caicos	Belly landed due to u/c failure	Saratosa, FL, USA	0	*
19.09.71	Beechcraft Queen Air B80	HK-1024	LD-397	Operator Unknown	Crashed	nr La Nubia, Colombia	*	*
27.09.71	Swearingen Merlin III	PT-DUX	T-215	Operator Unknown	Written off	Sao Paulo, Brazil	*	*
27.09.71	de Havilland Canada Otter	C-FMPZ	328	RCMP Air Services	Written off	Deer Lake, NF, Canada	*	*
28.09.71	Douglas DC-3	PP-CBV	4977	Cruzeiro	Crashed	Sena Madureira, Brazil	32	0
02.10.71	Vickers Vanguard 951	G-APEC	706	British European Airways	Crashed due to structural failure in tail	Ghent, Belgium	63	0
02.10.71	Douglas DC-3	N1981W	2232	H.B.Merser	Crashed	Off US Virgin Is	*	*
10.10.71	Tupolev TU-104B	SSSR-42490	021603	Aeroflot	Crashed after take-off	Moscow, RSFSR, USSR	25	*
12.10.71	Antonov AN-10	SSSR-11137	*	Aeroflot	Crashed on landing	Kishiniev, Moldavia, USSR	*	*
16.10.71	Swearingen Merlin IIB	N100NL	T26-168	Operator Unknown	Written off	Hot Springs, VA, USA	*	*
17.10.71	Douglas DC-3	HK-595	19238	Taxi Aero Opita	Crashed	San Vincente de Caguan, Colombia	22	2
19.10.71	Douglas DC-6B	HI-146	43270	Ladeco	Crashed	nr Mendoza, Argentina	3	0
20.10.71	Lockheed 1049H Super Constellation	N564E	4834	Balair	Crashed in sea	Off Grand Inagua, Bahamas	*	0
22.10.71	Douglas DC-6B	F-BNUZ	45173	Europe Aero Services	Damaged in heavy landing	Nice, France	*	*
24.10.71	Beechcraft 99	N986MA	U044	Monmouth Airlines	Crashed	Bath, PA, USA	*	*
oo.10.71	Britten-Norman BN-2A-7 Islander	HP-550	0282	Aviones de Panama	Written off	Panama	*	*
01.11.71	Vickers Viscount 749	YV-C-AMZ	096	Linea Aeropostal Venezolana	Crashed on take-off	Maracaibo, Venezuela	4	0
03.11.71	Douglas DC-3	HC-ANJ	20719	Aero Amazonas	Crashed	nr Cali, Colombia	3	0
07.11.71	NAMC YS-11A-212	PP-SML	2076	VASP	U/c collapsed on landing	Aragarcas, Brazil	*	*
10.11.71	Vickers Viscount 828	PK-MVS	448	Merpati Nusantara Airlines	Crashed	Off Pedang, Philippines	69	0
12.11.71	Antonov AN-24	SSSR-46809	*	Aeroflot	Crashed	Vinnitsa, Ukraine, USSR	47	0
13.11.71	Antonov AN-24	SSSR-46378	07306101	Aeroflot	Crashed on approach after striking cable	Kerch, Ukraine, USSR	5	0
15.11.71	Antonov AN-24RV	YR-AMA	17306904	Tarom	Crashed on landing	Bucharest, Romania	0	*
19.11.71	Aerospatiale 330C Puma	7T-WUC	1014	Algerian Air Force	Written off	Algeria	*	*
21.11.71	Aerospatiale Caravelle 3	B-1852	122	China Airlines	Crashed	Off Pescadores Is, Taiwan	25	0
23.11.71	Fokker F-27 Friendship 500	9V-BCU	10463	Malaysia-Singapore Airlines	Crashed on landing	Kota Kinabalu, Malaysia	0	*
29.11.71	Cessna 402B	OY-SAW	402B-0112	Sterling Airways	Crashed	Billund, Denmark	*	*
01.12.71	Antonov AN-24	SSSR-46788	57301705	Aeroflot	Crashed on approach	Saratov, RSFSR, USSR	57	0
05.12.71	de Havilland Canada Twin Otter 300	AP-AWH	293	Pakistan International Airlines	Destroyed during Indian air raid	Dacca, Pakistan	*	*
05.12.71	Nord 262A-25	F-BNMO	027	Rousseau Aviation	Crashed	Lanien, France	2	*

Date	Type	Reg'n	C/n	Operator	Accident	Location	F	S
05.12.71	Rockwell Turbo Commander 680V	N78D	1580-33	Operator Unknown	Written off	New Orleans, LA, USA	*	*
06.12.71	Fokker F-27 Friendship 200	ST-AAY	10238	Sudan Airways	Forced landing during hijack	Tirkaka, Sudan	10	32
09.12.71	Hindustan 748 2-224	VT-DXG	512	Indian Airlines	Crashed	Madurai, India	20	11
13.12.71	Fokker F-27 Friendship 200	AP-ALX	10188	Pakistan International Airlines	Crashed	nr Iranian border, Pakistan	4	0
15.12.71	Boeing 707-340C	AP-AVZ	20487	Pakistan International Airlines	Crashed	Urumchi, China	0	*
16.12.71	Convair 440-11	YU-ADV	429	Pan Adria	Crashed on landing	Belgrade, Yugoslavia	*	*
16.12.71	Beechcraft Queen Air B80	HK-844	LD-307	Operator Unknown	Written off	Location Unknown	*	*
21.12.71	Douglas DC-3	XW-TFC	*	Lao Airlines	Crashed	Ban Boum, Laos	2	*
21.12.71	Ilyushin IL-18	LZ-BES	185008104	Balkan Bulgarian Airlines	Crashed on take-off in rain	Sofia, Bulgaria	28	45
21.12.71	Britten-Norman BN-2 Islander	N589JA	0025	Vieques Air Link	Crashed	Puerto Rico	*	*
24.12.71	Lockheed Electra 188A	OB-R-941	1086	Lansa	Crashed after explosion. Found after two weeks	nr Puerto Inca, Peru	91	1
27.12.71	Fairchild C-123K Provider	57-6293	20303	Air America	Crashed	Laos	5	*
27.12.71	Beechcraft King Air B90	N480K	LJ-0439	Operator Unknown	Written off	Off Bahamas	*	*
28.12.71	Vickers Viscount 708	F-BOEA	012	Air Inter	Crash landed	Clermont Ferrand, France	0	*
28.12.71	Rockwell Turbo Commander 680W	N9019N	1844-43	Operator Unknown	Written off	Elkhart, IN, USA	*	*
oo.oo.71	Curtiss C-46	LV-GXB	22332	Aerovias Halcon	Destroyed by fire started by pilot	Buenos Aires, Argentina	*	*
oo.oo.71	Lockheed 1049H Super Constellation	N45515	4843	Unum Inc	Wing exploded on ground	Kingman, AZ, USA	0	*
05.01.72	Douglas DC-3	CF-KAH	15739/27184	McKenzie Air	Damaged beyond repair	Norman Wells, NWT, USA	*	*
05.01.72	Piper PA-27-250 Aztec E	G-AZIF	27-4633	Air London	Crashed	Stansted, Essex, UK	*	*
06.01.72	Hawker Siddeley HS.748 2	XA-SEV	1598	Saesa	Crashed after fire	North of Bacalar, Mexico	23	0
07.01.72	Aerospatiale Caravelle 6R	EC-ATV	163	Iberia	Crashed into mountain on descent	Ibiza, Balearic Is, Spain	104	0
07.01.72	Convair 340-68B	HZ-AAU	182	Saudi Arabian Airlines	Crashed on landing	Jeddah, Saudi Arabia	*	*
09.01.72	Lockheed Electra 188A	PI-C1060	1021	Air Manila	Written off	Manila, Philippines	*	*
18.01.72	Gates Learjet 25	N658TC	25-044	Tandy Corporation	Crashed	Victoria, TX, USA	9	0
20.01.72	Hawker Siddeley HS.748 1	LV-HHH	1546	Aerolineas Argentinas	Crashed	Samiento, Argentina	*	*
21.01.72	Douglas DC-3	FAC.661	*	Satena	Crashed	San Nicolas, Colombia	39	0
21.01.72	McDonnell Douglas DC-9-32	TC-JAC	47213	Turk Hava Yollari	Crashed in snowstorm	Adana, Turkey	1	4
21.01.72	Vickers Viscount 837	HK-1347	442	Lineas Aereas La Urraca	Exploded in mid-air	nr Bogota, Colombia	20	0
23.01.72	Hughes 269B	B-15105	20-0446	Great China Airlines	Crashed	Taiwan	*	*
25.01.72	Yakovlev YAK-40	YA-KAD	9120517	Bakhtar Afghan Airlines	Crashed short of runway	Khost, Afghanistan	0	*
26.01.72	McDonnell Douglas DC-9-32	YU-AHT	47482	JAT Yugoslav Airlines	Crashed due to bomb explosion	nr Prague, Czechoslovakia	27	1
28.01.72	Vickers Viscount 814	G-AZNP	343	Airwork	Broke back on landing	Hurn, Hants, UK	0	*
30.01.72	de Havilland Canada Twin Otter 200	N6767	189	Interior Airways	Destroyed in hangar fire	Fairbanks, AK, USA	*	*
01.02.72	VFW 614	D-BABA	G1	VFW-Fokker	Crashed on test flight	nr Bremen, West Germany	1	*
01.02.72	Douglas DC-6	XW-PEH	43126	Penas	Crashed in swamp	nr Tegal, Indonesia	5	*
01.02.72	Avia 14-40	OK-MCG	805109	Ceskoslovenske Aerolinie	Crashed	Karlovy Vary, Czechoslovakia	*	*
02.02.72	Dornier Do.28D-1 Skyservant	YV-C-FLF	4010	AVSA	Written off	Pista la Salvacion, Venezuela	*	*
02.02.72	Dornier Do.28D-1 Skyservant	YV-C-FLG	4013	AVSA	Written off	Pista la Salvacion, Venezuela	*	*
04.02.72	Convair 340-68B	HZ-AAT	174	Saudi Arabian Airlines	Crashed on road	Sanaa, Yemen Arab Republic	0	*
04.02.72	Hawker Siddeley HS.748 2	PP-VDU	1632	Varig	Crashed	Porte Alegre, Brazil	*	*
05.02.72	Fairchild F-27	HK-1139	0075	TAC Colombia	Crashed	nr Valledupar, Colombia	19	0
10.02.72	Douglas DC-3	*	*	Bangladesh Biman	Crashed on landing	Dacca, Bangladesh	5	0
11.02.72	Douglas C-54A	XW-TDE	3098	Royal Air Lao	Shot down	nr Vientiane, Laos	23	0
11.02.72	Boeing B-17G	CP-936	9300	Frigorificos Reyes	Crashed	San Ignacio de Moxos, Bolivia	*	*
16.02.72	Antonov AN-12	SSSR-11374	*	Aeroflot	Overran runway & crashed	Vorkuta, RSFSR, USSR	*	*
18.02.72	Gates Learjet 25B	SX-ASO	25B-074	Olympic Airways	Crashed	Antibes, France	2	0
20.02.72	Dassault Falcon 20D	HB-VCG	231	Travelair	Crashed	St Moritz, Switzerland	*	*
22.02.72	Antonov AN-24	SSSR-46732	69900905	Aeroflot	Crashed on approach	Lipetsk, RSFSR, USSR	*	*
27.02.72	Convair 240-23	PK-GCB	172	Garuda Indonesian Airlines	Crashed	Palembang, Indonesia	*	*
27.02.72	Antonov AN-24	SSSR-46418	07304103	Aeroflot	Crashed on approach	Mineralnye Vodny, RSFSR, USSR	*	*
28.02.72	BAC VC-10 1109	G-ARTA	803	British Caledonian Airways	Bounced & damaged on landing	Gatwick, Sussex, UK	0	*
01.03.72	Dassault Falcon 20F	OH-FFW	243	Finnwings	Crashed due to double engine failure	Montreal, PQ, Canada	*	*
03.03.72	Fairchild-Hiller FH.227B	N7818M	541	Mohawk Airlines	Crashed into houses on approach	Albany, NY, USA	16{1}	32
08.03.72	Boeing 707-331	N761TW	17673	Trans World Airlines	Damaged by bomb explosion in cockpit	Las Vegas, NV, USA	0	*

Date	Type	Reg'n	C/n	Operator	Accident	Location	F	S
10.03.72	Tupolev TU-104B	SSSR-42408	*	Aeroflot	Crashed short of runway on approach	Omsk, RSFSR, USSR	*	*
14.03.72	Aerospatiale Caravelle 10B3	OY-STL	267	Sterling Airways	Crashed in rain	nr Dubai, UAE	112	0
14.03.72	Douglas DC-3	HC-SJE	4425	Ecuatoriana	Crashed	Sangai, Ecuador	*	*
19.03.72	Lockheed Electra 188CF	N851V	2001	Universal Airlines	Crashed	Hill AFB, UT, USA	*	*
19.03.72	McDonnell Douglas DC-9-32	YU-AHR	47503	EgyptAir	Crashed on approach	Khormaksar, Yemen PDR	30	*
21.03.72	Douglas DC-3	N163J	19402	Aircraft Charter	Written off	Location Unknown	*	*
28.03.72	Swearingen Merlin IIB	N411X	T26-126	Operator Unknown	Written off	Nashville, TN, USA	*	*
06.04.72	Curtiss C-46	YV-C-EVF	22577	Avensa	Crashed	San Fernando, Venezuela	2	0
09.04.72	Aerospatiale 330F Puma	PK-PHY	1124	Pelita Air Service	Written off	Location Unknown	*	*
10.04.72	Douglas DC-6B	HP-539	43526	Internacional de Aviacion	Broke in two on landing	Manaus, Brazil	*	*
11.04.72	Douglas DC-3	VH-PNB	15344/26789	Trans Australia Airlines	Overran into sea on landing	Madang, Papua New Guinea	0	*
12.04.72	NAMC YS-11A-211	PP-SMI	2059	VASP	Crashed on approach	Rio de Janeiro, Brazil	25	0
14.04.72	Short Skyvan 2	N725R	SH.1841	Viking International Air Freight	Crashed	La Crosse, WI, USA	1	0
14.04.72	Douglas C-84	TAM-01	1934	Transporte Aereo Militar	Written off	Bolivia	*	*
16.04.72	Fokker F-27 Friendship 200	I-ATIP	10251	Aero Transporti Italiani	Crashed	nr Foggia, Italy	18	0
16.04.72	Mitsubishi MU-2G	N132MA	503	Operator Unknown	Written off	Atlantic City, NJ, USA	*	*
18.04.72	BAC Super VC-10 1154	5X-UVA	881	East African Airways	Crashed on take-off	Addis Ababa, Ethiopia	41	66
20.04.72	Douglas DC-3	OB-R-653	17102/34369	Satco	Crashed	Mt Killukichu, Peru	*	*
20.04.72	de Havilland Riley Dove	N50S	04461	Trans Isles Airways	Destroyed by fire	Rock Sound, Bahamas	*	*
22.04.72	Curtiss C-46	CP-940	30225	TABSA	Crashed	Bolivia	*	*
01.05.72	Beechcraft King Air A90	N295X	LJ-0244	Operator Unknown	Written off	Location Unknown	*	*
04.05.72	Yakovlev YAK-40	SSSR-87778	*	Aeroflot	Crashed on approach	Bratsk, RSFSR, USSR	18	0
06.05.72	McDonnell Douglas DC-8-43	I-DIWB	45625	Alitalia	Crashed on approach	Palermo, Sicily, Italy	115	0
07.05.72	Handley Page Dart Herald 101	HK-721	152	Lineas Aereas La Urraca	Written off	Valledupar, Colombia	*	*
08.05.72	Douglas DC-3	YV-C-GAI	15168/26613	Aerotechnica	Crashed	Venezuela	7	0
10.05.72	Fokker F-27 Friendship 400M	ST-ADX	10273	Sudan Airways	Overran on landing	El Obeid, Sudan	0	*
12.05.72	Lockheed 18 Lodestar	N211L	*	Carolina Aircraft Corporation	Crashed	Florida, USA	8	0
18.05.72	McDonnell Douglas DC-9-31	N8961E	45870	Eastern Air Lines	Crash landed	Fort Lauderdale, FL, USA	0	*
21.05.72	Fokker F-27 Friendship 200	CR-LLD	10439	DTA	Crashed	Off Lobito, Angola	23	0
27.05.72	de Havilland Canada Twin Otter 100	D-IDHC	031	General Air	Crashed on take-off	Heligoland, West Germany	8	5
28.05.72	Curtiss C-46	CP-752	22544	TABSA	Crashed	San Pedro Richard, Bolivia	*	*
29.05.72	Lockheed 049 Constellation	PP-PDG	2037	Amazonense	Crashed after total engine failure	Cruzeiro do Sul Acre, Brazil	14	0
30.05.72	McDonnell Douglas DC-9-14	N3305L	45700	Delta Air Lines	Crashed	Fort Worth, TX, USA	4	0
30.05.72	Cessna 402A	JA5162	402A-0021	Operator Unknown	Written off	Taikigata-cho, Japan	*	*
03.06.72	Curtiss C-46	*	*	China Airlines	Crashed	South Vietnam	31	*
13.06.72	Curtiss C-46	CC-CDU	33369	Austral	Crashed	nr Santiago, Chile	3	0
15.06.72	Convair 880-22M-21	VR-HFZ	53	Cathay Pacific Airways	Crashed due to bomb explosion	Pleiku, South Vietnam	81	0
15.06.72	McDonnell Douglas DC-8-53	JA8012	45680	Japan Air Lines	Crashed	nr New Delhi, India	86(4)	3
15.06.72	IRMA BN-2A-3 Islander	CR-AMX	0636	Transportes Aereos de Tete	Crashed	Baue, Mozambique	*	*
16.06.72	Ilyushin IL-62	SU-ARN	00801	EgyptAir	Overran on landing at wrong airport	nr Cairo, Egypt	0	*
18.06.72	Antonov AN-10A	SSSR-11215	*	Aeroflot	Crashed	Kharkov, Ukraine, USSR	122	0
18.06.72	Hawker Siddeley Trident 1C	G-ARPI	2109	British European Airways	Stalled on take-off & crashed	nr Staines, Middx, UK	118	0
21.06.72	Rockwell Turbo Commander 690	D-INIX	11013	Operator Unknown	Written off	Greenland	*	*
23.06.72	Piper PA-31-350 Chieftain	n/a	31-7305002	Piper Aircraft Corporation	Destroyed in flood	Lock Haven, PA, USA	0	0
24.06.72	de Havilland Heron 2B	N554PR	14085	Prinair	Crashed	Mercedita, Puerto Rico	5	*
29.06.72	de Havilland Canada Twin Otter 100	N4043B	013	Air Wisconsin	Mid-air collision with North Central A/L CV.580 N90858	Lake Winnebago, WI, USA	8(5)	0
29.06.72	Convair 580	N90858	083	North Central Airlines	Mid-air collision with Air Wisconsin Twin Otter N4043B	Lake Winnebago, WI, USA	5(8)	0
29.06.72	MBB HFB.320 Hansa	D-CASY	1029	Inter City Flug	Crashed	Blackpool, Lancs, UK	7	1
02.07.72	Douglas DC-3	F-WSGU	15420/26865	Rousseau Aviation	Crashed	Kulusuk, Greenland	*	*
03.07.72	Beechcraft Queen Air 65	PI-C825	LC-049	A.Soriano y Cia	Written off	Location Unknown	*	*
06.07.72	McDonnell Douglas DC-8-52	EC-ARA	45617	Aviaco	Crashed	Off Las Palmas, Canary Is, Spain	10	0
07.07.72	Douglas DC-3	XW-PHW	*	Cambodia Air Commercial	Crashed	Kompong Som, Khmer Republic	*	*
10.07.72	Douglas DC-3	HZ-AAK	16231/32979	Saudi Arabian Airlines	Crashed	Tabouk, Saudi Arabia	*	*
12.07.72	Boeing B-17G	N73648	32505	Black Hills Aviation	Crashed	Silver City, NM, USA	*	*

Date	Type	Reg'n	C/n	Operator	Accident	Location	F	S
17.07.72	Douglas DC-3	VH-MAE	11917	Ansett Airlines of Papua New Guinea	Damaged beyond repair	Wapenamunda, Papua New Guinea	*	*
17.07.72	Tupolev TU-134A	SSSR-65607	48560	Aeroflot	Written off	USSR	*	*
20.07.72	Canadair CL-44-6	LV-JYR	007	Aerotransportes Entre Rios	Crashed	Between Montevideo & Santiago	5	0
21.07.72	Douglas DC-3	N39393	4943	K.Knight	Damaged by fire	Pivijai, Colombia	*	*
25.07.72	de Havilland Canada Twin Otter 300	N5662	326	Air America	Crashed	nr Vientiane, Laos	3	1
29.07.72	Douglas DC-3	HK-1341X	11716	Avianca	Mid-air collision with Avianca DC-3 HK-107	Villavicencio, Colombia	17(21)	0
29.07.72	Douglas DC-3	HK-107	11723	Avianca	Mid-air collision with Avianca DC-3 HK-1341X	Villavicencio, Colombia	21(17)	0
04.08.72	Douglas DC-3	N31538	6317	Mercer Airlines	Destroyed by fire after emergency landing	Point Mugu, CA, USA	0	*
04.08.72	Westland WS-55 Srs.1	G-ANUK	WA.39	Bristow Helicopters	Crashed	Location Unknown	*	*
11.08.72	Britten-Norman BN-2A-6 Islander	EP-PAE	0297	Pars Air	Crashed	Gunareh, Iran	*	*
12.08.72	Fokker F-27 Friendship 100	VT-DME	10175	Indian Airlines	Crashed on approach	nr Delhi, India	18	0
14.08.72	Ilyushin IL-62	DM-SEA	00702	Interflug	Crashed on take-off after fire	East Berlin, East Germany	156	0
14.08.72	Rockwell Turbo Commander 690	N1NR	11024	Operator Unknown	Written off	Wellsburg, WV, USA	*	*
20.08.72	Douglas DC-3	PK-ZDD	2123	Zamrud Airlines	Crashed	Sumbawa Besar, Indonesia	*	*
21.08.72	Ford 4-AT-B Tri-Motor	N7684	4-AT-42	Island Air Lines	Crashed on take-off	Port Clinton, OH, USA	0	15
24.08.72	Vickers Viscount 761D	XY-ADF	188	Union of Burma Airways	Damaged on landing	Akyab, Burma	0	*
26.08.72	Ilyushin IL-18	SSSR-75663	188000702	Aeroflot	Crashed on landing in fog	Arkhangelsk, RSFSR, USSR	*	*
27.08.72	Douglas DC-3	YV-C-AKE	4705	Avensa	Crashed	Canaima, Venezuela	26	0
28.08.72	Gates Learjet 23	HB-VAM	23-044	Vodavia	Crashed	Innsbruck, Austria	2	0
29.08.72	Curtiss C-46	AN-AMR	175	Lanica	Belly landed	Managua, Nicaragua	*	*
31.08.72	Ilyushin IL-18	SSSR-74298	*	Aeroflot	Crashed after in-flight fire	nr Magnitogorsk, RSFSR, USSR	101	0
01.09.72	Short Skyvan 3	VH-PNI	SH.1840	Ansett Airlines of Papua New Guinea	Crashed into mountain	Papua New Guinea	4	0
07.09.72	Curtiss C-46	CP-959	26903	Servicios Aereos Virgen	Crashed	Beni, Bolivia	2	*
09.09.72	Westland Wessex 1	G-ATCA	462	Bristow Helicopters	Crashed & caught fire	Rhoose, Cardiff, UK	*	*
10.09.72	Douglas DC-3	ET-ABQ	4325	Ethiopian Airlines	Crashed after wing failure	Gondar, Ethiopia	11	0
13.09.72	Douglas C-47A	9N-RF10	9950	Royal Nepalese Air Force	Crashed	Dhulikhel, Nepal	31	0
14.09.72	Boeing 707-331C	N15712	20068	Trans World Airlines	Overran into bay	San Francisco, CA, USA	0	*
14.09.72	Beechcraft Queen Air B80	HK-1069	LD-364	Operator Unknown	Written off	Location Unknown	*	*
14.09.72	Piper PA-27-250 Aztec B	G-ASER	27-2283	Bon-Air	Crashed on landing	Nigg Bay, Aberdeenshire, UK	0	*
16.09.72	Hughes 269B	B-15104	*	Great China Airlines	Crashed	Taiwan	*	*
18.09.72	Fokker F-28 Fellowship 1000	PH-FPT	11994	Nigeria Airways	Crashed on landing	Port Harcourt, Nigeria	0	*
24.09.72	Douglas C-54D	XV-NUH	10588	Air Vietnam	Crashed on landing	Ben Cat, South Vietnam	10	3
24.09.72	McDonnell Douglas DC-8-53	JA8013	45681	Japan Air Lines	Crashed on landing on wrong airfield	Juhu, India	0	*
25.09.72	Douglas C-47A	TAM-24	9207	Transporte Aereo Militar	Written off	Location Unknown	*	*
26.09.72	Fokker F-27 Friendship 600	PK-GFP	10462	Garuda Indonesian Airlines	Crashed on take-off	Kemajoran, Indonesia	3	0
28.09.72	Douglas DC-3	TAM-23	*	Transporte Aereo Militar	Written off	Location Unknown	*	*
30.09.72	Douglas DC-3	EC-AQE	14196/25641	Spantax	Crashed on take-off	Madrid, Spain	1	5
01.10.72	Ilyushin IL-18V	SSSR-75507	*	Aeroflot	Crashed after take-off	Sochi, Georgia, USSR	109	0
02.10.72	Douglas DC-3	XW-TDA	13729	Cambodia Air Commercial	Shot down on approach	Kampot, Khmer Republic	9	0
13.10.72	Fairchild-Hiller FH.227D/LCD	T-571	572	TAMU	Crashed into mountains [Survivors not found until 22.12.72]	nr San Fernando, Chile	29	16
13.10.72	Ilyushin IL-62	SSSR-86671	70301	Aeroflot	Crashed on third approach	nr Moscow, RSFSR, USSR	176	0
18.10.72	NAMC YS-11A-202	PP-CTG	2063	Cruzeiro	Crashed	Sao Paulo, Brazil	*	*
21.10.72	NAMC YS-11A-500	SX-BBQ	2155	Olympic Airways	Crashed on approach	Off Athens, Greece	37	18
22.10.72	Yakovlev YAK-40	SSSR-87819	*	Aeroflot	Crashed on take-off	Krasnoyarsk, RSFSR, USSR	*	*
23.10.72	Britten-Norman BN-2A-6 Islander	F-OCRH	0221	Air Melanesie	Crashed	Tana, New Hebrides	*	*
27.10.72	Vickers Viscount 724	F-BMCH	050	Air Inter	Crashed	nr Clermont Ferrand, France	60	8
30.10.72	Fokker F-27 Friendship 200	I-ATIR	10301	Aero Transporti Italiani	Crashed	Pioggiorsini, Italy	27	0
30.10.72	Tupolev TU-134	DM-SCA	8350502	Interflug	Crashed	nr Dresden, East Germany	*	*
31.10.72	Dassault Falcon 10	F-WFAL	001	Avions Marcel Dassault	Crashed	Romorantin, France	*	*
01.11.72	Douglas DC-3	4W-ABJ	*	Yemen Airlines	Crashed on landing	Beihan, Yemen Arab Republic	*	*
02.11.72	Avro Anson I	G-AMDA	-	Skyfame	Damaged on landing	Staverton, Glos, UK	0	*
04.11.72	Ilyushin IL-14	LZ-ILA	146001046	Bulair	Crashed in poor weather	Plovdiv, Bulgaria	33	0
04.11.72	Antonov AN-24V	SSSR-46202	*	Aeroflot	Crashed into trees	Kursk, RSFSR, USSR	*	*

Date	Type	Reg'n	C/n	Operator	Accident	Location	F	S
04.11.72	Hughes 269B	B-15102	*	Great China Airlines	Crashed	Taiwan	*	*
17.11.72	Douglas DC-3	CF-FOL	14038/25483	S-H Aviation Sales	Crashed	Atlantic Ocean	3	*
20.11.72	Mitsubishi MU-2F	N757Q	151	Operator Unknown	Written off	Manning, SC, USA	*	*
21.11.72	Antonov AN-12	SSSR-11360	*	Aeroflot	Crashed on approach	Vorkuta, RSFSR, USSR	*	*
22.11.72	de Havilland Canada Caribou	*	*	Air America	Shot down	Laos	*	*
28.11.72	McDonnell Douglas DC-8-62	JA8040	46057	Japan Air Lines	Caught fire on take-off	Moscow, USSR	62	14
28.11.72	Hawker Siddeley HS.748 2	PI-C1027	1609	Philippine Air Lines	Damaged on landing	Bislig, Philippines	0	*
oo.11.72	IRMA BN-2A-9 Islander	F-BRGH	0649	Rousseau Aviation	Crashed	Dinard, France	*	*
01.12.72	Douglas DC-3	CF-TQW	12598	Reindeer Air Services	Crashed	Norman Wells, NWT, Canada	*	*
02.12.72	Curtiss C-46	HC-AMV	174	ANDES	U/c collapsed on landing	Panama City, Panama	*	*
03.12.72	Convair 990-30-5	EC-BZR	25	Spantax	Crashed on take-off	Tenerife, Canary Is, Spain	155	0
05.12.72	Boeing 707-366C	SU-AOW	19845	EgyptAir	Shot down by Egyptian forces in error	Beni Sueif, Egypt	6	0
06.12.72	Douglas DC-3	CF-AUQ	15281/26726	Superior Airways	Crashed	Lac Randall, PQ, Canada	*	*
06.12.72	Fairchild C-123 Provider	*	*	Air America	Shot down	Laos	0	4
08.12.72	Boeing 737-222	N9031U	19069	United Air Lines	Crashed into houses on approach	Chicago, IL, USA	43(2)	18
08.12.72	Fokker F-27 Friendship 400	AP-AUS	10314	Pakistan International Airlines	Crashed	N.E. of Rawalpindi, Pakistan	33	0
12.12.72	Hawker Siddeley HS.125-3A	N521M	25129	Marathon Oil Co	Crashed	Findlay, OH, USA	*	*
15.12.72	Gates Learjet 23	N20M	23-094	Operator Unknown	Crashed	Detroit, MI, USA	*	*
15.12.72	Dassault Flamant	5R-MPF	198	Malagasy Air Force	Written off	Madagascar	*	*
20.12.72	Convair 880-22-2	N8807E	29	Delta Air Lines	Struck by North Central Airlines DC-9 N954N taking off	Chicago, IL, USA	0(9)	*
20.12.72	McDonnell Douglas DC-9-31	N954N	47159	North Central Airlines	Crashed into Delta CV.880 N8807E on take-off	Chicago, IL, USA	9(0)	*
20.12.72	Curtiss C-46	CF-IHV	22551	Nordair	Crashed	Lac Randall, PQ, Canada	*	*
21.12.72	de Havilland Canada Twin Otter 300	F-OGFE	258	Air Guadeloupe	Crashed	Off St Marten, Netherlands Antilles	*	*
23.12.72	Fokker F-28 Fellowship 1000	LN-SUY	11011	Braathens SAFE	Crashed on approach	nr Oslo, Norway	40	5
27.12.72	Lockheed Jetstar 6	N400M	5008	Fluor Corporation	Crashed	Saranac Lake, NY, USA	*	*
28.12.72	Fokker F-28 Fellowship 1000	EC-BVC	11023	Iberia	Crash landed	Bilbao, Spain	0	4
29.12.72	Lockheed Tristar 1	N310EA	1011	Eastern Air Lines	Crashed on approach at night	Miami, FL, USA	103	73
31.12.72	Douglas DC-7CF	N500AE	45130	American Express Leasing	Crashed	Off San Juan, Puerto Rico	5	0
oo.12.72	Fairchild C-123 Provider	*	*	Air America	Shot down	Laos	*	*
oo.oo.72	Scottish Aviation Twin Pioneer 3	PK-GTA	510	Garuda Indonesian Airlines	Written off	Indonesia	*	*
oo.oo.72	Consolidated Privateer	N6816D	*	Hawkins & Powers Aviation	Destroyed by fire on ground	Wenatchee, WA, USA	0	*
oo.oo.72	Douglas R5D-1	TT-DAA	3096	R.Garnier	Written off	Location Unknown	*	*
02.01.73	Boeing 707-321C	CF-PWZ	18326	Pacific Western Airlines	Crashed in snowstorm	nr Edmonton, Canada	5	0
03.01.73	Beechcraft King Air C90	N936K	LJ-0539	Operator Unknown	Written off	nr Cedar Rapids, IA, USA	*	*
19.01.73	Vickers Viscount 802	G-AOHI	158	British European Airways	Crashed into mountain	Ben More, Perthshire, UK	4	0
20.01.73	Curtiss C-46	CP-749	43-43340	Servicios Aereos Bolivianos	Crashed	Reyes, Bolivia	*	*
21.01.73	Antonov AN-24	SSSR-46276	77303609	Aeroflot	Crashed	nr Perm, RSFSR, USSR	*	*
22.01.73	Douglas DC-3	PK-EHC	15684/27129	Trans Nusantara Airways	Crashed	Pontianak, Indonesia	*	*
22.01.73	Boeing 707-3D3C	JY-ADO	20494	Alia	Crashed on landing	Kano, Nigeria	176	33
27.01.73	Douglas DC-6A	HR-TNO	45476	TAN	Crashed on approach	Tegucigalpa, Honduras	3	0
28.01.73	Beechcraft King Air A90	XC-ICP	LJ-0176	Operator Unknown	Written off	Veracruz, Mexico	*	*
29.01.73	Ilyushin IL-18D	SU-AOY	188011101	EgyptAir	Crashed into mountain	nr Kyrenia, Cyprus	37	0
29.01.73	Douglas DC-3	PP-SQA	4742	VASP	Damaged on landing	Rondonopolis, Brazil	*	*
30.01.73	McDonnell Douglas DC-9-21	LN-RLM	47304	Scandinavian Airlines System	Aborted take-off & crashed in sea	Oslo, Norway	0	33
oo.01.73	Curtiss C-46	CF-HQI	22497	Reindeer Air Services	Crash landed	Banks Is, NWT, Canada	*	*
05.02.73	de Havilland Canada Twin Otter 200	OH-KOA	166	Kar-Air	Crashed when icing caused engine failure	nr Pudasjarui, Finland	*	*
06.02.73	Douglas DC-3	CF-HTH	15555/27000	Nordair	Damaged by truck	Montreal, PQ, Canada	0	*
12.02.73	Fairchild C-123 Provider	*	*	Air America	Shot down	nr Thakhek, Laos	3	0
12.02.73	Douglas DC-3	CF-OOV	13300	Kenting Atlas Aviation	Crashed	Northern Canada	*	*
17.02.73	Antonov AN-12	SSSR-11341	401702	Aeroflot	Damaged in hard landing	Anderma, RSFSR, USSR	*	*
19.02.73	Tupolev TU-154	SSSR-85023	023	Aeroflot	Crashed short of runway	Prague, Czechoslovakia	66	28
21.02.73	Douglas DC-3	HP-560	19242	Aerovias La Urraca	Crashed	Cerro Horqueta, Panama	19	5
21.02.73	Boeing 727-224	5A-DAH	20244	Libyan Arab Airlines	Shot down by Israeli F-4	nr Ismailiya, Egypt	108	5
21.02.73	Curtiss C-46	N10427	30532	Joanne Fashions	Crashed	Pereira, Colombia	*	*

Date	Type	Reg'n	C/n	Operator	Accident	Location	F	S
23.02.73	Douglas DC-3	ZK-AOI	16966/34226	Southern Air	Crashed	Ure River, New Zealand	*	*
24.02.73	de Havilland Dove 8	G-ARFZ	04526	Fairflight Charters	Destroyed by fire	Biggin Hill, Kent, UK	*	*
24.02.73	Ilyushin IL-18	SSSR-75712	189001804	Aeroflot	Crashed	nr Leninabad, Tajikistan, USSR	79	0
26.02.73	Gates Learjet 24	N454RN	24-121	Operator Unknown	Crashed	Atlanta, GA, USA	*	*
27.02.73	Beechcraft 18S	TF-REE	A-0226	Vaengir	Damaged in belly landing	Reykjavik, Iceland	*	*
28.02.73	de Havilland Canada Twin Otter 100	PK-NUC	070	Merpati Nusantara Airlines	Crashed	nr Nabire, Indonesia	*	*
28.02.73	Yakovlev YAK-40	SSSR-87602	*	Aeroflot	Crashed on take-off	Semipalatinsk, Kazakhstan, USSR	32	0
oo.02.73	Aerospatiale Caravelle 3	YU-AJG	191	JAT Yugoslav Airlines	Damaged on landing	Belgrade, Yugoslavia	0	*
02.03.73	Douglas DC-3	N6574	4388	Arute International Air	Overran into sea	Bahamas	*	*
03.03.73	Ilyushin IL-18	LZ-BEM	182005602	Balkan Bulgarian Airlines	Crashed	Moscow, RSFSR, USSR	25	*
05.03.73	McDonnell Douglas DC-9-32	EC-BII	47077	Iberia	Mid-air collision Spantax CV.990 EC-BJC which landed safely	nr Nantes, France	68(0)	0
05.03.73	Aerospatiale Caravelle 10R	EC-BID	228	Aviaco	Crashed	Off Madeira, Portugal	3	0
07.03.73	Rockwell Sabre 40	N9503Z	282-010	Operator Unknown	Crashed	Blaine, MN, USA	*	*
09.03.73	MBB HFB.320 Hansa	N320MC	1034	Operator Unknown	Written off	Phoenix, AZ, USA	*	*
13.03.73	Beechcraft King Air A90	N791K	LJ-0253	Operator Unknown	Written off	Location Unknown	*	*
15.03.73	Hindustan 748 2-224	VT-EAU	541	Indian Airlines	Crashed	nr Hyderabad, India	3	0
19.03.73	Douglas C-54D	XV-NUI	22174	Air Vietnam	Crashed	Ben Me Thuot, South Vietnam	62	0
22.03.73	Curtiss C-46	CP-969	26513	Air Bolivia	Crashed	Cerro Picon, Bolivia	*	*
23.03.73	Ilyushin IL-62	*	*	CAAC	Crashed	China	*	*
25.03.73	de Havilland Canada Twin Otter 100	N7705	005	Air Central	Crashed	Savoy, IL, USA	*	*
oo.03.73	Tupolev TU-154	*	*	Aeroflot	Crashed	nr Kiev, Ukraine, USSR	*	*
03.04.73	Lockheed 1049 Super Constellation	N6906C	4020	Aircraft Airframe Inc	U/c collapsed on landing	Miami, FL, USA	0	*
04.04.73	Sikorsky S-61N	G-AZNE	61-467	Bristow Helicopters	Ditched	Off Aberdeen, UK	*	*
06.04.73	Curtiss C-46	CP-801	22566	Frigorifico Movima	Crashed	Bolivia	*	*
10.04.73	Vickers Vanguard 952	G-AXOP	745	Invicta International Airlines	Crashed after overshoot in snowstorm	nr Hochwald, Switzerland	108	37
10.04.73	Swearingen Merlin IIB	D-ILSE	T26-163E	Operator Unknown	Written off	Stuttgart, West Germany	*	*
10.04.73	Swearingen Merlin III	N5296M	T-219	Operator Unknown	Written off	Montreal, PQ, Canada	*	*
12.04.73	Convair 990-30-5	N711NA	01	NASA	Mid-air collision with USN P-3 157332	Sunnyvale, CA, USA	11(5)	0
13.04.73	Rockwell Sabre 60	N743R	306-011	Operator Unknown	Crashed	Montrose, CO, USA	*	*
17.04.73	Vickers Viscount 735	YI-ACL	068	Iraqi Airways	U/c collapsed on landing	Mosul, Iraq	0	*
18.04.73	de Havilland Canada Twin Otter 100	YA-GAT	111	Bakhtar Afghan Airlines	Crashed	Bamyan, Afghanistan	*	*
18.04.73	Nord Noratlas	9XR-KH	094	Portalia Air Transport	Crashed on take-off	Djibouti, Fr Terr of Afars & Issas	*	*
21.04.73	Hawker Siddeley HS.748 2	PI-C1022	1643	Philippine Air Lines	Crashed after possible bomb explosion	Patabangan, Philippines	33	0
22.04.73	Cessna 337A Skymaster	PK-OAP	337-1010	Airfast Services	Crashed	nr Watansoppeng, Indonesia	*	*
23.04.73	Tupolev TU-104	*	*	Aeroflot	Destroyed by sabotage	Leningrad, RSFSR, USSR	*	*
25.04.73	Curtiss C-46	HI-201	*	Aeromar	Crashed in sea	Punta Causedo, Dominican Republic	0	4
30.04.73	Curtiss C-46	HK-791	26805	Lineas Aereas Orientales	Crashed	Leticia, Colombia	*	*
01.05.73	Douglas DC-7BF	HK-1300	45232	Aerocosta	Damaged by fire	Miami, FL, USA	*	*
04.05.73	Douglas DC-3	*	*	Air Cambodge	Destroyed on ground	Kampot, Khmer Republic	*	*
04.05.73	Gates Learjet 24	PT-CXK	24-122	Operator Unknown	Crashed	Rio Galeon, Brazil	*	*
07.05.73	Tupolev TU-154	SSSR-85030	*	Aeroflot	Crashed on take-off	Moscow, RSFSR, USSR	0	*
10.05.73	Fairchild F-27	TC-KOC	0081	Turk Hava Yollari	Belly landed	Istanbul, Turkey	*	*
10.05.73	McDonnell Douglas DC-8-33	HS-TGU	45526	Thai Airways International	Crashed on landing	Khatmandu, Nepal	0{1}	10
10.05.73	Curtiss C-46	N446M	133	J.Guinn	Damaged on landing	Ellington AFB, TX, USA	*	*
10.05.73	Beechcraft King Air E90	YV-T-ADJ	LW-053	Operator Unknown	Written off	nr Pratt, KS, USA	*	*
11.05.73	Ilyushin IL-18	SSSR-75687	189001202	Aeroflot	Crashed	nr Semipalatinsk, Kazakhstan, USSR	61	0
15.05.73	Vickers Viscount 827	PP-SRD	398	VASP	Crashed on landing	Salvador, Brazil	0	*
16.05.73	Swearingen Merlin IIA	N1214S	T26-031	Operator Unknown	Written off	Deadhorse, AK, USA	*	*
18.05.73	Tupolev TU-104	*	*	Aeroflot	Crashed after explosion during attempted hijack	Chita, RSFSR, USSR	100	0
19.05.73	Douglas DC-3	XW-TDM	10078	Air Union	Shot down	Suay Rieng, Khmer Republic	11	*
28.05.73	Fokker F-27 Friendship 200	AP-AUW	10331	Pakistan International Airlines	Crashed on landing	Lyallpur, Pakistan	0	40
29.05.73	Douglas DC-3	CF-QBB	10081	Air Gaspe	Crashed	nr Rimouski, PQ, Canada	4	0

Date	Type	Reg'n	C/n	Operator	Accident	Location	F	S
31.05.73	Boeing 737-2A8	VT-EAM	20486	Indian Airlines	Crashed on approach	Delhi, India	48	17
oo.05.73	Britten-Norman BN-2A Islander	TR-LOC	0083	Air Gabon	Written off	Gabon	*	*
01.06.73	Aerospatiale Caravelle 6R	PP-PDX	126	Cruzeiro	Overshot on landing	Sao Luiz, Brazil	23	0
01.06.73	Douglas DC-3	HI-117	2172	Aerovias Quisqueyana	Written off	Santiago, Dominican Republic	*	*
03.06.73	Tupolev TU-144	SSSR-77102	01-2	Tupolev Design Bureau	Stalled & crashed during air display	Paris, France	6{7}	0
03.06.73	Mitsubishi MU-2F	N882Q	168	Operator Unknown	Written off	Mexico	*	*
09.06.73	Boeing 707-327C	PP-VLJ	19106	Varig	Crashed on landing & ran into sea	Rio de Janeiro, Brazil	2	2
09.06.73	Lockheed 1049H Super Constellation	N173W	4674	Aircraft Specialities	Crashed on take-off	Casey, PQ, Canada	*	*
11.06.73	Convair 440	N999JZ	040	Air Cambodge	Destroyed by rockets	Phnom Penh, Khmer Republic	*	*
11.06.73	Consolidated PBY-5A Catalina	HK-1020	1750	Operator Unknown	Written off	Location Unknown	*	*
16.06.73	Ford 4-AT-E Tri-Motor	N8407	4-AT-69	D.Glenn	Damaged beyond repair during thunderstorm	Burlington, WI, USA	0	*
18.06.73	Gates Learjet 24B	D-IHLZ	24B-225	Operator Unknown	Crashed	Mariensiel, West Germany	*	*
21.06.73	Douglas DC-7CF	N296	45466	Transair Cargo	Crashed	Miami, FL, USA	3	0
21.06.73	McDonnell Douglas DC-8-53	CF-TIJ	45962	Air Canada	Exploded during refuelling	Toronto, Ont, Canada	0	*
21.06.73	McDonnell Douglas DC-9-15	XA-SOC	47100	Aeromexico	Crashed after explosion	Puerto Vallarta, Mexico	27	0
26.06.73	Beechcraft C-45H	HK-1147G	AF-614	Operator Unknown	Written off	Location Unknown	*	*
30.06.73	Tupolev TU-134A	SSSR-65668	1351208	Aeroflot	Overshot & crashed into houses	Amman, Jordan	2{7}	76
oo.06.73	Britten-Norman BN-2A Islander	CF-XZS	0050	Arctic Air	Written off	Location Unknown	*	*
oo.06.73	Britten-Norman BN-2A Islander	TR-LOD	0102	Air Gabon	Written off	Location Unknown	*	*
03.07.73	Aerospatiale Caravelle 6N	VT-DPO	128	Indian Airlines	U/c collapsed on landing & caught fire	Bombay, India	0	*
05.07.73	Hawker Siddeley HS.748 2A	HK-1408	1657	Avianca	Overshot into houses	Bogota, Colombia	0{3}	42
05.07.73	Douglas DC-3	5H-AAK	14370/25815	East African Airways	Crashed	M'boya, Tanzania	*	*
09.07.73	Tupolev TU-124	SSSR-45062	*	Aeroflot	Crashed after take-off	Kuibyshev, RSFSR, USSR	2	*
10.07.73	Curtiss C-46	N1312V	22575	Fairbanks Air Service	Crashed on landing	Beluga, AK, USA	*	*
11.07.73	Boeing 707-345C	PP-VJZ	19841	Varig	Crashed on approach	Paris, France	123	11
14.07.73	Aerospatiale Caravelle 6R	OY-SAN	093	Sterling Airways	Damaged by taxiing into post	Stockholm, Sweden	0	*
17.07.73	Convair 640	HB-IMM	412	SATA	Damaged in heavy landing	Tromso, Norway	0	59
22.07.73	Boeing 707-321B	N417PA	18959	Pan American World Airways	Crashed due to birdstrike	Off Tahiti, French Polynesia	78	1
23.07.73	Fairchild-Hiller FH.227B	N4215	513	Ozark Air Lines	Crashed after being struck by lightning	St Louis, MO, USA	38	7
23.07.73	Rockwell Turbo Commander 681	SE-FGE	6033	Operator Unknown	Written off	Mestersvig, Greenland	*	*
24.07.73	Boeing 747-246B	JA8109	20503	Japan Air Lines	Blown up by hijackers	Benghazi, Libya	0	0
25.07.73	Canadair CL-215-1	F-ZBBM	1019	Securite Civile	Crashed	France	*	*
27.07.73	Hawker Siddeley HS.748 2A	XA-SAB	1673	Saesa	Damaged on landing	Acapulco, Mexico	0	3
31.07.73	McDonnell Douglas DC-9-31	N975NE	47075	Delta Air Lines	Crashed on approach in fog	Boston, MA, USA	89	0
oo.07.73	Beechcraft C-45H	HK-1112G	AF-661	Operator Unknown	Written off	Bogota, Colombia	*	*
02.08.73	Grumman TBM3 Avenger	N9083Z	*	Aero Union	Crashed	Chester, CA, USA	*	*
05.08.73	Lockheed 1049 Super Constellation	N6202C	4002	Happy Hour Air Travel Club	Damaged in forced landing	Tamarac, FL, USA	0	*
08.08.73	Yakovlev YAK-40	SSSR-87790	*	Aeroflot	Crashed on take-off	Archangelsk, RSFSR, USSR	1	*
11.08.73	Fokker F-27 Friendship 500	F-BSUM	10447	Air France	Crashed on landing	Strasbourg, France	*	*
13.08.73	Aerospatiale Caravelle 10R	EC-BIC	225	Aviaco	Crashed	Corunna, Spain	85{1}	0
15.08.73	de Havilland Canada Twin Otter 100	CF-WWP	012	Kenting Atlas Aviation	Crashed	nr Eureka, NWT, Canada	*	*
15.08.73	Britten-Norman BN-2A-6 Islander	N38JA	0211	Turks & Caicos Airways	Crashed	Dondon, Turks & Caicos Is	*	*
17.08.73	Pilatus PC-6/B1-H2 Porter	ST-AEU	616	National Agriculture Organisation	Crashed	Eddamazin, Sudan	*	*
18.08.73	Antonov AN-24	SSSR-46435	*	Aeroflot	Crashed due to engine failure on take-off	Baku, Azerbaijan, USSR	56	8
21.08.73	Aerospatiale Caravelle 3	YV-C-AVI	020	Avensa	Damaged when wing struck ground on landing	Barquisimento, Venezuela	*	*
22.08.73	Douglas DC-3	HK-111	4105	Avianca	Crashed	El Yopal, Colombia	16	*
22.08.73	Rockwell Turbo Commander 69CA	N333CA	11117	Operator Unknown	Written off	Oklahoma City, OK, USA	*	*
22.08.73	Piper PA-31 Navajo	HK-1591	31-379	Transportes Aereos Tropicales	Ran into ditch after ground loop on landing	Yavi, Colombia	0	*
27.08.73	Lockheed Electra 188A	HK-777	1115	Aerocondor	Crashed into mountain after take-off in fog	Bogota, Colombia	42	0
27.08.73	Beechcraft Queen Air B80	HK-1093X	LD-292	Operator Unknown	Written off	Location Unknown	*	*
29.08.73	Tupolev TU-104A	OK-MDE	86601202	Ceskoslovenske Aerolinie	Crashed on landing	Nicosia, Cyprus	0	70
31.08.73	Hughes 269B	B-15110	98-0387	Great China Airlines	Crashed	Taiwan	*	*
02.09.73	Beechcraft 99	F-BSRZ	U019	Avia Taxi France	Crashed	Auvers, France	*	*
06.09.73	Fairchild F-27	PI-C875	0010	Air Manila	Damaged beyond repair	Daet, Philippines	0	*

Date	Type	Reg'n	C/n	Operator	Accident	Location	F	S
08.09.73	McDonnell Douglas DC-8-63CF	N802WA	46146	World Airways	Crashed in fog	Cold Bay, AK, USA	6	0
10.09.73	Convair 990-30-5	N7876	04	California Airmotive	Crashed on landing	Guam	0	*
11.09.73	Aerospatiale Caravelle 6N	YU-AHD	151	JAT Yugoslav Airlines	Crashed	Moganik, Yugoslavia	44	0
12.09.73	Douglas DC-3	XW-PKD	*	Lane Xang Airlines	Damaged beyond repair	Kampot, Khmer Republic	0	*
23.09.73	Aerospatiale Caravelle 3	7T-VAI	028	Air Algerie	Damaged on landing	Algiers, Algeria	*	*
24.09.73	Lockheed 1049H Super Constellation	N566E	4838	The Holy Nation of Islam	Ran off runway & caught fire	Gary, IN, USA	0	*
25.09.73	Gates Learjet 25	N40LB	25-009	Operator Unknown	Crashed	Omaha, NB, USA	*	*
25.09.73	IAI 1121B Jet Commander	N200RC	140	Operator Unknown	Crashed	Tampa, FL, USA	*	*
27.09.73	Convair 600	N94230	056	Texas International Airlines	Crashed during storm	Rich Mt, AR, USA	11	0
29.09.73	Aerospatiale Caravelle 6R	EC-BBR	171	Iberia	Destroyed in hangar fire	Madrid, Spain	0	*
30.09.73	Douglas DC-3	PT-CEV	20182	Construtora Andrade Gutierrez	Crashed	nr Miritituba, Brazil	8	*
30.09.73	Tupolev TU-104B	SSSR-42506	021904	Aeroflot	Crashed after take-off	Sverdlovsk, RSFSR, USSR	108	0
02.10.73	Antonov AN-12	SSSR-12967	*	Aeroflot	Crashed into hill on go-around	Magadan, RSFSR, USSR	10	0
04.10.73	Britten-Norman BN-2A-7 Islander	PT-DVN	0259	Taxi Aero Cesar Aguiar	Crashed	Itaituba, Brazil	*	*
12.10.73	Hawker Siddeley HS.125-1A	XA-COL	25086	Operator Unknown	Crashed	Acapulco, Mexico	*	*
13.10.73	Tupolev TU-104B	SSSR-42486	021504	Aeroflot	Crashed on approach	Moscow, RSFSR, USSR	122	0
15.10.73	de Havilland Canada Twin Otter 300	9N-ABG	370	Royal Nepal Airlines	Crashed	Location Unknown	*	*
20.10.73	Boeing 727-14	XA-SEN	19398	Mexicana	Crashed short of runway	Mazatlan, Mexico	0	*
20.10.73	Tupolev TU-124	SSSR-45031	350901	Aeroflot	Crashed on landing	Kazan, RSFSR, USSR	0	*
23.10.73	NAMC YS-11A-211	PP-SMJ	2068	VASP	Crashed into bay after take-off	Rio de Janeiro, Brazil	7	53
25.10.73	Avia 14	OK-MCV	101807106	Ceskoslovenske Aerolinie	Destroyed by fire	Brno, Czechoslovakia	*	*
26.10.73	Douglas DC-6A	N614SE	45064	Span East Airlines	Crashed out of fuel	Off Miami, FL, USA	0	3
26.10.73	Curtiss C-46	HK-1383	22522	Aerocosta	Crashed in sea	Off Cartagena, Colombia	*	*
29.10.73	Britten-Norman BN-2A-6 Islander	N37JA	0210	Antillaise de Transport Aerien	Crashed	Mt Guinee, St Lucia	*	*
oo.10.73	Swearingen Merlin IIB	C-FHYX	T26-174	Operator Unknown	Destroyed in ground fire	Canada	*	*
02.11.73	Handley Page Dart Herald 101	HK-718	150	Lineas Aereas La Urraca	Crashed on landing	Villavicencio, Colombia	6	6
03.11.73	Boeing 707-321C	N458PA	19368	Pan American World Airways	Crashed making emergency landing after cargo of acid spilled	Boston, MA, USA	3	0
05.11.73	Aerospatiale Caravelle 6R	EC-BIA	226	Iberia	Caught fire on ground	Madrid, Spain	0	*
12.11.73	Nord 262B-11	F-BLHT	005	Rousseau Aviation	Crashed	Craon, France	0	5
17.11.73	Douglas DC-3	XV-NIE	14910/26355	Air Vietnam	Crashed	Bato, South Vietnam	26	0
27.11.73	McDonnell Douglas DC-9-31	N8967E	47267	Eastern Air Lines	Overran on landing & tail broke off	Akron-Canton, OH, USA	0	26
27.11.73	McDonnell Douglas DC-9-32	N3323L	47032	Delta Air Lines	Crashed on landing during storm	Chattanooga, TN, USA	0	77
28.11.73	Short Skyvan 200	N40DA	SH.1857	Delaware Air Freight	Damaged by hurricane	Huntsville, AL, USA	*	*
28.11.73	Cessna 402A	F-BRSA	*	Europair	Crashed on approach & caught fire	Angouleme-Ruelle, France	*	*
03.12.73	de Havilland Canada Twin Otter 100	8R-GCP	039	Guyana Airways	Crashed	300 miles from Georgetown, Guyana	*	*
03.12.73	Douglas DC-3	XW-PHV	*	Air Union	Damaged on take-off	Phnom Penh, Khmer Republic	0	*
04.12.73	BAC One-Eleven 521FH	LV-JNR	192	Austral	Damaged on emergency landing after engine failure	Bahia Blanca, Argentina	0	*
07.12.73	Curtiss C-46	CP-910	33234	Transportes Aereos Illimani	Caught fire on landing	Santa Ana, Bolivia	*	*
07.12.73	Tupolev TU-104B	SSSR-42503	021901	Aeroflot	Crashed when wing touched ground on landing	Moscow, RSFSR, USSR	16	59
12.12.73	Dassault Falcon 20C	LN-FOE	062	Operator Unknown	Crashed	Norwich, Norfolk, UK	*	*
13.12.73	Douglas DC-7	CP-1048	45453	ALCON	Crashed on landing	Trinidad, Bolivia	*	*
13.12.73	Douglas DC-3	4W-ABR	*	Yemen Airlines	Crashed	Taiz, Yemen Arab Republic	*	*
15.12.73	Curtiss C-46	XW-PKK	*	Air Union	U/c collapsed on landing	Phnom Penh, Khmer Republic	0	*
15.12.73	Lockheed 1049H Super Constellation	N6917C	4815	ANDES	Crashed on take-off	Miami, FL, USA	3{5}	0
16.12.73	Tupolev TU-124	SSSR-45061	*	Aeroflot	Crashed	nr Vilnius, Lithuania, USSR	51	0
17.12.73	Boeing 707-321B	N407PA	18838	Pan American World Airways	Destroyed by terrorists on ground	Rome, Italy	32	145
17.12.73	Curtiss C-46	CC-CCA	30576	Transportes Aereos Suravia	Crashed	Aysen, Chile	*	*
17.12.73	McDonnell Douglas DC-10-30	EC-CBN	46925	Iberia	Crashed into lights on landing & caught fire	Boston, MA, USA	1	*
19.12.73	Boeing 707-330B	D-ABOT	18463	Lufthansa	Crashed on landing	Delhi, India	0	109
20.12.73	Beechcraft King Air C90	N711FC	LJ-0516	Operator Unknown	Written off	Colombia, SC, USA	*	*
21.12.73	Convair 440-62	TAM-47	444	Transporte Aereo Militar	Crashed	Talara, Peru	6	*
21.12.73	Yakovlev YAK-40	SSSR-87629	*	Aeroflot	Damaged on landing	Yerevan, Armenia, USSR	*	*
22.12.73	Aerospatiale Caravelle 6N	OO-SRD	069	Royal Air Maroc	Crashed in bad weather	nr Tetuan, Morocco	106	0

Date	Type	Reg'n	C/n	Operator	Accident	Location	F	S
23.12.73	Aerospatiale Caravelle 6R	PP-PDV	120	Cruzeiro	Overshot on landing	Manaus, Brazil	0	57
23.12.73	Tupolev TU-124	SSSR-45004	*	Aeroflot	Crashed after take-off	Lvov, Ukraine, USSR	17	*
27.12.73	Douglas C-54B	HK-1027	18392	Avianca	Damaged by fire	Cartagena, Colombia	*	*
28.12.73	Douglas DC-3	ZS-DAK	1498	Executive Funds	Crashed	Umbogintwini, South Africa	1	2
29.12.73	Nord 262A-24	F-BNTT	026	Rousseau Aviation	Crashed	Dole, France	*	*
oo.12.73	Sikorsky S-58T	PK-UHV	58-1101	National Utility Helicopters	Written off	Muara Tewe, Indonesia	*	*
oo.oo.73	de Havilland Canada Caribou	*	*	Air America	Shot down	nr Savannakhet, Laos	1	3
oo.oo.73	Tupolev TU-134	*	*	Interflug	Crash landed	East Berlin, East Germany	*	*
oo.oo.73	Convair 240-6	ZP-CDN	050	Lineas Aereas Paraguayas	Wing torn off while parked by crashing Porter	Asuncion, Paraguay	0(0)	*
oo.oo.73	Pilatus PC-6 Porter	*	*	Fairchild Aircraft	Ran off runway on take-off & struck LAP CV.240 ZP-CDN	Asuncion, Paraguay	0	*
01.01.74	Fokker F-28 Fellowship 1000	I-TIDE	11015	Itavia	Crashed on approach in rain	Turin, Italy	38	4
02.01.74	Douglas DC-6B	OH-KDC	44169	Y.Cuthbertson	Destroyed by arson	Antwerp, Belgium	0	*
04.01.74	Rockwell Sabre 40	N34W	282-047	Midwest Oil Corporation	Crashed	Midland, TX, USA	*	*
04.01.74	Pilatus PC-6/B1-H2 Porter	ST-AEV	666	National Agriculture Organisation	Destroyed	Sudan	*	*
05.01.74	Lockheed 18 Lodestar	HK-1146	2327	Aeropesca	Written off	Location Unknown	*	*
06.01.74	Beechcraft 99A	N125AE	U125	Air East	Crashed	Johnstown, PA, USA	*	*
06.01.74	Curtiss C-46	CP-990	22490	Servicios Aereos Bolivianos	Crashed	Unduavi, Bolivia	4	0
06.01.74	Antonov AN-24	SSSR-46357	07305807	Aeroflot	Crashed on approach	Mukachevo, Ukraine, USSR	24	0
09.01.74	Hawker Siddeley HS.748 2A	FAC.1103	1704	Satena	Crashed after in-flight fire	Florencia, Colombia	31	0
10.01.74	Douglas DC-4	TAM-52	*	Transporte Aereo Militar	Crashed	Bolivia	24	0
15.01.74	Douglas C-54A	B-1811	10302	China Airlines	Damaged beyond repair	Battambang, Khmer Republic	*	*
15.01.74	Rockwell Sabre 40A	N5565	282-119	Operator Unknown	Crashed	Oklahoma City, OK, USA	*	*
16.01.74	Boeing 707-131B	N757TW	18395	Trans World Airlines	Nosewheel collapsed on landing & caught fire	Los Angeles, CA, USA	0	63
16.01.74	Dassault Falcon 20C	N7842M	042	Operator Unknown	Crashed	Fort Worth, TX, USA	*	*
17.01.74	Douglas DC-3	HK-1216	1905	Cessnyca	Crashed	Cigerdu, Colombia	12	0
19.01.74	Douglas DC-3	TAM-30	*	Transporte Aereo Militar	Written off	Location Unknown	*	*
21.01.74	Douglas DC-3	PK-GDC	20041	Burmah Oil Co	Crashed	Broome, NT, Australia	*	*
25.01.74	Antonov AN-24	SSSR-46277	77303610	Aeroflot	Crashed on approach	nr Rostov, RSFSR, USSR	4	0
26.01.74	Fokker F-28 Fellowship 1000	TC-JAO	11057	Turk Hava Yollari	Crashed on take-off	Izmir, Turkey	66	6
28.01.74	de Havilland Canada Twin Otter 300	CF-DIJ	268	Bradley Air Services	Destroyed in hangar fire	Carp, ON, Canada	*	*
28.01.74	Douglas DC-3	CF-TVK	15559/27004	Bradley Air Services	Damaged in hangar fire	Carp, ON, Canada	*	*
30.01.74	Boeing 707-321B	N454PA	19376	Pan American World Airways	Crashed on landing in rain	Pago Pago, US Samoa	97	4
02.02.74	BAC One-Eleven 520FN	PP-SDQ	228	Transbrasil	Overran on landing & broke in two	Sao Paulo, Brazil	0	*
06.02.74	Douglas DC-6A	CP-947	44076	Alcon	Damaged on landing	San Juan, Bolivia	*	*
13.02.74	Rockwell Turbo Commander 690	CP-1017	11054	Yacimientos Petroliferos Bolivianos	Written off	Lima, Peru	*	*
15.02.74	Douglas DC-3	*	*	Aeroservicio Puntarenas	Crash landed	Managua, Nicaragua	0	*
23.02.74	Curtiss C-46	CP-1052	30195	Savco	Crashed	San Francisco de Moxos, Bolivia	7	0
23.02.74	Douglas DC-3	HK-1333	15606/27051	Taxi Aereo El Llanero	Crashed	Cali, Colombia	*	*
27.02.74	Rockwell Sabre 40A	CF-BRL	282-107	Operator Unknown	Crashed	Frobisher Bay, NWT, Canada	*	*
02.03.74	Mitsubishi MU-2G	N711AH	523	Federated Capital Corporation	Crashed	Glenwood Springs, CO, USA	4	2
03.03.74	BAC Super VC-10 1151	G-ASGO	865	British Airways	Blown up on ground by hijackers	Amsterdam, Netherlands	0	102
03.03.74	McDonnell Douglas DC-10-10	TC-JAV	46704	Turk Hava Yollari	Crashed after explosive decompression on take-off	Senlis, France	346	0
03.03.74	Douglas DC-7CF	EI-AWG	45471	Aer Turas	Overran & damaged beyond repair	Luton, Beds, UK	0	*
03.03.74	Lockheed 18 Lodestar	CP-1024	2489	L.Eduardo	Written off	Normandia, Bolivia	*	*
04.03.74	Douglas DC-4	A2-ZER	27242	Wenela Air Services	Crashed on take-off	Francistown, Botswana	77	7
05.03.74	NAMC YS-11A-202	N208PA	2082	Pacific Southwest Airlines	Crashed	San Diego, CA, USA	*	*
14.03.74	Convair 440	N4819C	138	Sierra Pacific Airlines	Crashed	Bishop, CA, USA	36	0
15.03.74	Aerospatiale Caravelle 10B3	OY-STK	266	Sterling Airways	Caught fire on take-off & crashed	Tehran, Iran	14	82
22.03.74	Aerospatiale Caravelle 3	F-BSRY	258	Air Inter	Destroyed by bomb on ground	Bastia, Corsica, France	0	0
23.03.74	McDonnell Douglas DC-8-63CF	N6164A	46144	Airlift International	Exploded on ground	Travis AFB, CA, USA	0{1}	*
24.03.74	Mitsubishi MU-2K	N333MA	288	Operator Unknown	Written off	Gander, NF, Canada	*	*
31.03.74	Beechcraft 99	N848NS	U077	Air South	Crashed	St Simons Is, GA, USA	*	*
07.04.74	Douglas DC-4-1009	9Q-CBH	43095	Air Zaire	Crashed on landing	Gemena, Zaire	*	*
09.04.74	Yakovlev YAK-40	SSSR-87369	*	Aeroflot	Crashed on take-off	Kazan, RSFSR, USSR	*	*

Date	Type	Reg'n	C/n	Operator	Accident	Location	F	S
10.04.74	Tupolev TU-154	SU-AXB	048	EgyptAir	Exploded in flight	nr Cairo, Egypt	6	0
18.04.74	Piper PA-27-250 Aztec C	G-AYDE	27-3807	McAlpine Aviation	Collided with Court One-Eleven G-AXMJ on runway	Luton, Beds, UK	*	*
19.04.74	Lockheed Tristar 1	N31007	1026	Trans World Airlines	Damaged by fire on ground	Boston, MA, USA	0	*
19.04.74	Aerospatiale 330F Puma	5N-AKE	1147	Aero Contractors	Crashed	Port Harcourt, Nigeria	*	*
20.04.74	Douglas DC-3	XW-TFL	*	Cambodia Air Commercial	Crashed into buildings on landing	Suay Rieng, Laos	*{6}	*
22.04.74	Boeing 707-321C	N446PA	19268	Pan American World Airways	Caught fire & crashed	Bali, Indonesia	107	0
24.04.74	Ilyushin IL-18D	SSSR-75405	186009005	Aeroflot	Crashed after birdstrike	Tashkent, Uzbekistan, USSR	1	*
27.04.74	Ilyushin IL-18V	SSSR-75559	184007703	Aeroflot	Caught fire & crashed after take-off	Leningrad, RSFSR, USSR	118	0
28.04.74	de Havilland Canada Twin Otter 300	N389EX	251	Air America	Crashed on landing	Laos	*	*
30.04.74	Beechcraft 99	N853SA	U041	Houston Metro Airlines	Crashed	Galveston, TX, USA	*	*
30.04.74	Fokker F-27 Friendship 200	XY-ADM	10237	Burma Airways	Damaged when overran runway	Bassein, Burma	*	*
01.05.74	Antonov AN-12	SSSR-12950	*	Aeroflot	Caught fire after emergency landing	Polar Station SP-22, RSFSR, USSR	1	*
02.05.74	Douglas DC-3	HC-AUC	*	ATESA	Crashed into mountain after take-off	Ecuador	22	3
02.05.74	Yakovlev YAK-40	SSSR-87398	*	Aeroflot	Crashed on take-off	Rostov, RSFSR, USSR	1	*
06.05.74	Douglas DC-6A	TF-OAE	44069	Fratflug	Crashed on approach	Nuremburg, West Germany	3	0
09.05.74	Ilyushin IL-18	SSSR-75425	*	Aeroflot	Crashed on landing	Ivano-Frankovsk, Ukraine, USSR	*	*
19.05.74	Hawker Siddeley Argosy 101	N891U	6655	Department of the Interior	Crashed on take-off	Anchorage, AK, USA	*	*
23.05.74	Lockheed L-100 Hercules	N14ST	4225	Saturn Airways	Crashed after wing detached in storm	Springfield, IL, USA	4	0
23.05.74	Yakovlev YAK-40	SSSR-87579	*	Aeroflot	Crashed on approach	Kiev, Ukraine, USSR	29	*
25.05.74	Piper PA-34-200 Seneca	G-BBFF	34-50076	Airgo	Damaged beyond repair	Colonsay, UK	*	*
28.05.74	Douglas DC-3	XW-TFN	*	Air Union	Crashed on landing	Kompong Som, Khmer Republic	*	*
31.05.74	Fokker F-27 Friendship 100	VH-EWL	10344	East-West Airlines	Ran off runway	Bathurst, NSW, Australia	0	33
oo.05.74	IRMA BN-2A Islander	5Y-AMG	0085/601	Desert Locust Control Organisation	Crashed	Addis Ababa, Ethiopia	*	*
08.06.74	Vickers Viscount 785D	HK-1058	380	Aerolineas TAO	Crashed after fatigue failure of tailplane	nr Cucuta, Colombia	44	0
22.06.74	Aerospatiale Caravelle 6R	PH-TRH	096	Transavia	Damaged when wing touched ground on landing	Amsterdam, Netherlands	*	*
24.06.74	Grumman Gulfstream II	N720Q	058	Operator Unknown	Crashed	Kline, SC, USA	*	*
27.06.74	Boeing Stratoliner	XW-TFR	1999	Cambodia Air Commercial	Crashed on take-off	Battambang, Khmer Republic	19	6
03.07.74	Douglas DC-3	XW-PKT	*	Lane Xang Airlines	Written off	Kompong Som, Khmer Republic	*	*
08.07.74	Hawker Siddeley Argosy 101	N894U	6658	Duncan Aviation	Crashed	Port Hope, AK, USA	*	*
16.07.74	Beechcraft King Air 90	N113TC	LJ-0022	Operator Unknown	Written off	Knoxville, TN, USA	*	*
17.07.74	Cessna 337G Skymaster	EL-AHN	337-01525	Air Liberia	Crashed	Liberia	*	*
22.07.74	Hawker Siddeley Trident 2E	5B-DAB	2155	Cyprus Airways	Damaged during Turkish air raid	Nicosia, Cyprus	0	0
22.07.74	Hawker Siddeley Trident 1E	5B-DAE	2134	Cyprus Airways	Destroyed during Turkish air raid	Nicosia, Cyprus	0	0
24.07.74	Douglas DC-4	HK-728	10507	Aeronorte	Crashed	Colombia	*	*
24.07.74	Fokker F-27 Friendship 600	F-BPUI	10389	Air France	Crashed after striking overhead cables	Nantes, France	*	*
27.07.74	Fairchild C-123 Provider	*	*	China Airlines	Crashed	South Vietnam	*	*
31.07.74	Bell 47G-5	B-15115	15011	Great China Airlines	Crashed	Taiwan	*	*
02.08.74	Douglas DC-6B	C-FPWA	44698	Conair Aviation	Crashed	Kamloops, BC, Canada	3	0
05.08.74	Douglas DC-3	C-FTAT	11850	Laurentian Air Services	Crashed	Mt Apica, PQ, Canada	5	6
05.08.74	Fokker F-27 Friendship 500	F-BPNF	10376	Air Inter	Damaged by bomb	Quimper, France	0	*
05.08.74	Douglas DC-3	ET-ABE	16098/32846	Ethiopian Airlines	Damaged beyond repair	Mota, Ethiopia	*	*
07.08.74	Martin 404	HK-1485	14237	Aeroprooveduria	Crashed	Mariquita, Colombia	2	4
11.08.74	Ilyushin IL-18B	TZ-ABE	181003304	Air Mali	Crashed out of fuel	nr Ouagadougou, Upper Volta	48	12
12.08.74	Douglas DC-3	HK-508	4527	Avianca	Crashed	Tumaco, Venezuela	24	0
14.08.74	Vickers Viscount 749	YV-C-AMX	095	Linea Aeropostal Venezolana	Crashed in hurricane	Polamar, Venezuela	43	4
18.08.74	Grumman TBM3 Avenger	N9548Z	*	Hemet Valley Flying Service	Crashed	Tuolomne, CA, USA	*	*
18.08.74	Grumman TBM3 Avenger	N1366N	*	TBM Air Tankers	Crashed	Porterville, CA, USA	*	*
24.08.74	Britten-Norman BN-2A-3 Islander	ZS-IZZ	0317	Emric Air	Crashed	Richard's Bay, South Africa	*	*
26.08.74	Curtiss C-46	N9760Z	22574	Tri-9 Corporation	Crashed	Phnom Penh, Khmer Republic	0	*
30.08.74	Lockheed L-100 Hercules	N100AK	4209	Alaska International Air	Exploded on ground while unloading fuel	Galbraith Lake, AK, USA	0	*
31.08.74	Gates Learjet 25B	N366AA	25B-151	Operator Unknown	Crashed	Briggsdale, CO, USA	*	*
31.08.74	Beechcraft C-45H	N57948	AF-478	Operator Unknown	Written off	Location Unknown	*	*
01.09.74	Martin 404	N40427	14133	GSD Aircraft Leasing	Destroyed by fire	Norfolk, VA, USA	*	*

Date	Type	Reg'n	C/n	Operator	Accident	Location	F	S
01.09.74	Sikorsky S-67 Blackhawk	N671SA	67001	Sikorsky	Crashed during air display	Farnborough, Hants, UK	2	0
07.09.74	Aerospatiale SA.316B Alouette III	PK-DAI	1792	Derazona Air Service	Crashed	Tanjung Harapan, Indonesia	*	*
08.09.74	Boeing 707-331B	N8734	20063	Trans World Airlines	Crashed after bomb explosion	Off Corfu, Greece	88	0
08.09.74	Fokker F-27 Friendship 600	PK-GFJ	10422	Garuda Indonesian Airlines	Crashed into building on approach	Tandjung-karang, Indonesia	36	4
09.09.74	Curtiss C-46	TI-1010C	33348	TAISA	Crashed	Location Unknown	*	*
11.09.74	McDonnell Douglas DC-9-31	N8984E	47400	Eastern Air Lines	Crashed on landing	Charlotte, NC, USA	72	10
13.09.74	Boeing 720-025	OY-DSR	18243	Conair	Damaged when u/c collapsed	Kastrup, Denmark	0	*
15.09.74	Boeing 727-21C	XV-NJC	19819	Air Vietnam	Blown up on approach by hijacker	Phan Rang, South Vietnam	75	0
20.09.74	Mitsubishi MU-2D	N200HL	120	Operator Unknown	Written off	New Orleans, LA, USA	*	*
26.09.74	Grumman F7F-3 Tigercat	N6179C	*	Sis-Q Flying Service	Crashed	Fortuna, CA, USA	*	*
oo.09.74	Rockwell Turbo Commander 681	HL5223	6057	Operator Unknown	Written off	South Korea	*	*
02.10.74	Britten-Norman BN-2A Islander	N864JA	0175	North Cay Airways	Crashed	Puerto Rico	*	*
04.10.74	Douglas DC-6B	OO-VGB	43830	Delta Air Transport	Damaged beyond repair	Southend, Essex, UK	0	*
05.10.74	Douglas DC-3	*	*	Operator Unknown	Crashed	Guatemala	6	*
09.10.74	Bell 205A-1	N2970W	30112	Evergreen Helicopters	Crashed in snowstorm [Found 14.08.82]	nr Medfra, AK, USA	3	0
15.10.74	Curtiss C-46	XW-PBW	*	Royal Air Lao	Crashed	North of Vientiane, Laos	*	*
18.10.74	Douglas DC-3	PP-FOR	19230	Projeto Rondon	Crashed	Bias Fortes, Brazil	*	*
18.10.74	Antonov AN-12	SSSR-11030	*	Aeroflot	Crashed on approach	Enisseysk, RSFSR, USSR	1	*
20.10.74	Antonov AN-2	YR-APV	1G124-41	Operator Unknown	Crashed	Topralsar, Romania	*	*
21.10.74	Grumman F7F-3 Tigercat	N7238C	*	Sis-Q Flying Service	Crashed	Rohnerville, CA, USA	*	*
26.10.74	Piper PA-31-350 Chieftain	HP-909	31-7405155	Corp. Turistica Melia	Damaged beyond repair	Contadora, Panama	*	*
27.10.74	Lockheed L-100 Hercules	N102AK	4234	Alaska International Air	Crashed on approach	Old Man, AK, USA	4	0
29.10.74	Lockheed Electra 188PF	C-FPAB	1141	Pan Arctic Oil	Crashed	Rae Point, Canada	32	2
oo.10.74	Britten-Norman BN-2 Islander	TR-LNF	0016	Air Inter Gabon	Written off	Port Gentil, Gabon	*	*
05.11.74	Tupolev TU-104B	SSSR-42501	021804	Aeroflot	Crashed after overrunning on landing	Chita, RSFSR, USSR	0	*
06.11.74	Lockheed Electra 188PF	N7140C	1118	Reeve Aleutian Airlines	Destroyed in hangar fire	Anchorage, AK, USA	0	*
06.11.74	NAMC YS-11A-626	N172RV	2172	Reeve Aleutian Airlines	Destroyed in hangar fire	Anchorage, AK, USA	0	*
06.11.74	Douglas DC-3	N76	4279	Federal Aviation Administration	Damaged in hangar fire	Anchorage, AK, USA	*	*
11.11.74	Douglas DC-3	TAM-34	*	Transporte Aereo Militar	Crashed	nr Sorato Mt, Bolivia	*	*
12.11.74	Rockwell Turbo Commander 690A	N40MP	11116	Operator Unknown	Mid-air collision with USAF F-111 67-0055	Kingston, UT, USA	*(*)	*
15.11.74	Douglas DC-3	RP-C570	*	Oasis	Damaged beyond repair	Location Unknown	*	*
20.11.74	Boeing 747-130	D-ABYB	19747	Lufthansa	Crashed on take-off	Nairobi, Kenya	59	98
20.11.74	Douglas DC-3	ET-AAR	9465	Ethiopian Airlines	Crashed on take-off	Soddu, Ethiopia	2	0
21.11.74	Dassault Falcon 20E	EP-AGX	283	Operator Unknown	Crashed	Kermanshah, Iran	*	*
22.11.74	Cessna Citation I	EC-CGG	500-0108	Operator Unknown	Crashed	Barcelona, Spain	*	*
23.11.74	McDonnell Douglas DC-9-32	YU-AJN	47579	Inex-Adria Airways	Force-landed after in-flight fire & destroyed	Belgrade, Yugoslavia	0	*
30.11.74	Beechcraft Queen Air B80	9M-ASU	LD-473	Sabah Air	Written off	Sandakan, Malaysia	*	*
01.12.74	Boeing 727-231	N54328	20306	Trans World Airlines	Crashed during storm	Mt Weather, DC, USA	92	0
01.12.74	Boeing 727-251	N274US	20296	Northwest Airlines	Crashed in storm	Bear Mt, NY, USA	3	0
01.12.74	Beechcraft King Air A100	N50PC	B-019	Operator Unknown	Written off	Birmingham, AL, USA	*	*
04.12.74	McDonnell Douglas DC-8-55F	PH-MBH	45818	Garuda Indonesian Airlines	Crashed on approach	nr Colombo, Sri Lanka	191	0
04.12.74	Antonov AN-12	SSSR-12985	00347110	Aeroflot	Mid-air collision with Aeroflot AN-2	Irkutsk, RSFSR, USSR	*(*)	*
04.12.74	Antonov AN-2	*	*	Aeroflot	Mid-air collision with Aeroflot AN-12 SSSR-12985	Irkutsk, RSFSR, USSR	*(*)	*
06.12.74	Piper PA-31-350 Chieftain	G-BBJG	31-7405401	Operator Unknown	Crashed	Yeadon, UK	*	*
09.12.74	Ilyushin IL-18D	YR-IMK	186009104	Tarom	Crashed	Red Sea, off Egypt	9	0
11.12.74	Lockheed Electra 188AF	N5003K	1064	Fairbanks Air Service	Written off	Alaska, USA	*	*
11.12.74	Grumman G-21A Goose	N1583V	1125	Operator Unknown	Crashed	Off Alaska, USA	*	*
14.12.74	Yakovlev YAK-40	SSSR-87360	*	Aeroflot	Crashed on landing	Bukhara, RSFSR, USSR	7	*
15.12.74	Douglas DC-3	XW-TFI	4119	Khemara Air	Crashed	Takeo, Khmer Republic	*	*
17.12.74	Beechcraft King Air C90	F-BTDP	LJ-0560	Operator Unknown	Written off	Location Unknown	*	*
22.12.74	McDonnell Douglas DC-9-14	YV-C-AVM	47056	Avensa	Crashed after take-off	Maturin, Venezuela	75	0
22.12.74	Canadair CL-44D4-1	G-AWSC	026	Tradewinds Airways	Damaged by fire after nosewheel collapsed	Lusaka, Zambia	0	*
24.12.74	Handley Page Dart Herald 203	G-BBXJ	196	British Island Airways	Ground looped & broke in two	Jersey	0	54
25.12.74	Douglas DC-3	PK-RDB	16147/32895	Seulawah Air Services	Damaged by cyclone	Darwin, NT, Australia	0	*

Date	Type	Reg'n	C/n	Operator	Accident	Location	F	S
25.12.74	Curtiss C-46	XW-PKJ	26493	Cambodia International Airlines	Crashed	Bannak, Khmer Republic	*	*
25.12.74	de Havilland Dove 6	PK-LEA	04313	SAATAS-Eastindio	Destroyed on ground by cyclone	Darwin, NT, Australia	*	*
26.12.74	Grumman Gulfstream II	5V-TAA	149	Togolese Government	Crashed	Lome, Togo	*	*
26.12.74	Britten-Norman BN-2A Islander	N66HA	0031	Harbor Airlines	Crashed	Riverton Heights, WA, USA	*	*
27.12.74	Rockwell Sabre 60	N920G	306-074	Operator Unknown	Crashed	Lancaster, PA, USA	*	*
28.12.74	Lockheed 18 Lodestar	*	*	Operator Unknown	Crashed on take-off	Tikal, Guatemala	24	*
28.12.74	Piper PA-31-350 Chieftain	5Y-ASH	31-7405149	Kenya Air Charters	Written off	Location Unknown	*	*
29.12.74	Antonov AN-24RV	YR-AMD	27307606	Tarom	Crashed	Carpathian Mts, Romania	33	0
oo.oo.74	Nord Noratlas	HC-AXG	145	Aerotaxis Ecuatorianos	Damaged beyond repair	Montalvo, Ecuador	*	*
oo.oo.74	Antonov AN-24	*	*	Pathet Lao Airlines	Crashed	Laos	*	*
oo.oo.74	Convair 340-49	N18837	187	Tri-9 Corporation	Destroyed	Phnom Penh, Khmer Republic	*	*
oo.oo.74	Douglas C-54B	B-1801	10529	Air Cambodge	Destroyed	South Vietnam	*	*
01.01.75	Douglas DC-3	N9BC	9510	Air O'Hare	Crashed	Off Fort Lauderdale, FL, USA	*	*
02.01.75	Douglas C-54P	N39AP	10430	Transvall Corporation	Crashed on take-off	Tucson, AZ, USA	*	*
03.01.75	Tupolev TU-124	SSSR-45037	351002	Aeroflot	Crashed after take-off	Moscow, RSFSR, USSR	61	0
07.01.75	Convair 440-59	CP-961	467	Frigorifico Movima	Crashed on take-off	San Borja, Bolivia	1	28
08.01.75	Douglas DC-3	FAC.688	*	Satena	Crashed	Docello, Colombia	30	0
09.01.75	de Havilland Canada Twin Otter 100	N6383	083	Golden West Airlines	Mid-air collision with Cessna 150 N421	Whittier, CA, USA	*(*)	*
09.01.75	Fokker F-27 Friendship 600	9Q-CLM	10393	Air Zaire	Crashed on landing	Boende, Zaire	0{1}	*
15.01.75	Ilyushin IL-18B	HA-MOH	184007104	Malev	Crashed on landing	Budapest, Hungary	9	0
16.01.75	Dornier Do.28D-1 Skyservant	ET-AEN	4012	Ministry of Public Health	Written off	Dolo, Ethiopia	*	*
16.01.75	Antonov AN-2	*	*	Aeroflot	Crashed	Sam Neuq, Laos	16	0
17.01.75	Pilatus Porter	*	*	Thai Police	Crashed on landing	Umphang, Thailand	5	0
19.01.75	Douglas DC-3	XU-HAK	14792/26237	Khmer Hansa	Damaged by rocket	Phnom Penh, Khmer Republic	*	*
19.01.75	Douglas DC-3	XU-KAL	4811	Khmer Hansa	Damaged by rocket	Phnom Penh, Khmer Republic	*	*
19.01.75	Douglas DC-3	N86AC	19950	Southeast Asia Air Transport	Damaged in rocket attack	Phnom Penh, Khmer Republic	*	*
22.01.75	Curtiss C-46	N1663M	22548	Fairbanks Air Service	Skidded off runway	Arctic Village, AK, USA	*	*
25.01.75	Fokker F-27 Friendship 600	OY-APD	10437	Maersk Air	Damaged after overrunning on landing	Vagar, Faroe Islands	0	26
25.01.75	Beechcraft King Air A90	N57V	LJ-0268	Operator Unknown	Written off	Washington, DC, USA	*	*
25.01.75	Beechcraft TC-45H	TG-AMM	AF-077	G.M.Sanabria	Written off	Location Unknown	*	*
26.01.75	Sikorsky S-58T	PK-UHN	58-1126	National Utility Helicopters	Struck sea & crashed	nr Karimun, Indonesia	*	*
28.01.75	Yakovlev YAK-40	SSSR-87825	*	Aeroflot	Crashed on take-off	Zaporozhye, Ukraine, USSR	*	*
30.01.75	Fokker F-28 Fellowship 1000	TC-JAP	11058	Turk Hava Yollari	Overshot at night due to failure of airport lights	Istanbul, Turkey	41	0
30.01.75	Douglas DC-3	HI-222	2189	Lansa	Crashed on take-off	Santo Domingo, Dominican Republic	1	29
31.01.75	Rockwell Turbo Commander 680T	N399T	1532-2	Operator Unknown	Written off	Olanthe, KS, USA	*	*
oo.01.75	Avia 14-40	OK-MCM	83806106	Ceskoslovenske Aerolinie	Crashed	Prague, Czechoslovakia	*	*
oo.01.75	de Havilland Dove 6	G-ARTS	04369	Haywards Aviation	Damaged when struck by runaway Cessna 150	Biggin Hill, Kent, UK	0(0)	0
01.02.75	Vickers Viscount 806	PK-RVM	413	Seulawah-Mandala Airlines	Overshot & damaged beyond repair	Taipei, Taiwan	0	5
01.02.75	Douglas DC-3	N15HC	43080	Horizon Properties	Crashed	Houston, TX, USA	*	*
02.02.75	IRMA BN-2A-9 Islander	5U-AAN	0674	Transniger	Crashed	nr Agades, Niger	*	*
03.02.75	Hawker Siddeley HS.748 2	RP-C1028	1590	Philippine Air Lines	Crashed after take-off	Manila, Philippines	32	1
09.02.75	BAC One-Eleven 401AK	N711ST	058	Sahara Tahoe Hotel	Crashed on take-off & struck snowbank	Lake Tahoe, NV, USA	0	*
15.02.75	Beechcraft King Air B90	N2GG	LJ-0462	Operator Unknown	Written off	Joliet, IL, USA	*	*
17.02.75	Douglas DC-3	TG-AMA	13484	Aviateca	Damaged by fire	Tikal Petan, Guatemala	0	*
17.02.75	Douglas DC-6B	N77DG	43520	Pacific Alaska Airlines	Crashed on take-off	Fairbanks, AK, USA	*	*
19.02.75	Yakovlev YAK-40FG	D-BOBD	9230323	General Air	Overran into trees	Saarbruken, West Germany	0	16
22.02.75	Canadair CL-44-6	HK-1972	001	Aerocondor	Crashed in storm	Guarne, Colombia	5	0
22.02.75	Douglas DC-3	XU-GAJ	4559	Khmer Hansa	Destroyed in rocket attack	Phnom Penh, Khmer Republic	*	*
23.02.75	Rockwell Sabre 75A	N500NL	380-08	Operator Unknown	Written off	Location Unknown	*	*
23.02.75	Cessna 337G Skymaster	EL-AHM	337-01483	Air Liberia	Crashed	Liberia	*	*
27.02.75	Embraer Bandeirante 110C	PP-SBE	110.021	VASP	Crashed	Sao Paulo, Brazil	*	*
28.02.75	Douglas DC-3	N87805	16810/33558	J.V.Masin	Damaged beyond repair	Madrid, Spain	*	*
oo.02.75	Douglas C-47A	HC-AUR	20143	TAME	Written off [Also carried serial 15677]	Location Unknown	*	*

Date	Type	Reg'n	C/n	Operator	Accident	Location	F	S
05.03.75	Fairchild F-27	HK-1492	0005	TAC Colombia	Damaged when u/c collapsed while parked	Barranquilla, Colombia	0	*
06.03.75	Ilyushin IL-18	*	*	Aeroflot	Crashed	nr Voronezh, RSFSR, USSR	*	*
08.03.75	Dassault Falcon 20C	N990L	043	Operator Unknown	Crashed	Dallas NAS, TX, USA	*	*
10.03.75	Curtiss C-46	CP-992	26433	Aerovias Las Minas	Damaged beyond repair	La China, Bolivia	*	*
10.03.75	Douglas DC-3	*	*	Samaki Airlines	Destroyed by rocket attack	Phnom Penh, Khmer Republic	0	*
11.03.75	Douglas DC-3	*	*	Khmer Hansa	Destroyed in rocket attack	Phnom Penh, Khmer Republic	*	*
11.03.75	Cessna 402	N8416F	*	Wilbur's Flight Operations	Crashed on take-off	Anchorage, AK, USA	*	*
12.03.75	Douglas C-54D	XV-NUJ	10701	Air Vietnam	Shot down	Central Highlands, South Vietnam	26	0
13.03.75	Curtiss C-46	XW-PMF	*	Royal Air Lao	Crashed	Between Hong Kong & Laos	*	*
13.03.75	Rockwell 1121 Jet Commander	N711JT	091	Operator Unknown	Crashed	Tullahoma, TN, USA	*	*
14.03.75	Douglas DC-3	ET-ABR	4297	Ethiopian Airlines	Destroyed by rebel gunfire during landing	Lalibela, Ethiopia	1	*
16.03.75	Fokker F-27 Friendship 400M	TC-72	10404	Lineas Aereas del Estado	Crashed into mountain	nr Barito, Argentina	52	0
16.03.75	Cessna Citation I	PT-JXS	500-0162	Operator Unknown	Crashed	Belem, Brazil	*	*
18.03.75	de Havilland Canada Twin Otter 100	ST-ADB	035	Sudan Airways	Crashed	nr Khartoum, Sudan	*	*
26.03.75	Douglas DC-3	B-1553	20434	China Airlines	Mid-air collision	Kompong Chong, Khmer Republic	*	*
27.03.75	Douglas DC-3	N6	4146	Federal Aviation Administration	Crashed	Dubois, PA, USA	*	*
27.03.75	Britten-Norman BN-2A-3 Islander	9J-ACF	0261	Zambian Flying Doctor Service	Crashed	Kalengwa, Zambia	*	*
28.03.75	Curtiss C-46	N4860V	30240	Fairbanks Air Service	Damaged beyond repair	Deadhorse, AK, USA	0	*
29.03.75	Fairchild F-27	RP-C874	0017	Air Manila	Damaged beyond repair	Banguio City, Philippines	*	*
31.03.75	Boeing 737-247	N4527W	20131	Western Air Lines	Overran on landing	Casper, WY, USA	0	98
oo.03.75	Vickers Viscount 806	XW-TFK	396	Royal Air Lao	Crashed when non-pilot attempted to take-off	Phnom Penh, Khmer Republic	4	0
05.04.75	Aerospatiale SA.315B Lama	F-BXAD	*	Heli-Union	Crashed on landing	Bolivia	*	*
09.04.75	Fokker F-28 Fellowship 1000	I-TIDA	11014	Itavia	Damaged beyond repair	Bergamo, Italy	*	*
10.04.75	Douglas DC-4	XW-PKO	*	Angkor Indonesian Airlines	Destroyed on ground during Communist attack	Phnom Penh, Khmer Republic	0	*
11.04.75	Douglas DC-3	N48230	17033/34298	Tri-9 Corporation	Destroyed in rocket attack	Pochetong, Khmer Republic	*	*
11.04.75	Douglas DC-3	*	*	Air Cambodge	Destroyed in rocket attack	Pochetong, Khmer Republic	*	*
14.04.75	Swearingen Merlin IV	N960M	AT-005	Operator Unknown	Written off	Southern Pines, NC, USA	*	*
18.04.75	Beechcraft King Air C90	N4146S	LJ-0646	Operator Unknown	Written off	Grand Rapids, MI, USA	*	*
19.04.75	Douglas DC-3	EL-AAB	12054	Air Liberia	Crashed on take-off	Robertsfield, Liberia	0	25
24.04.75	Curtiss C-46	CP-1063	85	S.A. Virgen de Copacabana	Crashed	nr Sayari, Bolivia	3	0
24.04.75	Beechcraft 18	C-FAID	*	Miksoo Air Service	Damaged on landing	Saskatoon, SK, Canada	*	*
24.04.75	Britten-Norman BN-2A Islander	N591JA	0057	Munz Northern Airlines	Written off	Location Unknown	*	*
25.04.75	Antonov AN-24	SSSR-46476	2708004	Aeroflot	Crashed on approach	Poltava, Ukraine, USSR	*	*
26.04.75	Beechcraft King Air A100	N700SP	B-092	Operator Unknown	Written off	Hilton Head Is, SC, USA	*	*
30.04.75	Lockheed Electra 188AF	N283F	1039	Zantop International Airlines	Crashed	Deadhorse, AK, USA	*	*
03.05.75	Douglas DC-3	FAC.663	*	Satena	Crashed	Sardinata, Colombia	4	3
07.05.75	Beechcraft H-18	PK-BIB	BA-735	Indoavia	Crashed on landing	Kaimana, Indonesia	0	*
10.05.75	Bristol 170 Freighter 21E	VH-SJQ	12807	Air Express	Crashed	Bass Strait, Australia	2	0
10.05.75	Hawker Siddeley HS.748 2	RP-C1029	1586	Philippine Air Lines	Crashed after take-off	Manila, Philippines	0	*
11.05.75	Vickers Viscount 769D	CX-AQO	322	Pluna	Overran in rain	Buenos Aires, Argentina	0	57
11.05.75	Lockheed 1049H Super Constellation	N45516	4840	Aircraft Specialties	Crashed into trees after take-off	Mesa, AZ, USA	*	*
17.05.75	Curtiss C-46	N800FA	22595	Fairbanks Air Service	Crashed into bank when landing on frozen lake	nr Barrow, AK, USA	*	*
17.05.75	Douglas DC-3	PP-CDD	15373/26818	Motortec	Damaged in storm	Rio Jacarepagua, Brazil	*	*
28.05.75	NAMC YS-11-125	JA8680	2041	Toa Domestic Airlines	U/c collapsed on landing	Osaka, Japan	0	*
oo.05.75	Douglas C-54A	XW-PKH	7466	Royal Air Lao	Destroyed	Location Unknown	*	*
06.06.75	Curtiss C-46	CP-941	22446	Transportes Aereos Illimani	Damaged on take-off	San Borja, Bolivia	*	*
09.06.75	Curtiss C-46	CP-855	26948	Santa Rita	Crashed when u/c failed	Riberalta, Bolivia	*	*
09.06.75	Aerospatiale SA.319B Alouette I I	PK-PGD	2164	Pelita Air Service	Crashed on take-off	Tanjung Santan, Indonesia	*	*
12.06.75	Boeing 747-128	N28888	20542	Air France	Caught fire while taxiing & destroyed	Bombay, India	0	392
14.06.75	Rockwell Sabre 75A	N67KM	380-07	Operator Unknown	Crashed	Watertown, SD, USA	*	*
17.06.75	Aerospatiale Caravelle 6N	VT-DVJ	216	Indian Airlines	Undershot on landing	Bombay, India	0	92
17.06.75	Hawker Siddeley HS.748 2	PP-VDN	1625	Varig	Crashed into houses on landing	Pedro Afonso, Brazil	4	13
22.06.75	Cessna 310	D-INGY	*	Hamaland Flugdienst	Caught fire after belly landing	Stadtholn, West Germany	*	*
24.06.75	Boeing 727-225	N8845E	20443	Eastern Air Lines	Crashed on highway on landing due to windshear	New York, NY, USA	115	9

Date	Type	Reg'n	C/n	Operator	Accident	Location	F	S
27.06.75	Britten-Norman BN-2 Islander	D-IJAN	0022	Kurfiss Aviation	Crashed	Emden, West Germany	*	*
27.06.75	Beechcraft E-18S	N791A	*	Hamilton Aviation	Crashed after engine failure on take-off	Toledo, TN, USA	*	*
30.06.75	Douglas DC-4	HK-1309	10403	Taxi Aereo El Venado	Crashed into mountain	Saravena, Colombia	3	0
oo.06.75	Britten-Norman BN-2A Islander	CF-RDI	0035	Wilderness Airline	Written off	Canada	*	*
oo.06.75	Grumman G-73 Mallard	TR-LSW	J-52	Operator Unknown	Written off	Location Unknown	*	*
02.07.75	Beechcraft 99	F-BTQE	U061	Touraine Air Transport	Crashed	Nantes, France	*	*
09.07.75	Britten-Norman BN-2A-6 Islander	TU-TFW	0196	Interivoire	Written off	Location Unknown	*	*
10.07.75	Lockheed Electra 188AF	HK-1976	1087	Aerocondor	Crashed into Aerocosta DC-6 HK-756 on take-off	El Dorado, Colombia	2(0)	2
10.07.75	Douglas DC-6	HK-756	43117	Aerocosta	Struck by Aerocondor Electra HK-1976 taking-off	El Dorado, Colombia	0(2)	*
11.07.75	Grumman Gulfstream I	N71CR	163	Collins Radio Corporation	Crashed	Addison, TX, USA	*	*
15.07.75	Yakovlev YAK-40	SSSR-87364	*	Aeroflot	Crashed	nr Batum, Georgia, USSR	41	0
15.07.75	Yakovlev YAK-40	SSSR-87475	*	Aeroflot	Crashed into mountain	Batum, Georgia, USSR	*	*
17.07.75	Douglas DC-4	HK-654	18391	Aerotal	Damaged when u/c collapsed	Arauca, Colombia	*	*
18.07.75	Antonov AN-2	YR-ANE	113417	Aviatia Utilitara	Crashed	Mircea Voda, Romania	*	*
25.07.75	Douglas DC-3	C-GLUC	4760	St Felicien Air Services	Crashed into lake	Lake Mistassini, PQ, Canada	0	24
31.07.75	Vickers Viscount 837	B-2029	439	Far Eastern Air Transport	Crashed in rain	Taipei, Taiwan	27	48
oo.07.75	Boeing B-17G	N621L	8683	Aircraft Specialities	Crashed	USA	*	*
03.08.75	Boeing 707-321C	JY-AEE	18767	Alia	Crashed on approach in fog	nr Agadir, Morocco	188	0
03.08.75	Convair 240-23	N77WA	174	R.L.Vaughn	Damaged in belly landing	Belize City, Belize	*	*
07.08.75	Boeing 727-224	N88777	19798	Continental Airlines	Crashed on take-off due to windshear	Denver, CO, USA	0	131
07.08.75	IRMA BN-2A-7 Islander	9Q-CYB	0633	AMAZ	Crashed	Kassangulu, Zaire	*	*
08.08.75	Curtiss C-46	N4873V	22415	Rich International Airways	Crashed	Off Puerto Rico	0	2
08.08.75	Britten-Norman BN-2A Islander	HP-677	0049	Servicios Aereos S.A.	Dropped by helicopter while being salvaged for repair	Porvenir Island, Panama	0	0
14.08.75	Nord 262A-32	F-BPNV	039	Service dela Formation Aeronautique	Written off	Saone et Loire, France	*	*
14.08.75	Britten-Norman BN-2A Islander	P2-ATX	0126	Aerial Tours	Crashed	Naoro, Papua New Guinea	*	*
15.08.75	Yakovlev YAK-40	SSSR-87323	*	Aeroflot	Crashed on landing in bad weather	Krasnovodsk, Turkmenistan, USSR	23	*
16.08.75	Douglas DC-3	6O-SAC	20424	Somali Airlines	Crashed	Bosaso, Somalia	*	*
20.08.75	Ilyushin IL-62	OK-DBF	31502	Ceskoslovenske Aerolinie	Crashed	nr Damascus, Syria	126	2
22.08.75	Douglas DC-3	HK-1517E	4997	TANA	Crashed	Ipiales, Colombia	*	*
30.08.75	Fairchild F-27B	N4904	0021	Wien Air Alaska	Crashed short of runway	St Lawrence Is, AK, USA	10	23
30.08.75	Tupolev TU-104B	SSSR-42472	021205	Aeroflot	Damaged in hard landing	Novosibirsk, RSFSR, USSR	0	*
01.09.75	Tupolev TU-134	DM-SCD	9350702	Interflug	Crashed	Leipzig, East Germany	26	8
09.09.75	Sikorsky HSS-1N	TI-SPI	*	Costa Rican Ministry of Security	Crashed	La Sabana, Costa Rica	*	*
11.09.75	Douglas DC-3	ET-ABX	4292	Ethiopian Airlines	Crashed	nr Bahardar, Ethiopia	1	8
11.09.75	Douglas DC-3	N144A	9723	Stoney's Rainbow Lanes & Lounge	Crashed	Wakeman, OH, USA	*	*
12.09.75	Rockwell Turbo Commander 690A	N847CE	11223	Operator Unknown	Written off	Nemacolm, PA, USA	*	*
15.09.75	Hawker Siddeley Trident 1E	G-AVYD	2138	British Airways	Overran on take-off	Bilbao, Spain	0	110
15.09.75	Britten-Norman BN-2A-6 Islander	N122DW	0234	Dorado Wings	Crashed	San Juan, Puerto Rico	*	*
16.09.75	Douglas DC-3	7O-ABP	*	Alyemda	Crashed	Location Unknown	*	*
17.09.75	Convair 240-4	N8329C	110	Asiatic International Airways	Crashed	Off Seletar, Singapore	0	2
22.09.75	Antonov AN-2R	SP-WNZ	IG155-29	ZUA	Crashed on landing	Skopje, Yugoslavia	*	*
24.09.75	Fokker F-28 Fellowship 1000	PK-GVC	11039	Garuda Indonesian Airlines	Crashed	nr Palembang, Indonesia	23	38
25.09.75	Douglas DC-3	C-FECY	9264	Laurentian Air Services	Damaged beyond repair	Lac Guyere, PQ, Canada	*	*
26.09.75	Douglas DC-3	C-FAII	19353	Ilford Riverton Airways	Crashed	Fort Severn, PQ, Canada	3	0
27.09.75	Canadair CL-44-6	LV-JSY	005	Aerotransportes Entre Rios	Crashed on take-off	Miami, FL, USA	6	4
30.09.75	de Havilland Canada Twin Otter 200	C-FMHU	142	Northern Thunderbird Air	Crashed	365 mls Prince George, BC, Canada	*	*
30.09.75	Tupolev TU-154B	HA-LCI	053	Malev	Crashed	Off Beirut, Lebanon	60	0
30.09.75	Boeing 727-24C	HK-1272	19525	Avianca	Crashed on landing	Barranquilla, Colombia	4	0
06.10.75	Yakovlev YAK-40	SSSR-87328	*	Aeroflot	Crashed after engine failure on take-off	Kirov, RSFSR, USSR	*	*
07.10.75	IRMA BN-2A-3 Islander	PK-OAV	0639	Dirgantara Air Service	Crashed	Sawa Island, Indonesia	*	*
17.10.75	Britten-Norman BN-2A-26 Islander	EI-BBA	0444	Aer Arann	Crashed	Inishmore, Eire	*	*
19.10.75	Piper PA-31-350 Chieftain	G-BBPV	31-7305097	British Car Auctions	Crashed	Sandhurst, UK	*	*
22.10.75	Yakovlev YAK-40	SSSR-87458	*	Aeroflot	Crashed into building on approach	Novgorod, RSFSR, USSR	6(5)	0

Date	Type	Reg'n	C/n	Operator	Accident	Location	F	S
23.10.75	de Havilland Riley Heron	VH-CLS	14067	Connair	Crashed when pilot committed suicide	Cairns, Qld, Australia	1	0
23.10.75	de Havilland Heron 1B	J6-LBC	14047	St Lucia Airways	Destroyed in hurricane	St Lucia	*	*
25.10.75	GAF Nomad 22	VH-AUI	001	Government Aircraft Factories	Destroyed by tornado	Mazatlan, Mexico	*	*
27.10.75	Convair 440-12	TAM-44	328	Transporte Aereo Militar	Crashed after take-off	Tomonoco, Bolivia	67	0
30.10.75	McDonnell Douglas DC-9-32	YU-AJO	47457	Inex-Adria Airways	Crashed short of runway	Prague, Czechoslovakia	67	53
03.11.75	Douglas DC-3	C-FOOY	12411	Kenting Aviation	Crashed	North of Frobisher Bay, NWT, Canada	*	*
04.11.75	Beechcraft King Air C90	N221MJ	LJ-0512	Operator Unknown	Written off	Charleston, WY, USA	*	*
12.11.75	McDonnell Douglas DC-10-30CF	N1032F	46826	Overseas National Airlines	Destroyed by fire after aborted take-off due to birdstrike	New York, NY, USA	0	139
13.11.75	Mitsubishi MU-2K	N69QJ	254	Operator Unknown	Written off	Charleston, WV, USA	*	*
15.11.75	Fokker F-28 Fellowship 1000	LV-LOB	11086	Aerolineas Argentinas	Crashed on approach	Concordia, Argentina	0	60
15.11.75	Douglas DC-3	C-FCSC	6183	Nordair	Damaged by fire	La Grande, PQ, Canada	*	*
17.11.75	Antonov AN-24	SSSR-46467	27307905	Aeroflot	Crashed into hill	nr Sukhumi, Georgia, USSR	38	0
18.11.75	Douglas DC-3	TG-AGA	6142	Aviateca	Crashed	Peten State, Guatemala	15	6
20.11.75	Hawker Siddeley HS.125-600B	G-BCUX	6043	Hawker Siddeley Aviation	Crashed on take-off due to birdstrike & struck car	Dunsfold, Surrey, UK	0{6}	*
20.11.75	Antonov AN-24	SSSR-46349	97305708	Aeroflot	Crashed into hill	Kharkov, Ukraine, USSR	19	*
22.11.75	Antonov AN-24V	LZ-ANA	67302708	Balkan Bulgarian Airlines	Crashed on landing	Sofia, Bulgaria	2	*
25.11.75	Lockheed C-130H Hercules	4X-FBD/011	4533	Israeli Defence Force Air Force	Crashed	Jebel Halal, Israel	20	0
30.11.75	Mitsubishi MU-2K	XB-LIJ	259	Operator Unknown	Written off	Beloit, KS, USA	*	*
03.12.75	Britten-Norman BN-2A-8 Islander	VH-ISG	0018	Pacific Resorts	Crashed	Du Motu, Tonga	*	*
21.12.75	Britten-Norman BN-2A-21 Islander	RP-C2136	0440	Philippine Aero Transport	Crashed	Catabalogan, Philippines	*	*
21.12.75	Piper PA-31 Navajo	*	*	Pelita Air Service	Crashed in mountains [PK-PPD or PK-PPG]	Burangrang Mts, Indonesia	*	*
22.12.75	Boeing 707-331B	N18701	18978	Trans World Airlines	Crashed on landing in fog	Milan, Italy	0	122
26.12.75	Mitsubishi MU-2G	N133MA	506	Operator Unknown	Written off	Rollinsville, CO, USA	*	*
28.12.75	Hawker Siddeley Trident 1C	G-ARPC	2103	British Airways	Damaged by fire while parked	Heathrow, London, UK	0	*
oo.12.75	Rockwell Turbo Commander 690A	LV-LTA	11197	Operator Unknown	Written off	Argentina	*	*
oo.oo.75	Douglas DC-3	N481F	15016/26461	Amoco	Written off	Location Unknown	*	*
oo.oo.75	Antonov AN-12B	LZ-BAA	08346001	Bulair	Damaged beyond repair	Egypt	*	*
01.01.76	Boeing 720-023B	OD-AFT	18020	Middle East Airlines	Crashed due to bomb explosion	Al Qaysumah, Saudi Arabia	81	0
02.01.76	McDonnell Douglas DC-10-30CF	N1031F	46825	Overseas National Airlines	Crashed on landing	Istanbul, Turkey	0	373
03.01.76	Tupolev TU-134	*	*	Aeroflot	Crashed into houses after take-off	Moscow, RSFSR, USSR	87	0
06.01.76	Britten-Norman BN-2A-3 Islander	5Y-AUA	0275	Caspair	Crashed	Kimba Ngorongoro, Tanzania	*	*
07.01.76	Vickers Viscount 806	PK-RVK	260	Mandala Airlines	Crashed	Mando, Indonesia	*	*
08.01.76	Britten-Norman BN-2A-21 Islander	RP-C2135	0439	Philippine Aero Transport	Crashed	Mactan, Philippines	*	*
12.01.76	Bell 212	PK-DBU	30660	Derazona Air Service	Crashed	Badak, Indonesia	*	*
13.01.76	Antonov AN-24	SSSR-47280	07306410	Aeroflot	Crashed on approach	Leningrad, RSFSR, USSR	*	*
14.01.76	Rockwell Sabre 40	N85	282-097	Operator Unknown	Crashed	nr Recife, Brazil	*	*
15.01.76	Douglas C-54A	HK-172	10280	Taxi Aereo El Venado	Crashed into mountain	nr Bogota, Colombia	13	0
18.01.76	Douglas DC-3	CP-573	4682	Frigorifico Maniqui	Crashed into trees	San Borja, Bolivia	7	0
20.01.76	Hawker Siddeley HS.748 2A	HC-AUE/683	1683	TAME	Crashed	nr Guayaquil, Ecuador	33	8
20.01.76	Hughes 369HS	PK-PHL	91-0343S	Pelita Air Service	Crashed	Cepu Cepu, Indonesia	*	*
21.01.76	Antonov AN-24	*	*	CAAC	Crashed on approach	nr Shanghai, China	40	0
22.01.76	Embraer Bandeirante 110C	PT-TBD	110.011	Transbrasil	Crashed	Chapeco, Brazil	*	*
23.01.76	Hawker Siddeley HS.748 2A	PK-IHD	1700	Bouraq Indonesia Airlines	Damaged on landing after running into ditch	Palu, Indonesia	*	*
30.01.76	Ilyushin IL-18V	SSSR-75558	184007505	Aeroflot	Crashed on training flight	Frunze, Kirghizia, USSR	6	0
oo.01.76	Beechcraft King Air B90	7T-VSH	LJ-0423	Operator Unknown	Written off	Location Unknown	*	*
02.02.76	Aerospatiale 330F Puma	PK-PDW	1187	Pelita Air Service	Crashed	Bobonaro, Indonesia	*	*
04.02.76	Douglas DC-6B	HK-1389	43519	Lineas Aereas del Caribe	Crashed	Off Santa Marta, Colombia	3	0
06.02.76	Gates Learjet 24D	I-AMME	24D-310	Operator Unknown	Crashed	Bari, Italy	*	*
07.02.76	Hughes 369HS	PK-PDH	73-0497S	Pelita Air Service	Crashed	Tembuni, Indonesia	*	*
08.02.76	Douglas YC-112A	N901MA	36326	Mercer Airlines	Crashed after take-off	Burbank, CA, USA	3	3
08.02.76	Mitsubishi MU-2J	N300MA	596	Operator Unknown	Written off	Easton, MD, USA	*	*
09.02.76	Tupolev TU-104A	SSSR-42327	*	Aeroflot	Crashed on take-off	Irkutsk, RSFSR, USSR	24	*
16.02.76	Douglas C-47B	TT-LAG	18972	Chad Air Force	Crashed	Faya, Chad	*	*

Date	Type	Reg'n	C/n	Operator	Accident	Location	F	S
18.02.76	Mitsubishi MU-2F	N531MA	130	Operator Unknown	Written off	Argyle, NY, USA	*	*
18.02.76	MBB Bo.105C	PK-PGW	S-197	Pelita Air Service	Crashed	Dili, Timor, Indonesia	*	*
22.02.76	Grumman Gulfstream II	N397F	072	Operator Unknown	Crashed	Burlington, VT, USA	*	*
25.02.76	Curtiss C-46	AN-AOC	22343	Lanica	U/c collapsed on landing	Managua, Nicaragua	0	*
01.03.76	VEB 14P	YR-ILO	14803061	Tarom	Crashed	Sibiu, Romania	*	*
02.03.76	IAI Arava 201	TAM-76	024	Transporte Aereo Militar	Crashed	Bolivia	*	*
06.03.76	Ilyushin IL-18D	SSSR-75408	186009201	Aeroflot	Crashed	nr Voronezh, RSFSR, USSR	111{7}	0
08.03.76	Westland Wessex 1	G-ATSC	544	Bristow Helicopters	Crashed	North Sea	*	*
08.03.76	Beechcraft King Air 90	N2400X	LJ-0018	Operator Unknown	Written off	Off Akutan Is, AK, USA	*	*
10.03.76	Antonov AN-24	SSSR-46613	37308610	Aeroflot	Ran off runway & crashed	Saratov, RSFSR, USSR	*	*
12.03.76	Lockheed Electra 188AF	N401FA	1059	Great Northern Airlines	Damaged by skidding off runway	Udrivik Lake, AK, USA	*	*
13.03.76	Fokker F-27 Friendship 600	9Q-CLO	10395	Air Zaire	Destroyed on ground by rocket attack	Vila Gagocoutinho, Angola	*	*
18.03.76	McDonnell Douglas DC-8-43	CU-T1200	45638	Cubana	Mid-air collision with Cubana AN-24 CU-T-879. Landed but dbr	Havana, Cuba	0(5)	29
18.03.76	Antonov AN-24V	CU-T879	67302501	Cubana	Mid-air collision with Cubana DC-8 CU-T1200	Havana, Cuba	5(0)	0
19.03.76	Yakovlev YAK-40	YK-AQC	*	Syrian Government	Damaged by fire after rocket attack	Beirut, Lebanon	0	*
24.03.76	Curtiss C-46	XW-PBV	22232	Air America	Damaged in storm	Vientiane, Laos	*	*
24.03.76	Douglas DC-3	XW-TDR	16733/33481	Royal Air Lao	Damaged in storm	Vientiane, Laos	*	*
24.03.76	Douglas DC-3	XW-TDF	15660/27105	Royal Air Lao	Damaged in storm	Vientiane, Laos	*	*
24.03.76	Douglas DC-4	XW-TAF	*	Royal Air Lao	Damaged in storm	Vientiane, Laos	*	*
24.03.76	Douglas DC-4	XW-PNI	*	Royal Air Lao	Damaged in storm	Vientiane, Laos	*	*
24.03.76	Douglas DC-4	XW-PNF	*	Royal Air Lao	Damaged in storm	Vientiane, Laos	*	*
24.03.76	Douglas DC-4	XW-PND	*	Royal Air Lao	Damaged in storm	Vientiane, Laos	*	*
25.03.76	Lockheed Jetstar 6	N1EM	5077	Operator Unknown	Crashed	Chicago, IL, USA	*	*
26.03.76	Convair 440-86	CP-1078	415	Servicios Aereos San Francisco	Crashed	Off Chile	*	*
31.03.76	Britten-Norman BN-2A Islander	VH-EQK	0146	Unionair	Written off	Location Unknown	*	*
02.04.76	Douglas DC-3	FAC.676	*	Satena	Crashed on take-off	Puerto Liquizamo, Colombia	5	24
05.04.76	Boeing 727-81	N124AS	18821	Alaska Airlines	Overran on landing & crashed into ravine	Ketchikan, AK, USA	1	49
09.04.76	Antonov AN-2	YR-ANF	113419	Aviatia Utilitara	Crashed	Romania	*	*
10.04.76	Grumman G-21A Goose	N18CS	B-059	Operator Unknown	Crashed at sea	Off Avalon, CA, USA	*	*
15.04.76	Hawker Siddeley HS.748 1	LV-HHB	1540	Yacimientos Petroliferos Fiscales	Crashed after engine exploded	Neuquen, Argentina	36	0
21.04.76	Sikorsky S-58ET	G-BCRU	58-1092	Bristow Helicopters	Crashed	North Sea	*	*
22.04.76	Boeing 720-022	N37777	18044	United States Global	Crashed	Barranquilla, Colombia	0	4
23.04.76	Douglas DC-3	ET-AAS	13454	Ethiopian Airlines	Damaged by fire	Massawa, Ethiopia	*	*
26.04.76	Boeing 727-95	N1963	19837	American Airlines	Crashed on landing	St Thomas, US Virgin Islands	34	54
02.05.76	Douglas DC-6B	YS-35C	45323	TACA International Airlines	Crashed short of runway	Altaverapaz, Guatemala	0	*
02.05.76	Convair 640	7T-VAH	408	Air Algerie	Written off	Location Unknown	*	*
04.05.76	de Havilland Canada Twin Otter 300	C-GDHA	428	de Havilland Aircraft of Canada	Crashed on demonstration flight	nr Monze, Zambia	*	*
04.05.76	de Havilland Canada Caribou	5X-AAB	222	Uganda Airlines	Written off	Uganda	*	*
05.05.76	Dornier Do.28D-1 Skyservant	9Q-CDZ	4051	Fa. Danzer Furnierwerke Zaire	Written off	Zaire	*	*
13.05.76	de Havilland Canada Twin Otter 200	N1456T	212	ERA Helicopters	Damaged beyond repair	Fairbanks, AK, USA	*	*
15.05.76	Antonov AN-24	SSSR-46534	57310108	Aeroflot	Crashed	Chernigov, Ukraine, USSR	52	0
19.05.76	Lockheed 1049H Super Constellation	N468C	4846	F & B Livestock	Damaged on landing	Belize City, Belize	0	*
20.05.76	Douglas DC-3	C-FFKZ	9052	St Felicien Air Services	Damaged beyond repair	Asbestos Hill, PQ, Canada	*	*
23.05.76	BAC One-Eleven 527FK	RP-C1161	213	Philippine Air Lines	Destroyed by fire after hijacker exploded grenades in cabin	Zamboanga, Philippines	14	73
23.05.76	Antonov AN-26	SSSR-26567	5733601	Aeroflot	Crash landed on approach	Khandyga, RSFSR, USSR	*	*
28.05.76	Sikorsky S-58E/T	PK-OAO	58-1071	Airfast Services	Written off	Ujung Padang, Indonesia	*	*
31.05.76	Douglas DC-3	ET-ADC	14717/26162	Ethiopian Airlines	Destroyed by fire after explosion	Massawa, Ethiopia	*	*
01.06.76	Tupolev TU-154A	SSSR-85102	102	Aeroflot	Crashed into mountains	Macias Nguema, Equatorial Guinea	45	0
04.06.76	Lockheed Electra 188A	RP-C1061	1007	Air Manila	Crashed after take-off	Agana, Guam	45{1}	0
07.06.76	North American B-25J Mitchell	CP-970	*	Transaereos Beni	Written off	Location Unknown	*	*
11.06.76	Douglas DC-3	PP-AJC	20402	RICO	Crashed	Rio Manana, Brazil	*	*
23.06.76	McDonnell Douglas DC-9-31	N994VJ	47333	Allegheny Airlines	Crashed on landing	Philadelphia, PA, USA	0	104
27.06.76	Boeing 720-047B	OD-AGE	18963	Middle East Airlines	Destroyed on ground by shelling	Beirut, Lebanon	1	2

Date	Type	Reg'n	C/n	Operator	Accident	Location	F	S
28.06.76	Hughes 369HS	PK-PEY	113-0534S	Pelita Air Service	Crashed	Indonesia	*	*
29.06.76	Gates Learjet 24D	XB-JOY	24D-263	Operator Unknown	Crashed	Mexico City, Mexico	*	*
02.07.76	Lockheed Electra 188A	N5531	1055	Eastern Air Lines	Destroyed on ground by bomb explosion	Boston, MA, USA	0	*
12.07.76	Hughes 369HS	PK-PDL	53-0472S	Pelita Air Service	Crashed	nr Salawati Rig, Indonesia	*	*
17.07.76	Tupolev TU-104A	SSSR-42335	*	Aeroflot	Crashed on take-off	Chita, RSFSR, USSR	0	*
24.07.76	Fokker F-27 Friendship 100	VT-DMD	10174	Indian Airlines	Damaged in heavy landing	Bhuwaneswar, India	*	*
26.07.76	Bell 212	PK-DBX	30652	Derazona Air Service	Crashed	Tarakan, Indonesia	*	*
28.07.76	Ilyushin IL-18B	OK-NAB	189001605	Ceskoslovenske Aerolinie	Crashed after engine fire	Bratislava, Czechoslovakia	71	4
28.07.76	Britten-Norman BN-2A Islander	CS-AJQ	0068	Transportes Aereos Continentais	Crashed	Location Unknown	*	*
02.08.76	Boeing 707-373C	HL7412	19715	Korean Air Lines	Crashed	nr Tehran, Iran	5	0
03.08.76	MBB Bo.105C	PK-PGY	S-199	Pelita Air Service	Crashed	Indonesia	*	*
05.08.76	Beechcraft Queen Air 80	CP-1054	LD-014	A.Pinto	Written off	Location Unknown	*	*
05.08.76	Boeing B-17G	N4710C	*	Dothan Aviation Corporation	Crashed	Blakeley, GA, USA	*	*
06.08.76	GAF Nomad 24A	VH-DHU	010	Government Aircraft Factories	Crashed	Avalon, Vic, Australia	*	*
06.08.76	GAF Nomad 22B	9M-ATZ	014	Sabah Air	Crashed	Off Kota Kinabalu, Malaysia	*	*
06.08.76	Cessna 402	CS-AHP	*	Operator Unknown	Crashed	En route Jos–Port Harcourt, Nigeria	1	*
07.08.76	Dassault Falcon 20C	N888AR	033	Operator Unknown	Crashed	Acapulco, Mexico	*	*
08.08.76	Rockwell Turbo Commander 680T	N601G	1605-44	Operator Unknown	Written off	Alphaha, AL, USA	*	*
13.08.76	Antonov AN-24	SSSR-47734	69901002	Aeroflot	Crashed short off runway	Guryev, Kazakhstan, USSR	*	*
15.08.76	Vickers Viscount 785D	HC-ARS	377	Saeta	Crashed	Ecuador Andes	56	0
15.08.76	Mitsubishi MU-2G	OO-TBW	526	Operator Unknown	Written off	Angouleme, France	*	*
16.08.76	Beechcraft 99	N200WP	U003	Bar Harbor Airlines	Crashed on approach	Bar Harbor, ME, USA	*	*
16.08.76	Boeing 720-047B	HK-723	18061	Avianca	Damaged on landing	Mexico City, Mexico	0	*
18.08.76	de Havilland Canada Otter	C-FMPW	271	RCMP Air Services	Written off	Saskatchewan, Canada	*	*
21.08.76	Convair 880-22M-3	N48060	47	Orient Pacific Airways	Damaged beyond repair	Seletar, Singapore	*	*
27.08.76	Canadair CL-44-6	OB-R-1104	012	Aeronaves del Peru	Crashed	Shonisu River, Peru	7	0
28.08.76	Aerospatiale Caravelle 3	F-BSGZ	083	Air France	Damaged when hijacker exploded grenade in cockpit on ground	Ho Chi Minh City, Vietnam	1	*
28.08.76	Beechcraft King Air 90	C-FRCL	LJ-0033	Operator Unknown	Written off	Canada	*	*
02.09.76	McDonnell Douglas DC-9-15	XA-SOF	47124	Aeromexico	Damaged beyond repair	Leon, Mexico	*	*
04.09.76	Britten-Norman BN-2A-3 Islander	VQ-SAC	0287	Air Mahe	Crashed	Praslin, Seychelles	*	*
04.09.76	Bell 205A	PK-HBB	30004	Bristow Masayu Helicopters	Crashed	Off Mawa, Indonesia	*	*
06.09.76	Antonov AN-24	SSSR-46518	37308504	Aeroflot	Mid-air collision with Aeroflot YAK-40 CCCP-87772	nr Sochi, Georgia, USSR	52(38)	0
07.09.76	Boeing 707-328	F-BHSH	17620	Air France	Destroyed by fire on ground after bomb explosion	Ajaccio, Corsica, France	0	0
07.09.76	Douglas DC-3	C-GKFC	4200	Kelowna Flightcraft	Crash landed	nr Brockelt, Canada	*	*
08.09.76	Sikorsky S-58ET	N4371S	58-0279	Carson Helicopters	Written off	Saudi Arabia	*	*
09.09.76	Yakovlev YAK-40	SSSR-87772	*	Aeroflot	Mid-air collision with Aeroflot AN-24 CCCP-46518	nr Sochi, Georgia, USSR	18(52)	0
09.09.76	Cessna 310B	OO-SEE	310-35616	Linair	Crashed	Baalgem, Belgium	*	*
10.09.76	Hawker Siddeley Trident 3B	G-AWZT	2320	British Airways	Mid-air collision with Inex-Adria DC-9 YU-AJR	Zagreb, Yugoslavia	63(113)	0
10.09.76	McDonnell Douglas DC-9-32	YU-AJR	47649	Inex-Adria Airways	Mid-air collision with British Airways Trident G-AWZT	Zagreb, Yugoslavia	113(63)	0
16.09.76	Curtiss C-46	HK-1282	33345	Operator Unknown	Crashed	Location Unknown	2	*
17.09.76	Douglas DC-3	CP-565	19236	Aerolineas Abaroa	Crashed	La Paz, Bolivia	*	*
19.09.76	Boeing 727-2F2A	TC-JBH	20982	Turk Hava Yollari	Crashed into mountain	Karatepe, Turkey	155	0
22.09.76	de Havilland Canada Twin Otter 100	C-FAWF	067	AirWest Airlines	Crashed	nr Bella Coola, BC, Canada	*	*
23.09.76	Bell 212	PK-DBJ	30702	Derazona Air Service	Crashed	Indonesia	*	*
24.09.76	Curtiss C-46	*	*	Aerosucre	Crashed	Off Aruba, Netherlands Antilles	*	*
26.09.76	Grumman Gulfstream II	N500J	060	Operator Unknown	Crashed	Hot Springs, VA, USA	*	*
26.09.76	Gates Learjet 25C	PT-IBR	25C-072	Operator Unknown	Crashed	Sao Paulo, Brazil	*	*
04.10.76	Douglas DC-7C	TZ-ARC	45467	Emirates Air Transport	Crashed	Mt Kenya, Kenya	4	0
06.10.76	McDonnell Douglas DC-8-43	CU-T1201	45611	Cubana	Crashed after take-off due to bomb explosion	Off Bridgetown, Barbados	73	0
12.10.76	Aerospatiale Caravelle 6N	VT-DWN	231	Indian Airlines	Crashed on take-off	Bombay, India	95	0
13.10.76	Beechcraft King Air A100	XB-NUV	B-128	Operator Unknown	Written off	San Luis Potosi, Mexico	*	*
14.10.76	Boeing 707-131	N730JP	17671	Lloyd Aereo Boliviano	Crashed into buildings on take-off	Santa Cruz, Bolivia	3{110}	0
25.10.76	Douglas DC-3	HK-149	4593	Taxi Aereo El Venado	Crashed after take-off	El Yopal, Colombia	37	0

Date	Type	Reg'n	C/n	Operator	Accident	Location	F	S
26.10.76	Rockwell Turbo Commander 690	N568H	11027	Operator Unknown	Written off	Los Angeles, CA, USA	*	*
28.10.76	Embraer Bandeirante 110C	PT-TBA	110.004	Nordeste	Crashed on take-off	Petrolina, Brazil	2	4
30.10.76	Convair 440-88	N985	448	OMCO Petroleum Co	Crashed after engine fire on take-off	Cairo, Egypt	*	*
30.10.76	Ilyushin IL-18D	SSSR-75575	185008005	Aeroflot	Crashed on landing in bad weather	Tashkent, Uzbekistan, USSR	*	*
02.11.76	Douglas DC-6	XA-MUV	43103	Mexicana	Damaged beyond repair	Location Unknown	*	*
04.11.76	Fokker F-27 Friendship 100	PK-KFR	10142	Bali Air	Crashed on landing	Banjarmasin, Indonesia	27	11
04.11.76	Hughes 369HS	PK-PEA	64-0612S	Pelita Air Service	Crashed	Indonesia	*	*
09.11.76	Rockwell Grand Commander 680FL	PT-CGS	1334	Taxi Aereo Jao Jorge	Forced landed in river bed	nr Tapuruquara, Brazil	0	*
11.11.76	Douglas DC-6B	4W-ABL	44902	Yemen Airlines	Damaged when ran into ground power unit	Hodeida, Yemen Arab Republic	*	*
12.11.76	Dassault Falcon 20E	N27R	303	R.J.Reynolds Tobacco Co	Crashed due to bird ingestion	Naples, FL, USA	0	11
12.11.76	Gates Learjet 25B	PT-DVL	25B-077	Taxi Aereo Marilia	Crashed	Sao Paulo, Brazil	0	*
12.11.76	Cessna Citation I	PT-KIU	500-0172	Taxi Aereo Jaragua	Crashed	Aracatuba, Brazil	*	*
12.11.76	Piper PA-31T Cheyenne II	HB-LHT	75-20003	Aeroleasing	Crashed into fence	Shannon, Eire	5	0
16.11.76	McDonnell Douglas DC-9-14	N9104	47081	Texas International Airlines	Crashed after aborted take-off	Denver, CO, USA	0	86
17.11.76	Rockwell Turbo Commander 690A	N57186	11186	Operator Unknown	Written off	Independence, KS, USA	*	*
18.11.76	Cessna 337 Skymaster	*	*	Abbotsford Air Services	Crashed on landing & ran down embankment	Duncan, BC, Canada	0	5
21.11.76	Lockheed L-100-20 Hercules	C-FPWX	4361	Pacific Western Airlines	Crashed	nr Kisangani, Zaire	4	1
21.11.76	Cessna 180C	ET-ADD	50861	Ethiopian Airlines	Destroyed by fire	Sheik Hussein, Ethiopia	*	*
22.11.76	Short Skyvan 3	A4O-SI	SH.1865	Gulf Air	Crashed	Off Das Island, UAE	0	2
23.11.76	NAMC YS-11A-500	SX-BBR	2156	Olympic Airways	Crashed into high ground	Kozani, Greece	50	0
23.11.76	Douglas DC-3	CP-755	4294	Aerolineas La Paz	Damaged beyond repair	Location Unknown	*	*
28.11.76	Tupolev TU-104B	SSSR-42471	*	Aeroflot	Crashed on take-off	Moscow, RSFSR, USSR	73	0
28.11.76	Cessna 402	SE-FRO	*	Globeaero	Crashed on take-off	Sumburgh, Shetlands, UK	*	*
28.11.76	Bell 212	PT-HIF	*	Lider Taxi Aereo	Crashed	Amapa, Brazil	*	*
29.11.76	Beechcraft King Air E90	N6843S	LW-137	Operator Unknown	Crashed	Cordova, AK, USA	*	*
01.12.76	Hughes 369HS	PK-PHQ	61-0327S	Pelita Air Service	Crashed	Indonesia	*	*
04.12.76	Lockheed C-130H Hercules	CN-AOB/4537	4537	Moroccan Air Force	Shot down by rebels	Western Sahara, Morocco	*	*
07.12.76	Yakovlev YAK-40	SSSR-87756	*	Aeroflot	Crashed out of fuel	Armavir, RSFSR, USSR	*	*
10.12.76	Douglas DC-3	C-FIAX	19499	Austin Airways	Crashed	Fort George, PQ, Canada	*	*
10.12.76	Cessna 402	5Y-WAW	*	Miwani Sugar Mills	Crashed into lake	Lake Victoria, Kenya	10	0
11.12.76	Cessna 337 Skymaster	C-GRAM	*	On Air	Crashed	nr Thunder Bay, ON, Canada	1	0
12.12.76	de Havilland Canada Twin Otter 300	N101AC	262	Atlantic City Airlines/Allegheny	Crashed in fog	Wildwood, NJ, USA	2	*
13.12.76	Sikorsky S-64	*	*	Erickson Air Crane	Crashed	nr Laramie, WY, USA	*	*
14.12.76	Douglas DC-3	ET-AEJ	15545/26990	Ethiopian Airlines	Damaged beyond repair	Oborso, Ethiopia	*	*
16.12.76	de Havilland Canada Twin Otter 100	C-FAJB	019	AirWest Airlines	Crashed & sank	Straits of Juan de Fuca, BC, Canada	0	16
16.12.76	Convair 880-22M-22	N5865	57	Air Trine	Crashed on take-off	Miami, FL, USA	2	1
16.12.76	Yakovlev YAK-40	SSSR-87638	*	Aeroflot	Crashed	Zaporozhye, Ukraine, USSR	5	0
17.12.76	Antonov AN-24V	SSSR-46722	*	Aeroflot	Crashed on approach in fog	Kiev, Ukraine, USSR	48	7
17.12.76	Yakovlev YAK-40	SSSR-88208	*	Aeroflot	Crashed into trees after take-off	Ust-Kut, RSFSR, USSR	7	0
23.12.76	Beechcraft 18	A2-AOS	*	African Overland Safaris	Crashed on take-off	Lanseria, South Africa	*	*
23.12.76	Bell 47G-5	B-15109	7852	Great China Airlines	Damaged beyond repair	Pingtung, Taiwan	*	*
25.12.76	Boeing 707-366C	SU-AXA	20763	EgyptAir	Crashed into buildings	Bangkok, Thailand	53{19}	0
28.12.76	Beechcraft 18	N3128B	CA-173	Operator Unknown	Crashed	Cairo, IL, USA	*	*
30.12.76	IRMA BN-2A-3 Islander	PK-KNC	0663	Bali Air	Written off	Location Unknown	*	*
30.12.76	Hughes 369HS	PK-PEC	74-0617S	Pelita Air Service	Crashed	Pendopo, Indonesia	*	*
31.12.76	Douglas C-54A	OB-R-247	7462	Faucett	Crashed into mountain	Trujillo, Peru	19	0
oo.oo.76	Douglas DC-3	C-FHPM	4989	Atlantic Central Airlines	Damaged beyond repair	St Johns, NB, Canada	*	*
oo.oo.76	Convair 440-86	CP-1008	437	San Francisco Servicios Aereos	Damaged beyond repair	Location Unknown	*	*
02.01.77	Tupolev TU-134A	OK-CFD	2351505	Ceskoslovenske Aerolinie	Collided on landing with CSA IL-18 OK-NAA	Prague, Czechoslovakia	0(0)	*
02.01.77	Ilyushin IL-18B	OK-NAA	189001604	Ceskoslovenske Aerolinie	Struck by CSA TU-134 OK-CFD on landing	Prague, Czechoslovakia	0(0)	*
03.01.77	IRMA BN-2A-21 Islander	5T-MAR	0787	Mauritanian Air Force	Written off	Location Unknown	*	*
05.01.77	BAC One-Eleven 520FN	PP-SDS	236	Transbrasil	Damaged on landing	Sao Paulo, Brazil	0	*
05.01.77	Cessna 206 Super Skywagon	PT-IBM	206-0246	Taxi Aereo Fortaleza	Crashed	nr Russas, Brazil	2	0

Date	Type	Reg'n	C/n	Operator	Accident	Location	F	S
06.01.77	Douglas DC-3	CP-728	19689	Transportes Aereos Itenez	Crash landed	La Senda, Bolivia	0	*
06.01.77	Gates Learjet 24B	N12MK	24B-192	Jet Avia	Crashed	Palm Springs, CA, USA	4	*
06.01.77	Gates Learjet 23	N332PC	23-056	Jet Avia	Crashed in snowstorm	Flint, MI, USA	2	*
07.01.77	Mitsubishi MU-2D	N854Q	107	Operator Unknown	Written off	Rochester, MN, USA	*	*
09.01.77	Bell 206B JetRanger II	G-BAYA	01035	PLM Helicopters	Crashed after tail rotor failure	nr Aviemore, UK	0	1
10.01.77	Britten-Norman Trislander	PK-KTD	1018	Bali Air	Crashed	Samarinda, Indonesia	*	*
12.01.77	Beechcraft King Air A100	G-BABX	B-141	Marchwiel Plant & Engineering	Crashed on approach	Sturgate, UK	0	*
13.01.77	McDonnell Douglas DC-8-62AF	JA8054	46148	Japan Air Lines	Crashed on take-off in fog	Anchorage, AK, USA	5	0
13.01.77	Tupolev TU-104A	SSSR-42369	*	Aeroflot	Crashed on approach	nr Alma Ata, Kazakhstan, USSR	90	0
14.01.77	de Havilland Canada Twin Otter 300	C-GNTB	463	Northern Thunderbird Air	Crashed into mountain	Terrace, BC, Canada	12	0
15.01.77	Vickers Viscount 838	SE-FOZ	372	Skyline Sweden	Crashed due to ice on tail	nr Stockholm, Sweden	22	0
15.01.77	Douglas DC-3	N73KW	2252	Air Sunshine	Damaged on take-off	Miami, FL, USA	*	*
16.01.77	Beechcraft C-45H	N9497Z	AF-390	Operator Unknown	Crash landed in fog	Sonoma, CA, USA	2	*
18.01.77	Gates Learjet 25B	YU-BJH	25B-186	Yugoslav Government	Crashed	Sarajevo, Yugoslavia	8	*
20.01.77	Martin 404	CP-1317	14163	CAMBA	Crashed	Location Unknown	*	*
22.01.77	Cessna 185	*	*	West Coast Air Services	Crashed	Richmond, BC, Canada	*	*
22.01.77	Hughes 300	HB-XFL	*	Schwyz Helikopter	Crashed	Faulhorn, Switzerland	0	1
24.01.77	de Havilland Canada Twin Otter 300	VP-FAP	333	British Antarctic Survey	Crashed on landing	Gomez Nunatak, Br Antarctic Terr	0	*
26.01.77	Douglas R5D-3	CP-1208	10651	Frigorificos Reyes	Damaged beyond repair	Bolivia	*	*
27.01.77	Fairchild C-82 Packet	CP-983	10147	Transportes Aereos Itenez	Crashed on take-off	San Ramon, Bolivia	6	*
27.01.77	Cessna 421B Golden Eagle	D-IAGA	*	Alpha Flug	Crashed	nr Solothurn, Switzerland	5	0
29.01.77	de Havilland Canada Twin Otter 200	CF-BQJ	143	Gateway Aviation	Damaged beyond repair	Antarctica	*	*
31.01.77	Chase C-122 Avitruc	N5904V	*	Transnorthern Aviation	Crashed	Anchorage, AK, USA	1	2
01.02.77	Cessna 401	5Y-AJP	*	Caspair	Damaged on landing	Dar-es-Salaam, Tanzania	0	*
02.02.77	Sikorsky S-58DT	N90936	58-1148	Carson Helicopters	Written off	Jeddah, Saudi Arabia	*	*
03.02.77	Swearingen Merlin IIIA	N34SM	T-263	Operator Unknown	Crashed on approach at night	San Antonio, TX, USA	2	*
04.02.77	Britten-Norman BN-2A-21 Defender	7Q-YAZ	0492	Malawi Police Air Wing	Crashed	Malawi	*	*
04.02.77	Piper PA-23 Aztec	CF-ULL	*	Kenting Aviation	Crashed on approach	Arrabida Mts, Portugal	*	*
07.02.77	Douglas DC-3	PK-NDH	19694	Merpati Nusantara Airlines	Crashed	Santan, Indonesia	*	*
08.02.77	Curtiss C-46	HI-208	30685	Argo	Crashed	Off San Juan, Puerto Rico	*	*
09.02.77	Hawker Siddeley HS.748 2	PK-IHK	1633	Bouraq Indonesia Airlines	Crashed	Ujung Pandang, Indonesia	*	*
10.02.77	SIAI-Marchetti S.208	ET-ADG	002	Admas Air Service	Crashed	Gojam Province, Ethiopia	*	*
11.02.77	Avia 14T	OK-OCA	190013167	Ceskoslovenske Aerolinie	Crashed in lake	Bratislava, Czechoslovakia	4	1
14.02.77	Beechcraft D18S	N32LD	A-0413	Operator Unknown	Crashed on take-off	Covington, KY, USA	0	*
15.02.77	Ilyushin IL-18V	SSSR-75520	183006703	Aeroflot	Crashed after aborting landing	Mineralnye Vody, RSFSR, USSR	77	0
17.02.77	Douglas C-47B	FAC.1125	14531/25976	Satena	Crashed into trees on take-off	Camanaos, Colombia	*	*
19.02.77	Beechcraft D18S	N762D	A-0803	Operator Unknown	Crashed on take-off	McAllen, TX, USA	1	*
22.02.77	Britten-Norman BN-2A-8 Islander	VP-HCD	0374	Maya Airways	Crashed on approach	Hill Bank, Belize	0	1
22.02.77	Piaggio P.166	VH-GOC	052	G.R.Board	Crashed	Marulan, NSW, Australia	1	*
25.02.77	Cessna 180	HK-429	30180	Aerolineas Especiales de Colombia	Crashed	Acevedo, Colombia	0	*
28.02.77	Douglas DC-3	C-FNAR	13154	Survair	Crashed on landing	Saglouc, BC, Canada	4	6
28.02.77	Douglas DC-3	C-FIQR	11876	Kenn Borek Air	Crashed	Saglone, PQ, Canada	*	*
01.03.77	Douglas DC-3	7O-ABF	13475	Alyemda	Crashed in sea	Off Aden, Yemen PDR	19	1
01.03.77	Cessna 402	P2-GKC	402-0144	Talair	Crashed into school on landing	Brugam, Papua New Guinea	0{5}	9
01.03.77	Cessna 188	ZS-ENE	*	Avexair	Crashed into trees	Koster, South Africa	0	1
03.03.77	Swearingen Merlin III	N5329M	T-243	Operator Unknown	Crashed on approach in rain	Nassau, Bahamas	1	*
04.03.77	McDonnell Douglas DC-8-63CF	N8635	46050	Overseas National Airlines	Crashed short of runway	Niamey, Niger	2	2
04.03.77	Douglas C-54E	N174DP	27263	Interamerica Air Leases	Crashed on drug smuggling flight	Monroe Station, FL, USA	*	*
05.03.77	Cessna 402	N69378	*	Operator Unknown	Crashed into sea	Off Highbourn Cay, Bahamas	4	0
10.03.77	Beechcraft King Air A90	N34F	LJ-0119	Operator Unknown	Written off	Kankanee, IL, USA	*	*
15.03.77	Beechcraft F33 Bonanza	N7307R	*	Pacific Southwest Airlines	Mid-air collision with Mooney	Needles, CA, USA	2(1)	*
15.03.77	Cessna U206G Super Skywagon	ZK-MCH	*	Mount Cook Airlines	Crashed	Earshell Cove, New Zealand	*	*
16.03.77	IAI Arava 201	TAM-77	026	Transporte Aereo Militar	Crashed	Bolivia	*	*
16.03.77	Cessna 182	ET-ADP	182-54139	Admas Air Service	Crashed	Djimma, Ethiopia	*	*

Date	Type	Reg'n	C/n	Operator	Accident	Location	F	S
17.03.77	Boeing 707-436	G-APFK	17712	British Airtours	Crashed on landing	Prestwick, Strathclyde, UK	0	*
18.03.77	Mitsubishi MU-2J	N777MA	559	Operator Unknown	Crashed	nr Austin, TX, USA	1	*
18.03.77	Beechcraft 18	N9929Z	*	Operator Unknown	Crashed	Kenosha, WI, USA	0	*
18.03.77	Aerospatiale SA.318C Alouette II	D-HAKA	*	Luft-Transport-Dienst	Crashed after hitting power cables	Dusseldorf, West Germany	3	0
25.03.77	Douglas DC-3	N692A	7318	Island Traders	Damaged in heavy landing	St Thomas, US Virgin Islands	0	*
27.03.77	Boeing 747-121	N736PA	19643	Pan American World Airways	Struck by KLM B.747 PH-BUF taking-off in fog	Tenerife, Canary Is, Spain	335 (248)	77
27.03.77	Boeing 747-206B	PH-BUF	20400	KLM Royal Dutch Airlines	Collided with Pan American B.747 N736PA while taking-off	Tenerife, Canary Is, Spain	248 (335)	0
28.03.77	Douglas DC-3	N57131	19040	Pinehurst Airlines	Destroyed in hangar fire	Chicago, IL, USA	*	*
29.03.77	de Havilland Canada Twin Otter 300	PK-NUP	486	Merpati Nusantara Airlines	Crashed	Bainalia Valley, Indonesia	1	23
29.03.77	de Havilland Canada Beaver	ZS-DRG	*	Avexair	Crashed & caught fire	Warmbad, South Africa	3	0
30.03.77	Yakovlev YAK-40	SSSR-87738	*	Aeroflot	Crashed on landing in fog	Zhadanof, RSFSR, USSR	8	19
30.03.77	de Havilland Canada Beaver	ZS-CMI	*	Avexair	Crashed	nr Springbok, South Africa	3	0
31.03.77	Lockheed Electra 188C	C-FNAZ	1132	Nordair	Struck by crashing CAF Argus 10737	Summerside, PEI, Canada	0(3)	*
oo.03.77	Bristol 170 Freighter 31E	C-FQWJ	13078	Lambair	Crashed	Rankin Inlet, Canada	*	*
01.04.77	Mitsubishi MU-2G	N100SW	539	Operator Unknown	Written off	En route Atlanta–Miami, USA	*	*
02.04.77	Sikorsky S-58DT	N90939	58-1402	Carson Helicopters	Written off	Jeddah, Saudi Arabia	*	*
02.04.77	Tupolev TU-134A-3	YU-AJS	6348370	Aviogenex	Crashed on landing	Libreville, Gabon	8	0
02.04.77	Beechcraft Queen Air B80	HK-1067X	LD-442	Taxi Aereo El Venado	Damaged beyond repair	Yopal, Colombia	*	*
03.04.77	Dassault Falcon 10	N60MB	015	Mountain States Telephone & Telecom	Crashed	Denver, CO, USA	4	*
04.04.77	McDonnell Douglas DC-9-31	N1335U	47393	Southern Airlines	Crashed on road after both engines failed in storm	New Hope, GA, USA	63{9}	22
04.04.77	Mitsubishi MU-2K	N321MA	276	Operator Unknown	Written off	Double Springs, AL, USA	*	*
04.04.77	Bell 206B JetRanger II	TG-KEZ	*	Helicopteros de Guatemala	Crashed	Chixov, Guatemala	1	4
05.04.77	Douglas DC-3	VT-EEL	13290	National Remote Sensing Agency	Crashed in fog	nr Ongole, India	10	0
05.04.77	Mitsubishi MU-2G	N888RJ	542	Mount Victory Flying Service	Crashed on approach in fog	New York, NY, USA	7	*
08.04.77	Piper PA-24 Comanche	5Y-AAW	*	Sight by Wings	Crashed on take-off	Kilimatinde, Kenya	*	*
09.04.77	Sikorsky S-58	ZS-HCX	*	Court Helicopters	Crashed	Off Cape Town, South Africa	0	*
09.04.77	Nord 262A-27	N7886A	047	Altair	Mid-air collision with Cessna 195 N4377N	Reading, PA, USA	4(*)	0
09.04.77	Convair 240-0	N1CAV	008	American Velodour Metal Inc	Crashed on beach	Barnstaple, MA, USA	*	*
10.04.77	Douglas DC-3	HK-556	4958	Taxi Aereo El Venado	Crashed	100 miles SW of Bogota, Colombia	32	0
11.04.77	Douglas DC-3	C-FXXT	15767/27212	Superior Airways	Crashed	Location Unknown	*	*
16.04.77	Douglas DC-3	B-247	19904	Far Eastern Air Transport	Damaged beyond repair	Tainan, Taiwan	*	*
18.04.77	McDonnell Douglas DC-8-53	RP-C803	45937	Philippine Air Lines	Ran off runway & destroyed	Tokyo, Japan	0	*
18.04.77	Beechcraft Super King Air 200	N256TM	BB-0096	Operator Unknown	Written off	New Orleans, LA, USA	*	*
21.04.77	Ilyushin IL-18B	YR-IMI	185008302	Tarom	Crashed	Otopeni, Romania	*	*
23.04.77	Rockwell Turbo Commander 690A	N847	11140	Operator Unknown	Written off	Chicago, IL, USA	*	*
25.04.77	Fokker F-27 Friendship 200	5N-AAW	10217	Nigeria Airways	Damaged when ran off runway	Sokoto, Nigeria	0	*
25.04.77	Hughes 500	ZK-HIA	*	Mountain Helicopters	Crashed after engine failed	Tarawera, New Zealand	0	1
27.04.77	Convair 440	TG-ACA	143	Aviateca	Crashed after take-off	nr Guatemala City, Guatemala	*	*
28.04.77	Gates Learjet 35	JY-AEW	35-052	Arab Wings	Crashed	Riyadh, Saudi Arabia	*	*
28.04.77	British Aerospace 125-600A	N40PC	6010	Southern Services Inc	Crashed	McLean, VA, USA	*	*
29.04.77	NAMC YS-11A-202	PP-CTI	2080	Cruzeiro	Crash landed	Santa Catarina, Brazil	*	*
06.05.77	Curtiss C-46	N355W	22523	Inter Air	Crashed	Off Hollywood, FL, USA	*	*
09.05.77	de Havilland Heron 1B	ZK-EJM	14005	Air North	Damaged when ran into ditch	Ardmore, New Zealand	0	*
12.05.77	Douglas DC-3	C-FBKV	4441	Patricia Air Services	Crashed	Pickle Lake, ON, Canada	*	*
12.05.77	Britten-Norman BN-2A-21 Islander	PT-KUO	0512	Geofoto S.A.	Crashed into mountain in poor weather	nr Curitaba, Brazil	1	0
13.05.77	Antonov AN-12B	SP-LZA	6344307	LOT Polish Airlines	Crashed in rain	nr Beirut, Lebanon	9	0
14.05.77	Boeing 707-321C	G-BEBP	18579	IAS Cargo	Crashed on approach due to fatigue failure of tail	Lusaka, Zambia	5	0
21.05.77	GAF Nomad 22B	P2-DNJ	029	Douglas Airways	Crashed	Wewak, Papua New Guinea	*	*
26.05.77	Gates Learjet 25B	N501PS	25B-153	Gates Learjet Acceptance Corp	Crashed	Detroit, MI, USA	0	*
26.05.77	Cessna 310	VH-ROC	*	Rundell Air Service	Crashed	Townsville, Qld, Australia	5	0
27.05.77	Ilyushin IL-62	SSSR-86614	51903	Aeroflot	Crashed into power lines	Havana, Cuba	69	1
27.05.77	Cessna 206 Super Skywagon	8R-GEF	*	Inair	Crashed	Essequibo, Guyana	*	*

Date	Type	Reg'n	C/n	Operator	Accident	Location	F	S
28.05.77	Yakovlev YAK-40EC	I-JAKE	9141418	Avio Ligure	Ran off runway on landing	Genoa, Italy	0	*
28.05.77	Mitsubishi MU-2J	C-GODI	649	Athabaska Airways	Crashed	Portage la Praine, MN, Canada	6	*
28.05.77	Bell 206A JetRanger	N2299W	*	Campbell Air Service	Crashed after engine failure	Franklin, GA, USA	*	*
31.05.77	Cessna 206 Super Skymaster	HK-1737	206-02798	RANSA	Crash landed after engine failure	Arauca, Colombia	0	2
01.06.77	Piper PA-34 Seneca	ZP-PGZ	34-7350325	Aeronorte	Crashed into ditch on take-off after tyre burst	Jejui, Paraguay	0	*
03.06.77	Beechcraft 18	N68A	*	Operator Unknown	Crashed	nr Springfield, OH, USA	1	*
06.06.77	Fokker F-27 Friendship 400M	ST-ADW	10282	Sudan Airways	Written off	El Fasher, Sudan	*	*
10.06.77	Douglas DC-3	5U-AAJ	4505	Air Ivoire	Damaged beyond repair	Founkoueye, Niger	0	*
12.06.77	Douglas DC-3	N33649	4809	T.Perez	Forced landed on drug smuggling flight	Vero Beach, FL, USA	*	*
15.06.77	Britten-Norman BN-2A-20 Islander	YV-O-MAR-6	0203	Operator Unknown	Written off	Location Unknown	*	*
16.06.77	Cessna 402B	OH-CFM	*	Finnwings	Crashed	nr Helsinki, Finland	3	*
17.06.77	Douglas DC-3	HK-1511E	6138	Taxi Aereo Nacional	Destroyed	Condoto, Colombia	*	*
19.06.77	Fairchild-Hiller FH.227B	YU-ALA	525	Pan Adria	Damaged while taxiing	Zagreb, Yugoslavia	0	*
21.06.77	Cessna 402	9Q-CFJ	*	Air Mediterranee	Crashed	nr Boteka, Zaire	*	*
21.06.77	Cessna 182B	HK-670	182-52053	Aerolineas Regionales de Faz	Crashed	Pore, Colombia	*	*
24.06.77	Cessna 182	6Y-JHJ	*	Trans Jamaican Airlines	Crashed	Kentish, Jamaica	4	0
26.06.77	Embraer Bandeirante 110C	CX-BJE/T584	110.083	TAMU	Crashed	nr Salto, Uruguay	5	0
27.06.77	IRMA BN-2A-27 Islander	YR-BNI	0776	Aviatia Utilitara	Written off	Nucet, Romania	*	*
30.06.77	Lockheed Electra 188CF	N126US	1105	Co-operativa de Montecillos	Crashed	Off Bocas del Toro, Panama	4	0
oo.06.77	Antonov AN-22A	SSSR-09349	*	Aeroflot	Crashed on take-off	nr Bransk, RSFSR, USSR	0	*
02.07.77	Cessna 404 Titan	HC-BDF	*	Aeroservicios Ecuatorianos	Crashed	Guaymaral, Colombia	2	*
06.07.77	Lockheed Electra 188AF	N280F	1076	Fleming International	Crashed on take-off	St Louis, MS, USA	3	0
07.07.77	Cessna 421 Golden Eagle	*	*	Operator Unknown	Crashed after take-off	Smith's Skyranch, CA, USA	1	0
08.07.77	Antonov AN-24	SSSR-46847	27307505	Aeroflot	Crashed in sea after take-off	Off Kirovograd, Ukraine, USSR	6	1
17.07.77	NAMC YS-11A-301	RP-C1419	2107	Philippine Air Lines	Crashed	Off Mactan, Philippines	0	*
19.07.77	Douglas DC-3	HK-166	12560	Lineas Aereas Orientales	Crashed on landing	Mitu, Colombia	0	*
20.07.77	Douglas DC-3	ET-ABF	6069	Ethiopian Airlines	Crashed	nr Jimma, Ethiopia	*	*
20.07.77	Beechcraft 18	*	*	Operator Unknown	Crashed on take-off	Oshawa, ON, Canada	2	*
21.07.77	Douglas DC-3	ET-AGI	19006	Ethiopian Airlines	Shot down by Somali Air Force	nr Jimma, Ethiopia	4	0
21.07.77	Britten-Norman BN-2A-6 Islander	N22JA	0264	Andy's Flying Service	Written off	Location Unknown	*	*
21.07.77	IRMA BN-2A-21 Islander	5T-MAT	0765	Mauritanian Air Force	Written off	Location Unknown	*	*
25.07.77	MBB HFB.320 Hansa	5N-AMF	1028	Motor Parts Manufacturers	Crashed on approach after first flight in two years	Abidjan, Ivory Coast	3	0
27.07.77	Beechcraft Super King Air 200	D-IBAF	BB-0093	Alfa Flug	Crashed	Bourgas, Bulgaria	6	0
28.07.77	Beechcraft King Air C90	PT-IBE	LJ-0531	Operator Unknown	Written off	Location Unknown	*	*
31.07.77	Beechcraft King Air E90	N4207S	LW-207	Operator Unknown	Written off	Sitka, AK, USA	*	*
oo.07.77	Douglas DC-3	ET-AGR	11711	Ethiopian Airlines	Destroyed on ground by rebels	Jiggigia, Ethiopia	*	*
oo.07.77	Britten-Norman BN-2A-7 Islander	C-FAZM	0114	Peace Air	Written off	Location Unknown	*	*
02.08.77	Piper PA-23 Aztec	N14007	27-4625	New England Airlines	Crashed at sea	Delaware Bay, DE, USA	1	1
08.08.77	Cessna 188	VH-RBR	*	Narrabari Air Taxis	Crashed	Narrabari, NSW, Australia	0	1
09.08.77	Boeing 707-430	9Q-CRT	17718	Pearl Air	Damaged on landing	Sanaa, Yemen Arab Republic	0	*
13.08.77	Beechcraft H-18	C-GWUY	BA-655	Operator Unknown	Crashed into mountain	175 miles S of Juneau, AK, USA	6	0
17.08.77	Mil Mi-8	SSSR-25840	*	Aeroflot	Crashed	Spitzbergen, Norway	20	*
17.08.77	Beechcraft 18	N75FA	BA-498	Flight Express	Crashed into houses on take-off	Coraopolis, PA, USA	0	2
19.08.77	Grumman G-21A Goose	*	*	Catalina Airlines	Crashed	Catalina Island, CA, USA	2	*
20.08.77	Convair 880-22-2	N8817E	65	Monarch Aviation	Crashed after take-off	San Jose, Costa Rica	3	0
23.08.77	Douglas DC-3	N74689	*	Societe Quarter Wins	Crashed	Off Le Raizet, Guadeloupe	*	*
23.08.77	Britten-Norman BN-2A-9 Islander	TR-LSF	0387	Air Inter Gabon	Written off	Location Unknown	*	*
25.08.77	Short Skyvan 3	N4917	SH.1850	Island Airways	Crashed	Keahole, HI, USA	*	*
oo.08.77	Douglas DC-3	ET-AAP	13181	Ethiopian Airlines	Shot down by Somali forces	Ogaden, Ethiopia	*	*
02.09.77	Canadair CL-44D4-2	G-ATZH	021	Transmeridian Air Cargo	Crashed	Off Wanglan Is, Hong Kong	5	0
04.09.77	Vickers Viscount 764D	HC-BCL	185	Servicios Aereos Nacionales	Crashed	nr Cuenca, Ecuador	33	0
06.09.77	de Havilland Canada Twin Otter 200	N563MA	196	Alaska Aeronautical Industries	Crashed	Mt Iliama, AK, USA	13	0
08.09.77	de Havilland Canada Twin Otter 300	XY-AEH	540	Burma Airways	Crashed	Keng Tung, Burma	22	0
08.09.77	Gates Learjet 25B	N999HG	25B-178	Champion Home Builders	Crashed on take-off	Sanford, NC, USA	5	*

Date	Type	Reg'n	C/n	Operator	Accident	Location	F	S
11.09.77	Douglas DC-7BF	N6314J	45359	Safe Air Cargo	Crashed on take-off	Yakutat, AK, USA	4	0
14.09.77	Aerospatiale SA.316B Alouette III	5N-AKC	1775	Aero Contractors	Crashed at sea	Texaco Pennington Field, Nigeria	5	0
14.09.77	de Havilland Canada Beaver	HK-249	982	Aerolineas Especiales de Colombia	Crashed	Cartagena del Chaira, Colombia	1	5
14.09.77	Sikorsky S-55	VR-BDB	*	Bristow Helicopters	Crashed	Dubai Creek, United Arab Emirates	*	*
18.09.77	Bell 47G-4	HK-744E	2415	Petroleum Helicopters de Colombia	Crashed	Simacota, Colombia	*	*
21.09.77	Tupolev TU-134	HA-LBC	8350605	Malev	Crashed on approach	nr Bucharest, Romania	29	24
21.09.77	Douglas DC-3	N723A	4395	NJ Airlines	Crashed on approach	Narasaruaq, Greenland	*	*
21.09.77	Gates Learjet 36A	JY-AFC	36A-020	Arab Wings	Crashed on take-off	Amman, Jordan	4	*
23.09.77	Beechcraft King Air C90	N23796	LJ-0737	Operator Unknown	Crashed	Pontiak, IL, USA	2	0
23.09.77	Hughes 300	ZK-HJJ	*	Marine Helicopters	Crashed after striking cables	Kaipara, New Zealand	*	*
24.09.77	IRMA BN-2A-21 Islander	PK-ZAD	0732	Sabang Merauke Raya Air Charter	Crashed	Off Lhokseumawe, Indonesia	4	6
25.09.77	Hughes 500	RP-C1272	*	Tropical Airways	Crashed	Barrio Malagdao, Philippines	0	3
25.09.77	Piper PA-31 Navajo	LN-PAA	*	Partnair	Crashed at sea	Off Fornebu, Norway	*	*
26.09.77	Dornier Do.28D-1 Skyservant	PK-VDH	4038	State Aerial Survey Corporation	Crashed	nr Bawean Is, Indonesia	*	1
27.09.77	McDonnell Douglas DC-8-62	JA8051	46152	Japan Air Lines	Crashed on approach	Kuala Lumpur, Malaysia	33	46
28.09.77	Pilatus PC-6C/H-2 Porter	ST-AGY	600	National Agriculture Organisation	Damaged while taxiing	nr Port Sudan, Sudan	0	*
29.09.77	Curtiss C-46	C-FCZH	22515	North Coast Air Services	Crashed on landing	Thompson, MN, Canada	0	*
30.09.77	Sikorsky S-58	D-HAUB	*	Meravo Luftreederei Flug	Crashed	Garmisch-Partenkirchen, W Germany	1	1
30.09.77	Bristol Britannia 253	EI-BBY	13455	Interconair	Crashed & caught fire on landing	Shannon, Eire	0	*
30.09.77	Douglas DC-3	TG-AKA	13327	Aviateca	Damaged on landing	Santa Elena el Peten, Guatemala	1	*
02.10.77	Douglas DC-3	N65121	20061	J.Lenhardt	Forced down on smuggling flight by Colombian Air Force	Villavicencio, Colombia	*	*
05.10.77	Beechcraft 18	PT-KXO	*	Operator Unknown	Crashed	Bridgetown, Barbados	0	1
06.10.77	Douglas DC-3	CP-1336	44617	Aerovias Las Minas	Written off	La China, Bolivia	*	*
08.10.77	Britten-Norman Trislander	ZS-JYF	1031	Southern Aviation	Crashed during air display	Lanseria, South Africa	*	*
18.10.77	British Aerospace 748 2	PK-RHS	1610	Seulawah-Mandala Airlines	Crashed	Manila, Philippines	5	2
20.10.77	Convair 300	N55VM	003	L & J Company	Crashed out of fuel [Rock group Lynyrd Skynryd killed]	McComb, MS, USA	6	20
20.10.77	Beechcraft Super King Air 200	N17530	BB-0204	Operator Unknown	Written off	Valparaiso, IN, USA	*	*
21.10.77	Cessna 182M	HK-1436	182-59910	AVES	Crashed	Medellin, Colombia	5	0
22.10.77	Lockheed 749A Constellation	N273R	2650	CIM Associates	Destroyed by fire	Lome, Togo	0	*
23.10.77	Douglas DC-3	C-FSAW	4644	Uniran	Crashed	Sabzevar, Iran	3	0
28.10.77	de Havilland Canada Otter	TI-SPF	*	Costa Rican Ministry of Security	Crashed	Costa Rica	*	*
30.10.77	Cessna 180	*	*	Yellowhead Air Service	Crashed	nr Likely, BC, Canada	*	*
30.10.77	de Havilland Canada Beaver	C-FODF	*	AirWest Airlines	Sank after losing float	False Bay, BC, Canada	0	*
03.11.77	Britten-Norman BN-2A-8 Islander	XA-FUA	0388	Servicios Aereos Martinez Leon	Exploded & crashed on approach	San Cristobal de las Casas, Mexico	13	0
07.11.77	Rockwell Sabre 40	N77AP	282-037	Mechanical Equipment Co	Crashed	Lake Pontchartrain, LA, USA	2	*
07.11.77	Britten-Norman BN-2A-9 Islander	8R-GEH	0348	M.C.Correia Holdings	Crashed on landing	Ogle, Guyana	*	*
12.11.77	Sikorsky S-58T	LN-OSD	*	Operator Unknown	Crashed	nr Bodo, Norway	*	*
15.11.77	Cessna 441 Conquest II	N9971G	0006	Operator Unknown	Crashed	nr Demopolis, AL, USA	7	0
16.11.77	Douglas DC-3	RP-C647	9786	Commercial Air Transport	Written off	Balesia Is, Philippines	*	*
19.11.77	Boeing 727-282A	CS-TBR	20972	Transportes Aereos Portugueses	Overran on landing & crashed over cliff	Madeira, Portugal	131	33
19.11.77	Boeing 707-360C	ET-ACD	19736	Ethiopian Airlines	Crashed on take-off	Rome, Italy	5	0
19.11.77	Aerospatiale SA.315B Lama	EP-HSV	*	Schreiner Airways	Crashed after rotor fouled rope	nr Reza Shah Kabir, Iran	2	3
20.11.77	Douglas C-47B	FAC.1127	16290/33038	Satena	Crashed	Location Unknown	*	*
20.11.77	Bristol 170 Freighter 31M	C-FWAD	13253	Wardair	Crashed on take-off	Hay River, NWT, Canada	0	*
20.11.77	Douglas C-47A	FAC.1120	12446	Satena	Damaged beyond repair	Llanos del Yori, Colombia	0	*
21.11.77	Britten-Norman BN-2A-8 Islander	N36MN	0546	Munz Northern Airlines	Forced landed on ice & sank	Off Alaska, USA	*	*
21.11.77	North American B-25J Mitchell	CP-808	5204	F.Garcia	Written off	La Paz, Bolivia	*	*
22.11.77	Tupolev TU-134	DM-SCM	8351904	Interflug	Crashed on landing	East Berlin, East Germany	0	*
22.11.77	BAC One-Eleven 420EL	LV-JGY	155	Austral	Crashed into mountain	nr Bariloche, Argentina	46	33
23.11.77	Sikorsky S-61N	LN-OSZ	*	Helikopter Service	Crashed	North Sea	12	0
23.11.77	Ilyushin IL-18B	HA-MOF	183006301	Malev	Damaged while taxiing	Budapest, Hungary	*	*
23.11.77	Piper PA-31 Navajo	*	*	Textafrica	Shot down in error by Mozambique troops	Cimoio, Mozambique	8	0

Date	Type	Reg'n	C/n	Operator	Accident	Location	F	S
26.11.77	Douglas C-54B	9Q-CAM	10441	African Lux	Shot down by Mozambique forces	Tete Province, Mozambique	*	*
26.11.77	Beechcraft King Air A90	N55MG	LJ-0303	Operator Unknown	Written off	Charleston, SC, USA	*	*
26.11.77	Britten-Norman BN-2A Islander	TR-LNG	0013	Bureau de Prospection Forestiere	Written off	Location Unknown	*	*
28.11.77	Cessna 180	C-GHAQ	*	Island Airlines	Crashed	Blowhole Bay, BC, Canada	4	0
01.12.77	de Havilland Canada Twin Otter 100	C-GPBO	100	AirWest Airlines	Crashed	Saturna Island, BC, Canada	0	*
01.12.77	Cessna A185F	HK-1918	185-03098	Vias Aereas Nacionales	Crashed	Cabuyare, Colombia	*	*
02.12.77	Tupolev TU-154B	LZ-BTN	054	Balkan Bulgarian Airlines	Crashed	nr Al Bayda, Lebanon	59	106
04.12.77	Boeing 737-2H6A	9M-MBD	20585	Malaysian Airline System	Exploded during hijack attempt & crashed	Kampong Ladang, Malaysia	100	0
08.12.77	Aerospatiale Puma	*	*	Petroleum Helicopters	Crashed	Gulf of Mexico	17	2
08.12.77	Rockwell Shrike Commander 500	PT-BVZ	*	Lider Taxi Aereo	Crashed on approach	Conceicao do Araguia, Brazil	2	0
09.12.77	Aerospatiale Caravelle 6N	F-BYAU	192	Aerotour	U/c collapsed on take-off	Oujda, Morocco	0	*
09.12.77	British Aerospace 125-400A	C-FCFL	25213	Churchill Falls Corp	Crashed	Labrador City, Nfd, Canada	*	*
09.12.77	Antonov AN-24	SSSR-47695	27307602	Aeroflot	Crashed	Tarko-Saley, RSFSR, USSR	17	*
11.12.77	McDonnell Douglas DC-8-33F	N8170A	45270	Charlotte Aircraft Corporation	Destroyed by fire during refuelling	Lake City, FL, USA	0	*
11.12.77	CASA 2.111	G-BFFS	-	D.Arnold	Crashed into mountains	El Escorial, Spain	4	0
13.12.77	Douglas DC-3	N51071	4837	Air Indiana	Crashed	nr Evansville, IN, USA	36	21
14.12.77	Vickers Viscount 837	HK-1267	441	Lineas Aereas La Urraca	Damaged beyond repair	Bucaramanga, Colombia	*	*
14.12.77	Grumman G-21A Goose	*	*	Operator Unknown	Crashed on approach	Opa-Locka, FL, USA	0	*
18.12.77	Aerospatiale Caravelle 10R	HB-ICK	200	SATA	Crashed in sea	Off Madeira, Portugal	36	21
18.12.77	McDonnell Douglas DC-8-54F	N8047U	45880	United Air Lines	Crashed in storm out of fuel	Salt Lake City, UT, USA	3	0
19.12.77	Britten-Norman BN-2A-6 Islander	N862JA	0184	Vieques Air Link	Crashed	Off Vieques Island, Puerto Rico	5	5
21.12.77	de Havilland Canada Twin Otter 300	C-FABW	278	Kenn Borek Air	Crashed	Nanisivik, NWT, Canada	8	0
22.12.77	Cessna 404 Titan	N404SA	*	Operator Unknown	Crashed	Ontario, Canada	1	*
22.12.77	Antonov AN-22	SSSR-09318	*	Aeroflot	Crashed after spin	nr Bransk, RSFSR, USSR	*	0
24.12.77	Type Unknown	*	*	Valley Air Service	Crashed after engine failure	Off St Maarten, Neth Antilles	10	0
25.12.77	Bell 47G-4	HK-1307	6539	Petroleum Helicopters de Colombia	Crashed	Cucuta, Colombia	1	0
29.12.77	Vickers Viscount 764D	HC-BEM	183	Servicios Aereos Nacionales	Crashed	nr Cuenca, Ecuador	24	0
31.12.77	de Havilland Canada Twin Otter 300	C-FTVP	335	NorOntair	Crashed	Kenora, Canada	*	*
00.00.77	Consolidated PBY-6A Catalina	N6458C	*	Hemet Valley Flying Service	Destroyed while refuelling	Stockton, CA, USA	*	*
00.00.77	Douglas DC-7CF	N73675	44878	Consolidated Air	Crashed	South Carolina, USA	*	*
00.00.77	Scottish Aviation Twin Pioneer 3	N48207	582	Murryair Aviation	Damaged beyond repair	Merril Field, AK, USA	*	*
01.01.78	Boeing 747-237B	VT-EBD	19959	Air India	Crashed	Off Bombay, India	213	0
02.01.78	Douglas DC-3	N15598	2258	Aero Virgin Islands	Crashed	Luquilla, Puerto Rico	0	*
03.01.78	Cessna 402	*	*	Mariksche Luftfahrtgesellschaft	Crashed into woods	Leitkirsch, West Germany	4	1
03.01.78	Cessna 421 Golden Eagle	*	*	Operator Unknown	Crashed	Great Smokey Mts, TN, USA	4	0
06.01.78	Fokker F-27 Friendship 600	9Q-CLR	10406	Air Zaire	Crashed & exploded on take-off	Kisangani, Zaire	3	0
09.01.78	Britten-Norman Trislander	HK-1711	1002	Tavina	Crashed in lake	nr Cienga Grande, Colombia	*	*
10.01.78	Beechcraft King Air B90	N388MC	LJ-0442	Operator Unknown	Crashed into house short of runway	Yazoo City, MI, USA	5	*
11.01.78	Piper PA-23 Aztec	VH-PYS	*	Emu Air Services	Crashed after striking ship's mast	Off Cairns, Qld, Australia	2	0
14.01.78	Antonov AN-2	YR-PVC	1G175-03	Operator Unknown	Crashed	Arad, Romania	*	*
15.01.78	Bell 206A JetRanger	9M-AUL	01815	Sabah Air	Crashed in sea	Kuala Paitan, Malaysia	1	4
18.01.78	de Havilland Canada Twin Otter 300	N982FL	465	Frontier Airlines	Crashed	Pueblo, CO, USA	3	0
20.01.78	Britten-Norman BN-2A Islander	N869JA	0120	Island Contractors	Written off	Location Unknown	*	*
21.01.78	Hughes 369HS	RP-C1280	15-0693S	Tropical Airways	Crashed into power cables	nr Manila, Philippines	4	0
22.01.78	Aerospatiale SA.319B Alouette III	OO-PCB	2151	Heliflight	Crashed in gale	Brugge, Belgium	*	*
24.01.78	Convair 440-86	TAM-45	406	Transporte Aereo Militar	Swerved into ditch on landing after engine failure	San Ramon, Bolivia	0{1}	*
26.01.78	Agusta-Bell 205A-1	LN-ORO	30058	Lufttransport	Struck building & crashed in snowstorm	nr Tromso, Norway	0	*
27.01.78	Douglas DC-3	HK-1351X	42958	Sadelca	Crashed	nr San Vincente, Colombia	13	0
27.01.78	Cessna 188	ET-AEG	188-00802	Admas Air Service	Crashed	Assayita, Ethiopia	*	*
27.01.78	Enstrom 280	HB-XET	*	Heli AG	Crashed after striking cable	Disentis, Switzerland	*	*
28.01.78	Douglas DC-3	TT-EAB	9157	Air Chad	Crashed – Possibly shot down by rebels	Tibesti, Chad	*	*
29.01.78	Douglas DC-4-1009	TT-NAA	42936	Chad Air Force	Shot down by rebels	nr Faya Largeau, Chad	*	*
31.01.78	Embraer Bandeirante 110P	PT-GKW	110.128	TABA	Crashed after take-off	Eirunepe, Brazil	2	12
31.01.78	Embraer Bandeirante 110P	PT-GKT	110.130	Rio Sul	Crashed	Eirunepe, Brazil	*	*

Date	Type	Reg'n	C/n	Operator	Accident	Location	F	S
31.01.78	Bell 206B JetRanger II	ZS-HCP	*	Court Helicopters	Crashed	nr Johannesburg, South Africa	*	*
06.02.78	Beechcraft Queen Air	N40SB	*	Transcommuter Airlines	Crashed on landing	Virgin Gorda, US Virgin Is	*	*
10.02.78	Beechcraft 99	N199EA	U037	Columbia Pacific Airlines	Crashed after take-off	Richland, WA, USA	17	0
10.02.78	Douglas C-47A	CX-BJH/T511	19301	TAMU	Crashed	Artigas, Uruguay	31	0
11.02.78	Boeing 737-275	C-FPWC	20142	Pacific Western Airlines	Crashed on landing while trying to avoid vehicle	Cranbrook, BC, Canada	41	7
12.02.78	Mitsubishi MU-2J	N888MA	550	Operator Unknown	Written off	nr Neiva, Colombia	*	*
12.02.78	Bell 205A	C-GWLI	*	Okanagan Helicopters	Crashed into mountain	Mica Creek, BC, Canada	4	0
13.02.78	Cessna 402	SE-GGR	*	Dicro	Crashed on approach	Gaevle, Sweden	4	0
15.02.78	Boeing 707-329	OO-SJE	17627	Sabena	Destroyed by fire after nosewheel collapsed on landing	Tenerife, Canary Is, Spain	0	*
15.02.78	Beechcraft King Air A90	XA-FOT	LJ-0168	Operator Unknown	Written off	Mexico	*	*
16.02.78	Beechcraft 99A	F-BRUX	U122	Air Alpes	Crashed	Clermont-Ferrand, France	*	*
17.02.78	Douglas DC-6B	N6523C	43523	Skyways International	Crashed	Grasias de Dias, Honduras	0	*
17.02.78	Beechcraft E-18S	N180X	*	Flight Express	Crashed	Harrisburg, PA, USA	*	*
18.02.78	Piper PA-25 Pawnee	ZS-CPB	*	Avexair	Crashed	Ceres, South Africa	*	*
19.02.78	Lockheed L-100-20 Hercules	OB-R-1004	4364	Satco	Crashed on take-off	Tarapota, Peru	*	*
19.02.78	Lockheed C-130H Hercules	SU-BAA/1270	4707	Egyptian Air Force	Damaged by Cypriot troops in hijack hostage rescue attempt	Larnaca, Cyprus	0	*
20.02.78	Aerospatiale 330C Puma	TR-KCD	1293	Gabon Air Force	Crashed	Bees Forest, Gabon	*	*
21.02.78	Douglas DC-3	FAC.668	*	Satena	Crashed	Location Unknown	*	*
22.02.78	Gates Learjet 35A	I-MCSA	35A-099	Maniglia Construzioni	Crashed on approach	Palermo, Sicily, Italy	3	*
24.02.78	Douglas DC-6B	N6103C	44103	Int. Aircraft Sales & Lease	Damaged when u/c collapsed after overrunning	San Juan, Puerto Rico	0	*
27.02.78	Beechcraft King Air A90	N878T	LJ-0246	Operator Unknown	Written off	Big Piney, NY, USA	*	*
28.02.78	de Havilland Canada Twin Otter 100	P2-RDE	084	Talair	Crashed	Garaing, Papua New Guinea	1	0
28.02.78	Mitsubishi MU-2J	N297MA	593	Operator Unknown	Crashed	Gulf of Mexico	5	0
01.03.78	McDonnell Douglas DC-10-10	N68045	46904	Continental Airlines	Destroyed by fire after tyre burst on take-off	Los Angeles, CA, USA	4	196
02.03.78	Fokker F-28 Fellowship 1000	5N-ANA	11993	Nigeria Airways	Mid-air collision with Nigerian Air Force MIG-21	Kano, Nigeria	18(*)	0
02.03.78	Fairchild F-27J	N747L	0038	Saudia	Damaged when u/c retracted while parked	Jeddah, Saudi Arabia	0	*
03.03.78	McDonnell Douglas DC-8-63	EC-BMX	45930	Iberia	Overran & destroyed by fire	Santiago, Spain	0	*
03.03.78	British Aerospace 748 2A	YV-45C	1744	Aeropostal	Crashed in sea after take-off	Caracas, Venezuela	47	0
04.03.78	Bell 206L Long Ranger	C-GERD	*	Heli-Quebec	Crashed	Cabot Island, Nfld, Canada	0	2
08.03.78	Rockwell Turbo Commander 681	N5NP	6042	Operator Unknown	Written off	Greenup, KY, USA	*	*
12.03.78	de Havilland Dove 5BA	N4959N	04311	Aircraft Brokers Inc	Crashed in sea	Off Santa Marta, Colombia	2	0
15.03.78	Hughes 500	PT-HIR	*	VOTEC	Crashed after striking power lines	Parana State, Brazil	4	0
16.03.78	Tupolev TU-134	LZ-TUB	8350501	Balkan Bulgarian Airlines	Crashed after take-off	Vratsa, Bulgaria	73	0
17.03.78	Beechcraft Queen Air 70	N8431N	*	Vernair Transport	Crashed into mountain due to navigation error	nr Kulusuk, Greenland	2	0
17.03.78	Bell 205A	HK-1495E	30148	Helicol	Crashed	Gachala, Colombia	0	1
19.03.78	Beechcraft King Air 90	N2MF	LJ-0096	Operator Unknown	Written off	Houston, TX, USA	*	*
21.03.78	Convair 440	N4807C	084	Florida Aircraft Leasing	Crash landed after engine failure	nr Elma, IN, USA	*	*
23.03.78	Douglas DC-3	N1546A	20191	Dominican Services	Crashed after take-off	Grand Turk, Turks & Caicos Is	*	*
23.03.78	Tupolev TU-154	LZ-BTB	027	Balkan Bulgarian Airlines	Crashed	nr Damascus, Syria	4	*
25.03.78	Fokker F-27 Friendship 200	XY-ADK	10235	Burma Airways	Crashed	nr Rangoon, Burma	48	0
27.03.78	Beechcraft Queen Air 80	N28BL	*	B.Lisle	Crashed	Labrador, Canada	0	1
01.04.78	Convair 300	N777DC	141	Thrifty Threads Inc	Crashed into lagoon	Unguia, Colombia	0	*
03.04.78	Boeing 737-2A1A	PP-SMX	20969	VASP	Belly landed & caught fire	Sao Paulo, Brazil	0	*
04.04.78	Boeing 737-229CA	OO-SDH	20914	Sabena	Crashed on take-off	Gosselies, Belgium	0	*
04.04.78	Bell 212	*	*	Air Logistics	Crashed trying to land on ship *Glomar Java Sea*	Off Galveston, TX, USA	3	0
05.04.78	Grumman G-21A Goose	N8777A	1152	Antilles Air Boats	Crashed after engine failure	Off St Croix, US Virgin Is	2	*
07.04.78	Douglas DC-3	N189UM	6262	Aero Service Corporation	Crashed on landing	Oran, Algeria	*	*
08.04.78	Yakovlev YAK-40	SSSR-87911	*	Aeroflot	Crashed on take-off	Aldan, RSFSR, USSR	*	*
10.04.78	Britten-Norman BN-2A-21 Islander	N97JA	0447	Digital Equipment Corporation	Written off	Location Unknown	*	*
16.04.78	Bell 206B JetRanger II	N49757	*	Sea Airmotive	Crashed	Alaska, USA	2	0
17.04.78	de Havilland Canada Twin Otter 300	YV-30C	526	Linea Aeropostal Venezolana	Crashed on take-off	Vrima, Venezuela	*	*
18.04.78	Douglas DC-4	N88909	10466	Panavia Cargo	Crashed short of runway	Bottle Creek, Turks & Caicos Is	*	*
18.04.78	Piper PA-34 Seneca	N44356	*	Troy Air Service	Crashed after being refuelled with jet fuel	Anchorage, AK, USA	0	4
19.04.78	de Havilland Canada Beaver	N4747S	1142	Chitina Air Service	Crashed	Cordova, AK, USA	2	0

Date	Type	Reg'n	C/n	Operator	Accident	Location	F	S
20.04.78	Boeing 707-321B	HL7429	19363	Korean Air Lines	Shot down by Soviet fighter & crash landed on frozen lake	Kem, RSFSR, USSR	2	109
20.04.78	Beechcraft King Air E90	TR-LYA	LW-247	Operator Unknown	Written off	Libreville, Gabon	*	*
24.04.78	Cessna 310	EP-JBC	*	Pars Air	Crashed	Ferdowsi, Iran	1	1
26.04.78	Swearingen Merlin IIIA	OY-ATW	T-261	Merlin Flite	Crashed	Gronholt, Denmark	*	*
27.04.78	Rockwell 1121A Jet Commander	N250UA	121	Universal Air Leasing	Crashed on take-off	Flatwood, LA, USA	2	*
28.04.78	Cessna 402A	ST-ADK	402A-0119	National Agriculture Organisation	Crashed	Malakal, Sudan	4	3
28.04.78	Cessna 402B	N3SP	402B-0930	South Pacific Island Airways	Crashed into mountain	nr Apia, Western Samoa	10	0
29.04.78	Douglas DC-6B	HK-1705	43565	Lineas Aereas del Caribe	Crashed after take-off	Bogota, Colombia	8	5
30.04.78	Douglas DC-7CF	N356AL	45228	J.McGeorge	Damaged on landing	Miami, FL, USA	0	*
05.05.78	Douglas C-118A Liftmaster	N3493F	44630	Surinam Airways	Crashed on approach	Zanderij, Surinam	0	*
05.05.78	Cessna 421 Golden Eagle	F-BOXS	*	Operator Unknown	Crashed onto road on approach	nr Milan, Italy	*	*
07.05.78	Aerospatiale 330J Puma	N49496	1463	Petroleum Helicopters	Crashed	Off Atlantic City, NJ, USA	2	*
08.05.78	Boeing 727-235	N4744	19464	National Airlines	Crashed	Pensacola Bay, FL, USA	3	55
10.05.78	Cessna 182	VH-UDM	*	Peninsula Air Services	Crashed	Tooraweenah, NSW, Australia	2	0
12.05.78	Convair 440-86	N9302	416	Argosy Airlines	Crashed after engine failure	Skippingport, PA, USA	*	*
16.05.78	Cessna 402B	N98720	402B-1065	Bar Harbor Airlines	Crashed short of runway	Trenton, ME, USA	4	0
18.05.78	Dassault Falcon 20C	N121GW	004	Flight Safety International	Crashed	Memphis, TN, USA	*	*
19.05.78	Douglas DC-3	VT-DEU	9952	Civil Aviation Department	Crashed	Barh Khalsa, India	7{1}	*
19.05.78	Tupolev TU-154B	SSSR-85169	*	Aeroflot	Crashed	Pochinok, RSFSR, USSR	4	130
21.05.78	Vickers PBY-5A Catalina	CF-NTL	CV383	Flying Fireman	Crashed	nr Snow Lake, MN, Canada	2	*
23.05.78	Douglas DC-6B	CP-1338	43566	Aerovias Las Minas	Crashed on take-off	Beni, Bolivia	3	2
23.05.78	Tupolev TU-144D	SSSR-77111	06-2	Aeroflot	Damaged on emergency landing after in-flight fire	Jegoriewskiem, RSFSR, USSR	3	0
25.05.78	Convair 880-22-2	N8815E	63	Groth Air	Crashed	Miami, FL, USA	0	*
25.05.78	Hughes 300	VH-THI	*	North Australia Helicopters	Crashed	Cooinda, NT, Australia	0	1
26.05.78	Rockwell 1121 Jet Commander	C-FEYG	081	Comstock International	Crashed on approach	Winnipeg, MN, Canada	0	2
27.05.78	Rockwell Turbo Commander 690A	N299F	11112	Operator Unknown	Written off	Calumet, OK, USA	*	*
29.05.78	Grumman TBM3 Avenger	C-FKCL	53638	Conair Aviation	Crashed after wing struck water	Oromcoto Lake, NB, Canada	0	*
29.05.78	Bell 206B JetRanger II	G-BAVI	00960	Trent Helicopters	Crashed	English Channel	4	0
30.05.78	Douglas DC-3	TG-LAM	14618/26063	Oneida	Crashed	nr Santo Tomas, Guatemala	*	*
30.05.78	Grumman TBM3 Avenger	C-GOBK	*	Conair Aviation	Crashed	Minto, NB, Canada	1	*
oo.05.78	Hamilton Westwind	5Y-ASF	BA-368	Caspair	Written off	Sudan	*	*
03.06.78	Bell 212	A6-BBJ	30800	Abu Dhabi Helicopters	Crashed into sea	Off Abu Dhabi, United Arab Emirates	15	0
04.06.78	Convair T-29C	RP-C12	412	Commercial Air Transport	Damaged when overran on landing	Roxas City, Philippines	*	*
08.06.78	Douglas DC-6B	TG-ADA	43531	Aviateca	Crashed & caught fire	Aurora, Guatemala	3	*
10.06.78	Vickers Viscount 814	9G-ACL	342	West African Air Cargo	Damaged when u/c collapsed on landing	Monrovia, Liberia	*	*
10.06.78	Fairchild C-119 Flying Boxcar	N3560	*	Hawkins & Powers Aviation	Belly landed	nr Greybull, WY, USA	3	0
10.06.78	Agusta-Bell 204B	HB-XCQ	*	Heliswiss	Crashed into cables	Disentis, Switzerland	*	*
14.06.78	Piper PA-28R-201T Cherokee Arrow	HK-1872I	28R-7703069	Aerocentro de Colombia	Crashed	nr Cali, Colombia	3	0
16.06.78	Noorduyn UC-64 Norseman	C-FISM	*	Operator Unknown	Crashed on take-off	Witchai Lake, MN, Canada	0	*
16.06.78	Piper PA-23-250E Aztec	S7-AAL	27-7305172	Inter Island Airways	Crashed in sea	Off Seychelles	*	*
22.06.78	Beechcraft King Air A100	N941K	B-111	Tennessee Valley Authority	Crashed	Muscle Shoals, AL, USA	0	5
22.06.78	Cessna 402	*	*	Operator Unknown	Crashed after take-off	Pottstown, PA, USA	5	0
23.06.78	Beechcraft Queen Air 80	C-GGAL	LD-233	Gander Aviation	Crashed after take-off	St Johns, NF, Canada	1	0
26.06.78	Sikorsky S-61N	LN-OQS	*	Helikopter Service	Crashed	Off Bergen, Norway	18	0
26.06.78	McDonnell Douglas DC-9-32	C-FTLV	47197	Air Canada	Crashed after aborted take-off	Malton, ON, Canada	2	105
30.06.78	Bell 206B JetRanger II	G-AZVN	00759	Gleneagles Helicopters	Crashed	Kippen, Stirlingshire, UK	*	*
oo.06.78	Douglas DC-6B	N111AQ	44871	Rosenbalm Aviation	Damaged in hangar explosion	Detroit, IL, USA	0	*
04.07.78	Cessna 180	EL-AFT	*	Monrovia Air Line	Crashed on landing	Kumbo, Liberia	0	*
06.07.78	Canadair CL-44D4-6	G-BCWJ	028	Tradewinds Airways	Damaged when u/c collapsed on landing	Nairobi, Kenya	0	*
07.07.78	Sikorsky S-62A	N54516	62079	Catalina Airlines	Crashed in sea	Off San Pedro, CA, USA	*	*
09.07.78	Douglas DC-3	N45873	12458	Operator Unknown	Crashed on take-off	Richmond, IN, USA	*	*
09.07.78	BAC One-Eleven 203AE	N1550	044	Allegheny Airlines	Damaged after overrunning on landing	Rochester, NY, USA	0	*
09.07.78	Beechcraft 18	HK-2114X	*	Lineas Aereas Orientales	Crashed	nr Esquinas, Colombia	2	0
10.07.78	Beechcraft King Air A90	N278DU	LJ-0243	Operator Unknown	Written off	Denver, CO, USA	*	*

Date	Type	Reg'n	C/n	Operator	Accident	Location	F	S
13.07.78	de Havilland Canada Twin Otter 300	N76214	236	Coastair	Crashed	Candor, NC, USA	5	0
14.07.78	Convair 440	N4809C	095	09 Charlie Inc	Crashed	Off Turks & Caicos Islands	*	*
14.07.78	Piper PA-31 Navajo	HC-BEP	*	Ecuavia	Crashed	nr El Coca, Ecuador	8	0
15.07.78	Westland-Bell 47G-3B1	HB-XFA	WA.584	Heliswiss	Mid-air collision with Pilatus B4-PC11 glider HB-1259	Sanetsch Pass, Switzerland	2(1)	0
17.07.78	de Havilland Canada Beaver	C-FTEB	*	La Sarre Air Services	Crashed into hill	nr Quebec, PQ, Canada	0	*
19.07.78	Lockheed 18 Lodestar	*	*	Operator Unknown	Landed on road & set on fire by drug smugglers	nr Hastings, FL, USA	0	0
20.07.78	Douglas DC-3	TG-PAW	10127	Aero Express	Crash landed	Lake Peten Itza, Guatemala	*	*
22.07.78	Curtiss C-46	N157K	436	R.A.Sayre	Crashed on single engine flight	nr Opa Locka, FL, USA	*	*
24.07.78	Britten-Norman Trislander	5Y-CMC	1032	Amphibians Ltd	Crashed	Nyeri Hill, Kenya	5	7
24.07.78	Convair 580	N4825C	380	North Central Airlines	Crashed on take-off due to engine failure	Kalamazoo, MI, USA	*	*
25.07.78	Grumman CS2F-1 Tracker	C-GHQZ	*	Conair Aviation	Crashed during demonstration flight	Castlegar, BC, Canada	1	*
26.07.78	Douglas DC-3	TG-ATA	*	Aviateca	Crash landed in swamp	nr Flores, Guatemala	*	*
28.07.78	Douglas DC-3	F-BIEE	14597/26042	M.Tesseydre	Crashed	Off Italy	*	*
31.07.78	Fairchild-Hiller FH.227B	C6-BDQ	518	Bahamasair	Crashed on take-off	Berry Is, Bahamas	0	*
oo.07.78	IRMA BN-2A-9 Islander	TN-ACO	0708	Department of Forests & Mines	Written off	Location Unknown	*	*
03.08.78	Boeing 707-351B	CC-CCX	18584	LAN-Chile	Crashed & caught fire on landing	Buenos Aires, Argentina	0	*
07.08.78	Piper PA-31 Navajo	N9093Y	31-128	Montauk-Caribbean Airways	Crashed short of runway	East Hampton, USA	*	*
10.08.78	IRMA BN-2A-21 Islander	PT-KRP	0743	ENCAL	Written off	Location Unknown	*	*
10.08.78	Piper PA-28 Cherokee	*	*	Crown International Airlines	Crashed	Off Cape Henry, VA, USA	0	*
11.08.78	Beechcraft King Air A100	N81MD	B-203	McDermott Inc	Damaged in forced landing after engine failure	nr Lagos, Nigeria	0	*
13.08.78	Swearingen 226TC Metro II	N300TL	TC-238E	Tejas Airlines	Crashed	Austin, TX, USA	*	*
13.08.78	Cessna U206A Super Skywagon	B-11102	U206-00635	Taiwan Aviation	Blown over on landing in storm	Green Island, Taiwan	1	5
14.08.78	Curtiss C-46	HK-1350	22557	Aeropesca	Crashed	Sogamoso, Bolivia	18	0
14.08.78	Grumman G-21 Goose	C-FGEC	B-098	West Coast Air Services	Crashed into bank	Powell River, BC, Canada	0	*
16.08.78	Cessna 402B	ZS-JDD	402B-0862	Suidwes Lugdiens	Crashed on take-off	Opuwa, Namibia	0	*
17.08.78	Douglas DC-3	G-AMSM	15764/27209	Skyways Cargo Airline	Overturned on landing	Lydd, Kent, UK	0	*
17.08.78	Rockwell Turbo Commander 680V	YV-O-MAR-2	1683-64	Operator Unknown	Written off	Venezuela	*	*
25.08.78	Mitsubishi MU-2J	N178MA	554	Operator Unknown	Written off	Raton, NJ, USA	*	*
25.08.78	Grumman G-21 Goose	N1045	1195	Webber Air	Crashed	Sumner Strait, AK, USA	11	0
26.08.78	de Havilland Canada Twin Otter 300	XY-AEI	541	Burma Airways	Crashed	Papun, Burma	14	*
26.08.78	Cessna 421B Golden Eagle	G-BAEI	421B-0259	Kenton Utilities	Crashed	Guecho, Spain	*	*
27.08.78	Douglas DC-6B	N122A	45327	New World Air Charter	Crashed into mountain	Mt Hameen, Oman	4	0
28.08.78	de Havilland Canada Twin Otter 300	C-FQDG	246	Bradley Air Services	Crashed into antenna	Frobisher Bay, Canada	1	*
28.08.78	Mitsubishi MU-2P	N765MA	372SA	Operator Unknown	Written off	nr Bedford, NH, USA	*	*
30.08.78	Piper PA-31-350 Chieftain	N44LV	*	Las Vegas Airlines	Crashed on take-off	Las Vegas, NV, USA	10	0
01.09.78	de Havilland Canada Beaver	C-FGCW	198	Airgava	Damaged in forced landing	Indian House Lake, PQ, Canada	0	*
02.09.78	de Havilland Canada Twin Otter 200	C-FAIV	215	AirWest Airlines	Crashed & sank	Coal Harbour, BC, Canada	11	2
02.09.78	Grumman G-21A Goose	N7777V	B-111	Antilles Air Boats	Crash landed after engine failure	Off St Thomas, US Virgin Is	4	0
03.09.78	Vickers Viscount 782D	VP-WAS	297	Air Rhodesia	Shot down by guerrillas [10 survivors shot after crash]	nr Kariba, Rhodesia	48	8
03.09.78	Ilyushin IL-18	3X-GAX	197009803	Air Guinee	Crashed	nr Bamako, Mali	15	2
04.09.78	Convair 240-8	N7177B	038	Mission Air Lift	Crashed on take-off due to fuel contamination	Clewiston, FL, USA	2	*
04.09.78	Cessna 421B Golden Eagle	G-AYMM	421B-0033	Pye of Cambridge	Crashed	Stansted, Essex, UK	1	*
05.09.78	Douglas DC-7CF	N244B	44876	Advance Aviation	Crashed & caught fire on drug smuggling flight	Farmerville, LA, USA	1	3
06.09.78	Convair 440-86	CP-924	425	North East Bolivian Airways	Crashed making emergency landing	Yacuma, Bolivia	*	*
06.09.78	Bell 206A JetRanger	LN-OQW	08287	Helitourist	Crashed into hill	Storefjell, Norway	*	*
07.09.78	British Aerospace 748 2	4R-ACJ	1571	Air Ceylon	Destroyed by terrorists	Ratmalana, Sri Lanka	0	*
09.09.78	de Havilland Canada Twin Otter 100	XA-BOP	018	Lineas Aereas del Centro	Crashed	nr Mexico City, Mexico	3	*
13.09.78	Beechcraft 18	HK-1850	BA-53	A.E.Colombia	Crashed	Isla de Providencia, Colombia	*	*
18.09.78	Douglas DC-3	C-FCRW	18958	Kenn Borek Air	Damaged beyond repair	Komakuk, NWT, Canada	*	*
21.09.78	Douglas DC-3	N407D	2244	Argosy Airlines	Crashed	Off Fort Lauderdale, FL, USA	*	*
24.09.78	Grumman Gulfstream I	N9'G	037	Continental Oil Corporation	Crashed	Houston, TX, USA	*	*
25.09.78	Douglas DC-3	G-BFPU	15247/26692	S.Macey	Forced landed & caught fire	Merowe, Sudan	0	*
25.09.78	Boeing 727-214	N533PS	19688	Pacific Southwest Airlines	Mid-air collision with Gibbs Flite Center C.172 N7711G	San Diego, CA, USA	135{7} (2)	0

Date	Type	Reg'n	C/n	Operator	Accident	Location	F	S
26.09.78	Beechcraft D18S	N500L	*	Mather Co	Crashed after being caught in wake of Tristar N335EA	Isla Verde, Puerto Rico	8	0
01.10.78	Douglas DC-3	N74Z	14508/25953	Evergreen Air	Crashed out of fuel	Off Fort Walton Beach, FL, USA	1	*
02.10.78	Yakovlev YAK-40	SSSR-87544	*	Aeroflot	Damaged in belly landing	Tblisi, Georgia, USSR	0	*
03.10.78	Fokker F-27 Friendship 600	XY-ADY	10572	Burma Airways	Crashed after take-off	Mandalay, Burma	2	43
05.10.78	Douglas DC-3	PK-NDI	19154	Merpati Nusantara Airlines	Caught fire while parked	Denpasar, Indonesia	*	*
07.10.78	Douglas DC-3	PT-KVU	12356	Con. Tec. Operacional de Aviacao	Overran & crashed	Belo Horizonte, Brazil	*	*
07.10.78	PADC BN-2A-21 Islander	RP-C2152	0487	Acme Plywood & Veneer Co	Crashed into mountain	Divilican Peak, Philippines	8	2
07.10.78	Yakovlev YAK-40	SSSR-87437	*	Aeroflot	Crashed after engine failure on take-off	Sverdlovsk, RSFSR, USSR	38	0
13.10.78	de Havilland Canada Twin Otter 200	N4048B	125	Arctic Guide	Crashed on approach	Barrow, AK, USA	*	*
15.10.78	Douglas DC-3	ET-AGK	15020/26465	Ethiopian Airlines	Crashed on landing	Sodo, Ethiopia	*	*
15.10.78	Lockheed 1049H Super Constellation	N6924C	4852	Operator Unknown	Crashed due to premature u/c retraction on take-off	Rio Hacha, Colombia	1	2
17.10.78	Gates Learjet 24	N123RE	24-154	Martin Aviation	Crashed	Lancaster, CA, USA	1	1
17.10.78	Britten-Norman BN-2A-27R Islander	HC-BFI	0588	Operator Unknown	Written off	Location Unknown	*	*
21.10.78	Gates Learjet 25	N100MK	25-019	M.J.Kelly & Co	Crashed	Sandusky, OH, USA	3	*
22.10.78	IRMA BN-2A Islander	H4-AAC	0613	Solomon Islands Airlines	Crashed	Off Bellona, Solomon Islands	11	0
23.10.78	Antonov AN-24	SSSR-46327	97305504	Aeroflot	Crashed	Sivash Gulf, Ukraine, USSR	26	*
25.10.78	Douglas DC-3	ET-AGQ	12278	Ethiopian Airlines	Ground looped & hit ditch after brake failure	Degahabour, Ethiopia	*	*
31.10.78	Cessna 402	PT-JXL	*	Taxi Aereo Kovacs	Crashed	nr Belem, Brazil	9	0
oo.10.78	Beechcraft King Air A100	CN-ANA	B-180	Moroccan Government	Written off	Morocco	*	*
03.11.78	Cessna 402B	YV-O-CDO-2	402B-0223	Operator Unknown	Written off	Location Unknown	*	*
03.11.78	Cessna 421 Golden Eagle	D-IDAS	*	Operator Unknown	Crashed in fog	Schwabische Hall, West Germany	4	*
04.11.78	Embraer Bandeirante 110C	PT-TBF	110.018	Nordeste	Crashed	Montes Claros, Brazil	*	*
05.11.78	Douglas DC-3	*	*	Nile Delta Air Services	Crashed	Off Alexandria, Egypt	18	*
05.11.78	Grumman G-21A Goose	N74676	1172	Antilles Air Boats	Crashed after engine failure	Off St Croix, US Virgin Is	0	3
06.11.78	Sikorsky S-55BT	C-GHKR	55750	Quasar Aviation	Crashed after tail rotor failure	nr Quesnel, BC, Canada	0	*
10.11.78	Martin 404	N13415	14290	J.Whaley	Crashed	Off Punta Fija, Venezuela	*	*
11.11.78	Rockwell Turbo Commander 680W	N94HD	1811-28	Operator Unknown	Written off	Location Unknown	*	*
13.11.78	Piper PA-31-350 Chieftain	TR-LTQ	31-7405480	Air Inter Gabon	Crashed & exploded	Ghana/Ivory Coast border	4	0
14.11.78	Douglas DC-3	4W-ABY	13174	Yemen Airlines	Damaged in heavy landing	Marib, Yemen Arab Republic	*	*
16.11.78	McDonnell Douglas DC-8-63CF	TF-FLA	46020	Loftleidir	Crashed into trees on approach	Colombo, Sri Lanka	184	78
16.11.78	Beechcraft 18	N901PC	BA-555	Festus Flying Service	Crashed	nr Hays, KS, USA	2	*
18.11.78	de Havilland Canada Twin Otter 300	F-OGHD	469	Air Guadeloupe	Crashed	Off Marie Galante Island,	15	5
21.11.78	Douglas DC-3	HK-1393	19053	Aerotal	Crashed	Judio, Venezuela	27	0
21.11.78	Beechcraft 18	N204CC	BA-733	Operator Unknown	Crashed on approach in fog	Brownsville, TX, USA	*	*
21.11.78	Cessna A185F	HK-1720	185-02620	Lineas Aereas del Uraba	Crashed	San Jeronimo, Colombia	6	0
22.11.78	Swearingen Merlin IIA	N2301N	T26-002	Operator Unknown	Crashed	Olive Branch, MS, USA	1	*
22.11.78	Bell 212	C-GBHL	30716	Bow Helicopters	Crashed into mountain	Castlegar, BC, Canada	1	0
29.11.78	Convair 240	LV-MMR	*	J.M.Cuadros	Crashed on take-off	Tamiami, FL, USA	*	*
02.12.78	Douglas DC-3	N41447	12987	SMB Stage Lines	Crashed on landing	Des Moins, IA, USA	*	*
04.12.78	de Havilland Canada Twin Otter 300	N25RM	387	Rocky Mountain Airways	Crashed due to icing	Steamboat Springs, CO, USA	2	20
04.12.78	Gates Learjet 25C	N77RS	25C-094	R.Sykes	Crashed on landing in high winds	Anchorage, AK, USA	5	2
06.12.78	Douglas DC-3	N25656	4845	Caribe Air Sales	Crashed on take-off	Lorida, FL, USA	3	*
08.12.78	Douglas DC-6B	HK-1707	44687	Lineas Aereas del Caribe	Crashed	Sierra Cocuy, Colombia	3	0
08.12.78	Douglas C-118A Liftmaster	N96040	44659	Aerovias Las Minas	Crashed	Colombia	*	*
09.12.78	Antonov AN-26	SSSR-26547	*	Aeroflot	Crashed on take-off	Chersky, RSFSR, USSR	5	*
11.12.78	Douglas DC-3	N133AC	6260	Aircraft Sales & Leasing	Crashed out of fuel on smuggling flight	Port Macaya, FL, USA	2	*
14.12.78	Douglas DC-3	N4996E	12141	J.Rodriguez	Ground looped on smuggling flight	Battle Creek, FL, USA	*	*
14.12.78	IRMA BN-2A-6 Islander	G-BELN	0830	Britten-Norman	Damaged in storm	Bembridge, IoW, UK	0	*
14.12.78	IRMA BN-2A-6 Islander	G-BESE	0844	Britten-Norman	Damaged in storm	Bembridge, IoW, UK	0	*
14.12.78	IRMA BN-2A-6 Islander	G-BESK	0850	Britten-Norman	Damaged in storm	Bembridge, IoW, UK	0	*
14.12.78	IRMA BN-2A-6 Islander	G-BFNL	0871	Britten-Norman	Damaged in storm	Bembridge, IoW, UK	0	*
16.12.78	Cessna 421 Golden Eagle	I-ASON	*	Air 70	Crashed	Selvapiana, Italy	10	0
17.12.78	Fokker F-27 Friendship 200	AP-ATO	10250	Pakistan International Airlines	Crashed	Karachi, Pakistan	1	1
17.12.78	Boeing 737-2A8	VT-EAL	20485	Indian Airlines	Crashed & caught fire	Hyderabad, India	0(3)	126

Date	Type	Reg'n	C/n	Operator	Accident	Location	F	S
18.12.78	Cessna 421 Golden Eagle	D-INUR	*	Operator Unknown	Crashed into sea	Off Palermo, Sicily, Italy	*	*
18.12.78	de Havilland Riley Heron	N3FB	14111	Fischer Brothers Aviation	Crashed	Cleveland, OH, USA	*	*
19.12.78	Antonov AN-24V	SSSR-46299	77303901	Aeroflot	Crashed on single engine approach	Samarkand, Uzbekistan, USSR	5	0
23.12.78	McDonnell Douglas DC-9-32	I-DIKQ	47227	Alitalia	Crashed in sea on approach	Palermo, Sicily, Italy	108	21
26.12.78	Gates Learjet 25C	PT-JDX	25C-131	Hidroservice Engenharia de Projetos	Crashed on take-off	Congonhas, Brazil	*	*
26.12.78	Britten-Norman BN-2A-21 Islander	HH-CNB	0442	Haiti Air Inter	Crashed	Off Turks & Caicos Is	*	*
29.12.78	McDonnell Douglas DC-8-61	N8082U	45972	United Air Lines	Crashed out of fuel	Portland, OR, USA	10	179
30.12.78	Beechcraft King Air C90	N2029N	LJ-0798	Operator Unknown	Written off	Houston, TX, USA	*	*
00.00.78	Douglas DC-3	F-BCYX	10144	Trans Europe Air	Written off	Dinard, France	*	*
00.00.78	Consolidated Privateer	N6813D	*	Hawkins & Powers Aviation	Ran off runway on landing & ran into sea	Port Hardy, BC, Canada	0	*
00.00.78	Sikorsky HSS-1N	TI-SPJ	*	Costa Rican Ministry of Security	Crashed	Costa Rica	*	*
01.01.79	Beechcraft Queen Air	N777AE	*	Universal Air Taxi	Crashed into swamp after take-off	Gulfport, MS, USA	7	0
02.01.79	Ilyushin IL-14	*	*	Aeroflot	Crashed	Moldezhnaya, Antarctica	2	5
02.01.79	Antonov AN-2R	HA-MDJ	IG181-41	Air Service Hungary	Crashed	Hungary	*	*
05.01.79	Lockheed Electra 188PF	N403GN	1127	Great Northern Airlines	Crashed	North Slope, AK, USA	*	*
07.01.79	Beechcraft King Air E90	N777EC	LW-037	Operator Unknown	Destroyed in hangar fire	New York, USA	*	*
10.01.79	Douglas DC-3	N9025R	4998	Waggoner Aircraft	Damaged on landing	Southbay, FL, USA	*	*
12.01.79	Douglas C-54D	CP-1352	10761	Transportes Aereos Kentuta	Crashed	San Borja, Bolivia	0	*
12.01.79	Britten-Norman BN-2A-8 Islander	D-IEDA	0437	Frisia Luftwerkhe Norddeich	Written off	Location Unknown	*	*
15.01.79	Beechcraft King Air C90	OY-AZA	LJ-0593	Danish Inter Flight	Crashed	Kongelunden, Denmark	*	*
15.01.79	Antonov AN-24V	SSSR-46807	*	Aeroflot	Crashed	nr Minsk, Byelorussia, USSR	13	0
16.01.79	Beechcraft King Air C90	N88CR	LJ-0514	Operator Unknown	Crashed on approach in bad weather	Houston, TX, USA	1	*
18.01.79	LET 410M Turbolet	SSSR-67210	760513	Aeroflot	Crashed	nr Belgorod, RSFSR, USSR	3	0
19.01.79	Gates Learjet 25D	N137GL	25D-237	Operator Unknown	Crashed	Detroit, MI, USA	6	*
19.01.79	Mitsubishi MU-2G	N115S	518	Operator Unknown	Written off	Hawesville, KY, USA	*	*
21.01.79	Pilatus Porter	*	*	Thai Police	Crashed & caught fire	Sakhon, Thailand	4	0
23.01.79	Sikorsky S-58	EC-CYJ	*	Operator Unknown	Damaged on deck of *Macoma*	Off Punta de Gando, Spain	*	*
23.01.79	Mitsubishi MU-2J	N5NW	597	Operator Unknown	Written off	Searcy, AR, USA	*	*
24.01.79	Nord 262A-44	7T-VSU	019	Air Algerie	Crashed	Algeria	13	14
26.01.79	British Aerospace 125-1A-522	N3MF	25093	Big Six General Partnership	Damaged beyond repair	New Mexico, USA	*	*
28.01.79	Fokker F-27 Friendship 500	F-BYAH	10570	Air Rouergue	Crashed	nr Rodez, France	5	1
28.01.79	Douglas DC-3	ET-AGP	15030/26475	Ethiopian Airlines	Crashed	Tessenei, Ethiopia	*	*
30.01.79	Boeing 707-323C	PP-VLU	19235	Varig	Crashed	Off Japan	6	0
05.02.79	Antonov AN-2P	SP-BSF	*	Polish Agricultural Aviation	Crashed	Mt Bjelasnica, Yugoslavia	3	0
08.02.79	Embraer Bandeirante 110C	PP-SBB	110.010	TAM Linha Aerea Regional	Crashed	nr Agudos, Brazil	18	0
09.02.79	McDonnell Douglas DC-9-14	N8910E	45771	Eastern Air Lines	Crashed during touch-and-go landing	Dade-Collier, FL, USA	0	*
12.02.79	Vickers Viscount 748D	VP-YND	101	Air Rhodesia	Shot down by guerrillas	nr Kariba, Rhodesia	59	0
12.02.79	Mohawk 298	N29824	048	Allegheny Airlines	Crashed on take-off in snowstorm	Clarksburg, WV, USA	2	23
13.02.79	de Havilland Canada Twin Otter 200	VH-PAQ	227	Pan-Air	Crashed out of fuel	King Island, Tas, Australia	*	*
14.02.79	Rockwell Turbo Commander 690	OB-M-1031	11008	Operator Unknown	Written off	Peru	*	*
17.02.79	Fokker F-27 Friendship 500	ZK-NFC	10456	Air New Zealand	Crashed	Auckland Harbour, New Zealand	2	2
19.02.79	Douglas DC-3	ET-AFW	16681/33429	Ethiopian Airlines	Crashed after bomb explosion	Barentu, Ethiopia	5	0
19.02.79	Boeing 707-123B	C-GQBH	17650	Quebecair	Damaged on landing	Hewanorra, St Lucia	0	*
21.02.79	Lockheed 18-56 Lodestar	N100GP	2571	Operator Unknown	Crashed due to icing	Truckee, CA, USA	*	*
24.02.79	Beechcraft 58 Baron	N17574	TH-800	Catskill Airways	Crashed on approach	Oneonta, NY, USA	*	*
26.02.79	Douglas DC-6B	TR-LXN	45108	Air Gabon	Crashed	nr Moanda, Gabon	3	0
27.02.79	Beechcraft E-18S	N711TL	BA-317	Burlington Airways	Written off	Indianapolis, IN, USA	*	*
07.03.79	Fokker F-28 Fellowship 1000	PK-GVP	11094	Garuda Indonesian Airlines	Crashed in storm	Mt Bromo, Indonesia	4	0
10.03.79	Nord 262A-33	N418SA	041	Swift Aire	Crashed after double engine failure	Off Los Angeles, CA, USA	3	4
12.03.79	Aerospatiale Caravelle 3	F-BHRL	031	Air France	Damaged in collision with fence	Frankfurt, West Germany	0	*
13.03.79	Cessna 340A	HK-2064	340A-0446	Tavina	Crashed	San Francisco, Colombia	4	0
14.03.79	Boeing 727-2D3A	JY-ADU	20886	Alia	Crashed on approach in storm	Doha, Qatar	45	16
14.03.79	Hawker Siddeley Trident 2E	B-274	2172	CAAC	Crashed after being stolen by unqualified pilot	Beijing, China	12{32}	0
17.03.79	de Havilland Canada Caribou	C-GVYW	*	Operator Unknown	Crashed due to engine failure	Off Bridgetown, Barbados	3	0

Date	Type	Reg'n	C/n	Operator	Accident	Location	F	S
17.03.79	Tupolev TU-104B	SSSR-42444	*	Aeroflot	Crashed attempting forced landing	Moscow, RSFSR, USSR	59	0
20.03.79	Yakovlev YAK-40	SSSR-87930	*	Aeroflot	Crashed on approach after being caught in wake of Mi-6	Chardzhov, Turkmenistan, USSR	*	*
22.03.79	Tupolev TU-134	SSSR-65031	*	Aeroflot	Crashed on approach	Liepaya, Latvia, USSR	4	1
22.03.79	SIAI-Marchetti S.208	ET-ADK	1-08	Admas Air Service	Damaged in belly landing	Dire Dawa, Ethiopia	*	*
25.03.79	Antonov AN-26	SSSR-26569	*	Aeroflot	Crashed on approach	Baykit, RSFSR, USSR	4	*
26.03.79	Ilyushin IL-18D	DM-STL	186009402	Interflug	Crashed on take-off	Luanda, Angola	6	0
28.03.79	Bell 206B JetRanger II	A6-BCC	*	Abu Dhabi Helicopters	Overturned & sank	Off Abu Dhabi, United Arab Emirates	*	*
29.03.79	de Havilland Heron 2D	N19D	14109	Air Pacific	Crashed	Pacific Ocean	*	*
29.03.79	Fairchild F-27	C-FQBL	0047	Quebecair	Crashed on go-around after engine failure on take-off	Ste Foy, PQ, Canada	17	7
30.03.79	Aerospatiale Corvette	TN-ADB	22	Aero Service Corporation	Crashed	Nkayi, Congo	*	*
01.04.79	Boeing 707-321C	5X-UAL	18580	Uganda Airlines	Damaged by gunfire during Tanzanian attack	Entebbe, Uganda	*	*
04.04.79	Beechcraft G18S	N149PA	*	Providence Air Charter	Crashed on approach	Stewart AFB, NY, USA	*	*
05.04.79	Beechcraft G18S	N145PA	*	Providence Air Charter	Crashed off runway on take-off	Newburgh, NY, USA	*	*
09.04.79	Mitsubishi MU-2B	N251M	013	Operator Unknown	Written off	Gardnerm KS, USA	*	*
14.04.79	Grumman G-21A Goose	*	*	Catalina Airlines	Crashed	Off Santa Catalina Is, CA, USA	1	10
17.04.79	Sikorsky S-61	N618PA	61-426	New York Airways	Crashed	Newark, NJ, USA	3	15
18.04.79	Vickers PBY-5A Catalina	CC-CDS	CV281	Aeroservicios Parrague	Crashed	Chiguayante, Chile	*	*
18.04.79	Piper PA-23 Aztec	C-GPCA	*	Pacific Coastal Airlines	Crashed	Cassidy, BC, Canada	6	0
20.04.79	Fairchild F-27A	CC-CBR	0055	Aero Nortesur	Crash landed after engine failure on take-off	Iquique, Chile	0	*
20.04.79	Howard 250	N48RM	*	Operator Unknown	Crashed	nr Tampico, Mexico	*	*
21.04.79	Mitsubishi MU-2F	N304L	137	Operator Unknown	Crashed after take-off	Marsh Harbour, Bahamas	1	*
23.04.79	Vickers Viscount 785D	HC-AVP	329	Saeta	Crashed	nr Cuenca, Ecuador	57	0
23.04.79	Aerospatiale SA.316B Lama	TS-HSU	2321	Tunisavia	Exploded & crashed	Off Sfax, Tunisia	4	0
26.04.79	Boeing 737-2A8A	VT-ECR	20962	Indian Airlines	Overshot on landing after explosion	Madras, India	0	67
26.04.79	IRMA BN-2A-21 Islander	PK-KNG	0749	Bali Air	Crashed	Beoganon, Indonesia	*	*
01.05.79	Beechcraft King Air 90	C-FCAS	LJ-0023	Operator Unknown	Crashed when wing broke-up	Sherrington, PQ, Canada	2	*
05.05.79	Agusta-Bell 206B JetRanger II	HB-XDP	*	Heliba Helikopter	Crashed when skid got caught on take-off	Les Mosses Pass, Switzerland	0	1
07.05.79	Douglas DC-3	TG-SAB	*	Tapsa	Crashed	Location Unknown	*	*
10.05.79	Ilyushin IL-18	SSSR-75414	186009303	Aeroflot	Crashed after aborting take-off	Sochi, RSFSR, USSR	*	*
15.05.79	Douglas DC-3	CC-CBO	6190	Aerolineas Cordillera	Force-landed	Coyhaique, Chile	*	*
15.05.79	Douglas C-54Q	N44905	22159	Globe Air	Overran on take-off & caught fire	Mesa-Falcon, AZ, USA	*	*
15.05.79	Britten-Norman Trislander	G-BCYC	1011	Loganair	Crashed	Aberdeen, UK	*	*
16.05.79	Lockheed L-100-30 Hercules	D2-FAF	4176	TAAG Angola Airlines	Crashed on landing	Sao Tome, Sao Tome & Principe	0	*
17.05.79	Douglas DC-4	*	*	Bush Aviation	Crashed after fire	Gulf of Mexico	0	3
19.05.79	Tupolev TU-134A	SSSR-65839	*	Aeroflot	Caught fire after overrunning on landing	Ufa, RSFSR, USSR	0	*
25.05.79	McDonnell Douglas DC-10-10	N110AA	46510	American Airlines	Crashed after engine detached on take-off	Chicago, IL, USA	271{2}	0
25.05.79	Beechcraft D18S	N1812D	A-0826	Operator Unknown	Crashed	nr Charleston, WV, USA	*	*
26.05.79	SAI KZ.IV	OY-DIZ	43	Aero-Kort	Crashed	Geding Mose, Denmark	*	*
27.05.79	de Havilland Canada Buffalo 5D	5T-MAX	088	Mauritanian Air Force	Crashed [Often reported as Caravelle 5T-RIM in error]	Off Dakar, Senegal	12	0
28.05.79	Hughes 500	PT-HIP	*	VOTEC	Crashed after striking power lines	nr Itabirito, Brazil	4	0
30.05.79	Cessna 402B	*	*	Business Jets	Crashed into forest	nr Mt Sorrell, Tas, Australia	0	*
31.05.79	Tupolev TU-134A	SSSR-65649	0351005	Aeroflot	U/c collapsed on take-off	Tumen, RSFSR, USSR	0	*
31.05.79	Swearingen Merlin IIIB	N5654M	T-303	Operator Unknown	Written off	San Marcos, TX, USA	*	*
01.06.79	Douglas C-54A	C-FQIX	7476	Aero Trades Western	Destroyed after engine caught fire on take-off	Thomson, MN, USA	0	*
06.06.79	Douglas DC-6B	AN-BFN	45322	Operator Unknown	Crash landed & caught fire on drug smuggling flight	Kanawha, WV, USA	0	8
09.06.79	Beechcraft 99	N454SA	U054	Skystream Airlines	Crashed	nr Chicago, IL, USA	*	*
11.06.79	Douglas DC-3	N148Z	20422	US Forest Service	Crashed	Selway River, ID, USA	10	2
11.06.79	Cessna 404 Titan	HB-LKO	404-0246	Jonathan Airways	Crashed into building on approach	Annemasse, France	1	*
11.06.79	de Havilland Canada Beaver	N68084	*	Kenmore Air Harbor	Crashed at sea	Maurelle Is, BC, Canada	1	0
12.06.79	Douglas DC-3	N427W	13825/43073	Bradley Aviation	Crashed on take-off	Fort Lauderdale, FL, USA	2	0
12.06.79	Britten-Norman BN-2A-6 Islander	PT-IJE	0304	VOTEC	Written off	Location Unknown	*	*
13.06.79	Aerospatiale SA.315B Lama	OE-EXI	2451	Heliaustria Helikoptergesellschaft	Crashed into mountains	nr Salzburg, Austria	1	2
14.06.79	Douglas C-54Q	N44904	10862	Globe Air	Crashed after fire	Eagle Lake, ME, USA	0	*

Date	Type	Reg'n	C/n	Operator	Accident	Location	F	S
15.06.79	Grumman TBM3 Avenger	C-FAXS	*	Conair Aviation	Crashed into trees	nr Serogle, NB, Canada	*	*
20.06.79	Cessna 206 Super Skywagon	HK-1289	*	Aerotaxi Casanare	Crashed	Vanpes, Colombia	2	0
21.06.79	Lockheed C-121A Constellation	C-GXKS	2609	Beaver Air Spray	Overran & caught fire	Riviere du Loup, PQ, Canada	0	*
24.06.79	Douglas DC-7CF	N357AL	45229	Go Transportation	Crashed after take-off	Barstow, CA, USA	5	1
28.06.79	Consolidated Catalina	N101CS	*	J.Cousteau	Crashed on landing [Explorer Phillipe Cousteau killed]	Nr Alverca, Portugal	1	*
oo.06.79	Hawker Siddeley Argosy C.1	9Q-CCE	6778	OTRAG Range Air Services	Damaged beyond repair	Lubumbashi, Zaire	*	*
oo.06.79	Cessna Citation I	YV-O-MAC-1	500-0336	Ministerio de Agricultura y Cria	Crashed	Caracas, Venezuela	*	*
01.07.79	Zlin Z-37 Cmelak	OK-ZSO	*	Slovair	Crashed	Roudnice, Czechoslovakia	1	0
05.07.79	Fairchild F-27A	F-GBRS	0108	Touraine Air Transport	Damaged beyond repair	Paris, France	0	*
06.07.79	Gates Learjet 25B	N40BC	25B-128	Chapman Commodities	Crashed	Pueblo, CO, USA	*	*
08.07.79	Beechcraft Queen Air A80	G-BDKG	LD-194	Vernair Transport	Damaged beyond repair	Karachi, Pakistan	*	*
11.07.79	Fokker F-28 Fellowship 1000	PK-GVE	11055	Garuda Indonesian Airlines	Crashed in bad weather	Mt Sibayak, Indonesia	61	0
12.07.79	Britten-Norman BN-2A-7 Islander	DQ-FBO	0195	Fiji Air	Crashed into jungle	nr Bua, Fiji	9	0
15.07.79	British Aerospace 748 2A	C-GPAA	1675	Austin Airways	Destroyed by fire after explosion on ground	Moosonee, ON, Canada	0	*
20.07.79	Douglas C-118A Liftmaster	N43865	44657	Kimex Inc	Crashed	Off Kingston, Jamaica	2	2
20.07.79	Aerospatiale Caravelle 6R	HK-1778	140	Aerotal	Broke in two on landing	Bogota, Colombia	0	*
20.07.79	Douglas DC-3	N63250	17062/34329	Trans National Airlines	Crashed	Between California & Hawaii, USA	2	0
23.07.79	GAF Nomad 22B	PK-MAJ	028	Missionary Aviation Fellowship	Crashed	West Irian, Indonesia	*	*
23.07.79	Boeing 707-327C	OD-AFX	19107	Trans Mediterranean Airways	Crashed on landing	Beirut, Lebanon	6	0
24.07.79	de Havilland Heron 2D	N575PR	14125	Prinair	Crashed on take-off	St Croix, US Virgin Islands	9	11
25.07.79	Douglas DC-3	N1047G	4812	Universal Pictures	Destroyed for film purposes	Bahamas	0	*
26.07.79	Boeing 707-330C	D-ABUY	20395	Lufthansa	Caught fire & crashed after take-off	Serra dos Macacos, Brazil	3	0
27.07.79	de Havilland Canada Twin Otter 100	TF-JME	098	Flugfelag Nordurlands	Damaged by fire while refuelling	Dane Berg, Greenland	*	*
31.07.79	British Aerospace 748 1	G-BEKF	1542	Dan-Air	Crashed in sea after overrunning	Sumburgh, Shetlands, UK	17	30
31.07.79	Bell 212	LN-CRL	30579	Helikopter Service	Crashed in sea	Off Stavanger, Norway	3	0
oo.07.79	Douglas DC-6B	N19CA	43744	New World Air Charter	Damaged beyond repair	Larnaca, Cyprus	*	*
02.08.79	Cessna Citation I	N15NY	501-0110	Operator Unknown	Crashed	Akron, OH, USA	*	*
03.08.79	Mitsubishi MU-2B	N208MA	016	Operator Unknown	Crashed on approach	Fort Hayes, KS, USA	7	0
03.08.79	LET 410M Turbolet	SSSR-67206	760509	Aeroflot	Crashed due to engine failure on approach	Leningrad, RSFSR, USSR	14	*
04.08.79	Hindustan 748 2-224	VT-DXJ	515	Indian Airlines	Crashed into hill	nr Panvel, India	45	0
05.08.79	Beechcraft King Air C90	N6040M	LJ-0840	Operator Unknown	Crashed out of fuel	Indianapolis, IN, USA	1	*
07.08.79	Britten-Norman BN-2A Islander	G-AXWG	0135	Harvest Air	Sank in snow on landing & abandoned	Greenland	0	*
08.08.79	Sikorsky S-62	*	*	Court Helicopters	Crashed after engine failure	Off Algoa Bay, South Africa	1	9
08.08.79	Westland SA.341G Gazelle	HB-XFW	WA.1124	Air Grischa	Crashed	San Bernadino, Switzerland	*	*
09.08.79	Mitsubishi MU-2P	D-IHAN	396SA	Operator Unknown	Written off	Steinhausen, West Germany	*	*
09.08.79	Beechcraft B55 Baron	N205AC	TE-614	Southern Jersey Airways	Crashed on take-off	La Guardia, NY, USA	3	0
10.08.79	Agusta-Bell 206B JetRanger II	LN-ORQ	*	Lufttransport	Crashed	nr Hornsund, Svalbard, Norway	1	1
11.08.79	Tupolev TU-134A	SSSR-65735	2351516	Aeroflot	Mid-air collision with Aeroflot TU-134 CCCP-65816	nr Donetsk, Ukraine, USSR	84(94)	0
11.08.79	Tupolev TU-134A	SSSR-65816	*	Aeroflot	Mid-air collision with Aeroflot TU-134 CCCP-65735	nr Donetsk, Ukraine, USSR	94(84)	0
11.08.79	Gates Learjet 35	N711AF	35-029	Bahri Aviation	Crashed [Found 06.03.87]	South of Katab, Egypt	*	*
15.08.79	Sikorsky S-55T	SE-HHY	55-1186	Norrlandsflyg	Crashed into lake	Sitasjaure, Sweden	6	0
19.08.79	Boeing 707-123B	5B-DAM	17628	Cyprus Airways	Damaged on landing	Manama, Bahrain	0	*
20.08.79	Bell 47J-2A	5N-ACS	2854	Pan African Airlines	Crashed	Nigeria	1	0
22.08.79	British Aerospace 748 2A	FAC.1101	1702	Satena	Crashed after being stolen by unqualified pilot	Bogota, Colombia	1(3)	0
23.08.79	Gates Learjet 24D	PT-DZU	24D-244	Lider Taxi Aereo	Crashed	Sao Paulo, Brazil	*	*
23.08.79	Antonov AN-12	SSSR-12963	*	Aeroflot	Crashed in wood	nr Enisseysk, RSFSR, USSR	11	5
25.08.79	de Havilland Canada Caribou	N531PA	253	Sea Airmotive	Crashed	nr Bullen Point, AK, USA	3	*
29.08.79	de Havilland Canada Twin Otter 300	C-GROW	415	Bradley Air Services	Crashed on landing	Frobisher Bay, NWT, Canada	9	*
29.08.79	Tupolev TU-124	SSSR-45038	3351003	Aeroflot	Crashed	nr Kirsanov, RSFSR, USSR	63	0
30.08.79	Grumman G-21A Goose	C-FUVJ	B-006	Trans Provincial Airlines	Crashed	nr Prince Rupert, BC, Canada	7	0
30.08.79	de Havilland Canada Otter	*	*	Newfoundland Labrador Air Transport	Crashed into hill on approach	Frobisher Bay, NWT, Canada	9	0
31.08.79	Douglas DC-3	HI-237	2107	Alas del Caribe	Damaged beyond repair by hurricane	Dominican Republic	0	*
31.08.79	Curtiss C-46	HI-189	101	A.Canaan	Damaged by being blown onto roof of building by hurricane	Santo Domingo, Dominican Republic	0	*

Date	Type	Reg'n	C/n	Operator	Accident	Location	F	S
31.08.79	Lockheed 049 Constellation	HI-260	2070	Aerovias Quisqueyana	Damaged beyond repair by hurricane	Santo Domingo, Dominican Republic	0	*
03.09.79	Aerospatiale Corvette	CY-SBS	21	Sterling Airways	Crashed on approach	Nice, France	10	*
03.09.79	Beechcraft King Air 90	N332K	LJ-0079	Operator Unknown	Written off	Laredo, TX, USA	*	*
03.09.79	Antonov AN-24	SSSR-46269	77303602	Aeroflot	Crash landed	Aderma, RSFSR, USSR	40	3
03.09.79	Aerospatiale AS.350 Ecureuil	SE-HIP	*	Norrlandsflyg	Crashed in mountains	Arjeplog, Sweden	1	0
05.09.79	Douglas DC-7	N4SW	44287	Butler Aviation	Crashed	nr Klamath Falls, OR, USA	12	0
09.09.79	Britten-Norman BN-2A-8 Islander	B-11107	0335	Taiwan Airlines	Collided with Yung Shing Ce.404 B-12204 on take-off	Lan-yu, Taiwan	0(*)	*
11.09.79	Boeing 707-324C	B-1834	18887	China Airlines	Crashed in sea after take-off	Off Taipei, Taiwan	6	0
12.09.79	Curtiss C-46	N7768B	467	Rich International Airways	Crashed in shallow water	Off Bahamas	0	3
12.09.79	Aerospatiale Caravelle 6R	HC-BFN	137	Servicios Aereos Nacionales	Damaged beyond repair	Ecuador	*	*
14.09.79	McDonnell Douglas DC-9-32	I-ATJC	47667	Aero Transporti Italiani	Crashed into mountain	nr Cagliari, Sardinia, Italy	31	0
14.09.79	IRMA BN-2A-20 Islander	P2-ISL	0806	Talair	Dropped by RAAF Chinook while being airlifted for repair	nr Wanuma, Papua New Guinea	0	0
15.09.79	Beechcraft 18	N600NA	AF-726	Operator Unknown	Crashed after wing fire	nr Hastings, MI, USA	4	0
18.09.79	Britten-Norman BN-2A-7 Islander	C-FZVV	0238	Pacific Coastal Airlines	Crashed	Blink Horn Point, BC, Canada	4	5
21.09.79	Douglas DC-3	ET-AGU	13026	Ethiopian Airlines	Crashed on landing	Barentu, Ethiopia	*	*
25.09.79	Beechcraft Super King Air 200	G-BGHR	BB-0508	Eagle Aircraft Services	Crashed after crew became incapaciatated	nr Nantes, France	2	0
28.09.79	Lockheed C-130H Hercules	CP-1375	4744	Transporte Aereo Boliviano	Crashed on take-off	Tocumen, Panama	4	0
28.09.79	Curtiss C-46	N10624	*	Miami Air Lease	Crashed	Off San Andros Is, Bahamas	0	*
30.09.79	de Havilland Canada Twin Otter 200	C-FWAF	122	West Coast Air Services	Crashed	Porpoise Bay, BC, Canada	1	6
oo.09.79	Cessna 441 Conquest II	N88832	0071	Operator Unknown	Stolen & written off	Location Unknown	*	*
01.10.79	Rockwell Turbo Commander 690A	N57233	11247	Operator Unknown	Written off	Columbus, OH, USA	*	*
05.10.79	Britten-Norman BN-2A Islander	P2-ATU	0119	Douglas Airways	Written off	Location Unknown	*	*
07.10.79	McDonnell Douglas DC-8-62	HB-IDE	45919	Swissair	Overran & crashed	Athens, Greece	14	140
08.10.79	Grumman G-21A Goose	C-FBXR	*	Trans Provincial Airlines	Hit log on take-off & later sank	Fern Passage, BC, Canada	0	*
08.10.79	Piper PA-31 Navajo	N5642L	31-580	Comair Air Taxi	Crashed after take-off	Cincinnati, OH, USA	9	0
08.10.79	Cessna 207 Skywagon	N6424H	*	Spernak Airways	Crashed into hangar	Anchorage, AK, USA	4	0
09.10.79	Canadair CL-44-6	CX-BXD	008	ALAS	U/c collapsed on landing & broken up to clear runway	Montevideo, Uruguay	0	*
09.10.79	de Havilland Canada Beaver	C-GPVE	*	Great Shield Air	Crashed	Otter Lake, SK, Canada	6	0
16.10.79	Rockwell Commander 680E	C-GFAC	837-68	Futura Airlines	Crashed	nr Quesnel, BC, Canada	0	1
19.10.79	Swearingen Merlin IIB	N65103	T26-140E	Operator Unknown	Written off	Palo Alto, CA, USA	*	*
20.10.79	IRMA BN-2A-21 Islander	PK-VIQ	0754	Dirgantara Air Service	Crashed	Indonesia	*	*
21.10.79	Cessna A188B	C-GHNM	188-02089T	Conair Aviation	Crashed into mountain	nr Hope, BC, Canada	1	0
23.10.79	Antonov AN-2	YR-APF	1G124-26	Operator Unknown	Crashed	Campina, Romania	*	*
25.10.79	Vickers Viscount 735	G-BFYZ	069	Guernsey Airlines	Ran off runway & u/c collapsed	Kirkwall, Orkneys, UK	0	*
28.10.79	Beechcraft Super King Air 200	XC-PGR	BB-0317	Operator Unknown	Written off	nr Tijuana, Mexico but in USA	*	*
28.10.79	de Havilland Canada Twin Otter 300	XC-BOS	519	Procuradoria General de la Republica	Crashed	Otay Mesa, Mexico	*	*
30.10.79	Douglas DC-3	N99663	16719/33467	Frontier Flying Service	Crashed	Bettles, AK, USA	*	*
30.10.79	Ilyushin IL-14P	SSSR-61683	*	Aeroflot	Damaged by fire aboard MV *Olyenok* after collision	Baltic Sea	*	*
30.10.79	Antonov AN-2	*	*	Aeroflot	Total 2 destroyed by fire aboard MV *Olyenok* after collision	Baltic Sea	0	*
31.10.79	McDonnell Douglas DC-10-10	N903WA	46929	Western Air Lines	Crashed after landing in error on runway under repair	Mexico City, Mexico	72{1}	17
31.10.79	Yakovlev YAK-40	SSSR-87648	*	Aeroflot	Crashed out of fuel	Krasnodar, RSFSR, USSR	0	*
01.11.79	de Havilland Canada Twin Otter 300	C-GTJA	630	Austin Airways	Crashed into beacon	Big Trout Lake, ON, Canada	3	*
01.11.79	Mitsubishi MU-2F	N873Q	160	Operator Unknown	Written off	Nashville, TN, USA	*	*
02.11.79	Piper PA-23-250 Aztec	HK-1607	27-4826	Aeroexpreso Velez Angel	Crashed	Off Colombia	7	0
03.11.79	de Havilland Canada Beaver	C-GAJU	*	Stewart Lake Air Service	Crashed after engine failure	McKinstry Lakes, ON, Canada	0	2
05.11.79	de Havilland Canada Twin Otter 300	N23BC	431	South Pacific Island Airways	Crashed on landing	Tau Is, US Samoa	*	*
05.11.79	Beechcraft 18	N145DC	AF-564	Operator Unknown	Crashed in sea out of fuel	Off Hawaii, USA	1	*
05.11.79	Beechcraft 18	N925YC	BA-273	Operator Unknown	Crashed at sea	Off South Caicos Islands	2	*
06.11.79	Britten-Norman BN-2A-20 Islander	YV-269C	2003	Transmandu	Written off	Location Unknown	*	*
07.11.79	Douglas DC-3	ST-AHH	15880/32628	National Agriculture Organisation	Crashed	Kadugli, Sudan	*	*
13.11.79	Curtiss C-46	C-GYHT	22375	Lambair	Crashed on approach	Churchill, MN, Canada	0	*
13.11.79	Douglas DC-3	PT-KVT	12147	Con. Tec. Operacional de Aviacao	Crashed	Cascavel, Brazil	*	*
15.11.79	Hughes 500	VH-THX	*	Great Northern Helicopters	Crashed after engine failure	nr Fitzroy Crossing, WA, Australia	0	1

Date	Type	Reg'n	C/n	Operator	Accident	Location	F	S
16.11.79	Martin 404	N40438	14173	Nevada Airlines	Crashed	nr Grand Canyon, AZ, USA	0	44
16.11.79	Yakovlev YAK-40	SSSR-87454	*	Aeroflot	Crashed on approach	Vologda, RSFSR, USSR	3	*
18.11.79	Fokker F-27 Friendship 200	S2-ABG	10308	Bangladesh Biman	Crash landed	nr Dacca, Bangladesh	0	4
18.11.79	Lockheed Electra 188CF	N859U	2016	Transamerica Airlines	Crashed	nr Salt Lake City, UT, USA	3	0
19.11.79	Douglas C-54D	N8060C	10563	Tiburon Aircraft	Crashed after fire on smuggling flight	McCormick, SC, USA	2	*
19.11.79	Cessna Citation I	N555AJ	500-0007	Nautilus Aviation Management	Crashed	Denver, CO, USA	*	*
21.11.79	IAI Arava 102	LV-MRX	054	Yacimientos Petroliferos Fiscales	Crashed	Navarion Is, Argentina	*	*
24.11.79	Convair 440-86	N444JM	419	Mackey International Airlines	Crashed after engine detached due to fire	Off Freeport, Bahamas	0	*
26.11.79	Boeing 707-340C	AP-AWZ	20275	Pakistan International Airlines	Crashed after fire	nr Jeddah, Saudi Arabia	156	0
26.11.79	de Havilland Canada Otter	C-FJIK	*	Smithers Air Service	Crashed after take-off	Takla Narrows, BC, Canada	3	1
26.11.79	Mitsubishi MU-2K	N234MA	252	Operator Unknown	Written off	Jacksboro, TX, USA	*	*
28.11.79	McDonnell Douglas DC-10-30	ZK-ZNP	46910	Air New Zealand	Crashed in snowstorm off course	Mt Erebus, Antarctica	257	0
28.11.79	Hughes 500	C-GPHN	*	Viking Helicopters	Crashed & caught fire after engine failure	Canada	0	*
28.11.79	Hughes 300	VH-MYF	*	Bristow Helicopters	Written off	Croydon, Qld, Australia	*	*
30.11.79	Grumman G-21A Goose	HK-2059	1019	Aerolineas La Gaviola	Crashed	Off Isla de San Andres, Colombia	9	0
oo.11.79	Boeing 707-373C	HZ-ACE	18582	Saudia	Damaged on landing	Jeddah, Saudi Arabia	0	*
02.12.79	Gates Learjet 24D	N300JA	24D-282	ERA Helicopters	Crashed	Dutch Harbor, AR, USA	*	*
03.12.79	de Havilland Canada Twin Otter 300	N8061V	294	Evergreen Helicopters	Crashed	Alaska, USA	4	0
07.12.79	Cessna 150	C-GPBS	*	Lumar Air Toronto	Crashed after being stolen	Claremont, ON, Canada	2	0
10.12.79	Gates Learjet 36A	I-AIFA	36A-021	Ferruzzi s.p.a.	Crashed into houses	Forli, Italy	3{2}	0
12.12.79	Martin 404	CP-1440	14114	CAMBA	Crashed after take-off	Apolo, Bolivia	10	1
13.12.79	de Havilland Dove 1B	VH-DSM	04120	Nicholson Air Service	Damaged beyond repair	Lismore, NSW, Australia	*	*
14.12.79	Piper PA-23-250 Aztec	C-FVWA	27-3639	Sabourin Lake Airways	Crashed	Ontario, Canada	*	*
15.12.79	de Havilland Dragon 1	VH-AGC	2045	J.O'Connell	Crashed after take-off	Point Cook, Australia	1	*
18.12.79	Douglas C-54D	FAC.1106	10853	Satena	Crashed	Cerro Toledo Mt, Colombia	21	0
19.12.79	de Havilland Canada Twin Otter 300	HK-1710W	252	Am-Son Drilling Co	Crashed	nr Orocue, Colombia	4	0
21.12.79	Mitsubishi MU-2F	N200BR	205	Operator Unknown	Written off	Provo, UT, USA	*	*
22.12.79	Beechcraft King Air 90	N724N	LJ-0082	Operator Unknown	Written off	Location Unknown	*	*
22.12.79	Beechcraft 18	*	*	Operator Unknown	Crashed	Lake Eola, FL, USA	*	*
22.12.79	Bell 206B JetRanger II	HB-XIM	*	Heli Trans Pilatus	Crashed	Lucerne, Switzerland	*	*
23.12.79	GAF Nomad 22B	P2-DNL	039	Douglas Airways	Crashed	Menari, Papua New Guinea	15	*
23.12.79	Fokker F-28 Fellowship 1000	TC-JAT	11071	Turk Hava Yollari	Crashed	nr Ankara, Turkey	39	4
23.12.79	Curtiss C-46	CP-777	33479	Frimo Transaereos	Crash landed	nr La Paz, Bolivia	*	*
27.12.79	Cessna 421 Golden Eagle	N100RV	421-0549	Design for Living Inc	Crashed on take-off	Eagle, CO, USA	5	0
oo.oo.79	Antonov AN-24B	SP-LTN	97305005	LOT Polish Airlines	Written off	Location Unknown	*	*
oo.oo.79	Rockwell Turbo Commander 690A	EP-AHN	11147	Operator Unknown	Written off	Location Unknown	*	*
oo.oo.79	Rockwell Turbo Commander 690A	L-7C1	11157	Ministry of National Defence	Written off	Lebanon	*	*
oo.oo.79	Douglas DC-7C	N302G	45190	R.A.Armstrong	Crashed	Colombia	*	*
oo.oo.79	IRMA BN-2A-8 Islander	F-OGGL	0680	Air Martinique	Written off	Location Unknown	*	*

1980–1989

By the 1980s air travel was routine and safe, even boring for the regular traveller. The statistics will show that this was probably the safest decade covered in this volume, but accidents nevertheless continued. In fact, some of the most notorious disasters occurred in this period.

Hostile action was becoming more than an occasional reason for a crash. The following pages show that over a hundred aircraft were lost to this cause in its various forms during this decade. Bombings, terrorism, war and hijackings all feature. In addition, smuggling activities led to an ever growing loss rate.

There were four highly publicized examples of this deliberate targeting of civilian airliners. In 1985 an Air India 747 was bombed, killing 329, and this was followed in 1988 by the infamous bomb which brought down a Pan American 747 over Lockerbie with 270 fatalities.

Even disciplined military units made tragic errors of judgement. The Soviets shot down a South Korean 747 and the Americans brought down an Iranian A.300, killing 559 between them. Both tragedies were the result of identification errors which should have been impossible in today's world.

There was one disaster which is still a mystery. In 1980 an Itavia DC-9 crashed off Palermo, Sicily. Ever since there have been rumours that the aircraft was brought down by a missile, with both the Libyans and NATO being accused by various parties. No conclusive proof has yet been given of the true cause of the crash, which killed 81 passengers and crew.

The 1980s were also years of military activity in many parts of the globe. Aircraft were lost during fighting in the Iran-Iraq War, Angola, Lebanon, the

On 2 June 1983 an Air Canada DC-9 (C-FTLU) caught fire in flight. Though it managed to land at Cincinnati, Ohio, 23 people unfortunately died. (Popperfoto)

Falklands, Western Sahara, Afghanistan, Libya, Mozambique, Sri Lanka, the Solomon Islands, Panama, Yugoslavia and even Northern Ireland – the list is depressingly long.

There were also disasters resulting from the more usual risks attached to aviation. The worst ever accident to date involving a single aircraft occurred in 1985, when a Japan Air Lines 747 crashed following a terrifying struggle to stay aloft after losing the major part of its vertical fin. A total of 520 people were killed in this one accident. The miracle was that four survived.

Probably even more tragic were the deaths of 301 people in a Saudia Tristar in August 1980. This aircraft suffered an in-flight fire but landed safely at Riyadh, Saudi Arabia. However, a combination of errors led to a delay in the aircraft's doors being opened and by then it was too late as fire, toxic fumes and smoke had overcome everyone on board.

British air transport fared a little better during this period with only four major accidents. The worst of these was the crash of a Dan-Air 727 into a mountain on Tenerife killing 146. A British Airtours 737 caught fire during take-off at Manchester and again smoke and toxic fumes led to 55 fatalities. An unusual accident occurred when 45 people died in a helicopter crash – a British International Chinook off the Shetlands in 1986. Finally, a BMA 737 crashed in 1989 at Kegworth after the crew inadvertantly shut down a functioning engine instead of the one that had failed, resulting in 47 fatalities.

First write-offs 1980–1989

Canadair Challenger	03.04.80
Short 330	03.06.80
McDonnell Douglas MD-81	18.06.80
Ilyushin IL-76	23.09.80
Potez 840	29.03.81
Airbus A.300	17.03.82
Dornier Do.228	26.03.82
DHC Dash 7	09.05.82
Yakovlev YAK-42	28.06.82
Westland WG.30	18.11.83
SIAI-Marchetti Canguro	08.02.85
Dassault Falcon 50	12.05.85
Cessna Caravan	29.09.85
Short 360	22.10.85
Mitsubishi Diamond	23.07.86
Embraer Brasilia	19.09.86
Antonov AN-28	14.08.87
ATR.42	15.10.87
Beechcraft 1900	23.11.87
BAe 146	07.12.87
DHC Dash 8	15.04.88
Airbus A.320	26.06.88
Beechcraft 1300	10.05.89

Only the structural strength of this Boeing 737 (N73711) of Aloha Airlines averted a tragedy when part of the fuselage blew off in flight near Hawaii on 29 April 1988. Unfortunately, one member of the crew was lost but the aircraft landed safely. (Popperfoto/Reuter)

Date	Type	Reg'n	C/n	Operator	Accident	Location	F	S
02.01.80	Britten-Norman BN-2A-21 Islander	HH-CNC	0474	Haiti Air Inter	Crashed into high ground	Grande Riviere du Nord, Haiti	9	0
07.01.80	McDonnell Douglas DC-9-32	I-DIKB	47118	Alitalia	Destroyed in hangar fire	Rome, Italy	*	*
08.01.80	Beechcraft 18	N641E	*	Skyranch Aviation	Crashed	Honolulu, HI, USA	2	0
09.01.80	Bell 206L Long Ranger	C-GUGP	*	Trans-Quebec Helicopters	Crashed	Opinaca, PQ, Canada	*	*
11.01.80	Convair 440-11	CP-1358	414	Carga Aerea Transportada	Destroyed by fire on take-off	Camiare, Bolivia	0	*
11.01.80	Cessna 441 Conquest II	N441NC	0099	Operator Unknown	Written off	Location Unknown	*	*
12.01.80	Bell 206B JetRanger II	C-FKOC	01218	Athabaska Airways	Crashed into lake	Montreal Lake, SK, Canada	4	0
13.01.80	McDonnell Douglas DC-9-32	PK-GND	47463	Garuda Indonesian Airlines	Damaged in hard landing	Banjarmasin, Indonesia	0	126
14.01.80	Bell 206B JetRanger II	HB-XCP	00033	Heliswiss	Crashed	Fribourg, Switzerland	2	0
15.01.80	IAI Arava 102	3D-DAB	060	Royal Swazi Defence Force	Crashed	nr Songe, Malawi	*	*
15.01.80	Rockwell Turbo Commander 690	N182	11048	Operator Unknown	Written off	Canton, MD, USA	*	*
21.01.80	Boeing 727-86	EP-IRD	19817	Iran Air	Crashed	nr Tehran, Iran	128	0
22.01.80	Fairchild F-27J	CP-1175	0121	Lloyd Aereo Boliviano	Ran into ditch & caught fire	Yacuma, Bolivia	0	30
23.01.80	Tupolev TU-134	SP-LGB	8350603	LOT Polish Airlines	Overran & caught fire	Warsaw, Poland	0	*
24.01.80	Douglas DC-3	HK-2214X	11627	Aerotal	Crashed after take-off due to engine failure	Bogota, Colombia	4	0
26.01.80	Aerospatiale AS.350 Ecureuil	C-GBVS	*	Associated Helicopters	Crashed into lake	Heaven Lake, ON, Canada	1	1
27.01.80	Boeing 720-059B	HK-725	18087	Avianca	Damaged when overran	Quito, Ecuador	0	*
29.01.80	Cessna 404 Titan II	PH-JAL	404-0218	Luycks Executive Flight	Crashed	St Aignan de Grandlieu, France	*	*
30.01.80	Dassault Falcon 10	N253K	010	Kellogg Co	Crashed	Meigs, IL, USA	*	*
30.01.80	Rockwell Turbo Commander 690A	XB-AEA	11199	Operator Unknown	Written off	Oklahoma City, OK, USA	*	*
02.02.80	MBB Bo.105	PT-HHC	S.134	Lider Taxi Aereo	Crashed & caught fire	Caraurari, Brazil	*	*
03.02.80	Yakovlev YAK-40	CU-T1219	9840959	Cubana	Crashed on landing	Baracoa, Cuba	1	36
04.02.80	Cessna 404 Titan	G-WING	404-0442	Euroair	Ran off runway on landing in snowstorm	Leeds, UK	0	*
06.02.80	Grumman Gulfstream II TT	TR-KHB	127	Gabon Government	Crashed	Ngaoundere, Gabon	*	*
08.02.80	Fokker F-27 Friendship 600	9Q-CLP	10402	Air Zaire	Crashed after take-off	Ndjili, Zaire	3	0
14.02.80	Mitsubishi MU-2J	N346MA	613	Operator Unknown	Crashed into trees on approach	Houston, TX, USA	4	0
14.02.80	Agusta-Bell 47G-3B-1	HB-XHS	1577	Heliswiss	Crashed on take-off when rotor struck ground	Bern, Switzerland	*	*
15.02.80	Convair 240-0	N8330C	109	W.J.Evans	Crash landed after engine fire on smuggling flight	Port-au-Prince, Haiti	0	2
15.02.80	Beechcraft 18	N729F	BA-706	Operator Unknown	Crashed on approach	Johnson, KS, USA	*	*
17.02.80	Bristol Britannia 253	G-BRAC	13448	Redcoat Air Cargo	Crashed after take-off due to icing	Boston, MA, USA	7	1
19.02.80	Bell 206B JetRanger II	PK-DBM	00674	Derazona Air Service	Crashed	Java Sea, Indonesia	2	0
21.02.80	Beechcraft Super King Air 200	VH-AAV	BB-0245	Advance Airlines	Crashed into sea wall on landing	Sydney, NSW, Australia	13	0
23.02.80	Mitsubishi MU-2P	N962MA	401SA	Operator Unknown	Crashed on approach in fog	Lake Pontchatrain, LA, USA	7	0
24.02.80	Britten-Norman BN-2A-20 Islander	PK-VIT	0595	Dirgantara Air Service	Crashed	Banjarmasin, Indonesia	*	*
26.02.80	Cessna 421 Golden Eagle	VH-EGT	*	Codds Air Service	Crashed	Dysart, Qld, Australia	1	*
27.02.80	Boeing 707-309C	B-1826	20262	China Airlines	Crashed on landing	Manila, Philippines	2	133
oo.02.80	Lockheed Electra 188AF	YS-07C	1069	TACA International Airlines	Damaged beyond repair	Location Unknown	*	*
01.03.80	Tupolev TU-154A	SSSR-85103	103	Aeroflot	Damaged in hard landing	Orenburg, RSFSR, USSR	0	*
03.03.80	Gates Learjet 25	N211MB	25-059	Merchant Bank	Crashed on approach	Port-au-Prince, Haiti	4	*
06.03.80	Piper PA-31-350 Chieftain	G-BGIN	31-7405433	Airmore Aviation	Crashed	Off Nice, France	*	*
10.03.80	Beechcraft King Air E90	N4GN	LW-038	Operator Unknown	Crashed on approach in fog	La Guardia, NY, USA	3	0
11.03.80	de Havilland Canada Beaver	C-GZBE	1082	Athabaska Airways	Crashed after hitting power lines	Buffalo Narrows, SK, Canada	1	5
13.03.80	Douglas DC-3	CP-1243	15861/32609	Aerolineas La Paz	Crashed after take-off	San Borja, Bolivia	0	*
14.03.80	Ilyushin IL-62	SP-LAA	11004	LOT Polish Airlines	Crashed on landing after engine explosion	Warsaw, Poland	87	0
17.03.80	McDonnell Douglas DC-9-14	N9103	45796	Texas International Airlines	Crashed	Baton Rouge, LA, USA	*	*
18.03.80	Douglas DC-3	ET-AGM	20874	Ethiopian Airlines	Crashed & destroyed by fire	Bole, Ethiopia	0	*
21.03.80	Piper PA-31-350 Chieftain	N59932	31-7552046	Eagle Commuter Airline	Crashed into three aircraft on ground	Houston, TX, USA	7(0)	0
21.03.80	Sikorsky S-76	PT-HKB	760008	VOTEC	Crashed in sea	Off Macae, Brazil	14	0
24.03.80	Cessna 402	C-FEIA	*	Tomahawk Airways	Crashed & caught fire	Deer Lake, ON, Canada	6	3
25.03.80	Gates Learjet 36	D-CDFA	36-006	Diskont & Kredit AG	Crashed	Libya	*	*
25.03.80	Cessna 310	C-FWPC	*	Miramichi Air Service	Crashed	nr Chatham, NB, Canada	4	0
27.03.80	Beechcraft Super King Air A200	N456L	BB-0112	Operator Unknown	Written off	Denver, CO, USA	*	*
29.03.80	Convair 880-22-2	HP-821	41	Inair	Damaged on take-off	Panama City, Panama	*	*
30.03.80	Meridionali Chinook	MM80825	M004	Agusta Helicopters	Crashed into hangar	Abu Dhabi, UAE	12	3

Date	Type	Reg'n	C/n	Operator	Accident	Location	F	S
30.03.80	IRMA BN-2A-9 Islander	PT-JSC	0695	VOTEC	Stalled & crashed on take-off	Cuiaba, Brazil	0	*
31.03.80	Antonov AN-24B	3X-GAU	87304210	Air Guinee	Damaged beyond repair	Conakry, Guinee	*	*
oo.03.80	Beechcraft Super King Air 200	N1KA	BB-0411	Operator Unknown	Destroyed in hangar fire	Location Unknown	*	*
01.04.80	Cessna 441 Conquest II	N36941	0018	Operator Unknown	Struck ridge on approach	Butte, MT, USA	2	0
02.04.80	Hughes 369HS	PT-HFE	1020426S	VOTEC	Crashed into power lines	Colombia	0	1
03.04.80	Canadair Challenger 600	C-GCGR-X	1001	Canadair	Crashed after brake parachute failed following stall	Mojave, CA, USA	1	3
03.04.80	Sikorsky S-58T	PT-HGK	58-1458	VOTEC	Crashed on landing	nr Belem, Brazil	1	*
03.04.80	Boeing 707-373C	S2-ABQ	19441	Bangladesh Biman	Crash landed after take-off	Singapore	0	78
07.04.80	Mitsubishi MU-2B	C-FQMS	009	Operator Unknown	Written off	Athabaska, AB, Canada	*	*
09.04.80	Agusta-Bell 47G-2	HB-XAW	2180	Heliswiss	Crashed into power cables	Kiesen, Switzerland	2	0
11.04.80	Douglas DC-3	N64490	13915/25360	C.A.Hackney	Crashed on take-off	Athol, IN, USA	3	3
11.04.80	Gates Learjet 25B	N25TA	25B-196	Jet East	Crashed	New Mexico, USA	*	*
12.04.80	Boeing 727-27QC	PT-TYS	19111	Transbrasil	Crashed on approach	nr Florianopolis, Brazil	55	3
14.04.80	Antonov AN-24	SSSR-47732	69900905	Aeroflot	Crashed on take-off	Krasy, RSFSR, USSR	2	*
18.04.80	Antonov AN-24	SSSR-46220	*	Aeroflot	Crashed on take-off	Moscow, RSFSR, USSR	*	*
23.04.80	Mitsubishi MU-2B	N307MA	007	Operator Unknown	Crashed out of fuel	Las Vegas, NV, USA	*	0
24.04.80	Douglas B-26 Invader	C-FBVH	28003	Air Spray	Crashed into trees	Slave Lake, AB, Canada	1	*
24.04.80	Douglas DC-3	N709Z	15737/27182	Florida Preferred Equity Inc	Crashed into trees on landing	Fort Lauderdale, FL, USA	0	*
25.04.80	Boeing 727-46	G-BDAN	19279	Dan-Air	Crashed into mountain on approach	Tenerife, Canary Islands, Spain	146	0
27.04.80	British Aerospace 748 2	HS-THB	1568	Thai Airways	Crashed in storm	Don Muang, Thailand	40	11
27.04.80	Cessna 404 Titan	N5237J	*	Faraday Industries	Crashed on approach out of fuel	New Orleans, LA, USA	1	*
28.04.80	Beechcraft 99	F-BTMO	U086	Compagnie Aerienne du Languedoc	Crashed	Paris, France	*	*
oo.04.80	Convair 440	N94436	102	A.Morales	Damaged beyond repair	Location Unknown	*	*
06.05.80	Gates Learjet 23	N866JS	23-018	Teterboro Aircraft Service	Crashed on landing	Richmond, VA, USA	2	*
06.05.80	Cessna 172	PZ-TAB	*	Gonimi Air Service	Crashed after take-off	Ladoanie, Surinam	4	0
11.05.80	Boeing 707-329C	OO-SJH	18890	Zaire International Airlines	Crashed on landing	Douala, Cameroons	0	3
11.05.80	Piper PA-32-300 Cherokee Six	CC-CEE	*	Transportes Aereos Costa Brava	Crashed during storm	nr Peumo, Chile	4	0
13.05.80	Swearingen 226TC Metro II	VH-SWO	TC-275	Skywest Airlines	Crashed short of runway	Esperance, WA, Australia	*	*
13.05.80	Ilyushin IL-14	*	*	Cubana	Crashed	Veradero Beach, Cuba	3	0
13.05.80	Britten-Norman BN-2A-6 Islander	PT-KHK	0208	VOTEC	Crashed	nr Viracopos, Brazil	7	0
13.05.80	Britten-Norman BN-2A-3 Islander	PK-OAB	0291	Airfast Services	Written off	Location Unknown	*	*
16.05.80	Curtiss C-46	YN-BVL	*	Lanica	Crashed after striking log on landing	Bonanza, Nicaragua	*	*
20.05.80	Bell 206B JetRanger II	*	*	Magnum Airlines	Crashed	Germiston, South Africa	1	0
21.05.80	Gates Learjet 25D	N125NE	25D-271	Northeast Jet Co	Crashed	Gulf of Mexico	2	*
24.05.80	Convair 240-0	N300GR	115	C.Clay	Crashed after take-off	nr Daytona Beach, FL, USA	3	0
28.05.80	Douglas DC-3	HR-SAC	4232	Sahsa	Crashed after u/c struck wall on approach	Utila, Honduras	*	*
02.06.80	Fairchild F-27J	CP-1117	0118	Lloyd Aereo Boliviano	Crashed	nr Yachiba, Bolivia	13	0
02.06.80	Antonov AN-22A	SSSR-09311	*	Aeroflot	Crashed on landing	Moscow, RSFSR, USSR	*	*
03.06.80	Short 330-100	N844SA	SH.3041	Suburban Airlines	Damaged when overturned by strong winds	Allentown, PA, USA	0	*
04.06.80	Westland Wessex 1	5N-AJP	463	Bristow Helicopters (Nigeria) Ltd	Crashed in sea	Off Nigeria	1	*
04.06.80	Pilatus Porter	*	*	Thai Police	Crashed	Umphang, Thailand	9	0
06.06.80	Ilyushin IL-18	*	*	Aeroflot	Crashed after engine fire	nr Moscow, RSFSR, USSR	*	*
08.06.80	Yakovlev YAK-40FG	D2-TYC	9721753	TAAG Angola Airlines	Crashed – Possibly shot down during SAAF raid	Southern Angola	29	0
12.06.80	Swearingen 226TC Metro II	N6505	TC-228	Air Wisconsin	Crashed during storm	Valley, NB, USA	12	0
12.06.80	Yakovlev YAK-40	SSSR-87689	*	Aeroflot	Crashed on landing on road	nr Dushanbe, Tajikistan, USSR	29	0
15.06.80	Rockwell Commander 560A	HP-776	*	Aviones de Panama	Stolen & crashed on gun running flight	San Miguel, Panama	*	*
18.06.80	McDonnell Douglas MD-81	N1002G	48001	McDonnell Douglas Aircraft	U/c collapsed on landing & damaged by crane during recovery	Yuma, AZ, USA	0	*
19.06.80	Aerospatiale Caravelle 6R	N805MW	095	Midwest Air Charter	Landed short of runway	Atlanta, GA, USA	0	*
21.06.80	British Aerospace 748 2	HS-THG	1693	Thai Airways	Veered off runway & ran into ditch	Chiang Rai, Thailand	0	21
22.06.80	Lockheed 1049H Super Constellation	N74CA	4850	Air Traders International	Crashed on take-off	Columbus, IN, USA	3	0
24.06.80	Piper PA-31-350 Chieftain	TJ-AFO	31-7752109	Air Affaires Afrique	Crashed after take-off	Douala, Cameroons	3	0
27.06.80	McDonnell Douglas DC-9-15	I-TIGI	45724	Itavia	Crashed – Possibly shot down by missile	Off Palermo, Sicily, Italy	81	0
27.06.80	Britten-Norman BN-2A-6 Islander	I-BADE	0237	Transavio	Forced landed in sea & sank	Off Elba, Italy	0	3
03.07.80	Bell 206B JetRanger II	C-GSHE	*	Vancouver Island Helicopters	Crashed	Snippacker Creek, BC, Canada	4	0

Date	Type	Reg'n	C/n	Operator	Accident	Location	F	S
04.07.80	Bell 47G-3B	C-GTNB	6768	Trans-North Turbo Air	Crashed with underslung load	nr Ross River, YK, Canada	1	0
05.07.80	Fairchild C-119 Flying Boxcar	N90268	*	Gifford Aviation	Caught fire on approach	King Salmon, AK, USA	*	*
07.07.80	Embraer Bandeirante 110P1	XC-DAK	110.242	IMSS	Crashed	nr Tepic, Mexico	13	0
07.07.80	Tupolev TU-154B-2	SSSR-85355	355	Aeroflot	Crashed on take-off	nr Alma Ata, Kazakhstan, USSR	166	0
07.07.80	Britten-Norman BN-2A-26 Islander	EI-BBR	0472	Aer Arann	Overran into wall after aborted take-off	Cornmore, Eire	0	*
12.07.80	Douglas DC-3	*	*	Operator Unknown	Crashed on landing at night after engine trouble	Port-au-Prince, Haiti	3	*
13.07.80	Bell 204B	C-FAHL	*	Transwest Helicopters	Crashed after breaking up in air	nr Armstrong, ON, Canada	2	0
14.07.80	Vickers Viscount 745D	HC-BHB	205	Aerolineas Condor	Written off	La Toma, Ecuador	*	*
17.07.80	Vickers Viscount 708	G-ARBY	010	Alidair	Crash landed out of fuel	Ottery St Mary, Devon, UK	0	62
18.07.80	Beechcraft D18S	N1824D	A-0812	Operator Unknown	Crashed out of fuel	Yap Is, USTT of the Pacific	0	*
18.07.80	Yakovlev YAK-40	SSSR-87893	*	Aeroflot	Crashed after crew shut down engines on approach	Archangelsk, RSFSR, USSR	0	*
19.07.80	Beechcraft Baron	*	*	Talair	Crashed into mountain	Tari, Papua New Guinea	6	0
21.07.80	Cessna 404 Titan	N2683S	404-0606	Scenic Airlines	Crashed on take-off	nr Grand Canyon, AZ, USA	7	1
23.07.80	Convair 340-62	HI-899	236	Operator Unknown	Written off while drug smuggling	Florida, USA	*	*
23.07.80	Rockwell Commander 500B	HK-869	1095-58	Aerotaxi Americano	Damaged in belly landing	Barrancabermeja, Colombia	0	*
24.07.80	Nord Noratlas	HC-AXK	137	Aerotaxis Ecuatorianos	Crashed	nr Rio Amazonas, Ecuador	2	0
25.07.80	Piper PA-31-350 Chieftain	N5MS	31-7405138	Air Pennsylvania	Crashed on approach after being caught in jet wake	Philadelphia, PA, USA	3	0
27.07.80	Douglas DC-7CF	CP-1291	45470	Lambda Air Cargo	Destroyed by fire on ground	Trujillo, Peru	*	*
29.07.80	Transavia PL-12 Airtruk	B-15118	*	Great China Airlines	Crashed	Hsing Woo, Taiwan	1	0
30.07.80	Cessna 404 Titan	N37097	404-0105	Operator Unknown	Crashed after striking trees on drug smuggling flight	Fort White, FL, USA	0	*
oo.07.80	Consolidated Privateer	N2870G	*	Hawkins & Powers Aviation	Ran off runway due to tyre burst	Ramona, CA, USA	0	2
oo.07.80	Beechcraft King Air C90	YV-164CP	LJ-0905	W.Morales y Cia	Written off	Location Unknown	*	*
01.08.80	McDonnell Douglas DC-8-43F	OB-R-1143	45598	Aeronaves del Peru	Crashed into hill in fog	nr Mexico City, Mexico	3	4
01.08.80	Douglas DC-3	N45864	9304	J.Rule	Ran off runway & crashed into trees	New Smyrna Beach, FL, USA	*	*
07.08.80	Sikorsky S-58	N4247	58-0807	Queen City Helicopters	Crashed onto building during lifting operation	Bellevue, WA, USA	*	*
07.08.80	Tupolev TU-154B-1	YR-TPH	272	Tarom	Crashed in sea on approach	Nouadhibou, Mauritania	1	168
11.08.80	IRMA BN-2A-6 Islander	PT-KAC	0644	Prospec	Crashed after take-off	Rio de Janeiro, Brazil	3	*
13.08.80	Gates Learjet 35A	EC-DFA	35A-196	Spantax	Crashed on approach	Palma, Spain	4	*
13.08.80	Fairchild FH-1100	PT-HFM	248	Castelo Taxi Aereo	Crashed	nr Sao Paulo, Brazil	2	0
19.08.80	Fokker F-27 Friendship 400	XY-ADO	10313	Burma Airways	Crashed	Moulmein, Burma	*	*
19.08.80	Piper PA-31-350 Chieftain	CX-BMT	*	Taxis Aereos Uruguayos	Crashed when passenger attempted to land after pilot fainted	Montevideo, Uruguay	2	*
20.08.80	Lockheed Tristar 200	HZ-AHK	1169	Saudia	Destroyed by fire after emergency landing	Riyadh, Saudi Arabia	301	0
20.08.80	Piper PA-23-250 Aztec	C-GWVO	*	Superior Airways	Crashed	nr Wawa, ON, Canada	2	0
25.08.80	Britten-Norman Trislander	9L-LAQ	0363	Sierra Leone Airways	Damaged by another aircraft on ground	Hastings Field, Sierra Leone	*	*
25.08.80	Beechcraft King Air E90	N908CM	LW-233	Operator Unknown	Written off	Hotham Inlet, AK, USA	*	*
26.08.80	Vickers Viscount 812	PK-IVS	353	Bouraq Indonesia Airlines	Crashed	nr Djakarta, Indonesia	37	0
28.08.80	Vickers Viscount 768D	VT-DJC	296	Huns Air	Damaged beyond repair on landing	Gannavaram, India	0	*
02.09.80	de Havilland Canada Twin Otter 300	HC-BAV/453	453	TAME	Written off	Location Unknown	*	*
03.09.80	Boeing 727-21	N327PA	19036	Pan American World Airways	Damaged by skidding off runway	San Jose, Costa Rica	0	73
04.09.80	Aerospatiale SA.315B Lama	HB-XEO	2321	Air Glaciers	Crashed	Jungfraujoch, Switzerland	0	2
07.09.80	Beechcraft Queen Air 80	N242Q	LD-042	Operator Unknown	Crashed in lake in unknown circumstances	Keenansville, FL, USA	0	*
10.09.80	Douglas DC-3	HK-329	4404	Aeronorte	Crashed	nr Puerto Berrio, Colombia	3	0
10.09.80	Grumman G-21A Goose	N33S	*	Operator Unknown	Destroyed by crashing Beech 18 N43L	Location Unknown	*(*)	*
10.09.80	Beechcraft 18	N43L	BA-228	Operator Unknown	Crashed on take-off & struck Q Air N2030 & Goose N33S	Location Unknown	*(*)	*
10.09.80	Beechcraft Queen Air	N2030	*	Q Air	Struck by crashed Beech 18 N43L with two other aircraft	Location Unknown	*	*
11.09.80	McDonnell Douglas DC-8-33F	N715UA	45386	Aeronaves del Peru	Crashed	Between Lima & Iquitos, Peru	4	0
11.09.80	de Havilland Canada Beaver	C-FMPM	*	Air Mount Laurier	Crashed into trees	nr Lac des Comes, PQ, Canada	1	2
12.09.80	Douglas DC-3	N75KW	4861	Florida Commuter Airlines	Crashed	Off Freeport, Bahamas	34	0
14.09.80	Rockwell Turbo Commander 690A	LV-MBR	11266	Operator Unknown	Written off	Buenos Aires, Argentina	*	*
15.09.80	Douglas DC-6B	N9018N	44425	JMG Inc	Crashed	Off Haiti	4	1
18.09.80	de Havilland Canada Beaver	C-FITW	*	Northwestern Flying Services	Crashed after take-off	Populus lake, ON, Canada	0	*
21.09.80	Douglas A-26 Invader	N3710G	18759	Cavalier Air Force	Crashed during air display	Biggin Hill, Kent, UK	7	0
22.09.80	Convair 240	*	*	Operator Unknown	Crashed in trees on landing after illegal flight	Okeechobee, FL, USA	*	*
22.09.80	Britten-Norman BN-2A Islander	TF-RTO	0142	Flugfelag Austurlands	Crashed	mt Smjorfjell, Iceland	3	*

Date	Type	Reg'n	C/n	Operator	Accident	Location	F	S
23.09.80	Ilyushin IL-76T	YI-AIO	073410315	Iraqi Airways	Shot down by Iranian aircraft on approach	Baghdad, Iraq	*	*
24.09.80	Piper PA-31-350 Chieftain	G-CTHS	31-7952100	T.Hampson-Silk	Crashed	nr St Agreve, France	2	*
24.09.80	Antonov AN-24TV	YI-AEM	1022805	Iraqi Airways	Destroyed by missile during Iranian air raid	Kirkuk, Iraq	*	*
26.09.80	Beechcraft 18	N9724Y	BA-656	Operator Unknown	Crashed on landing out of fuel on drug smuggling flight	nr Paraguadron, Colombia	*	*
28.09.80	Beechcraft D18S	N704D	A-0596	Operator Unknown	Crashed on hurried take-off when police arrived	Frostproof, FL, USA	0	2
01.10.80	Cessna Citation I	G-BPCP	500-0403	Penarth Commercial Properties	Crashed into houses on approach	Jersey, Channel Islands	1	*
01.10.80	Piper PA-31-350 Chieftain	5N-AKO	31-7512067	Aero Contractors	Crashed	En route Lagos-Benin	4	0
03.10.80	Douglas DC-3	*	*	G.Kurfiss	Missing – Presumed crashed	Mediterranean Sea	*	*
04.10.80	Beechcraft 18	N333FL	BA-029	Operator Unknown	Crashed on take-off from slush covered runway	Candle, AK, USA	*	*
08.10.80	Tupolev TU-154B-2	SSSR-85321	321	Aeroflot	Damaged in hard landing	Chita, RSFSR, USSR	0	*
13.10.80	Fokker F-27 Friendship 400	PK-PFC	10339	Pelita Air Service	Crashed out of fuel in bad weather	Misool Is, Indonesia	*	*
17.10.80	Beechcraft Super King Air 200	F-GBRP	BB-0368	Est. Economique du Casino	Written off	Colmar, France	7	0
18.10.80	Sikorsky S-58	N94523	*	Operator Unknown	Crashed	nr Pole Langow, NV, USA	3	*
28.10.80	Antonov AN-12B	SSSR-11104	01347710	Aeroflot	Crashed into hill on approach	Kabul, Afghanistan	6	0
oo.10.80	Britten-Norman BN-2A Islander	N851JA	0071	Trans Island Airways	Written off	Location Unknown	*	*
01.11.80	Cessna 206 Super Skywagon	EL-AFG	*	Monrovia Air Line	Crashed	Cocopa, Liberia	3	0
03.11.80	Convair 880-22-2	YV-145C	64	Latincarga	Crashed on take-off	Caracas, Venezuela	4	0
03.11.80	Douglas DC-3	TG-BAC	14330/25775	Aero Express	Crashed & caught fire	Yaxchibal, Guatemala	7	*
04.11.80	Canadair CL-44D4-1	5B-DAN	030	Cyprus Airways	Crash landed	Akrotiri, Cyprus	0	3
05.11.80	Boeing 737-2M2CA	D2-TAA	21172	TAAG Angola Airlines	Landed short of runway & damaged during recovery on 10.11.80	Benguela, Angola	0	*
06.11.80	Cessna 441 Conquest II	D-IAAY	0144	Atlas Air Service	Written off	Location Unknown	*	*
06.11.80	Cessna U206 Super Skywagon	N6446X	*	Kodiak Western Airlines	Crashed	nr Wainwright, AK, USA	1	0
07.11.80	Aerospatiale AS.350C Astar	C-GBEB	*	Okanagan Helicopters	Crashed	nr Fort Nelson, BC, Canada	3	0
13.11.80	Douglas DC-3	FAC.1131	*	Satena	Crashed	Subchoque, Colombia	0	23
13.11.80	Douglas DC-6B	YN-BVI	44117	Lanica	U/c collapsed on landing	Tocumen, Panama	0	*
15.11.80	Curtiss C-46	N355BY	30243	BWI Leasing	Crashed	Off Norman Cay, Bahamas	0	*
17.11.80	Britten-Norman Trislander	VH-BSG	0279	Provincial Air Services	Damaged beyond repair	Annanberg, Australia	*	*
18.11.80	Beechcraft 18	N700CC	BA-740	Moonlight Express	Crashed	nr Selingsgrove, PA, USA	1	0
19.11.80	Boeing 747-2B5B	HL7445	21773	Korean Air Lines	Crashed on landing in fog	Seoul, South Korea	14	198
20.11.80	de Havilland Dove 8	G-ASHW	04532	Fishing & Marine Salvage	Crashed on take-off	Cherbourg, France	0	*
20.11.80	Bell 47G-2	HB-XFB	2195	Heliswiss	Crashed during auto-rotation training	Bern, Switzerland	0	*
20.11.80	Bell 206L Long Ranger	C-GXKA	45025	Heli Voyageur	Crashed into lake	Lake Cordier, PQ, Canada	1	0
21.11.80	Boeing 727-92C	N18479	19174	Air Micronesia	U/c collapsed on landing & caught fire	Yap Island, USTT of the Pacific	0	70
22.11.80	Soloy Hiller UH-12E	HB-XLF	*	Helitrans Pilatus	Crashed into trees	nr Alpnach, Switzerland	*	*
24.11.80	Douglas DC-3	HK-1221G	9703	Colombian Customs	Crashed	El Chocho Mts, Colombia	20	0
26.11.80	Cessna 421B Golden Eagle	N200SM	421B-0649	Operator Unknown	Crash landed & caught fire after take-off	Detroit, MI, USA	*	*
26.11.80	Cessna 310Q	C-GYLK	310Q-0472	Boardaire	Crashed	Sioux Narrows, ON, Canada	5	0
28.11.80	Fokker F-27 Friendship 400	5A-DBE	10275	Libyan Arab Airlines	Damaged on landing	Kufra, Chad	0	*
28.11.80	Douglas DC-7B	N816D	45085	Central Air Services	Crashed after take-off	nr Pecos, TX, USA	2	*
28.11.80	Douglas DC-6A/C	N844TA	44421	Miami Air Lease	Crashed	Off South Bimini, Bahamas	2	*
30.11.80	Boeing 707-131B	N797TW	18760	Trans World Airlines	Belly landed	San Francisco, CA, USA	0	133
30.11.80	Mitsubishi MU-2J	N44MR	611	Operator Unknown	Force-landed after engine failure	Port Arnsas, TX, USA	0	*
02.12.80	Swearingen Merlin IIB	N177MF	T26-179	Operator Unknown	Crashed in mountains	nr Albany, KY, USA	3	0
04.12.80	Cessna 421 Golden Eagle	YV-314P	421-0040	E.J.Leal Marques	Crashed after take-off	Lisbon, Portugal	7	0
05.12.80	Piper PA-31-350 Chieftain	5H-TAL	31-7652016	Tanzania Aviation	Crashed	nr Dar-es-Salaam, Tanzania	10	0
06.12.80	Mitsubishi MU-2P	N969MA	408SA	Solitaire	Crashed on approach	Ramsey, MN, USA	5	0
07.12.80	Beechcraft King Air E90	N2181L	LW-181	Operator Unknown	Crashed on approach	Lake Michigan, IN, USA	4	0
13.12.80	Beechcraft 18	N9684R	BA-500	Operator Unknown	Crashed on take-off due to being overloaded	Fulton, GA, USA	*	*
16.12.80	Britten-Norman Trislander	VH-EGU	1030	Eagle Airways	Crashed	Snowy Mts, NSW, Australia	2	*
19.12.80	Rockwell 1121 Jet Commander	N29LP	061	Langham Petroleum Corporation	Crashed into trees on approach	Many, LA, USA	3	*
20.12.80	Boeing 707-321	HK-2410X	17605	Aerotal	Crashed on landing & caught fire	El Dorado, Colombia	0	*
21.12.80	Aerospatiale Caravelle 6R	HK-1810	165	Transportes Aereos del Caribe	Exploded after take-off	Rio Hacha, Colombia	70	0
22.12.80	Sikorsky S-58	N4375S	*	Airfast Services	Crashed	Off Madras, India	*	*
26.12.80	British Aerospace 125-400A	XA-CUZ	25279	Servicios Aereos Regiomontanos	Crashed	Cancun, Mexico	*	*

Date	Type	Reg'n	C/n	Operator	Accident	Location	F	S
27.12.80	Douglas DC-3	N54605	16191/32939	Visionair International	Damaged by storm	Reykjavik, Iceland	*	*
29.12.80	Cessna 421B Golden Eagle	N9394A	421B-0531	Operator Unknown	Crashed	Lake Michigan, MI, USA	5	0
oo.12.80	Ilyushin IL-86	*	*	Aeroflot	Reported as crashed	USSR	*	*
oo.oo.80	IPTN 212 Aviocar 100	PK-XCE	045/3N	Pelita Air Service	Crashed into mountains	Location Unknown	*	*
oo.oo.80	Douglas DC-7CF	N8219H	45214	Aero Services	Shot down on smuggling flight by Colombian forces	Colombia	*	*
oo.oo.80	Curtiss C-46	HI-197	26716	Operator Unknown	Crashed short of runway on smuggling flight	Rio Hacha, Colombia	*	*
oo.oo.80	Convair 440-38	N102US	378	Farm-Kem Inc	Crashed on smuggling flight	Colombia	*	*
oo.oo.80	Rockwell Sabre 40	XA-EEU	282-054	Servicios Internacionales	Damaged beyond repair	Mexico	*	*
oo.oo.80	Douglas DC-7C	N75000	45094	K.L.Meek	Crashed	Colombia	*	*
06.01.81	Tupolev TU-134A	SSSR-65698	*	Aeroflot	Damaged on landing	Sochi, RSFSR, USSR	0	*
07.01.81	Rockwell Turbo Commander 690B	N81521	11351	Operator Unknown	Written off	Burns, OR, USA	*	*
08.01.81	Lockheed Electra 188A	HR-SAW	1018	Sahsa	Crashed after taking-off on three engines	Guatemala City, Guatemala	6	0
08.01.81	Boeing 720-047B	AP-AXK	18590	Pakistan International Airlines	Damaged beyond repair	Quetta, Pakistan	0	*
11.01.81	Douglas DC-3	ET-AGW	12981	Ethiopian Airlines	U/c collapsed on landing	Bahar Dar, Ethiopia	0	*
12.01.81	Douglas DC-3	N137H	42965	Sun Valley Aviation	Crashed	nr Cruillas, Mexico	*	*
14.01.81	Bristol 170 Freighter 31E	ZK-CAM	13155	Safe Air	Damaged on landing	Blenheim, New Zealand	0	*
15.01.81	McDonnell Douglas DC-8-61	N913R	46128	Overseas National Airlines	Destroyed in hangar fire	Luxembourg	0	*
19.01.81	Cessna 402A	C-GDTW	402A-0037	Kenting Aviation	Crashed	En route to Iceland	2	0
21.01.81	Cessna Citation I	N501GP	500-0026	Operator Unknown	Crashed	Bluefield, WV, USA	*	*
22.01.81	Short Skyvan 3M	8R-GFF	SH.1966	Guyana Defence Force	Crashed	Guyana	4	*
23.01.81	Grumman G-21A Goose	N95468	1140	Peninsula Airways	Crashed in poor weather	nr Dutch Harbour, AK, USA	2	*
26.01.81	Piper PA-31 Navajo	VH-POC	31-7952087	Northwest Skyways	Crashed	nr Portland, VC, Australia	1	0
27.01.81	Rockwell Turbo Commander 681	N500JP	6003	Operator Unknown	Written off	Winnemucca, NV, USA	*	*
28.01.81	Douglas DC-3	PP-ZNU	20126	Sudene	Written off	Petrolina, Brazil	*	*
28.01.81	Beechcraft H-18S	N787Q	BA-662	Operator Unknown	Crashed into mountains after engine failure	nr Van Nuys, CA, USA	2	0
02.02.81	McDonnell Douglas DC-10-30	AP-AXE	46935	Pakistan International Airlines	Destroyed in hangar fire	Karachi, Pakistan	*	*
02.02.81	Beechcraft C-45H	N45437	AF-452	Express Airways	Crash landed in field	Dillsburg, PA, USA	*	*
07.02.81	Tupolev TU-134	*	*	Aeroflot	Crashed	nr Leningrad, RSFSR, USSR	73	0
09.02.81	Douglas DC-3	RP-C141	19251	Trans Air Service	Crashed	Panay Is, Philippines	*	*
10.02.81	Curtiss C-46	CP-1588	32831	Universal Ltd	Crash landed	Caravani, Bolivia	0	*
11.02.81	Lockheed Jetstar 731	N520S	5084	Texas Gulf Aviation	Crashed on approach	Westchester, NY, USA	7	*
15.02.81	Pilatus PC-6/B2-H2 Turbo Porter	G-BHCR	732	Peterborough Parachute Centre	Crashed after take-off	Sibson, Cambs, UK	*	*
17.02.81	Boeing 737-293	N468AC	20334	Air California	Crashed on landing	John Wayne, CA, USA	0	109
17.02.81	Cessna 421 Golden Eagle	PT-KRW	*	J.P.dos Santos	Crashed on take-off	Zavala, Paraguay	4	0
21.02.81	Rockwell Turbo Commander 690B	D-IKOC	11498	Operator Unknown	Written off	Paris, France	*	*
24.02.81	Embraer Bandeirante 110P	PT-GLB	110.144	VOTEC	Crashed into boat on approach	Belem, Brazil	11	*
27.02.81	de Havilland Canada Twin Otter 300	C-FCSV	354	Department of Transport	Crashed	Galt, ON, Canada	2	*
oo.02.81	Beechcraft C-45J	N68392	*	Operator Unknown	Crashed on drug smuggling flight	San Clemente Is, CA, USA	1	0
02.03.81	Beechcraft D18S	N80162	A-0123	Operator Unknown	Crashed out of fuel on approach	Claxton, GA, USA	*	*
02.03.81	Beechcraft King Air E90	XA-FEX	LW-113	Operator Unknown	Written off	Monterrey, Mexico	*	*
05.03.81	Douglas DC-3	HK-2497	15634/27079	LAPA	Crash landed after engine failure	Anapoima, Colombia	0	*
08.03.81	Antonov AN-24RT	SSSR-46280	77303703	Aeroflot	Crashed short of runway	Kursk, RSFSR, USSR	*	*
09.03.81	Pilatus PC-6/B Turbo-Porter	HB-FCX	*	Zimex Aviation	Crashed	Libya	*	*
10.03.81	Aerospatiale 330G Puma	PK-PEP	1253	Pertambangan Minjak Nasiona	Crashed	Off Natuna Is, Indonesia	0	17
11.03.81	Fokker F-28 Fellowship 2000	9G-ACA	11077	Ghana Airways	Crash landed	Accra, Ghana	0	*
11.03.81	Mitsubishi MU-2G	JA8753	504	Nihon Naigai Koku	Crashed	Kagoshima, Japan	*	*
11.03.81	Piper PA-31-310 Navajo	TF-RTR	31-86	Flugfelag Austurlands	Crashed into river	nr Hofn, Iceland	*	*
12.03.81	Sikorsky S-76A	G-BGXY	760021	Bristow Helicopters	Crashed	nr Peterhead, UK	4	0
13.03.81	Bell 212	PT-HKP	*	Lider Taxi Aereo	Crash landed in sea & sank on tow	Off Amape, Brazil	*	*
15.03.81	de Havilland Canada Twin Otter 200	C-FDHT	130	Bradley Air Services	Sank through ice	Station Nord, Greenland	*	*
16.03.81	Douglas DC-3	C-FIRW	9834	Air Inuit	Sank through ice	Lac Bienville, PQ, Canada	0	2
18.03.81	Beechcraft King Air A100	N999CR	B-012	Operator Unknown	Written off	Houston, TX, USA	*	*
18.03.81	Beechcraft 18	C-GRJE	3992	North Cariboo Flying Service	Crashed on approach	Beatty, NV, USA	2	0
24.03.81	Fairchild Merlin IIIB	N1011R	T-303E	Operator Unknown	Written off	Location Unknown	*	*

Date	Type	Reg'n	C/n	Operator	Accident	Location	F	S
25.03.81	Douglas DC-3	N3VB	2220	Sun Valley Aviation	Crashed	nr Salinas, Mexico	*	*
26.03.81	Fokker F-27 Friendship 400	5A-DBR	10517	Libyan Arab Airlines	Damaged on landing	Kufra, Chad	0	*
26.03.81	Antonov AN-24V	SP-LTU	07306007	LOT Polish Airlines	Crashed after propeller failure on approach	Slupsk, Poland	1	46
28.03.81	Douglas C-54S	N98AS	10431	Caribbean Air Cargo	Crashed	Off St Croix, Puerto Rico	1	1
29.03.81	Boeing 707-329	OO-SJA	17623	Sobelair	Crash landed with engine fire	Brussels, Belgium	0	109
29.03.81	Lockheed Jetstar 6	N267L	5067	W.Hilmer	Overshot on landing & caught fire	Luton, Beds, UK	0	9
29.03.81	Potez 840	F-BMCY	02	Paris Flying Club	Belly landed	Sumburgh, Shetlands, UK	0	*
oo.03.81	Beechcraft Super King Air 200	YV-257CP	BB-0517	Operator Unknown	Written off	Location Unknown	*	*
01.04.81	Cessna 402A	P2-GKJ	402A-0081	Talair	Crashed	nr Mt Hagen, Papua New Guinea	8	0
02.04.81	Fairchild 226TC Metro II	VH-BPL	TC-272	Bush Pilots Airways	Crashed	Emerald, Vic, Australia	*	*
02.04.81	Douglas DC-3	N258M	9555	Skytrain Air	Crashed	nr Veracruz, Mexico	2	0
03.04.81	Noorduyn UC-64 Norseman	N55555	*	Operator Unknown	Crashed on take-off	Prince George, BC, Canada	*	*
06.04.81	Douglas DC-3	CP-1470	19395	Urcupina	Crashed in bad weather	Laguna Soliz, Bolivia	7	*
10.04.81	Beechcraft Queen Air 80	N3768Z	LD-300	Operator Unknown	Crashed on take-off	Pine Knot, KY, USA	2	0
14.04.81	de Havilland Canada Beaver	C-FAWA	1430	Air BC	Crashed after engine failure	Fraser River, BC, Canada	0	1
15.04.81	Sikorsky S-61L	ZS-HGU	61-363	Court Helicopters	Crashed	Cape Town, South Africa	0	*
17.04.81	Handley Page Jetstream 1	N11360	238	Air US	Mid-air collision with Cessna 206 N4862F	Loveland, CO, USA	13(2)	0
19.04.81	Mitsubishi MU-2J	N500GL	579	Operator Unknown	Written off	Texas, USA	*	*
21.04.81	Douglas DC-3	F-BJBY	7390	Hemet Exploration	Crashed	Western Mediterranean Sea	4	0
22.04.81	Mitsubishi MU-2F	N9JS	178	Operator Unknown	Written off	Alpena, MI, USA	*	*
28.04.81	Douglas DC-3	PK-OBK	12209	Airfast Services	Crashed on approach	Simpang Tiga, Indonesia	9	8
01.05.81	Vickers Viscount 832	PK-RVN	415	Mandala Airlines	Crashed	Semarang, Indonesia	*	*
02.05.81	British Aerospace 125-700A	XA-KEW	257096	Servicios Aereos Regiomontanos	Crashed	Monterrey, Mexico	*	*
07.05.81	BAC One-Eleven 529FR	LV-LOX	212	Austral	Crashed in bad weather	River Plate, Argentina	30	0
09.05.81	Douglas DC-3	N60705	4638	Skytrain Air	Crash landed & caught fire	Vicente Guerreo, Mexico	0	*
13.05.81	Mitsubishi MU-2B	N92JR	006	Operator Unknown	Written off	Miami, FL, USA	*	*
13.05.81	Bell 206B JetRanger II	C-FAAN	01274	Aero Arctic	Crashed on landing	Amoga-Booga Lake, NWT, Canada	*	*
16.05.81	Cessna 206 Super Skywagon	8R-GEK	*	Toucan Air Services	Crashed	Essequibo, Guyana	6	0
16.05.81	Cessna U206G Super Skywagon	HK-2578	U206-05916	ALAS	Crashed	nr Miraflores, Colombia	2	0
18.05.81	Hughes 369HS	PT-HKU	827S	VOTEC	Crashed into mountain	Rio de Janeiro, Brazil	1	0
19.05.81	Bell 206B JetRanger II	N49746	*	Petroleum Helicopters	Crashed taking off from oil platform	Gulf of Mexico	*	*
21.05.81	de Havilland Canada Twin Otter 300	HC-BAX/457	457	TAME	Written off	Location Unknown	*	*
21.05.81	Convair 440-11	XA-KEH	327	Aerolineas Leon	Crashed into mountain	Pinarete Mt, Mexico	21	0
23.05.81	Beechcraft 18	N79LA	BA-543	Air Cape	Crashed after take-off	USA	2	0
24.05.81	Beechcraft Super King Air 200	HC-BHG/723	BB-0723	TAME	Crashed in poor weather [President of Ecuador killed]	nr Guachanama, Ecuador	9	0
27.05.81	Cessna 402	N2AQ	402-0210	Operator Unknown	Crashed after in-flight fire	Cliff, NM, USA	*	*
29.05.81	Lockheed C-130H Hercules	SU-BAH/1276	4792	Egyptian Air Force	Crashed after take-off	nr Cairo, Egypt	17	0
30.05.81	Dassault Falcon 20C	7T-VRE	156	Algerian Government	Crashed	Bamako, Mali	3	2
31.05.81	Cessna 402B	5Y-AZZ	402B-0915	Safari Air Services	Overshot on landing & crashed	Nairobi, Kenya	*	*
01.06.81	Hughes 369D	C-GRYK	190446D	Viking Helicopters	Crashed with underslung load	Swift River, YK, Canada	*	*
02.06.81	Cessna R172K	HK-2564	R172-3393	Aerotaxi Colombia	Crashed	La Balsa, Colombia	3	0
03.06.81	Convair C-131E	N121CA	342	Command Aviation	Crashed after engine failure on take-off	Dillingham, AK, USA	0	*
04.06.81	Britten-Norman BN-2A-7 Islander	N28377	0141	Pinders Charter Service	Crashed	Off Ship Channel Cay, Bahamas	0	*
04.06.81	Mitsubishi MU-2N	YV-174CP	695	Immobiliaria Uracoa	Mid-air collision with PA-31T YV-215CP	Off Caracas, Venezuela	5(5)	0
05.06.81	Sikorsky S-64	N6965R	64060	Silver Grizzle Timber Co	Crashed	Kitsault Village, BC, Canada	1	1
06.06.81	Fokker F-27 Friendship 600	AP-AXF	10354	Pakistan International Airlines	Damaged beyond repair	Gilgit, Pakistan	*	*
06.06.81	de Havilland Canada Beaver	C-FFHX	060	Lakeland Airways	Crashed into hill	Maple Mt, ON, Canada	3	0
10.06.81	Fairchild Merlin III	N555AM	T-201	Operator Unknown	Crashed in lake on drug smuggling flight	nr Cameron, LA, USA	2	0
11.06.81	Boeing 707-341C	PP-VJT	19322	Varig	Damaged on landing	Manaus, Brazil	0	*
12.06.81	de Havilland Canada Otter	C-FRHW	445	Trans Provincial Airlines	Crashed into hill on take-off	Smithers, BC, Canada	0	*
12.06.81	Beechcraft G18S	N547DA	BA-599	Aero Taxi	Crashed on take-off	Location Unknown	*	*
12.06.81	Beechcraft 95 Baron D55	P2-GKO	TE-478	Talair	Crashed after overrunning runway	Rakunda, Papua New Guinea	0	*
13.06.81	IRMA BN-2A-8 Islander	B-11108	0701	Taiwan Airlines	Crashed into cliff during typhoon	Hualien, Taiwan	2	0

Date	Type	Reg'n	C/n	Operator	Accident	Location	F	S
13.06.81	Tupolev TU-154	SSSR-85029	*	Aeroflot	Damaged after overrunning on landing	Bratsk, RSFSR, USSR	0	*
13.06.81	Aerospatiale SA.319B Alouette III	VH-FLH	2255	Helitrans	Crashed	Gladstone, Qld, Australia	*	*
15.06.81	IRMA BN-2A-20 Islander	P2-ISA	0703	Talair	Crashed short of runway	Lakunai, Papua New Guinea	*	*
16.06.81	Lockheed L-100-20 Hercules	D2-EAS	4830	TAAG Angola Airlines	Shot down by rebels	Mongua, Angola	*	*
16.06.81	Hindustan 748 2-224	VT-DXI	514	Indian Airlines	Crashed after take-off	Tirupati, India	0	21
17.06.81	Douglas DC-3	HK-1078	9884	Taxi Aereo El Venado	Crashed after engine failure	Miraflores, Colombia	3	10
17.06.81	Mitsubishi MU-2D	N3ED	101	Operator Unknown	Written off	Riverton, WY, USA	*	*
17.06.81	Beechcraft Queen Air	N6867Q	LD-223	Operator Unknown	Destroyed by fire after landing on drug smuggling flight	nr Gerlach, NV, USA	0	*
22.06.81	Aerospatiale SA.341G Gazelle	C-GXQE	*	Totem Air	Crashed & caught fire on landing	nr Fort Simpson, NWT, Canada	0	*
24.06.81	Douglas DC-3	N18949	2013	Nathaniel Hawthorne College	Crashed into trees on take-off	Deering, NH, USA	*	*
25.06.81	Douglas DC-3	FAC.1129	*	Satena	Damaged beyond repair	Barroblanca, Colombia	*	*
27.06.81	British Aerospace 748 1	G-ASPL	1560	Dan-Air	Crashed after cargo door detached & struck tail	Nailstone, Leics, UK	3	0
27.06.81	Fairchild C-119 Flying Boxcar	N8682	*	Hawkins & Powers Aviation	Crashed due to fire	Kayokuk River, AK, USA	0	1
28.06.81	Tupolev TU-134A	SSSR-65871	*	Aeroflot	Crashed on landing due to u/c failure	Simferopol, Ukraine, USSR	0	*
28.06.81	Beechcraft King Air F90	HK-2484	LA-054	Operator Unknown	Written off	Palanquera, Colombia	*	*
29.06.81	Fokker F-27 Friendship 400	XY-ADN	10312	Burma Airways	Crashed	Sandoway, Burma	*	*
30.06.81	Cessna 404 Titan	N6819N	*	Operator Unknown	Crashed after pilot suffered heart attack	Belmont, KS, USA	1	0
oo.06.81	Britten-Norman BN-2A-8 Islander	TN-ADS	0127	Societe Aero-Service Afrigo	Written off	Location Unknown	*	*
01.07.81	Douglas DC-3	N111ST	4661	United Aircraft Services	Crashed after take-off	Muskegon, MI, USA	3	*
05.07.81	Boeing 707-327C	OD-AGW	19440	Trans Mediterranean Airways	Destroyed by bomb while parked	Beirut, Lebanon	0	*
09.07.81	Howard 500	C-GKFN	107	Kelowna Flightcraft	Crashed on take-off	Toronto, ON, Canada	3	0
14.07.81	Douglas DC-4	N3373F	36061	Aero Union	Caught fire on take-off & crashed in sea	Off Kenai, AK, USA	3	*
15.07.81	Martin 404	CP-1318	14134	CAMBA	Crashed short of runway	Pista El Peru, Bolivia	0	*
15.07.81	Beechcraft Super King Air 200	N631SR	BB-0244	Operator Unknown	Crashed into mountain in poor weather	King Cove, AK, USA	5	*
18.07.81	Canadair CL-44D4-6	LV-JTN	C34	Transporte Aereo Rioplatense	Mid-air collision with Soviet AF fighter	nr Yerevan, Armenia, USSR	4(*)	0
20.07.81	Fokker F-27 Friendship 600	6O-SAY	10557	Somali Airlines	Crashed after take-off	Mogadishu, Somalia	50	0
20.07.81	Britten-Norman BN-2A-6 Islander	N116DW	0202	Dorado Wings	Stalled on take-off & crashed	San Juan, Puerto Rico	0	6
21.07.81	Antonov AN-2	YR-PVJ	1G175-09	Operator Unknown	Crashed	Romania	*	*
22.07.81	Bell 212	PT-HKW	*	Lider Taxi Aereo	Crashed after take-off from oil platform	Off Macae, Brazil	0	4
24.07.81	Type Unknown	*	*	Air Madagascar	Crashed	Malagasy Republic	19	0
25.07.81	Douglas DC-3	HK-772	11743	Transamazonica	Crashed	nr Caruru, Colombia	3	*
25.07.81	Volpar-Beechcraft 18	HB-GFT	*	Ciba-Pilatus Aerial Spraying	Belly landed	Khartoum, Sudan	*	*
27.07.81	McDonnell Douglas DC-9-32	XA-DEN	47621	Aeromexico	Crashed on landing in storm	Chihuahua, Mexico	32	34
28.07.81	Beechcraft Queen Air B80	N1028C	LD-355	Operator Unknown	Crashed on take-off	Groveland, FL, USA	2	0
01.08.81	Douglas DC-3	F-BJHC	14311/25756	Hemet Exploration	Shot down by missile in error by Mozambique forces	Mozambique	6	0
01.08.81	Beechcraft D18	N9826Z	AF-305	Operator Unknown	Crashed into mountain	nr Minto, AK, USA	*	0
02.08.81	Embraer Bandeirante 110P1	HK-2651	110.206	Taxi Aereo El Venado	Crashed after take-off	Paipa, Colombia	20	2
03.08.81	Douglas DC-3	FAC.1128	4824	Satena	Crashed	Cali, Colombia	*	*
07.08.81	Douglas DC-3	CC-CBW	15259/26704	Aerocor	Crashed	nr Coyhaique, Chile	*	*
07.08.81	Beechcraft Queen Air 65	N805Q	LC-015	Operator Unknown	Crashed on approach	Spirit Lake, IA, USA	*	*
10.08.81	Ford 5-AT-B Tri-Motor	N76GC	5-AT-011	Grand Canyon Airlines	Damaged by strong winds	Las Vegas, NV, USA	0	*
10.08.81	Bell 47G-4A	C-FAUR	7707	Athabaska Airways	Crashed	nr Buffalo Narrows, SK, Canada	*	*
11.08.81	Douglas DC-4	HK-136	10407	Sadelca	Crashed	nr Neiva, Colombia	*	*
12.08.81	Bell 212	G-BIJF	31163	Bristow Helicopters	Crashed in sea	North Sea	1	0
13.08.81	Westland Wessex 1	G-ASWI	199	Bristow Helicopters	Crashed	Off Cromer, Norfolk, UK	13	0
13.08.81	Beechcraft H-18	N518K	BA-622	M.Martin	Crashed on touch & go	Fort Lauderdale, FL, USA	*	*
18.08.81	Hindustan 748 2-224	VT-DXF	511	Indian Airlines	Overshot & crashed	Mangalore, India	0	21
18.08.81	Beechcraft King Air E90	F-GCJN	LW-335	Operator Unknown	Written off	Location Unknown	*	*
22.08.81	Boeing 737-222	B-2603	19939	Far Eastern Air Transport	Exploded & crashed due to structural failure	nr Miao-Li, Taiwan	110	0
24.08.81	Antonov AN-24	SSSR-46653	*	Aeroflot	Mid-air collision with Soviet Air Force TU-16	nr Zavitinsk, RSFSR, USSR	31(*)	1
24.08.81	Hughes 369D	C-GCTV	960005D	Terr-Air	Crashed	nr Philomena, AB, Canada	1	0
25.08.81	Britten-Norman BN-2A-21 Islander	7P-LAE	0556	Lesotho Airways	Crashed after take-off	Sekakes, Lesotho	0	*
26.08.81	Rockwell Turbo Commander 690C	LV-OEV	11628	Operator Unknown	Written off	Location Unknown	*	*
30.08.81	Cessna 421 Golden Eagle	N6867R	*	Operator Unknown	Crashed	nr Rutland, OH, USA	*	*

Date	Type	Reg'n	C/n	Operator	Accident	Location	F	S
31.08.81	Boeing 720-023B	OD-AFR	18018	Middle East Airlines	Blown up by bomb on ground	Beirut, Lebanon	0	*
02.09.81	Mitsubishi MU-2K	N233MA	251	Operator Unknown	Crashed	McCleod, TX, USA	4	*
07.09.81	Britten-Norman Trislander	C-GSZI	0360	Questor Surveys	Damaged beyond repair	Canada	*	*
07.09.81	Piper PA-23-250 Aztec	YJ-RV9	*	Air Melanesie	Crashed after engine failure	Port Vila, Vanuatu	1	0
12.09.81	Bell 206 JetRanger	C-FROO	*	Northern Mountain Helicopters	Crashed on take-off	nr Chetwynd, BC, Canada	1	0
15.09.81	Beechcraft King Air C90	N101LR	LJ-0802	Operator Unknown	Written off	Quito, Ecuador	*	*
15.09.81	Piper PA-28RT-201 Cherokee	HB-RET	*	Aeroleasing	Crashed into mountain	Weiss Horn Mt, Switzerland	2	0
16.09.81	Rockwell Turbo Commander 690C	ZS-KRS	11644	Operator Unknown	Written off	Location Unknown	*	*
16.09.81	de Havilland Canada Beaver	C-FEYT	487	Air Kipawa	Crashed into hill	Poste la Baleine, PQ, Canada	2	0
17.09.81	Bell 206B JetRanger II	C-GOOM	*	Delta Helicopters	Crashed into river	John d'Or Prairie, AB, Canada	2	1
18.09.81	Britten-Norman BN-2A-21 Islander	G-BDNP	0496	Jersey European Airways	Force-landed after engine failure	Guernsey, Channel Is	0	*
18.09.81	Yakovlev YAK-40	SSSR-87455	*	Aeroflot	Collided with Aeroflot Mi-8 on approach	Zheleznogorsk, RSFSR, USSR	33(*)	0
18.09.81	Mil Mi-8	*	*	Aeroflot	Mid-air collision with Aeroflot YAK-40 CCCP-87455	Zheleznogorsk, RSFSR, USSR	*(33)	*
24.09.81	Beechcraft 18	*	*	Hangar 2 Corporation	Crashed in storm	nr Port-au-Prince, Haiti	*	*
27.09.81	Cessna 185	C-GGQU	*	Fort Smith Air Service	Destroyed by fire	Porter Lake, NWT, Canada	*	*
28.09.81	Britten-Norman BN-2A Islander	N457SA	0027	Valley Air Service	Written off	Location Unknown	*	*
29.09.81	Sikorsky S-76	PT-HKC	760020	VOTEC	Overturned by high winds	Macae, Brazil	0	0
30.09.81	Agusta-Bell 206B JetRanger II	LN-ORJ	08374	Lufttransport	Damaged being transported aboard MV *Polastar*	Off Svalbard, Norway	0	0
oo.09.81	Fairchild F-27J	N777DG	0013	Pacific Alaska Airlines	Written off	Fairbanks, AK, USA	*	*
01.10.81	Gates Learjet 24	N44CJ	24-146	Precision Flite Inc	Crashed	Felt, OK, USA	3	0
04.10.81	Beechcraft 18	N6675	CA-256	Operator Unknown	Crashed on landing	nr Fraser, MI, USA	1	0
06.10.81	Fokker F-28 Fellowship 4000	PH-CHI	11141	NLM CityHopper	Crashed in storm	nr Rotterdam, Netherlands	21	0
06.10.81	Westland-Bell 47G-4A	G-AXKT	WA.724	Bristow Helicopters	Mid-air collision with AAC Scout	Middle Wallop, UK	0	2
07.10.81	Douglas DC-3	ET-AHR	13311	Ethiopian Airlines	Crashed & two months later struck by crashing Army Mi-24	Kombolcha, Ethiopia	*(*)	*
09.10.81	Soloy Bell 47G-3B-1	C-FYJP	6561	Alpine Helicopters	Crashed into trees	Alpine Base, BC, Canada	0	2
15.10.81	Cessna 404 Titan	OE-FCT	*	Oefag-Flugdienst	Crashed into mountain	Kufstein, Austria	9	0
16.10.81	Rockwell Turbo Commander 690C	N5926K	11674	Operator Unknown	Written off	Location Unknown	*	*
17.10.81	de Havilland Heron 1B	ZK-EKO	14044	Rotorua Airlines	Destroyed by fire	Rotorua, New Zealand	0	*
21.10.81	Tupolev TU-154B	HA-LCF	126	Malev	Broke in two on landing	Prague, Czechoslovakia	0	81
21.10.81	Curtiss C-46	HK-388	26796	Aeropesca	Hijacked & crashed	Orteganza River, Colombia	0	*
22.10.81	Boeing 707-331C	OD-AGT	19213	Trans Mediterranean Airways	Damaged in emergency landing after in-flight fire	Narita, Tokyo, Japan	0	*
23.10.81	Curtiss C-46A	CP-1617	253	Eldorado	Damaged on landing	El Tiboy, Bolivia	*	*
26.10.81	Lockheed C-121A Constellation	HI-328	2607	Argo	Crashed in rainstorm	Off St Thomas, US Virgin Islands	3	*
26.10.81	Beechcraft King Air E90	N114K	LW-122	Operator Unknown	Crashed when wing broke off after take-off	Mineral Wells, TX, USA	1	*
28.10.81	Britten-Norman Trislander	EL-AIC	1014	Air Liberia	Written off	Location Unknown	*	*
29.10.81	Bell 212	PT-HJU	30909	Lider Taxi Aereo	Crashed at sea	Off Salinopolis, Brazil	5	0
31.10.81	de Havilland Canada Twin Otter 300	TJ-CBC	416	Cameroon Airlines	Crashed on take-off	Bafoussom, Cameroons	1	*
oo.10.81	Beechcraft King Air B90	C-GWCY	LJ-0345	Operator Unknown	Written off	Lynn Lake, Canada	*	*
05.11.81	Mitsubishi MU-2 Marquise	N53AD	776SA	Operator Unknown	Written off	Saratoga, WY, USA	*	*
09.11.81	McDonnell Douglas DC-9-32	XA-DEO	47622	Aeromexico	Crashed into mountain	nr Altamirano, Mexico	18	0
13.11.81	Gates Learjet 55	N57TA	55-010	Gates Learjet	Crashed on take-off	Waterkloof, South Africa	2	0
16.11.81	Aerospatiale Corvette	TY-BBK	29	Benin Government	Crashed	Lagos, Nigeria	*	*
16.11.81	Tupolev TU-154B-2	SSSR-85480	480	Aeroflot	Crashed on landing	Norilsk, RSFSR, USSR	99	68
18.11.81	de Havilland Canada Twin Otter 300	VP-FAW	546	British Antarctic Survey	Damaged beyond repair during gale	Rothera Station, Br Antarctic Terr	0	0
18.11.81	Mitsubishi MU-2J	N444AR	555	Operator Unknown	Crashed out of fuel on drug smuggling flight	Walcott, CO, USA	7	0
19.11.81	Mitsubishi MU-2P	N750MA	365SA	Operator Unknown	Written off	Location Unknown	*	*
19.11.81	Pilatus PC-6/B2-H2 Turbo-Porter	9N-ABJ	746	Royal Nepal Airlines	Crashed after take-off	Biratnagar, Nepal	10	0
21.11.81	Cessna 421C Golden Eagle	N8369G	421C-0309	Operator Unknown	Crashed into mountain at night	nr Gooding, ID, USA	3	0
21.11.81	Cessna 172	C-GJIS	*	Medley Airways	Crashed	nr Saskatoon, SK, Canada	3	0
22.11.81	Mitsubishi MU-2G	N109TW	543	Operator Unknown	Crashed into sea	Off Pago Pago, US Samoa	*	*
30.11.81	Douglas DC-6A	N3486F	43683	Guyana Airways	Crashed & caught fire	Vigie, St Lucia	2	0
01.12.81	McDonnell Douglas MD-82	YU-ANA	48047	Inex-Adria Airways	Crashed into mountain	Corsica, France	180	0
01.12.81	Rockwell Turbo Commander 690A	D-IOET	11142	Operator Unknown	Written off	West Germany	*	*
05.12.81	Beechcraft 18	N8185H	AF-381	Jump Hawaii Club	Crashed after engine failure	Pearl Harbor Bay, HI, USA	11	0

Date	Type	Reg'n	C/n	Operator	Accident	Location	F	S
06.12.81	Mitsubishi MU-2J	C-GLOW	624	Operator Unknown	Crashed into hospital on approach	Edmonton, Alb, Canada	0	*
07.12.81	Bell 206B JetRanger	PT-HBY	00255	Lider Taxi Aereo	Crashed	Para, Brazil	1	0
12.12.81	Boeing 707-124	HI-384HA	17610	Hispaniola Airways	U/c collapsed on landing	Miami, FL, USA	0	*
13.12.81	Rockwell Turbo Commander 690C	N5860K	11608	Operator Unknown	Written off	Location Unknown	*	*
13.12.81	Rockwell Commander 500B	PT-BVX	1281-109	Lider Taxi Aereo	Damaged beyond repair	nr Anapuera, Brazil	*	*
15.12.81	Bell 206B JetRanger	JA9286	03242	Osaka Airways	Crashed into lake	Lake Biwa, Japan	3	0
16.12.81	Aerospatiale Puma	9M-SSC	1481	Bristow Helicopters	Crashed	Kuala Belait, Brunei	12	*
18.12.81	de Havilland Canada Twin Otter 300	HK-2217	609	ACES Colombia	Crashed into mountain	nr Covenas, Colombia	12	0
23.12.81	Antonov AN-26	SSSR-26505	*	Aeroflot	Crashed short of runway	Enisseysk, RSFSR, USSR	2	*
23.12.81	Hughes 369HS	PT-HIT	760835S	VOTEC	Crashed after engine failure	Jacareacanga, Brazil	4	1
29.12.81	British Aerospace 748 2A	C-GEPH	1635	Eastern Provincial Airways	Written off	Sydney, NS, Canada	*	*
31.12.81	Piper PA-31 Navajo	N41070	*	Sun West Airlines	Crashed in snowstorm	Durango La Plata, CO, USA	4	2
oo.12.81	Douglas DC-4-1009	C-FJRW	42983	Aero Trades Western	Crashed short of runway	Spence Bay, NWT, Canada	0	*
oo.oo.81	Douglas DC-3	5N-ARA	16294/33042	Arax Airlines	Damaged beyond repair	Lagos, Nigeria	*	*
oo.oo.81	Aerospatiale Caravelle 6R	TT-AAM	100	Chad Government	Damaged beyond repair during civil war	Chad	*	*
oo.oo.81	Antonov AN-2	OK-KIM	1G190-08	Slovair	Crashed after hijack attempt	Znojmo, Czechoslovakia	*	*
oo.oo.81	Douglas DC-4	N122AC	10748	Southern Aero Trades	Destroyed	Colombia	*	*
oo.oo.81	Douglas C-118A Liftmaster	N2949F	44629	GAF International Service	Crashed	Bahamas	*	*
03.01.82	Cessna 402B	5Y-ANY	402B-0204	Sunbird Aviation	Crashed	Kichwa Tembo, Kenya	*	*
07.01.82	LET 410M Turbolet	SSSR-67290	731101	Aeroflot	Crashed into hill	Gelendzhik, RSFSR, USSR	18	*
08.01.82	Bell 206B JetRanger	VH-AJD	*	Jayrow Helicopters	Crashed	Melbourne, Vic, Australia	4	0
10.01.82	Fairchild Merlin IIIB	N336SA	T-336	Operator Unknown	Written off	Texas, USA	*	*
11.01.82	Gates Learjet 25XR	HZ-GP5	25XR-199	Management Jets International	Crashed on landing	Narssarssuaq, Greenland	2	0
13.01.82	Boeing 737-222	N62AF	19556	Air Florida	Crashed on take-off due to icing	Potomac River, Washington, DC, USA	74{4}	5
13.01.82	de Havilland Canada Beaver	C-GUWC	*	Air Mistassini	Crashed after in-flight fire	Cache Lake, PQ, Canada	0	*
15.01.82	Cessna 172E	JA3212	172-51099	Nippon Sangyo Airways	Crashed	Lake Biwa, Japan	3	0
16.01.82	Yakovlev YAK-40	SSSR-87902	*	Aeroflot	Belly landed out of fuel	Shevchenko, Kazakhstan, USSR	0	3
17.01.82	Convair 440-75	N21DR	325	Island Airlines Hawaii	Crashed after take-off	Pearl Harbor, HI, USA	0	*
18.01.82	Mitsubishi MU-2M	C-GFRU	343	Kelowna Flightcraft	Crashed into mountain	Kelowna, BC, Canada	2	0
22.01.82	Hughes 500	C-GQCA	*	Queen Charlotte Helicopters	Crashed	nr Lyell Island, BC, Canada	3	0
24.01.82	McDonnell Douglas DC-10-30CF	N113WA	47821	World Airways	Overran into sea on landing & broke in two	Boston, MA, USA	2	208
24.01.82	Cessna 402B	N4244Z	*	S & N Construction Co	Crashed on approach	Laredo, TX, USA	7	0
25.01.82	Antonov AN-24RV	YR-BMD	57310202	Tarom	Crashed after wing struck ground on approach	Constanta, Romania	7	*
25.01.82	Antonov AN-2R	HA-MBI	1G166-27	Air Service Hungary	Crashed	Hungary	*	*
26.01.82	Boeing 707-348C	7O-ACJ	18737	Alyemda	Damaged on landing after being fired upon by fighter	Damascus, Syria	0	*
oo.01.82	Curtiss C-46	N7560U	22475	Casair	Crashed on landing	San Juan, Puerto Rico	0	*
01.02.82	Beechcraft 99	N451C	U066	Pilgrim Airlines	Crashed on approach	Groton, OK, USA	*	*
04.02.82	Beechcraft Super King Air 200	YV-426P	BB-0142	Operator Unknown	Written off	nr Caracas, Venezuela	*	*
04.02.82	Beechcraft King Air C90	YV-994P	LJ-0693	Operator Unknown	Written off	Caracas, Venezuela	*	*
04.02.82	Bell 206L Long Ranger	C-GSHU	45023	Shirley Air Services	Crashed & caught fire	nr Inuvik, AB, Canada	1	0
05.02.82	Canadair CL-44J	TR-LVO	020	Affretair	Destroyed by fire on ground	Salisbury, Zimbabwe	0	*
08.02.82	Douglas DC-3	HK-1212	4987	Sadelca	Damaged by bomb explosion	Miraflores, Colombia	1	*
09.02.82	McDonnell Douglas DC-8-61	JA8061	45889	Japan Air Lines	Crashed in sea on approach due to pilot sickness	Tokyo Bay, Japan	24	150
11.02.82	Cessna 421 Golden Eagle	N24CC	421-0043	Operator Unknown	Crashed due to wrong fuel being used	nr Miami, FL, USA	2	0
19.02.82	Douglas DC-6B	HK-1706	44168	Lineas Aereas del Caribe	Crashed	Cerro el Tablazo, Colombia	4	*
20.02.82	Britten-Norman BN-2A-9 Islander	G-BBRP	0371	Army Parachute Association	Crashed on take-off	Netheravon, Wilts, UK	0	9
20.02.82	Grumman G-21A Goose	N2845D	B-112	Operator Unknown	Sank after emergency landing	Cape Yakataga, AK, USA	0	2
21.02.82	de Havilland Canada Twin Otter 300	N127PM	105	Pilgrim Airlines	Crash landed on ice after fire & sank when heat melted ice	nr Scituate, RI, USA	*	*
03.03.82	Britten-Norman BN-2A-27R Islander	HC-BFJ	0590	Atesa	Written off	Location Unknown	*	*
08.03.82	Beechcraft 18	N700W	*	Operator Unknown	Crashed on take-off on drug smuggling flight	San Miguel Ranch, TX, USA	*	*
10.03.82	Beechcraft King Air C90	N6272C	LJ-1025	Operator Unknown	Crashed at sea	Off Azores, Portugal	0	1
10.03.82	IRMA BN-2A-20 Islander	P2-HAC	0762	Heron Air Charter	Written off	Location Unknown	*	*
11.03.82	de Havilland Canada Twin Otter 300	LN-BNK	568	Wideroe	Crashed	Off Norway	15	0

Date	Type	Reg'n	C/n	Operator	Accident	Location	F	S
11.03.82	Scottish Aviation Twin Pioneer 3	G-BBVF	558	Flight One	Damaged during gale	Shobdon, Hereford, UK	0	*
15.03.82	Beechcraft C-45	N9846Z	AF-397	Operator Unknown	Crashed short of runway	McAllen, TX, USA	1	0
17.03.82	Airbus A.300B4-203	F-BVGK	070	Air France	Aborted take-off after engine fire & damaged beyond repair	Sanaa, Yemen Arab Republic	0	124
20.03.82	Fokker F-28 Fellowship 1000	PK-GVK	11078	Garuda Indonesian Airlines	Crashed on landing in heavy rain	Branti, Indonesia	24	2
21.03.82	Lockheed Electra 188AF	N5504	1009	Zantop International Airlines	Destroyed in hangar collapse	Macon, GA, USA	0	*
21.03.82	Lockheed Electra 188AF	N5516	1022	Zantop International Airlines	Destroyed in hangar collapse	Macon, GA, USA	0	*
23.03.82	Vickers Viscount 745D	HK-2382	212	Aeropesca	Crashed into mountain during storm	Queate, Bolivia	22	0
26.03.82	Dornier Do.228-100	D-IFNS	4358	Dornier	Crashed	nr Augsburg, West Germany	3	0
29.03.82	Rockwell Turbo Commander 690C	N5957K	11720	Operator Unknown	Written off	Location Unknown	*	*
30.03.82	Bell 206B JetRanger II	C-FNMQ	00765	Northern Mountain Helicopters	Crashed	nr Quesnel, NC, Canada	*	*
05.04.82	Piper PA-31-350 Chieftain	N123CB	31-7752161	Operator Unknown	Crash landed & burned in field	Baconton, GA, USA	*	*
11.04.82	Lockheed L-100 Hercules	C-FPWK	4170	NWT Air	Destroyed by fire while unloading fuel	Canada	*	*
14.04.82	Fairchild 226TC Metro II	ZS-KYA	TC-331	Magnum Airlines	Crashed	South Africa	*	*
17.04.82	Hawker Siddeley Argosy 101	G-APRN	6654	Air Bridge Carriers	Damaged on landing	Belfast, UK	0	*
20.04.82	Mitsubishi MU-2G	N165MA	541	Operator Unknown	Crashed into high ground in fog	Lookout Mt, GA, USA	5	0
20.04.82	Piper PA-32 Cherokee Six	N2477U	32-7940254	Crown Airways	Crashed	Youngstown, OH, USA	0	1
21.04.82	Aerospatiale 330F Puma	6W-SHI	1336	Senegalese Air Force	Crashed	Banjul, Gambia	1	13
22.04.82	Antonov AN-24V	YI-AEO	87304602	Iraqi Airways	Crashed on approach when wing struck ground	H3, Iraq	*	*
24.04.82	Antonov AN-12B	SSSR-11107	01347809	Aeroflot	Crashed on take-off	Urengoy, RSFSR, USSR	0	7
26.04.82	Hawker Siddeley Trident 2E	B-266	2170	CAAC	Crashed in rain	nr Guilin, China	112	0
29.04.82	Beechcraft G18S	N6911	BA-445	Operator Unknown	Crashed after engine failure	nr Hakalau, HI, USA	2	0
30.04.82	Sikorsky S-76	C-GIMF	760038	Okanagan Helicopters	Crashed	Gulf of Thailand	13	0
01.05.82	Douglas DC-7B	N823D	45332	Kinney Air Tankers	Destroyed by fire	Glendive, MT, USA	0	*
01.05.82	IRMA BN-2A-27 Islander	VP-FAY	0872	FIGAS	Destroyed during British air raid	Port Stanley, Falkland Islands	0	0
03.05.82	Short Skyvan 3M	PA-54	SH.1891	Argentine Coast Guard	Destroyed on ground by British naval gunfire	Port Stanley, Falkland Islands	*	*
03.05.82	Aerospatiale 330L Puma	PA-12	*	Argentine Coast Guard	Destroyed on ground by British naval gunfire	Port Stanley, Falkland Islands	0	*
03.05.82	Grumman Gulfstream II	7T-VHB	230	Algerian Government	Crashed	nr Qotur, Iran	14	0
05.05.82	Convair 440	CP-1725	*	Transportes Aereos Unidos	Crashed after take-off	Rio Seco, Bolivia	0	*
05.05.82	Beechcraft King Air B90	N98949	LJ-0407	Operator Unknown	Written off	Location Unknown	*	*
06.05.82	Gates Learjet 23	N100TA	23-045	Ibex Corporation	Crashed	Savannah, GA, USA	4	0
07.05.82	Douglas DC-3	C-FQHF	13392	Kenn Borek Air	Crashed into ditch	Calgary, Canada	*	*
09.05.82	de Havilland Canada Twin Otter 300	C-GKBO	547	Pan Arctic Oil	Crashed	North Pole	*	*
09.05.82	de Havilland Canada Dash 7-103	7O-ACK	015	Alyemda	Crashed in sea on approach	Off Aden, Yemen PDR	47	2
11.05.82	Antonov AN-2R	HA-ANL	IG187-34	Air Service Hungary	Crashed	Hungary	*	*
11.05.82	Antonov AN-2	SSSR-07399	IG150-34	Aeroflot	Crashed	Sputendorf, East Germany	*	*
14.05.82	Piper PA-31-350 Chieftain	HK-2203	31-7852123	Lineas Aereas Petroleras	Crashed	nr Cimitarra, Colombia	6	0
15.05.82	Short Skyvan 3M	PA-50	SH.1887	Argentine Coast Guard	Destroyed by British troops on ground	Pebble Is, Falkland Islands	*	*
15.05.82	Martin 404	N40445	14230	Frontier Airways	Crashed after take-off due to engine failure	Madera, CA, USA	0	*
16.05.82	de Havilland Canada Caribou	N103AQ	*	Operator Unknown	Crashed on approach	Hooper Bay, AK, USA	0	8
16.05.82	Gates Learjet 25B	PT-KZY	25B-204	Taxi Aereo Marilia	Crashed	Uberaba, Brazil	0	10
16.05.82	de Havilland Canada Twin Otter 200	N103AQ	183	Kodiak Aviation	Crashed on approach	Hooper Bay, AK, USA	*	*
19.05.82	Cessna Citation II	D-IJHM	551-0033	J.Hurler Flugdienst	Crashed	Kassel, West Germany	*	*
19.05.82	de Havilland Canada Beaver	C-FTYB	397	Tyee Airways	Crashed into trees	Narrows Inlet, BC, Canada	2	0
22.05.82	Aerospatiale SA.318C Alouette II	G-FILM	1648	Alan Mann Helicopters	Crashed into power cables	Grobnik, Yugoslavia	3	0
23.05.82	Gates Learjet 23	N808JA	23-050A	Jet America International	Destroyed in ground fire	Location Unknown	*	*
24.05.82	Embraer Bandeirante 110P	PT-GKC	110.092	Rio Sul	Crashed	nr Florianopolis, Brazil	0	4
24.05.82	Boeing 737-2A1A	PP-SMY	20970	VASP	Broke in two in hard landing	Brasilia, Brazil	2	117
24.05.82	de Havilland Canada Beaver	C-GSKY	1358	Wilderness Airline	Sank while taxiing	Hardy Bay, BC, Canada	1	*
28.05.82	Aerospatiale 330G Puma	PK-PDU	1258	Pelita Air Service	Crashed	Off Naturna Is, Indonesia	10	0
31.05.82	Yakovlev YAK-40	SSSR-87485	*	Aeroflot	Damaged after overrunning runway	Dnepropretovsk, RSFSR, USSR	0	35
oo.05.82	Beechcraft Queen Air 65	OB-T-1211	*	Operator Unknown	Crashed	Peru	*	*
02.06.82	McDonnell Douglas DC-9-32	C-FTLY	47200	Air Canada	Destroyed by fire after fuel explosion in hangar	Montreal, PQ, Canada	0	*
06.06.82	Douglas DC-3	N95C	20139	Fromhagen Aviation	Crashed on landing	St Petersburg, FL, USA	0	5
08.06.82	Boeing 727-212A	PP-SRK	21347	VASP	Crashed in bad weather	Serra da Pacatuba Mts, Brazil	137	0

Date	Type	Reg'n	C/n	Operator	Accident	Location	F	S
08.06.82	Grumman TBM3 Avenger	C-GFPQ	53592	Forest Protection	Crashed	nr Edmunston, NB, Canada	1	0
09.06.82	Fokker F-27 Friendship 600	VH-TQQ	10388	Trans Australia Airlines	Damaged when struck arrester gear on landing	RAAF Amberley, NSW, Australia	0	*
11.06.82	Cessna 441 Conquest II	D-IAAE	0047	Operator Unknown	Written off	Location Unknown	*	*
11.06.82	Cessna 421 Golden Eagle	G-BFEM	421-0316	Brush Electrical Machines	Crashed on motorway & caught fire	nr Lausanne, Switzerland	0	4
12.06.82	Boeing 720-023B	OD-AFP	18017	Middle East Airlines	Destroyed in hangar during Israeli raid	Beirut, Lebanon	*	*
16.06.82	Fairchild-Hiller FH.227B/LCD	PT-LBV	536	TABA	Crashed into tower on approach in poor visibility	Tabatinga, Brazil	44	0
16.06.82	Boeing 720-023B	OD-AFU	18029	Middle East Airlines	Destroyed by Israeli shelling	Beirut, Lebanon	*	*
16.06.82	Boeing 720-023B	OD-AFW	18026	Middle East Airlines	Destroyed by Israeli shelling	Beirut, Lebanon	*	*
16.06.82	Boeing 707-323C	OD-AGN	18938	Trans Mediterranean Airways	Damaged by Israeli shelling	Beirut, Lebanon	*	*
16.06.82	Boeing 720-047B	OD-AGR	19161	Middle East Airlines	Damaged by Israeli shelling	Beirut, Lebanon	*	*
16.06.82	Boeing 707-384C	OD-AFB	20224	Middle East Airlines	Destroyed by Israeli attack	Beirut, Lebanon	*	*
16.06.82	Boeing 720-023B	OD-AFO	18035	Middle East Airlines	Damaged by Israeli attack	Beirut, Lebanon	*	*
18.06.82	Bell 206L Long Ranger	C-GMHS	*	Eagle Helicopters	Crashed after engine failure	Jervis Inlet, BC, Canada	0	*
22.06.82	Boeing 707-437	VT-DJJ	17723	Air India	Skidded off runway in monsoon & crashed into ditch	Bombay, India	19	92
22.06.82	Noorduyn Norseman V	C-FECD	N29-31	Operator Unknown	Damaged in forced landing	Dogskin Lake, MN, Canada	*	*
28.06.82	Yalovlev YAK-42	SSSR-42529	8040104	Aeroflot	Crashed due to structural failure	Mozyr, Bylorussia, USSR	132	0
01.07.82	Douglas A-26 Invader	C-GWJG	28860	Air Spray	Crashed	nr Watson Lake, YK, Canada	1	*
03.07.82	Cessna 404 Titan	TR-LYQ	404-0425	Operator Unknown	Crashed	nr Ndjole-Booue, Gabon	12	0
06.07.82	Ilyushin IL-62M	SSSR-86513	4037536	Aeroflot	Crashed after take-off when engine exploded	nr Moscow, RSFSR, USSR	90	0
06.07.82	IRMA BN-2A-8 Islander	9M-MDD	0684	Malaysian Airline System	Crashed	Malaysia	*	*
09.07.82	Boeing 727-235	N4737	19457	Pan American World Airways	Crashed into houses after take-off due to windshear	New Orleans, LA, USA	145(8)	0
09.07.82	Piper PA-23-250 Aztec	9Q-CFN	*	Transportes Aereos de Zambesia	Crashed on take-off	Binga, Zaire	6	0
11.07.82	British Aerospace 748 2	RP-C1014	1636	Philippine Air Lines	Crashed into bulldozer after overrunning on take-off	Jolo, Philippines	4	25
13.07.82	Mitsubishi MU-2B	N27GP	027	Operator Unknown	Written off	Schellville, CA, USA	*	*
17.07.82	Beechcraft 18	N4758N	*	Operator Unknown	Crashed & caught fire on landing	Sheridan, OR, USA	*	*
19.07.82	Piper 601 Aerostar	C-GDMI	*	Kenn Borek Air	Crashed	nr Dease Lake, BC, Canada	2	0
22.07.82	Cessna 421A Golden Eagle	N4567L	421A-0167	Operator Unknown	Crashed on take-off	Georgetown, Bahamas	0	*
24.07.82	de Havilland Canada Twin Otter 300	5R-MGB	327	Air Madagascar	Crashed	Madagascar	*	*
29.07.82	Agusta-Bell 206G JetRanger II	EI-BMP	08564	Irish Helicopters	Crashed	Off Lough Corrib, Eire	5	0
29.07.82	Bell 206L Long Ranger	C-GTEJ	45462	Alpine Helicopters	Crashed	Coleman, AB, Canada	*	*
30.07.82	Lockheed HC-130H Hercules	1600	4757	United States Coast Guard	Crashed on landing	nr Attu, AK, USA	2	9
30.07.82	Douglas DC-3	N102BL	15906/32654	Pronto Aviation Services	Crashed after take-off due to engine failure	El Paso, TX, USA	*	*
01.08.82	Boeing 720-047B	OD-AGG	18828	Middle East Airlines	Destroyed during Israeli air raid	Beirut, Lebanon	*	*
04.08.82	Boeing 727-21	HK-2559	13994	Aerotal	Crashed	Santa Marta, Colombia	0	*
05.08.82	Beechcraft King Air 90	N895K	LJ-0025	Operator Unknown	Written off	Billings, MT, USA	*	*
08.08.82	Beechcraft Queen Air 65	N35PK	LC-123	Operator Unknown	Crashed	Off Nassau, Bahamas	0	*
12.08.82	de Havilland Canada Twin Otter 300	XY-AEB	501	Burma Airways	Crashed	Mindat Sakan, Burma	8	*
13.08.82	Beechcraft E18S	N380MA	BA-237	Operator Unknown	Crashed avoiding collision with another aircraft on landing	Lakewood, NJ, USA	0	*
14.08.82	LET 410UVP Turbolet	SSSR-67101	841327	Aeroflot	Struck by Aeroflot TU-134 CCCP-65836 on take-off	Sukhumi, Georgia, USSR	11(0)	0
14.08.82	Tupolev TU-134A	SSSR-65836	*	Aeroflot	Collided with Aeroflot LET.410 on take-off	Sukhumi, Georgia, USSR	0(11)	*
14.08.82	Yakovlev YAK-40	SSSR-98102	*	Aeroflot	Crashed after in-flight fire	nr Kazan, RSFSR, USSR	0	4
20.08.82	Britten-Norman BN-2A Islander	VP-LAE	0160	Inter Island Air Services	Crashed	Off St Lucia	6	0
24.08.82	Douglas DC-3	ET-AHP	12210	Ethiopian Airlines	Crashed on take-off	Makele, Ethiopia	*	*
25.08.82	Convair 440	N477KW	210	National Flight Services	Crashed into high ground	Wolf Creek Pass, CO, USA	0	*
25.08.82	Antonov AN-2R	OK-JIK	1G186-25	Slovair	Crashed	Smedava, Czechoslovakia	*	*
25.08.82	Bell 205	LN-ORX	*	Helitourist	Crashed into lake	Hardanger, Norway	2	3
26.08.82	Boeing 737-2Q3A	JA8444	21477	Southwest Air Lines	Overran & caught fire on landing	Ishigaki Is, Japan	0	138
27.08.82	Antonov AN-24T	YI-ALN	1022810	Iraqi Airways	U/c collapsed on take-off	Nasiriyah, Iraq	*	*
29.08.82	Yakovlev YAK-40	SSSR-87346	*	Aeroflot	Crashed in bad weather	Zeya, RSFSR, USSR	3	31
01.09.82	de Havilland Canada Caribou	HC-BHZ	249	Aerolineas Condor	Crashed in mountains during bad weather	nr Valladolid, Ecuador	44	0
04.09.82	Gates Learjet 25B	PT-JBQ	253-119	Cia Brasiliera de Tratores	Crashed	Rio Branco, Brazil	10	0
05.09.82	Piper PA-28-161 Cherokee	HB-PGH	*	Aeroleasing	Crashed	Langenthal, Switzerland	0	4
10.09.82	Boeing 707-348C	ST-AIM	19410	Sudan Airways	Crashed on landing	Khartoum, Sudan	0	3
14.09.82	McDonnell Douglas DC-10-30CF	EC-DEG	46962	Spantax	Crashed when nose tyres burst & pilot aborted take-off	Malaga, Spain	51	342

Date	Type	Reg'n	C/n	Operator	Accident	Location	F	S
14.09.82	Bell 212	G-BDIL	30715	Bristow Helicopters	Crashed	North Sea	6	0
15.09.82	Beechcraft 18	N469DM	AF-341	Operator Unknown	Crashed on drug smuggling flight	nr Lehigh, FL, USA	*	*
16.09.82	Antonov AN-2	*	*	Operator Unknown	Crashed	Opole, Poland	11	14
17.09.82	McDonnell Douglas DC-8-61	JA8048	46160	Japan Air Lines	Overran on emergency landing after hydraulic failure	Shanghai, China	0	124
18.09.82	Beechcraft Super King Air B200C	OY-BEP	BL-43	Operator Unknown	Crashed on approach	Roodt-Syr, Luxembourg	3	0
19.09.82	Cessna 188	ET-ACP	188-00300	Admas Air Service	Crashed	Nura Era, Ethiopia	*	*
24.09.82	Cessna 421B Golden Eagle	N8091Q	421B-0019	Operator Unknown	Crashed	nr Afton, OK, USA	1	0
29.09.82	Ilyushin IL-62	SSSR-86470	72503	Aeroflot	Crashed on landing	Luxembourg	7	71
oo.09.82	de Havilland Canada Otter	C-FDJA	*	Central Mountain Air	Crashed	Two Bridge Lake, BC, Canada	5	0
03.10.82	Volpar Turbo 18	HB-GGC	AF-509	Ciba-Pilatus Aerial Spraying	Destroyed by arson	Stans, Switzerland	0	0
03.10.82	Pilatus PC-6/B Turbo-Porter	HB-FET	*	Ciba-Pilatus Aerial Spraying	Destroyed by arson	Stans, Switzerland	0	0
03.10.82	Beechcraft 18	N215H	AF-405	Panorama Air Tours	Crashed	Off Makapuu Beach, HI, USA	3	0
05.10.82	Fokker F-27 Friendship 200	ST-AAS	10194	Sudan Airways	Crashed on landing	nr Khartoum, Sudan	*	*
08.10.82	Vickers Viscount 828	HC-ATV	458	Servicios Aereos Nacionales	Damaged beyond repair	Cuenca, Ecuador	*	*
09.10.82	Douglas DC-3	ZS-EJK	19484	Comair	Crashed	nr Graskop, South Africa	0	30
10.10.82	Aerospatiale 330J Puma	G-BJWS	1517	Bristow Helicopters	Crashed	nr Aberdeen, Grampian, UK	2	0
14.10.82	Boeing-Vertol 107	N6676D	6	Columbia Helicopters	Crashed	nr Cascade, ID, USA	2	*
17.10.82	Boeing 707-366C	SU-APE	20342	EgyptAir	Undershot on landing & caught fire	Geneva, Switzerland	0	184
17.10.82	Beechcraft 18	N403SE	AF-701	Operator Unknown	Crashed after take-off due to being overloaded	Taft, CA, USA	14	0
27.10.82	Aerospatiale SE.3160 Alouette II	HB-XCM	1443	Air Glaciers	Crashed after striking cables	Les Diablerets, Switzerland	5	0
28.10.82	Lockheed 18 Lodestar	N1040G	2549	Operator Unknown	Crashed on drug smuggling flight	nr Kosciusko, MS, USA	3	*
31.10.82	Curtiss C-46	C-GIXZ	22453	Ilford Riverton Airways	Crashed	Shamattawa, MN, Canada	*	*
31.10.82	Piper PA-31-350 Chieftain	N41045	31-8252020	Operator Unknown	Crashed after take-off	Baton Rouge, LA, USA	3	0
01.11.82	Cessna 402B	N402DL	402B-0598	Darne Inc	Crashed after overshooting runway	Meadville, PA, USA	*	*
01.11.82	Britten-Norman Trislander	HP-947	1005	Aviation Distributors	Damaged beyond repair	Location Unknown	*	*
03.11.82	Britten-Norman BN-2A-21 Islander	EP-PBE	0581	Pars Air	Written off	Location Unknown	*	*
05.11.82	Beechcraft Queen Air B80	N1HQ	LD-275	Operator Unknown	Crashed	Off Bahamas	*	*
06.11.82	Gates Learjet 24D	N13MJ	24D-314	MJI	Crashed	Elizabeth City, NC, USA	*	*
08.11.82	IPTN 212 Aviocar 100	PK-DCR	128/20N	Deraya Air Taxi	Crashed	Bontang, Indonesia	*	*
12.11.82	Fairchild Merlin IV	OY-AUI	AT-015	Danair	Destroyed by fire	Copenhagen, Denmark	0	15
12.11.82	Cessna Citation I	N2627U	501-0247	Operator Unknown	Crashed	Wichita, KS, USA	*	*
12.11.82	Piper PA-31-350 Chieftain	N59771	31-7652401	Operator Unknown	Crashed on approach	Asheville, NC, USA	1	0
12.11.82	Piper 601P Aerostar	N3641T	08188063427	Purolater Courier	Crashed after take-off	Fountain, CO, USA	2	0
15.11.82	Rockwell Turbo Commander 680V	N89DA	1702-78	Operator Unknown	Written off	Jamaica	*	*
17.11.82	Bell 212	B-2311	30757	Far Eastern Air Transport	Crashed	Off Taiwan	15	0
20.11.82	Rockwell Turbo Commander 680W	N5058E	1787-17	Operator Unknown	Written off	Atlanta, GA, USA	*	*
29.11.82	de Havilland Canada Twin Otter 300	HK-2536	713	ACES Colombia	Crashed	nr San Juanito, Colombia	*	*
29.11.82	Antonov AN-26	D2-TAB	*	TAAG Angola Airlines	Damaged beyond repair	Lubango, Angola	15	*
oo.11.82	Britten-Norman BN-2A Islander	CS-AJO	0125	Penina	Written off	Location Unknown	*	*
01.12.82	Mitsubishi MU-2 Solitaire	N149JP	402SA	Operator Unknown	Written off	Location Unknown	*	*
04.12.82	Boeing 707-323B	N8434	20173	Global International	Damaged in emergency ldg after striking lights on take-off	Brasilia, Brazil	0	*
05.12.82	Douglas DC-3	N163E	7394	P.Grossman	Crashed into hangar while taxiing	Burbank, CA, USA	*	*
06.12.82	Gates Learjet 35A	HB-VFO	35A-184	Transair	Aborted take-off due to bidstrike & overran	Le Bourget, France	0	*
07.12.82	Fairchild 227AC Metro III	N30093	AC-449	Pioneer Airlines	Crashed	nr Pueblo, CO, USA	*	*
09.12.82	Fairchild F-27J	CC-CJE	0063	Aeronor Chile	Crashed on approach due to smoke drifting across runway	La Serena, Chile	46	0
09.12.82	de Havilland Canada Beaver	*	*	Seair Alaska Airlines	Crashed into mountain	Wolf Lake, AK, USA	8	0
11.12.82	Cessna 421B Golden Eagle	N8001Q	421B-0001	Operator Unknown	Crashed on night approach	Savannah, GA, USA	4	0
12.12.82	Douglas DC-3	HK-2580	19127	Transportes Aereos Latinamericanos	Crashed on training flight	Mariquita City, Colombia	5	0
15.12.82	Beechcraft King Air E90	F-GBDZ	LW-295	Operator Unknown	Written off	Paris, France	*	*
15.12.82	Mitsubishi MU-2F	N5589S	150	Operator Unknown	Written off	Louisville, KY, USA	*	*
16.12.82	Antonov AN-24	SSSR-46567	*	Aeroflot	Damaged in forced landing	Sakhanskoe, Ukraine, USSR	*	*
18.12.82	Cessna Citation II	N2CA	551-0024	Coin Acceptors Inc	Crashed	Mountain View, MO, USA	*	*
22.12.82	Piper PA-31-350 Chieftain	PH-TSM	31-7852161	Rijnmond Air Services	Crashed	Mesvres, France	10	0
23.12.82	Antonov AN-26	SSSR-26627	*	Aeroflot	Crashed on take-off	Rostov-on-Don, RSFSR, USSR	16	*

Date	Type	Reg'n	C/n	Operator	Accident	Location	F	S
23.12.82	Bell 212	LN-OQS	30913	Lufttransport	Crashed	Spitzbergen, Norway	*	*
24.12.82	Ilyushin IL-18	B-202	189001401	CAAC	Crash landed after in-flight fire	Baiyun, China	23	46
24.12.82	Piper PA-31-350 Chieftain	N4091U	31-8152159	Operator Unknown	Crashed on night approach	Dubuque, IA, USA	2	0
28.12.82	Dornier Do.128-6 Skyservant	9Q-COT	6005	SOMINIKI	Damaged beyond repair	Kalima, Zaire	*	*
oo.12.82	Type Unknown	*	*	Bakhtar Afghan Airlines	Shot down by rebels	Afghanistan	*	*
oo.oo.82	de Havilland Canada Twin Otter 300	5A-DCW	639	Ministry of Agriculture	Written off	Location Unknown	*	*
oo.oo.82	Sikorsky S-58	OD-AGK	*	Lebanese Helicopters	Destroyed during civil war	Beirut, Lebanon	*	*
oo.oo.82	Sikorsky S-58	OD-AGL	*	Lebanese Helicopters	Destroyed during civil war	Beirut, Lebanon	*	*
oo.oo.82	Douglas DC-3	RP-C3	14764/26209	Bangko Sentral Na Philipinas	Destroyed by fire while refuelling	Manila, Philippines	0	*
oo.oo.82	Mitsubishi MU-2K	N66U	309	Operator Unknown	Written off	Hayden, CA, USA	*	*
oo.oo.82	Mitsubishi MU-2M	YV-94CP	347	C.A.Bienes	Written off	Location Unknown	*	*
oo.oo.82	Douglas C-54Q	N111AV	22186	Florida Aircraft Leasing	Destroyed by fire	Great Abaco, Bahamas	*	*
02.01.83	Bell 212	OY-HMC	30864	Maersk Air	Crashed during storm	North Sea	3	0
03.01.83	Canadair Challenger 600	N805C	1037	A.E.Stanley Manufacturing Co	Crashed	Hailey, ID, USA	*	*
03.01.83	Piper PA-31 Navajo	C-GBSG	31-841	Voyageur Airways	Crashed into trees on approach	North Bay, ON, Canada	*	*
07.01.83	Boeing 727-86	EP-IRA	19171	Iran Air	Damaged while taxiing	Tehran, Iran	*	*
10.01.83	Beechcraft 99	N390CA	U101	Cascade Airways	Crashed on approach	Spokane, WA, USA	*	*
11.01.83	Lockheed 18 Lodestar	N520R	2183	Operator Unknown	Crashed on take-off in high winds	Madison, GA, USA	*	*
11.01.83	McDonnell Douglas DC-8-54F	N8053U	46010	United Air Lines	Crashed on take-off due to over rotation	Detroit, MI, USA	3	0
11.01.83	Rockwell Sabre 65	N99S	465-64	Sun Co Inc	Crashed on approach	Toronto, ON, Canada	5	*
16.01.83	Boeing 727-2F2A	TC-JBR	21603	Turk Hava Yollari	Crashed on landing in snowstorm	Ankara, Turkey	47	20
16.01.83	Douglas DC-3	TG-SAB	*	Operator Unknown	Crash landed on beach after smuggling flight	Bay City, TN, USA	0	*
16.01.83	Lockheed Jetstar 2	5A-DAR	5221	Libyan Government	Crashed	En route Tripoli-Algeria	*	*
16.01.83	Bell 214B-1	C-GBHH	28007	Alpine Helicopters	Crashed into mountain	Bugaboo Pass, BC, Canada	2	1
21.01.83	Beechcraft C-45H	N69K	AF-625	Operator Unknown	Crashed into lake after engine failure	nr Leesburg, FL, USA	*	*
27.01.83	Mitsubishi MU-2 Marquise	N440MA	1524SA	Operator Unknown	Crashed on approach	Scottsdale, AZ, USA	6	*
27.01.83	Dornier Do.128-6 Skyservant	TJ-XBO	6002	Cameroun Air Force	Written off	Cameroun	*	*
28.01.83	de Havilland Canada Twin Otter 200	T-81	155	Lineas Aereas del Estado	Damaged beyond repair	Rio Gallegos, Argentina	*	*
28.01.83	Agusta-Bell 206B JetRanger II	SE-HCG	03037	Lapplandsflyg	Crashed	Ria Fjall, Sweden	2	0
11.02.83	Cessna 310	5Y-MBP	*	Pioneer Airlines	Crashed	Nairobi National Park, Kenya	4	0
14.02.83	Gates Learjet 35A	N482U	35A-482	ARMCO Pacific	Crashed	Straits of Malacca, Malaysia	6	0
14.02.83	Rockwell Turbo Commander 690A	N81416	11306	Operator Unknown	Written off	Winter Haven, FL, USA	*	*
15.02.83	de Havilland Canada Twin Otter 300	N361V	361	Sierra Pacific Airlines	Crashed	Sun Valley, ID, USA	*	*
15.02.83	Douglas DC-3	C-FBKX	16065/32813	Ontario Central Airlines	Crashed	nr Gillam, MN, Canada	*	*
19.02.83	Aerospatiale AS.350B Ecureuil	JA9222	1051	Aero Asahi	Crashed	nr Okadama, Japan	0	4
21.02.83	Cessna 402	VH-DIL	*	Sunshine Coast Air Charter	Crashed	nr Gladstone, Qld, Australia	1	*
22.02.83	Boeing 737-2A1CA	PP-SNC	21187	VASP	Crashed after take-off	Manaus, Brazil	2	0
24.02.83	de Havilland Canada Twin Otter 300	TY-BBL	737	Air Benin	Crashed	Koko, Benin	*	*
27.02.83	Hawker Siddeley Trident 2E	B-260	2167	CAAC	Damaged beyond repair	Fuzhou, China	0	*
05.03.83	Douglas B-26 Invader	N4060A	44-34102A	Operator Unknown	Crashed into trees fighting forest fire	Hubbards Fork, KY, USA	1	*
07.03.83	Aerospatiale SA.315B Lama	LN-OSQ	2578	Westwing Helikopter	Crashed after striking cables	Suldal, Norway	0	1
09.03.83	Cessna 402C	N26506	402C-0340	Operator Unknown	Crashed after engine failure	Off Fort Lauderdale, FL, USA	0	*
09.03.83	Bell 212	PT-HJN	30761	Aeroleo Taxi Aereo	Crashed into sea	Off Macae, Brazil	11	0
10.03.83	de Havilland Canada Twin Otter 300	YA-GAZ	395	Bakhtar Afghan Airlines	Crashed	nr Shach Goan, Afghanistan	19	*
11.03.83	NAMC YS-11A-208	JA8693	2060	Nihon Kinkyori Airways	Belly landed short of runway & broke up	Nakashibetsu, Japan	0	53
11.03.83	McDonnell Douglas DC-9-32	YV-67C	47025	Avensa	Destroyed by fire following hard landing	Barquisimeto, Venezuela	22	28
14.03.83	Boeing 707-338C	5A-DJO	18955	Jamahiriya Air Transport	Crashed after take-off due to engine failure	Sebha, Libya	5	0
17.03.83	de Havilland Canada Buffalo 5A	ET-AHJ	102A	Ethiopian Air Force	Shot down	Degahabour, Ethiopia	*	*
17.03.83	Britten-Norman BN-2A-3 Islander	EP-PAC	0273	Pars Air	Written off	Location Unknown	*	*
18.03.83	IRMA BN-2A-21 Defender	7Q-YAX	0792	Malawi Police Air Wing	Crashed	Chikala Hillas, Malawi	*	*
18.03.83	Mitsubishi MU-2 Marquise	N473MA	1547SA	Operator Unknown	Crashed	nr North Adams, MA, USA	2	*
24.03.83	Mitsubishi MU-2 Marquise	N72B	735SA	Operator Unknown	Broke-up in flight	Jeffersonville, GA, USA	4	0
28.03.83	Boeing 737-2B1	C9-BAB	20281	Linhas Aereas de Mocambique	Crashed short of runway	Quelimane, Mozambique	0	*
29.03.83	LET 410M Turbolet	SSSR-67190	781119	Aeroflot	Crashed into hill on landing	Poty, Georgia, USSR	6	*

Date	Type	Reg'n	C/n	Operator	Accident	Location	F	S
30.03.83	de Havilland Canada Twin Otter 300	5A-DCP	605	Ministry of Agriculture	Destroyed by strong winds	Benghazi, Libya	0	*
30.03.83	Gates Learjet 25	N51CA	25-030	Chatham Corporation	Crashed on landing	Newark, NJ, USA	2	*
01.04.83	de Havilland Canada Twin Otter 200	N922MA	161	Metro Airlines	Destroyed by tornado	Lawton, OK, USA	*	*
01.04.83	Cessna Citation I	N700CW	500-0205	Winn Exploration Co	Crashed	Eagle Pass, TX, USA	*	*
03.04.83	Beechcraft Super King Air 200	F-BVRP	BB-0038	Operator Unknown	Written off	Canton, China	*	*
06.04.83	IRMA BN-2A-26 Islander	HP-945	0914	Operator Unknown	Written off	Location Unknown	*	*
07.04.83	Britten-Norman BN-2A-8 Islander	N37MN	0558	Munz Northern Airlines	Crashed during snowstorm. Located by Soviet satellite	nr Selawik, AK, USA	2	1
12.04.83	Antonov AN-26	SSSR-26686	8738806	Aeroflot	Overran on landing	Minsk, Bylorussia, USSR	*	*
13.04.83	Aerospatiale SA.319B Alouette III	HB-XIX	2035	Swiss Air Ambulance	Crashed in bad weather	Gotthard Pass, Switzerland	*	*
14.04.83	Gates Learjet 24D	N302EJ	24D-302	Operator Unknown	Crashed	Puerta Vallarta, Mexico	*	*
14.04.83	Beechcraft 18	N444PV	*	Operator Unknown	Crashed after take-off	Hollywood, FL, USA	*	*
16.04.83	British Aerospace 748 2A	EL-AIH	1755	Air Liberia	Crashed into houses after engine failure on take-off	Khartoum, Sudan	8{9}	0
18.04.83	British Aerospace 125-1A	C-FHLL	25034	Labrador Mining & Exploration Co	Damaged beyond repair	Gaspe, PQ, Canada	*	*
19.04.83	Yakovlev YAK-40	SSSR-87291	*	Aeroflot	Crashed into mountain on approach	Leninakan, Armenia, USSR	21	0
20.04.83	de Havilland Canada Twin Otter 300	G-STUD	545	Air Ecosse	Damaged when ran off runway	Flotta, Orkneys, UK	0	12
20.04.83	Type Unknown	*	*	Tonga Air Services	Crashed on landing	Nuku'Alofa, Tonga	*	*
26.04.83	Cessna Citation I	N22FM	500-0229	Federal Mogul Corporation	Crashed	Wichita, KS, USA	*	*
26.04.83	IRMA BN-2A-9 Islander	HK-2687X	0841	Aviones Ejectivos	Forced landed with engine fire & exploded	nr Barranca de Upia, Colombia	0	*
28.04.83	Beechcraft 18	N213S	*	Operator Unknown	Crashed into trees on go-around	Dania, FL, USA	*	*
29.04.83	Aerospatiale Caravelle 6R	HC-BAT	125	Servicios Aereos Nacionales	Crashed after engine failure on take-off	Guayaquil, Ecuador	8	92
29.04.83	Britten-Norman BN-2A-21 Islander	PK-OBE	0429	Airfast Services	Crashed after aborting take-off	Landitma, Indonesia	*	*
03.05.83	Douglas C-47B	FAC.1126	16860/33608	Satena	Crashed in mountains	Palmaseca, Colombia	0	*
08.05.83	Fairchild C-119 Flying Boxcar	N13626	*	Supra International	Sank through ice while taxiing & abandoned	River Kagoak, AK, USA	0	*
14.05.83	de Havilland Canada Twin Otter 100	C-FVTL	026	Simpson Air	Damaged in hangar fire	Calgary, Canada	*	*
18.05.83	Gates Learjet 25B	D-CDPD	25B-177	P.Dreidoppel	Crashed	Atlantic Ocean	*	*
18.05.83	Britten-Norman BN-2 Islander	D-IOLT	0021	Frisia Luftwerkhe Norddeich	Written off	Location Unknown	*	*
19.05.83	Bell 206B JetRanger II	JA9109	01167	Aero Asahi	Crashed at sea	Off Niigata, Japan	0	4
20.05.83	Short 330-100	N935MA	SH.3032	Metro Airlines	Damaged beyond repair during storm	Beaumont, TX, USA	0	*
24.05.83	Mitsubishi MU-2 Marquise	VH-MLU	1527SA	Interair	Crashed	Bargo, NSW, Australia	1	*
30.05.83	Noorduyn UC-64 Norseman	C-FFJB	022	La Tuque Air Service	Crashed	nr La Tuque, PQ, Canada	3	0
30.05.83	Bell 212	A6-BBX	30802	Abu Dhabi Helicopters	Crash landed in sea & sank	Persian Gulf	0	*
oo.05.83	Convair 880-22-2	N880SR	07	Groth Air	Written off	USA	*	*
02.06.83	McDonnell Douglas DC-9-32	C-FTLU	47196	Air Canada	Caught fire in flight & destroyed on landing	Cincinnati, OH, USA	23	23
02.06.83	Fokker F-28 Fellowship 3000RC	PK-GFV	11132	Garuda Indonesian Airlines	Stalled on take-off & crashed into mound	Tanjungkarang, Indonesia	3	58
02.06.83	Piper PA-31-350 Chieftain	HK-2456P	31-8052145	J.R.Silva	Crashed after take-off	Guaymaral, Colombia	9	0
05.06.83	Cessna 402B	ZS-KVG	*	Operator Unknown	Crashed on road after take-off	Cape Town, South Africa	7	2
08.06.83	Douglas VC-54Q	CP-1404	10576	Frigorificos Reyes	Caught fire & crashed	nr Trinidad, Bolivia	5	0
21.06.83	de Havilland Canada Twin Otter 300	TZ-ACH	394	Air Mali	Crashed	Niela, Mali	7	*
21.06.83	Cessna 421A Golden Eagle	N2960Q	421A-0060	Operator Unknown	Crashed into trees after engine failure	Atmore, AL, USA	8	0
21.06.83	Beechcraft 18	N576M	BA-576	Operator Unknown	Crashed	nr Veracruz, Mexico	1	0
21.06.83	de Havilland Canada Beaver	C-GVHS	733	Central Air Transport	Crashed on take-off	nr Pickle Lake, ON, Canada	1	0
22.06.83	Douglas DC-3	C-GUBT	12424	Skycraft Air Charter	Crashed	Toronto, ON, Canada	2	0
23.06.83	Lockheed 18 Lodestar	N333FB	2467	Operator Unknown	Crashed on smuggling flight	Millhaven, GA, USA	2	0
24.06.83	Bell 214B-1	LN-OSR	28047	Helikopter Service	Crashed	Gaustadtoppen, Norway	*	*
24.06.83	de Havilland Dove 7XC	D-IFSC	04527	Operator Unknown	Crashed on take-off after engine failure	Munich, West Germany	0	*
29.06.83	CASA 212 Aviocar 200	YN-BYZ	298	Aeronica	Damaged in heavy landing	Managua, Nicaragua	*	*
29.06.83	Douglas C-54G	N300JT	36072	Pacific Air Express	Damaged in belly landing after fire	Kahuliu, HI, USA	0	*
29.06.83	British Aerospace 125-1A-522	N125E	25110	Erasmus Inc	Ran off runway on landing & struck light aircraft	Hobby-Houston, TX, USA	0(2)	*
29.06.83	Yakovlev YAK-40	SSSR-87808	*	Aeroflot	Crashed	Kazarman, Kirgizia, USSR	0	*
30.06.83	Beechcraft G18S	N215W	BA-581	Operator Unknown	Crashed into high ground	nr Keyser, WV, USA	1	0
01.07.83	Ilyushin IL-62	889	*	Chosonminhang	Crashed	Fouta Djall Mts, Guinea-Bissau	23	0
02.07.83	Aerospatiale Caravelle 3	I-GISO	054	Altair	Caught fire on take-off	Malpensa, Milan, Italy	0	89
04.07.83	British Aerospace 748 2A	9J-ADM	1706	Zambia Airways	Damaged beyond repair	Kasaba Bay, Zambia	*	*
04.07.83	Aerospatiale 332L Super Puma	G-TIGD	2026	Bristow Helicopters	Written off	Dyce, Aberdeen, UK	*	*

Date	Type	Reg'n	C/n	Operator	Accident	Location	F	S
04.07.83	de Havilland Canada Beaver	C-FDVK	705	Labrador Air Safari	Crashed	nr Comeau Bay, PQ, Canada	5	0
09.07.83	de Havilland Sea Devon C.20	G-AMYP	04421	Southernair	Crashed after engine failure on take-off	Shoreham, W Sussex, UK	1	0
11.07.83	Boeing 737-2V2A	HC-BIG/607	22607	TAME	Crashed on approach	Cuenca, Ecuador	119	0
12.07.83	Britten-Norman BN-2A Islander	P2-FHP	0168	Cloudlands Aviation Development	Written off	Location Unknown	*	*
15.07.83	Grumman Gulfstream I	N68TG	068	Orion Air	Caught fire on landing	Blountville, TN, USA	0	2
16.07.83	Sikorsky S-61N-II	G-BEON	61-770	British Airways Helicopters	Crashed	Off Scilly Islands, UK	20	6
18.07.83	Cessna 402C	OB-T-1252	402C-0649	Taxi Aereo Selva	Crashed in bad weather	nr Tarapoto, Peru	2	0
19.07.83	Douglas DC-3	N480F	9719	Chevron Oil	Crashed	nr Khartoum, Sudan	0	24
21.07.83	Britten-Norman Trislander	N29929	1013	Cen-Tex Airlines	Destroyed in hangar fire	Brownwood, TX, USA	0	*
21.07.83	Britten-Norman BN-2A-9R Islander	N2718W	0331	Eagle Airlines	Destroyed in hangar fire	Brownwood, TX, USA	0	0
22.07.83	Gates Learjet 25D	5N-ASQ	25D-344	Imani & Sons	Crashed	Lagos, Nigeria	*	*
26.07.83	Cessna 404 Titan	PK-KCA	404-0006	Bali Air	Crashed	nr Ambon, Indonesia	7	4
29.07.83	Aerospatiale AS.350 Ecureuil	F-GBTG	*	Air Provence	Crashed & caught fire	St Rambert d'Albon, France	6	0
31.07.83	Aerospatiale SA.319B Alouette III	HB-XMZ	2385	Air Zermatt	Crashed	Mt Weiss Horn, Switzerland	1	2
oo.07.83	Douglas DC-3	N91378	12296	Operator Unknown	Destroyed by fire during air display	Missoula, MT, USA	0	*
04.08.83	Boeing 747-121	N738PA	19645	Pan American World Airways	Damaged beyond repair on landing	Karachi, Pakistan	0	*
04.08.83	de Havilland Riley Heron	VH-CLY	14122	Airlines of Tasmania	Damaged on landing	Launceston, Tas, Australia	*	*
05.08.83	IRMA BN-2A-21 Islander	PK-KNF	0745	Bali Air	Crashed	Off Bula, Indonesia	2	0
07.08.83	British Aerospace 748 2A	FAC.1104	1705	Satena	Crashed	Pasto, Colombia	*	*
11.08.83	Beechcraft G18S	N400NA	BA-591	Operator Unknown	Crashed after take-off	Evart, MI, USA	2	0
16.08.83	Cessna 421 Golden Eagle	N386G	*	Operator Unknown	Crashed	Centerto, IN, USA	*	*
17.08.83	Piper PA-31-350 Chieftain	N88LV	31-7752118	Las Vegas Airlines	Crashed into cliff	Grand Canyon, AZ, USA	10	0
17.08.83	Beechcraft King Air A100	N129D	B-134	Operator Unknown	Written off	Dieques, Puerto Rico	*	*
20.08.83	Boeing-Vertol 107-II	N190CH	2002	Columbia Helicopters	Crashed after rotor failure	Shaver Lake, CA, USA	2	*
20.08.83	Cessna 421 Golden Eagle	N2239Q	*	Operator Unknown	Crashed	West Jordan, UT, USA	1	0
21.08.83	Lockheed 18 Lodestar	N116CA	2472	Operator Unknown	Crashed on road	nr Stanwood, WA, USA	11	0
25.08.83	Sikorsky S-58	PT-HGO	58-1565	VOTEC	Crashed	Off Macae, Brazil	*	*
25.08.83	Yakovlev YAK-40	SSSR-87201	*	Aeroflot	Crashed on take-off	Omsukchan, RSFSR, USSR	0	*
27.08.83	Fairchild 226TC Metro II	N503SS	TC-229E	Skyways	Caught fire & cockpit destroyed	Hot Springs, AR, USA	0	*
27.08.83	Lockheed L-100-30 Hercules	N17ST	4333	Transamerica Airlines	Crashed	nr Dundo, Angola	7	0
28.08.83	Beechcraft Super King Air 200	VH-KTE	BB-0320	Moore's Air Charter	Crashed	Adavale, Qld, Australia	5	*
28.08.83	Hiller UH-12E	C-FOKQ	2206	Yukon Airways	Crashed after rotors struck mountain	nr Klukshu, YK, Canada	*	*
30.08.83	Tupolev TU-134A	SSSR-65129	*	Aeroflot	Crashed into mountain on approach	Alma Ata, Kazakhstan, USSR	90	0
30.08.83	Soloy Bell 47G-4A	JA9297	7666	Nihon Helicopters	Crashed after tail struck ground on take-off	Komatsu, Japan	*	*
01.09.83	Boeing 747-230B	HL7442	20559	Korean Air Lines	Shot down by Soviet Air Force Su-15 while off course	Off Sakhalin Is, RSFSR, USSR	269	0
02.09.83	Britten-Norman BN-2A-21 Islander	C-GIPF	0274	Central Mountain Air	Crashed	nr Smithers, BC, Canada	9	0
04.09.83	Cessna 421C Golden Eagle	N111FN	421C-0321	Operator Unknown	Crashed after take-off	Altus, OK, USA	7	0
08.09.83	Bell 206B JetRanger II	OY-HBH	01637	Greenlandair	Crashed into ravine	nr Nanortalik, Greenland	*	*
08.09.83	Beechcraft 18	N2990F	*	Operator Unknown	Crashed in sea after engine failure	Off Kailua-Kona, HI, USA	*	*
10.09.83	Beechcraft King Air B90	N400AM	LJ-0354	Operator Unknown	Written off	Location Unknown	*	*
14.09.83	Hawker Siddeley Trident 2E	B-264	2169	CAAC	Struck by Chinese Air Force aircraft while taxiing	Guilin, China	11	*
14.09.83	Sikorsky S-76	N521AC	*	Operator Unknown	Crashed into lake	Lake Michigan, IL, USA	*	*
17.09.83	Rockwell Turbo Commander 690A	N111QL	11312	Operator Unknown	Written off	Nacogdoches, TX, USA	*	*
19.09.83	Beechcraft Queen Air 80	N55ED	LD-003	Operator Unknown	Engine failed on landing & cartwheeled into ditch	Opa Locka, FL, USA	0	2
20.09.83	Cessna 402	5X-LCP	*	Larco Concrete Products	Crashed on take-off from waterlogged runway	Moyo, Uganda	*	*
23.09.83	Boeing 737-2P6A	A4O-BK	21734	Gulf Air	Crashed – possibly due to sabotage	nr Abu Dhabi, UAE	111	0
25.09.83	Boeing 707-336C	5N-ARO	18924	RN Cargo	Destroyed on landing after fire bomb exploded	Accra, Ghana	0	4
26.09.83	Cessna 172M	HK-1754	172-66341	Taxi Aereo del Guaviare	Crashed due to engine failure	Villavicencio, Colombia	0	2
27.09.83	Bell 214B	PT-HKQ	28038	Lider Taxi Aereo	Crashed after slung cargo hit tail	Caruari, Brazil	*	*
28.09.83	Britten-Norman BN-2A-26 Islander	B-11109	0518	Taiwan Airlines	Crashed in sea	Off Lanyu Island, Taiwan	10	0
29.09.83	Canadair CL-215	C-GKEE	1078	Canadair	Crashed on demonstration flight	Montreal, PQ, Canada	0	2
oo.09.83	Douglas DC-3	N401JB	3299	Swift Delivery Air Freight	Damaged by storm	Honolulu, HI, USA	*	*
04.10.83	Beechcraft King Air C90	EC-COJ	LJ-0664	Operator Unknown	Written off	Salamanca, Spain	*	*
06.10.83	Fairchild Merlin IIIB	9Q-COI	T-302	Operator Unknown	Written off	Zaire	*	*

Date	Type	Reg'n	C/n	Operator	Accident	Location	F	S
07.10.83	Sikorsky S-61	YV-323C	61-472	Aerotechnica	Crash landed	Palm Beach, FL, USA	*	*
07.10.83	Vickers Viscount 812	PK-RVW	389	Mandala Airlines	Crashed	Semarang, Indonesia	*	*
07.10.83	Embraer Bandeirante 110C	PP-SBH	110.026	TAM Linha Aerea Regional	Crashed	Aracatuba, Brazil	*	*
07.10.83	Embraer Bandeirante 110P1	PT-SFH	110.390	Embraer	Written off	Brazil	*	*
08.10.83	de Havilland Canada Twin Otter 300	XY-AEE	512	Burma Airways	Crashed on take-off	Lonkin, Burma	9	5
08.10.83	Douglas DC-6	*	*	Operator Unknown	Crashed on drug smuggling flight	Monterrubio, Colombia	7	*
08.10.83	Cessna Citation I	G-UESS	500-0326	Brencham Ltd	Crashed	Stornaway, Shetlands, UK	*	*
09.10.83	Britten-Norman BN-2A-8 Islander	B-12202	0380	Yung Shing Airlines	Damaged on landing	Lan Yu, Taiwan	0	*
11.10.83	British Aerospace 748 2A	N748LL	1716	Air Illinois	Crashed into hill in bad weather	nr Pickeyville, IL, USA	9	0
13.10.83	Boeing 707-436	N4465D	18411	Coastal Airways	Destroyed by fire while parked	Perpignan, France	0	*
19.10.83	LET 410UVP Turbolet	SSSR-67315	820815	Aeroflot	Damaged after running off runway	Kansk, RSFSR, USSR	*	*
20.10.83	Mitsubishi MU-2L	N444PA	691SA	Operator Unknown	Crashed into trees on approach	Patterson, LA, USA	3	*
24.10.83	Beechcraft King Air C90	N4TS	LJ-0541	Operator Unknown	Crashed	Fort Wayne, IN, USA	1	0
26.10.83	de Havilland Canada Buffalo 5D	TJ-XBS	121	Cameroun Air Force	Written off	Cameroun	*	*
28.10.83	Curtiss C-46	CP-916	30394	Transportes Aereos Bolivar	Crash landed & caught fire	nr Beni, Bolivia	0	4
31.10.83	Douglas DC-3	N44896	9665	FBN Flying Service	Destroyed after cargo caught fire on take-off	Laredo, TX, USA	*	*
07.11.83	Sikorsky S-76	PT-HKD	760023	VOTEC	Crashed after take-off from oil platform	Off Macae, Brazil	0	13
08.11.83	Sikorsky S-76	TF-RAN	760081	Icelandic Coast Guard	Crashed in fjord	Iceland	4	0
09.11.83	Boeing 737-2M2A	D2-TBN	22775	TAAG Angola Airlines	Shot down after take-off by rebels	Lubango, Angola	130	0
10.11.83	Curtiss C-46	CP-1077	32968	Trans Aereos Skorpio	Damaged in belly landing on road	nr San Borja, Bolivia	0	3
13.11.83	Sikorsky S-76	N4252S	760034	Houston Helicopters	Sank after emergency landing due to engine failure	Off Singapore	*	*
18.11.83	Westland WG.30	N5830T	005	Airspur	Crashed	Long Beach, CA, USA	0	2
20.11.83	Mitsubishi MU-2J	XA-DIS	608	Operator Unknown	Written off	El Paso, TX, USA	*	*
23.11.83	de Havilland Canada Twin Otter 300	C-GTLA	632	Austin Airways	Crashed short of runway	Lansdowne House, ON, Canada	4	1
25.11.83	Beechcraft H-18	N105PE	BA-672	Operator Unknown	Crashed after engine failure	Allentown, PA, USA	1	0
26.11.83	Beechcraft King Air B100	N1910L	BE-010	Operator Unknown	Crashed after go-around	Midland, TX, USA	8	0
27.11.83	Boeing 747-283B/SCD	HK-2910	21381	Avianca	Crashed on approach	nr Madrid, Spain	181	11
28.11.83	Fokker F-28 Fellowship 2000	5N-ANF	11090	Nigeria Airways	Crashed on approach	Enugu, Nigeria	52	6
oo.11.83	Mitsubishi MU-2G	VH-CJP	505	Operator Unknown	Written off	Location Unknown	*	*
03.12.83	Douglas DC-7	N6310J	45150	Jamaican Government	Set on fire – abandoned after smuggling flight in 1979	Vernam Field, Jamaica	0	0
04.12.83	Piper PA-31-350 Chieftain	N4115K	*	Operator Unknown	Crashed on test flight	Lakeland, FL, USA	2	0
05.12.83	Beechcraft D18S	N44609	A-0017	Operator Unknown	Crashed into power lines on emergency landing	Brownsville, TX, USA	1	0
05.12.83	Beechcraft TC-45J	N705M	BA-353	Operator Unknown	Crashed on approach in bad weather	Kansas City, KS, USA	1	0
07.12.83	Boeing 727-256A	EC-CFJ	20820	Iberia	Struck Aviaco DC-9 EC-CGS on take-off in fog	Madrid, Spain	51(42)	42
07.12.83	McDonnell Douglas DC-9-32	EC-CGS	47645	Aviaco	Struck by Iberia B.727 EC-CFJ when taxiing across runway	Madrid, Spain	42(51)	0
07.12.83	Cessna 402A	5Y-AJZ	402A-0113	ZB Air	Crashed	Ngong Hills, Kenya	*	*
11.12.83	Vickers Varsity T.1	N65388	*	Operator Unknown	Crashed on landing	El Paso, TX, USA	*	*
13.12.83	Douglas DC-3	RP-C287	14673/26118	Philair	Crashed	nr Zapote, Philippines	0	10
15.12.83	Boeing 707-373C	HK-2401X	18707	Tampa	Crashed into factory after take-off	Bogota, Colombia	3{50}	0
17.12.83	de Havilland Canada Twin Otter 200	C-FGJK	213	Inuvik Coastal Airways	Crashed on landing	Paulatuk, NWT, Canada	2	8
18.12.83	Airbus A.300B2-120	OY-KAA	122	Malaysian Airline System	Crashed on approach & caught fire	Kuala Lumpur, Malaysia	0	247
18.12.83	Pilatus PC-6/B2-H2 Turbo Porter	G-BIZP	812	Peterborough Parachute Centre	Damaged beyond repair	Yarwell, UK	*	*
23.12.83	McDonnell Douglas DC-10-30CF	HL7339	46960	Korean Air Lines	Collided on runway with South Central Air Navajo N35206	Anchorage, AK, USA	0(*)	*
23.12.83	Piper PA-31 Navajo	N35206	*	South Central Air	Collided on runway with Korean DC-10 HL7339	Anchorage, AK, USA	*(0)	*
24.12.83	Antonov AN-24	SSSR-46617	37308704	Aeroflot	Crashed on approach in bad weather	Leshukonskoye, RSFSR, USSR	44	5
26.12.83	Beechcraft King Air C90	G-BKID	LJ-0604	Airmore Aviation	Crashed after double engine failure	Off Kastrup, Denmark	0	1
30.12.83	de Havilland Canada Beaver	C-FRQW	618	Air BC	Crashed on take-off from water	Port McNeill, BC, Canada	1	0
oo.12.83	Boeing 727-21	HK-1804	19037	SAM Colombia	Damaged in belly landing	Colombia	*	*
oo.oo.83	Fairchild Merlin III	N4BC	T-205E	Caribbean Ventures Leasing	Written off	Location Unknown	*	*
10.01.84	Tupolev TU-134A	LZ-TUR	4352308	Balkan Bulgarian Airlines	Crashed on approach	Sofia, Bulgaria	50	0
10.01.84	Douglas DC-3	C-GSCA	15745/27190	Skycraft Air Transport	Force landed after engine failure due to wrong fuel	St Louis, MO, USA	1	*
13.01.84	Douglas C-54G	CP-1090	36036	North East Bolivian Airways	Caught fire after u/c collapsed on landing	Cochabamba, Bolivia	1	2
13.01.84	Fokker F-27 Friendship 100	N148PM	10108	Pilgrim Airlines	Crashed on take-off	New York, NY, USA	0	*
14.01.84	IRMA BN-2A-20 Islander	P2-ISH	0757	Talair	Crashed	nr Karimui, Papua New Guinea	10	0

Date	Type	Reg'n	C/n	Operator	Accident	Location	F	S
16.01.84	Douglas DC-3	9Q-CYD	9010	Transport Aerien Zaire	Destroyed when grass set on fire by engine	Kissidougou, Guinea	0	*
17.01.84	Rockwell Turbo Commander 690B	N81717	11445	Operator Unknown	Written off	Greenville, SC, USA	*	*
19.01.84	Type Unknown	*	*	ERA Helicopters	Blown off oilrig in high winds [Bell?]	Gulf of Mexico	*	*
20.01.84	Douglas DC-6B	YS-37C	44255	ALAS	Blown up by terrorist mine on landing	San Miguel, El Salvador	1	*
20.01.84	Rockwell Turbo Commander 690A	N83MC	11124	Operator Unknown	Written off	Location Unknown	*	*
24.01.84	CASA 212 Aviocar 200	PK-PCL	218/58N	Pelita Air Service	Crashed	Mt Lohon, Indonesia	6	3
24.01.84	Mitsubishi MU-2F	N123AX	220	Operator Unknown	Written off	Location Unknown	*	*
26.01.84	Aerospatiale SA.315B Lama	OE-EXV	2400	Tyrolean Airways	Crashed	Austria	*	*
28.01.84	Antonov AN-24	SSSR-47358	67310607	Aeroflot	Crashed on approach	Izhevsk, RSFSR, USSR	4	*
30.01.84	Fairchild 226TC Metro II	N63Z	TC-240	Britt Airways	Crashed on take-off	Terre Haute, IN, USA	3	0
30.01.84	Gates Learjet 24	N44GA	24-129	Gee Bee Aero Inc	Crashed	Santa Catalina, CA, USA	*	*
02.02.84	Piper PA-28-236 Dakota	HK-2641	28-8111069	Aerolineas Regionales de Paz	Crashed	Ariporo, Colombia	2	0
03.02.84	Cessna 402C	N6814G	402C-0647	Operator Unknown	Crashed into mountain	nr Jaffrey, NH, USA	2	0
03.02.84	Bell 206B JetRanger II	PT-HQC	03133	Aeroleo Taxi Aereo	Crashed after explosion	Off Natal, Brazil	4	0
05.02.84	Sikorsky S-61	N6981R	*	Operator Unknown	Collided with hangar door	Medford, OR, USA	1	*
09.02.84	Boeing 737-2M2A	D2-TBV	22626	TAAG Angola Airlines	Damaged by missile on take-off – landed safely but dbr	Huambo, Angola	0	135
11.02.84	Antonov AN-12	*	*	Aeroflot	Shot down by rebels	Cuenca Sul, Angola	*	*
16.02.84	Sikorsky S-58	C-GMMR	58-1272	Operator Unknown	Crashed	Indian Arm, Canada	2	*
20.02.84	Cessna Citation I	VH-FSA	500-0237	Operator Unknown	Crashed	Prosperpine, Qld, Australia	*	*
24.02.84	Cessna 404 Titan	HK-2685	404-0685	Taxi Aereo del Guaviare	Crashed	Colombia	7	0
05.03.84	Hindustan 748 2-224	VT-DUO	506	Indian Airlines	Crashed into wall on take-off	Begumpet, India	0	3
05.03.84	Cessna 421B Golden Eagle	N3291Q	421B-0911	Operator Unknown	Crashed short of runway	Cullman, AL, USA	6	0
05.03.84	Piper PA-31-310 Navajo	N6629L	31-565	Cumberland Airlines	Crashed on approach in fog	Beans Cove, PA, USA	3	0
10.03.84	McDonnell Douglas DC-8-63PF	F-BOLL	46096	UTA	Destroyed by bombs on ground	N'djamena, Chad	0	*
13.03.84	Curtiss C-46	HK-1322	444	Aerosucre	Crashed on landing after smuggling flight	Barranquilla, Colombia	3	2
14.03.84	Beechcraft Super King Air 200C	CP-1849	BL-52	Operator Unknown	Written off	Location Unknown	*	*
15.03.84	Convair VT-29B	XA-JOV	261	Aero Cozumel	Crash landed after engine failure on take-off	Cancun, Mexico	0	*
16.03.84	Lockheed 18 Lodestar	N77777	2373	Operator Unknown	Crashed on smuggling flight	Oneonta, NY, USA	2	0
16.03.84	Fairchild F-27M	CP-862	0127	Lloyd Aereo Boliviano	Crashed	nr San Borja, Bolivia	23	0
19.03.84	Beechcraft 18	N218X	3A-689	Operator Unknown	Crashed on take-off at night in icing conditions	Morrisonville, NY, USA	1	0
21.03.84	Piper PA-31-350 Chieftain	N27886	31-7952024	Operator Unknown	Crashed into forest on approach	Oneonta, NY, USA	5	0
22.03.84	Boeing 737-275A	C-GQPW	22265	Pacific Western Airlines	Destroyed by fire prior to take-off	Calgary, Canada	0	118
24.03.84	Douglas C-54S	CP-1206	10559	Frigorificos Reyes	Crashed after take-off in bad weather	Rurrenabaque, Bolivia	5	0
24.03.84	de Havilland Canada Otter	C-FAGM	400	Operator Unknown	Crashed on snow covered lake	Goose Bay, NF, Canada	3	0
24.03.84	Cessna 441 Conquest II	SE-IHX	0291	Swedair	Destroyed in hangar fire	Location Unknown	*	*
26.03.84	Douglas DC-3	N62WS	12005	Central Intelligence Agency	Crashed on gun running flight. [Carried fictitious CF-ETE]	Nicaragua	*	*
26.03.84	Beechcraft Super King Air 200	F-GCCC	BB-0504	Sinair	Crashed on approach	Bergamo, Italy	*	*
26.03.84	Cessna 402C	N620AC	402C-0455	Operator Unknown	Crashed into trees at night	Warm Mineral Springs, FL, USA	4	0
31.03.84	Cessna 402B	N44NC	402B-0852	State Airlines	Crashed at sea	Between Miami & Bahamas	6	0
04.04.84	Gates Learjet 24D	PT-LCN	24D-287	Lider Taxi Aereo	Crashed	Florianapolis, Brazil	*	*
07.04.84	Beechcraft 18	N719MS	A-0320	Operator Unknown	Crashed due to engine icing	Off Egekik, AK, USA	0	2
07.04.84	Cessna U206 Super Skywagon	CP-1486	U206-04787	El Peto Air Taxi	Crashed	nr San Borja, Bolivia	1	*
08.04.84	Bell 206B JetRanger II	PT-HPF	03522	Lider Taxi Aereo	Crashed	nr Macae, Brazil	1	2
18.04.84	Embraer Bandeirante 110E(J)	PT-GJZ	110.088	VOTEC	Mid-air collision with Votec Bandeirante PT-GKL	Imperatriz, Brazil	18(0)	0
18.04.84	Embraer Bandeirante 110P	PT-GKL	110.107	VOTEC	Mid-air collision with Votec Bandeirante PT-GJZ	Imperatriz, Brazil	0(18)	15
19.04.84	Mitsubishi MU-2 Marquise	N466MA	1540SA	Operator Unknown	Written off	Burlington, CT, USA	*	*
21.04.84	Fairchild C-119 Flying Boxcar	N15509	*	Hawkins & Powers Aviation	Crashed into snowbank on take-off	Venetie, AK, USA	0	2
25.04.84	Cessna U206F Super Skywagon	HK-1665	U206-02259	Aerolineas del Este	Crashed	Barrancominas, Colombia	*	*
28.04.84	Douglas C-118A Liftmaster	N92860	44619	Intercontinental Air Lease	Overran on landing & caught fire	San Manuel, AZ, USA	0	*
05.05.84	Beechcraft Super King Air 200	XA-LIG	BB-0802	Operator Unknown	Crashed on approach	Poza Rica, Mexico	7	*
06.05.84	Curtiss C-46	CP-974	22363	Transportes Aereos San Martin	Crash landed after engine fire	San Borja, Bolivia	0	*
15.05.84	Gates Learjet 35A	LV-TDF	35A-478	Tierra del Fuego Province	Crashed in bad weather	Ushuaia, Argentina	11	*
18.05.84	Beechcraft King Air F90	YV-288CP	LA-008	Inversiones Fizo	Written off	Location Unknown	*	*
24.05.84	Beechcraft Queen Air	N404C	*	Operator Unknown	Forced landed after double engine failure	nr Zapata, TX, USA	*	*

Date	Type	Reg'n	C/n	Operator	Accident	Location	F	S
30.05.84	Lockheed Electra 188AF	N5523	1034	Zantop International Airlines	Crashed	Chalkhill, PA, USA	4	0
30.05.84	Britten-Norman Trislander	HP-946	0305	Aviones de Panama	Damaged beyond repair	Panama	*	*
30.05.84	Antonov AN-2R	HA-MBM	IG166-31	Air Service Hungary	Crashed	Hungary	*	*
oo.05.84	Britten-Norman Trislander	XA-KOQ	1045	Aerocozumel	Written off	Mexico	*	*
01.06.84	Grumman Gulfstream I	N181TG	181	Orion Air	Destroyed by fire after landing	Nashville, TN, USA	2	0
01.06.84	Britten-Norman BN-2A-26 Islander	G-BDVW	0522	Loganair	Crashed on overshoot	Sanday, Orkney, UK	0	*
04.06.84	Gates Learjet 23	N101PP	23-085	Knight Air	Crashed	Windsor Locks, CT, USA	3	*
06.06.84	Aerospatiale SA.315B Lama	HB-XLT	2020	Air Glaciers	Crashed into telephone lines	Fully, Switzerland	*	*
07.06.84	Handley Page Dart Herald 203	G-BBXI	184	Channel Express	Damaged beyond repair when struck by lorry	Hurn, Hants, UK	0	*
07.06.84	Aerospatiale SA.315B Lama	CC-CKA	2529	Helicopteros Andes	Crashed	nr Santiago, Chile	*	*
11.06.84	McDonnell Douglas DC-9-32	PK-GNE	47561	Garuda Indonesian Airlines	Skidded off runway & broke in two	Kemayoran, Indonesia	0	*
11.06.84	MBB HFB.320 Hansa	XC-TIJ	1049	Baja California State Government	Crashed	San Diego, CA, USA	*	*
16.06.84	Ilyushin IL-18D	LZ-BEP	185008105	Balkan Bulgarian Airlines	Overran runway on landing	Sanaa, Yemen Arab Republic	*	*
20.06.84	Rockwell Turbo Commander 695	ZS-KVB	95005	Operator Unknown	Written off	Location Unknown	*	*
23.06.84	IRMA BN-2A-8 Islander	F-BVTD	0710	Delmotte Aviation	Crashed	Ajaccio, Corsica, France	*	*
26.06.84	Cessna 210K Centurion	9J-ABT	210-59204	Transcarriers	Crash landed	nr N'dola, Zambia	*	*
28.06.84	Embraer Bandeirante 110C	PP-SBC	110.013	TAM Linha Aerea Regional	Crashed	nr Bao Pedro d'Aldeia, Brazil	18	0
30.06.84	Cessna 402C	N120PB	402C-0473	Provincetown-Boston Airlines	Crashed	Boston Harbor, MA, USA	1	1
01.07.84	Beechcraft 18	*	*	Coval Air	Crashed	Port Hardy, BC, Canada	9	0
04.07.84	LET 410M Turbolet	SSSR-67276	781007	Aeroflot	Damaged on landing	Chulman, RSFSR, USSR	*	*
04.07.84	Bell 206B JetRanger II	ZS-HEA	01323	Republic Helicopters	Crashed on take-off	Tabatseka, Lesotho	*	*
06.07.84	Cessna 421B Golden Eagle	AP-AYQ	*	Operator Unknown	Crashed	Mankera, Pakistan	3	1
11.07.84	Rockwell Turbo Commander 680T	N932E	1588-39	Operator Unknown	Written off	Kelso, WA, USA	*	*
13.07.84	de Havilland Canada Twin Otter 300	7P-LAA	622	Air Lesotho	Crashed when engine failed on take-off	Mokhotlong, Lesotho	0	*
13.07.84	Douglas A-26C Invader	C-FFIM	28496	Air Spray	Crashed	nr Calgary, AB, Canada	1	0
16.07.84	Bell 204	PK-VBR	2058	Dirgantara Air Service	Crashed	Irian Jaya, Indonesia	*	*
17.07.84	Beechcraft 18	N21S	BA-690	Operator Unknown	Crashed after engine failure	Off Honolulu, HI, USA	0	1
20.07.84	Cessna 421 Golden Eagle	N14TC	421-0105	Operator Unknown	Crashed into woods	nr Birchwood, WI, USA	3	0
21.07.84	de Havilland Canada Twin Otter 300	N43SP	669	South Pacific Island Airways	Crashed into terminal on landing	Tau Is, US Samoa	1	13
21.07.84	Grumman G-21A Goose	N2021A	B-114	Operator Unknown	Crashed	Off Ouzinkie, AK, USA	4	0
22.07.84	Rockwell Turbo Commander 680V	HS-TFB	1573-28	Operator Unknown	Written off	Location Unknown	*	*
24.07.84	Antonov AN-26	SSSR-26009	*	Aeroflot	Overran runway & crashed	Krasnoselkap, RSFSR, USSR	*	*
24.07.84	MBB Bo.105D	G-AZOM	S-21	Bristow Helicopters	Crashed	North Sea	0	2
25.07.84	Cessna U206G Stationair 6	OB-T-1197	U206-05590	Servicios Aereos	Crashed after take-off	Pucallpa, Peru	2	2
26.07.84	Beechcraft D18S	C-FBCD	A-0611	Northern Thunderbird Air	Overshot into ravine on landing	Germanson, BC, Canada	0	4
27.07.84	IRMA BN-2B-27 Islander	HK-2822X	2109	Tavina	Struck horse on landing & crashed	Isla de Providencia, Colombia	0	*
28.07.84	Gates Learjet 25B	N1JR	25B-188	Panorama Flight Service	Damaged beyond repair	Waterville, ME, USA	*	*
oo.07.84	Vickers Viscount 756D	Z-YNI	374	Air Zimbabwe	Damaged in ground accident	Harare, Zimbabwe	*	*
01.08.84	Cessna 421C Golden Eagle	N6231G	421C-0262	Operator Unknown	Crashed after structural failure in thunderstorm	Fort Lupton, CO, USA	3	0
02.08.84	Britten-Norman BN-2A Islander	N589SA	0038	Vieques Air Link	Crashed due to water in fuel	Off Isla de Vieques, Puerto Rico	9	0
02.08.84	Piper PA-31-350 Chieftain	N27948	*	Operator Unknown	Crashed. [Not found until 18.11.84]	nr Petros, TN, USA	2	0
04.08.84	Fokker F-27 Friendship 600	S2-ABJ	10453	Bangladesh Biman	Crashed on approach in bad weather	Dacca, Bangladesh	49	0
04.08.84	BAC One-Eleven 527FK	RP-C1182	246	Philippine Air Lines	Damaged when overran runway into sea	Tacloban, Philippines	0	75
05.08.84	Antonov AN-12	SSSR-10232	*	Aeroflot	Crashed in storm	nr Nawabshah, Pakistan	17	0
06.08.84	Fokker F-27 Friendship 200	PT-LCZ	10291	Rio Sul	Skidded off runway & ran into sea	Rio de Janeiro, Brazil	0	*
07.08.84	Cessna 402A	5Y-AMS	402A-0038	Pioneer Airlines	Crashed	Machakos, Kenya	9	0
08.08.84	Cessna 421C Golden Eagle	N98457	421C-0050	Operator Unknown	Crashed into trees after take-off	Kennesaw, GA, USA	4	0
10.08.84	IRMA BN-2A-21 Islander	PK-ZAL	0780	Sabang Merauke Raya Air Charter	Written off	Aceh, Indonesia	*	*
11.08.84	Douglas DC-3	N70003	12938	River City Airways	Crashed into building	nr Memphis, TN, USA	3	0
11.08.84	Sikorsky S-76	N63WW	760188	Operator Unknown	Crashed after engine failure	Fort Dix, NJ, USA	1	1
15.08.84	Douglas DC-3	PK-OBC	12485	Airfast Services	Crashed in bad weather	Between Santani-Jayapura, Indonesia	*	*
19.08.84	Vickers Varsity T.1	G-BDFT	620	Leicester Aft. Preservation Society	Crashed into power lines after engine failure	Marchington, Staffs, UK	11	3
21.08.84	Piper PA-32-300 Cherokee Six	5H-MOE	32-40506	Tanzanian Air Services	Crashed	Dar-es-Salaam, Tanzania	2	0

Date	Type	Reg'n	C/n	Operator	Accident	Location	F	S
22.08.84	Sikorsky S-58	F-BVJI	58-0956	Air Affaires	Crashed	Off Cherbourg, France	1	*
24.08.84	Beechcraft C99	N6399U	U187	Wings West Airlines	Mid-air collision with Rockwell 112	nr San Luis Obispo, CA, USA	15(2)	0
24.08.84	Antonov AN-12B	LZ-BAD	6344001	Balkan Bulgarian Airlines	Overran runway on landing	Addis Ababa, Ethiopia	*	*
25.08.84	Saunders ST-27	C-FCNT	14141/007	Labrador Airways	Damaged when u/c collapsed	St John's, NF, Canada	*	*
25.08.84	Rockwell Turbo Commander 690	N9150N	11063	Operator Unknown	Written off	Little America, WY, USA	*	*
28.08.84	Douglas DC-3	*	*	Central Intelligence Agency	Crashed	nr Quilali, Nicaragua	*	*
28.08.84	Vickers Viscount 757	9Q-CPD	303	Zaire Aero Service	Crashed & caught fire after take-off	Kinshasa, Zaire	0	*
30.08.84	Boeing 737-2H7CA	TJ-CBD	21295	Cameroon Airlines	Destroyed by fire on ground when bomb exploded	Douala, Cameroons	2	114
30.08.84	IRMA BN-2A-26 Islander	S7-AAE	0603	Air Seychelles	Written off	Location Unknown	*	*
31.08.84	Piper PA-31-350 Chieftain	N4469R	*	Operator Unknown	Crashed on drug smuggling flight	St Petersburg, FL, USA	0	1
31.08.84	Cessna 402	N55LP	*	Operator Unknown	Crashed on approach	Albertville, AL, USA	1	0
oo.08.84	Lear Learstar II	C-FOZO	2209	Geoterrex	U/c collapsed on landing	Nanisivik, NWT, Canada	0	*
03.09.84	Rockwell Turbo Commander 680V	N100CT	1618-50	Operator Unknown	Written off	Bridgeport, CA, USA	*	*
04.09.84	de Havilland Canada Buffalo 5D	C-GCTC	103	de Havilland Aircraft of Canada	Crashed on runway during air display	Farnborough, Hants, UK	0	3
04.09.84	Aerospatiale SA.315B Lama	HB-XNC	2632	Air Grischa	Crashed	Arequipa, Peru	*	*
06.09.84	IRMA BN-2A-20 Islander	P2-ISG	0756	Talair	Crashed into mountain	Mt Musaka, Papua New Guinea	9	2
06.09.84	Piper PA-31-350 Chieftain	N4499B	31-7552105	Operator Unknown	Found floating after ditching on drug smuggling flight	Off Marathon, FL, USA	*	*
07.09.84	Fairchild F-27	ZS-LPI	0058	Wonderair	Destroyed by fire while taxiing	Omega, Namibia	0	*
07.09.84	Cessna 402C	N89PB	402C-0650	Operator Unknown	Forced landing & caught fire	nr Naples, FL, USA	0	*
11.09.84	Handley Page Dart Herald 202	9Q-CAH	159	MMM Aero Services	Crashed	nr River Kwango, Zaire	30	*
12.09.84	Beechcraft Queen Air B80	N30276	*	Operator Unknown	Crashed	Vera Cruz, Mexico	2	0
12.09.84	Rockwell Turbo Commander 690B	LV-MAV	11397	Operator Unknown	Written off	Argentina	*	*
15.09.84	Cessna 210 Centurion	N731FT	*	Tigra Air Taxi	Ran off runway & crashed	Point Hope, AK, USA	0	4
15.09.84	Pilatus Porter	1607	*	Thai Police	Crashed on take-off	Tak, Thailand	8	0
16.09.84	Antonov AN-2	SP-AMK	1G168-04	Opolskie Aero Club	Crashed	Opolskie, Poland	11	*
18.09.84	McDonnell Douglas DC-8-54F	HK-2380X	45879	Lineas Aereas del Caribe	Damaged when ran off runway in rain	Barranquilla, Colombia	0	*
18.09.84	McDonnell Douglas DC-8-55F	HC-BKN	45754	AECA Cargo	Crashed into buildings on take-off	Quito, Ecuador	4{85}	0
19.09.84	Antonov AN-12	D2-EAD	*	Angolan Government	Crashed	Angola	*	*
19.09.84	Fairchild 226TC Metro II	OE-LSA	TC-315	Austrian Air Services	Damaged beyond repair	Vienna, Austria	*	*
24.09.84	Piper PA-31 Navajo	PT-BKB	31-482	Mecon Taxi Aereo	Crashed after take-off	Aripuana, Brazil	8	0
26.09.84	Cessna Citation I	C-GXFZ	500-0032	Air Niagara	Crashed	Orillia, ON, Canda	*	*
28.09.84	Rockwell Grand Commander 680FL	OB-T-805	1486-92	Aerotour	Crashed	nr Satipo, Peru	*	*
05.10.84	MBB HFB.320 Hansa	N127MW	1027	McCollum Aviation	Crashed on take-off	Aberdeen, SD, USA	3	*
06.10.84	Cessna Citation I	OE-FAP	500-0300	Grondmet Handels	Written off	Greece	*	*
09.10.84	de Havilland Canada Twin Otter 100	C-FPPL	115	Nahanni Air Services	Crashed into pole in poor visibility	Fort Franklin, NWT, Canada	7	0
09.10.84	Gates Learjet 24B	N864CL	24B-229	C.Lacey	Crashed on take-off	San Francisco, CA, USA	3	*
09.10.84	Rockwell Turbo Commander 695A	N81502	96000	Operator Unknown	Written off	Location Unknown	*	*
11.10.84	de Havilland Canada Twin Otter 100	C-FAUS	034	Labrador Airways	Crashed	nr Goose Bay, NF, Canada	4	0
11.10.84	Tupolev TU-154B-1	SSSR-85243	243	Aeroflot	Crashed into vehicles on runway while landing	Omsk, RSFSR, USSR	174{4}	1
13.10.84	Consolidated Catalina	N16KL	*	Confederate Air Force	Crashed on low level photographic flight	nr Brownsville, TX, USA	6	4
18.10.84	Cessna 421 Golden Eagle	N121BT	*	Mission Air	Crashed on approach	Addison, TX, USA	1	0
20.10.84	Piper PA-28 Cherokee	*	*	Pacific Airways	Crashed in sea	Off San Juan, Philippines	6	0
22.10.84	Convair 440-12	TAM-46	373	Transporte Aereo Militar	Crashed on approach	La Paz, Bolivia	0	*
23.10.84	de Havilland Canada Caribou	N5488R	216	Newcal Aviation	Crashed out of fuel	Off Sable Is, NF, Canada	1	*
28.10.84	Antonov AN-22	SSSR-08837	7340106	Aeroflot	Crashed after possible mid-air collision	nr Kabul, Afghanistan	240(*)	0
29.10.84	de Havilland Canada Otter	N778L	*	J.Munoz	Crashed on take-off	San Juan, Puerto Rico	1	0
31.10.84	Douglas DC-3	RP-C138	20811	Village Airways	Crashed	En route Davao–Manila, Philippines	4	0
31.10.84	Rockwell Turbo Commander 690C	N2937A	11670	Operator Unknown	Written off	Location Unknown	*	*
oo.10.84	Lockheed VC-121A Constellation	HI-393	2603	Argo	Struck by Dominicana DC-6 HI-92 blown into it by DC-8	Santo Domingo, Dominican Republic	0(0)	*
oo.10.84	Douglas DC-6B	HI-92	43532	Dominicana	Blown into Argo Constellation HI-393 by DC-8	Santo Domingo, Dominican Republic	0(0)	*
oo.10.84	Boeing 707-458	9Q-CWR	18357	Wolf Aviation	Damaged in hard landing	Isiro, Zaire	0	*
01.11.84	Beechcraft 18	N32809	*	Operator Unknown	Crashed into trees on take-off	Laconia, NH, USA	*	*

Date	Type	Reg'n	C/n	Operator	Accident	Location	F	S
01.11.84	Sikorsky S-76	*	*	Petroleum Helicopters	Crashed	Off Hainan, China	5	0
03.11.84	IRMA BN-2T Islander	C9-TAI	2122	TTA	Crashed on approach	Tete, Mozambique	0	7
10.11.84	Gates Learjet 24F	N81MC	24F-344	Macton Corporation	Crashed	St Thomas, British Virgin Is	1	*
13.11.84	Rockwell Turbo Commander 690B	EI-BGL	11507	Flight Line	Written off	Location Unknown	*	*
19.11.84	Embraer Bandeirante 110P1	G-HGGS	110.294	Euroair	Crashed into hill	nr Inverness, Highland, UK	1	0
20.11.84	de Havilland Canada Twin Otter 300	HC-BCG/446	446	TAME	Crashed into mountain	En route Loja-Zumba, Peru	14	0
20.11.84	Bell 212	G-BJJR	32142	Bristow Helicopters	Crashed	North Sea	0	*
21.11.84	Beechcraft King Air A100	C-GVCE	B-135	Operator Unknown	Written off	Calgary, Canada	*	*
22.11.84	Douglas DC-3	N2204S	12798	G.Williams	Crashed	nr Salinas, Mexico	0	2
25.11.84	Britten-Norman BN-2A-21 Islander	VH-ISI	0329	Snowy Mts Hydro Electric Authority	Crashed after take-off	Wilton, NSW, Australia	*	*
oo.11.84	Douglas DC-3	F-BYCU	12720	Stellair	Written off	Location Unknown	*	*
01.12.84	Boeing 720-027	N833NA	18066	NASA	Crashed by remote control to test fuel fire retardant	Edwards AFB, CA, USA	0	0
01.12.84	Mitsubishi MU-2J	N112SK	651	Operator Unknown	Written off	Location Unknown	*	*
04.12.84	LET 410M Turbolet	SSSR-67225	770706	Aeroflot	Crashed	Kostroma, RSFSR, USSR	10	*
06.12.84	Embraer Bandeirante 110P1	N96PB	110.365	Provincetown-Boston Airlines	Crashed on take-off after tail failed	Jacksonville, MA, USA	13	0
13.12.84	Beechcraft 18	N8517Z	*	Operator Unknown	Crashed on approach	Norfolk, VA, USA	*	*
16.12.84	Convair 440-62	N44828	468	Air Resorts Airlines	Destroyed by fire on landing	Jasper, AL, USA	*	*
20.12.84	Gates Learjet 35	N95TC	35-020	Jet East	Crashed	Waco, TX, USA	1	*
20.12.84	Rockwell Turbo Commander 690A	N9229Y	11122	Operator Unknown	Written off	Location Unknown	*	*
21.12.84	de Havilland Canada Twin Otter 300	5H-MRD	581	Air Tanzania	Crashed	nr Dar-es-Salaam, Tanzania	3	0
22.12.84	de Havilland Canada Twin Otter 300	9N-ABH	376	Royal Nepal Airlines	Crashed into mountain	nr Bhojpur, Nepal	15	8
22.12.84	Beechcraft King Air B90	C-GPPN	LJ-0389	Operator Unknown	Crashed	Iles Belcher, PQ, Canada	7	0
22.12.84	Cessna 402	N8064Q	*	Operator Unknown	Crashed after door opened in flight	Rochester, NY, USA	1	0
23.12.84	Tupolev TU-154B-2	SSSR-85338	338	Aeroflot	Crashed after engine fire on take-off	Krasnoyarsk, RSFSR, USSR	110	0
25.12.84	Cessna 441 Conquest II	N441CM	0169	Operator Unknown	Written off	Location Unknown	*	*
26.12.84	Cessna 402	N114EA	*	Operator Unknown	Crashed into trees after take-off	Troy, MI, USA	*	*
29.12.84	Lockheed L-100-30 Hercules	N24ST	4101	Transamerica Airlines	Destroyed by rebel gunfire on ground	Kafunfo, Angola	0	20
29.12.84	LET 410UVP Turbolet	SSSR-67140	800406	Aeroflot	Damaged in forced landing	Astrakhan, RSFSR, USSR	*	*
30.12.84	McDonnell Douglas DC-9-32	PK-GNI	47636	Garuda Indonesian Airlines	Crashed & caught fire on landing	Ngurah Rai, Indonesia	0	*
oo.oo.84	Rockwell Turbo Commander 690B	HL5261	11437	Operator Unknown	Written off	Location Unknown	*	*
oo.oo.84	Douglas DC-6A/B	HP-1018	45131	Operator Unknown	Crashed	Bahamas	*	*
oo.oo.84	Embraer Bandeirante 110P2	P2-RDL	110.300	Talair	Written off	Papua New Guinea	*	*
oo.oo.84	Tupolev TU-134A	SSSR-65807	3352108	Aeroflot	Written off	Georgia, USSR	*	*
01.01.85	Boeing 727-225A	N819EA	22556	Eastern Air Lines	Crashed into mountains	nr La Paz, Bolivia	29	0
05.01.85	Mitsubishi MU-2K	N275MA	255	Operator Unknown	Crashed on approach	West Point, VA, USA	1	*
05.01.85	Bell 206B JetRanger II	G-AVIG	08004	Bristow Helicopters	Crashed into sea	Weddell Sea, Antarctica	0	*
08.01.85	de Havilland Canada Twin Otter 300	YA-GAY	332	Bakhtar Afghan Airlines	Crashed on approach	Bamyan, Afghanistan	*	*
09.01.85	Lockheed Electra 188AF	N357Q	1044	TPI International Airways	Crashed into lake	nr Kansas City, MO, USA	4	0
10.01.85	Bell 206B JetRanger II	N59619	01681	Alaska Helicopters	Crashed	Off Arness, AK, USA	2	2
11.01.85	Vickers Viscount 828	PK-MVG	445	Merpati Nusantara Airlines	Crashed on landing	Ambon, Indonesia	*	*
11.01.85	Aerospatiale SA.315B Lama	OE-EXH	*	Helikopter Air Transport	Crashed into hangar	St Anton, Austria	3	0
13.01.85	Vickers Viscount 806	PK-RVT	268	Mandala Airlines	Damaged in belly landing	Adisutjipto, Indonesia	0	49
15.01.85	Bell 206L Long Ranger	ZS-HHF	*	National Airways	Crashed after engine exploded	nr Ermelo, South Africa	3	3
18.01.85	GAF Nomad 22B	VH-BFH	035	Barrier Reef Airways	Damaged in hailstorm	Brisbane, Qld, Australia	*	*
19.01.85	Ilyushin IL-18D	CU-T899	188011102	Cubana	Crashed after take-off	Havana, Cuba	40	0
19.01.85	Antonov AN-24	B-434	*	CAAC	Crashed on overshoot	Jinan, China	38	3
21.01.85	Lockheed Electra 188A	N5532	1121	Galaxy Airlines	Crashed on take-off	Reno, NV, USA	71	1
23.01.85	de Havilland Canada Twin Otter 300	HK-1910	497	ACES Colombia	Crashed into trees	En route Quibdo-Medellin, Colombia	23	0
23.01.85	Embraer Bandeirante 110P1	HK-2638	110.341	AIRES	Crashed into mountains	nr Buga, Colombia	17	0
24.01.85	Cessna 404 Titan	N302SP	*	Southern Cross Aviation	Crashed after take-off	Johannesburg, South Africa	1	0
28.01.85	Britten-Norman BN-2A Islander	HP-659	0064	Aviones de Panama	Crashed after engine failure	Off Taboga Is, Panama	0	4
29.01.85	Lockheed Electra 188CF	N854U	2009	Galaxy Airlines	Damaged beyond repair	USA	*	*
30.01.85	Rockwell Turbo Commander 695	D-IBAR	95054	Operator Unknown	Written off	Location Unknown	*	*

Date	Type	Reg'n	C/n	Operator	Accident	Location	F	S
31.01.85	Beechcraft 18	N95HA	*	Operator Unknown	Crashed	Huntington, WV, USA	*	*
31.01.85	Fairchild Merlin IVC	N568UP	AT-568	United Parcel Service	Written off	Location Unknown	*	*
01.02.85	Tupolev TU-134A	SSSR-65910	63971	Aeroflot	Crashed on take-off due to icing	Minsk, Bylorussia, USSR	58	22
01.02.85	Piper PA-31-350 Chieftain	N27522	*	LADCO	Crashed on approach	Whitefield, NJ, USA	5	0
01.02.85	Beechcraft King Air B100	N4213S	BE-013	Operator Unknown	Written off	Location Unknown	*	*
02.02.85	Beechcraft King Air A100	N72BS	B-113	Lisa Flite Corporation	Crashed in rain	Milleville, NJ, USA	2	*
04.02.85	Beechcraft Queen Air A80	N50NP	LD-231	North Pacific Airlines	Crash landed in swamp on approach	Soldotna, AK, USA	9	0
06.02.85	McDonnell Douglas DC-9-15	N926AX	47002	Airborne Express	Crashed on take-off after wing touched runway	Philadelphia, PA, USA	0	*
06.02.85	Cessna 402B	N5780M	402B-0358	Altus Airlines	Crashed after engine fire	Altus, OK, USA	2	0
07.02.85	Canadair Challenger 601	N779XX	3018	TAG Aviation	Undershot on landing	Milan, Italy	0	*
08.02.85	SIAI-Marchetti SF.600TP Canguro	I-CANG	001	SIAI-Marchetti	Crashed	Mt Tolfa, Italy	*	*
11.02.85	Cessna 421C Golden Eagle	N6866K	*	Special Coating Systems	Crashed after take-off	Albuquerque, NM, USA	6	0
13.02.85	Beechcraft King Air C90	N2019U	LJ-0792	Operator Unknown	Written off	St Mary's, PA, USA	*	*
14.02.85	IRMA BN-2A-3 Islander	PK-VIO	0693	Dirgantara Air Service	Crashed during storm	Banjarmasin, Indonesia	9	1
14.02.85	Beechcraft Queen Air C90	N2019U	*	Beechwoods Flying Service	Crashed	nr St Mary's, PA, USA	2	0
14.02.85	Piper PA-31-310 Navajo	N63719	31-7712042	Peninsula Airways	Crashed in high winds	Nelson Lagoon, AK, USA	1	0
17.02.85	Beechcraft King Air B90	N444SR	LJ-0416	Operator Unknown	Written off	Location Unknown	*	*
19.02.85	Boeing 727-256A	EC-DDU	21777	Iberia	Struck TV mast on approach & crashed into mountain	nr Bilbao, Spain	148	0
19.02.85	Sikorsky S-76	N31223	*	Petroleum Helicopters	Crashed	Houma, LA, USA	*	*
22.02.85	Antonov AN-24V	TZ-ACT	87304104	Air Mali	Crashed after take-off	Timbuktu, Mali	50	1
24.02.85	Dornier Do.228-100	D-IGVN	7039	Alfred Wegener Institute	Shot down by Polisario guerrillas	Off Western Sahara	3	0
26.02.85	Douglas DC-3	ZS-GPL	9581	Sandrivier Safaris	Crashed on take-off	Mala Mala, South Africa	0	3
26.02.85	Cessna 210 Centurion	N6803B	*	Tampa Airways	Crashed after engine failure	nr Jacksonville, LA, USA	1	0
27.02.85	de Havilland Canada Twin Otter 300	HK-2763	789	ACES Colombia	Set on fire by protesters at mass meeting	El Bagre, Colombia	0	0
09.03.85	Bell 206L Long Ranger	N16841	*	Petroleum Helicopters	Crashed in bad weather	nr Dauphin Island, AL, USA	4	0
12.03.85	de Havilland Canada Twin Otter 300	N540N	401	Seair Alaska Airlines	Crashed	Alaska, USA	1	3
14.03.85	Bell 214	*	*	Operator Unknown	Crashed	Off Fox Island, NF, Canada	6	*
16.03.85	Boeing 747-3B3	F-GDUA	22870	UTA	Destroyed by fire while being cleaned	Paris, France	0	*
17.03.85	Douglas A-26 Invader	N142ER	*	Operator Unknown	Crashed	Lawton, OK, USA	0	*
21.03.85	Britten-Norman BN-2A-3 Islander	PK-OAN	0235	Airfast Services	Crashed	Irian Jaya, Indonesia	*	*
28.03.85	Fokker F-28 Fellowship 3000	FAC.1140	11165	Satena	Crashed into mountain	nr San Vicente de Caguan, Colombia	46	0
28.03.85	Rockwell Turbo Commander 681	N772CB	6050	Operator Unknown	Written off	Calhoun, CO, USA	*	*
28.03.85	Piper PA-31-350 Chieftain	N3517W	*	Operator Unknown	Crashed into sea after take-off	Staniel Key, Bahamas	3	0
02.04.85	Cessna 421B Golden Eagle	N5407J	*	Bradley Machine Co	Crashed on take-off	Binghampton, NY, USA	2	0
10.04.85	Aerospatiale SA.315B Lama	HB-XGE	2284	Air Zermatt	Crashed	Rothorngletscher, Switzerland	1	3
11.04.85	British Aerospace 125-700B	LV-ALW	7133	Yacimientos Petroliferos Fiscales	Crashed into mountains	Salta, Argentina	7	*
14.04.85	Mitsubishi MU-2J	N808W	609	Operator Unknown	Written off	Location Unknown	*	*
15.04.85	Boeing 737-2P5A	HS-TBB	21810	Thai Airways	Crashed into mountains	North of Phuket, Thailand	11	0
20.04.85	Sikorsky S-58	N65526	58-0750	Carson Helicopters	Crashed	Off Key West, FL, USA	5	0
20.04.85	Fokker F-27 Friendship 100	YN-BZF	10118	Aeronica	Crashed out of fuel	Kulusuk, Greenland	2	3
20.04.85	Convair 440-35	CP-1489	319	Carga Aerea Transportada	Crashed after take-off	Santa Rosa, Bolivia	4	0
20.04.85	Bell 214B	JA9276	*	Aero Asahi	Crashed into mountains	Hino, Japan	*	*
20.04.85	Cessna U206G Stationair	N5442Z	*	Island Air Service	Crashed	Paramanof Bay, AK, USA	*	*
22.04.85	Douglas DC-6B	F-ZBAE	43834	Securite Civile	Crashed into cliff in fog	nr Fitow, France	5	0
22.04.85	Beechcraft King Air E90	G-BHUL	LW-083	Cega Aviation	Crashed	Goodwood, W Sussex, UK	*	*
28.04.85	Aerospatiale AS.360C Dauphin	N49505	1006	New York Helicopters	Crashed on take-off	34th St Helipad, New York, NY, USA	1	*
oo.04.85	Bell 214ST	*	*	Universal Helicopters	Crashed at night	Off St Johns, NF, Canada	6	0
oo.04.85	Fairchild Merlin IIIA	F-GEBK	T-272	Operator Unknown	Written off	Location Unknown	*	*
01.05.85	Lockheed PV-2D Harpoon	N7415C	151608	Globe Air	Crashed on test flight after engine failure	Mesa, AZ, USA	0	2
03.05.85	Tupolev TU-134A	SSSR-65856	*	Aeroflot	Mid-air collision with Soviet Air Force AN-26 on approach	Lvov, Ukraine, USSR	71(8)	0
03.05.85	Fairchild Merlin IIA	N444LM	T-295	Operator Unknown	Crashed on landing	Livermore, CA, USA	*	*
04.05.85	Douglas DC-3	N157U	4132	Perris Valley Parachute Center	Destroyed by fire on take-off	Perris Valley, CA, USA	0	33

Date	Type	Reg'n	C/n	Operator	Accident	Location	F	S
09.05.85	Consolidated Catalina	N84857	1522	Diversified Drilling Muds	Ran off runway after brake failure & fell over cliff	Lewistown, MT, USA	2	2
12.05.85	Dassault Falcon 50	N1181G	072	W.M.Wrigley Co	Crashed	Lake Geneva, WI, USA	0	*
12.05.85	IRMA BN-2A-21 Islander	PK-KNE	0675	Bali Air	Crashed	Maluku, Indonesia	*	*
14.05.85	Britten-Norman BN-2A Islander	*	*	TTA	Crashed	nr Xai Xai, Mozambique	5	0
15.05.85	Cessna 402	N402CS	*	Operator Unknown	Crashed after wing detached	Pocatello, ID, USA	1	0
16.05.85	Ilyushin IL-18	*	*	Aeroflot	Crashed	Off Sakhalin Is, RSFSR, USSR	*	0
16.05.85	Cessna 402A	*	*	Regional Express	Crashed	Boise, ID, USA	1	0
18.05.85	Piper PA-31-350 Chieftain	N66892	31-7405191	Cumberland Airlines	Crashed on approach	Latrobe, PA, USA	0	7
19.05.85	Beechcraft King Air E90	N575HC	LW-067	Operator Unknown	Written off	Pine Bluff, AR, USA	*	*
21.05.85	Cessna Citation I	N10GE	501-0022	Acme Air	Crashed	nr Harrison, AR, USA	*	*
23.05.85	Britten-Norman BN-2A-8 Islander	C-GPCF	0039	Chilcotin Cariboo Aviation	Crashed on landing	Ten Mile Creek, BC, Canada	*	*
28.05.85	Convair 580	YV-84C	157	Avensa	Crashed after take-off	Oro Negro, Venezuela	2	11
oo.05.85	Britten-Norman BN-2A Islander	N865JA	0176	Trans Island Airways	Written off	Bahamas	*	*
oo.05.85	IRMA BN-2A-9 Islander	TZ-ACS	0910	Operator Unknown	Written off	Location Unknown	*	*
05.06.85	Beechcraft E18S	C-FFLC	BA-365	Operator Unknown	Crashed into Lake Erie	Off Cleveland, OH, USA	1	0
05.06.85	Bell 47G-4	HK-1158	0677	Lineas Aereas Petroleras	Crashed	San Juan, Colombia	*	*
05.06.85	Bell 206L Long Ranger	C-GIZQ	*	Ranger Helicopters	Crashed on landing after engine failure	Whitecourt, AB, Canada	0	*
08.06.85	Cessna F152	EI-BDO	152-01457	Iona National Airways	Crashed out of fuel	Off Youghal, Eire	1	0
09.06.85	Beechcraft Super King Air 200	N148CP	BB-0129	Operator Unknown	Written off	Hampton, NY, USA	*	*
10.06.85	Gates Learjet 24B	F-BSRL	24B-210	Euralair International	Crashed	Provins, France	*	*
11.06.85	Rockwell 1121 Jet Commander	N69GT	044	Sultan Industries	Ran off runway	Van Nuys, CA, USA	0	2
12.06.85	Boeing 727-2D3A	JY-AFW	22271	Alia	Blown up on ground by hijackers & caught fire	Beirut, Lebanon	0	0
13.06.85	Boeing 707-336B	TY-BBR	20457	Benin Government	Crashed on take-off	Sebha, Libya	0	*
15.06.85	Cessna A188B	ET-AHE	188-03247T	Admas Air Service	Crashed	Awash, Ethiopia	*	*
15.06.85	Cessna U206G Stationair 6	N9828M	*	Seagull Air Service	Crashed on take-off	Eek, AK, USA	0	6
17.06.85	Cessna 402B	N100HK	*	Neilson Leasing	Exploded and crashed	nr Denver, CO, USA	8	0
19.06.85	Convair VT-29B	N155PA	322	Combs Airways	Engine exploded & crashed	Trenton, NJ, USA	0	*
19.06.85	Fairchild Merlin IIB	N199TA	T26-110	Telco Systems	Crashed after tail broke off	Del Rio, TX, USA	1	*
20.06.85	Bell 214B-1	N214RM	28001	Rocky Mountain Helicopters	Crashed	Squaw Valley, CA, USA	2	*
20.06.85	Beechcraft E18S	N19T	BA-147	Airborne Express	Destroyed when struck by crashing USAF F-4 on runway	Birmingham, AL, USA	1(*)	*
23.06.85	Boeing 747-237B	VT-EFO	21473	Air India	Crashed following bomb explosion	Off Irish Republic	329	0
23.06.85	Embraer Bandeirante 110P	PT-GJN	110.063	TABA	Crashed into vehicle on emergency landing	Juara, Brazil	17	0
28.06.85	Piper PA-42 Cheyenne III	N542TW	42-8001052	Operator Unknown	Written off	Charlotte, NC, USA	*	*
29.06.85	Bell 206L-1 Long Ranger	C-GDBR	45573	Vernon Helicopters	Crashed	Revelstoke, BC, Canada	5	0
30.06.85	Douglas DC-3	N168Z	20850	Northern Peninsular Airlines	Crashed out of fuel	King Salmon, AK, USA	0	*
30.06.85	Beechcraft King Air A90	N28SE	LJ-0239	Operator Unknown	Crashed	nr Apalachicola, FL, USA	*	*
02.07.85	Fokker F-27 Friendship 200	ST-AAR	10193	Sudan Airways	Damaged in heavy landing	Ed Debba, Sudan	*	*
06.07.85	Douglas DC-3	HK-1340	11704	LACOL	Crashed on take-off	Villavicencio, Colombia	2	4
06.07.85	Douglas C-118A Liftmaster	N2878F	44660	Northern Pacific Transport	Crashed on take-off	Egegik, AK, USA	0	3
10.07.85	Tupolev TU-154B-2	SSSR-85311	311	Aeroflot	Crashed	nr Uch Kuduk, Uzbekistan, USSR	200	0
11.07.85	Aerospatiale AS.350D Astar	N3594N	1093	Petroleum Helicopters	Crashed	Matagorda Island, TX, USA	0	1
15.07.85	Bell 206L-1 Long Ranger	N32GT	45663	Lone Star Helicopters	Crashed after striking wires	nr Fort Worth, TX, USA	0	4
18.07.85	Convair 990-30-5	N712NA	37	NASA	Crashed on take-off due to tyre bursts	March AFB, CA, USA	0	19
19.07.85	Cessna 421 Golden Eagle	N5473G	*	Operator Unknown	Crashed into trees on take-off	Kennesaw, GA, USA	1	4
20.07.85	Cessna 421 Golden Eagle	C-FFEL	421-0156	Operator Unknown	Crash landed & caught fire	Invermore, Canada	*	*
23.07.85	Claudius Dornier Seastar CD.2	D-ICDS	VT-01	Claudius Dornier Seastar	Overturned after landing with wheels lowered	Lake Constance, West Germany	0	2
29.07.85	Consolidated Catalina	N2886D	*	Operator Unknown	Crashed & sank while fire fighting	Northport, WA, USA	2	*
29.07.85	Aerospatiale AS.350D Astar	N3607C	*	Petroleum Helicopters	Crashed into cables after take-off	Houma, LA, USA	1	0
30.07.85	Britten-Norman BN-2A Islander	Z-WHE	*	International Red Cross	Shot down on take-off by rebels	Luabo, Zimbabwe	1	*
02.08.85	Lockheed Tristar 1	N726DA	1163	Delta Air Lines	Crashed on approach due to windshear	Dallas, TX, USA	136{1}	30
04.08.85	Embraer Bandeirante 110P1	HK-2593	110.302	AIRES	Crashed on take-off	Mocoa, Colombia	0	5
07.08.85	Beechcraft Queen Air	VH-FDR	LD-234	Norfolk Island Airways	Crashed	nr Biloela, Qld, Australia	*	*
09.08.85	Bell 412	*	*	Aero Asahi	Crashed near oil platform	Off Tanggu, China	4	0
12.08.85	Boeing 747SR-46	JA8119	20783	Japan Air Lines	Crashed following structural failure of tail	nr Tokyo, Japan	520	4

Date	Type	Reg'n	C/n	Operator	Accident	Location	F	S
12.08.85	de Havilland Canada Twin Otter 300	PK-NUG	346	Merpati Nusantara Airlines	Crashed	Mulia, Indonesia	2	17
12.08.85	Beechcraft Super King Air 200	N100HC	BB-0098	Jet Fleet	Mid-air collision with Jet Fleet Cessna U206 N33177	Greenville, TX, USA	0(3)	2
12.08.85	Cessna U206 Super Skywagon	N33177	*	Jet Fleet	Mid-air collision with Jet Fleet Beech 200 N100HC	Greenville, TX, USA	3(0)	0
13.08.85	Antonov AN-2	YR-PVU	1G175-19	Operator Unknown	Crashed	Romania	*	*
16.08.85	Cessna 404 Titan	N404EX	*	Wolverine Air Charter	Crashed	nr Detroit, MI, USA	1	0
19.08.85	Martin 404	CP-1704	14172	Compania Aerea Nacional	Crashed after take-off due to engine failure	La Paz, Bolivia	0	*
20.08.85	Gates Learjet 24XR	N455JA	24XR-300	ERA Helicopters	Crashed on approach	Gulkana, AK, USA	3	*
20.08.85	Grumman S-2 Tracker	*	*	Securite Civile	Crashed	nr Marseilles, France	2	0
21.08.85	Boeing 720-047B	OD-AGQ	19160	Middle East Airlines	Damaged by shelling	Beirut, Lebanon	*	*
21.08.85	Boeing 720-023B	OD-AFL	18034	Middle East Airlines	Destroyed by shelling	Beirut, Lebanon	*	*
22.08.85	Boeing 737-236A	G-BGJL	22033	British Airtours	Caught fire after aborting take-off due to engine explosion	Manchester, UK	55	83
25.08.85	Beechcraft 99	N300WP	U022	Bar Harbor Airlines	Crashed on approach	Auburn, ME, USA	8	*
25.08.85	Britten-Norman BN-2 Islander	P2-DNI	0028	Douglas Airways	Written off	Location Unknown	*	*
28.08.85	Beechcraft C99	N992SB	U170	Sunbird Airlines	Crashed	Conover, NC, USA	*	*
30.08.85	Britten-Norman BN-2A Islander	P2-DNW	0067	Douglas Airways	Crashed	Kokoda, Papua New Guinea	3	2
30.08.85	Beechcraft King Air 90	C-FCAU	LJ-0024	Operator Unknown	Written off	nr Quebec, PQ, Canada	*	*
31.08.85	Beechcraft Queen Air B80	9J-AAW	*	Sunair	Crashed	Lanseria, South Africa	5	0
04.09.85	Antonov AN-26	YA-BAM	57314106	Ariana Afghan Airlines	Shot down by rebels	Kandahar, Afghanistan	52	*
06.09.85	McDonnell Douglas DC-9-14	N100ME	47309	Midwest Express	Crashed after take-off	Milwaukee, WI, USA	31	0
10.09.85	Douglas DC-3	*	*	Collier County Mosquito Control	Crashed after engine failure	East Naples, FL, USA	0	2
15.09.85	de Havilland Canada Twin Otter 300	AP-BCH	768	Pakistan International Airlines	Collided on ground in bad weather with PIA Twin Otter AP-BCG	Islamabad, Pakistan	0(*)	*
17.09.85	Fairchild Merlin III	N3RB	T-214	Operator Unknown	Crashed off	Gulf of Mexico	*	*
22.09.85	Gates Learjet 35A	N873LP	35A-104	Louisiana Pacific Corporation	Mid-air collision with ultralight of Auburn University	Auburn, AL, USA	2	5
23.09.85	Beechcraft B99	N339HA	U156	Henson Airlines	Crashed in fog	Blue Ridge Mts, VA, USA	14	0
23.09.85	Dassault Falcon 10	N700DK	191	Durakool Inc	Crashed	Pal-Waukee, IL, USA	*	*
23.09.85	Cessna 402	N402V	*	Operator Unknown	Crashed at sea	Off Fort Lauderdale, FL, USA	*	*
24.09.85	Cessna 402B	N684LT	*	Operator Unknown	Missing & presumed crashed	Off Nassau, Bahamas	*	*
25.09.85	Beechcraft D18S	N25Q	*	Transtar Aviation	Crashed on approach	Huntington, WV, USA	1	0
25.09.85	Antonov AN-12	SSSR-69321	*	Aeroflot	Crashed	nr Kharkov, Ukraine, USSR	9	0
26.09.85	de Havilland Canada Beaver	N5317G	*	Willow Air Service	Crashed	Merrill Pass, AK, USA	3	0
29.09.85	Cessna 208 Caravan I	N551CC	208-00017	Air Carrier Express Services	Crashed on parachute drop	nr Jenkinsburg, GA, USA	17	0
01.10.85	Cessna 441 Conquest II	N400BG	0069	Operator Unknown	Written off	Location Unknown	*	*
04.10.85	Cessna 402B	ZK-EHT	402B-0340	Air Albatross	Crashed into power lines	Tory Channel, New Zealand	8	1
06.10.85	Cessna 402	*	*	Executive Air Services	Crashed	Cayman Brac, Cayman Islands	1	0
08.10.85	IAI Arava 101B	EL-AJH	078	Air Liberia	Damaged beyond repair	Sasstown, Liberia	*	*
09.10.85	Aerospatiale Caravelle 6N	9Q-CMD	074	African Air Charter	Damaged beyond repair	Mbuji-Maji, Zaire	*	*
10.10.85	de Havilland Canada Twin Otter	N3251	*	Operator Unknown	Crashed into hill	Homer City, PA, USA	1	*
10.10.85	IAI 1124 Westwind	VH-IWJ	371	Transexecutive Airlines	Crashed	nr Botany Bay, NSW, Australia	2	*
11.10.85	Embraer Bandeirante 110C	PT-GKA	110.090	Nordeste	Crashed on take-off	Vitoria da Conquista, Brazil	2	0
11.10.85	Curtiss C-46	CP-1593	32936	Sabeni	Crashed into mountains	nr Beni, Bolivia	*	*
11.10.85	Cessna 441 Conquest II	LN-VIP	441-0279	Operator Unknown	Written off	Location Unknown	*	*
11.10.85	de Havilland Canada Twin Otter 200	N3257	192	Mountain Air Cargo	Crashed	Homer City, PA, USA	*	*
11.10.85	Yakovlev YAK-40	SSSR-87803	*	Aeroflot	Crashed into mountain	Kutayissi, RSFSR, USSR	14	0
11.10.85	Cessna 206 Super Skywagon	HK-3067	*	Aerovias del Llano	Crashed & caught fire after take-off	nr Villavicencio, Colombia	0	*
12.10.85	Fokker F-27 Friendship 600	XY-ADS	10501	Burma Airways	Crashed	nr Putao, Burma	2	2
14.10.85	Beechcraft King Air B90	SE-GUU	LJ-0470	Operator Unknown	Written off	Sindal, Denmark	*	*
17.10.85	Mitsubishi MU-2F	N23CD	142	Air Exchange	Crashed into mountain	El Paso, TX, USA	1	0
19.10.85	Vickers Viscount 818	N923RC	320	Ray Charles Enterprises	Skidded off wet runway & broke up	Bloomington, IN, USA	0	*
22.10.85	Short 360-100	B-3606	SH.3673	CAAC	Damaged beyond repair	Enshi, China	*	*
24.10.85	Gates Learjet 24XR	N456JA	24XR-265	ERA Helicopters	Crashed on approach	nr Juneau, AK, USA	4	*
24.10.85	Bell 222UT	*	*	Pumkin Air	Crashed on landing on oil platform	Off Louisiana, USA	2	0
28.10.85	Beechcraft Super King Air 200	HK-2489	BB-0393	Operator Unknown	Written off	El Dorado, Colombia	*	*
oo.10.85	Bell 214ST	*	*	Okanagan Helicopters	Crashed on test flight	Edmonton, Canada	2	0
01.11.85	Cessna 208 Caravan I	N9241F	208-00006	Hermens Air	Crashed	nr Bethel, AK, USA	4	0

Date	Type	Reg'n	C/n	Operator	Accident	Location	F	S
03.11.85	Cessna 402	8R-GEP	*	Guyana Mining Co	Crashed into mountains	Rupununi, Guyana	1	0
05.11.85	Aerospatiale 330J Puma	PT-HRV	*	Helijet Aero Taxi	Crashed	Porto Sergio, Brazil	0	3
05.11.85	Beechcraft H18S	N1461G	*	Starflight	Crashed into power lines after take-off	Expressway Air Park, OK, USA	2	0
07.11.85	Mitsubishi MU-2M	N727MA	342	Operator Unknown	Written off	Location Unknown	*	*
07.11.85	Hawker Siddeley HS.125-731	N984HF	25183	Operator Unknown	Written off	Sparta, TN, USA	*	*
08.11.85	Cessna 421C Golden Eagle II	G-SHOE	421C-0123	Shuimpex (Services) Ltd	Damaged beyond repair	Deauville, France	*	*
10.11.85	Dassault Falcon 50	N784B	118	Nabisco	Crashed	nr Teterboro, NJ, USA	*	*
10.11.85	Piper PA-25 Pawnee	ET-AEY	25-5480	Admas Air Service	Crashed into tree	Amibara, Ethiopia	1	0
11.11.85	Cessna 441 Conquest II	N59MD	0177	Hyflight Associates	Crashed	Derry, PA, USA	5	0
12.11.85	Cessna 402C	N6788Y	*	Gateway Toyota	Crashed short of runway	Taylor, MI, USA	1	0
12.11.85	Cessna 206 Super Skywagon	CC-CET	*	Transportes Aereos Coyahique	Crashed at sea	Off Puerto Montt, Chile	2	0
21.11.85	Cessna 421C Golden Eagle	D-IFLY	*	Operator Unknown	Crashed into school	Dortmund, West Germany	4	0
24.11.85	Boeing 737-266A	SU-AYH	21191	EgyptAir	Destroyed when Egyptian troops stormed hijackers	Luqa, Malta	60	28
27.11.85	Cessna 404 Titan	G-BKTJ	404-0236	Donington Aviation	Crashed on take-off	Birmingham, UK	0	*
27.11.85	Beechcraft King Air C90	N220F	LJ-0981	Operator Unknown	Written off	Location Unknown	*	*
30.11.85	Lockheed Electra 188C	PK-RLG	2008	Mandala Airlines	Crashed on landing after wheels fell off	Medan, Indonesia	0	45
30.11.85	Bell 206L-1 Long Ranger II	N3913Z	45650	Helitrans	Mid-air collision with Island Express B206 N5759Y	Los Angeles, CA, USA	0(1)	6
30.11.85	Bell 206L Long Ranger	N5759Y	*	Island Express	Mid-air collision with Helitrans B206 N3913Z	Los Angeles, CA, USA	1(0)	5
02.12.85	Boeing 747-228B/SCD	F-GCBC	22427	Air France	Ran off runway & broke in two	Rio de Janeiro, Brazil	0	282
03.12.85	Rockwell Turbo Commander 680V	N17690	1577-31	Operator Unknown	Written off	Location Unknown	*	*
04.12.85	Fairchild 226TC Metro II	D-IASN	TC-297	Delta Air	Damaged on landing	Friedrichshafen, West Germany	*	*
04.12.85	Pilatus PC-6/B2-H2 Turbo-Porter	HB-FIP	*	Zimex Aviation	Crashed on approach in turbulence	Al Furt, Yemen PDR	0	1
08.12.85	Gates Learjet 35A	N15TW	35A-106	National Tire Wholesalers	Crashed on approach	Minneapolis, MN, USA	3	*
12.12.85	McDonnell Douglas DC-8-63PF	N950JW	46058	Arrow Air	Crashed after take-off	Gander, NF, Canada	256	0
12.12.85	Gates Learjet 35A	N723GL	35A-107	General Telephone Co	Crashed	Esterwood, TX, USA	2	*
13.12.85	Aerospatiale Puma	9M-SSG	1484	Malaysian Helicopter Services	Crashed	nr Bintulu, Malaysia	0	4
13.12.85	IRMA BN-2A-26 Islander	TN-AEQ	2147	Aero Service Corporation	Crashed	Accra, Ghana	*	*
23.12.85	Rockwell Turbo Commander 690B	N700R	11434	Operator Unknown	Destroyed in hangar fire	Location Unknown	*	*
26.12.85	Beechcraft 58 Baron	A2-ACT	TH-614	Kalahari Air Services	Damaged by storm on ground	Gaberone, Botswana	0	0
26.12.85	Cessna 182	A2-AEJ	*	Okavango Air Services	Damaged by storm on ground	Gaberone, Botswana	0	0
31.12.85	Douglas DC-3	N711Y	13658	Century Equipment	Crashed after cockpit fire [Singer Rick Nelson killed]	nr de Kalb, TX, USA	7	0
31.12.85	British Aerospace 125-700B	5N-AXP	7203	Nigerian Government	Crashed	Kaduna, Nigeria	7	*
31.12.85	Cessna 404 Titan	*	*	Linea Aerea Aeropetrel	Crashed into mountain	Nelson Is, South Shetland Is	10	0
oo.12.85	Gates Learjet 24B	F-BRNL	24B-183	Air Provence	Crashed	Toulouse, France	*	*
oo.oo.85	Embraer Bandeirante 110P1	HK-2743	110.366	Tavina	Crashed	Colombia	*	*
oo.oo.85	Antonov AN-24V	3X-GCG	7735805	Air Guinee	Damaged when nosewheel collapsed on landing	Siguiri, Guinea	0	*
oo.oo.85	Ilyushin IL-76M	5A-DKK	*	Libyan Air Force	Damaged in hard landing	Sheba, Libya	*	*
02.01.86	Cessna 207 Skywagon	ZK-WED	207-00009	Outdoor Aviation	Crashed after take-off	nr Picton, New Zealand	7	0
04.01.86	Piper PA-31P-350 Chieftain	N9253Y	31-8414030	Operator Unknown	Crashed into trees in fog	Bonne Carre, LA, USA	2	0
05.01.86	Sikorsky S-76	*	*	Air Logistics	Crashed on landing on barge in high winds	nr Houma, LA, USA	3	5
10.01.86	Aerospatiale SA.315B Lama	HK-2609	2585	Lineas Aereas Petroleras	Crashed	Nevado del Ruiz, Colombia	5	0
15.01.86	Dassault Falcon 10	F-GBTC	124	Air BG	Crashed	Chalons-Vatry, France	2	*
16.01.86	Cessna 402	C-GVBS	*	Operator Unknown	Crashed through frozen lake	Little Grand Rapids, Canada	2	0
18.01.86	Aerospatiale Caravelle 6N	HC-BAE	040	Saeta	Crashed on go-around	Santa Elena, Guatemala	87	0
19.01.86	Douglas DC-3	C-GNNA	12483	Austin Airways	Crashed into tower on approach	Sachigo Lake, Canada	*	*
19.01.86	Bell 206L Long Ranger	ZS-HLI	45700	Court Republic Helicopters	Crashed after striking power lines	Vaal River, South Africa	0	4
24.01.86	Beechcraft King Air B90	HB-GDV	LJ-0433	Luftfahrtzeug-Finanz	Crashed after take-off	Kleinobir, Austria	*	*
27.01.86	Boeing 707-387C	LV-JGR	19961	Aerolineas Argentinas	Damaged when overran on landing	Buenos Aires, Argentina	0	*
27.01.86	Consolidated Catalina	CC-CCS	2043	Operator Unknown	Sank in lake	Lago Gutierrez, Argentina	*	*
28.01.86	Rockwell Space Shuttle	n/a	*	NASA	Exploded after take-off [Challenger]	Off Cape Canaveral, FL, USA	7	0
28.01.86	Boeing 737-2A1	PP-SME	20096	VASP	Crashed on take-off	Sao Paulo, Brazil	0	*
29.01.86	Douglas DC-3	XA-IOR	1547	Aero California	Crashed into hill on landing	Las Lomitas, Mexico	21	0
29.01.86	Cessna 421 Golden Eagle	N68653	*	Operator Unknown	Crashed	Birmingham, AL, USA	2	0
31.01.86	Short 360-100	EI-BEM	SH.3642	Aer Lingus	Crashed into trees on approach	East Midlands Airport, Derbs, UK	0	36

Date	Type	Reg'n	C/n	Operator	Accident	Location	F	S
oo.01.86	Douglas DC-6BF	HR-AIV	43266	Operator Unknown	Damaged beyond repair	Location Unknown	*	*
02.02.86	Dassault Falcon 10	N821LG	170	Seneca Sawmill Co	Crashed	nr West Chester, PA, USA	*	*
05.02.86	Lockheed Electra 188AF	9Q-CWT	1045	Zaire Air Cargo	Damaged in forced landing	120km from Kinshasa, Zaire	2	6
05.02.86	Hughes 500	G-HSKY	490036M	Skyline Helicopters	Mid-air collision with Bristow B.47 G-AXKO which landed OK	Tudeley, Kent, UK	0	*
06.02.86	Antonov AN-26	SSSR-26095	*	Aeroflot	Crashed into hill	Saransk, RSFSR, USSR	0	6
08.02.86	Douglas DC-3	HK-3031	10202	SAEP	Crashed on take-off	Bogota, Colombia	0	4
13.02.86	Beechcraft 18	N30Y	*	Operator Unknown	Crashed on take-off	Kalaupapa, HI, USA	*	*
16.02.86	Boeing 737-281	B-1870	20226	China Airlines	Crashed on go-around after aborted landing	Off Pescadores Is, Taiwan	13	0
16.02.86	Mitsubishi MU-2K	SE-IOU	304	Operator Unknown	Written off	Sweden	*	*
20.02.86	Fokker F-27 Friendship	EP-ASN	*	Iran Asseman Airlines	Shot down by Iraqi fighter	nr Ahvaz, Iran	49	0
21.02.86	McDonnell Douglas DC-9-31	N961VJ	47506	US Air	Damaged when skidded off runway in snow	Erie, PA, USA	0	23
22.02.86	Beechcraft 18	N74FA	*	Operator Unknown	Crashed	nr Copperhill, TN, USA	1	0
25.02.86	Piper PA-31-350 Chieftain	PH-ASU	31-7752046	XP Airlines	Damaged beyond repair	Basle, Switzerland	*	*
26.02.86	Beechcraft 18	N723T	*	Operator Unknown	Destroyed	Janesville, WI, USA	*	*
oo.02.86	Ilyushin IL-14	*	*	Aeroflot	Crashed out of fuel	Antarctica	6	0
oo.02.86	Gates Learjet 25D	I-COTO	25D-285	Operator Unknown	Damaged beyond repair	Le Bourget, Paris, France	*	*
02.03.86	Antonov AN-24V	SSSR-46423	07304108	Aeroflot	Crashed	Bulgulma, RSFSR, USSR	38	*
02.03.86	Aerospatiale SA.316B Alouette III	HB-XOT	1781	Rhein-Helikopter	Crashed when tail rotor detached on landing	Malbun, Switzerland	*	*
04.03.86	Partenavia P.68	OY-PRY	102	Muk Air	Crashed into cables during snowstorm	Malmoe, Denmark	1	0
05.03.86	Gates Learjet 35	N39DM	35-040	Flight International	Mid-air collision with Flight Int. Learjet N97DM	San Clemente Island, CA, USA	2(2)	0
05.03.86	Gates Learjet 24D	N97DM	24D-253	Flight International	Mid-air collision with Flight Int. Learjet N39DM	San Clemente Island, CA, USA	2(2)	0
05.03.86	Mitsubishi MU-2P	N513DQ	321	Air Hi-Ho	Crashed after entering spin	Aurora, IL, USA	5	0
06.03.86	Beechcraft 99	CP-1804	U180	Operator Unknown	Overran on landing in bad weather	La Gloria, Bolivia	*	*
07.03.86	Lockheed C-130A Hercules	TT-PAB	3020	Chad Air Force	Crashed on take-off	Chad	*	*
13.03.86	Embraer Bandeirante 110P1	N1356P	110.370	Simmons Airlines	Crashed on approach	Alpena-Phelps Collins, MI, USA	3	6
13.03.86	Rockwell Turbo Commander 681	HK-2217P	6053	Inversiones GJ Restrepo y F. Estrada	Written off	Colombia	*	*
13.03.86	Bell 212	B-11120	*	Taiwan Airlines	Crashed	nr Taipei, Taiwan	0	10
15.03.86	Mitsubishi MU-2M	SE-IOX	331	Nyge-Aero	Shot down in error by anti-aircraft fire during practice	Ringenaes, Sweden	2	0
23.03.86	Britten-Norman BN-2A-21 Islander	C-GYTC	0554	Phaega Corporation	Written off	Location Unknown	*	*
25.03.86	IPTN 212 Aviocar 100	PK-NCF	108/15N	Merpati Nusantara Airlines	Crashed into hill	Naha, Indonesia	2	0
25.03.86	Antonov AN-12	SSSR-11795	*	Aeroflot	Crashed on approach	Omsk, RSFSR, USSR	9	0
31.03.86	Boeing 727-264A	XA-MEM	22414	Mexicana	Crashed into mountain after tyres burst in wheel bay	Maravatio, Mexico	167	0
03.04.86	Mil Mi-8	*	*	Operator Unknown	Crashed on oil rig	Off East Germany	4	*
03.04.86	McDonnell Douglas DC-8-33F	C-GSWX	45388	Aviation Technology & Resources	Exploded after spark ignited fuel while parked	Abbotsford, BC, Canada	0	0
04.04.86	IAI 1124A Westwind Two	N50SK	309	Drayton Associates	Crashed in storm	nr Texarkana, TX, USA	7	*
05.04.86	Beechcraft Queen Air	N810Q	*	Operator Unknown	Crashed	Montague, TX, USA	1	0
08.04.86	Aerospatiale AS.355F Ecureuil 2	G-BIKH	5246	McAlpine Helicopters	Crashed after engine failure	Swalcliffe, Oxon, UK	6	0
09.04.86	Cessna U206G Stationair	OB-T-1174	U206-04880	Servicios Aereos	Crashed	nr Obenteni, Peru	2	0
15.04.86	Fokker F-27 Friendship 600	5A-DLP	10645	Libyan Arab Airlines	Destroyed by US air raid	Benina, Libya	*	*
15.04.86	Ilyushin IL-76TD	5A-DNF	*	Libyan Arab Airlines	Destroyed by US air raid	Benina, Libya	*	*
15.04.86	Ilyushin IL-76M	5A-DZZ	*	Libyan Arab Airlines	Destroyed by US air raid	Benina, Libya	*	*
15.04.86	Ilyushin IL-76	*	*	Libyan Arab Airlines	Destroyed by US air raid	Benina, Libya	*	*
15.04.86	de Havilland Canada Twin Otter 300	5A-DCS	621	Ministry of Agriculture	Damaged in US air-raid	Tripoli, Libya	*	*
17.04.86	Curtiss C-46	HK-3205X	22275	Lineas Aereas Suramericanas	Tyre burst & collided with Cessna 172 on take-off	Mitu, Colombia	0(*)	*
18.04.86	Yakovlev YAK-40	SSSR-87236	9530243	Aeroflot	Crashed after structural failure	Kazan, RSFSR, USSR	*	*
24.04.86	Short Skyvan 3M	7Q-YAY	SH.1973	Malawi Police Air Wing	Crashed	nr Mombasa, Kenya	*	*
27.04.86	de Havilland Canada Twin Otter 300	HK-2761	780	ACES Colombia	Crashed	nr Saravena, Colombia	13	0
oo.04.86	Hawker Siddeley Trident 3B	9Q-CTZ	2307	Air Charter Services	Damaged beyond repair	Zaire	*	*
01.05.86	Cessna U206G Stationair	OB-T-1273	U206-06690	Aerovias SA	Crashed	nr Obenteni, Peru	*	*
03.05.86	Lockheed Tristar 1	4R-ULD	1061	Air Lanka	Blown up by bomb on ground	Colombo, Sri Lanka	16	*
07.05.86	Fairchild Merlin IV	N577KA	AT-008	Career Aviation Services	Crashed on approach	Billings. MT, USA	1	*
07.05.86	Rockwell Turbo Commander 690D	N200PR	15029	Operator Unknown	Written off	Location Unknown	*	*
07.05.86	Fuji-Bell 204B-2	JA9230	CH-49	Nihon Norin Helicopters	Crashed into mountain	Yoshino, Japan	2	0
09.05.86	Pilatus PC-6/B2-H4 Turbo Porter	HB-FKC	*	Gromex	Crashed after parachutist damaged stabiliser on exit	Haun, West Germany	1	0

Date	Type	Reg'n	C/n	Operator	Accident	Location	F	S
17.05.86	Douglas DC-3	C-FGHL	12475	Nunasi Central Airlines	Fell through ice on frozen lake	Nejanilini Lake, ON, Canada	0	*
17.05.86	Yakovlev YAK-40	SSSR-87301	*	Aeroflot	Crashed on test flight after repairs	Hanty-Mansiyesk, RSFSR, USSR	5	0
21.05.86	Tupolev TU-154B-2	SSSR-85327	327	Aeroflot	Crashed	nr Moscow, RSFSR, USSR	0	*
30.05.86	Douglas DC-3	N3433U	9959/43087	Atorie Air	Damaged by ground loop	Las Vegas, NV, USA	0	*
06.06.86	Mitsubishi MU-2J	N8CC	569	Operator Unknown	Crashed	Bartlett, TX, USA	1	*
06.06.86	Bell 212	C-GFQI	30559	Viking Helicopters	Crashed	El Muglad, Sudan	2	0
08.06.86	Lockheed L-100-30 Hercules	D2-THA	4832	TAAG Angola Airlines	Caught fire after belly landing	Dondo, Angola	*	*
11.06.86	Fokker F-27 Friendship 500	SU-GAD	10659	Air Sinai	Crashed on landing during sandstorm with engine fire	Cairo, Egypt	23	3
11.06.86	Piper PA-31 Navajo	G-BFON	31-405	Airways International Cymru	Crashed attempting emergency landing	nr Brize Norton, Oxon, UK	0	3
12.06.86	de Havilland Canada Twin Otter 300	G-BGPC	635	Loganair	Crashed into hill on approach	Port Ellen, Islay, UK	1	15
13.06.86	MBB Bo.105S	N2784E	S-620	Evergreen Helicopters	Crashed	Houma, LA, USA	1	0
14.06.86	PADC BN-2A-26 Islander	G-BMDT	3012	Air Furness	Overran in poor visibility	Walney Is, Cumbria, UK	0	*
14.06.86	de Havilland Canada Twin Otter 200	C-FZZM	156	La Ronge Aviation	Crashed	Canada	*	*
16.06.86	Beechcraft King Air C90	N114CM	LJ-0709	J.B.McKee	Crashed into mountain	nr Jackson, WY, USA	1	0
18.06.86	de Havilland Canada Twin Otter 300	N76GC	248	Grand Canyon Airlines	Crashed	nr Grand Canyon, AZ, USA	*	*
19.06.86	Douglas C-54D	HK-1808	10669	Lineas Aereas Suramericanas	Crashed after take-off due to engine failure	La Macarena, Colombia	3	0
19.06.86	de Havilland Canada Twin Otter 300	N74GC	559	Grand Canyon Airlines	Mid-air collision with Grand Canyon H/C Jet Ranger N6TC	Grand Canyon, AZ, USA	20(5)	0
19.06.86	Bell 206B Jet Ranger II	N6TC	*	Grand Canyon Helicopters	Mid-air collision with Grand Canyon A/L Twin Otter N74GC	Grand Canyon, AZ, USA	5(20)	0
22.06.86	Tupolev TU-134A	SSSR-65142	*	Aeroflot	Crashed on take-off	Penza, RSFSR, USSR	38	0
22.06.86	de Havilland Canada Twin Otter 300	ET-AIQ	819	Ethiopian Airlines	Crashed on approach	Dembidollo, Ethiopia	*	*
27.06.86	Martin 404	N40443	14228	Frontier Airways	Crashed on take-off	Buffalo, WY, USA	3	*
29.06.86	Cessna 206 Super Skywagon	YV-229C	*	RUTACA	Crashed	Mt Roraima, Venezuela	6	0
01.07.86	Piasecki Heli-Stat	*	*	Piasecki Aircraft	Crashed when pilot applied excessive power to one rotor	Lakehurst, NJ, USA	1	4
02.07.86	Tupolev TU-134A	SSSR-65120	*	Aeroflot	Crashed after in-flight fire	nr Syktyvkar, RSFSR, USSR	54	38
16.07.86	Cessna 441 Conquest II	N6857E	0244	Operator Unknown	Written off	Location Unknown	*	*
19.07.86	Douglas DC-6B	F-ZBBU	45219	Securite Civile	Crashed	Mont de la Ponge, Spain	4	0
19.07.86	Cessna 421 Golden Eagle	N6VR	*	Operator Unknown	Crashed on take-off	Addison, TX, USA	4	0
22.07.86	Douglas DC-3	N27PR	11776	Borinquen Air	Crashed on take-off after engine failure	San Juan, Puerto Rico	1	1
23.07.86	Mitsubishi Diamond 1A	JA8246	A092SA	Shin Mitsubishi Jukogyo	Crashed	Sado Island, Japan	*	*
25.07.86	Fokker F-27 Friendship 600	TU-TIF	10573	Air Ivoire	Crashed after take-off	Tabou, Ivory Coast	*	*
29.07.86	Cessna 421B Golden Eagle	OY-BUS	*	Dansk Totalenterprise	Crashed at sea in thunderstorm	Off Kalundborg, Denmark	5	0
30.07.86	Fuji-Bell 204B-2	JA9172	CH-41	Naka Nihon Air Service	Crashed into trees	Kutchan, Japan	0	2
31.07.86	Britten-Norman BN-2A-21 Islander	RP-C850	0469	Atlas Consolidated Mining	Crashed	Mt Canlandog, Philippines	4	0
02.08.86	British Aerospace 125-1A-522	N50HH	25022	American Agronomics Corporation	Overshot & crashed	Bedford, IN, USA	2	*
04.08.86	de Havilland Canada Twin Otter 300	V2-LCJ	785	Leeward Islands Air Transport	Crashed in sea	Off St Vincent	13	0
06.08.86	Aerospatiale Caravelle 3	5N-AWK	050	Kabo Air	Damaged after overshooting	Calabar, Nigeria	*	*
06.08.86	Gates Learjet 55	N921FP	55-103	Federal Paper Board Co	Aborted take-off & ran through wall	Rutland, VT, USA	0	*
10.08.86	McDonnell Douglas DC-10-40	N184AT	46751	American Trans Air	Destroyed by fire on ground	Chicago, IL, USA	0	*
15.08.86	Grumman CS2F-2 Firecat	C-GHQY	DHC-35	Conair Aviation	Crashed	McBride, BC, Canada	1	*
16.08.86	Fokker F-27 Friendship 400M	ST-ADY	10277	Sudan Airways	Shot down by rebels after take-off	Malakal, Sudan	60	0
17.08.86	Douglas B-26 Invader	N190M	*	Operator Unknown	Crashed into trees on first flight for two years	Pattonville, TX, USA	*	*
28.08.86	Beechcraft King Air A100	F-GEFR	B-220	Operator Unknown	Written off	Lille, France	*	*
29.08.86	Cessna 441 Conquest II	N2727A	0201	Nolan's RV	Crashed after take-off	Lander, WY, USA	7	0
31.08.86	McDonnell Douglas DC-9-32	XA-JED	47356	Aeromexico	Mid-air collision with Cherokee N4891F on approach	Los Angeles, CA, USA	64{15} (3)	0
31.08.86	Cessna 404 Titan II	OH-CIG	404-0242	Wasawings	Crashed on landing	Ylivieska, Finland	0	1
02.09.86	de Havilland Canada Otter	C-FBER	086	Operator Unknown	Forced landed in swamp & caught fire	Pickle Lake, ON, Canada	*	*
03.09.86	Cessna 402	VH-RED	402-0130	Peninsula Air Services	Crashed due to engine failure after take-off	Tullamarine, SA, Australia	6	0
09.09.86	Fairchild Merlin III	N66KS	T-209	ORD Inc	Crashed	nr McLainstown, Bahamas	*	*
11.09.86	de Havilland Heron 2	DQ-FEC	14078	Fiji Air	Crashed into trees on take-off	Vanua Mbalavu, Fiji	1	2
14.09.86	Britten-Norman Trislander	G-BDTP	1028	Kondair	Crashed on approach	Amsterdam, Netherlands	1	0
16.09.86	Bell 206L Long Ranger	SE-HRD	45058	Osterman Helikopter	Crashed into sea	Off Gothenburg, Sweden	1	0
19.09.86	Embraer Brasilia 120	N219AS	120.019	Atlantic Southeast Airlines	Crashed into hill on delivery flight	Sao Jose dos Campos, Brazil	5	0
25.09.86	Bell 214B	JA9293	28060	Naka Nihon Air Service	Crashed	Shin Totsugawa-machi, Japan	0	2

Date	Type	Reg'n	C/n	Operator	Accident	Location	F	S
26.09.86	Beechcraft Super King Air B200	N551TR	BB-1033	Operator Unknown	Written off	Location Unknown	*	*
28.09.86	Beechcraft E18S	N101VE	BA-190	Viking Express	Crashed into houses after take-off	Chicago, IL, USA	1	0
29.09.86	Airbus A.300B2-1C	VT-ELV	022	Indian Airlines	Damaged beyond repair	Madras, India	0	*
oo.09.86	Rockwell Sabre 75A	N64	380-35	Federal Aviation Administration	Written off	USA	*	*
oo.09.86	IRMA BN-2A-21 Islander	N455JH	2163	Operator Unknown	Written off	Location Unknown	*	*
oo.09.86	Britten-Norman Trislander	VQ-TAJ	1009	Turks & Caicos National Airlines	Written off	Location Unknown	*	*
03.10.86	Short Skyvan 3	PK-ESC	SH.1851	East Indonesia Air Taxi	Crashed into high ground	nr Manado, Indonesia	13	0
03.10.86	Dassault Falcon 10	3D-ART	061	Rembrandt Tobacco	Crashed	Magoebaskloof, South Africa	4	*
03.10.86	Sikorsky UH-60A Blackhawk	*	*	Sikorsky	Damaged in heavy landing	West Palm Beach, FL, USA	*	*
03.10.86	Short Skyvan 3	PK-ESC	SH.1923	Eastindo Air Taxi	Crashed	Mt Tarawiran, Indonesia	*	*
04.10.86	Lockheed L-100-30 Hercules	N15ST	4391	Southern Air Transport	Crashed on take-off & exploded	Kelly AFB, TX, USA	3	0
09.10.86	Douglas DC-7C	N5903	45071	T & G Aviation	Crashed	Off Dakar, Senegal	3	0
11.10.86	Beechcraft Queen Air B80	YV-247P	LD-316	Operator Unknown	Crashed on take-off	La Carlota, Venezuela	*	0
14.10.86	LET 410MU Turbolet	SSSR-67264	780905	Aeroflot	Crashed into river after take-off	Ust-Maya, RSFSR, USSR	14	*
15.10.86	Boeing 737-286A	EP-IRG	20499	Iran Air	Damaged by Iraqi aircraft on ground	Shiraz, Iran	3	*
19.10.86	Tupolev TU-134A	C9-CAA	63457	Mozambique Air Force	Crashed in storm [Prime Minister Samora Machel killed]	Lembombo Mts, South Africa	33	10
20.10.86	Tupolev TU-134A	SSSR-65766	*	Aeroflot	Crashed when pilot attempted needless blind landing	Kuybyshev, RSFSR, USSR	70	24
22.10.86	Piper PA-31-350 Chieftain	SE-IDU	31-8152036	Travelair	Crashed	nr Borlaenge, Sweden	1	*
23.10.86	Fokker F-27 Friendship 600	AP-AUX	10335	Pakistan International Airlines	Crashed short of runway	Peshawar, Pakistan	13	40
23.10.86	Cessna 441 Conquest II	*	*	Operator Unknown	Crashed after take-off	Du Page, IL, USA	*	*
24.10.86	Gates Learjet 25XR	N51DB	25XR-246	Sheikh Salim bin Laden	Crashed	nr Medina, Saudi Arabia	2	*
24.10.86	Grumman G-73 Mallard	N604SS	*	Virgin Islands Seaplane Shuttle	Crashed after take-off	Off St Croix, US Virgin Is	3	0
25.10.86	Boeing 737-222	N752N	19073	Piedmont Airlines	Skidded off runway on landing & struck embankment	Charlotte, NC, USA	0	118
oo.10.86	Gates Learjet 24A	N88JF	24A-110	Operator Unknown	Written off	Detroit, MI, USA	*	*
02.11.86	Sikorsky H-3 Pelican	1473	*	United States Coast Guard	Crashed	Akhiok, AK, USA	5	0
02.11.86	Beechcraft King Air E90	F-GBRD	LW-091	Operator Unknown	Written off	Barcelonette, France	*	*
03.11.86	Beechcraft Super King Air 200	CN-CDE	BB-0567	Royal Air Maroc	Written off	Casablanca, Morocco	*	*
04.11.86	Sikorsky S-58	N42475	*	North American Helicopter Service	Crashed	Becker, MN, USA	1	*
06.11.86	Boeing-Vertol Chinook	G-BWFC	MJ004	British International Helicopters	Crashed after rotor failed	Off Sumburgh, Shetlands, UK	45	2
06.11.86	Cessna Citation II	N711WM	551-0388	Barbary Coast Hotel & Casino	Written off	Location Unknown	*	*
06.11.86	Cessna 421 Golden Eagle	N421AR	*	Operator Unknown	Crashed	nr Butte, MT, USA	1	0
07.11.86	Beechcraft 18	N149AA	*	Operator Unknown	Crashed in bad weather	Texarkana, AR, USA	1	0
08.11.86	Beechcraft Queen Air 80	N304D	*	Operator Unknown	Crashed during emergency landing	Baltimore, MD, USA	1	0
08.11.86	Beechcraft King Air A100	N78L	B-167	Operator Unknown	Written off	Brookville, FL, USA	*	*
12.11.86	Beechcraft 18	N925J	*	Operator Unknown	U/c collapsed on landing & caught fire	Pittsburgh, PA, USA	*	*
19.11.86	Cessna U206G Stationair	OB-T-1292	U206-03813	Aerotour	Crashed after take-off	Atalya, Peru	1	7
23.11.86	Cessna 441 Conquest II	N241FW	*	Operator Unknown	Crashed into high ground after take-off	Chicago, IL, USA	1	0
27.11.86	Aerospatiale Caravelle 11R	HK-2850X	261	Aerosucre	Damaged after overrunning runway	Arauca, Colombia	*	*
28.11.86	Cessna T210N Centurion	OB-T-1294	T210-63291	Airvas Air Taxi	Crashed attempting emergency landing	Urpay, Peru	3	*
30.11.86	British Aerospace Jetstream 31	N830JS	714	Jetstream International Airlines	Struck by Cessna 441 on ground & caught fire	Erie, PA, USA	*(*)	*
oo.11.86	Douglas DC-6A	HI-251	45520	Carga Aerea Dominicana	Overran on emergency landing	Congotown, Bahamas	0	*
07.12.86	Antonov AN-26	SSSR-88288	*	Aeroflot	Crash landed short of runway out of fuel	Moscow, RSFSR, USSR	*	*
10.12.86	Beechcraft Super King Air 200	C-GKRL	BB-0878	Syncrude Canada	Crashed	Fort McMurray, AB, Canada	*	*
10.12.86	Beechcraft King Air A100	N65TD	B-050	Teledyne Post of South Bend	Crashed on approach	Pittsfield, MA, USA	6	0
12.12.86	Tupolev TU-134A	SSSR-65795	*	Aeroflot	Crashed on landing after approach to wrong runway	Berlin, East Germany	72	9
14.12.86	Piper PA-31-350 Chieftain	N37490	*	Operator Unknown	Shot down on smuggling flight by Dominican Rep. AF A-37	Off Cabo Rojo, Dominican Republic	*	0
15.12.86	Antonov AN-24	B-444	*	CAAC	Crashed during storm	Lanzhou, China	6	38
17.12.86	CASA 212 Aviocar 200	N431CA	269	Latin Air Service	Crashed	Caribbean Sea	0	*
23.12.86	Douglas C-54R	N96361	27368	Central Air Service	Crashed due to engine fire	Off Arlington, WA, USA	0	*
25.12.86	Boeing 737-270CA	YI-AGJ	21183	Iraqi Airways	Crashed after grenades exploded during hijack attempt	Arar, Saudi Arabia	62	44
27.12.86	de Havilland Heron 2B	DQ-FEF	14056	Sunflower Airlines	Crashed short of runway	Nasaso, Fiji	11	3
28.12.86	Cessna 402B	OH-CDU	402B-0034	Siimes Aviation	Crashed	nr Joensuu, Finland	1	0
29.12.86	Aerospatiale Puma	VH-WOA	1526	Mayne-Bristow Helicopters	Crashed	Off Dampier, WA, Australia	2	15
31.12.86	British Aerospace 125-600B	5N-AWS	6042	Radio Communications Corporation	Crashed into house	Casablanca, Morocco	4	*

Date	Type	Reg'n	C/n	Operator	Accident	Location	F	S
31.12.86	LET 410UVP Turbolet	SSSR-67428	831119	Aeroflot	Damaged on ground	Chernenko, RSFSR, USSR	*	*
31.12.86	Cessna 310	N5462J	*	Buffalo Express Airlines	Crashed	Lake Erie, USA	1	0
oo.oo.86	Fokker F-27 Friendship 600	5A-DLR	10647	Libyan Arab Airlines	Damaged beyond repair	Gialo, Libya	*	*
oo.oo.86	Yakovlev YAK-42	SSSR-42536	*	Aeroflot	Damaged by fire on ground	Bykovo, RSFSR, USSR	*	*
oo.oo.86	Rockwell Turbo Commander 690D	N5889N	15019	Operator Unknown	Written off	Location Unknown	*	*
oo.oo.86	Britten-Norman Trislander	5Y-AOY	0320	Cooper Skybird Air Charters	Written off	Location Unknown	*	*
oo.oo.86	Tupolev TU-154B-2	7O-ACN	501	Alyemda	Destroyed during civil war	Aden, Yemen PDR	*	*
03.01.87	Boeing 707-379C	PP-VJK	19822	Varig	Crashed on take-off due to engine fire	Abidjan, Ivory Coast	51	2
06.01.87	Aerospatiale Caravelle 10R	SE-DEC	263	Transwede	Crashed on landing due to fire	Stockholm, Sweden	0	27
07.01.87	Boeing 707-323C	OD-AHB	19588	Middle East Airlines	Destroyed by shelling	Beirut, Lebanon	0	*
07.01.87	Douglas C-54D	9Q-CAG	10640	Kinair Cargo	Destroyed after engine caught fire	Zaire	*	*
10.01.87	Sikorsky HH-3F Pelican	*	*	United States Coast Guard	Crashed	Off California, USA	*	*
10.01.87	McDonnell Douglas DC-10-30	5N-ANR	46968	Nigeria Airways	Overran on landing & caught fire	Ilorin, Nigeria	0	9
10.01.87	Sikorsky S-58	N47782	58-0879	Carson Helicopters	Crashed	Off Georgetown, Bahamas	0	*
11.01.87	Cessna 421C Golden Eagle	JA5273	*	Kitaro Takahashi Sanko Kensetsu	Crashed after engine failure	Wada, Japan	4	0
12.01.87	Britten-Norman BN-2A-20 Islander	C-GIRH	0404	Operator Unknown	Written off	Location Unknown	*	*
13.01.87	NAMC YS-11A-213	N906TC	2154	Mid Pacific Air	Crash landed in field	Jasper County, IN, USA	0	*
14.01.87	Gates Learjet 35A	HB-VGC	35A-259	Fidinam Fiduciara	Crashed on landing	Lugano, Switzerland	*	*
15.01.87	Fairchild 226TC Metro II	N163SW	TC-327	Skywest Airlines	Mid-air collision with Mooney 21 N6485U on approach	Salt Lake City, UT, USA	10(*)	0
16.01.87	Yakovlev YAK-40	SSSR-87618	*	Aeroflot	Crashed on take off due to wake turbulence of IL-76	Tashkent, Uzbekistan, USSR	5	0
18.01.87	Fokker F-27 Friendship 200	G-BMAU	10241	British Midland Airways	Crashed on approach	Donnington Park, Derbs, UK	0	3
21.01.87	Piper PA-31 Navajo	TF-ORN	*	Ernir Airlines	Crashed into sea on approach	Isafjord, Iceland	1	0
25.01.87	Yakovlev YAK-40	SSSR-87696	9910105	Aeroflot	Crashed on take-off	Tarnoga, RSFSR, USSR	0	26
28.01.87	Cessna 207 Skywagon	N7393U	207-00436	South Central Air	Crashed on approach	Anchorage, AK, USA	*	*
31.01.87	Sikorsky S-58T	N5594C	58692	Aris Helicopters	Crashed on landing	Los Angeles, CA, USA	0	*
31.01.87	Bell 205A-1	HK-1495	30148	Helicopteros Nacionales de Colombia	Set on fire by guerillas on ground	Arauca, Colombia	0	*
02.02.87	Curtiss C-46	CP-909	22467	Trans Aereos San Miguel	Belly landed in swamp	San Ignacio de Moxos, Bolivia	0	5
02.02.87	Cessna 402	VH-TLQ	*	Gold-Air	Crashed into forest in poor weather	Mt Diane, Qld, Australia	5	0
04.02.87	Sikorsky S-76	N767AL	760030	Air Logistics	Crashed	nr Angleton, TX, USA	2	0
05.02.87	Fairchild Merlin IV	D-IEWK	AT-042	Regionalflug	U/c collapsed on landing	Munich, West Germany	0	*
05.02.87	Gates Learjet 55	F-GDHR	55-070	Aero France	Crashed	nr Jakiri, Cameroons	9	*
06.02.87	Embraer Bandeirante 110P2	P2-RDM	110.262	Talair	Crashed	Off Papua New Guinea	14	3
07.02.87	de Havilland Canada Twin Otter 300	8Q-GIA	341	Inter Atoll Air	Lost float on landing & sank	Felvoru, Maldive Islands	0	*
09.02.87	Britten-Norman Trislander	G-OCME	0262	Aviation West	Crashed out of fuel	nr Widnes, Cheshire, UK	0	1
09.02.87	Antonov AN-26	*	*	Aeroflot	Shot down by rebels	Khost, Afghanistan	36	*
16.02.87	Convair 240-26	N93218	167	Israel Aircraft Industries	Destroyed by fire in store	Tel Aviv, Israel	0	*
17.02.87	Beechcraft Super King Air 200T	JA8825	BT-19	Japan Maritime Safety Agency	Written off	Location Unknown	*	*
21.02.87	Cessna 441 Conquest II	N6858S	*	Operator Unknown	Crashed on approach	Flagstaff, AZ, USA	*	*
24.02.87	Britten-Norman BN-2A-23 Islander	PK-VIR	0392	Dirgantara Air Service	Crashed	Kaltim, Indonesia	*	*
25.02.87	Cessna 185F	OB-T-1040	185-02132	TASA	Crashed into radio mast on take-off	Ucayali River, Peru	0	*
oo.02.87	McDonnell Douglas DC-9-41	SE-DAT	47625	Scandinavian Airlines System	Damaged in heavy landing	Trondheim, Norway	0	*
oo.02.87	Grumman Gulfstream I	N720X	073	K.E.Molhook	Damaged after being buried in sand after smuggling flight	Arizona, USA	*	*
oo.02.87	IRMA BN-2A-26 Islander	B-12207	0831	Yung Shing Airlines	Written off	Location Unknown	*	*
01.03.87	Cessna U206G Stationair 6	OB-T-1262	*	Iberico Aerotaxi	Crashed into mountain in bad weather	Lamas, Peru	2	5
04.03.87	CASA 212 Aviocar 200	N160FB	160	Fischer Brothers Aviation	Crashed into buildings on landing	Detroit, MI, USA	10	9
06.03.87	Antonov AN-26	SSSR-26007	*	Aeroflot	Crashed into mountain	nr Alma Ata, Kazakhstan, USSR	9	*
08.03.87	Piper PA-31-350 Chieftain	5Y-AST	31-7405206	Cooper Skybird Air Charters	Crashed on take-off	Nairobi, Kenya	0	9
09.03.87	Douglas DC-3	N49454	10177	Aero Express	Shot down by Honduran forces on drug smuggling flight	El Paraiso, Honduras	3	0
09.03.87	Douglas DC-3	N78B	4140	Operator Unknown	Crashed on illegal flight	Venezuela	3	0
17.03.87	Bell 206B JetRanger II	N9AR	*	Heli-Lift	Crashed	nr Valdez, AK, USA	1	1
29.03.87	Bell 206B JetRanger II	N90153	01610	Kona Helicopters	Crashed in sea	Off Honokaa, HI, USA	1	4
30.03.87	Antonov AN-26	*	*	Bakhtar Afghan Airlines	Shot down by Pakistani F-16s	Parachinar, Pakistan	40	0
31.03.87	Antonov AN-2	SP-DNM	1G107-60	Polish Agricultural Aviation	Crashed into mountain	Hungary	2	*
oo.03.87	Antonov AN-26	*	*	Bakhtar Afghan Airlines	Shot down by rebels	Between Kabul & Logar, Afghanistan	30	0

Date	Type	Reg'n	C/n	Operator	Accident	Location	F	S
oo.03.87	Gates Learjet 24	N31SK	24-118	Connie Kalitta Services	Crashed into mountain	Eagle County, USA	*	*
02.04.87	Beechcraft King Air C90	LN-KCR	LJ-0793	Scanex Air	Crashed on approach	nr Skien, Norway	10	0
04.04.87	McDonnell Douglas DC-9-32	PK-GNQ	47741	Garuda Indonesian Airlines	Crashed in heavy rain	Polonia, Indonesia	30	15
08.04.87	Lockheed L-100-30 Hercules	N517SJ	4558	Southern Air Transport	Crashed when wing struck ground on landing	Travis AFB, CA, USA	5	0
08.04.87	Beechcraft E18S	ET-AFE	BA-288	Admas Air Service	Damaged in ground loop on landing	Wondo Tika, Ethiopia	0	*
11.04.87	Boeing 707-330C	PT-TCO	18932	Transbrasil	Skidded off runway & damaged during recovery	Manaus, Brazil	0	*
13.04.87	Boeing 707-351C	N144SP	19209	Burlington Air Express	Crashed on landing in poor weather & cargo exploded	Kansas City, MO, USA	3	0
13.04.87	Beechcraft Super King Air 200	ZS-KMT	BB-0767	Barlow Rand	Crashed	nr Germiston, South Africa	3	2
20.04.87	de Havilland Canada Otter	C-FRWK	450	Propair	Damaged after rolling off runway	Lac Placier, PQ, Canada	*	*
23.04.87	Fairchild 226TC Metro II	N505LB	TC-202	Air-Lift Commuter	Crashed on take-off	Wilmington, DE, USA	2	0
26.04.87	Cessna 441 Conquest II	G-MOXY	0154	Brown Air Services	Crashed on approach	Blackbushe, Hants, UK	1	0
26.04.87	Cessna 401B	OH-CDT	401-0054	Starwings	Destroyed by arson in attempted insurance fraud	Sodankylae, Finland	0	0
27.04.87	Airship Industries Skyship 500	G-BIHN	1214/2	Airship Industries	Damaged beyond repair in gale	Cardington, Beds, UK	0	*
28.04.87	British Aerospace 748 2	HS-THI	1708	Thai Airways	Damaged on landing	Chiang Rai, Thailand	*	*
oo.04.87	Britten-Norman BN-2A-26 Islander	B-11111	2001	Taiwan Airlines	Written off	Location Unknown	*	*
05.05.87	Cessna 404 Titan	ST-AIJ	404-0612	SASCO Air Charter	Shot down by rebels after take-off	Malakal, Sudan	13	0
08.05.87	Douglas DC-6B	CP-1650	45505	Frigorificos Reyes	U/c collapsed on landing & caught fire	La Paz, Bolivia	0	*
08.05.87	CASA 212 Aviocar 200	N432CA	271	Executive Air Charter	Undershot on landing	Mayaguez-El Mani, Puerto Rico	2	4
09.05.87	Ilyushin IL-62M	SP-LBG	3344942	LOT Polish Airlines	Crashed after engine fire	nr Warsaw, Poland	182	0
11.05.87	Douglas DC-3	C-FADD	14879/26324	Northland Air Manitoba	Crashed when wing broke off	nr Pickle Lake, ON, Canada	2	0
11.05.87	Gates Learjet 35A	N100EP	35A-150	Eagle Jet	Crashed on take-off	Allegheny County, USA	2	*
12.05.87	Piper PA-31-350 Chieftain	G-BASU	31-7305023	Streamline Aviation	Crashed	Dounray, UK	*	*
20.05.87	de Havilland Canada Twin Otter 300	CP-1018	363	YPFB Transportes Aereos	Crashed into hill in bad weather	Santa Cruz, Bolivia	14	2
23.05.87	de Havilland Canada Twin Otter 300	PK-NUW	474	Merpati Nusantara Airlines	Crashed on approach	Flores, Indonesia	23	0
25.05.87	de Havilland Canada Twin Otter 100	PK-MAM	076	Missionary Aviation Fellowship	Crashed	Ilaga, Indonesia	2	*
26.05.87	British Aerospace Jetstream 31	N331CY	742	Air New Orleans	Crashed on take-off	New Orleans, LA, USA	0	13
27.05.87	Antonov AN-2	SSSR-70501	1G83-34	Aeroflot	Crashed after being stolen	Off Gotland, Sweden	0	1
01.06.87	Cessna Citation I	D-IAEC	501-0203	Travel Air Flug	Crashed on landing	Blankensee, West Germany	3	1
09.06.87	Boeing 727-90C	N766AS	19728	Alaska Airlines	Taxiied into loading ramp & caught fire	Anchorage, AK, USA	0	*
11.06.87	Antonov AN-26	YA-BAL	57314105	Bakhtar Afghan Airlines	Shot down by rebels	Khost, Afghanistan	53	0
13.06.87	de Havilland Canada Twin Otter 100	C-FWGE	058	Athabaska Airways	Crashed into trees on landing	Maudsley Lake, SK, Canada	0	*
13.06.87	Grumman CS2F-1 Firecat	F-ZBEZ	135409	Securite Civile	Crashed	La Roque d'Antheron, France	1	0
16.06.87	Martin 404	CP-1570	14167	CAMBA	Belly landed & caught fire	Beni, Bolivia	0	3
16.06.87	Douglas DC-4-1009	C-GPFG	42917	Calm Air International	Damaged by undershooting runway	Hidden Bay, SK, Canada	*	*
19.06.87	Yakovlev YAK-40	SSSR-87826	*	Aeroflot	Crashed on landing too fast	Berdiansk, Ukraine, USSR	8	22
20.06.87	IRMA BN-2A-20 Islander	P2-KAD	0800	Kiunga Aviation	Crashed	nr Lae, Papua New Guinea	2	0
20.06.87	Mitsubishi MU-2F	N184MA	218	Cavenaugh Aviation	Crashed	Broward County, FL, USA	2	0
21.06.87	Fokker F-27 Friendship 200	XY-ADP	10357	Burma Airways	Crashed into hill	Heho, Burma	45	0
21.06.87	Cessna 402C	VH-WBQ	402C-0627	Operator Unknown	Crashed into trees on take-off	Bundaberg, Qld, Australia	4	1
21.06.87	Rockwell Turbo Commander 690	N662DM	11015	Operator Unknown	Written off	Bridgeport, CT, USA	*	*
23.06.87	Beechcraft Super King Air B200	N8590D	BB-0859	Operator Unknown	Written off	Jasper, AL, USA	*	*
24.06.87	IRMA BN-2A-26 Islander	VP-FBG	2126	FIGAS	Crashed	Brookfield Farm, Falkland Islands	*	*
24.06.87	Rockwell Turbo Commander 690A	N57169	11203	Bankair	Written off	Jacksonville, FL, USA	*	*
24.06.87	Beechcraft Super King Air 200C	N617MS	BL-35	Operator Unknown	Written off	Madisonville, KY, USA	*	*
25.06.87	Pilatus PC-6/B2-H2 Turbo Porter	FAC.1114	823	Satena	Crashed	nr Guapi, Colombia	*	*
26.06.87	British Aerospace 748 2	RP-C1015	1637	Philippine Air Lines	Crashed into mountain	Mt Pugo, Philippines	49	0
10.07.87	Antonov AN-2	YR-PBE	1G177-28	Operator Unknown	Crashed	Romania	*	*
10.07.87	Antonov AN-2R	HA-MBS	1G172-52	Air Service Hungary	Crashed	Hungary	*	*
13.07.87	Douglas DC-3	N28364	4108	KDD Aviation	Crashed & caught fire on landing	Ciudad del Camargo, Mexico	1	*
20.07.87	GAF Nomad 24A	ZK-NMD	036	Air Safaris	Crashed	Lake Tekapo, New Zealand	*	*
23.07.87	Westland Sea King 42B	ZF527	951	Westland Helicopters	Ditched & sank on tow	Off St Raphael, France	0	6
28.07.87	Douglas DC-3	N39DT	4871	Operator Unknown	Crashed	Laredo, TX, USA	*	*
29.07.87	Pilatus PC-6/B2-H2 Turbo Porter	HB-FIM	*	Amani Ltd	Crashed after damage caused by parachute opening inside	Grenchen, Switzerland	0	*
30.07.87	Boeing C-97 Stratofreighter	HI-481	16687	Agro Air International	Crashed on road after take-off in storm	Mexico City, Mexico	1{54}	5

Date	Type	Reg'n	C/n	Operator	Accident	Location	F	S
31.07.87	Gates Learjet 23	N28ST	23-013	Dolphin Aviation	Crashed	Guatemala City, Guatemala	2	1
oo.07.87	British Aerospace 748 2A	HC-BAZ/738	1738	TAME	Damaged beyond repair	Ecuador	*	*
03.08.87	Antonov AN-2	*	*	MIAT Mongolian Airlines	Crashed	Khubsugul Province, Mongolia	*	*
05.08.87	Boeing 737-2A1A	CC-CHJ	22602	LAN-Chile	Crashed on landing & caught fire	Calamas, Chile	2	33
06.08.87	Bell 206B JetRanger II	JA9123	01283	Naka Nihon Air Service	Crashed after take-off	Wakayanagi, Japan	*	*
14.08.87	Antonov AN-28	SSSR-28741	*	Aeroflot	Damaged in hard landing	Ust-Nem, RSFSR, USSR	*	*
15.08.87	Bell 206B JetRanger III	JA9246	02820	Shin Nihon Domestic Air	Crashed after striking rope	Aomori, Japan	0	1
16.08.87	McDonnell Douglas MD-82	N312RC	48090	Northwest Airlines	Crashed on take-off	Detroit, MI, USA	154{2}	1
17.08.87	Douglas DC-3	5Y-DAK	16206/32954	Air Kenya	Crashed on landing	Kilaguni Lodge, Kenya	8	*
18.08.87	Piper PA-31-350 Chieftain	G-BGEO	31-7405489	Oxaero Ltd	Crashed into mountain	nr Autun, France	4	3
20.08.87	Type Unknown	*	*	Aeroflot	Crash landed on mountain	USSR	0	*
21.08.87	IRMA BN-2A-27 Islander	G-BLDX	2181	Air Furness	Forced landed on beach & damaged during recovery	Southport, Lancs, UK	0	*
28.08.87	Grumman G-21A Goose	N742PC	37782	Operator Unknown	Destroyed by bomb in hangar	Long Beach, CA, USA	*	*
29.08.87	Cessna 404 Titan	D-ILEP	404-0688	Cologne Commercial Flight	Crashed into tower in fog	nr Feldberg, West Germany	1	0
31.08.87	Boeing 737-2P5A	HS-TBC	22267	Thai Airways	Crashed	Off Phuket, Thailand	83	0
02.09.87	Type Unknown	*	*	Aeroflot	Crashed	Afghanistan	6	*
11.09.87	Sikorsky S-61N	OY-HAN	61-487	Greenlandair	Damaged by hard landing & rotor striking cockpit	Holsteinborg, Greenland	1	*
12.09.87	Beechcraft Super King Air 200	G-WSJE	BB-0484	National Airways	Crashed after take-off	Rayleigh, Essex, UK	1	0
13.09.87	Antonov AN-26	*	*	Aeroflot	Shot down by rebels on approach	Kunduz, Afghanistan	15	*
16.09.87	Fairchild C-119 Flying Boxcar	*	*	Hawkins & Powers Aviation	Crashed	Castle Crags State Park, CA, USA	3	0
18.09.87	Britten-Norman BN-2A-6 Islander	C-GTPB	0223	Operator Unknown	Crashed after take-off	Cariboo Horn Lake, NWT, Canada	*	*
21.09.87	Airbus A.300B4-203	SU-BCA	115	EgyptAir	Crashed on touch and go landing	Luxor, Egypt	5	0
23.09.87	Cessna 340A	TU-TKS	340A-0776	Air Transivoire	Crashed after take-off	Yamoussoukro, Ivory Coast	4	*
24.09.87	LET 410MU Turbolet	SSSR-67249	770815	Aeroflot	Crashed on take-off	Magan, RSFSR, USSR	*	*
25.09.87	Fairchild 227AC Metro III	N2689E	AC-653	Horizon Air	Crashed after take-off	Joslin Field, ID, USA	*	*
25.09.87	Beechcraft D18S	N76Q	*	Air Cargo America	Crashed on take-off	Miami, FL, USA	2	0
26.09.87	Cessna 441 Conquest II	N1210Y	0338	Africair	Crashed	Maiduguri, Nigeria	0	4
30.09.87	Dassault Falcon 20DC	EC-ECB	210	Operator Unknown	Written off	Location Unknown	*	*
30.09.87	Beechcraft King Air B100	N32RL	BE-117	Operator Unknown	Written off	Gold Beach, OR, USA	*	*
30.09.87	Cessna 340	XA-KOA	*	Aero Sonora	Crashed	Otay Mesa, CA, USA	6	0
07.10.87	Grumman S-2 Tracker	*	*	Operator Unknown	Crashed	nr Weott, CA, USA	1	*
07.10.87	Cessna 421 Golden Eagle	*	*	Operator Unknown	Crashed after take-off	Deland, FL, USA	5	0
07.10.87	Piper PA-31-350 Chieftain	OY-BGK	31-7305019	Operator Unknown	Crashed on approach	Aarhus, Denmark	1	0
08.10.87	Rockwell Turbo Commander 690B	N711TT	11362	Operator Unknown	Written off	Albuquerque, NM, USA	*	*
09.10.87	Volpar Turboliner	N9231	*	Connie Kalitta Services	Crashed after taking off with gust lock on tail	Memphis, TN, USA	1	0
11.10.87	Fokker F-27 Friendship 600	XY-AEL	10689	Burma Airways	Crashed	nr Pagan, Burma	49	0
11.10.87	de Havilland Canada Twin Otter 300	HK-2920	419	Aeroservicios Ejectivos	Crashed making emergency landing	El Poleo, Colombia	2	7
11.10.87	Dassault Falcon 20	EC-EFI	189	Drenair	Crashed	Off Keflavik, Iceland	0	6
14.10.87	Lockheed L-100-30 Hercules	HB-ILF	4701	Zimex Aviation	Crashed on take-off	Kuito, Angola	6	0
15.10.87	Aerospatiale-Alenia ATR.42-312	I-ATRH	046	Aero Transporti Italiani	Crashed in bad weather	Mt Crezzo, Italy	37	0
15.10.87	Dassault Falcon 10	N121FJ	192	Falcon Jet Corporation	Crashed	nr Sacremento, CA, USA	3	*
18.10.87	LET 410UVP Turbolet	SSSR-67334	820834	Aeroflot	Damaged in belly landing	nr Saratov, RSFSR, USSR	*	*
19.10.87	Beechcraft Super King Air B200	G-MDJI	BB-1162	Artix Ltd	Crashed	Ottleychevin Hill, UK	*	*
19.10.87	Antonov AN-12	SSSR-12162	*	Antonov Design Bureau	Crashed	nr Kiev, Ukraine, USSR	9	0
20.10.87	Cessna 421B Golden Eagle	G-HAST	421B-0828	Hastingwood Hotels	Crashed after take-off due to engine failure	Stansted, Essex, UK	6	0
22.10.87	Cessna 172	JA3887	*	Aero Asahi	Crashed into buildings	Sapporo, Japan	3	0
23.10.87	Cessna 208A Caravan I	N828FE	208A-00073	Federal Express	Crashed	nr Travis AFB, CA, USA	1	0
27.10.87	Aerospatiale 330J Puma	F-GEBJ	1395	Heli-Union	Rotor struck Lider Bell 212 PT-HOW & caught fire	Carraveri, Brazil	0	*
28.10.87	Convair 640	N3411	031	SMB Stage Lines	Skidded off runway making emergency landing & struck trees	Bartlesville, OK, USA	0	*
oo.10.87	IRMA BN-2A-216 Islander	TZ-ADN	2161	Operator Unknown	Written off	Location Unknown	*	*
06.11.87	Short Skyvan 3	7Q-YMB	SH.1971	Air Malawi	Shot down by Mozambique Army	nr Malawi–Mozambique border	10	0
07.11.87	Fairchild Merlin IIIB	F-GFMS	T-296	Operator Unknown	Written off	Vannes, France	*	*
09.11.87	Sikorsky S-58T	PK-OBL	58-1612	Airfast Services	Crashed in bad weather	Off Madura Island, Indonesia	0	5
14.11.87	Type Unknown	*	*	Aeroflot	Shot down by rebels [Ilyushin ?]	nr Huambo, Angola	*	0

Date	Type	Reg'n	C/n	Operator	Accident	Location	F	S
15.11.87	McDonnell Douglas DC-9-14	N626TX	45726	Continental Airlines	Overturned on take-off in snowstorm	Denver, CO, USA	28	54
15.11.87	Cessna 441 Conquest II	*	*	US Customs Service	Crashed	nr Calexico, CA, USA	2	0
16.11.87	Beechcraft Super King Air 200	N334DP	BB-1188	Danpar Aviation	Broke up & crashed	Fort Atkinson, WI, USA	8	0
19.11.87	Cessna Citation I	OH-CAR	500-0144	Air Carelia	Force landed out of fuel	Tuusula, Finland	0	*
19.11.87	Volpar Turboliner	N10AS	*	Connie Kalitta Services	Crashed after engine failure	nr Detroit, MI, USA	*	*
20.11.87	Piper PA-31-350 Chieftain	N27512	31-7852035	Panorama Air	Crash landed on sports field	Kapaulei, HI, USA	0(*)	*
23.11.87	Beechcraft 1900C	N401RA	UB-58	Ryan Air Service	Crashed on approach	Homer, AK, USA	17	0
27.11.87	Cessna 208 Caravan I	ZK-SFB	208-00059	Flynn's Ferry Service	Crashed	nr Kaikoura, New Zealand	*	*
28.11.87	Boeing 747-244B/SCD	ZS-SAS	22171	South African Airways	Crashed after in-flight fire in cargo hold	Off Mauritius	159	0
29.11.87	Boeing 707-3B5C	HL7406	20522	Korean Air	Crashed following bomb explosion	Off Burma	115	0
30.11.87	Beechcraft King Air C90	N4463W	LJ-0633	J.R.Leon	Crashed	Beaufort, GA, USA	2	0
oo.11.87	Antonov AN-2	YU-BOD	IG218-30	PA Osijek	Crashed	Yugoslavia	*	*
03.12.87	Cessna 404 Titan	5Y-EJS	*	Cooper Skybird Air Charters	Crashed	nr Kishwati, Rwanda	14	0
04.12.87	Britten-Norman BN-2A-6 Islander	C-GOMC	0010	Whiteshell Air Services	Written off	Location Unknown	*	*
05.12.87	British Aerospace 125-400A	N400PH	25180	Scott Cable Communications	Crashed after striking power cables on approach	Lexington, KY, USA	4	*
06.12.87	Beechcraft King Air E90	D-IMWH	LA-114	Operator Unknown	Written off	Dusseldorf, West Germany	*	*
06.12.87	MBB Bo.105D	A6-ALT	S-137	Aerogulf Services	Crashed onto deck of ship during rescue flight	Off Dubai, United Arab Emirates	0	*
07.12.87	British Aerospace 146-200A	N350PS	E-2027	Pacific Southwest Airlines	Crashed after disgruntled ex-employee shot crew	nr Paso Robles, CA, USA	43	0
07.12.87	Cessna 421B Golden Eagle	HB-LMI	*	Operator Unknown	Crashed after becoming lost in fog	nr Moedling, Austria	2	0
08.12.87	Douglas DC-3	CP-1059	2173	Transportes Aereos San Miguel	Crashed on take-off	San Ignacio, Bolivia	0	*
08.12.87	Britten-Norman BN-2A-2 Islander	P2-MIB	0217	Talair	Crashed after take-off	Kanabea, Papua New Guinea	1	3
10.12.87	Cessna 402B	N969JW	402B-0328	Wilburs Inc	Crashed on landing	Anchorage, AK, USA	0	5
13.12.87	Short 360-300	EI-BTJ	SH.3719	Philippine Air Lines	Crashed	nr Iligan, Philippines	15	0
14.12.87	British Aerospace Jetstream 31	N331PX	700	Express Airlines	Crashed into snowbank on landing	Joplin, MO, USA	0	*
21.12.87	Embraer Brasilia 120	F-GEGH	120.033	Air Littoral	Crashed short of runway after fog diversion	Bordeaux, France	16	0
21.12.87	Aerospatiale 330J Puma	N3596N	1588	Petroleum Helicopters	Crashed into drilling rig *Penrod 18*	Off Morgan City, LA, USA	14	1
21.12.87	Douglas DC-6BF	YN-BFO	45324	Aeronica	Struck by missile & force landed	Corral de Batalla, Costa Rica	0	6
23.12.87	Piper PA-31 Navajo	N496SC	31-7752077	South Central Air	Crashed into trees on emergency landing	Kenai, AK, USA	7	0
23.12.87	Piper PA-31 Navajo	N712AN	31-7652151	Panorama Air Tours	Crashed in sea	Off Honolulu, HI, USA	8	0
26.12.87	Douglas DC-3	ET-AGO	15287/26732	Ethiopian Airlines	Written off	Goba, Ethiopia	*	*
28.12.87	McDonnell Douglas DC-9-31	N8948E	47184	Eastern Air Lines	Fuselage broke in two on landing	Pensacola, FL, USA	0	100
30.12.87	de Havilland Canada Twin Otter 300	PK-NUY	459	Merpati Nusantara Airlines	Missing – presumed crashed	Between Samarinda & Berau, Indonesia	17	0
oo.12.87	IRMA BN-2A-20 Islander	P2-COG	0843	Co-Air	Written off	Location Unknown	*	*
oo.12.87	Antonov AN-2	SSSR-06324	IG68-39	Aeroflot	Crashed	USSR	*	*
oo.oo.87	Ilyushin IL-14	SSSR-04243	*	Aeroflot	Written off	Mirny, Antarctica	*	*
oo.oo.87	IRMA BN-2A-26 Islander	XA-MAO	2104	Aero Taxco	Written off	Location Unknown	*	*
oo.oo.87	Fairchild Merlin IIB	N18SE	T26-134	Operator Unknown	Written off	Location Unknown	*	*
oo.oo.87	Douglas DC-3	VT-DFM	20269	Operator Unknown	Damaged by fire	Jaisalmer, India	*	*
oo.oo.87	Beechcraft King Air B90	C-GQOD	LJ-0328	Operator Unknown	Written off	Location Unknown	*	*
02.01.88	Boeing 737-230A	D-ABHD	22635	Condor	Crashed on approach in poor weather	Izmir, Turkey	16	0
05.01.88	Cessna U206F Stationair	OB-T-144	U206-02056	Aero Chasqui	Crashed	En route Quiteni–San Ramon, Peru	3	0
07.01.88	IPTN Bo.105CB	PK-PIW	N82/S-569	Pelita Air Service	Mid-air collision with Derazona Air Service B206 PK-DBE	Pabelokan Island, Indonesia	3(0)	*
08.01.88	Learjet 36A	N79SF	36A-041	Phoenix Air	Crashed on approach	Monroe, LA, USA	2	0
08.01.88	Yakovlev YAK-40	D2-TYD	9721853	TAAG Angola Airlines	Crashed	Luanda, Angola	*	*
10.01.88	Fairchild Merlin IIIB	N800AW	T-403	American Way Service Corp	Crashed after take-off	Pontiac, MI, USA	3	0
10.01.88	NAMC YS-11-109	JA8662	2022	Toa Domestic Airlines	Overran into lake on landing	Lake Nakaumi, Japan	0	*
11.01.88	Vickers Viscount 806	G-APIM	412	British Air Ferries	Damaged when struck by taxiing Fairflight S.330 G-BHWT	Southend, Essex, UK	0(0)	*
11.01.88	Short 330-200	G-BHWT	SH.3049	Fairflight	Damaged by taxiing into BAF Viscount G-APIM	Southend, Essex, UK	0(0)	*
12.01.88	Fairchild Merlin IV	C-GJWW	AT-013	Air Toronto	Damaged beyond repair	Hamilton, ON, Canada	*	*
15.01.88	Dassault Falcon 20	VR-BJB	244	Segas International Ltd	Overran into embankment after aborted take-off	Lugano, Switzerland	*	*
18.01.88	Ilyushin IL-18D	B-222	187009901	CAAC	Crashed on approach after engine failure	nr Chungching, China	108	0
18.01.88	Tupolev TU-154B-2	SSSR-85254	254	Aeroflot	Broke in two after heavy landing	Krosnovodsk, Turkmenistan, USSR	11	135
18.01.88	British Aerospace 125-600B	XA-KUT	256028	Aero Astra	Crashed into power cables on approach	Houston, TX, USA	1	*

Date	Type	Reg'n	C/n	Operator	Accident	Location	F	S
18.01.88	Curtiss C-46	CP-1244	246	Empresa Transportes Aereos	Crashed into mountain	Colorado Mt, Bolivia	9	0
19.01.88	Fairchild 227AC Metro III	N68TC	AC-457	Trans Colorado Airlines	Crashed on approach	Durango, CO, USA	9	8
19.01.88	Britten-Norman BN-2A-26 Islander	B-11125	2029	Taiwan Airlines	Crashed in mountains	Green Island, Taiwan	10	1
19.01.88	de Havilland Canada Twin Otter 200	N996SA	159	Mountain Air Cargo	Crashed into trees on approach in fog	Charlotte, NC, USA	*	*
23.01.88	Douglas DC-6	*	*	Operator Unknown	Shot down by Nicaraguan forces on rebel supply flight	Loma el Arenal, Guatemala	4	0
24.01.88	Yakovlev YAK-40	SSSR-87549	*	Aeroflot	Crashed on take-off	nr Nizhnevartovsk, RSFSR, USSR	27	4
25.01.88	Beechcraft King Air C90	G-BNAT	LJ-0614	National Airways	Crashed on go-around	East Midlands, Derbs, UK	1	0
29.01.88	Vickers Merchantman 953C	F-GEJF	715	Intercargo Service	Crashed on take-off	Toulouse, France	0	4
02.02.88	Convair 580	N5808	348	Aspen Airways	Skidded off runway & damaged beyond repair	Durango, CO, USA	0	*
08.02.88	Fairchild 227AC Metro III	D-CABB	AC-500	Nurnberger Flugdienst	Crashed in thunderstorm	nr Mulheim, West Germany	21	0
08.02.88	Cessna 404 Titan	ZS-LUI	*	Impala Air	Crashed on take-off	El Mirador, South Africa	*	*
09.02.88	British Aerospace Jetstream 31	N823JS	623	Jetstream International Airlines	Crashed	Springfield, OH, USA	3	0
10.02.88	Piper PA-34 Seneca	CC-CAU	*	Servicios Aereos Sudamericanos	Crashed into mountain	Villarica, Chile	7	0
11.02.88	Fairchild 226TC Metro II	C-GJDX	TC-211EE	Air Niagara Express	Crashed on approach	Lake Ontario, ON, Canada	2	0
12.02.88	Fairchild 227AC Metro III	N622AV	AC-622	Avair	Crashed into woods after take-off	nr Raleigh-Durham, VA, USA	12	0
13.02.88	Dassault Flamant	F-AZEP	286	Musee SV-4 Aero	Crashed during air display	nr Montceau les Mines, France	3{3}	0
17.02.88	Tupolev TU-134A	VN-A108	6348430	Hang Khong Vietnam	Crashed	Hanoi, Vietnam	*	*
19.02.88	Piper PA-31-325 Navajo	N27400	*	Atlantic Air Taxi	Crashed into woods	nr Ponoma, NJ, USA	3	0
24.02.88	Learjet 24F	PT-LMA	24F-353	Operator Unknown	Written off	Location Unknown	*	*
26.02.88	Cessna U206G Stationair	OB-T-1304	U206-05682	Amazonica	Caught fire after emergency landing	Yurimaguas, Peru	0	*
27.02.88	Tupolev TU-134A	SSSR-65675	1351501	Aeroflot	Crashed on approach	Surgut, RSFSR, USSR	20	11
27.02.88	Boeing 727-2H9A	TC-AKD	20930	Talia Airways	Crashed into mountain on approach	nr Ercan, Cyprus	15	0
27.02.88	Bell 212	HK-3377	*	Helitaxi	Crashed	Villavicencio, Colombia	1	0
oo.02.88	Boeing 707-349C	D2-TOI	18975	TAAG Angola Airlines	Damaged beyond repair in hard landing	Luanda, Angola	0	*
01.03.88	Embraer Bandeirante 110P1	ZS-LGP	110.402	Comair	Destroyed when passenger exploded bomb	Germiston, South Africa	17	0
04.03.88	Fairchild-Hiller FH.227B	F-GCPS	546	Transport Aerien Transregional	Crashed into power cables on approach in bad weather	Paris, France	23	0
05.03.88	Cessna 182	EL-AGZ	*	Weasua Air Transport	Crashed	nr Cape Palmas, Liberia	*	*
08.03.88	Tupolev TU-154B-2	SSSR-85413	413	Aeroflot	Hijackers exploded bomb when troops stormed aircraft	nr Leningrad, RSFSR, USSR	4	*
10.03.88	Beechcraft 18	N900WP	*	Lafayette Aviation	Crashed into buildings after engine failure	Detroit, MI, USA	3	0
17.03.88	Boeing 727-21	HK-1716	18999	Avianca	Crashed into mountain after take-off	Zulia, Colombia	139	0
19.03.88	Bell 206B JetRanger III	TC-HBJ	08703	Sancak Air	Crashed in bad weather	Antalya Bay, Turkey	5	0
25.03.88	British Aerospace Jetstream 31	N411AE	671	Chaparral Airlines	Crash landed in field	nr Decatur, TX, USA	0	2
29.03.88	Bell 214ST	VH-LAO	28116	Lloyd Helicopters	Ditched and sank in cyclone	300 mls off Darwin, NT, Australia	0	15
30.03.88	Cessna 402	5H-GTS	*	Tanzania Game Trackers	Crashed on take-off	Rubondo Island, Tanzania	5	0
oo.03.88	Fairchild 226TC Metro II	F-GCTE	TC-365	Compagnie Aerienne du Languedoc	Damaged beyond repair	France	*	*
01.04.88	McDonnell Douglas DC-8-55F	5N-ARH	45859	Arax Airlines	Crashed on take-off	Cairo, Egypt	4	0
01.04.88	Beechcraft 18	N989B	*	Air Cargo Express	Crashed	Kansas City, KS, USA	1	0
12.04.88	Douglas DC-3	ZS-UAS	6154	United Air	Crashed after in-flight fire	nr Henneman, South Africa	23	0
15.04.88	de Havilland Canada Dash 8-102	N819PH	061	Horizon Air	Crashed on landing with engine fire	Seattle, WA, USA	0	40
16.04.88	Mitsubishi MU-2L	F-GERA	701SA	Chaillotine Air Service	Crashed	St Just, France	6	0
19.04.88	LET 410UVP Turbolet	SSSR-67518	851422	Aeroflot	Crashed into mountain	Bagdarin, RSFSR, USSR	17	0
21.04.88	Douglas DC-3	N47FE	19536	African Air Carriers	Crashed on take-off – possibly shot down	Quelimane, Mozambique	2	0
24.04.88	Pilatus PC-6 Turbo-Porter	*	*	Operator Unknown	Crashed after take-off due to engine failure	Lens, France	8	0
29.04.88	Boeing 737-297	N73711	20209	Aloha Airlines	Damaged when fuselage roof blew off in flight. Landed safely	Off Maui, HI, USA	1	94
01.05.88	Bell 206B JetRanger II	N7094J	00727	Island Helicopter	Crashed	East River, NY, USA	*	*
02.05.88	Douglas DC-3	ET-AGT	13843/25288	Ethiopian Airlines	Destroyed when airfield attacked by EAF MIG-23s	Axum, Ethiopia	*	*
06.05.88	de Havilland Canada Dash 7-102	LN-WFN	028	Wideroe	Crashed on approach	Broennoysund, Norway	36	0
10.05.88	Cessna 205	ET-AEZ	205-0007	Admas Air Service	Destroyed by gunfire from rebels	Asmara, Ethiopia	*	*
10.05.88	Cessna T207 Turbo Skywagon	ET-ADB	207-00094	Admas Air Service	Destroyed by gunfire from rebels	Asmara, Ethiopia	*	*
16.05.88	Bell 206B JetRanger II	ZS-HIF	*	Court Helicopters	Crashed on landing	Champagne Castle, Lesotho	0	*
17.05.88	Rockwell Turbo Commander 690A	N660RB	11305	Operator Unknown	Written off	Little Rock, AR, USA	*	*
21.05.88	McDonnell Douglas DC-10-30	N136AA	47846	American Airlines	Damaged after aborting take-off & nosewheel collapsed	Dallas, TX, USA	0	254
23.05.88	Boeing 727-22	TI-LRC	18856	Lacsa	Crashed on take-off	San Jose, Costa Rica	0	28
24.05.88	Embraer Bandeirante 110P1	N65DA	110.389	Atlantic Southeast Airlines	Caught fire & crashed after take-off	Lawton, OK, USA	0	8

Date	Type	Reg'n	C/n	Operator	Accident	Location	F	S
24.05.88	Gates Learjet 35A	N500RW	35A-148	United Executive	Crashed into wood after take-off	Teterboro, NJ, USA	4	0
24.05.88	Douglas DC-6BF	YN-CBE	*	Aeronica	Crashed into high ground	Puerto Limon, Costa Rica	6	0
25.05.88	Cessna U206 Super Skywagon	N4882U	U206-05140	Manokotauk Airways	Mid-air collision with ERA AS.350 N353EH	nr Dillingham, AK, USA	1(1)	0
25.05.88	Aerospatiale AS.350D Astar	N353EH	1338	ERA Helicopters	Mid-air collision with Manokotauk Cessna U206 N4882U	nr Dillingham, AK, USA	1(1)	0
26.05.88	Fokker F-27 Friendship 600	OY-APE	10443	Star Air	Crashed on approach	Hanover, West Germany	2	0
26.05.88	Cessna 402B	N8493A	402B-0236	Midnite Express	Crashed after take-off	Columbia, SC, USA	1	0
oo.05.88	Beechcraft King Air A90	N611VP	LJ-0171	Operator Unknown	Written off	Narssarsuaq, Greenland	*	*
09.06.88	Aerospatiale SA.319B Alouette III	HB-XOM	1991	Air Zermatt	Crashed	nr Zermatt, Switzerland	*	0
10.06.88	Cessna 404 Titan	N8827K	*	Air Today	Crashed due to fuel starvation	Aurora, CO, USA	0	1
12.06.88	McDonnell Douglas MD-81	N1003G	48050	Austral	Crashed on approach in bad weather	Posadas, Argentina	22	0
13.06.88	de Havilland Dove	*	*	I.B.Ibanez	Crashed after engine failure on take-off	Plata, Argentina	8	*
16.06.88	Fokker F-27 Friendship 600	XY-ADQ	10452	Burma Airways	Crashed into high ground	Putao, Burma	4	4
17.06.88	Aerospatiale-Alenia ATR.42-200	F-WEGA	001	Aerospatiale	Crashed after take-off	Toulouse, France	0	3
17.06.88	de Havilland Canada Twin Otter 100	N202RH	068	Samoa Aviation	Crashed on approach	Tau Manua Is, US Samoa	0	6
21.06.88	Bristol 170 Freighter 31M	C-GYQY	13134	Trans Provincial Airlines	Skidded off runway & damaged beyond repair on landing	Bronson Creek, BC, Canada	0	*
26.06.88	Airbus A.320-110	F-GFKC	009	Air France	Crashed after low pass during air display	Habsheim, France	3	133
29.06.88	Douglas DC-6BF	YS-05C	45537	AESA Airlines	Crashed after take-off	Comalapa, El Salvador	2	0
29.06.88	Northrop YC-125B Raider	N2562B	2504	Frank Ambrose Aviation	Crashed onto road after take-off	Tulsa, OK, USA	0	2
30.06.88	Type Unknown	*	*	Air Glaciers	Crashed after being stolen by mechanic	nr Jungfrau, Switzerland	1	0
03.07.88	Airbus A.300B2-203	EP-IBU	186	Iran Air	Shot down in error by missile fired by USS *Vincennes*	Off Bandar Abbas, Iran	290	0
06.07.88	Canadair CL-44J	HK-3148X	039	Lineas Aereas Suramericanas	Crashed attempting to land after engine failure	Barranquilla, Colombia	3	0
08.07.88	Antonov AN-24	SSSR-46669	*	Aeroflot	Overran on take-off & crashed	Khabarovsk, RSFSR, USSR	0	46
10.07.88	Fokker F-27 Friendship 200	5Y-BBS	10213	Kenya Airways	Damaged in belly landing	Kisumu, Kenya	0	43
13.07.88	Sikorsky S-61N	G-BEID	61-223	British International Helicopters	Ditched & sank after engine fire	North Sea	0	21
13.07.88	Sikorsky S-58T	N94AH	58-0692	Aris Helicopters	Crashed while lifting building material	Marina del Rey, CA, USA	*	*
14.07.88	Aerospatiale 330J Puma	N47307	1402	Petroleum Helicopters	Crashed	Gulf of Mexico	0	15
14.07.88	de Havilland Canada Twin Otter 300	C-GKBM	417	Empire Airways	Crashed into high ground	nr John Day, OR, USA	1	0
20.07.88	de Havilland Canada Twin Otter 200	N7267	195	Fairways Corporation	Crashed after take-off	Washington, DC, USA	1	0
21.07.88	Boeing 707-328C	D2-TOV	18881	Angola Air Charter	Crashed into river on approach	Matogun, Nigeria	6	0
21.07.88	Douglas C-118A Liftmaster	N33VX	44615	TACA International Airlines	Crashed	nr New Orleans, LA, USA	3	0
26.07.88	Gates Learjet 35A	N442NE	35A-442	IJA Inc	Crashed short of runway	Morristown, NJ, USA	1	1
30.07.88	Learjet 23	N745F	23-077	Jet Management	Crashed	Perris, CA, USA	2	*
31.07.88	Bell 204B	N9173N	*	Servicios Generales Aereos	Crashed into hill	Sabadell, Spain	2	0
02.08.88	Yakovlev YAK-40	LZ-DOK	9620247	Hemus Air	Crashed after aborting take-off due to engine fire	Sofia, Bulgaria	25	12
02.08.88	CASA 212 Aviocar 200	C-GILU	245	Terra Surveys	Crashed short of runway	Reykjavik, Iceland	3	0
11.08.88	Cessna A188B	ET-AHD	188-03243T	Admas Air Service	Crashed	Abaya, Ethiopia	*	*
15.08.88	Cessna 402B	ZS-KPF	402B-0602	Citi Air	Crashed on approach	Durban, South Africa	0	8
20.08.88	Britten-Norman BN-2A Islander	5W-FAF	0109	Polynesian Airlines	Overran runway into sea	Asau, Western Samoa	*	*
21.08.88	de Havilland Riley Heron	DQ-FDY	14108	Sunflower Airlines	Damaged by fire while refuelling	Nadi, Fiji	0	12
23.08.88	Douglas C-54B	9Q-CBK	10452	Kinair Cargo	Crashed	M'Bamou Island, Zaire	5	0
26.08.88	LET 410MU Turbolet	SSSR-67235	770801	Aeroflot	Crashed on approach	Irkutsk, RSFSR, USSR	4	*
27.08.88	Antonov AN-12BP	SSSR-11514	*	Aeroflot	Destroyed in rebel missile attack	Kabul, Afghanistan	*	*
27.08.88	Antonov AN-24RV	*	*	Ariana Afghan Airlines	Damaged by shrapnel in rebel rocket attack	Kabul, Afghanistan	*	*
27.08.88	Boeing 727-31	N852TW	18571	Trans World Airlines	Damaged beyond repair in belly landing	Chicago, IL, USA	*	*
31.08.88	Hawker Siddeley Trident 2E	B-2218	2159	CAAC	Crashed into bay on landing in bad weather	Hong Kong	7	80
31.08.88	Boeing 727-232A	N473DA	20750	Delta Air Lines	Crashed on take-off	Dallas, TX, USA	13	95
31.08.88	Embraer Bandeirante 110P1	XC-COX	110.192	Transporte Aereo Federal	Crashed	nr Cerro de la Calera, Mexico	20	0
31.08.88	Convair 240	XA-HUL	229	Aerocaribe	Crashed on take-off	Merida, Mexico	1	19
06.09.88	Cessna Citation S/II	PT-LGJ	S550-0025	Operator Unknown	Written off	Rio de Janeiro, Brazil	*	*
08.09.88	Tupolev TU-134A	VN-A102	*	Hang Khong Vietnam	Crashed on approach in heavy rain	Bangkok, Thailand	75	6
09.09.88	Douglas C-54A	CP-1653	10285	Frigorificos Reyes	Belly landed & caught fire after take-off	La Paz, Bolivia	0	3
11.09.88	Beechcraft Super King Air 200	N1283	BB-0090	Operator Unknown	Written off	Location Unknown	*	*
12.09.88	Lockheed Electra 188A	HC-AZY/1052	1052	TAME	Crashed after take-off	Lago Agrio, Ecuador	7	0
12.09.88	Mitsubishi MU-2 Marquise	PH-DRX	1555SA	Rijnmond Air Services	Crashed	nr Eindhoven, Netherlands	2	0

Date	Type	Reg'n	C/n	Operator	Accident	Location	F	S
13.09.88	Britten-Norman BN-2A-26 Islander	YJ-RV20	0585	Dovair	Written off	Emae, Vanuatu	*	*
15.09.88	British Aerospace 748 2B	C-GFFA	1789	Bradley Air Services	Crashed on approach	nr Hammond, ON, Canada	2	0
16.09.88	Boeing 737-260A	ET-AJA	23914	Ethiopian Airlines	Broke in two on forced landing after birdstrike on take-off	Bahar Dar, Ethiopia	33	30
20.09.88	Douglas DC-3	Z-WRJ	11989	Crest Breeders	Damaged beyond repair in forced landing	Harare, Zimbabwe	*	*
20.09.88	Bell 206L JetRanger	HL9105	*	Air Korea	Crashed into sea	Busan, South Korea	0	4
22.09.88	Hindustan Do.228-200	VT-EJT	8060/1002	Vayudoot	Crashed	Purangabad, India	*	*
24.09.88	Tupolev TU-154B-2	SSSR-85479	479	Aeroflot	Crashed on landing	Aleppo, Syria	0	168
26.09.88	Boeing 737-287A	LV-LIU	20964	Aerolineas Argentinas	Veered off runway on landing & ran into sea	Ushuara, Argentina	0	56
30.09.88	Antonov AN-2	YR-PVS	1G175-17	Operator Unknown	Crashed	Romania	*	*
oo.09.88	Britten-Norman Trislander	6Y-JQF	1058	Trans Jamaican Airlines	Destroyed by hurricane Gilbert	Montego Bay, Jamaica	*	*
oo.09.88	Britten-Norman BN-2A-2 Islander	N111VA	0215	San Juan Air	Written off	Location Unknown	*	*
02.10.88	Beechcraft King Air F90	PT-LJR	LA-093	Aramar	Crashed	Sao Pedro da Aldeia, Brazil	8	*
04.10.88	Antonov AN-12BP	SSSR-11418	*	Aeroflot	Crashed into high ground	Batagay, RSFSR, USSR	6	0
08.10.88	Ilyushin IL-14	B-4218	6341406	Shanxi Airlines	Crashed after take-off	Linfen, China	42	4
08.10.88	de Havilland Canada Twin Otter 300	XT-AAX	490	Air Burkina	Crashed on take-off	Dori, Burkina Faso	*	*
10.10.88	Boeing 737-2F9A	5N-ANW	22771	Nigeria Airways	Crash landed & badly damaged	Port Harcourt, Nigeria	0	36
10.10.88	Boeing 707-347C	D2-TOM	19965	TAAG Angola Airlines	Destroyed by fire	Luanda, Angola	0	*
12.10.88	Bell 212	JA9537	30891	Aero Asahi	Crashed	Mizhuho, Japan	*	*
13.10.88	Rockwell Commander 560	*	*	Pacific Airways	Crashed on landing	Clark AFB, Philippines	1	1
16.10.88	Beechcraft King Air B90	C-GDOM	LJ-0368	Simpson Air	Crashed on approach	Fort Simpson, NWT, Canada	3	0
17.10.88	Boeing 707-338C	5X-UBC	19630	Uganda Airlines	Crashed after striking building on landing in fog	Rome, Italy	33	19
17.10.88	Sikorsky S-61N	G-BDII	61-750	Bristow Helicopters	Crashed	Off Handa Island, UK	0	4
19.10.88	Boeing 737-2A8	VT-EAH	20481	Indian Airlines	Crashed on approach in fog	Ahmedabad, India	130	5
19.10.88	Fokker F-27 Friendship 100	VT-DMC	10173	Vayudoot	Crashed into hillside during rainstorm	Guwahati, India	34	0
25.10.88	Fokker F-28 Fellowship 1000	OB-R-1020	11059	Aero Peru	Crashed into mountain after take-off	Juliaca, Peru	12	57
25.10.88	Cessna 185	OB-T-594	185-00095	Aero San Martin	Crashed in river in bad weather	Ucayali River, Peru	2	3
26.10.88	Cessna Citation I	OE-FFK	501-0124	Aero Technik	Mid-air collision with Cessna 172 OE-LCH	Salzburg, Austria	2(4)	0
28.10.88	Britten-Norman BN-2A-21 Islander	F-OGHL	0283	Air Guadeloupe	Written off	Location Unknown	*	*
oo.10.88	Fairchild Merlin IIB	C-GYMR	T26-177	Operator Unknown	Written off	Canada	*	*
01.11.88	Douglas DC-3	C-FBJE	13453	Air Ontario	Crashed into lake	Pikangikum Lake, ON, Canada	2	0
02.11.88	Antonov AN-24V	SP-LTD	67302209	LOT Polish Airlines	Force-landed in field	Rzeszow, Poland	1	*
02.11.88	Rockwell 1121A Jet Commander	N44	130	Federal Aviation Administration	Written off	Location Unknown	*	*
04.11.88	Aerospatiale AS.355F Ecureuil 2	N355EH	5137	ERA Helicopters	Crashed in sea	Gulf of Mexico	4	0
08.11.88	de Havilland Canada Buffalo 5D	ET-AHI	101	Ethiopian Airlines	Ran off runway on landing & broke in two	Gondar, Ethiopia	1	*
10.11.88	Sikorsky S-61N	G-BDES	61-747	British International Helicopters	Ditched & sank	Off Aberdeen, UK	0	13
10.11.88	Beechcraft Queen Air B80	DQ-FER	*	Sunflower Airlines	Crash landed after overshoot	Matei, Fiji	0	9
13.11.88	Grumman Gulfstream I	N750BR	099	Berlin Regional	Crashed	Niedernberg, West Germany	*	*
13.11.88	Vickers Viscount 843	PK-IVW	452	Bouraq Indonesia Airlines	Damaged after aquaplaning on landing	Balikpapan, Indonesia	0	*
14.11.88	Embraer Bandeirante 110P1	OH-EBA	110.226	Wasawings	Crashed on approach	Ilmajoki, Finland	5	7
14.11.88	Agusta-Bell 206B JetRanger II	OO-COD	08378	Publi-Air	Crashed	Kobbegem, Belgium	*	*
17.11.88	Cessna 441 Conquest II	F-GFHR	*	JC Air	Crashed after take-off	Toussus, France	7	0
17.11.88	Mitsubishi MU-2 Marquise	N271MA	797SA	Corporate Aviation	Crashed after take-off	Chicago, IL, USA	1	*
18.11.88	Fairchild 226TC Metro II	F-GCPG	TC-334E	Air Littoral	Crashed on take-off	Montlucon, France	4	0
18.11.88	Beechcraft King Air E90	N308PS	LW-092	Operator Unknown	Crashed on approach in rain & fog	Batesville, AR, USA	7	0
18.11.88	Fairchild 226TC Metro II	ZS-LKG	TC-291	Magnum Airlines	Damaged in forced landing after engine failure on take-off	nr Benoni, South Africa	0	12
18.11.88	Type Unknown	*	*	Air Littoral	Crashed after catching fire on take-off	Lepaud, France	4	0
20.11.88	Cessna 425	C-GBMI	425-0031	Air St Hubert	Crashed	Lac Larouche, PQ, Canada	1	0
23.11.88	Vickers Viscount 807	G-BBVH	281	GB Airways	Damaged when nosewheel collapsed on landing	Tangier, Morocco	0	*
29.11.88	Beechcraft King Air A100	C-GJUL	B-218	Voyageur Airways	Crashed on approach	Chapleau, ON, Canada	4	0
30.11.88	de Havilland Canada Twin Otter 300	5A-DDD	670	Aero Club of Libya	Crashed	Hamada, Libya	*	*
oo.11.88	Boeing 707-330B	Z-WKT	18929	Air Zimbabwe	Damaged in hangar accident	Harare, Zimbabwe	0	*
03.12.88	British Aerospace 748 2A	C-GQSV	1618	Air Creebec	Damaged when landed short of runway	Waskaganish, PQ, Canada	0	3
04.12.88	Bell 206B JetRanger III	VH-CIH	03031	Lloyd Helicopters	Crashed into hill at night	nr Moomba, SA, Australia	*	*
07.12.88	LET 410UVP Turbolet	SSSR-67127	790323	Aeroflot	Crashed on approach	Kodinsk, RSFSR, USSR	6	*

Date	Type	Reg'n	C/n	Operator	Accident	Location	F	S
08.12.88	Douglas DC-7CF	N284	45203	T & G Aviation	Shot down by guerilla missile	nr Bir Moghreim, Mauritania	5	0
09.12.88	Mitsubishi MU-2J	N296MA	592	Sunny Moon Association	Crashed into sea	Off Cairns, Qld, Australia	*	*
11.12.88	Ilyushin IL-76	*	*	Aeroflot	Mid-air collision with Soviet AF Mi-8 on relief flight	Leninakan, Armenia, USSR	78(0)	0
12.12.88	Antonov AN-12B	YU-AID	02348010	JAT Yugoslav Airlines	Crashed on approach during earthquake relief flight	Yerevan, Armenia, USSR	7	0
14.12.88	Boeing 707-321C	5N-AYJ	19168	GAS Air	Crashed on landing in poor weather	nr Luxor, Egypt	8{20}	0
16.12.88	Learjet 24B	N234CM	24B-214	Crown Center Aviation	Crashed	nr Monclova, Mexico	2	0
16.12.88	Mitsubishi MU-2 Marquise	VH-BBA	782SA	Broughton Air Services	Crashed	nr Leonora, WA, Australia	10	0
21.12.88	Boeing 747-121A/SCD	N739PA	19646	Pan American World Airways	Crashed following bomb explosion	Lockerbie, Dumfries, UK	259{11}	0
23.12.88	Piper PA-31-350 Chieftain	RP-C2662	31-7405186	LBC Air Cargo	Crashed in bad weather	Cebu, Philippines	2	0
oo.12.88	Britten-Norman BN-2A-26 Islander	N851JA	0011	Trans Island Airways	Written off	Bahamas	*	*
oo.oo.88	Ilyushin IL-18V	HA-MOE	182005505	Malev	Damaged on ground	Bucharest, Romania	*	*
oo.oo.88	Vickers Viscount 757	9Q-CTS	310	Filair	Damaged on landing	Tschikapa, Zaire	*	*
oo.oo.88	Grumman Gulfstream I	XB-CIJ	010	Operator Unknown	Written off in landing accident	Mexico	*	*
oo.oo.88	Lockheed 749A Constellation	HI-422	2667	Aerochago	Damaged in heavy landing	Santo Domingo, Dominican Republic	0	*
oo.oo.88	Beechcraft King Air 90	S9-NAA	LJ-0050	Operator Unknown	Written off	Location Unknown	*	*
oo.oo.88	Beechcraft Super King Air 200	VH-IBC	BB-0074	Operator Unknown	Written off	Location Unknown	*	*
oo.oo.88	Antonov AN-2R	HA-MHS	1G145-44	Air Service Hungary	Crashed	Kaposvar, Hungary	*	*
01.01.89	Fairchild 226TC Metro II	OY-ARI	TC-317	Fox Delta	Damaged beyond repair	Oernskoeldsvik, Sweden	*	*
02.01.89	Mitsubishi MU-2P	N50VS	379SA	Operator Unknown	Crashed	nr Falkoeping, Sweden	*	*
04.01.89	British Aerospace 748 2	PK-IHA	1614	Bouraq Indonesia Airlines	Damaged in belly landing	Banjarmasin, Indonesia	0	*
05.01.89	Cessna 208B Caravan I	N945FE	208B-0046	Federal Express	Crashed	nr Aspen, CO, USA	0	2
08.01.89	Boeing 737-4Y0	G-OBME	23867	British Midland Airways	Crashed on motorway after engine fire	nr Kegworth, Leics, UK	47	78
09.01.89	Agusta-Bell 206B JetRanger I	G-BAKF	08339	Dollar Helicopters	Crashed into power lines	Malmesbury, Glos, UK	0	2
12.01.89	British Aerospace 748 2A	C-GDOV	1582	Bradley Air Services	Crashed on take-off	Dayton, OH, USA	2	0
12.01.89	Beechcraft Super King Air 200	YV-597C	BB-0394	Operator Unknown	Crashed after take-off	Chavallave, Venezuela	2	0
13.01.89	Tupolev TU-154A	SSSR-85067	067	Aeroflot	Crashed on take-off	Monrovia, Liberia	0	*
13.01.89	Antonov AN-12	SSSR-12997	*	Aeroflot	Overran on landing & caught fire	Sverdlovsk, RSFSR, USSR	*	*
15.01.89	de Havilland Canada Otter	N11250	171	Temesco Airlines	Crashed	nr Ketchikan, AK, USA	*	*
16.01.89	Douglas DC-3	CP-1418	19344	Aerolineas La Paz	Missing – presumed crashed	En route La Paz–Apolo, Bolivia	5	0
19.01.89	Douglas DC-3	XB-DYP	*	Operator Unknown	Crashed & caught fire on take-off	Laredo, TX, USA	0	2
19.01.89	Convair 580	N73160	336	Aspen Airways	Crash landed in field after double engine failure	nr Buena Vista, CO, USA	0	29
19.01.89	Piper PA-23-250 Aztec	OY-BDP	27-4527	Fyn Air Taxi	Crashed on approach	Sindal, Denmark	4	0
27.01.89	Canadair CL-215-1A10	I-CFSS	1071	Securite Civile	Crashed into mountain during water drop	Quiliano, Italy	2	0
30.01.89	Learjet 23	F-GDAV	23-017	Air Enterprise	Damaged in belly landing	Lisbon, Portugal	*	*
03.02.89	Fokker F-27 Friendship 600	XY-AEK	10325	Burma Airways	Crashed on take-off	Rangoon, Burma	26	3
05.02.89	de Havilland DH.89A Dragon Rapide	G-AJHO	6835	Proteus Petroleum Aviation	Destroyed by fire after emergency landing	nr Kidlington, Oxon, UK	0	*
06.02.89	Vickers Merchantman 952C	F-GEJE	730	Intercargo Service	Crashed into lagoon after take-off	Marseilles, France	3	0
07.02.89	Westland WG.30-160	VT-EKR	033	Pawan Hans	Crashed	Marema, India	3	*
08.02.89	Boeing 707-331B	N7231T	19572	Independent Air	Crashed into mountain on approach	Santa Maria, Azores, Portugal	144	0
09.02.89	Boeing 737-2B1A	C9-BAD	20786	Linhas Aereas de Mocambique	Damaged when skidded off runway during rainstorm	Lichinga, Mozambique	0	108
09.02.89	Tupolev TU-154B-2	YR-TPJ	408	Tarom	Crashed on take-off on training flight	Bucharest, Romania	5	0
10.02.89	Beechcraft King Air C90	I-KWYR	LJ-0873	Operator Unknown	Written off	Location Unknown	*	*
13.02.89	Short 330-200	G-BPMA	SH.3067	Gill Air	Overturned & damaged by gale	Glasgow, UK	0	0
14.02.89	Piper PA-31-350 Chieftain	N41169	31-8452009	Operator Unknown	Crashed at sea	En route Pago Pago–Norfolk Island	0	1
14.02.89	Bell 206B JetRanger II	ZK-HKE	01982	Alpine Helicopters	Crashed	nr Queenstown, New Zealand	5	0
15.02.89	Dassault Falcon 20DC	N232RA	232	Reliant Airlines	Overran on landing & broke in half	Binghamton, NY, USA	0	2
17.02.89	Dassault Falcon 10	PT-ASJ	095	Serv-jet	Crashed on approach	Guanabara Bay, Brazil	0	2
18.02.89	Boeing 747-249F/SCD	N807FT	21828	Flying Tigers	Crashed into hill on approach	Puchong, Malaysia	4	0
19.02.89	Cessna 402	N69383	*	Las Vegas Flyers	Crashed into forest	Cleveland, CA, USA	10	0
23.02.89	Rockwell Turbo Commander 690D	OE-FCS	15036	Rheintalflug Seewald	Crashed into lake	Lake Constance, Austria	11	0
23.02.89	Fairchild Merlin III	N26RT	T-216	Predator	Crashed into trees on approach	Helsinki, Finland	7	0
25.02.89	Douglas DC-6AB	HR-AKZ	*	Albiacion Circulo G	Crashed into mountain on approach	Tegucigalpa, Honduras	10	0
28.02.89	Douglas DC-3	C-FBZN	13845/25290	Transfair	Crashed after take-off	Quebec, PQ, Canada	2	0

Date	Type	Reg'n	C/n	Operator	Accident	Location	F	S
28.02.89	Mitsubishi MU-2F	N701DM	149	Operator Unknown	Written off	California, USA	*	*
03.03.89	Beechcraft Super King Air 300	N3107W	FA-150	Operator Unknown	Written off	Location Unknown	*	*
05.03.89	Cessna Citation S/II	N29X	S550-0096	NYNEX Corporation	Written off	Location Unknown	*	*
07.03.89	Bell 206B JetRanger II	PT-HJI	01438	Aeroleo Taxi Aereo	Crashed	Natal, Brazil	5	0
10.03.89	Fokker F-28 Fellowship 1000	C-FONF	11060	Air Ontario	Crashed after take-off in heavy snow	Dryden, ON, Canada	24	41
10.03.89	IRMA BN-2A Islander	OB-T-1271	0604	Aero Condor	Crashed after striking radio mast in fog on approach	Lima, Peru	10	0
15.03.89	NAMC YS-11A-300	N128MP	2139	Phoenix Airlines	Crashed short of runway	Lafayette, LA, USA	2	0
15.03.89	Cessna 402	LV-JOD	*	Operator Unknown	Crashed after take-off	La Rioja, Argentina	2	5
18.03.89	McDonnell Douglas DC-9-33RC	N931F	47192	Evergreen International Airlines	Crashed after taking off with open cargo door	Carswell AFB, TX, USA	2	0
19.03.89	Britten-Norman BN-2A-21 Islander	ZK-SFE	0406	Operator Unknown	Written off	Location Unknown	*	*
21.03.89	Boeing 707-349C	PT-TCS	19354	Transbrasil	Crashed into houses on approach	Sao Paulo, Brazil	3{18}	0
21.03.89	IRMA BN-2B-26 Islander	P2-BAB	0846	Bougair	Destroyed by terrorists	Bougainville, Solomon Islands	*	*
24.03.89	Ilyushin IL-76	*	*	Aeroflot	Shot down by UNITA forces	Angola	*	*
29.03.89	Bell 206B JetRanger II	JA9238	02721	Aero Asahi	Crashed	Minami Aiza-gun, Japan	*	*
03.04.89	Britten-Norman Trislander	PK-KTI	1021	Bali Air	Aborted take-off & overran	Senipah, Indonesia	*	*
03.04.89	Boeing 737-248	OB-R-1314	19425	Faucett	Damaged after skidding off runway on landing in storm	Iquitos, Peru	0	*
03.04.89	Aerospatiale 330P Puma	5V-MAK	1323	Togolese Air Force	Crashed	Dakar, Senegal	*	*
04.04.89	de Havilland Riley Heron	DQ-FED	14061	Fiji Air	Crashed on take-off	Suva, Fiji	0	*
08.04.89	Lockheed L-382E Hercules	S9-NAI	4303	Transafrik	Crashed on approach after engine fires	Luena, Angola	0	*
10.04.89	Beechcraft Super King Air 200	N30PC	BB-0702	Operator Unknown	Written off	Pensacola, FL, USA	*	*
12.04.89	Fairchild-Hiller FH.227B	F-GGDM	532	Uni-Air	Crashed into cliff while off course	nr Valence, France	22	0
19.04.89	Pilatus PC-6/B2-H2 Turbo Porter	FAC.1110	819	Satena	Crashed	En route Cucuta-Arauca, Colombia	11	0
19.04.89	Cessna 310D	RP-C789	310D-39219	Air Link International Airways	Crashed after take-off	Manila, Philippines	4	0
20.04.89	Cessna 404 Titan II	N5274J	404-0631	Aero Service Corporation	Damaged in emergency landing after engine failure	Santa Cruz, Bolivia	1	*
26.04.89	Aerospatiale Caravelle 11R	HK-3325X	215	Aerosucre	Crashed into houses after engine failure on take-off	Barranquilla, Colombia	5{2}	0
01.05.89	Antonov AN-2	*	*	Aeroflot	Crashed into trees while making low leaflet drop	Sechenovo, RSFSR, USSR	5	0
02.05.89	Douglas DC-3	N28889	20520	Monroe County Mosquito Control	Crashed on spraying flight	Summerland Key, FL, USA	2	0
03.05.89	Piper PA-23-250 Aztec B	C-FJAI	27-2185	Aquila Air	Crashed after take-off	Nanimo, BC, Canada	5	0
05.05.89	Britten-Norman Trislander	XA-JPE	1051	Aerocozumel	Crashed	Cancun, Mexico	6	13
06.05.89	Embraer Bandeirante 110P1	N95PB	110.330	Southern Express	Crashed on approach	Mount Pleasant, TN, USA	*	*
06.05.89	Douglas DC-3	RP-C82	20209	Manila Aero Transport System	Crashed on take-off with 16 unauthorized passengers	Manila, Philippines	*	*
08.05.89	Beechcraft 99	SE-IZO	U048	Holmstroem Air	Crashed on approach due to being wrongly loaded	Oskarshamn, Sweden	16	0
09.05.89	Bell 412	JA9596	33070	Aero Asahi	Crashed	nr Tainjin, China	10	*
10.05.89	Beechcraft 1300	N139YV	*	Mesa Airlines	Crashed	San Gabriel Mts, USA	1	*
12.05.89	Beechcraft Super King Air 200	N39YV	BB-0039	Operator Unknown	Written off	Pasadena, CA, USA	*	*
17.05.89	Boeing 707-330B	6O-SBT	19316	Somali Airlines	Aborted take-off & skidded off runway into marsh	Nairobi, Kenya	0	*
17.05.89	Pilatus PC-6 Porter	*	*	Malaysian Police	Crashed into car making forced landing on road	Kuala Lumpur, Malaysia	6	0
18.05.89	Boeing C-97G Stratofreighter	N4580Q	17005	Stratolift	Crashed	Unalakleet, AK, USA	*	*
19.05.89	Dornier Do.228-201	VT-ESQ	8006	Jagson Airlines	Damaged beyond repair	Paro, Bhutan	*	*
20.05.89	Cessna 208 Caravan I	PNP-021	208-00145	Peruvian Police	Crashed	Olmos, Peru	5	0
21.05.89	Aerospatiale 332L Super Puma	G-TIGN	2056	Bristow Helicopters	Crashed into hillside	En route from Shenzen, China	3	0
21.05.89	Douglas DC-3	C-GWYX	13343	Central Mountain Air	Destroyed by engine fire on ground	Bronson Creek, BC, Canada	*	*
22.05.89	Douglas DC-3	N47CE	13456	Condor Enterprise	Crashed	nr De Kalb, IL, USA	3	0
22.05.89	Consolidated PBY-5A Catalina	N285NJ	*	E.Recchi	Overran into buildings on landing	Turin, Italy	2	3
26.05.89	IRMA BN-2A-27 Islander	YR-BNJ	0777	Aviatia Utilitara	Written off	Bubocu, Romania	*	*
27.05.89	de Havilland Canada Twin Otter 300	C-FMPH	319	RCMP Air Services	Crashed on take-off	Coleville Lake, NWT, Canada	*	*
31.05.89	Beechcraft King Air E90	N987GM	LW-098	Operator Unknown	Crashed	Tuba City, AZ, USA	0	2
oo.05.89	Britten-Norman BN-2A Islander	OB-T-1272	0105	Aero Condor	Crashed after take-off	Puerto Maldonado, Peru	*	*
oo.05.89	PADC BN-2A-27 Islander	VH-BSN	3005	Cockatoo Island Airways	Crashed in sea	Off Derby, Australia	*	*
06.06.89	McDonnell Douglas DC-8-62	N1809E	46107	Surinam Airways	Crashed on approach in fog	Paramaribo, Surinam	177	10
06.06.89	Fokker F-27 Friendship 600	5A-DDV	10588	Libyan Arab Airlines	Crashed after engine failure	nr Zella, Libya	0	*
07.06.89	Douglas DC-3	EC-EIS	16066/32814	Transporte Aereo de Mercania	Damaged when u/c collapsed on landing	Palma, Spain	0	*
11.06.89	de Havilland Canada Twin Otter 300	HK-2486	676	Aerotaxi Casanare	Crashed in poor weather after aborted landing	Caribabare, Colombia	5	12
11.06.89	Beechcraft 18	*	*	Scenic Air Tours	Crashed	Waipio Valley, HI, USA	11	0

Date	Type	Reg'n	C/n	Operator	Accident	Location	F	S
15.06.89	Cessna 310R II	OE-FCM	310R-1839	Austrian Airlines	Crashed into power cables	Koeneuburg, Austria	0	3
17.06.89	Ilyushin IL-62MK	DDR-SEW	2850324	Interflug	Overran on take-off & caught fire	East Berlin, East Germany	16{1}	89
18.06.89	Antonov AN-26	YA-BAK	57314104	Ariana Afghan Airlines	Pilot shot by security guard after fight & crash landed	Zabol, Iran	6	38
18.06.89	Grumman CS2F-1 Firecat	F-ZBEG	413	Securite Civile	Crashed while fire-fighting	Saint Martin-Vesubie, France	1	0
26.06.89	Douglas C-118A Liftmaster	C-GBYA	43717	Conifair Aviation	Crashed while spraying chemicals	nr St-Anne-des-Monts, PQ, Canada	4	0
26.06.89	Douglas DC-3	N8042X	19041	California Air Tours	Crashed	Scow Bay, AK, USA	0	2
27.06.89	Cessna 404 Titan Courier II	B-12206	404-0418	Formosa Airlines	Crashed into house after take-off	Kaohsiung, Taiwan	12	1
28.06.89	British Aerospace 748 2B	TJ-CCF	1804	Cameroon Airlines	Crashed on landing in bad weather	Yaounde, Cameroons	3	*
28.06.89	Fokker F-27 Friendship 600RF	6O-SAZ	10559	Somali Airlines	Crashed after take-off	nr Borama, Somalia	30	0
29.06.89	Dassault Falcon 20DC	N125CA	208	Phoenix Air Group	Struck power lines and crashed	Cartersville, GA, USA	2	0
06.07.89	Beechcraft Queen Air 70	VH-XAE	LB-073	Air Eastern	Crashed	N.E. Victoria, Australia	1	0
11.07.89	Boeing 707-351B	5Y-BBK	19872	Kenya Airways	Damaged in crash landing	Addis Ababa, Ethiopia	0	*
11.07.89	Aerospatiale AS.350D Astar	N3595B	*	Petroleum Helicopters	Mid-air collision with Offshore B206 N1082H	nr Galveston, TX, USA	1(1)	0
11.07.89	Bell 206L-1 Long Ranger	N1082H	*	Offshore Logistics	Mid-air collision with Petroleum Helicopters AS.350D N3595B	nr Galveston, TX, USA	1(1)	0
13.07.89	de Havilland Canada Beaver	N5354G	887	Uyak Air Service	Crashed into mountain	Kodiak, AK, USA	*	*
18.07.89	Britten-Norman BN-2A Islander	P2-ISJ	C089	Talair	Written off	Location Unknown	*	*
19.07.89	McDonnell Douglas DC-10-10	N1819U	46618	United Air Lines	Crashed on landing after engine & hydraulic failure	Sioux City, IA, USA	112	184
19.07.89	Antonov AN-26	SSSR-26685	*	Aeroflot	Crashed into hill	Talourow Island, RSFSR, USSR	10	0
20.07.89	BAC One-Eleven 516FP	RP-C1193	231	Philippine Air Lines	Skidded off runway on landing in storm & crashed into cars	Manila, Philippines	0{8}	98
21.07.89	de Havilland Canada Twin Otter 300	P2-RDW	366	Talair	Crashed on take-off	Porgera, Papua New Guinea	2	20
22.07.89	Cessna 208 Caravan I	HB-CKW	208-00046	Zimex Aviation	Crashed	nr Mocuba, Mozambique	*	*
25.07.89	Boeing B-17G	F-BEEA	8552	Institute Geographique Nationale	Crashed on take-off after engine failure during filming	Binbrook, Humberside, UK	0	10
26.07.89	Mil Mi-8	*	*	Aeroflot	Crashed into mountains	Sochi, Georgia, USSR	5	0
26.07.89	Beechcraft D18S	RP-C719	*	Commuter Air Philippines	Crashed & overturned on landing	Manila, Philippines	0	2
27.07.89	McDonnell Douglas DC-10-30	HL7328	47887	Korean Air	Crashed on approach in fog	Tripoli, Libya	72{6}	127
27.07.89	Sikorsky S-58T	HL9239	*	Air Universal	Crashed into sea	Off Ullung Do, South Korea	13	6
28.07.89	Cessna 182E	ET-ACO	132-54301	Admas Air Service	Collided with G-164B ET-AJJ on landing	Meki, Ethiopia	*	*
29.07.89	Pilatus PC-6 Porter	*	*	Operator Unknown	Struck parachutist and crashed	La Ferte-Gaucher, France	3	0
31.07.89	Convair 580	ZK-FTB	130	Air Freight New Zealand	Crashed into sea after take-off	Off Auckland, New Zealand	3	0
01.08.89	Lockheed L-382G Hercules	7T-VHK	4883	Air Algerie	Damaged when ground looped on landing	Tamanrasset, Algeria	0	*
02.08.89	Type Unknown	*	*	Ariana Afghan Airlines	Crashed into hangar	Qala Nua, Afghanistan	0	32
03.08.89	Short 330-200	SX-BGE	SH.3083	Olympic Aviation	Crashed into mountain in bad weather	Samos, Greece	34	0
04.08.89	Convair 600	N94253	1[illegible]4	International Turbine Service	Overshot runway on landing	Augusta, MN, USA	*	*
08.08.89	Britten-Norman BN-2A-26 Islander	ZK-EVK	0583	Aspiring Air	Crashed into mountain	nr Milford Sound, New Zealand	10	0
10.08.89	McDonnell Douglas DC-8-33F	OB-1316	45384	APISA	Overran on landing in heavy rain	Iquitos, Peru	0	*
12.08.89	de Havilland Canada Twin Otter 300	ET-AIL	699	RRC Air Service	Crashed in mountains	nr Fugnido, Ethiopia	17	0
13.08.89	Kavanagh E-160 Hot-Air Balloon	VH-NMS	KB-078	Toddy's Balloon Safaris	Mid-air collision with another balloon which landed safely	nr Alice Springs, NT, Australia	13(0)	0
15.08.89	Antonov AN-24	B-3417	37309006	CAAC	Crashed into river after aborting take-off	Shanghai, China	33	7
16.08.89	Fokker F-28 Fellowship 1000C	TC-51	11076	Lineas Aereas del Estado	Overran on snow & struck embankment	Bariloche, Argentina	*	*
21.08.89	Beechcraft King Air C90	N25ST	LJ-0507	Operator Unknown	Crashed	Gold Beach, OR, USA	0	3
22.08.89	Canadair CL-215-3	YV-O-INC-2	1063	Instituto Nacional de Canalizations	Crashed after take-off	Puerto Ordaz, Venezuela	3	0
25.08.89	Fokker F-27 Friendship 200	AP-BBF	10207	Pakistan International Airlines	Crashed	nr Gilgit, Pakistan	54	0
25.08.89	Boeing 727-247	TC-AJV	20265	Toros Air	Struck antenna on take-off & damaged – Landed safely	Ankara, Turkey	0	165
28.08.89	LET 410UVP Turbolet	SSSR-67104	841330	Aeroflot	Damaged in forced landing	Labinsk, RSFSR, USSR	*	*
02.09.89	Yakovlev YAK-40	SSSR-87509	*	Aeroflot	Damaged in belly landing	Bishkek, Kirghizia, USSR	0	43
03.09.89	Ilyushin IL-62M	CU-T1281	3850453	Cubana	Crashed on take-off in storm	Havana, Cuba	126{34}	0
03.09.89	Boeing 737-241A	PP-VMK	21006	Varig	Crash landed in jungle when lost	Para, Brazil	13	41
03.09.89	Fairchild C-123K Provider	*	*	US Drug Enforcement Administration	Destroyed by bomb on ground	Monteria, Colombia	0	*
04.09.89	Fokker F-27 Friendship 600	C-GSFS	10473	Conair Aviation	Crashed while fire-fighting	nr Ales, France	2	0
04.09.89	Lockheed Electra 188C	HC-AZJ/2004	2004	TAME	Damaged in belly landing	Taura, Ecuador	*	*
05.09.89	Bell 214B	JA9325	28043	Aero Asahi	Crashed while making emergency landing	Ooi, Japan	2	2
07.09.89	BAC One-Eleven 320L-AZ	5N-AOT	133	Okada Air	Damaged in heavy landing	Port Harcourt, Nigeria	0	*

Date	Type	Reg'n	C/n	Operator	Accident	Location	F	S
08.09.89	Convair 580	LN-PAA	056	Partnair	Crashed in sea	Off Denmark	55	0
15.09.89	de Havilland Canada Twin Otter 300	PK-NUE	345	Merpati Nusantara Airlines	Crashed	nr Bencuni, Indonesia	22	0
15.09.89	Beechcraft King Air 100	N887PE	B-049	Operator Unknown	Written off	Mayfield, KY, USA	*	*
15.09.89	Yakovlev YAK-40	SSSR-87391	*	Aeroflot	Damaged on landing	Dzhalal-Abad, Kirghizia, USSR	0	30
16.09.89	Beechcraft King Air 100	N204AJ	B-010	Operator Unknown	Written off	Location Unknown	*	*
17.09.89	Douglas DC-3	N4425N	1963	Aero Virgin Islands	Destroyed in hurricane	St Thomas, US Virgin Is	*	*
17.09.89	Douglas DC-3	N4471J	6187	Aero Virgin Islands	Destroyed in hurricane	St Thomas, US Virgin Is	*	*
17.09.89	Douglas DC-3	N28346	6259	Aero Virgin Islands	Destroyed in hurricane	St Thomas, US Virgin Is	*	*
17.09.89	Douglas DC-3	N4577Z	9795	Aero Virgin Islands	Destroyed in hurricane	St Thomas, US Virgin Is	*	*
17.09.89	Douglas DC-3	N100SD	12853	Aero Virgin Islands	Destroyed in hurricane	St Thomas, US Virgin Is	*	*
17.09.89	Martin 404	N40425	14131	Aero Virgin Islands	Destroyed in hurricane	St Thomas, US Virgin Is	*	*
17.09.89	Grumman G-73 Mallard	N628SS	J-28	Virgin Islands Seaplane Shuttle	Destroyed in hurricane	St Croix, US Virgin Is	*	*
17.09.89	Grumman G-73 Turbo Mallard	N632SS	J-32	Virgin Islands Seaplane Shuttle	Destroyed in hurricane	St Croix, US Virgin Is	*	*
17.09.89	Grumman G-73 Mallard	N655SS	J-55	Virgin Islands Seaplane Shuttle	Destroyed in hurricane	St Croix, US Virgin Is	*	*
17.09.89	Lockheed 18 Lodestar	N1046	*	Eagle Wings Air Service	Destroyed when struck by Cessna in hurricane	St Croix, US Virgin Is	0	*
17.09.89	Douglas DC-3	N100DW	*	Four Star Aviation	Destroyed by hurricane	St Croix, US Virgin Is	*	*
19.09.89	McDonnell Douglas DC-10-30	N54629	46852	UTA	Crashed after bomb explosion	nr Termit Mts, Niger	170	0
20.09.89	Boeing 737-401	N416US	23884	US Air	Overran into river on take-off	New York, NY, USA	2	59
23.09.89	Learjet 23D	LV-MMV	25D-259	Misiones Provincial Government	Crashed into river in bad weather	Parana, Argentina	2	5
23.09.89	Piper T-1040	C-GBDH	31-8375003	Aklak Air	Crashed in lake on attempting to land in fog	Banks Island, NWT, Canada	5	0
24.09.89	Dornier Do.228-201	VT-EJF	8052	Vayudoot	Exploded and crashed	Ujani Dam, India	11	0
26.09.89	Fairchild 227AC Metro III	C-GSLB	AC-481	Skylink Airlines	Crashed on approach	Terrace, BC, Canada	7	0
26.09.89	Cessna 404 Titan II	ST-AIW	404-0458	Nile Safari Aviation	Crashed into houses after take-off	Nyala, Sudan	6	0
27.09.89	de Havilland Canada Twin Otter 300	N75GC	439	Grand Canyon Airlines	Crashed	Grand Canyon National Pk, AZ, USA	10	11
28.09.89	Antonov AN-32	SSSR-48095	*	Aeroflot	Crashed in swamp	Chernigevski, Ukraine, USSR	9	0
oo.09.89	Britten-Norman BN-2A-26 Islander	N112JC	0514	Vieques Air Link	Written off	Location Unknown	*	*
oo.09.89	Britten-Norman BN-2A Islander	N290VL	0062	Vieques Air Link	Written off	Location Unknown	*	*
01.10.89	Beechcraft King Air C90	N43GT	LJ-0652	Operator Unknown	Written off	Location Unknown	*	*
02.10.89	Cessna 404 Titan Courier II	PK-KCC	404-0077	Bali Air	Crashed into houses on approach	Sjamsudin Noor, Indonesia	4	3
02.10.89	Cessna Citation II	N53CC	550-0400	GTE South Inc	Undershot runway at night & crashed	Roxboro, NC, USA	2	*
04.10.89	Antonov AN-24	SSSR-46525	47310004	Aeroflot	Overshot on landing & crashed	Stepnogorsk, RSFSR, USSR	0	51
06.10.89	Cessna 208 Caravan I	N208W	208-00115	Westchester Air	Crashed on take-off	Texas, USA	*	*
10.10.89	Cessna 402C Utililiner II	OB-T-1254	402C-0638	TAUSA	Crashed into mountain after take-off	Urpay, Peru	12	0
14.10.89	Boeing 727-232A	N530DA	21813	Delta Air Lines	Damaged in ground fire	Salt Lake City, UT, USA	*	*
18.10.89	Ilyushin IL-76MD	SSSR-76569	*	Aeroflot	Crashed after engine fire	Caspian Sea, USSR	57	0
20.10.89	Britten-Norman BN-2A-3 Islander	TC-KUN	0272	Tapu Kadastro Genel Mudurlugu	Shot down by Syrian Air Force MIG-21	Hatay, Turkey	5	0
20.10.89	Ilyushin IL-76TD	SSSR-76466	*	Aeroflot	Crashed into mountain on approach	nr Leninakan, Armenia, USSR	15	0
21.10.89	Boeing 727-224	N88705	19514	TAN	Crashed into mountain	nr Tegucigalpa, Honduras	131	19
21.10.89	Antonov AN-24	*	*	Aeroflot	Crashed on landing	nr Tyumen, RSFSR, USSR	*	*
24.10.89	Mitsubishi MU-2 Marquise	I-IDMA	769SA	Bestit Company	Crashed at sea	Off Orosei, Sardinia, Italy	2	0
26.10.89	Boeing 737-209A	B-180	23795	China Airlines	Crashed into mountain	Chia Min, Taiwan	56	0
26.10.89	Antonov AN-26	*	*	Aeroflot	Crashed into mountain on approach	Petropavlosk-Kamchatskiy, RSFSR,USSR	36	0
26.10.89	Rockwell Sabre 75A	XC-UJC	380-67	Mexican Air Force	Crashed [Also carried TP-101]	Mexico City, Mexico	0	*
27.10.89	Cessna 414A	VH-SDV	*	Skybird Aviation Services	Crashed	nr North Wonthaggi, Vic, Australia	0	7
29.10.89	de Havilland Canada Twin Otter 300	N707PV	400	Aloha Island Air	Crashed into mountain on approach	Halawa Valley, HI, USA	20	0
oo.10.89	Curtiss C-46F	C-GTPO	22556	Northland Air Manitoba	Overran on take-off	Pickle Lake, ON, Canada	0	*
01.11.89	Short Skyvan 3	OH-SBB	SH.1838	RV Aviation	Crashed at sea out of fuel	Off Aaland, Finland	0	2
02.11.89	Antonov AN-26	SSSR-26038	*	Aeroflot	Damaged on landing on runway under construction	Nurba, RSFSR, USSR	*	*
03.11.89	Curtiss C-46F	C-FFNC	22388	Northland Air Manitoba	Damaged by fire	Winnipeg, MN, Canada	*	*
04.11.89	Learjet 25C	PT-ISN	25C-113	Belair Taxi Aereo	Crashed into hill	nr Ribiero das Neves, Brazil	4	0
05.11.89	Handley Page Dart Herald 401	HK-2702	180	Aerosucre	Crashed into mountains	Between Bogota–Cali, Colombia	6	0
05.11.89	Beechcraft King Air C90	N3804F	LJ-0947	Operator Unknown	Written off	Location Unknown	*	*

Date	Type	Reg'n	C/n	Operator	Accident	Location	F	S
07.11.89	IRMA BN-2A-26 Islander	9L-LAV	0767	Weasua Air Transport	Crashed in sea on approach	nr Sinoe, Sierra Leone	2	8
14.11.89	Antonov AN-2	YR-PMG	1G227-17	Operator Unknown	Crashed	Sanmartin, Romania	*	*
15.11.89	Cessna Citation II/SP	LN-AAE	551-0245	Air Express	Crashed on approach	Bardufoss, Norway	4	0
15.11.89	Douglas DC-3	RP-C14	14643/26088	Victoria Air	Crashed at sea	Off Barualite, Philippines	0	5
19.11.89	Cessna U206F Super Skymaster	OB-T-1191	U206-01880	Aerovias SA	Crashed	nr Atalaya, Peru	4	0
21.11.89	Antonov AN-24	SSSR-46335	97305602	Aeroflot	Crashed on landing	nr Tyumem, RSFSR, USSR	34	8
25.11.89	Fokker F-28 Fellowship 4000	HL7285	11223	Korean Air	Crashed on take-off in fog	Seoul, South Korea	0	54
25.11.89	Britten-Norman BN-2A-26 Islander	V3-HCT	0571	Maya Airways	Damaged beyond repair	Belize	*	*
27.11.89	Boeing 727-21	HK-1803	19035	Avianca	Crashed after take-off due to bomb explosion	nr Bogota, Colombia	107{3}	0
27.11.89	Short 360-100	G-ROOM	SH.3600	Short Bros	Destroyed on ground by terrorist bomb	Belfast Harbour, UK	0	0
27.11.89	Lockheed L-100-20 Hercules	N9205T	4129	Tepper Aviation	Crashed on approach delivering arms to UNITA rebels	Jamba, Angola	5	0
27.11.89	Short 330-100	G-OATD	SH.3096	Short Bros	Damaged on ground by terrorist bomb	Belfast Harbour, UK	0	*
28.11.89	Cessna 402	YV-478C	*	Lineas Aereas CAVE	Crashed into mountains	Charallave, Venezuela	3	4
02.12.89	Sikorsky UH-60A Blackhawk	*	*	US Customs Service	Crashed while chasing smugglers	Off Marathon, FL, USA	1	5
02.12.89	Douglas DC-6A/B	N371	44057	Gomes & Warra Aircraft Corp	Crashed	Bahamas	*	*
09.12.89	Beechcraft King Air F90	N9PU	LA-057	Operator Unknown	Written off	Ruldoso, NM, USA	*	*
11.12.89	Westland WG.30-160	VT-EKQ	032	Pawan Hans	Crashed after take-off	Bombay, India	0	13
14.12.89	Antonov AN-2	*	*	Aeroflot	Crashed in fog	Kazakhstan, USSR	1	11
15.12.89	Aerospatiale AS.365N Dauphin 2	VT-ELO	6255	Pawan Hans	Crashed into river	nr Patna, India	7	0
18.12.89	Bell 206B JetRanger III	G-SHBB	02291	Starline Helicopters	Crashed in bad weather	Berry's Hill, Kent, UK	5	0
19.12.89	Piper PA-32-260 Cherokee Six	ZK-CUV	32-673	Great Barrier Airlines	Crashed	Haururu Falss, New Zealand	*	*
21.12.89	Britten-Norman BN-2A Islander	*	*	Medecins Sans Frontieres	Shot down by rebels	Aweil, Sudan	4	0
21.12.89	Learjet 35A	HP-1141P	*	Panamanian Government	Damaged by invading US troops	Paitilla, Panama	*	*
26.12.89	British Aerospace Jetstream 31	N410UE	776	North Pacific Airlines	Crashed on landing	Pasco, WA, USA	5	0
27.12.89	Cessna 421B Golden Eagle	9H-ABN	421B-0007	Eagle Aviation	Crashed on approach	Zurich, Switzerland	*	*
28.12.89	Antonov AN-24RV	YR-BMJ	77310801	Tarom	Crashed after take-off	Bucharest, Romania	7	0
30.12.89	Fokker F-28 Fellowship 4000	TU-TIK	11121	Air Ivoire	Overran runway on landing	Man, Ivory Coast	0	*
30.12.89	Cessna 207 Skywagon	ZK-DAX	*	Air Fiordland	Mid-air collision with Milford Sound Cessna 207 ZK-DQF	Milford Sound, New Zealand	5(0)	0
oo.12.89	Lockheed C-130H Hercules	TJ-XAC	4747	Cameroun Air Force	Destroyed by fire	Marseilles, France	*	*
oo.12.89	Britten-Norman BN-2A-6 Islander	HP-572OL	0226	Aerolineas Colon	Written off during US invasion	Panama	*	*
oo.12.89	IRMA BN-2A-7 Islander	HP-1002	0629	Aerolineas Nacionales	Written off during US invasion	Panama	*	*
oo.12.89	IRMA BN-2A-27 Islander	HP-1133	0750	Istmena de Aviacion	Written off during US invasion	Panama	*	*
oo.12.89	Boeing 737-204	N198AW	19710	America West Airlines	Damaged beyond repair when overran runway	Tucson, AZ, USA	0	*
oo.12.89	Learjet 35A	N930GL	35A-330	Air Pacific NC Inc	Damaged during US invasion	Panama	*	*
oo.oo.89	Aerospatiale 330J Puma	PK-PDV	1193	Pelita Air Service	Written off	Indonesia	*	*
oo.oo.89	British Aerospace 125-3A	N66HA	25126	Operator Unknown	Damaged beyond repair	Houston, TX, USA	*	*
oo.oo.89	Sikorsky S-58D	C-GUNI	58-1787	Operator Unknown	Damaged beyond repair	Canada	*	*
oo.oo.89	Antonov AN-2	YU-BBM	260805	PA Osijek	Destroyed in Federal air-raid	Varazdin, Yugoslavia	*	*

1990–1995

Even though this decade is only half-way through, there have been momentous changes affecting air transport.

This period will be remembered for the final collapse of Communism and the break-up of the Soviet Union. The end of the 1980s had already seen Eastern Europe gain its freedom, but in December 1991 the USSR finally ceased to exist and became 15 separate nations.

Each of these quickly generated its own airlines, mainly from the Aeroflot division based in its territory. In Russia, Aeroflot fragmented and literally hundreds of new airlines emerged. Some of these operated with only one aircraft and many lasted only a short time.

With changes in the political system and the economic disruption that followed these events, the safety of Russian and other CIS operators has been called into question. The listings on the following pages will show a dramatic increase in the number of accidents being recorded from this part of the world. Much of this increase must be due to the fact that accident reports now freely reach the West. However, this cannot be the sole reason.

There are many other factors also affecting their operations. Lack of money has led to fuel shortages, poor maintenance, and cutbacks in training. One thing not in short supply is aircraft. While many surplus Aeroflot aircraft exist, relatively minor accidents are leading to machines being

A Tristar (N11002) of Trans World, burnt out at New York after aborting its take-off on 30 July 1992. There were no fatalities amongst those on board. (Popperfoto/Reuter)

written off. Although the operators concerned are trying to rectify the situation, it will be a long time before standards reach an acceptable level with all airlines.

Probably the most graphic illustration of the state of the industry was given by the crash of an Aeroflot A.310 in 1994 after the pilot allegedly allowed his son to handle the controls. The subsequent crash killed 75 people. The fact that this could happen to the newly reformed Aeroflot Russian International Airlines with its experienced crews, on board their modern, western-built aircraft, is indicative of the breakdown in discipline which must have occurred.

A booming airline system has also led to problems in China. There have been a number of serious accidents in the past few years that have made the Chinese authorities clamp down on operators and restrict the formation of new airlines to help maintain safety. The first five years of the decade have seen 15 Chinese aircraft written off in fatal accidents.

Elsewhere the air transport business continues to be plagued by losses to hostile and criminal activities. The conflicts in Afghanistan, Angola, Iraq and Sri Lanka continue to cause aircraft to be lost. To these have been added Liberia, Somalia, Rwanda, Azerbaijan, Georgia, Yemen, Chechnya and Bosnia – in many of which the fighting still continues.

However, despite all these problems air travel continues to improve its overall safety record. There have been only 17 crashes involving more than a hundred fatalities up to November 1995. This compares with 41 in the previous decade.

First write-offs 1990–1995

(*military example crashed earlier)

Saab 340	21.02.90
Boeing 757	02.10.90
Antonov AN-8	10.10.90
Boeing 767	00.02.91
Antonov AN-74	16.09.91
Beechcraft Beechjet	27.11.91
Airbus A.310	31.07.92
Harbin Y-12	26.09.92
CASA CN.235	18.10.92*
Airbus A.340	22.01.93
Fokker 100	05.03.93
Ilyushin IL-114	05.07.93
Canadair Regional Jet	26.07.93
Antonov AN-124	13.10.93
BAe Jetstream 41	07.01.94
Beechcraft Starship	22.02.94
Airbus A.330	30.06.94
Antonov AN-72	23.10.94
ATR.72	31.10.94
Antonov AN-70	10.02.95
Fokker 50	15.09.95

Even the most modern airliner can suffer a mishap. This empty Airbus A.340 of Air France (F-GNIA) was burnt out on the ground at Paris-Roissy in January 1994. (Popperfoto/Reuter)

Date	Type	Reg'n	C/n	Operator	Accident	Location	F	S
02.01.90	IPTN 212 Aviocar 200	PK-PCM	217/57N	Pelita Air Service	Crashed	Off Sumatra, Indonesia	7	7
03.01.90	Britten-Norman Trislander	YJ-RV3	0349	Vanair	Crashed	Vanuatu	*	*
05.01.90	Fokker F-28 Fellowship 4000	LV-MZD	11127	Aerolineas Argentinas	Overran on landing & caught fire	Villa Gesell, Argentina	0	90
05.01.90	Lockheed L-100-30 Hercules	D2-THB	4222	TAAG Angola Airlines	Destroyed on landing after being struck by missile	Menogue, Angola	*	*
06.01.90	Lockheed Jetstar 731	N96GS	5068	Pan Aviation	Crashed on take-off	Miami, FL, USA	1	1
07.01.90	Curtiss C-46	CP-746	26417	Transportes Aereos Universal	Crashed after take-off due to engine failure	La Paz, Bolivia	*	*
13.01.90	Tupolev TU-134A	SSSR-65951	2351703	Aeroflot	Crashed on approach	Pervouralsk, RSFSR, USSR	27	44
15.01.90	CASA 212 Aviocar 200	TI-SAB	163	SANSA	Crashed after take-off	San Jose, Costa Rica	23	0
15.01.90	Fairchild 227AC Metro III	N2721M	AC-716	Skywest Airlines	Crashed into mountain on approach	Elko, UT, USA	0	16
17.01.90	Cessna 402B II	N87163	402B-1005	Superior Aviation	Crashed on approach	Appleton, WI, USA	1	*
17.01.90	Cessna 208A Caravan I	N835FE	208A-00091	PM Air	Crashed	nr Leadville, CO, USA	*	*
18.01.90	Learjet 23	N331DP	23-067	Aeroflite Services	Crashed	nr Dayton, OH, USA	2	0
18.01.90	Beechcraft King Air A100	N44UE	B-140	Epps Air Service	Damaged when struck by landing Eastern B.727	Atlanta, GA, USA	1(0)	*
19.01.90	Grumman Gulfstream II	N46TE	243	Eastman Kodak	Crashed short of runway	Little Rock, AR, USA	7	0
20.01.90	Cessna 208 Caravan I	N835FE	208-00091	Federal Express	Crashed in bad weather	nr Leadville, CO, USA	*	*
21.01.90	Beechcraft Super King Air 300	HI-578SP	FA-180	Operator Unknown	Written off after being stolen 04.12.89	Location Unknown	*	*
23.01.90	Piper PA-31-350 Chieftain	SE-IAA	31-7952113	Kungsair	Crashed into high ground on approach	Hudiksvall, Sweden	3	*
24.01.90	Britten-Norman BN-2A Islander	*	*	North Solomons Air Services	Set on fire by rebels after landing	Wakunai, Papua New Guinea	0	10
24.01.90	Bell 206B JetRanger III	G-EYEI	00597	Clyde Helicopters	Crashed into building	Glasgow, UK	*	*
25.01.90	Boeing 707-321B	HK-2016	19276	Avianca	Crashed on approach out of fuel	Long Island, NY, USA	73	85
25.01.90	British Aerospace 748 2	PK-OBW	1567	Airfast Services	Crashed into mountain	Mt Rijani, Lombok Is, Indonesia	19	0
25.01.90	Grumman Gulfstream III	HZ-AFS	450	Saudia	Damaged by hangar door blowing onto fuselage in storm	Le Bourget, France	0	*
26.01.90	Mitsubishi MU-2 Marquise	VH-MUA	746SA	Operator Unknown	Crashed	Meekathara, WA, Australia	2	0
26.01.90	Britten-Norman BN-2A-27 Islander	C-GSAF	0263	Western Arctic Air	Written off	Inuvik, Canada	*	*
27.01.90	Nord 262C-66	TN-230	103	Congolese Air Force	Crashed in rain storm	nr Brazzaville, Congo	23	0
27.01.90	Aerospatiale AS.350B Ecureuil	JA9315	1536	Nihon Norin Helicopters	Crashed into car park	Togari, Japan	*	*
29.01.90	Cessna 208B Caravan I	N854FE	208B-0172	Federal Express	Crashed	nr Plattsburgh, NY, USA	1	0
29.01.90	Cessna 208B Caravan I	N4688B	208B-0169	Airborne Express	Crashed	nr Burlington, VT, USA	*	*
30.01.90	British Aerospace 125-3B	G-OBOB	25069	Slender You (UK) Ltd	Crashed	nr Columbia, MO, USA	1	2
30.01.90	Mitsubishi MU-2L	OB-1219	730SA	TAUSA	Crashed out of fuel in storm	nr Santa Maria, Peru	*	*
oo.01.90	IRMA BN-2A-6 Islander	VH-BAY	0620	Bougair	Destroyed by rebels on ground	Wakunai, Papua New Guinea	*	*
oo.01.90	Yakovlev YAK-40	*	*	Liberia Air Transport	Total 2 damaged during civil war	Monrovia, Liberia	*	*
04.02.90	Cessna U206G Stationair	OB-T-1199	U206-05615	TAAPSA	Crashed	San Francisco, Peru	0	*
05.02.90	Grumman Gulfstream I	HK-3315X	024	Helicopteros Nacionales de Colombia	Crashed into mountains	nr Ibague, Colombia	15	0
07.02.90	Bell 205A-1	C-GNMJ	30264	Northern Mountain Helicopters	Crashed	Wrangell, Canada	4	0
09.02.90	Mitsubishi MU-2 Marquise	N64MD	747SA	Operator Unknown	Written off	Rapid City, SD, USA	*	*
12.02.90	Fokker F-27 Friendship 200	PT-LCG	10206	Brasil Central	Crashed into houses after aborting landing	Bauru, Brazil	0{2}	40
13.02.90	Beechcraft King Air C90	N110LT	LJ-0729	Holt Manufacturing Co	Crashed into wood	Burlington, NC, USA	2	0
13.02.90	Fokker F-27 Friendship 400M	*	*	Transporte Aereo Militar	Crashed	nr Sao Paolo, Bolivia	20	18
14.02.90	Airbus A.320-231	VT-EPN	079	Indian Airlines	Crashed short of runway	Bangalore, India	92	54
14.02.90	Mitsubishi MU-2 Marquise	N300CW	795SA	Williams Aviation	Crashed	nr Putnam, TX, USA	5	0
14.02.90	Ilyushin IL-14	SSSR-41803	*	Aeroflot	Crashed	Antarctica	*	*
18.02.90	McDonnell Douglas DC-9-32	EC-BIQ	47092	Aviaco	Made heavy landing but took off again. Landed safely but dbr	Mahon, Minorca, Spain	0	*
20.02.90	Antonov AN-2	SSSR-56472	IG182-29	Aeroflot	Crashed	Siauliai, Lithuania, USSR	*	*
21.02.90	Saab 340A	HB-AHA	005	Crossair	Damaged when u/c collapsed	Zurich, Switzerland	0	*
23.02.90	Douglas DC-3	VH-MMA	9583	Air North	Badly damaged when blown into RAAF DC-3 during gale	Darwin, NT, Australia	*(0)	*
24.02.90	Fokker F-27 Friendship 600	D-AELB	10562	Air Service Flugcharter	Damaged in forced landing after double engine fire	nr Bergitsch Gladbach, W Germany	0	2
25.02.90	Learjet 31	N984JD	31-001	Learjet Corporation	Belly landed & caught fire	Taiyuan, China	0	7
27.02.90	Cessna 208A Caravan I	N820FE	208A-00043	Federal Express	Crashed on approach	Colorado, USA	*	*
27.02.90	Bell 205A-1	C-GRUW	30097	Paramount Air	Crashed after take-off	Oliver, BC, Canada	0	*
28.02.90	Piper PA-31T Turbo Navajo	OB-S-1176	31T-8020010	Aero San Martin	Crashed on take-off	Tocache, Peru	2	0
oo.02.90	IRMA BN-2A-27 Islander	P2-BAC	0716	Bougair	Damaged when struck by vehicle	Papua New Guinea	*	*
01.03.90	Boeing 707-329C	9Q-CVG	19162	Katale Aero Transport	Damaged in heavy landing	Goma, Zaire	0	*

Date	Type	Reg'n	C/n	Operator	Accident	Location	F	S
01.03.90	Antonov AN-26	*	*	MIAT Mongolian Airlines	Crashed	Mongolia	30	0
12.03.90	Sikorsky S-58ET	EC-DDR	58-1617	Helicsa	Crashed into sea after take-off	Off Freetown, Sierra Leone	11	2
14.03.90	Antonov AN-2	HA-MER	IG194-27	Air Service Hungary	Damaged in forced landing after engine failure	Jazjakohalma, Hungary	*	*
18.03.90	Douglas DC-3	HR-SAZ	19495	Sahsa	Blown into sea on landing in high winds	Roatan Island, Honduras	0	32
21.03.90	Lockheed Electra 188CF	HR-TNL	1134	TAN	Crashed	Las Mesitas, Honduras	3	0
22.03.90	Rockwell Turbo Commander 695A	HK-3278	*	Aerovias del Caucia	Crashed	Colombia	7	0
22.03.90	Hawker Siddeley Trident 2E	B-2208	2165	Air China	Overran & damaged beyond repair	Guilin, China	*	*
22.03.90	Gulfstream Commander 1000	HK-3278	*	Aerocauca	Crashed into mountain	Colombia	7	0
23.03.90	Antonov AN-26	CU-T111	7207	Cubana	Struck ditch & caught fire on take-off	Santiago de Cuba, Cuba	0	*
23.03.90	Cessna 404 Titan	HK-3382P	404-0671	Operator Unknown	Written off	Alto de la Cabra, Colombia	*	*
23.03.90	Bell 206B JetRanger II	JA9058	00613	Aero Asahi	Crashed	Lake Towada, Japan	*	*
27.03.90	Ilyushin IL-76MD	SSSR-78781	*	Aeroflot	Crashed on approach	nr Kabul, Afghanistan	9	0
28.03.90	Beechcraft King Air 100	N696JB	B-013	Operator Unknown	Written off	Garner, TX, USA	*	*
29.03.90	Douglas C-54G	C-FIQM	36088	Kenn Borek Air	Damaged beyond repair	Calgary, AB, Canada	*	*
oo.03.90	Cessna 404 Titan	HK-2686P	404-0852	Operator Unknown	Bombed by Colombian Air Force	Panorama City, Colombia	*	*
01.04.90	Hawker Siddeley Argosy 222	ZK-SAF	6801	Safe Air	U/c collapsed on landing	Woodbourne, New Zealand	*	*
02.04.90	Learjet 35	N51FN	35-059	Flight International	Crashed on take-off	Carlsbad, CA, USA	0	2
03.04.90	de Havilland Canada Twin Otter 300	PK-NUQ	488	Merpati Nusantara Airlines	Crashed into hill	Lebuhanraio, Indonesia	*	*
04.04.90	de Havilland Canada Twin Otter	HR-ALH	*	Islenas de Inversiones	Undershot and crashed into sea	Utila Is, Honduras	*	*
05.04.90	Lockheed EC-121S S Constellation	HI-515CT	4192	Aerolineas Mundo	Crashed into sea after tail broke off	Off San Juan, Puerto Rico	1	*
06.04.90	Learjet 25C	PT-CMY	25C-108	Transamerica Taxi Aereo	Overran on landing & caught fire	Juiz de Fora, Brazil	*	*
07.04.90	Martin 404	CP-1738	14137	Transportes Aereos Samuel Selum	Ran off runway on emergency landing	Yacuma, Bolivia	0	*
12.04.90	de Havilland Canada Twin Otter 300	LN-BNS	536	Wideroe	Crashed into sea after take-off	Vaeroey, Lofoten Is, Norway	5	0
17.04.90	Bell 212	C-GBHT	*	Canadian Helicopters	Crashed on take-off	Cariboo Mt, Canada	*	*
18.04.90	de Havilland Canada Twin Otter 200	N187SA	131	Aeroperlas	Crashed after birdstrike shortly following take-off	Contadora Is, CA, USA	20	2
22.04.90	Cessna Citation 1/SP	N2652Z	501-0145	Operator Unknown	Written off	Lord Howe Island, NSW, Australia	*	*
26.04.90	Douglas DC-3	RP-C81	13880/25325	Manila Aero Transport System	Crashed after take-off	Manila, Philippines	6	17
30.04.90	Beechcraft C99	C-FGAW	U197	Frontier Air	Crashed	Ship Sands Is, ON, Canada	*	*
30.04.90	IPTN 332C Super Puma	PK-PUF	NSP1/2019	Pelita Air Service	Crashed into sea on approach	nr Matak, Indonesia	*	*
30.04.90	Douglas DC-4	N67109	10459	Aero Union	Crashed on runway during training flight	Chico, CA, USA	0	2
02.05.90	Grumman Gulfstream I	HK-3316X	059	Helicopteros Nacionales de Colombia	Crashed on landing	Montoria, Colombia	0	6
03.05.90	Cessna TU206D Super Skymaster	OB-1331	U206-01331	Aerovias SA	Crashed	En route Uchiza–Satipo, Peru	*	*
04.05.90	GAF Nomad N24A	N418NE	089	Tar Heel Aviation	Crashed on approach	Wilmington, NC, USA	*	*
05.05.90	Douglas DC-6BF	N84BL	43739	Aerial Transit Co	Crashed after take-off	Guatamala City, Guatemala	3{23}	0
07.05.90	Boeing 747-237B	VT-EBO	20558	Air India	Engine detached on landing and damaged by fire in wing	New Delhi, India	0	*
10.05.90	Fairchild F-27J	F-GHXA	0101	Aviacsa	Crashed on approach	Tuxtla Gutierrez, Mexico	27	17
11.05.90	Boeing 737-3Y0	EI-BZG	24466	Philippine Air Lines	Damaged when bomb exploded in cabin before take-off	Manila, Philippines	7	112
11.05.90	Cessna Citation I	VH-ANQ	500-0283	Air North Queensland	Crashed into mountains in bad weather	nr Mt Emerald, Qld, Australia	11	0
15.05.90	Sikorsky S-76A	9M-AXW	760057	Malaysian Helicopter Services	Crashed in sea	South China Sea	0	10
18.05.90	Beechcraft 1900C-1	RP-C314	UC-46	Aerolift Philippines	Crashed into houses after take-off	Manila, Philippines	21{4}	0
19.05.90	Douglas DC-3	N1FN	11685	K & K Aircraft	Crashed into overhead cables	nr Winchester, VA, USA	*	*
29.05.90	Beechcraft King Air 90	N707CE	LJ-0314	Operator Unknown	Crashed on approach	Tamanrasset, Algeria	6	*
30.05.90	Beechcraft King Air C90A	N34134	LJ-1186	Taboca Mining Company	Crashed after colliding with tower	Manaus, Brazil	*	*
30.05.90	Cessna TU206G Stationair	OB-1189	U206-05547	Aerovias Peruanas	Crashed	Biabo, Peru	3	0
31.05.90	Cessna 404 Titan	G-DAFS	404-0872	Dept. of Ag. & Fish. for Scotland	Crashed after engine failure	Off Jura, UK	0	3
oo.05.90	Britten-Norman BN-2A-26 Islander	P2-IST	0130	Talair	Damaged beyond repair	Wan-Morobe, Papua New Guinea	*	*
oo.05.90	Antonov AN-2	YU-BKE	IG167-17	Operator Unknown	Crashed	Yugoslavia	*	*
01.06.90	Cessna 402B	OB-1318	402B-0403	Aero Sur	Crashed in bad weather [Found 28.08.90]	nr Ayacucho, Peru	4	0
02.06.90	Boeing 737-2X6C	N670MA	23121	Markair	Crashed into hillside	nr Unalakleet, AK, USA	0	4
02.06.90	Antonov AN-24	SSSR-46551	87304503	Aeroflot	Crashed on approach	Ken-Kiyak, Kazakhstan, USSR	*	*
06.06.90	Fairchild-Hiller FH.227B	PT-ICA	570	TABA	Crashed on approach	Altamira, Brazil	23	19
06.06.90	de Havilland Canada Twin Otter 300	C-FWAB	349	Ptarmigan Airways	Crashed on take-off	Thistle Lake, NWT, Canada	2	0
06.06.90	Cessna 208A Caravan I	N803FE	208A-00015	Federal Express	Crashed	Fresno, CA, USA	0	1
07.06.90	Bell 222B	JA9687	47144	Royal Airline Co	Crashed into mountain	Toyohira-Cho, Japan	0	*

Date	Type	Reg'n	C/n	Operator	Accident	Location	F	S
12.06.90	Ilyushin IL-76MD	SSSR-86905	*	Aeroflot	Shot down on approach by rebel missile	Kabul, Afghanistan	0	8
15.06.90	Rockwell Turbo Commander 690C	HK-2478P	11609	Operator Unknown	Written off	Location Unknown	*	*
23.06.90	Short Skyvan	N50GA	SH.1856	North Star Air Cargo	Ran off runway and crashed	Russian Mission, AK, USA	0	*
23.06.90	Boeing 707-321B	CC-CEI	20021	LAN-Chile	Damaged while being towed	Santiago, Chile	0	*
30.06.90	de Havilland Canada Otter	N17689	*	Operator Unknown	Crashed	Beaver, WA, USA	2	*
oo.06.90	Lockheed C-121J Super Constellation	HI-532CT	4155	Aerochago	Damaged when nosewheel collapsed on landing	Santo Domingo, Dominican Republic	0	*
05.07.90	IRMA BN-2B-21 Islander	P2-DNJ	0857	Douglas Airways	Crashed	nr Port Moresby, Papua New Guinea	8	5
12.07.90	Britten-Norman BN-2A-8 Islander	J6-SLW	0006	Eagle Air Services	Crashed	Off Union Island, St Lucia	*	*
13.07.90	Kamov Ka-26	HA-MMR	7303306	Air Service Hungary	Crashed after striking ground	Celldomolk, Hungary	*	*
14.07.90	Boeing 707-349C	ST-ALK	18976	Trans Arabian Air Transport	U/c collapsed on landing	Khartoum, Sudan	*	*
14.07.90	Lockheed Electra 188F	N4465F	1096	TPI International Airways	Dbr when prop broke off & struck fuselage – landed safely	off Aruba, Netherlands Antilles	0	3
14.07.90	PZL Mi-2	SP-SSD	*	Provincial Helicopter Services	Crashed	nr Freetown, Sierra Leone	4	0
17.07.90	de Havilland Canada Caribou	HC-BFH	064	TAME	Crashed & caught fire on landing	Calgary, Canada	*	*
19.07.90	Fokker F-27 Friendship 200	G-BCDO	10234	Air UK	Damaged when u/c collapsed on landing	Amsterdam, Netherlands	0	25
22.07.90	Boeing 737-222	N210US	19555	US Air	Damaged beyond repair after u/c collapse on take-off	Kinston, NC, USA	0	*
24.07.90	Douglas DC-3	RP-C140	19253	Commuter Airlines	Damaged in crash landing	San Juan, Philippines	0	3
25.07.90	Sikorsky S-61N	G-BEWL	61-769	British International Helicopters	Crashed into sea after striking oil rig	North Sea	6	7
25.07.90	Boeing 707-379C	ET-ACQ	19820	Ethiopian Airlines	Ran off runway after aborting take-off	Addis Ababa, Ethiopia	0	*
25.07.90	Beechcraft King Air E90	VH-LFH	LW-255	Operator Unknown	Written off	nr Kingaroy, QL, Australia	*	*
26.07.90	Antonov AN-2	*	*	Aero Manu	Crashed on landing	Iberia, Peru	0	10
31.07.90	Beechcraft King Air B90	OB-1362	LJ-0448	Servicio Expreso Nacional	Crashed on emergency landing	nr Huanuco, Peru	9	0
31.07.90	Aerospatiale Corvette	F-BTTU	37	DGAC/SFACT	Written off	St Yan, France	*	*
01.08.90	Yakovlev YAK-40	SSSR-87453	*	Aeroflot	Crashed into mountain	Stepanakert, Azerbaijan, USSR	47	0
01.08.90	Sikorsky S-76A	JA9943	*	Aero Asahi	Crashed & caught fire	Hakone, Japan	2	0
04.08.90	Boeing-Vertol 107-II	N6672D	2	Columbia Helicopters	Crashed while water bombing	nr Wenatchee, USA	*	*
04.08.90	Bell 204	EC-EKB	345	Sergasa Helicopters	Crashed after hitting trees	Layo, Spain	0	*
05.08.90	Rockwell Turbo Commander 690V	N444GB	1565-21	International Airboats	Crashed on approach out of fuel	Keflavik, Iceland	0	*
09.08.90	Beechcraft E.18S	N563W	*	Operator Unknown	Crashed after take-off	Greenwood, SC, USA	1	*
12.08.90	Lockheed L-382G Hercules	N911SJ	4384	Southern Air Transport	Overran on emergency landing & caught fire	Juba, Sudan	0	*
13.08.90	Rockwell 1121 Jet Commander	N301AJ	048	Operator Unknown	Crashed into ILS equipment on approach	Cozumel, Mexico	1	*
14.08.90	Dornier Do.228-201	B-12268	8129	Formosa Airlines	Undershot on landing	Orchard Island, Taiwan	0	*
15.08.90	Bell 205A-1	C-FJTF	30012	Nationwide Helicopters	Crashed	nr Dillon, SK, Canada	0	*
17.08.90	Sikorsky S-55BT	C-FALA	55546	Athabaska Airways	Crashed	nr La Loche, SK, Canada	1	*
18.08.90	Aerospatiale SA.341G Gazelle	C-GXRS	1319	Northland Helicopters	Crashed after take-off	Edmonton, AB, Canada	4	0
20.08.90	Short 360-300	N730CC	SH.3730	CC Air	Blown into power vehicle by gale & caught fire	Charlotte, NC, USA	0	0
20.08.90	Bell 206L-3 Long Ranger	JA9365	51068	Aero Asahi	Crashed in sea	Okinawa, Japan	4	0
23.08.90	Grumman Gulfstream I	N80RD	198	Rowan Drilling Company	Crashed on take-off	Houston, TX, USA	3	12
27.08.90	Bell 206B JetRanger III	N16933	02338	Omniflight Helicopters	Crashed	East Troy, WI, USA	5	0
04.09.90	Piper PA-31-350 Chieftain	N59783	31-7612024	Frontier Flying Service	Crashed into trees after engine failure	Kaitag, AK, USA	3	0
06.09.90	Mitsubishi MU-2L	N82MA	665	International Flight Center	Crashed after take-off	Nashville, TN, USA	1	*
07.09.90	MBB Bo.105CB	A6-ALE	S-108	Aerogulf Services	Crashed in sea	Off Jebel Ali, United Arab Emirates	0	3
09.09.90	Yakovlev YAK-40	SSSR-87914	*	Aeroflot	Crashed into Aeroflot YAK-40 on landing	Pavlodar, Kazakhstan, USSR	0(0)	*
09.09.90	Yakovlev YAK-40	*	*	Aeroflot	Struck by crashing YAK-40 CCCP-87914	Pavlodar, Kazakhstan, USSR	0(0)	*
11.09.90	Boeing 727-247	OB-1303	20266	Faucett	Crashed out of fuel	Off Newfoundland, Canada	15	0
12.09.90	Cessna 441 Conquest II	OY-CGM	0229	Nuna Air	Crashed	Off Sondre Stromfjord, Greenland	8	0
12.09.90	Cessna U206F Super Skywagon	LN-ASC	*	Fjellfly	Crashed into lake	nr Rogeland, Norway	5	0
14.09.90	Yakovlev YAK-42	SSSR-42351	*	Aeroflot	Crashed on approach	Sverdlovsk, RSFSR, USSR	4	125
16.09.90	Learjet 24	N500P	24-119	Connie Kalitta Services	Overran runway on ldg after being stolen by drunken pilot	Morristown, TN, USA	0	*
16.09.90	Antonov AN-26	YN-BYX	27312405	Aeronica	Written off	Nicaragua	*	*
20.09.90	Boeing 707-321B	N720MJ	20028	Omega Air	Crashed on take-off	Marana, AZ, USA	1	2
20.09.90	Antonov AN-2	OB-1349	*	Aero Manu	Overturned on emergency landing	Saylla Chico, Peru	0	7
21.09.90	Piper PA-31-350 Chieftain	N3558W	31-8052072	PM Air	Crashed	nr Flagstaff, AZ, USA	1	*

Date	Type	Reg'n	C/n	Operator	Accident	Location	F	S
22.09.90	Rockwell Turbo Commander 690B	N81628	11396	Westport Air Travel	Crashed	Byram Reservoir, NY, USA	0	6
24.09.90	Conair Firecat	F-ZBAT	DHC-29	Securite Civile	Crashed into mountain	nr Calvi, Corsica, France	1	*
24.09.90	Cessna Citation I	N79DD	500-0254	Hi-Tech Helicopters	Crashed on approach	San Luis Obispo, CA, USA	4	*
24.09.90	Cessna TU206G Stationair	OB-1265	U206-06565	Aero Taxi Rios	Crashed into mountain	nr Tabalosos, Peru	0	2
26.09.90	Embraer Bandeirante 110P1	PT-FAW	110.368	Pernambuco District Government	Crashed after take-off	Off Fernando do Noronha, Brazil	11	0
27.09.90	Type Unknown	*	*	Aero Asahi	Crashed into mountain	Kyushu Island, Japan	10	0
29.09.90	Lockheed PV-2V Harpoon	N7250	*	Operator Unknown	Crashed after take-off	Clear Lake, CA, USA	7	0
29.09.90	Cessna 402	N82922	*	Victoria Air	Crashed out of fuel	off Santo Domingo, Dominican Rep	1	*
oo.09.90	Convair 240-23	HI-376CT	177	Aerochago	Crashed	Location Unknown	*	*
02.10.90	Boeing 737-247	B-2510	23189	Xiamen Airlines	Crashed on landing after hijack & struck 707 & 757	Guangzhou, China	84{1} (48)	20
02.10.90	Boeing 707-3J6B	B-2402	20714	China Southwest Airlines	Struck by crashing Xiamen Airlines B737 B-2510	Guangzhou, China	1{1} (131)	0
02.10.90	Boeing 757-21B	B-2812	24758	China Southern Airlines	Struck by crashing Xiamen Airlines B737 B-2510	Guangzhou, China	47{1} (85)	71
02.10.90	Bell 214ST	LN-OML	28135	Helikopter Service	Crashed into mountain on rescue flight	Alden Island, Norway	5	0
02.10.90	Antonov AN-32	SSSR-69306	*	Aeroflot	Damaged after taxiing into hole in runway	Ufa, RSFSR, USSR	0	*
04.10.90	Fokker F-27 Friendship 600	EP-ANA	10554	Iran Asseman Airlines	Overran on landing & crashed into wall	Ramsar, Iran	*	*
05.10.90	Cessna 172	DQ-FEH	*	Sunflower Airlines	Crashed	Bua, Fiji	*	*
10.10.90	Antonov AN-8	*	*	Aeroflot	Crashed on approach	Novosibirsk, RSFSR, USSR	5	0
11.10.90	Grumman Gulfstream I	XB-ESO	015	Operator Unknown	Damaged on landing	Mexico	*	*
12.10.90	LET 410UVP Turbolet	SSSR-67331	820831	Aeroflot	Damaged in hard landing	Odessa, Ukraine, USSR	*	*
12.10.90	Rockwell Turbo Commander 690C	N45Q	11623	Operator Unknown	Written off	Location Unknown	*	*
19.10.90	Douglas DC-3	CP-735	16805/33553	Bolivian Air Flight International	Missing – presumed crashed	nr Bella Vista, Bolivia	*	*
20.10.90	Tupolev TU-154	SSSR-85268	268	Aeroflot	Crashed on take-off after nosewheel failed	Kutayissi, Georgia, USSR	0	171
20.10.90	Partenavia P.68B	G-BMCB	156	Air Kilroe	Crashed	nr Castle Donington, UK	1	0
22.10.90	Cessna U206F Stationair	OB-1262	U206-02209	Aero Lima	Caught fire after emergency landing	Aucallacu, Peru	*	*
24.10.90	Yakovlev YAK-40	CU-T1202	9631449	Cubana	Crashed on approach	Santiago de Cuba, Cuba	10	0
oo.10.90	Lockheed PV-2 Harpoon	N7428C	*	Operator Unknown	Crashed & caught fire	Conroy, TX, USA	*	*
03.11.90	Rockwell Turbo Commander 690V	N541F	1509-45	M.L.Bryan	Crashed after take-off	Fort Lauderdale, FL, USA	2	0
04.11.90	IRMA BN-2B-21 Islander	OB-T-1207	0359	Aero Bellavista	Crashed into mountain	La Escalera, Peru	0	12
07.11.90	Mitsubishi MU-2G	VH-WMU	512	Operator Unknown	Written off	Bathurst, Australia	*	*
09.11.90	de Havilland DH.9B	G-EAQN	P.37E	Aircraft Transport & Travel	Crashed	Le Bourget, France	*	*
09.11.90	Beechcraft King Air C90	7Q-YMM	LJ-0880	Operator Unknown	Crashed into dam after engine failure	nr Blantyre, Malawi	*	*
13.11.90	Beechcraft King Air A90	N2EP	LJ-0284	Flight Safety International	Ran off runway on attempted go-around	Crestview, FL, USA	3	0
14.11.90	McDonnell Douglas DC-9-32	I-ATJA	47641	Alitalia	Crashed on approach	Zurich, Switzerland	46	0
16.11.90	Boeing 727-2J0	6Y-JMO	21107	Air Jamaica	Damaged on landing	Curacao, Netherlands Antilles	0	*
17.11.90	Tupolev TU-154M	SSSR-85664	818	Aeroflot	Caught fire in air & crash landed	Trutnov, Czechoslovakia	0	6
18.11.90	CASA 212 Aviocar 200	FAC.1150	304	Satena	Crashed into jungle	SW of Medellin, Colombia	15	0
19.11.90	Mil Mi-8	*	*	Aeroflot	Crash landed after engine failure	nr Ashkhabad, Turkmenistan, USSR	15	*
19.11.90	Cessna T210N Centurion	OB-1358	T210-63675	America de Aviacion	Crashed in heavy rain	Pinata Mt, Peru	6	0
21.11.90	de Havilland Canada Dash 8-103	HS-SKI	172	Bangkok Airways	Crashed in heavy rain	Koh Samui, Thailand	36	0
21.11.90	Ilyushin IL-62M	SSSR-86546	62301	Aeroflot	Crashed on approach	Yakutsk, RSFSR, USSR	176	0
21.11.90	Beechcraft Super King Air 200	D-IGSW	BB-0669	GSW Charterflug	Crashed	Keller Joch Mt, Austria	3	0
21.11.90	Fokker F-27 Friendship 600	5A-DBN	10436	Libyan Red Crescent	Crashed on landing	Labrak, Libya	*	*
21.11.90	Ilyushin IL-62	SSSR-86613	51901	Aeroflot	Damaged beyond repair	Yakutsk-Magan, RSFSR, USSR	*	*
23.11.90	Bell 206B JetRanger II	HC-BFR	00430	Helipet	Crashed on take-off	Shushufindi, Ecuador	*	*
25.11.90	Aerospatiale 330J Puma	I-EHPA	1133	Elitos	Crashed at sea in storm	Off Ravenna, Italy	13	0
28.11.90	Aerospatiale 330J Puma	A4O-AX	1631	Omani Royal Flight	Crashed	Seeb, Oman	1	0
29.11.90	Cessna Citation II	N97QS	550-0097	Daily Variety	Crashed on approach in fog	Sebring, FL, USA	0	*
29.11.90	Nord 262C-62	TR-KJB	090	Gabon Air Force	Crashed	Libreville, Gabon	*	*
29.11.90	Cessna T210N Centurion	OB-1255	T210-64770	Aero Pacifico	Crashed in emergency landing	nr Iquitos, Peru	1	1
30.11.90	Yakovlev YAK-40	SSSR-87934	*	Aeroflot	Broke in half on landing	Dixon, RSFSR, USSR	0	35

Date	Type	Reg'n	C/n	Operator	Accident	Location	F	S
oo.11.90	Dornier Do.228-201	5N-ARF	8047	Afrimex	Damaged beyond repair	Nigeria	*	*
01.12.90	Rockwell Turbo Commander 690A	N400N	11156	Aero Air	Crashed into mountain	nr Kelso, WA, USA	*	*
03.12.90	McDonnell Douglas DC-9-14	N3313L	45708	Northwest Airlines	Struck by Northwest B.727 N278US after entering runway	Detroit, MI, USA	8(0)	29
03.12.90	Antonov AN-32	SSSR-69310	*	Aeroflot	Damaged in crash landing	Ufa, RSFSR, USSR	0	*
04.12.90	Boeing 707-321C	ST-SAC	19377	Trans Arabian Air Transport	Crashed on approach	Nairobi, Kenya	10	0
04.12.90	Cessna 441 Conquest II	F-ODUK	0270	Tahiti Conquest Airlines	Crashed on emergency landing	Papeete, French Polynesia	3	0
06.12.90	IPTN 332C Super Puma	PK-PUI	NSP4/2022	Pelita Air Service	Crashed into sea	nr Matak, Indonesia	10	2
10.12.90	Cessna 337 Skymaster	AP-BDW	*	Raji Aviation	Crash landed	Karachi, Pakistan	0	*
12.12.90	Antonov AN-12	SSSR-29110	*	Aeroflot	Crashed out of fuel	nr Kiev, Ukraine, USSR	*	*
14.12.90	Antonov AN-24	SSSR-47164	89901706	Aeroflot	Crashed short of runway	Shakhtyorsk, RSFSR, USSR	*	*
15.12.90	Embraer Bandeirante 110P1	HK-3195X	110.414	AIRES	Siezed by rebels on landing and set on fire	Villa Garzon, Colombia	0	*
19.12.90	Bell 206B JetRanger III	HC-BHO	15002	Helipet	Crashed with underslung load	Tarapoa, Ecuador	*	*
21.12.90	Cessna 208 Caravan I	N9444F	208-00104	Markair Express	Crashed into mountain	False Pass, AK, USA	*	*
27.12.90	Mil Mi-8	*	*	MAS Air	Crashed on landing in fog	Bursa, Turkey	0	17
oo.oo.90	IRMA BN-2A-9 Islander	F-OGSM	0688	Aviation Sans Frontiers	Written off	Location Unknown	*	*
oo.oo.90	Douglas DC-6B	CP-1953	45516	Frigorificos Santa Rita	Crashed into swamp after belly landing	San Ignace, Bolivia	0	*
oo.oo.90	Mitsubishi MU-2G	VH-UZD	513	Operator Unknown	Written off	Location Unknown	*	*
oo.oo.90	LET 410M Turbolet	OK-FDC	750408	Aero Vodochody	Damaged beyond repair	Lecany, Czechoslovakia	*	*
oo.oo.90	Antonov AN-2	SSSR-07308	IG149-12	Aeroflot	Crashed after mid-air collision	USSR	*	*
05.01.91	Cessna 421 Golden Eagle	N421H	*	R.Shanks	Crashed in bad weather	Muskogee, OK, USA	6	0
05.01.91	Douglas DC-3	EC-EQH	16310/33058	Transporte Aereo de Mercania	Damaged by fire on landing	Palma, Spain	0	*
05.01.91	Piper PA-31 Navajo	9Y-PIA	*	Nealco Air Services	Crashed	River Demerara, Trinidad & Tobago	2	*
10.01.91	Boeing 707-3K1C	YR-ABD	21651	Tarom	Wing hit runway on landing and aircraft caught fire	Bucharest, Romania	0	*
11.01.91	Learjet 25C	PT-KKV	25C-172	Belair Taxi Aereo	Crashed in heavy rain	nr Belo Horizonte, Brazil	5	0
11.01.91	Mil Mi-8	*	*	Polish Police	Crashed during storm	nr Cisna, Poland	10	0
11.01.91	Beechcraft King Air F90	N311DS	LA-041	Ridgaire	Crashed after take-off	Mangham, TX, USA	*	*
12.01.91	Tupolev TU-134A-1	VN-A126	60435	Vietnam Airlines	Damaged in hard landing	Ho Chi Minh City, Vietnam	0	*
15.01.91	Dornier Do.228-101	D-CICE	7073	Alfred Wegener Institute	Crashed on landing short	Antarctica	*	*
17.01.91	Cessna 402C	OY-SUM	402C-0505	Muk Air	Crashed on approach	Roenne, Denmark	1	0
17.01.91	Antonov AN-32	SSSR-48109	*	Liberia Air Cargo	Crashed on take-off when u/c retracted in error	Freetown, Sierra Leone	0	*
30.01.91	IPTN 212 Aviocar 200	PK-NCY	258/78N	Merpati Nusantara Airlines	Crashed in jungle on emergency landing	Jalaludin, Indonesia	1	20
30.01.91	British Aerospace Jetstream 31	N167PC	710	CC Air	Crashed on landing in poor weather	Beckley, WV, USA	0	19
31.01.91	Beechcraft King Air B90	OB-1361	LJ-0451	Aero Huaylas	Crashed on take-off	Peru	0	2
31.01.91	Cessna 402C	N5775C	402C-0040	Aero Coach	Damaged beyond repair when struck by vehicle during taxiing	Miami, FL, USA	0	*
31.01.91	Cessna T206F Stationair	OB-1311	206-03132	Aero Huaylas	Shot down by FAP Tucano on drug smuggling flight	Peru	0	3
01.02.91	Boeing 737-3B7	N388US	23310	US Air	Crashed into Skywest Metro N683AV on landing	Los Angeles, CA, USA	21(12)	68
01.02.91	Fairchild 227AC Metro III	N683AV	AC-683	Skywest Airlines	Struck by landing US Air B.737 N388US	Los Angeles, CA, USA	12(21)	0
05.02.91	Antonov AN-26	*	*	Air Guinee	Crashed on approach	Monrovia, Liberia	0	65
08.02.91	Cessna 208B Caravan I	C-FPEZ	208B-0120	Labrador Airways	Crashed	Goose Bay, Labrador, Canada	*	*
08.02.91	Beechcraft Super King Air 200	F-GHBE	BB-0500	Operator Unknown	Written off	Location Unknown	*	*
10.02.91	Douglas DC-6A	HK-1702	44670	Air Colombia	Crashed after two engines failed on take-off	nr Bogota, Colombia	0	85
14.02.91	Learjet 35A	N535PC	35A-291	Seanaire	Crashed	nr Aspen, CO, USA	3	0
14.02.91	de Havilland Canada Twin Otter 300	447	832	TAME	Crashed into mountain	Mt Paso Macuna, Ecuador	22	0
14.02.91	Antonov AN-2	OB-1350	*	Aero Manu	Crash landed after engine failure	nr Iquitos, Peru	0	15
15.02.91	Airbus A.300C4-620	9K-AHF	327	Kuwait Airways	Destroyed by allied bombing	Baghdad, Iraq	*	*
15.02.91	Airbus A.300C4-620	9K-AHG	332	Kuwait Airways	Destroyed by allied bombing	Baghdad, Iraq	*	*
17.02.91	McDonnell Douglas DC-9-15F	N565PC	47240	Emery Air Freight	Crashed on take-off	Cleveland, OH, USA	2	0
17.02.91	LET 410UVP Turbolet	SSSR-67145	800411	Tatar Airlines	Crashed on take-off	Muslumovo, RSFSR, USSR	*	*
18.02.91	de Havilland Canada Twin Otter 300	HK-2758	770	ACES Colombia	Set on fire by rebels after landing	Otu, Colombia	0	0
20.02.91	British Aerospace 146-200A	CC-CET	E-2061	LAN-Chile	Crashed on landing	Puerta Williams, Chile	20	52
22.02.91	Mitsubishi MU-2 Marquise	N274MA	786SA	Operator Unknown	Written off	Tulsa, OK, USA	*	*
25.02.91	Embraer Bandeirante 110C	CX-BJK/T581	110.079	TAMU	Crash landed out of fuel	nr Montevideo, Uruguay	0	*
27.02.91	Boeing 747-136	G-AWND	19764	British Airways	Destroyed by allied attack on airport	Kuwait City, Kuwait	0	0
oo.02.91	Boeing 767-269ER	9K-AIC	23282	Kuwait Airways	Destroyed by allied bombing	Baghdad, Iraq	*	*

Date	Type	Reg'n	C/n	Operator	Accident	Location	F	S
oo.02.91	Boeing 767-269ER	9K-AIB	23281	Kuwait Airways	Destroyed by allied bombing	Baghdad, Iraq	*	*
oo.02.91	Grumman Gulfstream III	YI-AKI	408	Iraqi Government	Destroyed by allied bombing	Baghdad, Iraq	*	*
oo.02.91	Grumman Gulfstream III	YI-AKJ	419	Iraqi Government	Destroyed by allied bombing	Baghdad, Iraq	*	*
oo.02.91	British Aerospace 125-700B	YI-AKH	257187	Iraqi Government	Destroyed by allied bombing	Muthana, Iraq	*	*
03.03.91	Bell 206L Long Ranger	*	*	Sea World Aviation	Crashed	South Stradbroke Is, Qld, Australia	7	0
04.03.91	Boeing 737-291	N999UA	22742	United Air Lines	Crashed on approach	Colorado Springs, CO, USA	25	0
04.03.91	Antonov AN-24	*	*	Aeroflot	Cockpit destroyed when hijacker set off grenade	Leningrad, RSFSR, USSR	1	*
05.03.91	McDonnell Douglas DC-9-32	YV-23C	47720	Aeropostal	Crashed after take-off	nr Trujillo, Venezuela	43	0
11.03.91	Cessna 402B	D-ICLW	402B-0859	Luft-Taxi Emsland	Crashed in fog	Hassfurt, Germany	6	0
12.03.91	McDonnell Douglas DC-8-62F	N730PL	46161	Air Transport International	Crashed after aborting take-off	New York, NY, USA	0	5
15.03.91	Learjet 35	PT-LIH	35A-433	Lider Taxi Aereo	Crashed near runway	Uberlandia, Brazil	0	*
16.03.91	British Aerospace 125-1A	N831LC	25095	Duncan Aircraft Sales	Crashed after take-off	San Diego, CA, USA	9	0
16.03.91	Lockheed L-382G Hercules	CP-1564	4833	Transafrik	Shot down by rebel missile	Melanje, Angola	9	0
18.03.91	Learjet 25D	PT-LLL	25D-258	Aero Consul	Crashed	Brasilia, Brazil	4	0
18.03.91	Cessna 402C	N5785C	402C-0043	Aero Coach	Crashed on approach	Treasure City, Bahamas	5	0
20.03.91	Piper PA-42-1000 Cheyenne IV	HL5204	42-5527043	Korean Air Lines	Written off	South Korea	*	*
23.03.91	Antonov AN-24B	SSSR-46472	27307910	Aeroflot	Crashed after veering off runway on landing	Tashkent, Uzbekistan, USSR	31	25
23.03.91	Fairchild-Hiller FH.227B	F-GCPZ	561	Transport Aerien Transregional	Destroyed by fire during repainting	Dinard, France	0	0
25.03.91	Boeing 707-385C	ET-AJZ	19433	Ethiopian Airlines	Destroyed by rebel shelling on ground	Asmara, Ethiopia	*	*
31.03.91	Vickers Viscount 745D	HK-1708	138	Intercontinental	Overstressed during violent loss of height	nr Medellin, Colombia	0	*
04.04.91	Douglas DC-3	C-FQNF	15198/26643	Central Mountain Air	Crashed on frozen lake	Thutade Lake, BC, Canada	6	1
05.04.91	Embraer Brasilia 120RT	N270AS	120.218	Atlantic Southeast Airlines	Crashed on approach	Brunswick, GA, USA	23	0
05.04.91	Sikorsky S-61N	ZS-HHN	61-702	Heliavia Aero Taxi	Rotor touched tail on landing in river & capsized under tow	Tesse, Brazil	0	*
07.04.91	Mil Mi-8	TC-HSB	25188	MAS Air	Crashed on landing	Atakoy, Turkey	1	2
07.04.91	Cessna T210N Centurion	OB-1310	T210-63189	Airvas Air Taxi	Crashed in river after engine failure	Caymba River, Peru	3	2
15.04.91	Grumman Gulfstream III	HZ-AFM	324	Saudia	Damaged during high winds on ground	Jeddah, Saudi Arabia	*	*
19.04.91	Dornier Do.228-212	F-OHAB	8196	Air Tahiti	Crashed in sea after engine failure	Off Nuka Hiva, French Polynesia	10	8
22.04.91	Antonov AN-24RV	RDPL-34008	67310702	Lao Aviation	Crashed into buildings on take-off	Luangnamtha, Laos	0	*
25.04.91	Bell 212	SU-CAT	31295	Petroleum Air Services	Crashed	Ras Gharib, Egypt	2	0
oo.04.91	Fairchild 226TC Metro II	OY-BZW	TC-328	Muk Air	Damaged when nosewheel collapsed	Copenhagen, Denmark	0	*
03.05.91	Boeing 727-22C	N425EX	19095	Emery Worldwide	Aborted take-off and damaged by fire	Windsor Locks, CT, USA	0	3
04.05.91	GAF Nomad N22B	N5590M	083	Johnson Inc	Damaged in forced landing	Ricardsville, KY, USA	*	*
05.05.91	Cessna 404 Titan	ST-AHX	404-0657	Nile Safari Aviation	Shot down and crashed	nr Aweil, Sudan	8	0
06.05.91	Grumman G-21A Goose	C-GHAV	1045	Oakley Air	Crashed on approach	Squamish, BC, Canada	2	0
06.05.91	Learjet 25B	N20DL	25B-263	Petrolift Aviation	Damaged when hangar collapsed during tornado	Shreveport, LA, USA	0	*
06.05.91	Cessna Citation I	N41JP	501-0090	Petrolift Aviation	Damaged when hangar collapsed during tornado	Shreveport, LA, USA	0	*
06.05.91	British Aerospace 125-731	N101AD	25284	Franks Petroleum	Damaged when hangar collapsed during tornado	Shreveport, LA, USA	0	*
06.05.91	Beechcraft King Air B90	C-GBTI	LJ-0352	Operator Unknown	Written off	Location Unknown	*	*
07.05.91	Mitsubishi MU-2F	N106MA	184	Operator Unknown	Written off	Lake Texoma, TX, USA	*	*
08.05.91	de Havilland Canada Otter	C-FQRI	326	Harbour Air	Crashed	Cameron Lake, BC, Canada	0	*
09.05.91	Fokker F-27 Friendship 600	PK-MFD	10399	Merpati Nusantara Airlines	Crashed into mountain on approach	Sulawesi, Indonesia	13	0
09.05.91	Mitsubishi MU-2P	F-GGRZ	395SA	Operator Unknown	Written off	Location Unknown	*	*
10.05.91	Douglas DC-3	N134FS	16551/33299	Four Star Air Cargo	Crashed on approach	Aguadilla, Puerto Rico	2	0
12.05.91	Aerospatiale 330J Puma	VH-WOF	1508	Bristow Helicopters	Crashed at sea	Off Dampier, WA, Australia	*	*
12.05.91	Aerospatiale SA.315B Lama	C-GLAY	2500	Liftair International	Crashed	nr Geladin, Ethiopia	2	0
15.05.91	Douglas DC-3	HK-3177	15330/26775	Aerolineas del Este	Crashed on take-off	Villavicencio, Colombia	3	11
18.05.91	Antonov AN-8	*	*	Ministry of Aviation Industry	Crashed	Irkutsk, RSFSR, USSR	1	6
20.05.91	Cessna TU206G Stationair	OB-1434	U206-00229	Peruana de Aviacion	Crashed	nr Palma de Espino, Peru	2	0
21.05.91	Cessna Citation II	5N-AMR	550-0045	Ashaka Cement Company	Crashed	Ashaka, Nigeria	3	0
21.05.91	Mitsubishi MU-2 Marquise	F-GDHS	1532SA	Operator Unknown	Crashed	Macey, France	3	0
21.05.91	Bell 204	N87966	64-13968	Papillon Airways	Crashed	Koyuktolik Bay, AK, USA	1	0
23.05.91	Tupolev TU-154B-1	SSSR-85097	097	Aeroflot	Crashed & broke in half on landing	Leningrad, RSFSR, USSR	13	168
24.05.91	Ilyushin IL-76TD	LZ-INK	0093494835	Metro Cargo Airlines	Crashed into mountain	nr Bakhtaran, Iran	6	4

Date	Type	Reg'n	C/n	Operator	Accident	Location	F	S
26.05.91	Boeing 767-3Z9ER	OE-LAV	24628	Lauda Air	Crashed after engine failure	nr Ban Nong Rong, Thailand	223	0
04.06.91	Rockwell Turbo Commander 690C	ZS-KOF	11617	Operator Unknown	Written off	Location Unknown	*	*
05.06.91	Fokker F-27 Friendship 600	PK-JFF	10410	Sempati Air Transport	Crashed after wing fire	Gresik, Indonesia	0	2
05.06.91	PZL M-18A Dromader	OK-TGE	12018-14	Slovair	Crashed after engine failure	Banska Bystrica, Czechoslovakia	*	*
07.06.91	Douglas DC-3	N102AP	2257	Victoria Air	Crash landed in field after engine failure	Puerto Plato, Dominican Repuiblic	0	*
09.06.91	de Havilland Canada Twin Otter 300	9N-ABA	301	Royal Nepal Airlines	Ran off runway on landing	Lukla, Nepal	*	*
10.06.91	Lockheed L-382B Hercules	J6-SLQ	3099	Carib Air Transport	Crashed on take-off	Luanda, Angola	10	0
10.06.91	PZL M-18 Dromader	HA-MUM	IZ010-10	Air Service Hungary	Crashed after striking ground	Jasztelek, Hungary	*	*
11.06.91	Bell-Boeing V-22 Osprey	163915	*	Bell Aircraft Corporation	Crashed on first test flight	New Castle, DE, USA	0	2
12.06.91	GAF Nomad N24A	N8071L	044	Agape Flights	Crashed at sea	Off Great Inagua, Bahamas	2	0
16.06.91	de Havilland Canada Beaver	C-GJKA	1481	Superior North Air	Crashed after take-off	Sandridge Lake, ON, Canada	4	0
17.06.91	Grumman Gulfstream II	N204RC	034	Castor Trading Co	Crashed into hill on approach	Caracas, Venezuela	4	0
17.06.91	Sikorsky S-76	N541BN	760209	Petroleum Helicopters	Crashed attempting to land on oil platform	Gulf of Mexico	*	*
18.06.91	Grumman Turbo Goose	*	*	Airways Corporation	Crashed into mountain	Caracas, Venezuela	4	0
19.06.91	Canadair CL-215-5	C-GFQA	1091	Transport Canada	Written off	Quebec, Canada	*	*
20.06.91	Douglas DC-6A	HK-3511	45132	Aerosucre	Crashed on landing	Barranquilla, Colombia	2	11
21.06.91	Cessna 404 Titan II	ZS-LUI	404-0100	AOC Surveys	Destroyed by fire	Kameeldrift, South Africa	*	*
25.06.91	Aerospatiale AS.350D Astar	VH-NBN	*	Jayrow Helicopters	Crashed	Bass Strait, Australia	0	1
26.06.91	BAC One-Eleven 402AP	5N-AOW	094	Okada Air	Crash landed after airport failed to open	Sokoto, Nigeria	3	22
27.06.91	Lockheed Tristar 1	D-AERI	1114	LTU International Airways	Destroyed by fire on ground during maintenance	Dusseldorf, Germany	0	4
27.06.91	Sikorsky S-64E	N6959R	64002	Erickson Air Crane	Became airborne while refuelling and crashed into vehicles	USA	*	*
27.06.91	Aerospatiale AS.360 Dauphin	*	*	Securite Civile	Crashed into power lines	Chateaulin, France	4	0
28.06.91	Mitsubishi MU-2B-36A	*	*	Operator Unknown	Crashed after avoiding collision with Skywest aircraft	Off Goleta, CA, USA	4	0
30.06.91	de Havilland DH.89A Dragon Rapide	G-AHGD	6862	P.A. & A.Wood	Crashed during air display	Audley End, Essex, UK	1	0
01.07.91	Learjet 25XR	N458J	25XR-106	New Creations	Written off	Location Unknown	*	*
02.07.91	Learjet 23	N500FM	23-088	American International Airways	Crashed on landing	Columbia, TN, USA	0	*
04.07.91	de Havilland Canada Twin Otter 300	HK-2889X	606	Helicol	Crashed into mountain in bad weather	nr El Yopal, Colombia	3	0
09.07.91	CASA 212 Aviocar 200	OB-1218	232	Aero Chasqui	Shot down by drunken police in mistake for drug runner	Bellavista, Peru	17	0
09.07.91	Aerospatiale AS.350B Ecureuil	JA9272	1416	Imperial Airlines	Crashed into power cables	Ichihara, Japan	1	0
10.07.91	Beechcraft C99	N7217L	U226	L'Express Airlines	Crashed on landing in thunderstorm	Birmingham, AL, USA	13{4}	15
10.07.91	Aerospatiale SA.341G Gazelle	F-GKYC	*	Heli Ocean	Crashed into river	nr St Nazaire, France	*	*
11.07.91	McDonnell Douglas DC-8-61	C-GMXQ	45982	Nigeria Airways	Crashed on emergency landing due to fire	Jeddah, Saudi Arabia	261	0
23.07.91	Learjet 23	N959SC	23-045A	Bard Air Corporation	Crashed on take-off	Detroit, MI, USA	3	*
25.07.91	Britten-Norman BN-2A-6 Islander	YJ-RV4	0220	Vanair	Crashed	Espirirtu Santo, Vanuatu	9	0
25.07.91	Fokker F-27 Friendship 400M	7T-VRM	10496	Air Algerie	Damaged when nosewheel collapsed on landing	Inguezzam, Algeria	*	*
oo.07.91	Aerospatiale SA.316B Alouette III	F-ZBAG	1517	Securite Civile	Crashed into mountains	Nr Ajaccio, Corsica, France	*	*
02.08.91	Cessna R172K	OB-1417	*	America de Aviacion	Crashed	nr Satipo, Peru	0	2
04.08.91	Kamov Ka-26	HA-MNP	7505206	Air Service Hungary	Crashed after rotor failure	Budakeszi, Hungary	*	*
06.08.91	IRMA BN-2A-27 Islander	DQ-FCN	0676	Fiji Air	Crashed on approach	Rarotonga, Cook Islands	6	4
06.08.91	Canadair CL-215-1A10	I-CFSV	1077	Securite Civile	Crashed while fire bombing	nr Savona, Italy	2	0
10.08.91	Bell 212	LN-OSC	31210	Helikopter Service	Crashed after rotor struck flame tower on oil rig	North Sea	3	0
11.08.91	Grumman G-164B AgCat	ET-AJE	001E	Admas Air Service	Crashed after engine failure	Ataki, Ethiopia	*	*
14.08.91	Ilyushin IL-18V	YR-IMH	185008301	Tarom	Crashed in bad weather	Uricani, Romania	9	0
14.08.91	Beechcraft E18S	RP-C707	BA-126	Commuter Air Philippines	Crashed in sea after take-off	Masbate, Philippines	*	*
14.08.91	British Aerospace 748 2A	C-FKTL	1613	Kelner Airways	Destroyed by fire during cargo transfer	Big Trout Lake, ON, Canada	0	0
15.08.91	Fokker F-27 Friendship 100	J5-GBB	10119	Air Bissau	Crashed	nr Dori, Burkina Faso	2	0
16.08.91	Boeing 737-2A8	VT-EFL	21497	Indian Airlines	Crashed on approach	Imphal, India	69	0
20.08.91	Britten-Norman BN-2A-26 Islander	N68HA	2009	Temesco Airlines	Crashed	Ketchikan, AK, USA	4	*
20.08.91	Beechcraft E18S	N63B	BA-119	Northern Airmotive	Forced landed & caught fire	Martinsville, OH, USA	*	*
21.08.91	LET 410UVP Turbolet	SSSR-67091	810732	Far East Corporation	Damaged after aborting take-off	Polina Osopemko, RSFSR, USSR	*	*
21.08.91	Grumman G-164B AgCat	ET-AJM	*	Admas Air Service	Badly damaged on landing	Harere, Ethiopia	*	*
26.08.91	Boeing 727-281	HL7350	20469	Korean Air	Damaged when belly landed by mistake	Taegu, South Korea	0	*
26.08.91	Bell 412	N3909F	*	Petroleum Helicopters	Crashed into sea after rotor failure	Off Cameron, LA, USA	0	12
27.08.91	LET 410UVP Turbolet	SSSR-67099	841325	Aeroflot	Damaged in forced landing	nr Guriev, Kazakhstan, USSR	*	*

Date	Type	Reg'n	C/n	Operator	Accident	Location	F	S
31.08.91	Boeing 707-323C	CP-1365	18692	Lloyd Aereo Boliviano	Destroyed in hangar fire during repainting	Dothan, AL, USA	0	0
02.09.91	Lockheed L-100-20 Hercules	N521SJ	4250	Southern Air Transport	Blown up by mine on take-off	Wau, Sudan	0	5
03.09.91	IRMA BN-2A-21 Islander	PK-VIP	0752	Dirgantara Air Service	Crashed after take-off	Sampit, Indonesia	3	5
03.09.91	Short Skyvan 3	9M-AZB	SH.1975	ADTEC Rajawari Udara	Crashed after engine failure	Long Seridan, Sarawak, Malaysia	14	6
04.09.91	Grumman Gulfstream II	N204C	143	Du Pont Co Inc	Crashed into mountains on approach	Kota Kinabalu, Malaysia	12	0
08.09.91	Antonov AN-2	YU-BOC	IG216-03	PA Osijek	Destroyed in Federal air raid	Osijek, Yugoslavia	*	*
08.09.91	Rockwell Turbo Commander 690A	HK-2415	11100	Occidental de Aviacion	Crashed on landing	Bolivar Quay, Colombia	7	0
10.09.91	Fokker F-27 Friendship 400M	9Q-CBE	10655	Scibe Airlift	Damaged by rebel Rwandan gunfire	Goma, Zaire	*	*
11.09.91	Embraer Brasilia 120RT	N33071	120.077	Continental Express	Crashed due to structural failure	nr Laredo, TX, USA	14	0
13.09.91	Hindustan Do.228-101	VT-EPV	7099/2017	UB Air	Damaged beyond repair	Madras, India	*	*
14.09.91	Tupolev TU-154B-2	CU-T1227	541	Cubana	Crashed on landing	Mexico City, Mexico	0	*
15.09.91	Antonov AN-2	YU-BOZ	1G225-30	PA Osijek	Destroyed in Federal air raid	Varazdin, Yugoslavia	*	*
15.09.91	Antonov AN-2	YU-BBN	IG51-26	Operator Unknown	Damaged by Federal air raid	Varazdin, Yugoslavia	*	*
15.09.91	Antonov AN-2	YU-BFP	IG99-13	Privredna Avijacija	Destroyed in Federal air raid	Varazdin, Yugoslavia	*	*
16.09.91	BAC One-Eleven 204AF	5N-KBG	082	Kabo Air	Damaged in belly landing	Port Harcourt, Nigeria	0	*
16.09.91	Handley Page Dart Herald 401	HK-2701	178	Lineas Aereas Colombianas	Crashed on approach	Barranquilla, Colombia	5	0
16.09.91	Antonov AN-74	*	*	Aeroflot	Caught fire and crashed on take-off	Petropavlosk-Kamchatskiy, RSFSR,USSR	13	0
18.09.91	Lockheed L-100-30 Hercules	ET-AJL	5029	Ethiopian Airlines	Crashed into mountains after take-off	nr Djibouti, Djibouti	4	0
19.09.91	Convair 580	C-FICA	098	Canair Cargo	Crashed	nr Burlington, VT, USA	2	0
19.09.91	Antonov AN-2	YU-BFS	IG99-15	PA Osijek	Destroyed in Federal air raid	Osijek, Yugoslavia	*	*
19.09.91	Antonov AN-2R	YU-BHU	IG135-44	PA Osijek	Destroyed in Federal air raid	Osijek, Yugoslavia	0	2
22.09.91	Antonov AN-2	*	*	Operator Unknown	Crashed on emergency landing	Lombok, Indonesia	0	7
23.09.91	Antonov AN-12	SSSR-13320	07345407	Aeroflot	Crashed out of fuel	Khatanga, RSFSR, USSR	1	15
24.09.91	Bell 206B JetRanger II	EI-BST	01584	Celtic Helicopters	Crashed during filming	nr Dunquin, Eire	0	2
25.09.91	Dassault Falcon 20C	I-NLAE	134	Grup-Air	Overshot on landing and crashed into trees	Kiel, Germany	1	*
25.09.91	Cessna 185	*	*	Missionary Aviation Fellowship	Crashed on landing	Pontianak Supadio, Indonesia	*	*
26.09.91	Antonov AN-24	SSSR-46724	*	Aeroflot	Crashed in sea after take-off	St Petersburg, RSFSR, USSR	10	0
27.09.91	de Havilland Canada Twin Otter 300	H4-SIA	271	Solomon Islands Airlines	Crashed after take-off	Guadalcanal Is, Solomon Islands	15	0
27.09.91	Embraer Bandeirante 110P1	PT-LRJ	110.384	Nordeste	Crashed on take-off	Sao Paulo, Brazil	0	*
29.09.91	Aerospatiale Caravelle IIR	HK-3288X	219	Aerosucre	U/c collapsed on take-off	Bogota, Colombia	0	*
29.09.91	Curtiss C-46C	HK-3238	30268	CORAL	Crashed short of runway	Villavicencio, Colombia	*	*
04.10.91	Aerospatiale AS.350B Ecureuil	*	*	Pacific Helicopters	Crashed into mountains after take-off	nr Kopi, Papua new Guinea	3	0
08.10.91	Embraer Bandeirante 110P1	N731A	110.275	BAC Charter	Crashed in poor weather	nr Narssarssuaq, Greenland	*	*
08.10.91	Cessna 402A	PK-WWE	402-0002	Deraya Air Taxi	Crashed on approach	Ketapang, Indonesia	1	8
11.10.91	Beechcraft King Air A90	OB-1305	LJ-0302	STAT	Crashed into mountain	nr Rio Diamante, Peru	4	0
11.10.91	Curtiss C-46D	HK-750	22230	LANSA	Crashed on drug smuggling flight with false regn N500	Quirigua, Guatemala	6	0
13.10.91	Bell 214ST	YV-O-CVG-4	28181	EDELCA	Crashed into hill	Aponguao Falls, Venezuela	12	0
17.10.91	Lockheed P-3A Orion	N924AU	5072	Aero Union	Crashed into mountain	nr Missoula, MT, USA	2	0
19.10.91	Beechcraft 99	N299GL	U102	Frontier Flying Service	Damaged beyond repair	Unalakleet, AK, USA	*	*
23.10.91	Antonov AN-28	SSSR-28924	*	Aeroflot	Damaged in hard landing	Shelopugino, RSFSR, USSR	*	*
25.10.91	Britten-Norman Trislander	PK-KTC	1017	Bali Air	Crashed	Tumbang Miri, Indonesia	17	0
26.10.91	de Havilland Canada Twin Otter 300	N724CA	793	Markair Express	Crashed on take-off	Chevak, AK, USA	0	*
27.10.91	Rockwell Turbo Commander 690C	HC-BHU	11634	Transporte Aereo Ejecutvo	Believed crashed after being hijacked	nr Lago Agrio, Ecuador	*	*
29.10.91	Antonov AN-2	*	*	Yevlakh Air Transport	Crashed in fog	Khanabad, Azerbaijan, USSR	3	0
oo.10.91	Fairchild Merlin IIB	N61PH	T26-143	Operator Unknown	Written off	Location Unknown	*	*
02.11.91	Rockwell Turbo Commander 690B	N799V	11407	Operator Unknown	Crashed after pilot suffered heart attack	Wichita, KS, USA	2	0
02.11.91	Mil Mi-8	*	*	Aeroflot	Crashed into cliff	nr Irkutsk, RSFSR, USSR	9	0
07.11.91	Yakovlev YAK-40	SSSR-87526	*	Aeroflot	Crashed into mountain	Makhachkala, RSFSR, USSR	51	0
08.11.91	Bell 206B JetRanger II	JA9127	01344	Aero Asahi	Crashed on forced landing	Rubishibe, Japan	0	1
10.11.91	Boeing 727-25	YN-BXW	18284	Aeronica	Destroyed in oxygen fire on ground	Managua, Nicaragua	*	*
11.11.91	Embraer Bandeirante 110P1	PT-SCU	110.314	Nordeste	Crashed after take-off	Recife, Brazil	15(2)	0
16.11.91	Antonov AN-22	*	*	Aeroflot	Crashed on landing	Amderma, RSFSR, USSR	*	*
17.11.91	Boeing 737-2K6	EI-CBL	20957	TAN-SAHSA	Overran on landing	San Jose, Costa Rica	0	*

Date	Type	Reg'n	C/n	Operator	Accident	Location	F	S
20.11.91	Mil Mi-8	*	*	Aeroflot	Crashed on approach	Martunisikiy, RSFSR, USSR	22	0
21.11.91	Yakovlev YAK-40	*	*	Azerbaijan Airlines	Crashed	nr Khodzavend, RSFSR, USSR	20	0
22.11.91	Bell 214ST	VH-HOQ	28121	Lloyd Helicopters	Crashed after take-off from tanker *Skua Venture*	Off Darwin, NT, Australia	0	17
22.11.91	Beechcraft King Air B100	N24169	BE-038	Ligon Brothers	Crashed on approach in poor weather	Romeo, MI, USA	3	0
25.11.91	Douglas DC-3	C9-STD	*	Scan Air Charter	Crashed	Sena, Mozambique	1	2
26.11.91	Antonov AN-24	SSSR-47823	17307204	Tartarstan Airlines	Crashed on landing	Bugulma, RSFSR, USSR	41	0
26.11.91	Boeing 707-369C	7O-ACS	20547	Alyemda	U/c collapsed on landing	Amman, Jordan	0	*
27.11.91	Beechcraft Beechjet 400A	I-ALSU	RK-11	Aliseirio	Crashed on landing	Palma, Majorca, Spain	0	2
28.11.91	Convair 240-52	N450GA	52-83	Rhoades International	Crashed on take-off	Akron, OH, USA	*	*
28.11.91	Britten-Norman BN-2A Islander	N127JL	0069	New England Airlines	Crashed at sea	Off Block Is, RI, USA	8	0
oo.11.91	Beechcraft Beechjet 400	N3123T	RJ-23	Transair America	Crashed into tower on landing	Bucharest, Romania	0	*
07.12.91	Boeing 707-351C	5A-DJT	18888	Libyan Arab Airlines	Damaged by fire after aborting take-off	Tripoli, Libya	0	199
10.12.91	Piper PA-31-350 Chieftain	N350MR	31-7652100	Las Vegas Airlines	Crashed in bad weather	Mt Wilson, NV, USA	5	0
11.12.91	Beechcraft Beechjet 400	N25BR	RJ-57	BR Air	Crashed into mountain	Rome, GA, USA	9	0
11.12.91	Curtiss C-46F	HK-2716	22478	Lineas Aereas Suramericanas	Crashed into hill	nr Bogota, Colombia	4	0
15.12.91	de Havilland Heron 2B	DQ-FEE	14057	Fiji Air	Damaged in belly landing	Suva, Fiji	0	*
17.12.91	McDonnell Douglas DC-9-32	I-RIBN	47339	Alitalia	Damaged overrunning on landing	Warsaw, Poland	0	96
22.12.91	Douglas DC-3	D-CCCC	7353	Classic Wings	Crashed in fog	nr Heidelberg, Germany	28	4
27.12.91	McDonnell Douglas MD-81	OY-KHO	53003	Scandinavian Airlines System	Crashed after take-off	nr Stockholm, Sweden	0	129
27.12.91	Piper PA-31-310 Navajo	5Y-SRV	31-7300902	Eagle Aviation	Crashed after colliding with vulture	Maasai Mara Reserve, Kenya	9	0
28.12.91	Beechcraft 1900C	N811BE	UB-49	Business Express	Crashed at sea	Off Block Island, RI, USA	3	0
29.12.91	Boeing 747-2R7F	B-198	22390	China Airlines	Crashed after take-off	nr Taipei, Taiwan	5	0
oo.12.91	de Havilland Canada Twin Otter 300	C-GBJE	566	Air Inuit	Damaged beyond repair	Canada	*	*
oo.oo.91	Rockwell 1121 Jet Commander	LV-BDB	012	Operator Unknown	Written off	Moron, Argentina	*	*
oo.oo.91	Beechcraft Super King Air 300	N2614C	FA-100	Operator Unknown	Written off	Location Unknown	*	*
03.01.92	Beechcraft 1900C-1	N55000	UC-135	Commutair	Crashed on approach	Saranak Lake, NY, USA	2	2
03.01.92	Antonov AN-28	SSSR-28706	*	Tajikistan Directorate	Damaged when landed short of runway	Lyahsh, Tajikistan	0	*
04.01.92	Cessna 421C Golden Eagle	N2654M	*	F.Gearhart	Crashed into mountain in snow	Red Mountain, CA, USA	4	0
05.01.92	Piper PA-31-350 Chieftain	5H-IAS	31-7852064	Island Air Services	Damaged beyond repair	Shinyanga, Tanzania	*	*
06.01.92	Douglas DC-3	C9-ATH	9410	African Air Carriers	Damaged beyond repair	Mozambique	*	*
11.01.92	Britten-Norman BN-2A-26 Islander	P2-DWA	0113	Heli Niugini	Damaged beyond repair on landing	Komo, Papua New Guinea	*	*
13.01.92	Cessna 210 Centurion	N22592	*	Air Vegas	Crashed	Temple Bar, AZ, USA	2	0
15.01.92	Beechcraft King Air B90	HR-IAI	LJ-0489	Islena Airlines	Undershot on landing	La Ceiba, Honduras	0	2
18.01.92	McDonnell Douglas DC-9-31	N964VJ	47373	US Air	Dbr in heavy landing	Elmira, NY, USA	0	37
20.01.92	Airbus A.320-111	F-GGED	015	Air Inter	Crashed into mountain in fog	nr Strasbourg, France	87	9
24.01.92	Beechcraft 99	N42AK	U148	Nature Island Express	Crashed at sea	Off Canefield, Dominica	2	0
25.01.92	Cessna 421C Golden Eagle	D-IBHH	421C-0162	Air Boniats	Crashed after engine fire on approach	Munich, Germany	5	0
26.01.92	Antonov AN-2R	YU-BKF	IG167-27	Operator Unknown	Crashed into cables	Sinj, Yugoslavia	*	*
27.01.92	Beechcraft C18S	C-FRVR	6148	Air Rainbow	Crashed on take-off	Nanaimo, BC, Canada	7	2
30.01.92	Bell 212	PK-HMZ	30662	Gatari Air Service	Crashed in sea	Off Terbang, Indonesia	0	3
02.02.92	El Gavilan 358	*	*	El Gavilan	Crashed on approach	Columbus, MI, USA	0	*
02.02.92	Piper PA-18-150 Super Cub	I-BALR	*	Transavio	Crashed in mountains	nr Carrara, Italy	1	0
03.02.92	Embraer Bandeirante 110	PT-TBB	110.005	Nordeste	Crashed into mountain	Caetite, Brazil	12	0
03.02.92	Douglas DC-4	N74AF	10460	West Indies Air Transport	Ran away on ground & collided with Constellation HI-542CT	Borinquen, Puerto Rico	0(0)	1
03.02.92	Lockheed C-121A Super Constellation	HI-542CT	4825	AMSA	Damaged when struck by DC-4 N74AF on ground	Borinquen, Puerto Rico	0(0)	0
06.02.92	Beechcraft E18S	C-FRGT	BA-154	Ministic Air	Crashed	nr Garden Hill, MN, Canada	*	*
08.02.92	Lockheed P2H Neptune	N70600	726-7227	Hawkins & Powers Aviation	Crashed	nr Dixon, WY, USA	2	0
09.02.92	Convair 640	N862FW	009	Gambcrest	Crashed into swamp on mistaking building lights for runway	Cap Skirring, Senegal	29	25
13.02.92	Fairchild Merlin IIB	N26JB	T26-163	Western Aviators	Crashed into mountain	Colorado, USA	0	4
14.02.92	Beechcraft H18	N33AP	BA-748	Polynesian Airways	Crashed	nr Lanai, HI, USA	*	*
15.02.92	McDonnell Douglas DC-8-55F	9G-MKB	45860	MK Air Cargo	Crashed on approach	Kano, Nigeria	0	5
15.02.92	McDonnell Douglas DC-8-63F	N794AL	45923	Burlington Air Express	Crashed on landing in bad weather	Toledo, OH, USA	4	0
15.02.92	Bell 206L-3 Long Ranger	N3120X	51532	Petroleum Helicopters	Crashed near oil rig	Gulf of Mexico	0	*
18.02.92	Curtiss C-46D	CP-1655	33294	Servicios Aereos Cochabamba	Damaged on landing	Cochabamba, Bolivia	*	*

Date	Type	Reg'n	C/n	Operator	Accident	Location	F	S
20.02.92	Boeing 707-349C	D2-TOJ	19355	TAAG Angola Airlines	Nosewheel collapsed on engine start-up & fuselage buckled	Luanda, Angola	0	*
22.02.92	Antonov AN-24RV	OB-1439	27307804	Trans Amazon	Overran & broke in two	Arequipa, Peru	0	2
22.02.92	Cessna 172	*	*	Sunflower Airlines	Crash landed when low on fuel	Seagaga, Fiji	*	*
23.02.92	Bell 214B-1	N814RM	28067	Rocky Mountain Helicopters	Crashed	nr Hobart Bay, AK, USA	6	5
23.02.92	Bell 206B JetRanger III	ZS-HIW	03044	Court Helicopters	Crashed after striking power lines	Witdraal, South Africa	1	0
26.02.92	Beechcraft H18	N347G	BA-654	Piedmont Air Cargo	Crashed on approach	nr Morganton, NC, USA	1	*
27.02.92	Bell 206B JetRanger II	N3185G	00721	Air Chile	Damaged beyond repair	nr Puerto Mont, Chile	*	*
29.02.92	Douglas DC-3	CP-529	4980	Frigorificos Santa Rita	Destroyed after engine caught fire on ground	Trinidad, Bolivia	*	*
29.02.92	Bell 212	N92AL	*	Offshore Logistics	Crashed	nr Morgan City, LA, USA	1	0
oo.02.92	IRMA BN-2A-8 Islander	P2-MBF	0646	Milne Bay Air	Written off	Papua New Guinea	*	*
oo.02.92	Douglas DC-3	5Y-BBN	16097/32845	Air Kenya	Crashed	Mara, Kenya	*	*
02.03.92	Curtiss C-46F	CP-754	22570	Frigorificos Santa Rita	Crashed on take-off	Beni, Bolivia	0	5
02.03.92	Bell 206B JetRanger II	N59613	01502	Smith Helicopters	Crashed in lake	Maricopa, AZ, USA	*	*
03.03.92	Vickers Viscount 757	9Q-CTU	277	Filair	Damaged on landing	N'Djili, Zaire	0	*
05.03.92	Mitsubishi MU-2 Marquise	N303CA	1518SA	S.R.Neece	Crashed	nr Rifle, CO, USA	6	0
05.03.92	Douglas DC-6BF	N151	45174	Everts Air Fuel	Crashed short of ice runway	Selowick, AK, USA	0	3
06.03.92	Bell 214B-1	N314RM	28041	Rocky Mountain Helicopters	Crashed into ravine after engine failure	Hobart Bay, AK, USA	*	*
06.03.92	NAMC YS-11A-205	N918AX	2112	ABX Air	Damaged beyond repair	Wilmington, OH, USA	*	*
12.03.92	British Aerospace Jetstream 31	N165PC	683	CC Air	Crashed after propeller touched ground	Knoxville, TN, USA	2	0
12.03.92	de Havilland Canada Twin Otter 300	TN-ACX	452	Lina Congo	Crashed during storm	Etsouali, Congo	3	5
13.03.92	Fairchild-Hiller FH.227C	XA-RSV	510	Aerocaribe	Damaged beyond repair	Acapulco, Mexico	*	*
13.03.92	LET 410UVP-E Turbolet	OK-PDI	851527	Slovair	Damaged on landing	Zilina, Czechoslovakia	*	*
14.03.92	Aerospatiale 332B Super Puma	G-TIGH	2034	Bristow Helicopters	Crashed in bad weather	North Sea	11	6
19.03.92	de Havilland Canada Twin Otter 300	C-GQKZ	532	Air Dale	Crashed on take-off	Red Lake, ON, Canada	2	0
19.03.92	Yakovlev YAK-40	SSSR-87385	*	Kamchatavia	Damaged in heavy landing	Russia	0	*
22.03.92	Antonov AN-30	*	*	Miatchkovo Aviation	Crashed following structural failure	nr Nizhneiansk, Russia	11	0
22.03.92	Fokker F-28 Fellowship 4000	N485US	11235	US Air	Crashed into bay on take-off in snowstorm	La Guardia, NY, USA	27	24
24.03.92	Boeing 707-321C	ST-ALX	18715	Golden Star Air Cargo	Crashed on approach	Athens, Greece	7	0
25.03.92	Aerospatiale 332 Super Puma	XC-UJH/04	*	Mexican Air Force	Crashed into hill	Huautla de Jiminez, Mexico	10	0
26.03.92	McDonnell Douglas DC-9-15	HK-2864X	45721	Intercontinental	Damaged in heavy landing	Tumaco, Colombia	0	92
26.03.92	Dassault Falcon 10	F-GJHK	108	Operator Unknown	Written off	Brest, France	*	*
27.03.92	Yakovlev YAK-40	*	*	Armenian Airlines	Damaged beyond repair by Azeri gunfire – Landed safely	nr Yerevan, Armenia	0	*
28.03.92	McDonnell Douglas DC-8-33F	OB-1456	45272	Export Air Cargo	Damaged when nosewheel collapsed on landing	Iquitos, Peru	0	*
30.03.92	McDonnell Douglas DC-9-32	EC-BYH	47556	Aviaco	Broke in half on landing	Granada, Spain	0	99
30.03.92	Antonov AN-26	*	*	Aeroflot	Crashed out of fuel on football pitch	Swaroop Nagar, India	*	*
30.03.92	Antonov AN-2	SSSR-55607	*	Magadan Avia	Crashed	nr Magadan, Russia	*	*
31.03.92	Boeing 707-321C	5N-MAS	18718	Kabo Air	Damaged when two engines fell off – Landed safely	Istres, France	0	*
03.04.92	Mil Mi-2	SSSR-20973	549646026	Operator Unknown	Crashed	Off St Petersburg, Russia	*	*
04.04.92	LET 410UVP Turbolet	SSSR-67130	800326	Kamchatavia	Crashed on approach	Baykovo, Kuril Is, Russia	1	11
07.04.92	Antonov AN-24RV	J5-GAE	*	Transportes Aereos da Guine-Bissau	Crashed in sandstorm [PLO leader Yasser Arafat survived]	nr Al Sarah, Libya	3	10
09.04.92	Beechcraft King Air C90	N105FL	LJ-1215	Florida State Government	Crashed into trees on approach	St Augustine, FL, USA	2	0
09.04.92	Bell 206L-3 Long Ranger	N6610L	51423	Petroleum Helicopters	Crashed	Venice, LA, USA	2	0
10.04.92	Britten-Norman BN-2A-26 Islander	B-11116	2007	Taiwan Airlines	Crashed into sea after take-off	Off Orchid Island, Taiwan	7	3
13.04.92	Bell 206B JetRanger III	OY-HDI	02828	Greenlandair	Crashed	nr Sardloq, Greenland	2	0
14.04.92	Antonov AN-2	SSSR-35546	*	Aeroflot	Crashed	Kyshik, Russia	*	*
15.04.92	Embraer Bandeirante 110P1	P2-RDS	110.355	Talair	Crashed into mountains	nr Goroka, Papua New Guinea	11	3
22.04.92	de Havilland Canada Twin Otter 100	N141PV	141	Perris Valley Skydivers	Crashed on take-off due to fuel contamination	Perris Valley Airport, CA, USA	15	0
23.04.92	Beechcraft E18S	N342E	BA-308	Scenic Air Tours	Crashed near top of volcano	Maui, HI, USA	9	0
26.04.92	Fokker F-27 Friendship 400M	5-8815	10499	Saha Airlines	Crashed in bad weather	nr Saweh, Iran	39	0
29.04.92	Boeing 707-351C	9G-RBO	18746	GAS Air	Damaged in belly landing	Lagos, Nigeria	0	*
29.04.92	Agusta A109A-II	SX-HDB	7423	Olympic Aviation	Crashed onto deck of MV *Pallas* & fell into sea	Off Pylos, Greece	0	5
02.05.92	Learjet 35A	PT-OEF	35A-102	Transamerica Taxi Aereo	Crashed on landing after suspected smuggling flight	Cumuatillo, Mexico	2	0
06.05.92	Antonov AN-2	SSSR-50585	IG131-27	Krasnoyarskavia	Crashed	Lake Taymyr, Russia	*	*
07.05.92	Rockwell Turbo Commander 690A	OB-1212	11222	Operator Unknown	Written off	Peru	*	*

Date	Type	Reg'n	C/n	Operator	Accident	Location	F	S
11.05.92	Convair 580	N73107	008	R G Aviation	Collided with JBQ Electra N360WS after brakes failed	Opa Locka, FL, USA	0(0)	*
11.05.92	Yakovlev YAK-40	*	*	Operator Unknown	Reported as shot down	Nagorno-Karabakh, Azerbaijan	*	*
12.05.92	Bell 204B	C-GBHB	2061	Canadian Helicopters	Crashed	Oakville, Canada	1	0
13.05.92	Yakovlev YAK-40	SSSR-88235	*	Turkmen Avia	Caught fire on landing after wing struck mast	Chardzhev, Turkmenistan	0	38
14.05.92	Mitsubishi MU-2K	OB-1284	282	Transportes Aereo Maranon	Crashed	nr Campanilla, Peru	2	0
18.05.92	Mitsubishi MU-2L	N742DM	670	United States Navy	Crashed on runway	Edwards AFB, CA, USA	2	0
18.05.92	Cessna 414	5H-TZS	414-0951	Tanzanian Air Services	Crashed after fuel starvation	Off Changuu Is, Tanzania	1	*
21.05.92	Aerospatiale SA.315B Lama	VR-HJE	2618	Heliservices	Crashed after take-off	nr Castle Peak, Hong Kong	1	0
21.05.92	Bell 206L-3 Long Ranger	7T-WUI	*	Air Algerie	Crashed on landing	Rhoud Bahira, Algeria	3	0
27.05.92	Bell 212	C-GRNR	30999	Alpine Helicopters	Crashed after tail struck ground	Invermere, BC, Canada	*	*
29.05.92	Tupolev TU-154M	YA-TAP	747	Ariana Afghan Airlines	Struck by missile in nose – landed OK – Destroyed 02.08.92	Kabul, Afghanistan	0	*
29.05.92	Aerospatiale AS.350B Ecureuil	N5806K	1989	Rocky Mountain Helicopters	Crashed into trees in fog	Winnsboro, SC, USA	0	3
30.05.92	Mil Mi-2	OK-PIN	529307065	Slovair	Crashed	Trebisov, Czechoslovakia	*	*
04.06.92	Bell 212	PT-HQF	31121	Aeroleo Taxi Aereo	Crashed in sea after engine fire	Off Campos Basin, Brazil	1	0
05.06.92	Tupolev TU-154B	LZ-BTD	058	Balkan Bulgarian Airlines	Damaged beyond repair after overrunning	Varna, Bulgaria	0	127
06.06.92	Bell 206L-3 Long Ranger	EC-FAO	*	Heliarcos	Crashed	nr Vistabella, Spain	6	0
07.06.92	Boeing 737-204	HP-1205CMP	22059	COPA Panama	Crashed	nr Tucuti, Panama	47	0
07.06.92	CASA 212 Aviocar 200	N355CA	234	Executive Airlines	Crashed on landing in heavy rain	Mayaguez, Puerto Rico	5	0
07.06.92	Bell 222	N5007L	47008	Rogers Helicopters	Crashed after take-off	Mariposa, CA, USA	*	*
08.06.92	Beechcraft C99	N118GP	U185	GP Express Airlines	Crashed on approach	Anniston, AL, USA	3	3
09.06.92	Beechcraft Super King Air 200	N162PA	BB-0232	Aero Lima	Hijacked & possibly crashed	Peru	*	2
10.06.92	Antonov AN-32	SSSR-48058	2807	Aero Pulse	Crashed on landing during relief flight	Marromeu, Mozambique	0	7
12.06.92	Learjet 25B	N38DJ	25B-191	Jet Charter Group	Crashed on take-off	Sheboygan, WI, USA	2	0
13.06.92	Cessna 402	*	*	Aerojet	Caught fire & crashed	Off Bahamas	0	2
15.06.92	Embraer Bandeirante 110P1	YV-245C	110.325	RUTACA	Crashed	nr Anaco, Venezuela	*	*
16.06.92	Beechcraft Super King Air 200	N32HG	BB-0146	Omega Air	Crashed on approach	Wilmington, DE, USA	4	0
17.06.92	Aerospatiale AS.350B1 Ecureuil	HB-XTE	2156	Heli-Linth	Damaged in heavy landing	nr Mollis, Switzerland	0	*
19.06.92	Cessna 402C	N2715X	402C-0215	Adventure Airlines	Crashed after take-off due to engine failure	Grand Canyon, AZ, USA	10	0
19.06.92	Grumman S-2F Tracker	N451DF	027	California Dept of Forestry	Crashed during fire fighting	Railroad Flat, CA, USA	1	0
19.06.92	Mil Mi-6	SSSR-21882	*	Tumenavia	Crashed in emergency landing	nr Hanty-Mansiysk, Russia	6	*
21.06.92	Piper PA-31-350 Chieftain	OB-1458	31-8052012	Aero Star	Shot down by police after being stolen	nr Uribe, Peru	3	0
21.06.92	Antonov AN-2	SSSR-32544	*	Aeroflot	Crashed	Poitavsky, Russia	*	*
21.06.92	MBB BK.117A-3	N117HH	7015	Rocky Mountain Helicopters	Crashed into power lines	Middletown, CT, USA	1	0
22.06.92	Boeing 737-2A1C	PP-SND	21188	VASP	Crashed	Moa River, Brazil	3	0
22.06.92	Antonov AN-12	SSSR-11896	*	Krasnoyarskavia	Crashed beside runway	Norlisk, Russia	10	2
24.06.92	Mitsubishi MU-2G	N108SC	545	Operator Unknown	Written off	Location Unknown	*	*
25.06.92	IPTN 212 Aviocar 100	PK-VSM	116/17N	Dirgantara Air Service	Crashed	nr Datu Island, Indonesia	3	0
25.06.92	Rockwell Turbo Commander 690B	N690JC	11479	Prine Inc	Crashed	nr Konowa, OK, USA	1	0
27.06.92	Cessna 185C	ZK-CVG	185-0681	Mount Cook Airlines	Crashed after colliding with Glacier AS.350D ZK-HEA	Fox Glacier, New Zealand	*	*
oo.06.92	Tupolev TU-154B-1	SSSR-85234	234	Aeroflot	Destroyed by fire in refuelling accident with SSSR-85282	Bratsk, Russia	*	*
oo.06.92	Tupolev TU-154B-1	SSSR-85282	282	Aeroflot	Destroyed by fire in refuelling accident with SSSR-85234	Bratsk, Russia	*	*
01.07.92	Beechcraft King Air E90	N45RM	LW-174	Aerolineas JLJ	Crash landed after engine fire	Pongo de Caynarachi, Peru	0	2
01.07.92	Short 330-100	G-CGIL	SH.3068	Gill Air	Taxied into vehicle & hangar striking 330 G-BIFH	Newcastle-upon-Tyne, UK	0(0)	*
03.07.92	Antonov AN-2	SSSR-40237	IG221-42	Aeroflot	Crashed	Sosnovsky, Russia	*	*
03.07.92	Hughes 500D	HK-3427	110890D	Aero Expreso Bogota	Crashed	Lebrija, Colombia	*	*
05.07.92	de Havilland Canada Twin Otter 300	9N-ABB	302	Royal Nepal Airlines	Crashed on take-off	Jumla, Nepal	*	*
05.07.92	Mil Mi-8	SSSR-22384	*	Yakutavia	Crashed on landing	Tiksi, Russia	0	3
07.07.92	Bell 206B JetRanger III	ZS-HKA	03356	Court Helicopters	Crashed	nr Kokstad, South Africa	*	*
08.07.92	Antonov AN-2	SSSR-07816	*	Aeroflot	Crashed	Ukrainsky, Russia	*	*
09.07.92	Mitsubishi MU-2 Solitaire	N220MA	441SA	RRH Inc	Crashed after take-off	Concord, NH, USA	2	0
11.07.92	Beechcraft 18	*	*	Pacific Airways	Crashed after engine failure on take-off	Lumbia, Philippines	0	4
11.07.92	Mil Mi-8	SSSR-06165	*	Far East Avia	Crashed after striking water sprinkler	Sinelnikovo, Russia	0	4
11.07.92	Mil Mi-8	SSSR-22831	*	Magadan Avia	Crashed into hill	nr Zyryanka, Russia	6	0
13.07.92	Short Skyvan 3	N20086	SH.1918	Arctic Circle Air Service	Crashed on take-off	Bethel, AK, USA	1	0

Date	Type	Reg'n	C/n	Operator	Accident	Location	F	S
16.07.92	Piper PA-38-112 Tomahawk	RP-C1071	*	Philippine Air Lines	Crashed after striking power lines	Apalit, Philippines	0	2
17.07.92	Antonov AN-12B	SSSR-11111	01347903	Magadan Avia	Crashed after four engines failed	nr Irkutsk, Russia	0	7
20.07.92	Tupolev TU-154B-1	SSSR-85222	222	Georgian Airlines	Crashed into buildings on take-off	Tblisi, Georgia	24{4}	0
20.07.92	Bell-Boeing V-22 Osprey	163914	*	Bell Aircraft Corporation	Crashed on approach	nr Quantico, VA, USA	7	0
20.07.92	Cessna 207A Skywagon	N9975M	207-00772	Markair Express	Crashed into hill	nr Dillingham, AK, USA	*	*
21.07.92	Douglas DC-3	LX-DKT	10253	Legend Air	Broken in two by gale	Ostend, Belgium	0	*
22.07.92	Mil Mi-6	SSSR-21896	*	Komiavia	Crashed after engine fire	nr Mutny Materic, Russia	0	5
22.07.92	de Havilland Canada Otter	N41755	339	Woods Air Service	Damaged in forced landing after in-flight fire	nr McGrath, AK. USA	0	*
24.07.92	Vickers Viscount 816	PK-RVU	434	Mandala Airlines	Crashed into hill on approach	Mt Liliboy, Ambon, Indonesia	70	0
24.07.92	Antonov AN-12	SSSR-11342	00347607	Volga-Dnepr Cargo Airlines	Crashed into mountain in storm	nr Veles, Macedonia	6	0
27.07.92	Vickers Viscount 798D	XA-SCM	392	Aero Eslava	Crashed into mountain	nr Puebla, Mexico	4	0
28.07.92	Antonov AN-24V	LZ-ANN	77302906	Balkan Bulgarian Airlines	Damaged beyond repair when crane fell onto it	Sofia, Bulgaria	0	*
28.07.92	Learjet 25C	PT-LHU	25C-099	Crasa Taxi Aereo	Crashed	Icuape, Brazil	6	0
30.07.92	Lockheed Tristar 1	N11002	1014	Trans World Airlines	Caught fire and aborted take-off	New York, NY, USA	0	287
30.07.92	Mil Mi-8	SSSR-27043	*	Kazakhstan Directorate	Crashed into hill	Soldatova, Kazakhstan	5	0
31.07.92	Airbus A.310-304	HS-TID	438	Thai Airways International	Crashed into mountain on approach	Mt Talaku Shir, Nepal	113	0
31.07.92	Yakovlev YAK-42D	B-2755	2116644	China General Aviation	Crashed on take-off due to engine failure	Nanjing, China	109	17
oo.07.92	Beechcraft King Air C90	F-BUTV	LJ-0602	Operator Unknown	Written off	Location Unknown	*	*
01.08.92	Yakovlev YAK-40	YA-KAB	9120417	Ariana Afghan Airlines	Destroyed on ground in rocket attack	Kabul, Afghanistan	*	*
01.08.92	Yakovlev YAK-40	YA-KAF	9120617	Ariana Afghan Airlines	Destroyed on ground in rocket attack	Kabul, Afghanistan	*	*
04.08.92	Cessna 207A Skywagon	N70364	*	Markair Express	Crashed into lake	St Marys, AK, USA	0	*
06.08.92	Beechcraft King Air C90	N90RG	LJ-0546	Roy Green Associates	Crashed out of fuel on approach	Oakland, MI, USA	*	*
07.08.92	Beechcraft 18	N3657G	*	EXA Inc	Crashed after take-off	Hinckley, IL, USA	12	0
07.08.92	Sikorsky S-76	N50KY	*	Kentucky State Government	Crashed after take-off	nr Frankfurt, KY, USA	*	*
08.08.92	MBB Bo.105S	N30SV	S.755	Rocky Mountain Helicopters	Crashed	Lake Madison, SD, USA	*	*
10.08.92	Cessna 441 Conquest II	N920C	0020	Air Travel Services	Crashed after birdstrike on take-off	Gainsville, GA, USA	*	*
11.08.92	Mil Mi-8	*	*	Beijing Lianhe Hangkong Luyou Gongsi	Crashed	nr Juyongguan, China	16	8
13.08.92	Aerospatiale AS.365N Dauphin 2	HL9244	*	Air Korea	Crashed	Soguipo, South Korea	1	0
14.08.92	Hughes 369	JA9454	*	Tohoku Air Service	Crashed in mountains	Fukushima, Japan	3	0
14.08.92	Cessna A188B	N4807Q	02545T	Briko Air Services	Crashed into HT cables	Trinidad	*	*
16.08.92	MBB Bo.105CBS	N295EH	S.847	ERA Aviation	Crashed	Gulf of Mexico	*	*
19.08.92	Cessna 185F	N1867Q	185-03497	Hammonds Air Service	Crashed on take-off	Houma, LA, USA	0	4
21.08.92	Convair 440-80	CP-1961	405	Servicios Aereos Santa Ana	Crashed into lake in bad weather	Colorado, Bolivia	10	0
22.08.92	Beechcraft 65 Queen Air 80	CP-1039	LD-143	J.Guzman	Crashed landed in field	La Ponderosa, Moxos, Bolivia	*	*
22.08.92	Piper PA-32-301 Saratoga	N8402S	32-8106075	Peninsula Airways	Crashed on take-off	Togiak, AK, USA	*	*
22.08.92	Bell 206L-3 Long Ranger	EC-EJM	51193	Helisureste	Crashed during fire fighting	Montaverner, Spain	2	0
23.08.92	BAC One-Eleven 204AF	5N-KBA	179	Kabo Air	Overshot on landing at disused airfield	Sokoto, Nigeria	0	57
24.08.92	Sikorsky UH-60A Blackhawk	*	*	US Customs Service	Destroyed by hurricane	Homestead AFB, FL, USA	0	*
24.08.92	Fairchild F-27	N273RD	0011	Airlift International	Damaged by hurricane	Miami, FL, USA	0	0
24.08.92	Douglas DC-6BF	N94BL	43842	Bellomy Lawson Aviation	Damaged by hurricane	Miami, FL, USA	*	*
24.08.92	Douglas R5D-3	N62433	10685	J.Balboa	Damaged by hurricane	Miami, FL, USA	*	*
24.08.92	Curtiss C-46	N67977	22533	Mayo Aviation	Damaged by hurricane	New Tamiami, FL, USA	0	*
24.08.92	Curtiss C-46	N625CL	33254	International Flight Center	Damaged by hurricane	New Tamiami, FL, USA	0	*
24.08.92	Learjet 24	N881FC	24-175	International Flight Center	Damaged by hurricane	New Tamiami, FL, USA	0	*
24.08.92	Ford 4-AT-B Tri-Motor	N7584	4-AT-38	K.Weeks	Destroyed by hurricane	Homestead, FL, USA	0	0
24.08.92	Fairchild F-27M	N276RD	0128	Airlift International	Damaged by hurricane	Miami, FL, USA	0	0
24.08.92	Beechcraft 18	N112L	BA-420	Operator Unknown	Destroyed by hurricane	Homestead, FL, USA	*	*
24.08.92	Hughes 369D	C-FBVG	*	Trans North Air	Crashed	nr Exeter Lake, AB, Canada	1	0
25.08.92	Fairchild 227AC Metro III	N342AE	AC-545	Lone Star Airlines	Crashed on take-off	Hot Springs, AR, USA	3	0
26.08.92	Beechcraft King Air A90	HR-IAG	*	Islena Airlines	Overran on landing & crashed into building	Palacios, Honduras	0	*
26.08.92	Fokker F-27 Friendship 600	D2-TFP	10424	TAAG Angola Airlines	Damaged beyond repair	Dundo, Angola	*	*
27.08.92	Tupolev TU-134A	SSSR-65058	*	Aeroflot	Crashed on landing	Ivanovo, Russia	84	0
27.08.92	de Havilland Canada Turbo Caribou	N400NC	240	Newcal Aviation	Crashed on take-off	Gimli, MN, Canada	3	0
27.08.92	Beechcraft Super King Air B200	VT-EHK	BB-0985	Border Security Force	Crashed after take-off	Delhi, India	1	0

Date	Type	Reg'n	C/n	Operator	Accident	Location	F	S
28.08.92	Ilyushin IL-76MD	SSSR-78780	*	Aeroflot	Destroyed by fire during rocket attack by rebels	Kabul, Afghanistan	0	*
28.08.92	Vickers Viscount 843	PK-IVX	454	Bouraq Indonesia Airlines	Caught fire on landing	Banjarmasin, Indonesia	0	70
28.08.92	Short 330-100	N74F	SH.3016	Freedom Air	Destroyed by typhoon	Guam	0	*
29.08.92	BAC One-Eleven 208AL	5N-HTA	051	Hold Trade Air Services	Damaged after running off runway on landing	Kaduna, Nigeria	0	*
31.08.92	Douglas Turbo DC-3	ZS-DHX	15908/32656	Professional Aviation Services	Crashed after take-off	Jamba, Angola	3	17
31.08.92	Cessna T210L Centurion	OB-1464	T210-61278	Aerolineas SARA	Crashed	Huallaga, Peru	4	0
05.09.92	Tupolev TU-154B-1	SSSR-85269	269	Aeroflot	Damaged beyond repair	Kiev, Ukraine	*	*
09.09.92	Mil Mi-8	SSSR-25475	95629	Tumenavia	Crashed on landing	Bugang, Papua New Guinea	6	15
10.09.92	Fokker F-27 Friendship 500	OB-1443	10533	Expresso Aereo	Crashed on landing	Bellavista, Peru	1	42
11.09.92	Mitsubishi MU-2 Marquise	N74FB	770SA	Solar Sources	Mid-air collision with PA-32 N82419	Greenwood, IN, USA	5(1)	0
12.09.92	Mil Mi-8	SSSR-22738	*	Kamchatavia	Crashed into trees	Kozyrevsk, Russia	10	0
12.09.92	Cessna TU206C Stationair	C-GOPB	U206-01004	Mountain Air Services	Crashed into river	nr Silver Hilton Lodge, BC, Canada	3	0
14.09.92	Yakovlev YAK-40	SSSR-87411	9402334	Yakutavia	Caught fire on take-off – Landed safely but dbr	Neryungry, Russia	0	*
17.09.92	Sikorsky S-61N	ZS-HRU	61-466	Court Helicopters	Crashed on deck of *Darya Shubh*	Off Cape Town, South Africa	0	*
18.09.92	Douglas DC-6A	YV-502C	44656	Aeroejecutivos	Crashed into sea	Off Curacao, Netherlands Antilles	3	0
18.09.92	Fairchild 227AC Metro III	N2183A	AC-422	Fairchild Aircraft	Damaged in heavy landing	San Antonio, TX, USA	0	*
18.09.92	Antonov AN-2	SSSR-40670	*	Far East Avia	Crashed in lake on approach due to engine failure	Ekimchan, Russia	0	2
18.09.92	Beechcraft B55 Baron	TR-LUF	TH-630	Air Affaires Gabon	U/c torn off on landing	Gabon	0	*
19.09.92	Curtiss C-46F	HK-3468	22436	Avesca	Crashed after engine fire on take-off	Bogota, Colombia	11	10
21.09.92	IAI 1124 Westwind	SE-DLK	197	Time Air	Damaged by fire when engine exploded on take-off	Umeaa, Sweden	0	*
21.09.92	Mil Mi-8	SSSR-22651	*	Yakutavia	Crashed into power lines	nr Kular, Russia	10	0
22.09.92	Bell 206L-3 Long Ranger	HK-3353	51177	Helitaxi	Damaged in hard landing	El Turnaco, Colombia	0	*
23.09.92	Mil Mi-8	SSSR-25909	*	Tumenavia	Crashed into vehicles on forced landing	nr Megion, Russia	0	6
25.09.92	Mil Mi-8	SSSR-25491	*	Sibavia	Crashed in bad weather	nr Karakoksha, Russia	7	0
26.09.92	Mil Mi-17	*	*	United Nations Organisation	Crashed	Uige, Angola	16	1
26.09.92	Harbin Y-12	9N-ACI	069	Royal Nepal Airlines	Damaged when nosewheel collapsed on landing	Lukla, Nepal	0	*
26.09.92	Mil Mi-2	14398	535532028	Tumenavia	Crashed after take-off	nr Urengoy, Russia	1	0
28.09.92	Airbus A.300B4-2C	AP-BCP	025	Pakistan International Airlines	Crashed into mountain in bad weather	Teenpane, Nepal	167	0
29.09.92	Mil Mi-8	SSSR-25356	*	Far East Avia	Struck trees on approach & crashed into lake	Toko Lake, Russia	0	6
01.10.92	Fairchild Merlin III	5Y-TNT	T-211	Eagle Aviation	Crashed after aborting take-off due to nosewheel collapse	Nairobi, Kenya	0	2
01.10.92	Douglas DC-7B	N848D	45454	TBM Inc	Crashed while fire fighting	Union Valley Reservoir, CA, USA	2	0
04.10.92	Boeing 747-258F	4X-AXG	21737	El Al Israel Airlines	Engines caught fire on take-off & crashed into flats	Amsterdam, Netherlands	4{47}	0
06.10.92	British Aerospace Jetstream 32	G-SUPR	956	British Aerospace	Crashed on take-off	Prestwick, UK	2	0
07.10.92	Kamov Ka-32	SSSR-31016	*	Leningrad Civil Aviation Assoc	Crashed into crane	Cheluskin Cope, Russia	4	0
08.10.92	Avia 14-40	B-4211	807113	Wuhan Air Lines	Crashed after engine failure	Huajia, China	14	21
09.10.92	Antonov AN-32	SSSR-48088	2905	African Airlines International	Crashed on landing	Mogadishu, Somalia	1	12
09.10.92	Mil Mi-8	SSSR-24443	*	Magadan Avia	Crashed after take-off	nr Vesenny, Russia	1	12
13.10.92	Antonov AN-124-100	SSSR-82002	19530501003	Antonov Design Bureau	Crashed when nose cargo door opened in flight	Kodry, Ukraine	8	2
13.10.92	Tupolev TU-154B-2	SSSR-85528	528	Belarus Airlines	Crashed after aborting take-off when overloaded	Vladivostok, Russia	0	68
14.10.92	Antonov AN-2	07840	*	Kazakhstan Directorate	Crashed	Kustanay, Kazakhstan	0	3
15.10.92	McDonnell Douglas DC-8-55F	HK-3753X	45765	Lineas Aereas del Caribe	Ran off runway on landing	Medellin, Colombia	0	*
15.10.92	Mil Mi-8	SSSR-24565	*	Department of Aviation Industry	Crashed into pylon after take-off	nr Kondon, Russia	*	*
15.10.92	Hughes 369E	N16008	0215E	Evergreen Helicopters	Crashed	Tamale, Ghana	2	0
18.10.92	IPTN-CASA CN.235-10	PK-MNN	013N	Merpati Nusantara Airlines	Crashed into mountain	Mt Papandayan, Indonesia	31	0
19.10.92	Antonov AN-28	SSSR-28785	IAJ005-18	Komiavia	Crashed after engine failure on take-off	nr Usti Nem, Russia	15	1
19.10.92	Rockwell Turbo Commander 695	XC-AA38	95020	P.G.R.	Crashed after take-off	Monterrey, Mexico	8	0
23.10.92	Convair 580F	OO-DHD	135	European Air Transport	Damaged on landing with retracted nosewheel	Brussels, Belgium	0	*
25.10.92	Fairchild 226TC Metro II	5Y-DNT	TC-299	Eagle Aviation	Ran off runway on landing	Mogadishu, Somalia	0	10
27.10.92	Cessna 402B	C9-MJB	402B-0553	Sky Tours	Crashed in lake after reported engine fire	Lake Malawi, Malawi	0	*
27.10.92	Cessna 310R II	N5074J	310R-0194	Pacific Island Aviation	Crashed and overturned on landing	Saipan, Northern Marianas	3	0
28.10.92	Mil Mi-8MTV1	RA-70869	*	Kazan Helicopters	Crashed	Bugulma, Russia	*	*
29.10.92	Antonov AN-8	SSSR-69346	OD-3430	Aeroflot	Crashed on landing	Chita, Russia	14	1
oo.10.92	de Havilland Canada Turbo Otter	N53JH	131	Ketchikan Air Service	Destroyed in gale	Patriot Hills Camp, Antarctica	0	0
oo.10.92	Ilyushin IL-62	RA-86703	41601	Aeroflot	Destroyed by fire while refuelling	Moscow, Russia	0	*

Date	Type	Reg'n	C/n	Operator	Accident	Location	F	S
02.11.92	Douglas DC-3	CP-1960	18993	Transportes Aereos San Jorge	Crashed short of runway on test flight	San Juan, Bolivia	0	*
05.11.92	Mil Mi-8	SSSR-27070	*	Aeroflot	Crash landed after being hit by rebel gunfire	nr Ankor-Wat, Cambodia	0	11
05.11.92	Mil Mi-17	*	*	CAAC	Crashed into building while leaflet dropping	Yuanyang, China	*{33}	0
06.11.92	Douglas DC-7CF	HI-619SP	45158	Aerochago	Crashed in sea after engine failure on take-off	Dania Beach, FL, USA	0	5
07.11.92	Rockwell Sabre 60	N169RF	306-045	H. & V.Price	Overran on landing & caught fire	Phoenix, AZ, USA	0	*
07.11.92	Cessna 207 Skywagon	N1686U	207-00286	Harbor Air Service	Crashed	nr Patton Bay, AK, USA	2	0
09.11.92	Cessna 402C II	N67941	402C-0633	Baker Aviation	Crashed	nr Kiana, AK, USA	3	0
11.11.92	Antonov AN-22A	SSSR-09303	053483299	Aeroflot	Crashed after take-off due to poor loading	Nekrasovo, Russia	23	0
11.11.92	IRMA BN-2A-27 Islander	YR-BNS	0812	Operator Unknown	Written off	Tulcea, Romania	*	*
12.11.92	Fairchild 227AC Metro III	N3044J	AC-466	Aerodinos	Damaged after veering off runway on take-off	Trinidad, Bolivia	*	*
14.11.92	Yakovlev YAK-40	VN-A449	9631848	Vietnam Airlines	Crashed on landing	Nha Trang, Vietnam	29	1
15.11.92	Ilyushin IL-18D	CU-T1270	187010301	Aero Caribbean	Crashed into hill on approach	nr Puerta Plata, Dominican Republic	34	0
20.11.92	Boeing 737-287C	LV-JNE	20408	Aerolineas Argentinas	Overran after tyre burst on take-off & caught fire	San Luis, Argentina	0	100
21.11.92	Antonov AN-24	SSSR-46306	97305206	Yugavia	U/c collapsed on landing	Krasnodar, Russia	0	*
24.11.92	Boeing 737-3YO	B-2523	24913	China Southern Airlines	Crashed into mountain on approach	nr Guilin, China	141	0
25.11.92	Boeing 707-321C	5X-DAR	18825	DAS Air Services	Crashed on approach	Kano, Nigeria	0	5
26.11.92	Boeing 707-365C	PT-TCP	19416	Aerobrasil	Crashed on take-off	Manaus, Brazil	0	4
27.11.92	McDonnell Douglas DC-9-34CF	YV-37C	47752	Aeropostal	Damaged by missile on ground during coup attempt	Baraquisimeto, Venezuela	*	*
01.12.92	Cessna Citation S/II	PT-LKT	S550-0117	Taxi Aereo Marilia	Overran on landing	Sao Paulo, Brazil	*	*
01.12.92	Aerospatiale SA.316B Alouette III	F-BRQI	1915	Air Reunion	Rolled into volcano crater after hard landing	Mt La Fournaise, Reunion	0	*
02.12.92	Mil Mi-8	SSSR-22334	*	Sibavia	Damaged in forced landing	Kedrovy, Russia	0	*
02.12.92	Cessna 207 Skywagon	D-EBSD	*	Berliner Spezialflug	Crashed	nr Perleberg, Germany	2	0
05.12.92	Antonov AN-26	SSSR-26618	5735102	Yugavia	U/c retracted in error on take-off	Volgograd, Russia	0	7
05.12.92	Tupolev TU-154A	85105	105	Armenian Airlines	Damaged after running off runway on landing	Yerevan, Armenia	0	154
08.12.92	de Havilland Canada Twin Otter 100	PK-YPG	049	Trigana Air Service	Damaged by running off runway & down embankment on take-off	Pogapa, Indonesia	0	*
09.12.92	IRMA BN-2B-27 Islander	XA-RML	0864	Aero Sud Pacifico	Crashed after take-off	Tancitaro, Mexico	8	0
10.12.92	Volpar Turbo 18	N7770B	AF-320	Kalitta Flying Service	Crashed on approach	Baltimore, MD, USA	1	0
11.12.92	Kaman HH-43F	N100PL	59-1583	ERA Aviation	Crashed after rotor struck trees	Lugoff, SC, USA	*	*
11.12.92	Fairchild FH-1100	N5046F	192	West Florida Helicopters	Crashed after rotor struck ground	nr Forney, TX, USA	1	0
13.12.92	Fokker F-27 Friendship 400M	9Q-CBH	10649	Scibe Airlift	Crashed into hill	nr Goma, Zaire	37	0
13.12.92	Cessna 402B	N17CH	402B-0519	Dwyer Air	Crashed short of runway on second approach	Cedar Rapids, IA, USA	*	*
13.12.92	McDonnell Douglas DC-8-33	LV-LTP	45255	TRAFE	Destroyed by fire on ground	Buenos Aires, Argentina	*	*
15.12.92	Britten-Norman BN-2A-26 Islander	P2-MBE	0194	Milne Bay Air	Crashed into mountain	Alotau, Papua New Guinea	6	0
15.12.92	Volpar Turboliner	N706M	4251	Mohican Air Services	Crashed on take-off	Cleveland, OH, USA	1	0
16.12.92	Grumman G-21A Goose	N3116Y	B-109	Provo Air Charter	Crashed on landing	Caicos Island, Turks & Caicos Is	0	*
16.12.92	Bell 212	OY-HEA	30914	SL Helicopters	Crashed on approach	Off Klasvik, Faroe Islands	5	0
18.12.92	Cessna Citation II	N6887Y	550-0293	US Department of Energy	Crashed into warehouse on approach	Billings, MT, USA	8	0
18.12.92	Antonov AN-12	SSSR-12975	9346509	Balkan Bulgarian Airlines	Damaged beyond repair after running off runway	Norilsk, Bulgaria	0	8
19.12.92	Beechcraft Queen Air 65	N555GC	LC-164	W.J.Edwards	Crashed after engine failure	nr Orlando, FL, USA	5	0
20.12.92	Hughes 500E	VH-LLD	0133E	Masling Helicopters	Crashed after striking power cables	nr Yass, NSW, Australia	3	0
21.12.92	McDonnell Douglas DC-10-30F	PH-MBN	46924	Martinair	Crashed on landing in thunderstorm	Faro, Portugal	54	287
22.12.92	Boeing 727-2L5	5A-DIA	21050	Libyan Arab Airlines	Mid-air collision on approach with Libyan AF MiG-23	nr Tripoli, Libya	157(0)	0
23.12.92	Rockwell Turbo Commander 690C	N81TR	11690	Casper Air Service	Crashed after structural failure	nr Denver, CO, USA	1	0
24.12.92	Mil Mi-2	23463	524104045	Tumenavia	Crashed	nr Ishim, Russia	*	*
26.12.92	Beechcraft King Air B90	ZS-IHZ	LJ-0497	Operator Unknown	Written off	Cape Town, South Africa	*	*
27.12.92	Cessna T210N Centurion	SE-INL	T210-64692	Holmstroem Air	Crashed	Ridoen, Sweden	1	0
31.12.92	Rockwell Turbo Commander 690B	N300CP	11374	Medic Air	Crashed after breaking up	nr Susanville, CA, USA	2	0
00.00.92	Antonov AN-12	LZ-SFC	402913	Air Afrique	Damaged on landing	Abidjan, Ivory Coast	*	*
00.00.92	Beechcraft 99A	C-FHIE	U093	Sabourin Lake Airways	Damaged in ground fire	Canada	*	*
00.00.92	Tupolev TU-154M	YN-CBT	821	Aeronica	Damaged beyond repair	Managua, Nicaragua	*	*
00.00.92	Beechcraft King Air 90	F-GDMM	LJ-0054	Operator Unknown	Written off	Location Unknown	*	*
02.01.93	Dornier Do.228-101	CG-75	*	Indian Coast Guard	Crashed at sea	Off Paradip, India	4	2

Date	Type	Reg'n	C/n	Operator	Accident	Location	F	S
02.01.93	Saab 340A	N342PX	147	Express Airlines	Badly damaged when u/c collapsed on landing	Hibbing, MN, USA	0	*
06.01.93	de Havilland Canada Dash 8-311	D-BEAT	210	Contact Air	Overran on landing & crashed into trees	Paris, France	4	15
06.01.93	Mitsubishi MU-2J	N900YH	584	Bering Air	Crashed landed due to fuel starvation	Nome, AK, USA	0	*
08.01.93	Learjet 35A	XA-LAN	35A-267	AVEMEX	Crashed into hill	nr Hermosillo, Mexico	9	0
09.01.93	Tupolev TU-154B-2	85533	533	Indian Airlines	Overshot on landing & crashed	New Delhi, India	0	167
09.01.93	British Aerospace 748 2A	PK-IHE	1620	Bouraq Indonesia Airlines	Crashed after take-off due to engine failure	Surabaya, Indonesia	17	27
10.01.93	Beechcraft Super King Air 200	C-FSSU	BB-0633	Operator Unknown	Destroyed in hangar fire	Quebec, PQ, Canada	*	*
12.01.93	Mitsubishi MU-2N	VH-SSL	712SA	Operator Unknown	Written off	Tullamarine, Vic, Australia	*	*
13.01.93	Embraer Bandeirante 110P1	G-ZAPE	110.391	Titan Airways	Crashed into hillside	Ponsonby Fell, Cumbria, UK	2	0
14.01.93	Douglas DC-3C	C-FAAM	9862	Central Mountain Air	Crashed after take-off	Bronson Creek, BC, Canada	2	0
15.01.93	Boeing 707-321C	YR-ABM	19272	Air Afrique	Crashed short of runway	Abidjan, Ivory Coast	0	3
16.01.93	Antonov AN-24	46478	*	Kazakhstan Airlines	Crashed short of runway on approach & struck CIS AF AN-24	Kustanay, Kazakhstan	0(0)	23
21.01.93	EH Industries EH.101	PP.2	PP.2	EH Industries	Crashed due to rotor brake failure	nr Cameri, Italy	4	0
22.01.93	Lockheed L-382G-44K-30 Hercules	D2-EHD	4839	Diamang	Shot down by Angolan forces	nr Huambo, Angola	*	*
22.01.93	Airbus A.340-311	F-WWAS	002	Airbus Industrie	Damaged in landing accident	Toulouse, France	0	*
23.01.93	Britten-Norman BN-2A-20 Islander	P2-ISF	0281	Island Airways	Written off	Location Unknown	*	*
25.01.93	Fairchild-Hiller FH.227B	PT-LCS	522	TABA	Crashed	nr Altamira, Brazil	3	0
27.01.93	Nord 262A-12	9Q-CJK	011	Trans Service Airlift	Crashed into building on take-off [8 looters shot by troops]	Kinshasa, Zaire	9{8}	12
30.01.93	Short Skyvan 3-100	9M-PID	SH.1961	Pan Malaysian Air Transport	Crashed into high ground in bad weather	Sumatra, Indonesia	16	0
31.01.93	Boeing 707-387B	LV-ISA	19238	Lineas Aereas del Estado	Damaged when u/c collapsed on landing	Recife, Brazil	0	167
01.02.93	Aerospatiale AS.350B Ecureuil	ZK-HNH	1285	Helicopters (NZ) Ltd	Crashed	Mt Fyffe, New Zealand	*	*
03.02.93	Lockheed L-100-20 Hercules HTTB	N130X	4412	Lockheed Corporation	Crashed after becoming airborne in high speed ground test	Dobbins AFB, GA, USA	7	0
03.02.93	Short Skyvan 3	9M-PIF	SH.1963	Pan Malaysian Air Transport	Damaged in hard landing when nosewheel collapsed	Padang, Malaysia	0	2
03.02.93	Antonov AN-24B	RA-47180	99901905	Aeroflot	Damaged beyond repair	Ut-Kulga, Russia	*	*
07.02.93	Beechcraft King Air	PT-OOP	*	Taxi Aereo Florianopolis	Crashed	Foz do Iguacu, Brazil	6	0
08.02.93	Tupolev TU-154M	EP-ITD	903	Iran Air Tours	Mid-air collision with Iranian AF Su-17 after take-off	Tehran, Iran	132(2)	0
08.02.93	Piper PA-42-720 Cheyenne III	OB-1234	42-8001007	Aero Transporte	Crashed	Pucallpa, Peru	*	*
09.02.93	Antonov AN-32	*	*	Aeroflot	Crashed after take-off	Nairobi National Park, Kenya	0	4
10.02.93	Antonov AN-12	*	*	Ariana Afghan Airlines	Crash landed out of fuel	nr Termez, Uzbekistan	0	119
15.02.93	Rockwell Turbo Commander 690V	C-FFEO	1693-72	Operator Unknown	Destroyed in hangar fire	Hamilton, ON, Canada	0	0
17.02.93	Britten-Norman BN-2A-21 Islander	LN-MAF	0441	Air Norving	Written off	Location Unknown	*	*
17.02.93	Dassault Falcon 10	N85JM	085	Operator Unknown	Written off	Aurillac, France	*	*
18.02.93	Douglas DC-7CF	HI-599CT	45208	Aerochago	Exploded on take-off	Santo Domingo, Dominican Republic	0	3
19.02.93	Bell 214B-1	N114CR	28034	CRI Helicopters	Crashed	Dora Bay, AK, USA	2	0
20.02.93	Convair 440-11	HP-1200CTH	413	Panama Cargo Three	Crashed after engine fire on take-off	Bogota, Colombia	2	0
24.02.93	Beechcraft E18S	N47E	BA-183	Centre Airlines	Crashed on approach	Mt Nittany, PA, USA	1	0
24.02.93	Bell 206B JetRanger II	C-FDDL	00789	Trans North Air	Crashed	nr MacMillan Pass, YK, Canada	*	*
26.02.93	Learjet 31	PT-OFK	31-017	Lider Taxi Aereo	Crashed into water short of runway in heavy rain	Rio de Janeiro, Brazil	0	*
28.02.93	Dornier Do.228-201	B-12238	8111	Formosa Airlines	Crashed at sea	Off Green Island, Taiwan	6	0
oo.02.93	Beechcraft Super King Air 200	C-GCSL	BB-0118	Les Constructions du St Laurent	Destroyed by fire on ground	Beauport, PQ, Canada	*	*
01.03.93	Bell 212	OY-HCT	31154	Greenlandair	Crashed	nr Innarsuit, Greenland	4	0
02.03.93	Douglas DC-3	EC-FAH	9336	Palfe	Crashed on take-off	Palma, Majorca, Spain	2	0
05.03.93	Fokker 100	PH-KXL	11393	Palair Macedonian Airlines	Crashed after take-off due to icing	nr Skopje, Macedonia	85	14
05.03.93	Mil Mi-8	RA-24728	*	Tumenavia	Crashed with underslung load after gearbox failure	nr Sovetsky, Russia	0	4
06.03.93	de Havilland Canada Twin Otter 100	C-FQBT	095	Kenn Borek Air	Damaged in ground loop on take-off	Baffin Island, NWT, Canada	0	2
06.03.93	Bell 205A-1	C-GFHT	30032	Frontier Helicopters	Crash landed after being caught in downdraught	Mamina, Chile	0	*
07.03.93	Bell 206B JetRanger III	C-GDFA	03120	Huisson Aviation	Crashed onto frozen sea	nr Charlottetown, PEI, Canada	0	*
08.03.93	Douglas DC-6	CP-1654	43035	Compania Aerea Nacional	Crashed on take-off & caught fire	Beni, Bolivia	0	4
08.03.93	Mil Mi-8	RA-25904	*	Kamchatavia	Crashed on take-off in snow	Kalygir Bay, Russia	0	4
11.03.93	Antonov AN-26	RA-26529	*	Ural Airlines	Crashed short of runway on approach	Harasavey, Russia	0	5
12.03.93	Mil Mi-8	RA-24472	*	Krasnoyarskavia	Crashed on approach	nr Igarka, Russia	0	*
13.03.93	Mitsubishi MU-2F	PT-ICD	215	Sete Taxi Aereo	Ran off runway and damaged on landing	Araxa, Brazil	0	7
17.03.93	Aerospatiale AS.350D Astar	ZK-HGV	*	Glacier Helicopters	Damaged in hard landing	Fox Glacier, New Zealand	0	*

Date	Type	Reg'n	C/n	Operator	Accident	Location	F	S
18.03.93	Beechcraft King Air E90	N102RB	LW-019	Aero Taxi Icuitos	Crashed into mountain	nr Juica, Peru	4	0
19.03.93	Beechcraft Super King Air 200	LN-TSA	BB-0308	West Aviation	Crashed in bad weather	nr Geilo, Norway	3	3
20.03.93	Mil Mi-8	RA-70914	*	Aeroflot	Crashed after losing tail rotor on landing	Siem Reap, Cambodia	0	23
22.03.93	Piper PA-32 Cherokee Six	YS-23C	*	Transportes Aereos de El Salvador	Crashed on approach	nr San Salvador, El Salvador	5	0
23.03.93	Cessna 402B	N405PC	402B-1381	Springfield Air Service	Crashed into HT cables on take-off	Tullahoma, TN, USA	1	0
23.03.93	Fokker F-27 Friendship 300	ST-AWA	10186	Air West Express	Crashed on emergency landing out of fuel	nr Addis Ababa, Ethiopia	0	35
23.03.93	Embraer Bandeirante 110C	PP-SBJ	110.037	Oseste Linhas Aereas	Crashed after take-off	Tangara de Serra, Brazil	6	0
24.03.93	Douglas DC-7C	HR-ALY	45230	Caicos Aircraft Leasing	Exploded during maintenance	Miami, FL, USA	0	0
25.03.93	Cessna 421C Golden Eagle	HA-ACA	421C-0615	Phoenix 2000 Air Taxi	Crashed	Budapest, Hungary	0	2
31.03.93	Airbus A.300B2-1C	F-BUAE	004	Air Inter	Damaged when towed into pylon	Montpelier, France	0	*
31.03.93	Cessna 152	*	*	Austrian Airlines	Crashed into mountain – pilot froze to death	nr Murau, Austria	1	0
oo.03.93	Douglas DC-6	N1125J	44888	Operator Unknown	Damaged beyond repair by high winds	Tamiami, FL, USA	0	0
01.04.93	Fairchild 227AT Metro IIIC	N500AK	TT-527	R.Brooks	Crashed on approach at night	Sullivan County, TN, USA	4	0
02.04.93	Sikorsky S-61N	C-FWYN	61743	Coulson Air Crane	Crashed during logging operations	Canoe Creek, BC, Canada	0	2
02.04.93	McDonnell Douglas DC-9-15	YV-03C	47000	Aeropostal	Crashed in sea on test flight	Off Margarita Island, Venezuela	11	0
03.04.93	Cessna 207A Skywagon	N6467H	207-00531	Ryan Air Service	Crashed	nr Nome, AK, USA	2	0
04.04.93	Mil Mi-2	14235	5311122030	Arkhangelsk Airlines	Crashed in bad weather	nr Varandey, Russia	*	*
06.04.93	Mitsubishi MU-2J	N96JP	556	Casper Air Service	Crashed on approach	Casper, WY, USA	4	0
06.04.93	Antonov AN-24RV	47309	*	Latavio	Damaged after overrunning on landing	Stepanevan, Armenia	0	32
06.04.93	Beechcraft C-45H	N492DM	*	Eagle Airways	Crashed into power lines on landing	Morringsport, LA, USA	1	0
06.04.93	Mil Mi-2	13343	*	Central Region Directorate	Crashed	nr Oktyabrsky, Russia	*	*
08.04.93	Mil Mi-8	25349	*	Air Ukraine	Crashed after engine failure	nr Simferopol, Ukraine	0	3
14.04.93	McDonnell Douglas DC-10-30	N139AA	46711	American Airlines	Damaged when u/c collapsed on landing	Dallas, TX, USA	0	202
14.04.93	Fairchild 226TC Metro II	VH-UZS	TC-320	Jetcraft	Ran off runway during emergency landing	Mackay, Qld, Australia	0	1
18.04.93	McDonnell Douglas DC-9-41	JA8448	47767	Japan Air System	Crashed and caught fire on landing	Hanamaki, Japan	0	77
19.04.93	Mitsubishi MU-2 Marquise	N86SD	765SA	South Dakota State Government	Crashed in fog after propeller failure	nr Dubuque, IA, USA	8	0
19.04.93	British Aerospace Jetstream 31	N131CA	787	Westair	Crashed into trees after take-off	Merced, CA, USA	0	3
20.04.93	Douglas DC-3	N8056	14563/26008	Phoenix Air	Forced landed after engine fire	Zephyr Hills, FL, USA	0	40
20.04.93	Douglas DC-3	CP-1622	13336	Trans Aereos Cochabamba	Crashed	Florencia, Colombia	2	0
21.04.93	Ilyushin IL-76TD	76794	0093498954	Uzbekistan Airways	Ran into buildings on emergency landing	Peshawar, Pakistan	0	*
21.04.93	Mil Mi-8	RA-24721	*	Kamchatavia	Struck trees and crashed	Ivuvovchan River, Russia	0	2
21.04.93	Mil Mi-6	RA-21170	*	Tumenavia	Destroyed by fire after emergency landing	nr Tarkosale, Russia	0	5
23.04.93	Mil Mi-8	RA-24450	*	Aerovolga	Crashed into TV mast in fog	nr Cheboksary, Russia	7	0
23.04.93	Antonov AN-26	*	*	MIAT Mongolian Airlines	Crashed into mountain [Not found until 01.05.93]	nr Dzavkhan, Mongolia	36	0
26.04.93	Boeing 737-2A8	VT-ECQ	20961	Indian Airlines	Crashed after striking truck on take-off	nr Aurangabad, India	55	63
26.04.93	Antonov AN-12	RA-11121	02348103	Aeroflot	Struck by missile & crashed in minefield	nr Luena, Angola	1	6
29.04.93	Beechcraft C99	N115GP	U228	GP Express Airlines	Crashed at night	nr Grand Island, NE, USA	2	0
29.04.93	Embraer Brasilia 120RT	N24706	120.093	Continental Express	Crash landed after losing propeller during spin	Pine Bluff, AR, USA	0	30
01.05.93	Beechcraft King Air A90	N530N	LJ-0141	Operator Unknown	Written off	USA	*	*
02.05.93	Short 330-100	VP-LVR	SH.3006	Atlantic Air BVI	Crashed into water after aborting take-off	Beef Island, British Virgin Islands	0	30
04.05.93	Beechcraft E18S	N80CB	BA-257	Viking Express	Crashed on approach	Lone Rock, WI, USA	*	*
06.05.93	Aerospatiale Caravelle 10B	HK-3835X	182	SERCA Colombia	Crashed when u/c collapsed in hard landing	Cayenne, French Guiana	0	4
08.05.93	Bell 214B-1	N314CR	28055	CRI Helicopters	Crash landed after engine failure	Prince of Wales Is, AK, USA	0	2
08.05.93	Bell 212	LN-OPX	30546	Lufttransport	Crashed into sea	Off Tromso, Norway	*	*
11.05.93	Britten-Norman BN-2A-6 Islander	DQ-FEO	0009	Fiji Air	Crashed into vehicle after undershooting runway	Nausori, Fiji	2	0
12.05.93	Embraer Brasilia 120RT	PT-SLI	120.044	Rio Sul	Crashed on landing	Rio de Janeiro, Brazil	0	17
13.05.93	Mil Mi-8	RA-24104	*	Tumenavia	Crashed after rotors touched	nr Surgut, Russia	1	3
14.05.93	Harbin Y-12-II	*	*	TANS	Crashed on landing	Atalya, Peru	0	*
15.05.93	Douglas DC-6BF	XA-SEA	43825	Carga del Caribe	Crashed on take-off	Cancun, Mexico	3	2
15.05.93	Mil Mi-8	RA-22912	*	Magadan Avia	Crashed in snowstorm	nr Nutepelmen, Russia	9	11
17.05.93	Rockwell Turbo Commander 690A	N28AD	11291	Lineas Aereas Covitrans	Crashed after take-off	Sepahua, Peru	1	1
17.05.93	Yakovlev YAK-40	RA-88244	*	Tumenavia	Damaged by running off runway when u/c collapsed on landing	Hanty-Mansiysk, Russia	*	*
18.05.93	Mil Mi-17	HK-3733X	95619	Helitaxi	Crashed on take-off	Tunja, Colombia	0	13

Date	Type	Reg'n	C/n	Operator	Accident	Location	F	S
19.05.93	Boeing 727-46	HK-2422X	18876	SAM Colombia	Crashed in mountains on approach	Medellin, Colombia	132	0
22.05.93	de Havilland Canada Otter	C-GKPB	274	Loon Air	Crashed on take-off on delivery flight	Villeneve, AB, Canada	2	0
22.05.93	Mil Mi-8	RA-22554	*	Tumenavia	Damaged in hard landing	nr Tolka, Russia	*	*
22.05.93	Beechcraft C-18S	N67E	*	Operator Unknown	Crashed on landing & caught fire	North Branch, MN, USA	*	*
23.05.93	Mil Mi-8	RA-24459	*	Yakutavia	Damaged in hard landing and rolled over	nr Nurba, Russia	*	*
25.05.93	Fairchild Merlin III	N241DT	T-242	Peacock's Flying Service	Crashed into trees on approach	Santa Fe, NM, USA	4	0
26.05.93	Cessna Citation II	G-JETB	550-0288	City Air	Crashed onto motorway after overrunning on landing in rain	Eastleigh, Hants, UK	0	2
27.05.93	Aerospatiale AS.350D Astar	N782LF	1487	Rocky Mountain Helicopters	Crashed	nr Cameron, MO, USA	2	2
31.05.93	Beechcraft King Air E90	N3177W	LW-077	Aero Taxi Iquitos	Caught fire landing on unauthorised airstrip after hijack	Bellavista, Colombia	*	*
03.06.93	Britten-Norman BN-2A-20 Islander	P2-ISC	0394	North Coast Airlines	Crashed due to engine failure	Kiriwina, Papua New Guinea	*	*
03.06.93	Bell 206B JetRanger II	G-BNIT	00641	Dollar Helicopters	Crashed into power cables	Fordoun, Aberdeenshire, UK	3	0
06.06.93	de Havilland Canada Twin Otter 300	HK-2759X	771	Aerotaca	Crashed into hillside	nr El Yopal, Colombia	2	0
07.06.93	Learjet 35A	D-COCO	35A-466	Aero-Dienst	Crashed after take-off	Cologne, Germany	4	0
07.06.93	Cessna 404 Titan	ST-AID	404-0455	Sasco Air Lines	Crashed attempting forced landing	nr Ariab, Sudan	11	0
08.06.93	Hamilton Westwind 1	N51FG	BA-324	Active Aero Charter	Crashed after take-off in bad weather	Ypsilanti, MI, USA	1	0
08.06.93	Mil Mi-2	23414	548936114	Kyrgys Airlines	Crashed	Osh, Kirghizia	1	0
09.06.93	Convair 580	N580HH	500	Texas Instruments	Damaged by running off runway during landing	Greenville, TX, USA	0	15
11.06.93	Piper PA-31-350 Chieftain	VH-NDU	31-8152083	Monarch Air Service	Crashed into hillside	Young, NSW, Australia	6	1
14.06.93	Sikorsky S-76B	HL9245	*	Sunkyung Engineering	Crashed whilst undertaking aerial filming	nr Seoul, South Korea	7	1
14.06.93	Dornier Do.228-201	B-12298	8151	Formosa Airlines	Undershot runway on landing	Green Island, Taiwan	0	22
15.06.93	Mil Mi-8	RA-22285	*	Sibavia	Damaged in heavy landing while overloaded	Akta, Russia	0	8
16.06.93	de Havilland Canada Twin Otter 300	PK-NUL	391	Merpati Nusantara Airlines	Crashed due to cargo shifting	Nibire, Indonesia	1	2
17.06.93	Antonov AN-26	26035	*	Tajikistan National Airlines	Crashed into mountains	nr Choporti, Georgia	24	0
17.06.93	PADC BN-2T Islander	RP-C766	3007	National Power Corporation	Crash landed after double engine failure	Manila, Philippines	0	3
18.06.93	Mil Mi-8	RA-25345	*	Krasnoyarskavia	Crashed after heavy rain caused engine failure	Boguchany, Russia	1	5
19.06.93	Grumman TS-2F Tracker	N427DF	*	California Dept of Forestry	Crashed into trees on water drop	Columbia, CA, USA	1	*
19.06.93	Cessna 207A Skywagon	N9869M	207-00744	Markair Express	Crashed on landing	Grayling, AK, USA	*	*
20.06.93	Douglas DC-6B	CP-1651	*	Frigorificos Reyes	Damaged by in-flight fire – Landed safely	Laja, Bolivia	0	*
21.06.93	Pilatus PC-6/B2-H4 Turbo Porter	HB-FKS	875	Farner Air Transport	Crashed	Aousard, Western Sahara	1	3
21.06.93	Antonov AN-24	RA-47708	69900403	Yakutavia	Ran into ditch on landing after engine failure	Yakutsk, Russia	0	38
22.06.93	Mil Mi-8	RA-24527	*	Baikal Air	Crashed into mountain	Kirensk, Russia	0	6
22.06.93	Douglas B-26 Invader	N8036E	*	Collings Foundation	Crashed due to engine failure on take-off during air display	Kanakee, IL, USA	*	*
23.06.93	Agusta-Bell 206A JetRanger	G-BHYW	08043	Lakeside Helicopters	Mid-air collision with RAF Tornado which landed OK	nr Kendal, Cumbria, UK	2(0)	0
24.06.93	Pilatus PC-6/B2-H2 Turbo Porter	FAC.1112	821	Satena	Crashed on approach in bad weather	nr Mitu, Colombia	3	0
24.06.93	Antonov AN-26	RA-26090	*	Omsk Production	Overran on landing	Samara, Russia	0	4
28.06.93	Beechcraft Super King Air 200	ZS-NEP	BB-0838	Trans Namibia Aviation	Crashed after night take-off	Windhoek, Namibia	3	0
29.06.93	Britten-Norman BN-2T Islander	9Q-CLW	2030	Shabair	Crashed into hill on approach	Mitwaba, Zaire	0	4
oo.06.93	Piper PA-31-350 Chieftain	VH-LIC	31-7652173	Augusta Airways	Crash landed after engine failure	Innamincka, SA, Australia	0	*
01.07.93	Fokker F-28 Fellowship 3000	PK-GFU	11131	Merpati Nusantara Airlines	Crashed into sea on approach in rain	Off Sorong, Indonesia	42	2
02.07.93	Cessna U206F Stationair	N1801Q	U206-02925	Alaska Bush Carrier	Crashed into sandbar on landing	Skwentna, AK, USA	*	*
05.07.93	Ilyushin IL-114	RA-54001	*	Ilyushin Design Bureau	Crashed after take-off on test flight	Zhukovsky, Russia	5	4
06.07.93	Bell 212	SU-CAP	31261	Petroleum Air Services	Crashed into sea	Off Alexandria, Egypt	3	0
08.07.93	Mil Mi-8	UR-25445	*	Ukrainian Airlines	Crashed	nr Noyabrsky, Ukraine	1	*
12.07.93	Cessna 402C	N818AN	402C-0324	Air Nevada	Crashed	nr Las Vegas, NV, USA	3	0
12.07.93	Mil Mi-2	14134	5210906049	Kazakhstan Directorate	Crashed	nr Guriev, Kazakhstan	*	*
12.07.93	de Havilland Canada Beaver	C-FPQB	166	Wilderness Airline	Crashed after take-off	Eucott Bay, BC, Canada	5	0
14.07.93	Sikorsky UH-60A Blackhawk	81-23577	*	US Customs Service	Crashed after striking power lines	nr Jesup, GA, USA	4	0
15.07.93	Beechcraft Super King Air 300	VT-EQM	FA-128	National Remote Sensing Agency	Crashed into hill	nr Taloja, India	4	0
18.07.93	Boeing 737-2H6	N401FH	20584	Sahsa	U/c collapsed after overrunning on landing in heavy rain	Managua, Nicaragua	0	*
19.07.93	McDonnell Douglas DC-9-32	YV-613C	47104	Servivensa	Overran runway on landing	Ciudad Bolivar, Bolivia	0	*
20.07.93	Cessna T-47A Citation	N12855	552-0001	Cessna Aircraft Co	Destroyed in hangar fire	Topeka, KS, USA	0	0
20.07.93	Cessna T-47A Citation	N12756	552-0002	Cessna Aircraft Co	Destroyed in hangar fire	Topeka, KS, USA	0	0
20.07.93	Cessna T-47A Citation	N12757	552-0003	Cessna Aircraft Co	Destroyed in hangar fire	Topeka, KS, USA	0	0
20.07.93	Cessna T-47A Citation	N12058	552-0004	Cessna Aircraft Co	Destroyed in hangar fire	Topeka, KS, USA	0	0

Date	Type	Reg'n	C/n	Operator	Accident	Location	F	S
20.07.93	Cessna T-47A Citation	N12859	552-0005	Cessna Aircraft Co	Destroyed in hangar fire	Topeka, KS, USA	0	0
20.07.93	Cessna T-47A Citation	N12660	552-0006	Cessna Aircraft Co	Destroyed in hangar fire	Topeka, KS, USA	0	0
20.07.93	Cessna T-47A Citation	N12761	552-0007	Cessna Aircraft Co	Destroyed in hangar fire	Topeka, KS, USA	0	0
20.07.93	Cessna T-47A Citation	N12762	552-0008	Cessna Aircraft Co	Destroyed in hangar fire	Topeka, KS, USA	0	0
20.07.93	Cessna T-47A Citation	N12763	552-0009	Cessna Aircraft Co	Destroyed in hangar fire	Topeka, KS, USA	0	0
20.07.93	Cessna T-47A Citation	N12564	552-0010	Cessna Aircraft Co	Destroyed in hangar fire	Topeka, KS, USA	0	0
20.07.93	Cessna T-47A Citation	N12065	552-0011	Cessna Aircraft Co	Destroyed in hangar fire	Topeka, KS, USA	0	0
20.07.93	Cessna T-47A Citation	N12967	552-0013	Cessna Aircraft Co	Destroyed in hangar fire	Topeka, KS, USA	0	0
20.07.93	Cessna T-47A Citation	N12669	552-0015	Cessna Aircraft Co	Destroyed in hangar fire	Topeka, KS, USA	0	0
23.07.93	British Aerospace 146-300	B-2716	E-3215	China Northwest Airlines	Crashed into lake after aborting take-off	Yinchuan, China	55	58
24.07.93	Cessna 404 Titan	HK-3001G	*	Aerocivil	Crashed after take-off	Bogota, Colombia	13{6}	0
24.07.93	Aerospatiale AS.350B Ecureuil	C-FTPH	1375	Corporate Helicopters	Forced landed & caught fire	Whistler Mt, BC, Canada	0	*
26.07.93	Boeing 737-5L9	HL7229	24805	Asiana Airlines	Crashed into mountain in bad weather	nr Mokpo, South Korea	68	46
26.07.93	Canadair Regional Jet 100ER	C-FCRJ	7001	Bombardier Aerospace	Crashed during test flight	Wichita, KS, USA	3	0
26.07.93	Boeing 707-327C	OD-AFY	19108	Trans Mediterranean Airways	U/c collapsed during taxiing for take-off	Amsterdam, Netherlands	0	*
26.07.93	de Havilland Canada Beaver	C-FRQW	618	Wagair	Crashed on approach	Klemtu, BC, Canada	5	0
27.07.93	Convair T-29B	N156PA	324	Cool Air	Damaged in belly landing	Boise, ID, USA	0	*
28.07.93	de Havilland Canada Beaver	C-FIUS	901	Aero Golfe	Crashed after take-off	Lac Allard, PQ, Canada	5	0
30.07.93	Short Skyvan 3	9M-AXM	SH.1967	Hornbill Skyways	Crashed into mountain on approach in bad weather	Long Loyanga, Malaysia	1	16
31.07.93	Dornier Do.228-101	9N-ACL	7029	Everest Air	Crashed into hill	Devghat, Nepal	19	0
31.07.93	Rockwell Turbo Commander 690A	N707BP	11326	Operator Unknown	Mid-air collision with PA-28	Location Unknown	*(*)	*
oo.07.93	Beriev Be-12	*	*	Tikhookeanskiy Aviarabotnik	Crashed on landing	Yuzhno-Sakhalinsk, Russia	0	*
02.08.93	Cessna 208 Caravan I	N9526F	208-00085	Markair Express	Crashed after landing on lake with wheels extended	Geographic Harbor, AK, USA	*	*
03.08.93	Cessna 207 Skywagon	*	*	Aeroservicios Ecuatorianos	Crashed in mountains	Ecuador	4	3
04.08.93	Boeing 727-46	HK-2421X	18875	SAM Colombia	Damaged by engine fire on ground	Bogota, Colombia	0	0
07.08.93	Antonov AN-12B	RA-11110	01347902	Aviakor	Crashed out of fuel after becoming lost	El Fasher, Sudan	0	23
09.08.93	Mil Mi-8	RA-22315	*	Tumenavia	Crashed after rotor struck tree on take-off	Saranpatil, Russia	0	9
16.08.93	Cessna 208B Super Cargomaster	N1037D	208B-0332	Aviation & Services Europe	Crashed after engine failure	nr Valensole, France	1	0
17.08.93	Fairchild 226TC Metro II	N220KC	TC-231	Aviation Services	Crashed into river on approach	Hartford, CN, USA	2	0
18.08.93	McDonnell Douglas DC-8-61F	N814CK	46127	American International Airways	Crashed when wing touched ground on landing	Guantanamo, Cuba	0	3
20.08.93	Antonov AN-12	RA-11375	402405	Komiavia	Forced landed & caught fire	Slavgorod, Russia	0	7
25.08.93	Cessna 402C	N206RH	402C-0206	Air Sunshine	Crash landed	West Broward, FL, USA	0	5
25.08.93	Mil Mi-8	RA-22347	*	Magadan Avia	Crashed	nr Magadan, Russia	9	0
26.08.93	LET 410UVP-E Turbolet	RA-67656	902509	Sakha Avia	Crashed after aborting landing	Aldan, Russia	24	0
26.08.93	Cessna 208A Caravan I	PT-OGN	208A-00020	Brasil Central	Hijacked and set on fire after emergency landing	Sinop, Brazil	0	0
27.08.93	Yakovlev YAK-40	87995	*	Tajikistan National Airlines	Crashed on take-off while overloaded	Khorog, Tajikistan	75	5
28.08.93	Antonov AN-28	HA-LAJ	IAJ005-11	Avia Special	Crashed after take-off due to engine failure	Weston-on-the-Green, Oxon, UK	0	19
28.08.93	Antonov AN-26	RA-26549	57302907	Magnitogorsk Avia	Crashed into buildings after running off runway	Donetsk, Ukraine	0	4
31.08.93	Curtiss C-46F	HK-400	22468	Aerosol	Crashed on landing	La Colma, Colombia	0	*
31.08.93	Douglas DC-3	HK-3220	11808	Trans Oriente	Crashed into river on landing	Rio Guaviare, Colombia	*	*
02.09.93	Learjet 25D	XA-NOG	25D-349	TAESA	Ran off runway on landing when tyre burst	Mexico City, Mexico	0	6
03.09.93	Rockwell Sabre 40A	OB-1319	282-127	Aero Condor	Overran on landing & crashed into vehicle	Buenos Aires, Argentina	0	4
05.09.93	Learjet 25D	N999BH	25D-318	Cambridge Aviation	Crashed into high ground	Rowe Mera, TX, USA	7	0
06.09.93	Boeing 727-281	HI-617CA	20726	Dominicana	Caught fire in flight & made emergency landing	Santo Domingo, Dominican Republic	0	*
12.09.93	Mil Mi-8	RA-22813	*	Krasnoyarskavia	Crashed short of runway in poor weather due to fuel shortage	Khatanga, Russia	0	12
13.09.93	Curtiss C-46A	CP-1848	26999	Frigorificos Santa Rita	Crashed after engine failure on take-off	Angora, Bolivia	0	3
13.09.93	LET T-37T	OK-XJI	*	Air Special	Crashed	Kutna Hora, Czech Republic	*	*
14.09.93	Airbus A.320-211	D-AIPN	105	Lufthansa	Crashed on landing in heavy rain and caught fire	Warsaw, Poland	2	68
14.09.93	Convair 440	CP-2256	447	SASA	Damaged in forced belly landing	nr Colquemarca, Peru	0	3
14.09.93	Antonov AN-2	07562	*	Turkmenistan Airlines	Crashed	Dzhebela, Turkmenistan	*	*
15.09.93	Antonov AN-2	RA-07624	1G156-64	Far East Avia	Crashed	nr Vladivostok, Russia	*	*
17.09.93	Piper PA-31-350 Chieftain	VH-WGI	*	Operator Unknown	Crashed into power lines on approach	Launceston, Tas, Australia	6	4
19.09.93	Fairchild 227AC Metro III	F-GILN	AC-458	Regional Airlines	Overran after engine failure on take-off	Troyes, France	0	*

Date	Type	Reg'n	C/n	Operator	Accident	Location	F	S
21.09.93	Tupolev TU-134A	4L-65893	5340120	Transair Georgia	Shot down on approach by Abkhazi rebels	Off Sukhumi, Georgia	27	0
22.09.93	Tupolev TU-154B	4L-85163	*	Transair Georgia	Crash landed after being struck by Abkhazi missile	Sukhumi, Georgia	106	26
23.09.93	Tupolev TU-134A	4L-65001	42235	Transair Georgia	Destroyed by Abkhazi shelling on ground	Sukhumi, Georgia	1	*
23.09.93	Tupolev TU-134A	4L-65809	3352110	ORBI Georgian Airways	Destroyed during Abkhazi attack	Sukhumi, Georgia	*	*
23.09.93	Tupolev TU-134A	4L-65053	49838	ORBI Georgian Airways	Damaged beyond repair	Sukhumi, Georgia	*	*
23.09.93	Tupolev TU-154B-2	4L-85359	359	ORBI Georgian Airways	Damaged beyond repair	Sukhumi, Georgia	*	*
25.09.93	Antonov AN-12	RA-13387	*	Rostov Helicopter Factory	Crash landed out of fuel	Roshino, Russia	0	7
26.09.93	Antonov AN-2	RA-68150	IG196-43	Aeroflot	Crashed	Novoalekseevskaya, Russia	*	*
30.09.93	Cessna 421 Golden Eagle	I-STMO	421-0410	Comet Leasing	Crashed on approach in bad weather	nr Genoa, Italy	5	0
30.09.93	Dassault Falcon 10	F-GJGB	047	G.Bourgoin	Written off	Besancon, France	0	*
30.09.93	Mil Mi-2	23578	*	Air Ukraine	Crashed & caught fire on landing	Poltava, Ukraine	*	*
06.10.93	Fokker F-27 Friendship 600	XY-AEP	10593	Myanma Airways	Overran into river on landing	Kawthaung, Myanmar	0	*
09.10.93	Douglas DC-4	N811E	36080	Brooks Air Fuel	Overran on landing in icy conditions	Point Lay, AK, USA	0	3
12.10.93	Cessna 402B	N7093L	*	Operator Unknown	Crashed after take-off searching for crashed aircraft	Congo Town, Bahamas	2	0
13.10.93	IRMA BN-2A-20 Islander	P2-HBE	0815	Heli Niugini	Crashed into hill	Jimi Valley, Papua New Guinea	4	0
13.10.93	Antonov AN-2T	YV-511C	IG231-21	Aero Transportes La Montana	Crashed after take-off	La Paragua, Venezuela	0	2
15.10.93	Mil Mi-8	YS-1005P	*	South Pacific Heli Logging	Crashed	Westlands, New Zealand	3	0
15.10.93	Mil Mi-26	RA-06043	*	Tumenavia	Crashed	Wyuganst, Russia	*	*
16.10.93	Aerospatiale AS.365N Dauphin 2	B-7104	6060	China Ocean Helicopter Co	Crashed in sea attempting to land on oil platform	South China Sea	3	0
16.10.93	Cessna 207A Skywagon	N208SC	207-00445	South Central Air	Crashed into mountain	nr Kenai, AK, USA	1	0
16.10.93	Kamov Ka-26	HA-MPG	7706306	Air Service Hungary	Crashed into hill	Herceghalom, Hungary	*	*
18.10.93	Fairchild 226TC Metro II	EC-FHB	TC-355	Swiftair	U/c collapsed on landing	Madrid, Spain	0	2
24.10.93	Aerospatiale 332L Super Puma	B-7952	2159	China Ocean Helicopter Co	Crashed at sea	Off Lintin Island, China	*	*
25.10.93	McDonnell Douglas MD-82	B-28003	53065	Far Eastern Air Transport	U/c collapsed & wing torn off in hard landing	Kaohsiung, Taiwan	0	*
25.10.93	GAF Nomad N22	ZK-NOM	004	Hibiscus Air	Crashed onto glacier	Franz Josef Glacier, New Zealand	9	0
26.10.93	McDonnell Douglas MD-82	B-2103	49355	China Eastern Airlines	Crashed after overrunning on landing	Fuzhou, China	2	79
26.10.93	Beechcraft Super King Air 300	N82	FF-17	Federal Aviation Administration	Crashed into trees	High Knob, VA, USA	3	0
27.10.93	Beechcraft Queen Air 65	RP-C999	LC-156	Operator Unknown	Crashed into mountain	Mauban, Philippines	5	0
27.10.93	de Havilland Canada Twin Otter 300	LN-BNM	408	Wideroe	Crashed on approach in bad weather	Namsos, Norway	6	*
27.10.93	LET 410UVP Turbolet	UR-67536	820916	Air Ukraine	Damaged while taxiing for take-off	Roshino, Ukraine	0	*
01.11.93	Beriev Be-12	*	*	Tikhookeanskiy Aviarabotnik	Crashed on landing in storm	Yuzhno-Sakhalinsk, Russia	0	*
04.11.93	Boeing 747-409	B-165	24313	China Airlines	Overran & crashed into bay on landing	Hong Kong	0	*
04.11.93	Convair 440-12	CP-2212	*	CAMBA	Damaged on landing with engine fire	El Triunfo, Bolivia	0	3
06.11.93	Cessna 421B Golden Eagle	N41010	421B-0569	Operator Unknown	Crashed short of runway	Greenburg, IN, USA	5	0
07.11.93	Douglas Turbo DC-3	ZS-KCV	15268/26713	Professional Aviation Services	Collided on take-off with Cessna 208 ZS-NIH	Lokiohogtio, Kenya	0(0)	*
07.11.93	Cessna 208 Caravan I	ZS-NIH	208-00057	King Air Services	Struck by DC-3 ZS-KCV during its take-off run	Lokiohogtio, Kenya	0(0)	*
08.11.93	Harbin Y-12-II	9N-ACS	044	Royal Nepal Airlines	Overshot on landing and ran into river	Jomsom, Nepal	0	19
10.11.93	British Aerospace 748 2A	C-GQTH	1617	Air Manitoba	Crashed after take-off	Sandy Lake, ON, Canada	7	0
11.11.93	Cessna 208 Caravan I	5Y-MAK	*	Falcon Air Charter	Crashed into train after aborting take-off	Ariat, Sudan	0	*
11.11.93	Antonov AN-2	EZ-07469	*	Turkmenistan Airlines	Damaged in forced landing after engine failure	nr Bekdash, Turkmenistan	0	4
13.11.93	McDonnell Douglas MD-82	B-2141	49849	China Northern Airlines	Crash landed & caught fire	nr Urumqi, China	12	90
14.11.93	Bell 206B JetRanger III	C-GDBP	02463	Heli-Plus	Crashed on landing after tail rotor failure	nr Luskville, PQ, Canada	*	*
15.11.93	Antonov AN-124	RA-82071	*	Magistralnye Avialinii	Crashed into mountains when short of fuel	nr Kerman, Iran	17	0
15.11.93	Airbus A.300B2-1C	VT-EDV	034	Indian Airlines	Crash landed in field while short of fuel	Tirupati, India	0	263
19.11.93	Boeing 737-112	HP-873CMP	19768	COPA Panama	Ran off runway on landing & nosewheel collapsed	Panama City, Panama	0	92
20.11.93	Yakovlev YAK-42	RA-42390	4016557	Avioimpex	Crashed in mountains on approach	nr Ohrid, Macedonia	115	1
20.11.93	Cessna 421 Golden Eagle	*	*	Operator Unknown	Crashed on roadway attempting to land	Avignon, France	2	0
21.11.93	Beechcraft Queen Air 80	TG-ACP	*	Aerovias SA	Crashed into mountain	nr Palencia, Guatemala	13	0
22.11.93	Douglas DC-3	C9-STE	19006	Scan Transportes Aereos	Crashed after engine failure	nr Chemba, Mozambique	2	1
23.11.93	Antonov AN-28	RA-28716	*	Kamchatavia	Damaged in heavy landing	Palana, Russia	0	2
23.11.93	Piper PA-31 Navajo	OB-1453	31-7812067	Transportes Aereos Maranon	Damaged in crash landing	Constitucion, Peru	*	*
26.11.93	Douglas DC-6B	N1597F	43700	Allcair Air Transport	Crashed into rising ground on approach	Patriot Hills, Antarctica	0	8
01.12.93	British Aerospace Jetstream 31	N334PX	706	Northwest Airlink	Crashed in poor weather	Minneapolis, MN, USA	18	0
01.12.93	Short 330-300	C-FPQE	SH.3124	Government of Quebec Air Service	Crashed due to icing on approach	Umiujaq, PQ, Canada	0	13

Date	Type	Reg'n	C/n	Operator	Accident	Location	F	S
02.12.93	Short Skyvan 3	LX-UGO	SH.1945	CAE Aviation	Landed short & crashed into trees	Vahun, Liberia	0	13
03.12.93	de Havilland Dove 5	VH-DHD	04104	Rudge Air	Crashed into houses after take-off	Melbourne, Vic, Australia	0	10
03.12.93	Mil Mi-8	RA-25740	*	Far East Avia	Crashed & caught fire attempting emergency landing	Chuguevka, Russia	0	*
03.12.93	Bell 412	N356EH	33072	ERA Aviation	Crashed on approach	Cameron, LA, USA	*	*
04.12.93	Grumman G-21A Goose	C-FUMG	B-145	Waglisla Air	Crashed into lake after take-off	Prince Rupert, BC, Canada	6	0
05.12.93	Britten-Norman BN-2A-20 Islander	C-GMOP	0398	Arctic Wings & Rotors	Crashed into lake	nr Tuktoyaktuk, NWT, Canada	7	0
06.12.93	Cessna 208A Caravan I	PT-OGM	208A-00069	Taxi Aereo Marilia	Damaged in forced landing on approach	Tucuma, Brazil	0	*
06.12.93	Antonov AN-26	RA-26515	*	Krasnoyarskavia	Damaged after running off runway	Tura-Gorny, Russia	*	*
10.12.93	de Havilland Canada Twin Otter 300	6V-ADE	393	Air Senegal	Mid-air collision with Gambia A/W YS-11 C5-GAA	Off Dakar, Senegal	3(0)	0
10.12.93	Britten-Norman BN-2A-20 Islander	P2-ALL	0448	Airlink	Crashed	Namatanai, Papua New Guinea	*	*
12.12.93	Antonov AN-8	13323	OE-3430	Kadvi Company	Undershot on landing	Yerevan, Armenia	0	8
13.12.93	Harbin Y-12-II	*	*	Lao Aviation	Crashed on approach after striking trees	Phonesavanh, Laos	18	0
13.12.93	Beechcraft Super King Air 200T	9M-CAM	BT-24	Malaysian Dept. of Civil Aviation	Damaged after leaving runway on landing	Ipoh, Malaysia	0	*
14.12.93	Antonov AN-2	RA-62599	*	Krasnoyarskavia	Crashed & caught fire on take-off	Vorogovo, Russia	0	17
15.12.93	IAI 1124 Westwind Two	N309CK	350	Management Activities	Crashed on approach after flying into B757 wake	Irvine, CA, USA	5	0
15.12.93	Mitsubishi Diamond 1	N710MB	AO78SA	Whitham Farms Feed Yard	Crashed & caught fire	Goodland, KS, USA	3	0
17.12.93	Beechcraft King Air C90A	RP-C2446	LJ-1102	Air Link International Airways	Crashed in bad weather	Palawan, Philippines	2	0
19.12.93	Antonov AN-12	RA-12187	*	Sibavia	Undershot & ran off runway on landing	Lensk, Russia	0	10
19.12.93	MBB Bo.105CBS	EC-DSU	S.623	TAF Helicopteres	Crashed into mountain	Sierra del Calde, Spain	3	0
21.12.93	Tupolev TU-134A	UN-65787	*	Kazair	Landed off runway & u/c collapsed	Alma Ata, Kazakhstan	0	6
22.12.93	Antonov AN-2	RA-01410	IG230-01410	Tumenavia	Crash landed in woods after engine failure	nr Uray, Russia	0	10
23.12.93	Cessna A185F	ZK-EHM	185-03427	Mount Cook Airlines	Crashed on landing	Quinton, New Zealand	0	*
24.12.93	Britten-Norman BN-2A-26 Islander	P2-ISR	0015	Transniugini Airways	Crashed	Mt Hagan, Papua New Guinea	*	*
25.12.93	Tupolev TU-154B-1	RA-85295	295	Vnukovo Production Association	Ran off runway after landing in fog	Grozny, Russia	0	172
25.12.93	Mil Mi-2	RA-23201	5310122037	North West Directorate	Crashed after striking power lines	nr Kirovsk, Russia	0	*
26.12.93	Antonov AN-26	26141	*	Krasnodar Air Enterprises	Crashed at night on approach while overloaded	Gyumri, Armenia	36	0
28.12.93	Short Skyvan 3	G-OVAN	SH.1892	Peterborough Parachute Centre	Veered off runway & crashed into tree on landing	Ampuriabrava, Spain	0	*
29.12.93	Tupolev TU-154B-2	RA-85358	358	Sibavia	U/c collapsed on landing	Omsk, Russia	0	8
oo.oo.93	Canadair CL-44D4-6	N100BB	029	Tradewinds	Badly damaged during thunderstorm – landed safely	nr Santo Domingo, Dominica	0	*
oo.oo.93	Mil Mi-8	HA-BCN	528229063	Do-Air Trade	Crashed into chimney in bad weather	Tiszaujvaros, Hungary	*	*
01.01.94	Bell 206L-3 Long Ranger	C-GPRM	51316	Pyramid Helicopters	Slid backwards over cliff	nr Kalso, BC, Canada	0	1
02.01.94	Britten-Norman BN-2A Islander	YV-2349P	*	JSCTD	Crashed after take-off	Elorza, Venezuela	2	0
03.01.94	Tupolev TU-154M	RA-85656	801	Baikal Air	Crashed after engine failure on take-off	Irkutsk, Russia	124(1)	0
06.01.94	Beechcraft King Air B90	N230TW	LJ-0445	Kimura International	Crashed after engine failure on take-off	Kissimmee, FL, USA	10	0
06.01.94	IRMA BN-2A-21 Islander	PK-VIV	0852	Dirgantara Air Service	Damaged in forced landing after engine failure	Kuala Kapuas, Indonesia	0	10
07.01.94	British Aerospace Jetstream 41	N304UE	41016	Atlantic Coast Airlines	Crashed on approach	Columbus, OH, USA	5	0
08.01.94	Mil Mi-8P	LZ-CAP	10320	Hummingbird Helicopters	Crashed at sea due to tail rotor failure	Kandholhudu, Maldives	9	2
08.01.94	Short Skyvan 3	OY-JRK	SH.1901	Danish Air Transport	Crashed landed in desert	Mauritania	0	*
08.01.94	Beechcraft King Air A100	OO-TLS	B-188	Travair	Damaged in heavy landing	nr Bacau, Romania	0	*
10.01.94	Mil Mi-2	RA-20945	528645044	Central Region Directorate	Crashed	nr Cherusty, Russia	3	0
12.01.94	Beechcraft 99	C-FKHD	U011	North-Wright Air	Crashed into snowbank on landing	Fort Franklin, NWT, Canada	0	*
13.01.94	Beechcraft King Air A90	N46WA	LJ-0065	Operator Unknown	Crashed at sea	Off Marseilles, France	*	*
13.01.94	Aerospatiale AS.350D Astar	N902BA	1414	Bulldog Airlines	Crashed after engine failure	nr Lakeland, FL, USA	0	2
14.01.94	Rockwell Turbo Commander 690	VH-BSS	11044	Newcastle Aviation	Crashed at sea	Off Sydney, NSW, Australia	1	0
15.01.94	Bell 206B JetRanger II	G-BODW	00784	Delta Helicopters	Crashed on take-off after rotor struck ground	Luton, Beds, UK	1	0
16.01.94	Consolidated PBY-5A Catalina	N5404J	22022	The Catalina Company	Sank after forced landing with engine problems	Off Christmas Is, Pacific Ocean	0	7
17.01.94	Mil Mi-8	RA-22793	*	Krasnoyarskavia	Crashed into snowbank on take-off	Vamava, Russia	0	10
17.01.94	Kamov Ka-26	RA-24309	*	Bashkirian Airlines	Damaged in forced landing	Priyutovo, Russia	0	5
18.01.94	Antonov AN-22	RA-09331	*	Aeroflot	Crashed following explosion on take-off	nr Tver, Russia	7	3
18.01.94	Learjet 24D	9Q-CBC	24D-248	Scibe Airlift	Crashed on approach out of fuel	Kinshasa, Zaire	2	0
20.01.94	Airbus A.340-211	F-GNIA	010	Air France	Destroyed by fire on ground	Paris, France	0	0
21.01.94	Lockheed Electra 188A	9Q-CCV	1126	Trans Service Airlift	Damaged when nose u/c collapsed on landing	Kinshasa, Zaire	0	*
23.01.94	FMA Guarani II	LV-LAE	27	Lineas Aereas Entre Rios	U/c collapsed on second landing	Santa Elena, Argentina	0	2
24.01.94	Cessna 425	D-IEFW	425-0228	Aerowest	Crashed into lake on purpose	Lake Constance, Switzerland	0	*

Date	Type	Reg'n	C/n	Operator	Accident	Location	F	S
24.01.94	Cessna TU206G Stationair 6	OB-1341	U206-04906	Transportes Aereos	Sank in river after forced landing	River Ucayali, Peru	0	*
25.01.94	Yakovlev YAK-42	RA-42331	*	Southern Directorate	Damaged by running into tug while on tow	Russia	0	84
26.01.94	Cessna 421C Golden Eagle	N5468G	421C-0215	Sky Harbor Air Service	Crashed on approach	McCook, NE, USA	2	5
27.01.94	IAI 1124 Westwind Two	C-FMWW	380	Millar Western Industries	Crashed on approach in bad weather	Meadow Lake, SK, Canada	2	0
28.01.94	Sikorsky S-58T	N4995G	58-1561	Air One Helicopters	Crashed onto roof of building	San Jose, CA, USA	1	0
28.01.94	Hughes 500E	C-FGSU	0012E	Great Slave Helicopters	Crashed in snowstorm	Aylmer Lake, NWT, Canada	0	3
29.01.94	Bell 206B JetRanger III	C-GRAH	03304	Westland Helicopters	Crashed after take-off	Houston, BC, Canada	5	0
30.01.94	Curtiss C-46A	HK-1856	369	Lineas Aereas Suramericanas	Crashed on landing	Puerto Inirita, Colombia	*	*
01.02.94	Antonov AN-24	RA-47718	69900701	Kolyma Avia	Crashed into snowbank on take-off	Omsukchan, Russia	0	53
05.02.94	Britten-Norman BN-2A Islander	G-AXHE	0086	North West Parachute Centre	Damaged after running off runway on landing	Cark, Cumbria, UK	0	1
08.02.94	Antonov AN-12	RA-11340	*	Privolzhskoye Directorate	Damaged by overrunning on landing	Anadyr, Russia	0	11
14.02.94	Bell 206L-3 Long Ranger	N1077N	45349	Aspen Helicopters	Crashed after hard landing	Barstow, CA, USA	0	1
16.02.94	Beechcraft E18S	N49K	BA-519	H & G Import & Export Corp	Crashed	nr Fort Lauderdale, FL, USA	0	*
20.02.94	Bell 212	C-GKTL	32124	Canadian Helicopters	Crashed in snowstorm	Eldorado Mt, BC, Canada	0	13
21.02.94	Sikorsky S-58T	N581BG	58-1487	Air One Helicopters	Crashed into hill	Walnut Creek, CA, USA	3	0
22.02.94	Beechcraft 2000A Starship	N8149S	*	Operator Unknown	Damaged in aborted take-off	Roskilde, Denmark	*	*
22.02.94	Tupolev TU-134A-3	HA-LBP	63560	Malev	Damaged by cockpit fire on ground	Budapest, Hungary	0{1}	0
23.02.94	Aerospatiale AS.350B Ecureuil	N766MP	1301	Papillon Hawaiian Helicopters	Crashed	nr Humuula, HI, USA	0	7
24.02.94	Antonov AN-12B	RA-11118	01348002	North Western Air Transport	Crashed	Nalchik, Russia	13	0
25.02.94	Vickers Viscount 813	G-OHOT	349	British World Airlines	Crashed after engine failure	Drointon, Staffs, UK	1	1
25.02.94	Yakovlev YAK-40	OB-1559	*	Expresso Aereo	Crashed in mountains after take-off	Tingo Maria, Peru	31	0
26.02.94	Bell 206L-3 Long Ranger	N2753U	*	Classic Helicopters	Rolled down mountain after landing	nr Salt Lake City, UT, USA	*	*
27.02.94	Bell 206B JetRanger II	N50PE	*	Helinet	Damaged in hard landing	Agua Dulce, CA, USA	0	2
01.03.94	Bell 206B JetRanger III	P2-HBA	2891	Heli Niugini	Crashed on approach	Mt Notuku, Papua New Guinea	4	1
02.03.94	McDonnell Douglas MD-82	N18835	49439	Continental Airlines	Overran after aborting take-off	Denver, CO, USA	0	116
02.03.94	Bell 412	PK-HMR	33104	Gatari Air Service	Crash landed on beach out of fuel	Nias Island, Indonesia	0	10
03.03.94	Douglas DC-6	CP-2251	*	Aerobeni	Destroyed on ground by fuel fire	Tumbes, Peru	0	*
04.03.94	Piper PA-31-350 Chieftain	N78DE	31-7852087	Ameriflight	Crashed into mountain	nr Mt Pinos, CA, USA	1	*
08.03.94	Boeing 737-2R4C	VT-SIA	21763	Sahara India Airlines	Crashed on take-off and struck Aeroflot IL-86 RA-86119	New Delhi, India	4(3)	0
08.03.94	Ilyushin IL-86	RA-86119	*	Aeroflot	Destroyed on ground by crashing Sahara Air B.737 VT-SIA	New Delhi, India	3(4)	4
09.03.94	Fairchild Merlin IVA	VH-SWP	AT-033	Jetcraft	Crashed on approach	Tamworth, NSW, Australia	1	0
10.03.94	Mil Mi-8	RA-25203	*	Tumenavia	Destroyed by fire on ground	Russia	*	*
10.03.94	Bell 206B JetRanger III	N57340	02998	Evergreen Helicopters	Crashed on take-off	nr Cameron, LA, USA	0	1
12.03.94	LET Z-37A	OK-WJJ	0220	Air Special	Crashed	Pardubice, Czech Republic	1	0
15.03.94	Aerospatiale Caravelle 10B3	HK-3855	265	SEC Colombia	Crashed	Bogota, Colombia	0	6
16.03.94	IRMA BN-2A-21 Islander	D2-ECE	0903	Mavewa	Damaged during emergency landing	nr Cabinda, Angola	0	*
18.03.94	Grumman G-73 Turbo Mallard	N150FB	J-51	Chalks International Airlines	Crashed on take-off	Key West, FL, USA	2	0
18.03.94	Douglas DC-3	N3433Y	43089	Salair	Crashed attempting to land after engine failure	Spokane, OR, USA	2	0
18.03.94	Fairchild Merlin IIB	N20PT	T26-128	Eagle Aviation	Crashed on approach	Winchester, VA, USA	1	*
18.03.94	Mil Mi-2	RA-14131	*	Privolzhskoye Air Transport	Crashed on landing in high winds	Rishevo, Russia	0	3
18.03.94	Aerospatiale AS.350B Ecureuil	C-GAHG	1047	Canadian Helicopters	Struck trees on emergency landing	Golden, BC, Canada	0	5
19.03.94	de Havilland Canada Twin Otter 300	*	*	Light Air Transport	Crashed	nr Tripoli, Libya	1	1
19.03.94	CASA 212 Aviocar 200	FAC.1154	317	Satena	Damaged in forced landing after engine failure	La Macarena, Colombia	0	29
20.03.94	Canadair Challenger 3A	N88HA	5072	Crystal Aviation	Damaged in forced landing after engine failure	Bassett-Rock, NE, USA	0	2
21.03.94	McDonnell Douglas DC-9-32	EC-CLE	47678	Aviaco	Landed short of runway & caught fire	Vigo, Spain	0	116
22.03.94	Airbus A.310-308	F-OGQS	596	Aeroflot Russian International A/L	Crashed after pilot allowed his son to handle controls	nr Mezhdurechensk, Russia	75	0
22.03.94	IRMA BN-2A-21 Islander	VH-JUU	0632	Aurukun Aboriginal Community	Crashed after engine failure on take-off	Weipa, Qld, Australia	6	0
23.03.94	Cessna Citation VI	PT-OMV	650-0200	Orion Aero Taxi	Crashed into mountain on approach	Facatativa, Colombia	4	0
23.03.94	Aerospatiale SA.341G Gazelle	9Y-TFN	1044	National Helicopter Services	Crashed at sea on approach	Chaguaramas, Trinidad & Tobago	0	4
24.03.94	IAR Alouette III	YR-ELV	102	Aviatia Utilitara	Crashed after passenger knocked controls	Brasov, Romania	7	0
26.03.94	Bell 206L-1 Long Ranger	F-GJGP	45619	Helijet Vietnam	Crashed in bad weather	Bao Yan, Vietnam	5	0
27.03.94	Beechcraft King Air E90	YV-726CP	LW-182	Multi Servicios Lujal	Crashed on emergency approach	Caracas, Venezuela	*	*
27.03.94	Mil Mi-2	RA-15362	*	Yuzhnoye Air Transport	Damaged in hard landing	nr Makop, Russia	0	1
30.03.94	Mil Mi-8	RA-22226	*	Komiavia	Crashed	Pechora, Russia	2	18

Date	Type	Reg'n	C/n	Operator	Accident	Location	F	S
31.03.94	Mil Mi-8	*	*	Algerian Police	Crashed after rotor failure	Djanet, Algeria	14	2
01.04.94	Learjet 35A	XC-PGR	35A-460	Procuraduria General de la Republica	Damaged in belly landing	Mexico City, Mexico	0	*
03.04.94	Bell 206B JetRanger III	N27736	02773	El Aero Services	Crashed	nr Lamoille, NV, USA	3	2
04.04.94	Saab 340B	PH-KSH	195	KLM Cityhopper	Crashed on emergency landing after engine failure	Amsterdam, Netherlands	3	21
04.04.94	Aerospatiale AS.350B Ecureuil	C-FHBG	1440	Turbowest Helicopters	Rolled over after landing on beaver dam	nr High Prairie, AB, Canada	0	2
06.04.94	Dassault Falcon 50	9XR-NN	006	Rwanda Government	Shot down by missile [Presidents of Rwanda & Burundi killed]	Kigali, Rwanda	9	0
06.04.94	Hughes 500D	OE-XAA	1090587D	Helijet Airways	Crashed into power cables	St Michael, Austria	3	0
07.04.94	Lockheed L-100-30 Hercules	D2-THC	4679	Angola Air Charter	Destroyed by wheel fire after landing	Angola	0	*
11.04.94	Aerospatiale SA.315B Lama	I-ELTA	2507	ETI 2000	Crashed in fog	Zermatt, Switzerland	5	0
18.04.94	Hughes 500D	N1103N	410945D	Inter-Island Helicopters	Crashed into stream after engine failure	Waimea Falls, HI, USA	1	4
22.04.94	Bell 412	N70AM	*	Air Methods	Crashed on approach	East River Mt, WV, USA	4	0
23.04.94	Sikorsky S-76A	PK-PUD	760195	Pelita Air Service	Crashed attempting to land on oil platform	Off Matak Island, Indonesia	*	*
23.04.94	Curtiss C-46F	C-GIXZ	22495	Relief Air Transport	Crashed after engine failure on take-off	Lokichoggio, Kenya	*	*
24.04.94	Douglas DC-3	VH-EDC	12874	South Pacific Airmotive	Crashed after take-off due to engine failure	Botany Bay, NSW, Australia	0	25
24.04.94	Mil Mi-8	HA-BCU	*	Horex	Crashed after striking ground in turn	Soltvadkert, Hungary	0	5
25.04.94	IRMA BN-2A-21 Islander	PK-ZAA	0730	Dirgantara Air Service	Crashed into mountain	Nanga Pinoh, Indonesia	11	0
26.04.94	Airbus A.300B4-622R	B-1816	580	China Airlines	Crashed after attempting to abort landing	Nagoya, Japan	263	8
26.04.94	Mil Mi-8	RA-25613	*	Kamchatavia	Damaged in forced landing after rotor failure	nr Esso, Russia	0	8
27.04.94	Boeing 727-44F	S9-TAN	18893	Air Transafrik	Crashed on landing	M'Banza-Congo, Angola	0{7}	3
27.04.94	Piper PA-31-350 Chieftain	N990RA	31-7405417	Action Air	Crashed on approach	Stratford, CT, USA	8	1
29.04.94	Cessna 208 Caravan I	HK-3470	*	Lineas Aereas de los Libertadores	Crashed into mountain on approach	Cerro el Vino Mts, Colombia	8	1
03.05.94	Aerospatiale SA.319B Alouette III	HB-XOL	2211	Air Zermatt	Damaged in heavy landing	Switzerland	0	1
05.05.94	Sikorsky S-58ET	PK-OBS	58-1111	Airfast Services	Crashed	En route Jen to Tabang, Indonesia	2	0
05.05.94	Mil Mi-2	*	*	Operator Unknown	Crashed after striking power lines	Aktyubinsk, Kazakhstan	1	2
07.05.94	Tupolev TU-134A	RA-65976	3352007	Arkhangelsk Airlines	Damaged when u/c collapsed on landing	Arkhangelsk, Russia	0	62
07.05.94	Beechcraft King Air	*	*	SNEL	Crashed on approach	Kinshasa, Zaire	9	0
07.05.94	Embraer Bandeirante 110E	PT-GJW	110.072	Rico Taxi Aereo	Damaged in forced landing	San Gabriel, Brazil	0	*
07.05.94	Mil Mi-2	RA-20314	527520022	Central Region Directorate	Crashed after take-off	Trockurovo, Russia	0	1
08.05.94	IRMA BN-2A-28 Islander	CS-DAF	0691	Aerocondor Transportes Aereos	Crashed into trees attempting forced landing on road	nr Braganca, Portugal	0	4
11.05.94	Mil Mi-2	RA-23462	*	West Siberian Directorate	Crashed after take-off	Novosibirsk, Russia	3	0
12.05.94	Antonov AN-28	RA-28713	1AJ006-23	Kamchatavia	Damaged in hard landing	Palana, Russia	0	12
15.05.94	Aerospatiale AS.350B Ecureuil	SE-HNG	1752	Norrlandsflyg	Crashed after striking rocks	nr Hoigancorru, Sweden	0	*
20.05.94	Sikorsky S-58E	C-GIMO	58-0067	Cypress Helicopters	Crash landed in trees after engine failure	Slave Lake, AB, Canada	0	1
21.05.94	McDonnell Douglas DC-8-51F	HK-3816X	45685	Fine Air	Damaged when nosewheel collapsed on take-off	Medellin, Colombia	0	3
21.05.94	Douglas DC-6A/B	HK-1276W	44056	Inv. Agropecuarias del Casanare	Damaged in forced landing	Mitu, Colombia	0	9
21.05.94	Mil Mi-2	RA-20110	543011063	Central Region Directorate	Crashed after tail struck ground	nr Zmeevo, Russia	1	1
22.05.94	Bell 206B JetRanger III	G-STST	3755	Central Helicopters	Crashed into mountain	Mt Moel Goch, UK	3	1
23.05.94	IRMA BN-2B-27 Islander	HK-2890	2111	Aerolineas Llaneras	Crashed attempting emergency landing	Loma Linda, Colombia	4	7
23.05.94	Mil Mi-8	RA-25329	*	North West Directorate	Crashed after engine failure after take-off	nr Vorkuta, Russia	0	3
24.05.94	Antonov AN-2	RA-07330	*	Far East Directorate	Damaged in forced landing in swamp	nr Oktyabrsky, Russia	0	*
27.05.94	Beechcraft King Air C90	D-IHNA	LJ-0926	Burkhart Grob Luft-und-Raumfahrt	Crashed after take-off	Mindelheim, Germany	1	0
27.05.94	Mitsubishi MU-2B-60 Marquise	F-GDHV	779SA	Air Oceania Tahiti	Crashed into sea on approach	Off Papeete, French Polynesia	5	0
27.05.94	Bell 204B	N911SW	2025	Horizon Helicopters	Crashed after engine failure	nr Libby, MT, USA	0	1
28.05.94	Douglas DC-3	HK-2213	11752	Trans Oriente	Crashed after take-off	Villa Vicencio, Colombia	4	25
30.05.94	British Aerospace 125-3A	N900CD	25111	DB Aviation	Damaged in hard landing	Waukegan, IL, USA	0	*
31.05.94	Fairchild Merlin IIA	C-FFYC	T26-036	Keewatin Air	Crashed on night approach	nr Thompson, MN, Canada	2	1
01.06.94	Bell 205A-1	HK-1772E	30066	Helicol	Crashed on landing & fell down slope	Orito, Colombia	1	2
05.06.94	Mil Mi-2	RA-28756	*	AS Airlines	Crashed into lake after take-off	nr Nakhodka, Russia	0	1
06.06.94	Tupolev TU-154M	B-2610	740	China Northwest Airlines	Crashed after take-off	nr Mighu, China	160	0
13.06.94	Fairchild 226TC Metro II	XA-SLU	TC-401	Aero Cuahonte	Crashed on landing in rain	Uruapan, Mexico	9	0
14.06.94	Bell 206B JetRanger II	C-FLIL	00800	Vancouver Island Helicopters	Crashed after rotors struck tree	King Island, BC, Canada	0	*
18.06.94	Fokker F-27 Friendship 500F	PK-MFI	10624	Merpati Nusantara Airlines	Crashed into mountain in bad weather	Multiara, Indonesia	12	0
18.06.94	Learjet 25D	XA-BBA	25D-223	TAESA	Crashed on approach in poor weather	Washington, DC, USA	12	0
22.06.94	Mil Mi-8	RA-27076	*	TAN Airlines	Crashed after engine fire	nr Kazan, Russia	8	3

Date	Type	Reg'n	C/n	Operator	Accident	Location	F	S
22.06.94	Bell 206B JetRanger III	HB-XUT	02272	Air Glaciers	Mid-air collision with Swiss AF SA.332 T-318 which landed OK	nr Grindelwald, Switzerland	3(0)	0
23.06.94	de Havilland Canada Otter	N13GA	179	Wings of Alaska	Crashed and sank	Taku Inlet, AK, USA	8	2
23.06.94	de Havilland Canada Beaver	C-FDTI	037	Harbour Air	Crashed	nr Hunter Point, BC, Canada	*	*
25.06.94	Bell 206A JetRanger	N7881S	00068	Orion Helicopters	Damaged in hard landing	Rocky Mountain National Pk, CO, USA	*	*
25.06.94	Antonov AN-2	RA-70263	IG139-22	East Siberian Directorate	Crashed on take-off & caught fire	Kirensk, Russia	0	8
26.06.94	Fokker F-27 Friendship 400M	TU-TIP	10577	Air Ivoire	Crashed on approach	Abidjan, Ivory Coast	16	1
26.06.94	Douglas DC-3	C-FROD	12307	Buffalo Airways	Crashed in forced landing on road	Fort Simpson, NWT, Canada	0	2
26.06.94	Hughes 500D	LV-WBL	280262D	Andes Aviacion	Crashed after striking rock outcrop	Cerro Bayo, Argentina	0	4
27.06.94	Mil Mi-2	UN-14229	5311116020	Kazakhstan Airlines	Crashed into power lines	Aktyubinsk, Kazakhstan	1	1
28.06.94	Grumman Gulfstream I	F-GIIX	128	Air Provence	Crashed on landing & caught fire	Lyon, France	0	27
30.06.94	Airbus A.330-321	F-WWKH	042	Airbus Industrie	Crashed after simulated engine failure on take-off	Toulouse, France	7	0
oo.06.94	Douglas DC-6	HK-3531X	43708	Transamazonica	Crashed	Colombia	*	*
01.07.94	Fokker F-28 Fellowship 4000	5T-CLF	11092	Air Mauritanie	Crashed on landing in sandstorm	Tidjikja, Mauretania	94	7
01.07.94	Mil Mi-6	RA-21040	*	Tyumen Directorate	Caught fire after hard landing	nr Nadym, Russia	0	6
01.07.94	Bell 206B JetRanger III	N10800	2910	PJ Helicopters	Crashed after underslung load struck rocks	nr Tucson, AZ, USA	0	2
03.07.94	McDonnell Douglas DC-9-31	N954VJ	47590	US Air	Crashed on landing	Charlotte, NC, USA	37	15
06.07.94	Antonov AN-32P	UR-48018	*	Antonov Design Bureau	Crashed while fighting forest fire	nr Valencia, Spain	5	1
06.07.94	Fokker F-27 Friendship 200	AP-ALN	10164	Pakistan International Airlines	Forced landed after engine failure on approach	Dera Ismail Khan, Pakistan	0	42
06.07.94	Aerospatiale AS.350B2 Ecureuil	N901BA	2452	Bulldog Airlines	Crashed after tail struck water	Off Caryville, FL, USA	0	1
07.07.94	Rockwell Turbo Commander 680	SE-GUO	535-204	Varmlandsflyg	Crashed into mast	Roslags Bro, Sweden	2	0
09.07.94	Aerospatiale AS.350B2 Ecureuil	N95LG	2389	Rocky Mountain Helicopters	Crashed into mountain	nr Granite, CO, USA	2	0
09.07.94	Beechcraft Super King Air 200	VT-EUJ	BB-1456	Operator Unknown	Crashed after hitting trees in fog	Runda, India	13	0
09.07.94	Antonov AN-2	OK-NYA	113902	Operator Unknown	Damaged beyond repair	Ried-Kirchheim, Austria	*	*
10.07.94	Hughes 500HS	G-HSAA	109-0203S	Redhill Helicopter Centre	Crashed	Old Stratford, Northants, UK	0	3
12.07.94	Beechcraft King Air C90	N9066N	LJ-0557	TATSA	Ran off runway on take-off	Ciudad Constitucion, Peru	0	11
13.07.94	Agusta A109A	RP-C1109	7177	Airspan Helicopters	Crashed on take-off in high winds	Makati, Philippines	0	2
14.07.94	LET 410UVP Turbolet	RA-67470	841235	Far East Directorate	Damaged after taxiing into ditch	Blagoveschensk, Russia	0	14
14.07.94	Hughes 500D	N8648F	180257D	Temesco Helicopters	Crashed into lake	Ketchikan, AK, USA	0	2
14.07.94	Aerospatiale AS.350D Astar	N151BH	1298	Papillon Hawaiian Helicopters	Crashed in sea	Off Kauai, HI, USA	3	4
14.07.94	Bell 206B JetRanger II	C-FXAL	00198	Great Slave Helicopters	Crashed	nr Copper Mine, NWT, Canada	0	1
14.07.94	Bell 206B JetRanger III	JA9211	2478	Aero Asahi	Crashed after striking wires	Shariki-mura, Japan	0	1
15.07.94	Hughes 500D	C-GLHS	1100853D	Northern Mountain Helicopters	Damaged in crash landing	Goose Lake, NWT, Canada	0	1
17.07.94	Yakovlev YAK-40	RA-87256	9311326	Sankuru Air Service	Overran on landing & caught fire	Boma, Zaire	5	4
17.07.94	Beechcraft King Air C90	F-ZBBF	LJ-0518	Securite Civile	Crashed after take-off due to engine failure	Ajaccio, Corsica, France	2{1}	0
17.07.94	IRMA BN-2B-26 Islander	8P-TAD	2152	Trans Island Air	Crashed on approach	ne Bellefontaine, Martinique	6	0
17.07.94	Antonov AN-24B	RA-46575	87304901	Central Region Directorate	Damaged when u/c retracted on take-off	Kherson, Ukraine	0	32
19.07.94	Embraer Bandeirante 110P1	HP-1202AC	110.375	Alas Chiricanas	Crashed after bomb explosion following take-off	Colon, Panama	21	0
20.07.94	Boeing 737-3W0	B-2540	27139	Yunnan Airlines	Overran on landing & u/c collapsed	Kunming, China	0	*
24.07.94	Bell 206B JetRanger II	N820CW	02948	Classic Helicopters	Crashed	nr Syracuse, UT, USA	1	0
26.07.94	Sikorsky S-58ET	PK-OBT	58-1098	Airfast Services	Crashed	East Kalimantan, Indonesia	18	0
26.07.94	Bell 206B JetRanger II	C-GLGF	02421	Frontier Helicopters	Crashed	nr Watson Lake, YK, Canada	1	2
27.07.94	Antonov AN-26	*	*	Kiev Airlines	Shot down and crashed in minefield	Bihac, Bosnia-Herzegovina	7	0
29.07.94	Lockheed P2V-7 Neptune	N918AP	726-7186	Black Hills Aviation	Crashed during firefighting	Squaw Mt, MT, USA	2	0
29.07.94	Bell 206B JetRanger II	N90315	01863	Alaska West Air	Crashed	Mt Spur, AK, USA	0	5
oo.07.94	BAC One-Eleven 201AC	9Q-CSJ	013	Shabair	Damaged beyond repair	Zaire	*	*
oo.07.94	Beechcraft 1900C-1	OY-GEG	UC-132	Aviation Assistance	Damaged on ground by shrapnel during civil war	Aden, Yemen	0	0
oo.07.94	Douglas DC-6A	V5-WAC	44668	West Air Aviation	Crashed on landing short of runway	Namibia	*	*
01.08.94	Antonov AN-2	RA-50582	*	Arkhangelsk Airlines	Crashed on approach	Turnema, Russia	0	17
01.08.94	Mil Mi-2	RA-20357	529803076	Southern Directorate	Damaged in forced landing	El Mahmudie, Egypt	0	1
02.08.94	Bell 206B JetRanger III	LN-OSL	03430	Helilift	Crashed after tail rotor failure	Aas, Norway	0	*
02.08.94	Mil Mi-2	RA-23407	548929104	Sakhalin Air Routes	Caught fire after hard landing	Sakhalin, Russia	0	5
03.08.94	Cessna 421C Golden Eagle III	C-GVPB	421C-0484	Les Ailes de Charlevoix	Crashed into hill after take-off	St Irenee, PQ, Canada	6	0
04.08.94	Beechcraft King Air A100	N7GA	B-119	Westchester Air	Crashed after take-off	Williamstown, MA, USA	1	0

Date	Type	Reg'n	C/n	Operator	Accident	Location	F	S
04.08.94	Antonov AN-30	RA-30037	0704	West Siberian Directorate	Damaged when landed off runway and ran into mound	Russia	0	23
08.08.94	Cessna 406 Caravan II	5Y-JJC	406-0040	Tawakel Airlines	Crashed on take-off after window opened	Nairobi, Kenya	0	3
08.08.94	de Havilland Canada Beaver	N126UA	1493	Uyak Air Service	Crashed	Kodiak, AK, USA	6	1
09.08.94	Airbus A.300B4-622R	HL7296	533	Korean Air	Overran on landing in bad weather & caught fire	Cheju, South Korea	0	160
09.08.94	Bell 204B	TG-HUI	*	Servicios Aereos	Crashed	Baja Verpaz, Guatemala	5	0
12.08.94	Bell 206L-4 Long Ranger	N124NH	52089	New York Helicopters	Crashed	Whiting, NJ, USA	3	0
13.08.94	Lockheed L-182 Hercules	N135FF	3148	Hemet Valley Flying Service	Crashed after explosion	nr Palmdale, CA, USA	3	0
17.08.94	Bell 206B JetRanger III	N8NU	03346	Hillsboro Helicopters	Crashed after tail rotor failure	Siskiyou Mts, CA, USA	0	1
18.08.94	McDonnell Douglas DC-9-31	5N-BBE	45872	ADC Airlines	Crashed on landing in rainstorm	Monrovia, Liberia	0	72
18.08.94	Hughes 500D	C-GPDH	270083D	Northern Mountain Helicopters	Crashed	nr Dawson Creek, BC, Canada	0	1
19.08.94	Piper PA-46-310P Malibu	C-GSEV	46-8408035	Simo-Air	Crashed into hill on approach	Killarney, ON, Canada	6	0
21.08.94	Aerospatiale-Alenia ATR.42-300	CN-CDT	127	Royal Air Maroc	Crashed into mountain by pilot committing suicide	nr Agadir, Morocco	44	0
22.08.94	de Havilland Canada Twin Otter 300	N141Z	803	US Forest Service	Damaged after landing short in soft ground	McCall, ID, USA	0	1
26.08.94	Dassault Falcon 200	XA-SKO	505	Aerocorp	Crashed into lake after aborting take-off	New Orleans, LA, USA	0	*
27.08.94	CASA 212 Aviocar 200	N119CA	357	US Drug Enforcement Administration	Crashed in mountains in bad weather	nr Puerto Pisana, Peru	5	0
27.08.94	Boeing 737-4Q8	TC-JEL	26300	Turkish Airlines	Damaged after overrunning on landing	Istanbul, Turkey	0	176
28.08.94	Grumman S2F Firecat	C-GHNU	351	Conair Aviation	Force-landed in river after engine failure	nr Quesnel, BC, Canada	0	*
30.08.94	Bell 206B JetRanger II	N382EH	01635	ERA Aviation	Crashed into water	Reed Inlet, AK, USA	0	1
31.08.94	HAI Alouette III	RA-01187	263	Tropuf Avia	Crashed	nr Krasnogorsk, Russia	6	0
01.09.94	Sikorsky S-64	N165AC	64085	Erickson Air Crane	Crashed	Hanging Flower Lake, MT, USA	0	3
02.09.94	British Aerospace Jetstream 31	HB-AEB	882	Zimex Aviation	Destroyed in terrorist attack	Aden, Yemen	*	*
02.09.94	Bell 206B JetRanger II	C-FPQS	03231	Great Slave Helicopters	Crashed	Walmsely Lake, NWT, Canada	0	1
03.09.94	Bell UH-1E	N6204D	154757	Aeronorte	Crashed after being caught in forest fire	Rio del Mar, Portugal	*	*
08.09.94	Boeing 737-3B7	N513AU	23699	US Air	Crashed on approach	Hopewell, PA, USA	132	0
09.09.94	Tupolev TU-134A	RA-65760	62187	Gromov Aviation Research Institute	Mid-air collision with Gromov TU-22	Yegorevsk, Russia	7(0)	0
10.09.94	Learjet 24D	PT-LAU	24D-239	Thor Taxi Aereo	Struck by vehicle & caught fire	Brasilia, Brazil	0	*
13.09.94	de Havilland Canada Twin Otter 300	5N-ATQ	538	Aero Contractors	Crashed on approach in heavy rain	Abuja, Nigeria	2	3
15.09.94	Bell 206L Long Ranger	C-FUHL	45040	Universal Helicopters	Crashed on landing on beach & covered by tide	Porcupine Point, Nfld, Canada	0	6
17.09.94	Learjet 35A	B-98181	35A-675	Golden Eagle Aviation	Shot down in error by Taiwanese Navy while target towing	Off Taiwan	4	0
17.09.94	de Havilland Canada Twin Otter 100	C-FDMR	036	Pacific Coastal Airlines	Crashed on water take-off	Illahie Inlet, BC, Canada	3	1
18.09.94	BAC One-Eleven 515FB	5N-IMO	229	Oriental Airlines	Crashed during emergency landing	Tamanrasset, Algeria	4	35
19.09.94	Cessna 402A	P2-ALC	402A-0118	Airlink	Damaged on ground by ash after volcanic eruption	Rabaul, Papua New Guinea	0	0
19.09.94	Cessna 402B	P2-ALD	402B-0110	Airlink	Damaged on ground by ash after volcanic eruption	Rabaul, Papua New Guinea	0	0
19.09.94	Britten-Norman BN-2A-26 Islander	P2-ALF	0395	Airlink	Damaged on ground by ash after volcanic eruption	Rabaul, Papua New Guinea	0	0
19.09.94	Bell 206B JetRanger III	P2-FHE	01322	Pacific Helicopters	Damaged on ground by ash after volcanic eruption	Rabaul, Papua New Guinea	0	0
19.09.94	Aerospatiale AS.350B Ecureuil	P2-PHB	1516	Pacific Helicopters	Damaged on ground by ash after volcanic eruption	Rabaul, Papua New Guinea	0	0
19.09.94	Beechcraft 58 Baron	P2-ALE	TH-51	Airlink	Damaged on ground by ash after volcanic eruption	Rabaul, Papua New Guinea	0	0
21.09.94	Bell 206B JetRanger II	C-FAHQ	00246	Canadian Air Crane	Crashed after centre of gravity shifted	nr Port Alberni, BC, Canada	0	3
22.09.94	Mitsubishi MU-2B-60 Marquise	HB-LLP	767SA	Air Material	Crashed into woods after engine failure	Urnasch, Switzerland	1	0
22.09.94	Cessna A185E Skywagon	C-FVZP	185-1191	Tel Air Services	Crashed	nr Snettisham, AK, USA	*	*
22.09.94	McDonnell Douglas 520N	D-HDAS	*	SP Helicopter Service	Crashed after fuel starvation	Suhl Thuringen, Germany	0	1
23.09.94	Lockheed L-382G Hercules	PK-PLV	4826	Pelita Air Service	Ran off runway into sea on take-off	Hong Kong	6	6
24.09.94	Bell 212	PK-HML	30540	Gatari Air Service	Crash landed in sea after engine failure	Off Parigi, Indonesia	5	0
26.09.94	Yakovlev YAK-40	RA-87468	*	Cheremshanka Airlines	Crashed out of fuel	Vanavarva, Russia	28	0
28.09.94	Rockwell 1121B Jet Commander	LV-WEN	126	Radeair	Crashed on take-off	Buenos Aires, Argentina	7	0
28.09.94	Douglas DC-3	2009	*	Transporte Aereo Militar	Crashed on take-off due to engine failure	Bahia Negra, Paraguay	1	26
29.09.94	Antonov AN-8	RA-59504	OE-3480	Kadvi Company	Caught fire and destroyed on landing	Elista, Russia	0	23
30.09.94	Antonov AN-8	RA-27209	OE-3460	Arseniev Air Wing	Crashed on take-off	Chaibukha, Russia	8	13
oo.09.94	Britten-Norman BN-2A-27 Islander	8R-GGU	0251	Kayman Sankar Aviation	Written off	Guyana	*	*
02.10.94	Rockwell Turbo Commander 690B	VH-SVQ	11380	Seaview Air	Crashed at sea	Off Lord Howe Is, NSW, Australia	9	0
06.10.94	Kamov Ka-26	UK-19633	*	Kokand Aviation	Crashed into power cables	Kokand, Uzbekistan	1	0
06.10.94	Bell 206L Long Ranger III	D-HHSB	51410	Hubschrauber-Sonder-Dienst	Crashed into crane on take-off	Neubranden, Germany	2	0
08.10.94	Rockwell Turbo Commander 690B	N27MT	11533	B.B.Limbaugh	Crashed after take-off	Springfield, MO, USA	1	0
08.10.94	Pilatus PC-6/B2-H2 Turbo Porter	FAC.1115	820	Satena	Damaged by Selva AN-32 HK-3929X which veered off runway	Mitu, Colombia	*	*

Date	Type	Reg'n	C/n	Operator	Accident	Location	F	S
08.10.94	Antonov AN-32B	HK-3929X	3301	Selva	Ran into vehicles & Satena PC-6 1115 after landing short	Mitu, Colombia	10	*
09.10.94	Boeing 707-324C	HK-3355X	18886	Tampa	U/c collapsed on emergency landing	Sao Paulo, Colombia	0	5
11.10.94	Aerospatiale AS.350B Squirrel	ZK-HZP	1243	The Helicopter Line	Crashed at sea	Off Whitianga, New Zealand	2	3
12.10.94	Fokker F-28 Fellowship 1000	EP-PAV	11070	Iran Asseman Airlines	Crashed into mountain after suspected bomb explosion	nr Nantanz, Iran	66	0
13.10.94	Bell 206B JetRanger III	PT-HPD	03514	Lider Taxi Aereo	Crashed after striking power lines	Guratingueta, Brazil	0	2
14.10.94	Short Skyvan 3	8R-GRR	SH.1976	Guyana Government	Ran off runway & u/c collapsed	Maiwak, Guyana	0	*
16.10.94	Antonov AN-2	OB-1542	*	Operator Unknown	Crashed on drug smuggling flight	Huanco, Peru	3	0
19.10.94	Beechcraft King Air C90A	F-GLRA	LJ-1105	Mono Max Aviation	Crashed on approach	nr Saumur, France	7	0
22.10.94	Mil Mi-2	HA-BFD	528604024	Horex	Crashed by pilot with no licence	nr Oroshaza, Hungary	10	0
22.10.94	Airbus A.300B4-103	HS-THO	072	Thai Airways International	Damaged by Thai MD-11 HS-TMD which jumped chocks on test	Bangkok, Thailand	0(0)	*
22.10.94	Mil Mi-8	RA-22752	*	Western Siberian Directorate	Rolled over on take-off	New Vasyugan, Russia	0	4
23.10.94	Antonov AN-72	RA-72960	*	Federal Frontier Guards	Ran off runway during take-off	Vorkuta, Russia	34	0
27.10.94	Yakovlev YAK-40	RA-88254	*	Don Avia	Damaged when hijacker exploded grenade in cabin on ground	Makhachkala, Russia	1	0
27.10.94	Beechcraft Super King Air 200	PH-ATM	BB-0123	Tulip Air	Damaged in emergency landing after engine failure	nr Rotterdam, Netherlands	0	6
29.10.94	Antonov AN-2	RA-33008	*	Yakutavia	Crashed on take-off while overweight	Batagay, Russia	6	17
29.10.94	Antonov AN-12	RA-11790	*	Aero Nika	Crashed on approach	nr Ust Ilimsk, Russia	21	0
29.10.94	Aerospatiale AS.350B Squirrel	ZK-HWV	1813	The Helicopter Line	Crashed into high ground	Fox Glacier, New Zealand	7	0
30.10.94	Mil Mi-2	RA-23240	5210246067	Far East Directorate	Missing – presumed crashed but was carrying cargo of gold	nr Fevralsk, Russia	8	0
31.10.94	Aerospatiale-Alenia ATR.72-212	N401AM	401	Simmons Airlines/American Eagle	Crashed on approach in bad weather	nr Thayer, IN, USA	68	0
01.11.94	Bell 212	XA-SVS	*	Transportes Aereos Pegaso	Crashed	nr Cozumel, Mexico	14	0
01.11.94	MBB Bo.105CBS-4	SE-JBS	S.643	SOS Helikoptern Gotland	Crashed at sea	Off Gotland, Sweden	3	0
04.11.94	de Havilland Canada Twin Otter 100	PK-YNM	055	Trigana Air Service	Crashed into mountain	nr Kebu, Irian Jaya, Indonesia	4	0
04.11.94	MBB Bo.105CS	N911LF	S-740	Omniflight Helicopters	Crashed after striking power lines	nr Perry, FL, USA	2	1
05.11.94	Yakovlev YAK-40	OB-1569	*	Servicios Aereos Amazonicos	Crashed dry in river bed	Saposoa River, Peru	8	20
06.11.94	Antonov AN-26	RA-88286	*	KIT Airline	Crash landed on frozen river out of fuel	River Omulyovka, Russia	0	9
08.11.94	Sikorsky S-76	N2620	760211	Mobil Oil	Crashed at sea	Off Cameron, LA, USA	1	2
09.11.94	Learjet 55	PT-LIG	55-111	Lider Taxi Aereo	Crashed into bay on landing	Rio de Janeiro, Brazil	0	5
10.11.94	Aerospatiale 332L Super Puma	TJ-AAR	2119	Cameroun Government	Damaged in hard landing	nr Bamako, Mali	0	4
13.11.94	Bell 206B JetRanger II	C-GHHV	1983	Highland Helicopters	Damaged in hard landing	nr Fort McMurray, AB, Canada	0	1
13.11.94	Bell 206B JetRanger III	JA9464	3961	Kagoshima Kokusai Air	Crashed	Amami, Japan	2	0
16.11.94	Beechcraft C99	N63995	U178	Ameriflight	Crashed	Avenal, CA, USA	1	0
17.11.94	Aerospatiale AS.350B Ecureuil	I-ELMR	1751	Eliliguria	Crashed after hitting power cables	Isoverde, Italy	5	0
18.11.94	Cessna 402C	N402BK	402C-0223	Island Airlines	Crashed after striking power cables	Hyannis, FL, USA	1	0
21.11.94	Mil Mi-8	RA-24102	*	Tyumenaviatrans	Damaged in crash landing	nr Surgut, Russia	0	3
22.11.94	Cessna 441 Conquest II	N441KM	0196	Superior Aviation	Struck by TWA MD-82 N954U which was taking off	St Louis, MO, USA	2(0)	0
22.11.94	IRMA BN-2A-20 Islander	P2-SWC	0835	Southwest Air	Crashed into mountain in bad weather	nr Tabubil, Papua New Guinea	7	0
24.11.94	de Havilland Canada Twin Otter 300	C-GKBD	314	Kenn Borek Air	Crashed after take-off in high winds	Rothera, Br Antarctic Territory	4	0
24.11.94	Douglas DC-3	2028	16667/33415	Transporte Aereo Militar	Damaged on take-off	Puerto la Victoria, Paraguay	0	3
29.11.94	Tupolev TU-134	*	*	Chechen National Airlines	Destroyed during air raid by Russian Mi-24 helicopters	Grozny, Chechnya, Russia	*	*
30.11.94	Tupolev TU-134	*	*	Chechen National Airlines	Total 3 destroyed when bombed by Russian Su-25s	Grozny, Chechnya, Russia	*	*
30.11.94	Cessna 421B Golden Eagle	PH-SYG	421B-0368	Operator Unknown	Destroyed on ground by arson	Coburg, Germany	0	0
30.11.94	Fokker F-28 Fellowship 4000	PK-GKU	11210	Merpati Nusantara Airlines	Damaged after overrunning on landing	Semarang, Indonesia	0	77
30.11.94	Tupolev TU-154	*	*	Armenian Airlines	Destroyed in air-raid by Russian Su-25s	Grozny, Chechnya, Russia	*	*
30.11.94	Mil Mi-2	RA-23555	*	Tumenaskoe Directorate	Crashed	nr Pokur, Russia	0	2
02.12.94	Piper PA-31-350 Chieftain	5Y-SMR	31-8252001	Trans World Safaris	Crashed	nr Nairobi, Kenya	5	0
02.12.94	IRMA BN-2B-20 Islander	N61VM	2204	Southern Cross Aviation	Crashed at sea	200m north of Majuro, Marshall Is	0	1
03.12.94	Cessna U206 Super Skywagon	N5282U	U206-0282	South Central Air	Crashed	nr Homer, AK, USA	1	0
04.12.94	Mil Mi-8MTV-1	*	*	Bosnia-Herzegovina Government	Exploded after emergency landing	Luckno, Croatia	0	6
04.12.94	Mil Mi-8MTV-1	T9-HAI	*	Bosnia-Herzegovina Government	Destroyed when Mi-8 exploded on landing	Luckno, Croatia	*	*
04.12.94	Mil Mi-2	RA-23639	*	Aero Air	Crashed attempting forced landing	Kanakajevo, Russia	2	3
05.12.94	Dornier Do.28D-2 Skyservant	D-IDNG	4112	Operator Unknown	Crash landed after engine failure	Nuuk, Greenland	0	*
06.12.94	Antonov AN-8	D2-FVA	*	Von Haaf Air	Veered off runway & struck power lines on take-off	Dundo, Angola	0	5
07.12.94	Aerospatiale AS.350B2 Ecureuil	G-PLMG	2513	PLM Helicopters	Crashed	nr Ballahulish, UK	2	0

Date	Type	Reg'n	C/n	Operator	Accident	Location	F	S
07.12.94	Aerospatiale AS.355F1 Ecureuil 2	D-HEAD	5072	Heli Bavaria	Crashed on take-off and caught fire	Basl Wiefsee, Germany	0	1
08.12.94	Beechcraft E18S	N5647D	BA-364	Cape Central Airways	Crashed on approach	Kansas City, MO, USA	1	0
08.12.94	Aerospatiale-Alenia ATR.72-201	F-OHOC	318	Air Gabon	Ran off runway into ditch on landing	Oyem, Gabon	0	21
08.12.94	Aerospatiale SA.319B Alouette II	HB-XOI	2196	Swiss Air Ambulance	Crashed after tail struck hangar	Untervaz, Switzerland	*	*
09.12.94	Lockheed L-382G Hercules	D2-THE	4673	Angola Air Charter	Damaged when u/c collapsed on landing	Luena, Angola	0	*
11.12.94	Cessna 402C III	N1238K	402C-1019	Ryan Air Service	Crashed into hill in snowstorm	nr Elim, AK, USA	5	0
12.12.94	Bell 212	EC-EHH	30682	Helisureste	Crashed after striking object while hovering	Candelaria, Canary Is, Spain	0	3
13.12.94	British Aerospace Jetstream 31	N918AE	918	Flagship Airlines/American Eagle	Crashed on approach	Raleigh-Durham, NC, USA	15	5
13.12.94	Kamov Ka-26	RA-24083	*	Bashkirian Airlines	Crashed on approach	Durtuli, Russia	*	*
13.12.94	Cessna T207A Skywagon	N7340U	207-00407	Hageland Aviation Services	Crashed in snowstorm	St Marys, AK, USA	*	*
14.12.94	Learjet 35A	N521PA	35A-239	Phoenix Air	Crashed into buildings making emergency landing	Fresno, CA, USA	2{1}	0
14.12.94	Learjet 35A	D-CATY	35A-114	Air Charter	Crashed on take-off	Moscow, Russia	1	5
15.12.94	Mil Mi-6	RA-21001	*	Tyumenaviatrans	Crashed in forced landing during bad weather	Noyabrsk, Russia	0	*
15.12.94	Mil Mi-2	UN-14211	*	Kazakhstan Airlines	Damaged in hard landing in fog	Kul-Sary, Kazakhstan	0	*
16.12.94	Douglas Turbo DC-3	N96BF	13321	SL Aviation Services	Crashed on take-off	Lobito, Angola	2	0
17.12.94	de Havilland Canada Twin Otter 300	P2-MFS	187	Missionary Aviation Fellowship	Crashed into hills	nr Tabubil, Papua New Guinea	28	0
17.12.94	Douglas DC-3	YV-761C	2476	Servivensa	Crashed on approach	Cerro Hiaiche, Venezuela	7	2
19.12.94	Boeing 707-3F9C	5N-ABK	20669	Nigeria Airways	Crashed	nr Hadejia, Nigeria	3	2
21.12.94	Boeing 737-2D6C	7T-VEE	20758	Air Algerie	Crashed on approach after striking pylon	Willenhall, West Midlands, UK	5	0
21.12.94	Mitsubishi MU-2B-30	VH-IAM	517	Newcastle Aviation	Crashed on approach in bad weather	Melbourne, Vic, Australia	1	0
21.12.94	Rockwell Sabre 40	N747E	282-022	Servicios Aereos Facchini	Crashed after aborting take-off	Buenos Aires, Argentina	0	*
22.12.94	Fokker F-27 Friendship 600	CP-2165	10592	Lloyd Aereo Boliviano	Crashed into trees after aborting take-off	Guayaramerin, Bolivia	0	40
23.12.94	Aerospatiale SA.315B Lama	G-AZNI	06-2014	Dollar Helicopters	Damaged in hard landing	nr Tambubamba, Peru	0	2
23.12.94	Mil Mi-2	*	*	Riaxan Aviation	Crashed	nr Turlatovo, Russia	0	*
29.12.94	Boeing 737-4Y0	TC-JES	26074	Turkish Airlines	Crashed on approach in snowstorm	nr Van, Turkey	57	29
31.12.94	Ilyushin IL-76TD	EW-76836	1013409305	Belair	Damaged when nose u/c collapsed on landing	Sarajevo, Bosnia-Herzegovina	0	*
31.12.94	Aerospatiale SA.315B Lama	G-BOUY	2468	Dollar Helicopters	Struck by winds and crashed	Artouste, Peru	0	3
oo.oo.94	Rockwell Sabre 60	XC-AA26	306-012	Operator Unknown	Damaged by flooding	Mexico	*	*
oo.oo.94	Fairchild Merlin IIB	N1221S	T26-109	Operator Unknown	Written off	Location Unknown	*	*
02.01.95	Cessna 208 Caravan I	N242CS	208-0158	Taquan Air Service	Caught fire after striking log with float	Craig, AK, USA	0	8
02.01.95	Boeing 737-298C	9Q-CNI	20793	Air Zaire	Damaged after running off runway in bad weather	Kinshasa, Zaire	0	*
03.01.95	Beechcraft King Air 90	N101GA	LJ-0011	Kel-Air	Crashed after take-off	nr Hot Springs, AR, USA	2	0
03.01.95	de Havilland Canada Twin Otter 310	P2-IAA	244	Islands Aviation	Ran off runway on take-off and u/c collapsed	Billi, Papua New Guinea	0	*
08.01.95	Aerospatiale AS.350B Ecureuil	I-GLPB	2331	Elistar	Crashed in mountains	Trentino-Alto Adige, Italy	6	0
09.01.95	Cessna 402B	5Y-PAL	402-0584	Equator Airlines	Crashed	nr Mombasa, Kenya	1	2
09.01.95	Piper PA-31-350 Chieftain	N50WT	31-7952018	Operator Unknown	Crashed on landing	Brownsville, TX, USA	*	*
10.01.95	de Havilland Canada Twin Otter 300	PK-NUK	390	Merpati Nusantara Airlines	Missing – presumed crashed	Off Flores Island, Indonesia	14	0
10.01.95	Beechcraft King Air B95	N673Q	TD-313	Operator Unknown	Crashed on approach	Hot Springs, AR, USA	3	0
10.01.95	Rockwell Sabre 60	N771WW	306-29	Wallace's Bookstores	Destroyed in ground fire	Lexington, KY, USA	0	*
11.01.95	McDonnell Douglas DC-9-14	HK-3839X	45742	Intercontinental	Crashed on approach	Cartagena, Colombia	51	1
11.01.95	Learjet 35	C-GPUN	35-058	Canada Jet Charters	Crashed in sea on approach	Off Masset, BC, Canada	5	0
11.01.95	Cessna 208B Caravan I	N746FE	208B-0236	Empire Airlines/Federal Express	Crashed after take-off	Flagstaff, AZ, USA	1	0
12.01.95	Cessna 208B Caravan I	N754FE	208B-0249	Westair/Federal Express	Crashed into hillside	nr Oakland, CA, USA	1	0
13.01.95	Cessna 414	N13SE	414-0437	Panorama Flight Service	Crashed into buildings after double engine failure	Augusta, GA, USA	4	0
14.01.95	Yakovlev YAK-40	RA-87565	9211721	Chelyabinsk Air	Damaged after running off runway on landing	Tobolsk, Russia	0	*
15.01.95	Hughes 369D	LV-WDL	*	Andes Aviacion	Crashed on mountain during rescue flight	Mt Tronador, Argentina	1	0
17.01.95	de Havilland Canada Twin Otter 300	9N-ABI	392	Royal Nepal Airlines	Crashed on take-off	Kathmandu, Nepal	2	22
18.01.95	Cessna 208B Caravan I	N9471B	208B-0081	Martinaire	Crashed after take-off	Lubbock, TX, USA	0	1
19.01.95	Aerospatiale 332L Super Puma	G-TIGK	2044	Bristow Helicopters	Ditched after lightning strike & later sank	North Sea	0	18
20.01.95	Dassault Falcon 20E	F-GDLU	314/516	Leadair	Crashed after take-off	Le Bourget, France	10	0
20.01.95	LET 410UVP Turbolet	RA-67120	790316	Abakan Avia	Crashed after take-off	nr Krasnoyarsk, Russia	3	13
20.01.95	Beechcraft King Air E90	N47WM	LW-307	Aviation Holdings	Crashed on approach	nr Kingston, ON, Canada	0	2
20.01.95	Bell 205A-1	C-FFHB	30294	Frontier Helicopters	Crashed	nr Williams Lake, BC, Canada	*	*
23.01.95	LET 410UVP Turbolet	UR-67115	790311	Ukraine Airlines	Crashed on approach after wing struck frozen lake	Providenya, Russia	0	3

Date	Type	Reg'n	C/n	Operator	Accident	Location	F	S
24.01.95	Beechcraft C-45H	N618K	AF-759	Operator Unknown	Crashed into building on take-off	New Hudson, MI, USA	*	*
25.01.95	Britten-Norman BN-2A-27 Islander	C-GSGK	0383	Northway Aviation	Crashed on approach	nr Atpaungassi, MN, Canada	0	*
25.01.95	Yakovlev YAK-40	RA-87464	9430337	Volga Airlines	Overran and crashed on landing	Rostov, Russia	0	10
25.01.95	Cessna Citation II	D-CHVB	550-0629	Viessman Werke	Crashed on landing	Allendorf, Germany	2	*
26.01.95	Antonov AN-26	UN-26080	*	Kazakhstan Airlines	Crashed on take-off	Sambailo, Guinea	*	*
27.01.95	Cessna 421B Golden Eagle	C-GPAT	421B-0263	Excel Air	Crashed in mountains during high winds	Rocky Mountain House, AB, Canada	0	5
27.01.95	Beechcraft 18S	N250RP	BA-47	Operator Unknown	Crashed	nr Butte, MT, USA	1	*
28.01.95	Beechcraft Super King Air 200	D2-ECH	BB-345	Aviacao Ligeira	Crashed after explosion – possibly shot down by missile	nr Cafunfo, Angola	2	4
30.01.95	Aerospatiale-Alenia ATR.72-202	B-22717	435	Transasia Airways	Crashed into hill	nr Linkou, Taiwan	4	0
31.01.95	Boeing 727-21F	D2-TJB	19005	Angola Air Charter	Damaged after overrunning into minefield in wet weather	Huambo, Angola	0	3
oo.01.95	Antonov AN-8	*	*	Von Haaf Air	Crashed	Angola	*	*
oo.01.95	Ilyushin IL-22M11	UN-75915	2964111701	Kazakhstan Government	Damaged in ground collision with AN-12	Almaty, Kazakhstan	0	*
01.02.95	Boeing 737-2A4	PP-SMV	20968	VASP	Overran on landing after hydraulics failure	Sao Paulo, Brazil	0	126
01.02.95	Antonov AN-28	RA-28797	IAJ006-05	Chaunskoe Air	Undershot on landing	Schmidt Cape, Russia	0	10
04.02.95	IPTN Bo.105CB	PK-PGP	N60/S-458	Pelita Air Service	Crashed on landing	nr Blang Dalam, Indonesia	*	*
10.02.95	Antonov AN-70	n/a	*	Antonov Design Bureau	Mid-air collision with AN-72 chase plane which landed safely	nr Kiev, Ukraine	7(0)	0
10.02.95	Boeing 737-2M2	D2-TBP	23220	TAAG Angola Airlines	Overran runway on landing & nose u/c collapsed	Dundo, Angola	0	*
11.02.95	Bell 206B JetRanger II	C-FBHR	313	High Terrain Helicopters	Crashed on approach	Kokanee, BC, Canada	*	*
12.02.95	Rockwell Turbo Commander 690A	N69TM	11322	T.McMullen	Crashed	Guthrie, OK, USA	2	*
13.02.95	Piper PA-31-350 Chieftain	N27245	31-7752121	Las Vegas Airlines	Crashed after engine failure	nr Tusayan, AZ, USA	8	2
13.02.95	Sikorsky S-58JT	N1099T	581646	Glacier Helicopters	Crashed	nr Marblemount, WA, USA	*	*
14.02.95	Bell 206L Long Ranger IV	N172AL	*	Air Logistics	Crashed at sea	Off Vermilion Bay, LA, USA	5	0
15.02.95	Cessna Citation Jet	N63HB	525-0019	M & M Air	Crashed on landing	Wauchula, FL, USA	0	*
16.02.95	McDonnell Douglas DC-8-63F	N782AL	45929	Air Transport International	Crashed on take-off and caught fire	Kansas City, MO, USA	3	0
20.02.95	Cessna 208B Caravan II	LV-VGE	*	Goyayke	Damaged after overrunning on landing	nr Rio Gallegos, Argentina	0	*
21.02.95	Beechcraft King Air A100	C-GYQT	B-189	Bearskin Airlines	Crashed on approach	Big Trout Lake, ON, Canada	0	*
21.02.95	IAI 1124 Westwind	N66JE	326	Professional Jet Management	Destroyed by fire on ground	Denver, CO, USA	0	*
24.02.95	Mil Mi-2	HA-BFC	549245065	Etjoernyos Iskol Godollo	Overturned on landing	Delegyhaza, Hungary	*	*
26.02.95	Bell 206B JetRanger III	B-6622	*	Asia Pacific Airlines	Crashed on landing	nr Chiaya, Taiwan	*	*
27.02.95	Cessna 402B	5H-TZB	402B-0444	Tanzanair	Crashed on take-off	Tabora, Tanzania	0	6
27.02.95	Cessna U206F Stationair	OB-1030	U206-02465	Lineas Aereas del Sur	Crashed on approach	Pucallpa, Peru	1	1
oo.02.95	Piper PA-42-720 Cheyenne IIIA	*	*	CAAC Flying College	Crashed	Taiyuan, China	4	0
01.03.95	Mitsubishi Diamond 1A	C-GLIG	A076SA	Lignum	Crashed on landing	Jasper Hinton, CA, USA	0	*
02.03.95	Cessna 208B Caravan I	N9448B	208B-0121	Martinaire	Crashed in fog on approach	nr Ardmore, OK, USA	0	1
03.03.95	Cessna 208B Caravan II	N227DM	208B-0364	DMC Flying Service	Crashed into trees on approach	Gainsville, GA, USA	2	0
04.03.95	Harbin Y-12	PNP 224	*	Peruvian Police	Damaged in forced landing & bombed by Brazilian Air Force	Bon Jesus, Brazil	0	8
04.03.95	IAI 1124A Westwind 2	N311BR	344	Kennecott Corporation	Undershot runway on landing	Gilette, WY, USA	*	*
12.03.95	Douglas DC-3	C-FDTT	14170/25615	Transfair	Crashed after striking ridge on landing	Lac Manitou, PQ, Canada	0	3
13.03.95	Lockheed Electra 188A	9Q-CDG	1119	Blue Airlines	Damaged in crash landing	Kinshasa, Zaire	0	*
14.03.95	Antonov AN-12	RA-11337	3341204	Penaza Air Unit	Crashed on emergency approach while low on fuel	nr Baku, Azerbaijan	0	16
16.03.95	Antonov AN-26	UR-26084	11806	Ukraine Flight Academy	Crashed into hill on approach	Kossora, Russia	6	3
16.03.95	de Havilland Canada Twin Otter 200	N37ST	207	T.McGill	Crashed at sea on ferry flight	300km NE of Honolulu, HI, USA	0	3
17.03.95	McDonnell Douglas DC-9-15	HK-3564X	47127	Intercontinental	Destroyed by fire on ground	Barranquilla, Colombia	0	0
18.03.95	Convair 440	N137CA	317	Gulf and Caribbean Cargo	Ran off runway after tyre burst & struck US Army UH-60	Cap Haitien, Haiti	0(0)	32
20.03.95	Mil Mi-2	RA-14146	*	Bransk Flight Unit	Damaged in forced landing	nr Nizhnevartovsk, Russia	0	4
20.03.95	Cessna 208B Caravan I	9M-PMN	208B-0295	Transmile Air Services	Overran runway on take-off	Tawau, Malaysia	0	2
21.03.95	Noorduyn UC-64A Norseman	C-FKAS	367	Hanna's Air Saltspring	Crashed	Kuper Island, BC, Canada	*	*
21.03.95	Bell 206A JetRanger II	C-FALP	0654	Provincial Helicopters	Crashed into frozen lake	Lake Winnipeg, MN, Canada	*	*
22.03.95	Cessna 208B Caravan II	N9417B	*	Union Flights	Crashed into mountain	nr Reno, NV, USA	1	0
23.03.95	Xian Y-7-100	*	*	CAAC Flying College	Crashed after striking mountain	nr Jinan, China	7	0
23.03.95	Beechcraft 18	N8111	BA-113	Operator Unknown	Crashed on approach	Walkers Cay, Bahamas	*	*
23.03.95	Douglas DC-3	C-GCXD	14167/25612	Aviation Boreal	Crashed on take-off	Lac Bondesir, PQ, Canada	0	2
25.03.95	Cessna Citation I	XA-SMH	500-0084	Operator Unknown	Crashed	nr Vera Cruz, Mexico	*	*

Date	Type	Reg'n	C/n	Operator	Accident	Location	F	S
26.03.95	Antonov AN-12	RA-13340	00347504	Amuraviatrans Airlines	Destroyed after engine fire on take-off	Bunia, Zaire	0	*
26.03.95	Mil Mi-2	RA-23801	*	Yashen Airlines	Damaged after rolling over on start up	Bogatye Sady, Russia	0	*
29.03.95	Beechcraft Excalibur Queenaire 8800	ZK-TIK	LD-249	Kiwi West Aviation	Crashed after engine failure	nr Hamilton, New Zealand	6	0
29.03.95	Hughes 369D	CS-HCE	0080	Heli Portugal	Destroyed in ground accident	Cascais, Portugal	0	*
30.03.95	Douglas DC-3	C-FQBC	15581/27026	Aviation Boreal	Crashed on landing on frozen lake	James Bay, PQ, Canada	0	2
31.03.95	Airbus A.310-324	YR-LCC	450	Tarom	Crashed after take-off in snowstorm	Balotesti, Romania	60	0
oo.03.95	Mil Mi-26	*	*	Air Troika	Crashed into building on landing after engine failure	Skopje, Macedonia	0	*
01.04.95	Antonov AN-2	*	*	African Air Charter	Crashed in bad weather	nr Tongo, Sierra Leone	1	0
04.04.95	Antonov AN-26	*	*	Korovograd Airlines	Crashed after take-off	Palana, Russia	0	9
07.04.95	Westland EH.101 Merlin	ZF644	PP.4	Westland Helicopters	Crashed	Yarcombe, Devon, UK	0	4
07.04.95	Bell 206B JetRanger II	C-GWGS	0447	Vancouver Island Helicopters	Crashed after take-off	King Island, BC, Canada	*	*
07.04.95	Hawker Siddeley HS.125 Srs.400	N41953	25268	Delass Americanas	Damaged in crash landing	Santo Domingo, Dominican Republic	*	*
07.04.95	Bell 214ST	VH-LAT	28131	Lloyd Helicopters	Crashed at sea	Off Darwin, NT, Australia	*	*
08.04.95	Bell 206B JetRanger II	C-GXWR	0462	Pemberton Helicopters	Crashed on landing	Inrig Bay, BC, Canada	*	*
12.04.95	Beechcraft Super King Air 200	P2-IAH	BB-297	Island Nationair	Crashed on landing	Lae Nadzab, Papua New Guinea	*	*
13.04.95	Cessna T210 Centurion	OB-1589	*	Aviasa	Crashed [Survivors found after one week]	Pampa Hermosa, Peru	0	*
19.04.95	Westland-Bell 47G-4A	G-OEMH	WA.716	East Midlands Helicopters	Crashed while hovering	Leicester, UK	0	2
23.04.95	de Havilland Canada Twin Otter 300	5N-AJQ	607	Bristow Helicopters (Nigeria) Ltd	Crashed into Nigerian AF F-27 908 on landing in heavy rain	Lagos, Nigeria	1(0)	7
24.04.95	Cessna Citation I/SP	N120ES	501-0041	TACA International Airlines	Crashed after undershooting runway	San Salvador, El Salvador	0	*
26.04.95	Cessna Citation II	N7RC	550-0019	Ring Can Corporation	Crashed into trees on landing short	Walkers Cay, Bahamas	0	5
27.04.95	IAI 1124 Westwind	VH-AJS	221	Pel-Air	Crashed	nr Alice Springs, NT, Australia	3	0
27.04.95	Bell 206B JetRanger III	HB-XLR	3170	Mountain Flyers 80	Crashed after take-off	Berne, Switzerland	*	*
28.04.95	Douglas DC-8F-54	N43UA	45677	Millon Air	Overran on landing and crashed into buildings	Guatemala City, Guatemala	0(6)	3
28.04.95	British Aerospace 748 Srs.2A	4R-HVB/835	1757	Helitours	Shot down by Tamil missile after take-off	Palaly, Sri Lanka	45	0
29.04.95	British Aerospace 748 Srs.2B/SCD	4R-HVA/834	1768	Helitours	Shot down by Tamil missile on approach	Palaly, Sri Lanka	52	0
29.04.95	McDonnell Douglas MD.520N	HB-XUJ	LN011	Fuchs Helikopter	Crashed on take-off	nr Felskopf, Switzerland	*	*
01.05.95	Piper PA-31-325 Chieftain	C-GYPZ	31-7652168	Air Sandy	Mid-air collision with Bearskin Metro C-GYYB	nr Sioux Lookout, ON, Canada	5(3)	0
01.05.95	Fairchild 227CC Metro 23	C-GYYB	CC-827B	Bearskin Airlines	Mid-air collision with Air Sandy PA-31 C-GYPZ	nr Sioux Lookout, ON, Canada	3(5)	0
02.05.95	Bell 206L-3 Long Ranger III	N347AL	51381	Air Logistics	Crashed in sea	Off Venice, LA, USA	1	2
03.05.95	Grumman Gulfstream II	N409MA	083	American Jet	Crashed into mountain on approach	nr Quito, Ecuador	7	0
03.05.95	Mitsubishi MU-2B-60	LV-MOP	742SA	TAPSA	Crashed at night	nr Chimpay, Argentina	2	0
04.05.95	Antonov AN-2	*	*	Magnitogosk Enterprise	Crashed & caught fire on take-off	Sebai, Russia	3	4
04.05.95	Bell 206L-3 Long Ranger	HK-3171	*	Taxi Aereo del Tulima	Crashed into hill	nr Buenavista, Colombia	4	0
05.05.95	Aerospatiale AS.350B Ecureuil	G-PLMA	1049	PLM Helicopters	Crashed	Lochgilphead, UK	1	0
07.05.95	Mil Mi-8	*	*	Bosnia-Herzegovina Government	Shot down by Bosnian Serb forces	nr Zepa, Bosnia-Herzegovina	12	11
07.05.95	Beechcraft E18S	N8711	BA-384	Viking Express	U/c collapsed on landing	Sugar Grove, IL, USA	0	*
08.05.95	Fokker F-27 Friendship 600	PK-YPL	10435	Trigana Air Service	Crashed on landing	Sentani, Indonesia	0	28
09.05.95	Curtiss C-46F	HK-3079G	22538	ADES Colombia	Crashed on approach	Restrepo, Colombia	9	0
09.05.95	Antonov AN-12	RA-11127	02348202	Pulkovo Airlines	Badly damaged when nose u/c collapsed on landing	Lukapa, Angola	0	*
17.05.95	Piper PA-34-200T Seneca II	N2883D	34-7970323	Sky Harbor Air Service	Crashed on approach	Cheyenne, WY, USA	1	0
19.05.95	Convair 580	EC-899	354	Swiftair	Damaged in belly landing	Vitoria, Spain	0	*
20.05.95	de Havilland Canada Otter	N108CA	*	Operator Unknown	Crashed at sea	Off Anathahan Is, Northern Marianas	3	0
21.05.95	Boeing B-29 Superfortress	N70887	*	D.Greenamyer	Destroyed by fire while taxiing for first flight in 48 years	Greenland	0	*
22.05.95	Convair 440	CP-2142	120	Servicios Aereos Santa Ana	Belly landed after engine failure and broke up	San Borja, Bolivia	1	*
24.05.95	Embraer Bandeirante 110P1	G-OEAA	110.256	Knight Air	Crashed after take-off in bad weather	nr Harewood, S Yorks, UK	12	0
25.05.95	Douglas DC-3	HK-3215	26111	LACOL	Crashed on approach	Miraflores, Colombia	5	8
28.05.95	Mil Mi-8	*	*	Bosnia-Herzegovina Government	Shot down by Bosnian Serb missile	nr Slunj, Bosnia-Herzegovina	7	0
29.05.95	Piper PA-31-310 Navajo	6V-AGH	31-205	Senegalair	Crashed at sea	Off Dakar, Senegal	1	4
29.05.95	Bell 206L-1 Long Ranger II	C-FMZE	45622	North Central Helicopters	Crashed after take-off	Glansberg Lake, SK, Canada	*	*
30.05.95	Cessna 182	CS-APG	*	Heliservico	Crashed	Lisbon, Portugal	3	0
31.05.95	Fokker F-28 Fellowship 1000	P2-ANB	11049	Air Niugini	Ran off runway on landing & crashed into harbour	Madang, Indonesia	0	*
31.05.95	Aerospatiale AS.355F TwinStar	N5781D	5038	Rogers Helicopters	Crashed on landing	Lost Hills, CA, USA	*	*

Date	Type	Reg'n	C/n	Operator	Accident	Location	F	S
31.05.95	Kamov Ka-26	RA-19616	*	Saak Avia	Crashed	nr Stavropol, Russia	*	*
01.06.95	Bell UH-1L	N27FL	6439	Intermountain Helicopters	Crashed	nr Sutherlin, OR, USA	*	*
02.06.95	Cessna 402B II	LV-MIU	402B-1332	Lineas Aereas Entre Rios	Crashed after take-off	River Plate, Argentina	6	1
03.06.95	Boeing 747-238B	N706CK	20010	Kalitta American International Airways	Crashed on approach	Panama City, Panama	0	*
07.06.95	Short Skyvan 3-100	OE-FDL	SH.1904	Pink Aviation Services	Crash landed after take-off	Hohenems, Austria	0	*
09.06.95	de Havilland Canada Dash 8-102	ZK-NEY	055	Ansett New Zealand	Crashed on approach in bad weather	nr North Palmerston, New Zealand	4	17
09.06.95	McDonnell Douglas DC-9-32	N908VJ	47321	Valujet	Damaged by fire after engine explosion while taxiing	Atlanta, GA, USA	0	55
09.06.95	Eurocopter SA.315B Lama	VR-HJH	2611	Heliservices Hong Kong	Crashed while carrying underslung load	Sek Kong, Hong Kong	0	1
13.06.95	McKinnon G-21E Goose	N121H	1211	Air Classic Museum	Crashed and caught fire after take-off	West Chicago, IL, USA	2	0
13.06.95	Bell 212	C-FNMP	30759	Northern Mountain Helicopters	Crashed after take-off	nr Fort Vermilion, AL, Canada	0	*
14.06.95	Douglas DC-3	YV-610C	9894	Servivensa	Crashed on approach	Kavac, Venezuela	0	*
15.06.95	Dornier Do.228-201	B-12288	8142	Formosa Airlines	Damaged in belly landing	Taitung, Taiwan	0	*
16.06.95	Antonov AN-74	RA-74041	36547096924	Aviacor	Crashed on landing	Keprveen, Russia	*	*
16.06.95	Antonov AN-2	RA-07743	*	Far East Directorate	Crashed in bad weather	nr Poliny Osipenko, Russia	12	1
16.06.95	Fokker F-27 Friendship 400M	TC-73	10407	Lineas Aereas del Estado	Crashed into building on landing	Port-au-Prince, Haiti	0	35
18.06.95	de Havilland Canada Beaver 1	C-FGBC	199	White River Air Services	Crashed after take-off	Pine Lake, ON, Canada	5	0
19.06.95	Aerospatiale AS.350B Ecureuil	C-GSKI	1040	Blackcomb Helicopters	Damaged on landing	Brokelbank, SK, Canada	*	*
20.06.95	Bell 206L-1 Long Ranger	C-GSHZ	45352	Heli-Transport	Crashed into cables on take-off	Chapais, PQ, Canada	*	*
21.06.95	Douglas C-54G	N4989P	36082	Aero Union	Mid-air collision with Beechcraft 55 N156Z on approach	Ramona, CA, USA	2(1)	0
23.06.95	Beechcraft 58 Baron	N4403Q	TH-809	Air Orlando Charter	Crashed after take-off due to engine failure	Orlando, FL, USA	2	0
23.06.95	Learjet 35A	XA-SWF	35A-391	Aereo Reservaciones Ejecutivas	Crashed on approach	Tepico, Mexico	2	5
24.06.95	Tupolev TU-134A	RA-65617	4308068	Harka Air Services	Crashed after overshooting on landing	Lagos, Nigeria	15	65
26.06.95	Hughes 369D	N1089N	51-0966D	Western Helicopters	Crashed into mountain	Highland, CA, USA	*	*
27.06.95	Convair 440-98(F)	N356SA	432	Salair	Crashed after engine failure	nr La Romana, Dominican Republic	2	1
28.06.95	Bell 205A-1	C-GNMR	30015	Northern Mountain Helicopters	Crashed into river	nr Leaf Rapids, MN, Canada	*	*
29.06.95	Eurocopter SA.315B Lama	VR-HJG	2601	Heliservices Hong Kong	Crashed while carrying underslung load	nr Yuen Long, Hong Kong	0	1
29.06.95	Agusta-Bell 206B JetRanger III	G-BHXU	8595	Castle Air	Crashed at sea	Off Alderney, Channel Islands	0	2
29.06.95	Bell 206B JetRanger II	OH-HSR	1494	Copter Action	Crashed	Vihtij, Finland	*	*
29.06.95	Bell 206B JetRanger II	C-GRAA	2071	Aero Arctic	Crashed in bad weather	Taloyoak, NWT, Canada	*	*
30.06.95	Rockwell Turbo Commander 681	N70RF	6013	EM Travel & Sales	Crashed on landing	Nassau, Bahamas	0	*
01.07.95	de Havilland Canada Caribou	P2-VTC	013	Garamut Aviation	Crashed on approach	nr Kiunga, Papua New Guinea	2	1
04.07.95	Bell 206L-1 Long Ranger	C-GLBA	45017	Air Alma	Crashed on take-off	Fontagnes, PQ, Canada	*	*
06.07.95	Boeing 737-3J6	B-2536	25079	Air China International	Crashed after aborting take-off	Guangzhou, China	0	*
07.07.95	Piper PA-32R-300 Lance	N6281J	32R-7680348	LAB Flying Service	Crashed into mountain	Haines, AK, USA	6	0
08.07.95	IRMA BN-2B-27 Islander	TR-LBJ	2127	Air Inter Gabon	Crashed on approach	Medouneu, Gabon	0	8
10.07.95	Bell 206B JetRanger	C-GBPB	0321	Denendeh Helicopters	Crashed on landing	nr Copper Mine, NWT, Canada	0	*
12.07.95	de Havilland Canada Twin Otter 300	P2-MBI	275	Milne Bay Air	Crashed on beach after take-off	Gurney, Papua New Guinea	17	0
17.07.95	de Havilland Canada Twin Otter 300	PK-NUT	473	Merpati Nusantara Airlines	Crashed on take-off	Bentuni, Indonesia	1	*
17.07.95	Piper PA-34-200T Seneca	N2883D	34-7970323	Sky Harbor Air Service	Crashed on approach	Cheyenne, WY, USA	1	0
18.07.95	Douglas C-47A	*	*	Malagasy Air Force	Crashed on approach	Antananarivo, Madagascar	34	6
19.07.95	Douglas DC-3	N54NA	19475	Business Air	Crashed into hill	Whitesville, MO, USA	1	1
22.07.95	Douglas DC-6A	HK-1776	45499	Lineas Aereas del Norte de Colombia	Crashed	nr Puerto Inride, Colombia	0	*
24.07.95	Grumman Gulfstream IV	N400UP	1054	Union Pacific Aviation	Damaged in hard landing	Englewood, CO, USA	0	*
24.07.95	Sikorsky S-76A	VR-BQD	760136	Operator Unknown	Destroyed in hangar fire	Aspropirgos, Greece	0	*
25.07.95	Britten-Norman BN-2A-20 Islander	P2-TNT	0393	Transniugini Airways	Crashed after take-off	Bomai, Papua New Guinea	2	0
25.07.95	Mil Mi-2	RA-23518	*	Abakan State Aviation	Crashed on approach	nr Norilsk, Russia	*	*
26.07.95	McDonnell Douglas DC-9-31	5N-BBA	47217	ADC Airlines	Crash landed after fire and burnt out	Monrovia, Liberia	0	91
26.07.95	Piper PA-42 Cheyenne	*	*	Confortair	Crashed in sea after double engine failure	Off Seven Islands, PQ, Canada	0	7
27.07.95	Eurocopter AS.350B2 Ecureuil	F-ZBFR	2100	Securite Civile	Crashed into mountain	nr St Etienne de Tinee, France	4	0
29.07.95	Britten-Norman BN-2A Islander	P2-MBM	*	Provincial Air Transport	Crashed on approach	Fane, Papua New Guinea	0	12
01.08.95	Cessna 310	*	*	RegionAir	Crashed in mountains during hurricane	nr Kingston, Jamaica	5	0
02.08.95	Antonov AN-2	RA-05708	1G153-21	Aero Air	Crashed into pylon on take-off	Johannesburg, South Africa	3	0
02.08.95	Westinghouse Sentinel 1000-001	*	*	Westinghouse	Destroyed in hangar fire	Weeksville, NC, USA	0	*

Date	Type	Reg'n	C/n	Operator	Accident	Location	F	S
09.08.95	Boeing 737-2H6	N125GU	23849	Aviateca	Crashed into mountain	nr San Salvador, El Salvador	65	0
09.08.95	Hawker Siddeley HS.748 2A	PK-KHL	1735	Bouraq Indonesia Airlines	Crashed into mountain [Found 14.08.95]	nr Kaimana, Indonesia	10	0
10.08.95	Antonov AN-2	*	*	Operator Unknown	Crashed after striking power line whilst overloaded	Mezhdurechenskly, Russia	0	25
14.08.95	Embraer Bandeirante 110P1	HK-2594	110.310	AIRES	Crashed into mountain	nr Cali, Colombia	7	0
17.08.95	Britten-Norman BN-2 Islander	*	*	Operator Unknown	Crashed on take-off due to engine failure	Haifa, Israel	0	8
17.08.95	Boeing 707-321C	YR-ABN	19379	Tarom	Damaged on landing	N'Djamena, Chad	0	6
19.08.95	Douglas DC-3	C-GZOF	20833	Air North	Crashed after engine failure	nr Richmond, BC, Canada	0	3
21.08.95	Embraer Brasilia 120ER	N256AS	120.122	Atlantic Southeast Airlines	Crashed & caught fire after engine failure	nr Carrollton, GA, USA	5	24
24.08.95	Lockheed Tristar 1	N781DL	1003	Delta Air Lines	Damaged by explosive decompression [One more ferry flight]	Off Los Angeles, CA, USA	0	*
28.08.95	Beechcraft E18S	N171LG	BA-427	Operator Unknown	Crashed after in-flight fire	Off Freeport, Bahamas	*	*
01.09.95	Short Skyvan 3-200	N30GA	SH 1839	Air Cargo Carriers	Crashed into mountain	nr Farewell, AK, USA	*	*
02.09.95	Cessna 421C Golden Eagle	N6234G	421C-0265	Adventure Airlines	Crashed after engine failure	Mesquite, NV, USA	8	0
02.09.95	Cessna 421C Golden Eagle	N3911C	421C-0138	Operator Unknown	Crashed on approach	Phoenix, AZ, USA	*	*
05.09.95	Dassault Falcon 20F	5N-EPN	273	Aero Contractors	Damaged in belly landing	Lagos, Nigeria	0	11
09.09.95	CASA 212 Aviocar 200	FAC.1152	306	Satena	Crashed into mountain in bad weather	nr La Macarena, Colombia	21	1
11.09.95	Antonov AN-26	*	*	Ariana Afghan Airlines	Crashed due to fuel starvation	nr Jalalabad, Afghanistan	3	43
12.09.95	Beechcraft Queen Air 65	N19CR	*	Peninsula Skydiving	Crashed into building	West Point, WV, USA	11	0
12.09.95	Mil Mi-2	B-2929	5310929069	Czech Police	Crashed	Czech Republic	*	*
13.09.95	Cessna 402B	N69303	402B-0423	Operator Unknown	Crashed	nr Marsh Harbor, Bahamas	5	*
15.09.95	Fokker 50	9M-MGH	20174	Malaysia Airlines	Overran on landing & crashed into buildings	Tawau, Sabah, Malaysia	35	18
18.09.95	Antonov AN-2	Z3-BGE	1G111-14	Aviotransport	Crashed	Macedonia	*	*
18.09.95	Fairchild Merlin III	N693PG	T-207	Operator Unknown	Crashed & caught fire	nr Chino, CA, USA	*	*
19.09.95	Boeing 727-214	*	*	Harco Air Services	Overshot runway after crash landing	Kaduna, Nigeria	0	70
21.09.95	Antonov AN-24	BNMAU-10103	57310103	MIAT Mongolian Airlines	Crashed into mountain	nr Moreon, Mongolia	42	1
21.09.95	Mitsubishi MU-2	N309MA	602	Operator Unknown	Crashed after take-off	nr Smyrna, TX, USA	*	*
21.09.95	Cessna 421B Golden Eagle	N14A	421B-0373	Operator Unknown	Crashed	Coldwater, MI, USA	*	*
22.09.95	de Havilland Canada Otter	*	*	Operator Unknown	Crashed on landing	Salvesen Lake, ON, Canada	5	1
24.09.95	Mil Mi-8	*	*	Dikson Air	Crashed and sank	Off Taymyr, Russia	9	0
27.09.95	de Havilland Canada Otter	*	*	Western Straits Air	Crashed on forced landing in fog	Vancouver Is, BC, Canada	8	2
28.09.95	Martin B-26C Marauder	N5546N	2253	Confederate Air Force	Crashed while practising for air display	Odessa, TX, USA	5	0
oo.09.95	Britten-Norman Trislander	N127LB	1010	Virgin Air	Crashed	Off St Thomas, US Virgin Is	*	*
03.10.95	CASA 212 Aviocar 100	PK-ZAG	28N/158	Sabang Merauke Raya Air Charter	Crashed	Gunung Antara, Indonesia	1	13
05.10.95	Mil Mi-8	*	*	Operator Unknown	Crashed into mountain	Kirghizia	15	0
10.10.95	Mil Mi-8T	*	*	Operator Unknown	Crashed	Almaty, Kazakhstan	1	15
16.10.95	Antonov AN-2	*	*	Tyumenaviatrans	Crashed on emergency landing	Konstantinov Kamen, Russia	2	6
25.10.95	Antonov AN-32	*	*	Operator Unknown	Undershot on landing in snowstorm	Tyumen, Russia	7	6
08.11.95	Fokker F-27 Friendship	*	*	Lineas Aereas del Estado	Crashed into mountain in rain	nr Luyaba, Argentina	53	0
13.11.95	Boeing 737	*	*	Nigeria Airways	Crashed on landing	Kaduna, Nigeria	77	52
oo.oo.95	Antonov AN-26	UR-26049	10902	Ukraine Flight Academy	Damaged after attempting take-off with locked brakes	Palana, Ukraine	*	*
oo.oo.95	Yakovlev YAK-40	UN-88181	9620148	Kazakhstan Airlines	Damaged after running off runway on landing	Jambyl, Kazakhstan	*	*

Appendix A
Crashes with no known date

The following aircraft are known to have been written off in accidents but no date has been traced as yet. All other information is in the same format as that in the main listings.

Type	Reg'n	C/n	Operator	Accident	Location	F	S
Lockheed Vega 1	*	017	Argentine Government	Crashed in early 1930s	Argentina	*	*
Lockheed C-69	43-10314	1966	War Assets Administration	Damaged beyond repair	Location Unknown	*	*
de Havilland Riley Dove 400	5N-AGF	04246	Biafran Air Force	Destroyed during civil war	Nigeria	*	*
IRMA BN-2A-21 Islander	5T-MAQ	0786	Mauritanian Air Force	Written off	Location Unknown	*	*
Britten-Norman BN-2A-21 Islander	5T-MBA	0577	Mauritanian Air Force	Written off	Location Unknown	*	*
Britten-Norman BN-2A-3 Islander	5Y-ANV	0284	Caspair	Written off	Location Unknown	*	*
Beechcraft Queen Air 70	7T-VSB	LB-007	Air Algerie	Written off	Location Unknown	*	*
Britten-Norman BN-2A-27 Islander	8R-GES	0482	Guyana Defence Force	Written off	Guyana	*	*
Britten-Norman BN-2A Islander	9Q-CRF	0157	Enterprise Generale M.Forrest	Written off	Location Unknown	*	*
Douglas DC-3	C-68	9388	Lansa	Crashed	Location Unknown	*	*
Scottish Aviation Twin Pioneer 1	C-FSTX	516	Vancouver Air Services	Crashed	Yukon, Canada	*	*
Beechcraft Super King Air 200	C-GJCM	BB-0450	Operator Unknown	Written off	Location Unknown	*	*
Scottish Aviation Twin Pioneer 1	C-GSTX	508	Terr-Air	Crashed	Yukon, Canada	*	*
Lockheed 18 Lodestar	CC-CLC	2602	LAN-Chile	Crashed	Location Unknown	*	*
Rockwell Turbo Commander 690	CP-1016	11053	Operator Unknown	Written off	Bolivia	*	*
Curtiss C-46A	CP-1333	45	Transportes Aereos Luwior	Written off	Cochabamba, Bolivia	*	*
Avro Anson I	CR-AAT	–	Transportes Aereos de Timor	Written off	Location Unknown	*	*
de Havilland Dove 1	CR-ACJ	04148	DETA	Written off	Location Unknown	*	*
de Havilland Dove 1	CR-ACM	04158	DETA	Written off	Location Unknown	*	*
Beechcraft D18S	CX-BAI	A-1004	J.B.Varela	Crashed	Paraguay	*	*
Dornier Merkur	D-1465	126	Deruluft	Crashed post 1931	Location Unknown	*	*
Junkers F.13	D-368	725	Deutsche Lufthansa	Crashed	Location Unknown	*	*
Junkers F.13	D-550	688	Deutsche Lufthansa	Crashed	Location Unknown	*	*
Junkers G.38	D-APIS	3302	Deutsche Lufthansa	Destroyed by RAF bombing	Athens, Greece	*	*
de Havilland DH.89A Dragon Rapide	ET-P-22	6700	C.Tonna	Written off	Location Unknown	*	*
Farman F.63bis Goliath	F-AEGP	9	Air Union	Crashed	UK	*	*
Breguet 14A.2	F-AEJA	*	Lignes Aeriennes Latecoere	Crashed	Morocco	*	*
CAMS 56	F-AIOY	04	Aeropostale	Lost at sea	Location Unknown	*	*
CAMS 53	F-AISZ	09	Aeropostale	Destroyed in harbour	Algiers, Algeria	*	*
Latecoere 28-1	F-AJIP	905	Aeropostale	Written off	Location Unknown	*	*
CAMS 53	F-AJJQ	16	Aeropostale	Crashed at sea	Location Unknown	*	*
CAMS 53	F-AJKB	17	Aeropostale	Lost at sea	Location Unknown	*	*
CAMS 53	F-AJKF	18	Aeropostale	Crashed at sea	Location Unknown	*	*
Latecoere 28	F-AJOZ	*	Aeropostale	Written off	Location Unknown	*	*
Latecoere 28-0	F-AJUZ	932	Air France	Written off	Location Unknown	*	*
Latecoere 28-0	F-AJVH	924	Aeropostale	Written off	Location Unknown	*	*
CAMS 53	F-ALCG	31	Aeropostale	Crashed at sea	Location Unknown	*	*
Dewoitine D.338	F-AQBN	14	Air France	Damaged beyond repair	Hanoi, French Indo-China	*	*
Farman F.2200	F-AQCY	4	Air France	Destroyed	Location Unknown	*	*
Latecoere 631	F-BDRB	05	Latecoere	Damaged when hangar collapsed in snowstorm	France	*	*
Beechcraft King Air C90	F-BXAR	LJ-0658	Operator Unknown	Written off	Location Unknown	*	*
IRMA BN-2A-3 Islander	F-ODHU	0867	Operator Unknown	Written off	Location Unknown	*	*
IRMA BN-2A-9 Islander	F-ODSF	0740	Operator Unknown	Written off	Location Unknown	*	*
Mitsubishi MU-2L	HK-2245W	684	Centro Int. de Agricultura Tropical	Written off	Location Unknown	*	*
Rockwell Turbo Commander 695A	HK-3376	96083	Operator Unknown	Written off	Mexico	*	*
Britten-Norman BN-2A Islander	HP-658	0106	Turismo Aereo	Written off	Location Unknown	*	*
Britten-Norman BN-2A-6 Islander	HP-676	0186	Turismo Aereo	Written off	Panama	*	*
Britten-Norman BN-2A-3 Islander	HP-680	0328	Aviones de Panama	Written off	Location Unknown	*	*
Mitsubishi MU-2P	I-FRUT	413SA	Operator Unknown	Written off	Location Unknown	*	*
de Havilland Dove 1	LQ-XWW	04094	Civil Aeronautics Board	Crashed on take-off	Formosa, Taiwan	7	0
Macchi C.94	LV-AAE	94012	Corporacion Sudamericana	Crashed post 1939	Location Unknown	*	*
Noorduyn Norseman VI	LV-AAW	798	ALFA	Written off post 1947	Location Unknown	*	*
Noorduyn Norseman VI	LV-AAY	341	ALFA	Written off post 1947	Location Unknown	*	*
Beechcraft C18S	LV-AAZ	4958	ALFA	Written off post 1947	Location Unknown	*	*

Type	Reg'n	C/n	Operator	Accident	Location	F	S
Avro Lancastrian 4	LV-ACS	1382	FAMA	Crashed	Location Unknown	*	*
de Havilland DH.89A Dragon Rapide	LV-AEO	6789	ZONDA	Written off post 1948	Location Unknown	*	*
Noorduyn Norseman VI	LV-AFR	768	ALFA	Written off post 1947	Location Unknown	*	*
de Havilland DH.90 Dragonfly	LV-KAB	7563	Operator Unknown	Mid-air collision with Ju.52/3m PP-SPF	Rio de Janeiro, Brazil	*(*)	*
de Havilland Dove 1	LV-XZY	04144	Civil Aeronautics Board	Crashed	Location Unknown	*	*
de Havilland Dove 1	LV-YAE	04149	Civil Aeronautics Board	Crashed	Location Unknown	*	*
de Havilland Dove 1	LV-YBL	04238	Civil Aeronautics Board	Crashed	Location Unknown	*	*
de Havilland Dove 1	LV-YBP	04242	Civil Aeronautics Board	Crashed	Location Unknown	*	*
Avia 14T	LZ-ILF	197014101	Balkan Bulgarian Airlines	Crashed	Provadia, Bulgaria	*	*
Avia 14T	LZ-ILG	198014102	Balkan Bulgarian Airlines	Damaged beyond repair	Sofia, Bulgaria	*	*
Rockwell Turbo Commander 695A	N17ZD	96017	Operator Unknown	Written off	Location Unknown	*	*
Rockwell Turbo Commander 690B	N23LS	11372	Operator Unknown	Written off	Location Unknown	*	*
Fairchild 227AC Metro III	N31138	AC-579	Chautauqua Airlines	Damaged beyond repair	Hagerstown, MD, USA	*	*
Cessna 441 Conquest II	N36962	0033	Operator Unknown	Damaged in ground accident	Location Unknown	*	*
Convair 300	N558	075	Executive Aviation	Written off	Location Unknown	*	*
Douglas DC-7	N6302C	44266	APA Services	Destroyed by fire	Wildwood, NJ, USA	*	*
Boeing B-17G	N66573	*	Black Hills Aviation	Crashed	Location Unknown	*	*
Britten-Norman BN-2A Islander	N856JA	0108	Sun Air	Written off	Location Unknown	*	*
Britten-Norman BN-2A Islander	N857JA	0092	International Sky Cab Airlines	Written off	Location Unknown	*	*
Britten-Norman BN-2A-8 Islander	N94CA	0315	Harbor Airlines	Written off	Location Unknown	*	*
Fokker F.32	NC130M	1202	Fokker	Crashed before delivery	Location Unknown	*	*
Boeing 314A	NC18609	2083	Universal Airlines	Damaged by storm	Location Unknown	*	*
Lockheed Vega 5	NC392H	084	Corp Aeronautica de Transportes	Crashed	Mexico	*	*
Ford 4-AT-B Tri-Motor	NC9609	4-AT-52	E.L.Fulton	Destroyed in hurricane	Boca Chica, Mexico	*	*
Fokker Super Universal	NC9786	*	Pan American Airways	Sunk and destroyed	Brazil	*	*
Faucett F.19	OA-BBK	02	Faucett	Written off post 1934	Location Unknown	*	*
Faucett F.19	OA-BBL	03	Faucett	Written off post 1934	Location Unknown	*	*
Faucett F.19	OA-BBN	05	Faucett	Written off post 1934	Location Unknown	*	*
Faucett F.19	OA-BBO	06	Faucett	Written off post 1934	Location Unknown	*	*
Faucett F.19	OA-BBS	10	Faucett	Written off post 1934	Location Unknown	*	*
Faucett F.19	OA-BBU	12	Faucett	Written off post 1934	Location Unknown	*	*
Faucett F.19	OA-BBX	15	Faucett	Written off post 1934	Location Unknown	*	*
Faucett F.19	OB-PAA-104	07	Faucett	Written off post 1934	Location Unknown	*	*
Faucett F.19	OB-PAB-105	08	Faucett	Written off post 1934	Location Unknown	*	*
Faucett F.19	OB-PAD-120	14	Faucett	Written off post 1934	Location Unknown	*	*
Faucett F.19	OB-PAE-132	18	Faucett	Written off post 1934	Location Unknown	*	*
Faucett F.19	OB-PAK-144	28	Faucett	Written off post 1934	Location Unknown	*	*
Faucett F.19	OB-PAR-148	30	Faucett	Written off post 1934	Location Unknown	*	*
LET 410A Turbolet	OK-DKD	720205	VZLU	Destroyed by fire	Czechoslovakia	*	*
Sikorsky S-38	P-BDAD	214-10	Panair do Brasil	Written off	Location Unknown	*	*
Beechcraft D18S	PK-SVA	*	Standard Vacuum Petrol	Written off	Kemayoran, Indonesia	*	*
Lockheed 14 Super Electra	PP-AVA	1405	Aerovias Brasil	Written off	Location Unknown	*	*
Junkers W.34	PP-CAN	2593	Syndicato Condor	Crashed	Location Unknown	*	*
Junkers W.34	PP-CAP	2595	Syndicato Condor	Crashed	Location Unknown	*	*
Junkers W.34	PP-CAR	2711	Syndicato Condor	Crashed	Location Unknown	*	*
Junkers G.24	PP-CAS	961	Syndicato Condor	Crashed	Location Unknown	*	*
Lockheed 10A Electra	PP-NBC	1073	Aeronorte	Written off	Location Unknown	*	*
Lockheed 10A Electra	PP-NBD	1074	Aeronorte	Written off	Location Unknown	*	*
Sikorsky S-43	PP-PAU	4308	Panair do Brasil	Written off	Location Unknown	*	*
Sikorsky S-43	PP-PBA	4303	Panair do Brasil	Written off	Location Unknown	*	*
Consolidated PBY-5A Catalina	PP-PDB	22021	Panair do Brasil	Written off	Location Unknown	*	*
Consolidated PBY-5A Catalina	PP-PEC	91	Cruzeiro	Written off post 1965	Location Unknown	*	*
Junkers Ju.52/3m	PP-SPD	5459	VASP	Written off	Location Unknown	*	*
Junkers Ju.52/3m	PP-SPF	5869	VASP	Written off	Location Unknown	*	*

Type	Reg'n	C/n	Operator	Accident	Location	F	S
Noorduyn Norseman VI	PP-VBE	623	Varig	Written off post 1947	Location Unknown	*	*
Britten-Norman BN-2A-8 Islander	PT-JYC	0385	VOTEC	Written off	Location Unknown	*	*
Dornier Do.28D-1 Skyservant	PZ-TBB	4006	Gum Air	Damaged	Zorg en Hoop, Surinam	*	*
Ilyushin IL-14	SSSR-41807	*	Aeroflot	Written off	Mirny, Antarctica	*	*
Tupolev TU-134	SSSR-65612	7350205	Aeroflot	Written off [Prior to 04.91]	Leningrad, RSFSR, USSR	*	*
Tupolev TU-134	SSSR-65642	C350926	Aeroflot	Written off	St Petersburg, Russia	*	*
LET 410M Turbolet	SSSR-67191	781120	Aeroflot	Crashed	USSR	*	*
Antonov AN-2	SSSR-70087	IG136-13	Aeroflot	Crashed	Tver, Russia	*	*
Mil Mi-4	SSSR-N968	*	Aeroflot	Damaged beyond repair	Mirny, Antarctica	*	*
de Havilland Canada Twin Otter 200	T-84	172	Lineas Aereas del Estado	Written off [Pre 04.82]	Location Unknown	*	*
Mil Mi-4	TJ-XAP	*	Cameroun Air Force	Written off [Prior to 1975]	Cameroun	*	*
de Havilland Canada Caribou	TJ-XAT	298	Cameroun Air Force	Written off [Prior to 1980]	Cameroun	*	*
Aerospatiale 330H Puma	TN-231	1294	Congolese Air Force	Crashed	Congo	*	*
Britten-Norman BN-2A Islander	TR-LXW	0151	Rougier Gabon	Written off	Location Unknown	*	*
Britten-Norman BN-2A-8 Islander	TZ-ASC	0397	Operator Unknown	Written off	Location Unknown	*	*
Lockheed 14H Super Electra	VP-TAF	1439A	British West Indian Airways	Written off	Surinam	*	*
Lockheed 414-56 Hudson IIIA	VP-TAK	7569	British West Indian Airways	Written off	Location Unknown	*	*
de Havilland DH.89A Dragon Rapide	VR-LAD	6963	Sierra Leone Airways	Destroyed by fire	Hastings, Sierra Leone	*	*
de Havilland DH.89A Dragon Rapide	VR-LAE	6827	Sierra Leone Airways	Destroyed by fire	Hastings, Sierra Leone	*	*
Lockheed 10E Electra	XA-BAU	1041	Mexicana	Written off	Location Unknown	*	*
Lockheed 10C Electra	XA-BEO	1007	Mexicana	Written off	Location Unknown	*	*
Lockheed 10C Electra	XA-BEQ	1022	Mexicana	Written off	Location Unknown	*	*
Avro Anson V	XA-YEO	M-1553	Cia Impulsora de Aviacion	Crashed	Mexico	*	*
Britten-Norman BN-2A-9R Islander	XC-UPJ	0307	Operator Unknown	Written off	Location Unknown	*	*
Britten-Norman BN-2A-6 Islander	XU-BAE	0190	Air Cambodge	Written off	Location Unknown	*	*
Scottish Aviation Twin Pioneer 2	XW-PBJ	564	Continental Air Services	Lost on covert mission	S.E.Asia	*	*
Scottish Aviation Twin Pioneer 2	XW-PBN	565	Continental Air Services	Lost on covert mission	S.E.Asia	*	*
Scottish Aviation Twin Pioneer 2	XW-PBP	567	Continental Air Services	Lost on covert mission	S.E.Asia	*	*
Antonov AN-26	YA-BAN	14304	Ariana Afghan Airlines	Destroyed	Kabul, Afghanistan	*	*
Antonov AN-2	YU-BGI	IG111-13	Operator Unknown	Written off	Yugoslavia	*	*
Cessna 421B Golden Eagle	YV-270P	421B-0517	Operator Unknown	Written off	Location Unknown	*	*
Lockheed 14 Super Electra	YV-ADO	1510	Linea Aeropostal Venezolana	Written off	Location Unknown	*	*

Appendix B

Crashes by aircraft type

This appendix provides a cross reference to the main listings. All crashes are listed here under a simplified type name giving the registration and date for each accident suffered. Reference to this date in the main text will furnish the full accident details. If the date reads 'oo.oo.oo', the entry will be found in Appendix A.

AAC.1 Toucan

F-BAJB 04.10.47
F-BAJP 10.09.45
F-BAJS 29.06.46
F-BAJT 08.08.46
F-BAKL 23.11.45
F-BAKM 20.03.47
F-BAKO 04.02.46
F-BAKP 05.03.47
F-BAKV 07.06.47
F-BALE 10.04.53
F-BALF 01.07.47
F-BALK 02.02.46
F-BAMQ 01.01.52
F-BANB 05.06.47
F-BANK 05.12.52
F-BANO 10.11.45
F-BANP 13.01.46
F-BANQ 21.08.49
F-BBOF 17.03.55
F-BBYA oo.oo.48
F-BBYC 03.03.48
F-BBYF 26.07.51
F-BBYG 30.04.47
F-BBYH 30.05.47
F-BBYK 06.01.47
F-BBYL 26.10.46
F-BBZC 02.01.48
F-BBZL 11.05.53
F-BCAA 10.10.46
F-BCAD 01.11.46
F-BCHD 23.10.46
F-BCHH 14.07.47
F-BCHQ 30.08.47
F-BDYE 12.05.51
F-BDYH 13.11.47
YU-ACE 29.06.51

AEG K

D-74 14.06.28

ATR.42/72

B-22717 30.01.95
CN-CDT 21.08.94
F-OHOC 08.12.94
F-WEGA 17.06.88
I-ATRH 15.10.87
N401AM 31.10.94

Aermacchi AL.60B

G-ARZG 07.07.65
VQ-ZBM 02.01.65

Aerospatiale Alouette

C-GLAY 12.05.91
CC-CKA 07.06.84
D-HAKA 18.03.77
EP-HSV 19.11.77
F-BXAD 05.04.75
G-FILM 22.05.82
HB-XCM 27.10.82
HB-XEO 04.09.80
HB-XGE 10.04.85
HB-XLT 06.06.84
HB-XNC 04.09.84
HB-XOI 08.12.94
HK-2609 10.01.86
LN-OSQ 07.03.83
OE-EXH 11.01.85
OE-EXI 13.06.79
OE-EXV 26.01.84
TS-HSU 23.04.79
VQ-ZBG 20.05.60
VR-HJE 21.05.92

Aerospatiale Alouette III

5N-AKC 14.09.77
F-BRQI 01.12.92
F-ZBAG oo.07.91
HB-XIX 13.04.83
HB-XMZ 31.07.83
HB-XOL 03.05.94
HB-XOM 09.06.88
HB-XOT 02.03.86
OO-PCB 22.01.78
PK-DAI 07.09.74
PK-PGD 09.06.75
RA-01187 31.08.94
VH-FLH 13.06.81
YR-ELV 24.03.94

Aerospatiale Caravelle

5N-AWK 06.08.86
7T-VAI 23.09.73
7T-VAK 26.07.69
9Q-CMD 09.10.85
B-1852 21.11.71
CN-CCV 01.04.70
EC-ATV 07.01.72
EC-BBR 29.09.73
EC-BDD 04.11.67
EC-BIA 05.11.73
EC-BIC 13.08.73
EC-BID 05.03.73
F-BHRL 12.03.79
F-BJTB 12.09.61
F-BNKI 04.01.71
F-BOHB 11.09.68
F-BSGZ 28.08.76
F-BSRY 22.03.74
F-BYAU 09.12.77
HB-ICK 18.12.77
HB-ICV 04.09.63
HC-BAE 18.01.86
HC-BAT 29.04.83
HC-BFN 12.09.79
HK-1778 20.07.79
HK-1810 21.12.80
HK-2850X 27.11.86
HK-3288X 29.09.91
HK-3325X 26.04.89
HK-3835X 06.05.93
HK-3855 15.03.94
HS-TGI 29.06.67
HS-TGK 09.07.69
I-DABF 02.08.69
I-GISO 02.07.83
LV-HGY 03.07.63
N805MW 19.06.80
OD-AEE 28.12.68
OD-AEF 28.12.68
OD-AEM 17.04.64
OO-SRD 22.12.73
OY-KRB 19.01.60
OY-SAN 14.07.73
OY-STK 15.03.74
OY-STL 14.03.72
PH-TRH 22.06.74
PP-PDU 06.09.63
PP-PDV 23.12.73
PP-PDX 01.06.73
PP-VJD 27.09.61
SE-DEC 06.01.87
TT-AAM oo.oo.81
VT-DPO 03.07.73
VT-DPP 15.02.66
VT-DSB 04.09.66
VT-DVJ 17.06.75
VT-DWN 12.10.76
XU-JTA 22.01.71
YU-AHD 11.09.73
YU-AJG oo.02.73
YV-C-AVI 21.08.73

Aerospatiale Corvette

F-BTTU 31.07.90
F-WRSN 23.03.71
OY-SBS 03.09.79
TN-ADB 30.03.79
TY-BBK 16.11.81

Aerospatiale Dauphin

* 27.06.91
B-7104 16.10.93
HL9244 13.08.92
N49505 28.04.85
VT-ELO 15.12.89

Aerospatiale Ecureuil

* 04.10.91
C-FHBG 04.04.94
C-FTPH 24.07.93
C-GAHG 18.03.94
C-GBEB 07.11.80
C-GBVS 26.01.80
C-GSKI 19.06.95
D-HEAD 07.12.94
F-GBTG 29.07.83
F-ZBFR 27.07.95
G-BIKH 08.04.86
G-PLMA 05.05.95
G-PLMG 07.12.94
HB-XTE 17.06.92
I-ELMR 17.11.94
I-GLPB 08.01.95
JA9222 19.02.83
JA9272 09.07.91
JA9315 27.01.90
N151BH 14.07.94
N353EH 25.05.88
N355EH 04.11.88
N3594N 11.07.85
N3595B 11.07.89
N3607C 29.07.85
N5781D 31.05.95
N5806K 29.05.92
N766MP 23.02.94
N782LF 27.05.93
N901BA 06.07.94
N902BA 13.01.94
N95LG 09.07.94
P2-PHB 19.09.94
SE-HIP 03.09.79
SE-HNG 15.05.94
VH-NBN 25.06.91
ZK-HGV 17.03.93
ZK-HNH 01.02.93
ZK-HWV 29.10.94
ZK-HZP 11.10.94

Aerospatiale Gazelle

9Y-TFN 23.03.94
C-GXQE 22.06.81
C-GXRS 18.08.90
F-GKYC 10.07.91
HB-XFW 08.08.79

Aerospatiale Lama

G-AZNI 23.12.94
G-BOUY 31.12.94
I-ELTA 11.04.94
VR-HJG 29.06.95
VR-HJH 09.06.95

Aerospatiale Puma

* 08.12.77
5N-AKE 19.04.74
5V-MAK 03.04.89
6W-SHI 21.04.82
7T-WUC 19.11.71
7T-WUD 01.04.71
9M-SSC 16.12.81
9M-SSG 13.12.85
A4O-AX 28.11.90
B-7952 24.10.93
F-GEBJ 27.10.87
G-BJWS 10.10.82
G-TIGD 04.07.83
G-TIGH 14.03.92
G-TIGK 19.01.95
G-TIGN 21.05.89
I-EHPA 25.11.90
N3596N 21.12.87
N47307 14.07.88
N49496 07.05.78
PA-12 03.05.82
PK-PDU 28.05.82
PK-PDV oo.oo.89
PK-PDW 02.02.76
PK-PEP 10.03.81
PK-PHY 09.04.72
PK-PUF 30.04.90
PK-PUI 06.12.90
PT-HRV 05.11.85
TJ-AAR 10.11.94
TN-231 oo.oo.oo

TR-KCD 20.02.78
VH-WOA 29.12.86
VH-WOF 12.05.91
XC-UJH/04 25.03.92

Aerospatiale Super Frelon

F-WMCU 30.05.65

Agusta A109A

RP-C1109 13.07.94
SX-HDB 29.04.92

Airbus A.300

9K-AHF 15.02.91
9K-AHG 15.02.91
AP-BCP 28.09.92
B-1816 26.04.94
EP-IBU 03.07.88
F-BUAE 31.03.93
F-BVGK 17.03.82
HL7296 09.08.94
HS-THO 22.10.94
OY-KAA 18.12.83
SU-BCA 21.09.87
VT-EDV 15.11.93
VT-ELV 29.09.86

Airbus A.310

F-OGQS 22.03.94
HS-TID 31.07.92
YR-LCC 31.03.95

Airbus A.320

D-AIPN 14.09.93
F-GFKC 26.06.88
F-GGED 20.01.92
VT-EPN 14.02.90

Airbus A.330

F-WWKH 30.06.94

Airbus A.340

F-GNIA 20.01.94
F-WWAS 22.01.93

Airship Industries Skyship

G-BIHN 27.04.87

Airspeed Ambassador

G-ALZR 26.07.69
G-ALZS 14.09.67
G-ALZU 06.02.58
G-ALZX 14.04.66
G-AMAB 08.04.55
G-AMAD 03.07.68
G-AMAG 30.09.68

Airspeed Consul

F-BCJF 04.03.54
F-BDPV 28.06.49
F-BDPX 16.03.49
F-BDPY 18.05.49
F-BEDP 26.10.50
G-AFFM 20.11.39
G-AFVS 03.09.39
G-AGVY 11.02.49
G-AHFT 14.06.52
G-AHGU 11.10.60
G-AHJX 12.05.50
G-AHMA 23.12.46
G-AHYW 16.10.46
G-AIDY 14.06.48
G-AIIO 17.07.48
G-AIIS 01.11.49
G-AIOM 24.01.48
G-AIOO 27.11.47
G-AIOU 24.05.48
G-AIOZ 15.08.47
G-AIRZ 18.07.52
G-AIUZ 02.09.48
G-AJGC 13.11.47
G-AJGD 15.07.49
G-AJGE 27.02.48
G-AJGI 14.11.47
G-AJLH 25.10.50
G-AJLJ 25.10.50
G-AJXE 21.11.59
G-ALTP 01.01.62
G-ALTR 14.08.61
G-ALTZ 04.06.57
OO-GVP 06.01.47
SE-BTU 24.11.54
TF-RPM 12.04.51
TJ-ABA 31.10.50
VR-TAR 04.03.48

Airspeed Courier

G-ACLS 17.10.34
G-ACSY 29.09.34
G-ACSZ 29.05.37

Airspeed Envoy

* 28.08.36
* 27.10.37
* 22.06.38
F-APPQ oo.oo.37
G-ACVH oo.05.36
G-ADBZ 22.01.37
G-AENA 01.10.36
PH-ARK 10.05.40
PH-ARL 10.05.40
VH-UXY 04.12.34
VT-AHR 22.03.42

Airspeed Ferry

VT-AFO 01.10.36

Albatros L58

D-576 oo.06.28

Antonov AN-10

SSSR-11137 12.10.71
SSSR-11145 31.03.71
SSSR-11148 27.01.62
SSSR-11149 15.05.70
SSSR-11167 16.11.59
SSSR-11172 08.08.68
SSSR-11180 26.02.60
SSSR-11185 28.06.62
SSSR-11188 08.08.70
SSSR-11189 12.10.69
SSSR-11193 08.02.63
SSSR 11215 10.06.72

Antonov AN-12

* 02.04.63
* 07.12.63
* 11.09.65
* 14.01.67
* 03.03.67
* 04.06.67
* 29.01.68
* 02.11.68
* 25.06.69
* 12.08.69
* 13.11.69
* 06.12.69
* 11.02.84
* 10.02.93
CU-T827 09.02.67
D2-EAD 19.09.84
LZ-BAA oo.oo.75
LZ-BAD 24.08.84
LZ-SFC oo.oo.92
RA-11110 07.08.93
RA-11118 24.02.94
RA-11121 26.04.93
RA-11127 09.05.95
RA-11337 14.03.95
RA-11340 08.02.94
RA-11375 20.08.93
RA-11790 29.10.94
RA-12187 19.12.93
RA-13340 26.03.95
RA-13387 25.09.93
SP-LZA 13.05.77
SSSR-10232 05.08.84
SSSR-11000 22.01.71
SSSR-11024 25.05.71
SSSR-11030 18.10.74
SSSR-11031 01.10.70
SSSR-11104 28.10.80
SSSR-11107 24.04.82
SSSR-11111 17.07.92
SSSR-11341 17.02.73
SSSR-11342 24.07.92
SSSR-11360 21.11.72
SSSR-11374 16.02.72
SSSR-11418 04.10.88
SSSR-11514 27.08.88
SSSR-11795 25.03.86
SSSR-11896 22.06.92
SSSR-12162 19.10.87
SSSR-12950 01.05.74
SSSR-12963 23.08.79
SSSR-12966 26.02.70
SSSR-12967 02.10.73
SSSR-12975 18.12.92
SSSR-12985 04.12.74
SSSR-12993 29.07.71
SSSR-12996 31.01.71
SSSR-12997 13.01.89
SSSR-13320 23.09.91
SSSR-29110 12.12.90
SSSR-69321 25.09.85
YU-AID 12.12.88

Antonov AN-124

RA-82071 15.11.93
SSSR-82002 13.10.92

Antonov AN-2

* 04.12.74
* 16.01.75
* 30.10.79
* 16.09.82
* 03.08.87
* 01.05.89
* 14.12.89
* 26.07.90
* 22.09.91
* 29.10.91
* 01.04.95
* 04.05.95
* 10.08.95
* 16.10.95
07562 14.09.93
07840 14.10.92
DM-SKS 26.07.64
EZ-07469 11.11.93
HA-ANL 11.05.82
HA-MBI 25.01.82
HA-MBM 30.05.84
HA-MBS 10.07.87
HA-MDJ 02.01.79
HA-MER 14.03.90
HA-MHS oo.oo.88
OB-1349 20.09.90
OB-1350 14.02.91
OB-1542 16.10.94
OK-JIK 25.08.82
OK-KHD 31.07.69
OK-KIM oo.oo.81
OK-MYC 11.07.68
OK-NYA 09.07.94
RA-01410 22.12.93
RA-05708 02.08.95
RA-07330 24.05.94
RA-07624 15.09.93
RA-07743 16.06.95
RA-33008 29.10.94
RA-50582 01.08.94
RA-62599 14.12.93
RA-68150 26.09.93
RA-70263 25.06.94
SP-AMK 16.09.84
SP-BSF 05.02.79
SP-DNM 31.03.87
SP-WNZ 22.09.75
SSSR-06324 oo.12.87
SSSR-07308 oo.oo.90
SSSR-07399 11.05.82
SSSR-07816 08.07.92
SSSR-32544 21.06.92
SSSR-35546 14.04.92
SSSR-40237 03.07.92
SSSR-40670 18.09.92
SSSR-50585 06.05.92
SSSR-55607 30.03.92
SSSR-56472 20.02.90
SSSR-70087 oo.oo.oo
SSSR-70501 27.05.87
YR-AND 29.07.62
YR-ANE 18.07.75
YR-ANF 09.04.76
YR-ANO 09.04.62
YR-APF 23.10.79
YR-APV 20.10.74
YR-PBE 10.07.87
YR-PMG 14.11.89
YR-PVC 14.01.78
YR-PVJ 21.07.81
YR-PVS 30.09.88
YR-PVU 13.08.85
YU-BBJ oo.oo.66
YU-BBM oo.oo.89
YU-BBN 15.09.91
YU-BFP 15.09.91
YU-BFS 19.09.91
YU-BGI oo.oo.oo
YU-BHU 19.09.91
YU-BKE oo.05.90
YU-BKF 26.01.92
YU-BOC 08.09.91
YU-BOD oo.11.87
YU-BOZ 15.09.91
YV-511C 13.10.93
Z3-BGE 18.09.95

Antonov AN-22

* 16.11.91
RA-09331 18.01.94
SSSR-08837 28.10.84
SSSR-09303 18.07.70
SSSR-09303 11.11.92
SSSR-09305 19.12.70
SSSR-09311 02.06.80
SSSR-09318 22.12.77
SSSR-09349 oo.06.77

Antonov AN-24/26

* 29.07.62
* 20.03.65
* 30.12.66
* 06.01.68
* 06.10.68
* 24.03.69
* 03.08.69
* oo.oo.74
* 21.01.76
* 09.02.87
* 30.03.87
* oo.03.87
* 13.09.87
* 27.08.88
* 21.10.89
* 26.10.89
* 01.03.90
* 05.02.91
* 04.03.91
* 22.03.92
* 30.03.92
* 23.04.93
* 27.07.94
* 23.03.95
* 04.04.95
* 11.09.95
26035 17.06.93
26141 26.12.93
3X-GAU 31.03.80
3X-GCG oo.oo.85
46478 16.01.93
47309 06.04.93
B-3417 15.08.89
B-434 19.01.85
B-444 15.12.86
BNMAU-10103 21.09.95
CU-T111 23.03.90
CU-T879 18.03.76
D2-TAB 29.11.82
J5-GAE 07.04.92
LZ-ANA 22.11.75
LZ-ANN 28.07.92
OB-1439 22.02.92
RA-26090 24.06.93
RA-26515 06.12.93
RA-26529 11.03.93
RA-26549 28.08.93
RA-30037 04.08.94
RA-46575 17.07.94
RA-47180 03.02.93
RA-47708 21.06.93
RA-47718 01.02.94
RA-88286 06.11.94
RDPL-34008 22.04.91
SP-LTD 02.11.88
SP-LTE 24.01.69
SP-LTF 02.04.69
SP-LTN oo.oo.79
SP-LTU 26.03.81
SSSR-26007 06.03.87
SSSR-26009 24.07.84
SSSR-26038 02.11.89
SSSR-26095 06.02.86
SSSR-26505 23.12.81
SSSR-26547 09.12.78
SSSR-26567 23.05.76
SSSR-26569 25.03.79

SSSR-26618 05.12.92
SSSR-26627 23.12.82
SSSR-26685 19.07.89
SSSR-26686 12.04.83
SSSR-46201 31.12.67
SSSR-46202 04.11.72
SSSR-46220 18.04.80
SSSR-46269 03.09.79
SSSR-46276 21.01.73
SSSR-46277 25.01.74
SSSR-46280 08.03.81
SSSR-46299 19.12.78
SSSR-46306 21.11.92
SSSR-46327 23.10.78
SSSR-46335 21.11.89
SSSR-46349 20.11.75
SSSR-46357 06.01.74
SSSR-46378 13.11.71
SSSR-46418 27.02.72
SSSR-46423 02.03.86
SSSR-46435 18.08.73
SSSR-46467 17.11.75
SSSR-46472 23.03.91
SSSR-46476 25.04.75
SSSR-46518 06.09.76
SSSR-46525 04.10.89
SSSR-46534 15.05.76
SSSR-46551 02.06.90
SSSR-46567 16.12.82
SSSR-46613 10.03.76
SSSR-46617 24.12.83
SSSR-46653 24.08.81
SSSR-46669 08.07.88
SSSR-46722 17.12.76
SSSR-46724 26.09.91
SSSR-46732 22.02.72
SSSR-46747 31.03.71
SSSR-46788 01.12.71
SSSR-46807 15.01.79
SSSR-46809 12.11.71
SSSR-46847 08.07.77
SSSR-47164 14.12.90
SSSR-47280 13.01.76
SSSR-47358 28.01.84
SSSR-47695 09.12.77
SSSR-47701 28.01.70
SSSR-47729 01.06.71
SSSR-47732 14.04.80
SSSR-47734 13.08.76
SSSR-47751 01.04.70
SSSR-47772 13.10.69
SSSR-47823 26.11.91
SSSR-88288 07.12.86
SU-ANZ 19.07.70
SU-AOA 18.03.66
SU-AOB 02.02.66
SU-AOC 14.03.70
SU-AOK 13.01.70
SU-AOL 18.08.68
SU-AOM 30.09.66
TZ-ACT 22.02.85
UN-26080 26.01.95
UR-26049 oo.oo.95
UR-26084 16.03.95
YA-BAK 18.06.89
YA-BAL 11.06.87
YA-BAM 04.09.85
YA-BAN oo.oo.oo
YI-AEM 24.09.80
YI-AEO 22.04.82
YI-ALN 27.08.82
YN-BYX 16.09.90
YR-AMA 15.11.71
YR-AMD 29.12.74
YR-AMT 04.02.70
YR-BMD 25.01.82
YR-BMJ 28.12.89

Antonov AN-28

HA-LAJ 28.08.93
RA-28713 12.05.94
RA-28716 23.11.93
RA-28797 01.02.95
SSSR-28706 03.01.92
SSSR-28741 14.08.87
SSSR-28785 19.10.92
SSSR-28924 23.10.91

Antonov AN-32

* 09.02.93
* 25.10.95
HK-3929X 08.10.94
SSSR-48058 10.06.92
SSSR-48088 09.10.92
SSSR-48095 28.09.89
SSSR-48109 17.01.91
SSSR-69306 02.10.90
SSSR-69310 03.12.90
UR-48018 06.07.94

Antonov AN-70

n/a 10.02.95

Antonov AN-72/74

* 16.09.91
RA-72960 23.10.94
RA-74041 16.06.95

Antonov AN-8

* 10.10.90
* 18.05.91
* oo.01.95
13323 12.12.93
D2-FVA 06.12.94
RA-27209 30.09.94
RA-59504 29.09.94
SSSR-69346 29.10.92

Arado V 1

D-1594 19.12.29

Armstrong Whitworth AW.23

G-AFRX 18.08.40

Armstrong Whitworth Argosy

G-AACH 22.04.31
G-AACI 28.03.33
G-EBLO 16.06.31

Armstrong Whitworth Atalanta

G-ABTG 27.07.38
G-ABTH oo.06.39
G-ABTK 29.09.36

Armstrong Whitworth Ensign

G-ADSZ 23.05.40
G-ADTA 23.05.40
G-ADTC 24.11.40

Armstrong Whitworth F.K.8

G-AUCF 25.02.23
G-AUDE 13.09.23
G-EAET oo.08.19
G-EALW 16.08.20

Armstrong Whitworth Whitley

G-AGCI 26.09.42
G-AGDU 12.08.42

Auster Autocrat

G-AIBS 22.05.51
G-AIGY 01.08.50
G-AKTF 07.02.60
PH-FCB 03.06.49

Avia B.H.25

L-BABD 09.05.29

Avro 504K

G-AASS 01.08.31
G-EAFQ 26.11.21
G-EAGV oo.09.20
G-EAGW oo.07.20
G-EANN oo.oo.20

Avro 642

VH-UXD oo.03.42

Avro Anson

AP-AGA 26.03.55
CF-BCA 24.05.62
CF-DTO 15.10.48
CF-DTS 26.10.57
CF-DTW 03.03.69
CF-EFZ 27.01.58
CF-EIG 06.12.54
CF-EJX oo.oo.52
CF-EKJ 06.02.51
CF-EKL 02.02.52
CF-ESA 10.12.54
CF-ESB 06.12.53
CF-ETG 17.01.58
CF-FEO 02.02.49
CF-FGM 05.12.52
CF-FJL 08.10.58
CF-FOF 20.08.58
CF-FVZ 06.01.55
CF-FYI 26.06.48
CF-FZE 06.04.53
CF-GDZ 14.10.52
CF-GFP oo.04.48
CF-GHI 05.04.50
CF-GJV 13.04.51
CF-GML 24.08.64
CF-GOA 16.04.63
CF-GRU 14.06.57
CF-GSA 07.04.51
CF-ICQ oo.04.57
CF-INT 25.03.63
CR-AAT oo.oo.oo
EC-ALF oo.oo.61
EP-CAA 24.09.60
F-BGOG 26.03.58
G-AGNI 11.06.48
G-AGPB 22.09.50
G-AGUE 16.08.46
G-AGZS 04.01.52
G-AGZT 03.01.57
G-AHFV 03.07.47
G-AHIG 06.08.55
G-AHKJ 12.02.47
G-AHXM 05.11.51
G-AHYO 31.10.46
G-AIEZ oo.oo.48
G-AIIC 13.11.46
G-AIKM 21.04.49
G-AIRN 22.02.52
G-AIWW 20.11.47
G-AIXE 07.01.48
G-AIXT 18.07.47
G-AIXW 26.04.50
G-AIXZ 05.02.51
G-AJBA 10.02.50
G-AJFX 10.07.51
G-AKDU 30.07.50
G-AKDV 02.03.50
G-AKFL 18.12.49
G-ALFD 17.02.52
G-ALFJ 08.03.49
G-ALXH 09.04.63
G-AMDA 02.11.72
G-ANWW 08.07.58
G-AWMG 03.09.68
G-AWMH 20.06.69
HC-SJN-014 11.06.54
HC-SJO oo.10.57
OB-ABO-341 18.06.54
OB-QAH-202 30.08.47
OH-ANA 01.05.55
OO-APG 29.07.56
OO-APN 20.03.47
OO-CCA 06.07.53
OO-CED 01.05.54
OO-CFB 07.04.48
OO-SRA 14.08.49
OY-DYC 16.02.56
OY-DYY 16.02.56
OY-DZI 05.10.56
OY-FAD 22.06.56
PP-ATC 21.04.46
PP-ATD 05.11.45
PP-ETD 09.07.50
PP-MTA 19.12.45
PP-MTB 06.03.46
PP-MTC 08.03.46
SE-BRP 04.12.50
SE-BRS 23.09.50
SU-ACX 26.10.45
SU-ADB 28.12.45
SU-ADJ 24.08.46
SU-ADN oo.06.48
SX-BDA 25.12.50
TF-RVF 27.07.51
TF-RVL 07.03.48
TG-CES-40 26.08.56
TI-16 oo.04.47
VH-AJP 10.02.51
VH-AKH 01.03.47
VH-ARL oo.08.51
VH-AVQ 24.04.47
VH-AVS 07.11.52
VH-AVZ 22.11.46
VH-AYD 24.05.47
VH-AYE 09.12.50
VH-AYN 04.02.56
VH-BAB 14.07.51
VH-BAB 12.04.60
VH-BAK 24.01.48
VH-BAX oo.08.51
VH-BBZ 11.05.49
VH-BCH 08.08.47
VH-BDD 04.02.53
VH-BDO 12.10.49
VH-BDX 06.02.50
VH-BEP oo.12.47
VH-BES 05.06.48
VH-BET 05.06.48
VH-BFC 31.08.51
VH-BFI 13.01.52
VH-BGO 05.06.48
VH-BIU 29.06.48
VH-BIX 22.03.61
VH-BKL 05.12.50
VH-BKT 20.02.53
VH-BKZ 17.01.53
VH-BLG oo.oo.59
VH-BMC oo.11.49
VH-BMD 18.12.54
VH-BMN 22.12.54
VH-BMS 14.10.49
VH-BNS 03.04.53
VH-FIB 10.02.60
VH-GVB 13.03.55
VH-ICA 04.02.56
VO-ABP 14.02.49
VP-KDI 26.01.49
VP-KDJ 20.01.48
VP-KDW 01.07.48
VP-KEM oo.06.48
VP-KEO 31.12.49
VP-KHS 09.07.54
VP-KHT 01.08.51
VP-KJK 01.10.56
VP-RCJ 24.09.52
VP-YKF 25.07.54
VP-YKT 10.01.54
VR-HDX 09.02.48
VR-SDL 10.04.53
VR-TAT 03.01.50
VT-CJZ oo.oo.47
VT-CXX 20.02.50
XA-DUU 02.02.46
XA-FOU 15.06.49
XA-FUG 11.02.49
XA-HEC oo.02.49
XA-HIM 13.10.49
XA-KED 24.04.54
XA-NEI oo.oo.63
XA-YEO oo.oo.oo
YV-P-APY 15.02.51
ZK-BCL oo.06.59

Avro Lancastrian

AP-ACM 01.08.48
CF-CMU 30.12.44
G-AGLF 11.05.47
G-AGLU 15.08.46
G-AGLX 24.03.46
G-AGMB 27.08.48
G-AGMC 02.05.46
G-AGMF 20.08.46
G-AGMH 17.05.46
G-AGMM 07.11.49
G-AGUL 23.10.47
G-AGWG 13.11.47
G-AGWH 02.08.47
G-AGWJ 30.08.46
G-AGWK 05.09.47
G-AHBU 03.10.47
G-AHCA 08.12.46
G-AHJW 22.11.48
G-AKDP 10.05.49
G-AKFH 26.06.49
I-AHBX 23.12.49
LV-ACS oo.oo.oo
VH-EAS 07.04.49
VH-EAV 17.11.51

Avro Shackleton

WL799 18.12.55

Avro Tudor

G-AGRE 17.01.49
G-AGRG 27.01.59

G-AGRH	23.04.59
G-AGSU	23.08.47
G-AHNP	30.01.48
G-AKBY	12.03.50
G-AKCC	26.10.51

Avro York

CF-HAS	oo.oo.67
CF-HFP	25.06.57
CF-HFQ	13.09.56
CF-HIQ	08.01.57
CF-HMU	24.01.56
CF-HMV	29.09.55
CF-HMW	26.09.56
CF-HMX	12.05.55
CF-HMY	26.05.55
CF-HMZ	11.04.55
EP-ADA	14.09.55
EP-ADB	17.09.56
EP-ADE	05.07.59
G-AGJD	01.02.49
G-AGNR	16.07.47
G-AGNS	22.04.56
G-AGNY	26.06.54
G-AGNZ	24.08.52
G-AGSN	oo.08.51
G-AHEW	06.09.46
G-AHEX	05.01.49
G-AHEZ	13.04.47
G-AHFA	02.02.53
G-AHFI	16.03.49
G-AIUP	25.07.47
G-ALBX	10.06.49
G-AMGL	11.03.52
G-AMGM	27.11.52
G-AMUL	30.04.56
G-AMUM	13.04.54
G-AMUN	23.12.57
G-AMUT	20.05.58
G-AMUV	25.05.58
G-ANRC	22.09.54
LV-XIG	23.12.46
LV-XIH	25.07.47
OD-ACD	27.05.60
OD-ACE	05.01.59
OD-ACJ	11.08.58
OD-ACN	06.04.62
OD-ACO	25.05.61
OD-ACP	08.10.58
OD-ACZ	15.03.63
OD-ADA	09.09.62
OD-ADB	29.09.58
XG920	18.02.56

B.E.2c

RRODD	oo.oo.27

BAC 1-11

5N-AOT	07.09.89
5N-AOW	26.06.91
5N-HTA	29.08.92
5N-IMO	18.09.94
5N-KBA	23.08.92
5N-KBG	16.09.91
9Q-CSJ	oo.07.94
D-ALAR	06.09.71
G-ASHG	22.10.63
G-ASJB	18.03.64
G-ASJJ	14.01.69
LV-JGY	22.11.77
LV-JNR	04.12.73
LV-LOX	07.05.81
N1116J	23.06.67
N1550	09.07.78
N1553	06.08.66
N711ST	09.02.75
PI-C1131	12.09.69
PP-SDQ	02.02.74
PP-SDS	05.01.77
RP-C1161	23.05.76
RP-C1182	04.08.84
RP-C1193	20.07.89
YR-BCA	07.12.70

BAC VC-10

5N-ABD	20.11.69
5X-UVA	18.04.72
9G-ABP	28.12.68
G-ARTA	28.02.72
G-ASGN	13.09.70
G-ASGO	03.03.74

BAT F.K.26

G-EAPK	31.07.22

BAe 146

B-2716	23.07.93
CC-CET	20.02.91
N350PS	07.12.87

BAe Jetstream

D-INAH	06.03.70
G-AXEL	29.09.69
G-SUPR	06.10.92
HB-AEB	02.09.94
N11360	17.04.81
N131CA	19.04.93
N165PC	12.03.92
N167PC	30.01.91
N331CY	26.05.87
N331PX	14.12.87
N334PX	01.12.93
N410UE	26.12.89
N411AE	25.03.88
N823JS	09.02.88
N830JS	30.11.86
N918AE	13.12.94

BAe Jetstream 41

N304UE	07.01.94

BN Islander

*	14.05.85
*	21.12.89
*	24.01.90
*	17.08.95
5T-MAQ	oo.oo.oo
5T-MAR	03.01.77
5T-MAT	21.07.77
5T-MBA	oo.oo.oo
5U-AAN	02.02.75
5W-FAF	20.08.88
5Y-AMG	oo.05.74
5Y-ANV	oo.oo.oo
5Y-AUA	06.01.76
7P-LAE	25.08.81
7Q-YAX	18.03.83
7Q-YAZ	04.02.77
8P-TAD	17.07.94
8R-GEH	07.11.77
8R-GES	oo.oo.oo
8R-GGU	oo.09.94
9J-ACF	27.03.75
9L-LAV	07.11.89
9M-APE	05.12.69
9M-MDD	06.07.82
9Q-CLW	29.06.93
9Q-CRF	oo.oo.oo
9Q-CTS	20.07.70
9Q-CYB	07.08.75
A2-ZEV	26.01.71
B-11107	09.09.79
B-11108	13.06.81
B-11109	28.09.83
B-11111	oo.04.87
B-11116	10.04.92
B-11125	19.01.88
B-12202	09.10.83
B-12207	oo.02.87
C-FAZM	oo.07.77
C-FZVV	18.09.79
C-GIPF	02.09.83
C-GIRH	12.01.87
C-GMOP	05.12.93
C-GOMC	04.12.87
C-GPCF	23.05.85
C-GSAF	26.01.90
C-GSGK	25.01.95
C-GTPB	18.09.87
C-GYTC	23.03.86
C9-TAI	03.11.84
CF-RDI	oo.06.75
CF-XZS	oo.06.73
CR-AMX	15.06.72
CS-AJO	oo.11.82
CS-AJQ	28.07.76
CS-DAF	08.05.94
D-IEDA	12.01.79
D-IJAN	27.06.75
D-IOLT	18.05.83
D2-ECE	16.03.94
DQ-FBO	12.07.79
DQ-FCN	06.08.91
DQ-FEO	11.05.93
EI-BBA	17.10.75
EI-BBR	07.07.80
EP-PAC	17.03.83
EP-PAE	11.08.72
EP-PBE	03.11.82
F-BRGH	oo.11.72
F-BVTD	23.06.84
F-OCRH	23.10.72
F-ODHU	oo.oo.oo
F-ODSF	oo.oo.oo
F-OGDR	oo.03.70
F-OGGL	oo.oo.79
F-OGHL	28.10.88
F-OGSM	oo.oo.90
G-ATCT	09.11.66
G-AXHE	05.02.94
G-AXRJ	07.04.70
G-AXWG	07.08.79
G-BBRP	20.02.82
G-BDNP	18.09.81
G-BDVW	01.06.84
G-BELN	14.12.78
G-BESE	14.12.78
G-BESK	14.12.78
G-BFNL	14.12.78
G-BLDX	21.08.87
G-BMDT	14.06.86
H4-AAC	22.10.78
HC-BFI	17.10.78
HC-BFJ	03.03.82
HH-CNB	26.12.78
HH-CNC	02.01.80
HK-2687X	26.04.83
HK-2822X	27.07.84
HK-2890	23.05.94
HP-1002	oo.12.89
HP-1133	oo.12.89
HP-550	oo.10.71
HP-572OL	oo.12.89
HP-658	oo.oo.oo
HP-659	28.01.85
HP-676	oo.oo.oo
HP-677	08.08.75
HP-680	oo.oo.oo
HP-945	06.04.83
I-BADE	27.06.80
J6-SLW	12.07.90
LN-MAF	17.02.93
N111VA	oo.09.88
N112JC	oo.09.89
N116DW	20.07.81
N122DW	15.09.75
N127JL	28.11.91
N22JA	21.07.77
N2718W	21.07.83
N28377	04.06.81
N290VL	oo.09.89
N36MN	21.11.77
N37JA	29.10.73
N37MN	07.04.83
N38JA	15.08.73
N455JH	oo.09.86
N457SA	28.09.81
N584JA	13.01.69
N587JA	03.01.69
N589JA	21.12.71
N589SA	02.08.84
N591JA	24.04.75
N61VM	02.12.94
N66HA	26.12.74
N68HA	20.08.91
N851JA	oo.10.80
N851JA	oo.12.88
N852JA	11.10.69
N855JA	09.09.70
N856JA	oo.oo.oo
N857JA	oo.oo.oo
N862JA	19.12.77
N864JA	02.10.74
N865JA	oo.05.85
N869JA	20.01.78
N94CA	oo.oo.oo
N97JA	10.04.78
OB-T-1207	04.11.90
OB-T-1271	10.03.89
OB-T-1272	oo.05.89
P2-ALF	19.09.94
P2-ALL	10.12.93
P2-ATU	05.10.79
P2-ATX	14.08.75
P2-BAB	21.03.89
P2-BAC	oo.02.90
P2-COG	oo.12.87
P2-DNI	25.08.85
P2-DNJ	05.07.90
P2-DNW	30.08.85
P2-DWA	11.01.92
P2-FHP	12.07.83
P2-HAC	10.03.82
P2-HBE	13.10.93
P2-ISA	15.06.81
P2-ISC	03.06.93
P2-ISF	23.01.93
P2-ISG	06.09.84
P2-ISH	14.01.84
P2-ISJ	18.07.89
P2-ISL	14.09.79
P2-ISR	24.12.93
P2-IST	oo.05.90
P2-KAD	20.06.87
P2-MBE	15.12.92
P2-MBF	oo.02.92
P2-MBM	29.07.95
P2-MIB	08.12.87
P2-SWC	22.11.94
P2-TNT	25.07.95
PH-NVA	30.08.70
PK-KNC	30.12.76
PK-KNE	12.05.85
PK-KNF	05.08.83
PK-KNG	26.04.79
PK-OAB	13.05.80
PK-OAN	21.03.85
PK-OAV	07.10.75
PK-OBE	29.04.83
PK-VIO	14.02.85
PK-VIP	03.09.91
PK-VIQ	20.10.79
PK-VIR	24.02.87
PK-VIT	24.02.80
PK-VIV	06.01.94
PK-ZAA	25.04.94
PK-ZAD	24.09.77
PK-ZAL	10.08.84
PT-DVN	04.10.73
PT-IJE	12.06.79
PT-JSC	30.03.80
PT-JYC	oo.oo.oo
PT-KAC	11.08.80
PT-KHK	13.05.80
PT-KRP	10.08.78
PT-KUO	12.05.77
RP-C2135	08.01.76
RP-C2136	21.12.75
RP-C2152	07.10.78
RP-C766	17.06.93
RP-C850	31.07.86
S7-AAE	30.08.84
TC-KUN	20.10.89
TF-RTO	22.09.80
TI-1063C	08.10.68
TN-ACO	oo.07.78
TN-ADS	oo.06.81
TN-AEQ	13.12.85
TR-LBJ	08.07.95
TR-LNF	oo.10.74
TR-LNG	26.11.77
TR-LOC	oo.05.73
TR-LOD	oo.06.73
TR-LSF	23.08.77
TR-LXW	oo.oo.oo
TU-TFW	09.07.75
TZ-ACS	oo.05.85
TZ-ADN	oo.10.87
TZ-ASC	oo.oo.oo
V3-HCT	25.11.89
VH-ATK	20.11.69
VH-BAY	oo.01.90
VH-BSN	oo.05.89
VH-EQK	31.03.76
VH-ISG	03.12.75
VH-ISI	25.11.84
VH-JUU	22.03.94
VP-FAY	01.05.82
VP-FBG	24.06.87
VP-HCD	22.02.77
VP-LAE	20.08.82
VQ-SAC	04.09.76
XA-FUA	03.11.77
XA-MAO	oo.oo.87
XA-RML	09.12.92
XC-UPJ	oo.oo.oo
XU-BAE	oo.oo.oo
YJ-RV20	13.09.88
YJ-RV4	25.07.91
YR-BNI	27.06.77

YR-BNJ 26.05.89
YR-BNS 11.11.92
YV-2349P 02.01.94
YV-269C 06.11.79
YV-O-MAR-6 15.06.77
Z-WHE 30.07.85
ZK-EVK 08.08.89
ZK-SFE 19.03.89
ZS-IZZ 24.08.74

BN Trislander

5Y-AOY oo.oo.86
5Y-CMC 24.07.78
6Y-JQF oo.09.88
9L-LAQ 25.08.80
C-GSZI 07.09.81
EL-AIC 28.10.81
G-BCYC 15.05.79
G-BDTP 14.09.86
G-OCME 09.02.87
HK-1711 09.01.78
HP-946 30.05.84
HP-947 01.11.82
N127LB oo.09.95
N29929 21.07.83
PK-KTC 25.10.91
PK-KTD 10.01.77
PK-KTI 03.04.89
VH-BSG 17.11.80
VH-EGU 16.12.80
VQ-TAJ oo.09.86
XA-JPE 05.05.89
XA-KOQ oo.05.84
YJ-RV3 03.01.90
ZS-JYF 08.10.77

Barkley-Grow T8P-1

CF-BLV oo.01.60
CF-BMG 01.02.47
CF-BMV oo.12.42
CF-BMW oo.oo.56
CF-BTX oo.11.45

Beech 1300

N139YV 10.05.89

Beech 17

VT-AKJ 23.02.39

Beech 18

* 20.07.77
* 22.12.79
* 24.09.81
* 01.07.84
* 11.06.89
* 11.07.92
4R-AAR 04.04.58
4R-AAS 25.08.58
5Y-ASF oo.05.78
9Q-CXA 24.07.64
9Q-CXC 15.12.70
A2-AOS 23.12.76
C-FAID 24.04.75
C-FBCD 26.07.84
C-FFLC 05.06.85
C-FRGT 06.02.92
C-FRVR 27.01.92
C-GRJE 18.03.81
C-GWUY 13.08.77
CF-BGY 07.01.41
CF-BMI 05.09.41
CF-BQG 29.01.52
CF-BQH 29.09.61
CF-BQQ 12.04.53
CF-BVC 11.09.41
CF-BVM 23.01.42
CF-MPA 26.02.67
CR-LCJ 28.08.54
CX-BAI oo.oo.oo
EL-AFO 19.09.66
ET-ABM 01.03.67
ET-AFE 08.04.87
F-OGCA 10.02.69
G-AIYI 24.08.49
G-APBX 05.08.59
HB-GFT 25.07.81
HB-GGC 03.10.82
HC-ACR oo.07.58
HK-1112G oo.07.73
HK-1147G 26.06.73
HK-1850 13.09.78
HK-2114X 09.07.78
HP-319 23.09.66
JA5002 25.09.54
JA5012 24.08.54
JA5020 19.12.69
JA5028 16.03.64
JA5034 05.02.63
JA5035 14.09.61
JA5036 16.04.58
JA5037 26.07.60
JA5137 05.10.67
JA5164 14.02.71
JA5169 14.02.71
LV-AAZ oo.oo.oo
N101VE 28.09.86
N102S 18.01.67
N105PE 25.11.83
N10AS 19.11.87
N112L 24.08.92
N145DC 05.11.79
N145PA 05.04.79
N1461G 05.11.85
N149AA 07.11.86
N149PA 04.04.79
N171LG 28.08.95
N180X 17.02.78
N1812D 25.05.79
N1824D 18.07.80
N19T 20.06.85
N204CC 21.11.78
N213S 28.04.83
N215H 03.10.82
N215W 30.06.83
N218X 19.03.84
N21S 17.07.84
N250RP 27.01.95
N25Q 25.09.85
N2990F 08.09.83
N30Y 13.02.86
N3128B 28.12.76
N32809 01.11.84
N32LD 14.02.77
N333FL 04.10.80
N33AP 14.02.92
N342E 23.04.92
N347G 26.02.92
N3657G 07.08.92
N380MA 13.08.82
N400NA 11.08.83
N403SE 17.10.82
N43L 10.09.80
N444PV 14.04.83
N44609 05.12.83
N45437 02.02.81
N469DM 15.09.82
N4758N 17.07.82
N47E 24.02.93
N492DM 06.04.93
N49K 16.02.94
N500L 26.09.78
N518K 13.08.81
N51FG 08.06.93
N547DA 12.06.81
N563W 09.08.90
N5647D 08.12.94
N576M 21.06.83
N57948 31.08.74
N600NA 15.09.79
N618K 24.01.95
N63B 20.08.91
N641E 08.01.80
N6675 04.10.81
N67E 22.05.93
N68392 oo.02.81
N68A 03.06.77
N6911 29.04.82
N69K 21.01.83
N700CC 18.11.80
N700W 08.03.82
N704D 28.09.80
N705M 05.12.83
N706M 15.12.92
N711TL 27.02.79
N719MS 07.04.84
N723T 26.02.86
N729F 15.02.80
N74FA 22.02.86
N75FA 17.08.77
N762D 19.02.77
N76Q 25.09.87
N7770B 10.12.92
N787Q 28.01.81
N791A 27.06.75
N79LA 23.05.81
N80162 02.03.81
N80CB 04.05.93
N8111 23.03.95
N8185H 05.12.81
N8517Z 13.12.84
N8711 07.05.95
N900WP 10.03.88
N901PC 16.11.78
N9231 09.10.87
N925J 12.11.86
N925YC 05.11.79
N9497Z 16.01.77
N95HA 31.01.85
N9684R 13.12.80
N9724Y 26.09.80
N9826Z 01.08.81
N9846Z 15.03.82
N989B 01.04.88
N9929Z 18.03.77
PH-UBS 13.11.47
PH-UBV 16.01.47
PH-UBW 30.12.60
PH-UDI 26.04.49
PK-BIB 07.05.75
PK-SVA oo.oo.oo
PP-CCF 11.10.56
PP-CCG 25.12.55
PT-KXO 05.10.77
PZ-TAR 23.06.65
PZ-TAT 14.04.67
RP-C707 14.08.91
RP-C719 26.07.89
SU-ADK 26.07.49
SU-ADM 02.03.50
SU-ADZ 26.08.48
SU-AEA 10.12.46
SU-AEB 30.12.51
SU-AEC 23.04.47
SU-AED 24.03.47
SU-AEE 10.11.48
SU-ANH 20.03.66
TF-AIS oo.01.66
TF-ISL 09.07.45
TF-REE 27.02.73
TG-AMM 25.01.75
VP-RCA oo.11.51
VT-CIS oo.oo.50
YV-C-LBL 16.06.59
ZS-BVR 12.02.67

Beech 1900

N401RA 23.11.87
N55000 03.01.92
N811BE 28.12.91
OY-GEG oo.07.94
RP-C314 18.05.90

Beech 99

C-FGAW 30.04.90
C-FHIE oo.oo.92
C-FKHD 12.01.94
CP-1804 06.03.86
F-BRUF 15.01.70
F-BRUX 16.02.78
F-BSRZ 02.09.73
F-BTMO 28.04.80
F-BTQE 02.07.75
N115GP 29.04.93
N118GP 08.06.92
N125AE 06.01.74
N12RA 12.01.71
N199EA 10.02.78
N200WP 16.08.76
N2550A 20.06.69
N299GL 19.10.91
N300WP 25.08.85
N339HA 23.09.85
N390CA 10.01.83
N42AK 24.01.92
N451C 01.02.82
N454SA 09.06.79
N63995 16.11.94
N6399U 24.08.84
N7217L 10.07.91
N844NS 06.07.69
N848NS 31.03.74
N853SA 30.04.74
N986MA 24.10.71
N992SB 28.08.85
SE-IZO 08.05.89

Beech Baron

* 19.07.80
A2-ACT 26.12.85
N17574 24.02.79
N205AC 09.08.79
N4403Q 23.06.95
P2-ALE 19.09.94
P2-GKO 12.06.81
TR-LUF 18.09.92

Beech Bonanza

* 03.02.59
N7307R 15.03.77
N8765A 21.08.52

Beech King Air

* 07.05.94
7Q-YMM 09.11.90
7T-VSH oo.01.76
C-FCAS 01.05.79
C-FCAU 30.08.85
C-FRCL 28.08.76
C-GBTI 06.05.91
C-GDOM 16.10.88
C-GJUL 29.11.88
C-GPPN 22.12.84
C-GQOD oo.oo.87
C-GVCE 21.11.84
C-GWCY oo.10.81
C-GYQT 21.02.95
CN-ANA oo.10.78
D-IHNA 27.05.94
D-ILMA 13.08.69
D-ILNI 21.09.67
D-ILNU 16.02.67
D-ILTU 22.01.71
D-IMWH 06.12.87
EC-COJ 04.10.83
F-BTDP 17.12.74
F-BUTV oo.07.92
F-BXAR oo.oo.oo
F-GBDZ 15.12.82
F-GBRD 02.11.86
F-GCJN 18.08.81
F-GDMM oo.oo.92
F-GEFR 28.08.86
F-GLRA 19.10.94
F-ZBBF 17.07.94
G-BABX 12.01.77
G-BHUL 22.04.85
G-BKID 26.12.83
G-BNAT 25.01.88
HB-GDV 24.01.86
HK-2484 28.06.81
HR-IAG 26.08.92
HR-IAI 15.01.92
I-KWYR 10.02.89
LN-KCR 02.04.87
LN-VIP 28.06.68
N101GA 03.01.95
N101LR 15.09.81
N102RB 18.03.93
N105FL 09.04.92
N110LT 13.02.90
N113TC 16.07.74
N114CM 16.06.86
N114K 26.10.81
N129D 17.08.83
N129GP 16.04.67
N1910L 26.11.83
N2019U 13.02.85
N2029N 30.12.78
N204AJ 16.09.89
N2181L 07.12.80
N220F 27.11.85
N221MJ 04.11.75
N230TW 06.01.94
N23796 23.09.77
N2400X 08.03.76
N24169 22.11.91
N25ST 21.08.89
N278DU 10.07.78
N28SE 30.06.85
N295X 01.05.72
N2EP 13.11.90
N2GG 15.02.75
N2MF 19.03.78
N308PS 18.11.88
N311DS 11.01.91
N3177W 31.05.93
N32RL 30.09.87
N332K 03.09.79
N34134 30.05.90
N34F 10.03.77

N3804F	05.11.89
N388MC	10.01.78
N400AM	10.09.83
N4146S	18.04.75
N4207S	31.07.77
N4213S	01.02.85
N43GT	01.10.89
N444SR	17.02.85
N4463W	30.11.87
N44UE	18.01.90
N45RM	01.07.92
N46WA	13.01.94
N47WM	20.01.95
N480K	27.12.71
N4GN	10.03.80
N4TS	24.10.83
N500X	26.11.69
N50PC	01.12.74
N529N	11.03.66
N530N	01.05.93
N55MG	26.11.77
N575HC	19.05.85
N57V	25.01.75
N6040M	05.08.79
N611VP	oo.05.88
N6272C	10.03.82
N65TD	10.12.86
N673Q	10.01.95
N6843S	29.11.76
N696JB	28.03.90
N700SP	26.04.75
N703WC	18.10.68
N707CE	29.05.90
N711FC	20.12.73
N724N	22.12.79
N72BS	02.02.85
N777EC	07.01.79
N78L	08.11.86
N791K	13.03.73
N7GA	04.08.94
N81MD	11.08.78
N878T	27.02.78
N887PE	15.09.89
N88CR	16.01.79
N895K	05.08.82
N9066N	12.07.94
N908CM	25.08.80
N90RG	06.08.92
N936K	03.01.73
N941K	22.06.78
N987GM	31.05.89
N98949	05.05.82
N999CR	18.03.81
N9PU	09.12.89
OB-1305	11.10.91
OB-1361	31.01.91
OB-1362	31.07.90
OO-TLS	08.01.94
OY-AZA	15.01.79
PT-IBE	28.07.77
PT-LJR	02.10.88
PT-OOP	07.02.93
RP-C2446	17.12.93
S9-NAA	oo.oo.88
SE-GUU	14.10.85
TR-LYA	20.04.78
VH-LFH	25.07.90
XA-FEX	02.03.81
XA-FOT	15.02.78
XB-NUV	13.10.76
XC-ICP	28.01.73
YV-164CP	oo.07.80
YV-288CP	18.05.84
YV-726CP	27.03.94
YV-994P	04.02.82
YV-T-ADJ	10.05.73
ZS-IHZ	26.12.92

Beech Queen Air

7T-VSB	oo.oo.oo
7T-VSD	16.10.65
7T-VSI	21.01.71
9J-AAW	31.08.85
9M-ASU	30.11.74
C-GGAL	23.06.78
CP-1039	22.08.92
CP-1054	05.08.76
DQ-FER	10.11.88
G-BDKG	08.07.79
HK-1024	19.09.71
HK-1067X	02.04.77
HK-1069	14.09.72
HK-1093X	27.08.73
HK-1095X	17.09.69
HK-844	16.12.71
N1028C	28.07.81
N19CR	12.09.95
N1HQ	05.11.82
N2019U	14.02.85
N2030	10.09.80
N242Q	07.09.80
N28BL	27.03.78
N30276	12.09.84
N304D	08.11.86
N35PK	08.08.82
N3768Z	10.04.81
N404C	24.05.84
N40SB	06.02.78
N50NP	04.02.85
N555GC	19.12.92
N55ED	19.09.83
N6867Q	17.06.81
N777AE	01.01.79
N805Q	07.08.81
N810Q	05.04.86
N8431N	17.03.78
OB-T-1211	oo.05.82
OO-CHG	12.07.70
PI-C825	03.07.72
PI-C835	02.02.62
PK-LEB	15.12.70
RP-C999	27.10.93
TG-ACP	21.11.93
VH-FDR	07.08.85
VH-XAE	06.07.89
YV-247P	11.10.86
ZK-TIK	29.03.95

Beech Starship

N8149S	22.02.94

Beech Super King Air

9M-CAM	13.12.93
C-FSSU	10.01.93
C-GCSL	oo.02.93
C-GJCM	oo.oo.oo
C-GKRL	10.12.86
CN-CDE	03.11.86
CP-1849	14.03.84
D-IBAF	27.07.77
D-IGSW	21.11.90
D2-ECH	28.01.95
F-BVRP	03.04.83
F-GBRP	17.10.80
F-GCCC	26.03.84
F-GHBE	08.02.91
G-BGHR	25.09.79
G-MDJI	19.10.87
G-WSJE	12.09.87
HC-BHG/723	24.05.81
HI-578SP	21.01.90
HK-2489	28.10.85
JA8825	17.02.87
LN-TSA	19.03.93
N100HC	12.08.85
N1283	11.09.88
N148CP	09.06.85
N162PA	09.06.92
N17530	20.10.77
N1KA	oo.03.80
N256TM	18.04.77
N2614C	oo.oo.91
N30PC	10.04.89
N3107W	03.03.89
N32HG	16.06.92
N334DP	16.11.87
N39YV	12.05.89
N456L	27.03.80
N551TR	26.09.86
N617MS	24.06.87
N631SR	15.07.81
N82	26.10.93
N8590D	23.06.87
OY-BEP	18.09.82
P2-IAH	12.04.95
PH-ATM	27.10.94
VH-AAV	21.02.80
VH-IBC	oo.oo.88
VH-KTE	28.08.83
VT-EHK	27.08.92
VT-EQM	15.07.93
VT-EUJ	09.07.94
XA-LIG	05.05.84
XC-PGR	28.10.79
YV-257CP	oo.03.81
YV-426P	04.02.82
YV-597C	12.01.89
ZS-KMT	13.04.87
ZS-NEP	28.06.93

Beech Twin Quad

NX90521	17.01.40

Bell 204

C-FAHL	13.07.80
C-GBHB	12.05.92
EC-EKB	04.08.90
HB-XCQ	10.06.78
JA9172	30.07.86
JA9230	07.05.86
N6204D	03.09.94
N87966	21.05.91
N911SW	27.05.94
N9173N	31.07.88
PK-VBR	16.07.84
TG-HUI	09.08.94

Bell 205

C-FFHB	20.01.95
C-FJTF	15.08.90
C-GFHT	06.03.93
C-GNMJ	07.02.90
C-GNMR	28.06.95
C-GRUW	27.02.90
C-GWLI	12.02.78
HK-1495	31.01.87
HK-1495E	17.03.78
HK-1772E	01.06.94
LN-ORO	26.01.78
LN-ORX	25.08.82
N27FL	01.06.95
N2970W	09.10.74
PK-HBA	26.04.69
PK-HBB	04.09.76

Bell 212

*	04.04.78
A6-BBJ	03.06.78
A6-BBX	30.05.83
B-11120	13.03.86
B-2311	17.11.82
C-FNMP	13.06.95
C-GBHL	22.11.78
C-GBHT	17.04.90
C-GFQI	06.06.86
C-GKTL	20.02.94
C-GRNR	27.05.92
EC-EHH	12.12.94
G-BDIL	14.09.82
G-BIJF	12.08.81
G-BJJR	20.11.84
HK-3377	27.02.88
JA9537	12.10.88
LN-OPX	08.05.93
LN-OQS	23.12.82
LN-ORL	31.07.79
LN-OSC	10.08.91
N92AL	29.02.92
OY-HCT	01.03.93
OY-HEA	16.12.92
OY-HMC	02.01.83
PK-DBJ	23.09.76
PK-DBU	12.01.76
PK-DBX	26.07.76
PK-HML	24.09.94
PK-HMZ	30.01.92
PT-HIF	28.11.76
PT-HJN	09.03.83
PT-HJU	29.10.81
PT-HKP	13.03.81
PT-HKW	22.07.81
PT-HQF	04.06.92
SU-CAP	06.07.93
SU-CAT	25.04.91
XA-SVS	01.11.94

Bell 214

*	14.03.85
*	oo.04.85
*	oo.10.85
C-GBHH	16.01.83
JA9276	20.04.85
JA9293	25.09.86
JA9325	05.09.89
LN-OML	02.10.90
LN-OSR	24.06.83
N114CR	19.02.93
N214RM	20.06.85
N314CR	08.05.93
N314RM	06.03.92
N814RM	23.02.92
PT-HKQ	27.09.83
VH-HOQ	22.11.91
VH-LAO	29.03.88
VH-LAT	07.04.95
YV-O-CVG-4	13.10.91

Bell 222

*	24.10.85
JA9687	07.06.90
N5007L	07.06.92

Bell 412

*	09.08.85
JA9596	09.05.89
N356EH	03.12.93
N3909F	26.08.91
N70AM	22.04.94
PK-HMR	02.03.94

Bell 47

5N-ACS	20.08.79
B-12105	17.07.71
B-15109	23.12.76
B-15115	31.07.74
C-FAUR	10.08.81
C-FYJP	09.10.81
C-GTNB	04.07.80
ET-AAF	19.04.61
ET-ABB	06.08.71
ET-H-1	01.04.59
ET-H-2	02.03.58
ET-H-6	28.12.59
G-AKFA	04.01.55
G-AXKT	06.10.81
G-OEMH	19.04.95
HB-XAW	09.04.80
HB-XFA	15.07.78
HB-XFB	20.11.80
HB-XHS	14.02.80
HK-1158	05.06.85
HK-1307	25.12.77
HK-744E	18.09.77
JA9297	30.08.83

Bell JetRanger

*	20.05.80
*	03.03.91
7T-WUI	21.05.92
9M-AUL	15.01.78
A6-BCC	28.03.79
B-6622	26.02.95
C-FAAN	13.05.81
C-FAHQ	21.09.94
C-FALP	21.03.95
C-FBHR	11.02.95
C-FDDL	24.02.93
C-FKOC	12.01.80
C-FLIL	14.06.94
C-FMZE	29.05.95
C-FNMQ	30.03.82
C-FPQS	02.09.94
C-FROO	12.09.81
C-FUHL	15.09.94
C-FXAL	14.07.94
C-GBPB	10.07.95
C-GDBP	14.11.93
C-GDBR	29.06.85
C-GDFA	07.03.93
C-GERD	04.03.78
C-GHHV	13.11.94
C-GIZQ	05.06.85
C-GLBA	04.07.95
C-GLGF	26.07.94
C-GMHS	18.06.82
C-GOOM	17.09.81
C-GPRM	01.01.94
C-GRAA	29.06.95
C-GRAH	29.01.94
C-GSHE	03.07.80
C-GSHU	04.02.82
C-GSHZ	20.06.95
C-GTEJ	29.07.82
C-GUGP	09.01.80
C-GWGS	07.04.95
C-GXKA	20.11.80
C-GXWR	08.04.95
D-HHSB	06.10.94
EC-EJM	22.08.92
EC-FAO	06.06.92

EI-BMP	29.07.82
EI-BST	24.09.91
F-GJGP	26.03.94
G-AVIG	05.01.85
G-AZVN	30.06.78
G-BAKF	09.01.89
G-BAVI	29.05.78
G-BAYA	09.01.77
G-BHXU	29.06.95
G-BHYW	23.06.93
G-BNIT	03.06.93
G-BODW	15.01.94
G-EYEI	24.01.90
G-SHBB	18.12.89
G-STST	22.05.94
HB-XCP	14.01.80
HB-XDP	05.05.79
HB-XIM	22.12.79
HB-XLR	27.04.95
HB-XUT	22.06.94
HC-BFR	23.11.90
HC-BHO	19.12.90
HK-3171	04.05.95
HK-3353	22.09.92
HL9105	20.09.88
JA9058	23.03.90
JA9109	19.05.83
JA9123	06.08.87
JA9127	08.11.91
JA9211	14.07.94
JA9238	29.03.89
JA9246	15.08.87
JA9286	15.12.81
JA9365	20.08.90
JA9464	13.11.94
LN-OQW	06.09.78
LN-ORJ	30.09.81
LN-ORQ	10.08.79
LN-OSL	02.08.94
N1077N	14.02.94
N10800	01.07.94
N1082H	11.07.89
N124NH	12.08.94
N16841	09.03.85
N16933	27.08.90
N172AL	14.02.95
N2299W	28.05.77
N2753U	26.02.94
N27736	03.04.94
N3120X	15.02.92
N3185G	27.02.92
N32GT	15.07.85
N347AL	02.05.95
N382EH	30.08.94
N3913Z	30.11.85
N49746	19.05.81
N49757	16.04.78
N50PE	27.02.94
N57340	10.03.94
N5759Y	30.11.85
N59613	02.03.92
N59619	10.01.85
N6610L	09.04.92
N6TC	19.06.86
N7094J	01.05.88
N7881S	25.06.94
N820CW	24.07.94
N8NU	17.08.94
N90153	29.03.87
N90315	29.07.94
N9AR	17.03.87
OH-HSR	29.06.95
OO-COD	14.11.88
OY-HBH	08.09.83
OY-HDI	13.04.92
P2-FHE	19.09.94
P2-HBA	01.03.94
PK-DBM	19.02.80
PK-HBE	12.06.70
PT-HBY	07.12.81
PT-HJI	07.03.89
PT-HPD	13.10.94
PT-HPF	08.04.84
PT-HQC	03.02.84
SE-HCG	28.01.83
SE-HRD	16.09.86
TC-HBJ	19.03.88
TG-KEZ	04.04.77
VH-AJD	08.01.82
VH-CIH	04.12.88
ZK-HKE	14.02.89
ZS-HCP	31.01.78
ZS-HEA	04.07.84
ZS-HHF	15.01.85
ZS-HIF	16.05.88
ZS-HIW	23.02.92
ZS-HKA	07.07.92
ZS-HLI	19.01.86

Bell-Boeing Osprey

163914	20.07.92
163915	11.06.91

Bellanca Skyrocket

RX-15	17.09.38

Beriev Be-12

*	oo.07.93
*	01.11.93

Blackburn B.2

G-ABWI	09.10.36

Blackburn Dart

G-EBKF	07.01.32

Blackburn Kangaroo

G-EADE	29.06.19
G-EADF	31.05.19
G-EAIT	05.05.25
G-EAOW	08.12.19
G-EBOM	25.09.28

Bleriot 155

F-AICQ	oo.oo.26
F-AIEB	18.08.26

Bleriot Spad 33

F-AIMO	23.08.28
F-FREJ	24.08.25
F-FREM	26.06.25
O-BAHE	27.09.21

Bleriot Spad 46

F-AEBL	oo.oo.27
F-AEGS	31.07.24

Bleriot Spad 56/4

F-AIMN	31.10.28

Bleriot Spad 66

F-AEAY	30.05.30
F-AEHX	31.12.28

Bloch 120

F-ANJX	16.11.38

Bloch 220

F-AOHA	03.03.40
F-AQNL	01.09.41

Boeing 247

42-68367	17.11.42
AN-ACB	29.11.46
C-138	oo.oo.43
C-140	29.09.45
C-144	24.10.42
C-146	27.02.44
C-149	15.03.39
C-79	29.02.40
D-AGAR	24.05.35
D-AKIN	13.08.37
N41813	oo.oo.52
NC13302	07.06.34
NC13304	10.10.33
NC13314	01.09.35
NC13315	12.01.37
NC13317	07.10.35
NC13319	23.11.36
NC13320	12.05.33
NC13323	30.10.35
NC13324	24.11.33
NC13339	12.01.41
NC13345	09.11.33
NC13355	27.12.36
NC13357	23.02.34
NC13359	16.04.41
NC13370	15.12.36
NR13352	27.05.50
XA-BFK	oo.oo.50
XA-CAB	07.01.50
XA-DEZ	26.08.50
XA-DUA	09.09.47
XA-DUY	01.08.45
XA-GUV	oo.oo.57
XA-GUW	23.02.52
XA-JUV	05.05.52

Boeing 314

N18611	oo.oo.51
NC18601	04.11.45
NC18603	22.02.43
NC18609	oo.oo.oo
NC18612	14.10.47

Boeing 40B

NC10348	02.06.32
NC273	07.02.32
NC5589	16.05.32
NC742K	09.02.32
NC830M	30.05.32
NC842M	13.12.32

Boeing 707/720

5A-DJO	14.03.83
5A-DJT	07.12.91
5B-DAM	19.08.79
5N-ABK	19.12.94
5N-ARO	25.09.83
5N-AYJ	14.12.88
5N-MAS	31.03.92
5X-DAR	25.11.92
5X-UAL	01.04.79
5X-UBC	17.10.88
5Y-BBK	11.07.89
6O-SBT	17.05.89
7O-ACJ	26.01.82
7O-ACS	26.11.91
9G-RBO	29.04.92
9Q-CRT	09.08.77
9Q-CVG	01.03.90
9Q-CWR	oo.10.84
AP-AMH	20.05.65
AP-AVZ	15.12.71
AP-AWZ	26.11.79
AP-AXK	08.01.81
B-1826	27.02.80
B-1834	11.09.79
B-2402	02.10.90
C-GQBH	19.02.79
CC-CCX	03.08.78
CC-CEI	23.06.90
CF-PWZ	02.01.73
CP-1365	31.08.91
D-ABOK	04.12.61
D-ABOP	15.07.64
D-ABOT	19.12.73
D-ABUY	26.07.79
D2-TOI	oo.02.88
D2-TOJ	20.02.92
D2-TOM	10.10.88
D2-TOV	21.07.88
ET-AAG	09.01.68
ET-ACD	19.11.77
ET-ACQ	25.07.90
ET-AJZ	25.03.91
F-BHSA	27.07.61
F-BHSH	07.09.76
F-BHSM	03.06.62
F-BHST	22.06.62
F-BHSZ	03.12.69
F-BLCJ	05.03.68
G-APFE	05.03.66
G-APFK	17.03.77
G-ARWE	08.04.68
G-BEBP	14.05.77
HI-384HA	12.12.81
HK-2016	25.01.90
HK-2401X	15.12.83
HK-2410X	20.12.80
HK-3355X	09.10.94
HK-723	16.08.76
HK-725	27.01.80
HL7406	29.11.87
HL7412	02.08.76
HL7429	20.04.78
HZ-ACE	oo.11.79
JY-ADO	22.01.73
JY-AEE	03.08.75
LV-ISA	31.01.93
LV-JGR	27.01.86
N144SP	13.04.87
N15712	14.09.72
N18701	22.12.75
N3166	31.03.71
N37777	22.04.76
N407PA	17.12.73
N417PA	22.07.73
N4465D	13.10.83
N446PA	22.04.74
N454PA	30.01.74
N458PA	03.11.73
N461PA	25.07.71
N494PA	12.12.68
N7071	19.10.59
N70773	01.07.65
N70775	22.05.62
N708PA	17.09.65
N709PA	08.12.63
N720MJ	20.09.90
N7231T	08.02.89
N724US	12.02.63
N730JP	14.10.76
N742TW	06.11.67
N743TW	22.04.70
N7502A	28.01.61
N7506A	01.03.62
N7514A	15.08.59
N757TW	16.01.74
N761TW	08.03.72
N769TW	23.11.64
N779PA	07.04.64
N787TW	26.07.69
N790TW	30.11.70
N791SA	07.02.68
N797TW	30.11.80
N798PA	13.06.68
N799PA	26.12.68
N833NA	01.12.84
N8434	04.12.82
N8715T	13.09.70
N8734	08.09.74
OD-AFB	16.06.82
OD-AFC	28.12.68
OD-AFL	21.08.85
OD-AFO	16.06.82
OD-AFP	12.06.82
OD-AFR	31.08.81
OD-AFT	01.01.76
OD-AFU	16.06.82
OD-AFW	16.06.82
OD-AFX	23.07.79
OD-AFY	26.07.93
OD-AGE	27.06.76
OD-AGG	01.08.82
OD-AGN	16.06.82
OD-AGQ	21.08.85
OD-AGR	16.06.82
OD-AGT	22.10.81
OD-AGW	05.07.81
OD-AHB	07.01.87
OO-SJA	29.03.81
OO-SJB	15.02.61
OO-SJE	15.02.78
OO-SJH	11.05.80
OO-SJK	13.07.68
OY-DSR	13.09.74
PP-VJA	27.11.62
PP-VJK	03.01.87
PP-VJR	07.09.68
PP-VJT	11.06.81
PP-VJZ	11.07.73
PP-VLJ	09.06.73
PP-VLU	30.01.79
PT-TCO	11.04.87
PT-TCP	26.11.92
PT-TCS	21.03.89
S2-ABQ	03.04.80
ST-AIM	10.09.82
ST-ALK	14.07.90
ST-ALX	24.03.92
ST-SAC	04.12.90
SU-AOW	05.12.72
SU-APE	17.10.82
SU-AXA	25.12.76
TY-BBR	13.06.85
VT-DJI	23.01.71
VT-DJJ	22.06.82
VT-DMN	24.01.66
YR-ABD	10.01.91
YR-ABM	15.01.93
YR-ABN	17.08.95
Z-WKT	oo.11.88
ZS-EUW	20.04.68

Boeing 727

*	19.09.95
5A-DAH	21.02.73
5A-DIA	22.12.92

6Y-JMO 16.11.90
B-1018 16.02.68
CC-CAQ 28.04.69
CS-TBR 19.11.77
D2-TJB 31.01.95
EC-CFJ 07.12.83
EC-DDU 19.02.85
EP-IRA 07.01.83
EP-IRD 21.01.80
G-BDAN 25.04.80
HI-617CA 06.09.93
HK-1272 30.09.75
HK-1716 17.03.88
HK-1803 27.11.89
HK-1804 oo.12.83
HK-2421X 04.08.93
HK-2422X 19.05.93
HK-2559 04.08.82
HL7350 26.08.91
JA8302 04.02.66
JA8329 30.07.71
JY-ADU 14.03.79
JY-AFW 12.06.85
N124AS 05.04.76
N18479 21.11.80
N1963 26.04.76
N1996 08.11.65
N274US 01.12.74
N2969G 04.09.71
N317PA 15.11.66
N327PA 03.09.80
N425EX 03.05.91
N4737 09.07.82
N473DA 31.08.88
N4744 08.05.78
N530DA 14.10.89
N533PS 25.09.78
N54328 01.12.74
N68650 19.07.67
N7030U 11.11.65
N7036U 16.08.65
N7425U 21.03.68
N7434U 18.01.69
N766AS 09.06.87
N819EA 01.01.85
N852TW 27.08.88
N8790R 28.12.70
N8845E 24.06.75
N88705 21.10.89
N88777 07.08.75
OB-1303 11.09.90
PP-SRK 08.06.82
PT-TYS 12.04.80
S9-TAN 27.04.94
TC-AJV 25.08.89
TC-AKD 27.02.88
TC-JBH 19.09.76
TC-JBR 16.01.83
TI-LRC 23.05.88
XA-MEM 31.03.86
XA-SEJ 21.09.69
XA-SEL 04.06.69
XA-SEN 20.10.73
XV-NJC 15.09.74
YA-FAR 05.01.69
YN-BXW 10.11.91

Boeing 737

* 13.11.95
5N-ANW 10.10.88
7T-VEE 21.12.94
9M-MBD 04.12.77
9Q-CNI 02.01.95
A4O-BK 23.09.83
B-180 26.10.89
B-1870 16.02.86
B-2510 02.10.90
B-2523 24.11.92
B-2536 06.07.95
B-2540 20.07.94
B-2603 22.08.81
C-FPWC 11.02.78
C-GQPW 22.03.84
C9-BAB 28.03.83
C9-BAD 09.02.89
CC-CHJ 05.08.87
D-ABHD 02.01.88
D2-TAA 05.11.80
D2-TBN 09.11.83
D2-TBP 10.02.95
D2-TBV 09.02.84
EI-BZG 11.05.90
EI-CBL 17.11.91
EP-IRG 15.10.86
ET-AJA 16.09.88
G-BGJL 22.08.85
G-OBME 08.01.89
HC-BIG/607 11.07.83
HL7229 26.07.93
HP-1205CMP 07.06.92
HP-873CMP 19.11.93
HS-TBB 15.04.85
HS-TBC 31.08.87
JA8444 26.08.82
LV-JNE 20.11.92
LV-LIU 26.09.88
N125GU 09.08.95
N198AW oo.12.89
N210US 22.07.90
N388US 01.02.91
N401FH 18.07.93
N416US 20.09.89
N4527W 31.03.75
N468AC 17.02.81
N513AU 08.09.94
N62AF 13.01.82
N670MA 02.06.90
N73711 29.04.88
N752N 25.10.86
N9005U 19.07.70
N9031U 08.12.72
N999UA 04.03.91
OB-R-1314 03.04.89
OO-SDH 04.04.78
PP-SME 28.01.86
PP-SMV 01.02.95
PP-SMX 03.04.78
PP-SMY 24.05.82
PP-SNC 22.02.83
PP-SND 22.06.92
PP-VMK 03.09.89
SU-AYH 24.11.85
TC-JEL 27.08.94
TC-JES 29.12.94
TJ-CBD 30.08.84
VT-EAH 19.10.88
VT-EAL 17.12.78
VT-EAM 31.05.73
VT-ECQ 26.04.93
VT-ECR 26.04.79
VT-EFL 16.08.91
VT-SIA 08.03.94
YI-AGJ 25.12.86

Boeing 747

4X-AXG 04.10.92
B-165 04.11.93
B-198 29.12.91
D-ABYB 20.11.74
F-GCBC 02.12.85
F-GDUA 16.03.85
G-AWND 27.02.91
HK-2910 27.11.83
HL7442 01.09.83
HL7445 19.11.80
JA8109 24.07.73
JA8119 12.08.85
N28888 12.06.75
N706CK 03.06.95
N736PA 27.03.77
N738PA 04.08.83
N739PA 21.12.88
N752PA 06.09.70
N807FT 18.02.89
PH-BUF 27.03.77
VT-EBD 01.01.78
VT-EBO 07.05.90
VT-EFO 23.06.85
ZS-SAS 28.11.87

Boeing 757

B-2812 02.10.90

Boeing 767

9K-AIB oo.02.91
9K-AIC oo.02.91
OE-LAV 26.05.91

Boeing 80

* 10.07.32

Boeing 95

NC415E 16.09.33
NC419E 24.02.30
NC420E 21.01.30
NC425E 25.02.33

Boeing B-17

CP-570 21.09.55
CP-571 16.01.62
CP-579 29.12.58
CP-580 07.02.65
CP-588 02.05.63
CP-597 05.09.55
CP-622 18.02.57
CP-623 28.07.58
CP-624 23.02.63
CP-625 17.11.59
CP-626 25.10.59
CP-640 17.08.67
CP-686 04.11.65
CP-694 18.12.63
CP-741 30.10.64
CP-742 21.02.65
CP-762 16.12.64
CP-767 13.04.67
CP-936 11.02.72
F-BDAT 12.12.50
F-BEEA 25.07.89
F-BEEB 11.03.49
N1340N 18.08.70
N4710C 05.08.76
N5116N 10.11.52
N5845N oo.oo.58
N621L oo.07.75
N66573 oo.oo.oo
N73648 12.07.72
N9324Z 12.07.71
OY-DFE 30.01.46
SE-BAM 04.12.45

Boeing B-29

N70887 21.05.95

Boeing C-97

4X-FPR/033 17.09.71
4X-FPS/037 30.11.70
HI-481 30.07.87
N4580Q 18.05.89
N52676 26.09.69
N52679 08.05.69

Boeing Monomail

NC10225 oo.oo.35
NC725W 29.05.35

Boeing Stratocruiser

G-ALSA 25.12.54
N1023V 02.06.58
N1032V 26.03.55
N1033V 10.04.59
N1039V 29.04.52
N111AS 12.05.70
N31230 12.09.51
N74607 14.08.59
N74608 02.04.56
N90941 09.07.59
N90942 oo.08.67
N90943 16.10.56
N90944 09.11.57

Boeing Stratoliner

F-BELV 18.10.65
F-BELZ 29.12.62
F-BHHR 22.05.61
N75385 10.05.58
NX19901 18.03.39
XW-PGR 27.02.71
XW-TFR 27.06.74

Boeing-Canada Thunderbird

CF-ALD 30.07.35

Boeing-Vertol Chinook

G-BWFC 06.11.86
MM80825 30.03.80

Bolkow Bo.208

G-ATRI 01.08.70

Boulton & Paul P.64

G-ABYK 21.10.33

Boulton & Paul P.71A

G-ACOX 25.09.36
G-ACOY 25.10.35

Breguet 14

F-ADBM 29.09.25
F-AEEJ 03.10.28
F-AEEN 11.12.25
F-AEGZ 17.10.25
F-AEHD 25.12.25
F-AEIS oo.oo.25
F-AEJA oo.oo.oo
F-AFAX 11.11.26
F-AFBB 25.05.25
F-AFBE 17.10.26
F-AFBG 01.09.25
F-AFBI 20.07.25
F-AFEF 05.02.26
F-AFHN 27.01.28
F-AGBN oo.oo.27
F-AGBS 11.11.26
F-AGBT oo.oo.26
F-AGBY oo.oo.25
F-AGCD 21.06.25
F-AHEM 22.05.26
F-AHEP oo.oo.26
F-AHEQ 22.01.28
F-ALKU oo.oo.27
F-ALSE oo.oo.27
F-FYMS 13.03.26

Breguet 284

F-AIYB 19.02.29

Breguet 391

* oo.07.31

Breguet Atlantic

02 19.04.62

Bristol 170

C-FQWJ oo.03.77
C-FWAD 20.11.77
C-GYQY 21.06.88
CF-FZU 13.02.56
CF-GBT 17.09.55
CF-TFY 18.06.56
CF-TFZ 30.05.56
CF-WAG 03.05.70
EC-ADH 13.03.59
EC-ADI 09.05.57
EC-ADK 24.11.49
EC-AEG 04.12.53
EC-AEH 11.09.57
EC-AHJ 19.04.62
EC-AHK 01.10.61
EI-APM 12.06.67
F-BCJA 25.01.48
F-BCJN 16.10.47
F-BECR 10.03.50
F-BENF 29.07.50
F-BENG 10.04.48
F-BLHH 11.06.69
F-OAOU oo.11.56
F-VNAI 16.08.54
G-AGVB 04.11.58
G-AGVC 30.06.62
G-AHJB 04.07.46
G-AHJJ 21.03.50
G-AICM 19.01.53
G-AICS 27.02.58
G-AIFF 06.05.49
G-AIMC 23.11.47
G-AMWA 24.09.63
G-ANWL 01.11.61
HC-SBU 06.08.49
HZ-AAB 25.03.58
HZ-AAC 08.10.57
SE-BNG 18.11.47
VH-AAH 18.12.61
VH-SJQ 10.05.75
VR-NAD 05.02.55
VR-NAX 27.07.51
ZK-AYH 21.11.57
ZK-CAM 14.01.81
ZK-CPU 10.04.68

Bristol 173

G-AMJI 16.09.56

Bristol Britannia

CF-CZB 22.07.62
EI-BBY 30.09.77
G-ALRX 04.02.54
G-ANBB 31.08.66

G-ANBC	11.11.60
G-ANCA	06.11.57
G-ANCG	20.04.67
G-AOVD	24.12.58
G-AOVO	29.02.64
G-BRAC	17.02.80
HB-ITB	20.04.67
LV-JNL	12.07.70
XA-MEC	09.07.65

Bristol Sycamore

G-AMWH	15.08.64
VH-INO	11.01.60
VH-INQ	04.09.61

Bristol Tourer 28

G-AUDF	27.01.25

Budd Conestoga

HC-SBE	15.05.46
HC-SBF	23.07.46
HC-SBG	26.08.46
HC-SBH	25.03.47
HK-344X	oo.oo.57

CAMS 53

F-AIOX	09.12.31
F-AIOY	oo.oo.oo
F-AIQY	12.08.32
F-AISV	11.01.33
F-AISX	22.05.29
F-AISZ	oo.oo.oo
F-AJIR	21.01.36
F-AJJQ	oo.oo.oo
F-AJKB	oo.oo.oo
F-AJKF	oo.oo.oo
F-AJZX	oo.12.35
F-ALCE	23.04.33
F-ALCF	20.01.35
F-ALCG	oo.oo.oo
F-ALCH	17.12.33
F-ALFF	09.02.34

CASA Aviocar

C-GILU	02.08.88
FAC.1150	18.11.90
FAC.1152	09.09.95
FAC.1154	19.03.94
N119CA	27.08.94
N160FB	04.03.87
N355CA	07.06.92
N431CA	17.12.86
N432CA	08.05.87
OB-1218	09.07.91
PK-DCR	08.11.82
PK-NCF	25.03.86
PK-NCY	30.01.91
PK-PCL	24.01.84
PK-PCM	02.01.90
PK-VSM	25.06.92
PK-XCE	oo.oo.80
PK-ZAG	03.10.95
TI-SAB	15.01.90
YN-BYZ	29.06.83

Canadair C-4

CF-CPR	09.02.50
CF-TEL	12.08.48
CF-TFD	09.12.56
CF-TFJ	27.08.64
CF-TFQ	27.08.64
CF-TFW	08.04.54
CF-UXB	17.09.71
G-ALHE	24.06.56
G-ALHG	04.06.67
G-ALHL	21.09.55
I-ACOA	11.10.66
VP-KNY	11.04.62
YV-C-LBU	27.08.64
YV-C-LBV	06.07.62

Canadair CL-215

C-GFQA	19.06.91
C-GKEE	29.09.83
F-ZBAX	04.07.70
F-ZBBG	03.09.71
F-ZBBM	25.07.73
I-CFSS	27.01.89
I-CFSV	06.08.91
YV-O-INC-2	22.08.89

Canadair CL-44

5B-DAN	04.11.80
CX-BXD	09.10.79
G-ATZH	02.09.77
G-AWSC	22.12.74
G-BCWJ	06.07.78
HK-1972	22.02.75
HK-3148X	06.07.88
LV-JSY	27.09.75
LV-JTN	18.07.81
LV-JYR	20.07.72
N100BB	oo.oo.93
N228SW	24.12.66
N446T	01.05.69
N453T	21.03.66
OB-R-1104	27.08.76
TF-LLG	02.12.70
TR-LVO	05.02.82

Canadair Challenger

C-GCGR-X	03.04.80
N779XX	07.02.85
N805C	03.01.83
N88HA	20.03.94

Canadair Regional Jet

C-FCRJ	26.07.93

Canadian Vickers Stranraer

CF-BYI	oo.oo.48
CF-BYJ	24.12.48
CF-BYL	31.08.46
CF-BYM	01.10.57

Cant Z.506

I-DENO	07.09.38
I-RODI	27.09.36

Caproni CA-60

n/a	oo.03.21

Caproni Ca.133

I-DIRE	13.10.39

Carley Werkspoor

PH-AFI	10.05.40

Castel-Mauboussin CM-10

n/a	05.05.48

Caudron C.61

F-AEHQ	oo.08.23
F-AFAO	09.07.27
F-AFBT	03.07.26
F-AFCP	04.05.23

Caudron C.74

F-ESAB	oo.11.22

Caudron C.81

F-AGFU	30.05.25

Caudron Goeland

F-AOMR	04.08.41
F-AOMT	10.07.38
F-BAAE	03.09.41
F-BAPE	oo.06.56
F-BAPI	21.12.57
F-BAPJ	22.05.47
F-BAPQ	25.11.58
F-BAQJ	11.05.47
F-BAQT	08.07.47
F-BCCK	13.08.47
OO-CCJ	24.08.48
OO-CCK	27.11.58
OO-CCR	24.08.48

Caudron Simoun

F-ANRI	22.01.38
F-ANRK	04.12.35
F-AOOT	03.04.39

Cessna 150/172

*	22.02.92
*	31.03.93
C-GJIS	21.11.81
C-GPBS	07.12.79
DQ-FEH	05.10.90
EI-BDO	08.06.85
HK-1754	26.09.83
HK-2564	02.06.81
JA3212	15.01.82
JA3887	22.10.87
OB-1417	02.08.91
PZ-TAB	06.05.80

Cessna 180

*	30.10.77
C-GHAQ	28.11.77
EL-AFT	04.07.78
ET-AAC	04.08.63
ET-ABK	03.09.64
ET-ABL	21.11.67
ET-ABO	14.10.70
ET-ADD	21.11.76
HK-429	25.02.77

Cessna 182/185

*	22.01.77
*	25.09.91
6Y-JHJ	24.06.77
A2-AEJ	26.12.85
C-FVZP	22.09.94
C-GGQU	27.09.81
CS-APG	30.05.95
EL-AGZ	05.03.88
ET-ACO	28.07.89
ET-ADP	16.03.77
HK-1436	21.10.77
HK-1720	21.11.78
HK-1918	01.12.77
HK-670	21.06.77
N1867Q	19.08.92
OB-T-1040	25.02.87
OB-T-594	25.10.88
VH-UDM	10.05.78
ZK-CVG	27.06.92
ZK-EHM	23.12.93

Cessna 188

C-GHNM	21.10.79
ET-ACP	19.09.82
ET-AEG	27.01.78
ET-AHD	11.08.88
ET-AHE	15.06.85
N4807Q	14.08.92
VH-RBR	08.08.77
ZS-ENE	01.03.77

Cessna 206/207

*	03.08.93
8R-GEF	27.05.77
8R-GEK	16.05.81
B-11102	13.08.78
C-GOPB	12.09.92
CC-CET	12.11.85
CP-1486	07.04.84
D-EBSD	02.12.92
EL-AFG	01.11.80
ET-ADB	10.05.88
ET-AEZ	10.05.88
HK-1289	20.06.79
HK-1665	25.04.84
HK-1737	31.05.77
HK-2578	16.05.81
HK-3067	11.10.85
LN-ASC	12.09.90
N1686U	07.11.92
N1801Q	02.07.93
N208SC	16.10.93
N33177	12.08.85
N4882U	25.05.88
N5282U	03.12.94
N5442Z	20.04.85
N6424H	08.10.79
N6446X	06.11.80
N6467H	03.04.93
N70364	04.08.92
N7340U	13.12.94
N7393U	28.01.87
N9828M	15.06.85
N9869M	19.06.93
N9975M	20.07.92
OB-1030	27.02.95
OB-1189	30.05.90
OB-1262	22.10.90
OB-1265	24.09.90
OB-1311	31.01.91
OB-1331	03.05.90
OB-1341	24.01.94
OB-1434	20.05.91
OB-T-1174	09.04.86
OB-T-1191	19.11.89
OB-T-1197	25.07.84
OB-T-1199	04.02.90
OB-T-1262	01.03.87
OB-T-1273	01.05.86
OB-T-1292	19.11.86
OB-T-1304	26.02.88
OB-T-144	05.01.88
PT-IBM	05.01.77
YV-229C	29.06.86
ZK-DAX	30.12.89
ZK-MCH	15.03.77
ZK-WED	02.01.86

Cessna 208

5Y-JJC	08.08.94
5Y-MAK	11.11.93
9M-PMN	20.03.95
C-FPEZ	08.02.91
HB-CKW	22.07.89
HK-3470	29.04.94
LV-VGE	20.02.95
N1037D	16.08.93
N208W	06.10.89
N227DM	03.03.95
N242CS	02.01.95
N4688B	29.01.90
N551CC	29.09.85
N746FE	11.01.95
N754FE	12.01.95
N803FE	06.06.90
N820FE	27.02.90
N828FE	23.10.87
N835FE	17.01.90
N835FE	20.01.90
N854FE	29.01.90
N9241F	01.11.85
N9417B	22.03.95
N9444F	21.12.90
N9448B	02.03.95
N945FE	05.01.89
N9471B	18.01.95
N9526F	02.08.93
PNP-021	20.05.89
PT-OGM	06.12.93
PT-OGN	26.08.93
ZK-SFB	27.11.87
ZS-NIH	07.11.93

Cessna 210

9J-ABT	26.06.84
N22592	13.01.92
N6803B	26.02.85
N731FT	15.09.84
OB-1255	29.11.90
OB-1310	07.04.91
OB-1358	19.11.90
OB-1464	31.08.92
OB-1589	13.04.95
OB-T-1294	28.11.86
SE-INL	27.12.92

Cessna 310

*	01.08.95
5Y-MBP	11.02.83
C-FWPC	25.03.80
C-GYLK	26.11.80
D-INGY	22.06.75
EP-JBC	24.04.78
N5074J	27.10.92
N5462J	31.12.86
OE-FCM	15.06.89
OO-CUA	26.05.61
OO-SEA	17.01.67
OO-SEC	22.06.61
OO-SEE	09.09.76
RP-C789	19.04.89
VH-ROC	26.05.77

Cessna 337

*	18.11.76
AP-BDW	10.12.90
C-GRAM	11.12.76
EL-AHM	23.02.75
EL-AHN	17.07.74
PK-OAP	22.04.73

Cessna 340

HK-2064	13.03.79
TU-TKS	23.09.87
XA-KOA	30.09.87

Cessna 402/404

*	03.01.78
*	22.06.78

*	30.05.79
*	16.05.85
*	06.10.85
*	31.12.85
*	13.06.92
5H-GTS	30.03.88
5H-TZB	27.02.95
5X-LCP	20.09.83
5Y-AJP	01.02.77
5Y-AJZ	07.12.83
5Y-AMS	07.08.84
5Y-ANY	03.01.82
5Y-AZZ	31.05.81
5Y-EJS	03.12.87
5Y-PAL	09.01.95
5Y-WAW	10.12.76
8R-GEP	03.11.85
9Q-CFJ	21.06.77
B-12206	27.06.89
C-FEIA	24.03.80
C-GDTW	19.01.81
C-GVBS	16.01.86
C9-MJB	27.10.92
CN-MBI	03.01.70
CS-AHP	06.08.76
D-ICLW	11.03.91
D-ILEP	29.08.87
F-BRSA	28.11.73
G-BKTJ	27.11.85
G-DAFS	31.05.90
G-WING	04.02.80
HB-LKO	11.06.79
HC-BDF	02.07.77
HK-2685	24.02.84
HK-2686P	oo.03.90
HK-3001G	24.07.93
HK-3382P	23.03.90
JA5162	30.05.72
LV-JOD	15.03.89
LV-MIU	02.06.95
N100HK	17.06.85
N114EA	26.12.84
N120PB	30.06.84
N1238K	11.12.94
N17CH	13.12.92
N206RH	25.08.93
N26506	09.03.83
N2683S	21.07.80
N2715X	19.06.92
N2AQ	27.05.81
N302SP	24.01.85
N37097	30.07.80
N3SP	28.04.78
N402BK	18.11.94
N402CS	15.05.85
N402DL	01.11.82
N402V	23.09.85
N404EX	16.08.85
N404SA	22.12.77
N405PC	23.03.93
N4244Z	24.01.82
N44NC	01.03.84
N5237J	27.04.80
N5274J	20.04.89
N55LP	31.08.84
N5775C	31.01.91
N5780M	06.02.85
N5785C	18.03.91
N620AC	26.03.84
N6788Y	12.11.85
N67941	09.11.92
N6814G	03.02.84
N6819N	30.06.81
N684LT	24.09.85
N69303	13.09.95
N69378	05.03.77
N69383	19.02.89
N7093L	12.10.93
N8064Q	22.12.84
N818AN	12.07.93
N82922	29.09.90
N8416F	11.03.75
N8493A	26.05.88
N87163	17.01.90
N8827K	10.06.88
N89PB	07.09.84
N969JW	10.12.87
N98720	16.05.78
OB-1318	01.06.90
OB-T-1252	18.07.83
OB-T-1254	10.10.89
OE-FCT	15.10.81
OH-CDT	26.04.87
OH-CDU	28.12.86
OH-CFM	16.06.77
OH-CIG	31.08.86
OY-SAW	29.11.71
OY-SUM	17.01.91
P2-ALC	19.09.94
P2-ALD	19.09.94
P2-GKC	01.03.77
P2-GKJ	01.04.81
PH-JAL	29.01.80
PK-KCA	26.07.83
PK-KCC	02.10.89
PK-WWE	08.10.91
PT-JXL	31.10.78
SE-FRO	28.11.76
SE-GGR	13.02.78
ST-ADK	28.04.78
ST-AHX	05.05.91
ST-AID	07.06.93
ST-AIJ	05.05.87
ST-AIW	26.09.89
TR-LYQ	03.07.82
TS-DAA	20.09.70
VH-DIL	21.02.83
VH-RED	03.00.86
VH-TLQ	02.02.87
VH-WBQ	21.06.87
YV-478C	28.11.89
YV-O-CDO-2	03.11.78
ZK-EHT	04.10.85
ZS-JDD	16.08.78
ZS-KPF	15.08.88
ZS-KVG	05.06.83
ZS-LUI	08.02.88
ZS-LUI	21.06.91

Cessna 414

5H-TZS	18.05.92
N13SE	13.01.95
VH-SDV	27.10.89

Cessna 421

*	07.07.77
*	03.01.78
*	07.10.87
*	20.11.93
9H-ABN	27.12.89
AP-AYQ	06.07.84
C-FFEL	20.07.85
C-GPAT	27.01.95
C-GVPB	03.08.94
D-IAGA	27.01.77
D-IBHH	25.01.92
D-IDAS	03.11.78
D-IFLY	21.11.85
D-INUR	18.12.78
F-BOXS	05.05.78
G-AYMM	04.09.78
G-BAEI	26.08.78
G-BFEM	11.06.82
G-HAST	20.10.87
G-SHOE	08.11.85
HA-ACA	25.03.93
HB-LMI	07.12.87
I-ASON	16.12.78
I-STMO	30.09.93
JA5273	11.01.87
N100RV	27.12.79
N111FN	04.09.83
N121BT	18.10.84
N14A	21.09.95
N14TC	20.07.84
N200SM	26.11.80
N2239Q	20.08.83
N24CC	11.02.82
N2654M	04.01.92
N2960Q	21.06.83
N3291Q	05.03.84
N386G	16.08.83
N3911C	02.09.95
N41010	06.11.93
N421AR	06.11.86
N421H	05.01.91
N4567L	22.07.82
N5407J	02.04.85
N5468G	26.01.94
N5473G	19.07.85
N6231G	01.08.84
N6234G	02.09.95
N68653	29.01.86
N6866K	11.02.85
N6867R	30.08.81
N6VR	19.07.86
N8001Q	11.12.82
N8091Q	24.09.82
N8369G	21.11.81
N9394A	29.12.80
N98457	08.08.84
OY-DU3	29.07.86
PH-SYG	30.11.94
PT-KRW	17.02.81
VH-EGT	26.02.80
YV-270P	oo.oo.oo
YV-314P	04.12.80

Cessna 425

C-GBMI	20.11.88
D-IEFW	24.01.94

Cessna 441

*	23.10.86
*	15.11.87
D-IAAE	11.06.82
D-IAAY	06.11.80
F-GFHR	17.11.88
F-ODUK	04.12.90
G-MOXY	26.04.87
LN-VIP	11.10.85
N1210Y	26.09.87
N241FW	23.11.86
N2727A	29.08.86
N36941	01.04.80
N36962	oo.oo.oo
N400BG	01.10.85
N441CM	25.12.84
N441KM	22.11.94
N441NC	11.01.80
N59MD	11.11.85
N6857E	16.07.86
N6858S	21.02.87
N88832	oo.09.79
N920C	10.08.92
N9971G	15.11.77
OY-CGM	12.09.90
SE-IHX	24.03.84

Cessna Citation

5N-AMR	21.05.91
C-GXFZ	26.09.84
D-CHVB	25.01.95
D-IAEC	01.06.87
D-IJHM	19.05.82
EC-CGG	22.11.74
G-BPCP	01.10.80
G-JETB	26.05.93
G-UESS	08.10.83
LN-AAE	15.11.89
N10GE	21.05.85
N12058	20.07.93
N12065	20.07.93
N120ES	24.04.95
N12564	20.07.93
N12660	20.07.93
N12669	20.07.93
N12756	20.07.93
N12757	20.07.93
N12761	20.07.93
N12762	20.07.93
N12763	20.07.93
N12855	20.07.93
N12859	20.07.93
N12967	20.07.93
N15NY	02.08.79
N22FM	26.04.83
N2627U	12.11.82
N2652Z	22.04.90
N29X	05.03.89
N2CA	18.12.82
N41JP	06.05.91
N501GP	21.01.81
N53CC	02.10.89
N555AJ	19.11.79
N63HB	15.02.95
N6887Y	18.12.92
N700CW	01.04.83
N711WM	06.11.86
N79DD	24.09.90
N7RC	26.04.95
N97QS	29.11.90
OE-FAP	06.10.84
OE-FFK	26.10.88
OH-CAR	19.11.87
PT-JXS	16.03.75
PT-KIU	12.11.76
PT-LGJ	06.09.88
PT-LKT	01.12.92
PT-OMV	23.03.94
VH-ANQ	11.05.90
VH-FSA	20.02.84
XA-SMH	25.03.95
YV-O-MAC-1	oo.06.79

Chase C-122

N5904V	31.01.77

Cierva Air Horse

G-ALCV	13.06.50

Clark GA-43

HB-ITU	30.04.36
M-701	18.05.34

Claudius Dornier Seastar

D-ICDS	23.07.85

Consolidated Catalina

*	18.04.56
*	20.03.60
*	12.05.62
C-406	20.12.46
CC-CCS	27.01.86
CC-CDS	18.04.79
CF-CRV	11.05.53
CF-FOQ	17.10.51
CF-HFL	oo.10.57
CF-NTL	21.05.78
G-AGDA	23.03.43
HK-1000E	31.01.55
HK-1001E	15.03.61
HK-1020	11.06.73
HK-133	08.12.56
HK-811	07.06.58
HP-425	11.07.67
N101CS	28.06.79
N1096M	19.06.49
N16KL	13.10.84
N285NJ	22.05.89
N2886D	29.07.85
N5404J	16.01.94
N6458C	oo.oo.77
N6459C	18.07.70
N84857	09.05.85
PK-AKC	02.12.49
PK-AKR	28.08.50
PK-CTA	08.03.48
PP-PCW	01.12.66
PP-PDB	oo.oo.oo
PP-PEC	oo.oo.oo
VP-BAO	09.04.50
VP-JAT	21.08.51
VP-JAW	02.01.52
VR-HDT	16.07.48
YV-C-AQA	oo.10.47
YV-P-APJ	15.07.48

Consolidated Commodore

NC660M	16.04.35
NC668M	24.09.43
VP-BAA	oo.oo.49

Consolidated Fleetster

N704Y	oo.oo.33
NC13212	26.01.35

Consolidated Liberator

*	19.02.52
*	14.04.57
CC-CAH	21.02.55
CC-CAN	21.02.55
CP-575	08.02.64
CP-589	17.09.61
CP-618	21.05.60
G-AGDR	15.02.42
G-AGEM	21.02.46
G-AHYC	13.11.48
G-AHZP	13.10.48
N2870G	oo.07.80
N6813D	oo.oo.78
N6816D	oo.oo.72
N7974A	oo.07.68

Convair 240-600

*	22.09.80
AP-AEG	14.03.53

AP-AEH	15.05.58
D-BELU	31.07.60
HB-IRW	19.06.54
HI-376CT	oo.09.90
JA5088	29.05.65
JA5098	27.02.64
JY-ACB	22.01.59
LV-ADM	12.12.59
LV-ADQ	16.10.54
LV-MMR	29.11.78
N1015G	14.05.71
N10AV	09.04.77
N155PA	19.06.85
N156PA	27.07.93
N270L	17.01.70
N278E	22.08.68
N300GR	24.05.80
N450GA	28.11.91
N558	oo.oo.oo
N55VM	20.10.77
N7177B	04.09.78
N741J	20.02.70
N777DC	01.04.78
N77WA	03.08.75
N8329C	17.09.75
N8330C	15.02.80
N8405H	13.02.58
N8407H	26.02.54
N8410H	oo.oo.69
N90662	02.09.51
N90664	27.02.51
N90670	15.08.58
N91238	14.01.52
N91239	22.08.68
N91241	11.08.49
N93218	16.02.87
N94213	01.03.58
N94221	04.08.55
N94229	22.01.52
N94230	27.09.73
N94234	20.03.55
N94244	20.01.54
N94247	06.01.57
N94253	04.08.89
N94255	16.09.53
N94256	19.02.61
N94266	22.06.49
N94273	15.03.59
OO-AWO	19.12.53
OO-AWQ	14.10.53
PH-TEI	25.05.53
PK-GCB	27.02.72
PK-GCE	17.08.62
PP-CEV	15.01.65
PP-CEZ	09.05.62
PP-CFD	20.08.65
PP-VCK	22.09.58
PP-VCQ	22.12.62
RP-C12	04.06.78
SP-LPB	11.04.58
XA-HUL	31.08.88
XA-JOV	15.03.84
XB-DOK	25.01.70
ZP-CDN	oo.oo.73
ZP-CDP	26.05.67

Convair 340-640

7T-VAH	02.05.76
C-FICA	19.09.91
CC-C-LCA	07.05.62
CF-PWR	18.09.69
CP-1008	oo.oo.76
CP-1078	26.03.76
CP-1358	11.01.80
CP-1489	20.04.85
CP-1725	05.05.82
CP-1961	21.08.92
CP-2142	22.05.95
CP-2212	04.11.93
CP-2256	14.09.93
CP-924	06.09.78
CP-961	07.01.75
D-ACAT	28.01.66
EC-899	19.05.95
EC-ATB	12.11.62
EC-ATH	31.03.65
HB-IMD	17.07.56
HB-IMF	10.02.67
HB-IMM	17.07.73
HI-899	23.07.80
HP-1200CTH	20.02.93
HZ-AAT	04.02.72
HZ-AAU	07.01.72
HZ-AAZ	08.07.68
LN-PAA	08.09.89
N102US	oo.oo.80
N121CA	03.06.81
N137CA	18.03.95
N18837	oo.oo.74
N2045	27.12.68
N21DR	17.01.82
N3408	23.01.67
N3411	28.10.87
N3414	29.11.66
N3422	17.07.55
N356SA	27.06.95
N444JM	24.11.79
N44828	16.12.84
N477KW	25.08.82
N4807C	21.03.78
N4809C	14.07.78
N4819C	14.03.74
N4820C	20.03.68
N4825C	24.07.78
N5802	24.12.68
N5808	02.02.88
N580HH	09.06.93
N5825	06.01.69
N5832	07.06.71
N5844	20.08.71
N73107	11.05.92
N73130	21.12.62
N73130	05.03.67
N73135	04.11.68
N73160	19.01.89
N7601	21.12.63
N8415H	23.07.65
N8420H	oo.oo.55
N862FW	09.02.92
N90853	16.03.54
N90858	29.06.72
N9302	12.05.78
N94436	oo.04.80
N985	30.10.76
N999JZ	11.06.73
OO-DHD	23.10.92
PP-AQE	18.09.57
PP-CDW	03.05.63
PP-CDY	22.01.63
PP-CEP	16.06.58
PP-YRB	24.06.60
SE-BSU	01.11.69
SE-CCK	20.11.64
TAM-44	27.10.75
TAM-45	24.01.78
TAM-46	22.10.84
TAM-47	21.12.73
TG-ACA	27.04.77
XA-KEH	21.05.81
YU-ADA	22.12.56
YU-ADC	10.10.55
YU-ADL	04.02.61
YU-ADO	oo.oo.70
YU-ADV	16.12.71
YV-84C	28.05.85
ZK-FTB	31.07.89

Convair 880

HP-821	29.03.80
JA8023	27.02.65
JA8028	25.06.69
JA8030	26.08.66
N48060	21.08.76
N5865	16.12.76
N820TW	13.09.65
N821TW	20.11.67
N8804E	23.05.60
N8807E	20.12.72
N880SR	oo.05.83
N8815E	25.05.78
N8817E	20.08.77
VR-HFX	05.11.67
VR-HFZ	15.06.72
YV-145C	03.11.80

Convair 990

EC-BNM	05.01.70
EC-BZR	03.12.72
HB-ICD	21.02.70
N5603	08.08.70
N5616	30.05.63
N711NA	12.04.73
N712NA	18.07.85
N7876	10.09.73
OD-AEW	28.12.68
OD-AEX	28.12.68
PK-GJA	28.05.68

Couzinet 27

F-AMBI	08.08.28

Curtiss C-46

*	13.07.46
*	25.12.46
*	28.01.47
*	10.12.47
*	20.01.48
*	05.01.49
*	22.02.49
*	04.05.49
*	04.12.49
*	09.12.49
*	10.12.49
*	05.02.50
*	28.10.51
*	22.01.55
*	09.09.56
*	19.06.57
*	20.09.57
*	13.08.61
*	04.02.62
*	06.04.62
*	05.09.63
*	03.02.67
*	13.09.67
*	03.06.72
*	24.09.76
4X-ACG	26.06.49
9T-PLK	15.07.70
AN-AIN	05.04.60
AN-AKY	22.07.64
AN-AMR	29.08.72
AN-AOC	25.02.76
AN-AOE	15.12.61
B-148	17.07.63
B-1535	28.04.66
B-1543	01.11.70
B-908	20.06.64
C-FCZH	29.09.77
C-FFNC	03.11.89
C-GIXZ	31.10.82
C-GIXZ	23.04.94
C-GTPO	oo.10.89
C-GYHT	13.11.79
CB-37	10.08.49
CB-38	09.10.50
CB-39	29.07.51
CB-42	oo.oo.46
CB-43	29.09.51
CB-45	23.10.56
CB-47	08.11.50
CB-51	24.04.50
CC-CAH-0331	03.11.56
CC-CAN	29.12.64
CC-CAZ	25.05.71
CC-CDI	18.07.68
CC-CDU	13.06.72
CC-CIA-0497	21.05.59
CC-CIB-0504	24.11.64
CC-CNC-0466	11.04.57
CC-COA	17.12.73
CC-CYA-0141	28.04.51
CF-FBJ	20.06.66
CF-HEI	09.08.61
CF-HQI	oo.01.73
CF-HTI	11.01.63
CF-HVJ	18.06.55
CF-HZI	oo.oo.56
CF-HZL	oo.oo.56
CF-IHQ	25.03.60
CF-IHR	23.09.56
CF-IHV	20.12.72
CF-NAD	15.05.67
CF-NAE	oo.06.71
CF-PWD	29.01.60
CP-1052	23.02.74
CP-1063	24.04.75
CP-1077	10.11.83
CP-1244	18.01.88
CP-1333	oo.oo.oo
CP-1588	10.02.81
CP-1593	11.10.85
CP-1617	23.10.81
CP-1655	18.02.92
CP-1848	13.09.93
CP-541	22.01.62
CP-549	20.09.55
CP-552	12.03.59
CP-687	12.09.61
CP-712	02.05.67
CP-730	03.08.66
CP-745	01.02.69
CP-746	15.10.66
CP-746	07.01.90
CP-749	20.01.73
CP-752	28.05.72
CP-754	02.03.92
CP-760	23.08.68
CP-769	03.06.67
CP-777	23.12.79
CP-786	15.09.66
CP-791	11.11.68
CP-800	12.12.69
CP-801	06.04.73
CP-825	31.01.70
CP-834	06.09.69
CP-855	09.06.75
CP-908	02.03.71
CP-909	02.02.87
CP-910	07.12.73
CP-914	15.07.70
CP-916	28.10.83
CP-940	22.04.72
CP-941	06.06.75
CP-959	07.09.72
CP-969	22.03.73
CP-974	06.05.84
CP-990	06.01.74
CP-992	10.03.75
CU-C556	17.05.54
CU-C644	14.04.60
CU-P198	10.07.48
CU-T607	10.08.61
CX-AYI	28.01.62
F-DAAR	13.03.54
F-OAFI	02.03.65
HC-AMC	20.09.68
HC-AMV	02.12.72
HC-SIB	13.05.49
HC-SJA	27.03.53
HI-16	17.07.58
HI-170	07.05.70
HI-189	31.08.79
HI-197	oo.oo.80
HI-201	25.04.73
HI-208	08.02.77
HI-36	oo.09.56
HI-39	oo.10.68
HK-1282	16.09.76
HK-1322	13.03.84
HK-1350	14.08.78
HK-1383	26.10.73
HK-1856	30.01.94
HK-2716	11.12.91
HK-3079G	09.05.95
HK-3205X	17.04.86
HK-3238	29.09.91
HK-330	24.11.50
HK-333	14.02.51
HK-3468	19.09.92
HK-354X	26.11.62
HK-388	21.10.81
HK-391	26.06.50
HK-400	31.08.93
HK-459	29.12.54
HK-489	17.06.54
HK-489E	08.04.61
HK-512	04.11.66
HK-513	25.07.57
HK-514	16.09.58
HK-515	08.12.59
HK-516	20.03.60
HK-527	11.07.66
HK-603	31.01.54
HK-605	29.01.53
HK-682	oo.oo.69
HK-683	13.02.69
HK-750	11.10.91
HK-758	04.03.67
HK-790	oo.03.70
HK-791	30.04.73
HK-792	28.10.70
HP-312	11.01.62
HR-196P	21.05.62
HR-SAL	07.06.62
JY-ABV	09.09.56
LV-FTO	10.10.59
LV-FTP	11.11.58
LV-GEB	17.12.69
LV-GED	16.01.59

LV-GFW 27.01.66
LV-GGJ 18.05.60
LV-GGN 07.12.65
LV-GLA 18.08.66
LV-GXB oo.oo.71
LV-HIJ 07.12.65
LX-LAA 19.06.58
N10012 10.02.71
N10415 16.06.66
N10427 21.02.73
N10624 28.09.79
N1210W 23.11.65
N1240N 14.01.59
N1243N 07.05.69
N1244N 22.10.60
N1245N 20.03.66
N1247N 23.05.69
N1248N 05.06.50
N1300N 15.10.60
N1301N 16.11.58
N1302N 31.05.58
N1308V 22.01.61
N1309V 13.09.67
N1312V 10.07.73
N1386N 25.11.68
N157K 22.07.78
N1648M 07.01.53
N1662M 12.12.56
N1663M 22.01.75
N1669M 22.05.53
N1678M 16.12.51
N1693M 23.04.53
N1697M 19.07.53
N1823M 27.08.64
N1911M 05.04.52
N2028A 16.12.56
N355BY 15.11.80
N355W 06.05.77
N3908B 11.08.51
N3914 02.04.69
N3944C 29.12.51
N3971B 20.11.64
N446M 10.05.73
N46Q 13.02.60
N4717N 04.03.53
N4860V 28.03.75
N4873V 08.08.75
N5075N 19.07.49
N5132B 13.09.65
N5133B 04.02.69
N5140B 02.09.59
N51424 02.04.55
N5160V 09.12.63
N5615V 27.05.49
N59485 09.10.49
N59490 23.02.51
N608Z 30.12.64
N609Z 07.12.63
N616Z 16.02.63
N625CL 24.08.92
N66534 28.09.53
N66559 20.03.53
N67933 26.02.63
N67937 18.09.62
N67941 14.08.63
N67960 30.07.50
N67977 24.08.92
N68823 18.02.59
N68963 30.12.51
N68966 19.11.66
N74170 15.06.50
N74176 08.08.51
N7560U oo.01.82
N7768B 12.09.79
N7840B 30.03.59
N79097 04.08.52
N79978 12.07.49
N79982 04.01.51
N800FA 17.05.75
N8013E 19.06.57
N8404C 18.04.52
N92857 07.06.49
N9406H 27.07.50
N9473Z 13.08.67
N9760Z 26.08.74
N9885F 24.11.64
N9903F 27.08.64
N9904F 17.12.55
N9905F 28.07.66
N9995F 18.03.56
NC1241N 26.01.49
NC1664M 26.03.49
NC59486 14.02.47
NC59488 21.08.47
NC59489 16.05.48
NC59495 17.09.47
OB-OAD-233 17.01.49
OB-QAL-487 04.01.59
OB-QAM-488 08.05.59
OB-R-577 18.03.65
OB-R-606 23.02.66
OB-WBP-507 13.05.59
OD-ACK 03.10.57
PP-AKF 07.12.60
PP-BTA 06.05.59
PP-BTB 31.05.58
PP-BTE 27.06.62
PP-BTF 22.09.60
PP-BTH 12.08.65
PP-BTJ 24.08.60
PP-ITF 21.02.51
PP-ITI 23.09.59
PP-LDB 08.09.50
PP-LDC 15.04.51
PP-LDD 17.12.50
PP-LDE 24.05.52
PP-LDH 06.01.59
PP-LDL 21.03.64
PP-LDM 14.09.53
PP-LDQ 19.12.65
PP-LDX 05.09.58
PP-LPH 04.03.54
PP-NMD 03.05.60
PP-NME oo.oo.68
PP-NMF 16.08.64
PP-VBI 25.09.49
PP-VBJ 22.03.65
PP-VBM 12.12.61
PP-VBZ 04.06.54
PP-VCB 21.02.52
PP-VCF 07.04.57
PP-VCT 18.12.60
PT-BEE 15.07.59
PT-BVG 07.04.64
SE-CFB 08.06.62
SE-CFF 13.01.64
SE-CFG 06.03.66
TAM-60 17.02.71
TG-ACA-A 11.05.71
TG-AQA 15.12.53
TI-1010C 09.09.74
TI-1019 30.03.58
TI-1022 10.07.59
TI-1024C 18.11.60
TI-1065 25.02.70
XA-GOT oo.oo.53
XA-LID 18.06.55
XA-LOS 22.02.66
XA-MIS 17.04.59
XT-44 19.06.48
XT-520 02.06.49
XT-538 05.12.48
XT-822 29.07.48
XW-PBV 24.03.76
XW-PBW 15.10.74
XW-PKJ 26.12.74
XW-PKK 15.12.73
XW-PMF 13.03.75
YN-BVL 16.05.80
YS-012C 13.02.65
YV-C-AMK 22.05.70
YV-C-ARC 21.12.52
YV-C-ARE 03.06.49
YV-C-EVF 06.04.72
YV-C-EVL 05.09.55
YV-C-LBG 19.05.60
YV-C-LBH 02.11.62
ZP-CAI 17.01.62
ZP-CAP 06.12.66
ZP-CBM 22.12.57
ZP-CCE oo.oo.63

Curtiss Condor

* 29.07.36
CH-170 27.07.34
NC12354 09.06.34
NC12373 21.09.33
NC12393 27.07.35
NC12395 19.12.34
NC185H 14.01.33
NC728K 09.07.36

DH Albatross

G-AFDI 20.12.40
G-AFDK 06.07.43
G-AFDL 06.10.40

DH Comet

CF-CUN 03.03.53
F-BGSC 25.06.53
G-ALYP 10.01.54
G-ALYR 25.07.53
G-ALYV 02.05.53
G-ALYY 08.04.54
G-ALYZ 26.10.52
G-APDH 22.03.64
G-APDL 07.10.70
G-APDN 03.07.70
G-ARCO 12.10.67
G-ARJM 21.12.61
LV-AHO 20.02.60
LV-AHP 27.08.59
LV-AHR 23.11.61
OD-ADQ 28.12.68
OD-ADR 28.12.68
OD-ADS 28.12.68
SA-R-7 20.03.63
SU-ALC 02.01.71
SU-ALD 28.07.63
SU-ALE 09.02.70
SU-AMW 19.07.62
SU-ANI 14.01.70

DH Dove

* 13.06.88
5N-AGF oo.oo.oo
CF-EYM 06.12.54
CR-ACJ oo.oo.oo
CR-ACM oo.oo.oo
CR-CAC 14.06.57
CR-CAD 07.09.61
D-IFSC 24.06.83
EP-ACF 24.09.58
G-AGUC 14.08.46
G-AHRA 13.03.47
G-AHYX 24.09.49
G-AJHL 09.02.48
G-AJLW 26.04.65
G-AJOU 13.05.48
G-AJZT 09.06.51
G-AKJG 20.01.65
G-AKSK 23.07.55
G-AKST 31.10.60
G-ALEC 06.05.59
G-ALMR 12.04.60
G-ALTM 22.06.55
G-AMKT 19.02.60
G-AMYP 09.07.83
G-ANDY 29.05.62
G-ANGE 26.02.64
G-AOCE 15.01.58
G-ARFZ 24.02.73
G-ARTS oo.01.75
G-ASHW 20.11.80
G-AVHV 09.04.70
I-TURI 14.08.69
JA5003 18.02.63
JA5008 14.11.61
LQ-XWW oo.oo.oo
LQ-YAU 06.04.60
LV-GIT 28.11.59
LV-XZT 01.07.71
LV-XZY oo.oo.oo
LV-YAE oo.oo.oo
LV-YAZ oo.12.48
LV-YBL oo.oo.oo
LV-YBP oo.oo.oo
N13114 11.09.69
N1515V 02.10.52
N1542V oo.oo.69
N2300H 28.01.70
N26W 02.07.56
N4040B 08.10.68
N420D 16.04.70
N4267C 09.01.64
N4272C 04.08.53
N4276C oo.oo.60
N4277C 09.12.52
N4278C 23.07.54
N4914V 09.07.68
N4922V 06.05.71
N4952N oo.oo.51
N4957N 25.09.68
N4959N 12.03.78
N4962N oo.oo.53
N4964N 29.02.52
N50S 20.04.72
N6503D 15.07.65
N6533D 21.09.68
N669R 03.11.69
N880JG 23.02.69
N88G 25.07.69
N91827 oo.oo.63
N999NJ 08.03.68
OE-FAC 16.12.57
OO-CBM 20.12.53
OO-CFD 01.05.54
OO-DAL 19.06.59
PK-LEA 25.12.74
ST-AAB oo.oo.61
TJ-ACC 21.01.67
VH-AQO 15.10.51
VH-CTS 17.11.68
VH-DHD 01.12.54
VH-DHD 03.12.93
VH-DSM 13.12.79
VP-YER 22.01.50
VR-NAG 02.05.49
VR-NAY 26.09.58
VR-NEW 14.11.50
VT-CQA 17.01.48
VT-CTX 08.05.51
XY-ABO 14.03.49
XY-ABP 23.04.49
XY-ABR 22.11.50
YI-ABJ 04.02.55
ZS-AVZ 18.08.56
ZS-BTM 09.01.52
ZS-DDW 12.01.51

DH Dragon

F-AMUZ 13.06.38
G-ACAN 21.05.41
G-ACAP 26.03.36
G-ACCE 29.08.34
G-ACCR 22.01.36
G-ACCV 23.07.33
G-ACGK 08.01.35
G-ACGU 16.07.35
G-ACHX 25.04.38
G-ACJM 12.08.34
G-ACJT 20.12.39
G-ACMP 23.07.35
G-ACNG 19.04.40
G-ACPY 03.06.41
G-ACRH 13.07.34
G-ADCR 25.06.38
G-ADCT 14.02.40
G-ADED 01.07.35
G-ADEE 26.10.35
G-ADFI 03.07.37
SU-ABI 15.03.35
SU-ABJ 22.06.38
VH-AGC 15.12.79
VH-URE 11.12.57
VH-URO 01.10.35
VH-UVN 07.01.42
VH-UXG 19.04.54
VH-UXK 29.08.38
VH-UZX 26.02.38
VP-KAW 08.12.33
VP-KBG 14.04.37
VT-AEL 28.08.39
ZK-AHT 30.06.44
ZK-AXI 23.04.67
ZS-AEF 26.09.33

DH Drover

VH-DHA 16.04.52
VH-EBQ 16.07.51
VQ-FAO oo.08.54
VQ-FAQ 30.12.55

DH Flamingo

G-AFYE 15.02.43
G-AFYG 18.11.42
G-AFYI 13.09.42

DH Heron

C-FCNT 25.08.84
CR-TAI 26.01.60
DQ-FDY 21.08.88
DQ-FEC 11.09.86
DQ-FED 04.04.89
DQ-FEE 15.12.91
DQ-FEF 27.12.86
EC-ANJ 14.04.58
EC-ANZ 15.11.57
EC-AOA 26.10.57
F-BGOI 18.04.55

F-OECD 27.01.68
G-AMTS 16.07.61
G-AMYU 15.08.58
G-AOFY 28.09.57
G-APJS 19.02.58
HR-ASN 26.05.70
I-AOMU 14.10.60
J6-LBC 23.10.75
JA6155 17.08.63
JA6158 23.02.62
LN-NPH 04.09.68
LN-SUR 07.11.56
N19D 29.03.79
N3FB 18.12.78
N554PR 24.06.72
N575PR 24.07.79
PK-GHP 10.12.58
PP-SLG 27.03.53
TN-ABA 11.07.69
VH-CLS 23.10.75
VH-CLY 04.08.83
VP-BAO 23.08.59
VP-WAM oo.11.67
VQ-FAL 11.12.65
VQ-FAX 09.11.66
ZK-EJM 09.05.77
ZK-EKO 17.10.81

DH Mosquito

G-AGGD 03.01.44
G-AGGF 17.08.43
G-AGGG 25.10.43
G-AGKP 19.08.44
G-AGKR 29.08.44

DH.16

G-EACT oo.03.20

DH.18

G-EARI 16.08.20
G-EAUF 13.05.21
G-EAWO 07.04.22
G-EAWW 02.05.24

DH.34

G-EBBQ oo.08.23
G-EBBR 27.05.24
G-EBBS 14.09.23
G-EBBU 03.11.22
G-EBBX 24.12.24
G-EBCX 23.09.24

DH.4

G-EAHF 11.12.19
G-EAHG 29.10.19
G-EAVL oo.04.21
O-BADO 27.09.21
O-BAIN 25.01.21
O-BALO 05.05.24
O-BARI 27.09.21
O-BATO 27.09.21

DH.50

G-EBKZ 23.10.28
G-EBOP 30.12.26
VH-UER 08.12.35
VH-UHE 03.10.34
VH-UMC 01.03.32

DH.54 Highclere

G-EBKI 01.02.27

DH.60 Moth

LN-ABU 02.08.35
VP-KAC 04.08.35

DH.61 Giant Moth

CF-OAK 23.05.36
G-AAEV 19.01.30
G-AUHW 02.11.34
G-AUJB 09.05.38
G-AUJC 23.10.35
G-CAJT 23.10.28

DH.66 Hercules

G-ABCP 23.11.35
G-EBMW 19.04.31
G-EBMZ 06.09.29
G-EBNA 14.02.30
VH-UJO 06.02.41
VH-UJP oo.oo.42

DH.80A Puss Moth

G-ABSB 07.05.33
HS-PAA 22.06.33
VH-UPM 18.09.32
VP-YAR 04.08.42

DH.83 Fox Moth

G-ACEY 08.07.40
VO-ABC 25.08.35

DH.85 Leopard Moth

VP-KBE 08.06.38
VP-YAY 02.07.39

DH.86

G-ACVZ 15.03.37
G-ACWC 17.06.41
G-ACZN 04.11.38
G-ACZP 21.09.58
G-ADCM 22.10.35
G-ADCN 03.12.38
G-ADEB 12.08.36
G-ADUH oo.06.51
G-ADYF 15.09.36
G-AEFH oo.06.40
G-AEWR oo.06.40
OH-IPA 02.05.40
VH-URN 19.10.34
VH-URT 02.10.35
VH-USC 09.10.44
VH-USE 20.02.42
VH-USF 24.06.45
VH-USG 15.11.34
VH-USW 13.12.35
VH-UYW 15.03.40

DH.89 Dragon Rapide

5H-AAM 13.09.66
5R-MAN oo.oo.68
5Y-KLB 07.08.68
9O-CJT 06.10.60
9Q-CJE oo.oo.62
CF-AEO 18.07.35
CF-AVJ 17.05.39
CF-BBH 19.03.47
CF-BNG 09.03.46
CR-ADM 15.03.55
CR-LBH 10.05.57
EI-AEA 04.09.49
ET-P-16 03.09.53
ET-P-22 oo.oo.oo
F-BGOL oo.oo.60
F-BGPM 13.02.53
F-LAAC oo.oo.58
F-LAAE oo.oo.58
F-LAAF 02.05.58
F-OAUH 14.11.56
F-OAVZ oo.09.56
F-OBKH oo.08.61
F-OBOD 27.04.65
F-OBRU 08.06.62
G-ACPM 02.10.34
G-ACPR 19.02.40
G-ADBU oo.11.36
G-ADBX 16.05.36
G-ADNG oo.08.36
G-AEAK 18.05.39
G-AEBW 18.06.40
G-AEBX 03.07.38
G-AEGS 30.12.36
G-AEMM 03.05.40
G-AEPF 18.06.40
G-AERE 20.06.39
G-AERZ 01.04.46
G-AESR 22.09.56
G-AFEY 18.03.40
G-AFFF 27.09.46
G-AFIA 20.08.42
G-AFMF 19.02.54
G-AGDH 25.11.41
G-AGED 02.02.43
G-AGJF 06.08.47
G-AGLN 15.12.46
G-AGLR 07.10.56
G-AGOJ 01.05.61
G-AGOP 25.06.48
G-AGPH 06.12.51
G-AGPI 16.06.49
G-AGUF 29.06.57
G-AGUR 02.08.54
G-AGUV 26.04.54
G-AHGD 30.06.91
G-AHIA 05.03.51
G-AHJA oo.oo.68
G-AHKR 15.04.47
G-AHLL 21.05.59
G-AHLM 20.07.63
G-AHPT 07.07.59
G-AHTR 10.07.50
G-AHTS 29.04.47
G-AHXV 15.01.49
G-AHXY 27.12.48
G-AHXZ 28.08.51
G-AIUI 10.06.48
G-AIWZ 30.07.49
G-AIYP 05.07.53
G-AIZI 14.09.52
G-AJFN 04.12.47
G-AJFO 04.12.47
G-AJGZ 16.07.49
G-AJHO 05.02.89
G-AJKW 07.05.67
G-AJSJ 18.09.47
G-AKLA 15.06.54
G-AKME 30.06.50
G-AKOF 11.11.48
G-AKSF 23.07.49
G-AKTZ 27.05.57
G-AKZB 12.12.61
G-ALBB 01.08.52
G-ALBC 30.12.63
G-ALEJ 14.09.56
G-ALGO 10.07.51
G-ALWY 19.04.52
G-ALXA 04.06.52
G-ALXJ 10.07.51
LV-AEO oo.oo.oo
LV-FEP 03.11.52
OO-ARN 20.06.60
OO-CMS 08.07.56
OO-ITI 29.12.62
OY-DZY 16.07.60
PK-AKU 16.08.38
PK-AKV oo.oo.42
PK-AKW 07.03.36
SU-ABP 06.02.45
SU-ABQ 09.10.41
SU-ACS 27.07.48
SU-ACT 25.02.51
VH-ADE 26.01.44
VH-UBN 20.07.44
VH-UUO 23.05.52
VH-UVS 12.05.37
VP-KCJ 07.10.62
VP-KCU 28.06.46
VP-KEA 24.01.54
VP-KEB 15.10.51
VP-KEC 12.05.50
VP-KFV 29.11.49
VP-KFW 08.08.48
VP-KHF 23.01.55
VP-KND 18.03.55
VP-RCP 30.08.53
VP-UAW 21.09.47
VP-YEZ 06.01.55
VP-YLV 06.01.55
VP-YOY 25.11.57
VQ-FAL 26.04.54
VR-LAD oo.oo.oo
VR-LAE oo.oo.oo
VR-OAC 21.12.60
VR-SAV 18.12.41
VR-SAW 10.02.42
VT-AHB 30.12.45
VT-AJA 20.11.38
VT-ART 08.04.46
VT-ARY 09.02.59
VT-ARZ oo.oo.51
ZK-AKS 15.06.65
ZK-AKT 15.04.67
ZK-ALC 15.01.50
ZK-BAU 22.04.64
ZP-TDH oo.10.62
ZS-ATV 05.06.51
ZS-ATW 11.12.46
ZS-AYG 31.10.46
ZS-BCI 06.09.52
ZS-BEA 22.02.55
ZS-BZU 10.09.54
ZS-DJT 11.10.63

DH.9

3 oo.11.28
6 oo.06.28
C6054 01.05.19
DL-10 22.06.28
G-AUED 24.03.27
G-EAGX oo.08.20
G-EAOP oo.09.20
G-EAPO oo.09.20
G-EAPU oo.11.20
G-EAQA oo.01.21
G-EAQN 09.11.90
G-EBIX oo.01.29
H-NABE 30.05.22
H-NABF oo.02.26
H-NABO 17.11.22
H-NABP 02.09.21
T-DOBC 17.10.21

DH.90 Dragonfly

G-AEEK 17.08.37
G-AEHC 02.02.37
G-AEWZ 03.03.61
G-AEXN 21.07.39
G-ANYK 22.06.61
LV-KAB oo.oo.oo
R326 25.11.37
VP-YAX 20.12.38
VP-YBR 01.01.39
VR-SAX 20.01.42
ZK-AFB 12.02.62
ZK-AGP 21.12.42

DHC Beaver

* 09.12.82
C-FAWA 14.04.81
C-FDTI 23.06.94
C-FDVK 04.07.83
C-FEYT 16.09.81
C-FFHX 06.06.81
C-FGBC 18.06.95
C-FGCW 01.09.78
C-FITW 18.09.80
C-FIUS 28.07.93
C-FMPM 11.09.80
C-FODF 30.10.77
C-FPQB 12.07.93
C-FRQW 30.12.83
C-FRQW 26.07.93
C-FTEB 17.07.78
C-FTYB 19.05.82
C-GAJU 03.11.79
C-GJKA 16.06.91
C-GPVE 09.10.79
C-GSKY 24.05.82
C-GUWC 13.01.82
C-GVHS 21.06.83
C-GZBE 11.03.80
F-OAMH 04.03.54
F-OAMI 04.03.54
HK-249 14.09.77
JZ-PAB 16.11.57
N126UA 08.08.94
N4747S 19.04.78
N5317G 26.09.85
N5354G 13.07.89
N68084 11.06.79
ZS-CMI 30.03.77
ZS-DRG 29.03.77

DHC Buffalo

5T-MAX 27.05.79
C-GCTC 04.09.84
ET-AHI 08.11.88
ET-AHJ 17.03.83
TJ-XBS 26.10.83

DHC Caribou

* 24.03.70
* 22.11.72
* oo.oo.73
5X-AAB 04.05.76
C-GVYW 17.03.79
CF-LKI-X 24.02.59
HC-BFH 17.07.90
HC-BHZ 01.09.82
N103AQ 16.05.82
N400NC 27.08.92
N5488R 23.10.84
N581PA 25.08.79
P2-VTC 01.07.95
TJ-XAT oo.oo.oo

DHC Dash 7

7O-ACK 09.05.82
LN-WFN 06.05.88

DHC Dash 8

D-BEAT	06.01.93
HS-SKI	21.11.90
N819PH	15.04.88
ZK-NEY	09.06.95

DHC Otter

*	30.08.79
*	22.09.95
*	27.09.95
C-FAGM	24.03.84
C-FBER	02.09.86
C-FDJA	oo.09.82
C-FJIK	26.11.79
C-FMPW	18.08.76
C-FMPZ	27.09.71
C-FQRI	08.05.91
C-FRHW	12.06.81
C-FRWK	20.04.87
C-GKPB	22.05.93
JA3115	01.05.63
N108CA	20.05.95
N11250	15.01.89
N13GA	23.06.94
N17689	30.06.90
N41755	22.07.92
N58JH	oo.10.92
N778L	29.10.84
OO-HAD	09.02.70
PI-51	20.05.64
PI-52	21.06.57
PI-55	21.02.64
PI-56	21.05.57
PK-PHA	25.09.55
PK-PHB	09.01.65
TI-SPF	28.10.77
VP-FAJ	28.12.64
VP-FAM	03.03.69

DHC Twin Otter

*	19.03.94
447	14.02.91
5A-DCP	30.03.83
5A-DCS	15.04.86
5A-DCW	oo.oo.82
5A-DDD	30.11.88
5H-MRD	21.12.84
5N-AJQ	23.04.95
5N-ATQ	13.09.94
5R-MGB	24.07.82
6V-ADE	10.12.93
7P-LAA	13.07.84
8Q-GIA	07.02.87
8R-GCP	03.12.73
9N-ABA	09.06.91
9N-ABB	05.07.92
9N-ABG	15.10.73
9N-ABH	22.12.84
9N-ABI	17.01.95
9N-RF9	27.02.70
AP-AWH	05.12.71
AP-BCH	15.09.85
C-FABW	21.12.77
C-FAIV	02.09.78
C-FAJB	16.12.76
C-FAUS	11.10.84
C-FAWF	22.09.76
C-FCSV	27.02.81
C-FDHT	15.03.81
C-FDMR	17.09.94
C-FGJK	17.12.83
C-FMHU	30.09.75
C-FMPH	27.05.89
C-FPPL	09.10.84
C-FQBT	06.03.93
C-FQDG	28.08.78
C-FTVP	31.12.77
C-FVTL	14.05.83
C-FWAB	06.06.90
C-FWAF	30.09.79
C-FWGE	13.06.87
C-FZZM	14.06.86
C-GBJE	oo.12.91
C-GDHA	04.05.76
C-GKBD	24.11.94
C-GKBM	14.07.88
C-GKBO	09.05.82
C-GNTB	14.01.77
C-GPBO	01.12.77
C-GQKZ	19.03.92
C-GROW	29.08.79
C-GTJA	01.11.79
C-GTLA	23.11.83
CF-BQJ	29.01.77
CF-DIJ	28.01.74
CF-WWP	15.08.73
CP-1018	20.05.87
D-IDHC	27.05.72
ET-AIL	12.08.89
ET-AIQ	22.06.86
F-OGFE	21.12.72
F OGHD	18.11.78
G-BGPC	12.06.86
G-STUD	20.04.83
H4-SIA	27.09.91
HC-BAV/453	02.09.80
HC-BAX/457	21.05.81
HC-BCG/446	20.11.84
HK-1710W	19.12.79
HK-1910	23.01.85
HK-2217	18.12.81
HK-2486	11.06.89
HK-2536	29.11.82
HK-2758	18.02.91
HK-2759X	06.06.93
HK-2761	27.04.86
HK-2763	27.02.85
HK-2889X	04.07.91
HK-2920	11.10.87
HR-ALH	04.04.90
I-CLAI	11.03.67
LN-BNK	11.03.82
LN-BNM	27.10.93
LN-BNS	12.04.90
N101AC	12.12.76
N103AQ	16.05.82
N124PM	10.02.70
N127PM	21.02.82
N141PV	22.04.92
N141Z	22.08.94
N1456T	13.05.76
N187SA	18.04.90
N202RH	17.06.88
N23BC	05.11.79
N25RM	04.12.78
N2711N	06.09.69
N3251	10.10.85
N3257	11.10.85
N361V	15.02.83
N37ST	16.03.95
N389EX	28.04.74
N4043B	29.06.72
N4048B	13.10.78
N43SP	21.07.84
N540N	12.03.85
N558MA	15.07.69
N563MA	06.09.77
N5662	25.07.72
N6383	09.01.75
N6767	30.01.72
N707PV	29.10.89
N724CA	26.10.91
N7267	20.07.88
N74GC	19.06.86
N75GC	27.09.89
N76214	13.07.78
N7666	23.11.68
N76GC	18.06.86
N7705	25.03.73
N8061V	03.12.79
N922MA	01.04.83
N956SM	09.11.70
N982FL	18.01.78
N996SA	19.01.88
OH-KOA	05.02.73
P2-IAA	03.01.95
P2-MBI	12.07.95
P2-MFS	17.12.94
P2-RDE	28.02.78
P2-RDW	21.07.89
PK-MAM	25.05.87
PK-NUC	28.02.73
PK-NUE	15.09.89
PK-NUG	12.08.85
PK-NUK	10.01.95
PK-NUL	16.06.93
PK-NUP	29.03.77
PK-NUQ	03.04.90
PK-NUT	17.07.95
PK-NUW	23.05.87
PK-NUY	30.12.87
PK-YNM	04.11.94
PK-YPG	08.12.92
ST-ADB	18.03.75
T-81	28.01.83
T-84	oo.oo.oo
TF-JME	27.07.79
TJ-CBC	31.10.81
TN-ACX	12.03.92
TY-BBL	24.02.83
TZ-ACH	21.06.83
V2-LCJ	04.08.86
VH-PAQ	13.02.79
VH-TGR	28.04.70
VP-FAP	24.01.77
VP-FAW	18.11.81
XA-BOP	09.09.78
XC-BOS	28.10.79
XT-AAX	08.10.88
XY-AEB	12.08.82
XY-AEE	08.10.83
XY-AEH	08.09.77
XY-AEI	26.08.78
YA-GAT	18.04.73
YA-GAY	08.01.85
YA-GAZ	10.03.83
YV-30C	17.04.78

Dassault Falcon

3D-ART	03.10.86
5N-EPN	05.09.95
7T-VRE	30.05.81
EC-ECB	30.09.87
EC-EFI	11.10.87
EP-AGX	21.11.74
F-GBTC	15.01.86
F-GDLU	20.01.95
F-GJGB	30.09.93
F-GJHK	26.03.92
F-WFAL	31.10.72
HB-VAP	01.10.67
HB-VCG	20.02.72
I-NLAE	25.09.91
LN-FOE	12.12.73
N121FJ	15.10.87
N121GW	18.05.78
N125CA	29.06.89
N1846	13.03.68
N232RA	15.02.89
N253K	30.01.80
N27R	12.11.76
N60MB	03.04.77
N700DK	23.09.85
N7842M	16.01.74
N805F	05.07.71
N821LG	02.02.86
N85JM	17.02.93
N888AR	07.08.76
N990L	08.03.75
OH-FFW	01.03.72
PT-ASJ	17.02.89
VR-BJB	15.01.88
XA-SKO	26.08.94

Dassault Falcon 50

9XR-NN	06.04.94
N1181G	12.05.85
N784B	10.11.85

Dassault Flamant

5R-MPF	15.12.72
F-AZEP	13.02.88

Desoutter II

ZK-ACA	08.02.31

Dewoitine D.332

F-AMMY	14.01.34
F-ANQA	27.10.37

Dewoitine D.338

F-AOZA	05.04.44
F-AQBA	07.07.40
F-AQBB	23.03.38
F-AQBF	oo.oo.41
F-AQBH	oo.oo.40
F-AQBJ	11.10.40
F-AQBL	05.04.44
F-AQBN	oo.oo.oo
F-AQBO	oo.oo.41
F-AQBS	oo.oo.41
F-ARIA	oo.oo.41
F-ARIC	03.05.39
F-ARIZ	27.09.42
F-ARTD	20.06.40
FL-ARI	oo.11.42

Dornier Delphin

D-1620	29.06.29

Dornier Do.128

TJ-XBO	27.01.83

Dornier Do.18

D-AROZ	01.10.38

Dornier Do.228

5N-ARF	oo.11.90
9N-ACL	31.07.93
B-12238	28.02.93
B-12268	14.08.90
B-12288	15.06.95
B-12298	14.06.93
CG-75	02.01.93
D-CICE	15.01.91
D-IFNS	26.03.82
D-IGVN	24.02.85
F-OHAB	19.04.91
VT-EJF	24.09.89
VT-EJT	22.09.88
VT-EPV	13.09.91
VT-ESQ	19.05.89

Dornier Do.27

VQ-ZBL	27.09.66

Dornier Do.28

9Q-CDZ	05.05.76
9Q-COT	28.12.82
D-IDNG	05.12.94
ET-AEN	16.01.75
PK-VDH	26.09.77
PZ-TBB	oo.oo.oo
TR-LOS	oo.06.71
YV-C-FLF	02.02.72
YV-C-FLG	02.02.72

Dornier Merkur

D-1079	oo.11.32
D-1101	oo.oo.28
D-1465	oo.oo.oo
D-585	23.09.27
D-OKES	16.05.36
RRUAA	oo.oo.28
RRUAH	28.07.27
SSSR-201	15.05.29
SSSR-210	30.01.31
URSS-D306	oo.oo.33

Dornier Wal

*	06.04.27
A20	oo.oo.26
D-861	06.10.31
D-864	07.07.30
D-ADYS	15.02.36
D-ARIP	oo.08.35
G-CAJI	02.08.26
I-AYZZ	oo.09.28
I-AZDA	25.01.29
I-AZDB	24.12.29
I-AZDH	10.06.30
I-AZDL	03.11.32
I-AZEA	16.02.32
I-AZEE	18.07.33
I-CITO	25.05.33
I-DAER	oo.07.28
I-DEOR	21.08.24
I-RATA	11.08.33
I-RIDE	12.04.29
I-RONY	21.11.30
N-24	oo.oo.25
P-BACA	03.12.28
P-BADA	11.02.28
PP-CAL	12.09.31
SSSR-N2	oo.08.37
SSSR-N3	08.09.32
SSSR-N9	oo.oo.34

Douglas B-26

C-FBVH	24.04.80
C-FFIM	13.07.84
C-GWJG	01.07.82
N142ER	17.03.85
N190M	17.08.86
N3710G	21.09.80
N4060A	05.03.83
N65Y	10.01.54
N8036E	22.06.93

Douglas C-74

HP-385 09.10.63

Douglas DC-1

EC-AAE oo.12.40

Douglas DC-2

* 08.12.38
* 29.10.40
C-157 01.03.46
CX-AEG 18.01.46
EC-AAA oo.04.46
EC-AAB oo.10.45
EC-AAC 03.02.44
EC-AAD oo.08.40
EC-AGK oo.oo.38
EC-BFF oo.04.37
G-AGBH 03.10.46
HB-ISI 09.08.44
HB-ITA 07.01.39
HB-ITI 28.02.36
J-BBOI 12.02.40
LV-AHI 02.12.54
LV-GGT 17.05.60
NC13715 01.01.47
NC13721 07.04.36
NC13722 03.08.35
NC13727 26.03.39
NC13730 25.03.37
NC13732 19.12.36
NC13734 18.02.37
NC13735 19.10.38
NC13739 10.08.37
NC13785 06.05.35
NC13786 03.04.40
NC13789 01.03.38
NC14269 25.12.36
NC14272 19.07.38
NC14273 11.10.36
NC14274 14.01.36
NC14279 02.08.41
NC14285 06.10.35
NC14292 oo.oo.42
NC14298 23.08.37
NC14979 31.05.36
OK-AIA 21.04.36
PH-AJU 20.12.34
PH-AKG 20.07.35
PH-AKK 10.05.40
PH-AKL 09.12.36
PH-AKM 17.07.35
PH-AKN 10.05.40
PH-AKO 10.05.40
PH-AKP 10.05.40
PH-ALD 10.05.40
PH-ALF 28.07.37
PK-AFJ oo.12.41
PP-AVG 05.02.47
PP-MGA 29.03.49
SP-ASJ 23.11.37
URSS-M25 06.08.37
VH-AEN 09.05.48
VH-ARC 16.03.49
VH-UYC 25.10.38
XA-DOB 14.07.55
XA-DOQ 27.11.51
XA-DOT 11.08.45
XA-GEE 28.12.47
XA-KIC oo.oo.61
ZS-DFW 29.08.52

Douglas DC-3

* 10.11.38
* 23.08.40
* 19.06.41
* 07.01.45
* 15.12.46
* 25.12.46
* 25.12.46
* 25.01.47
* 13.02.47
* 16.10.47
* 17.10.47
* 27.10.47
* 02.11.47
* 19.11.47
* 23.12.47
* 27.08.48
* 12.12.48
* 29.01.49
* 13.06.49
* 27.02.50
* 24.07.50
* 21.09.50
* 14.01.54
* 19.12.55
* 18.01.56
* 08.09.59
* 14.07.60
* 15.12.60
* oo.09.61
* 22.01.66
* 04.07.66
* 11.08.67
* 24.10.67
* 06.01.69
* 18.01.69
* 10.02.72
* 04.05.73
* 15.02.74
* 05.10.74
* 10.03.75
* 11.03.75
* 11.04.75
* 05.11.78
* 12.07.80
* 03.10.80
* 28.08.84
* 10.09.85
* 18.07.95
2009 28.09.94
2028 24.11.94
42-38257 10.03.42
4W-AAS 19.03.69
4W-ABI 16.09.71
4W-ABJ 01.11.72
4W-ABR 13.12.73
4W-ABY 14.11.78
5H-AAK 05.07.73
5N-AAK 06.11.67
5N-AAL 17.01.68
5N-ARA oo.oo.81
5R-MAJ 16.07.63
5U-AAJ 10.06.77
5W-FAB 11.05.66
5W-FAC 13.01.70
5Y-ADI 24.12.68
5Y-BBN oo.02.92
5Y-DAK 17.08.87
5Y-DCA 06.04.71
6O-SAC 16.08.75
6V-AAA 06.07.65
6V-AAP 24.07.71
7O-ABF 01.03.77
7O-ABP 16.09.75
8P-AAC 09.09.71
9G-AAF 24.04.69
9G-GAD oo.08.67
9M-AMU 30.01.67
9N-AAD 05.11.60
9N-AAH 01.08.62
9N-AAO 12.07.69
9N-AAP 12.07.69
9N-RF10 13.09.72
9Q-CUD 19.02.70
9Q-CUM 18.08.68
9Q-CUP 15.02.70
9Q-CUS 29.03.63
9Q-CYD 16.01.84
AN-ACZ 27.08.48
AN-ADQ oo.02.60
AN-AEC 23.01.57
AP-AAC 22.03.61
AP-AAD 02.08.53
AP-AAF 13.10.54
AP-AAH 26.03.65
AP-AAZ 22.10.52
AP-ACE 26.11.48
AP-ACZ 25.02.56
AP-ADI 12.12.49
AP-AJS 01.07.57
B-112 25.07.67
B-1523 21.08.67
B-1553 26.03.75
B-241 15.02.69
B-243 21.02.70
B-247 16.04.77
B-251 24.04.69
B-304 22.08.71
B-305 30.09.70
B-308 25.04.70
B-309 02.01.69
B-811 20.10.54
C-1002 15.03.48
C-108 22.01.47
C-110 29.12.48
C-119 10.11.48
C-204 22.01.47
C-307 24.05.50
C-310 15.12.48
C-400 09.03.47
C-68 oo.oo.oo
C-FAAM 14.01.93
C-FADD 11.05.87
C-FAII 26.09.75
C-FBJE 01.11.88
C-FBKV 12.05.77
C-FBKX 15.02.83
C-FBZN 28.02.89
C-FCRW 18.09.78
C-FCSC 15.11.75
C-FDTT 12.03.95
C-FECY 25.09.75
C-FFKZ 20.05.76
C-FGHL 17.05.86
C-FHPM oo.oo.76
C-FIAX 10.12.76
C-FIQR 28.02.77
C-FIRW 16.03.81
C-FNAR 28.02.77
C-FOOY 03.11.75
C-FQBC 30.03.95
C-FQHF 07.05.82
C-FQNF 04.04.91
C-FROD 26.06.94
C-FSAW 23.10.77
C-FTAT 05.08.74
C-FXXT 11.04.77
C-GCXD 23.03.95
C-GKFC 07.09.76
C-GLUC 25.07.75
C-GNNA 19.01.86
C-GSCA 10.01.84
C-GUBT 22.06.83
C-GWYX 21.05.89
C-GZOF 19.08.95
C9-ATH 06.01.92
C9-STD 25.11.91
C9-STE 22.11.93
CB-31 01.01.51
CB-32 28.05.47
CB-33 29.08.49
CC-C-LDP 03.04.61
CC-CBM 08.04.68
CC-CBO 15.05.79
CC-CBT 12.02.70
CC-CBW 07.08.81
CC-CBY 05.12.69
CC-CLH-0184 29.05.54
CF-AAC 19.06.70
CF-AAL 09.11.69
CF-AUQ 06.12.72
CF-BXZ 22.03.52
CF-BZH 14.02.56
CF-CUA 09.09.49
CF-CUF 22.12.50
CF-DGJ 04.12.57
CF-DXR 18.10.51
CF-ECN 02.01.51
CF-EPI 23.06.57
CF-FAJ 03.04.65
CF-FKQ 15.04.61
CF-FKY 24.07.48
CF-FOL 17.11.72
CF-GKV 10.12.57
CF-GOC 21.11.64
CF-GVZ 17.01.56
CF-GXE 12.04.61
CF-HTH 06.02.73
CF-HTP 25.10.55
CF-ILQ 09.01.64
CF-ILY 19.03.57
CF-IQF 15.01.62
CF-JNR 04.04.61
CF-JRY 30.08.70
CF-KAH 05.01.72
CF-OOV 12.02.73
CF-PQG 16.03.65
CF-QBB 29.05.73
CF-QBD 13.07.58
CF-QBE 13.07.58
CF-QBF 13.07.58
CF-QBG 13.07.58
CF-QBH 13.07.58
CF-TAR 07.10.70
CF-TET 25.09.58
CF-TQW 01.12.72
CF-TVK 28.01.74
CF-UZA oo.oo.69
CN-CCJ 14.11.58
CP-1059 08.12.87
CP-1243 13.03.80
CP-1336 06.10.77
CP-1418 16.01.89
CP-1470 06.04.81
CP-1622 20.04.93
CP-1960 02.11.92
CP-529 29.02.92
CP-535 18.03.57
CP-536 21.08.62
CP-565 17.09.76
CP-568 04.02.64
CP-573 18.01.76
CP-584 31.12.59
CP-600 03.11.53
CP-605 25.08.56
CP-639 08.12.64
CP-645 29.10.65
CP-680 22.08.64
CP-691 22.11.67
CP-695 06.12.62
CP-710 10.09.62
CP-728 06.01.77
CP-729 06.06.64
CP-734 19.04.68
CP-735 19.10.90
CP-755 23.11.76
CR-LBK 18.07.50
CS-TDB 27.01.48
CS-TDF 08.06.48
CU-T138 01.09.61
CU-T172 15.04.60
CU-T7 25.11.50
CX-AGE 09.10.62
CX-BJH/T511 10.02.78
D-AAIE 14.08.44
D-AAIF oo.oo.43
D-AAIG 21.04.44
D-AAIH 29.10.40
D-ABBF 09.12.42
D-CCCC 22.12.91
EC-ABC 29.04.57
EC-ABK 23.12.48
EC-ABN 10.04.58
EC-ABO 12.06.46
EC-ACG 22.12.47
EC-ACH 28.10.57
EC-ACX 16.09.66
EC-AGO 19.09.62
EC-AQE 30.09.72
EC-AQH 21.06.64
EC-ARZ 07.12.65
EC-EIS 07.06.89
EC-EQH 05.01.91
EC-FAH 02.03.93
EI-ACA 18.06.46
EI-ACF 01.01.53
EI-AFL 10.01.52
EL-AAB 25.06.70
EL-AAB 19.04.75
EP-AAG 14.09.50
EP-AAJ 01.12.50
EP-ABB 02.01.62
EP-ACI 26.12.48
EP-ACJ 25.12.52
EP-ACL 25.04.59
EP-ACV 30.06.53
EP-ADG 13.06.71
EP-ADI 04.05.64
EP-AEF 17.03.67
EP-AEI 20.02.62
EP-AGZ 13.04.70
ET-AAP oo.08.77
ET-AAQ 10.04.69
ET-AAR 20.11.74
ET-AAS 23.04.76
ET-AAT 30.11.63
ET-ABE 05.08.74
ET-ABF 20.07.77
ET-ABI 14.09.65
ET-ABQ 10.09.72
ET-ABR 14.03.75
ET-ABX 11.09.75
ET-ADC 31.05.76
ET-AEJ 14.12.76
ET-AFW 19.02.79
ET-AGI 21.07.77
ET-AGK 15.10.78
ET-AGM 18.03.80
ET-AGO 26.12.87

ET-AGP	28.01.79	F-VNAE	17.10.53	HK-111	22.08.73	I-LAIL	26.01.53	N19928	02.03.51
ET-AGQ	25.10.78	F-WSGU	02.07.72	HK-116	29.08.50	I-LEDA	02.01.57	N19941	01.09.53
ET-AGR	oo.07.77	FAC.1120	20.11.77	HK-118	17.10.65	I-LENT	10.04.54	N19963	30.07.49
ET-AGT	02.05.88	FAC.1125	17.02.77	HK-120	02.05.50	I-LETR	28.11.51	N1FN	19.05.90
ET-AGU	21.09.79	FAC.1126	03.05.83	HK-1200	13.08.49	I-LINC	22.12.56	N200	21.04.61
ET-AGW	11.01.81	FAC.1127	20.11.77	HK-1212	08.02.82	I-REGI	20.02.48	N2204S	22.11.84
ET-AHP	24.08.82	FAC.1128	03.08.81	HK-1216	17.01.74	I-TAVI	30.03.63	N25656	06.12.78
ET-AHR	07.10.81	FAC.1129	25.06.81	HK-1221G	24.11.80	JA5018	16.03.60	N25691	12.12.49
ET-T-1	13.01.62	FAC.1131	13.11.80	HK-123	11.03.50	JA5024	29.10.63	N258M	02.04.81
ET-T-16	05.09.61	FAC.661	21.01.72	HK-126	09.07.51	JA5039	30.04.63	N27PR	22.07.86
ET-T-18	16.07.60	FAC.663	03.05.75	HK-1270	12.03.70	JA5040	10.05.63	N28324	02.08.59
ET-T-5	22.07.48	FAC.668	21.02.78	HK-1333	23.02.74	JA5045	12.08.58	N28343	oo.oo.70
F-BAIF	oo.11.46	FAC.676	02.04.76	HK-1340	06.07.85	JA5080	14.02.65	N28345	17.05.53
F-BAII	30.04.59	FAC.685	08.09.69	HK-1341X	29.07.72	KA-DFN	oo.12.61	N28346	17.09.89
F-BAOA	08.01.58	FAC.688	08.01.75	HK-1351X	27.01.78	LN-NAD	05.05.52	N28360	21.12.67
F-BAOB	03.09.46	G-AGBB	01.06.43	HK-1393	21.11.78	LN-NAE	04.04.52	N28364	13.07.87
F-BAOD	16.02.50	G-AGBC	21.09.40	HK-142	02.04.51	LN-PAS	05.03.64	N28889	02.05.89
F-BAOE	30.07.62	G-AGBE	18.11.46	HK-143	19.09.53	LQ-IPC	05.05.69	N29086	04.11.49
F-BAXB	11.08.51	G-AGBI	24.11.40	HK-149	25.10.76	LR-AAA	30.01.48	N31538	04.08.72
F-BAXC	06.01.48	G-AGFZ	21.04.44	HK-1511E	17.06.77	LV-ABX	oo.oo.53	N33649	12.06.77
F-BAXD	04.09.46	G-AGHK	17.04.46	HK-1517E	22.08.75	LV-ACD	16.07.56	N3433U	30.05.86
F-BAXL	18.03.55	G-AGHP	16.05.58	HK-153	11.03.65	LV-ACH	30.12.50	N3433Y	18.03.94
F-BAXM	13.10.50	G-AGHR	24.10.45	HK-155	09.03.57	LV-ACL	12.06.50	N34417	15.09.57
F-BAXO	14.03.47	G-AGHT	14.08.46	HK-160	11.01.54	LV-ACM	14.07.59	N34963	27.08.64
F-BAXQ	01.02.47	G-AGIR	28.08.44	HK-161	24.12.66	LV-ACQ	20.05.55	N3588	18.04.62
F-BAXT	24.01.56	G-AGIW	17.10.50	HK-166	19.07.77	LV-ACX	23.04.54	N386T	29.11.63
F-BAXY	08.12.50	G-AGIX	30.07.48	HK-167	24.06.53	LV-ACY	26.03.51	N38G	05.11.59
F-BCCL	08.06.54	G-AGIY	23.01.46	HK-2213	28.05.94	LV-ADD	30.07.47	N39393	21.07.72
F-BCYF	12.12.47	G-AGJU	03.01.47	HK-2214X	24.01.80	LV-AFW	15.05.59	N39DT	28.07.87
F-BCYI	13.03.54	G-AGJX	11.01.47	HK-2497	05.03.81	LV-AGE	03.06.51	N3VB	25.03.81
F-BCYJ	25.04.54	G-AGKD	23.12.46	HK-2580	12.12.82	LV-FYJ	09.01.64	N401JB	oo.09.83
F-BCYK	28.01.56	G-AGKM	08.04.45	HK-303	22.01.56	LV-JTC	25.02.71	N407D	21.09.78
F-BCYL	05.11.51	G-AGKN	14.07.48	HK-3031	08.02.86	LX-DKT	21.07.92	N410D	09.03.64
F-BCYO	08.01.49	G-AGNA	01.05.45	HK-306	07.12.48	N100DW	17.09.89	N41447	02.12.78
F-BCYP	07.07.48	G-AGZA	19.12.46	HK-308	09.08.56	N100SD	17.09.89	N41718	12.01.52
F-BCYU	21.09.55	G-AGZB	06.05.62	HK-309	15.04.50	N102AP	07.06.91	N427W	12.06.79
F-BCYX	oo.oo.78	G-AHCS	07.08.46	HK-311	31.01.51	N102BL	30.07.82	N4296	15.04.69
F-BEFG	17.03.53	G-AHCW	19.02.49	HK-315	21.03.51	N1047G	25.07.79	N4425N	17.09.89
F-BEFK	22.08.49	G-AHCY	19.08.49	HK-3177	15.05.91	N111ST	01.07.81	N4471J	17.09.89
F-BEFQ	10.01.50	G-AJBG	20.05.48	HK-319	15.09.64	N12978	oo.oo.70	N44896	31.10.83
F-BEFS	24.01.54	G-AJVZ	27.03.51	HK-3215	25.05.95	N133AC	11.12.78	N45335	01.11.63
F-BEIA	04.12.54	G-AMRB	28.03.56	HK-3220	31.08.93	N134FS	10.05.91	N4577Z	17.09.89
F-BEIB	04.05.52	G-AMSF	05.03.62	HK-326	26.04.67	N137H	12.01.81	N45864	01.08.80
F-BEIH	30.01.50	G-AMOL	18.02.50	HK-328	09.03.55	N139D	10.07.69	N45873	09.07.78
F-BEIK	08.04.57	G-AMSM	17.08.78	HK-329	10.09.80	N14273	14.05.71	N47	01.10.70
F-BEIO	04.09.54	G-AMSW	07.10.61	HK-385	17.11.56	N142D	20.03.69	N47CE	22.05.89
F-BEIP	21.05.54	G-AMVB	22.10.58	HK-437E	06.12.62	N144A	11.09.75	N47FE	21.04.88
F-BEIV	07.11.51	G-AMVC	17.10.61	HK-502	25.02.62	N148Z	11.06.79	N480F	19.07.83
F-BEIZ	12.09.51	G-AMWX	17.12.65	HK-503	23.05.57	N150A	06.04.65	N481F	oo.oo.75
F-BESS	16.04.53	G-AMYW	08.04.67	HK-504	15.06.51	N1546A	23.03.78	N48230	11.04.75
F-BEST	16.06.53	G-AMZC	22.12.55	HK-507	01.03.50	N1549V	22.09.64	N485	27.11.65
F-BFGD	24.01.50	G-AMZD	19.08.59	HK-508	12.08.74	N154R	03.07.70	N49319	26.03.71
F-BFGH	22.10.49	G-ANTB	14.04.65	HK-524	22.04.62	N15569	29.06.53	N49454	09.03.87
F-BFGL	09.07.50	G-AOFZ	17.08.66	HK-556	10.04.77	N15570	18.02.69	N49551	20.01.54
F-BFGN	14.03.55	G-BFPU	25.09.78	HK-595	17.10.71	N15598	02.01.78	N49553	04.06.58
F-BGXD	31.01.54	HA-TSA	06.08.61	HK-772	25.07.81	N157U	04.05.85	N4994E	27.07.66
F-BHKU	26.09.63	HB-IRK	18.06.57	HK-794	23.08.62	N15HC	01.02.75	N4996E	14.12.78
F-BHKV	31.05.58	HC-ACL	07.04.58	HK-862	08.03.64	N16030	09.06.50	N4997E	18.03.65
F-BIEE	28.07.78	HC-AFQ	16.09.65	HP-560	21.02.73	N16067	04.03.63	N51071	13.12.77
F-BJBY	21.04.81	HC-ALC	02.03.71	HR-ANA	25.11.69	N16088	28.04.51	N51359	15.06.54
F-BJHC	01.08.81	HC-ALK	25.08.69	HR-SAC	28.05.80	N163E	05.12.82	N525W	29.02.68
F-BYCU	oo.11.84	HC-ANJ	03.11.71	HR-SAZ	18.03.90	N163J	21.02.70	N541S	oo.oo.61
F-OABJ	27.11.49	HC-AUC	02.05.74	HS-000	24.07.66	N163J	21.03.72	N54370	24.03.67
F-OABK	12.02.51	HC-AUR	oo.02.75	HS-SAE	09.04.51	N168Z	30.06.85	N54605	27.12.80
F-OABX	20.07.51	HC-AUX	12.09.71	HS-SAF	20.08.51	N17085	21.12.60	N54NA	19.07.95
F-OACA	12.09.50	HC-SJE	14.03.72	HS-TA-180	17.11.49	N17109	04.12.51	N55V	30.10.59
F-OAFP	01.05.50	HI-117	01.06.73	HS-TDH	27.12.67	N17314	01.02.59	N57131	28.03.77
F-OAFR	03.02.53	HI-159	18.05.69	HZ-AAE	09.02.68	N17337	27.06.66	N57372	05.04.71
F-OAHY	13.02.53	HI-222	30.01.75	HZ-AAJ	11.06.67	N17891	30.11.54	N6	27.03.75
F-OANH	04.03.54	HI-237	31.08.79	HZ-AAK	10.07.72	N18936	04.09.50	N60256	07.12.49
F-OAPC	04.03.54	HI-6	11.01.48	HZ-AAM	24.06.67	N18941	08.01.59	N60705	09.05.81
F-OAVR	22.05.63	HK-107	29.07.72	HZ-AAN	13.06.64	N18949	24.06.81	N61350	19.08.64
F-OCKT	23.07.69	HK-1078	17.06.81	HZ-AAO	16.02.56	N189UM	07.04.78	N61442	12.03.64
F-VNAD	30.07.53	HK-109	22.03.65	I-ETNA	06.12.48	N1981W	02.10.71	N61451	22.08.54

N62WS	26.03.84	NC19947	11.11.46	OH-LCA	08.11.63	PK-AFZ	26.02.42	PP-SPK	06.06.64
N63250	20.07.79	NC19970	18.01.46	OH-LCC	03.01.61	PK-ALN	29.12.41	PP-SPL	18.05.51
N63439	06.04.51	NC206	21.01.48	OK-WDB	25.01.47	PK-ALO	03.03.42	PP-SPM	13.05.52
N64423	29.09.68	NC20750	10.11.46	OO-AUI	23.05.40	PK-DPA	09.05.52	PP-SPP	14.09.69
N64490	11.04.80	NC21712	20.10.41	OO-AUQ	18.12.49	PK-DPB	17.11.50	PP-SPQ	08.09.51
N65121	02.10.77	NC21714	12.05.42	OO-AUR	17.09.46	PK-DPD	25.11.54	PP-SPR	11.01.69
N65134	07.03.69	NC21727	03.04.41	OO-AUX	08.05.70	PK-EHC	22.01.73	PP-SPT	13.12.50
N65276	21.12.67	NC21746	05.01.47	OO-AWH	02.03.48	PK-GDC	21.01.74	PP-SPU	15.01.65
N6574	02.03.73	NC21767	10.02.44	OO-CBA	24.07.51	PK-GDE	01.01.66	PP-SPV	26.05.50
N692A	25.03.77	NC21786	06.01.46	OO-CBK	27.08.49	PK-GDI	24.01.61	PP-SPW	14.12.50
N7	04.01.71	NC21788	02.02.42	OO-CBN	04.02.52	PK-GDM	05.04.62	PP-SPX	07.05.56
N70003	11.08.84	NC21789	31.08.40	OO-CBO	07.01.47	PK-GDU	01.01.66	PP-SPZ	27.05.64
N709Z	24.04.80	NC21799	03.03.46	OO-SBH	28.03.69	PK-GDV	24.12.59	PP-SQA	29.01.73
N711Y	31.12.85	NC25647	12.07.45	OO-UBL	31.08.48	PK-GDY	05.02.61	PP-SQP	26.11.64
N723A	21.09.77	NC25663	30.10.41	OY-AEB	17.02.47	PK-GDZ	29.12.61	PP-VAY	20.04.66
N73KW	15.01.77	NC25675	31.01.46	OY-DCI	12.02.48	PK-NDH	07.02.77	PP-VBH	14.10.67
N74139	08.06.68	NC25678	04.12.40	OY-DNP	17.10.67	PK-NDI	05.10.78	PP-VBV	01.07.63
N74663	08.09.55	NC25684	10.01.45	PH-ALP	03.04.37	PK-OBC	15.08.84	PP-VCS	18.10.57
N74689	23.08.77	NC25692	14.04.45	PH-ALS	06.10.37	PK-OBK	28.04.81	PP-VDL	03.01.58
N74844	16.07.71	NC28310	04.11.44	PH-ALU	10.05.40	PK-RDB	25.12.74	PP-YPK	23.06.66
N74Z	01.10.78	NC28383	02.07.46	PH-ARX	10.05.40	PK-REA	10.02.48	PP-YPM	01.12.49
N75391	16.01.58	NC28384	13.01.48	PH-ARY	14.04.38	PK-ZDD	20.08.72	PP-YPT	15.07.66
N75430	21.05.70	NC28394	26.02.41	PH-ASP	10.05.40	PK-ZDF	04.06.70	PP-YPX	17.08.51
N75KW	12.09.80	NC33611	04.06.45	PH-AST	10.05.40	PP-AJA	15.03.53	PP-YPZ	06.03.55
N76	06.11.74	NC33621	24.04.46	PH-DAA	26.10.68	PP-AJB	03.08.49	PP-YQK	23.08.53
N78B	09.03.87	NC33631	07.09.45	PH-MOA	03.06.71	PP-AJC	11.06.76	PP-YQN	03.03.62
N8042X	26.06.89	NC33645	22.01.43	PH-TBO	06.11.46	PP-AJE	08.08.65	PP-YQS	15.03.61
N8056	20.04.93	NC33646	24.02.47	PH-TBW	14.11.46	PP-ANH	12.08.52	PP-ZNU	28.01.81
N85B	06.12.54	NC33657	15.09.43	PH-TCR	26.01.47	PP-ANK	06.09.56	PT-ATP	06.02.64
N86AC	19.01.75	NC36480	28.01.48	PH-TCV	27.12.47	PP-ANO	31.05.54	PT-BJC	04.03.61
N8744R	17.04.66	NC36498	25.02.48	PH-TEU	02.02.50	PP-ANX	10.04.57	PT-CEV	30.09.73
N87805	28.02.75	NC38942	17.10.46	PH-TFA	20.11.49	PP-ASB	20.04.49	PT-KVT	13.11.79
N9025R	10.01.79	NC39188	08.03.46	PI-C1	14.12.46	PP-ASS	01.03.67	PT-KVU	07.10.78
N90627	27.06.71	NC41798	08.03.46	PI-C10	oo.oo.48	PP-AVL	06.09.61	RP-C138	31.10.84
N91003	30.09.67	NC45395	24.12.46	PI-C11	16.06.47	PP-AVM	22.05.47	RP-C14	15.11.89
N91008	08.08.54	NC49657	22.04.47	PI-C12	25.01.47	PP-AVO	14.07.48	RP-C140	24.07.90
N91016	29.05.65	NC50040	08.08.46	PI-C126	22.12.60	PP-AVY	27.08.59	RP-C141	09.02.81
N91375	01.04.66	NC51878	21.08.46	PI-C133	23.11.60	PP-AVZ	30.05.50	RP-C287	13.12.83
N91378	oo.07.83	NC52710	04.04.47	PI-C14	20.04.48	PP-AXD	25.02.60	RP-C3	oo.oo.82
N95C	06.06.82	NC53210	06.01.49	PI-C142	15.10.53	PP-AXG	19.12.49	RP-C570	15.11.74
N96BF	16.12.94	NC53218	16.05.46	PI-C143	17.05.48	PP-AXJ	14.10.52	RP-C647	16.11.77
N99663	30.10.79	NC54335	06.02.49	PI-C144	20.10.65	PP-BTU	28.06.64	RP-C81	26.04.90
N999B	12.01.55	NC54451	05.02.47	PI-C145	21.01.48	PP-BTX	27.03.68	RP-C82	06.05.89
N99H	19.02.71	NC57667	07.12.48	PI-C15	19.11.60	PP-CBS	05.02.46	RX-76	26.11.46
N9BC	01.01.75	NC57850	05.09.46	PI-C16	14.07.60	PP-CBV	28.09.71	SE-BAF	28.08.43
NC12919	11.12.46	NC58024	28.12.46	PI-C17	29.06.66	PP-CBX	13.03.48	SE-BAG	22.10.43
NC14941	25.02.46	NC58121	04.10.48	PI-C184	18.01.50	PP-CBY	26.08.55	SE-BAY	09.08.47
NC15577	28.12.46	NC59398	14.02.47	PI-C22	24.01.50	PP-CBZ	14.04.69	SE-BBM	01.04.51
NC16002	28.12.48	NC60331	07.01.48	PI-C262	22.03.58	PP-CCA	21.04.46	SE-BBN	22.01.49
NC16008	15.10.43	NC64722	08.03.48	PI-C270	30.03.52	PP-CCC	01.12.55	SP-LCC	28.03.50
NC16014	28.07.43	NC65350	06.08.47	PI-C3	oo.oo.48	PP-CCD	28.04.46	SP-LCG	14.11.51
NC16017	23.10.42	NC66637	04.11.48	PI-C36	oo.oo.48	PP-CCK	26.07.51	SP-LCH	13.03.53
NC16060	15.12.42	NC75402	07.09.48	PI-C38	30.12.52	PP-CCL	22.08.70	ST-AAM	21.02.67
NC16064	18.11.42	NC79024	13.07.47	PI-C485	13.10.62	PP-CCP	21.10.54	ST-AHH	07.11.79
NC16066	29.11.38	NC79025	02.01.49	PI-C489	02.03.63	PP-CCX	22.03.51	SU-AJG	15.01.68
NC16072	12.01.41	NC79042	12.06.48	PI-C5	10.03.52	PP-CDD	17.05.75	SU-AJM	15.05.62
NC16073	09.02.37	NC88804	14.03.47	PI-C53	26.12.47	PP-CDH	06.12.70	SU-AJW	oo.06.65
NC16074	17.10.37	NC88826	25.08.46	PI-C568	20.05.64	PP-CDI	19.08.58	SU-AJX	12.05.63
NC16086	04.11.40	NC88872	12.01.47	PI-C569	21.12.64	PP-CDJ	12.09.54	SU-ALP	06.05.61
NC16090	11.01.43	NC88873	31.12.46	PI-C59	13.09.47	PP-CDS	12.05.60	SX-BAB	03.09.47
NC17315	23.01.41	NC88876	17.12.46	PI-C648	14.10.47	PP-FOR	18.10.74	SX-BAD	29.10.59
NC17322	01.12.44	NC91006	20.01.49	PI-C854	23.05.67	PP-IBC	04.11.50	SX-BAF	23.04.49
NC17335	20.09.48	NC95486	27.11.47	PI-C856	16.12.65	PP-LPB	07.10.48	SX-BAI	06.06.49
NC17645	05.05.48	NX88787	08.08.47	PI-C9	19.11.70	PP-LPC	15.05.51	TAM-01	14.04.72
NC17713	27.01.49	OB-PAM-146	20.03.60	PI-C92	16.10.46	PP-LPG	12.07.51	TAM-03	15.10.58
NC18108	24.05.38	OB-PAU-201	23.11.50	PI-C942	11.09.65	PP-NAL	06.06.51	TAM-04	21.01.58
NC18114	15.07.38	OB-PAV-223	10.02.49	PI-C944	19.11.70	PP-NAR	22.09.58	TAM-05	08.11.58
NC18123	30.12.45	OB-PAY-226	15.12.48	PI-C945	20.01.65	PP-NAZ	22.11.59	TAM-09	01.08.60
NC18142	23.02.45	OB-PBH-530	04.02.62	PI-C947	23.04.69	PP-PCH	27.09.46	TAM-11	12.02.70
NC18146	02.05.42	OB-PBN-659	25.08.62	PI-C948	08.03.65	PP-PCN	28.02.52	TAM-17	14.07.70
NC18645	13.11.46	OB-R-568	30.11.66	PI-C97	21.02.64	PP-PEE	22.01.65	TAM-22	04.05.71
NC18951	04.11.42	OB-R-653	20.04.72	PI-C98	05.05.49	PP-SAD	20.10.68	TAM-23	28.09.72
NC1946	17.01.42	OB-XAU-654	24.12.64	PK-AFV	03.03.42	PP-SDD	15.08.52	TAM-24	25.09.72
NC19470	04.01.45	OE-FDA	02.05.59	PK-AFW	24.01.42	PP-SLL	04.08.63	TAM-30	19.01.74

TAM-34	11.11.74
TC-ACA	19.11.51
TC-ARK	03.04.54
TC-BAG	05.01.54
TC-BAL	25.03.50
TC-EFE	28.06.62
TC-EGE	25.09.53
TC-ETI	03.02.64
TF-AIO	03.05.67
TF-ISA	23.02.67
TF-ISG	31.01.51
TF-ISI	29.05.47
TG-AGA	18.11.75
TG-AHA	24.05.56
TG-AJA	08.10.54
TG-AKA	30.09.77
TG-AMA	17.02.75
TG-APA	05.04.62
TG-ATA	26.07.78
TG-BAC	03.11.80
TG-LAM	30.05.78
TG-PAW	20.07.78
TG-SAB	07.05.79
TG-SAB	16.01.83
TI-1002	15.06.53
TI-1005C	15.08.59
TI-1006C	12.05.61
TI-1023	25.05.60
TI-107	01.07.47
TI-161	24.04.48
TL-KAA	20.01.66
TT-EAB	28.01.78
TT-LAG	16.02.76
UN-202	20.09.62
UN-203	oo.oo.61
URSS-C	25.04.41
VH-ACB	19.03.43
VH-AET	10.03.46
VH-ANJ	01.04.65
VH-ANK	02.09.48
VH-ANM	07.09.46
VH-AOG	15.12.55
VH-AOH	03.06.47
VH-BBV	14.03.54
VH-BZA	12.01.56
VH-CAQ	27.03.51
VH-CDC	13.11.45
VH-EDC	24.04.94
VH-INI	11.12.60
VH-MAE	17.07.72
VH-MMA	23.02.90
VH-MME	02.07.49
VH-PAT	08.04.61
VH-PNB	11.04.72
VH-SMH	12.10.50
VH-TAT	08.08.51
VH-UZJ	29.12.48
VH-UZK	08.11.48
VP-BBN	21.11.60
VP-CAT	21.12.49
VP-KJT	29.08.63
VP-KKH	18.05.55
VP-YFD	25.01.47
VP-YKO	23.02.55
VP-YRX	22.11.61
VR-AAA	26.03.65
VR-AAM	12.04.64
VR-AAN	23.11.66
VR-HDG	24.02.49
VR-HDQ	11.07.49
VR-HDW	13.09.49
VR-HEP	13.01.51
VT-ARH	20.08.57
VT-ATI	13.11.47
VT-ATS	17.07.50
VT-ATT	26.03.71
VT-ATU	25.02.54
VT-AUA	01.09.57
VT-AUD	09.05.53
VT-AUF	10.01.47
VT-AUG	27.12.47
VT-AUJ	14.04.53
VT-AUL	03.06.63
VT-AUN	30.04.52
VT-AUO	21.11.51
VT-AUQ	17.10.65
VT-AUV	05.05.57
VT-AXA	26.08.61
VT-AXD	09.05.53
VT-AXE	19.02.52
VT-AYG	24.05.62
VT-AZC	21.06.47
VT-AZV	07.12.61
VT-AZX	30.08.55
VT-AZZ	oo.02.49
VT-CCA	15.09.51
VT-CCD	18.05.56
VT-CDZ	16.01.49
VT-CFB	13.05.57
VT-CFK	13.12.50
VT-CFL	18.09.47
VT-CGB	15.09.52
VT-CGG	03.01.60
VT-CGI	29.03.59
VT-CGM	18.04.50
VT-CGN	21.03.56
VT-CHB	17.05.50
VT-CHF	12.12.53
VT-CHT	12.07.51
VT-CJD	05.04.50
VT-CKU	14.11.51
VT-CLA	21.10.47
VT-CLE	12.11.52
VT-CMD	07.04.64
VT-COA	31.12.51
VT-COI	25.11.50
VT-COJ	25.06.58
VT-COK	08.02.52
VT-COU	02.04.64
VT-COZ	21.01.55
VT-CPQ	25.01.50
VT-CUZ	29.03.55
VT-CVB	01.02.55
VT-CYH	12.03.59
VT-CYM	09.07.58
VT-CYN	24.03.58
VT-CZC	05.12.70
VT-DAT	26.09.50
VT-DBA	15.05.56
VT-DCM	31.03.56
VT-DDR	25.04.66
VT-DEM	30.04.54
VT-DEU	19.05.78
VT-DFM	oo.oo.87
VT-DFN	10.04.52
VT-DFZ	16.07.62
VT-DGK	19.10.56
VT-DGO	15.05.54
VT-DGP	03.08.59
VT-DGS	10.07.60
VT-DGX	21.09.62
VT-DTH	17.01.69
VT-EEL	05.04.77
XA-DEE	28.07.46
XA-DIK	08.03.55
XA-DUH	26.09.49
XA-DUK	16.12.49
XA-FOZ	11.11.46
XA-FUW	12.06.67
XA-GAM	12.09.49
XA-GEV	10.04.68
XA-GIC	14.09.53
XA-GOC	13.01.48
XA-GOR	08.10.51
XA-GUN	25.03.54
XA-HOU	10.10.49
XA-HUS	28.09.60
XA-IOR	29.01.86
XA-SAE	31.12.68
XB-DYP	19.01.89
XC-BII	17.05.67
XC-CFE	22.03.70
XH-SAA	06.01.59
XH-SAF	29.08.57
XH-SAG	17.12.55
XH-TAR	08.09.53
XT-T72	10.02.49
XU-GAJ	22.02.75
XU-HAK	19.01.75
XU-KAL	19.01.75
XV-NIC	16.09.65
XV-NID	10.11.62
XV-NIE	17.11.73
XW-PAD	oo.oo.61
XW-PFM	07.12.67
XW-PGJ	02.01.70
XW-PHV	03.12.73
XW-PHW	07.07.72
XW-PKD	12.09.73
XW-PKT	03.07.74
XW-TAD	24.02.68
XW-TDA	02.10.72
XW-TDC	23.07.70
XW-TDF	24.03.76
XW-TDI	30.06.71
XW-TDJ	23.12.69
XW-TDM	19.05.73
XW-TDO	29.06.70
XW-TDR	24.03.76
XW-TFC	21.12.71
XW-TFI	15.12.74
XW-TFL	20.04.74
XW-TFN	28.05.74
XY-ACC	13.11.49
XY-ACL	10.01.53
XY-ACQ	02.09.55
XY-ACR	24.05.69
XY-ACS	10.06.63
XY-ADB	19.03.57
XY-ADC	08.08.56
YA-AAA	oo.oo.63
YA-AAB	15.01.69
YA-AAD	02.11.59
YE-AAB	03.11.58
YK-AAE	24.02.56
YK-AAF	21.12.53
YK-ACB	06.02.67
YS-22	03.06.45
YS-30	30.04.47
YU-ABC	27.11.47
YU-ABE	08.06.51
YU-ABH	25.08.62
YU-ABK	08.01.68
YU-ACB	20.02.65
YU-ACC	22.10.51
YV-610C	14.06.95
YV-761C	17.12.94
YV-AGU	23.02.48
YV-AVN	20.04.48
YV-C-AFA	12.04.57
YV-C-AFE	28.04.60
YV-C-AGI	10.12.54
YV-C-AHI	26.06.48
YV-C-AKE	27.08.72
YV-C-AKU	01.12.59
YV-C-ALU	21.05.55
YV-C-AMP	18.12.54
YV-C-AMU	20.03.47
YV-C-AQC	21.06.48
YV-C-ARG	30.06.50
YV-C-AVG	03.09.57
YV-C-AVU	15.12.50
YV-C-AVX	25.12.52
YV-C-AZQ	10.03.61
YV-C-AZU	29.03.52
YV-C-GAI	08.05.72
Z-WRJ	20.09.88
ZK-AOE	09.08.48
ZK-AOI	23.02.73
ZK-AQT	22.05.54
ZK-AXS	06.11.70
ZK-AYZ	03.07.63
ZS-AVI	15.09.52
ZS-AVJ	15.10.51
ZS-AYB	12.01.49
ZS-BNB	19.04.47
ZS-BWX	20.11.48
ZS-BWY	15.05.48
ZS-BWZ	12.10.48
ZS-BYX	31.12.48
ZS-DAK	28.12.73
ZS-DFB	27.07.52
ZS-DHX	31.08.92
ZS-DJC	06.03.62
ZS-DKR	06.10.70
ZS-EJK	09.10.82
ZS-GPL	26.02.85
ZS-KCV	07.11.93
ZS-UAS	12.04.88

Douglas DC-4

*	05.01.47
*	22.09.66
*	14.04.70
*	17.05.79
41-107452	21.04.45
41-32939	15.01.43
4X-ACA	02.01.49
4X-ACD	05.02.50
4X-ADN	24.11.51
5R-MAD	19.07.67
7T-VAC	11.06.65
7T-VAU	11.04.67
9Q-CAG	07.01.87
9Q-CAM	26.11.77
9Q-CBH	07.04.74
9Q-CBK	23.08.88
A2-ZER	04.03.74
B-1801	oo.oo.74
B-1811	15.01.74
C-114	15.02.47
C-FIQM	29.03.90
C-FJRW	oo.12.81
C-FQIX	01.06.79
C-GPFG	16.06.87
CF-CPC	21.07.51
CF-EDN	13.11.50
CF-EPU	28.09.68
CF-ILI	04.11.59
CF-MCF	11.08.57
CP-1090	13.01.84
CP-1206	24.03.84
CP-1208	26.01.77
CP-1352	12.01.79
CP-1404	08.06.83
CP-1653	09.09.88
CP-609	05.02.60
CP-717	29.05.64
CP-747	29.05.64
CS-TSB	oo.oo.48
CU-T188	25.04.51
CU-T397	06.12.52
D-ABEB	17.06.61
D-ALAF	03.11.57
EP-ADK	04.08.61
F-BBDB	22.01.50
F-BBDC	10.04.48
F-BBDE	12.06.50
F-BBDL	12.07.48
F-BBDM	14.05.50
F-BBDO	03.02.51
F-BBDS	20.10.49
F-BDRI	18.07.51
F-BELB	08.12.50
F-BELK	20.04.58
F-BELL	01.05.69
F-BELO	28.11.49
F-BFCP	28.05.69
F-BFGQ	04.04.54
F-BFGR	07.02.53
F-BFVO	06.11.52
F-BFVT	03.06.55
F-BHKY	02.11.57
F-BMHU	08.03.67
F-OCNU	oo.07.69
FAC.1106	18.12.79
G-AJPL	04.02.49
G-APIN	17.09.61
G-APNH	18.03.71
G-APYK	03.06.67
G-ARJY	19.06.61
G-ARLF	08.10.61
G-ARSF	28.12.62
G-ASOG	21.01.67
HB-ILA	15.05.60
HB-ILE	13.12.50
HB-ILO	14.12.51
HC-AON	14.04.70
HI-168	23.06.69
HK-1027	27.12.73
HK-130	28.01.62
HK-1309	30.06.75
HK-135	23.06.59
HK-136	11.08.81
HK-171	21.01.70
HK-172	15.01.76
HK-1808	19.06.86
HK-654	17.07.75
HK-728	24.07.74
HK-730	15.01.66
HP-382	10.07.63
HS-POA	13.07.51
HS-POS	11.03.51
HZ-AAF	25.09.59
JA6003	10.04.62
JA6011	30.09.57
LV-ABI	27.09.49
LV-ABL	12.08.47
LV-ABQ	17.06.53
LV-AFG	13.01.48
LV-AHZ	08.12.57
LV-JPG	19.02.71
N111AV	oo.oo.82
N122AC	oo.oo.81
N174DP	04.03.77
N188S	30.06.64
N229A	27.03.53
N30061	14.11.61
N30062	06.10.55
N30070	15.06.54

N300JT 29.06.83
N3373F 14.07.81
N37474 oo.02.58
N3821 07.03.69
N384 10.03.64
N39AP 02.01.75
N44904 14.06.79
N44905 15.05.79
N45342 19.01.52
N4726V 28.03.64
N480G 10.11.69
N48762 28.10.60
N4989P 21.06.95
N54083 oo.oo.48
N5519V 22.03.61
N62433 24.08.92
N63396 24.09.59
N65143 26.03.52
N67109 30.04.90
N68736 13.05.57
N74644 30.03.51
N74685 14.01.51
N74AF 03.02.92
N79992 17.11.51
N79998 15.08.49
N8060C 19.11.79
N811E 09.10.93
N8342C 21.12.48
N86574 07.01.53
N88727 01.11.49
N88839 18.04.57
N88852 17.11.55
N88899 11.04.52
N88900 12.09.59
N88909 18.04.78
N88942 20.03.53
N90426 oo.oo.48
N90427 28.09.68
N90433 24.09.55
N90449 02.03.57
N95425 23.06.50
N96361 23.12.86
N98AS 28.03.81
N9982H 24.05.69
NC30046 29.05.47
NC30050 24.12.46
NC30051 08.10.46
NC37478 10.03.48
NC44567 06.02.47
NC45345 28.09.48
NC56743 02.12.46
NC88729 11.10.46
NC88785 27.10.48
NC88814 30.05.47
NC88842 13.06.47
NC88911 20.09.47
NC88920 26.10.47
NC90904 03.10.46
NC91009 30.11.47
NC91068 12.09.46
NC91077 23.07.47
NC91086 23.07.47
NC95412 06.01.47
NC95422 12.03.48
NX30065 29.05.46
OB-PAZ-228 02.10.55
OB-R-148 08.12.67
OB-R-247 31.12.76
OB-R-769 04.08.65
OB-R-778 14.01.70
OB-SAF-175 12.12.48
OD-ADI 28.12.68
OD-ADO 21.01.63
OD-AEB 12.12.63
OD-AEC 09.07.62
OO-ADN 15.09.61
OO-CBE 13.05.48
OO-CBG 18.09.46
OO-DEP 29.11.64
OO-SBL 22.04.60
PH-TAE 05.11.46
PH-TCF 16.06.48
PI-C100 11.01.47
PI-C107 28.10.49
PP-AXS 04.11.57
PP-BTQ 04.04.64
PP-BTR 05.05.63
PP-LEM 01.02.58
PP-LEQ 12.08.58
PP-LET 02.04.69
PP-LEW 06.11.68
SE-BBG 26.10.47
TAM-52 10.01.74
TF-IST 23.10.63
TF-RVC 14.09.50
TF-RVH 27.01.52
TJ-ABC 13.06.61
TT-DAA oo.oo.72
TT-NAA 29.01.78
VH-ANA 26.06.50
VH-AND 16.10.52
VH-TAA 24.05.61
VP-YTY oo.oo.68
VR-HEU 23.07.54
VT-CYK 30.12.49
VT-CZT 03.05.62
VT-DIA 08.09.58
VT-DIC 07.05.62
XA-FOW 25.06.46
XA-GUU 22.09.48
XA-HEG 15.11.56
XV-NUG 20.09.69
XV-NUH 24.09.72
XV-NUI 19.03.73
XV-NUJ 12.03.75
XW-PKH oo.05.75
XW-PKO 10.04.75
XW-PND 24.03.76
XW-PNF 24.03.76
XW-PNI 24.03.76
XW-TAF 24.03.76
XW-TDE 11.02.72
YA-BAG 21.11.59
YK-AAR 01.09.60
YK-ADA 02.10.64
ZS-CIG 03.09.60

Douglas DC-5

VH-CXA oo.oo.42

Douglas DC-6

* 08.10.83
* 23.01.88
4W-ABL 11.11.76
AN-BFN 06.06.79
B-2005 22.12.69
C-FPWA 02.08.74
C-GBYA 26.06.89
CC-CCG 06.02.65
CF-CUP 29.08.56
CF-CUQ 08.07.65
CP-1338 23.05.78
CP-1650 08.05.87
CP-1651 20.06.93
CP-1654 08.03.93
CP-1953 oo.oo.90
CP-2251 03.03.94
CP-698 26.09.69
CP-707 15.03.63
CP-926 17.06.71
CP-947 06.02.74
ET-AAY 12.03.70
F-BGOD 20.02.56
F-BGTZ 26.12.58
F-BHMS 02.10.64
F-BIAO 03.05.63
F-BNUZ 22.10.71
F-ZBAE 22.04.85
F-ZBBU 19.07.86
G-APOM 26.03.61
HB-IBT 07.05.69
HI-146 19.10.71
HI-251 oo.11.86
HI-92 oo.10.84
HK-1276W 21.05.94
HK-1389 04.02.76
HK-1702 10.02.91
HK-1705 29.04.78
HK-1706 19.02.82
HK-1707 08.12.78
HK-1776 22.07.95
HK-3511 20.06.91
HK-3531X oo.06.94
HK-756 10.07.75
HP-1018 oo.oo.84
HP-539 10.04.72
HR-AIV oo.01.86
HR-AKZ 25.02.89
HR-SAG 20.02.67
HR-TNG 30.06.66
HR-TNO 27.01.73
I-DIMO 08.03.62
I-LEAD 24.11.56
I-LINE 18.12.54
I-LUCK 23.12.51
LN-FOM 02.11.69
LV-ADS 07.09.60
LV-ADV 10.06.58
LV-ADW 19.07.61
N111AQ oo.06.78
N1125J oo.03.93
N11817 22.02.60
N122A 27.08.78
N151 05.03.92
N1597F 26.11.93
N19CA oo.07.79
N2878F 06.07.85
N2949F oo.oo.81
N33VX 21.07.88
N3486F 30.11.81
N3493F 05.05.78
N34954 01.02.57
N371 02.12.89
N37512 04.04.55
N37519 17.10.65
N37543 30.06.51
N37550 24.08.51
N37559 01.11.55
N43865 20.07.79
N5026K 22.06.59
N575 28.08.58
N6103C 24.02.78
N6113C 16.11.70
N6118C 21.07.61
N614SE 26.10.73
N640NA 31.01.67
N6523C 17.02.78
N6541C 23.04.65
N6579C 18.06.65
N74841 24.01.67
N77DG 17.02.75
N8224H 24.02.67
N8225H 06.01.60
N8228H 15.11.61
N844TA 28.11.80
N84BL 05.05.90
N9018N 15.09.80
N901MA 08.02.76
N90728 29.11.49
N90773 10.09.61
N90779 18.09.60
N90806 12.07.53
N90891 11.02.52
N90893 14.02.53
N91303 20.04.53
N92860 28.04.84
N94BL 24.08.92
N96040 08.12.78
NC37506 17.06.48
NC37510 24.10.47
OB-R-920 oo.oo.69
OD-AEL 10.03.66
OD-AEY 28.12.68
OH-KDC 02.01.74
OO-ABG 18.02.66
OO-CTL 20.12.70
OO-SDB 13.02.55
OO-VGB 04.10.74
OY-EAN 23.12.67
OY-EAP 13.04.63
PH-DFO 23.08.54
PH-TKW 01.05.48
PH-TPJ 22.03.52
PI-C291 15.11.48
PI-C294 14.01.54
PI-C950 06.06.65
SE-BDA 04.07.48
SE-BDP 28.11.57
SE-BDY 18.09.61
SU-ANL 24.01.67
SX-DAE 08.12.69
SX-DAI 05.11.70
TF-AAE 02.06.69
TF-OAE 06.05.74
TG-ABA-C oo.03.71
TG-ADA 08.06.78
TR-LXN 26.02.79
V5-WAC oo.07.94
VH-BPE 29.10.53
XA-JOR 01.09.51
XA-LAU 30.01.67
XA-MOO 20.08.69
XA-MUV 02.11.76
XA-NAH 29.06.67
XA-SAR 25.08.70
XA-SEA 15.05.93
XV-NUC 02.04.69
XW-PEH 01.02.72
YK-AEB 07.04.63
YN-BFO 21.12.87
YN-BVI 13.11.80
YN-CBE 24.05.88
YS-05C 29.06.88
YS-35C 02.05.76
YS-37C 20.01.84
YV-502C 18.09.92

Douglas DC-7

5T-TAR 03.10.68
CP-1048 13.12.73
CP-1291 27.07.80
EC-ATQ 02.10.70
EC-BEO 29.06.69
EI-AWG 03.03.74
F-BIAP 24.09.59
G-ARUD 04.03.62
G-ASID 28.09.64
HC-AIP oo.03.66
HI-599CT 18.02.93
HI-619SP 06.11.92
HK-1300 01.05.73
HR-ALY 24.03.93
I-DUVO 26.02.60
JY-ACO 05.06.67
JY-ACP 05.06.67
N2282 12.09.66
N244B 05.09.78
N284 08.12.88
N285 22.10.62
N290 03.06.63
N292 14.07.60
N296 21.06.73
N302G oo.oo.79
N312A 20.06.61
N317A 26.09.61
N356AL 30.04.78
N357AL 24.06.79
N4059K 30.12.66
N4871C 16.12.61
N4891C 15.11.59
N4SW 05.09.79
N500AE 31.12.72
N51702 29.10.62
N5903 09.10.86
N5904 25.03.58
N5905 19.11.61
N6302C oo.oo.oo
N6310J 03.12.83
N6314J 11.09.77
N6324C 30.06.56
N6328C 21.04.58
N6339C 18.05.66
N68N 24.04.64
N73675 oo.oo.77
N740PA 20.02.59
N745PA 18.02.61
N7466 27.09.68
N75000 oo.oo.80
N762Z 02.07.68
N808D 28.06.57
N809D 17.07.64
N815D 30.11.62
N816D 28.11.80
N8210H 31.01.57
N8219H oo.oo.80
N823D 01.05.82
N824D 16.10.65
N831D 20.07.64
N843D 29.07.63
N846D 10.03.58
N848D 01.10.92
N849D 08.02.65
OD-AEI 28.12.68
OD-AEK 28.12.68
OO-SFA 18.05.58
PP-PDL 14.10.61
PP-PDM 08.04.63
PP-PDO 01.11.61
SE-CCC 08.02.65
SE-ERC 20.01.68
SE-ERP 05.06.69
TZ-ARC 04.10.76
VR-BCT 26.07.70
VR-BCY 07.12.68

Douglas DC-8

5N-ARH 01.04.88
9G-MKB 15.02.92
C-GMXQ 11.07.91
C-GSWX 03.04.86

CF-CPK 04.03.66
CF-TIJ 21.06.73
CF-TIW 05.07.70
CF-TJM 19.05.67
CF-TJN 29.11.63
CU-T1200 18.03.76
CU-T1201 06.10.76
EC-ARA 06.07.72
EC-BMX 03.03.78
F-BOLL 10.03.84
HB-IDD 13.09.70
HB-IDE 07.10.79
HC-BKN 18.09.84
HK-2380X 18.09.84
HK-3753X 15.10.92
HK-3816X 21.05.94
HS-TGU 10.05.73
I-DIWB 06.05.72
I-DIWD 06.07.62
I-DIWF 02.08.68
I-DIWZ 15.09.70
JA8012 15.06.72
JA8013 24.09.72
JA8040 28.11.72
JA8048 17.09.82
JA8051 27.09.77
JA8054 13.01.77
JA8061 09.02.82
LN-MOO 13.01.69
LV-LTP 13.12.92
N1802 28.04.68
N1809E 06.06.89
N43UA 28.04.95
N4863T 08.09.70
N4909C 27.11.70
N6164A 23.03.74
N715UA 11.09.80
N730PI 12.03.91
N782AL 16.02.95
N785FT 27.07.70
N794AL 15.02.92
N8013U 16.12.60
N802E 30.03.67
N802WA 08.09.73
N8040U 11.07.61
N8047U 18.12.77
N8053U 11.01.83
N8082U 29.12.78
N814CK 18.08.93
N8170A 11.12.77
N8607 25.02.64
N8634 17.10.69
N8635 04.03.77
N8784R 24.11.65
N913R 15.01.81
N950JW 12.12.85
OB-1316 10.08.89
OB-1456 28.03.92
OB-R-1143 01.08.80
PH-DCH 29.06.68
PH-DCL 30.05.61
PH-MBH 04.12.74
PP-PDT 20.08.62
PP-PEA 04.03.67
RP-C803 18.04.77
SE-DBE 19.04.70
TF-FLA 16.11.78
XA-NUS 24.12.66
XA-PEI 13.08.66
XA-XAX 19.01.61
ZK-NZB 04.07.66

Douglas DF
J-ANES 10.08.38

Douglas Dolphin
NC12212 02.11.33
V111 05.12.36
V126 05.08.41
V130 oo.08.35

Douglas M-2
* 08.12.26
NC1476 10.12.27

EH.101
PP.2 21.01.93
ZF644 07.04.95

El Gavilan 358
* 02.02.92

Embraer Bandeirante
CX-BJE/T584 26.06.77
CX-BJK/T581 25.02.91
G-HGGS 19.11.84
G-OEAA 24.05.95
G-ZAPE 13.01.93
HK-2593 04.08.85
HK-2594 14.08.95
HK-2638 23.01.85
HK-2651 02.08.81
HK-2743 oo.oo.85
HK-3195X 15.12.90
HP-1202AC 19.07.94
N1356P 13.03.86
N65DA 24.05.88
N731A 08.10.91
N95PB 06.05.89
N96PB 06.12.84
OH-EBA 14.11.88
P2-RDL oo.oo.84
P2-RDM 06.02.87
P2-RDS 15.04.92
PP-SBB 08.02.79
PP-SBC 28.06.84
PP-SBE 27.02.75
PP-SBH 07.10.83
PP-SBJ 23.03.93
PT-FAW 26.09.90
PT-GJN 23.06.85
PT-GJW 07.05.94
PT-GJZ 18.04.84
PT-GKA 11.10.85
PT-GKC 24.05.82
PT-GKL 18.04.84
PT-GKT 31.01.78
PT-GKW 31.01.78
PT-GLB 24.02.81
PT-LRJ 27.09.91
PT-SCU 11.11.91
PT-SFH 07.10.83
PT-TBA 28.10.76
PT-TBB 03.02.92
PT-TBD 22.01.76
PT-TBF 04.11.78
XC-COX 31.08.88
XC-DAK 07.07.80
YV-245C 15.06.92
ZS-LGP 01.03.88

Embraer Brasilia
F-GEGH 21.12.87
N219AS 19.09.86
N24706 29.04.93
N256AS 21.08.95
N270AS 05.04.91
N33071 11.09.91
PT-SLI 12.05.93

Enstrom 280
HB-XET 27.01.78

FMA Guarani
LV-LAE 23.01.94

Fairchild 51
CF-AUX 27.05.38

Fairchild 71
CF-AJP 15.08.33
CF-AUJ 03.10.40
NC153H oo.02.34
NC9145 07.12.29
NC9170 06.01.34
NC9172 oo.11.33
NC9726 oo.06.29
NC9737 14.08.30
NC9765 20.09.33
VO-AFG oo.04.40

Fairchild 82
* 23.04.37

Fairchild C-119
* 11.03.54
* 06.05.54
* 16.09.87
N13626 08.05.83
N15509 21.04.84
N3560 10.06.78
N8682 27.06.81
N90268 05.07.80

Fairchild C-123
* 06.12.72
* oo.12.72
* 12.02.73
* 27.07.74
* 03.09.89
57-6293 27.12.71

Fairchild C-82
* 29.10.57
CP-665 24.08.60
CP-677 15.03.70
CP-678 26.11.60
CP-983 27.01.77
PP-CEF 16.01.58
PP-CEH 11.01.58
PP-CEM 26.01.60
PT-DNZ 28.10.70

Fairchild F-27/FH.227
C-FQBL 29.03.79
C6-BDQ 31.07.78
CC-CBR 20.04.79
CC-CJE 09.12.82
CF-GND 12.06.68
CF-GNG 20.12.69
CF-PAP 08.02.69
CP-1117 02.06.80
CP-1175 22.01.80
CP-862 16.03.84
F-GBRS 05.07.79
F-GCPS 04.03.88
F-GCPZ 23.03.91
F-GGDM 12.04.89
F-GHXA 10.05.90
HC-ADV 07.11.60
HK-1139 05.02.72
HK-1492 05.03.75
N1027 09.05.58
N2703 17.01.63
N2707 24.08.63
N2712 10.03.67
N273RD 24.08.92
N276RD 24.08.92
N2770R 07.05.64
N27W 04.05.68
N380NE 25.10.68
N4215 23.07.73
N4904 30.08.75
N4905 02.12.68
N712U 10.08.68
N745L 15.11.64
N747L 02.03.78
N757L 16.04.65
N777DG oo.09.81
N7811M 19.11.69
N7818M 03.03.72
PI-C870 14.04.69
PI-C871 08.03.68
PI-C873 09.05.68
PI-C875 06.09.73
PP-BUF 14.03.70
PT-ICA 06.06.90
PT-LBV 16.06.82
PT-LCS 25.01.93
RP-C874 29.03.75
T-571 13.10.72
TC-KOC 10.05.73
TC-KOP 08.03.62
XA-RSV 13.03.92
YU-ALA 19.06.77
YV-C-EVH 25.02.62
ZS-LPI 07.09.84

Fairchild FC.2
* 24.05.33
* 14.03.36
* 27.02.37
* 09.03.39
G-CAGC 12.08.30
G-CAIQ 09.01.29
G-CAJJ 05.02.35
G-CANB 20.12.37
G-CANC 29.04.30
G-CARA 19.06.37
G-CARH 31.07.32
G-CARI oo.05.29
G-CARJ 09.08.29
G-CARM 15.06.39
G-CATR 09.02.33
G-CAVL 04.08.30
NC8023 03.02.31
NC8026 oo.02.31
NC9723 11.03.33

Fairchild FH-1100
N5046F 11.12.92
PT-HFM 13.08.80

Fairchild Pilgrim
NC710Y 06.03.34
NC732N 16.03.33
NC737N oo.oo.36
NC742N oo.oo.36
NC982M 12.02.34

Fairey IIID
G-EBPZ 13.03.27

Farman 63
F-AEFC 11.03.28
F-GEAI 19.05.29

Farman F.190
F-AJDP 29.03.32

Farman F.2200
F-AQCY oo.oo.oo

Farman F.2234
F-AROA 27.11.40

Farman F.30
* 25.05.25

Farman F.303
F-AJIG 18.03.32
F-AJMI 31.10.33
F-AJVS 17.09.32
F-ALHO 01.04.35
YU-SAH 12.09.33

Farman Goliath
F-ADFN oo.05.27
F-AEGP oo.oo.oo
F-AEIE 23.05.28
F-FHMY 10.02.30
F-GEAD 07.04.22
O-BLAN 26.08.21
O-BLEU 27.09.21
O-BRUN 27.09.21

Farman Jabiru
F-AIBX 20.01.28
T-DOXD 20.04.27

Faucett F.19
OA-BBJ-261 18.09.44
OA-BBK oo.oo.oo
OA-BBL oo.oo.oo
OA-BBN oo.oo.oo
OA-BBO oo.oo.oo
OA-BBR 15.09.37
OA-BBS oo.oo.oo
OA-BBU oo.oo.oo
OA-BBX oo.oo.oo
OB-BBP-279 24.06.45
OB-PAA-104 oo.oo.oo
OB-PAB-105 oo.oo.oo
OB-PAD-120 oo.oo.oo
OB-PAE-132 oo.oo.oo
OB-PAF-133 10.09.45
OB-PAG-139 24.10.45
OB-PAK-144 oo.oo.oo
OB-PAR-148 oo.oo.oo

Fiat G.12
I-FELI 09.11.42

Fiat G.18
I-ELIO oo.11.40
I-ETRA oo.12.40

Fiat G.212
G-ANOE 29.07.54
I-ELSA 01.07.48
SU-AFF 02.11.56
SU-AFX 17.10.49

Fleet Freighter
CF-BDX oo.08.38
CF-BJT oo.02.39
CF-BJU oo.oo.44
CF-BJW oo.10.46
XA-DOE oo.oo.46

Focke-Wulf Condor

D-ABOD 22.04.40
D-ACON 06.12.38
D-ADHR oo.oo.41
D-AMHC oo.oo.43
D-ARHW 29.11.44
D-ASHH 21.04.45
OY-DEM 04.09.46
PP-CBI 08.03.47

Focke-Wulf Mowe

D-1380 oo.02.33
D-1388 oo.12.33
D-1430 oo.oo.36
D-1775 oo.08.31
D-1922 oo.oo.30

Fokker 100

PH-KXL 05.03.93

Fokker 50

9M-MGH 15.09.95

Fokker AF-14A

CF-AUD 24.05.34

Fokker C.IV

SSSR-155 29.07.30
SSSR-166 oo.04.29
SSSR-173 oo.02.31

Fokker F-10A

NC279E 23.02.30
NC393E 02.06.29
NC39N 21.12.32
NC5170 36.01.31
NC5358 36.12.29
NC591E 32.12.30
NC810H oo.11.30
NC9700 13.06.29
NC9716 08.09.32
NC999E 31.03.31
X-ABCR 07.08.31
X-ABCS 27.09.34
X-ABEA 24.11.33

Fokker F-27

* 13.02.90
* 08.11.95
5-8815 26.04.92
5A-DBE 28.11.80
5A-DBN 21.11.90
5A-DBR 26.03.81
5A-DDV 06.06.89
5A-DLP 15.04.86
5A-DLR oo.oo.86
5N-AAV 07.10.67
5N-AAW 25.04.77
5N-AAX 04.04.71
5Y-BBS 10.07.88
6O-SAY 20.07.81
6O-SAZ 28.06.89
7T-VRM 25.07.91
9N-AAR 25.01.70
9Q-CBE 10.09.91
9Q-CBH 13.12.92
9Q-CLM 09.01.75
9Q-CLO 13.03.76
9Q-CLP 08.02.80
9Q-CLR 06.01.78
9V-BCU 23.11.71
AP-ALM 06.08.70
AP-ALN 06.07.94
AP-ALO 25.06.64
AP-ALX 13.12.71
AP-ATO 17.12.78
AP-ATT 08.10.65
AP-AUS 08.12.72
AP-AUV 30.12.70
AP-AUW 28.05.73
AP-AUX 23.10.86
AP-AXF 06.06.81
AP-BBF 25.08.89
C-GSFS 04.09.89
CP-2165 22.12.94
CR-AIB 27.03.70
CR-LLD 21.05.72
D-AELB 24.02.90
D2-TFP 26.08.92
EC-BOD 05.01.70
EP-ANA 04.10.90
EP-ASN 20.02.86
EP-MRP 10.10.62
F-BPNF 05.08.74
F-BPUI 24.07.74
F-BSUM 11.08.73
F-BYAH 28.01.79
G-BCDO 19.07.90
G-BMAU 18.01.87
HB-AAI 13.09.64
HL5212 23.01.71
I-ATIP 16.04.72
I-ATIR 30.10.72
I-ATIT 24.05.69
J5-GBB 15.08.91
N148PM 13.01.84
OB-1443 10.09.92
OY-APB 27.12.69
OY-APD 25.01.75
OY-APE 26.05.88
PH-SAB 02.02.66
PI-C501 28.02.67
PI-C503 12.10.62
PI-C504 01.07.70
PI-C527 06.07.67
PI-C532 09.05.70
PK-GFJ 08.09.74
PK-GFP 26.09.72
PK-JFF 05.06.91
PK-KFR 04.11.76
PK-MFD 09.05.91
PK-MFI 18.06.94
PK-PFB 27.04.67
PK-PFC 13.10.80
PK-YPL 08.05.95
PT-LCG 12.02.90
PT-LCZ 06.08.84
S2-ABG 18.11.79
S2-ABJ 04.08.84
ST-AAR 02.07.85
ST-AAS 05.10.82
ST-AAY 06.12.71
ST-ADW 06.06.77
ST-ADX 10.05.72
ST-ADY 16.08.86
ST-AWA 23.03.93
SU-GAD 11.06.86
TC-72 16.03.75
TC-73 16.06.95
TC-75 10.06.70
TC-77 02.12.69
TC-TAY 23.09.61
TC-TEZ 17.02.70
TF-FIL 26.09.70
TU-TIF 25.07.86
TU-TIP 26.06.94
VH-EWL 31.05.74
VH-FNE 25.03.71
VH-FNH 17.03.65
VH-TFB 10.06.60
VH-TQQ 09.06.82
VT-DMA 30.01.71
VT-DMC 19.10.88
VT-DMD 24.07.76
VT-DME 12.08.72
VT-DOJ 21.04.69
VT-DVG 07.06.70
VT-DWT 29.08.70
XY-ADK 25.03.78
XY-ADL 25.06.66
XY-ADM 30.04.74
XY-ADN 29.06.81
XY-ADO 19.08.80
XY-ADP 21.06.87
XY-ADQ 16.06.88
XY-ADS 12.10.85
XY-ADY 03.10.78
XY-AEK 03.02.89
XY-AEL 11.10.87
XY-AEP 06.10.93
YN-BZF 20.04.85
ZK-NFC 17.02.79

Fokker F-28

5N-ANA 02.03.78
5N-ANF 28.11.83
5T-CLF 01.07.94
9G-ACA 11.03.81
C-FONF 10.03.89
EC-BVC 28.12.72
EP-PAV 12.10.94
FAC.1140 28.03.85
HL7285 25.11.89
I-TIDA 09.04.75
I-TIDE 01.01.74
LN-SUY 23.12.72
LV-LOB 15.11.75
LV-MZD 05.01.90
N485US 22.03.92
OB-R-1020 25.10.88
P2-ANB 31.05.95
PH-CHI 06.10.81
PH-FPT 18.09.72
PK-GFU 01.07.93
PK-GFV 02.06.83
PK-GKU 30.11.94
PK-GVC 24.09.75
PK-GVE 11.07.79
PK-GVK 20.03.82
PK-GVP 07.03.79
TC-51 16.08.89
TC-JAO 26.01.74
TC-JAP 30.01.75
TC-JAT 23.12.79
TU-TIK 30.12.89

Fokker F.32

NC130M oo.oo.oo
NX124M 27.11.29

Fokker F.III

CH-153 oo.oo.27
CH-156 oo.oo.26
D-1028 17.08.28
D-180 06.09.28
D-200 16.05.28
D-353 oo.07.35
D-378 oo.07.35
D-447 03.10.27
D-468 08.10.26
D-489 oo.11.28
D-516 30.06.26
D-533 30.06.26
D-575 oo.07.35
D-701 oo.07.35
D-729 22.04.27
D-743 03.06.33
D-OLYK oo.10.36
D-ORIP oo.10.36
D-OTIK oo.07.35
G-AALC 11.09.29
H-MABC 18.05.29
H-NABH 19.10.23
H-NABI 04.11.25
H-NABL 10.11.21
H-NABM oo.07.23
H-NABM 25.06.25
H-NABR 24.07.28
H-NABS 24.04.24
H-NABT 17.05.22
H-NABU 13.04.26
RR7 oo.06.27
RRUAW 11.10.28
T-DOFB 01.11.25
T-DOFD 19.09.27

Fokker F.IX

PH-AFK 04.08.31

Fokker F.VII

* 25.02.27
* oo.04.39
G-EBTQ 31.08.27
H-NACC 09.07.26
H-NACL 21.06.26
H-NACZ oo.oo.25
H-NADH 12.01.27
H-NADQ 12.07.27
NC776 17.09.27
NX703 06.09.27
OO-ADO 28.04.36
OO-AID oo.oo.30
OY-DAC 02.05.33
PH-ACJ 10.05.40
PH-ACT 10.05.40
PH-AEB 10.05.40
PH-AEZ 15.07.36
PH-AFO 06.12.31
PH-AGB 19.10.29
PH-EHE 27.07.37
SE-APR 01.02.48
SP-AAP oo.09.39
n/a 17.03.36
n/a 17.03.36

Fokker F.VII/3m

C3908 20.09.29
C7888 29.03.29
CH-161 30.10.30
CH-193 oo.oo.31
F-AIGT 15.09.31
F-AJBH 22.09.31
F-AJBJ 02.07.37
F-ALGT 23.11.35
G-AADZ 10.06.29
G-AASP 03.04.40
G-ABLU 30.12.33
G-CASC 04.03.31
G-EBYI oo.07.29
G-EBZJ 04.09.29
I-AAXZ 15.04.36
I-AFRO 06.03.39
I-UGRI oo.10.36
NC3080 18.02.29
NC3085 25.11.27
NC53 15.08.28
NC55 18.06.27
NC55 15.08.28
NR1661 oo.oo.33
NX206 30.06.27
OK-ABT oo.oo.35
OO-ADO 10.05.40
OO-AGK 21.04.35
OO-AIE 22.12.33
OO-AIF 21.04.36
OO-AII 07.12.34
OO-AIL 02.06.38
OO-AIN 11.09.30
OO-AIP 31.05.43
P-PAAA 31.07.28
PH-AEO 07.06.31
PH-TOL oo.05.40
PK-AFB 04.02.38
PK-AFD 20.12.38
PK-AFE 16.08.32
PK-AFF oo.10.39
PK-AFG 09.02.42
SE-APR 01.02.47
SP-ABG 35.11.34
SP-AOC oo.09.39
SP-AOE 12.01.38
SP-AOF 06.06.36
VH-UMF 21.03.31
VH-UMG 21.11.36
VH-UNA 06.11.31
X-ABCP oo.07.30
n/a oo.05.36

Fokker F.VIII

H-NADU 22.08.27
H-NAEE oo.04.28
PH-OTO 10.05.40

Fokker F.XII

G-ADZI 15.08.36
G-ADZK 16.08.36
G-AEOT 19.11.36
OY-DIG 17.12.45
PH-AFL 06.04.35
PK-AFI 19.02.42
SE-ACZ oo.oo.46

Fokker F.XVIII

PJ-AIO 25.07.46
VQ-PAF 13.01.39

Fokker F.XX

EC-45-E oo.02.38

Fokker F.XXII

PH-AJQ 14.07.35
SE-ABA 09.06.36

Fokker Universal

* 11.02.38
C-44 15.12.32
C-48 31.10.34
G-CAFU 17.12.39
G-CAGD 30.11.32
G-CAGE 05.01.28
G-CAHG 17.02.28
G-CAHH 29.08.28
G-CAIV 15.12.31
G-CAIX 12.03.31
G-CAIY 06.03.28
G-CAJD 10.12.31
G-CAJH 14.08.28
G-CASD 23.12.29
G-CASE 10.06.33
G-CASF 02.06.30

G-CASJ	13.07.29
G-CASK	31.03.33
G-CASL	29.06.32
G-CASM	04.03.31
G-CASN	04.03.31
G-CASO	16.11.29
G-CASP	26.08.29
G-CASQ	17.11.38
G-CAWB	21.03.37
NC122M	02.12.33
NC326N	28.11.33
NC7242	04.09.28
NC8011	03.12.33
NC9127	28.12.32
NC9129	01.09.34
NC9786	oo.oo.oo
NC9789	31.12.33
NR1776	30.05.32
VH-UJT	06.08.39
ZS-ABR	31.12.31

Fokker-Grulich F.II

D-175	16.06.31
D-757	24.08.29
D-758	26.07.30
D-765	02.05.32
D-766	23.11.31
D-780	22.07.29
D-784	03.08.27
D-OGOT	24.07.34
D-OJIP	24.06.36
D-OVYF	10.06.36

Fokker-Grulich V.1

D-902	oo.12.26

Ford 2-AT

NC2431	04.02.28
NC2432	oo.04.28

Ford Tri-Motor

*	22.12.30
*	29.10.34
*	07.05.35
*	09.12.35
*	oo.03.36
*	03.10.37
*	10.05.38
*	20.02.40
*	20.01.41
*	04.04.41
*	03.07.44
*	07.09.46
*	oo.oo.46
AN-AAR	12.06.45
C-207	oo.oo.48
C-31	24.06.34
C-60	oo.oo.38
CB-CAM-2	26.09.41
CF-AZB	oo.07.40
CF-BEP	02.03.39
CV-FAI	17.04.31
EC-BAB	oo.oo.48
F-31	24.06.34
G-CATX	25.08.28
HC-SBC	05.04.46
HC-SBD	15.11.46
HC-SBI	10.09.46
HC-SBJ	15.11.46
HC-SBK	16.07.47
HC-SBQ	oo.oo.48
LG-AAE	28.09.37
LG-AAH	oo.03.39
N69905	17.08.53
N7584	24.08.92
N7684	21.08.72
N76GC	10.08.81
N8400	14.07.53
N8407	16.06.73
N8419	04.08.59
N9606	06.05.53
N9610	03.07.54
N9642	19.06.56
NC1076	16.01.29
NC1492	12.05.28
NC2492	08.02.30
NC3443	29.12.28
NC403H	16.07.32
NC407H	22.03.34
NC421H	29.04.31
NC422H	20.01.37
NC427H	27.10.31
NC430H	08.09.35
NC431H	24.01.33
NC433H	24.12.34
NC435H	03.09.38
NC4805	15.03.32
NC4806	18.10.33
NC5092	30.01.40
NC5093	oo.oo.42
NC5493	10.06.42
NC5809	14.06.41
NC5811	08.08.36
NC6892	21.11.42
NC6894	15.11.41
NC7118	21.11.30
NC7119	19.12.31
NC7120	oo.oo.33
NC7416	24.06.29
NC7586	01.07.34
NC7683	17.03.29
NC7685	22.06.34
NC7686	31.03.33
NC7687	10.12.28
NC7739	25.06.30
NC7862	01.12.28
NC7863	28.04.35
NC7864	18.05.35
NC7865	20.10.38
NC8403	26.10.34
NC8404	29.05.37
NC8411	15.04.39
NC8413	11.08.38
NC8417	11.06.34
NC8418	01.04.31
NC880	13.10.28
NC9607	29.08.33
NC9609	oo.oo.oo
NC9611	20.12.30
NC9613	08.03.42
NC9636	21.04.29
NC9647	27.01.31
NC9649	03.09.29
NC9650	14.12.32
NC9651	oo.08.43
NC9655	02.09.34
NC9662	09.08.31
NC9664	02.10.32
NC9665	19.08.31
NC9666	10.02.33
NC9674	19.03.29
NC9675	05.06.30
NC9689	19.01.30
NM-7	10.12.34
NR9614	02.06.33
NR9648	21.08.37
NS-1	26.09.33
NX419H	24.11.30
OK-FOR	22.08.30
R-131	02.03.30
R-148	08.04.30
TI-33	25.02.40
TI-51	04.12.40
VH-USX	oo.01.42
VH-UTB	23.10.41
X-ABCO	26.03.36
XA-BCW	05.03.40
XA-DOL	12.05.47
XA-FOH	13.06.46
XA-FON	03.07.55
XA-FUP	06.12.46
XA-GIJ	16.08.49
XB-NET	oo.oo.55
XH-TAN	29.11.44
n/a	26.10.32
n/a	05.03.36
n/a	14.03.39

GAF Nomad

9M-ATZ	06.08.76
N418NE	04.05.90
N5590M	04.05.91
N8071L	12.06.91
P2-DNJ	21.05.77
P2-DNL	23.12.79
PK-MAJ	23.07.79
VH-AUI	25.10.75
VH-BFH	18.01.85
VH-DHU	06.08.76
ZK-NMD	20.07.87
ZK-NOM	25.10.93

GAL Monospar

G-ADIK	oo.05.36
G-ADLM	16.05.36
G-AEDY	10.01.40
VH-UTK	01.07.38
VH-UTZ	06.09.35

GAL Monospar ST-18

G-AECB	07.10.36

Gates Learjet

5A-DAD	05.06.67
5N-ASQ	22.07.83
9Q-CBC	18.01.94
B-98181	17.09.94
C-GPUN	11.01.95
D-CATY	14.12.94
D-CDFA	25.03.80
D-CDPD	18.05.83
D-COCO	07.06.93
D-IHAQ	12.12.65
D-IHLZ	18.06.73
EC-DFA	13.08.80
F-BRNL	oo.12.85
F-BSRL	10.06.85
F-GDAV	30.01.89
F-GDHR	05.02.87
HB-VAM	28.08.72
HB-VFO	06.12.82
HB-VGC	14.01.87
HP-1141P	21.12.89
HZ-GP5	11.01.82
I-AIFA	10.12.79
I-AMME	06.02.76
I-COTO	oo.02.86
I-MCSA	22.02.78
JY-AEW	28.04.77
JY-AFC	21.09.77
LV-MMV	23.09.89
LV-TDF	15.05.84
N100EP	11.05.87
N100MK	21.10.78
N100TA	06.05.82
N101PP	04.06.84
N1021B	06.11.69
N123CB	17.04.71
N123RE	17.10.78
N125NE	21.05.80
N12MK	06.01.77
N137GL	19.01.79
N13MJ	06.11.82
N15TW	08.12.85
N1JR	28.07.84
N20DL	06.05.91
N20M	15.12.72
N211MB	03.03.80
N234CM	16.12.88
N234F	14.11.65
N235R	23.04.66
N25TA	11.04.80
N28ST	31.07.87
N300JA	02.12.79
N302EJ	14.04.83
N316M	19.03.66
N31SK	oo.03.87
N331DP	18.01.90
N332PC	06.01.77
N366AA	31.08.74
N38DJ	12.06.92
N39DM	05.03.86
N40BC	06.07.79
N40LB	25.09.73
N432EJ	25.10.67
N434EJ	09.05.70
N442NE	26.07.88
N44CJ	01.10.81
N44GA	30.01.84
N454RN	26.02.73
N455JA	20.08.85
N456JA	24.10.85
N458J	01.07.91
N482U	14.02.83
N500FM	02.07.91
N500P	16.09.90
N500RW	24.05.88
N501PS	26.05.77
N515VW	17.04.69
N51CA	30.03.83
N51DB	24.10.86
N51FN	02.04.90
N521PA	14.12.94
N535PC	14.02.91
N57TA	13.11.81
N658TC	18.01.72
N690LJ	30.11.67
N711AF	11.08.79
N723GL	12.12.85
N745F	30.07.88
N77RS	04.12.78
N79SF	08.01.88
N801L	04.06.64
N804LJ	21.10.65
N808JA	23.05.82
N81MC	10.11.84
N822LJ	09.12.67
N864CL	09.10.84
N866JS	06.05.80
N873LP	22.09.85
N881FC	24.08.92
N88JF	oo.10.86
N921FP	06.08.86
N930GL	oo.12.89
N959SC	23.07.91
N95TC	20.12.84
N97DM	05.03.86
N984JD	25.02.90
N999BH	05.09.93
N999HG	08.09.77
PP-FMX	30.08.69
PT-CMY	06.04.90
PT-CXK	04.05.73
PT-DVL	12.11.76
PT-DZU	23.08.79
PT-IBR	26.09.76
PT-ISN	04.11.89
PT-JBQ	04.09.82
PT-JDX	26.12.78
PT-KKV	11.01.91
PT-KZY	16.05.82
PT-LAU	10.09.94
PT-LCN	04.04.84
PT-LHU	28.07.92
PT-LIG	09.11.94
PT-LIH	15.03.91
PT-LLL	18.03.91
PT-LMA	24.02.88
PT-OEF	02.05.92
PT-OFK	26.02.93
SX-ASO	18.02.72
XA-BBA	18.06.94
XA-LAN	08.01.93
XA-NOG	02.09.93
XA-SWF	23.06.95
XB-JOY	29.06.76
XC-PGR	01.04.94
YU-BJH	18.01.77

Grigorovich L-1

RRUOC	oo.oo.27

Grumman Avenger

C-FAXS	15.06.79
C-FKCL	29.05.78
C-GFPQ	08.06.82
C-GOBK	30.05.78
N1366N	18.08.74
N3356G	28.07.70
N6825C	04.09.71
N9082Z	28.07.70
N9083Z	02.08.73
N9548Z	18.08.74

Grumman G-164B

ET-AJE	11.08.91
ET-AJM	21.08.91

Grumman Goose

*	oo.oo.43
*	31.05.47
*	02.01.66
*	10.03.66
*	21.08.66
*	19.08.77
*	14.12.77
*	14.04.79
*	18.06.91
C-FBXR	08.10.79
C-FGEC	14.08.78
C-FUMG	04.12.93
C-FUVJ	30.08.79
C-GHAV	06.05.91
CF-BHL	27.01.53
HC-SBB	17.02.49
HC-SBL	03.12.46
HC-SBV	28.04.49
HK-2059	30.11.79
N101LB	oo.07.71
N1045	25.08.78

N121H 13.06.95
N1583V 11.12.74
N18CS 10.04.76
N2021A 21.07.84
N2845D 20.02.82
N3116Y 16.12.92
N33S 10.09.80
N68174 oo.03.64
N742PC 28.08.87
N74676 05.11.78
N7777V 02.09.78
N8777A 05.04.78
N95468 23.01.81
NC16917 oo.04.38
PK-AER 26.12.41
PK-AES 26.01.42
PK-AFS 26.01.42
PK-AKB 02.02.42
TF-RVI 13.03.47
VP-BAE 16.03.47

Grumman Gulfstream 1
F-GIIX 28.06.94
HK-3315X 05.02.90
HK-3316X 02.05.90
N129GP 11.07.67
N181TG 01.06.84
N205M 25.07.67
N68TG 15.07.83
N71CR 11.07.75
N720X oo.02.87
N750BR 13.11.88
N80RD 23.08.90
N91G 24.09.78
XB-CIJ oo.oo.88
XB-ESO 11.10.90

Grumman Gulfstream 2-4
5V-TAA 26.12.74
7T-VHB 03.05.82
HZ-AFM 15.04.91
HZ-AFS 25.01.90
N204C 04.09.91
N204RC 17.06.91
N397F 22.02.76
N400UP 24.07.95
N409MA 03.05.95
N46TE 19.01.90
N500J 26.09.76
N720Q 24.06.74
TR-KHB 06.02.80
YI-AKI oo.02.91
YI-AKJ oo.02.91

Grumman Mallard
JA5067 18.02.64
N150FB 18.03.94
N604SS 24.10.86
N628SS 17.09.89
N632SS 17.09.89
N655SS 17.09.89
PK-AKE 27.01.51
PK-AKH 06.05.70
TR-LSW oo.06.75

Grumman Tigercat
N6179C 26.09.74
N7238C 21.10.74

Grumman Tracker
* 20.08.85
* 07.10.87
C-GHNU 28.08.94
C-GHQY 15.08.86
C-GHQZ 25.07.78
F-ZBAT 24.09.90
F-ZBEG 18.06.89
F-ZBEZ 13.06.87
N427DF 19.06.93
N451DF 19.06.92

Gulfstream Commander 1000
HK-3278 22.03.90

HM Airship No.1
n/a 24.09.11

HS Argosy
9Q-COE oo.06.79
G-APRN 17.04.82
G-ASXL 04.07.65
G-ASXP 04.12.67
N601Z 14.10.65
N891U 19.05.74
N894U 08.07.74
ZK-SAF 01.04.90

HS Trident
5B-DAB 22.07.74
5B-DAE 22.07.74
9K-ACG 30.06.66
9Q-CTZ oo.04.86
B-2208 22.03.90
B-2218 31.08.88
B-260 27.02.83
B-264 14.09.83
B-266 26.04.82
B-274 14.03.79
G-ARPC 28.12.75
G-ARPI 18.06.72
G-ARPS 29.07.69
G-ARPT 03.07.68
G-ARPY 03.06.66
G-AVYD 15.09.75
G-AWZT 10.09.76

HS.125
5N-AWS 31.12.86
5N-AXP 31.12.85
C-FCFL 09.12.77
C-FHLL 18.04.83
F-BKMF 05.06.66
G-AVGW 23.12.67
G-AXPS 20.07.70
G-BCUX 20.11.75
G-OBOB 30.01.90
LV-ALW 11.04.85
N101AD 06.05.91
N1135K 24.02.66
N125E 29.06.83
N235KC 21.11.66
N36MK 28.12.70
N3MF 26.01.79
N400PH 05.12.87
N40PC 28.04.77
N41953 07.04.95
N50HH 02.08.86
N521M 12.12.72
N66HA oo.oo.89
N831LC 16.03.91
N900CD 30.05.94
N984HF 07.11.85
XA-COL 12.10.73
XA-CUZ 26.12.80
XA-KEW 02.05.81
XA-KUT 18.01.88
YI-AKH oo.02.91

HS.748
4R-ACJ 07.09.78
4R-HVA/834 29.04.95
4R-HVB/835 28.04.95
9G-ABW 22.01.71
9J-ADM 04.07.83
C-FKTL 14.08.91
C-GDOV 12.01.89
C-GEPH 29.12.81
C-GFFA 15.09.88
C-GPAA 15.07.79
C-GQSV 03.12.88
C-GQTH 10.11.93
EL-AIH 16.04.83
FAC.1101 22.08.79
FAC.1103 09.01.74
FAC.1104 07.08.83
G-ARMV 11.07.65
G-ASPL 27.06.81
G-BEKF 31.07.79
HC-AUE/683 20.01.76
HC-BAZ/738 oo.07.87
HK-1408 05.07.73
HS-THB 27.04.80
HS-THG 21.06.80
HS-THI 28.04.87
LV-HGW 04.02.70
LV-HHB 15.04.76
LV-HHH 20.01.72
LV-HHI 27.11.69
LV-IEV 15.07.69
N748LL 11.10.83
PI-C1022 21.04.73
PI-C1027 28.11.72
PK-IHA 04.01.89
PK-IHD 23.01.76
PK-IHE 09.01.93
PK-IHK 09.02.77
PK-KHL 09.08.95
PK-OBW 25.01.90
PK-RHS 18.10.77
PP-VDN 17.06.75
PP-VDQ 14.12.69
PP-VDU 04.02.72
RP-C1014 11.07.82
RP-C1015 26.06.87
RP-C1028 03.02.75
RP-C1029 10.05.75
TJ-CCF 28.06.89
XA-SAB 27.07.73
XA-SEV 06.01.72
YV-45C 03.03.78
YV-C-AMY 20.08.68

Handley Page HP.42
G-AAGX 01.03.40
G-AAUD 19.03.40
G-AAXC 19.03.40
G-AAXD 07.11.39
G-AAXE 31.05.37

Handley Page Halifax/Halton
AP-ABZ 09.05.48
F-BCJS 01.12.48
F-BCJX 13.05.48
F-BCJZ oo.12.47
G-AHDL 01.04.49
G-AHDP 09.04.49
G-AHDV 17.12.52
G-AHDX 16.04.50
G-AHWN 06.07.49
G-AHZJ 31.07.47
G-AHZM 16.09.46
G-AHZN 26.09.46
G-AIAP 25.11.50
G-AIHU 05.12.47
G-AIHW 05.06.47
G-AIHX 03.09.48
G-AIHY 28.12.49
G-AIOH 30.05.47
G-AIOI 15.02.49
G-AITC 20.01.50
G-AIWK oo.12.47
G-AIWT 05.09.47
G-AIZO 23.05.48
G-AJNZ 28.09.48
G-AJPJ 20.07.48
G-AJZY 08.03.51
G-AJZZ 21.03.49
G-AKAC 29.04.49
G-AKAD 17.05.48
G-AKBA 25.05.48
G-AKBB 11.02.49
G-AKBJ 01.06.49
G-AKEC 17.12.52
G-AKGN 17.12.52
G-AKGZ 08.10.48
G-ALBZ 10.05.49
PP285 13.02.48
PP325 08.07.46
VH-BDT oo.oo.48
ZS-BUL 25.11.47

Handley Page Hampstead
VH-ULK 31.05.30

Handley Page Harrow
G-AFRL 18.08.40

Handley Page Herald
9Q-CAH 11.09.84
B-2009 24.02.69
CF-NAF 17.03.65
G-AODE 30.08.58
G-BBXI 07.06.84
G-BBXJ 24.12.74
HK-2701 16.09.91
HK-2702 05.11.89
HK-718 02.11.73
HK-721 07.05.72
I-TIVE oo.04.71
JY-ACQ 10.04.65
PI-C869 oo.11.70
PP-SDJ 03.11.67

Handley Page Hermes
G-AGSS 03.12.45
G-ALDB 23.07.52
G-ALDC 09.10.60
G-ALDF 21.08.52
G-ALDH 08.03.60
G-ALDJ 05.11.56
G-ALDK 05.08.56
G-ALDN 28.05.52
G-ALDV 01.04.58
G-ALDW 04.03.56
G-ALEU 10.04.51
XD632 01.09.57

Handley Page Marathon
G-AGPD 28.05.48
XY-ACX 04.08.53

Handley Page O/7
* oo.oo.20
G-EAKE 30.06.20
G-EAMA 14.12.20
G-EAMC 25.02.20
G-EANV 23.02.20
G-EATL oo.04.21
G-EATM 30.12.21
G-EATN 14.01.22
G-IAAC oo.10.20

Handley Page W.10
G-EBMM 24.09.34
G-EBMR 22.09.34
G-EBMS 21.10.26
G-EBMT 17.06.29

Handley Page W.8
G-EAPJ 10.07.23
G-EBBG 15.02.28
G-EBIX 30.10.30
OO-AHK 19.10.29

Hanriot HD.1
CH-77 29.03.22

Harbin Y-12
* 14.05.93
* 13.12.93
9N-ACI 26.09.92
9N-ACS 08.11.93
PNP 224 04.03.95

Heinkel HD.24
D-1165 24.05.29

Heinkel He.111
D-ALIX 12.03.37
G-BFFS 11.12.77

Heinkel He.116
D-ATIO 27.05.38

Heinkel He.12
D-1717 06.10.31

Heinkel He.70
* 25.04.35
D-AHUX 03.11.34
D-UXUV 20.05.37

Heston Phoenix
G-AEHJ 13.02.40

Hiller UH-12
C-FOKQ 28.08.83
ET-AAD 18.03.60
HB-XLF 22.11.80

Hindustan 748
VT-DUO 05.03.84
VT-DXF 18.08.81
VT-DXG 09.12.71
VT-DXI 16.06.81
VT-DXJ 04.08.79
VT-EAU 15.03.73

Howard 250
C-GKFN 09.07.81
N48RM 20.04.79

Hughes 269B
B-15102 04.11.72
B-15103 28.08.70
B-15104 16.09.72
B-15105 23.01.72

- B-15106 28.04.71
- B-15110 31.08.73

Hughes 369

- C-FBVG 24.08.92
- C-GCTV 24.08.81
- C-GRYK 01.06.81
- CS-HCE 29.03.95
- HB-XFL 22.01.77
- JA9454 14.08.92
- LV-WDL 15.01.95
- N1089N 26.06.95
- N16008 15.10.92
- PK-PDH 07.02.76
- PK-PDL 12.07.76
- PK-PEA 04.11.76
- PK-PEC 30.12.76
- PK-PEY 28.06.76
- PK-PHL 20.01.76
- PK-PHQ 01.12.76
- PT-HFE 02.04.80
- PT-HIT 23.12.81
- PT-HKU 18.05.81
- RP-C1280 21.01.78
- VH-MYF 28.11.79
- VH-THI 25.05.78
- ZK-HJJ 23.09.77

Hughes 500

- C-FGSU 28.01.94
- C-GLHS 15.07.94
- C-GPDH 18.08.94
- C-GPHN 28.11.79
- C-GQCA 22.01.82
- D-HDAS 22.09.94
- G-HSAA 10.07.94
- G-HSKY 05.02.86
- HB-XUJ 29.04.95
- HK-3427 03.07.92
- LV-WBL 26.06.94
- N1103N 18.04.94
- N8648F 14.07.94
- OE-XAA 06.04.94
- PT-HIP 28.05.79
- PT-HIR 15.03.78
- RP-C1272 25.09.77
- VH-LLD 20.12.92
- VH-THX 15.11.79
- ZK-HIA 25.04.77

Hunting Percival Prince

- G-AMOT 06.06.58
- PP-NBA 09.03.52
- ZK-BMQ 04.12.60

Hurel-Dubois HD-321

- F-BHHA 30.10.56

IAI Arava

- 3D-DAB 15.01.80
- 4X-IAI 19.11.70
- EL-AJH 08.10.85
- LV-MRX 21.11.79
- TAM-76 02.03.76
- TAM-77 16.03.77

IPTN CN.235

- PK-MNN 18.10.92

Ilyushin IL-114

- RA-54001 05.07.93

Ilyushin IL-12

- OK-DBP 24.11.56
- SP-LHC 18.07.52
- SP-LHE oo.10.52

Ilyushin IL-14

- * 06.07.62
- * 02.01.79
- * 13.05.80
- * oo.02.86
- B-4211 08.10.92
- B-4218 08.10.88
- CU-T819 27.03.62
- DM-SBL oo.02.63
- HA-MAH 17.02.64
- LZ-ILA 04.11.72
- LZ-ILF oo.oo.oo
- LZ-ILG oo.oo.oo
- OK-MCG 01.02.72
- OK-MCJ 11.10.68
- OK-MCK 11.10.68
- OK-MCM oo.01.75
- OK-MCT 10.09.62
- OK-MCV 25.10.73
- OK-MCZ 02.01.61
- OK-OCA 11.02.77
- SP-LNF 14.06.57
- SSSR-04243 oo.oo.87
- SSSR-41803 14.02.90
- SSSR-41807 oo.oo.oo
- SSSR-61683 30.10.79
- SSSR-L1657 03.12.57
- SSSR-L1874 15.08.57
- TZ-ABH 05.11.66
- YR-ILB 09.10.64
- YR-ILL 16.06.63
- YR-ILO 01.03.76
- YR-PCC 04.11.57

Ilyushin IL-18

- * 13.12.59
- * 27.04.60
- * 28.12.60
- * 13.08.61
- * 17.12.61
- * 31.12.61
- * 26.02.63
- * 05.03.63
- * 04.04.63
- * 02.09.64
- * 19.10.64
- * 03.01.65
- * 27.08.66
- * 22.11.66
- * 06.04.67
- * 16.10.67
- * 04.11.67
- * 09.01.68
- * 24.02.68
- * 22.04.68
- * 20.10.68
- * 26.08.69
- * 10.09.69
- * 06.03.75
- * 06.06.80
- * 16.05.85
- 3X-GAB 09.07.67
- 3X-GAX 03.09.78
- B-202 24.12.82
- B-222 18.01.88
- CU-T1270 15.11.92
- CU-T830 10.07.66
- CU-T899 19.01.85
- DM-STF oo.01.67
- DM-STL 26.03.79
- HA-MOC 28.08.71
- HA-MOD 23.11.62
- HA-MOE oo.oo.88
- HA-MOF 23.11.77
- HA-MOH 15.01.75
- LZ-BED 18.01.71
- LZ-BEG 04.09.68
- LZ-BEM 03.03.73
- LZ-BEN 24.11.66
- LZ-BEP 16.06.84
- LZ-BES 21.12.71
- OK-NAA 02.01.77
- OK-NAB 28.07.76
- OK-OAD 28.03.61
- OK-PAF 11.07.61
- OK-WAI 05.09.67
- SSSR-74252 29.02.68
- SSSR-74298 31.08.72
- SSSR-75405 24.04.74
- SSSR-75408 06.03.76
- SSSR-75414 10.05.79
- SSSR-75425 09.05.74
- SSSR-75507 01.10.72
- SSSR-75520 15.02.77
- SSSR-75533 05.06.70
- SSSR-75558 30.01.76
- SSSR-75559 27.04.74
- SSSR-75575 30.10.76
- SSSR-75578 16.10.70
- SSSR-75663 26.08.72
- SSSR-75687 11.05.73
- SSSR-75705 17.08.60
- SSSR-75712 24.02.73
- SSSR-75773 31.12.70
- SSSR-75798 06.02.70
- SSSR-75823 23.08.70
- SSSR-75824 03.08.64
- SU-AOY 29.01.73
- SU-APC 20.03.69
- TZ-ABE 11.08.74
- UN-75915 oo.01.95
- YR-IMB 10.10.64
- YR-IMH 14.08.91
- YR-IMI 21.04.77
- YR-IMK 09.12.74

Ilyushin IL-62

- * 23.03.73
- 889 01.07.83
- CU-T1281 03.09.89
- DDR-SEW 17.06.89
- DM-SEA 14.08.72
- OK-DBF 20.08.75
- RA-86703 oo.10.92
- SP-LAA 14.03.80
- SP-LBG 09.05.87
- SSSR-06156 oo.oo.65
- SSSR-06300 oo.oo.64
- SSSR-86470 29.09.82
- SSSR-86513 06.07.82
- SSSR-86546 21.11.90
- SSSR-86613 21.11.90
- SSSR-86614 27.05.77
- SSSR-86671 13.10.72
- SU-ARN 16.06.72

Ilyushin IL-76

- * 15.04.86
- * 11.12.88
- * 24.03.89
- 5A-DKK oo.oo.85
- 5A-DNF 15.04.86
- 5A-DZZ 15.04.86
- 76794 21.04.93
- EW-76836 31.12.94
- LZ-INK 24.05.91
- SSSR-76466 20.10.89
- SSSR-76569 18.10.89
- SSSR-78780 28.08.92
- SSSR-78781 27.03.90
- SSSR-86905 12.06.90
- YI-AIO 23.09.80

Ilyushin IL-86

- * oo.12.80
- RA-86119 08.03.94

Ju.160

- XVI 25.12.35

Ju.21

- SSSR-122 oo.oo.29
- SSSR-124 oo.07.29
- SSSR-197 20.05.30

Ju.52

- D-2356 27.05.33

Ju.52/3m

- * 05.03.46
- * 23.02.57
- CB-17 03.11.40
- CB-18 15.12.37
- CX-ABB 24.12.40
- D-2201 29.07.32
- D-ABEW oo.oo.43
- D-ABUR 04.01.38
- D-ABVF oo.oo.42
- D-ACBE oo.oo.43
- D-ACBO oo.oo.40
- D-ADHF oo.oo.43
- D-ADQV 16.10.44
- D-AEAO oo.oo.41
- D-AFCD oo.oo.41
- D-AFES oo.oo.42
- D-AFOP 30.08.39
- D-AFYS oo.oo.41
- D-AGAV 26.11.37
- D-AGBI oo.oo.42
- D-AGDA 24.02.42
- D-AGEP oo.oo.42
- D-AGIS oo.oo.41
- D-AGUK oo.oo.42
- D-AHFN oo.oo.42
- D-AHIH oo.oo.41
- D-AHMS oo.oo.41
- D-AHUT oo.oo.41
- D-AJAN oo.oo.41
- D-AKEP oo.oo.42
- D-AKOK oo.oo.42
- D-AKUO oo.oo.41
- D-ALAM oo.oo.43
- D-ALAN oo.oo.42
- D-ALUN oo.oo.41
- D-ALUS 24.02.39
- D-ANAL oo.oo.41
- D-ANAZ oo.oo.43
- D-ANEN oo.oo.42
- D-ANJH 03.08.39
- D-ANOL oo.oo.41
- D-ANOY 02.12.38
- D-ANXG oo.oo.41
- D-ANYF oo.oo.41
- D-APAR 22.02.38
- D-APOO 01.11.36
- D-APXD oo.oo.43
- D-ARDS oo.oo.42
- D-AREN 31.01.35
- D-ARIW oo.oo.41
- D-ASIH 04.12.36
- D-ASLG oo.oo.42
- D-ASOR 24.04.36
- D-ASUI 17.11.36
- D-ATAK 28.11.36
- D-ATON oo.oo.42
- D-AUXZ oo.oo.41
- D-AVAJ oo.oo.41
- D-AVAN 06.11.34
- D-AVFB 01.10.38
- D-AXAT oo.oo.43
- D-AXES oo.oo.41
- D-AXFH oo.oo.42
- D-AYGX oo.oo.42
- G-AHOK 26.01.47
- HA-JUA 18.01.41
- HC-SAB 10.12.38
- HC-SND 02.04.58
- LN-DAE 16.06.36
- LN-LAB 22.05.46
- OA-HHB 26.06.38
- OE-LAL 16.03.36
- OH-ALL 14.06.40
- OH-LAK 31.10.45
- OO-AGU 25.03.44
- OO-AGW 16.11.37
- OO-AUA 14.03.39
- OO-AUB 16.11.37
- OO-AUF 03.04.44
- OO-AUG 01.01.43
- PP-CAT 15.08.38
- PP-CAU 05.02.36
- PP-CAY 13.01.39
- PP-CBC 22.05.38
- PP-SPD 27.08.43
- PP-SPD oo.oo.oo
- PP-SPF oo.oo.oo
- PP-VAL 28.02.42
- XV 11.12.41
- XVII 06.05.39
- XVIII 01.08.37
- XX 30.12.40
- XXI 10.07.00
- XXII 08.12.41
- XXIII 12.03.39
- XXIV 08.12.41
- XXV 26.10.40
- ZS-AJE 29.07.37
- ZS-AKY 16.06.37
- n/a 17.01.36

Ju.86

- * 14.03.39
- * 16.03.39
- HB-IXA 10.07.39

Ju.90

- D-AALU 06.02.38
- D-AIVI 26.11.38
- D-AURE oo.09.44

Junkers A 20

- D-404 oo.oo.34
- D-443 oo.oo.28
- D-IBUX oo.oo.37

Junkers A.50

- P-BAAE 25.04.31

Junkers F.13

- A-3 03.09.30
- A10 03.09.26
- A12 02.09.30
- A16 08.06.24

- A2 00.00.23
- A32 00.00.34
- A4 00.00.27
- A9 05.06.27
- C-30 00.00.29
- C-31 00.00.29
- C-36 00.00.33
- C-40 06.08.36
- C-41 00.00.29
- D-206 27.07.27
- D-207 00.00.34
- D-232 00.00.33
- D-272 00.00.26
- D-290 00.00.26
- D-368 00.00.00
- D-409 00.00.25
- D-422 00.00.30
- D-534 00.00.33
- D-550 00.00.00
- D-560 00.00.27
- D-583 26.05.28
- D-724 02.11.32
- D-OBAZ 00.00.36
- D-OHIL 00.00.35
- D-ONIQ 00.00.27
- G-AAZK 21.07.30
- III 15.12.32
- IV 00.08.37
- J1 00.00.23
- K-SALA 28.05.27
- K-SALB 10.07.28
- K-SALD 16.11.27
- OH-ALI 09.10.35
- R-RECA 22.03.25
- SSSR-L19 00.00.35
- SSSR-L92 00.00.35
- n/a 00.01.26

Junkers G-1
- SSSR-L43 00.00.35

Junkers G.23
- SE-AAE 31.08.32

Junkers G.24
- D-1019 00.04.34
- D-1088 06.01.28
- D-896 00.00.38
- D-899 00.02.29
- D-903 06.11.29
- D-944 00.00.26
- D-946 00.09.28
- D-ALAB 00.00.39
- D-ULET 00.00.35
- D-UQAN 00.00.35
- D-USAH 00.00.35
- I-BAUS 30.04.38
- M-CAFF 17.10.29
- PP-CAB 00.00.38
- PP-CAH 10.11.30
- PP-CAS 00.00.00

Junkers G.31
- D-1137 00.12.28
- D-1427 25.09.28
- D-1473 11.12.28
- VH-UOU 00.00.42
- VH-UOV 00.00.42
- VH-UOW 00.00.42
- VH-URQ 00.00.42

Junkers G.38
- D-APIS 00.00.00
- D-AZUR 00.00.36

Junkers K.30
- SSSR-L718 22.02.32

Junkers W.33/34
- CB-20 13.03.37
- CF-ASI 12.03.32
- D-1649 07.04.30
- D-1826 00.00.30
- D-2017 29.10.32
- D-2018 13.01.33
- D-2072 13.09.31
- D-4 29.04.33
- D-OJIL 04.03.38
- D-OMYI 30.04.35
- I 26.08.32
- I 04.03.35
- II 00.00.45
- III 11.05.35
- PP-CAN 00.00.00
- PP-CAP 00.00.00
- PP-CAR 00.00.00
- SE-AEF 01.12.37
- SSSR-L20 00.00.35
- SSSR-L21 00.00.35
- SSSR-L416 00.07.36
- SSSR-L417 03.10.34
- V 27.11.35
- VH-UNR 22.05.31
- VI 01.09.32
- VI 08.12.41
- VII 08.12.41
- VIII 00.08.37
- ZS-AEB 14.12.33
- ZS-AEC 16.10.37
- n/a 00.03.35
- n/a 12.04.39

Kalinin AK-1
- R-RDAX 20.08.25

Kalinin K-4
- * 18.01.30
- SSSR-202 19.01.31
- SSSR-217 24.08.29
- SSSR-219 25.06.29
- SSSR-225 00.00.30
- SSSR-L47 07.03.32
- SSSR-L5 10.10.31
- SSSR-L52 19.04.32
- SSSR-L60 00.09.32

Kalinin K-7
- n/a 21.11.33

Kaman HH-43
- N100PL 11.12.92

Kamov Ka-26
- HA-MMR 13.07.90
- HA-MNP 04.08.91
- HA-MPG 16.10.93
- RA-19616 31.05.95
- RA-24083 13.12.94
- RA-24309 17.01.94
- UK-19633 06.10.94

Kamov Ka-32
- SSSR-31016 07.10.92

Kavanagh E-160
- VH-NMS 13.08.89

Khioni Konek-Gorbutnok
- RRODE 18.05.25
- RRUOA 25.09.25
- SSSR-107 00.07.29
- n/a 05.06.26

Koolhoven FK.43
- PH-AIL 26.05.33
- PH-AJJ 18.12.35
- PH-AJK 10.06.39
- PH-AJL 10.05.40
- PH-AKB 10.05.40
- PH-AKC 17.12.37
- PH-AKD 10.05.40

Koolhoven FK.48
- PH-AJX 10.05.40

Koolhoven FK.50
- EL-ADV 06.07.62
- HB-AMO 20.09.37

LET Turbolet
- OK-DKD 00.00.00
- OK-FDC 00.00.90
- OK-PDI 13.03.92
- RA-67120 20.01.95
- RA-67470 14.07.94
- RA-67656 26.08.93
- SSSR-67091 21.08.91
- SSSR-67099 27.08.91
- SSSR-67101 14.08.82
- SSSR-67104 28.08.89
- SSSR-67127 07.12.88
- SSSR-67130 04.04.92
- SSSR-67140 29.12.84
- SSSR-67145 17.02.91
- SSSR-67190 29.03.83
- SSSR-67191 00.00.00
- SSSR-67206 03.08.79
- SSSR-67210 18.01.79
- SSSR-67225 04.12.84
- SSSR-67235 26.08.88
- SSSR-67249 24.09.87
- SSSR-67264 14.10.86
- SSSR-67276 04.07.84
- SSSR-67290 07.01.82
- SSSR-67315 19.10.83
- SSSR-67331 12.10.90
- SSSR-67334 18.10.87
- SSSR-67428 31.12.86
- SSSR-67518 19.04.88
- UR-67115 23.01.95
- UR-67536 27.10.93

LET Z-37
- OK-WJJ 12.03.94
- OK-XJI 13.09.93

LTV XC-142
- 62-5921 10.05.67
- 62-5922 00.10.67
- 62-5923 03.01.66
- 62-5925 28.12.66

LVG C.VI
- RR14 00.10.24

Lasco Lascowl
- VH-UGF 14.07.31

Latecoere 25
- F-AISB 20.03.34
- F-AIUT 10.12.32

Latecoere 26
- F-AILG 11.06.34
- F-AIMU 01.02.29
- F-AINF 29.06.28
- F-AIXU 25.10.31
- F-AJCN 30.11.29
- F-AJOM 30.10.32
- F-AJIP 00.00.00

Latecoere 28
- F-AJIQ 02.11.35
- F-AJIX 09.05.33
- F-AJJM 12.10.32
- F-AJNQ 00.05.30
- F-AJOX 27.02.32
- F-AJOZ 00.00.00
- F-AJPA 26.02.34
- F-AJPB 11.11.35
- F-AJPD 10.05.30
- F-AJUU 12.10.30
- F-AJUZ 00.00.00
- F-AJVH 00.00.00
- F-AJVK 29.06.33
- R293 23.06.36

Latecoere 300
- F-AKCU 17.12.31
- F-AKGF 07.12.36
- F-AOIK 10.02.36

Latecoere 32
- F-AISN 15.11.28
- F-AITX 24.02.31

Latecoere 521
- F-NORD 00.08.44

Latecoere 522
- F-ARAP 00.08.44

Latecoere 631
- F-BANU 28.03.50
- F-BDRB 00.00.00
- F-BDRC 01.08.48
- F-BDRD 21.02.48
- F-BDRE 10.09.55

Laville ZIG-1
- n/a 29.11.35

LeO 13
- F-AFDH 14.08.25
- F-AFGP 11.04.25
- F-AGFY 10.02.25
- F-AHBF 19.12.25
- F-AHBI 02.01.28
- F-AHEU 13.01.26

LeO 196
- F-AIGM 12.12.27

LeO 213
- F-AIFD 16.11.33
- F-AIFE 17.09.32
- F-AIVG 31.05.34
- F-AJNS 13.01.33

LeO 45
- * 03.05.43

LeO H.242
- F-ANPB 09.02.38
- F-ANQG 00.00.36

LeO H.246
- F-AREJ 13.08.42
- F-AREK 00.00.44

LeO H.47
- n/a 19.05.37

Letov S-32
- OK-ADB 00.06.34

Lisunov Li-2
- * 04.12.46
- * 06.12.52
- HA-LIF 23.12.54
- HA-LII 23.12.54
- HA-LIK 19.09.49
- HA-LIL 02.10.52
- HA-LIM 09.06.57
- HA-LIO 24.04.68
- SP-LAE 14.04.55
- SP-LAH 19.03.54
- SP-LAL 15.08.60
- SP-LAO 07.10.52
- SP-LBA 29.03.50
- SP-LBC 26.09.46
- SP-LBD 19.05.52
- SP-LKA 15.11.54
- SSSR-04214 00.12.68
- YR-DAC 13.06.64
- YR-TAA 00.00.51
- YR-TAI 21.11.47
- YR-TAN 11.08.66
- YR-TAV 13.08.47
- YR-TAX 08.10.60

Lockheed 10 Electra
- * 00.00.41
- * 00.01.47
- * 27.08.67
- CC-CLE 04.08.47
- G-AEPP 13.12.37
- G-AEPR 14.04.44
- G-AESY 15.08.39
- G-AFCS 19.11.43
- NC14243 07.08.34
- NC14905 23.12.36
- NC14935 18.12.36
- NC16022 05.08.36
- NR16020 01.07.37
- PP-NBC 00.00.00
- PP-NBD 00.00.00
- PP-VAQ 20.06.44
- PP-VAS 07.03.48
- PP-VAU 18.10.52
- SP-AYA 28.12.36
- SP-AYB 01.12.36
- SP-AYD 11.11.37
- SP-BGJ 12.09.39
- VH-AEC 11.02.48
- XA-BAS 09.02.38
- XA-BAU 00.00.00
- XA-BEO 00.00.00
- XA-BEQ 00.00.00
- XH-TAB 17.10.46
- YV-ACE 01.12.41
- YV-ADA 09.02.46
- YV-ADE 14.10.41
- ZK-AFC 10.05.38
- ZK-AFE 07.05.42
- ZK-AGJ 19.04.48
- ZK-AGK 23.10.48
- ZK-BUT 18.02.59

Lockheed 14

*	10.11.44
AN-ACC	22.04.46
CF-TCL	21.11.38
CF-TCP	06.02.41
CR-AAV	23.02.44
CR-AAX	14.11.41
FK459	16.06.43
FK618	30.06.43
G-AFGN	11.08.39
G-AFGO	22.11.38
G-AFGP	04.08.41
G-AFGR	19.01.41
G-AFKD	22.04.40
G-AFMO	15.01.40
G-AFYU	21.12.39
G-AFZZ	24.07.40
G-AGAA	24.07.40
G-AGAR	29.05.41
G-AGDF	23.06.42
G-AKPD	29.10.48
NC17383	08.07.38
NC17389	13.01.39
NC17394	16.05.38
PH-APE	09.12.38
PJ-AIK	13.08.48
PJ-AIM	oo.08.49
PJ-AIP	22.08.42
PJ-AIT	13.08.48
PK-AFM	26.03.42
PK-AFN	13.02.44
PK-AFO	22.01.40
PP-AVA	oo.oo.oo
SE-BTN	14.07.51
SP-BNE	24.07.40
SP-BNG	22.07.38
SP-BNJ	18.08.38
SP-BPM	oo.06.40
VH-ABI	18.01.39
VH-ADT	22.01.47
VP-TAF	oo.oo.oo
VP-TAH	26.08.43
VP-TAK	oo.oo.oo
VP-TAL	18.02.46
YV-ADI	25.07.44
YV-ADO	oo.oo.oo

Lockheed Air Express

NC522K	27.04.34
NC7955	17.01.30
NC974Y	oo.oo.42

Lockheed Constellation

43-10314	oo.oo.oo
4X-AKC	27.07.55
5N-85H	28.11.69
5T-TAC	oo.01.68
5T-TAC	03.06.68
5T-TAG	01.07.68
C-GXKS	21.06.79
CF-NAJ	03.08.69
CF-NAK	17.12.69
CF-TGG	17.12.54
CX-BGP	oo.oo.69
D-ALAK	11.01.59
EC-AIN	05.05.65
EC-AIP	06.03.61
ET-T-35	10.07.57
F-BAZE	26.04.62
F-BAZG	17.12.55
F-BAZI	25.08.54
F-BAZM	11.01.63
F-BAZN	28.10.49
F-BAZS	03.08.53
F-BAZX	24.12.58
F-BAZZ	01.09.53
F-BGNA	03.08.54
F-BGNC	09.08.69
F-BHBC	29.08.60
F-BHBM	10.05.61
F-BHMK	06.12.57
G-ALAM	13.03.54
HH-ABA	11.11.61
HI-260	31.08.79
HI-328	26.10.81
HI-393	oo.10.84
HI-422	oo.oo.88
HI-515CT	05.04.90
HI-532CT	oo.06.90
HI-542CT	03.02.92
HK-163	09.08.54
HK-177	21.01.60
HP-467	30.03.68
LV-GLH	19.06.61
LX-IOK	02.10.64
N102R	24.11.59
N110A	03.01.60
N112A	21.12.55
N116	26.04.62
N119A	19.10.53
N120A	04.08.60
N1554V	14.06.60
N173W	09.06.73
N174W	05.05.70
N189S	29.05.63
N2735A	12.05.59
N2737A	08.11.61
N273R	22.10.77
N38936	22.01.53
N45515	oo.oo.71
N45516	11.05.75
N468C	19.05.76
N5595A	20.06.61
N564E	20.10.71
N566E	24.09.73
N6004C	31.08.50
N6202C	05.08.73
N6212C	28.06.57
N6214C	06.09.53
N6218C	04.12.65
N6219C	18.10.66
N6220C	03.08.61
N65	15.08.66
N6503C	10.11.58
N6901C	06.03.66
N6902C	30.06.56
N6906C	03.04.73
N6907C	16.12.60
N6911C	15.03.62
N6913C	14.12.62
N6914C	15.12.65
N6915C	24.12.64
N6917C	15.12.73
N6920C	09.09.58
N6921C	15.03.62
N6923C	23.09.62
N6924C	15.10.78
N6936C	22.06.67
N7101C	29.02.60
N7115C	26.01.66
N7125C	08.11.60
N7301C	18.12.66
N7307C	03.09.64
N7311C	26.03.69
N7313C	26.06.59
N7314C	09.12.68
N7324C	oo.oo.69
N74CA	22.06.80
N7777C	17.04.67
N8021	06.06.70
N8081H	28.09.68
N86504	01.03.64
N86511	01.09.61
N86523	06.06.66
N88846	22.06.51
N9719C	20.09.65
N9740Z	03.02.63
NC111A	21.01.48
NC86505	26.12.46
NC86507	18.11.47
NC86508	11.05.47
NC86510	29.03.46
NC86512	12.10.46
NC86513	11.07.46
NC88831	24.09.46
NC88845	19.06.47
NC88858	15.04.48
NC90824	25.11.48
OB-R-771	27.04.66
PH-LKM	14.08.58
PH-LKT	15.07.57
PH-LKY	05.09.54
PH-TDF	12.07.49
PH-TEN	20.10.48
PH-TER	23.06.49
PH-TFF	23.03.52
PP-PCF	14.07.62
PP-PCG	28.07.50
PP-PCR	03.03.62
PP-PDA	17.06.53
PP-PDC	26.01.61
PP-PDE	14.12.62
PP-PDG	29.05.72
PP-PDJ	16.06.55
PP-VDA	16.08.57
VH-EAC	24.08.60
VT-CQP	03.11.50
VT-DEP	11.04.55
VT-DIN	19.07.59
XA-MEV	02.06.58
YV-C-AMA	27.11.56
YV-C-AMS	20.06.56
YV-C-ANC	14.10.58

Lockheed Constitution

N7673C	14.07.63

Lockheed Electra

9Q-CCV	21.01.94
9Q-CDG	13.03.95
9Q-CWT	05.02.86
C-FNAZ	31.03.77
C-FPAB	29.10.74
HC-AZJ/2004	04.09.89
HC-AZY/1052	12.09.88
HK-1976	10.07.75
HK-777	27.08.73
HR-SAW	08.01.81
HR-TNL	21.03.90
N121US	17.03.60
N126US	30.06.77
N137US	16.09.61
N185H	22.04.66
N280F	06.07.77
N283F	30.04.75
N357Q	09.01.85
N401FA	12.03.76
N403GN	05.01.79
N4465F	14.07.90
N5003K	11.12.74
N5504	21.03.82
N5516	21.03.82
N5523	30.05.84
N5531	02.07.76
N5532	21.01.85
N5533	04.10.60
N6101A	03.02.59
N6102A	06.08.62
N6127A	14.09.60
N7140C	06.11.74
N851V	19.03.72
N854U	29.01.85
N855U	24.08.70
N859U	18.11.79
N9705C	29.09.59
N9707C	03.05.68
OB-R-939	09.08.70
OB-R-941	24.12.71
PH-LLM	12.06.61
PI-C1060	09.01.72
PK-GLB	16.02.67
PK-RLG	30.11.85
PP-VJP	05.02.70
RP-C1061	04.06.76
YS-07C	oo.02.80
ZK-TEC	27.03.65

Lockheed Harpoon

CP-648	03.12.58
N7250	29.09.90
N7415C	01.05.85
N7428C	oo.10.90

Lockheed Hercules

1600	30.07.82
4X-FBD/011	25.11.75
64-0506	oo.02.70
64-0507	oo.02.70
7T-VHK	01.08.89
9J-RBX	11.04.68
9J-RCY	11.04.68
C-FPWK	11.04.82
C-FPWX	21.11.76
CF-PWO	16.07.69
CN-AOB/4537	04.12.70
CP-1375	28.09.79
CP-1564	16.03.91
D2-EAS	16.06.81
D2-EHD	22.01.93
D2-FAF	16.05.79
D2-THA	08.06.86
D2-THB	05.01.90
D2-THC	07.04.94
D2-THE	09.12.94
ET-AJL	18.09.91
HB-ILF	14.10.87
J6-SLQ	10.06.91
N100AK	30.08.74
N102AK	27.10.74
N130X	03.02.93
N135FF	13.08.94
N14ST	23.05.74
N15ST	04.10.86
N17ST	27.08.83
N24ST	29.12.84
N517SJ	08.04.87
N521SJ	02.09.91
N760AL	24.12.68
N911SJ	12.08.90
N9205T	27.11.89
N9248R	11.10.70
N9267R	16.05.68
OB-R-1004	19.02.78
PK-PLV	23.09.94
S9-NAI	08.04.89
SU-BAA/1270	19.02.78
SU-BAH/1276	29.05.81
TJ-XAC	oo.12.89
TT-PAB	07.03.86

Lockheed Jetstar

5A-DAR	16.01.83
N1EM	25.03.76
N267L	29.03.81
N400M	27.12.72
N520S	11.02.81
N96GS	06.01.90

Lockheed Lodestar

*	09.08.46
*	oo.oo.47
*	15.06.52
*	07.03.55
*	04.09.62
*	02.04.67
*	05.02.69
*	28.12.74
*	19.07.78
C-202	19.03.47
C-801	10.05.47
C-FOZO	oo.08.84
CB-25	21.08.44
CB-26	oo.09.49
CC-CLC	oo.oo.oo
CC-CLD-0100	15.06.53
CF-ETC	11.07.51
CF-FYR	26.12.54
CF-TCU	04.11.49
CP-1024	03.03.74
F-ARTE	24.03.52
F-ARTL	02.07.42
F-BALV	25.12.45
G-AGBW	29.11.44
G-AGCR	13.05.42
G-AGCZ	21.12.41
G-AGDE	17.12.43
G-AGEJ	04.04.43
G-AGIH	29.08.44
G-AGLI	02.05.45
HK-1146	05.01.74
N100GP	21.02.79
N1040G	28.10.82
N1046	17.09.89
N116CA	21.08.83
N211L	12.05.72
N333FB	23.06.83
N520R	11.01.83
N77777	16.03.84
N94537	28.01.52
N94538	28.01.52
NC15555	11.10.45
NC18199	05.10.45
NC25636	27.08.45
NC25687	08.01.47
NC33349	13.09.45
OO-CAK	14.12.45
OO-CAR	24.12.47
OO-GVP	27.07.48
PJ-AKA	11.08.48
PJ-AKB	11.08.48
PP-NAE	15.02.45
PP-NAF	11.10.44
PP-PBD	18.08.41
PP-PBH	21.09.44
PP-PBI	30.08.44
PP-PBQ	22.10.46
SE-BUX	11.01.53
TI-84	04.05.47
VP-JBC	10.04.53
YS-28	17.03.47

YV-AFI	12.02.46
ZK-AHU	13.05.45
ZK-AKX	18.03.49
ZK-CGV	24.04.71
ZK-CMX	26.03.68
ZS-AST	28.03.41
ZS-ASV	01.02.59
ZS-ASW	05.01.48

Lockheed Neptune

N70600	08.02.92
N918AP	29.07.94

Lockheed Orion

NC12221	05.11.31
NC12226	25.03.33
NC12229	17.11.32
NC12277	28.07.33
NC12278	08.12.36
NC12285	15.11.34
NC12286	22.12.34
NC12287	10.01.35
NC13748	30.09.41
NC13749	24.10.36
NC229Y	21.11.33
NC799W	oo.11.47
NC960Y	02.06.33
NC991Y	05.02.32
NR12283	15.08.35
XA-BAY	03.08.36
XA-BDH	06.10.36
XA-BEJ	23.06.34

Lockheed P-3

N924AU	17.10.91

Lockheed Sirius

NC167W	24.12.35

Lockheed Tristar

4R-ULD	03.05.86
D-AERI	27.06.91
HZ-AHK	20.08.80
N11002	30.07.92
N31007	19.04.74
N310EA	29.12.72
N726DA	02.08.85
N781DL	24.08.95

Lockheed Vega

*	oo.oo.oo
AN-ABL	19.02.45
N161N	19.05.61
NC102N	26.03.30
NC102W	04.08.30
NC103W	28.10.30
NC106W	08.12.34
NC160W	01.08.30
NC162W	02.08.44
NC176W	28.09.36
NC194E	27.04.30
NC195E	22.04.33
NC196E	05.03.29
NC198E	05.03.29
NC239M	06.11.41
NC306H	17.10.34
NC31M	25.06.30
NC32E	09.07.34
NC35E	22.09.31
NC392H	oo.oo.oo
NC394H	10.07.30
NC396H	22.03.30
NC4097	24.06.34
NC433E	05.12.31
NC435E	22.11.30
NC46M	04.11.29
NC47M	15.01.58
NC483M	27.04.37
NC48610	09.06.45
NC48M	13.12.38
NC497H	31.01.34
NC49M	14.11.52
NC504K	27.05.30
NC513E	12.08.29
NC536M	04.03.30
NC537M	07.01.31
NC574E	01.03.30
NC5885	19.05.29
NC606	14.09.31
NC624E	20.01.37
NC657E	27.04.33
NC658E	19.08.33
NC7162	05.02.32
NC7425	21.04.35
NC7427	26.05.37
NC7428	17.02.36
NC7894	30.04.30
NC7896	10.02.30
NC8497	12.07.31
NC857E	11.05.31
NC870E	11.08.29
NC891E	01.05.35
NC892E	14.05.30
NC904Y	12.09.34
NC934Y	01.06.34
NC9424	08.05.35
NC959Y	29.09.36
NC965Y	26.08.43
NC972Y	10.10.43
NC974H	10.10.34
NC980Y	09.11.35
NR105N	15.01.37
NR12282	oo.oo.54
NR393H	04.08.29
NR496M	04.11.32
NR500V	03.08.30
NR625E	30.05.40
NR7426	15.05.37
NR7429	18.04.33
NR7805	11.07.33
NR7954	11.08.41
NR7973	05.01.32
NR859E	02.09.29
NR869E	06.07.32
NR869E	oo.06.33
NX308H	16.05.31
NX34E	04.08.29
NX3625	29.03.29
NX4769	03.11.28
NX7430	13.09.28
NX7441	25.07.29
NX913	16.08.27
R-48	oo.oo.48
XA-BAW	26.11.42
XA-BFP	oo.03.41
XA-BFR	05.05.38
XA-BFT	22.02.45
XA-BHG	15.05.37
XA-BHJ	08.01.38
XA-BKG	13.03.40
XA-BLZ	16.11.42
XA-DAH	11.05.44
XA-DAI	23.06.43
XA-DAY	oo.oo.46
XA-DEB	oo.oo.45
XB-KAQ	29.04.49

Loening Air Yacht

NC8042	29.10.28
NC9713	01.01.29
NC9717	03.04.32

Loening Lo-8

G-CARS	16.03.33

MBB BK.117

N117HH	21.06.92

MBB Bo.105

A6-ALE	07.09.90
A6-ALT	06.12.87
EC-DSU	19.12.93
G-AZOM	24.07.84
N2784E	13.06.86
N295EH	16.08.92
N30SV	08.08.92
N911LF	04.11.94
PK-PGP	04.02.95
PK-PGW	18.02.76
PK-PGY	03.08.76
PK-PIW	07.01.88
PT-HHC	02.02.80
SE-JBS	01.11.94

MBB Hansa

5N-AMF	25.07.77
D-CASY	29.06.72
D-CHFB	12.05.65
D-CIRO	18.12.70
N127MW	05.10.84
N320MC	09.03.73
XC-TIJ	11.06.84

Macchi C.100

I-PACE	30.07.41
I-PLUS	06.02.42

Macchi C.94

I-NILO	18.08.38
LV-AAE	oo.oo.oo

Martin 202/404

CP-1317	20.01.77
CP-1318	15.07.81
CP-1440	12.12.79
CP-1570	16.06.87
CP-1704	19.08.85
CP-1738	07.04.90
HK-1485	07.08.74
N13415	10.11.78
N174A	01.12.59
N177A	02.11.63
N251S	01.01.68
N40401	21.08.62
N40403	01.04.56
N40404	15.11.56
N40406	20.11.66
N40412	30.05.70
N40416	19.02.56
N40425	17.09.89
N40427	01.09.74
N40438	16.11.79
N40443	27.06.86
N40445	15.05.82
N40446	09.07.66
N445A	17.02.56
N449A	02.07.63
N453A	10.03.57
N464M	02.10.70
N492A	14.11.57
N496A	17.03.58
N93037	13.10.50
N93039	05.11.51
N93040	07.11.50
N93043	09.04.52
N93050	07.03.50
N93054	16.01.51
N93061	30.12.55
N93202	21.08.59
N93211	12.01.55
NC93044	29.08.48

Martin B-26

N1502	oo.oo.59
N5546N	28.09.95
XB-PEX	oo.oo.65

Martin M.130

NC14714	28.07.38
NC14715	21.01.43
NC14716	08.01.45

Martin Mariner

*	09.11.58

Martin Mars

CF-LYJ	23.06.61
CF-LYM	12.10.62

McDonnell Douglas DC-10

5N-ANR	10.01.87
AP-AXE	02.02.81
EC-CBN	17.12.73
EC-DEG	14.09.82
HL7328	27.07.89
HL7339	23.12.83
N1031F	02.01.76
N1032F	12.11.75
N110AA	25.05.79
N113WA	24.01.82
N136AA	21.05.88
N139AA	14.04.93
N1819U	19.07.89
N184AT	10.08.86
N54629	19.09.89
N68045	01.03.78
N903WA	31.10.79
PH-MBN	21.12.92
TC-JAV	03.03.74
ZK-ZNP	28.11.79

McDonnell Douglas DC-9

5N-BBA	26.07.95
5N-BBE	18.08.94
C-FTLU	02.06.83
C-FTLV	26.06.78
C-FTLY	02.06.82
EC-BII	05.03.73
EC-BIQ	18.02.90
EC-BYH	30.03.92
EC-CGS	07.12.83
EC-CLE	21.03.94
HI-177	15.02.70
HK-2864X	26.03.92
HK-3564X	17.03.95
HK-3839X	11.01.95
I-ATJA	14.11.90
I-ATJC	14.09.79
I-DIKB	07.01.80
I-DIKQ	23.12.78
I-RIBN	17.12.91
I-TIGI	27.06.80
JA8448	18.04.93
LN-RLM	30.01.73
N100ME	06.09.85
N1063T	09.03.67
N1335U	04.04.77
N3305L	30.05.72
N3313L	03.12.90
N3323L	27.11.73
N565PC	17.02.91
N626TX	15.11.87
N8910E	09.02.79
N8948E	28.12.87
N8961E	18.05.72
N8967E	27.11.73
N8984E	11.09.74
N908VJ	09.06.95
N9101	01.10.66
N9103	17.03.80
N9104	16.11.76
N926AX	06.02.85
N931F	18.03.89
N9345	06.06.71
N935F	02.05.70
N954N	20.12.72
N954VJ	03.07.94
N961VJ	21.02.86
N964VJ	18.01.92
N974Z	27.12.68
N975NE	31.07.73
N97S	14.11.70
N988VJ	09.09.69
N994VJ	23.06.76
PK-GND	13.01.80
PK-GNE	11.06.84
PK-GNI	30.12.84
PK-GNQ	04.04.87
SE-DAT	oo.02.87
TC-JAC	21.01.72
XA-DEN	27.07.81
XA-DEO	09.11.81
XA-JED	31.08.86
XA-SOC	21.06.73
XA-SOF	02.09.76
YU-AHR	19.03.72
YU-AHT	26.01.72
YU-AJN	23.11.74
YU-AJO	30.10.75
YU-AJR	10.09.76
YV-03C	02.04.93
YV-23C	05.03.91
YV-37C	27.11.92
YV-613C	19.07.93
YV-67C	11.03.83
YV-C-AVD	16.03.69
YV-C-AVM	22.12.74

McDonnell Douglas MD-81/82

B-2103	26.10.93
B-2141	13.11.93
B-28003	25.10.93
N1002G	18.06.80
N1003G	12.06.88
N18835	02.03.94
N312RC	16.08.87
OY-KHO	27.12.91
YU-ANA	01.12.81

Messerschmitt M.20

D-1928	14.04.31
D-1930	06.10.30
D-2059	oo.oo.35
D-UDAL	oo.oo.43
D-UFON	oo.oo.41
D-UHEN	oo.oo.41

D-UJAR	00.00.43
D-UKUM	00.00.42
D-UMOK	00.00.42
D-UNAH	00.00.36
D-UREK	00.00.42
D-UVOK	00.00.42
D-UXYN	00.00.37
n/a	26.02.28

Mil Mi-17

*	26.09.92
*	05.11.92
HK-3733X	18.05.93

Mil Mi-2

*	05.05.94
*	23.12.94
13343	06.04.93
14134	12.07.93
14235	04.04.93
14398	26.09.92
23414	08.06.93
23463	24.12.92
23578	30.09.93
B-2929	12.09.95
HA-BFC	24.02.95
HA-BFD	22.10.94
OK-PIN	30.05.92
RA-14131	18.03.94
RA-14146	20.03.95
RA-15362	27.03.94
RA-20110	21.05.94
RA-20314	07.05.94
RA-20357	01.08.94
RA-20945	10.01.94
RA-23201	25.12.93
RA-23240	30.10.94
RA-23407	02.08.94
RA-23462	11.05.94
RA-23518	25.07.95
RA-23555	30.11.94
RA-23639	04.12.94
RA-23801	26.03.95
RA-28756	05.06.94
SP-SSD	14.07.90
SSSR-20973	03.04.92
UN-14211	15.12.94
UN-14229	27.06.94

Mil Mi-26

*	00.03.95
RA-06043	15.10.93

Mil Mi-4

9G-OTP	00.00.70
SSSR-N968	00.00.00
TJ-XAP	00.00.00

Mil Mi-6

RA-21001	15.12.94
RA-21040	01.07.94
RA-21170	21.04.93
SSSR-06174	00.08.67
SSSR-21882	19.06.92
SSSR-21896	22.07.92

Mil Mi-8

*	18.09.81
*	03.04.86
*	26.07.89
*	19.11.90
*	27.12.90
*	11.01.91
*	02.11.91
*	20.11.91
*	11.08.92
*	31.03.94
*	04.12.94
*	07.05.95
*	28.05.95
*	24.09.95
*	05.10.95
*	10.10.95
25349	08.04.93
HA-BCN	00.00.93
HA-BCU	24.04.94
LZ-CAP	08.01.94
RA-22226	30.03.94
RA-22285	15.06.93
RA-22315	09.08.93
RA-22347	25.08.93
RA-22554	22.05.93
RA-22752	22.10.94
RA-22793	17.01.94
RA-22813	12.09.93
RA-22912	15.05.93
RA-24102	21.11.94
RA-24104	13.05.93
RA-24450	23.04.93
RA-24459	23.05.93
RA-24472	12.03.93
RA-24527	22.06.93
RA-24721	21.04.93
RA-24728	05.03.93
RA-25203	10.03.94
RA-25329	23.05.94
RA-25345	18.06.93
RA-25613	26.04.94
RA-25740	03.12.93
RA-25904	08.03.93
RA-27076	22.06.94
RA-70869	28.10.92
RA-70914	20.03.93
SSSR-06165	11.07.92
SSSR-22334	02.12.92
SSSR-22384	05.07.92
SSSR-22651	21.09.92
SSSR-22738	12.09.92
SSSR-22831	11.07.92
SSSR-24443	09.10.92
SSSR-24565	15.10.92
SSSR-25356	29.09.92
SSSR-25475	09.09.92
SSSR-25491	25.09.92
SSSR-25840	17.08.77
SSSR-25909	23.09.92
SSSR-27043	30.07.92
SSSR-27070	05.11.92
T9-HAI	04.12.94
TC-HSB	07.04.91
UR-25445	08.07.93
YS-1005P	15.10.93

Mil V 12

*	00.00.69

Miles Aerovan

EC-ACQ	04.09.52
G-AGWO	02.07.47
G-AHDM	28.06.58
G-AHTX	09.11.51
G-AIDJ	22.11.48
G-AIHK	02.10.49
G-AIHL	29.10.46
G-AIKV	12.01.47
G-AILF	20.08.50
G-AISF	29.04.57
G-AISG	14.06.47
G-AISJ	15.07.47
G-AJKJ	25.03.48
G-AJKM	03.05.49
G-AJKP	17.12.57
G-AJOB	27.06.47
G-AJOI	07.12.50
G-AJTC	23.09.55
G-AJTD	03.11.48
G-AJWD	26.08.56
G-AJWI	00.00.50
G-AJXK	03.12.50
G-AKHG	21.02.52
PH-EAB	00.00.62
VP-KEN	31.12.49
ZK-AWV	02.11.51
ZK-AWW	26.02.54

Mitsubishi Diamond

C-GLIG	01.03.95
I-ALSU	27.11.91
JA8246	23.07.86
N25BR	11.12.91
N3123T	00.11.91
N710MB	15.12.93

Mitsubishi MC-20

M-604	21.06.41

Mitsubishi MU-2

*	28.06.91
C-FQMS	07.04.80
C-GFRU	18.01.82
C-GLOW	06.12.81
C-GODI	28.05.77
D-IHAN	09.08.79
F-GDHS	21.05.91
F-GDHV	27.05.94
F-GERA	16.04.88
F-GGRZ	09.05.91
HB-LLP	22.09.94
HK-2245W	00.00.00
I-FRUT	00.00.00
I-IDMA	24.10.89
JA8753	11.03.81
LV-MOP	03.05.95
N100SW	01.04.77
N106MA	07.05.91
N108SC	24.06.92
N109TW	22.11.81
N112SK	01.12.84
N115S	19.01.79
N123AX	24.01.84
N132MA	16.04.72
N133MA	26.12.75
N149JP	01.12.82
N165MA	20.04.82
N178MA	25.08.78
N184MA	20.06.87
N200BR	21.12.79
N200HL	20.09.74
N208MA	03.08.79
N220MA	09.07.92
N233MA	02.09.81
N234MA	26.11.79
N23CD	17.10.85
N251M	09.04.79
N271MA	17.11.88
N274MA	22.02.91
N275MA	05.01.85
N27GP	13.07.82
N296MA	09.12.88
N297MA	28.02.78
N300CW	14.02.90
N300MA	08.02.76
N303CA	05.03.92
N304L	21.04.79
N307MA	23.04.80
N309MA	21.09.95
N321MA	04.04.77
N333MA	24.03.74
N346MA	14.02.80
N3550X	21.12.68
N3ED	17.06.81
N440MA	27.01.83
N444AR	18.11.81
N444PA	20.10.83
N44MR	30.11.80
N466MA	19.04.84
N473MA	18.03.83
N500GL	19.04.81
N50VS	02.01.89
N513DQ	05.03.86
N531MA	18.02.76
N53AD	05.11.81
N549LK	13.10.70
N5589S	15.12.82
N5NW	23.01.79
N64MD	09.02.90
N66U	00.00.82
N69QJ	13.11.75
N701DM	28.02.89
N711AH	02.03.74
N727MA	07.11.85
N72B	24.03.83
N742DM	18.05.92
N74FB	11.09.92
N750MA	19.11.81
N757Q	20.11.72
N758Q	15.04.69
N764Q	16.01.70
N765MA	28.08.78
N777MA	18.03.77
N808W	14.04.85
N82MA	06.09.90
N854Q	07.01.77
N86SD	19.04.93
N873Q	01.11.79
N882Q	03.06.73
N888MA	12.02.78
N888RJ	05.04.77
N8CC	06.06.86
N900YH	06.01.93
N92JR	13.05.81
N962MA	23.02.80
N969MA	06.12.80
N96JP	06.04.93
N9JS	22.04.81
OB-1219	30.01.90
OB-1284	14.05.92
OO-TBW	15.08.76
PH-DRX	12.09.88
PT-ICD	13.03.93
SE-IOU	16.02.86
SE-IOX	15.03.86
VH-BBA	16.12.88
VH-CJP	00.11.83
VH-IAM	21.12.94
VH-MLU	24.05.83
VH-MUA	26.01.90
VH-SSL	12.01.93
VH-UZD	00.00.90
VH-WMU	07.11.90
XA-DIS	20.11.83
XB-LIJ	30.11.75
YV-174CP	04.06.81
YV-94CP	00.00.82

NAMC YS-11

B-156	12.08.70
HL5208	11.12.69
JA8658	13.11.66
JA8662	10.01.88
JA8680	28.05.75
JA8693	11.03.83
JA8708	20.10.69
JA8764	03.07.71
N128MP	15.03.89
N172RV	06.11.74
N208PA	05.03.74
N906TC	13.01.87
N918AX	06.03.92
PK-MYN	01.04.71
PP-CTG	18.10.72
PP-CTI	29.04.77
PP-SMI	12.04.72
PP-SMJ	23.10.73
PP-SML	07.11.71
RP-C1419	17.07.77
SX-BBQ	21.10.72
SX-BBR	23.11.76

Noorduyn Norseman

C-FECD	22.06.82
C-FFJB	30.05.83
C-FISM	16.06.78
C-FKAS	21.03.95
CF-AYO	23.08.53
CF-BAW	03.01.44
CF-BDD	29.12.45
CF-BDG	22.02.42
CF-BXL	09.12.46
CF-GPB	19.09.51
CF-GPG	18.08.50
CF-MPE	00.00.39
CF-OBH	30.08.50
CF-PAA	09.05.52
ET-P-5	05.05.50
ET-T-30	11.06.50
HK-454	19.06.59
HS-SGF	00.00.51
LV-AAW	00.00.00
LV-AAY	00.00.00
LV-AFR	00.00.00
N55555	03.04.81
NC79822	20.05.48
PP-VBE	00.00.00
TF-RVD	26.06.46
TF-RVE	12.01.46
VO-ABL	20.06.47
VT-AYF	21.11.48
VT-AZE	21.11.48
VT-AZF	10.04.47
VT-AZK	12.05.47
VT-CBW	21.11.48
ZS-DMB	13.06.55

Nord 26

9Q-CJK	27.01.93

Nord 262

7T-VSU	24.01.79
F-BLHT	12.11.73
F-BNGB	31.12.70
F-BNMO	05.12.71
F-BNTT	29.12.73
F-BPNV	14.08.75
N29824	12.02.79
N418SA	10.03.79
N7886A	09.04.77
TN-230	27.01.90
TR-KJB	29.11.90

Nord Noratlas
- 9XR-KH 18.04.73
- F-BGZB 29.03.59
- F-WFUN 06.07.52
- HC-AXG oo.oo.74
- HC-AXK 24.07.80

North American B-25
- CP-718 02.03.66
- CP-796 18.02.67
- CP-808 21.11.77
- CP-970 07.06.76

Northrop Alpha
- NC127W 11.12.33
- NC947Y 11.12.33
- NC992Y 10.01.33
- NC994Y 31.01.35
- NC999Y 15.11.34

Northrop C-125
- CP-631 29.07.59
- CP-650 04.03.66
- N2562B 29.06.88
- NX8500H oo.02.48
- PZ-TAO 15.08.60

Northrop Delta
- NC12292 10.11.33
- NC14265 01.01.38
- SE-ADW 06.07.34
- X-ABED 05.05.34

Northrop F-15
- N9768Z 06.09.68

PZL Dromader
- HA-MUM 10.06.91
- OK-TGE 05.06.91

Partenavia P.68
- G-BMCB 20.10.90
- OY-PRY 04.03.86

Percival Gull Six
- VT-AJD 23.02.39

Percival Proctor
- G-AGSX 17.05.47
- G-AHMS 14.05.47
- G-AHWP 06.01.48
- G-AHWY 09.09.48
- G-AIAB 20.11.47

Percival Q.6
- G-AFIX 06.05.49
- G-AHTB 02.11.47

Piaggio P.166
- VH-GOC 22.02.77
- VH-PAU oo.03.61

Piaggio PD-808
- I-PIAI 18.06.68

Piasecki Heli-Stat
- * 01.07.86

Pilatus Porter
- * 20.04.71
- * oo.oo.73
- * 17.01.75
- * 21.01.79
- * 04.06.80
- * 24.04.88
- * 17.05.89
- * 29.07.89
- 1607 15.09.84
- 9N-ABJ 19.11.81
- FAC.1110 19.04.89
- FAC.1112 24.06.93
- FAC.1114 25.06.87
- FAC.1115 08.10.94
- G-BHCR 15.02.81
- G-BIZP 18.12.83
- HB-FCX 09.03.81
- HB-FET 03.10.82
- HB-FIM 29.07.87
- HB-FIP 04.12.85
- HB-FKC 09.05.86
- HB-FKS 21.06.93
- ST-AEU 17.08.73
- ST-AEV 04.01.74
- ST-AGY 28.09.77
- SX-AFB 22.07.69

Piper Aerostar
- C-GDMI 19.07.82
- N3641T 12.11.82

Piper PA-18
- ET-AAB 07.01.68
- I-BALR 02.02.92

Piper PA-22
- VQ-ZBA 08.11.55
- VQ-ZBF 22.01.58

Piper PA-23/27
- 9Q-CFN 09.07.82
- C-FJAI 03.05.89
- C-FVWA 14.12.79
- C-GPCA 18.04.79
- C-GWVO 20.08.80
- CF-ULL 04.02.77
- G-ASER 14.09.72
- G-ASHC 21.03.64
- G-ASTE 20.02.69
- G-ATCM 26.06.68
- G-ATFZ 01.09.66
- G-AYDE 18.04.74
- G-AZIF 05.01.72
- HK-1607 02.11.79
- N14007 02.08.77
- OY-BDP 19.01.89
- S7-AAL 16.06.78
- VH-PYS 11.01.78
- YJ-RV9 07.09.81

Piper PA-24
- 5Y-AAW 08.04.77

Piper PA-25
- ET-AEY 10.11.85
- ZS-CPB 18.02.78

Piper PA-28/32
- * 10.08.78
- * 20.10.84
- 5H-MOE 21.08.84
- CC-CEE 11.05.80
- HB-PGH 05.09.82
- HB-RET 15.09.81
- HK-1872I 14.06.78
- HK-2641 02.02.84
- N2477U 20.04.82
- N8402S 22.08.92
- YS-23C 22.03.93
- ZK-CUV 19.12.89

Piper PA-31
- * 21.12.75
- * 23.11.77
- 5Y-SRV 27.12.91
- 6V-AGH 29.05.95
- 9Y-PIA 05.01.91
- C-GBSG 03.01.83
- G-BFON 11.06.86
- HC-BEP 14.07.78
- HK-1591 22.08.73
- LN-PAA 25.09.77
- N27400 19.02.88
- N35206 23.12.83
- N41070 31.12.81
- N496SC 23.12.87
- N5642L 08.10.79
- N63719 14.02.85
- N6629L 05.03.84
- N712AN 23.12.87
- N9093Y 07.08.78
- OB-1453 23.11.93
- OB-S-1176 28.02.90
- PT-BKB 24.09.84
- TF-ORN 21.01.87
- TF-RTR 11.03.81
- VH-POC 26.01.81

Piper PA-31-350
- 5H-IAS 05.01.92
- 5H-TAL 05.12.80
- 5N-AKO 01.10.80
- 5Y-ASH 28.12.74
- 5Y-AST 08.03.87
- 5Y-SMR 02.12.94
- C-GYPZ 01.05.95
- CX-BMT 19.08.80
- G-BASU 12.05.87
- G-BBJG 06.12.74
- G-BBPV 19.10.75
- G-BGEO 18.08.87
- G-BGIN 06.03.80
- G-CTHS 24.09.80
- HK-2203 14.05.82
- HK-2456P 02.06.83
- HP-909 26.10.74
- N123CB 05.04.82
- N27245 13.02.95
- N27512 20.11.87
- N27522 01.02.85
- N27886 21.03.84
- N27948 02.08.84
- N350MR 10.12.91
- N3517W 28.03.85
- N3558W 21.09.90
- N37490 14.12.86
- N4091U 24.12.82
- N41045 31.10.82
- N4115K 04.12.83
- N41169 14.02.89
- N4469R 31.08.84
- N4499B 06.09.84
- N44LV 30.08.78
- N50WT 09.01.95
- N59771 12.11.82
- N59783 04.09.90
- N59932 21.03.80
- N5MS 25.07.80
- N66892 18.05.85
- N78DE 04.03.94
- N88LV 17.08.83
- N9253Y 04.01.86
- N990RA 27.04.94
- OB-1458 21.06.92
- OY-BGK 07.10.87
- PH-ASU 25.02.86
- PH-TSM 22.12.82
- RP-C2662 23.12.88
- SE-IAA 23.01.90
- SE-IDU 22.10.86
- TJ-AFO 24.06.80
- TR-LTQ 13.11.78
- VH-LIC oo.06.93
- VH-NDU 11.06.93
- VH-WGI 17.09.93
- n/a 23.06.72

Piper PA-31T
- HB-LHT 12.11.76

Piper PA-32
- N6281J 07.07.95

Piper PA-34
- CC-CAU 10.02.88
- G-BBFF 25.05.74
- N2883D 17.05.95
- N2883D 17.07.95
- N44356 18.04.78
- ZP-PGZ 01.06.77

Piper PA-38
- RP-C1071 16.07.92

Piper PA-42
- * oo.02.95
- * 26.07.95
- HL5204 20.03.91
- N542TW 28.06.85
- OB-1234 08.02.93

Piper PA-46
- C-GSEV 19.08.94

Piper T-1040
- C-GBDH 23.09.89

Pitcairn Mailwing
- * 04.06.33
- 4231 22.05.28
- 5564 26.05.28

Polikarpov AP
- SSSR-110 oo.oo.29
- SSSR-A11 25.10.33
- SSSR-A14 oo.08.31
- SSSR-A15 oo.10.31
- SSSR-A16 08.12.33
- SSSR-A26 oo.10.31
- SSSR-A27 oo.08.31
- SSSR-L78 oo.oo.35
- SSSR-N18 oo.oo.34
- SSSR-N5 oo.04.32

Polikarpov P-5
- SSSR-F48 oo.06.35
- SSSR-N43 03.05.36
- SSSR-N45 08.09.34
- SSSR-N6 15.08.32

Polikarpov PM-1
- RRUSS oo.07.26

Potez 56
- * 13.10.37
- * 18.02.43
- * 29.03.43
- 5 27.03.37

Potez 62
- F-ANPH 10.12.35
- F-ANPJ 27.01.39
- F-ANQR 07.03.38

Potez 621
- F-AOTZ 08.12.37

Potez 840
- F-BMCY 29.03.81

Putilov Stal'-2
- SSSR-L1196 oo.oo.35

R-BVZ Russkiy Vityaz
- n/a 26.09.13

Renard R35
- OO-ARM 01.04.38

Rockwell Commander
- * 13.10.88
- C-GFAC 16.10.79
- HK-869 23.07.80
- HP-776 15.06.80
- OB-T-805 28.09.84
- PT-BVX 13.12.81
- PT-BVZ 08.12.77
- PT-CGS 09.11.76

Rockwell Jet Commander
- 4X-COJ 21.01.70
- C-FEYG 26.05.78
- C-FMWW 27.01.94
- LV-BDB oo.oo.91
- LV-WEN 28.09.94
- N100RC 14.11.70
- N148E 13.09.68
- N196KC 01.07.68
- N200RC 25.09.73
- N236JP 31.10.69
- N250UA 27.04.78
- N29LP 19.12.80
- N301AJ 13.08.90
- N309CK 15.12.93
- N311BR 04.03.95
- N400CP 21.01.71
- N403M 16.12.69
- N44 02.11.88
- N500JR 26.09.66
- N50SK 04.04.86
- N66JE 21.02.95
- N69GT 11.06.85
- N711JT 13.03.75
- SE-DCY 04.12.69
- SE-DLK 21.09.92
- VH-AJS 27.04.95
- VH-IWJ 10.10.85

Rockwell Sabre
- CF-BRL 27.02.74
- N169RF 07.11.92
- N30W 21.12.67
- N34W 04.01.74
- N500NL 23.02.75
- N5565 15.01.74
- N64 oo.09.86
- N67KM 14.06.75
- N739R 16.05.67
- N743R 13.04.73
- N747E 21.12.94

N771WW 10.01.95
N77AP 07.11.77
N85 14.01.76
N920G 27.12.74
N9503Z 07.03.73
N99S 11.01.83
OB-1319 03.09.93
XA-EEU oo.oo.80
XC-AA26 oo.oo.94
XC-UJC 26.10.89

Rockwell Space Shuttle
n/a 28.01.86

Rockwell Turbo Commander
C-FFEO 15.02.93
CP-1016 oo.oo.oo
CP-1017 13.02.74
CP-894 18.06.71
D-IBAR 30.01.85
D-IKOC 21.02.81
D-INIX 21.06.72
D-IOET 01.12.81
EI-BGL 13.11.84
EP-AHN oo.oo.79
HC-BHU 27.10.91
HK-2217P 13.03.86
HK-2415 08.09.91
HK-2478P 15.06.90
HK-3278 22.03.90
HK-3376 oo.oo.oo
HL5223 oo.09.74
HL5261 oo.oo.84
HS-TFB 22.07.84
L-701 oo.oo.79
LV-LTA oo.12.75
LV-MAV 12.09.84
LV-MBR 14.09.80
LV-OEV 26.08.81
N100CT 03.09.84
N111QL 17.09.83
N17690 03.12.85
N17ZD oo.oo.oo
N182 15.01.80
N1NR 14.08.72
N200PR 07.05.86
N23LS oo.oo.oo
N27MT 08.10.94
N28AD 17.05.93
N2937A 31.10.84
N299F 27.05.78
N300CP 31.12.92
N333CA 22.08.73
N399T 31.01.75
N400N 01.12.90
N40MP 12.11.74
N444GB 05.08.90
N45Q 12.10.90
N500JP 27.01.81
N5058E 20.11.82
N541F 03.11.90
N541W 03.10.70
N568H 26.10.76
N57169 24.06.87
N57186 17.11.76
N57233 01.10.79
N5860K 13.12.81
N5889N oo.oo.86
N5926K 16.10.81
N5957K 29.03.82
N5NP 08.03.78
N601G 08.08.76
N660RB 17.05.88
N662DM 21.06.87
N690JC 25.06.92
N69TM 12.02.95
N700R 23.12.85
N707BP 31.07.93
N70RF 30.06.95
N711TT 08.10.87
N772CB 28.03.85
N78D 05.12.71
N799V 02.11.91
N81416 14.02.83
N81502 09.10.84
N81521 07.01.81
N81628 22.09.90
N81717 17.01.84
N81TR 23.12.92
N83MC 20.01.84
N847 23.04.77
N847CE 12.09.75
N89DA 15.11.82
N9001N 05.05.69
N9019N 28.12.71
N9060N 25.11.70
N9150N 25.08.84
N9202N 26.06.70
N9229Y 20.12.84
N932E 11.07.84
N94HD 11.11.78
OB-1212 07.05.92
OB-M-1031 14.02.79
OE-FCS 23.02.89
SE-FGE 23.07.73
SE-GUO 07.07.94
VH-BSS 14.01.94
VH-SVQ 02.10.94
XB-AEA 30.01.80
XC-AA38 19.10.92
YV-O-MAR-2 17.08.78
ZS-KOF 04.06.91
ZS-KRS 16.09.81
ZS-KVB 20.06.84

Rohrbach Roland
D-1338 07.03.31
D-1712 oo.03.35
D-AJYP 07.03.35
M-CCCC 19.04.28

Rohrbach Romar
D-1693 18.11.28
D-1734 10.09.29

Royal Airship Works R.101
G-FAAW 05.10.30

Royal Airship Works ZR-2
R38 24.08.21

SA Twin Pioneer
5N-ABQ 04.04.67
5N-ABR 16.01.63
9M-ANC 17.05.67
9M-ANO 03.03.67
C-FSTX oo.oo.oo
C-GSTX oo.oo.oo
G-ANTP 10.03.60
G-AOEN 12.12.59
G-AOEO 07.12.57
G-ARBA 10.01.71
G-BBVF 11.03.82
JZ-PPX 30.08.57
N48207 oo.oo.77
PI-C430 12.01.60
PK-GTA oo.oo.72
PK-GTB 20.09.63
PK-GTC 14.05.63
VH-BHJ 23.12.60
VR-OAE 07.09.63
XW-PBJ oo.oo.oo
XW-PBN oo.oo.oo
XW-PBO 20.09.64
XW-PBP oo.oo.oo

SAI KZ.IV
OY-DIZ 26.05.79

SIAI-Marchetti Canguro
I-CANG 08.02.85

SIAI-Marchetti S.208
ET-ADG 10.02.77
ET-ADK 22.03.79

SNCAC Cormoran
n/a 20.07.48

SNCAC Martinet
F-BAIP oo.oo.47
F-BAOP 13.10.46
F-BAOQ 25.10.47
F-BBFA 22.07.46
F-BBFO 26.06.47
F-BBFX 11.10.46
F-BDLG 08.01.48
F-BDLR 28.07.48

SNCASE Armagnac
F-BAVG 29.01.57
F-WAVA 30.06.50

SNCASE Languedoc
EC-AKV 29.09.56
EC-ANR 04.12.58
F-BATB 07.04.52
F-BATG 14.06.48
F-BATH 10.02.48
F-BATK 04.02.48
F-BATM 23.11.48
F-BATO 29.08.48
F-BATU 09.04.49
F-BATY 07.10.47
F-BCUC 26.01.48
F-BCUI 30.07.50
F-BCUM 03.03.52
OD-ABU 06.01.54
SU-AHH 23.12.51
SU-AHX 30.07.52
SU-AHZ 24.04.54

SNCASE SE.1010
F-WEEE 01.10.49

SNCASE SE.200
F-BAIY 18.10.49

SNCASO Bretagne
F-BEHA oo.oo.52
F-BEHS 30.08.54
F-DABD 10.10.53
F-OAIY 30.10.51
F-OAMA 30.04.54

SNCASO Corse
F-BBAP 23.07.46

SPCA Meteore 63
F-AIPA 09.12.28

Saab 340
HB-AHA 21.02.90
N342PX 02.01.93
PH-KSH 04.04.94

Saab Scandia
PP-SQE 30.12.58
PP-SQS 15.08.60
PP-SQV 23.09.59
PP-SQY 08.03.64
PP-SRA 26.11.62

Sabca S.73
OO-AGS 23.05.40

Sablatnig P.III
D-171 21.04.27
D-395 23.08.28
D-453 31.05.27
D-50 17.10.26
D-727 07.08.26
D-730 23.07.25
D-962 23.09.27
D-984 30.07.27

Saro Cloud
G-ABHG oo.06.41
G-ABXW 31.07.36

Saro Windhover
VH-UPB 14.05.36

Savoia FBA
CH-18 31.08.20

Savoia Marchetti S.66
I-NAVE oo.08.37
I-VOLO 14.07.38

Savoia Marchetti S.70
I-ALAN oo.oo.41

Savoia Marchetti SM.95
I-DALO 17.01.51
I-LATI oo.11.49

Savoia-Marchetti S.55
I-AASZ 12.10.29
I-DINI 01.07.33
I-TACO 20.11.29
NC105H oo.05.34
NC20K 30.09.37
NC379N oo.oo.31
SSSR-L840 oo.09.35

Savoia-Marchetti SM.73
I-DOUL oo.11.42
I-SUSA 02.08.37
OK-BAG 23.08.38
OO-AGM 07.11.35
OO-AGN 10.12.35
OO-AGP oo.05.40
OO-AGR 20.02.37
OO-AGT 10.10.38

Savoia-Marchetti SM.75
I-BAYR 15.01.41
I-BELO 07.05.43
I-BETA 18.08.43
I-BONI 10.04.43
I-BURA 28.03.42
I-TELO 15.11.42

Savoia-Marchetti SM.83
I-AMER oo.02.41
I-ANDE 16.08.42
I-AREM 10.01.41
I-ARGE 18.06.42
I-ARMA 07.07.43
I-ARPA 24.12.39
I-ASTA 20.12.40
I-BAIA oo.02.41
I-BENI 25.03.42
I-BRAZ 09.06.42

Schutte-Lanz S.L.1
S.L.1 17.07.13

Short 330
C-FPQE 01.12.93
G-BHWT 11.01.88
G-BPMA 13.02.89
G-OATD 27.11.89
G-OGIL 01.07.92
N74F 28.08.92
N844SA 03.06.80
N935MA 20.05.83
SX-BGE 03.08.89
VP-LVR 02.05.93

Short 360
B-3606 22.10.85
EI-BEM 31.01.86
EI-BTJ 13.12.87
G-ROOM 27.11.89
N730CC 20.08.90

Short Calcutta
G-AADN 26.10.29
G-AASJ 31.12.35
G-EBVG 28.12.36

Short Kent
G-ABFA 22.08.36
G-ABFB 09.11.35

Short L.17
G-ACJJ 14.09.40

Short S.21
G-ADHK 11.05.41

Short S.23-33
G-ADUU 21.01.39
G-ADUX 29.12.41
G-ADUY 12.03.39
G-ADUZ 05.12.37
G-ADVA 24.03.37
G-ADVC 01.10.37
G-ADVD 01.05.39
G-ADVE 12.06.39
G-AETW 27.11.38
G-AETX 01.12.42
G-AETZ 28.02.42
G-AEUC 03.03.42
G-AEUF 22.03.42
G-AEUH 30.01.42
G-AFCW 19.06.39
G-AFCX 15.02.41
G-AFCZ 24.09.42
VH-ACD 18.11.44
VH-ADU 22.04.43

Short S.26
G-AFCI 03.05.54

G-AFCK	09.01.43

Short Scion

G-ADDT	26.07.36
G-AEIL	25.04.40
G-AEOY	17.12.37
G-AETT	13.02.40

Short Scion Senior

G-AENX	oo.08.39

Short Sealand

AP-AGB	26.03.55
AP-AGC	26.03.55
G-AKLM	15.10.49
JZ-PTA	28.04.55
PK-CMA	oo.oo.53

Short Skyvan

7Q-YAY	24.04.86
7Q-YMB	06.11.87
8R-GFF	22.01.81
8R-GRR	14.10.94
9M-AXM	30.07.93
9M-AZB	03.09.91
9M-PID	30.01.93
9M-PIF	03.02.93
A4O-SI	22.11.76
G-OVAN	28.12.93
I-TORE	06.03.67
LX-UGO	02.12.93
N123PA	22.10.70
N20086	13.07.92
N21CK	02.07.70
N30GA	01.09.95
N40DA	28.11.73
N4917	25.08.77
N50GA	23.06.90
N725R	14.04.72
OE-FDL	07.06.95
OH-SBB	01.11.89
OY-JRK	08.01.94
PA-50	15.05.82
PA-54	03.05.82
PK-ESC	03.10.86
PK-ESC	03.10.86
VH-PNI	01.09.72

Short Solent

G-AHIX	01.02.50
G-AKNU	15.11.57
G-ANAJ	26.09.56
VH-TOA	28.01.51

Short Stirling

OO-XAC	22.12.47

Short Sunderland/ Sandringham

CX-AFA	11.09.56
CX-ANA	22.10.55
G-AGES	28.07.43
G-AGET	15.02.46
G-AGEV	04.03.46
G-AGEW	05.09.48
G-AGHV	10.03.46
G-AGHW	19.11.47
G-AGIB	06.11.43
G-AGJN	21.01.53
G-AGJO	21.02.49
G-AGKY	28.01.53
G-AHYZ	18.01.47
G-AHZB	22.08.47
G-ANAK	27.11.54
LN-IAU	15.05.50
LN-IAV	28.08.47
LN-IAW	02.10.48
LN-LAI	oo.11.52
LV-AAP	29.07.48
VH-BRD	31.10.52
VH-BRE	03.07.63

Sikorsky H-3

*	10.01.87
1473	02.11.86

Sikorsky H-60

*	03.01.86
*	02.11.89
*	24.08.92
81-23577	14.07.93

Sikorsky S-38

C-45	oo.oo.32
C-46	10.03.34
C-49	oo.oo.40
C-52	06.08.36
F-AOUC	12.08.39
NC113M	25.09.32
NC141M	11.06.33
NC16V	24.11.33
NC17V	10.04.34
NC197H	19.09.29
NC21V	11.12.41
NC306N	07.02.31
NC309N	oo.04.31
NC40V	13.08.35
NC5933	12.08.31
NC8020	30.12.29
NC8021	05.06.29
NC8044	26.05.33
NC944M	14.06.32
P-BDAD	oo.oo.oo
PK-AKS	19.02.42
PK-AKT	25.12.41
PP-PAL	oo.07.33
PP-PAM	oo.oo.38
n/a	27.09.35
n/a	10.10.41

Sikorsky S-41

n/a	14.02.36

Sikorsky S-42/43

*	02.06.37
NC15065	02.08.37
NC15066	03.08.45
NC15376	10.03.41
NC16734	11.01.38
NC16735	07.12.41
NC16736	27.07.43
NC16928	26.06.41
NC823M	08.08.44
NC824M	20.12.35
PK-AFT	26.12.41
PK-AFU	19.02.42
PK-AFX	19.02.42
PP-PAR	08.02.37
PP-PAU	oo.oo.oo
PP-PBA	oo.oo.oo
PP-PBL	25.04.38
PP-PBM	13.08.39
PP-PBN	03.01.47

Sikorsky S-51

G-AKCU	4.05.49

Sikorsky S-55

5N-AJP	04.06.80
C-FALA	17.08.90
C-GHKR	06.11.78
C-GIMO	20.05.94
C-GMMR	16.02.84
C-GUNI	oo.oo.89
D-HAUB	30.09.77
EC-CYJ	23.01.79
EC-DDR	12.03.90
F-BVJI	22.08.84
G-ANUK	04.08.72
G-ASWI	13.08.81
G-ATCA	09.09.72
G-ATSC	08.03.76
G-BCRU	21.04.76
HL9239	27.07.89
JA7067	10.05.66
LN-OSD	12.11.77
N1099T	13.02.95
N4247	07.08.80
N42475	04.11.86
N4371S	08.09.76
N4375S	22.12.80
N47782	10.01.87
N4995G	28.01.94
N5594C	31.01.87
N581BG	21.02.94
N65526	20.04.85
N879	27.07.60
N90936	02.02.77
N90939	02.04.77
N94523	18.10.80
N94AH	13.07.88
OD-AGK	oo.oo.82
OD-AGL	oo.oo.82
OO-SHK	05.05.61
PK-HBR	08.06.71
PK-OAO	28.05.76
PK-OBL	09.11.87
PK-OBS	05.05.94
PK-OBT	26.07.94
PK-UHN	26.01.75
PK-UHV	oo.12.73
PT-HGK	03.04.80
PT-HGO	25.08.83
SE-HHY	15.08.79
TI-SPI	09.09.75
TI-SPJ	oo.oo.78
VR-BDB	14.09.77
XS118	24.05.65
ZS-HCX	09.04.77

Sikorsky S-61

AP-AOA	10.12.66
AP-AOC	02.02.66
C-FWYN	02.04.93
G-ASNM	15.11.70
G-AZNE	04.04.73
G-BDES	10.11.88
G-BDII	17.10.88
G-BEID	13.07.88
G-BEON	16.07.83
G-BEWL	25.07.90
LN-OQS	26.06.78
LN-OSZ	23.11.77
N300Y	14.08.68
N303Y	22.05.68
N618PA	17.04.79
N6981R	05.02.84
OY-HAN	11.09.87
XV372	15.01.69
YV-323C	07.10.83
ZF527	23.07.87
ZS-HGU	15.04.81
ZS-HHN	05.04.91
ZS-HRU	17.09.92

Sikorsky S-62

*	08.08.79
N54516	07.07.78

Sikorsky S-64

*	13.12.76
N165AC	01.09.94
N6959R	27.06.91
N6965R	05.06.81

Sikorsky S-67

N671SA	01.09.74

Sikorsky S-76

*	01.11.84
*	05.01.86
9M-AXW	15.05.90
C-GIMF	30.04.82
G-BGXY	12.03.81
HL9245	14.06.93
JA9943	01.08.90
N2620	08.11.94
N31223	19.02.85
N4252S	13.11.83
N50KY	07.08.92
N521AC	14.09.83
N541BN	17.06.91
N63WW	11.08.84
N767AL	04.02.87
PK-PUD	23.04.94
PT-HKB	21.03.80
PT-HKC	29.09.81
PT-HKD	07.11.83
TF-RAN	08.11.83
VR-BQD	24.07.95

Sikorsky S.29A

n/a	oo.oo.28

Simmonds Spartan

ZK-AAY	12.02.37

Sopwith 1 1/2 Strutter

*	oo.oo.26

Spartan Cruiser

G-ABTY	11.05.35
G-ACDX	09.10.35
G-ACVT	23.03.36
G-ACYK	14.01.38
G-ADEM	20.11.36

Standard D-27

NC9124	21.10.32

Stearman C3B

NC11721	20.01.33
NC3709	07.05.29
NC3863	10.08.30
NC487W	24.10.35
NC490W	20.01.33
NC8820	06.01.30

Stinson L-5 Sentinel

VT-CAG	21.11.48

Stinson Model A

NC14141	26.05.36
NC14599	14.08.35
NC15134	27.08.36
NC15152	01.04.36
VH-UGG	28.03.37
VH-UHH	19.02.37
VT-AQW	04.08.43

Stinson Model U

NC12119	06.02.36
NC12121	03.09.38
NX12132	08.02.33

Stinson Reliant

CF-BEI	12.01.38

Stinson SM-6000B

CF-ATE	30.01.34
NC10894	28.05.35
NC11155	11.02.35
NC1118	31.08.34
NC976W	08.04.36

Supermarine Air Yacht

G-AASE	25.01.33

Supermarine Sea Eagle

G-EBFK	21.05.24
G-EBGS	10.01.27

Swearingen Merlin

5Y-TNT	01.10.92
9Q-COI	06.10.83
C-FFYC	31.05.94
C-FHYX	oo.10.73
C-GYMR	oo.10.88
D-ILSE	10.04.73
F-GEBK	oo.04.85
F-GFMS	07.11.87
N100NL	16.10.71
N1011R	24.03.81
N1214S	16.05.73
N1221S	oo.oo.94
N177MF	02.12.80
N18SE	oo.oo.87
N199TA	19.06.85
N20PT	18.03.94
N2301N	22.11.78
N239P	29.01.70
N241DT	25.05.93
N26JB	13.02.92
N26RT	23.02.89
N336SA	10.01.82
N34SM	03.02.77
N3RB	17.09.85
N411X	28.03.72
N444LM	03.05.85
N4BC	oo.oo.83
N5296M	10.04.73
N5329M	03.03.77
N555AM	10.06.81
N5654M	31.05.79
N61PH	oo.10.91
N65103	19.10.79
N66KS	09.09.86
N693PG	18.09.95
N800AW	10.01.88
OY-ATW	26.04.78
PT-DUX	27.09.71

Swearingen Metro

5Y-DNT	25.10.92
C-GJDX	11.02.88
C-GJWW	12.01.88
C-GSLB	26.09.89
C-GYYB	01.05.95
D-CABB	08.02.88

D-IASN 04.12.85
D-IEWK 05.02.87
EC-FHB 18.10.93
F-GCPG 18.11.88
F-GCTE oo.03.88
F-GILN 19.09.93
N163SW 15.01.87
N2183A 18.09.92
N220KC 17.08.93
N2689E 25.09.87
N2721M 15.01.90
N30093 07.12.82
N300TL 13.08.78
N3044J 12.11.92
N31138 oo.oo.oo
N342AE 25.08.92
N500AK 01.04.93
N503SS 27.08.83
N505LB 23.04.87
N568UP 31.01.85
N577KA 07.05.86
N622AV 12.02.88
N63Z 30.01.84
N6505 12.06.80
N683AV 01.02.91
N68TC 19.01.88
N960M 14.04.75
OE-LSA 19.09.84
OY-ARI 01.01.89
OY-AUI 12.11.82
OY-BZW oo.04.91
VH-BPL 02.04.81
VH-SWO 13.05.80
VH-SWP 09.03.94
VH-UZS 14.04.93
XA-SLU 13.06.94
ZS-KYA 14.04.82
ZS-LKG 18.11.88

Transavia Airtruk
B-15118 29.07.80

Tupolev ANT-20
SSSR-I20 18.05.35
SSSR-L760 12.12.42

Tupolev ANT-4
URSS-300 09.08.29

Tupolev ANT-9
D-2831 22.10.34
URSS-D311 06.11.36

Tupolev DB-A
URSS-N209 12.08.37

Tupolev TU-104
* 23.04.73
* 18.05.73
OK-LDB 16.08.63
OK-MDE 29.08.73
OK-NDD 01.06.70
SSSR-42327 09.02.76
SSSR-42335 17.07.76
SSSR-42357 01.02.61
SSSR-42362 17.10.58
SSSR-42366 02.09.62
SSSR-42369 13.01.77
SSSR-42370 30.06.62
SSSR-42388 17.09.61
SSSR-42405 25.07.71
SSSR-42408 10.03.72
SSSR-42436 28.04.69
SSSR-42438 16.03.61
SSSR-42444 17.03.79
SSSR-42447 10.07.61
SSSR-42452 20.10.60
SSSR-42471 28.11.76
SSSR-42472 30.08.75
SSSR-42476 09.06.64
SSSR-42483 18.05.63
SSSR-42486 13.10.73
SSSR-42490 10.10.71
SSSR-42491 04.06.62
SSSR-42492 13.07.63
SSSR-42495 25.10.62
SSSR-42501 05.11.74
SSSR-42503 07.12.73
SSSR-42504 02.11.61
SSSR-42506 30.09.73
SSSR-L5414 19.02.58
SSSR-L5442 15.08.58

Tupolev TU-114
SSSR-76457 02.12.66
SSSR-76462 oo.oo.63
SSSR-L5612 18.02.58

Tupolev TU-124
OK-TEB 18.08.70
SSSR-45004 23.12.73
SSSR-45012 02.09.70
SSSR-45017 12.03.66
SSSR-45019 07.03.68
SSSR-45021 21.08.63
SSSR-45028 08.03.65
SSSR-45031 20.10.73
SSSR-45037 03.01.75
SSSR-45038 29.08.79
SSSR-45061 16.12.73
SSSR-45062 09.07.73
SSSR-45083 29.01.70
SSSR-45086 10.11.65

Tupolev TU-134
* 10.04.71
* oo.oo.73
* 03.01.76
* 07.02.81
* 29.11.94
* 30.11.94
4L-65001 23.09.93
4L-65053 23.09.93
4L-65809 23.09.93
4L-65893 21.09.93
C9-CAA 19.10.86
DM-SCA 30.10.72
DM-SCD 01.09.75
DM-SCM 22.11.77
HA-LBA 19.11.69
HA-LBC 21.09.77
HA-LBD 16.09.71
HA-LBP 22.02.94
LZ-TUD 16.03.78
LZ-TUR 10.01.84
OK-CFD 02.01.77
RA-65617 24.06.95
RA-65760 09.09.94
RA-65976 07.05.94
SP-LGB 23.01.80
SSSR-65031 22.03.79
SSSR-65058 27.08.92
SSSR-65120 02.07.86
SSSR-65129 30.08.83
SSSR-65142 22.06.86
SSSR-65607 17.07.72
SSSR-65612 oo.oo.oo
SSSR-65642 oo.oo.oo
SSSR-65649 31.05.79
SSSR-65668 30.06.73
SSSR-65675 27.02.88
SSSR-65698 06.01.81
SSSR-65735 11.08.79
SSSR-65766 20.10.86
SSSR-65795 12.12.86
SSSR-65807 oo.oo.84
SSSR-65816 11.08.79
SSSR-65836 14.08.82
SSSR-65839 19.05.79
SSSR-65856 03.05.85
SSSR-65871 28.06.81
SSSR-65910 01.02.85
SSSR-65951 13.01.90
UN-65787 21.12.93
VN-A102 08.09.88
VN-A108 17.02.88
VN-A126 12.01.91
YI-AED 22.07.71
YU-AHZ 23.05.71
YU-AJS 02.04.77

Tupolev TU-144
SSSR-77102 03.06.73
SSSR-77111 23.05.78

Tupolev TU-154
* oo.03.73
* 30.11.94
4L-85163 22.09.93
4L-85359 23.09.93
7O-ACN oo.oo.86
85105 05.12.92
85533 09.01.93
B-2610 06.06.94
CU-T1227 14.09.91
EP-ITD 08.02.93
HA-LCF 21.10.81
HA-LCI 30.09.75
LZ-BTB 23.03.78
LZ-BTD 05.06.92
LZ-BTN 02.12.77
RA-85295 25.12.93
RA-85358 29.12.93
RA-85656 03.01.94
SSSR-85023 19.02.73
SSSR-85029 13.06.81
SSSR-85030 07.05.73
SSSR-85067 13.01.89
SSSR-85097 23.05.91
SSSR-85102 01.06.76
SSSR-85103 01.03.80
SSSR-85169 19.05.78
SSSR-85222 20.07.92
SSSR-85234 oo.06.92
SSSR-85243 11.10.84
SSSR-85254 18.01.88
SSSR-85268 20.10.90
SSSR-85269 05.09.92
SSSR-85282 oo.06.92
SSSR-85311 10.07.85
SSSR-85321 08.10.80
SSSR-85327 21.05.86
SSSR-85338 23.12.84
SSSR-85355 07.07.80
SSSR-85413 08.03.88
SSSR-85479 24.09.88
SSSR-85480 16.11.81
SSSR-85528 13.10.92
SSSR-85664 17.11.90
SU-AXB 10.04.74
YA-TAP 29.05.92
YN-CBT oo.oo.92
YR-TPH 07.08.80
YR-TPJ 09.02.89

Type Unknown
* 12.10.33
* 25.01.35
* 18.09.36
* 23.07.37
* 05.08.37
* 08.08.37
* 28.03.38
* 12.08.38
* 04.08.39
* 05.05.40
* 27.05.44
* 20.09.46
* 25.04.47
* 26.03.52
* 29.12.54
* 31.12.54
* 06.08.55
* 19.02.68
* 24.12.77
* 24.07.81
* oo.12.82
* 20.04.83
* 19.01.84
* 20.08.87
* 02.09.87
* 14.11.87
* 30.06.88
* 18.11.88
* 02.08.89
* 27.09.90

Udet U.8
D-670 oo.oo.26

V4 Airship
SSSR-V4 16.08.34

V6 Airship
SSSR-V6 06.02.38

VEB 152
DM-ZYA 04.03.59

VFW 614
D-BABA 01.02.72

Vertol 107
* 14.10.63
JA9501 04.09.65
JA9502 16.04.68
JA9503 05.08.67
N190CH 20.08.83
N6672D 04.08.90
N6676D 14.10.82

Vickers 103 Vanguard
G-EBCP 16.05.29

Vickers R.36
G-FAAF 21.06.21

Vickers Vanguard
F-GEJE 06.02.89
F-GEJF 29.01.88
G-APEC 02.10.71
G-APEE 27.10.65
G-AXOP 10.04.73

Vickers Vellox
G-ABKY 10.08.36

Vickers Viastra
VH-UOM 11.10.33

Vickers Viking
CR-IAD 02.11.57
D-ADEL 26.09.57
D-BALI 04.02.61
D-BELA 17.10.58
F-BFDN 05.09.59
F-BJEQ 08.02.65
F-BJER 12.09.63
G-AGOK 23.04.46
G-AGRT 26.02.58
G-AHON 27.07.52
G-AHOR 29.05.60
G-AHPD 08.05.51
G-AHPH 28.07.59
G-AHPI 16.02.52
G-AHPK 06.01.48
G-AHPL 02.08.65
G-AHPM 09.08.61
G-AHPN 31.10.50
G-AHPO 20.12.53
G-AIJE 02.09.58
G-AIVE 21.04.48
G-AIVG 12.08.53
G-AIVP 05.04.48
G-AIXS 15.08.54
G-AJBO 01.05.57
G-AJCE 14.08.61
G-AJDL 05.01.53
G-AMGG 22.12.59
G-AMNK 24.08.60
G-APAZ 27.03.63
G-APKR 21.09.63
G-BDFT 19.08.84
LV-AFL 14.05.48
N65388 11.12.83
OY-DLI 29.12.47
OY-DLU 08.02.49
SU-AFK 15.12.53
SU-AFO 15.09.54
SU-AGN 07.03.50
SU-AGO 05.08.54
VP-YEX 17.03.55
VP-YEY 29.03.53
VP-YMO 05.10.56
VT-CEJ 08.10.48
VT-CEL 27.03.48
VT-CIZ 07.04.49
VT-CLY 06.02.48
XB-FIP oo.oo.64
YI-ABQ 10.10.55
YI-ABR 13.06.49

Vickers Vimy Commercial
G-EAAV 27.02.20

Vickers Viscount
4X-AVC 26.10.69
6O-AAJ 06.05.70
9G-ACL 10.06.78
9Q-CPD 28.08.84
9Q-CTS oo.oo.88
9Q-CTU 03.03.92
AP-AJC 18.05.59
AP-AJE 14.08.59
B-2029 31.07.75
CF-TGL 10.11.58
CF-TGY 03.10.59
CF-THK 07.04.69
CF-THT 13.06.64
CU-T603 01.11.58

Registration	Date
CX-AQO	11.05.75
EI-AKK	21.09.67
EI-AOF	22.06.67
EI-AOM	24.03.68
EP-AHC	15.02.65
F-BGNK	12.12.56
F-BGNV	12.08.63
F-BMCH	27.10.72
F-BOEA	28.12.71
G-AHRF	27.08.52
G-ALWE	14.03.57
G-AMNY	05.01.60
G-AMOA	19.01.70
G-AMOL	20.07.65
G-AMOM	21.01.56
G-ANHC	22.10.58
G-ANRR	02.12.58
G-AODG	20.02.69
G-AODH	30.10.61
G-AOHI	19.01.73
G-AOHP	17.11.57
G-AOHU	07.01.60
G-AOJA	23.10.57
G-AORC	28.04.58
G-AOYF	20.10.57
G-APIM	11.01.88
G-APKJ	12.06.61
G-APNF	22.09.70
G-APPU	05.05.68
G-ARBY	17.07.80
G-ATFN	09.08.68
G-AVJA	20.03.69
G-AVJZ	03.05.67
G-AWXI	22.01.70
G-AZNP	28.01.72
G-BBVH	23.11.88
G-BFYZ	25.10.79
G-OHOT	25.02.94
HC-ARS	15.08.76
HC-ART	03.06.70
HC-ATV	08.10.82
HC-AVP	23.04.79
HC-BCL	04.09.77
HC-BEM	29.12.77
HC-BHB	14.07.80
HK-1058	08.06.74
HK-1267	14.12.77
HK-1347	21.01.72
HK-1708	31.03.91
HK-2382	23.03.82
I-LAKE	28.03.64
I-LIZT	21.12.59
JA8202	19.11.62
LX-LGC	22.12.69
N242V	28.01.63
N243V	08.07.62
N6592C	15.11.61
N7404	20.02.56
N7405	09.07.64
N7410	20.05.58
N7410	27.06.69
N7415	oo.08.71
N7429	11.12.67
N7430	23.11.62
N7431	19.01.67
N7437	06.04.58
N7462	18.01.60
N7463	12.05.59
N7465	28.11.67
N923RC	19.10.85
OD-ACT	28.12.68
OD-ACX	21.04.64
OD-ADE	01.02.63
OE-LAF	26.09.60
PK-IVS	26.08.80
PK-IVW	13.11.88
PK-IVX	28.08.92
PK-MVG	11.01.85
PK-MVS	10.11.71
PK-RVK	07.01.76
PK-RVM	01.02.75
PK-RVN	01.05.81
PK-RVT	13.01.85
PK-RVU	24.07.92
PK-RVW	07.10.83
PP-SRD	15.05.73
PP-SRE	15.09.68
PP-SRG	22.12.59
PP-SRM	31.10.66
PP-SRQ	03.03.65
PP-SRR	04.09.64
SE-FOZ	15.01.77
SP-LVA	20.08.65
SP-LVB	19.12.62
SU-AIC	01.10.56
SU-AID	16.03.62
SU-AKW	29.09.60
SU-AKX	23.02.64
TC-SET	02.02.69
TC-SEV	17.02.59
TF-ISU	14.04.63
VH-RMI	22.09.66
VH-RMQ	31.12.68
VH-TVA	31.10.54
VH-TVC	30.11.61
VP-WAS	03.09.78
VP-YND	12.02.79
VP-YNE	09.08.58
VR-AAV	30.06.67
VT-DIH	15.11.61
VT-DIO	11.09.63
VT-DIX	09.08.71
VT-DJC	28.08.80
VX217	oo.oo.58
XA-SCM	27.07.92
XW-TFK	oo.03.75
XY-ADF	24.08.72
YI-ACL	17.04.73
YI-ACU	19.03.65
YS-09C	05.03.59
YV-C-AMV	25.01.71
YV-C-AMX	14.08.74
YV-C-AMZ	01.11.71
Z-YNI	oo.07.84
ZS-CVA	13.03.67

Vickers Vulcan

Registration	Date
G-EBDH	oo.oo.22
G-EBEM	07.05.26
G-EBLB	13.07.28

Vickers-Supermarine Walrus

Registration	Date
G-AHFN	03.07.55
G-AIIB	oo.oo.47
LN-TAK	31.08.49

Vought-Sikorsky VS-44A

Registration	Date
CX-AIR	15.08.47
N41881	oo.01.69
NC41880	03.10.42

Vultee V-1

Registration	Date
*	15.08.37
*	oo.09.37
NC13767	29.01.36
NC14249	12.06.36
NC14250	24.02.38
NC22077	20.03.48

Waco RNF

Registration	Date
CF-BDZ	07.10.49
LN-BAN	07.04.36

Westinghouse Sentinel 1000

Registration	Date
*	02.08.95

Westland WG.30

Registration	Date
N5830T	18.11.83
VT-EKQ	11.12.89
VT-EKR	07.02.89

Westland Wessex

Registration	Date
G-ABEG	oo.oo.36
G-ABVB	30.05.36
G-ADEW	03.07.35

Wibault 280

Registration	Date
F-AMHO	22.12.34
F-AMHP	09.05.34
F-AMYD	24.12.37
F-ANBL	02.08.36

Wild WT-S

Registration	Date
CH-71	18.09.21

Yakovlev YAK-24

Registration	Date
*	oo.oo.52
*	oo.oo.53

Yakovlev YAK-40

Registration	Date
*	oo.01.90
*	09.09.90
*	21.11.91
*	27.03.92
*	11.05.92
87995	27.08.93
CU-T1202	24.10.90
CU-T1219	03.02.80
D-BOBD	19.02.75
D2-TYC	08.06.80
D2-TYD	08.01.88
I-JAKE	28.05.77
LZ-DOK	02.08.88
OB-1559	25.02.94
OB-1569	05.11.94
RA-87256	17.07.94
RA-87464	25.01.95
RA-87468	26.09.94
RA-87565	14.01.95
RA-88244	17.05.93
RA-88254	27.10.94
SSSR-87201	25.08.83
SSSR-87236	18.04.86
SSSR-87291	19.04.83
SSSR-87301	17.05.86
SSSR-87323	15.08.75
SSSR-87328	06.10.75
SSSR-87346	29.08.82
SSSR-87360	14.12.74
SSSR-87364	15.07.75
SSSR-87369	09.04.74
SSSR-87385	19.03.92
SSSR-87391	15.09.89
SSSR-87398	02.05.74
SSSR-87411	14.09.92
SSSR-87437	07.10.78
SSSR-87453	01.08.90
SSSR-87454	16.11.79
SSSR-87455	18.09.81
SSSR-87458	22.10.75
SSSR-87475	15.07.75
SSSR-87485	31.05.82
SSSR-87509	02.09.89
SSSR-87526	07.11.91
SSSR-87544	02.10.78
SSSR-87549	24.01.88
SSSR-87579	23.05.74
SSSR-87602	28.02.73
SSSR-87618	16.01.87
SSSR-87629	21.12.73
SSSR-87638	16.12.76
SSSR-87648	31.10.79
SSSR-87689	12.06.80
SSSR-87690	03.09.70
SSSR-87696	25.01.87
SSSR-87719	28.07.71
SSSR-87738	30.03.77
SSSR-87756	07.12.76
SSSR-87772	09.09.76
SSSR-87778	04.05.72
SSSR-87790	08.08.73
SSSR-87803	11.10.85
SSSR-87808	29.06.83
SSSR-87819	22.10.72
SSSR-87825	28.01.75
SSSR-87826	19.06.87
SSSR-87893	18.07.80
SSSR-87902	16.01.82
SSSR-87911	08.04.78
SSSR-87914	09.09.90
SSSR-87930	20.03.79
SSSR-87934	30.11.90
SSSR-88208	17.12.76
SSSR-88235	13.05.92
SSSR-98102	14.08.82
UN-88181	oo.oo.95
VN-A449	14.11.92
YA-KAB	01.08.92
YA-KAD	25.01.72
YA-KAF	01.08.92
YK-AQC	19.03.76

Yakovlev YAK-42

Registration	Date
B-2755	31.07.92
RA-42331	25.01.94
RA-42390	20.11.93
SSSR-42351	14.09.90
SSSR-42536	oo.oo.86
SSSR-42529	28.06.82

Zeppelin Airship

Registration	Date
D-LZ219	06.05.37
LZ10	28.06.12
LZ11	12.10.15
LZ2	17.01.06
LZ4	05.08.08
LZ6A	14.09.10
LZ7	28.06.10
LZ8	16.05.11

Zeppelin-Staaken E.4/20

Registration	Date
n/a	28.12.20

Zlin Z-37 Cmelak

Registration	Date
OK-ZSO	01.07.79

Appendix C

Crashes by operator

This appendix provides another cross reference to the main listings. All crashes are listed here under the operator's name, again giving the registration and date for each accident they have suffered. Reference to this date in the main text will furnish the full accident details. If the date reads 'oo.oo.oo', the entry will be found in Appendix A.

09 Charlie Inc
- N4809C 14.07.78

A.E.Colombia
- HK-1850 13.09.78

A.E.Stanley Manufacturing Co
- N805C 03.01.83

A.G.Mechin & Co
- VP-YKF 25.07.54
- VP-YKT 10.01.54

A.Soriano y Cia
- PI-C825 03.07.72

AB Aerotransport
- SE-AAE 31.08.32
- SE-ABA 09.06.36
- SE-ADW 06.07.34
- SE-BAF 28.08.43
- SE-BAG 22.10.43
- SE-BAM 04.12.45
- SE-BAY 09.08.47
- SE-BBG 26.10.47

ABX Air
- N918AX 06.03.92

ACES Colombia
- HK-1910 23.01.85
- HK-2217 18.12.81
- HK-2536 29.11.82
- HK-2758 18.02.91
- HK-2761 27.04.86
- HK-2763 27.02.85

ADC Airlines
- 5N-BBA 26.07.95
- 5N-BBE 18.08.94

ADES Colombia
- HK-3079G 09.05.95

ADTEC Rajawari Udara
- 9M-AZB 03.09.91

AECA Cargo
- HC-BKN 18.09.84

AERA
- OO-ADO 10.05.40

AESA Airlines
- YS-05C 29.06.88

AIDA
- HK-1000E 31.01.55
- HK-1001E 15.03.61
- HK-133 08.12.56

AIRES
- HK-2593 04.08.85
- HK-2594 14.08.95
- HK-2638 23.01.85
- HK-3195X 15.12.90

ALA
- CC-CAN 21.02.66

ALAS
- CX-BXD 09.10.79
- HK-2578 16.05.81
- YS-37C 20.01.84

ALCON
- CP-1048 13.12.73

ALFA
- CC-CDI 18.07.68
- LV-AAP 29.07.48
- LV-AAW oo.oo.oo
- LV-AAY oo.oo.oo
- LV-AAZ oo.oo.oo
- LV-AFR oo.oo.oo

ALI
- I-ETNA 06.12.48

ALM Antillean Airlines
- N935F 02.05.70

AMAMZ
- 9Q-CJE oo.oo.62

AMAZ
- 9Q-CXA 24.07.64
- 9Q-CXC 15.12.70
- 9Q-CYB 07.08.75

AMSA
- HI-542CT 03.02.92

ANDES
- HC-AMC 20.09.68
- HC-AMV 02.12.72
- N6917C 15.12.73
- OB-OAD-233 17.01.49

AOC Surveys
- ZS-LUI 21.06.91

APA Services
- N6302C oo.oo.oo

APISA
- OB-1316 10.08.89

ARCO Bermuda
- VR-BCT 26.07.70

AREA
- HC-ACL 07.04.58
- HC-ADV 07.11.60
- HC-SJA 27.03.53
- HC-SJN-014 11.06.54
- HC-SJO oo.10.57
- N9267R 16.05.68

ARMCO Pacific
- N482U 14.02.83

AS Airlines
- RA-28756 05.06.94

ATESA
- HC-AUC 02.05.74

AVEMEX
- XA-LAN 08.01.93

AVES
- HK-1436 21.10.77

AVSA
- YV-C-FLF 02.02.72
- YV-C-FLG 02.02.72

Aaxico Airlines
- N5140B 02.09.59
- N51424 02.04.55
- N6541C 23.04.65
- N6579C 18.06.65
- N67941 14.08.63

Abakan Avia
- RA-67120 20.01.95

Abakan State Aviation
- RA-23518 25.07.95

Abbotsford Air Services
- * 18.11.76

Aberdeen Airways
- G-ACAN 21.05.41
- G-ACRH 13.07.34
- G-ADFI 03.07.37

Abu Dhabi Helicopters
- A6-BBJ 03.06.78
- A6-BBX 30.05.83
- A6-BCC 28.03.79

Abyssinian Government
- n/a 17.03.36

Abyssinian Royal Flight
- n/a oo.05.36

Acme Air
- N10GE 21.05.85

Acme Plywood & Veneer Co
- RP-C2152 07.10.78

Action Air
- N990RA 27.04.94

Active Aero Charter
- N51FG 08.06.93

Ad Astra Aero
- CH-18 31.08.20
- CH-71 18.09.21
- CH-77 29.03.22

Adastra Airways
- VH-BGO 05.06.48
- VH-BKZ 17.01.53
- VH-BNS 03.04.53

Adastral Air Lines
- G-EANN oo.oo.20

Adelaide Airways
- VH-URE 11.12.57
- VH-UUO 23.05.52

Aden Airways
- VR-AAA 26.03.65
- VR-AAM 12.04.64
- VR-AAN 23.11.66
- VR-AAV 30.06.67

Admas Air Service
- ET-ACO 28.07.89
- ET-ACP 19.09.82
- ET-ADB 10.05.88
- ET-ADG 10.02.77
- ET-ADK 22.03.79
- ET-ADP 16.03.77
- ET-AEG 27.01.78
- ET-AEY 10.11.85
- ET-AEZ 10.05.88
- ET-AFE 08.04.87
- ET-AHD 11.08.88
- ET-AHE 15.06.85
- ET-AJE 11.08.91
- ET-AJM 21.08.91

Advance Airlines
- VH-AAV 21.02.80

Advance Aviation
- N244B 05.09.78

Adventure Airlines
- N2715X 19.06.92
- N6234G 02.09.95

Aer Arann
- EI-BBA 17.10.75
- EI-BBR 07.07.80

Aer Lingus
- EI-ACA 18.06.46
- EI-ACF 01.01.53

EI-AFL	10.01.52
EI-AKK	21.09.67
EI-AOF	22.06.67
EI-AOM	24.03.68
EI-BEM	31.01.86

Aer Turas

EI-APM	12.06.67
EI-AWG	03.03.74

Aeralpi

I-CLAI	11.03.67
I-TORE	06.03.67

Aereo Reservaciones Ejecutivas

XA-SWF	23.06.95

Aerial Surveys

VH-AVS	07.11.52
VH-BFC	31.08.51

Aerial Tours

P2-ATX	14.08.75
VH-ATK	20.11.69

Aerial Transit Co

N84BL	05.05.90
HS-PAA	22.06.33

Aero Air [1]

N400N	01.12.90

Aero Air [2]

RA-05708	02.08.95
RA-23639	04.12.94

Aero Amazonas

HC-ANJ	03.11.71

Aero Arctic

C-FAAN	13.05.81

Aero Asahi

*	09.08.85
*	27.09.90
JA3887	22.10.87
JA7067	10.05.66
JA9058	23.03.90
JA9109	19.05.83
JA9127	08.11.91
JA9211	14.07.94
JA9222	19.02.83
JA9238	29.03.89
JA9276	20.04.85
JA9325	05.09.89
JA9365	20.08.90
JA9537	12.10.88
JA9596	09.05.89
JA9943	01.08.90

Aero Astra

XA-KUT	18.01.88

Aero Aysen

CC-CBT	12.02.70

Aero Bellavista

OB-T-1207	04.11.90

Aero California

XA-IOR	29.01.86

Aero Cargo

F-BCJS	01.12.48
F-BCJZ	oo.12.47

Aero Caribbean

CU-T1270	15.11.92

Aero Chasqui

OB-1218	09.07.91
OB-T-144	05.01.88

Aero Club of Cabo Verde

CR-CAC	14.06.57
CR-CAD	07.09.61

Aero Club of Libya

5A-DDD	30.11.88

Aero Coach

N5775C	31.01.91
N5785C	18.03.91

Aero Condor

OB-1319	03.09.93
OB-T-1271	10.03.89
OB-T-1272	oo.05.89

Aero Consul

PT-LLL	18.03.91

Aero Contractors

5N-AKC	14.09.77
5N-AKE	19.04.74
5N-AKO	01.10.80
5N-ATQ	13.09.94
5N-EPN	05.09.95

Aero Cozumel

XA-JOV	15.03.84

Aero Cuahonte

XA-SLU	13.06.94

Aero Eslava

XA-SCM	27.07.92

Aero Expreso Bogota

HK-3427	03.07.92

Aero Express

N49454	09.03.87
TG-BAC	03.11.80
TG-PAW	20.07.78

Aero Flite

N1340N	18.08.70

Aero France

F-GDHR	05.02.87

Aero Golfe

C-FIUS	28.07.93

Aero Holland

PH-TFA	20.11.49

Aero Huaylas

OB-1311	31.01.91
OB-1361	31.01.91

Aero Lima

N162PA	09.06.92
OB-1262	22.10.90

Aero Llanos

HK-344X	oo.oo.57

Aero Lloyd

D-1620	29.06.29
D-180	06.09.28

Aero Manu

*	26.07.90
OB-1349	20.09.90
OB-1350	14.02.91

Aero Nika

RA-11790	29.10.94

Aero Nortesur

CC-CBR	20.04.79

Aero O/Y

K-SALA	28.05.27
K-SALB	10.07.28
K-SALD	16.11.27
OH-ALI	09.10.35
OH-ALL	14.06.40
OH-LAK	31.10.45
SE-AEF	01.12.37

Aero Pacifico

OB-1255	29.11.90

Aero Palas

LV-JPG	19.02.71

Aero Peru

OB-R-1020	25.10.88

Aero Propaganda

SE-BTU	24.11.54

Aero Pulse

SSSR-48058	10.06.92

Aero San Martin

OB-S-1176	28.02.90
OB-T-594	25.10.88

Aero Scandia

SE-BRP	04.12.50

Aero Service Corporation

N189UM	07.04.78
N5274J	20.04.89
N5845N	oo.oo.58
TN-ADB	30.03.79
TN-AEQ	13.12.85

Aero Services

N8219H	oo.oo.80

Aero Sonora

XA-KOA	30.09.87

Aero Spacelines

N111AS	12.05.70
N90942	oo.08.67

Aero Star

OB-1458	21.06.92

Aero Sud Pacifico

XA-RML	09.12.92

Aero Sur

OB-1318	01.06.90

Aero Survey

n/a	oo.03.35

Aero Taxco

XA-MAO	oo.oo.87

Aero Taxi

N547DA	12.06.81

Aero Taxi Iquitos

N102RB	18.03.93
N3177W	31.05.93

Aero Taxi Rios

OB-1265	24.09.90

Aero Technik

OE-FFK	26.10.88

Aero Teseo

I-REGI	20.02.48

Aero Trades Western

C-FJRW	oo.12.81
C-FQIX	01.06.79

Aero Transport

OE-FAC	16.12.57

Aero Transporte

OB-1234	08.02.93

Aero Transportes

XA-GOR	08.10.51

Aero Transportes La Montana

YV-511C	13.10.93

Aero Transporti Italiani

I-ATIP	16.04.72
I-ATIR	30.10.72
I-ATIT	24.05.69
I-ATJC	14.09.79
I-ATRH	15.10.87

Aero Union

N3373F	14.07.81
N4989P	21.06.95
N67109	30.04.90
N9083Z	02.08.73
N924AU	17.10.91
N9324Z	12.07.71

Aero Virgin Islands

N100SD	17.09.89
N15598	02.01.78
N28346	17.09.89
N40425	17.09.89
N4425N	17.09.89
N4471J	17.09.89
N4577Z	17.09.89

Aero Vodochody

OK-FDC	oo.oo.90

Aero-Dienst

D-COCO	07.06.93

Aero-Kort

OY-DIZ	26.05.79

Aerobeni

CP-2251	03.03.94

Aerobrasil

PT-TCP	26.11.92

Aerocarga

HK-512	04.11.66
XA-LOS	22.02.66
ZP-CAI	17.01.62

Aerocargo

F-BCHH	14.07.47

Aerocaribe

XA-HUL	31.08.88
XA-RSV	13.03.92

Aerocauca

HK-3278	22.03.90

Aerocentro de Colombia

HK-1872I	14.06.78

Aerochago

HI-376CT	oo.09.90
HI-422	oo.oo.88
HI-532CT	oo.06.90
HI-599CT	18.02.93
HI-619SP	06.11.92

Aerocivil

HK-3001G	24.07.93

Aerocondor

HK-1972	22.02.75
HK-1976	10.07.75
HK-758	04.03.67
HK-777	27.08.73
N7301C	18.12.66

Aerocondor Transportes Aereos

CS-DAF	08.05.94

Aerocor

CC-CBW	07.08.81

Aerocorp

XA-SKO	26.08.94

Aerocosta

HK-1300	01.05.73
HK-1383	26.10.73
HK-756	10.07.75
HK-792	28.10.70

Aerocozumel

XA-JPE	05.05.89
XA-KOQ	oo.05.84

Aerodinos

N3044J	12.11.92

Aerodyne Engineering Corporation

N74139	08.06.68

Aeroejecutivos

YV-502C	18.09.92

Aeroespresso

I-AZDA	25.01.29

I-AZDB	24.12.29
I-AZDH	10.06.30
I-AZEE	18.07.33

Aeroexpreso Velez Angel

HK-1607	02.11.79

Aeroflite Services

N331DP	18.01.90

Aeroflot

*	oo.oo.41
*	04.12.46
*	26.03.52
*	29.12.54
*	31.12.54
*	06.08.55
*	13.12.59
*	27.04.60
*	28.12.60
*	13.08.61
*	17.12.61
*	31.12.61
*	06.07.62
*	29.07.62
*	26.02.63
*	05.03.63
*	02.04.63
*	04.04.63
*	07.12.63
*	02.09.64
*	19.10.64
*	03.01.65
*	20.03.65
*	11.09.65
*	27.08.66
*	22.11.66
*	30.12.66
*	14.01.67
*	03.03.67
*	06.04.67
*	04.06.67
*	16.10.67
*	04.11.67
*	06.01.68
*	09.01.68
*	29.01.68
*	19.02.68
*	24.02.68
*	22.04.68
*	06.10.68
*	20.10.68
*	02.11.68
*	24.03.69
*	25.06.69
*	03.08.69
*	12.08.69
*	26.08.69
*	10.09.69
*	13.11.69
*	06.12.69
*	10.04.71
*	oo.03.73
*	23.04.73
*	18.05.73
*	04.12.74
*	16.01.75
*	06.03.75
*	03.01.76
*	02.01.79
*	30.10.79
*	06.06.80
*	oo.12.80
*	07.02.81
*	18.09.81
*	11.02.84
*	16.05.85
*	oo.02.86
*	09.02.87
*	20.08.87
*	02.09.87
*	13.09.87
*	14.11.87
*	11.12.88
*	24.03.89
*	01.05.89
*	26.07.89
*	21.10.89
*	26.10.89
*	14.12.89
*	09.09.90
*	10.10.90
*	19.11.90
*	04.03.91
*	16.09.91
*	02.11.91
*	16.11.91
*	20.11.91
*	30.03.92
*	09.02.93
RA-09331	18.01.94
RA-11121	26.04.93
RA-47180	03.02.93
RA-68150	26.09.93
RA-70914	20.03.93
RA-86119	08.03.94
RA-86703	oo.10.92
SSSR-04214	oo.12.68
SSSR-04243	oo.oo.87
SSSR-06174	oo.08.67
SSSR-06324	oo.12.87
SSSR-07308	oo.oo.90
SSSR-07399	11.05.82
SSSR-07816	08.07.92
SSSR-08837	28.10.84
SSSR-09303	18.07.70
SSSR-09303	11.11.92
SSSR-09305	19.12.70
SSSR-09311	02.06.80
SSSR-09318	22.12.77
SSSR-09349	oo.06.77
SSSR-10232	05.08.84
SSSR-11000	22.01.71
SSSR-11024	25.05.71
SSSR-11030	18.10.74
SSSR-11031	01.10.70
SSSR-11104	28.10.80
SSSR-11107	24.04.82
SSSR-11137	12.10.71
SSSR-11145	31.03.71
SSSR-11148	27.01.62
SSSR-11149	15.05.70
SSSR-11167	16.11.59
SSSR-11172	08.08.68
SSSR-11180	26.02.60
SSSR-11185	28.06.62
SSSR-11188	08.08.70
SSSR-11189	12.10.69
SSSR-11193	08.02.63
SSSR-11215	18.06.72
SSSR-11341	17.02.73
SSSR-11360	21.11.72
SSSR-11374	16.02.72
SSSR-11418	04.10.88
SSSR-11514	27.08.88
SSSR-11795	25.03.86
SSSR-12950	01.05.74
SSSR-12963	23.08.79
SSSR-12966	26.02.70
SSSR-12967	02.10.73
SSSR-12985	04.12.74
SSSR-12993	29.07.71
SSSR-12996	31.01.71
SSSR-12997	13.01.89
SSSR-13320	23.09.91
SSSR-25840	17.08.77
SSSR-26007	06.03.87
SSSR-26009	24.07.84
SSSR-26038	02.11.89
SSSR-26095	06.02.86
SSSR-26505	23.12.81
SSSR-26547	09.12.78
SSSR-26567	23.05.76
SSSR-26569	25.03.79
SSSR-26627	23.12.82
SSSR-26685	19.07.89
SSSR-26686	12.04.83
SSSR-27070	05.11.92
SSSR-28741	14.08.87
SSSR-28924	23.10.91
SSSR-29110	12.12.90
SSSR-32544	21.06.92
SSSR-35546	14.04.92
SSSR-40237	03.07.92
SSSR-41803	14.02.90
SSSR-41807	oo.oo.oo
SSSR-42327	09.02.76
SSSR-42335	17.07.76
SSSR-42351	14.09.90
SSSR-42357	01.02.61
SSSR-42362	17.10.58
SSSR-42366	02.09.62
SSSR-42369	13.01.77
SSSR-42370	30.06.62
SSSR-42388	17.09.61
SSSR-42405	25.07.71
SSSR-42408	10.03.72
SSSR-42436	28.04.69
SSSR-42438	16.03.61
SSSR-42444	17.03.79
SSSR-42447	10.07.61
SSSR-42452	20.10.60
SSSR-42471	28.11.76
SSSR-42472	30.08.75
SSSR-42476	09.06.64
SSSR-42483	18.05.63
SSSR-42486	13.10.73
SSSR-42490	10.10.71
SSSR-42491	04.06.62
SSSR-42492	13.07.63
SSSR-42495	25.10.62
SSSR-42501	05.11.74
SSSR-42503	07.12.73
SSSR-42504	02.11.61
SSSR-42506	30.09.73
SSSR-42529	28.06.82
SSSR-42536	oo.oo.86
SSSR-45004	23.12.73
SSSR-45012	02.09.70
SSSR-45017	12.03.66
SSSR-45019	07.03.68
SSSR-45021	21.08.63
SSSR-45028	08.03.65
SSSR-45031	20.10.73
SSSR-45037	03.01.75
SSSR-45038	29.08.79
SSSR-45061	16.12.73
SSSR-45062	09.07.73
SSSR-45083	29.01.70
SSSR-45086	10.11.65
SSSR-46201	31.12.67
SSSR-46202	04.11.72
SSSR-46220	18.04.80
SSSR-46269	03.09.79
SSSR-46276	21.01.73
SSSR-46277	25.01.74
SSSR-46280	08.03.81
SSSR-46299	19.12.78
SSSR-46327	23.10.78
SSSR-46335	21.11.89
SSSR-46349	20.11.75
SSSR-46357	06.01.74
SSSR-46378	13.11.71
SSSR-46418	27.02.72
SSSR-46423	02.03.86
SSSR-46435	18.08.73
SSSR-46467	17.11.75
SSSR-46472	23.03.91
SSSR-46476	25.04.75
SSSR-46518	06.09.76
SSSR-46525	04.10.89
SSSR-46534	15.05.76
SSSR-46551	02.06.90
SSSR-46567	16.12.82
SSSR-46613	10.03.76
SSSR-46617	24.12.83
SSSR-46653	24.08.81
SSSR-46669	08.07.88
SSSR-46722	17.12.76
SSSR-46724	26.09.91
SSSR-46732	22.02.72
SSSR-46747	31.03.71
SSSR-46788	01.12.71
SSSR-46807	15.01.79
SSSR-46809	12.11.71
SSSR-46847	08.07.77
SSSR-47164	14.12.90
SSSR-47280	13.01.76
SSSR-47358	28.01.84
SSSR-47695	09.12.77
SSSR-47701	28.01.70
SSSR-47729	01.06.71
SSSR-47732	14.04.80
SSSR-47734	13.08.76
SSSR-47751	01.04.70
SSSR-47772	13.10.69
SSSR-48095	28.09.89
SSSR-56472	20.02.90
SSSR-61683	30.10.79
SSSR-65031	22.03.79
SSSR-65058	27.08.92
SSSR-65120	02.07.86
SSSR-65129	30.08.83
SSSR-65142	22.06.86
SSSR-65607	17.07.72
SSSR-65612	oo.oo.oo
SSSR-65642	oo.oo.oo
SSSR-65649	31.05.79
SSSR-65668	30.06.73
SSSR-65675	27.02.88
SSSR-65698	06.01.81
SSSR-65735	11.08.79
SSSR-65766	20.10.86
SSSR-65795	12.12.86
SSSR-65807	oo.oo.84
SSSR-65816	11.08.79
SSSR-65836	14.08.82
SSSR-65839	19.05.79
SSSR-65856	03.05.85
SSSR-65871	28.06.81
SSSR-65910	01.02.85
SSSR-65951	13.01.90
SSSR-67099	27.08.91
SSSR-67101	14.08.82
SSSR-67104	28.08.89
SSSR-67127	07.12.88
SSSR-67140	29.12.84
SSSR-67190	29.03.83
SSSR-67191	oo.oo.oo
SSSR-67206	03.08.79
SSSR-67210	18.01.79
SSSR-67225	04.12.84
SSSR-67235	26.08.88
SSSR-67249	24.09.87
SSSR-67264	14.10.86
SSSR-67276	04.07.84
SSSR-67290	07.01.82
SSSR-67315	19.10.83
SSSR-67331	12.10.90
SSSR-67334	18.10.87
SSSR-67428	31.12.86
SSSR-67518	19.04.88
SSSR-69306	02.10.90
SSSR-69310	03.12.90
SSSR-69321	25.09.85
SSSR-69346	29.10.92
SSSR-70087	oo.oo.oo
SSSR-70501	27.05.87
SSSR-74252	29.02.68
SSSR-74298	31.08.72
SSSR-75405	24.04.74
SSSR-75408	06.03.76
SSSR-75414	10.05.79
SSSR-75425	09.05.74
SSSR-75507	01.10.72
SSSR-75520	15.02.77
SSSR-75533	05.06.70
SSSR-75558	30.01.76
SSSR-75559	27.04.74
SSSR-75575	30.10.76
SSSR-75578	16.10.70
SSSR-75663	26.08.72
SSSR-75687	11.05.73
SSSR-75705	17.08.60
SSSR-75712	24.02.73
SSSR-75773	31.12.70
SSSR-75798	06.02.70
SSSR-75823	23.08.70
SSSR-75824	03.08.64
SSSR-76457	02.12.66
SSSR-76462	oo.oo.63
SSSR-76466	20.10.89
SSSR-76569	18.10.89
SSSR-77111	23.05.78
SSSR-78780	28.08.92
SSSR-78781	27.03.90
SSSR-85023	19.02.73
SSSR-85029	13.06.81
SSSR-85030	07.05.73
SSSR-85067	13.01.89
SSSR-85097	23.05.91
SSSR-85102	01.06.76
SSSR-85103	01.03.80
SSSR-85169	19.05.78
SSSR-85234	oo.06.92
SSSR-85243	11.10.84
SSSR-85254	18.01.88
SSSR-85268	20.10.90
SSSR-85269	05.09.92
SSSR-85282	oo.06.92
SSSR-85311	10.07.85
SSSR-85321	08.10.80
SSSR-85327	21.05.86
SSSR-85338	23.12.84
SSSR-85355	07.07.80
SSSR-85413	08.03.88
SSSR-85479	24.09.88
SSSR-85480	16.11.81
SSSR-85664	17.11.90

SSSR-86470 29.09.82
SSSR-86513 06.07.82
SSSR-86546 21.11.90
SSSR-86613 21.11.90
SSSR-86614 27.05.77
SSSR-86671 13.10.72
SSSR-86905 12.06.90
SSSR-87201 25.08.83
SSSR-87236 18.04.86
SSSR-87291 19.04.83
SSSR-87301 17.05.86
SSSR-87323 15.08.75
SSSR-87328 06.10.75
SSSR-87346 29.08.82
SSSR-87360 14.12.74
SSSR-87364 15.07.75
SSSR-87369 09.04.74
SSSR-87391 15.09.89
SSSR-87398 02.05.74
SSSR-87437 07.10.78
SSSR-87453 01.08.90
SSSR-87454 16.11.79
SSSR-87455 18.09.81
SSSR-87458 22.10.75
SSSR-87475 15.07.75
SSSR-87485 31.05.82
SSSR-87509 02.09.89
SSSR-87526 07.11.91
SSSR-87544 02.10.78
SSSR-87549 24.01.88
SSSR-87579 23.05.74
SSSR-87602 28.02.73
SSSR-87618 16.01.87
SSSR-87629 21.12.73
SSSR-87638 16.12.76
SSSR-87648 31.10.79
SSSR-87689 12.06.80
SSSR-87690 03.09.70
SSSR-87696 25.01.87
SSSR-87719 28.07.71
SSSR-87738 30.03.77
SSSR-87756 07.12.76
SSSR-87772 09.09.76
SSSR-87778 04.05.72
SSSR-87790 08.08.73
SSSR-87803 11.10.85
SSSR-87808 29.06.83
SSSR-87819 22.10.72
SSSR-87825 28.01.75
SSSR-87826 19.06.87
SSSR-87893 18.07.80
SSSR-87902 16.01.82
SSSR-87911 08.04.78
SSSR-87914 09.09.90
SSSR-87930 20.03.79
SSSR-87934 30.11.90
SSSR-88208 17.12.76
SSSR-88288 07.12.86
SSSR-98102 14.08.82
SSSR-L1196 oo.oo.35
SSSR-L1657 03.12.57
SSSR-L1874 15.08.57
SSSR-L416 oo.07.36
SSSR-L417 03.10.34
SSSR-L5414 19.02.58
SSSR-L5442 15.08.58
SSSR-L5612 18.02.58
SSSR-L760 12.12.42
SSSR-L840 oo.09.35
SSSR-N968 oo.oo.oo
URSS-C 25.04.41
URSS-M25 06.08.37

Aeroflot Russian International A/L
F-OGQS 22.03.94

Aerogeodeziya
SSSR-F48 oo.06.35

Aerogulf Services
A6-ALE 07.09.90
A6-ALT 06.12.87

Aerojet
* 13.06.92

Aeroleasing
HB-LHT 12.11.76
HB-PGH 05.09.82
HB-RET 15.09.81

Aeroleo Taxi Aereo
PT-HJI 07.03.89
PT-HJN 09.03.83
PT-HQC 03.02.84
PT-HQF 04.06.92

Aerolift Philippines
RP-C314 18.05.90

Aerolineas Abaroa
CP-565 17.09.76
CP-639 08.12.64
CP-691 22.11.67
CP-695 06.12.62
CP-710 10.09.62
CP-729 06.06.64
CP-791 11.11.68

Aerolineas Argentinas
LV-ABQ 17.06.53
LV-ABX oo.oo.53
LV-ACD 16.07.56
LV-ACH 30.12.50
LV-ACL 12.06.50
LV-ACM 14.07.59
LV-ACQ 20.05.55
LV-ACX 23.04.54
LV-ACY 26.03.51
LV-ADM 12.12.59
LV-ADQ 16.10.54
LV-ADS 07.09.60
LV-ADV 10.06.58
LV-ADW 19.07.61
LV-AFW 15.05.59
LV-AGE 03.06.51
LV-AHO 20.02.60
LV-AHP 27.08.59
LV-AHR 23.11.61
LV-AHZ 08.12.57
LV-HGW 04.02.70
LV-HGY 03.07.63
LV-HHH 20.01.72
LV-HHI 27.11.69
LV-IEV 15.07.69
LV-JGR 27.01.86
LV-JNE 20.11.92
LV-LIU 26.09.88
LV-LOB 15.11.75
LV-MZD 05.01.90

Aerolineas Brasil
PP-AVZ 30.05.50

Aerolineas Carreras
LV-GGN 07.12.65
LV-HIJ 07.12.65

Aerolineas Colon
HP-572OL oo.12.89

Aerolineas Condor
HC-BHB 14.07.80
HC-BHZ 01.09.82

Aerolineas Cordillera
CC-CBO 15.05.79

Aerolineas El Salvador
YS-012C 13.02.65

Aerolineas Especiales de Colombia
HK-249 14.09.77
HK-429 25.02.77

Aerolineas JLJ
N45RM 01.07.92

Aerolineas La Gaviola
HK-2059 30.11.79

Aerolineas La Paz
CP-1243 13.03.80
CP-1418 16.01.89
CP-755 23.11.76

Aerolineas Leon
XA-KEH 21.05.81

Aerolineas Litoral Argentina
LV-FYJ 09.01.64

Aerolineas Llaneras
HK-2890 23.05.94

Aerolineas Moxi
XA-FUW 12.06.67

Aerolineas Mundo
HI-515CT 05.04.90

Aerolineas Nacionales [1]
TI-1019 30.03.58
TI-1023 25.05.60

Aerolineas Nacionales [2]
HP-1002 oo.12.89

Aerolineas Regionales de Paz
HK-2641 02.02.84
HK-670 21.06.77

Aerolineas SARA
OB-1464 31.08.92

Aerolineas TAO
HK-1058 08.06.74

Aerolineas Topografica
* 09.11.58

Aerolineas Vega
XA-KIC oo.oo.61

Aerolineas del Este
HK-1665 25.04.84
HK-3177 15.05.91

Aeromar
HI-201 25.04.73

Aeromaritime
F-AOMT 10.07.38

Aeromexico
XA-DEN 27.07.81
XA-DEO 09.11.81
XA-JED 31.08.86
XA-SOC 21.06.73
XA-SOF 02.09.76

Aeronaut Air Services
N17337 27.06.66

Aeronaves Nacionales
TI-1022 10.07.59

Aeronaves de Mexico
XA-FUG 11.02.49
XA-GUN 25.03.54
XA-MEC 09.07.65
XA-MEV 02.06.58
XA-NUS 24.12.66
XA-PEI 13.08.66
XA-XAX 19.01.61

Aeronaves de Panama
HP-382 10.07.63
HP-385 09.10.63

Aeronaves del Peru
N715UA 11.09.80
OB-R-1104 27.08.76
OB-R-1143 01.08.80

Aeronica
YN-BFO 21.12.87
YN-BXW 10.11.91
YN-BYX 16.09.90
YN-BYZ 29.06.83
YN-BZF 20.04.85
YN-CBE 24.05.88
YN-CBT oo.oo.92

Aeronor Chile
CC-CJE 09.12.82

Aeronorte [1]
PP-NBA 09.03.52
PP-NBC oo.oo.oo
PP-NBD oo.oo.oo
PP-YQS 15.03.61

Aeronorte [2]
HK-329 10.09.80
HK-728 24.07.74

Aeronorte [3]
ZP-PGZ 01.06.77

Aeronorte [4]
N6204D 03.09.94

Aeroperlas
N187SA 18.04.90

Aeropesca
HK-1146 05.01.74
HK-1350 14.08.78
HK-2382 23.03.82
HK-388 21.10.81
HK-527 11.07.66
HK-682 oo.oo.69
HK-683 13.02.69
HK-790 oo.03.70

Aeroporikai Metaphorai Ellados
SX-BDA 25.12.50

Aeroposta Argentina
F-AJPD 10.05.30
R293 23.06.36

Aeropostal
YV-03C 02.04.93
YV-23C 05.03.91
YV-37C 27.11.92
YV-45C 03.03.78

Aeropostale
F-AEEJ 03.10.28
F-AFHN 27.01.28
F-AHEQ 22.01.28
F-AIMU 01.02.29
F-AIOX 09.12.31
F-AIOY oo.oo.oo
F-AISN 15.11.28
F-AISV 11.01.33
F-AISX 22.05.29
F-AISZ oo.oo.oo
F-AITX 24.02.31
F-AIUT 10.12.32
F-AIXU 25.10.31
F-AJCN 30.11.29
F-AJIP oo.oo.oo
F-AJIX 09.05.33
F-AJJM 12.10.32
F-AJJQ oo.oo.oo
F-AJKB oo.oo.oo
F-AJKF oo.oo.oo
F-AJNQ oo.05.30
F-AJOM 30.10.32
F-AJOX 27.02.32
F-AJOZ oo.oo.oo
F-AJUU 12.10.30
F-AJVH oo.oo.oo
F-AJVK 29.06.33
F-ALCG oo.oo.oo

Aeroprooveduria
HK-1485 07.08.74

Aeroput
YU-SAH 12.09.33

Aeroservicio Puntarenas
* 15.02.74

Aeroservicios Ecuatorianos
* 03.08.93
HC-BDF 02.07.77

Aeroservicios Ejectivos
HK-2920 11.10.87

Aeroservicios Parrague
CC-CDS 18.04.79

Aeroservicios S. de R.L.
- HR-ASN 26.05.70

Aeroservicios de Emergencia
- TG-CES-40 26.08.56

Aerosol
- HK-400 31.08.93

Aerospatiale
- F-WEGA 17.06.88
- F-WMCU 30.05.65
- F-WRSN 23.03.71

Aerosucre
- * 24.09.76
- HK-1322 13.03.84
- HK-2702 05.11.89
- HK-2850X 27.11.86
- HK-3288X 29.09.91
- HK-3325X 26.04.89
- HK-3511 20.06.91

Aerotaca
- HK-2759X 06.06.93

Aerotal
- HK-1393 21.11.78
- HK-1778 20.07.79
- HK-2214X 24.01.80
- HK-2410X 20.12.80
- HK-2559 04.08.82
- HK-654 17.07.75

Aerotaxi Americano
- HK-869 23.07.80

Aerotaxi Casanare
- HK-1289 20.06.79
- HK-2486 11.06.89

Aerotaxi Colombia
- HK-2564 02.06.81

Aerotaxis Astro
- LV-XZT 01.07.71

Aerotaxis Ecuatorianos
- HC-AXG oo.oo.74
- HC-AXK 24.07.80

Aerotechnica [1]
- EC-ACQ 04.09.52

Aerotechnica [2]
- YV-323C 07.10.83
- YV-C-GAI 08.05.72

Aerotour [1]
- F-BYAU 09.12.77

Aerotour [2]
- OB-T-1292 19.11.86
- OB-T-805 28.09.84

Aerotransportes Entre Rios
- LV-JNL 12.07.70
- LV-JSY 27.09.75
- LV-JYR 20.07.72

Aerotransportes del Sureste
- XA-DUU 02.02.46

Aerovias Boliviana Transandina
- CP-712 02.05.67

Aerovias Brasil
- PP-AVA oo.oo.oo
- PP-AVM 22.05.47
- PP-AVO 14.07.48
- PP-AXG 19.12.49
- YS-22 03.06.45

Aerovias Centrales
- X-ABEA 24.11.33
- X-ABED 05.05.34
- XA-BEJ 23.06.34

Aerovias Coahuila
- XA-HOU 10.10.49

Aerovias Condor
- CP-678 26.11.60

Aerovias Condor de Colombia
- HK-503 23.05.57

Aerovias Contreras
- XA-GOT oo.oo.53

Aerovias Cubanas Internacionales
- * 27.08.48
- NC44567 06.02.47

Aerovias Darientas
- HP-319 23.09.66

Aerovias Guest
- XA-GUU 22.09.48
- XA-HEG 15.11.56

Aerovias Halcon
- LV-GFW 27.01.66
- LV-GLA 18.08.66
- LV-GXB oo.oo.71

Aerovias Inc
- CF-BZH 14.02.56

Aerovias La Urraca
- HP-560 21.02.73

Aerovias Las Minas
- CP-1336 06.10.77
- CP-1338 23.05.78
- CP-908 02.03.71
- CP-992 10.03.75
- N96040 08.12.78

Aerovias Latinas Americanas
- YS-30 30.04.47

Aerovias Los Andes
- CP-622 18.02.57

Aerovias Moxos
- CP-571 16.01.62
- CP-588 02.05.63

Aerovias Panama
- HP-312 11.01.62

Aerovias Peruanas
- OB-1189 30.05.90

Aerovias Pilotos Asociados Medellin
- HK-524 22.04.62

Aerovias Quisqueyana
- HI-117 01.06.73
- HI-260 31.08.79

Aerovias Reformas
- XA-FOU 15.06.49

Aerovias Rojas
- XA-GEV 10.04.68

Aerovias SA [1]
- PP-AVG 05.02.47
- PP-MGA 29.03.49

Aerovias SA [2]
- OB-1331 03.05.90
- OB-T-1191 19.11.89
- OB-T-1273 01.05.86

Aerovias SA [3]
- TG-ACP 21.11.93

Aerovias Sud Americana
- N1662M 12.12.56
- N66559 20.03.53

Aerovias del Caucia
- HK-3278 22.03.90

Aerovias del Llano
- HK-3067 11.10.85

Aerovias del Valle
- TI-1063C 08.10.68

Aerovolga
- RA-24450 23.04.93

Aerowest
- D-IEFW 24.01.94

Affretair
- TR-LVO 05.02.82

Africair
- N1210Y 26.09.87

African Air Carriers
- C9-ATH 06.01.92
- N47FE 21.04.88

African Air Cars
- VP-KDI 26.01.49
- VP-KDJ 20.01.48

African Air Charter
- * 01.04.95
- 9Q-CMD 09.10.85

African Airlines International
- SSSR-48088 09.10.92

African Lux
- 9Q-CAM 26.11.77

African Overland Safaris
- A2-AOS 23.12.76

Afrimex
- 5N-ARF oo.11.90

Agape Flights
- N8071L 12.06.91

Agar, C.
- EP-CAA 24.09.60

Agencia Interamericana de Aviada
- C-1002 15.03.48

Agro Air International
- HI-481 30.07.87

Aguinaldo Development Co
- PI-C648 14.10.47

Agusta Helicopters
- MM80825 30.03.80

Aid by Air
- TF-AAE 02.06.69

Aigle Azur
- F-BCJE 04.03.54
- F-BCYP 07.07.48
- F-BEFG 17.03.53
- F-BEHS 30.08.54
- F-BESS 16.04.53
- F-BEST 16.06.53
- F-BFGL 09.07.50
- F-BGPM 13.02.53
- F-BGXD 31.01.54
- F-BHHR 22.05.01
- F-DAAR 13.03.54
- F-OABJ 27.11.49
- F-OABK 12.02.51
- F-OAMH 04.03.54
- F-OAMI 04.03.54
- F-OAPC 04.03.54

Air 70
- I-ASON 16.12.78

Air Ads
- G-AJTC 23.09.55
- G-AJWD 26.08.56

Air Affaires
- F-BKMF 05.06.66
- F-BVJI 22.08.84

Air Affaires Afrique
- TJ-AFO 24.06.80

Air Affaires Gabon
- TR-LUF 18.09.92

Air Afrique
- F-AMUZ 13.06.38
- F-ANJX 16.11.38
- F-BIAO 03.05.63
- LZ-SFC oo.oo.92
- YR-ABM 15.01.93

Air Albatross
- ZK-EHT 04.10.85

Air Algerie
- 7T-VAC 11.06.65
- 7T-VAH 02.05.76
- 7T-VAI 23.09.73
- 7T-VAK 26.07.69
- 7T-VAU 11.04.67
- 7T-VEE 21.12.94
- 7T-VHK 01.08.89
- 7T-VRM 25.07.91
- 7T-VSB oo.oo.oo
- 7T-VSD 16.10.65
- 7T-VSI 21.01.71
- 7T-VSU 24.01.79
- 7T-WUI 21.05.92
- F-BAZE 26.04.62
- F-BAZG 17.12.55
- F-BCYF 12.12.47
- F-BCYO 08.01.49
- F-OAIY 30.10.51
- F-OAVR 22.05.63

Air Alma
- C-GLBA 04.07.95

Air Alpes
- F-BRUF 15.01.70
- F-BRUX 16.02.78

Air America
- * 13.08.61
- * 04.02.62
- * 06.04.62
- * 05.09.63
- * 18.01.69
- * 20.04.71
- * 22.11.72
- * 06.12.72
- * oo.12.72
- * 12.02.73
- * oo.oo.73
- 57-6290 27.12.71
- 64-0506 oo.02.70
- 64-0507 oo.02.70
- B-148 17.07.63
- B-1535 28.04.66
- B-811 20.10.54
- N1386N 25.11.68
- N389EX 28.04.74
- N5662 25.07.72
- XW-PBV 24.03.76

Air Associates
- NC5885 19.05.29

Air Atlas
- F-BAXM 13.10.50
- F-BAXY 08.12.50
- F-BCHQ 30.08.47

Air Azur
- F-BAQT 08.07.47

Air BC
- C-FAWA 14.04.81
- C-FRQW 30.12.83

Air BG
- F-GBTC 15.01.86

Air Benin
- TY-BBL 24.02.83

Air Bissau
J5-GBB 15.08.91

Air Bleu
F-ANRI 22.01.38
F-ANRK 04.12.35

Air Bolivia
CP-969 22.03.73

Air Boniats
D-IBHH 25.01.92

Air Bridge Carriers
G-APRN 17.04.82

Air Brousse
9O-CJT 06.10.60
OO-ARN 20.06.60
OO-CMS 08.07.56

Air Burkina
XT-AAX 08.10.88

Air Caicos
CF-UXB 17.09.71

Air California
N468AC 17.02.81

Air Cambodge
* 04.05.73
* 11.04.75
B-1801 00.00.74
N999JZ 11.06.73
XU-BAE 00.00.00
XU-JTA 22.01.71

Air Cameroun
F-OAFI 02.03.65
TJ-ABC 13.06.61

Air Canada
C-FTLU 02.06.83
C-FTLV 26.06.78
C-FTLY 02.06.82
CF-THK 07.04.69
CF-THT 13.06.64
CF-TIJ 21.06.73
CF-TIW 05.07.70
CF-TJM 19.05.67
CF-TJN 29.11.63

Air Cape
N79LA 23.05.81

Air Carelia
OH-CAR 19.11.87

Air Cargo America
N76Q 25.09.87

Air Cargo Carriers
N30GA 01.09.95

Air Cargo Express
N989B 01.04.88

Air Cargo Transport
NC39188 08.03.46
NC41798 08.03.46

Air Carrier
N12978 00.00.70

Air Carrier Express Services
N551CC 29.09.85

Air Carriers
VH-BDT 00.00.48
VR-HEP 13.01.51

Air Central
N7705 25.03.73

Air Ceylon
4R-ACJ 07.09.78
VP-CAT 21.12.49

Air Chad
TT-EAB 28.01.78

Air Charter [1]
G-AGRG 27.01.59
G-AGRH 23.04.59
G-AMGL 11.03.52
G-AMGM 27.11.52

Air Charter [2]
ZK-AFB 12.02.62

Air Charter [3]
D-CATY 14.12.94

Air Charter Services
9Q-CTZ 00.04.86

Air Chile
CC-CAH 21.02.55
N3185G 27.02.92

Air China
B-2208 22.03.90
B-2536 06.07.95

Air Classic Museum
N121H 13.06.95

Air Colombia
HK-1702 10.02.91

Air Commerce
G-AEPF 18.06.40

Air Commerciale
* 08.08.37

Air Comores
F-OECD 27.01.68

Air Congo
9Q-CUD 19.02.70
9Q-CUM 18.08.68
9Q-CUP 15.02.70
9Q-CUS 29.03.63
OO-CFB 07.04.48
OO-CUA 26.05.61

Air Contractors
G-AIHL 29.10.46
G-AIKV 12.01.47

Air Council
G-FAAF 21.06.21
G-FAAW 05.10.30

Air Courier
* 00.09.61
KA-DFN 00.12.61

Air Creebec
C-GQSV 03.12.88

Air Dale
C-GQKZ 19.03.92

Air Dispatch
G-ADBZ 22.01.37

Air Djibouti
F-OCKT 23.07.69

Air East
N125AE 06.01.74

Air Eastern
VH-XAE 06.07.89

Air Ecosse
G-STUD 20.04.83

Air Enterprise
F-GDAV 30.01.89

Air Enterprises
G-AGVY 11.02.49
G-AJLJ 25.10.50
G-ALWY 19.04.52

Air Exchange
N23CD 17.10.85

Air Express [1]
VH-SJQ 10.05.75

Air Express [2]
LN-AAE 15.11.89

Air Ferry
G-APYK 03.06.67
G-ASOG 21.01.67

Air Fiordland
ZK-DAX 30.12.89

Air Florida
N62AF 13.01.82

Air France
* 18.09.36
* 05.05.40
* 03.05.43
F-AIFD 16.11.33
F-AILG 11.06.34
F-AISB 20.03.34
F-AIVG 31.05.34
F-AJBJ 02.07.37
F-AJIQ 02.11.35
F-AJIR 21.01.36
F-AJMI 31.10.33
F-AJPA 26.02.34
F-AJPB 11.11.35
F-AJUZ 00.00.00
F-AJZX 00.12.35
F-AKGF 07.12.36
F-ALCF 20.01.35
F-ALCH 17.12.33
F-ALFF 09.02.34
F-ALHO 01.04.35
F-AMHO 22.12.34
F-AMHP 09.05.34
F-AMMY 14.01.34
F-AMYD 24.12.37
F-ANBL 02.08.36
F-ANPB 09.02.38
F-ANPH 10.12.35
F-ANPJ 27.01.39
F-ANQA 27.10.37
F-ANQG 00.00.36
F-ANQR 07.03.38
F-AOHA 03.03.40
F-AOIK 10.02.36
F-AOMR 04.08.41
F-AOOT 03.04.39
F-AOTZ 08.12.37
F-AOZA 05.04.44
F-AQBA 07.07.40
F-AQBB 23.03.38
F-AQBF 00.00.41
F-AQBH 00.00.40
F-AQBJ 11.10.40
F-AQBL 05.04.44
F-AQBN 00.00.00
F-AQBO 00.00.41
F-AQBS 00.00.41
F-AQCY 00.00.00
F-AQNL 01.09.41
F-ARAP 00.08.44
F-AREJ 13.08.42
F-ARIA 00.00.41
F-ARIC 03.05.39
F-ARIZ 27.09.42
F-AROA 27.11.40
F-ARTD 20.06.40
F-ARTL 02.07.42
F-BAIF 00.11.46
F-BAII 30.04.59
F-BAJB 04.10.47
F-BAJP 10.09.45
F-BAJS 29.06.46
F-BAJT 08.08.46
F-BAKL 23.11.45
F-BAKM 20.03.47
F-BAKO 04.02.46
F-BAKP 05.03.47
F-BAKV 07.06.47
F-BALE 10.04.53
F-BALF 01.07.47
F-BALK 02.02.46
F-BALV 25.12.45
F-BAMQ 01.01.52
F-BANB 05.06.47
F-BANK 05.12.52
F-BANO 10.11.45
F-BANP 13.01.46
F-BAOA 08.01.58
F-BAOB 03.09.46
F-BAOD 16.02.50
F-BAOE 30.07.62
F-BAPE 00.06.56
F-BAPI 21.12.57
F-BAPJ 22.05.47
F-BAPQ 25.11.58
F-BATB 07.04.52
F-BATG 14.06.48
F-BATH 10.02.48
F-BATK 04.02.48
F-BATM 23.11.48
F-BATO 29.08.48
F-BATU 09.04.49
F-BATY 07.10.47
F-BAXB 11.08.51
F-BAXC 06.01.48
F-BAXD 04.09.46
F-BAXL 18.03.55
F-BAXO 14.03.47
F-BAXQ 01.02.47
F-BAXT 24.01.56
F-BAZI 25.08.54
F-BAZN 28.10.49
F-BAZS 03.08.53
F-BAZX 24.12.58
F-BAZZ 01.09.53
F-BBDB 22.01.50
F-BBDC 10.04.48
F-BBDE 12.06.50
F-BBDL 12.07.48
F-BBDM 14.05.50
F-BBDO 03.02.51
F-BBDS 20.10.49
F-BBFA 22.07.46
F-BBYC 03.03.48
F-BBYG 30.04.47
F-BCUC 26.01.48
F-BCUI 30.07.50
F-BCUM 03.03.52
F-BCYK 28.01.56
F-BCYU 21.09.55
F-BDRC 01.08.48
F-BEIK 08.04.57
F-BELK 20.04.58
F-BELO 28.11.49
F-BFCP 28.05.69
F-BGNA 03.08.54
F-BGNK 12.12.56
F-BHBC 29.08.60
F-BHBM 10.05.61
F-BHKU 26.09.63
F-BHKV 31.05.58
F-BHKY 02.11.57
F-BHMK 06.12.57
F-BHRL 12.03.79
F-BHSA 27.07.61
F-BHSH 07.09.76
F-BHSM 03.06.62
F-BHST 22.06.62
F-BHSZ 03.12.69
F-BJTB 12.09.61
F-BLCJ 05.03.68
F-BOHB 11.09.68
F-BPUI 24.07.74
F-BSGZ 28.08.76
F-BSUM 11.08.73
F-BVGK 17.03.82
F-GCBC 02.12.85
F-GFKC 26.06.88
F-GNIA 20.01.94
N28888 12.06.75

Air Freight New Zealand
ZK-FTB 31.07.89

Air Fret
F-OCNU 00.07.69

Air Fret Transimax
F-BDYE 12.05.51

Air Furness
G-BLDX 21.08.87
G-BMDT 14.06.86

Air Gabon
F-OHOC 08.12.94
TR-LOC 00.05.73
TR-LOD 00.06.73
TR-LXN 26.02.79

Air Gaspe
CF-QBB 29.05.73

Air Glaciers
* 30.06.88
HB-XCM 27.10.82
HB-XEO 04.09.80
HB-XLT 06.06.84
HB-XUT 22.06.94

Air Grischa
HB-XFW 08.08.79
HB-XNC 04.09.84

Air Guadeloupe
F-OGFE 21.12.72
F-OGHD 18.11.78
F-OGHL 28.10.88

Air Guinee
* 05.02.91
3X-GAB 09.07.67
3X-GAU 31.03.80
3X-GAX 03.09.78
3X-GCG oo.oo.85

Air Haiti International
HH-ABA 11.11.61

Air Hi-Ho
N513DQ 05.03.86

Air Illinois
N748LL 11.10.83

Air India
VT-ATI 13.11.47
VT-AUD 09.05.53
VT-AUF 10.01.47
VT-AUG 27.12.47
VT-CCA 15.09.51
VT-CFK 13.12.50
VT-CIZ 07.04.49
VT-CLY 06.02.48
VT-CQP 03.11.50
VT-DAT 26.09.50
VT-DEP 11.04.55
VT-DIN 19.07.59
VT-DJI 23.01.71
VT-DJJ 22.06.82
VT-DMN 24.01.66
VT-EBD 01.01.78
VT-EBO 07.05.90
VT-EFO 23.06.85

Air Indiana
N51071 13.12.77

Air Inter
F-BGNV 12.08.63
F-BMCH 27.10.72
F-BNKI 04.01.71
F-BOEA 28.12.71
F-BPNF 05.08.74
F-BSRY 22.03.74
F-BUAE 31.03.93
F-GGED 20.01.92

Air Inter Gabon
TR-LBJ 08.07.95
TR-LNF oo.10.74
TR-LSF 23.08.77
TR-LTQ 13.11.78

Air Interamerica
5N-85H 28.11.69

Air Inuit
C-FIRW 16.03.81
C-GBJE oo.12.91

Air Ivoire
5U-AAJ 10.06.77
6V-AAP 24.07.71
TU-TIF 25.07.86
TU-TIK 30.12.89
TU-TIP 26.06.94

Air Jamaica
6Y-JMO 16.11.90

Air Jordan
G-AKFL 18.12.49
JY-ACB 22.01.59
TJ-ABA 31.10.50

Air Katanga
OO-ADN 15.09.61

Air Kenya
5Y-BBN oo.02.92
5Y-DAK 17.08.87

Air Kilroe
G-BMCB 20.10.90

Air Kipawa
C-FEYT 16.09.81

Air Korea
HL9105 20.09.88
HL9244 13.08.92

Air Kruise
G-AESR 22.09.56

Air Lanka
4R-ULD 03.05.86

Air Laos
F-BEIA 04.12.54
F-BFGN 14.03.55
F-OAMA 30.04.54
F-OAOU oo.11.56

Air Lesotho
7P-LAA 13.07.84

Air Liban
* 24.07.50
OD-ABU 06.01.54

Air Liberia
EL-AAB 19.04.75
EL-AHM 23.02.75
EL-AHN 17.07.74
EL-AIC 28.10.81
EL-AIH 16.04.83
EL-AJH 08.10.85

Air Link International Airways
RP-C2446 17.12.93
RP-C789 19.04.89

Air Littoral
* 18.11.88
F-GCPG 18.11.88
F-GEGH 21.12.87

Air Logistics
* 04.04.78
* 05.01.86
N172AL 14.02.95
N347AL 02.05.95
N767AL 04.02.87

Air London
G-AZIF 05.01.72

Air Madagascar
* 24.07.81
5R-MAD 19.07.67
5R-MAJ 16.07.63
5R-MGB 24.07.82

Air Mahe
VQ-SAC 04.09.76

Air Malawi
7Q-YMB 06.11.87

Air Mali
TZ-ABE 11.08.74
TZ-ABH 05.11.66
TZ-ACH 21.06.83
TZ-ACT 22.02.85

Air Manila
PI-C1060 09.01.72
PI-C854 23.05.67
PI-C856 16.12.65
PI-C869 oo.11.70
PI-C870 14.04.69
PI-C871 08.03.68
PI-C873 09.05.68
PI-C875 06.09.73
RP-C1061 04.06.76
RP-C874 29.03.75

Air Manitoba
C-GQTH 10.11.93

Air Maroc
F-BEHA oo.oo.52
F-DABD 10.10.53

Air Martinique
F-OGGL oo.oo.79

Air Material
HB-LLP 22.09.94

Air Mauritanie
5T-CLF 01.07.94
6V-AAA 06.07.65

Air Mediterranee
9Q-CFJ 21.06.77

Air Melanesie
F-OCRH 23.10.72
YJ-RV9 07.09.81

Air Methods
N70AM 22.04.94

Air Micronesia
N18479 21.11.80

Air Ministry
G-EAWW 02.05.24
G-EBCP 16.05.29

Air Mistassini
C-GUWC 13.01.82

Air Mount Laurier
C-FMPM 11.09.80

Air Nautic
F-BELZ 29.12.62
F-BFDN 05.09.59
F-BJEQ 08.02.65
F-BJER 12.09.63

Air Navigation & Trading
G-ALXJ 10.07.51
G-ARZG 07.07.65

Air Nevada
N818AN 12.07.93

Air New Orleans
N331CY 26.05.87

Air New Zealand
ZK-NFC 17.02.79
ZK-NZB 04.07.66
ZK-ZNP 28.11.79

Air Niagara
C-GJDX 11.02.88
C-GXFZ 26.09.84

Air Niugini
P2-ANB 31.05.95

Air Nolis
F-BEFQ 10.01.50
F-BEIH 30.01.50

Air North [1]
ZK-EJM 09.05.77

Air North [2]
VH-MMA 23.02.90

Air North [3]
C-GZOF 19.08.95

Air North Queensland
VH-ANQ 11.05.90

Air Norving
LN-MAF 17.02.93

Air O'Hare
N9BC 01.01.75

Air Ocean
F-BCAA 10.10.46

Air Oceania Tahiti
F-GDHV 27.05.94

Air One Helicopters
N4995G 28.01.94
N581BG 21.02.94

Air Ontario
C-FBJE 01.11.88
C-FONF 10.03.89

Air Orient [1]
PH-AEO 07.06.31

Air Orient [2]
F-AIQY 12.08.32
F-AJDP 29.03.32
F-AJIG 18.03.32
F-AJVS 17.09.32
F-ALCE 23.04.33

Air Orlando Charter
N4403Q 23.06.95

Air Outremer
F-BEIO 04.09.54
F-OABX 20.07.51
F-OACA 12.09.50
F-OAFR 03.02.53
F-OAHY 13.02.53

Air Pacific
N19D 29.03.79

Air Pacific NC Inc
N930GL oo.12.89

Air Pennsylvania
N5MS 25.07.80

Air Provence
F-BRNL oo.12.85
F-GBTG 29.07.83
F-GIIX 28.06.94

Air Pyrenees
F-APPQ oo.oo.37

Air Rainbow
C-FRVR 27.01.92

Air Resorts Airlines
N44828 16.12.84

Air Reunion
F-BRQI 01.12.92

Air Rhodesia
VP-WAS 03.09.78
VP-YND 12.02.79

Air Rouergue
F-BYAH 28.01.79

Air Safaris
G-AHOR 29.05.60
ZK-NMD 20.07.87

Air Sandy
C-GYPZ 01.05.95

Air Senegal
6V-ADE 10.12.93

Air Service Flugcharter
D-AELB 24.02.90

Air Service Hungary
HA-ANL 11.05.82
HA-MBI 25.01.82
HA-MBM 30.05.84
HA-MBS 10.07.87
HA-MDJ 02.01.79
HA-MER 14.03.90
HA-MHS oo.oo.88

HA-MMR 13.07.90
HA-MNP 04.08.91
HA-MPG 16.10.93
HA-MUM 10.06.91

Air Services of India
VT-AHB 30.12.45
VT-AXD 09.05.53
VT-CPQ 25.01.50

Air Seychelles
S7-AAE 30.08.84

Air Sinai
SU-GAD 11.06.86

Air South
N844NS 06.07.69
N848NS 31.03.74

Air Special
OK-WJJ 12.03.94
OK-XJI 13.09.93

Air Spray
C-FBVH 24.04.80
C-FFIM 13.07.84
C-GWJG 01.07.82

Air St Hubert
C-GBMI 20.11.88

Air Sunshine
N206RH 25.08.93
N73KW 15.01.77

Air Tahiti
F-OHAB 19.04.91

Air Tansport Charter
G-AJVZ 27.03.51

Air Tanzania
5H-MRD 21.12.84

Air Taxi Co
EP-ADG 13.06.71
EP-AGZ 13.04.70

Air Taxis
G-ACLS 17.10.34
G-EBIX oo.01.29

Air Today
N8827K 10.06.88

Air Toronto
C-GJWW 12.01.88

Air Traders
N7673C 14.07.63

Air Traders International
N74CA 22.06.80

Air Trans Africa
VP-WAM oo.11.67
VP-YTY oo.oo.68

Air Transafrik
S9-TAN 27.04.94

Air Transivoire
TU-TKS 23.09.87

Air Transport
OO-GVP 06.01.47
OO-GVP 27.07.48
OO-XAC 22.12.47

Air Transport Associates
N5075N 19.07.49

Air Transport Association
G-AHFV 03.07.47

Air Transport Charter
G-AJBG 20.05.48

Air Transport International
N730PL 12.03.91
N782AL 16.02.95

Air Travel
ZK-AGP 21.12.42
ZK-AHT 30.06.44

Air Travel Services
N920C 10.08.92

Air Trine
N5865 16.12.76

Air Troika
* oo.03.95

Air UK
G-BCDO 19.07.90

Air US
N11360 17.04.81

Air Ukraine
23578 30.09.93
25349 08.04.93
UR-67536 27.10.93

Air Union [1]
F-ADBM 29.09.25
F-AEFC 11.03.28
F-AEGP oo.oo.oo
F-AICQ oo.oo.26
F-AIEB 18.08.26
F-AIFE 17.09.32
F-AIGM 12.12.27
F-AIMN 31.10.28
F-AIMO 23.08.28
F-AIPA 09.12.28
F-AJNS 13.01.33
F-FHMY 10.02.30

Air Union [2]
XW-PHV 03.12.73
XW-PKK 15.12.73
XW-TDM 19.05.73
XW-TFN 28.05.74

Air Universal
HL9239 27.07.89

Air Vegas
N22592 13.01.92

Air Vietnam
B-1543 01.11.70
B-2005 22.12.69
B-304 22.08.71
B-305 30.09.70
F-BELL 01.05.69
F-VNAI 16.08.54
XV-NIC 16.09.65
XV-NID 10.11.62
XV-NIE 17.11.73
XV-NJC 15.09.74
XV-NUC 02.04.69
XV-NUG 20.09.69
XV-NUH 24.09.72
XV-NUI 19.03.73
XV-NUJ 12.03.75

Air West Express
ST-AWA 23.03.93

Air Wisconsin
N4043B 29.06.72
N6505 12.06.80

Air Zaire
9Q-CBH 07.04.74
9Q-CLM 09.01.75
9Q-CLO 13.03.76
9Q-CLP 08.02.80
9Q-CLR 06.01.78
9Q-CNI 02.01.95

Air Zermatt
HB-XGE 10.04.85
HB-XMZ 31.07.83
HB-XOL 03.05.94
HB-XOM 09.06.88

Air Zimbabwe
Z-WKT oo.11.88
Z-YNI oo.07.84

Air-Lift Commuter
N505LB 23.04.87

AirWest Airlines
C-FAIV 02.09.78
C-FAJB 16.12.76
C-FAWF 22.09.76
C-FODF 30.10.77
C-GPBO 01.12.77

Airborne Express
N19T 20.06.85
N4688B 29.01.90
N926AX 06.02.85

Airborne Transport
NC16002 28.12.48

Airbus Industrie
F-WWAS 22.01.93
F-WWKH 30.06.94

Aircraft Airframe Inc
N6906C 03.04.73

Aircraft Brokers Inc
N4959N 12.03.78

Aircraft Charter
N163J 21.03.72

Aircraft Disposals
VH-BMC oo.11.49

Aircraft Export Corporation
NC13748 30.09.41
NC9613 08.03.42

Aircraft Operating Co
ZS-AEF 26.09.33

Aircraft Sales & Leasing
N133AC 11.12.78

Aircraft Specialities
N173W 09.06.73
N45516 11.05.75
N621L oo.07.75

Aircraft Transport & Travel
C6054 01.05.19
G-EACT oo.03.20
G-EAGX oo.08.20
G-EAHF 11.12.19
G-EAHG 29.10.19
G-EAOP oo.09.20
G-EAPO oo.09.20
G-EAPU oo.11.20
G-EAQA oo.01.21
G-EAQN 09.11.90
G-EARI 16.08.20

Aircruise
G-AJLW 26.04.65
G-ATCM 26.06.68

Airfast Services
N4375S 22.12.80
PK-OAB 13.05.80
PK-OAN 21.03.85
PK-OAO 28.05.76
PK-OAP 22.04.73
PK-OBC 15.08.84
PK-OBE 29.04.83
PK-OBK 28.04.81
PK-OBL 09.11.87
PK-OBS 05.05.94
PK-OBT 26.07.94
PK-OBW 25.01.90

Airflight
G-AKBY 12.03.50

Airgava
C-FGCW 01.09.78

Airgo
G-BBFF 25.05.74

Airland (NZ) Ltd
ZK-CGV 24.04.71
ZK-CMX 26.03.68

Airlift Co
JA9501 04.09.65
JA9502 16.04.68
JA9503 05.08.67

Airlift International
N1823M 27.08.64
N2282 12.09.66
N273RD 24.08.92
N276RD 24.08.92
N4059K 30.12.66
N5132B 13.09.65
N6164A 23.03.74
N6936C 22.06.67
N9903F 27.08.64

Airline Transport Carriers
NC36480 28.01.48

Airlines (WA) Ltd
VH-AQO 15.10.51
VH-BIU 29.06.48

Airlines of Australia
VH-UGG 28.03.37
VH-UHH 19.02.37
VH-UTK 01.07.38
VH-UVS 12.05.37

Airlines of New South Wales
VH-ANJ 01.04.65
VH-INI 11.12.60

Airlines of Tasmania
VH-CLY 04.08.83

Airlink
P2-ALC 19.09.94
P2-ALD 19.09.94
P2-ALE 19.09.94
P2-ALF 19.09.94
P2-ALL 10.12.93

Airmore Aviation
G-BGIN 06.03.80
G-BKID 26.12.83

Airship Industries
G-BIHN 27.04.87

Airspan
G-AJGI 14.11.47

Airspan Helicopters
RP-C1109 13.07.94

Airspeed
G-ACVH oo.05.36
G-AFVS 03.09.39

Airspur
N5830T 18.11.83

Airtaco
SE-BTN 14.07.51

Airvas Air Taxi
OB-1310 07.04.91
OB-T-1294 28.11.86

Airways (India) Ltd
VT-AUJ 14.04.53
VT-CHB 17.05.50
VT-CKU 14.11.51
VT-CQA 17.01.48
VT-CUZ 29.03.55

Airways Corporation
* 18.06.91

Airways International Cymru
G-BFON 11.06.86

Airwork [1]
ZK-AWV 02.11.51

Airwork [2]
G-AIXS 15.08.54
G-ALDB 23.07.52
G-ALDF 21.08.52
G-AZNP 28.01.72
XD632 01.09.57

Airwork (East Africa) Ltd
VP-KEN 31.12.49
VP-KHS 09.07.54
VP-KHT 01.08.51
VP-KJK 01.10.56

Aklak Air
C-GBDH 23.09.89

Ala Littoria
I-AFRO 06.03.39
I-BAUS 30.04.38
I-DENO 07.09.38
I-DIRE 13.10.39
I-NAVE oo.08.37
I-PACE 30.07.41
I-PLUS 06.02.42
I-RODI 27.09.36
I-SUSA 02.08.37
I-UGRI oo.10.36
I-VOLO 14.07.38

Alan Mann Helicopters
G-FILM 22.05.82

Alares Developments
G-AMSF 05.03.62

Alas Chiricanas
HP-1202AC 19.07.94

Alas del Caribe
HI-237 31.08.79

Alaska Aeronautical Industries
N563MA 06.09.77

Alaska Airlines
N11817 22.02.60
N124AS 05.04.76
N2969G 04.09.71
N6118C 21.07.61
N766AS 09.06.87
N7777C 17.04.67
N90449 02.03.57
N91008 08.08.54
NC1241N 26.01.49
NC162W 02.08.44
NC91006 20.01.49
NC91009 30.11.47

Alaska Airways
NC20K 30.09.37

Alaska Bush Carrier
N1801Q 02.07.93

Alaska Coastal Airlines
* 21.08.66
NC47M 15.01.58
NC49M 14.11.52

Alaska Helicopters
N59619 10.01.85

Alaska International Air
N100AK 30.08.74
N102AK 27.10.74

Alaska Southern Airways
NC974H 10.10.34

Alaska West Air
N90315 29.07.94

Alaska-Washington Airways
NC102N 26.03.30
NC102W 04.08.30
NC103W 28.10.30

Albiacion Circulo G
HR-AKZ 25.02.89

Alcon
CP-947 06.02.74

Alfa Flug
D-IBAF 27.07.77

Alfred Wegener Institute
D-CICE 15.01.91
D-IGVN 24.02.85

Algerian Air Force
7T-WUC 19.11.71
7T-WUD 01.04.71

Algerian Government
7T-VHB 03.05.82
7T-VRE 30.05.81

Algerian Police
* 31.03.94

Alia
JY-ACO 05.06.67
JY-ACP 05.06.67
JY-ACQ 10.04.65
JY-ADO 22.01.73
JY-ADU 14.03.79
JY-AEE 03.08.75
JY-AFW 12.06.85

Alidair
G-ARBY 17.07.80

Aliseirio
I-ALSU 27.11.91

Alitalia
I-AHBX 23.12.49
I-ATJA 14.11.90
I-DABF 02.08.69
I-DALO 17.01.51
I-DIKB 07.01.80
I-DIKQ 23.12.78
I-DIWB 06.05.72
I-DIWD 06.07.62
I-DIWF 02.08.68
I-DIWZ 15.09.70
I-DUVO 26.02.60
I-LAKE 28.03.64
I-LEDA 02.01.57
I-LIZT 21.12.59
I-RIBN 17.12.91

All American Airways
N3908B 11.08.51

All Nippon Airways
G-APKJ 12.06.61
JA5003 18.02.63
JA5008 14.11.61
JA5018 16.03.60
JA5024 29.10.63
JA5039 30.04.63
JA5040 10.05.63
JA5045 12.08.58
JA8202 19.11.62
JA8302 04.02.66
JA8329 30.07.71
JA8658 13.11.66
JA8708 20.10.69

Allcair Air Transport
N1597F 26.11.93

Allegheny Airlines
N1550 09.07.78
N174A 01.12.59
N177A 02.11.63
N29824 12.02.79
N3414 29.11.66
N5802 24.12.68
N5825 06.01.69
N5832 07.06.71
N5844 20.08.71
N8415H 23.07.65
N988VJ 09.09.69
N994VJ 23.06.76

Aloha Airlines
N73711 29.04.88
N7410 27.06.69
N7415 oo.08.71

Aloha Island Air
N707PV 29.10.89

Alpar
HB-AMO 20.09.37

Alpes Provence
F-BEFK 22.08.49
F-BEIZ 12.09.51

Alpha Airways
G-AKBA 25.05.48

Alpha Flug
D-IAGA 27.01.77

Alpine Helicopters [1]
C-FYJP 09.10.81
C-GBHH 16.01.83
C-GRNR 27.05.92
C-GTEJ 29.07.82

Alpine Helicopters [2]
ZK-HKE 14.02.89

Altair [1]
N7886A 09.04.77

Altair [2]
I-GISO 02.07.83

Altus Airlines
N5780M 06.02.85

Alyemda
7O-ABF 01.03.77
7O-ABP 16.09.75
7O-ACJ 26.01.82
7O-ACK 09.05.82
7O-ACN oo.oo.86
7O-ACS 26.11.91

Am-Son Drilling Co
HK-1710W 19.12.79

Amani Ltd
HB-FIM 29.07.87

Amazonense
PP-PDG 29.05.72

Amazonia
PT-DNZ 28.10.70

Amazonica
OB-T-1304 26.02.88

Ambica Air Lines
VT-AYF 21.11.48
VT-CAG 21.11.48
VT-CBW 21.11.48

America West Airlines
N198AW oo.12.89

America de Aviacion
OB-1358 19.11.90
OB-1417 02.08.91

American Agronomics Corporation
N50HH 02.08.86

American Air Transport
N1693M 23.04.53

American Airlines
N110AA 25.05.79
N136AA 21.05.88
N139AA 14.04.93
N1963 26.04.76
N1996 08.11.65
N5616 30.05.63
N6101A 03.02.59
N6102A 06.08.62
N6127A 14.09.60
N7502A 28.01.61
N7506A 01.03.62
N7514A 15.08.59
N90426 oo.oo.48
N90728 29.11.49
N94213 01.03.58
N94221 04.08.55
N94229 22.01.52
N94234 20.03.55
N94244 20.01.54
N94247 06.01.57
N94255 16.09.53
N94266 22.06.49
N94273 15.03.59
NC11721 20.01.33
NC12119 06.02.36
NC12285 15.11.34
NC12286 22.12.34
NC12287 10.01.35
NC12354 09.06.34
NC12393 27.07.35
NC12395 19.12.34
NC13767 29.01.36
NC14141 26.05.36
NC14274 14.01.36
NC15152 01.04.36
NC15577 28.12.46
NC16008 15.10.43
NC16014 28.07.43
NC16017 23.10.42
NC18142 23.02.45
NC21746 05.01.47
NC21767 10.02.44
NC21799 03.03.46
NC229Y 21.11.33
NC25663 30.10.41
NC25684 10.01.45
NC33657 15.09.43
NC487W 24.10.35
NC490W 20.01.33
NC710Y 06.03.34
NC732N 16.03.33
NC88826 25.08.46
NC9127 28.12.32
NC9662 09.08.31
NC9716 08.09.32
NC982M 12.02.34
NX88787 08.08.47

American Export Airlines
41-107452 21.04.45
NC41880 03.10.42

American Express Leasing
N500AF 31.12.72

American Flyers Airline
N185H 22.04.66
N9719C 20.09.65

American International Airlines
NC18612 14.10.47
N500FM 02.07.91
N814CK 18.08.93

American Jet
N409MA 03.05.95

American Overseas Airlines
NC90904 03.10.46

American Trans Air
N184AT 10.08.86

American Velodour Metal Inc
N10AV 09.04.77

American Way Service Corp
N800AW 10.01.88

Ameriflight
N63995 16.11.94
N78DE 04.03.94

Amerine Turkey Breeding Farms
N54370 24.03.67

Amoco
N481F oo.oo.75

Amphibians Ltd
5Y-CMC 24.07.78

Amuraviatrans Airlines
RA-13340 26.03.95

Andes Aviacion
LV-WBL 26.06.94
LV-WDL 15.01.95

Andrade, E.R.
XA-SAR 25.08.70

Andrau Air Park
N4952N oo.oo.51

Andy's Flying Service
N22JA 21.07.77

Angel, J. & Baker, J.
AN-ABL 19.02.45

Angkor Indonesian Airlines
XW-PKO 10.04.75

Anglo Iranian Oil Co
G-AEMM 03.05.40
G-AFIA 20.08.42
G-AHYX 24.09.49

Angola Air Charter
D2-THC 07.04.94
D2-THE 09.12.94
D2-TJB 31.01.95
D2-TOV 21.07.88

Angolan Government
D2-EAD 19.09.84

Ansett Airlines of Australia
VH-FNE 25.03.71

Ansett Airlines of Papua New Guinea
VH-MAE 17.07.72
VH-PNI 01.09.72

Ansett Flying Boat Services
VH-BRD 31.10.52
VH-BRE 03.07.63

Ansett New Zealand
ZK-NEY 09.06.95

Ansett-ANA
VH-BZA 12.01.56
VH-FNH 17.03.65
VH-INQ 04.09.61
VH-RMI 22.09.66

Anson, C.R.
G-AECB 07.10.36

Antillaise de Transport Aerien
N37JA 29.10.73

Antilles Air Boats
N41881 oo.01.69
N74676 05.11.78
N7777V 02.09.78
N8777A 05.04.78

Antonov Design Bureau
SSSR-12162 19.10.87
SSSR-82002 13.10.92
UR-48018 06.07.94
n/a 10.02.95

Apache Airlines
N4922V 06.05.71

Aquila Air
C-FJAI 03.05.89

Aquila Airways
G-AGJN 21.01.53
G-AGKY 28.01.53
G-AKNU 15.11.57
G-ANAJ 26.09.56
G-ANAK 27.11.54

Arab Contracting & Trading Co
G-AHTX 09.11.51
G-AIDJ 22.11.48
G-AIHK 02.10.49
G-AKHG 21.02.52

Arab Wings
JY-AEW 28.04.77
JY-AFC 21.09.77

Arabian Airways
G-AEIL 25.04.40
G-AEOY 17.12.37

Arabian Desert Airlines
G-ANOE 29.07.54

Aramar
PT-LJR 02.10.88

Arax Airlines
5N-ARA oo.oo.81
5N-ARH 01.04.88

Arctic Air
CF-XZS oo.06.73

Arctic Circle Air Service
N20086 13.07.92

Arctic Guide
N4048B 13.10.78

Arctic Pacific Airlines
N1244N 22.10.60

Arctic Wings
CF-HMX 12.05.55

Arctic Wings & Rotors
C-GMOP 05.12.93

Argentine Coast Guard
PA-12 03.05.82
PA-50 15.05.82
PA-54 03.05.82

Argentine Government
* oo.oo.oo
R-48 oo.oo.48

Argo
HI-208 08.02.77
HI-328 26.10.81
HI-393 oo.10.84

Argosy Airlines
N407D 21.09.78
N9302 12.05.78

Ariana Afghan Airlines
* 27.08.88
* 02.08.89
* 10.02.93
* 11.09.95
YA-AAA oo.oo.63
YA-AAB 15.01.69
YA-AAD 02.11.59
YA-BAG 21.11.59
YA-BAK 18.06.89
YA-BAM 04.09.85
YA-BAN oo.oo.oo
YA-FAR 05.01.69
YA-KAB 01.08.92
YA-KAF 01.08.92
YA-TAP 29.05.92

Aris Helicopters
N5594C 31.01.87
N94AH 13.07.88

Arkhangelsk Airlines
14235 04.04.93
RA-50582 01.08.94
RA-65976 07.05.94

Arkia
4X-AVC 26.10.69

Armenian Airlines
* 27.03.92
* 30.11.94
85105 05.12.92

Armitage, G.H.
NC22077 20.03.48

Armstrong, R.A.
N302G oo.oo.79

Army Parachute Association
G-BBRP 20.02.82

Arnold, D.
G-BFFS 11.12.77

Arrow Air
N950JW 12.12.85

Arrow Airways [1]
CF-BAW 03.01.44

Arrow Airways [2]
N60256 07.12.49

Arseniev Air Wing
RA-27209 30.09.94

Artix Ltd
G-MDJI 19.10.87

Arute International Air
N6574 02.03.73

Ashaka Cement Company
5N-AMR 21.05.91

Ashland Oil & Refining Co
* 04.09.62

Asia Pacific Airlines
B-6622 26.02.95

Asiana Airlines
HL7229 26.07.93

Asiatic International Airways
N8329C 17.09.75

Aspen Airways
N270L 17.01.70
N5808 02.02.88
N73160 19.01.89

Aspen Helicopters
N1077N 14.02.94

Aspiring Air
ZK-EVK 08.08.89

Associated Air Transport
N1648M 07.01.53
N46Q 13.02.60

Associated Airways
CF-HMV 29.09.55
CF-HMY 26.05.55
CF-HMZ 11.04.55

Associated Aviation Industries
N1210W 23.11.65

Associated Aviators
NR859E 02.09.29

Associated Helicopters
C-GBVS 26.01.80

Atesa
HC-BFJ 03.03.82

Athabaska Airways
C-FALA 17.08.90
C-FAUR 10.08.81
C-FKOC 12.01.80
C-FWGE 13.06.87
C-GODI 28.05.77
C-GZBE 11.03.80

Atlantic & Pacific Airlines
NC59398 14.02.47

Atlantic Air BVI
VP-LVR 02.05.93

Atlantic Air Taxi
N27400 19.02.88

Atlantic Airmotive
NC5493 10.06.42
NC6892 21.11.42

Atlantic Central Airlines [1]
* 09.08.46

Atlantic Central Airlines [2]
C-FHPM oo.oo.76

Atlantic City Airlines/Allegheny
N101AC 12.12.76

Atlantic Coast Airlines
N304UE 07.01.94

Atlantic Coast Airways
NC9129 01.09.34

Atlantic Southeast Airlines
N219AS 19.09.86
N256AS 21.08.95
N270AS 05.04.91
N65DA 24.05.88

Atlas Air Service
D-IAAY 06.11.80

Atlas Aviation
G-AHMA 23.12.46

Atlas Consolidated Mining
RP-C850 31.07.86

Atorie Air
N3433U 30.05.86

Auckland Flying School
ZK-AXI 23.04.67

Augusta Airways
VH-LIC oo.06.93

Aurukun Aboriginal Community
VH-JUU 22.03.94

Austin Airways
C-FIAX 10.12.76
C-GNNA 19.01.86
C-GPAA 15.07.79
C-GTJA 01.11.79
C-GTLA 23.11.83
CF-AAC 19.06.70
CF-AAL 09.11.69
CF-BJW oo.10.46
CF-DTW 03.03.69
CF-EJX oo.oo.52

CF-GRU	14.06.57
CF-ILQ	09.01.64

Austral

CC-CAZ	25.05.71
CC-CDU	13.06.72
LV-GEB	17.12.69
LV-GED	16.01.59
LV-JGY	22.11.77
LV-JNR	04.12.73
LV-LOX	07.05.81
N1003G	12.06.88

Australian Aerial Services

VH-UGF	14.07.31

Australian Dept. of Civil Aviation

VH-CAQ	27.03.51
VH-DHA	16.04.52

Australian Iron & Steel Pty Ltd

VH-BHJ	23.12.60

Australian National Airways

VH-ACB	19.03.43
VH-ADE	26.01.44
VH-AET	10.03.46
VH-ANA	26.06.50
VH-AND	16.10.52
VH-ANK	02.09.48
VH-ANM	07.09.46
VH-CDC	13.11.45
VH-INO	11.01.60
VH-UMF	21.03.31
VH-UNA	26.11.31
VH-UYC	25.10.38
VH-UZJ	29.12.48
VH-UZK	08.11.48

Australian Trans-continental Airways

VH-UTZ	06.09.35

Austrian Air Services

OE-LSA	19.09.84

Austrian Airlines

*	31.03.93
OE-FCM	15.06.89
OE-FDA	02.05.59
OE-LAF	26.09.60

Autair

G-ALZS	14.09.67

Automovil Club Argentino

LV-JTC	25.02.71

Autrex

F-BBYF	26.07.51
F-BBZL	11.05.53
F-BCYI	13.03.54
F-BCYJ	25.04.54
F-BEFS	24.01.54
F-BEIP	21.05.54
F-BFGQ	04.04.54
F-BFGR	07.02.53

Avair

N622AV	12.02.88

Avensa

YV-67C	11.03.83
YV-84C	28.05.85
YV-AVN	20.04.48
YV-C-AKE	27.08.72
YV-C-AVG	03.09.57
YV-C-AVI	21.08.73
YV-C-AVM	22.12.74
YV-C-AVU	15.12.50
YV-C-AVX	25.12.52
YV-C-EVF	06.04.72
YV-C-EVH	25.02.62
YV-C-EVL	05.09.55

Avery Aviation

N7974A	oo.07.68

Avesca

HK-3468	19.09.92

Avexair

ZS-CMI	30.03.77
ZS-CPB	18.02.78
ZS-DRG	29.03.77
ZS-ENE	01.03.77

Avia Special

HA-LAJ	28.08.93

Avia Taxi France

F-BSRZ	02.09.73

Aviacao Ligeira

D2-ECH	28.01.95

Aviaco

EC-ADH	13.03.59
EC-ADI	09.05.57
EC-ADK	24.11.49
EC-AEG	04.12.53
EC-AEH	11.00.57
EC-AHJ	19.04.62
EC-AHK	01.10.61
EC-AKV	29.09.56
EC-ANJ	14.04.58
EC-ANR	04.12.58
EC-ANZ	15.11.57
EC-AOA	26.10.57
EC-ARA	06.07.72
EC-BIC	13.08.73
EC-BID	05.03.73
EC-BIQ	18.02.90
EC-BYH	30.03.92
EC-CGS	07.12.83
EC-CLE	21.03.94

Aviacor

RA-74041	16.06.95

Aviacsa

F-GHXA	10.05.90

Aviakhim

*	oo.oo.26
RRODD	oo.oo.27
RRODE	18.05.25
RRUOA	25.09.25
RRUOC	oo.oo.27
RRUSS	oo.07.26

Aviakor

RA-11110	07.08.93

Avianca

*	22.09.66
C-108	22.01.47
C-110	29.12.48
C-114	15.02.47
C-119	10.11.48
C-140	29.09.45
C-146	27.02.44
HK-1027	27.12.73
HK-107	29.07.72
HK-109	22.03.65
HK-111	22.08.73
HK-116	29.08.50
HK-118	17.10.65
HK-120	02.05.50
HK-123	11.03.50
HK-126	09.07.51
HK-1272	30.09.75
HK-130	28.01.62
HK-1341X	29.07.72
HK-135	23.06.59
HK-1408	05.07.73
HK-142	02.04.51
HK-143	19.09.53
HK-153	11.03.65
HK-155	09.03.57
HK-160	11.01.54
HK-161	24.12.66
HK-163	09.08.54
HK-167	24.06.53
HK-171	21.01.70
HK-1716	17.03.88
HK-177	21.01.60
HK-1803	27.11.89
HK-2016	25.01.90
HK-2910	27.11.83
HK-303	22.01.56
HK-308	09.08.56
HK-319	15.09.64
HK-326	26.04.67
HK-320	09.03.55
HK-502	25.02.62
HK-508	12.08.74
HK-723	16.08.76
HK-725	27.01.80
HK-730	15.01.66

Aviasa

OB-1589	13.04.95

Aviateca

N125GU	09.08.95
TG-ABA-C	oo.03.71
TG-ACA	27.04.77
TG-ACA-A	11.05.71
TG-ADA	08.06.78
TG-AGA	18.11.75
TG-AHA	24.05.56
TG-AJA	08.10.54
TG-AKA	30.09.77
TG-AMA	17.02.75
TG-APA	05.04.62
TG-AQA	15.12.53
TG-ATA	26.07.78

Aviatia Utilitara

YR-AND	29.07.62
YR-ANE	18.07.75
YR-ANF	09.04.76
YR-ANO	09.04.62
YR-BNI	27.06.77
YR-BNJ	26.05.89
YR-ELV	24.03.94

Aviation & Services Europe

N1037D	16.08.93

Aviation Assistance

OY-GEG	oo.07.94

Aviation Boreal

C-FQBC	30.03.95
C-GCXD	23.03.95

Aviation Distributors

HP-947	01.11.82

Aviation Enterprises

N4296	15.04.69

Aviation Holdings

N47WM	20.01.95

Aviation Sans Frontiers

F-OGSM	oo.oo.90

Aviation Services

N220KC	17.08.93

Aviation Technology & Resources

C-GSWX	03.04.86

Aviation Traders

G-AHDP	09.04.49

Aviation West

G-OCME	09.02.87

Avio Ligure

I-JAKE	28.05.77

Avio Linee Italiane

I-AAXZ	15.04.30
I-ELSA	01.07.48

Aviogenex

YU-AHZ	23.05.71
YU-AJS	02.04.77

Avioimpex

RA-42390	20.11.93

Avion

N142D	20.03.69

Avion S.A.

CU-C644	14.04.60

Aviones Ejectivos

HK-2687X	26.04.83

Aviones de Panama

HP-550	oo.10.71
HP-659	28.01.85
HP-680	oo.oo.oo
HP-776	15.06.80
HP-946	30.05.84

Avions Caudron

F-ESAB	oo.11.22

Avions Marcel Dassault

F-WFAL	31.10.72

Aviotransport

Z3-BGE	18.09.95

Avro

WL799	18.12.55

Ayling, J.R.

G-ACJM	12.08.34

Azerbaijan Airlines

*	21.11.91

B.F.Goodrich Company

NX308H	16.05.31

BAC Charter

N731A	08.10.91

BC Air Lines

*	02.01.66

BEA Helicopters

G-AKCU	24.05.49
G-AKFA	04.01.55
G-ASNM	15.11.70

BKS Air Survey

G-ALXH	09.04.63

BKS Air Transport

G-AMAD	03.07.68
G-AMVC	17.10.61
G-APNF	22.09.70

BR Air

N25BR	11.12.91

BWI Leasing

N355BY	15.11.80

Babb, C.H.

NC239M	06.11.41

Bahamas Airways

VP-BAA	oo.oo.49
VP-BAE	16.03.47
VP-BBN	21.11.60

Bahamas Government

CX-BGP	oo.oo.69

Bahamasair

C6-BDQ	31.07.78

Bahri Aviation

N711AF	11.08.79

Baikal Air

RA-24527	22.06.93
RA-85656	03.01.94

Baja California State Government

XC-TIJ	11.06.84

Baker Aviation

N67941	09.11.92

Bakhtar Afghan Airlines

*	oo.12.82
*	30.03.87
*	oo.03.87
YA-BAL	11.06.87

YA-GAT 18.04.73
YA-GAY 08.01.85
YA-GAZ 10.03.83
YA-KAD 25.01.72

Balair
CH-153 00.00.27
CH-156 00.00.26
CH-161 30.10.30
HB-AAI 13.09.64
HB-ILA 15.05.60
N564E 20.10.71

Balboa, J.
N62433 24.08.92

Bali Air
PK-KCA 26.07.83
PK-KCC 02.10.89
PK-KFR 04.11.76
PK-KNC 30.12.76
PK-KNE 12.05.85
PK-KNF 05.08.83
PK-KNG 26.04.79
PK-KTC 25.10.91
PK-KTD 10.01.77
PK-KTI 03.04.89

Balkan Bulgarian Airlines
LZ-ANA 22.11.75
LZ-ANN 28.07.92
LZ-BAD 24.08.84
LZ-BED 18.01.71
LZ-BEM 03.03.73
LZ-BEP 16.06.84
LZ-BES 21.12.71
LZ-BTB 23.03.78
LZ-BTD 05.06.92
LZ-BTN 02.12.77
LZ-ILF 00.00.00
LZ-ILG 00.00.00
LZ-TUB 16.03.78
LZ-TUR 10.01.84
SSSR-12975 18.12.92

Bangko Sentral Na Philipinas
RP-C3 00.00.82

Bangkok Airways
HS-SKI 21.11.90

Bangladesh Biman
* 10.02.72
S2-ABG 18.11.79
S2-ABJ 04.08.84
S2-ABQ 03.04.80

Bankair
N57169 24.06.87

Bar Harbor Airlines
N200WP 16.08.76
N300WP 25.08.85
N98720 16.05.78

Barbary Coast Hotel & Casino
N711WM 06.11.86

Bard Air Corporation
N959SC 23.07.91

Barlow Rand
ZS-KMT 13.04.87

Barrier Reef Airways
VH-BFH 18.01.85

Bashkirian Airlines
RA-24083 13.12.94
RA-24309 17.01.94

Basutair
VQ-ZBA 08.11.55
VQ-ZBF 22.01.58
VQ-ZBG 20.05.60
VQ-ZBL 27.09.66
VQ-ZBM 02.01.65

Battafsche Petroleum
PK-AKC 02.12.49
PK-AKE 27.01.51

Bavaria Flug
D-INAH 06.03.70

Beardsley & Piper
NC31M 25.06.30

Bearskin Airlines
C-GYQT 21.02.95
C-GYYB 01.05.95

Beaver Air Spray
C-GXKS 21.06.79

Beech Aircraft Corporation
NX90521 17.01.49

Beecham Group
G-AVGW 23.12.67

Beechwoods Flying Service
N2019U 14.02.85

Beijing Lianhe Hang-kong Luyou Gongsi
* 11.08.92

Belair
EW-76836 31.12.94

Belair Taxi Aereo
PT-ISN 04.11.89
PT-KKV 11.01.91

Belarus Airlines
SSSR-85528 13.10.92

Belgian Air Service
OO-SRA 14.08.49

Belgian International Air Services
OO-ABG 18.02.66
OO-DEP 29.11.64
OO-SBH 28.03.69

Bell Aircraft Corporation
163914 20.07.92
163915 11.06.91

Bellamy, V.H.
G-ACZP 21.09.58
G-AEWZ 03.03.61

Bellomy Lawson Aviation
N94BL 24.08.92

Benin Government
TY-BBK 16.11.81
TY-BBR 13.06.85

Bering Air
N900YH 06.01.93

Berlin Regional
N750BR 13.11.88

Berliner Spezialflug
D-EBSD 02.12.92

Bestit Company
I-IDMA 24.10.89

Bettison, F.C.
G-AFCI 03.05.54

Bharat Airways
VT-CGM 18.04.50
VT-CJZ 00.00.47
VT-CLE 12.11.52
VT-CYK 30.12.49

Biafran Air Force
5N-AAK 06.11.67
5N-AAV 07.10.67
5N-AGF 00.00.00

Bienes C.A.
YV-94CP 00.00.82

Big Six General Partnership
N3MF 26.01.79

Bihar State Government
VT-ARZ 00.00.51

Bird & Sons
XW-PAD 00.00.61
XW-PBO 20.09.64
XW-PGJ 02.01.70

Black Hills Aviation
N66573 00.00.00
N73648 12.07.72
N918AP 29.07.94

Blackburn Aeroplane & Motor Co
G-EAOW 08.12.19

Blackcomb Helicopters
C-GSKI 19.06.95

Blackpool & West Coast Air Services
G-ACGU 16.07.35
G-ADCR 25.06.38

Blair, R.
NC12278 08.12.36

Blue Airlines
9Q-CDG 13.03.95

Blue Bird Air Service
NC959Y 29.09.36

Board, G.R.
VH-GOC 22.02.77

Boardaire
C-GYLK 26.11.80

Boardman, R.B.
NC48610 09.06.45

Boeing Air Transport
* 10.07.32
NC842M 13.12.32

Boeing Airplane Company
N7071 19.10.59
NX19901 18.03.39

Bolivian Air Flight International
CP-735 19.10.90

Bolivian Air System
CP-745 01.02.69
CP-746 15.10.66
CP-762 16.12.64

Boliviana de Aviacion
CP-575 08.02.64
CP-589 17.09.61
CP-618 21.05.60
CP-640 17.08.67

Bombardier Aerospace
C-FCRJ 26.07.93

Bon-Air
G-ASER 14.09.72

Bonanza Airlines
N745L 15.11.64
N757L 16.04.65

Bond Air Services
G-AHMS 14.05.47
G-AIOH 30.05.47
G-AIOI 15.02.49
G-AIZO 23.05.48

Border Security Force
VT-EHK 27.08.92

Boreas Corporation
N34963 27.08.64

Borinquen Air
N27PR 22.07.86

Borneo Airways
VR-OAC 21.12.60
VR-OAE 07.09.63

Bosnia-Herzegovina Government
* 04.12.94
* 07.05.95
* 28.05.95
T9-HAI 04.12.94

Botswana Airways
A2-ZEV 26.01.71

Bougair
P2-BAB 21.03.89
P2-BAC 00.02.90
VH-BAY 00.01.90

Boulton & Paul
G-ABYK 21.10.33

Bouraq Indonesia Airlines
PK-IHA 04.01.89
PK-IHD 23.01.76
PK-IHE 09.01.93
PK-IHK 09.02.77
PK-IVS 26.08.80
PK-IVW 13.11.88
PK-IVX 28.08.92
PK-KHL 09.08.95

Bourgoin, G.
F-GJGB 30.09.93

Bow Helicopters
C-GBHL 22.11.78

Bowen Air Lines
NC160W 01.08.30
NC960Y 02.06.33

Braathens SAFE
LN-SUR 07.11.56
LN-SUY 23.12.72

Bradley Air Services
C-FDHT 15.03.81
C-FQDG 28.08.78
C-GDOV 12.01.89
C-GFFA 15.09.88
C-GROW 29.08.79
CF-DIJ 28.01.74
CF-TVK 28.01.74

Bradley Aviation
N427W 12.06.79

Bradley Machine Co
N5407J 02.04.85

Brain & Brown Airfreighters
VH-BAB 12.04.60
VH-BIX 22.03.61
VH-BKT 20.02.53

Braniff Airlines
N1553 06.08.66
N3422 17.07.55
N5904 25.03.58
N5905 19.11.61
N61451 22.08.54
N65143 26.03.52
N9705C 29.09.59
N9707C 03.05.68
NC106W 08.12.34
NC13727 26.03.39
NC14905 23.12.36
NC195E 22.04.33
NC433E 05.12.31
NC8497 12.07.31
NC9145 07.12.29
NC980Y 09.11.35

Bransk Flight Unit
RA-14146 20.03.95

Brasil Central
PT-LCG 12.02.90
PT-OGN 26.08.93

Breguet
* oo.07.31
02 19.04.62
F-AIYB 19.02.29

Brencham Ltd
G-UESS 08.10.83

Briko Air Services
N4807Q 14.08.92

Bristol Aeroplane Co
G-AHJB 04.07.46
G-AHJJ 21.03.50
G-AIFF 06.05.49
G-AIMC 23.11.47
G-ALRX 04.02.54
G-AMJI 16.09.56
G-ANCA 06.11.57

Bristow Helicopters
9M-SSC 16.12.81
G-ANUK 04.08.72
G-ASWI 13.08.81
G-ATCA 09.09.72
G-ATSC 08.03.76
G-AVIG 05.01.85
G-AXKT 06.10.81
G-AZNE 04.04.73
G-AZOM 24.07.84
G-BCRU 21.04.76
G-BDII 17.10.88
G-BDIL 14.09.82
G-BGXY 12.03.81
G-BIJF 12.08.81
G-BJJR 20.11.84
G-BJWS 10.10.82
G-TIGD 04.07.83
G-TIGH 14.03.92
G-TIGK 19.01.95
G-TIGN 21.05.89
VH-MYF 28.11.79
VH-WOF 12.05.91
VR-BDB 14.09.77

Bristow Helicopters (Nigeria) Ltd
5N-ABQ 04.04.67
5N-ABR 16.01.63
5N-AJP 04.06.80
5N-AJQ 23.04.95

Bristow Masayu Helicopters
PK-HBA 26.04.69
PK-HBB 04.09.76
PK-HBE 12.06.70
PK-HBR 08.06.71

Britannia Airways
G-ANBB 31.08.66

Britavia
G-ALDJ 05.11.56
G-ALDK 05.08.56

British Aerospace
G-SUPR 06.10.92

British Air Ferries
G-APIM 11.01.88
G-APNH 18.03.71

British Air Lines
G-AALC 11.09.29

British Air Transport
G-AIDY 14.06.48
G-AIWW 20.11.47

British Aircraft Corporation
G-ASHG 22.10.63
G-ASJB 18.03.64

British Airtours
G-APFK 17.03.77
G-BGJL 22.08.85

British Airways [1]
G-ACDX 09.10.35
G-ACVT 23.03.36
G-ADBX 16.05.36
G-ADEB 12.08.36
G-ADYF 15.09.36
G-ADZI 15.08.36
G-ADZK 16.08.36
G-AEOT 19.11.36
G-AEPP 13.12.37
G-AESY 15.08.39
G-AFFM 20.11.39
G-AFGN 11.08.39
G-AFGO 22.11.38
G-AFMO 15.01.40
G-AFYU 21.12.39

British Airways [2]
G-ARPC 28.12.75
G-ASGO 03.03.74
G-AVYD 15.09.75
G-AWND 27.02.91
G-AWZT 10.09.76

British Airways Helicopters
G-BEON 16.07.83

British American Air Services
G-AEHJ 13.02.40
G-AKAD 17.05.48
G-AKBB 11.02.49

British Antarctic Survey
VP-FAJ 28.12.64
VP-FAM 03.03.69
VP-FAP 24.01.77
VP-FAW 18.11.81

British Caledonian Airways
G-ARTA 28.02.72

British Car Auctions
G-BBPV 19.10.75

British Columbia Airways
G-CATX 25.08.28

British Commonwealth Pacific Airlines
VH-BPE 29.10.53

British Eagle Airways
G-ANCG 20.04.67
G-AOVO 29.02.64
G-ATFN 09.08.68

British European Airways
G-AGHP 16.05.58
G-AGIW 17.10.50
G-AGIX 30.07.48
G-AGJF 06.08.47
G-AGPH 06.12.51
G-AGUR 02.08.54
G-AGUV 26.04.54
G-AHCW 19.02.49
G-AHCY 19.08.49
G-AHKR 15.04.47
G-AHOK 26.01.47
G-AHPK 06.01.48
G-AHPN 31.10.50
G-AHXV 15.01.49
G-AHXY 27.12.48
G-AHXZ 28.08.51
G-AIVE 21.04.48
G-AIVG 12.08.53
G-AIVP 05.04.48
G-AJDL 05.01.53
G-AKZB 12.12.61
G-ALWE 14.03.57
G-ALZU 06.02.58
G-AMAB 08.04.55
G-AMNY 05.01.60
G-AMOM 21.01.56
G-AMWH 15.08.64
G-ANHC 22.10.58
G-AOFY 28.09.57
G-AOHI 19.01.73
G-AOHP 17.11.57
G-AOHU 07.01.60
G-AOJA 23.10.57
G-AORC 28.04.58
G-APEC 02.10.71
G-APEE 27.10.65
G-ARCO 12.10.67
G-ARJM 21.12.61
G-ARPI 18.06.72
G-ARPS 29.07.69
G-ARPT 03.07.68
G-ASXI 04.07.65
G-ASXP 04.12.67

British International Helicopters
G-BDES 10.11.88
G-BEID 13.07.88
G-BEWL 25.07.90
G-BWFC 06.11.86

British Island Airways
G-BBXJ 24.12.74

British Marine Air Navigation Co
G-EBFK 21.05.24

British Midland Airways
G-ALHG 04.06.67
G-AODG 20.02.69
G-AVJA 20.03.69
G-AWXI 22.01.70
G-BMAU 18.01.87
G-OBME 08.01.89

British Overseas Airways Corporation
FK459 16.06.43
FK618 30.06.43
G-AASP 03.04.40
G-ABHG oo.06.41
G-ACJJ 14.09.40
G-ACWC 17.06.41
G-ADHK 11.05.41
G-ADSZ 23.05.40
G-ADTA 23.05.40
G-ADTC 24.11.40
G-ADUX 29.12.41
G-AEPR 14.04.44
G-AETX 01.12.42
G-AETZ 28.02.42
G-AEUC 03.03.42
G-AEUF 22.03.42
G-AEUH 30.01.42
G-AFCK 09.01.43
G-AFCS 19.11.43
G-AFCX 15.02.41
G-AFCZ 24.09.42
G-AFDI 20.12.40
G-AFDK 06.07.43
G-AFDL 06.10.40
G-AFGP 04.08.41
G-AFGR 19.01.41
G-AFKD 22.04.40
G-AFYE 15.02.43
G-AFYG 18.11.42
G-AFYI 13.09.42
G-AFZZ 24.07.40
G-AGAA 24.07.40
G-AGBB 01.06.43
G-AGBC 21.09.40
G-AGBI 24.11.40
G-AGBW 29.11.44
G-AGCI 26.09.42
G-AGCR 13.05.42
G-AGCZ 21.12.41
G-AGDA 23.03.43
G-AGDE 17.12.43
G-AGDF 23.06.42
G-AGDR 15.02.42
G-AGDU 12.08.42
G-AGEJ 04.04.43
G-AGEM 21.02.46
G-AGES 28.07.43
G-AGET 15.02.46
G-AGEV 04.03.46
G-AGEW 05.09.48
G-AGFZ 21.04.44
G-AGGD 03.01.44
G-AGGF 17.08.43
G-AGGG 25.10.43
G-AGHK 17.04.46
G-AGHR 24.10.45
G-AGHT 14.08.46
G-AGHV 10.03.46
G-AGHW 19.11.47
G-AGIB 06.11.43
G-AGIH 29.08.44
G-AGIR 28.08.44
G-AGIY 23.01.46
G-AGJD 01.02.49
G-AGJO 21.02.49
G-AGJU 03.01.47
G-AGJX 11.01.47
G-AGKD 23.12.46
G-AGKM 08.04.45
G-AGKN 14.07.48
G-AGKP 19.08.44
G-AGKR 29.08.44
G-AGLI 02.05.45
G-AGLU 15.08.46
G-AGLX 24.03.46
G-AGMB 27.08.48
G-AGMC 02.05.46
G-AGMF 20.08.46
G-AGMH 17.05.46
G-AGMM 07.11.49
G-AGNA 01.05.45
G-AGNR 16.07.47
G-AGNS 22.04.56
G-AGUC 14.08.46
G-AHCS 07.08.46
G-AHIX 01.02.50
G-AHRA 13.03.47
G-AHYC 13.11.48
G-AHYZ 18.01.47
G-AHZB 22.08.47
G-AJHL 09.02.48
G-ALAM 13.03.54
G-ALDN 28.05.52
G-ALHE 24.06.56
G-ALHL 21.09.55
G-ALSA 25.12.54
G-ALTM 22.06.55
G-ALYP 10.01.54
G-ALYR 25.07.53
G-ALYV 02.05.53
G-ALYY 08.04.54
G-ALYZ 26.10.52
G-ANBC 11.11.60
G-AOVD 24.12.58
G-APFE 05.03.66
G-ARWE 08.04.68
G-ASGN 13.09.70
PP325 08.07.46

British South American Airways
G-AGHE 17.01.49
G-AGUL 23.10.47
G-AGWG 13.11.47
G-AGWH 02.08.47
G-AGWJ 30.08.46
G-AGWK 05.09.47
G-AHEW 06.09.46
G-AHEX 05.01.49
G-AHEZ 13.04.47
G-AHNP 30.01.48
G-AIKM 21.04.49

British Steel Corporation
G-AXEL 29.09.69

British United (C.I.) Airways
G-ANTB 14.04.65

British United Air Ferries
G-AMWA 24.09.63

British United Airways
G-AODH 30.10.61
G-ASJJ 14.01.69

British West Indian Airways
VP-TAF oo.oo.oo

VP-TAH 26.08.43
VP-TAK 00.00.00
VP-TAL 18.02.46

British World Airlines
G-OHOT 25.02.94

British Yukon Navigation Co
CF-AZB 00.07.40
CF-BVC 11.09.41

Brito, A.
XB-KAQ 29.04.49

Britt Airways
N63Z 30.01.84

Britten-Norman
G-ATCT 09.11.66
G-AXRJ 07.04.70
G-BELN 14.12.78
G-BESE 14.12.78
G-BESK 14.12.78
G-BFNL 14.12.78

Brooks Air Fuel
N811E 09.10.93

Brooks, R.
N500AK 01.04.93

Broughton Air Services
VH-BBA 16.12.88

Brown Air Services
G-MOXY 26.04.87

Brown, A.C & Odstone, L.C.S.
G-AIIB 00.00.47

Brown, E.W.
N99H 19.02.71

Bruning Aviation
NC36498 25.02.48

Brush Electrical Machines
G-BFEM 11.06.82

Bryan, M.L.
N541F 03.11.90

Buchans Mining Co
VO-ABL 20.06.47

Buffalo Airways
C-FROD 26.06.94

Buffalo Express Airlines
N5462J 31.12.86

Bulair
LZ-BAA 00.00.75
LZ-ILA 04.11.72

Bulldog Airlines
N901BA 06.07.94
N902BA 13.01.94

Bulolo Gold Dredging
VH-UOU 00.00.42
VH-UOV 00.00.42
VH-URQ 00.00.42

Bureau de Prospection Forestiere
TR-LNG 26.11.77

Burke Air Transport
NC79024 13.07.47

Burkhart Grob Luft- und-Raumfahrt
D-IHNA 27.05.94

Burlington Air Express
N144SP 13.04.87
N794AL 15.02.92

Burlington Airways
N711TL 27.02.79

Burma Airways
XY-ADK 25.03.78
XY-ADM 30.04.74
XY-ADN 29.06.81
XY-ADO 19.08.80
XY-ADP 21.06.87
XY-ADQ 16.06.88
XY-ADS 12.10.85
XY-ADY 03.10.78
XY-AEB 12.08.82
XY-AEE 08.10.83
XY-AEH 08.09.77
XY-AEI 26.08.78
XY-AEK 03.02.89
XY-AEL 11.10.87

Burmah Oil Co
G-AKST 31.10.60
PK-GDC 21.01.74

Burnstein, S.
N163J 21.02.70

Bush Aviation
* 17.05.79

Bush Pilots Airways
VH-BPL 02.04.81

Business Air
N54NA 19.07.95

Business Express
N811BE 28.12.91

Business Jets
* 30.05.79

Butler Air Transport
VH-AOG 15.12.55
VH-AOH 03.06.47
VH-BAB 14.07.51

Butler Aviation
N4SW 05.09.79

By Air
G-EALW 16.08.20

Byrd, R.E.
NX206 30.06.27

C.A. de Transports Indochinois
F-BCYL 05.11.51

C.D.Stoltzfus & Associates
N91375 01.04.66

CAAC
* 23.03.73
* 21.01.76
* 05.11.92
B-202 24.12.82
B-2218 31.08.88
B-222 18.01.88
B-260 27.02.83
B-264 14.09.83
B-266 26.04.82
B-274 14.03.79
B-3417 15.08.89
B-3606 22.10.85
B-434 19.01.85
B-444 15.12.86

CAAC Flying College
* 00.02.95
* 23.03.95

CAE Aviation
LX-UGO 02.12.93

CAFSSA
XA-BKG 13.03.40

CAMBA
CP-1317 20.01.77
CP-1318 15.07.81
CP-1440 12.12.79
CP-1570 16.06.87
CP-2212 04.11.93
CP-687 12.09.61

CANA
F-AEHQ 00.08.23

CATA
F-BDLG 08.01.48

CATI
F-BANQ 21.08.49

CATS
OY-DYC 16.02.56
OY-DYY 16.02.56
OY-FAD 22.06.56

CAUSA
CX-ABB 24.12.40
CX-AFA 11.09.56
CX-ANA 22.10.55

CC Air
N165PC 12.03.92
N167PC 30.01.91
N730CC 20.08.90

CFRA
F-AFCP 04.05.23

CGEA
F-AFDH 14.08.25
F-AFGP 11.04.25
F-AGFY 10.02.25
F-AHBF 19.12.25
F-AHBI 02.01.28
F-AHEU 13.01.26
F-AINF 29.06.28

CGT
* 25.01.35

CIDNA
F-AEAY 30.05.30
F-AEBL 00.00.27
F-AEGS 31.07.24
F-AEHX 31.12.28
F-AFAO 09.07.27
F-AFBT 03.07.26
F-AGFU 30.05.25
F-AIGT 15.09.31
F-AJBH 22.09.31
F-ALGT 23.11.35
F-FREJ 24.08.25
F-FREM 26.06.25

CIM Associates
N273R 22.10.77

CL Air Surveys
G-AHKJ 12.02.47

CLASSA
M-CAFF 17.10.29

CNAC
* 00.03.36
* 29.10.40
* 20.01.41
* 27.05.44
* 07.01.45
* 20.09.46
* 25.12.46
* 25.12.46
* 05.01.47
* 25.01.47
* 28.01.47
* 25.04.47
* 27.10.47
* 20.01.48
* 12.12.48
* 29.01.49
NC14269 25.12.36
NC16V 24.11.33
NC17V 10.04.34
NC40V 13.08.35
n/a 05.03.36

COHATA
* 22.01.66

COPA Panama
HP-1205CMP 07.06.92
HP-873CMP 19.11.93

CORAL
HK-3238 29.09.91

CRI Helicopters
N114CR 19.02.93
N314CR 08.05.93

CTA Languedoc Roussillon
F-BCAD 01.11.46

CTAI
F-BCJX 13.05.48

Cable Commuter
N7666 23.11.68

Caicos Aircraft Leasing
HR-ALY 24.03.93

Caledonian Airways
G-ARUD 04.03.62
G-ASID 28.09.64

California Air Freight
N1240N 14.01.59

California Air Tours
N8042X 26.06.89

California Airmotive
N7876 10.09.73

California Dept of Forestry
N427DF 19.06.93
N451DF 19.06.92

California Eastern Airlines
* 14.04.70
N229A 27.03.53
N37474 00.02.58

Calm Air International
C-GPFG 16.06.87

Calvert, E.M.
NC13715 01.01.47

Cambodia Air Commercial
XW-PHW 07.07.72
XW-TDA 02.10.72
XW-TFL 20.04.74
XW-TFR 27.06.74

Cambodia International Airlines
XW-PKJ 25.12.74

Cambrian Air Service
G-AKSK 23.07.55

Cambrian Airways
G-AIGY 01.08.50
G-AMOA 19.01.70
G-AMOL 20.07.65

Cambridge Aviation
N999BH 05.09.93

Cameroon Airlines
TJ-CBC 31.10.81
TJ-CBD 30.08.84
TJ-CCF 28.06.89

Cameroons Air Transport
TJ-ACC 21.01.67

Cameroun Air Force
TJ-XAC 00.12.89
TJ-XAP 00.00.00
TJ-XAT 00.00.00
TJ-XBO 27.01.83
TJ-XBS 26.10.83

Cameroun Government
TJ-AAR 10.11.94

Campbell Air Service
N2299W 28.05.77

Campbell Chain Corporation
N1515V 02.10.52

Canaan, A.
HI-189 31.08.79

Canada Jet Charters
C-GPUN 11.01.95

Canadair
C-GCGR-X 03.04.80
C-GKEE 29.09.83

Canadian Air Crane
C-FAHQ 21.09.94

Canadian Airways
CF-AEO 18.07.35
CF-ASI 12.03.32
CF-AUJ 03.10.40
CF-BBH 19.03.47
CF-BDD 29.12.45
CF-BDG 22.02.42
G-CARS 16.03.33
G-CASC 04.03.31

Canadian Colonial Airways
CF-ATE 30.01.34

Canadian Helicopters
C-GAHG 18.03.94
C-GBHB 12.05.92
C-GBHT 17.04.90
C-GKTL 20.02.94

Canadian Pacific Airlines
CF-BMG 01.02.47
CF-BTX oo.11.45
CF-BXL 09.12.46
CF-CPC 21.07.51
CF-CPK 04.03.66
CF-CPR 09.02.50
CF-CRV 11.05.53
CF-CUA 09.09.49
CF-CUF 22.12.50
CF-CUN 03.03.53
CF-CUP 29.08.56
CF-CUQ 08.07.65
CF-CZB 22.07.62
N791SA 07.02.68

Canair Cargo
C-FICA 19.09.91

Canairelief
CF-NAJ 03.08.69
CF-NAK 17.12.69

Candler, A.
NC536M 04.03.30

Cape Central Airways
N5647D 08.12.94

Cape Cod Airlines
* 23.07.37

Caperton, A.L.
NC141M 11.06.33

Capital Airlines
N2735A 12.05.59
N28324 02.08.59
N49553 04.06.58
N7404 20.02.56
N7410 20.05.58
N7437 06.04.58
N7462 18.01.60
N7463 12.05.59
N88839 18.04.57

Capitol Airlines
N1300N 15.10.60
N1301N 16.11.58
N1308V 22.01.61
N1309V 13.09.67
N1802 28.04.68
N25691 12.12.49
N4909C 27.11.70

Caproni
n/a oo.03.21

Cardiff & Peacock
NR7805 11.07.33

Career Aviation Services
N577KA 07.05.86

Carga Aerea Dominicana
HI-251 oo.11.86

Carga Aerea Transportada
CP-1358 11.01.80
CP-1489 20.04.85

Carga del Caribe
XA-SEA 15.05.93

Cargolux
TF-LLG 02.12.70

Carib Air Transport
J6-SLQ 10.06.91

Carib West Airways
8P-AAC 09.09.71

Caribair
N1549V 22.09.64
N3408 23.01.67

Caribbean Air Cargo
N98AS 28.03.81

Caribbean Airlines
* 02.04.67

Caribbean Atlantic Airlines
NC25687 08.01.47

Caribbean International Airways
VP-BAO 09.04.50
VP-JAT 21.08.51
VP-JAW 02.01.52
VP-JBC 10.04.53

Caribbean Ventures Leasing
N4BC oo.oo.83

Caribe Air Sales
N25656 06.12.78

Carolina Aircraft Corporation
N211L 12.05.72
N5133B 04.02.69
N5160V 09.12.63
N68966 19.11.66

Carson Helicopters
N4371S 08.09.76
N47782 10.01.87
N65526 20.04.85
N90936 02.02.77
N90939 02.04.77

Casair
N7560U oo.01.82

Cascade Airways
N2550A 20.06.69
N390CA 10.01.83

Caspair
5Y-AJP 01.02.77
5Y-ANV oo.oo.oo
5Y-ASF oo.05.78
5Y-AUA 06.01.76
VP-KCJ 07.10.62
VP-KHF 23.01.55
VP-KND 18.03.55

Caspar Air Charters
VP-KEO 31.12.49

Casper Air Service
N81TR 23.12.92
N96JP 06.04.93

Castel-Mauboussin
n/a 05.05.48

Castelo Taxi Aereo
PT-HFM 13.08.80

Castle Air
G-BHXU 29.06.95

Castleton Inc
N999B 12.01.55

Castor Trading Co
N204RC 17.06.91

Catair
F-BGNC 09.08.69

Catalina Airlines
* 19.08.77
* 14.04.79
N54516 07.07.78

Catalina Company, The
N5404J 16.01.94

Catalina Vegas Airlines
N4040B 08.10.68

Cathay Pacific Airways
VR-HDG 24.02.49
VR-HDT 16.07.48
VR-HDW 13.09.49
VR-HDX 09.02.48
VR-HEU 23.07.54
VR-HFX 05.11.67
VR-HFZ 15.06.72

Catholic Mission of the Holy Ghost
VH-UJT 06.08.39

Catskill Airways
N17574 24.02.79

Cavalier Air Force
N3710G 21.09.80

Cavenaugh Aviation
N184MA 20.06.87

Cavener, D.
N75430 21.05.70

Cega Aviation
G-BHUL 22.04.85

Celtic Helicopters
EI-BST 24.09.91

Cen-Tex Airlines
N29929 21.07.83

Center Aviation
N1542V oo.oo.69

Central Aerea
PP-IBC 04.11.50

Central African Airways
VP-YER 22.01.50
VP-YEX 17.03.55
VP-YEY 29.03.53
VP-YEZ 06.01.55
VP-YKO 23.02.55
VP-YMO 05.10.56
VP-YNE 09.08.58

Central African Republic Air Force
TL-KAA 20.01.66

Central Air Service
N96361 23.12.86

Central Air Services
N816D 28.11.80

Central Air Transport [1]
* 10.11.44
* 13.07.46
* 15.12.46
* 25.12.46
XT-520 02.06.49
XT-538 05.12.48

Central Air Transport [2]
C-GVHS 21.06.83

Central Airlines
N91003 30.09.67
NC904Y 12.09.34
NC934Y 01.06.34

Central BC Airways
CF-BHL 27.01.53

Central Helicopters
G-STST 22.05.94

Central Intelligence Agency
* 28.08.84
N62WS 26.03.84

Central Mining Corporation
ZS-BTM 09.01.52

Central Mountain Air
C-FAAM 14.01.93
C-FDJA oo.09.82
C-FQNF 04.04.91
C-GIPF 02.09.83
C-GWYX 21.05.89

Central Northern Airways
CF-ESA 10.12.54
CF-GFP oo.04.48
CF-GHI 05.04.50
CF-GJV 13.04.51

Central Region Directorate
13343 06.04.93
RA-20110 21.05.94
RA-20314 07.05.94
RA-20945 10.01.94
RA-46575 17.07.94

Central Vermont Airways
NC976W 08.04.36

Centre Airlines
N47E 24.02.93

Centro Int. de Agricultura Tropical
HK-2245W oo.oo.oo

Century Equipment
N711Y 31.12.85

Ceskoslovenska Letecka Spolecnost
L-BABD 09.05.29
OK-ABT oo.oo.35
OK-AIA 21.04.36

Ceskoslovenske Aerolinie
* 05.03.46
* 13.02.47
* 27.02.50
* 14.01.54
* 18.01.56
OK-ADB oo.06.34
OK-BAG 23.08.38
OK-CFD 02.01.77
OK-DBF 20.08.75
OK-DBP 24.11.56

OK-FOR	22.08.30
OK-LDB	16.08.63
OK-MCG	01.02.72
OK-MCJ	11.10.68
OK-MCK	11.10.68
OK-MCM	oo.01.75
OK-MCT	10.09.62
OK-MCV	25.10.73
OK-MCZ	02.01.61
OK-MDE	29.08.73
OK-NAA	02.01.77
OK-NAB	28.07.76
OK-NDD	01.06.70
OK-OAD	28.03.61
OK-OCA	11.02.77
OK-PAF	11.07.61
OK-TEB	18.08.70
OK-WAI	05.09.67
OK-WDB	25.01.47

Cessna Aircraft Co

N12058	20.07.93
N12065	20.07.93
N12564	20.07.93
N12660	20.07.93
N12669	20.07.93
N12756	20.07.93
N12757	20.07.93
N12761	20.07.93
N12762	20.07.93
N12763	20.07.93
N12855	20.07.93
N12859	20.07.93
N12967	20.07.93

Cessnyca
HK-1216 17.01.74

Chad Air Force

TT-LAG	16.02.76
TT-NAA	29.01.78
TT-PAB	07.03.86

Chad Government
TT-AAM oo.oo.81

Chaillotine Air Service
F-GERA 16.04.88

Chalks International Airlines
N150FB 18.03.94

Chamberlin Flying Services
NC728K 09.07.36

Champion Home Builders
N999HG 08.09.77

Channel Air Bridge
G-ARSF 28.12.62

Channel Airways

G-AGZB	06.05.62
G-APPU	05.05.68
G-AVJZ	03.05.67

Channel Express
G-BBXI 07.06.84

Chaparral Airlines
N411AE 25.03.88

Chapman Commodities
N40BC 06.07.79

Charlotte Aircraft Corporation
N8170A 11.12.77

Chartair

G-AIOM	24.01.48
G-AKGN	17.12.52

Charter Flite Aviation Service
VH-BMS 14.10.49

Chatham Corporation
N51CA 30.03.83

Chaunskoe Air
RA-28797 01.02.95

Chautauqua Airlines
N31138 oo.oo.oo

Chechen National Airlines

*	29.11.94
*	30.11.94

Chelyabinsk Air
RA-87565 14.01.95

Cheremshanka Airlines
RA-87468 26.09.94

Chevron Oil
N480F 19.07.83

Chicago & Southern Airlines

NC10894	28.05.35
NC11155	11.02.35
NC16022	05.08.36

Chicago Helicopter Airways
N879 27.07.60

Chicago-Detroit Airways
NC606 14.09.31

Chilcotin Cariboo Aviation
C-GPCF 23.05.85

China Airlines

*	24.10.67
*	03.06.72
*	27.07.74
B-1523	21.08.67
B-1553	26.03.75
B-156	12.08.70
B-165	04.11.93
B-180	26.10.89
B-1811	15.01.74
B-1816	26.04.94
B-1826	27.02.80
B-1834	11.09.79
B-1852	21.11.71
B-1870	16.02.86
B-198	29.12.91
B-309	02.01.69

China Eastern Airlines
B-2103 26.10.93

China General Aviation
B-2755 31.07.92

China Northern Airlines
B-2141 13.11.93

China Northwest Airlines

B-2610	06.06.94
B-2716	23.07.93

China Ocean Helicopter Co

B-7104	16.10.93
B-7952	24.10.93

China Southern Airlines

B-2523	24.11.92
B-2812	02.10.90

China Southwest Airlines
B-2402 02.10.90

Chinese Government
* oo.oo.20

Chitina Air Service
N4747S 19.04.78

Chosonminhang
889 01.07.83

Christian & Missionary Alliance

JZ-PTA	28.04.55
PK-CMA	oo.oo.53

Churchill Falls Corp
C-FCFL 09.12.77

Cia Aeronautica Francisco Sarabia

XA-BAW	26.11.42
XA-BFP	oo.03.41

Cia Aramayo de Mines
CB-CAM-2 26.09.41

Cia Brasiliera de Tratores
PT-JBQ 04.09.82

Cia Impulsora de Aviacion

XA-NEI	oo.oo.63
XA-YEO	oo.oo.oo

Cia Nacional de Aviacion Guatemala
NC430H 08.09.35

Ciba-Pilatus Aerial Spraying

HB-FET	03.10.82
HB-GFT	25.07.81
HB-GGC	03.10.82

Cie Air Transport

F-BENF	29.07.50
F-BENG	10.04.48
F-BLHH	11.06.69
F-BMHU	08.03.67

Cie Darienitas de Servicios
HP-425 11.07.67

Cie Veha-Akat

F-LAAC	oo.oo.58
F-LAAE	oo.oo.58
F-LAAF	02.05.58

Cie de Trans. Aer. et de Commerce
F-OANH 04.03.54

Cie des Chargeurs Reunis
F-AOUC 12.08.39

Cierva Autogyro Co
G-ALCV 13.06.50

Citi Air
ZS-KPF 15.08.88

City Air
G-JETB 26.05.93

City Centre Air Taxies
VH-CTS 17.11.68

Civil Aeronautics Board

LQ-XWW	oo.oo.oo
LV-XZY	oo.oo.oo
LV-YAE	oo.oo.oo
LV-YAZ	oo.12.48
LV-YBL	oo.oo.oo
LV-YBP	oo.oo.oo

Civil Air Training Centre
VT-CTX 08.05.51

Civil Air Transport

*	17.10.47
*	04.12.49
*	09.12.49
*	10.12.49
*	11.03.54
*	06.05.54
B-1018	16.02.68
B-908	20.06.64
II	oo.oo.45
N8342C	21.12.48
XT-44	19.06.48
XT-822	29.07.48

Civil Aviation Department
VT-DEU 19.05.78

Clairways

VP-KDW	01.07.48
VP-KEM	oo.06.48

Clanair
G-ANRR 02.12.58

Classic Helicopters

N2753U	26.02.94
N820CW	24.07.94

Classic Wings
D-CCCC 22.12.91

Claudius Dornier Seastar
D-ICDS 23.07.85

Clay, C.
N300GR 24.05.80

Clearo, N.L.
PT-BVG 07.04.64

Cloudlands Aviation Development
P2-FHP 12.07.83

Clyde Helicopters
G-EYEI 24.01.90

Co Boliviana de Rutas Aereas

CP-741	30.10.64
CP-742	21.02.65
CP-767	13.04.67

Co-Air
P2-COG oo.12.87

Co-operativa de Montecillos
N126US 30.06.77

Coastair
N76214 13.07.78

Coastal Airlines

*	23.12.47
NC60331	07.01.48

Coastal Airways
N4465D 13.10.83

Coastal Cargo
NC53210 06.01.49

Cobham Air Routes
G-ADEW 03.07.35

Cockatoo Island Airways
VH-BSN oo.05.89

Codds Air Service
VH-EGT 26.02.80

Cogeair
TN-ABA 11.07.69

Coin Acceptors Inc
N2CA 18.12.82

Collier County Mosquito Control
* 10.09.85

Collings Foundation
N8036E 22.06.93

Collins Radio Corporation
N71CR 11.07.75

Cologne Commercial Flight
D-ILEP 29.08.87

Coloma, F.
LV-AHI 02.12.54

Colombian Aido Canso
* 20.03.60

Colombian Customs
HK-1221G 24.11.80

Colonial Air Transport
NC55 18.06.27
NC9675 05.06.30

Colonial Airlines
NC17335 20.09.48

Colonial Corporation
* 13.09.67

Colonial Western Airways
NC7683 17.03.29

Columbia Air Cargo
NC95486 27.11.47

Columbia Helicopters
N190CH 20.08.83
N6672D 04.08.90
N6676D 14.10.82

Columbia Pacific Airlines
N199EA 10.02.78

Comair
ZS-FJK 09.10.82
ZS-LGP 01.03.88

Comair Air Taxi
N5642L 08.10.79

Combs Airways
N155PA 19.06.85

Comet Leasing
I-STMO 30.09.93

Comituri
OO-CED 01.05.54

Comm. Aereas de Veracruz
XA-FOZ 11.11.46

Command Aviation
N121CA 03.06.81

Commercial Air Hire
G-ABTY 11.05.35
G-ACAP 26.03.36
G-ACCR 22.01.36
G-ADLM 16.05.36

Commercial Air Transport
RP-C12 04.06.78
RP-C647 16.11.77

Commercial Aviation
VH-AYN 04.02.56

Commutair
N55000 03.01.92

Commuter Air Philippines
RP-C707 14.08.91
RP-C719 26.07.89

Commuter Airlines
RP-C140 24.07.90

Compagnie Aerienne du Languedoc
F-BTMO 28.04.80
F-GCTE oo.03.88

Compagnie Sila
F-VNAE 17.10.53

Companhia Meridional de Transportes
PP-MTA 19.12.45
PP-MTB 06.03.46
PP-MTC 08.03.46

Compania Aerea Nacional
CP-1654 08.03.93
CP-1704 19.08.85

Comstock International
C-FEYG 26.05.78

Con. Tec. Operacional de Aviacao
PT-KVT 13.11.79
PT-KVU 07.10.78

Conair
OY-DSR 13.09.74

Conair Aviation
C-FAXS 15.06.79
C-FKCL 29.05.78
C-FPWA 02.08.74
C-GHNM 21.10.79
C-GHNU 28.08.94
C-GHQY 15.08.86
C-GHQZ 25.07.78
C-GOBK 30.05.78
C-GSFS 04.09.89

Condor
D-ABHD 02.01.88

Condor Enterprise
N47CE 22.05.89

Confederate Air Force
N16KL 13.10.84
N5546N 28.09.95

Confortair
* 26.07.95

Congo Motor
OO-CCJ 24.08.48
OO-CCK 27.11.58

Congolese Air Force
TN-230 27.01.90
TN-231 oo.00.00

Conifair Aviation
C-GBYA 26.06.89

Connair
VH-CLS 23.10.75

Conner, C.J. & Chesher, A.C.
NC574E 01.03.30

Connie Kalitta Services
N10AS 19.11.87
N31SK oo.03.87
N500P 16.09.90
N9231 09.10.87

Consolidated Air
N73675 oo.oo.77

Constructions Aero-nautiques Renard
OO-ARM 01.04.38

Construtora Andrade Gutierrez
PT-CEV 30.09.73

Contact Air
D-BEAT 06.01.93

Container Corporation of America
N739R 16.05.67

Continental Air Express
C3908 20.09.29
* 06.01.69
N8744R 17.04.66
N9473Z 13.08.67
XW-PBJ oo.oo.oo
XW-PBN oo.oo.oo
XW-PBP oo.oo.oo

Continental Airlines
N18835 02.03.94
N242V 28.01.63
N243V 08.07.62
N626TX 15.11.87
N68045 01.03.78
N70773 01.07.65
N70775 22.05.62
N88777 07.08.75
N90853 16.03.54
NC25636 27.08.45

Continental Airways
NC991Y 05.02.32

Continental Can Co
N1502 oo.oo.59

Continental Charters
* 04.05.49
N3944C 29.12.51

Continental Express
N24706 29.04.93
N33071 11.09.91

Continental Oil Corporation
N91G 24.09.78

Continentale Deutsche Luftreederei
D-ABEB 17.06.61

Cookers & Geysers Ltd
G-AIEZ oo.oo.48

Cool Air
N156PA 27.07.93

Cooper Skybird Air Charters
5Y-AOY oo.oo.86
5Y-AST 08.03.87
5Y-EJS 03.12.87

Copter Action
C-GRAA 29.06.95
OH-HSR 29.06.95

Cordonez, C.C.
XA-HIM 13.10.49

Corio Air Engineers
VH-BAX oo.08.51

Corp Aeronautica de Transportes
NC392H oo.oo.oo
NC46M 04.11.29
NC504K 27.05.30

Corp. Turistica Melia
HP-909 26.10.74

Corporacion Boliviano de Fomento
CB-42 oo.oo.46
CP-549 20.09.55
CP-552 12.03.59
CP-624 23.02.63
CP-626 25.10.59

Corporacion Minera de Bolivia
CP-631 29.07.59
CP-894 18.06.71

Corporacion Sudamericana
LV-AAE oo.oo.oo

Corporate Aviation
N271MA 17.11.88

Corporate Helicopters
C-FTPH 24.07.93

Costa Rican Ministry of Security
TI-SPF 28.10.77
TI-SPI 09.09.75
TI-SPJ oo.oo.78

Costa, J.
NR105N 15.01.37

Cotton, F.S.
G-AGAR 29.05.41

Coulson Air Crane
C-FWYN 02.04.93

Court Helicopters
* 08.08.79
ZS-HCP 31.01.78
ZS-HCX 09.04.77
ZS-HGU 15.04.81
ZS-HIF 16.05.88
ZS-HIW 23.02.92
ZS-HKA 07.07.92
ZS-HRU 17.09.92

Court Republic Helicopters
ZS-HLI 19.01.86

Cousin Properties
N400CP 21.01.71

Cousteau, J.
N101CS 28.06.79

Coval Air
* 01.07.84

Crasa Taxi Aereo
PT-LHU 28.07.92

Crest Breeders
Z-WRJ 20.09.88

Crewsair
G-AHON 27.07.52

Crilly Airways
G-ACEY 08.07.40

Crosley Radio Corporation
NR496M 04.11.32

Cross Airways
NC394H 10.07.30

Crossair
HB-AHA 21.02.90

Crown Airways
N2477U 20.04.82

Crown Center Aviation
N234CM 16.12.88

Crown International Airlines
* 10.08.78

Cruzeiro
PP-CAT 15.08.38
PP-CAU 05.02.36
PP-CBC 22.05.38
PP-CBI 08.03.47
PP-CBS 05.02.46
PP-CBV 28.09.71
PP-CBX 13.03.48
PP-CBY 26.08.55
PP-CBZ 14.04.69
PP-CCA 21.04.46
PP-CCC 01.12.55
PP-CCD 28.04.46
PP-CCF 11.10.56
PP-CCG 25.12.55
PP-CCK 26.07.51

PP-CCL 22.08.70
PP-CCP 21.10.54
PP-CCX 22.03.51
PP-CDI 19.08.58
PP-CDJ 12.09.54
PP-CDW 03.05.63
PP-CDY 22.01.63
PP-CEF 16.01.58
PP-CEH 11.01.58
PP-CEM 26.01.60
PP-CEP 16.06.58
PP-CEV 15.01.65
PP-CEZ 09.05.62
PP-CFD 20.08.65
PP-CTG 18.10.72
PP-CTI 29.04.77
PP-PCW 01.12.66
PP-PDV 23.12.73
PP-PDX 01.06.73
PP-PEC 00.00.00
PP-SAD 20.10.68

Crystal Aviation
N88HA 20.03.94

Cuadros, J.M.
LV-MMR 29.11.78

Cubana
* 13.05.80
CU-C556 17.05.54
CU-T111 23.03.90
CU-T1200 18.03.76
CU-T1201 06.10.76
CU-T1202 24.10.90
CU-T1219 03.02.80
CU-T1227 14.09.91
CU-T1281 03.09.89
CU-T138 01.09.61
CU-T172 15.04.60
CU-T188 25.04.51
CU-T397 06.12.52
CU-T603 01.11.58
CU-T607 10.08.61
CU-T7 25.11.50
CU-T819 27.03.62
CU-T827 09.02.67
CU-T830 10.07.66
CU-T879 18.03.76
CU-T899 19.01.85
NM-7 10.12.34

Cumberland Airlines
N6629L 05.03.84
N66892 18.05.85

Cunard Eagle Airways
G-AHPM 09.08.61
G-APOM 26.03.61

Currey Air Transport
N74663 08.09.55

Curtiss Reid Flying Services
CF-EDN 13.11.50

Curtiss-Wright Flying Service
NC7118 21.11.30

Cuthbertson, Y.
OH-KDC 02.01.74

Cypress Helicopters
C-GIMO 20.05.94

Cyprus Airways
5B-DAB 22.07.74
5B-DAE 22.07.74
5B-DAM 19.08.79
5B-DAN 04.11.80

Czech Police
B-2929 12.09.95

D.A.C.
CP-665 24.08.60

D.G.Harris Productions
CF-JRY 30.08.70

DAS Air Services
5X-DAR 25.11.92

DB Aviation
N900CD 30.05.94

DDL
OY-AEB 17.02.47
OY-DAC 02.05.33
OY-DCI 12.02.48
OY-DEM 04.09.46
OY-DFE 30.01.46
OY-DIG 17.12.45
OY-DLI 29.12.47
SE-APR 01.02.48
T-DOBC 17.10.21
T-DOFB 01.11.25
T-DOFD 19.09.27
T-DOXD 20.04.27

DETA
CR-AAV 23.02.44
CR-AAX 14.11.41
CR-ACJ 00.00.00
CR-ACM 00.00.00
CR-ADM 15.03.55
CR-AIB 27.03.70

DGAC/SFACT
F-BTTU 31.07.90

DMC Flying Service
N227DM 03.03.95

DNL
LN-DAE 16.06.36
LN-IAU 15.05.50
LN-IAV 28.08.47
LN-IAW 02.10.48
LN-LAB 22.05.46

DTA
CR-LBH 10.05.57
CR-LCJ 28.08.54
CR-LLD 21.05.72

DVS
D-1165 24.05.29
D-ARIP oo.08.35

Dagens Nyheter
SE-BUX 11.01.53

Dai Nippon Airlines
J-ANES 10.08.38
J-BBOI 12.02.40

Daily Variety
N97QS 29.11.90

Daimler Hire
G-EAWO 07.04.22
G-EBBQ oo.08.23
G-EBBS 14.09.23
G-EBBU 03.11.22

Dalmia Jain Airways
VT-CDZ 16.01.49

Dan-Air
G-ALZR 26.07.69
G-ALZX 14.04.66
G-AMAG 30.09.68
G-AMUT 20.05.58
G-AMUV 25.05.58
G-APDL 07.10.70
G-APDN 03.07.70
G-ASPL 27.06.81
G-ATFZ 01.09.66
G-BDAN 25.04.80
G-BEKF 31.07.79

Danair
OY-AUI 12.11.82

Danforth, W.H.
NC14265 01.01.38

Danish Air Transport
OY-JRK 08.01.94

Danish Government
TF-IST 23.10.63

Danish Inter Flight
OY-AZA 15.01.79

Danpar Aviation
N334DP 16.11.87

Dansk Totalenterprise
OY-BUS 29.07.86

Darbhanga Aviation
VT-AYG 24.05.62
VT-DEM 30.04.54

Darne Inc
N402DL 01.11.82

de Campos, C.E.
PT-BJC 04.03.61

de Havilland Aircraft
VH-DHD 01.12.54

de Havilland Aircraft of Canada
C-GCTC 04.09.84
C-GDHA 04.05.76
CF-LKI-X 24.02.59
N4964N 29.02.52

de Kroonduif
JZ-PPX 30.08.57

de Paoli, R.
PP-ITI 23.09.59

De Zevende Bouw Mij
PH-TOL oo.05.40

DePonti Aviation
C422H 20.01.37

Decca Navigator Co
G-APKR 21.09.63

Deccan Airways
VT-AUN 30.04.52
VT-AUO 21.11.51
VT-AXE 19.02.52
VT-CJD 05.04.50

Delag
LZ10 28.06.12
LZ11 12.10.15
LZ6A 14.09.10
LZ7 28.06.10
LZ8 16.05.11

Delass Americanas
N41953 07.04.95

Delaware Air Freight
N40DA 28.11.73

Delmotte Aviation
F-BVTD 23.06.84

Delta Air
D-IASN 04.12.85

Delta Air Lines
N28345 17.05.53
N3305L 30.05.72
N3323L 27.11.73
N473DA 31.08.88
N4820C 20.03.68
N4871C 16.12.61
N4891C 15.11.59
N51359 15.06.54
N530DA 14.10.89
N726DA 02.08.85
N781DL 24.08.95
N802E 30.03.67
N8804E 23.05.60
N8807E 20.12.72
N975NE 31.07.73
N9885F 24.11.64
NC14599 14.08.35
NC15134 27.08.36
NC167W 24.12.35
NC20750 10.11.46
NC37478 10.03.48
NC49657 22.04.47

Delta Air Transport
OO-AUX 08.05.70
OO-VGB 04.10.74

Delta Helicopters [1]
C-GOOM 17.09.81

Delta Helicopters [2]
G-BODW 15.01.94

Denendeh Helicopters
C-GBPB 10.07.95

Dennis Aviation
G-AIXW 26.04.50
G-AIXZ 05.02.51

Dep Marina di Pisa
I-DEOR 21.08.24

Departamento de Transporte Aereo
CR-LBK 18.07.50

Department of Aviation Industry
SSSR-24565 15.10.92

Department of Forests & Mines
TN-ACO oo.07.78

Department of Public Works
CF-BCA 24.05.62

Department of Survey
4R-AAR 04.04.58
4R-AAS 25.08.58

Department of Transport
C-FCSV 27.02.81
CF-DTO 15.10.48
CF-GXE 12.04.61

Department of the Interior
N1015G 14.05.71
N891U 19.05.74

Dept. of Ag. & Fish. for Scotland
G-DAFS 31.05.90

Dept. of Transportation & Comm.
CF-PQG 16.03.65

Deraya Air Taxi
PK-DCR 08.11.82
PK-WWE 08.10.91

Derazona Air Service
PK-DAI 07.09.74
PK-DBJ 23.09.76
PK-DBM 19.02.80
PK-DBU 12.01.76
PK-DBX 26.07.76

Derby Aviation
G-AMSW 07.10.61

Deruluft
D-1079 oo.11.32
D-1465 oo.oo.oo
D-200 16.05.28
D-2831 22.10.34
D-902 oo.12.26
D-AJYP 07.03.35
D-AREN 31.01.35
D-OKES 16.05.36
RR14 oo.10.24
RR7 oo.06.27
URSS-D306 oo.oo.33
URSS-D311 06.11.36

Desert Locust Control Organisation
5Y-AMG oo.05.74

Design for Living Inc
N100RV 27.12.79

Deutsche Flugdienst
D-BELA 17.10.58
D-BELU 31.07.60

Deutsche Reichbahn-gesellschaft
D-AVAN 06.11.34

Deutsche Zeppelin-Reederei
D-LZ219 06.05.37

Devlet Hava Yollari
TC-ACA 19.11.51
TC-ARK 03.04.54
TC-BAG 05.01.54
TC-BAL 25.03.50
TC-EGE 25.09.53

Diamang
D2-EHD 22.01.93

Dicro
SE-GGR 13.02.78

Digital Equipment Corporation
N97JA 10.04.78

Dikson Air
* 24.09.95

Dirgantara Air Service
PK-OAV 07.10.75
PK-VBR 16.07.84
PK-VIO 14.02.85
PK-VIP 03.09.91
PK-VIQ 20.10.79
PK-VIR 24.02.87
PK-VIT 24.02.80
PK-VIV 06.01.94
PK-VSM 25.06.92
PK-ZAA 25.04.94

Diskont & Kredit AG
D-CDFA 25.03.80

Diversified Drilling Muds
N84857 09.05.85

Do-Air Trade
HA-BCN oo.oo.93

Dobrolet
3 oo.11.28
6 oo.06.28
DL-10 22.06.28
R-RDAX 20.08.25
SSSR-107 oo.07.29
SSSR-110 oo.oo.29
SSSR-122 oo.oo.29
SSSR-124 oo.07.29
SSSR-155 29.07.30
SSSR-166 oo.04.29
SSSR-173 oo.02.31
SSSR-197 20.05.30
SSSR-202 19.01.31
SSSR-L718 22.02.32
URSS-300 09.08.29
n/a 05.06.26

Dollar Helicopters
G-AZNI 23.12.94
G-BAKF 09.01.89
G-BNIT 03.06.93
G-BOUY 31.12.94

Dolphin Aviation
N28ST 31.07.87

Domaire
HI-170 07.05.70

Dominican Services
N1546A 23.03.78

Dominicana
HI-16 17.07.58
HI-168 23.06.69
HI-177 15.02.70
HI-36 oo.09.56
HI-39 oo.10.68
HI-6 11.01.48
HI-617CA 06.09.93
HI 92 oo.10.84

Dominion Air Lines
ZK-ACA 08.02.31

Don Avia
RA-88254 27.10.94

Don Everall Aviation
G-AGLR 07.10.56
G-AHPT 07.07.59
G-AMNK 24.08.60

Donington Aviation
G-BKTJ 27.11.85

Dorado Wings
N116DW 20.07.81
N122DW 15.09.75

Dornier
D-IFNS 26.03.82

dos Santos, J.P.
PT-KRW 17.02.81

Dothan Aviation Corporation
N4710C 05.08.76

Douglas Aircraft
N8210H 31.01.57
N846D 10.03.58

Douglas Airways
P2-ATU 05.10.79
P2-DNI 25.08.85
P2-DNJ 21.05.77
P2-DNJ 05.07.90
P2-DNL 23.12.79
P2-DNW 30.08.85

Dovair
YJ-RV20 13.09.88

Dowty Group Services
G-AVHV 09.04.70

Dragon Airways
G-AIYP 05.07.53

Drayton Associates
N50SK 04.04.86

Dreidoppel, P.
D-CDPD 18.05.83

Drenair
EC-EFI 11.10.87

Du Pont Co Inc
N204C 04.09.91

Duff, R.W.
NC57667 07.12.48

Duncan Aircraft Sales
N831LC 16.03.91

Duncan Aviation
N894U 08.07.74

Durakool Inc
N700DK 23.09.85

Dutch Continental Airlines
PH-NVA 30.08.70

Dwyer Air
N17CH 13.12.92

Dwyers Flying Service
* 03.02.59

E.J.Benes & Co
N6533D 21.09.68

EDELCA
YV-O-CVG-4 13.10.91

EH Industries
PP.2 21.01.93

EM Travel & Sales
N70RF 30.06.95

ENCAL
PT-KRP 10.08.78

ERA Aviation
N100PL 11.12.92
N295EH 16.08.92
N356EH 03.12.93
N382EH 30.08.94

ERA Helicopters
* 19.01.84
N1456T 13.05.76
N300JA 02.12.79
N353EH 25.05.88
N355EH 04.11.88
N455JA 20.08.85
N456JA 24.10.85

ETI 2000
I-ELTA 11.04.94

EXA Inc
N3657G 07.08.92

Eagle Air Freight
NC64722 08.03.48
NC79042 12.06.48

Eagle Air Services
J6-SLW 12.07.90
G-BGHR 25.09.79

Eagle Airlines
N2718W 21.07.83

Eagle Airways [1]
VH-EGU 16.12.80

Eagle Airways [2]
N492DM 06.04.93

Eagle Aviation [1]
G-AGNZ 24.08.52
G-AGRT 26.02.58
G-AHPO 20.12.53
G-AIAP 25.11.50
G-AJBO 01.05.57
G-AMGG 22.12.59

Eagle Aviation [2]
5Y-DNT 25.10.92
5Y-SRV 27.12.91
5Y-TNT 01.10.92

Eagle Aviation [3]
N20PT 18.03.94

Eagle Aviation [4]
9H-ABN 27.12.89

Eagle Commuter Airline
N59932 21.03.80

Eagle Helicopters
C-GMHS 18.06.82

Eagle Jet
N100EP 11.05.87

Eagle Wings Air Service
N1046 17.09.89

East African Airways
5H-AAK 05.07.73
5X-UVA 18.04.72
VP-KCU 28.06.46
VP-KEA 24.01.54
VP-KEB 15.10.51
VP-KEC 12.05.50
VP-KJT 29.08.63
VP-KKH 18.05.55
VP-KNY 11.04.62

East Anglian Flying Services
G-AHPH 28.07.59
G-AJKM 03.05.49
G-AOCE 15.01.58

East Coast Leasing
N278E 22.08.68
N91239 22.08.68

East Indonesia Air Taxi
PK-ESC 03.10.86

East Midlands Helicopters
G-OEMH 19.04.95

East Pakistan Government
AP-AGA 26.03.55
AP-AGB 26.03.55
AP-AGC 26.03.55

East Siberian Directorate
RA-70263 25.06.94

East-West Airlines
VH-BDO 12.10.49
VH-BKL 05.12.50
VH-EWL 31.05.74

Eastern Air Lines
N110A 03.01.60
N112A 21.12.55
N119A 19.10.53
N19963 30.07.49
N310EA 29.12.72
N445A 17.02.56
N453A 10.03.57
N492A 14.11.57
N496A 17.03.58
N5531 02.07.76
N5533 04.10.60
N6212C 28.06.57
N6218C 04.12.65
N6219C 18.10.66
N6220C 03.08.61
N808D 28.06.57
N809D 17.07.64
N815D 30.11.62
N819EA 01.01.85
N824D 16.10.65
N831D 20.07.64
N843D 29.07.63
N849D 08.02.65
N8607 25.02.64
N8845E 24.06.75
N88727 01.11.49
N8910E 09.02.79
N8948E 28.12.87
N8961E 18.05.72
N8967E 27.11.73
N8984E 11.09.74
NC111A 21.01.48
NC13732 19.12.36
NC13734 18.02.37
NC13735 19.10.38
NC13739 10.08.37
NC16072 12.01.41
NC18123 30.12.45
NC19970 18.01.46
NC21727 03.04.41
NC25647 12.07.45
NC28384 13.01.48
NC28394 26.02.41
NC33631 07.09.45
NC88729 11.10.46
NC88814 30.05.47
NC88872 12.01.47

Eastern Air Transport
* 04.06.33
NC12373 21.09.33
NC185H 14.01.33

Eastern Petroleum
SU-ANH 20.03.66

Eastern Provincial Airways
* 12.05.62
C-GEPH 29.12.81
CF-EPU 28.09.68
CF-FAJ 03.04.65

CF-GOC	21.11.64
CF-GSA	07.04.51
CF-HFL	oo.10.57
CF-JNR	04.04.61
CF-NAF	17.03.65

Eastex
N27W 04.05.68

Eastindo Air Taxi
PK-ESC 03.10.86

Eastman Kodak
N46TE 19.01.90

Ecuatoriana
HC-AIP oo.03.66
HC-AON 14.04.70
HC-SJE 14.03.72

Ecuavia
HC-BEP 14.07.78

Edde Airlines
N485 27.11.65

Eduardo, L.
CP-1024 03.03.74

Edwards, W.J.
N555GC 19.12.92

EgyptAir
SU-AOW 05.12.72
SU-AOY 29.01.73
SU-APE 17.10.82
SU-ARN 16.06.72
SU-AXA 25.12.76
SU-AXB 10.04.74
SU-AYH 24.11.85
SU-BCA 21.09.87
YU-AHR 19.03.72

Egyptian Air Force
SU-BAA/1270 19.02.78
SU-BAH/1276 29.05.81

Ehrenstrom Flyg
SE-DCY 04.12.69

El Aero Services
N27736 03.04.94

El Al Israel Airlines
* 13.06.49
4X-ACD 05.02.50
4X-ACG 26.06.49
4X-ADN 24.11.51
4X-AKC 27.07.55
4X-AXG 04.10.92

El Gavilan
* 02.02.92

El Peto Air Taxi
CP-1486 07.04.84

Elders Colonial Airways
G-AENX oo.08.39

Eldorado
CP-1617 23.10.81

Eldorado Aviation
CF-DGJ 04.12.57

Eliliguria
I-ELMR 17.11.94

Elistar
I-GLPB 08.01.95

Elitos
I-EHPA 25.11.90

Ellis Airlines
* 31.05.47
N4272C 04.08.53

Ellyou Goldfields Development Corp
VH-ULK 31.05.30

Embraer
PT-SFH 07.10.83

Emery Air Freight
N565PC 17.02.91

Emery Worldwide
N425EX 03.05.91

Emirates Air Transport
TZ-ARC 04.10.76

Empire Airlines/Federal Express
N746FE 11.01.95

Empire Airways
C-GKBM 14.07.88

Empresa Aviacion del Pacifico
HK-385 17.11.56

Empresa Transportes Aereos
CP-1244 18.01.88

Emric Air
ZS-IZZ 24.08.74

Emu Air Services
VH-PYS 11.01.78

English Electric Co
G-ALMR 12.04.60

Enterprise Generale M.Forrest
9Q-CRF oo.oo.oo

Epps Air Service
N44UE 18.01.90

Equator Airlines
5Y-PAL 09.01.95

Erasmus Inc
N125E 29.06.83

Erickson Air Crane
* 13.12.76
N165AC 01.09.94
N6959R 27.06.91

Ernir Airlines
TF-ORN 21.01.87

Est. Economique du Casino
F-GBRP 17.10.80

Ethiopian Air Force
ET-AHJ 17.03.83

Ethiopian Airlines
ET-AAB 07.01.68
ET-AAC 04.08.63
ET-AAD 18.03.60
ET-AAF 19.04.61
ET-AAP oo.08.77
ET-AAQ 10.04.69
ET-AAR 20.11.74
ET-AAS 23.04.76
ET-AAT 30.11.63
ET-AAY 12.03.70
ET-ABB 06.08.71
ET-ABE 05.08.74
ET-ABF 20.07.77
ET-ABI 14.09.65
ET-ABK 03.09.64
ET-ABL 21.11.67
ET-ABM 01.03.67
ET-ABO 14.10.70
ET-ABQ 10.09.72
ET-ABR 14.03.75
ET-ABX 11.09.75
ET-ACD 19.11.77
ET-ACQ 25.07.90
ET-ADC 31.05.76
ET-ADD 21.11.76
ET-AEJ 14.12.76
ET-AFW 19.02.79
ET-AGI 21.07.77
ET-AGK 15.10.78
ET-AGM 18.03.80
ET-AGO 26.12.87
ET-AGP 28.01.79
ET-AGQ 25.10.78
ET-AGR oo.07.77
ET-AGT 02.05.88
ET-AGU 21.09.79
ET-AGW 11.01.81
ET-AHI 08.11.88
ET-AHP 24.08.82
ET-AHR 07.10.81
ET-AIQ 22.06.86
ET-AJA 16.09.88
ET-AJL 18.09.91
ET-AJZ 25.03.91
ET-H-1 01.04.59
ET-H-2 02.03.58
ET-H-6 28.12.59
ET-T-1 13.01.62
ET-T-16 05.09.61
ET-T-18 16.07.60
ET-T-35 10.07.57
ET-T-5 22.07.48

Etjoernyos Iskol Godollo
HA-BFC 24.02.95

Euralair International
F-BSRL 10.06.85

Eurasia
I 26.08.32
I 04.07.35
III 15.12.32
III 11.05.35
IV oo.08.37
V 27.11.35
VI 01.09.32
VI 08.12.41
VII 08.12.41
VIII oo.08.37
XV 11.12.41
XVI 25.12.35
XVII 06.05.39
XVIII 01.08.37
XX 30.12.40
XXI 16.07.38
XXII 08.12.41
XXIII 12.03.39
XXIV 08.12.41
XXV 26.10.40

Eureka Aero Industries
N13114 11.09.69

Euroair
G-HGGS 19.11.84
G-WING 04.02.80

Europair
F-BRSA 28.11.73

Europe Aero Services
F-BNUZ 22.10.71

European Air Transport
OO-DHD 23.10.92

Evans, W.J.
N8330C 15.02.80

Everest Air
9N-ACL 31.07.93

Evergreen Air
N74Z 01.10.78

Evergreen Helicopters
N16008 15.10.92
N2784E 13.06.86
N2970W 09.10.74
N57340 10.03.94
N8061V 03.12.79

Evergreen International Airlines
N931F 18.03.89

Eversharp Inc
N148E 13.09.68

Everts Air Fuel
N151 05.03.92

Ex. Antartique Belgo-Neerlandaise
OO-HAD 09.02.70

Examiner Printing Co
NC14250 24.02.38

Excel Air
C-GPAT 27.01.95

Executive Air Charter
N432CA 08.05.87

Executive Air Services
* 06.10.85

Executive Airlines
N355CA 07.06.92

Executive Aviation
N558 oo.oo.oo

Executive Funds
ZS-DAK 28.12.73

Executive Jet Sales Inc
N432EJ 25.10.67
N434EJ 09.05.70

Export Air Cargo
OB-1456 28.03.92

Expreso Aereo Inter-Americano
CU-P198 10.07.48

Express Airlines
N331PX 14.12.87
N342PX 02.01.93

Express Airways
N45437 02.02.81

Expresso Aereo
OB-1443 10.09.92
OB-1559 25.02.94

Expresso Aereo Inter-Americano
* 07.09.46

Extractors (Hull) Ltd
G-AIIO 17.07.48

F & B Livestock
N468C 19.05.76

FAMA
LV-ABI 27.09.49
LV-ABL 12.08.47
LV-ACS oo.oo.oo
LV-AFG 13.01.48
LV-AFL 14.05.48
LV-XIG 23.12.46
LV-XIH 25.07.47

FBN Flying Service
N44896 31.10.83

FIGAS
VP-FAY 01.05.82
VP-FBG 24.06.87

Fa. Danzer Furnierwerke Zaire
9Q-CDZ 05.05.76

Facilities Management Corp
N4726V 28.03.64

Fairbanks Air Service
N1312V 10.07.73
N1663M 22.01.75
N4860V 28.03.75
N5003K 11.12.74
N800FA 17.05.75

Fairchild Aircraft
* 00.00.73
N1027 09.05.58
N2183A 18.09.92

Fairey Air Surveys
G-ANWW 08.07.58

Fairflight
G-BHWT 11.01.88

Fairflight Charters
G-ARFZ 24.02.73

Fairline
OY-DNP 17.10.67

Fairways
PI-C942 11.09.65
PI-C944 19.11.70
PI-C945 20.01.65
PI-C947 23.04.69
PI-C948 08.03.65

Fairways (Jersey) Ltd
G-AGZT 03.01.57
G-AHIG 06.08.55

Fairways Corporation
N7267 20.07.88

Falcon Air Charter
5Y-MAK 11.11.93

Falcon Airways
G-ALDC 09.10.60
G-APBX 05.08.59

Falcon Jet Corporation
N121FJ 15.10.87

Fales, H.G.
NR625E 30.05.40

Falk, L.H.
G-AERE 20.06.39

Far East Avia
RA-07624 15.09.93
RA-25740 03.12.93
SSSR-06165 11.07.92
SSSR-25356 29.09.92
SSSR-40670 18.09.92

Far East Corporation
SSSR-67091 21.08.91

Far East Directorate
RA-07330 24.05.94
RA-07743 16.06.95
RA-23240 30.10.94
RA-67470 14.07.94

Far Eastern Air Transport
B-2009 24.02.69
B-2029 31.07.75
B-2311 17.11.82
B-241 15.02.69
B-243 21.02.70
B-247 16.04.77
B-251 24.04.69
B-2603 22.08.81
B-28003 25.10.93
PI-C1 14.12.46
PI-C100 11.01.47

Faraday Industries
N5237J 27.04.80

Farm-Kem Inc
N102US 00.00.80

Farman Line
F-ADFN 00.05.27
F-AEIE 23.05.28

Farner Air Transport
HB-FKS 21.06.93

Faucett
OA-BBJ-261 18.09.44
OA-BBK 00.00.00
OA-BBL 00.00.00
OA-BBN 00.00.00
OA-BBO 00.00.00
OA-BBR 15.09.37
OA-BBS 00.00.00
OA-BBU 00.00.00
OA-BBX 00.00.00
OB-1303 11.09.90
OB-BBP-279 24.06.45
OB-PAA-104 00.00.00
OB-PAB-105 00.00.00
OB-PAD-120 00.00.00
OB-PAE-132 00.00.00
OB-PAF-133 10.09.45
OB-PAG-139 24.10.45
OB-PAK-144 00.00.00
OB-PAM-146 20.03.60
OB-PAR-148 00.00.00
OB-PAU-201 23.11.50
OB-PAV-223 10.02.49
OB-PAY-226 15.12.48
OB-PAZ-228 02.10.55
OB-PBH-530 04.02.62
OB-PBN-659 25.08.62
OB-R-1314 03.04.89
OB-R-148 08.12.67
OB-R-247 31.12.76
OB-R-778 14.01.70
OB-R-920 00.00.69

Federal Aviation Administration
N116 26.04.62
N200 21.04.61
N44 02.11.88
N47 01.10.70
N6 27.03.75
N64 00.09.86
N65 15.08.66
N68N 24.04.64
N7 04.01.71
N7307C 03.09.64
N76 06.11.74
N82 26.10.93

Federal Electricity Commission
XB-DOK 25.01.70
XC-CFE 22.03.70

Federal Express
N803FE 06.06.90
N820FE 27.02.90
N828FE 23.10.87
N835FE 20.01.90
N854FE 29.01.90
N945FE 05.01.89

Federal Frontier Guards
RA-72960 23.10.94

Federal Mogul Corporation
N22FM 26.04.83

Federal Paper Board Co
N921FP 06.08.86

Federated Capital Corporation
N711AH 02.03.74

Fender, J. & Partner
N4914V 09.07.68

Ferranti Ltd
G-ANDY 29.05.62

Ferruzzi s.p.a.
I-AIFA 10.12.79

Festus Flying Service
N901PC 16.11.78

Fetterman, F.O.Y.
NR7426 15.05.37

Fidinam Fiduciara
HB-VGC 14.01.87

Fiji Air
DQ-FBO 12.07.79
DQ-FCN 06.08.91
DQ-FEC 11.09.86
DQ-FED 04.04.89
DQ-FEE 15.12.91
DQ-FEO 11.05.93

Fiji Airways
VQ-FAL 26.04.54
VQ-FAL 11.12.65
VQ-FAO 00.08.54
VQ-FAQ 30.12.55
VQ-FAX 09.11.66

Filair
9Q-CTS 00.00.88
9Q-CTU 03.03.92

Filipinas Orient Airways
PI-C950 06.06.65

Findlay, M.H. & Waller, K.H.F.
G-AENA 01.10.36

Fine Air
HK-3816X 21.05.94

Finnair
OH-LCA 08.11.63
OH-LCC 03.01.61

Finnish Government
OH-IPA 02.05.40

Finnwings
OH-CFM 16.06.77
OH-FFW 01.03.72

Firth, Sir William
G-AEEK 17.08.37

Fischer Brothers Aviation
N160FB 04.03.87
N3FB 18.12.78

Fishing & Marine Salvage
G-ASHW 20.11.80

Fjellfly
LN-ASC 12.09.90

Flagship Airlines/ American Eagle
N918AE 13.12.94

Flamingo Air Services
NC54335 06.02.49

Fleming Airways System Transport
PI-C262 22.03.58
PI-C568 20.05.64
PI-C569 21.12.64

Fleming International
280F 06.07.77

Flight Express
N180X 17.02.78
N75FA 17.08.77

Flight International
N39DM 05.03.86
N51FN 02.04.90
N97DM 05.03.86

Flight Line
EI-BGL 13.11.84
G-BBVF 11.03.82

Flight Refuelling
G-AFRL 18.08.40
G-AFRX 18.08.40
G-AHJW 22.11.48
G-AKDP 10.05.49

Flight Safety International
N121GW 18.05.78
N2EP 13.11.90

Flinders Island Airways
VH-FIB 10.02.60

Florida Aircraft Leasing
N111AV 00.00.82
N4807C 21.03.78

Florida Commuter Airlines
N75KW 12.09.80

Florida Preferred Equity Inc
N709Z 24.04.80

Florida State Government
N105FL 09.04.92

Flugfelag Austurlands
TF-RTO 22.09.80
TF-RTR 11.03.81

Flugfelag Islands
TF-ISA 23.02.67
TF-ISI 29.05.47

Flugfelag Nordurlands
TF-JME 27.07.79

Flugsyn
TF-AIO 03.05.67
TF-AIS 00.01.66

Flugtransport
N16067 04.03.63

Fluor Corporation
N400M 27.12.72

Fly by Night Safaris
N7314C 09.12.68

Flying Fireman
CF-NTL 21.05.78

Flying Tiger Line
N228SW 24.12.66
N453T 21.03.66
N67960 30.07.50
N6911C 15.03.62
N6913C 14.12.62
N6914C 15.12.65
N6915C 24.12.64
N6920C 09.09.58
N6921C 15.03.62
N6923C 23.09.62
N705FT 27.07.70
N807FT 18.02.89
N86574 07.01.53
N90433 24.09.55
N9995F 18.03.56

Flying W Airways
N1243N 07.05.69

Flynn's Ferry Service
ZK-SFB 27.11.87

Fokker
H-NACZ 00.00.25
H-NADH 12.01.27
NC130M 00.00.00
NX124M 27.11.29
PK-PFB 27.04.67

Ford Air Freight Lines
NC1492 12.05.28

Ford Motor Co
N64423 29.09.68
NC9674 19.03.29
NX419H 24.11.30

Forderung-der Motorluft-Schiffahrt
LZ2 17.01.06
LZ4 05.08.08

Forest Industries Flying Tankers
CF-LYJ 23.06.61
CF-LYM 12.10.62

Forest Protection
C-GFPQ 08.06.82

Formosa Airlines
B-12206 27.06.89
B-12238 28.02.93
B-12268 14.08.90
B-12288 15.06.95
B-12298 14.06.93

Fort Smith Air Service
C-GGQU 27.09.81

Four Star Air Cargo
N134FS 10.05.91

Four Star Aviation
N100DW 17.09.89

Fox Delta
OY-ARI 01.01.89

Fr High Commisioner to Cameroons
F-OAFP 01.05.50

France Hydro
F-BDRE 10.09.55
LN-LAI oo.11.52

Frank Ambrose Aviation
N2562B 29.06.88

Franks Petroleum
N101AD 06.05.91

Fratflug
TF-OAE 06.05.74

Fred Olsen Air Transport
LN-NAD 05.05.52
LN-NAE 04.04.52

Free, F.
NC4806 18.10.33

Freedom Air
N74F 28.08.92

Freight Air
NC1664M 26.03.49

French Navy
F-AREK oo.oo.44
F-NORD oo.08.44

French Police
F-BBOF 17.03.55

Frigorifico Maniqui
CP-573 18.01.76

Frigorifico Movima
CP-801 06.04.73
CP-961 07.01.75

Frigorificos Ballivian
CB-47 08.11.50

Frigorificos Co-operativo Los Andes
CB-43 29.09.51
CB-45 23.10.56

Frigorificos Grigota
CP-579 29.12.58

Frigorificos Reyes
CP-1206 24.03.84
CP-1208 26.01.77
CP-1404 08.06.83
CP-1650 08.05.87
CP-1651 20.06.93
CP-1653 09.09.88
CP-936 11.02.72

Frigorificos Santa Rita
CP-1848 13.09.93
CP-1953 oo.oo.90
CP-529 29.02.92
CP-754 02.03.92

Frimo Transaereos
CP-777 23.12.79

Frisia Luftwerkhe Norddeich
D-IEDA 12.01.79
D-IOLT 18.05.83

Fromhagen Aviation
N95C 06.06.82

Frontier Air
C-FGAW 30.04.90

Frontier Airlines
N4994E 27.07.66
N61442 12.03.64
N65276 21.12.67
N73130 21.12.62
N982FL 18.01.78

Frontier Airways
N40443 27.06.86
N40445 15.05.82

Frontier Flying Service
N299GL 19.10.91
N59783 04.09.90
N99663 30.10.79

Frontier Helicopters
C-FFHB 20.01.95
C-GFHT 06.03.93
C-GLGF 26.07.94

Fuchs Helikopter
HB-XUJ 29.04.95

Fuji Airlines
JA5098 27.02.64

Fujita Airlines
JA6155 17.08.63

Fulford, C.
G-AHFN 03.07.55

Fulton, E.L.
NC9609 oo.oo.oo

Futura Airlines
C-GFAC 16.10.79

Fyn Air Taxi
OY-BDP 19.01.89

GAF International Service
N2949F oo.oo.81

GAS Air
5N-AYJ 14.12.88
9G-RBO 29.04.92

GB Airways
G-BBVH 23.11.88

GP Express Airlines
N115GP 29.04.93
N118GP 08.06.92

GSD Aircraft Leasing
40427 01.09.74

GSW Charterflug
D-IGSW 21.11.90

GTE South Inc
N53CC 02.10.89

GU-SMA
URSS-N209 12.08.37

Gabon Air Force
TR-KCD 20.02.78
TR-KJB 29.11.90

Gabon Government
TR-KHB 06.02.80

Galaxy Airlines
N5532 21.01.85
N854U 29.01.85

Gambcrest
N862FW 09.02.92

Gamez Calcan y Cia
YV-P-APY 15.02.51

Gander Aviation
C-GGAL 23.06.78

Garamut Aviation
P2-VTC 01.07.95

Garcia, F.
CP-808 21.11.77

Garnier, R.
TT-DAA oo.oo.72

Garuda Indonesian Airlines
PH-MBH 04.12.74
PK-DPA 09.05.52
PK-DPD 25.11.54
PK-GCB 27.02.72
PK-GCE 17.08.62
PK-GDE 01.01.66
PK-GDI 24.01.61
PK-GDM 05.04.62
PK-GDU 01.01.66
PK-GDV 24.12.59
PK-GDY 05.02.61
PK-GDZ 29.12.61
PK-GFJ 08.09.74
PK-GFP 26.09.72
PK-GFV 02.06.83
PK-GHP 10.12.58
PK-GJA 28.05.68
PK-GLB 16.02.67
PK-GND 13.01.80
PK-GNE 11.06.84
PK-GNI 30.12.84
PK-GNQ 04.04.87
PK-GTA oo.oo.72
PK-GTB 20.09.63
PK-GTC 14.05.63
PK-GVC 24.09.75
PK-GVE 11.07.79
PK-GVK 20.03.82
PK-GVP 07.03.79

Gasuden
* 22.06.38

Gatari Air Service
PK-HML 24.09.94
PK-HMR 02.03.94
PK-HMZ 30.01.92

Gates Learjet
N501PS 26.05.77
N57TA 13.11.81

Gateway Aviation
CF-BQJ 29.01.77

Gateway Toyota
N6788Y 12.11.85

Gearhart, F.
N2654M 04.01.92

Gee Bee Aero Inc
N44GA 30.01.84

General Air
D-BOBD 19.02.75
D-CIRO 18.12.70
D-IDHC 27.05.72

General Airlines
N587JA 03.01.69

General Airways [1]
CF-BEI 12.01.38

General Airways [2]
N17314 01.02.59
N41718 12.01.52

General Telephone Co
N723GL 12.12.85

General Tire & Rubber Co
NR393H 04.08.29

General Transportation Co
N805F 05.07.71

Geofoto S.A.
PT-KUO 12.05.77

Georgian Airlines
SSSR-85222 20.07.92

Geoterrex
C-FOZO oo.08.84

Germa Inc.
ZP-CAP 06.12.66

German Ministry of Transport
D-861 06.10.31

Ghana Airways
9G-AAF 24.04.69
9G-ABW 22.01.71
9G-ACA 11.03.81
9G-GAD oo.08.67

Gibb Coyne & Sager (Kariba) Ltd
VP-YOY 25.11.57

Gifford Aviation
N90268 05.07.80

Gill Air
G-BPMA 13.02.89
G-OGIL 01.07.92

Ginger Coote Airways
CF-AUX 27.05.38
CF-BNG 09.03.46

Glacier Helicopters
N1099T 13.02.95
ZK-HGV 17.03.93

Gleneagles Helicopters
G-AZVN 30.06.78

Glenn, D.
N8407 16.06.73

Global International
N8434 04.12.82

Globe Air [1]
HB-ITB 20.04.67

Globe Air [2]
N44904 14.06.79
N44905 15.05.79
N7415C 01.05.85

Globeaero
SE-FRO 28.11.76

Go Transportation
N357AL 24.06.79

Goilala Air Service
VH-BDD 04.02.53

Gold Belt Air Service
CF-PAA 09.05.52

Gold-Air
VH-TLQ 02.02.87

Golden Eagle Aviation [1]
N464M 02.10.70

Golden Eagle Aviation [2]
B-98181 17.09.94

Golden North Airlines
* 22.02.49

Golden Star Air Cargo
ST-ALX 24.03.92

Golden West Airlines
6383 09.01.75

Gomes & Warra Aircraft Corp
N371 02.12.89

Gonimi Air Service
PZ-TAB 06.05.80

Gor'ky Eskadril'ya
SSSR-I20 18.05.35

Gordon Air Services
N4278C 23.07.54

Government Aircraft Factories
VH-AUI 25.10.75
VH-DHU 06.08.76

Government of Quebec Air Service
C-FPQE 01.12.93

Goyayke
LV-VGE 20.02.95

Grahame-White Aviation
G-EADE 29.06.19
G-EADF 31.05.19

Grand Canyon Airlines
N74GC 19.06.86
N75GC 27.09.89
N76GC 10.08.81
N76GC 18.06.86

Grand Canyon Helicopters
N6TC 19.06.86

Grand Central Aircraft
N65Y 10.01.54

Grands Express Aeriens
F-GEAD 07.04.22

Great Barrier Airlines
ZK-CUV 19.12.89

Great China Airlines
B-15102 04.11.72
B-15103 28.08.70
B-15104 16.09.72
B-15105 23.01.72
B-15106 28.04.71
B-15109 23.12.76
B-15110 31.08.73
B-15115 31.07.74
B-15118 29.07.80

Great Northern Airlines
N401FA 12.03.76
N403GN 05.01.79

Great Northern Airways [1]
* 10.11.38

Great Northern Airways [2]
CF-GND 12.06.68
CF-GNG 20.12.69

Great Northern Helicopters
VH-THX 15.11.79

Great Shield Air
C-GPVE 09.10.79

Great Slave Helicopters
C-FGSU 28.01.94
C-FPQS 02.09.94
C-FXAL 14.07.94

Great Western & Southern Air Lines
G-ACPR 19.02.40

Greenamyer, D.
N70887 21.05.95

Greenlandair
OY-HAN 11.09.87
OY-HBH 08.09.83
OY-HCT 01.03.93
OY-HDI 13.04.92

Gregory, R.F.
NC6894 15.11.41

Gregory, W.N.
NR7429 18.04.33

Gromex
HB-FKC 09.05.86

Gromov Aviation Research Institute
RA-65760 09.09.94

Grondmet Handels
OE-FAP 06.10.84

Grossman, P.
N163E 05.12.82

Groth Air
N880SR oo.05.83
N8815E 25.05.78

Grup-Air
I-NLAE 25.09.91

Guernsey Airlines
G-BFYZ 25.10.79

Guernsey Airways
G-ABXW 31.07.36

Guinea Air Traders
VH-AKH 01.03.47
VH-ARC 16.03.49
VH-AVQ 24.04.47
VH-AYD 24.05.47

Guinea Airways
VH-ABI 18.01.39
VH-UNR 22.05.31
VH-UOW oo.oo.42
VH-USX oo.01.42
VH-UTB 23.10.41

Guinn, J.
N446M 10.05.73

Gulf Air
A4O-BK 23.09.83
A4O-SI 22.11.76

Gulf Aviation [1]
CF-BQG 29.01.52

Gulf Aviation [2]
G-ADUH oo.06.51
G-AOFZ 17.08.66
G-APJS 19.02.58
VT-DGS 10.07.60

Gulf and Caribbean Cargo
N137CA 18.03.95

Gum Air
PZ-TBB oo.oo.oo

Guyana Airways
8R-GCP 03.12.73
N3486F 30.11.81

Guyana Defence Force
8R-GES oo.oo.oo
8R-GFF 22.01.81

Guyana Government
8R-GRR 14.10.94

Guyana Mining Co
8R-GEP 03.11.85

Guyane Air Transport
F-OGDR oo.03.70

Guzman, J.
CP-1039 22.08.92

H & G Import & Export Corp
N49K 16.02.94

Hackney, C.A.
N64490 11.04.80

Hageland Aviation Services
N7340U 13.12.94

Haiti Air Inter
HH-CNB 26.12.78
HH-CNC 02.01.80

Hal Roach Studios
NC12229 17.11.32

Hall, T.M.S.
VH-AYE 09.12.50

Hamaland Flugdienst
D-INGY 22.06.75

Hamburger Flugzeugbau
D-CHFB 12.05.65

Hamilton Aviation
N791A 27.06.75

Hamilton, L.
G-EBEM 07.05.26

Hammonds Air Service
N1867Q 19.08.92

Hampson-Silk, T.
G-CTHS 24.09.80

Handley Page
G-AGSS 03.12.45
G-AJXK 03.12.50
G-AODE 30.08.58
PP285 13.02.48

Handley Page S.A. Transport Co
G-EANV 23.02.20

Handley Page Transport
G-EAKE 30.06.20
G-EAMA 14.12.20
G-EAMC 25.02.20
G-EAPJ 10.07.23
G-EATL oo.04.21
G-EATM 30.12.21
G-EATN 14.01.22
G-EAVL 00.04.21

Hanford Airlines
NC306H 17.10.34
NC624E 20.01.37

Hanfords Tri-State Airlines
NC9655 02.09.34

Hang Khong Vietnam
VN-A102 08.09.88
VN-A108 17.02.88

Hangar 2 Corporation
* 24.09.81

Hangar Six
NC5809 14.06.41

Hanna's Air Saltspring
C-FKAS 21.03.95

Hanratty, M.
XA-BHJ 08.01.38

Happy Hour Air Travel Club
N6202C 05.08.73

Harbor Air Service
N1686U 07.11.92

Harbor Airlines
N66HA 26.12.74
N94CA oo.oo.oo

Harbour Air
C-FDTI 23.06.94
C-FQRI 08.05.91

Harco Air Services
* 19.09.95

Hargreaves Airways
G-AIUI 10.06.48

Harka Air Services
RA-65617 24.06.95

Harrington's Inc
N29086 04.11.49

Harrys Moda
I-TURI 14.08.69

Harvest Air
G-AXWG 07.08.79

Hastingwood Hotels
G-HAST 20.10.87

Hawker Siddeley Aviation
G-ARPY 03.06.66
G-BCUX 20.11.75

Hawkins & Powers Aviation
* 16.09.87
N15509 21.04.84
N2870G oo.07.80
N3560 10.06.78
N6813D oo.oo.78
N6816D oo.oo.72
N70600 08.02.92
N8682 27.06.81

Hawthorne Nevada Airlines
N61350 19.08.64

Haywards Aviation
G-ARTS oo.01.75

Hearst, G.
NX913 16.08.27

Hearst, W.R.
NX703 06.09.27

Heli AG
HB-XET 27.01.78

Heli Bavaria
D-HEAD 07.12.94

Heli Niugini
P2-DWA 11.01.92
P2-HBA 01.03.94
P2-HBE 13.10.93

Heli Ocean
F-GKYC 10.07.91

Heli Portugal
CS-HCE 29.03.95

Heli Trans Pilatus
HB-XIM 22.12.79

Heli Voyageur
C-GXKA 20.11.80

Heli-Lift
N9AR 17.03.87

Heli-Linth
HB-XTE 17.06.92

Heli-Plus
C-GDBP 14.11.93

Heli-Quebec
C-GERD 04.03.78

Heli-Transport
C-GSHZ 20.06.95

Heli-Union
F-BXAD 05.04.75
F-GEBJ 27.10.87

Heliarcos
EC-FAO 06.06.92

Heliaustria Helikopter-gesellschaft
OE-EXI 13.06.79

Heliavia Aero Taxi
ZS-HHN 05.04.91

Heliba Helikopter
HB-XDP 05.05.79

Helicol
HK-1495E 17.03.78
HK-1772E 01.06.94
HK-2889X 04.07.91

Helicopter Line, The
ZK-HWV 29.10.94
ZK-HZP 11.10.94

Helicopteros Andes
CC-CKA 07.06.84

Helicopteros Nacionales de Colombia
HK-1495 31.01.87
HK-3315X 05.02.90
HK-3316X 02.05.90

Helicopteros de Guatemala
TG-KEZ 04.04.77

Helicopters (NZ) Ltd
ZK-HNH 01.02.93

Helicsa
EC-DDR 12.03.90

Heliflight
OO-PCB 22.01.78

Helijet Aero Taxi
PT-HRV 05.11.85

Helijet Airways
OE-XAA 06.04.94

Helijet Vietnam
F-GJGP 26.03.94

Helikopter Air Transport
OE-EXH 11.01.85

Helikopter Service
LN-OML 02.10.90
LN-OQS 26.06.78
LN-ORL 31.07.79
LN-OSC 10.08.91
LN-OSR 24.06.83
LN-OSZ 23.11.77

Helilift
LN-OSL 02.08.94

Helinet
N50PE 27.02.94

Helipet
HC-BFR 23.11.90
HC-BHO 19.12.90

Heliservices Hong Kong
VR-HJE 21.05.92
VR-HJG 29.06.95
VR-HJH 09.06.95

Heliservico
CS-APG 30.05.95

Helisureste
EC-EHH 12.12.94
EC-EJM 22.08.92

Heliswiss
HB-XAW 09.04.80
HB-XCP 14.01.80
HB-XCQ 10.06.78
HB-XFA 15.07.78
HB-XFB 20.11.80
HB-XHS 14.02.80

Helitaxi
HK-3353 22.09.92
HK-3377 27.02.88
HK-3733X 18.05.93

Helitourist
LN-OQW 06.09.78
LN-ORX 25.08.82

Helitours
4R-HVA/834 29.04.95
4R-HVB/835 28.04.95

Helitrans [1]
VH-FLH 13.06.81

Helitrans [2]
N3913Z 30.11.85

Helitrans Pilatus
HB-XLF 22.11.80

Hemet Exploration
F-BJBY 21.04.81
F-BJHC 01.08.81

Hemet Valley Flying Service
N135FF 13.08.94
N3356G 28.07.70
N6458C oo.oo.77
N6459C 18.07.70
N6825C 04.09.71
N9082Z 28.07.70
N9548Z 18.08.74

Hemus Air
LZ-DOK 02.08.88

Henson Airlines
N339HA 23.09.85

Hermens Air
N9241F 01.11.85

Heron Air Charter
P2-HAC 10.03.82

Hi-Tech Helicopters
N79DD 24.09.90

Hibiscus Air
ZK-NOM 25.10.93

Hidroservice Engenharia de Projetos
PT-JDX 26.12.78

High Terrain Helicopters
C-FBHR 11.02.95

Highland Airways
G-ACCE 29.08.34
G-ACGK 08.01.35

Highland Helicopters
C-GHHV 13.11.94

Hillman's Airways
G-ABSB 07.05.33
G-ACPM 02.10.34

Hillsboro Helicopters
N8NU 17.08.94

Hilmer, W.
N267L 29.03.81

Himalayan Airways
VT-AFO 01.10.36

Hindu Publications
VT-DTH 17.01.69

Hispaniola Airways
HI-384HA 12.12.81

Hold Trade Air Services
5N-HTA 29.08.92

Holden Air Transport
G-AUHW 02.11.34

Hollinger Ungava Transport
CF-DXR 18.10.51

Holmstroem Air
SE-INL 27.12.92
SE-IZO 08.05.89

Holt Manufacturing Co
N110LT 13.02.90

Holt, A.P.
G-EBZJ 04.09.29

Holy Nation of Islam, The
N566E 24.09.73

Holyman Airways
VH-URN 19.10.34
VH-URT 02.10.35
VH-USW 13.12.35

Honduras International
HR-196P 21.05.62

Honeywell Inc
N129GP 11.07.67

Hong Kong Airways
VR-HDQ 11.07.49

Horex
HA-BCU 24.04.94
HA-BFD 22.10.94

Horizon Air
N2689E 25.09.87
N819PH 15.04.88

Horizon Helicopters
N911SW 27.05.94

Horizon Properties
N15HC 01.02.75

Hornbill Skyways
9M-AXM 30.07.93

Hosmer, E.
G-CAJI 02.08.26

Houston Helicopters
N4252S 13.11.83

Houston Metro Airlines
N853SA 30.04.74

Hubschrauber-Sonder-Dienst
D-HHSB 06.10.94

Hudson Bay Company
CF-BMI 05.09.41
CF-BVM 23.01.42

Hughes Air West
N9345 06.06.71

Hughes Tool Co
N8410H oo.oo.69

Huisson Aviation
C-GDFA 07.03.93

Hummingbird Helicopters
LZ-CAP 08.01.94

Huns Air
VT-DJC 28.08.80

Hunting Air Travel
G-AGSX 17.05.47
G-AHPD 08.05.51
G-AHPI 16.02.52

Hunting Surveys
G-AIRZ 18.07.52
G-AMKT 19.02.60
G-AMOT 06.06.58
G-AMVB 22.10.58
G-AMYW 08.04.67

Hyflight Associates
N59MD 11.11.85

IAS Cargo
G-BEBP 14.05.77

IJA Inc
N442NE 26.07.88

IMSS
XC-DAK 07.07.80

ITAU
PP-ITF 21.02.51

Ibanez, I.B.
* 13.06.88

Iberia
EC-AAA oo.04.46
EC-AAB oo.10.45
EC-AAC 03.02.44
EC-AAD oo.08.40
EC-AAE oo.12.40
EC-ABC 29.04.57
EC-ABK 23.12.48
EC-ABN 10.04.58
EC-ABO 12.06.46
EC-ACG 22.12.47
EC-ACH 28.10.57
EC-AGO 19.09.62
EC-AIN 05.05.65
EC-AIP 06.03.61
EC-ATB 12.11.62
EC-ATH 31.03.65
EC-ATV 07.01.72
EC-BAB oo.oo.48
EC-BBR 29.09.73
EC-BDD 04.11.67
EC-BIA 05.11.73
EC-BII 05.03.73
EC-BMX 03.03.78
EC-BOD 05.01.70
EC-BVC 28.12.72
EC-CBN 17.12.73
EC-CFJ 07.12.83
EC-DDU 19.02.85
M-CCCC 19.04.28
N7125C 08.11.60

Iberico Aerotaxi
OB-T-1262 01.03.87

Ibex Corporation
N100TA 06.05.82

Icelandair
TF-FIL 26.09.70
TF-ISG 31.01.51

TF-ISL 09.07.45
TF-ISU 14.04.63

Icelandic Coast Guard
TF-RAN 08.11.83

Ilford Riverton Airways
C-FAII 26.09.75
C-GIXZ 31.10.82

Ilyushin Design Bureau
RA-54001 05.07.93
SSSR-06156 oo.oo.65
SSSR-06300 oo.oo.64

Imani & Sons
5N-ASQ 22.07.83

Immobiliaria Uracoa
YV-174CP 04.06.81

Impala Air
ZS-LUI 08.02.88

Imperial Airlines [1]
N2737A 08.11.61

Imperial Airlines [2]
JA9272 09.07.91

Imperial Airways
G-AACH 22.04.31
G-AACI 28.03.33
G-AADN 26.10.29
G-AAEV 19.01.30
G-AAGX 01.03.40
G-AASJ 31.12.35
G-AAUD 19.03.40
G-AAXC 19.03.40
G-AAXD 07.11.39
G-AAXE 31.05.37
G-ABCP 23.11.35
G-ABEG oo.oo.36
G-ABFA 22.00.30
G-ABFB 09.11.35
G-ABKY 10.08.36
G-ABLU 30.12.33
G-ABTG 27.07.38
G-ABTH oo.06.39
G-ABTK 29.09.36
G-ACOX 25.09.36
G-ACOY 25.10.35
G-ADCM 22.10.35
G-ADCN 03.12.38
G-ADUU 21.01.39
G-ADUY 12.03.39
G-ADUZ 05.12.37
G-ADVA 24.03.37
G-ADVC 01.10.37
G-ADVD 01.05.39
G-ADVE 12.06.39
G-AETW 27.11.38
G-AFCW 19.06.39
G-EBBG 15.02.28
G-EBBR 27.05.24
G-EBBX 24.12.24
G-EBCX 23.09.24
G-EBGS 10.01.27
G-EBIX 30.10.30
G-EBKI 01.02.27
G-EBKZ 23.10.28
G-EBLB 13.07.28
G-EBLO 16.06.31
G-EBMS 21.10.26
G-EBMT 17.06.29
G-EBMW 19.04.31
G-EBMZ 06.09.29
G-EBNA 14.02.30
G-EBVG 28.12.36
VO-ABC 25.08.35
VO-AFG oo.04.40

Imperial Tobacco Group
G-AXPS 20.07.70

Inair
8R-GEF 27.05.77
HP-821 29.03.80

Indamer
NC65350 06.08.47
VT-ARH 20.08.57
VT-CHT 12.07.51
VT-COI 25.11.50

Independent Air
N7231T 08.02.89

Independent Air Travel
G-AIJE 02.09.58

Indian Airlines
85533 09.01.93
PH-SAB 02.02.66
VT-ATU 25.02.54
VT-AUA 01.09.57
VT-AUL 03.06.63
VT-AUV 05.05.57
VT-AXA 26.08.61
VT-CCD 18.05.56
VT-CFB 13.05.57
VT-CGG 03.01.60
VT-CGI 29.03.59
VT-CGN 21.03.56
VT-CHF 12.12.53
VT-COJ 25.06.58
VT-COZ 21.01.55
VT-CVB 01.02.55
VT-CYH 12.03.59
VT-CYM 09.07.58
VT-CYN 24.03.58
VT-CZT 03.05.62
VT-DBA 15.05.56
VT-DDR 25.04.66
VT-DGO 15.05.54
VT-DIA 08.09.58
VT-DIC 07.05.62
VT-DIH 15.11.61
VT-DIO 11.09.63
VT-DIX 09.08.71
VT-DMA 30.01.71
VT-DMD 24.07.76
VT-DME 12.08.72
VT-DOJ 21.04.69
VT-DPO 03.07.73
VT-DPP 15.02.66
VT-DSB 04.09.66
VT-DUO 05.03.84
VT-DVG 07.06.70
VT-DVJ 17.06.75
VT-DWN 12.10.76
VT-DWT 29.08.70
VT-DXF 18.08.81
VT-DXG 09.12.71
VT-DXI 16.06.81
VT-DXJ 04.08.79
VT-EAH 19.10.88
VT-EAL 17.12.78
VT-EAM 31.05.73
VT-EAU 15.03.73
VT-ECQ 26.04.93
VT-ECR 26.04.79
VT-EDV 15.11.93
VT-EFL 16.08.91
VT-ELV 29.09.86
VT-EPN 14.02.90

Indian Coast Guard
CG-75 02.01.93

Indian Department of Civil Aviation
VT-CXX 20.02.50

Indian Government
N8013E 19.06.57

Indian National Airlines
VT-AEL 28.08.39
VT-AHR 22.03.42
VT-AJD 23.02.39
VT-AKJ 23.02.39
VT-ART 08.04.46
VT-ATS 17.07.50
VT-CEJ 08.10.48
VT-CEL 27.03.48
VT-COK 08.02.52

Indian Overseas Airlines
VT-AZE 21.11.48
VT-AZF 10.04.47
VT-AZK 12.05.47
VT-AZZ oo.02.49

Indo-Burmese Transport
G-IAAC oo.10.20

Indoavia
PK-BIB 07.05.75

Inex-Adria Airways
YU-AJN 23.11.74
YU-AJO 30.10.75
YU-AJR 10.09.76
YU-ANA 01.12.81

Ingalls, L.
NR7954 11.08.41

Inland Airlines
NC10225 oo.oo.35
NC725W 29.05.35

Inner Circle Air Line
G-ADIK oo.05.36

Ins. Geographique du Congo Belge
OO-CBM 20.12.53
OO-CCA 06.07.53

Inst. Brasileiro de Reforma Agraria
PP-FMX 30.08.69

Institute Geographique Nationale
F-BAOP 13.10.46
F-BAOQ 25.10.47
F-BAQJ 11.05.47
F-BDAT 12.12.50
F-BEEA 25.07.89
F-BEEB 11.03.49

Instituto Nacional de Canalizations
YV-O-INC-2 22.08.89

Instone Air Line
G-EAUF 13.05.21
G-EBDH oo.oo.22

Int. Aircraft Sales & Lease
N6103C 24.02.78

Inter Air
N355W 06.05.77

Inter Atoll Air
8Q-GIA 07.02.87

Inter City Flug
D-CASY 29.06.72

Inter Island Air Services
VP-LAE 20.08.82

Inter Island Airways
S7-AAL 16.06.78

Inter-Island Helicopters
N1103N 18.04.94

Interair
VH-MLU 24.05.83

Interamerica Air Leases
N174DP 04.03.77

Intercargo Service
F-GEJE 06.02.89
F-GEJF 29.01.88

Interconair
EI-BBY 30.09.77

Intercontinent Airways
N38936 22.01.53

Intercontinental
HK-1708 31.03.91
HK-2864X 26.03.92
HK-3564X 17.03.95
HK-3839X 11.01.95

Intercontinental Air Lease
N92860 28.04.04
NC88873 31.12.46

Interflug
* oo.oo.73
DDR-SEW 17.06.89
DM-SBL oo.02.63
DM-SCA 30.10.72
DM-SCD 01.09.75
DM-SCM 22.11.77
DM-SEA 14.08.72
DM-SKS 26.07.64
DM-STF oo.01.67
DM-STL 26.03.79

Interior Airways
N2711N 06.09.69
N6767 30.01.72
N760AL 24.12.68

Interior Enterprises
N75391 16.01.58

Interivoire
TU-TFW 09.07.75

Intermountain Helicopters
N27FL 01.06.95

Internacional de Aviacion
HP-539 10.04.72

International Aerodyne
N8021 06.06.70

International Air Freight
NC52710 04.04.47
NC54451 05.02.47

International Airboats
N444GB 05.08.90

International Aircraft Services
N5595A 20.06.61

International Airways
G-AIAB 20.11.47
G-AIIS 01.11.49

International Control Commission
F-BELV 18.10.65

International Flight Center
N625CL 24.08.92
N82MA 06.09.90
N881FC 24.08.92

International Products Corp
ZP-CCE oo.oo.63

International Red Cross
HB-IBT 07.05.69
Z-WHE 30.07.85
n/a 17.03.36

International Sky Cab Airlines
N857JA oo.oo.oo

International Turbine Service
N94253 04.08.89

Interocean Airways
LX-IOK 02.10.64

Interstate Air Services
VH-AVZ 22.11.46

Inuvik Coastal Airways
C-FGJK 17.12.83

Inv. Agropecuarias del Casanare
HK-1276W 21.05.94

Inversiones GJ Restrepo y R Estrada
HK-2217P 13.03.86

Inversiones Rizo
YV-288CP 18.05.84

Invicta Airways
G-AHPL 02.08.65

Invicta International Airlines
G-AXOP 10.04.73

Iona National Airways
EI-BDO 08.06.85

Iran Air
EP-AAG 14.09.50
EP-AAJ 01.12.50
EP-ABB 02.01.62
EP-ACF 24.09.58
EP-ACI 26.12.48
EP-ACJ 25.12.52
EP-ACL 25.04.59
EP-ACV 30.06.53
EP-ADI 04.05.64
EP-ADK 04.08.61
EP-AEF 17.03.67
EP-AEI 20.02.62
EP-AHC 15.02.65
EP-IBU 03.07.88
EP-IRA 07.01.83
EP-IRD 21.01.80
EP-IRG 15.10.86

Iran Air Tours
EP-ITD 08.02.93

Iran Asseman Airlines
EP-ANA 04.10.90
EP-ASN 20.02.86
EP-PAV 12.10.94

Iranian Royal Flight
EP-MRP 10.10.62

Iraq Petroleum Transport Co
G-ADNG oo.08.36
G-AEGS 30.12.36
G-ARBA 10.01.71

Iraqi Airways
YI-ABJ 04.02.55
YI-ABQ 10.10.55
YI-ABR 13.06.49
YI-ACL 17.04.73
YI-ACU 19.03.65
YI-AED 22.07.71
YI-AEM 24.09.80
YI-AEO 22.04.82
YI-AGJ 25.12.86
YI-AIO 23.09.80
YI-ALN 27.08.82

Iraqi Government
YI-AKH oo.02.91
YI-AKI oo.02.91
YI-AKJ oo.02.91

Irish Helicopters
EI-BMP 29.07.82

Island Air Lines
N7684 21.08.72

Island Air Service
N5442Z 20.04.85

Island Air Services [1]
G-ALBB 01.08.52

Island Air Services [2]
5H-IAS 05.01.92

Island Airlines [1]
C-GHAQ 28.11.77

Island Airlines [2]
N402BK 18.11.94

Island Airlines Hawaii
N21DR 17.01.82

Island Airways [1]
N4917 25.08.77

Island Airways [2]
P2-ISF 23.01.93

Island Contractors
N869JA 20.01.78

Island Express
N5759Y 30.11.85

Island Helicopter
N7094J 01.05.88

Island Nationair
P2-IAH 12.04.95

Island Traders
N692A 25.03.77

Islands Aviation
P2-IAA 03.01.95

Islands of the Bahamas Inc
N3914 02.04.69

Isle of Man Air Services
G-AEAK 18.05.39
G-AEBW 18.06.40

Islena Airlines
HR-IAG 26.08.92
HR-IAI 15.01.92

Islenas de Inversiones
HR-ALH 04.04.90

Israel Aircraft Industries
4X-COJ 21.01.70
4X-IAI 19.11.70
N93218 16.02.87

Israeli Defence Force Air Force
4X-ACA 02.01.49
4X-FBD/011 25.11.75
4X-FPR/033 17.09.71
4X-FPS/037 30.11.70

Istmena de Aviacion
HP-1133 oo.12.89

Italian Air Force
I-DINI 01.07.33

Itavia
I-AOMU 14.10.60
I-TAVI 30.03.63
I-TIDA 09.04.75
I-TIDE 01.01.74
I-TIGI 27.06.80
I-TIVE oo.04.71

J.Hurler Flugdienst
D-IJHM 19.05.82

JAT Yugoslav Airlines
* 21.09.50
YU-ABC 27.11.47
YU-ABE 08.06.51
YU-ABH 25.08.62
YU-ABK 08.01.68
YU-ACB 20.02.65
YU-ACC 22.10.51
YU-ACE 29.06.51
YU-ADA 22.12.56
YU-ADC 10.10.55
YU-ADL 04.02.61
YU-ADO oo.oo.70
YU-AHD 11.09.73
YU-AHT 26.01.72
YU-AID 12.12.88
YU-AJG oo.02.73

JC Air
F-GFHR 17.11.88

JMG Inc
N9018N 15.09.80

JSCTD
YV-2349P 02.01.94

Jacobs, C.E.
PH-EHE 27.07.37

Jagson Airlines
VT-ESQ 19.05.89

Jamahiriya Air Transport
5A-DJO 14.03.83

Jamaican Government
N6310J 03.12.83

Jamair
VT-ATT 26.03.71
VT-CZC 05.12.70

James, J.J.
G-AASE 25.01.33

Japan Air Lines
JA6003 10.04.62
JA6011 30.09.57
JA8012 15.06.72
JA8013 24.09.72
JA8023 27.02.65
JA8028 25.06.69
JA8030 26.08.66
JA8040 28.11.72
JA8048 17.09.82
JA8051 27.09.77
JA8054 13.01.77
JA8061 09.02.82
JA8109 24.07.73
JA8119 12.08.85
N93043 09.04.52

Japan Air System
JA8448 18.04.93

Japan Air Transport
* 05.08.37
* 28.03.38

Japan Aviation Corporation
* 08.12.38

Japan Domestic Airlines
JA5080 14.02.65
JA5088 29.05.65

Japan Maritime Safety Agency
JA8825 17.02.87

Jayrow Helicopters
VH-AJD 08.01.82
VH-NBN 25.06.91

Jersey Airlines
G-AMYU 15.08.58

Jersey Airways
G-ACZN 04.11.38

Jersey European Airways
G-BDNP 18.09.81

Jet America International
N808JA 23.05.82

Jet Avia
N12MK 06.01.77
N332PC 06.01.77

Jet Charter Group
N38DJ 12.06.92

Jet East
N25TA 11.04.80
N95TC 20.12.84

Jet Fleet
N100HC 12.08.85
N33177 12.08.85

Jet International
N690LJ 30.11.67
N741J 20.02.70
N822LJ 09.12.67

Jet Management
N745F 30.07.88

Jetco Aviation International
N21CK 02.07.70

Jetcraft
VH-SWP 09.03.94
VH-UZS 14.04.93

Jetstream International Airlines
N823JS 09.02.88
N830JS 30.11.86

Jim Robbins Airborne Division
N500JR 26.09.66

Joanne Fashions
N10427 21.02.73

John Fairfax & Sons
VH-SMH 12.10.50

John Mahieu Aviation
OO-APN 20.03.47

Johns, V.N.
NC7863 28.04.35

Johnson Airways
* 12.10.33

Johnson Flying Service
N69905 17.08.53
N8400 14.07.53
N8419 04.08.59
N9642 19.06.56
NC435H 03.09.38

Johnson Inc
N5590M 04.05.91

Johnson, L.B.
N94256 19.02.61

Joint Church Aid
LN-FOM 02.11.69

Jokai (Assam) Tea Co
VT-ARY 09.02.59

Jonathan Airways
HB-LKO 11.06.79

Jones, P.F. & McJunkin, J.B.
NC4097 24.06.34

Jordan International Airlines
JY-ABV 09.09.56

Jump Hawaii Club
N8185H 05.12.81

Junkers Flugzeug und Motorenwerke
D-AALU 06.02.38

K & K Aircraft
N1FN 19.05.90

KDD Aviation
N28364 13.07.87

KIT Airline
RA-88286 06.11.94

KLM Cityhopper
PH-KSH 04.04.94

KLM Royal Dutch Airlines
H-NABE 30.05.22
H-NABF oo.02.26
H-NABH 19.10.23
H-NABI 04.11.25
H-NABL 10.11.21
H-NABM oo.07.23
H-NABM 25.06.25
H-NABO 17.11.22
H-NABP 02.09.21
H-NABR 24.07.28
H-NABS 24.04.24
H-NABT 17.05.22
H-NABU 13.04.26
H-NACC 09.07.26
H-NACL 21.06.26
H-NADQ 12.07.27
H-NADU 22.08.27
H-NAEE oo.04.28
JZ-PAB 16.11.57
PH-ACJ 10.05.40
PH-ACT 10.05.40
PH-AEB 10.05.40
PH-AEZ 15.07.36
PH-AFI 10.05.40
PH-AFK 04.08.31
PH-AFL 06.04.35
PH-AFO 06.12.31
PH-AGB 19.10.29
PH-AIL 26.05.33
PH-AJJ 18.12.35
PH-AJK 10.06.39
PH-AJL 10.05.40
PH-AJQ 14.07.35
PH-AJU 20.12.34
PH-AJX 10.05.40
PH-AKB 10.05.40
PH-AKC 17.12.37
PH-AKD 10.05.40
PH-AKG 20.07.35
PH-AKK 10.05.40
PH-AKL 09.12.36
PH-AKM 17.07.35
PH-AKN 10.05.40
PH-AKO 10.05.40
PH-AKP 10.05.40
PH-ALD 10.05.40
PH-ALF 28.07.37
PH-ALP 03.04.37
PH-ALS 06.10.37
PH-ALU 10.05.40
PH-APE 09.12.38
PH-ARX 10.05.40
PH-ARY 14.04.38
PH-ASP 10.05.40
PH-AST 10.05.40
PH-BUF 27.03.77
PH-DAA 26.10.68
PH-DCH 29.06.68
PH-DCL 30.05.61
PH-DFO 23.08.54
PH-FCB 03.06.49
PH-LKM 14.08.58
PH-LKT 15.07.57
PH-LKY 05.09.54
PH-LLM 12.06.61
PH-OTO 10.05.40
PH-TAE 05.11.46
PH-TBO 06.11.46
PH-TBW 14.11.46
PH-TCF 16.06.48
PH-TCR 26.01.47
PH-TCV 27.12.47
PH-TDF 12.07.49
PH-TEI 25.05.53
PH-TEN 20.10.48
PH-TER 23.06.49
PH-TEU 02.02.50
PH-TFF 23.03.52
PH-TKW 01.05.48
PH-TPJ 22.03.52
PJ-AIO 25.07.46
PJ-AIP 22.08.42
PK-CTA 08.03.48
PK-REA 10.02.48

KNILM
PK-AFB 04.02.38
PK-AFD 20.12.38
PK-AFE 16.08.32
PK-AFF oo.10.39
PK-AFG 09.02.42
PK-AFI 19.02.42
PK-AFJ oo.12.41
PK-AFM 26.03.42
PK-AFN 13.02.44
PK-AFO 22.01.40
PK-AFS 26.01.42
PK-AFT 26.12.41
PK-AFU 19.02.42
PK-AFV 03.03.42
PK-AFW 24.01.42
PK-AFX 19.02.42
PK-AFZ 26.02.42
PK-AKU 16.08.38
PK-AKV oo.oo.42
PK-AKW 07.03.36
PK-ALN 29.12.41
PK-ALO 03.03.42
PK-DPB 17.11.50

Kabo Air
5N-AWK 06.08.86
5N-KBA 23.08.92
5N-KBG 16.09.91
5N-MAS 31.03.92

Kadvi Company
13323 12.12.93
RA-59504 29.09.94

Kagoshima Kokusai Air
JA9464 13.11.94

Kalahari Air Services
A2-ACT 26.12.85

Kalinga Airlines
VT-AUQ 17.10.65
VT-AZV 07.12.61
VT-AZX 30.08.55
VT-CGB 15.09.52
VT-CMD 07.04.64
VT-COA 31.12.51
VT-COU 02.04.64
VT-DFN 10.04.52
VT-DFZ 16.07.62
VT-DGK 19.10.56
VT-DGP 03.08.59
VT-DGX 21.09.62

Kalinin
n/a 21.11.33

Kalitta American International Airways
N706CK 03.06.95

Kalitta Flying Service
N7770B 10.12.92

Kamchatavia
RA-24721 21.04.93
RA-25613 26.04.94
RA-25904 08.03.93
RA-28713 12.05.94
RA-28716 23.11.93
SSSR-22738 12.09.92
SSSR-67130 04.04.92
SSSR-87385 19.03.92

Kansas City Life Insurance Co
N196KC 01.07.68

Kansas City Southern
NC58024 28.12.46

Kar-Air
OH-KOA 05.02.73

Karl Herfurtner
D-ADEL 26.09.57
D-ALAF 03.11.57

Katale Aero Transport
9Q-CVG 01.03.90

Kayman Sankar Aviation
8R-GGU oo.09.94

Kazair
UN-65787 21.12.93

Kazakhstan Airlines
46478 16.01.93
UN-14211 15.12.94
UN-14229 27.06.94
UN-26080 26.01.95
UN-88181 oo.oo.95

Kazakhstan Directorate
07840 14.10.92
14134 12.07.93
SSSR-27043 30.07.92

Kazakhstan Government
UN-75915 oo.01.95

Kazan Helicopters
RA-70869 28.10.92

Keegan Aviation
CF-TFQ 27.08.64

Keegan, T.D.
G-AJXE 21.11.59

Keewatin Air
C-FFYC 31.05.94

Keir Air Transport
CF-UZA oo.oo.69

Kel-Air
N101GA 03.01.95

Kellogg Co
N235KC 21.11.66
N253K 30.01.80

Kelner Airways
C-FKTL 14.08.91

Kelowna Flightcraft
C-GFRU 18.01.82
C-GKFC 07.09.76
C-GKFN 09.07.81

Kenmore Air Harbor
N68084 11.06.79

Kenn Borek Air
C-FABW 21.12.77
C-FCRW 18.09.78
C-FIQM 29.03.90
C-FIQR 28.02.77
C-FQBT 06.03.93
C-FQHF 07.05.82
C-GDMI 19.07.82
C-GKBD 24.11.94

Kennecott Corporation
N311BR 04.03.95

Kenting Atlas Aviation
CF-OOV 12.02.73
CF-WWP 15.08.73

Kenting Aviation
C-FOOY 03.11.75
C-GDTW 19.01.81
CF-ULL 04.02.77

Kenton Utilities
G-BAEI 26.08.78

Kentucky State Government
N50KY 07.08.92

Kenya Air Charters
5Y-ASH 28.12.74

Kenya Airways
5Y-BBK 11.07.89
5Y-BBS 10.07.88

Kenya Department of Civil Aviation
5Y-DCA 06.04.71

Kenya Police Air Wing
5Y-ADI 24.12.68

Kerkorian, R.R.
N88852 17.11.55

Ketchikan Air Service
N58JH oo.10.92

Khemara Air
XW-TFI 15.12.74

Khmer Hansa
* 11.03.75
XU-GAJ 22.02.75
XU-HAK 19.01.75
XU-KAL 19.01.75

Kidston, G.
G-EBYI oo.07.29

Kiev Airlines
* 27.07.94

Kimex Inc
N1247N 23.05.69
N43865 20.07.79

Kimura International
N230TW 06.01.94

Kinair Cargo
9Q-CAG 07.01.87
9Q-CBK 23.08.88

King Air Services
ZS-NIH 07.11.93

Kinney Air Tankers
N823D 01.05.82

Kitaro Takahashi Sanko Kensetsu
JA5273 11.01.87

Kiunga Aviation
P2-KAD 20.06.87

Kiwi West Aviation
ZK-TIK 29.03.95

Knight Air [1]
N101PP 04.06.84

Knight Air [2]
G-OEAA 24.05.95

Knight, K.
N39393 21.07.72

Knowles Flying Service
NC7864 18.05.35

Kodiak Aviation
N103AQ 16.05.82

Kodiak Western Airlines
N6446X 06.11.80

Kokand Aviation
UK-19633 06.10.94

Kolyma Avia
RA-47718 01.02.94

Komiavia
RA-11375 20.08.93
RA-22226 30.03.94
SSSR-21896 22.07.92
SSSR-28785 19.10.92

Kona Helicopters
N90153 29.03.87

Kondair
G-BDTP 14.09.86

Korda Kentucky Leasing
N30W 21.12.67

Korean Air Lines
HL5204 20.03.91
HL5208 11.12.69
HL5212 23.01.71
HL7285 25.11.89
HL7296 09.08.94
HL7328 27.07.89
HL7339 23.12.83
HL7350 26.08.91
HL7406 29.11.87
HL7412 02.08.76
HL7429 20.04.78
HL7442 01.09.83
HL7445 19.11.80

Korovograd Airlines
* 04.04.95

Krasnodar Air Enterprises
26141 26.12.93

Krasnoyarskavia
RA-22793 17.01.94
RA-22813 12.09.93
RA-24472 12.03.93
RA-25345 18.06.93
RA-26515 06.12.93
RA-62599 14.12.93
SSSR-11896 22.06.92
SSSR-50585 06.05.92

Kungsair
SE-IAA 23.01.90

Kurfiss Aviation
D-IJAN 27.06.75

Kurfiss, G.
* 03.10.80

Kuwait Airways
9K-ACG 30.06.66
9K-AHF 15.02.91
9K-AHG 15.02.91
9K-AIB oo.02.91
9K-AIC oo.02.91

Kuwait National Airways
G-AMSL 18.02.56

Kyrgys Airlines
23414 08.06.93

L & J Company
N55VM 20.10.77

L'Express Airlines
N7217L 10.07.91

L'Office General de l'Air
* 28.08.36

L.A. Patagonicas Argentinas
N6901C 06.03.66

L.A. Transcontinental Brasiliera
PP-ATC 21.04.46
PP-ATD 05.11.45
PP-NAL 06.06.51

L.M.Berner & Co
G-ALTZ 04.06.57

LAB Flying Service
N6281J 07.07.95

LACOL
HK-1340 06.07.85
HK-3215 25.05.95

LACSA
RX-76 26.11.46

LADCO
N27522 01.02.85

LAMS (South Africa) Ltd
ZS-BUL 25.11.47

LAN-Chile
* 22.12.30
* 24.05.33
* 14.03.36
* 29.07.36
* 27.02.37
* 02.06.37
* 13.10.37
* 10.05.38
* 09.03.39
* 14.03.39
* 18.02.43
* 29.03.43
* 15.06.52
5 27.03.37
CC-C-LCA 07.05.62
CC-C-LDP 03.04.61
CC-CAQ 28.04.69
CC-CBY 05.12.69
CC-CCG 06.02.65
CC-CCX 03.08.78
CC-CEI 23.06.90
CC-CET 20.02.91
CC-CHJ 05.08.87
CC-CLC oo.oo.oo
CC-CLD-0100 15.06.53
CC-CLE 04.08.47
CC-CLH-0184 29.05.54

LANSA
HK-750 11.10.91

LAPA
HK-2497 05.03.81

LAPE
EC-45-E oo.02.38
EC-AGK oo.oo.38
EC-BFF oo.04.37

LASA
PP-CDH 06.12.70

LATI
I-ALAN oo.oo.41
I-AMER oo.02.41
I-ANDE 16.08.42
I-AREM 10.01.41
I-ARGE 18.06.42
I-ARMA 07.07.43
I-ARPA 24.12.39
I-ASTA 20.12.40
I-BAIA oo.02.41
I-BAYR 15.01.41
I-BELO 07.05.43
I-BENI 25.03.42
I-BETA 18.08.43
I-BONI 10.04.43
I-BRAZ 09.06.42
I-BURA 28.03.42
I-DOUL oo.11.42
I-FELI 09.11.42
I-LATi oo.11.49
I-TELO 15.11.42

LBC Air Cargo
RP-C2662 23.12.88

LIDCA
HK-330 24.11.50

LOT Polish Airlines
P-PAAA 31.07.28
SP-AAP oo.09.39
SP-ABG 25.11.34
SP-AOC oo.09.39
SP-AOE 12.01.38
SP-AOF 06.06.36
SP-ASJ 23.11.37
SP-AYA 28.12.36
SP-AYB 01.12.36
SP-AYD 11.11.37
SP-BGJ 12.09.39
SP-BNE 24.07.40
SP-BNG 22.07.38
SP-BNJ 18.08.38
SP-BPM oo.06.40
SP-LAA 14.03.80
SP-LAE 14.04.55
SP-LAH 19.03.54
SP-LAL 15.08.60
SP-LAO 07.10.52
SP-LBA 29.03.50
SP-LBC 26.09.46
SP-LBD 19.05.52
SP-LBG 09.05.87
SP-LCC 28.03.50
SP-LCG 14.11.51
SP-LCH 13.03.53
SP-LGB 23.01.80
SP-LHC 18.07.52
SP-LHE oo.10.52
SP-LKA 15.11.54
SP-LNF 14.06.57
SP-LPB 11.04.58
SP-LTD 02.11.88
SP-LTE 24.01.69
SP-LTF 02.04.69
SP-LTN oo.oo.79
SP-LTU 26.03.81
SP-LVA 20.08.65
SP-LVB 19.12.62
SP-LZA 13.05.77

LTU International Airways
D-AERI 27.06.91

LTV Aerospace
62-5921 10.05.67
62-5922 oo.10.67
62-5923 03.01.66
62-5925 28.12.66

La Legion Caribe
N1096M 19.06.49

La Ronge Aviation
C-FZZM 14.06.86

La Sarre Air Services
C-FTEB 17.07.78

La Tuque Air Service
C-FFJB 30.05.83

Labrador Air Safari
C-FDVK 04.07.83

Labrador Airways
C-FAUS 11.10.84
C-FCNT 25.08.84
C-FPEZ 08.02.91

Labrador Mining & Exploration Co
C-FHLL 18.04.83
CF-BJU oo.oo.44

Lacey, C.
N864CL 09.10.84

Lacsa
TI-1002 15.06.53
TI-1005C 15.08.59
TI-1006C 12.05.61
TI-1024C 18.11.60
TI-LRC 23.05.88

Ladeco
CC-CBM 08.04.68
HI-146 19.10.71

Lafayette Aviation
N900WP 10.03.88

Lake Central Airlines
N45335 01.11.63
N73130 05.03.67
N8765A 21.08.52

Lake Riverside Estates
N90627 27.06.71

Lakeland Airways
C-FFHX 06.06.81

Lakeside Helicopters
G-BHYW 23.06.93

Lambair
C-FQWJ oo.03.77
C-GYHT 13.11.79

Lambda Air Cargo
CP-1291 27.07.80

Lancashire Aircraft Corporation
G-AGSN oo.08.51
G-AHDV 17.12.52
G-AHFA 02.02.53
G-AHWN 06.07.49
G-AIHU 05.12.47
G-AIHW 05.06.47
G-AIHX 03.09.48
G-AIHY 28.12.49
G-AJLH 25.10.50
G-AJZY 08.03.51
G-AJZZ 21.03.49
G-AKBJ 01.06.49
G-AKEC 17.12.52
G-ALBZ 10.05.49
G-ALEJ 14.09.56

Lane Xang Airlines
XW-PKD 12.09.73
XW-PKT 03.07.74

Langham Petroleum Corporation
N29LP 19.12.80

Lanica
AN-ACB 29.11.46
AN-ACZ 27.08.48
AN-ADQ oo.02.60
AN-AEC 23.01.57
AN-AIN 05.04.60
AN-AKY 22.07.64
AN-AMR 29.08.72
AN-AOC 25.02.76
AN-AOE 15.12.61
YN-BVI 13.11.80
YN-BVL 16.05.80

Lansa [1]
C-307 24.05.50
C-310 15.12.48
C-68 oo.oo.oo
HK-306 07.12.48
HK-309 15.04.50
HK-311 31.01.51
HK-315 21.03.51
HK-333 14.02.51

Lansa [2]
OB-R-771 27.04.66
OB-R-939 09.08.70
OB-R-941 24.12.71

Lansa [3]
HI-159 18.05.69
HI-222 30.01.75

Lao Airlines
XW-TDI 30.06.71
XW-TDO 29.06.70
XW-TFC 21.12.71

Lao Aviation
* 13.12.93
RDPL-34008 22.04.91

Lao Cathay Airlines
XW-PFM 07.12.67

Laos Air Charter
XW-TDJ 23.12.69

Lapplandsflyg
SE-HCG 28.01.83

Larco Concrete Products
5X-LCP 20.09.83

Lares
* 23.08.40
* 19.06.41

Las Vegas Airlines
N27245 13.02.95
N350MR 10.12.91
N44LV 30.08.78

N88LV 17.08.83

Las Vegas Flyers
N69383 19.02.89

Latavio
47309 06.04.93

Latecoere
F-AKCU 17.12.31
F-BDRB 00.00.00
F-BDRD 21.02.48

Latin Air Service
N431CA 17.12.86

Latincarga
YV-145C 03.11.80

Lauda Air
OE-LAV 26.05.91

Lauderdale Leasing Co
N28343 00.00.70

Laurentian Air Services
C-FECY 25.09.75
C-FTAT 05.08.74

Laville
n/a 29.11.35

Leadair
F-GDLU 20.01.95

Leal Marques, E.J.
YV-314P 04.12.80

Lear Jet Corporation
N801L 04.06.64

Learjet Corporation
N984JD 25.02.90

Lebanese Helicopters
OD-AGK 00.00.82
OD-AGL 00.00.82

Lebanese International Airways
OD-ACK 03.10.57
OD-AEI 28.12.68
OD-AEK 28.12.68
OD-AEW 28.12.68
OD-AEX 28.12.68

Lebca
YV-C-LBG 19.05.60
YV-C-LBH 02.11.62
YV-C-LBL 16.06.59

Lec Refrigeration
G-ALEC 06.05.59

Leeward Islands Air Transport
V2-LCJ 04.08.86
VP-BAO 23.08.59

Legend Air
LX-DKT 21.07.92

Lehigh Acres Development Co
N40412 30.05.70

Leicester Aft. Preservation Society
G-BDFT 19.08.84

Lekeu, L.
OO-APG 29.07.56

Lenhardt, J.
N65121 02.10.77

Leningrad Civil Aviation Assoc
SSSR-31016 07.10.92

Leon, J.R.
N4463W 30.11.87

Les Ailes de Charlevoix
C-GVPB 03.08.94

Les Constructions du St Laurent
C-GCSL 00.02.93

Lesotho Airways
7P-LAE 25.08.81

Lewis, J.
NC7427 26.05.37

Liberia Air Cargo
SSSR-48109 17.01.91

Liberia Air Transport
* 00.01.90

Liberian National Airlines
EL-AAB 25.06.70

Libyan Air Force
5A-DKK 00.00.85

Libyan Arab Airlines
* 15.04.86
5A-DAD 05.06.67
5A-DAH 21.02.73
5A-DBE 28.11.80
5A-DBR 26.03.81
5A-DDV 06.06.89
5A-DIA 22.12.92
5A-DJT 07.12.91
5A-DLP 15.04.86
5A-DLR 00.00.86
5A-DNF 15.04.86
5A-DZZ 15.04.86

Libyan Aviation Co
G-ANGE 26.02.64

Libyan Government
5A-DAR 16.01.83

Libyan Red Crescent
5A-DBN 21.11.90

Lider Taxi Aereo
PT-BVX 13.12.81
PT-BVZ 08.12.77
PT-DZU 23.08.79
PT-HBY 07.12.81
PT-HHC 02.02.80
PT-HIF 28.11.76
PT-HJU 29.10.81
PT-HKP 13.03.81
PT-HKQ 27.09.83
PT-HKW 22.07.81
PT-HPD 13.10.94
PT-HPF 08.04.84
PT-LCN 04.04.84
PT-LIG 09.11.94
PT-LIH 15.03.91
PT-OFK 26.02.93

Liftair International
C-GLAY 12.05.91

Light Air Transport
* 19.03.94

Lignes Aeriennes Latecoere
F-AEEN 11.12.25
F-AEGZ 17.10.25
F-AEHD 25.12.25
F-AEIS 00.00.25
F-AEJA 00.00.00
F-AFAX 11.11.26
F-AFBB 25.05.25
F-AFBE 17.10.26
F-AFBG 01.09.25
F-AFBI 20.07.25
F-AFEF 05.02.26
F-AGBN 00.00.27
F-AGBS 11.11.26
F-AGBT 00.00.26
F-AGBY 00.00.25
F-AGCD 21.06.25
F-AHEM 22.05.26
F-AHEP 00.00.26
F-ALKU 00.00.27
F-ALSE 00.00.27
F-FYMS 13.03.26

Lignes Aeriennes Militaire
FL-ARI 00.11.42

Lignum
C-GLIG 01.03.95

Ligon Brothers
N24169 22.11.91

Limbaugh, B.B.
N27MT 08.10.94

Lina Congo
TN-ACX 12.03.92

Linair
OO-SEE 09.09.76

Linea Aerea Aeropetrel
* 31.12.85

Linea Aerea Ala de Chile
* 03.02.67

Linea Aeropostal Venezolana
* 23.04.37
YV-30C 17.04.78
YV-ACE 01.12.41
YV-ADA 09.02.46
YV-ADE 14.10.41
YV-ADI 25.07.44
YV-ADO 00.00.00
YV-AFI 12.02.46
YV-AGU 23.02.48
YV-C-AFA 12.04.57
YV-C-AFE 28.04.60
YV-C-AGI 10.12.54
YV-C-AHI 26.06.48
YV-C-AKU 01.12.59
YV-C-ALU 21.05.55
YV-C-AMA 27.11.56
YV-C-AMK 22.05.70
YV-C-AMP 18.12.54
YV-C-AMS 20.06.56
YV-C-AMU 20.03.47
YV-C-AMV 25.01.71
YV-C-AMX 14.08.74
YV-C-AMY 20.08.68
YV-C-AMZ 01.11.71
YV-C-ANC 14.10.58
YV-C-AZQ 10.03.61

Linea Expresa Bolivar
CF-TFJ 27.08.64
YV-C-LBU 27.08.64
YV-C-LBV 06.07.62

Linea Interamericana Aerea
HK-603 31.01.54
HK-605 29.01.53

Lineas Aereas Brasil
PP-AJB 03.08.49

Lineas Aereas CAVE
YV-478C 28.11.89

Lineas Aereas Colombianas
HK-2701 16.09.91

Lineas Aereas Covitrans
N28AD 17.05.93

Lineas Aereas Entre Rios
LV-LAE 23.01.94
LV-MIU 02.06.95

Lineas Aereas Guerrero Oaxaca
XA-BFK 00.00.50
XA-CAB 07.01.50
XA-GIJ 16.08.49

Lineas Aereas Interpolar
CC-CIA-0497 21.05.59
CC-CIB-0504 24.11.64

Lineas Aereas La Urraca
HK-1267 14.12.77
HK-1270 12.03.70
HK-1347 21.01.72
HK-354X 26.11.62
HK-718 02.11.73
HK-721 07.05.72

Lineas Aereas Mexicanas
XA-BFT 22.02.45
XA-DAY 00.00.46
XA-DEB 00.00.45

Lineas Aereas Mineras
XA-BFR 05.05.38
XA-BLZ 16.11.42
XA-DAH 11.05.44
XA-DAI 23.06.43
XA-DUY 01.08.45

Lineas Aereas Orientales
HK-166 19.07.77
HK-2114X 09.07.78
HK-791 30.04.73

Lineas Aereas Paraguayas
ZP-CDN 00.00.73
ZP-CDP 26.05.67

Lineas Aereas Petroleras
HK-1158 05.06.85
HK-2203 14.05.82
HK-2609 10.01.86

Lineas Aereas Sud Americana
CC-CAN 29.12.64

Lineas Aereas Suramericanas
HK-1808 19.06.86
HK-1856 30.01.94
HK-2716 11.12.91
HK-3148X 06.07.88
HK-3205X 17.04.86

Lineas Aereas Unidas
XA-DOB 14.07.55
XA-DOQ 27.11.51
XA-HEC 00.02.49

Lineas Aereas de los Libertadores
HK-3470 29.04.94

Lineas Aereas del Caribe
HK-1389 04.02.76
HK-1705 29.04.78
HK-1706 19.02.82
HK-1707 08.12.78
HK-2380X 18.09.84
HK-3753X 15.10.92
HK-459 29.12.54
HK-489 17.06.54

Lineas Aereas del Centro
XA-BOP 09.09.78

Lineas Aereas del Estado
* 08.11.95
LV-ISA 31.01.93
T-81 28.01.83
T-84 00.00.00
TC-51 16.08.89
TC-72 16.03.75

TC-73 16.06.95
TC-75 10.06.70
TC-77 02.12.69

Lineas Aereas del Norte de Colombia
HK-1776 22.07.95

Lineas Aereas del Pacifico
N41813 oo.oo.52
NC13345 09.11.33

Lineas Aereas del Sur
OB-1030 27.02.95

Lineas Aereas del Uraba
HK-1720 21.11.78

Linee Aeree Italiane
I-LAIL 26.01.53
I-LEAD 24.11.56
I-LENT 10.04.54
I-LETR 28.11.51
I-LINC 22.12.56
I-LINE 18.12.54
I-LUCK 23.12.51

Linhas Aereas Paulistas
PP-LPB 07.10.48
PP-LPC 15.05.51
PP-LPH 04.03.54

Linhas Aereas de Mocambique
C9-BAB 28.03.83
C9-BAD 09.02.89

Linjeflyg
SE-BSU 01.11.69
SE-CCK 20.11.64

Liore et Olivier
n/a 19.05.37

Lisa Flite Corporation
N72BS 02.02.85

Lisle, B.
N28BL 27.03.78

Litchfield, E.H.
N999NJ 08.03.68

Lloyd Aereo Boliviano
CB-17 03.11.40
CB-18 15.12.37
CB-20 13.03.37
CB-25 21.08.44
CB-26 oo.09.49
CB-31 01.01.51
CB-32 28.05.47
CB-33 29.08.49
CB-37 10.08.49
CB-38 09.10.50
CB-39 29.07.51
CB-51 24.04.50
CP-1117 02.06.80
CP-1175 22.01.80
CP-1365 31.08.91
CP-2165 22.12.94
CP-535 18.03.57
CP-536 21.08.62
CP-541 22.01.62
CP-568 04.02.64
CP-570 21.09.55
CP-580 07.02.65
CP-584 31.12.59
CP-597 05.09.55
CP-600 03.11.53
CP-605 25.08.56
CP-609 05.02.60
CP-623 28.07.58
CP-625 17.11.59
CP-686 04.11.65
CP-698 26.09.69
CP-707 15.03.63
CP-730 03.08.66
CP-734 19.04.68
CP-862 16.03.84
N730JP 14.10.76
n/a 26.10.32
n/a 27.09.35
n/a 17.01.36
n/a 12.04.39
n/a 10.10.41

Lloyd Aereo Colombiano
HK-391 26.06.50

Lloyd Helicopters
VH-CIH 04.12.88
VH-HOQ 22.11.91
VH-LAO 29.03.88
VH-LAT 07.04.95

Lloyd International Airways
G-ARLF 08.10.61

Lloyd-Luftverkehr Sablatnig
D-171 21.04.27
D-395 23.08.28
D-453 31.05.27
D-50 17.10.26
D-727 07.08.26
D-730 23.07.25
D-962 23.09.27
D-984 30.07.27

Lockheed Aircraft
N130X 03.02.93
NC196E 05.03.29
NC198E 05.03.29
NC396H 22.03.30
NX34E 04.08.29

Loftleidir
TF-FLA 16.11.78
TF-RVC 14.09.50
TF-RVD 26.06.46
TF-RVE 12.01.46
TF-RVF 27.07.51
TF-RVH 27.01.52
TF-RVI 13.03.47
TF-RVL 07.03.48

Loganair
G-ATRI 01.08.70
G-BCYC 15.05.79
G-BDVW 01.06.84
G-BGPC 12.06.86

Logsdon, J.H.
N139D 10.07.69

Loide Aereo Nacional
PP-ANK 06.09.56
PP-LDC 15.04.51
PP-LDD 17.12.50
PP-LDE 24.05.52
PP-LDM 14.09.53
PP-LDX 05.09.58
PP-LEM 01.02.58
PP-LEQ 12.08.58
PP-LPG 12.07.51

London & Provincial Aviation
G-EAET oo.08.19

London Aero & Motor Services
G-AHWP 06.01.48
G-AHZJ 31.07.47
G-AHZM 16.09.46
G-AHZN 26.09.46
G-AIWK oo.12.47
G-AIWT 05.09.47

London Express Newspapers
G-AEHC 02.02.37

London Scottish & Provincial Airways
G-ACSY 29.09.34

Lone Star Airlines
N342AE 25.08.92

Lone Star Helicopters
N32GT 15.07.85

Loneragan, E.H.
VH-BLG oo.oo.59

Loomis, R.
NC7586 01.07.34

Loon Air
C-GKPB 22.05.93

Los Angeles Airlines
N300Y 14.08.68
N303Y 22.05.68

Louisiana Pacific Corporation
N873LP 22.09.85

Luft-Taxi Emsland
D-ICLW 11.03.91

Luft-Transport-Dienst
D-HAKA 18.03.77

Luftfahrtzeug-Finanz
HB-GDV 24.01.86

Lufthansa
* 25.04.35
* 16.03.39
* 04.08.39
D-1019 oo.04.34
D-1028 17.08.28
D-1088 06.01.28
D-1101 oo.oo.28
D-1137 oo.12.28
D-1338 07.03.31
D-1380 oo.02.33
D-1388 oo.12.33
D-1427 25.09.28
D-1430 oo.oo.36
D-1473 11.12.28
D-1594 19.12.29
D-1649 07.04.30
D-1693 18.11.28
D-1712 oo.03.35
D-1717 06.10.31
D-1734 10.09.29
D-175 16.06.31
D-1775 oo.08.31
D-1826 oo.oo.30
D-1922 oo.oo.30
D-1928 14.04.31
D-1930 06.10.30
D-2017 29.10.32
D-2018 13.01.33
D-2059 oo.oo.35
D-206 27.07.27
D-207 oo.oo.34
D-2072 13.09.31
D-2201 29.07.32
D-232 oo.oo.33
D-2356 27.05.33
D-272 oo.oo.26
D-290 oo.oo.26
D-353 oo.07.35
D-368 oo.oo.oo
D-378 oo.07.35
D-4 29.04.33
D-404 oo.oo.34
D-409 oo.oo.25
D-422 oo.oo.30
D-443 oo.oo.28
D-447 03.10.27
D-468 08.10.26
D-489 oo.11.28
D-516 30.06.26
D-533 30.06.26
D-534 oo.oo.33
D-550 oo.oo.oo
D-560 oo.oo.27
D-575 oo.07.35
D-576 oo.06.28
D-583 26.05.28
D-585 23.09.27
D-670 oo.oo.26
D-701 oo.07.35
D-724 02.11.32
D-729 22.04.27
D-74 14.06.28
D-743 03.06.33
D-757 24.08.29
D-758 26.07.30
D-765 02.05.32
D-766 23.11.31
D-780 22.07.29
D-784 03.08.27
D-864 07.07.30
D-896 oo.oo.38
D-899 oo.02.29
D-903 06.11.29
D-944 oo.oo.26
D-946 oo.09.28
D-AAIE 14.08.44
D-AAIF oo.oo.43
D-AAIG 21.04.44
D-AAIH 29.10.40
D-ABBF 09.12.42
D-ABEW oo.oo.43
D-ABOD 22.04.40
D-ABOK 04.12.61
D-ABOP 15.07.64
D-ABOT 19.12.73
D-ABUR 04.01.38
D-ABUY 26.07.79
D-ABVF oo.oo.42
D-ABYB 20.11.74
D-ACAT 28.01.66
D-ACBE oo.oo.43
D-ACBO oo.oo.40
D-ACON 06.12.38
D-ADHF oo.oo.43
D-ADHR oo.oo.41
D-ADQV 16.10.44
D-ADYS 15.02.36
D-AEAO oo.oo.41
D-AFCD oo.oo.41
D-AFES oo.oo.42
D-AFOP 30.08.39
D-AFYS oo.oo.41
D-AGAR 24.05.35
D-AGAV 26.11.37
D-AGBI oo.oo.42
D-AGDA 24.02.42
D-AGEP oo.oo.42
D-AGIS oo.oo.41
D-AGUK oo.oo.42
D-AHFN oo.oo.42
D-AHIH oo.oo.41
D-AHMS oo.oo.41
D-AHUT oo.oo.41
D-AHUX 03.11.34
D-AIPN 14.09.93
D-AIVI 26.11.38
D-AJAN oo.oo.41
D-AKEP oo.oo.42
D-AKIN 13.08.37
D-AKOK oo.oo.42
D-AKUO oo.oo.41
D-ALAB oo.oo.39
D-ALAK 11.01.59
D-ALAM oo.oo.43
D-ALAN oo.oo.42
D-ALIX 12.03.37
D-ALUN oo.oo.41
D-ALUS 24.02.39
D-AMHC oo.oo.43
D-ANAL oo.oo.41
D-ANAZ oo.oo.43
D-ANEN oo.oo.42
D-ANJH 03.08.39
D-ANOL oo.oo.41
D-ANOY 02.12.38
D-ANXG oo.oo.41
D-ANYF oo.oo.41
D-APAR 22.02.38
D-APIS oo.oo.oo
D-APOO 01.11.36
D-APXD oo.oo.43
D-ARDS oo.oo.42
D-ARHW 29.11.44
D-ARIW oo.oo.41
D-AROZ 01.10.38
D-ASHH 21.04.45
D-ASIH 04.12.36
D-ASLG oo.oo.42
D-ASOR 24.04.36
D-ASUI 17.11.36
D-ATAK 28.11.36
D-ATIO 27.05.38
D-ATON oo.oo.42
D-AURE oo.09.44

D-AUXZ 00.00.41
D-AVAJ 00.00.41
D-AVFB 01.10.38
D-AXAT 00.00.43
D-AXES 00.00.41
D-AXFH 00.00.42
D-AYGX 00.00.42
D-AZUR 00.00.36
D-IBUX 00.00.37
D-OBAZ 00.00.36
D-OGOT 24.07.34
D-OHIL 00.00.35
D-OJIP 24.06.36
D-OLYK 00.10.36
D-OMYI 30.04.35
D-ONIQ 00.00.27
D-ORIP 00.10.36
D-OTIK 00.07.35
D-OVYF 10.06.36
D-UDAL 00.00.43
D-UFON 00.00.41
D-UHEN 00.00.41
D-UJAR 00.00.43
D-UKUM 00.00.42
D-ULET 00.00.35
D-UMOK 00.00.42
D-UNAH 00.00.36
D-UQAN 00.00.35
D-UREK 00.00.42
D-USAH 00.00.35
D-UVOK 00.00.42
D-UXUV 20.05.37
D-UXYN 00.00.37
OA-HHB 26.06.38

Luftransport Union
D-BALI 04.02.61

Luftschiffbau Schutte-Lanz
S.L.1 17.07.13

Lufttransport
LN-OPX 08.05.93
LN-OQS 23.12.82
LN-ORJ 30.09.81
LN-ORO 26.01.78
LN-ORQ 10.08.79

Lumar Air Toronto
C-GPBS 07.12.79

Lundy & Atlantic Coast Air Lines
G-AETT 13.02.40

Lusaka Air Charter
VP-RCJ 24.09.52

Lutheran Mission
XT-T72 10.02.49

Luxair
LX-LAA 19.06.58
LX-LGC 22.12.69

Luycks Executive Flight
PH-JAL 29.01.80

Lyon Air
CC-CAH-0331 03.11.56
CC-CYA-0141 28.04.51

M & M Air
N63HB 15.02.95

M.C.Correia Holdings
8R-GEH 07.11.77

M.J.Kelly & Co
N100MK 21.10.78

MAS Air
* 27.12.90
TC-HSB 07.04.91

MIAT Mongolian Airlines
* 03.08.87
* 01.03.90
* 23.04.93
BNMAU-10103 21.09.95

MJI
N13MJ 06.11.82

MK Air Cargo
9G-MKB 15.02.92

MMM Aero Services
9Q-CAH 11.09.84

MacRobertson-Miller Airlines
VH-MME 02.07.49
VH-RMQ 31.12.68
VH-USF 24.06.45

Macchi
I-NILO 18.08.38

Macey, S.
G-BFPU 25.09.78

Macfadden Publications
NX7430 13.09.28

Macfadden, B.
NX3625 29.03.29

Mack Trucks Inc
N1021B 06.11.69

Mackenzie Air Services
CF-AUD 24.05.34

Mackey International Airlines
N444JM 24.11.79

Macton Corporation
N81MC 10.11.84

Maddux Airlines
NC9636 21.04.29
NC0689 19.01.30

Maersk Air
OY-APB 27.12.69
OY-APD 25.01.75
OY-HMC 02.01.83

Magadan Avia
RA-22347 25.08.93
RA-22912 15.05.93
SSSR-11111 17.07.92
SSSR-22831 11.07.92
SSSR-24443 09.10.92
SSSR-55607 30.03.92

Magistralnye Avialinii
RA-82071 15.11.93

Magnitogorsk Avia
RA-26549 28.08.93

Magnitogosk Enterprise
* 04.05.95

Magnum Airlines
* 20.05.80
ZS-KYA 14.04.82
ZS-LKG 18.11.88

Mair Inc
N1846 13.03.68

Major & White
EL-AFO 19.09.66

Malagasy Air Force
* 18.07.95
5R-MPF 15.12.72

Malawi Police Air Wing
7Q-YAX 18.03.83
7Q-YAY 24.04.86
7Q-YAZ 04.02.77

Malayan Volunteer Air Force
VR-SAV 18.12.41
VR-SAW 10.02.42
VR-SAX 20.01.42

Malaysia-Singapore Airlines
9M-AMU 30.01.67
9M-APE 05.12.69
9V-BCU 23.11.71

Malaysian Airline System
9M-MBD 04.12.77
9M-MDD 06.07.82
9M-MGH 15.09.95
OY-KAA 18.12.83

Malaysian Airlines
9M-ANC 17.05.67
9M-ANO 03.03.67
G-APDH 22.03.64

Malaysian Dept. of Civil Aviation
9M-CAM 13.12.93

Malaysian Helicopter Services
9M-AXW 15.05.90
9M-SSG 13.12.85

Malaysian Police
* 17.05.89

Malert
H-MABC 18.05.29
HA-JUA 18.01.41

Malev
HA-LBA 19.11.69
HA-LBC 21.09.77
HA-LBD 16.09.71
HA-LBP 22.02.94
HA-LCF 21.10.81
HA-LCI 30.09.75
HA-LIF 23.12.54
HA-LII 23.12.54
HA-LIM 09.06.57
HA-LIO 24.04.68
HA-MAH 17.02.64
HA-MOC 28.08.71
HA-MOD 23.11.62
HA-MOE 00.00.88
HA-MOF 23.11.77
HA-MOH 15.01.75
HA-TSA 06.08.61

Maluti Air Services
ZS-DMB 13.06.55

Management Activities
N309CK 15.12.93

Management Jets International
HZ-GP5 11.01.82

Manchurian Air Lines
M-604 21.06.41
M-701 18.05.34

Mandala Airlines
PK-RLG 30.11.85
PK-RVK 07.01.76
PK-RVN 01.05.81
PK-RVT 13.01.85
PK-RVU 24.07.92
PK-RVW 07.10.83

Mandated Airlines
VH-UXD 00.03.42

Maniglia Construzioni
I-MCSA 22.02.78

Manila Aero Transport System
RP-C81 26.04.90
RP-C82 06.05.89

Mannin Airways
G-AKOF 11.11.48

Mannix Ltd
CF-ESB 06.12.53

Manokotauk Airways
N4882U 25.05.88

Manx Airlines
G-AGVC 30.06.62
G-AMZC 22.12.55

Marathon Oil Co
N521M 12.12.72

Marchwiel Plant & Engineering
G-BABX 12.01.77

Marger, E.
N150A 06.04.65

Marikscho Luftfahrtgesellschaft
* 03.01.78

Marine Helicopters
ZK-HJJ 23.09.77

Maritime Central Airways
CF-BMV 00.12.42
CF-BXZ 22.03.52
CF-FKQ 15.04.61
CF-FZU 13.02.56
CF-HMU 24.01.56
CF-HMW 26.09.56
CF-HTI 11.01.63
CF-HTP 25.10.55
CF-MCF 11.08.57

Mark Hurd Mapping Co
N5116N 10.11.52

Markair
N670MA 02.06.90

Markair Express
N70364 04.08.92
N724CA 26.10.91
N9444F 21.12.90
N9526F 02.08.93
N9869M 19.06.93
N9975M 20.07.92

Marquess of Londonderry
G-AGWO 02.07.47

Marshall, T.H.
G-ALTP 01.01.62
G-ALTR 14.08.61

Martin Aviation
N123RE 17.10.78

Martin, M.
N518K 13.08.81

Martinair
PH-MBN 21.12.92

Martinaire
N9448B 02.03.95
N9471B 18.01.95

Maryland Flying Service
EL-ADV 06.07.62

Masin, J.V.
N87805 28.02.75

Masling Helicopters
VH-LLD 20.12.92

Maszovlet
HA-LIK 19.09.49
HA-LIL 02.10.52

Mather Co
N500L 26.09.78

Mattern, J.J.
NR869E 06.07.32
NR869E 00.06.33

Matthews Aviation
VH-UPB 14.05.36

Matthews, F.M.
NC965Y 26.08.43

Mauldin, L.
N161N 19.05.61

Mauritanian Air Force
5T-MAQ 00.00.00
5T-MAR 03.01.77
5T-MAT 21.07.77
5T-MAX 27.05.79
5T-MBA 00.00.00

Mavewa
D2-ECE 16.03.94

Maya Airways
V3-HCT 25.11.89
VP-HCD 22.02.77

Mayfair Air Services
G-AJWI 00.00.50

Mayflower Air Services
G-AHLM 20.07.63
G-AJPJ 20.07.48

Mayflower Airlines
NC12121 03.09.38

Mayne-Bristow Helicopters
VH-WOA 29.12.86

Mayo Aviation
N67977 24.08.92

McAlpine Aviation
G-AYDE 18.04.74

McAlpine Helicopters
G-BIKH 08.04.86

McCollum Aviation
N127MW 05.10.84

McDermott Inc
N81MD 11.08.78

McDonnell Douglas Aircraft
N1002G 18.06.80

McGeorge, J.
N356AL 30.04.78

McGill, T.
N37ST 16.03.95

McInnes Products Corp
CF-ECN 02.01.51

McKee, J.B.
N114CM 16.06.86

McKenzie Air
CF-KAH 05.01.72

McMullen, T.
N69TM 12.02.95

Mears, J.H.
NR500V 03.08.30

Meat Export & Supply Co
ET-P-16 03.09.53

Mechanical Equipment Co
N77AP 07.11.77

Mecon Taxi Aereo
PT-BKB 24.09.84

Medecins Sans Frontieres
* 21.12.89

Medic Air
N300CP 31.12.92

Medley Airways
C-GJIS 21.11.81

Meek, K.L.
N75000 00.00.80

Mellon Bank
N205M 25.07.67

Meravo Luftreederei Flug
D-HAUB 30.09.77

Mercer Airlines
N31538 04.08.72
N901MA 08.02.76

Merchant Bank
N211MB 03.03.80

Mercury Aviation
ZS-BNB 19.04.47
ZS-BWX 20.11.48
ZS-BWY 15.05.48
ZS-BWZ 12.10.48

Mercy Missions
G-AWMG 03.09.68
G-AWMH 20.06.69

Meridian Air Maps
G-AISF 29.04.57
G-AJKP 17.12.57

Merlin Flite
OY-ATW 26.04.78

Merpati Nusantara Airlines
PK-GFU 01.07.93
PK-GKU 30.11.94
PK-MFD 09.05.91
PK-MFI 18.06.94
PK-MNN 18.10.92
PK-MVG 11.01.85
PK-MVS 10.11.71
PK-MYN 01.04.71
PK-NCF 25.03.86
PK-NCY 30.01.91
PK-NDH 07.02.77
PK-NDI 05.10.78
PK-NUC 28.02.73
PK-NUE 15.09.89
PK-NUG 12.08.85
PK-NUK 10.01.95
PK-NUL 16.06.93
PK-NUP 29.03.77
PK-NUQ 03.04.90
PK-NUT 17.07.95
PK-NUW 23.05.87
PK-NUY 30.12.87

Merser, H.B.
N1981W 02.10.71

Mesa Airlines
N139YV 10.05.89

Messerschmitt
n/a 26.02.28

Metro Airlines
N922MA 01.04.83
N935MA 20.05.83

Metro Cargo Airlines
LZ-INK 24.05.91

Metropolitan Air Movements
G-AMTS 16.07.61
G-ANYK 22.06.61

Mexican Air Force
XC-UJC 26.10.89
XC-UJH/04 25.03.92

Mexicana
* 08.09.59
X-ABCO 26.03.36
X-ABCP 00.07.30
X-ABCR 07.08.31
X-ABCS 27.09.34
XA-BAS 09.02.38
XA-BAU 00.00.00
XA-BAY 03.08.36
XA-BCW 05.03.40
XA-BDH 06.10.36
XA-BEO 00.00.00
XA-BEQ 00.00.00
XA-DEE 28.07.46
XA-DIK 08.03.55
XA-DOL 12.05.47
XA-DOT 11.08.45
XA-DUH 26.09.49
XA-DUK 16.12.49
XA-FOW 25.06.46
XA-GAM 12.09.49
XA-HUS 28.09.60
XA-JOR 01.09.51
XA-LAU 30.01.67
XA-MEM 31.03.86
XA-MOO 20.08.69
XA-MUV 02.11.76
XA-SEJ 21.09.69
XA-SEL 04.06.69
XA-SEN 20.10.73

Miami Air Lease
N10624 28.09.79
N844TA 28.11.80

Miami Airlines
N1678M 16.12.51

Miami Aviation
N4997E 18.03.65

Miatchkovo Aviation
* 22.03.92

Michaelov, G.A.
VH-BDX 06.02.50

Mid Continent Airlines
N19928 02.03.51
N420D 16.04.70
N90664 27.02.51

Mid Pacific Air
N906TC 13.01.87

Middle East Airlines
9G-ABP 28.12.68
ET-AAG 09.01.68
LR-AAA 30.01.48
OD-ACT 28.12.68
OD-ACX 21.04.64
OD-ACZ 15.03.63
OD-ADA 09.09.62
OD-ADB 29.09.58
OD-ADE 01.02.63
OD-ADQ 28.12.68
OD-ADR 28.12.68
OD-ADS 28.12.68
OD-AEE 28.12.68
OD-AEF 28.12.68
OD-AEM 17.04.64
OD-AFB 16.06.82
OD-AFC 28.12.68
OD-AFL 21.08.85
OD-AFO 16.06.82
OD-AFP 12.06.82
OD-AFR 31.08.81
OD-AFT 01.01.76
OD-AFU 16.06.82
OD-AFW 16.06.82
OD-AGE 27.06.76
OD-AGG 01.08.82
OD-AGQ 21.08.85
OD-AGR 16.06.82
OD-AHB 07.01.87

Middle States Airlines
NC513E 12.08.29
NC870E 11.08.29

Midnite Express
N8493A 26.05.88

Midwest Air Charter
N805MW 19.06.80

Midwest Express
N100ME 06.09.85

Midwest Oil Corporation
N34W 04.01.74

Miguel, J.P.
OB-ABO-341 18.06.54

Miksoo Air Service
C-FAID 24.04.75

Mil Design Bureau
* 00.00.69

Milburnair
G-AIOZ 15.08.47

Miles Aircraft
G-AGPD 28.05.48
G-AHDM 28.06.58
G-AISJ 15.07.47

Millar Western Industries
C-FMWW 27.01.94

Millers Aviation
N525W 29.02.68

Millon Air
N43UA 28.04.95

Milne Bay Air
P2-MBE 15.12.92
P2-MBF 00.02.92
P2-MBI 12.07.95

Minchin, L.
G-EBTQ 31.08.27

Mineral County Airlines
N15570 18.02.69

Ministerio de Agricultura y Cria
YV-O-MAC-1 00.06.79

Ministic Air
C-FRGT 06.02.92

Ministry of Agriculture
5A-DCP 30.03.83
5A-DCS 15.04.86
5A-DCW 00.00.82

Ministry of Aviation
I-AASZ 12.10.29

Ministry of Aviation Industry
* 18.05.91

Ministry of Civil Aviation
G-AGPB 22.09.50
G-AGZS 04.01.52

Ministry of National Defence
L-701 00.00.79

Ministry of Public Health
ET-AEN 16.01.75

Ministry of Supply
G-AGSU 23.08.47
G-ALEU 10.04.51
VX217 00.00.58

Miramichi Air Service
C-FWPC 25.03.80

Misiones Provincial Government
LV-MMV 23.09.89

Misrair
SU-ABI 15.03.35
SU-ABJ 22.06.38
SU-ABP 06.02.45

SU-ABQ 09.10.41
SU-ACS 27.07.48
SU-ACT 25.02.51
SU-ACX 26.10.45
SU-ADB 28.12.45
SU-ADJ 24.08.46
SU-ADK 26.07.49
SU-ADM 02.03.50
SU-ADN oo.06.48
SU-ADZ 26.08.48
SU-AEA 10.12.46
SU-AEB 30.12.51
SU-AEC 23.04.47
SU-AED 24.03.47
SU-AEE 10.11.48
SU-AFK 15.12.53
SU-AFO 15.09.54
SU-AGN 07.03.58
SU-AGO 05.08.54
SU-AHH 23.12.51
SU-AHX 30.07.52
SU-AHZ 24.04.54
SU-AIC 01.10.56
SU-AOB 02.02.66
SU-AOC 14.03.70
SU-AOM 30.09.66

Mission Air
N121BT 18.10.84

Mission Air Lift
N7177B 04.09.78

Missionary Aviation Fellowship
* 25.09.91
P2-MFS 17.12.94
PK-MAJ 23.07.79
PK-MAM 25.05.87

Mississippi Valley Airlines
N956SM 09.11.70

Mistry Airways
VT-AZC 21.06.47

Mitsubishi Nainenki Seizo
* 27.10.37

Miwani Sugar Mills
5Y-WAW 10.12.76

Mobil Oil
N2620 08.11.94
N446T 01.05.69

Modern Air
N5603 08.08.70

Mohawk Airlines
N1116J 23.06.67
N449A 02.07.63
N7811M 19.11.69
N7818M 03.03.72

Mohican Air Services
706M 15.12.92

Molhook, K.E.
N720X oo.02.87

Mollison, A.
G-ACCV 23.07.33

Monarch Air Service
VH-NDU 11.06.93

Monarch Air Services
N79982 04.01.51

Monarch Aviation
N8817E 20.08.77

Monmouth Airlines
N986MA 24.10.71

Mono Max Aviation
F-GLRA 19.10.94

Monroe County Mosquito Control
N28889 02.05.89

Monrovia Air Line
EL-AFG 01.11.80
EL-AFT 04.07.78

Montauk-Caribbean Airways
N9093Y 07.08.78

Montgomery Construction Co
N4962N oo.oo.53

Moonlight Express
N700CC 18.11.80

Moore's Air Charter
VH-KTE 28.08.83

Moormanair
PH-MOA 03.06.71

Morales, A.
N94436 oo.04.80

Morgan Air Lines
NC7120 oo.oo.33

Moroccan Air Force
CN-AOB/4537 04.12.76

Moroccan Government
CN-ANA oo.10.78

Morrison, R.E.
NC7425 21.04.35

Morton Air Services
G-AHFT 14.06.52
G-AHJX 12.05.50
G-AIOU 24.05.48

Motor Parts Manufacturers
5N-AMF 25.07.77

Motortec
PP-CDD 17.05.75

Mount Cook Airlines
ZK-CVG 27.06.92
ZK-EHM 23.12.93
ZK-MCH 15.03.77

Mount Victory Flying Service
N888RJ 05.04.77

Mountain Air Cargo
N3257 11.10.85
N996SA 19.01.88

Mountain Air Services
C-GOPB 12.09.92

Mountain Flyers 80
HB-XLR 27.04.95

Mountain Helicopters
ZK-HIA 25.04.77

Mountain States Telephone & Telecom
N60MB 03.04.77

Mozambique Air Force
C9-CAA 19.10.86

Muk Air
OY-BZW oo.04.91
OY-PRY 04.03.86
OY-SUM 17.01.91

Multi Servicios Lujal
YV-726CP 27.03.94

Mulzer Flying Service
NC7685 22.06.34

Munoz, J.
N778L 29.10.84

Munz Airways
N26W 02.07.56

Munz Northern Airlines
N36MN 21.11.77
N37MN 07.04.83
N591JA 24.04.75

Murphy, D.J.
NR12282 oo.oo.54

Murryair Aviation
N48207 oo.oo.77

Musee SV-4 Aero
F-AZEP 13.02.88

Musleh, H.W.
NC7865 20.10.38

Mutual Benefit Health & Accident
N316M 19.03.66

Mutual Finance
G-AEXN 21.07.39

Myanma Airways
XY-AEP 06.10.93

NAAM
XA-FUP 06.12.46

NASA
N711NA 12.04.73
N712NA 18.07.85
N833NA 01.12.84
n/a 28.01.86

NJ Airlines
N723A 21.09.77

NLM CityHopper
PH-CHI 06.10.81

NV Mijnbouw
PK-AER 26.12.41
PK-AES 26.01.42

NWT Air
C-FPWK 11.04.82

NYNEX Corporation
N29X 05.03.89

Nabisco
N784B 10.11.85

Nachez, J.A.
CX-AYI 28.01.62

Nahanni Air Services
C-FPPL 09.10.84

Naka Nihon Air Service
JA9123 06.08.87
JA9172 30.07.86
JA9293 25.09.86

Nalson, K.J.
G-ALFJ 08.03.49

Nanyang Airways
VR-SDL 10.04.53

Narrabari Air Taxis
VH-RBR 08.08.77

Nastra Luchtreclame Service
PH-EAB oo.oo.62

Nathaniel Hawthorne College
N18949 24.06.81

National Aero Sales Corp
N38G 05.11.59

National Agriculture Organisation
ST-ADK 28.04.78
ST-AEU 17.08.73
ST-AEV 04.01.74
ST-AGY 28.09.77
ST-AHH 07.11.79

National Air Operators
VT-DCM 31.03.56

National Air Transport
NC13304 10.10.33
NC13320 12.05.33
NC13324 24.11.33
NC421H 29.04.31
NC425E 25.02.33
NC427H 27.10.31

National Air Transport Services
NC38942 17.10.46

National Airlines
N4744 08.05.78
N74685 14.01.51
N8225H 06.01.60
N8228H 15.11.61
N90891 11.02.52
N90893 14.02.53
NC15555 11.10.45
NC18199 05.10.45
NC33349 13.09.45

National Airways [1]
ZS-DKR 06.10.70
ZS-HHF 15.01.85

National Airways [2]
G-BNAT 25.01.88
G-WSJE 12.09.87

National Aviation Day Displays
G-EBMM 24.09.34
G-EBMR 22.09.34

National Executive Flight Service
N4267C 09.01.64

National Flight Services
N477KW 25.08.82

National Helicopter Services
9Y-TFN 23.03.94

National Parks Airways
NC326N 28.11.33
NC7242 04.09.28

National Power Corporation
RP-C766 17.06.93

National Remote Sensing Agency
VT-EEL 05.04.77
VT-EQM 15.07.93

National Tire Wholesalers
N15TW 08.12.85

National Utility Helicopters
PK-UHN 26.01.75
PK-UHV oo.12.73

Nationwide Helicopters
C-FJTF 15.08.90

Nature Island Express
N42AK 24.01.92

Nautilus Aviation Management
555AJ 19.11.79

Navegacao Aerea Brasiliera
PP-NAE 15.02.45
PP-NAF 11.10.44
PP-NAR 22.09.58
PP-NAZ 22.11.59
PP-NMD 03.05.60

Navin Air Transport
NC35E 22.09.31

Navin, T.R.
NC7162 05.02.32

Nealco Air Services
9Y-PIA 05.01.91

Ned. Nieuw Guinea Petroleum
PK-AKB 02.02.42
PK-AKS 19.02.42
PK-AKT 25.12.41

Neece, S.R.
N303CA 05.03.92

Neilson Leasing
N100HK 17.06.85

Nepalese Royal Flight
9N-RF9 27.02.70

Nevada Airlines
N40438 16.11.79

New Creations
N458J 01.07.91

New England Air Express
NC58121 04.10.48

New England Airlines
N127JL 28.11.91
N14007 02.08.77

New England Airways
VH-BCH 08.08.47
VH-UPM 18.09.32

New England Propeller Service
N74844 16.07.71

New Holland Airways
VH-AEN 09.05.48

New Tribes Mission
N16030 09.06.50

New World Air Charter
N122A 27.08.78
N19CA oo.07.79

New York Airways
* 14.10.63
N558MA 15.07.69
N618PA 17.04.79
NC944M 14.06.32

New York Helicopters
N124NH 12.08.94
N49505 28.04.85

New York, Philadelphia & Washington AW
NC12221 05.11.31

New York, Rio & Buenos Aires Airlines
R-131 02.03.30
R-148 08.04.30

New Zealand Airways
ZK-AAY 12.02.37

New Zealand Ministry of Transport
ZK-AXS 06.11.70

New Zealand National Airways
ZK-AGJ 19.04.48
ZK-AGK 23.10.48
ZK-AKX 18.03.49
ZK-ALC 15.01.50
ZK-AOE 09.08.48
ZK-AQT 22.05.54
ZK-AYZ 03.07.63

Newcal Aviation
N400NC 27.08.92
N5488R 23.10.84

Newcastle Aviation
VH-BSS 14.01.94
VH-IAM 21.12.94

Newfoundland Airways
CF-GPG 18.08.50
VO-ABP 14.02.49

Newfoundland Labrador Air Transport
* 30.08.79

Nicholson Air Service
VH-DSM 13.12.79

Nigeria Airways
* 13.11.95
5N-AAW 25.04.77
5N-AAX 04.04.71
5N-ABD 20.11.69
5N-ABK 19.12.94
5N-ANA 02.03.78
5N-ANF 28.11.83
5N-ANR 10.01.87
5N-ANW 10.10.88
C-GMXQ 11.07.91
PH-FPT 18.09.72

Nigerian Air Force
5N-AAL 17.01.68

Nigerian Government
5N-AXP 31.12.85

Nihon Helicopters
JA9297 30.08.83

Nihon Kinkyori Airways
JA8693 11.03.83

Nihon Naigai Koku
JA8753 11.03.81

Nihon Norin Helicopters
JA9230 07.05.86
JA9315 27.01.90

Nile Delta Air Services
* 05.11.78

Nile Safari Aviation
ST-AHX 05.05.91
ST-AIW 26.09.89

Nippon Air Transport
* 11.02.38

Nippon Sangyo Airways
JA3212 15.01.82

Nitto Airlines
JA5067 18.02.64

Nolan's RV
N2727A 29.08.86

Noon, E.M.
VP-KFV 29.11.49

NorOntair
C-FTVP 31.12.77

Nord Aviation
F-WFUN 06.07.52

Nordair
C-FCSC 15.11.75
C-FNAZ 31.03.77
CF-HEI 09.08.61
CF-HTH 06.02.73
CF-IHV 20.12.72
CF-IQF 15.01.62
CF-NAD 15.05.67
CF-NAE oo.06.71

Nordchurchaid
N52676 26.09.69
N52679 08.05.69

Nordeste
PT-GKA 11.10.85
PT-LRJ 27.09.91
PT-SCU 11.11.91
PT-TBA 28.10.76
PT-TBB 03.02.92
PT-TBF 04.11.78

Norflyselskap
LN-NPH 04.09.68

Norfolk Island Airways
VH-FDR 07.08.85

Norman, S.E.
G-AHTB 02.11.47

Norrlandsflyg
SE-HHY 15.08.79
SE-HIP 03.09.79
SE-HNG 15.05.94

Norsk Luftseiladsforenings
N-24 oo.oo.25

North American Aircraft Trading
5T-TAC oo.01.68
5T-TAC 03.06.68
5T-TAG 01.07.68
5T-TAR 03.10.68
VR-BCY 07.12.68

North American Helicopter Service
N42475 04.11.86

North Australia Helicopters
VH-THI 25.05.78

North Cariboo Flying Service
C-GRJE 18.03.81

North Cay Airways
N864JA 02.10.74

North Central Airlines
N2045 27.12.68
N4825C 24.07.78
N90858 29.06.72
N954N 20.12.72

North Central Helicopters
C-FMZE 29.05.95

North Coast Air Services
C-FCZH 29.09.77

North Coast Airlines
P2-ISC 03.06.93

North Continent Airlines
N8404C 18.04.52

North East Bolivian Airways
CP-1090 13.01.84
CP-924 06.09.78

North Eastern Airways
G-ACSZ 29.05.37

North Pacific Airlines
N410UE 26.12.89
N50NP 04.02.85

North Sea Aerial & General Transport
G-ABWI 09.10.36
G-EAIT 05.05.25
G-EBKF 07.01.32
G-EBOM 25.09.28
G-EBOP 30.12.26
G-EBPZ 13.03.27
G-EAGV oo.09.20
G-EAGW oo.07.20

North Sea Air Transport
G-AISG 14.06.47
G-AIWZ 30.07.49

North Slope Supply Co
N174W 05.05.70

North Solomons Air Services
* 24.01.90

North Star Air Cargo
N50GA 23.06.90

North West Directorate
RA-23201 25.12.93
RA-25329 23.05.94

North West Parachute Centre
G-AXHE 05.02.94

North Western Air Transport
RA-11118 24.02.94

North-Wright Air
C-FKHD 12.01.94

Northair
G-ASTE 20.02.69

Northeast Airlines
N17891 30.11.54
N34417 15.09.57
N34954 01.02.57
N380NE 25.10.68
N6592C 15.11.61
N8224H 24.02.67
N90670 15.08.58
N91238 14.01.52
N91241 11.08.49

Northeast Jet Co
N125NE 21.05.80

Northern & Scottish Airways
G-ACYK 14.01.38
G-ADBU oo.11.36
G-ADEM 20.11.36

Northern Airmotive
N63B 20.08.91

Northern Airways
CF-BDZ 07.10.49

Northern Mountain Helicopters
C-FNMP 13.06.95
C-FNMQ 30.03.82
C-FROO 12.09.81
C-GLHS 15.07.94
C-GNMJ 07.02.90
C-GNMR 28.06.95
C-GPDH 18.08.94

Northern Pacific Transport
N2878F 06.07.85

Northern Peninsular Airlines
N168Z 30.06.85

Northern Rhodesia Government
VP-RCP 30.08.53

Northern Thunderbird Air
C-FBCD 26.07.84
C-FMHU 30.09.75
C-GNTB 14.01.77

Northern Wings
CF-BQQ 12.04.53
CF-DTS 26.10.57
CF-GDZ 14.10.52
CF-GKV 10.12.57
CF-ILY 19.03.57

Northland Air Manitoba
C-FADD 11.05.87
C-FFNC 03.11.89
C-GTPO oo.10.89

Northland Airlines
CF-BMW oo.oo.56
CF-GOA 16.04.63
CF-INT 25.03.63

Northland Helicopters
C-GXRS 18.08.90

Northrop Aircraft
NX8500H oo.02.48

Northway Aviation
C-GSGK 25.01.95

Northwest Agricultural Aviation
N9606 06.05.53

Northwest Airlines
N121US 17.03.60
N137US 16.09.61
N274US 01.12.74
N285 22.10.62
N290 03.06.63
N292 14.07.60
N312RC 16.08.87
N3313L 03.12.90
N46342 19.01.52
N48762 28.10.60
N575 28.08.58
N6214C 06.09.53
N724US 12.02.63
N74607 14.08.59
N74608 02.04.56
N93037 13.10.50
N93040 07.11.50
N93050 07.03.50
N93054 16.01.51
N95425 23.06.50
NC14243 07.08.34
NC14935 18.12.36
NC17383 08.07.38
NC17389 13.01.39
NC17394 16.05.38
NC21712 20.10.41
NC21714 12.05.42
NC88785 27.10.48
NC93044 29.08.48
NC95412 06.01.47
NC95422 12.03.48

Northwest Airlink
N334PX 01.12.93

Northwest Airways
NC7416 24.06.29
NC7739 25.06.30

Northwest Skyways
VH-POC 26.01.81

Northwestern Flying Services
C-FITW 18.09.80

Nucleo Comunicazioni Avio Linee
I-ELIO oo.11.40
I-ETRA oo.12.40

Nuna Air
OY-CGM 12.09.90

Nunasi Central Airlines
C-FGHL 17.05.86

Nurnberger Flugdienst
D-CABB 08.02.88

Nyge-Aero
SE-IOX 15.03.86

O'Brien, J.H.
NC7686 31.03.33

O'Connell, J.
VH-AGC 15.12.79

ODVF
* 25.05.25

OMCO Petroleum Co
N985 30.10.76

ORBI Georgian Airways
4L-65053 23.09.93
4L-65809 23.09.93
4L-85359 23.09.93

ORD Inc
N66KS 09.09.86

OTRAG Range Air Services
9Q-COE oo.06.79

Oakley Air
C-GHAV 06.05.91

Oasis
RP-C570 15.11.74

Occidental de Aviacion
HK-2415 08.09.91

Oefag-Flugdienst
OE-FCT 15.10.81

Oergel, F.
XB-NET oo.oo.55

Offshore Logistics
N1082H 11.07.89
N92AL 29.02.92

Okada Air
5N-AOT 07.09.89
5N-AOW 26.06.91

Okanagan Helicopters
* oo.10.85
C-GBEB 07.11.80
C-GIMF 30.04.82
C-GWLI 12.02.78

Okavango Air Services
A2-AEJ 26.12.85

Oklahoma Pipe Line Construction
N85B 06.12.54

Olag
OE-LAL 16.03.36

Oldstead Airlines
G-AFMF 19.02.54

Olley Air Services
G-ACPY 03.06.41
G-AJGD 15.07.49

Olympic Airways
SX-ASO 18.02.72
SX-BAD 29.10.59
SX-BBQ 21.10.72
SX-BBR 23.11.76
SX-DAE 08.12.69
SX-DAI 05.11.70

Olympic Aviation
SX-BGE 03.08.89
SX-HDB 29.04.92

Omani Royal Flight
A4O-AX 28.11.90

Omega Air
N32HG 16.06.92
N720MJ 20.09.90

Omniflight Helicopters
N16933 27.08.90
N911LF 04.11.94

Omsk Production
RA-26090 24.06.93

On Air
C-GRAM 11.12.76

Oneida
TG-LAM 30.05.78

Ontario Central Airlines
C-FBKX 15.02.83

Ontario Provincial Govt Air Service
CF-OAK 23.05.36

Onzeair
AP-ACM 01.08.48

Operator Unknown
* 07.05.35
* 15.08.37
* oo.09.37
* oo.04.39
* oo.01.47
* 28.10.51
* 07.03.55
* 19.12.55
* 23.02.57
* 11.08.67
* 05.02.69
* 05.10.74
* 28.12.74
* 07.07.77
* 20.07.77
* 14.12.77
* 03.01.78
* 22.06.78
* 19.07.78
* 22.12.79
* 12.07.80
* 22.09.80
* 16.09.82
* 08.10.83
* 14.03.85
* 03.04.86
* 23.10.86
* 07.10.87
* 07.10.87
* 23.01.88
* 24.04.88
* 29.07.89
* 28.06.91
* 22.09.91
* 11.05.92
* 20.11.93
* 05.05.94
* 10.08.95
* 17.08.95
* 22.09.95
* 05.10.95
* 10.10.95
* 25.10.95
5H-AAM 13.09.66
5R-MAN oo.oo.68
5Y-KLB 07.08.68
7Q-YMM 09.11.90
7T-VSH oo.01.76
9G-OTP oo.oo.70
9Q-COI 06.10.83
A-3 03.09.30
AN-ACC 22.04.46
AN-BFN 06.06.79
AP-AYQ 08.07.84
C-202 19.03.47
C-207 oo.oo.48
C-406 20.12.46
C-801 10.05.47
C-FAGM 24.03.84
C-FBER 02.09.86
C-FCAS 01.05.79
C-FCAU 30.08.85
C-FECD 22.06.82
C-FFEL 20.07.85
C-FFEO 15.02.93
C-FFLC 05.06.85
C-FHYX oo.10.73
C-FISM 16.06.78
C-FQMS 07.04.80
C-FRCL 28.08.76
C-FSSU 10.01.93
C-GBTI 06.05.91
C-GIRH 12.01.87
C-GJCM oo.oo.oo
C-GLOW 06.12.81
C-GMMR 16.02.84
C-GPPN 22.12.84
C-GQOD oo.oo.87
C-GTPB 18.09.87
C-GUNI oo.oo.89
C-GVBS 16.01.86
C-GVCE 21.11.84
C-GVYW 17.03.79
C-GWCY oo.10.81
C-GWUY 13.08.77
C-GYMR oo.10.88
CC-CCS 27.01.86
CF-AYO 23.08.53
CF-BRL 27.02.74
CF-FYR 26.12.54
CF-GPB 19.09.51
CF-OBH 30.08.50
CN-MBI 03.01.70
CP-1016 oo.oo.oo
CP-1804 06.03.86
CP-1849 14.03.84
CS-AHP 06.08.76
D-IAAE 11.06.82
D-IBAR 30.01.85
D-IDAS 03.11.78
D-IDNG 05.12.94
D-IFLY 21.11.85
D-IFSC 24.06.83
D-IHAN 09.08.79
D-IHLZ 18.06.73
D-IKOC 21.02.81
D-ILMA 13.08.69
D-ILNI 21.09.67
D-ILNU 16.02.67
D-ILSE 10.04.73
D-ILTU 22.01.71
D-IMWH 06.12.87
D-INIX 21.06.72
D-INUR 18.12.78
D-IOET 01.12.81
EC-CGG 22.11.74
EC-COJ 04.10.83
EC-CYJ 23.01.79
EC-ECB 30.09.87
EP-AGX 21.11.74
EP-AHN oo.oo.79
F-BGOL oo.oo.60
F-BOXS 05.05.78
F-BTDP 17.12.74
F-BUTV oo.07.92
F-BVRP 03.04.83
F-BXAR oo.oo.oo
F-GBDZ 15.12.82
F-GBRD 02.11.86
F-GCJN 18.08.81
F-GDHS 21.05.91
F-GDMM oo.oo.92
F-GEAI 19.05.29
F-GEBK oo.04.85
F-GEFR 28.08.86
F-GFMS 07.11.87
F-GGRZ 09.05.91
F-GHBE 08.02.91
F-GJHK 26.03.92
F-OAUH 14.11.56
F-OAVZ oo.09.56
F-OBKH oo.08.61
F-OBOD 27.04.65
F-OBRU 08.06.62
F-ODHU oo.oo.oo
F-ODSF oo.oo.oo
F-OGCA 10.02.69
G-AGLN 15.12.46
G-AGOP 25.06.48
G-AGUF 29.06.57
G-AHJA oo.oo.68
G-AHLL 21.05.59
G-AHTR 10.07.50
G-AHTS 29.04.47
G-AIZI 14.09.52
G-AJFN 04.12.47

G-AJFO 04.12.47
G-AJGZ 16.07.49
G-AJKW 07.05.67
G-AJSJ 18.09.47
G-AKLA 15.06.54
G-AKTZ 27.05.57
G-ALGO 10.07.51
G-ALXA 04.06.52
G-BBJG 06.12.74
G-CAFU 17.12.39
G-CAGC 12.08.30
G-CAGD 30.11.32
G-CAGE 05.01.28
G-CAHG 17.02.28
G-CAHH 29.08.28
G-CAIQ 09.01.29
G-CAIV 15.12.31
G-CAIX 12.03.31
G-CAIY 06.03.28
G-CAJD 10.12.31
G-CAJH 14.08.28
G-CAJJ 05.02.35
G-CANB 20.12.37
G-CANC 29.04.30
G-CARA 19.06.37
G-CARH 31.07.32
G-CARI oo.05.29
G-CARJ 09.08.29
G-CARM 15.06.39
G-CASD 23.12.29
G-CASE 10.06.33
G-CASF 02.06.30
G-CASJ 13.07.29
G-CASK 31.03.33
G-CASL 29.06.32
G-CASM 04.03.31
G-CASN 04.03.31
G-CASO 16.11.29
G-CASP 26.08.29
G-CASQ 17.11.38
G-CATR 09.02.33
G-CAVL 04.08.30
G-CAWB 21.03.37
HB-LMI 07.12.87
HB-VAP 01.10.67
HC-ACR oo.07.58
HC-BFI 17.10.78
HI-197 oo.oo.80
HI-578SP 21.01.90
HI-899 23.07.80
HK-1020 11.06.73
HK-1024 19.09.71
HK-1069 14.09.72
HK-1093X 27.08.73
HK-1095X 17.09.69
HK-1112G oo.07.73
HK-1147G 26.06.73
HK-1282 16.09.76
HK-2478P 15.06.90
HK-2484 28.06.81
HK-2489 28.10.85
HK-2686P oo.03.90
HK-3376 oo.oo.oo
HK-3382P 23.03.90
HK-454 19.06.59
HK-844 16.12.71
HL5223 oo.09.74
HL5261 oo.oo.84
HP-1018 oo.oo.84
HP-945 06.04.83
HR-AIV oo.01.86
HS-TFB 22.07.84
I-AMME 06.02.76
I-COTO oo.02.86
I-FRUT oo.oo.oo
I-KWYR 10.02.89
JA3115 01.05.63
JA5002 25.09.54
JA5012 24.08.54
JA5020 19.12.69
JA5028 16.03.64
JA5034 05.02.63
JA5035 14.09.61
JA5036 16.04.58
JA5037 26.07.60
JA5137 05.10.67
JA5162 30.05.72
JA5164 14.02.71
JA5169 14.02.71
LN-FOE 12.12.73
LN-OSD 12.11.77
LN-VIP 28.06.68
LN-VIP 11.10.85
LV-BDB oo.oo.91
LV-FEP 03.11.52
LV-JOD 15.03.89
LV-KAB oo.oo.oo
LV-LTA oo.12.75
LV-MAV 12.09.84
LV-MBR 14.09.80
LV-OEV 26.08.81
N100CT 03.09.84
N100GP 21.02.79
N100NL 16.10.71
N100SW 01.04.77
N1011R 24.03.81
N101LB oo.07.71
N101LR 15.09.81
N1028C 28.07.81
N102S 18.01.67
N103AQ 16.05.82
N1040G 28.10.82
N105PE 25.11.83
N106MA 07.05.91
N108CA 20.05.95
N108SC 24.06.92
N109TW 22.11.81
N111FN 04.09.83
N111QL 17.09.83
N1125J oo.03.93
N112L 24.08.92
N112SK 01.12.84
N113TC 16.07.74
N114EA 26.12.84
N114K 26.10.81
N115S 19.01.79
N116CA 21.08.83
N1214S 16.05.73
N1221S oo.oo.94
N123AX 24.01.84
N123CB 17.04.71
N123CB 05.04.82
N1283 11.09.88
N129D 17.08.83
N129GP 16.04.67
N132MA 16.04.72
N133MA 26.12.75
N137GL 19.01.79
N142ER 17.03.85
N145DC 05.11.79
N148CP 09.06.85
N149AA 07.11.86
N149JP 01.12.82
N14A 21.09.95
N14TC 20.07.84
N1583V 11.12.74
N15NY 02.08.79
N165MA 20.04.82
N171LG 28.08.95
N17530 20.10.77
N17689 30.06.90
N17690 03.12.85
N177MF 02.12.80
N178MA 25.08.78
N17ZD oo.oo.oo
N1812D 25.05.79
N182 15.01.80
N1824D 18.07.80
N18611 oo.oo.51
N18CS 10.04.76
N18SE oo.oo.87
N190M 17.08.86
N1910L 26.11.83
N1EM 25.03.76
N1HQ 05.11.82
N1KA oo.03.80
N1NR 14.08.72
N200BR 21.12.79
N200HL 20.09.74
N200PR 07.05.86
N200RC 25.09.73
N200SM 26.11.80
N2019U 13.02.85
N2021A 21.07.84
N2029N 30.12.78
N204AJ 16.09.89
N204CC 21.11.78
N208MA 03.08.79
N20M 15.12.72
N213S 28.04.83
N215W 30.06.83
N2181L 07.12.80
N218X 19.03.84
N21S 17.07.84
N220F 27.11.85
N221MJ 04.11.75
N2239Q 20.08.83
N2301N 22.11.78
N233MA 02.09.81
N234MA 26.11.79
N23796 23.09.77
N239P 29.01.70
N23LS oo.oo.oo
N2400X 08.03.76
N241FW 23.11.86
N242Q 07.09.80
N24CC 11.02.82
N250RP 27.01.95
N251M 09.04.79
N256TM 18.04.77
N25ST 21.08.89
N2614C oo.oo.91
N2627U 12.11.82
N26506 09.03.83
N2652Z 22.04.90
N274MA 22.02.91
N275MA 05.01.85
N27886 21.03.84
N278DU 10.07.78
N27948 02.08.84
N27GP 13.07.82
N2845D 20.02.82
N2886D 29.07.85
N28SE 30.06.85
N2937A 31.10.84
N295X 01.05.72
N2960Q 21.06.83
N297MA 28.02.78
N2990F 08.09.83
N299F 27.05.78
N2AQ 27.05.81
N2GG 15.02.75
N2MF 19.03.78
N300MA 08.02.76
N301AJ 13.08.90
N30276 12.09.84
N302EJ 14.04.83
N304D 08.11.86
N304L 21.04.79
N307MA 23.04.80
N308PS 18.11.88
N309MA 21.09.95
N30PC 10.04.89
N30Y 13.02.86
N3107W 03.03.89
N3128B 28.12.76
N320MC 09.03.73
N321MA 04.04.77
N3251 10.10.85
N32809 01.11.84
N3291Q 05.03.84
N32LD 14.02.77
N32RL 30.09.87
N332K 03.09.79
N333CA 22.08.73
N333FB 23.06.83
N333FL 04.10.80
N333MA 24.03.74
N336SA 10.01.82
N33S 10.09.80
N346MA 14.02.80
N34F 10.03.77
N34SM 03.02.77
N3517W 28.03.85
N3550X 21.12.68
N35PK 08.08.82
N366AA 31.08.74
N36941 01.04.80
N36962 oo.oo.oo
N36MK 28.12.70
N37097 30.07.80
N37490 14.12.86
N3768Z 10.04.81
N3804F 05.11.89
N380MA 13.08.82
N386G 16.08.83
N388MC 10.01.78
N3911C 02.09.95
N397F 22.02.76
N399T 31.01.75
N39DT 28.07.87
N39YV 12.05.89
N3ED 17.06.81
N3RB 17.09.85
N400AM 10.09.83
N400BG 01.10.85
N400NA 11.08.83
N402CS 15.05.85
N402V 23.09.85
N403SE 17.10.82
N404C 24.05.84
N404SA 22.12.77
N4060A 05.03.83
N4091U 24.12.82
N40LB 25.09.73
N40MP 12.11.74
N41010 06.11.93
N41045 31.10.82
N4115K 04.12.83
N41169 14.02.89
N411X 28.03.72
N4146S 18.04.75
N4207S 31.07.77
N4213S 01.02.85
N421AR 06.11.86
N43GT 01.10.89
N43L 10.09.80
N440MA 27.01.83
N441CM 25.12.84
N441NC 11.01.80
N444AR 18.11.81
N444LM 03.05.85
N444PA 20.10.83
N444PV 14.04.83
N444SR 17.02.85
N44609 05.12.83
N4469R 31.08.84
N4499B 06.09.84
N44MR 30.11.80
N454RN 26.02.73
N455JH oo.09.86
N4567L 22.07.82
N456L 27.03.80
N45873 09.07.78
N45Q 12.10.90
N466MA 19.04.84
N469DM 15.09.82
N46WA 13.01.94
N473MA 18.03.83
N4758N 17.07.82
N480K 27.12.71
N48RM 20.04.79
N4GN 10.03.80
N4TS 24.10.83
N500GL 19.04.81
N500J 26.09.76
N500JP 27.01.81
N500NL 23.02.75
N500X 26.11.69
N501GP 21.01.81
N5058E 20.11.82
N50PC 01.12.74
N50VS 02.01.89
N50WT 09.01.95
N520R 11.01.83
N521AC 14.09.83
N5296M 10.04.73
N529N 11.03.66
N530N 01.05.93
N531MA 18.02.76
N5329M 03.03.77
N53AD 05.11.81
N541W 03.10.70
N542TW 28.06.85
N5473G 19.07.85
N549LK 13.10.70
N551TR 26.09.86
N55555 03.04.81
N555AM 10.06.81
N5565 15.01.74
N5589S 15.12.82
N55ED 19.09.83
N55LP 31.08.84
N55MG 26.11.77
N563W 09.08.90
N5654M 31.05.79
N568H 26.10.76
N57186 17.11.76
N57233 01.10.79
N575HC 19.05.85
N576M 21.06.83
N57948 31.08.74
N57V 25.01.75
N5860K 13.12.81
N5889N oo.oo.86
N5926K 16.10.81
N5957K 29.03.82
N59771 12.11.82
N5NP 08.03.78
N5NW 23.01.79

N600NA	15.09.79
N601G	08.08.76
N6040M	05.08.79
N611VP	oo.05.88
N617MS	24.06.87
N618K	24.01.95
N61PH	oo.10.91
N620AC	26.03.84
N6231G	01.08.84
N6272C	10.03.82
N631SR	15.07.81
N63WW	11.08.84
N64MD	09.02.90
N65103	19.10.79
N65388	11.12.83
N660RB	17.05.88
N662DM	21.06.87
N6675	04.10.81
N66HA	oo.oo.89
N66U	oo.oo.82
N673Q	10.01.95
N67E	22.05.93
N67KM	14.06.75
N6814G	03.02.84
N68174	oo.03.64
N6819N	30.06.81
N68392	oo.02.81
N6843S	29.11.76
N684LT	24.09.85
N6857E	16.07.86
N6858S	21.02.87
N68653	29.01.86
N6867Q	17.06.81
N6867R	30.08.81
N68A	03.06.77
N6911	29.04.82
N6924C	15.10.78
N69303	13.09.95
N69378	05.03.77
N693PG	18.09.95
N696JB	28.03.90
N6981R	05.02.84
N69K	21.01.83
N69QJ	13.11.75
N6VR	19.07.86
N700R	23.12.85
N700SP	26.04.75
N700W	08.03.82
N701DM	28.02.89
N703WC	18.10.68
N704D	28.09.80
N705M	05.12.83
N707BP	31.07.93
N707CE	29.05.90
N7093L	12.10.93
N711FC	20.12.73
N711JT	13.03.75
N711TT	08.10.87
N719MS	07.04.84
N720Q	24.06.74
N723T	26.02.86
N724N	22.12.79
N7250	29.09.90
N727MA	07.11.85
N729F	15.02.80
N72B	24.03.83
N7428C	oo.10.90
N742PC	28.08.87
N743R	13.04.73
N74FA	22.02.86
N750MA	19.11.81
N757Q	20.11.72
N758Q	15.04.69
N762D	19.02.77
N764Q	16.01.70
N765MA	28.08.78
N772CB	28.03.85
N77777	16.03.84
N777EC	07.01.79
N777MA	18.03.77
N7842M	16.01.74
N787Q	28.01.81
N78B	09.03.87
N78D	05.12.71
N78L	08.11.86
N791K	13.03.73
N799V	02.11.91
N8001Q	11.12.82
N80162	02.03.81
N805Q	07.08.81
N8064Q	22.12.84
N808W	14.04.85
N8091Q	24.09.82
N810Q	05.04.86
N8111	23.03.95
N81416	14.02.83
N8149S	22.02.94
N81502	09.10.84
N81521	07.01.81
N81717	17.01.84
N8369G	21.11.81
N83MC	20.01.84
N847	23.04.77
N847CE	12.09.75
N85	14.01.76
N8517Z	13.12.84
N854Q	07.01.77
N8590D	23.06.87
N85JM	17.02.93
N873Q	01.11.79
N878T	27.02.78
N882Q	03.06.73
N887PE	15.09.89
N88832	oo.09.79
N888AR	07.08.76
N888MA	12.02.78
N88CR	16.01.79
N88JF	oo.10.86
N895K	05.08.82
N89DA	15.11.82
N89PB	07.09.84
N8CC	06.06.86
N9001N	05.05.69
N9019N	28.12.71
N9060N	25.11.70
N908CM	25.08.80
N91378	oo.07.83
N9150N	25.08.84
N9202N	26.06.70
N920G	27.12.74
N9229Y	20.12.84
N9253Y	04.01.86
N925J	12.11.86
N925YC	05.11.79
N92JR	13.05.81
N932E	11.07.84
N936K	03.01.73
N9394A	29.12.80
N94523	18.10.80
N94537	28.01.52
N94538	28.01.52
N9497Z	16.01.77
N94HD	11.11.78
N9503Z	07.03.73
N95HA	31.01.85
N960M	14.04.75
N962MA	23.02.80
N9684R	13.12.80
N9724Y	26.09.80
N9826Z	01.08.81
N98457	08.08.84
N9846Z	15.03.82
N984HF	07.11.85
N987GM	31.05.89
N98949	05.05.82
N990L	08.03.75
N9929Z	18.03.77
N9971G	15.11.77
N999CR	18.03.81
N9JS	22.04.81
N9PU	09.12.89
NC105H	oo.05.34
NC14941	25.02.46
NC79822	20.05.48
NR13352	27.05.50
NR1776	30.05.32
OB-1212	07.05.92
OB-1542	16.10.94
OB-M-1031	14.02.79
OB-T-1211	oo.05.82
OK-NYA	09.07.94
OO-CCR	24.08.48
OO-TBW	15.08.76
OY-BEP	18.09.82
OY-BGK	07.10.87
PH-SYG	30.11.94
PI-51	20.05.64
PI-52	21.06.57
PI-55	21.02.64
PI-56	21.05.57
PI-C835	02.02.62
PJ-AIK	13.08.48
PJ-AIM	oo.08.49
PJ-AIT	13.08.48
PJ-AKA	11.08.48
PJ-AKB	11.08.48
PK-AKH	06.05.70
PK-AKR	28.08.50
PK-PHA	25.09.55
PK-PHB	09.01.65
PT-CXK	04.05.73
PT-DUX	27.09.71
PT-IBE	28.07.77
PT-IBR	26.09.76
PT-JXS	16.03.75
PT-KXO	05.10.77
PT-LGJ	06.09.88
PT-LMA	24.02.88
PZ-TAR	23.06.65
PZ-TAT	14.04.67
RP-C999	27.10.93
S9-NAA	oo.oo.88
SE-FGE	23.07.73
SE-GUU	14.10.85
SE-IOU	16.02.86
SSSR-20973	03.04.92
TF-RPM	12.04.51
TG-SAB	16.01.83
TR-LSW	oo.06.75
TR-LYA	20.04.78
TR-LYQ	03.07.82
TZ-ACS	oo.05.85
TZ-ADN	oo.10.87
TZ-ASC	oo.oo.oo
VH-CJP	oo.11.83
VH-FSA	20.02.84
VH-IBC	oo.oo.88
VH-LFH	25.07.90
VH-MUA	26.01.90
VH-SSL	12.01.93
VH-UBN	20.07.44
VH-UVN	07.01.42
VH-UXG	19.04.54
VH-UXK	29.08.38
VH-UZD	oo.oo.90
VH-UZX	26.02.38
VH-WBQ	21.06.87
VH-WGI	17.09.93
VH-WMU	07.11.90
VP-KFW	08.08.48
VP-RCA	oo.11.51
VQ-PAF	13.01.39
VR-BQD	24.07.95
VT-CIS	oo.oo.50
VT-DFM	oo.oo.87
VT-EUJ	09.07.94
XA-COL	12.10.73
XA-DIS	20.11.83
XA-DOE	oo.oo.46
XA-FEX	02.03.81
XA-FOT	15.02.78
XA-GOC	13.01.48
XA-LIG	05.05.84
XA-SMH	25.03.95
XB-AEA	30.01.80
XB-CIJ	oo.oo.88
XB-DYP	19.01.89
XB-ESO	11.10.90
XB-JOY	29.06.76
XB-LIJ	30.11.75
XB-NUV	13.10.76
XB-PEX	oo.oo.65
XC-AA26	oo.oo.94
XC-ICP	28.01.73
XC-PGR	28.10.79
XC-UPJ	oo.oo.oo
YR-APF	23.10.79
YR-APV	20.10.74
YR-BNS	11.11.92
YR-PBE	10.07.87
YR-PMG	14.11.89
YR-PVC	14.01.78
YR-PVJ	21.07.81
YR-PVS	30.09.88
YR-PVU	13.08.85
YS-28	17.03.47
YU-BBJ	oo.oo.66
YU-BBN	15.09.91
YU-BGI	oo.oo.oo
YU-BKE	oo.05.90
YU-BKF	26.01.92
YV-247P	11.10.86
YV-257CP	oo.03.81
YV-270P	oo.oo.oo
YV-426P	04.02.82
YV-597C	12.01.89
YV-994P	04.02.82
YV-O-CDO-2	03.11.78
YV-O-MAR-2	17.08.78
YV-O-MAR-6	15.06.77
YV-P-APJ	15.07.48
YV-T-ADJ	10.05.73
ZK-SFE	19.03.89
ZP-TDH	oo.10.62
ZS-ATV	05.06.51
ZS-ATW	11.12.46
ZS-AYG	31.10.46
ZS-BCI	06.09.52
ZS-BEA	22.02.55
ZS-BVR	12.02.67
ZS-BZU	10.09.54
ZS-DJT	11.10.63
ZS-IHZ	26.12.92
ZS-KOF	04.06.91
ZS-KRS	16.09.81
ZS-KVB	20.06.84
ZS-KVG	05.06.83

Opolskie Aero Club

SP-AMK	16.09.84

Orient Airways

AP-AAD	02.08.53
AP-AAF	13.10.54
AP-AAZ	22.10.52
AP-AEG	14.03.53

Orient Pacific Airways

N48060	21.08.76

Oriental Airlines

5N-IMO	18.09.94

Orion Aero Taxi

PT-OMV	23.03.94

Orion Air

N181TG	01.06.84
N68TG	15.07.83

Orion Helicopters

N7881S	25.06.94

Orissa State Government

VT-CLA	21.10.47

Osaka Airways

JA9286	15.12.81

Oseste Linhas Aereas

PP-SBJ	23.03.93

Osterman Helikopter

SE-HRD	16.09.86

Outdoor Aviation

ZK-WED	02.01.86

Overland Air Services

VH-ARL	oo.08.51
VH-BFI	13.01.52

Overseas Aviation

G-AHGU	11.10.60
G-AJCE	14.08.61

Overseas National Airlines

N1031F	02.01.76
N1032F	12.11.75
N312A	20.06.61
N317A	26.09.61
N79992	17.11.51
N8635	04.03.77
N913R	15.01.81

Oxaero Ltd

G-BGEO	18.08.87

Ozark Air Lines

N4215	23.07.73
N974Z	27.12.68

P.G.R.

XC-AA38	19.10.92

PA Osijek

YU-BBM	oo.oo.89
YU-BFS	19.09.91

YU-BHU 19.09.91
YU-BOC 08.09.91
YU-BOD oo.11.87
YU-BOZ 15.09.91

PAB
* 18.04.56

PJ Helicopters
N10800 01.07.94

PLM Helicopters
G-BAYA 09.01.77
G-PLMA 05.05.95
G-PLMG 07.12.94

PM Air
N3558W 21.09.90
N835FE 17.01.90

Pacific Air Express
N300JT 29.06.83

Pacific Air Lines
N2770R 07.05.64
N93202 21.08.59

Pacific Air Transport
NC10348 02.06.32
NC431H 24.01.33
NC5589 16.05.32

Pacific Airmotive Corporation
N4277C 09.12.52
NC974Y oo.oo.42

Pacific Airways
* 20.10.84
* 13.10.88
* 11.07.92

Pacific Alaska Air Express
NC66637 04.11.48

Pacific Alaska Airlines
N777DG oo.09.81
N77DG 17.02.75

Pacific Alaska Airways
NC153H oo.02.34
NC9170 06.01.34
NC9172 oo.11.33
NC9765 20.09.33

Pacific Aviation
VH-AAH 18.12.61

Pacific Coastal Airlines
C-FDMR 17.09.94
C-FZVV 18.09.79
C-GPCA 18.04.79

Pacific Helicopters
* 04.10.91
P2-FHE 19.09.94
P2-PHB 19.09.94

Pacific Island Aviation
N5074J 27.10.92

Pacific Northern Airlines
N1554V 14.06.60
N86523 06.06.66

Pacific Overseas Airways
HS-POS 11.03.51

Pacific Petroleum
CF-TCU 04.11.49

Pacific Resorts
VH-ISG 03.12.75

Pacific Southwest Airlines
N208PA 05.03.74
N350PS 07.12.87
N533PS 25.09.78
N7307R 15.03.77

Pacific Western Airlines
* 10.03.66
C-FPWC 11.02.78
C-FPWX 21.11.76
C-GQPW 22.03.84
CF-BLV oo.01.60
CF-BQH 29.09.61
CF-BYM 01.10.57
CF-EFZ 27.01.58
CF-FJL 08.10.58
CF-FOF 20.08.58
CF-GBT 17.09.55
CF-HFP 25.06.57
CF-PWD 29.01.60
CF-PWO 16.07.69
CF-PWR 18.09.69
CF-PWZ 02.01.73
CF-TFZ 30.05.56

Paget, K.K.
CF-EIG 06.12.54

Pak Air
AP-ACE 26.11.48
AP-ADI 12.12.49

Pakistan Airways
AP-ABZ 09.05.48

Pakistan International Airlines
AP-AAC 22.03.61
AP-AAH 26.03.65
AP-ACZ 25.02.56
AP-AEH 15.05.58
AP-AJC 18.05.59
AP-AJE 14.08.59
AP-AJS 01.07.57
AP-ALM 06.08.70
AP-ALN 06.07.94
AP-ALO 25.06.64
AP-ALX 13.12.71
AP-AMH 20.05.65
AP-AOA 10.12.66
AP-AOC 02.02.66
AP-ATO 17.12.78
AP-ATT 08.10.65
AP-AUS 08.12.72
AP-AUV 30.12.70
AP-AUW 28.05.73
AP-AUX 23.10.86
AP-AVZ 15.12.71
AP-AWH 05.12.71
AP-AWZ 26.11.79
AP-AXE 02.02.81
AP-AXF 06.06.81
AP-AXK 08.01.81
AP-BBF 25.08.89
AP-BCH 15.09.85
AP-BCP 28.09.92

Palair Macedonian Airlines
PH-KXL 05.03.93

Palfe
EC-FAH 02.03.93

Pan Adria
YU-ADV 16.12.71
YU-ALA 19.06.77

Pan African Air Charter
ZS-AYB 12.01.49
ZS-BYX 31.12.48

Pan African Airlines
5N-ACS 20.08.79
N480G 10.11.69
N90427 28.09.68
N9982H 24.05.69

Pan Alaska Airways
N123PA 22.10.70

Pan American Airways
* 12.08.38
42-38257 10.03.42
N1023V 02.06.58
N1032V 26.03.55
N1033V 10.04.59
N1039V 29.04.52
N317PA 15.11.66
N327PA 03.09.80
N407PA 17.12.73
N417PA 22.07.73
N446PA 22.04.74
N454PA 30.01.74
N458PA 03.11.73
N461PA 25.07.71
N4737 09.07.82
N494PA 12.12.68
N5026K 22.06.59
N704Y oo.oo.33
N708PA 17.09.65
N709PA 08.12.63
N736PA 27.03.77
N738PA 04.08.83
N739PA 21.12.88
N740PA 20.02.59
N74170 15.06.50
N74176 08.08.51
N745PA 18.02.61
N752PA 06.09.70
N779PA 07.04.64
N798PA 13.06.68
N799PA 26.12.68
N88846 22.06.51
N88899 11.04.52
N88900 12.09.59
N90662 02.09.51
N90941 09.07.59
N90943 16.10.56
N90944 09.11.57
NC113M 25.09.32
NC14714 28.07.38
NC14715 21.01.43
NC14716 08.01.45
NC15066 03.08.45
NC15376 10.03.41
NC16734 11.01.38
NC16735 07.12.41
NC16736 27.07.43
NC18114 15.07.38
NC18601 04.11.45
NC18603 22.02.43
NC197H 19.09.29
NC21V 11.12.41
NC33611 04.06.45
NC53 15.08.28
NC55 15.08.28
NC5933 12.08.31
NC660M 16.04.35
NC668M 24.09.43
NC737N oo.oo.36
NC742N oo.oo.36
NC8020 30.12.29
NC8042 29.10.28
NC8044 26.05.33
NC810H oo.11.30
NC823M 08.08.44
NC824M 20.12.35
NC88831 24.09.46
NC88845 19.06.47
NC88858 15.04.48
NC88911 20.09.47
NC88920 26.10.47
NC9664 02.10.32
NC9700 13.06.29
NC9713 01.01.29
NC9717 03.04.32
NC9786 oo.oo.oo

Pan Arctic Oil
C-FPAB 29.10.74
C-GKBO 09.05.82

Pan Aviation
N96GS 06.01.90

Pan Malaysian Air Transport
9M-PID 30.01.93
9M-PIF 03.02.93

Pan-Air
VH-PAQ 13.02.79

Panagra
N51702 29.10.62
NC14272 19.07.38
NC14273 11.10.36
NC14292 oo.oo.42
NC14298 23.08.37
NC15065 02.08.37
NC16928 26.06.41
NC19470 04.01.45
NC306N 07.02.31
NC33645 22.01.43
NC403H 16.07.32
NC407H 22.03.34
NC433H 24.12.34
NC8023 03.02.31
NC8026 oo.02.31
NC8417 11.06.34
NC8418 01.04.31
NC9424 08.05.35
NC9723 11.03.33
NC9726 oo.06.29
NC9737 14.08.30

Panair do Brasil
P-BDAD oo.oo.oo
PP-PAL oo.07.33
PP-PAM oo.oo.38
PP-PAR 08.02.37
PP-PAU oo.oo.oo
PP-PBA oo.oo.oo
PP-PBD 18.08.41
PP-PBH 21.09.44
PP-PBI 30.08.44
PP-PBL 25.04.38
PP-PBM 13.08.39
PP-PBN 03.01.47
PP-PBQ 22.10.46
PP-PCF 14.07.62
PP-PCG 28.07.50
PP-PCH 27.09.46
PP-PCN 28.02.52
PP-PCR 03.03.62
PP-PDA 17.06.53
PP-PDB oo.oo.oo
PP-PDC 26.01.61
PP-PDE 14.12.62
PP-PDJ 16.06.55
PP-PDL 14.10.61
PP-PDM 08.04.63
PP-PDO 01.11.61
PP-PDT 20.08.62
PP-PDU 06.09.63
PP-PEE 22.01.65

Panama Cargo Three
HP-1200CTH 20.02.93

Panamanian Government
HP-1141P 21.12.89

Panavia Cargo
N88909 18.04.78

Paninternational
D-ALAR 06.09.71

Panorama Air
N27512 20.11.87

Panorama Air Tours
N215H 03.10.82
N712AN 23.12.87

Panorama Flight Service
N13SE 13.01.95
N1JR 28.07.84

Papillon Airways
N87966 21.05.91

Papillon Hawaiian Helicopters
N151BH 14.07.94
N766MP 23.02.94

Papuan Air Transport
VH-BMD 18.12.54
VH-BMN 22.12.54
VH-PAT 08.04.61

Paradise Airlines
N86504 01.03.64

Paraense Transportes Aereos
- PP-BTA 06.05.59
- PP-BTB 31.05.58
- PP-BTE 27.06.62
- PP-BTF 22.09.60
- PP-BTH 12.08.65
- PP-BTJ 24.08.60
- PP-BTQ 04.04.64
- PP-BTR 05.05.63
- PP-BTU 28.06.64
- PP-BTX 27.03.68
- PP-BUF 14.03.70
- PP-LDH 06.01.59
- PT-BEE 15.07.59

Paraguay Air Services
- ZP-CBM 22.12.57

Paramount Air
- C-GRUW 27.02.90

Paris Flying Club
- F-BMCY 29.03.81

Pars Air
- EP-JBC 24.04.78
- EP-PAC 17.03.83
- EP-PAE 11.08.72
- EP-PBE 03.11.82

Partnair
- LN-PAA 25.09.77
- LN-PAA 08.09.89

Pasquelle, B.
- XB-FIP 00.00.64

Patair
- VH-PAU 00.03.61

Pathet Lao Airlines
- * 00.00.74

Patricia Air Services
- C-FBKV 12.05.77

Patrick Motors
- G-AJOI 07.12.50

Patterson McCarthy Leasing
- N14273 14.05.71

Paul Kelly Flying Service
- N234F 14.11.65

Pawan Hans
- VT-EKQ 11.12.89
- VT-EKR 07.02.89
- VT-ELO 15.12.89

Payloads
- G-AIOO 27.11.47

Peace Air
- C-FAZM 00.07.77

Peacock's Flying Service
- N241DT 25.05.93

Pearl Air
- 9Q-CRT 09.08.77

Pel-Air
- VH-AJS 27.04.95

Pelita Air Service
- * 21.12.75
- PK-PCL 24.01.84
- PK-PCM 02.01.90
- PK-PDH 07.02.76
- PK-PDL 12.07.76
- PK-PDU 28.05.82
- PK-PDV 00.00.89
- PK-PDW 02.02.76
- PK-PEA 04.11.76
- PK-PEC 30.12.76
- PK-PEY 28.06.76
- PK-PFC 13.10.80
- PK-PGD 09.06.75
- PK-PGP 04.02.95
- PK-PGW 18.02.76
- PK-PGY 03.08.76
- PK-PHL 20.01.76
- PK-PHQ 01.12.76
- PK-PHY 09.04.72
- PK-PIW 07.01.88
- PK-PLV 23.09.94
- PK-PUD 23.04.94
- PK-PUF 30.04.90
- PK-PUI 06.12.90
- PK-XCE 00.00.80

Pemberton Helicopters
- C-GXWR 08.04.95

Penarth Commercial Properties
- G-BPCP 01.10.80

Penas
- XW-PEH 01.02.72

Penaza Air Unit
- RA-11337 14.03.95

Penina
- CS-AJO 00.11.82

Peninsula Air Services
- VH-RED 03.09.86
- VH-UDM 10.05.78

Peninsula Airways
- N63719 14.02.85
- N8402S 22.08.92
- N95468 23.01.81

Peninsula Skydiving
- N19CR 12.09.95

Pennsylvania Air Lines
- NC9124 21.10.32

Pennsylvania Central Airlines
- NC12919 11.12.46
- NC13359 16.04.41
- NC21786 06.01.46
- NC21788 02.02.42
- NC21789 31.08.40
- NC25692 14.04.45
- NC88842 13.06.47
- NC91068 12.09.46

Perdigao SA Comercio y Industria
- PT-ATP 06.02.64

Perez, T.
- N33649 12.06.77

Pernambuco District Government
- PT-FAW 26.09.90

Perris Valley Parachute Center
- N157U 04.05.85

Perris Valley Skydivers
- N141PV 22.04.92

Persian Air Services
- EP-ADA 14.09.55
- EP-ADB 17.09.56
- EP-ADE 05.07.59

Pertambangan Minjak Nasional
- PK-PEP 10.03.81

Peruana de Aviacion
- OB-1434 20.05.91

Peruvian International Airways
- OB-SAF-175 12.12.48

Peruvian Police
- PNP 224 04.03.95
- PNP-021 20.05.89

Peterborough Parachute Centre
- G-BHCR 15.02.81
- G-BIZP 18.12.83
- G-OVAN 28.12.93

Petroleos Mexicanos
- XC-BII 17.05.67

Petroleum Air Services
- SU-CAP 06.07.93
- SU-CAT 25.04.91

Petroleum Helicopters
- * 08.12.77
- * 01.11.84
- N16841 09.03.85
- N3120X 15.02.92
- N31223 19.02.85
- N3594N 11.07.85
- N3595B 11.07.89
- N3596N 21.12.87
- N3607C 29.07.85
- N3909F 26.08.91
- N47307 14.07.88
- N49496 07.05.78
- N49746 19.05.81
- N541BN 17.06.91
- N6610L 09.04.92

Petroleum Helicopters de Colombia
- HK-1307 25.12.77
- HK-744E 18.09.77

Petrolift Aviation
- N20DL 06.05.91
- N41JP 06.05.91

Phaega Corporation
- C-GYTC 23.03.86

Philair
- RP-C287 13.12.83

Philippine Aero Transport
- RP-C2135 08.01.76
- RP-C2136 21.12.75

Philippine Air Express
- * 02.11.47

Philippine Air Lines
- EI-BTJ 13.12.87
- EI-BZG 11.05.90
- PI-C10 00.00.48
- PI-C1022 21.04.73
- PI-C1027 28.11.72
- PI-C107 28.10.49
- PI-C11 16.06.47
- PI-C1131 12.09.69
- PI-C12 25.01.47
- PI-C126 22.12.60
- PI-C133 23.11.60
- PI-C14 20.04.48
- PI-C142 15.10.53
- PI-C143 17.05.48
- PI-C144 20.10.65
- PI-C145 21.01.48
- PI-C15 19.11.60
- PI-C16 14.07.60
- PI-C17 29.06.66
- PI-C22 24.01.50
- PI-C270 30.03.52
- PI-C291 15.11.48
- PI-C294 14.01.54
- PI-C3 00.00.48
- PI-C36 00.00.48
- PI-C38 30.12.52
- PI-C430 12.01.60
- PI-C485 13.10.62
- PI-C489 02.03.63
- PI-C5 10.03.52
- PI-C501 28.02.67
- PI-C503 12.10.62
- PI-C504 01.07.70
- PI-C527 06.07.67
- PI-C53 26.12.47
- PI-C532 09.05.70
- PI-C59 13.09.47
- PI-C9 19.11.70
- PI-C92 16.10.46
- PI-C97 21.02.64
- PI-C98 05.05.49
- RP-C1014 11.07.82
- RP-C1015 26.06.87
- RP-C1028 03.02.75
- RP-C1029 10.05.75
- RP-C1071 16.07.92
- RP-C1161 23.05.76
- RP-C1182 04.08.84
- RP-C1193 20.07.89
- RP-C1419 17.07.77
- RP-C803 18.04.77

Phillips, S.J.
- N91827 00.00.63

Phoenix 2000 Air Taxi
- HA-ACA 25.03.93

Phoenix Air
- N521PA 14.12.94
- N79SF 08.01.88
- N8056 20.04.93

Phoenix Air Group
- N125CA 29.06.89

Phoenix Airlines [1]
- ZS-DFW 29.08.52

Phoenix Airlines [2]
- N128MP 15.03.89

Piasecki Aircraft
- * 01.07.86

Pickfords Ltd
- G-AILF 20.08.50

Piedmont Air Cargo
- N347G 26.02.92

Piedmont Airlines
- N40401 21.08.62
- N40406 20.11.66
- N40446 09.07.66
- N55V 30.10.59
- N68650 19.07.67
- N712U 10.08.68
- N752N 25.10.86

Piedra, L.A.
- * 05.01.49

Pieter Kiewit & Son
- N1135K 24.02.66

Pilgrim Airlines
- N124PM 10.02.70
- N127PM 21.02.82
- N148PM 13.01.84
- N451C 01.02.82

Pinders Charter Service
- N28377 04.06.81

Pinehurst Airlines
- N57131 28.03.77

Pink Aviation Services
- OE-FDL 07.06.95

Pinto, A.
- CP-1054 05.08.76

Pioneer Airlines [1]
- N30093 07.12.82

Pioneer Airlines [2]
- 5Y-AMS 07.08.84
- 5Y-MBP 11.02.83

Pioneer Airways
- CF-ALD 30.07.35

Piper Aircraft Corporation
- n/a 23.06.72

Pitcairn Aviation
4231 22.05.28
5564 26.05.28

Pittsburgh Airways
NC9611 20.12.30

Pittston Corporation
N236JP 31.10.69

Plane Speaking Corporation
NR1661 00.00.33
NR9614 02.06.33

Pluna
CX-AEG 18.01.46
CX-AGE 09.10.62
CX-AQO 11.05.75

Pobjoy Airmotors & Aircraft
G-ADDT 26.07.36

Polish Agricultural Aviation
SP-BSF 05.02.79
SP-DNM 31.03.87

Polish Police
* 11.01.91

Polyarnaya Aviatsiya
SSSR-N18 00.00.34
SSSR-N2 00.08.37
SSSR-N3 08.09.32
SSSR-N43 03.05.36
SSSR-N45 08.09.34
SSSR-N5 00.04.32
SSSR-N6 15.08.32
SSSR-N9 00.00.34

Polynesian Airlines
5W-FAB 11.05.66
5W-FAC 13.01.70
5W-FAF 20.08.88
ZK-BMQ 04.12.60

Polynesian Airways
N33AP 14.02.92

Portalia Air Transport
9XR-KH 18.04.73

Portsmouth Aviation
G-AHYW 16.10.46

Portsmouth, Southsea & IOW Aviation
G-ABVB 30.05.36

Portuguese Air Ministry
* 06.04.27

Post, W.
NR12283 15.08.35

Precision Flite Inc
N44CJ 01.10.81

Predator
N26RT 23.02.89

President Airlines
N90773 10.09.61

Price, H. & V.
N169RF 07.11.92

Prinair
N554PR 24.06.72
N575PR 24.07.79

Prince Aly Khan
G-AIYI 24.08.49
G-AJZT 09.06.51

Prince Bilbesco
CV-FAI 17.04.31

Prine Inc
N690JC 25.06.92

Privolzhskoye Air Transport
RA-14131 18.03.94

Privolzhskoye Directorate
RA-11340 08.02.94

Privredna Avijacija
YU-BFP 15.09.91

Procuradoria General de la Republica
XC-BOS 28.10.79

Procuraduria General de la Republica
XC-PGR 01.04.94

Professional Aviation Services
ZS-DHX 31.08.92
ZS-KCV 07.11.93

Professional Jet Management
N66JE 21.02.95

Projeto Rondon
PP-FOR 18.10.74

Pronto Aviation Services
N102BL 30.07.82

Propair
C-FRWK 20.04.87

Prospec
PT-KAC 11.08.80

Proteus Petroleum Aviation
G-AJHO 05.02.89

Providence Air Charter
N145PA 05.04.79
N149PA 04.04.79

Provincetown-Boston Airlines
* 27.08.67
N120PB 30.06.84
N96PB 06.12.84

Provincial Air Services
VH-BSG 17.11.80

Provincial Air Transport
P2-MBM 29.07.95

Provincial Helicopter Services
SP-SSD 14.07.90

Provincial Helicopters
C-FALP 21.03.95

Provo Air Charter
N3116Y 16.12.92

Ptarmigan Airlines
NC8403 26.10.34

Ptarmigan Airways
C-FWAB 06.06.90

Publi-Air
OO-COD 14.11.88

Puerto Rican American Airlines
N67937 18.09.62

Pulkovo Airlines
RA-11127 09.05.95

Pullman Airways
G-AJGE 27.02.48

Pumkin Air
* 24.10.85

Purdue Aeron Corp
N3588 18.04.62
N386T 29.11.63

Purdue Research Foundation
NR16020 01.07.37

Purolater Courier
N3641T 12.11.82

Pye of Cambridge
G-AYMM 04.09.78

Pyramid Helicopters
C-GPRM 01.01.94

Q Air
N2030 10.09.80

Qantas
G-AUCF 25.02.23
G-AUDE 13.09.23
G-AUED 24.03.27
VH-ACD 18.11.44
VH-ADT 22.01.47
VH-ADU 22.04.43
VH-AEC 11.02.48
VH-BBZ 11.05.49
VH-EAC 24.08.60
VH-EAS 07.04.49
VH-EAV 17.11.51
VH-EBQ 16.07.51
VH-UHE 03.10.34
VH-USC 09.10.44
VH-USE 20.02.42
VH-USG 15.11.34

Quaker City Airways
N75385 10.05.58

Quandt, H.
D-IHAQ 12.12.65

Quasar Aviation
C-GHKR 06.11.78

Quebec Airways
CF-AVJ 17.05.39

Quebecair
C-FQBL 29.03.79
C-GQBH 19.02.79
CF-GVZ 17.01.56
CF-QBD 13.07.58
CF-QBE 13.07.58
CF-QBF 13.07.58
CF-QBG 13.07.58
CF-QBH 13.07.58

Queen Charlotte Airlines
CF-BYI 00.00.48
CF-BYJ 24.12.48
CF-EPI 23.06.57
CF-FGM 05.12.52
CF-FOQ 17.10.51

Queen Charlotte Helicopters
C-GQCA 22.01.82

Queen City Helicopters
N4247 07.08.80

Queensland Airlines
VH-BBV 14.03.54

Questor Surveys
C-GSZI 07.09.81

R G Aviation
N73107 11.05.92

R.A.Brand & Co Ltd
G-AKPD 29.10.48

R.J.Reynolds Tobacco Co
N27R 12.11.76

RANSA
HK-1737 31.05.77
YV-C-ARC 21.12.52
YV-C-ARG 30.06.50

RCMP Air Services
C-FMPH 27.05.89
C-FMPW 18.08.76
C-FMPZ 27.09.71
CF-MPA 26.02.67
CF-MPE 00.00.39

REAL
PP-AKF 07.12.60
PP-ANX 10.04.57
PP-AQE 18.09.57
PP-AVL 06.09.61
PP-AVY 27.08.59
PP-AXD 25.02.60
PP-AXJ 14.10.52
PP-AXS 04.11.57
PP-YPM 01.12.49
PP-YPT 15.07.66
PP-YPX 17.08.51
PP-YPZ 06.03.55
PP-YQK 23.08.53
PP-YRB 24.06.60

RICO
PP-AJC 11.06.76

RN Cargo
5N-ARO 25.09.83

RRC Air Service
ET-AIL 12.08.89

RRH Inc
N220MA 09.07.92

RUTACA
YV-229C 29.06.86
YV-245C 15.06.92

RV Aviation
OH-SBB 01.11.89

Radeair
LV-WEN 28.09.94

Radio Communications Corporation
5N-AWS 31.12.86

Railway Air Services
G-ACVZ 15.03.37
G-ADED 01.07.35
G-ADEE 26.10.35
G-AEBX 03.07.38
G-AEFH 00.06.40
G-AERZ 01.04.46
G-AEWR 00.06.40
G-AFFF 27.09.46
G-AGUE 16.08.46
G-AGZA 19.12.46

Raji Aviation
AP-BDW 10.12.90

Ranger Helicopters
C-GIZQ 05.06.85

Rapid Air Transport
NC1118 31.08.34

Ray Charles Enterprises
N923RC 19.10.85

Recchi, E.
N285NJ 22.05.89

Redcoat Air Cargo
G-BRAC 17.02.80

Redhill Helicopter Centre
G-HSAA 10.07.94

Reeder Flying Service
N154R 03.07.70

Reeve Aleutian Airlines
N10012 10.02.71
N1302N 31.05.58
N172RV 06.11.74
N63396 24.09.59
N7140C 06.11.74
N91016 29.05.65

Regina Cargo Airlines
N19941 01.09.53
N9406H 27.07.50

RegionAir
* 01.08.95

Regional Airlines
F-GILN 19.09.93

Regional Express
* 16.05.85

Regionalflug
D-IEWK 05.02.87

Reindeer Air Services
CF-HQI oo.01.73
CF-TQW 01.12.72

Reinders, D.V.
PH-ARK 10.05.40
PH-ARL 10.05.40

Reliant Airlines
N232RA 15.02.89

Relief Air Transport
C-GIXZ 23.04.94

Rembrandt Tobacco
3D-ART 03.10.86

Rentavia
OO-CHG 12.07.70

Republic Helicopters
ZS-HEA 04.07.84

Republic Oil Co
NR9648 21.08.37

Resort Airlines
* 22.01.55
N1669M 22.05.53
N79097 04.08.52

Rexall Drug & Chemical Corporation
N235R 23.04.66

Reynolds Airways
NC3080 18.02.29
NC3085 25.11.27
NC776 17.09.27

Rhein-Helikopter
HB-XOT 02.03.86

Rheintalflug Seewald
OE-FCS 23.02.89

Rhoades International
N450GA 28.11.91

Rhodesia & Nyasaland Airways
VP-YAR 04.08.42
VP-YAX 20.12.38
VP-YAY 02.07.39
VP-YBR 01.01.39

Rhodesian Air Services
VP-YRX 22.11.61

Riaxan Aviation
* 23.12.94

Rich International Airways
N4873V 08.08.75
N7768B 12.09.79

Rico Taxi Aereo
PT-GJW 07.05.94

Riddle Airlines
N7840B 30.03.59
N9904F 17.12.55

Ridgaire
N311DS 11.01.91

Rigsby Truck Lines
N4276C oo.oo.60

Rijksluchtvaartschool
PH-UBS 13.11.47
PH-UBV 16.01.47
PH-UBW 30.12.60
PH-UDI 26.04.49

Rijnmond Air Services
PH-DRX 12.09.88
PH-TSM 22.12.82

Rimouski Airlines
CF-FKY 24.07.48

Rinaldo Piaggio
I-PIAI 18.06.68

Ring Can Corporation
N7RC 26.04.95

Rio Airways
N12RA 12.01.71

Rio Sul
PT-GKC 24.05.82
PT-GKT 31.01.78
PT-LCZ 06.08.84
PT-SLI 12.05.93

Risseghem, V.
OO-ITI 29.12.62

River City Airways
N70003 11.08.84

Riverton Airways
CF-EKL 02.02.52
CF-ETG 17.01.58

Robert J.Graf Inc
N804LJ 21.10.65

Robinson Airlines
N18936 04.09.50

Robinson, H.W.
NC5093 oo.oo.42

Rockhampton Aerial Services
VH-UER 08.12.35

Rocky Mountain Airways
N25RM 04.12.78

Rocky Mountain Helicopters
N117HH 21.06.92
N214RM 20.06.85
N30SV 08.08.92
N314RM 06.03.92
N5806K 29.05.92
N782LF 27.05.93
N814RM 23.02.92
N95LG 09.07.94

Rodriguez, J.
N4996E 14.12.78

Rogers Helicopters
N5007L 07.06.92
N5781D 31.05.95

Rolls Royce
XS118 24.05.65

Romanian Government
YR-PCC 04.11.57

Rosenbalm Aviation
N111AQ oo.06.78

Rostov Helicopter Factory
RA-13387 25.09.93

Rotorua Airlines
ZK-EKO 17.10.81

Rougier Gabon
TR-LXW oo.oo.oo

Rousseau Aviation
F-BLHT 12.11.73
F-BNGB 31.12.70
F-BNMO 05.12.71
F-BNTT 29.12.73
F-BRGH oo.11.72
F-WSGU 02.07.72

Rowan Drilling Company
N80RD 23.08.90

Roy Green Associates
N90RG 06.08.92

Royal Air Force
OO-AGS 23.05.40
OO-AUI 23.05.40

Royal Air Lao
* 15.12.60
XW-PBW 15.10.74
XW-PGR 27.02.71
XW-PKH oo.05.75
XW-PMF 13.03.75
XW-PND 24.03.76
XW-PNF 24.03.76
XW-PNI 24.03.76
XW-TAD 24.02.68
XW-TAF 24.03.76
XW-TDE 11.02.72
XW-TDF 24.03.76
XW-TDR 24.03.76
XW-TFK oo.03.75

Royal Air Maroc
CN-CCJ 14.11.58
CN-CCV 01.04.70
CN-CDE 03.11.86
CN-CDT 21.08.94
OO-SRD 22.12.73

Royal Airline Co
JA9687 07.06.90

Royal Airship Works
R38 24.08.21

Royal Australian Air Force
VH-CXA oo.oo.42

Royal Canadian Air Force
CF-BEP 02.03.39

Royal Crown Cola Corporation
N100RC 14.11.70

Royal Nepal Airlines
9N-AAD 05.11.60
9N-AAH 01.08.62
9N-AAO 12.07.69
9N-AAP 12.07.69
9N-AAR 25.01.70
9N-ABA 09.06.91
9N-ABB 05.07.92
9N-ABG 15.10.73
9N-ABH 22.12.84
9N-ABI 17.01.95
9N-ABJ 19.11.81
9N-ACI 26.09.92
9N-ACS 08.11.93

Royal Nepalese Air Force
9N-RF10 13.09.72

Royal Swazi Defence Force
3D DAB 15.01.80

Rubner Flying Service
NC857E 11.05.31

Rudd, C.R. & Murphy, W.R.
VH-BES 05.06.48
VH-BET 05.06.48

Rudge Air
VH-DHD 03.12.93

Rule, J.
N45864 01.08.80

Rundell Air Service
VH-ROC 26.05.77

Rundstrom, D.
ET-P-5 05.05.50

Russko-Baltiski Vagoni Zavrod
n/a 26.09.13

Rutas Aereas Panamenas
HP-467 30.03.68

Rutas Aereas Uncia
CP-769 03.06.67

Rutas Internacionales Peruanas
OB-R-769 04.08.65

Rwanda Government
9XR-NN 06.04.94

Ryan Air Service
N1238K 11.12.94
N401RA 23.11.87
N6467H 03.04.93

S & N Construction Co
N4244Z 24.01.82

S-H Aviation Sales
CF-FOL 17.11.72

S. Aerienne de Transports Tropicaux
F-ARTE 24.03.52

S.A. Rene Couzinet
F-AMBI 08.08.28

S.A. Tolima
HK-1200 13.08.49

S.A. Virgen de Copacabana
CP-1063 24.04.75

S.A. de Chiapas
XA-KED 24.04.54

S.Instone & Co
G-EAPK 31.07.22

SAATAS-Eastindio
PK-LEA 25.12.74
PK-LEB 15.12.70

SAEP
HK-3031 08.02.86

SAGETA
F-BAVG 29.01.57

SAIDE
SU-AFF 02.11.56
SU-AFX 17.10.49

SAM Colombia
HK-1804 oo.12.83
HK-2421X 04.08.93
HK-2422X 19.05.93

SAMSA
HK-516 20.03.60

SANA [1]
I-AYZZ 00.09.28
I-AZDL 03.11.32
I-AZEA 16.02.32
I-CITO 25.05.33
I-DAER 00.07.28
I-RATA 11.08.33
I-RIDE 12.04.29
I-RONY 21.11.30

SANA [2]
F-BDYH 13.11.47

SANIA
CP-796 18.02.67
CP-834 06.09.69

SANSA
TI-SAB 15.01.90

SASA
CP-2256 14.09.93

SASCO Air Charter
ST-AIJ 05.05.87

SATA
HB-ICK 18.12.77
HB-IMM 17.07.73

SATI
F-BBFO 26.06.47

SCADTA
A10 03.09.26
A12 02.09.30
A16 08.06.24
A2 00.00.23
A20 00.00.26
A32 00.00.34
A4 00.00.27
A9 05.06.27
C-138 00.00.43
C-144 24.10.42
C-149 15.03.39
C-30 00.00.29
C-31 00.00.29
C-31 24.06.34
C-36 00.00.33
C-40 06.08.36
C-41 00.00.29
C-44 15.12.32
C-45 00.00.32
C-46 10.03.34
C-48 31.10.34
C-49 00.00.40
C-52 06.08.36
C-60 00.00.38
C-79 29.02.40
J1 00.00.23
NC309N 00.04.31
n/a 00.01.26
n/a 14.02.36
n/a 14.03.39

SCLAM
F-BAAE 03.09.41

SEC Colombia
HK-3855 15.03.94

SEDTA
D-OJIL 04.03.38
HC-SAB 10.12.38

SEMAF
F-BANU 28.03.50

SERCA Colombia
HK-3835X 06.05.93

SGAC
F-BAZM 11.01.63

SGACC
F-BHHA 30.10.56

SGTA
F-AIBX 20.01.28

SIAI-Marchetti
I-CANG 08.02.85

SITA
F-BDPV 28.06.49
F-BDPX 16.03.49
F-BDPY 18.05.49
F-BEDP 26.10.50

SL Aviation Services
N96BF 16.12.94

SL Helicopters
OY-HEA 16.12.92

SMB Stage Lines
N3411 28.10.87
N41447 02.12.78

SNCAC
F-BAIP 00.00.47
F-BBFX 11.10.46
n/a 20.07.48

SNCASE
F-BAIY 18.10.49
F-WAVA 30.06.50
F-WEEE 01.10.49

SNCASO
F-BBAP 23.07.46

SNECMA
F-BDLR 28.07.48

SNEL
* 07.05.94

SNETA
O-BADO 27.09.21
O-BAHE 27.09.21
O-BAIN 25.01.21
O-BALO 05.05.24
O-BARI 27.09.21
O-BATO 27.09.21
O-BLAN 26.08.21
O-BLEU 27.09.21
O-BRUN 27.09.21

SOCOTRA
F-BBZC 02.01.48
F-BCHD 23.10.46

SODEMAC
9T-PLK 15.07.70

SOMINIKI
9Q-COT 28.12.82

SOS Helikoptern Gotland
SE-JBS 01.11.94

SP Helicopter Service
D-HDAS 22.09.94

STA
F-BBYA 00.00.48

STAAP
* 19.02.52

STARO
F-BCCK 13.08.47

STAT
OB-1305 11.10.91

Saak Avia
RA-19616 31.05.95

Sabah Air
9M-ASU 30.11.74
9M-ATZ 06.08.76
9M-AUL 15.01.78

Sabang Merauke Raya Air Charter
PK-ZAD 24.09.77
PK-ZAG 03.10.95
PK-ZAL 10.08.84

Sabena
OO-AGK 21.04.35
OO-AGM 07.11.35
OO-AGN 10.12.35
OO-AGP 00.05.40
OO-AGR 20.02.37
OO-AGT 10.10.38
OO-AGU 25.03.44
OO-AGW 16.11.37
OO-AHK 19.10.29
OO-AID 00.00.30
OO-AIE 22.12.33
OO-AIF 21.04.36
OO-AII 07.12.34
OO-AIL 02.06.38
OO-AIN 11.09.30
OO-AIP 31.05.43
OO-AUA 14.03.39
OO-AUB 16.11.37
OO-AUF 03.04.44
OO-AUG 01.01.43
OO-AUQ 18.12.49
OO-AUR 17.09.46
OO-AWH 02.03.48
OO-AWO 19.12.53
OO-AWQ 14.10.53
OO-CAK 14.12.45
OO-CAR 24.12.47
OO-CBA 24.07.51
OO-CBE 13.05.48
OO-CBG 18.09.46
OO-CBK 27.08.49
OO-CBN 04.02.52
OO-CBO 07.01.47
OO-CFD 01.05.54
OO-SDB 13.02.55
OO-SDH 04.04.78
OO-SEA 17.01.67
OO-SEC 22.06.61
OO-SFA 18.05.58
OO-SHK 05.05.61
OO-SJB 15.02.61
OO-SJE 15.02.78
OO-SJK 13.07.68
OO-UBL 31.08.48

Sabeni
CP-1593 11.10.85

Sabourin Lake Airways
C-FHIE 00.00.92
C-FVWA 14.12.79

Sadelca
HK-1212 08.02.82
HK-1351X 27.01.78
HK-136 11.08.81

Sadia
PP-ASS 01.03.67
PP-SDJ 03.11.67

Saesa
XA-NAH 29.06.67
XA-SAB 27.07.73
XA-SAE 31.12.68
XA-SEV 06.01.72

Saeta
HC-ARS 15.08.76
HC-ART 03.06.70
HC-AVP 23.04.79
HC-BAE 18.01.86

Safari Air Services
5Y-AZZ 31.05.81

Safe Air
ZK-CAM 14.01.81
ZK-CPU 10.04.68
ZK-SAF 01.04.90

Safe Air Cargo
N6314J 11.09.77

Saha Airlines
5-8815 26.04.92

Sahara India Airlines
VT-SIA 08.03.94

Sahara Tahoe Hotel
N711ST 09.02.75

Sahsa
HR-ANA 25.11.69
HR-SAC 28.05.80
HR-SAG 20.02.67
HR-SAL 07.06.62
HR-SAW 08.01.81
HR-SAZ 18.03.90
N401FH 18.07.93
XH-SAF 29.08.57
XH-SAG 17.12.55

Sakha Avia
RA-67656 26.08.93

Sakhalin Air Routes
RA-23407 02.08.94

Salair
N3433Y 18.03.94
N356SA 27.06.95

Salmita Consolidated Mines
CF-FZE 06.04.53

Saltzgaber, E.
NC5811 08.08.36

Samaki Airlines
* 10.03.75

Samoa Aviation
N202RH 17.06.88

San Francisco Servicios Aereos
CP-1008 00.00.76

San Juan Air
N111VA 00.09.88
N852JA 11.10.69
N855JA 09.09.70

Sanabria, G.M.
TG-AMM 25.01.75

Sancak Air
TC-HBJ 19.03.88

Sandrivier Safaris
ZS-GPL 26.02.85

Sankuru Air Service
RA-87256 17.07.94

Santa Rita
CP-855 09.06.75

Sargo S.A.
LV-GIT 28.11.59

Sasco Air Lines
ST-AID 07.06.93

Saskatchewan Government Airways
CF-FVZ 06.01.55

Satco
OB-R-1004 19.02.78
OB-R-568 30.11.66
OB-R-577 18.03.65
OB-R-653 20.04.72
OB-XAU-654 24.12.64

Satena
FAC.1101 22.08.79
FAC.1103 09.01.74
FAC.1104 07.08.83
FAC.1106 18.12.79
FAC.1110 19.04.89
FAC.1112 24.06.93
FAC.1114 25.06.87
FAC.1115 08.10.94
FAC.1120 20.11.77
FAC.1125 17.02.77
FAC.1126 03.05.83
FAC.1127 20.11.77
FAC.1128 03.08.81
FAC.1129 25.06.81
FAC.1131 13.11.80
FAC.1140 28.03.85
FAC.1150 18.11.90
FAC.1152 09.09.95
FAC.1154 19.03.94

FAC.661 21.01.72
FAC.663 03.05.75
FAC.668 21.02.78
FAC.676 02.04.76
FAC.685 08.09.69
FAC.688 08.01.75

Satroma
OO-DAL 19.06.59

Saturn Airways
N14ST 23.05.74
N640NA 31.01.67
N74841 24.01.67
N9248R 11.10.70

Saudi Arabian Royal Flight
SA-R-7 20.03.63

Saudia
HZ-AAB 25.03.58
HZ-AAC 08.10.57
HZ-AAE 09.02.68
HZ-AAF 25.09.59
HZ-AAJ 11.06.67
HZ-AAK 10.07.72
HZ-AAM 24.06.67
HZ-AAN 13.06.64
HZ-AAO 16.02.56
HZ-AAT 04.02.72
HZ-AAU 07.01.72
HZ-AAZ 08.07.68
HZ-ACE oo.11.79
HZ-AFM 15.04.91
HZ-AFS 25.01.90
HZ-AHK 20.08.80
N747L 02.03.78

Savco
CP-1052 23.02.74
CP-926 17.06.71

Sayre, R.A.
N157K 22.07.78

Scan Air Charter
C9-STD 25.11.91

Scan Transportes Aereos
C9-STE 22.11.93

Scandinavian Airlines System
LN-MOO 13.01.69
LN-RLM 30.01.73
OY-DLU 08.02.49
OY-KHO 27.12.91
OY-KRB 19.01.60
SE-BBM 01.04.51
SE-BBN 22.01.49
SE-BDA 04.07.48
SE-BDP 28.11.57
SE-CCC 08.02.65
SE-DAT oo.02.87
SE-DBE 19.04.70

Scanex Air
LN-KCR 02.04.87

Scenic Air Tours
* 11.06.89
N342E 23.04.92

Scenic Airlines
N2683S 21.07.80

Schlee-Brock Aircraft Corporation
NC7894 30.04.30
NC892E 14.05.30
NX7441 25.07.29

Schreiner Airways
EP-HSV 19.11.77

Schwyz Helikopter
HB-XFL 22.01.77

Scibe Airlift
9Q-CBC 18.01.94
9Q-CBE 10.09.91
9Q-CBH 13.12.92

Scott Cable Communications
N400PH 05.12.87

Scottish Airlines
G-AHZP 13.10.48
G-AKSF 23.07.49
G-AMUL 30.04.56
G-AMUM 13.04.54
G-AMUN 23.12.57
G-ANRC 22.09.54
G-ANTP 10.03.60
G-AOEN 12.12.59
G-AOEO 07.12.57
XG929 18.02.56

Scottish Airways
G-ACNG 19.04.40
G-ADCT 14.02.40
G-AFEY 18.03.40
G-AGDH 25.11.41
G-AGED 02.02.43

Sea Airmotive
N49757 16.04.78
N581PA 25.08.79

Sea World Aviation
* 03.03.91

Seaboard & Western Airlines
N6503C 10.11.58
N74644 30.03.51
NC91077 23.07.47
NC91086 23.07.47

Seaboard World Airlines
N8634 17.10.69

Seagull Air Service
N9828M 15.06.85

Seair Alaska Airlines
* 09.12.82
N540N 12.03.85

Seanaire
N535PC 14.02.91

Seattle Air Charter
NC79025 02.01.49

Seaview Air
VH-SVQ 02.10.94

Sec. de Aeronautica
LQ-IPC 05.05.69
LQ-YAU 06.04.60

Secretary of State for the Colonies
G-AKDU 30.07.50
G-AKDV 02.03.50

Securite Civile [1]
* 20.08.85
* 27.06.91
F-ZBAE 22.04.85
F-ZBAG oo.07.91
F-ZBAT 24.09.90
F-ZBAX 04.07.70
F-ZBBF 17.07.94
F-ZBBG 03.09.71
F-ZBBM 25.07.73
F-ZBBU 19.07.86
F-ZBEG 18.06.89
F-ZBEZ 13.06.87
F-ZBFR 27.07.95

Securite Civile [2]
I-CFSS 27.01.89
I-CFSV 06.08.91

Segas International Ltd
VR-BJB 15.01.88

Seitz, D.
NC2492 08.02.30

Selkhozaviatsiya
SSSR-A11 25.10.33
SSSR-A14 oo.08.31
SSSR-A15 oo.10.31
SSSR-A16 08.12.33
SSSR-A26 oo.10.31
SSSR-A27 oo.08.31

Selva
HK-3929X 08.10.94

Seminole Aircraft
N66534 28.09.53

Sempati Air Transport
PK-JFF 05.06.91

Seneca Sawmill Co
N821LG 02.02.86

Senegalair
6V-AGH 29.05.95

Senegalese Air Force
6W-SHI 21.04.82

Ser de Telecom. et de Signalisation
F-BBYH 30.05.47

Sergasa Helicopters
EC-EKB 04.08.90

Serv-jet
PT-ASJ 17.02.89

Service dela Formation Aeronautique
F-BPNV 14.08.75

Servicio Aereo Colombiano
F-31 24.06.34

Servicio Aereo Panini
XA-GEE 28.12.47

Servicio Expreso Nacional
OB-1362 31.07.90

Servicios Aereos [1]
OB-T-1174 09.04.86
OB-T-1197 25.07.84

Servicios Aereos [2]
TG-HUI 09.08.94

Servicios Aereos Amazonicos
OB-1569 05.11.94

Servicios Aereos Bolivianos
CP-749 20.01.73
CP-914 15.07.70
CP-990 06.01.74

Servicios Aereos Cochabamba
CP-1655 18.02.92
CP-680 22.08.64
CP-694 18.12.63

Servicios Aereos Curtiss
TI-1065 25.02.70

Servicios Aereos Facchini
N747E 21.12.94

Servicios Aereos Martinez Leon
XA-FUA 03.11.77

Servicios Aereos Medellin
HK-504 15.06.51
HK-507 01.03.50

Servicios Aereos Nacionales [1]
XA-DEZ 26.08.50
XA-FOH 13.06.46
XA-GUV oo.oo.57

Servicios Aereos Nacionales [2]
HC-ATV 08.10.82
HC-BAT 29.04.83
HC-BCL 04.09.77
HC-BEM 29.12.77
HC-BFN 12.09.79

Servicios Aereos Panini
XA-DUA 09.09.47

Servicios Aereos Regiomontanos
XA-CUZ 26.12.80
XA-KEW 02.05.81

Servicios Aereos S.A.
HP-677 08.08.75

Servicios Aereos San Francisco
CP-1078 26.03.76

Servicios Aereos Santa Ana
CP-1961 21.08.92
CP-2142 22.05.95

Servicios Aereos Sudamericanos
CC-CAU 10.02.88

Servicios Aereos Virgen
CP-959 07.09.72

Servicios Aereos de Chiapas
XA-FON 03.07.55

Servicios Aereos de Honduras
XH-SAA 06.01.59

Servicios Americanos
N1245N 20.03.66

Servicios Generales Aereos
N9173N 31.07.88

Servicios Internacionales
XA-EEU oo.oo.80

Servivensa
YV-610C 14.06.95
YV-613C 19.07.93
YV-761C 17.12.94

Sete Taxi Aereo
PT-ICD 13.03.93

Seulawah Air Services
PK-RDB 25.12.74

Seulawah-Mandela Airlines
PK-RHS 18.10.77
PK-RVM 01.02.75

Seven Seas Airlines
N5519V 22.03.61

Shabair
9Q-CLW 29.06.93
9Q-CSJ oo.07.94

Shackleton Aviation
G-AKJG 20.01.65

Shanks, R.
N421H 05.01.91

Shanxi Airlines
B-4218 08.10.88

Sheikh Salim bin Laden
N51DB 24.10.86

Shell Aviation
CF-EYM 06.12.54
NC657E 27.04.33

Shell Co of Ecuador
HC-SBB 17.02.49
HC-SBC 05.04.46
HC-SBD 15.11.46
HC-SBE 15.05.46
HC-SBF 23.07.46
HC-SBG 26.08.46
HC-SBH 25.03.47
HC-SBI 10.09.46
HC-SBJ 15.11.46
HC-SBK 16.07.47
HC-SBL 03.12.46
HC-SBQ 00.00.48
HC-SBU 06.08.49
HC-SBV 28.04.49

Shell Mex Argentina
R326 25.11.37

Shin Mitsubishi Jukogyo
JA8246 23.07.86

Shin Nihon Domestic Air
JA9246 15.08.87

Shirley Air Services
C-GSHU 04.02.82

Short Bros
G-OATD 27.11.89
G-ROOM 27.11.89

Short Brothers & Harland
G-AKLM 15.10.49

Shuimpex (Services) Ltd
G-SHOE 08.11.85

Siamese Airways
HS-POA 13.07.51
HS-SAE 09.04.51
HS-SAF 20.08.51
HS-SGF 00.00.51

Sibavia
RA-12187 19.12.93
RA-22285 15.06.93
RA-85358 29.12.93
SSSR-22334 02.12.92
SSSR-25491 25.09.92

Sierra Leone Airways
9L-LAQ 25.08.80
VR-LAD 00.00.00
VR-LAE 00.00.00

Sierra Pacific Airlines
N361V 15.02.83
N4819C 14.03.74

Sight by Wings
5Y-AAW 08.04.77

Siimes Aviation
OH-CDU 28.12.86

Sikorsky
* 03.10.86
N671SA 01.09.74

Silva, J.R.
HK-2456P 02.06.83

Silver City Airways
G-AGVB 04.11.58
G-AICM 19.01.53
G-AICS 27.02.58
G-ANWL 01.11.61

Silver Grizzle Timber Co
N6965R 05.06.81

Simmons Airlines
N1356P 13.03.86
N401AM 31.10.94

Simo-Air
C-GSEV 19.08.94

Simpson Air
C-FVTL 14.05.83
C-GDOM 16.10.88

Sinair
F-GCCC 26.03.84

Sinclair Petroleum Company
ET-T-30 11.06.50

Sinclair Somali Corp
N17085 21.12.60

Sis-Q Flying Service
N6179C 26.09.74
N7238C 21.10.74
N9768Z 06.09.68

Sivewright Airways
G-AIXE 07.01.48

Six T Ranch
N7324C 00.00.69

Skaneflyg
SE-APR 01.02.47

Sky Harbor Air Service
N2883D 17.05.95
N2883D 17.07.95
N5468G 26.01.94

Sky Tours
C9-MJB 27.10.92

Sky Tours Hawaii
N669R 03.11.69
N88G 25.07.69

Skybird Aviation Services
VH-SDV 27.10.89

Skycraft Air Charter
C-GUBT 22.06.83

Skycraft Air Transport
C-GSCA 10.01.84

Skyfame
G-AMDA 02.11.72

Skyline Helicopters
G-HSKY 05.02.86

Skyline Sweden
SE-FOZ 15.01.77

Skylink Airlines
C-GSLB 26.09.89

Skyloft
NC658E 19.08.33

Skyranch Aviation
N641E 08.01.80

Skystream Airlines
N454SA 09.06.79

Skytrain Air
N258M 02.04.81
N60705 09.05.81

Skyvan Airways
N67933 26.02.63

Skyway
NC4805 15.03.32

Skyways [1]
G-AGBE 18.11.46
G-AGLF 11.05.47
G-AGNY 26.06.54
G-AHBU 03.10.47
G-AHCA 08.12.46
G-AHFI 16.03.49
G-AHIA 05.03.51
G-AIUP 25.07.47
G-AJOU 13.05.48
G-AJPL 04.02.49
G-AKFH 26.06.49
G-ALBX 10.06.49
G-ALDH 08.03.60
G-ALDV 01.04.58
G-ALDW 04.03.56

Skyways [2]
N503SS 27.08.83

Skyways Cargo Airline
G-AMSM 17.08.78

Skyways Coach Air
G-AGOJ 01.05.61
G-AKTF 07.02.60
G-AMWX 17.12.65
G-ARMV 11.07.65

Skyways International
N6523C 17.02.78

Skywest Airlines [1]
VH-SWO 13.05.80

Skywest Airlines [2]
N163SW 15.01.87
N2721M 15.01.90
N683AV 01.02.91

Slender You (UK) Ltd
G-OBOB 30.01.90

Slick Airways
* 10.12.47
N384 10.03.64
N4717N 04.03.53
N59485 09.10.49
N59490 23.02.51
N9740Z 03.02.63
NC59486 14.02.47
NC59488 21.08.47
NC59489 16.05.48
NC59495 17.09.47

Slovair
OK-JIK 25.08.82
OK-KHD 31.07.69
OK-KIM 00.00.81
OK-PDI 13.03.92
OK-PIN 30.05.92
OK-TGE 05.06.91
OK-ZSO 01.07.79

Smith Helicopters
N59613 02.03.92

Smithers Air Service
C-FJIK 26.11.79

Smiths Aviation
G-APAZ 27.03.63

Snow Valley Ski Lines
N410D 09.03.64

Snowy Mts Hydro Electric Authority
VH-ISI 25.11.84

Sobelair
OO-CTL 20.12.70
OO-SBL 22.04.60
OO-SJA 29.03.81

Soc Indochinoise de Transports Aer.
F-BCJA 25.01.48
F-BECR 10.03.50

Sociedad Aeronautica Medellin
HK-513 25.07.57
HK-514 16.09.58
HK-515 08.12.59

Societa Aerea Mediterranea
I-DIMO 08.03.62
I-TACO 20.11.29

Societe Aera
OO-ADO 28.04.36

Societe Aerienne du Littoral
F-BCJN 16.10.47

Societe Aero-Service Afrigo
TN-ADS 00.06.81

Societe General Photo-Topographie
F-BGOG 26.03.58

Societe Quarter Wins
N74689 23.08.77

Societe Transatlantique Aerienne
F-BFGD 24.01.50
F-BFGH 22.10.49

Solair Flying Services
G-ALBC 30.12.63

Solar Sources
N74FB 11.09.92

Solitaire
N969MA 06.12.80

Solomon Islands Airlines
H4-AAC 22.10.78
H4-SIA 27.09.91

Somali Airlines
6O-AAJ 06.05.70
6O-SAC 16.08.75
6O-SAY 20.07.81
6O-SAZ 28.06.89
6O-SBT 17.05.89

Somerton Airways
G-AGPI 16.06.49
G-AHWY 09.09.48
G-AIBS 22.05.51

South African Airways
ZS-AEC 16.10.37
ZS-AJE 29.07.37
ZS-AKY 16.06.37
ZS-AST 28.03.41
ZS-ASV 01.02.59
ZS-ASW 05.01.48
ZS-AVI 15.09.52
ZS-AVJ 15.10.51
ZS-CVA 13.03.67
ZS-DJC 06.03.62
ZS-EUW 20.04.68
ZS-SAS 28.11.87

South American Gulf Oil Co
NC8411 15.04.39

South American Placers
CP-650 04.03.66

South Central Air
N208SC 16.10.93
N35206 23.12.83
N496SC 23.12.87
N5282U 03.12.94
N7393U 28.01.87

South Coast Airways
VH-AJP 10.02.51

South Dakota State Government
N86SD 19.04.93

South Pacific Airmotive
VH-EDC 24.04.94

South Pacific Heli Logging
YS-1005P 15.10.93

South Pacific Island Airways
N23BC 05.11.79
N3SP 28.04.78
N43SP 21.07.84

South Wales Airways
G-AASS 01.08.31

Southampton Air Service
G-AGBH 03.10.46

Southeast Airlines
N18941 08.01.59

Southeast Asia Air Transport
N86AC 19.01.75

Southern Aero Trades
N122AC oo.oo.81

Southern Aerowork
G-AIXT 18.07.47

Southern Air
ZK-AOI 23.02.73

Southern Air Transport
N15ST 04.10.86
N1697M 19.07.53
N517SJ 08.04.87
N521SJ 02.09.91
N911SJ 12.08.90
YV-C-ARE 03.06.49

Southern Airlines [1]
VH-GVB 13.03.55

Southern Airlines [2]
N1335U 04.04.77
N251S 01.01.68
N97S 14.11.70

Southern Aviation
ZS-JYF 08.10.77

Southern Cross Airways
N68823 18.02.59

Southern Cross Aviation
N302SP 24.01.85
N61VM 02.12.94

Southern Directorate
RA-20357 01.08.94
RA-42331 25.01.94

Southern Express
N95PB 06.05.89

Southern Jersey Airways
N205AC 09.08.79

Southern Scenic Air Services
ZK-AKS 15.06.65
ZK-AKT 15.04.67
ZK-BAU 22.04.64

Southern Services Inc
N40PC 28.04.77

Southernair
G-AMYP 09.07.83

Southland Aerial Fertilisers
ZK-AWW 26.02.54

Southland Scenic Air Services
ZK-BCL oo.06.59

Southwest Air
P2-SWC 22.11.94

Southwest Air Lines
JA8444 26.08.82

Southwest Airlines
N63439 06.04.51
N93061 30.12.55

Southwick, O.K.
NC8404 29.05.37

Span East Airlines
N614SE 26.10.73

Spantax
EC-ACX 16.09.66
EC-ALF oo.oo.61
EC-AQE 30.09.72
EC-ARZ 07.12.65
EC-ATQ 02.10.70
EC-BNM 05.01.70
EC-BZR 03.12.72
EC-DEG 14.09.82
EC-DFA 13.08.80

Spartan Air Services
CF-FYI 26.06.48
CF-GML 24.08.64
CF-ICQ oo.04.57

Special Coating Systems
N6866K 11.02.85

Spencer Airways
VP-YFD 25.01.47

Spernak Airways
N6424H 08.10.79

Sperry Gyroscope Co
G-AHXM 05.11.51

Spilsbury & Hepburn
CF-BYL 31.08.46

Springfield Air Service
N405PC 23.03.93

St Felicien Air Services
C-FFKZ 20.05.76
C-GLUC 25.07.75

St Lawrence Airways
CF-FEO 02.02.49

St Lucia Airways
J6-LBC 23.10.75

Stack, W.J.
N4957N 25.09.68

Stallard Airways
G-EAFQ 26.11.21

Stanair
CF-PAP 08.02.69

Standard Airlines
C7888 29.03.29
N79978 12.07.49

Standard Airways
N189S 29.05.63

Standard Oil of California
NC14285 06.10.35

Standard Vacuum Petrol
PK-SVA oo.oo.oo

Star Air
OY-APE 26.05.88

Star Air Lines
NC9651 oo.08.43

Starflight
N1461G 05.11.85

Starline Helicopters
G-SHBB 18.12.89

Starratt Airways & Transportation
CF-BGY 07.01.41

Starways
G-AFIX 06.05.49
G-AMRB 28.03.56
G-APIN 17.09.61
G-ARJY 19.06.61

Starwings
OH-CDT 26.04.87

State Aerial Survey Corporation
PK-VDH 26.09.77

State Airlines
N44NC 31.03.84

Ste Air Service
TR-LOS oo.06.71

Ste des Tran. Aer. Camerounais
F-BEIV 07.11.51

Ste des Tran. Aer. d'Extreme Orient
F-BCCL 08.06.54
F-BEIB 04.05.52

Steiner, D.L.
G-AJGC 13.11.47

Stellair
F-BYCU oo.11.84

Stephens Aviation
G-AUJB 09.05.38
VH-UJO 06.02.41
VH-UJP oo.oo.42

Sterling Airways
OY-EAN 23.12.67
OY-EAP 13.04.63
OY-SAN 14.07.73
OY-SAW 29.11.71
OY-SBS 03.09.79
OY-STK 15.03.74
OY-STL 14.03.72

Steward, F.H. & Gibson, T.M.
NC799W oo.11.47

Stewart & Lloyds Ltd
ZS-AVZ 18.08.56

Stewart Lake Air Service
C-GAJU 03.11.79

Stewart, R.
NR7973 05.01.32

Stinson
NX12132 08.02.33

Stoney's Rainbow Lanes & Lounge
N144A 11.09.75

Stout Air Services
NC1076 16.01.29
NC2431 04.02.28
NC2432 oo.04.28
NC880 13.10.28

Straights Air Freight Express
ZK-AYH 21.11.57

Strato Freight
* 16.10.47
N92857 07.06.49

Stratolift
N4580Q 18.05.89

Streamline Aviation
G-BASU 12.05.87

Suburban Airlines
N844SA 03.06.80

Sud Aviacion
N584JA 13.01.69

Sudair
CF-FBJ 20.06.66

Sudan Airways
ST-AAB oo.oo.61
ST-AAM 21.02.67
ST-AAR 02.07.85
ST-AAS 05.10.82
ST-AAY 06.12.71
ST-ADB 18.03.75
ST-ADW 06.06.77
ST-ADX 10.05.72
ST-ADY 16.08.86
ST-AIM 10.09.82

Sudene
PP-ZNU 28.01.81

Suidwes Lugdiens
ZS-JDD 16.08.78

Sultan Industries
N69GT 11.06.85

Sun Air
N856JA oo.oo.oo

Sun Co Inc
N99S 11.01.83

Sun Valley Aviation
N137H 12.01.81
N3VB 25.03.81

Sun West Airlines
N41070 31.12.81

Sunair
9J-AAW 31.08.85

Sunbeam Air Transport Co
NC7862 01.12.28

Sunbird Airlines
N992SB 28.08.85

Sunbird Aviation
5Y-ANY 03.01.82

Sunflower Airlines
* 22.02.92
DQ-FDY 21.08.88
DQ-FEF 27.12.86
DQ-FEH 05.10.90
DQ-FER 10.11.88

Sunkyung Engineering
HL9245 14.06.93

Sunny Moon Association
N296MA 09.12.88

Sunshine Coast Air Charter
VH-DIL 21.02.83

Superior Airways
C-FXXT 11.04.77
C GWVO 20.08.80
CF-AUQ 06.12.72

Superior Aviation
N441KM 22.11.94
N87163 17.01.90

Superior North Air
C-GJKA 16.06.91

Superior Oil Corporation
- NC17645 05.05.48
- NC75402 07.09.48

Supra International
- N13626 08.05.83

Surinam Airways
- N1809E 06.06.89
- N3493F 05.05.78
- PZ-TAO 15.08.60

Survair
- C-FNAR 28.02.77

Svazarm
- OK-MYC 11.07.68

Svensk Flygtjanst
- SE-ACZ oo.oo.46

Svenska Aero
- SE-BRS 23.09.50

Swedair
- SE-IHX 24.03.84

Swedish Red Cross
- SE-ERP 05.06.69

Swiflight Aircraft Corporation
- NC522K 27.04.34

Swift Aire
- N418SA 10.03.79

Swift Delivery Air Freight
- N401JB oo.09.83

Swiftair
- EC-899 19.05.95
- EC-FHB 18.10.93

Swiss Air Ambulance
- HB-XIX 13.04.83
- HB-XOI 08.12.94

Swissair
- CH-170 27.07.34
- CH-193 oo.oo.31
- HB-ICD 21.02.70
- HB-ICV 04.09.63
- HB-IDD 13.09.70
- HB-IDE 07.10.79
- HB-ILE 13.12.50
- HB-ILO 14.12.51
- HB-IMD 17.07.56
- HB-IMF 10.02.67
- HB-IRK 18.06.57
- HB-IRW 19.06.54
- HB-ISI 09.08.44
- HB-ITA 07.01.39
- HB-ITI 28.02.36
- HB-ITU 30.04.36
- HB-IXA 20.07.39

Sykes, R.
- N77RS 04.12.78

Syncrude Canada
- C-GKRL 10.12.86

Syndicato Condor
- P-BACA 03.12.28
- P-BADA 11.02.28
- PP-CAB oo.oo.38
- PP-CAH 10.11.30
- PP-CAL 12.09.31
- PP-CAN oo.oo.oo
- PP-CAP oo.oo.oo
- PP-CAR oo.oo.oo
- PP-CAS oo.oo.oo
- PP-CAY 13.01.39

Synetairistikon Propsidevtikon Eno.
- SX-AFB 22.07.69

Syrian Airways
- YK-AAE 24.02.56
- YK-AAF 21.12.53
- YK-AAR 01.09.60

Syrian Arab Airlines
- YK-ACB 06.02.67
- YK-ADA 02.10.64
- YK-AEB 07.04.63

Syrian Government
- YK-AQC 19.03.76

Syrota Brothers
- CF-HAS oo.oo.67

T & G Aviation
- N284 08.12.88
- N5903 09.10.86

T.A. Intercontinentaux
- F-BELB 08.12.50
- F-BIAP 24.09.59

T.A. da Indias Portugueses
- CR-IAD 02.11.57

T.Eaton Co
- CF-ETC 11.07.51

TAAG Angola Airlines
- D2-EAS 16.06.81
- D2-FAF 16.05.79
- D2-TAA 05.11.80
- D2-TAB 29.11.82
- D2-TBN 09.11.83
- D2-TBP 10.02.95
- D2-TBV 09.02.84
- D2-TFP 26.08.92
- D2-THA 08.06.86
- D2-THB 05.01.90
- D2-TOI oo.02.88
- D2-TOJ 20.02.92
- D2-TOM 10.10.88
- D2-TYC 08.06.80
- D2-TYD 08.01.88

TAAPSA
- OB-T-1199 04.02.90

TABA
- PT-GJN 23.06.85
- PT-GKW 31.01.78
- PT-ICA 06.06.90
- PT-LBV 16.06.82
- PT-LCS 25.01.93

TABSA
- CP-752 28.05.72
- CP-940 22.04.72

TAC Colombia
- HK-1139 05.02.72
- HK-1492 05.03.75

TACA
- * 29.10.34
- * 09.11.35
- * 03.10.37
- * 20.02.40
- * 04.04.41
- * 03.07.44
- * oo.oo.46
- AN-AAR 12.06.45
- C-157 01.03.46
- C-204 22.01.47
- LG-AAE 28.09.37
- LG-AAH oo.03.39
- TI-33 25.02.40
- TI-51 04.12.40
- TI-84 04.05.47
- XH-TAB 17.10.46
- XH-TAN 29.11.44
- XH-TAR 08.09.53
- YV-C-AZU 29.03.52

TACA International Airlines
- N120ES 24.04.95
- N33VX 21.07.88
- YS-07C oo.02.80
- YS-09C 05.03.59
- YS-35C 02.05.76

TACI
- CX-AIR 15.08.47

TAESA
- XA-BBA 18.06.94
- XA-NOG 02.09.93

TAF Helicopteres
- EC-DSU 19.12.93

TAG Aviation
- N779XX 07.02.85

TAI
- F-BBYK 06.01.47
- F-BBYL 26.10.46
- F-BDRI 18.07.51

TAISA
- TI-1010C 09.09.74

TALA
- HK-811 07.06.58

TAM Linha Aerea Regional
- PP-SBB 08.02.79
- PP-SBC 28.06.84
- PP-SBH 07.10.83

TAME
- 447 14.02.91
- HC-AUE/683 20.01.76
- HC-AUR oo.02.75
- HC-AUX 12.09.71
- HC-AZJ/2004 04.09.89
- HC-AZY/1052 12.09.88
- HC-BAV/453 02.09.80
- HC-BAX/457 21.05.81
- HC-BAZ/738 oo.07.87
- HC-BCG/446 20.11.84
- HC-BFH 17.07.90
- HC-BHG/723 24.05.81
- HC-BIG/607 11.07.83
- TAM-60 17.02.71

TAMSA
- * 14.04.57
- * 29.10.57
- XA-GIC 14.09.53

TAMU
- CX-BJE/T584 26.06.77
- CX-BJH/T511 10.02.78
- CX-BJK/T581 25.02.91
- T-571 13.10.72

TAN [1]
- N88705 21.10.89
- TI-107 01.07.47
- TI-16 oo.04.47
- TI-161 24.04.48

TAN [2]
- EI-CBL 17.11.91
- HR-TNG 30.06.66
- HR-TNL 21.03.90
- HR-TNO 27.01.73

TAN Airlines
- RA-27076 22.06.94

TANA
- HK-1517E 22.08.75

TANS
- * 14.05.93

TAPSA
- LV-MOP 03.05.95
- OB-QAL-487 04.01.59

TARS
- YR-TAA oo.oo.51
- YR-TAI 21.11.47
- YR-TAV 13.08.47

TASA
- OB-T-1040 25.02.87

TASSA
- EC-AQH 21.06.64

TATSA
- N9066N 12.07.94

TAUSA
- OB-1219 30.01.90
- OB-T-1254 10.10.89

TBM Air Tankers
- N1366N 18.08.74

TBM Inc
- N848D 01.10.92

THY Turkish Airlines
- SE-ERC 20.01.68
- TC-EFE 28.06.62
- TC-ETI 03.02.64
- TC-JAC 21.01.72
- TC-JAO 26.01.74
- TC-JAP 30.01.75
- TC-JAT 23.12.79
- TC-JAV 03.03.74
- TC-JBH 19.09.76
- TC-JBR 16.01.83
- TC-JEL 27.08.94
- TC-JES 29.12.94
- TC-KOC 10.05.73
- TC-KOP 08.03.62
- TC-SET 02.02.69
- TC-SEV 17.02.59
- TC-TAY 23.09.61
- TC-TEZ 17.02.70

TPI International Airways
- N357Q 09.01.85
- N4465F 14.07.90

TRAFE
- LV-LTP 13.12.92

TTA
- * 14.05.85
- C9-TAI 03.11.84

Taboca Mining Company
- N34134 30.05.90

Tabso
- * 06.12.52
- LZ-BEG 04.09.68
- LZ-BEN 24.11.66

Tag Airlines
- N2300H 28.01.70

Tahiti Conquest Airlines
- F-ODUK 04.12.90

Taiwan Airlines
- B-11107 09.09.79
- B-11108 13.06.81
- B-11109 28.09.83
- B-11111 oo.04.87
- B-11116 10.04.92
- B-11120 13.03.86
- B-11125 19.01.88

Taiwan Aviation
- B-11102 13.08.78
- B-112 25.07.67

Tajikistan Directorate
- SSSR-28706 03.01.92

Tajikistan National Airlines
- 26035 17.06.93
- 87995 27.08.93

Talair
- * 19.07.80
- P2-GKC 01.03.77
- P2-GKJ 01.04.81
- P2-GKO 12.06.81
- P2-ISA 15.06.81
- P2-ISG 06.09.84
- P2-ISH 14.01.84
- P2-ISJ 18.07.89
- P2-ISL 14.09.79

P2-IST oo.05.90
P2-MIB 08.12.87
P2-RDE 28.02.78
P2-RDL oo.oo.84
P2-RDM 06.02.87
P2-RDS 15.04.92
P2-RDW 21.07.89

Talia Airways
TC-AKD 27.02.88

Tampa
HK-2401X 15.12.83
HK-3355X 09.10.94

Tampa Airways
N6803B 26.02.85

Tampereen Lentoliikenne
OH-ANA 01.05.55

Tandy Corporation
N658TC 18.01.72

Tanganyika Government
G-AIIC 13.11.46

Tanzanair
5H-TZB 27.02.95

Tanzania Aviation
5H-TAL 05.12.80

Tanzania Game Trackers
5H-GTS 30.03.88

Tanzanian Air Services
5H-MOE 21.08.84
5H-TZS 18.05.92

Tapsa
TG-SAB 07.05.79

Tapu Kadastro Genel Mudurlugu
TC-KUN 20.10.89

Taquan Air Service
N242CS 02.01.95

Tar Heel Aviation
N418NE 04.05.90

Tarom
YR-ABD 10.01.91
YR-ABN 17.08.95
YR-AMA 15.11.71
YR-AMD 29.12.74
YR-AMT 04.02.70
YR-BCA 07.12.70
YR-BMD 25.01.82
YR-BMJ 28.12.89
YR-DAC 13.06.64
YR-ILB 09.10.64
YR-ILL 16.06.63
YR-ILO 01.03.76
YR-IMB 10.10.64
YR-IMH 14.08.91
YR-IMI 21.04.77
YR-IMK 09.12.74
YR-LCC 31.03.95
YR-TAN 11.08.66
YR-TAX 08.10.60
YR-TPH 07.08.80
YR-TPJ 09.02.89

Tartarstan Airlines
SSSR-47823 26.11.91

Tasman Empire Airways
ZK-TEC 27.03.65

Tata Airlines
VT-AJA 20.11.38
VT-AQW 04.08.43
VT-CFL 18.09.47

Tatar Airlines
SSSR-67145 17.02.91

Tavina
HK-1711 09.01.78
HK-2064 13.03.79
HK-2743 oo.oo.85
HK-2822X 27.07.84

Tawakel Airlines
5Y-JJC 08.08.94

Taxader
HK-437E 06.12.62
HK-794 23.08.62

Taxi Aereo El Llanero
HK-1333 23.02.74

Taxi Aereo El Venado
HK-1067X 02.04.77
HK-1078 17.06.81
HK-1309 30.06.75
HK-149 25.10.76
HK-172 15.01.76
HK-2651 02.08.81
HK-556 10.04.77

Taxi Aereo Florianopolis
PT-OOP 07.02.93

Taxi Aereo Fortaleza
PT-IBM 05.01.77

Taxi Aereo Jao Jorge
PT-CGS 09.11.76

Taxi Aereo Jaragua
PT-KIU 12.11.76

Taxi Aereo Kovacs
PT-JXL 31.10.78

Taxi Aereo Marilia
PT-DVL 12.11.76
PT-KZY 16.05.82
PT-LKT 01.12.92
PT-OGM 06.12.93

Taxi Aereo Nacional
HK-1511E 17.06.77

Taxi Aereo Selva
OB-T-1252 18.07.83

Taxi Aereo de Santander
HK-862 08.03.64

Taxi Aereo del Guaviare
HK-1754 26.09.83
HK-2685 24.02.84

Taxi Aereo del Tulima
HK-3171 04.05.95

Taxi Aero Cesar Aguiar
PT-DVN 04.10.73

Taxi Aero Opita
HK-595 17.10.71

Taxis Aereos Nacionales
XA-JUV 05.05.52

Taxis Aereos Uruguayos
CX-BMT 19.08.80

Tech. & Aeronautical Exploitation
SX-BAB 03.09.47
SX-BAF 23.04.49
SX-BAI 06.06.49

Tejas Airlines
N300TL 13.08.78

Tel Air Services
C-FVZP 22.09.94

Telco Systems
N199TA 19.06.85

Teledyne Post of South Bend
N65TD 10.12.86

Temesco Airlines
N11250 15.01.89
N68HA 20.08.91

Temesco Helicopters
N8648F 14.07.94

Tennessee Valley Authority
N941K 22.06.78

Tepper Aviation
N9205T 27.11.89

Terr-Air
C-GCTV 24.08.81
C-GSTX oo.oo.oo

Terra Surveys
C-GILU 02.08.88

Territorio de Acre
PP-ETD 09.07.50

Tesseydre, M.
F-BIEE 28.07.78

Teterboro Aircraft Service
N866JS 06.05.80

Tex Johnston Inc
N73135 04.11.68

Texaco
HK-489E 08.04.61
NC3443 29.12.28

Texas Co, The
NC7955 17.01.30

Texas Gulf Aviation
N520S 11.02.81

Texas Instruments
N580HH 09.06.93

Texas International Airlines
N9103 17.03.80
N9104 16.11.76
N94230 27.09.73

Texas Pipe Line Co
NC435E 22.11.30

Texas Worth Tool Co
C194E 27.04.30

Textafrica
* 23.11.77

Thai Airways
HS-TBB 15.04.85
HS-TBC 31.08.87
HS-TDH 27.12.67
HS-THB 27.04.80
HS-THG 21.06.80
HS-THI 28.04.87

Thai Airways International
HS-TGI 29.06.67
HS-TGK 09.07.69
HS-TGU 10.05.73
HS-THO 22.10.94
HS-TID 31.07.92

Thai Government
HS-000 24.07.66

Thai Police
* 24.03.70
* 17.01.75
* 21.01.79
* 04.06.80
1607 15.09.84

Thor Taxi Aereo
PT-LAU 10.09.94

Thrifty Threads Inc
N777DC 01.04.78

Tiburon Aircraft
N8060C 19.11.79

Tierra del Fuego Province
LV-TDF 15.05.84

Tigra Air Taxi
N731FT 15.09.84

Tigres Voladores
XA-LID 18.06.55
XA-MIS 17.04.59

Tikhookeanskiy Aviarabotnik
* oo.07.93
* 01.11.93

Tilghman, J.
XA-GUW 23.02.52

Time Air
SE-DLK 21.09.92

Titan Airways
G-ZAPE 13.01.93

Toa Airways
JA6158 23.02.62

Toa Domestic Airlines
JA8662 10.01.88
JA8680 28.05.75
JA8764 03.07.71

Toddy's Balloon Safaris
VH-NMS 13.08.89

Togolese Air Force
5V-MAK 03.04.89

Togolese Government
5V-TAA 26.12.74

Tohoku Air Service
JA9454 14.08.92

Tomahawk Airways
C-FEIA 24.03.80

Tonga Air Services
* 20.04.83

Tonna, C.
ET-P-22 oo.oo.oo

Toros Air
TC-AJV 25.08.89

Totem Air
C-GXQE 22.06.81

Toucan Air Services
8R-GEK 16.05.81

Touraine Air Transport
F-BTQE 02.07.75
F-GBRS 05.07.79

Townsville & Country Airways
VH-BAK 24.01.48

Tradeastern Ltd
G-AIRN 22.02.52

Tradewinds
N100BB oo.oo.93

Tradewinds Airways
G-AWSC 22.12.74
G-BCWJ 06.07.78

Trafik-Turist-Transportflyg
SE-BNG 18.11.47

Tramaco Services
9Q-CTS 20.07.70

Trans Aereos Cochabamba
CP-1622 20.04.93

Trans Aereos San Miguel
CP-909 02.02.87

Trans Aereos Skorpio
CP-1077 10.11.83

Trans Air
CF-TAR 07.10.70

Trans Air Service
RP-C141 09.02.81

Trans Amazon
OB-1439 22.02.92

Trans American Leasing
N7311C 26.03.69

Trans Arabia Air Services
G-AJFX 10.07.51

Trans Arabian Air Transport
ST-ALK 14.07.90
ST-SAC 04.12.90

Trans Asiatic Airlines
HS-TA-180 17.11.49
PI-C184 18.01.50

Trans Australia Airlines
VH-PNB 11.04.72
VH-TAA 24.05.61
VH-TAT 08.08.51
VH-TFB 10.06.60
VH-TGR 28.04.70
VH-TQQ 09.06.82
VH-TVA 31.10.54
VH-TVC 30.11.61

Trans Canada Airlines
* 00.00.47
CF-CMU 30.12.44
CF-TCL 21.11.38
CF-TCP 06.02.41
CF-TEL 12.08.48
CF-TFD 09.12.56
CF-TFW 08.04.54
CF-TGG 17.12.54
CF-TGL 10.11.58
CF-TGY 03.10.59

Trans Caribbean Air Cargo Line
NC50040 08.08.46

Trans Caribbean Airlines
N8784R 24.11.65
N8790R 28.12.70
N54083 00.00.48

Trans Colorado Airlines
N68TC 19.01.88

Trans Europe Air
F-BCYX 00.00.78

Trans International Airlines
N4863T 08.09.70

Trans Island Air
8P-TAD 17.07.94

Trans Island Airways
N851JA 00.10.80
N851JA 00.12.88
N865JA 00.05.85

Trans Isles Airways
N50S 20.04.72
N880JG 23.02.69

Trans Jamaican Airlines
6Y-JHJ 24.06.77
6Y-JQF 00.09.88

Trans Mediterranean Airways
OD-ACD 27.05.60
OD-ACE 05.01.59
OD-ACJ 11.08.58
OD-ACN 06.04.62
OD-ACO 25.05.61
OD-ACP 08.10.58
OD-ADI 28.12.68
OD-ADO 21.01.63
OD-AEB 12.12.63
OD-AEC 09.07.62
OD-AEL 10.03.66
OD-AEY 28.12.68
OD-AFX 23.07.79
OD-AFY 26.07.93
OD-AGN 16.06.82
OD-AGT 22.10.81
OD-AGW 05.07.81

Trans Namibia Aviation
ZS-NEP 28.06.93

Trans National Airlines
N63250 20.07.79

Trans North Air
C-FBVG 24.08.92
C-FDDL 24.02.93

Trans Nusantara Airways
PK-EHC 22.01.73

Trans Oceanic Airways
VH-TOA 28.01.51

Trans Oriente
HK-2213 28.05.94
HK-3220 31.08.93

Trans Peruana
OB-R-606 23.02.66

Trans Provincial Airlines
C-FBXR 08.10.79
C-FRHW 12.06.81
C-FUVJ 30.08.79
C-GYQY 21.06.88

Trans Service Airlift
9Q-CCV 21.01.94
9Q-CJK 27.01.93

Trans Southern Corporation
N120A 04.08.69

Trans World Airlines
N102R 24.11.59
N1063T 09.03.67
N11002 30.07.92
N15712 14.09.72
N18701 22.12.75
N31007 19.04.74
N40403 01.04.56
N40404 15.11.56
N40416 19.02.56
N54328 01.12.74
N6004C 31.08.50
N6902C 30.06.56
N6907C 16.12.60
N7101C 29.02.60
N7115C 26.01.66
N7313C 26.06.59
N742TW 06.11.67
N743TW 22.04.70
N757TW 16.01.74
N761TW 08.03.72
N769TW 23.11.64
N787TW 26.07.69
N790TW 30.11.70
N797TW 30.11.80
N820TW 13.09.65
N821TW 20.11.67
N852TW 27.08.88
N86511 01.09.61
N8715T 13.09.70
N8734 08.09.74
N93211 12.01.55

Trans World Safaris
5Y-SMR 02.12.94

Trans-Air Hawaii
N5615V 27.05.49

Trans-Island Airways
ZK-BUT 18.02.59

Trans-Luxury Airlines
NC51878 21.08.46
NC57850 05.09.46

Trans-North Turbo Air
C-GTNB 04.07.80

Trans-Quebec Helicopters
C-GUGP 09.01.80

TransAir
CF-HFQ 13.09.56
CF-HIQ 08.01.57

Transa Chile
CC-CNC-0466 11.04.57

Transaer
LV-GGT 17.05.60

Transaereos Beni
CP-970 07.06.76

Transafrik
CP-1564 16.03.91
S9-NAI 08.04.89

Transair [1]
G-AIUZ 02.09.48
G-AJBA 10.02.50
G-ALFD 17.02.52
G-AMZD 19.08.59

Transair [2]
CF-HZI 00.00.56
CF-HZL 00.00.56
CF-TET 25.09.58
CF-TFY 18.06.56

Transair [3]
HB-VFO 06.12.82

Transair America
N3123T 00.11.91

Transair Cargo
N296 21.06.73

Transair Congo
SE-CFF 13.01.64
SE-CFG 06.03.66

Transair Georgia
4L-65001 23.09.93
4L-65893 21.09.93
4L-85163 22.09.93

Transair Sweden
* 19.11.47

Transamazonica
HK-3531X 00.06.94
HK-772 25.07.81

Transamerica Airlines
N17ST 27.08.83
N24ST 29.12.84
N859U 18.11.79

Transamerica Taxi Aereo
PT-CMY 06.04.90
PT-OEF 02.05.92

Transamerican Air Transport
LV-GGJ 18.05.60

Transandina Ecuador
HC-SIB 13.05.49

Transasia Airways
B-22717 30.01.95

Transatlantica Argentina
LV-GLH 19.06.61

Transavia
PH-TRH 22.06.74

Transaviatsiya
SSSR-L19 00.00.35
SSSR-L20 00.00.35
SSSR-L21 00.00.35
SSSR-L43 00.00.35
SSSR-L60 00.09.32
SSSR-L78 00.00.35
SSSR-L92 00.00.35

Transavio
I-BADE 27.06.80
I-BALR 02.02.92

Transbrasil
PP-SDQ 02.02.74
PP-SDS 05.01.77
PT-TBD 22.01.76
PT-TCO 11.04.87
PT-TCS 21.03.89
PT-TYS 12.04.80

Transcarriers
9J-ABT 26.06.84

Transcommuter Airlines
N40SB 06.02.78

Transcontinental & Western Air
41-32939 15.01.43
42-68367 17.11.42
NC12277 28.07.33
NC12292 10.11.33
NC127W 11.12.33
NC13212 26.01.35
NC13721 07.04.36
NC13722 03.08.35
NC13730 25.03.37
NC13785 06.05.35
NC13786 03.04.40
NC13789 01.03.38
NC14979 31.05.36
NC17315 23.01.41
NC17322 01.12.44
NC18951 04.11.42
NC1946 17.01.42
NC28310 04.11.44
NC28383 02.07.46
NC45345 28.09.48
NC497H 31.01.34
NC7119 19.12.31
NC8413 11.08.38
NC86505 26.12.46
NC86507 18.11.47
NC86508 11.05.47
NC86510 29.03.46
NC86512 12.10.46
NC86513 11.07.46
NC90824 25.11.48
NC947Y 11.12.33
NC9607 29.08.33
NC9647 27.01.31
NC9650 14.12.32
NC9665 19.08.31
NC9666 10.02.33
NC992Y 10.01.33
NC994Y 31.01.35
NC999E 31.03.31
NC999Y 15.11.34

Transcontinental Air Transport
NC9649 03.09.29

Transcontinental Airlines
LV-FTO 10.10.59
LV-FTP 11.11.58

Transcontinental Airways
VH-UMG 21.11.36

Transexecutive Airlines
VH-IWJ 10.10.85

Transfair
C-FBZN 28.02.89
C-FDTT 12.03.95

Transmandu
YV-269C 06.11.79

Transmeridian Air Cargo
G-ATZH 02.09.77

Transmile Air Services
9M-PMN 20.03.95

Transniger
5U-AAN 02.02.75

Transniugini Airways
P2-ISR 24.12.93
P2-TNT 25.07.95

Transnorthern Aviation
N5904V 31.01.77

Transocean Airlines
N68963 30.12.51
N79998 15.08.49
N88942 20.03.53
N90806 12.07.53
N93039 05.11.51

Transport Aerien Intercontinentaux
F-BGOD 20.02.56

Transport Aerien Transregional
F-GCPS 04.03.88
F-GCPZ 23.03.91

Transport Aerien Zaire
9Q-CYD 16.01.84

Transport Canada
C-GFQA 19.06.91

Transporte Aereo Boliviano
CP-1375 28.09.79

Transporte Aereo Ejecutvo
HC-BHU 27.10.91

Transporte Aereo Federal
XC-COX 31.08.88

Transporte Aereo Militar [1]
* 04.07.66
* 13.02.90
TAM-01 14.04.72
TAM-03 15.10.58
TAM-04 21.01.58
TAM-05 08.11.58
TAM-09 01.08.60
TAM-11 12.02.70
TAM-17 14.07.70
TAM-22 04.05.71
TAM-23 28.09.72
TAM-24 25.09.72
TAM-30 19.01.74
TAM-34 11.11.74
TAM-44 27.10.75
TAM-45 24.01.78
TAM-46 22.10.84
TAM-47 21.12.73
TAM-52 10.01.74
TAM-76 02.03.76
TAM-77 16.03.77

Transporte Aereo Militar [2]
2009 28.09.94
2028 24.11.94

Transporte Aereo Rioplatense
LV-JTN 18.07.81

Transporte Aereo Transandino
* 05.02.50
YV-C-AQA oo.10.47
YV-C-AQC 21.06.48

Transporte Aereo de Mercania
EC-EIS 07.06.89
EC-EQH 05.01.91

Transportes Aereas Bandeirantes
PP-LDR 08.09.60

Transportes Aereo Maranon
OB-1284 14.05.92

Transportes Aereos
OB-1341 24.01.94

Transportes Aereos Acre
CP-645 29.10.65

Transportes Aereos Benianos
CP-677 15.03.70
CP-717 29.05.64
CP-747 29.05.64
CP 760 23.08.68

Transportes Aereos Bolivar
CP-916 28.10.83

Transportes Aereos Catarinense
PP-AJA 15.03.53
PP-AJE 08.08.65

Transportes Aereos Continentais
CS-AJQ 28.07.76

Transportes Aereos Costa Brava
CC-CEE 11.05.80

Transportes Aereos Coyahique
CC-CET 12.11.85

Transportes Aereos Espanoles
EC-BEO 29.06.69

Transportes Aereos Gelabert
RX-15 17.09.38

Transportes Aereos Illimani
CP-910 07.12.73
CP-941 06.06.75

Transportes Aereos Itenez
CP-728 06.01.77
CP-983 27.01.77

Transportes Aereos Kentuta
CP-1352 12.01.79

Transportes Aereos Latin America
N6113C 16.11.70

Transportes Aereos Latinamericanos
HK-2580 12.12.82

Transportes Aereos Litoral
CP-800 12.12.69
CP-825 31.01.70

Transportes Aereos Luwior
CP-1333 oo.oo.oo

Transportes Aereos Maranon
OB-1453 23.11.93

Transportes Aereos Mexico-Cuba
NC379N oo.oo.31

Transportes Aereos Nacionales
PP-ANH 12.08.52
PP-ANO 31.05.54

Transportes Aereos Orientales
HC-AFQ 16.09.65
HC-ALC 02.03.71
HC-ALK 25.08.69
HC-SND 02.04.58

Transportes Aereos Pegaso
XA-SVS 01.11.94

Transportes Aereos Peruanas
OB-QAH-202 30.08.47
OB-QAM-488 08.05.59
OB-WBP-507 13.05.59

Transportes Aereos Portugueses
CS-TBR 19.11.77
CS-TDB 27.01.48
CS-TDF 08.06.48
CS-TSB oo.oo.48

Transportes Aereos Salvador
PP-SLG 27.03.53
PP-SLL 04.08.63

Transportes Aereos Samuel Selum
CP-1738 07.04.90

Transportes Aereos San Jorge
CP-1960 02.11.92

Transportes Aereos San Martin
CP-974 06.05.84

Transportes Aereos San Miguel
CP-1059 08.12.87

Transportes Aereos Suravia
CC-COA 17.12.73

Transportes Aereos Tropicales
HK-1591 22.08.73

Transportes Aereos Unidos
CP-1725 05.05.82

Transportes Aereos Universal
CP-746 07.01.90

Transportes Aereos da Guine-Bissau
J5-GAE 07.04.92

Transportes Aereos de El Salvador
YS-23C 22.03.93

Transportes Aereos de Tete
CR-AMX 15.06.72

Transportes Aereos de Timor
CR-AAT oo.oo.oo
CR-TAI 26.01.60

Transportes Aereos de Zambesia
9Q-CFN 09.07.82

Transportes Aereos del Caribe
HK-1810 21.12.80

Transportes Carga Aerea
PP-ASB 20.04.49

Transtar Aviation
N25Q 25.09.85

Transvall Corporation
N39AP 02.01.75

Transwede
SE-DEC 06.01.87

Transwest Helicopters
C-FAHL 13.07.80

Travair
OO-TLS 08.01.94

Travel Air Flug
D-IAEC 01.06.87

Travelair [1]
HB-VCG 20.02.72

Travelair [2]
SE-IDU 22.10.86

Travelair Taxi
N9610 03.07.54

Trek Airways
ZS-CIG 03.09.60

Trent Helicopters
G-BAVI 29.05.78

Tri-9 Corporation
N18837 oo.oo.74
N48230 11.04.75
N9760Z 26.08.74

Trigana Air Service
PK-YNM 04.11.94
PK-YPG 08.12.92
PK-YPL 00.05.95

Tropic Airways
ZS-DFB 27.07.52

Tropical Airways
RP-C1272 25.09.77
RP-C1280 21.01.78

Tropuf Avia
RA-01187 31.08.94

Troy Air Service
N44356 18.04.78

TsAGI
SSSR-V4 16.08.34
SSSR-V6 05.02.38

Tucker, H.J.
NX4769 03.11.28

Tulip Air
PH-ATM 27.10.94

Tumenaskoe Directorate
RA-23555 30.11.94

Tumenavia
14398 26.09.92
23463 24.12.92
RA-01410 22.12.93
RA-06043 15.10.93
RA-21170 21.04.93
RA-22315 09.08.93
RA-22554 22.05.93
RA-24104 13.05.93
RA-24728 05.03.93
RA-25203 10.03.94
RA-88244 17.05.93
SSSR-21882 19.06.92
SSSR-25475 09.09.92
SSSR-25909 23.09.92

Tunis Air
TS-DAA 20.09.70

Tunisavia
TS-HSU 23.04.79

Tupolev Design Bureau
SSSR-77102 03.06.73

Turbowest Helicopters
C-FHBG 04.04.94

Turismo Aereo
HP-658 00.00.00
HP-676 00.00.00

Turkmen Avia
SSSR-88235 13.05.92

Turkmenistan Airlines
07562 14.09.93
EZ-07469 11.11.93

Turks & Caicos Airways
N38JA 15.08.73

Turks & Caicos National Airlines
VQ-TAJ 00.09.86

Turner, R.
n/a 00.00.28

Tyee Airways
C-FTYB 19.05.82

Tyrolean Airways
OE-EXV 26.01.84

Tyumen Directorate
RA-21040 01.07.94

Tyumenaviatrans
* 16.10.95
RA-21001 15.12.94
RA-24102 21.11.94

UAT
F-BFVO 06.11.52
F-BFVT 03.06.55
F-BGOI 18.04.55
F-BGSC 25.06.53
F-BGTZ 26.12.58
F-BGZB 29.03.59

UB Air
VT-EPV 13.09.91

US Air
N210US 22.07.90
N388US 01.02.91
N416US 20.09.89
N485US 22.03.92
N513AU 08.09.94
N954VJ 03.07.94
N961VJ 21.02.86
N964VJ 18.01.92

US Airlines
N1911M 05.04.52
NC88804 14.03.47

US Civil Aeronautics Authority
NC206 21.01.48

US Commerce Department
NS-1 26.09.33

US Customs Service
* 15.11.87
* 02.12.89
* 24.08.92
81-23577 14.07.93

US Department of Energy
N6887Y 18.12.92

US Drug Enforcement Administration
* 03.09.89
N119CA 27.08.94

US Engineers Office
NC972Y 10.10.43

US Forest Service
N141Z 22.08.94
N148Z 11.06.79

US Mission to Colombia
* 14.07.60

US Overseas Airlines
N68736 13.05.57

US Steel Co
N541S 00.00.61

US Treasury
NC14279 02.08.41

UTA
F-BHMS 02.10.64
F-BOLL 10.03.84
F-GDUA 16.03.85
N54629 19.09.89

Uganda Airlines
5X-AAB 04.05.76
5X-UAL 01.04.79
5X-UBC 17.10.88

Uganda Co Ltd
VP-UAW 21.09.47

Ukraine Airlines
UR-67115 23.01.95

Ukraine Flight Academy
UR-26049 00.00.95
UR-26084 16.03.95

Ukrainian Airlines
UR-25445 08.07.93

Ukrvozdukhput
* 18.01.30
RRUAA 00.00.28
RRUAH 28.07.27
RRUAW 11.10.28
SSSR-201 15.05.29
SSSR-217 24.08.29
SSSR-219 25.06.29
SSSR-225 00.00.30

Ulm, C.T.P.
VH-UXY 04.12.34

Ulster Aviation
G-AJKJ 25.03.48
G-AJOB 27.06.47
G-AJTD 03.11.48

Uni-Air
F-GGDM 12.04.89

Union Airways
ZS-ABR 31.12.31
ZS-AEB 14.12.33

Union Airways of New Zealand
ZK-AFC 10.05.38
ZK-AFE 07.05.42
ZK-AHU 13.05.45

Union Flights
N9417B 22.03.95

Union Oil Co of California
N7601 21.12.63

Union Pacific Aviation
N400UP 24.07.95

Union Producing Co
N8420H 00.00.55

Union of Burma Airways
XY-ABO 14.03.49
XY-ABP 23.04.49
XY-ABR 22.11.50
XY-ACC 13.11.49
XY-ACL 10.01.53
XY-ACQ 02.09.55
XY-ACR 24.05.69
XY-ACS 10.06.63
XY-ACX 04.08.53
XY-ADB 19.03.57
XY-ADC 08.08.56
XY-ADF 24.08.72
XY-ADL 25.06.66

Unionair
VH-EQK 31.03.76

Uniran
C-FSAW 23.10.77

United Air
ZS-UAS 12.04.88

United Air Lines
N16088 28.04.51
N17109 04.12.51
N1819U 19.07.89
N30062 06.10.55
N30070 15.06.54
N31230 12.09.51
N37512 04.04.55
N37519 17.10.65
N37543 30.06.51
N37550 24.08.51
N37559 01.11.55
N6324C 30.06.56
N6328C 21.04.58
N6339C 18.05.66
N7030U 11.11.65
N7036U 16.08.65
N7405 09.07.64
N7425U 21.03.68
N7429 11.12.67
N7430 23.11.62
N7431 19.01.67
N7434U 18.01.69
N7465 28.11.67
N8013U 16.12.60
N8040U 11.07.61
N8047U 18.12.77
N8053U 11.01.83
N8082U 29.12.78
N9005U 19.07.70
N9031U 08.12.72
N999UA 04.03.91
NC13302 07.06.34
NC13317 07.10.35
NC13319 23.11.36
NC13323 30.10.35
NC13355 27.12.36
NC13357 23.02.34
NC16064 18.11.42
NC16066 29.11.38
NC16073 09.02.37
NC16074 17.10.37
NC16086 04.11.40
NC16090 11.01.43
NC17713 27.01.49
NC18108 24.05.38
NC18146 02.05.42
NC19947 11.11.46
NC25675 31.01.46
NC25678 04.12.40
NC273 07.02.32
NC30046 29.05.47
NC30050 24.12.46
NC30051 08.10.46
NC33646 24.02.47
NC37506 17.06.48
NC37510 24.10.47
NC415E 16.09.33
NX30065 29.05.46

United Air Services [1]
NC32E 09.07.34
NC48M 13.12.38
NC7428 17.02.36

United Air Services [2]
VR-TAR 04.03.48
VR-TAT 03.01.50

United Air Transport
CF-BDX 00.08.38
CF-BJT 00.02.39

United Aircraft Services
N111ST 01.07.81

United Airways
ZS-DDW 12.01.51

United Arab Airlines
SU-AID 16.03.62
SU-AJG 15.01.68
SU-AJM 15.05.62
SU-AJW 00.06.65
SU-AJX 12.05.63
SU-AKW 29.09.60
SU-AKX 23.02.64
SU-ALC 02.01.71
SU-ALD 28.07.63
SU-ALE 09.02.70
SU-ALP 06.05.61
SU-AMW 19.07.62
SU-ANI 14.01.70
SU-ANL 24.01.67
SU-ANZ 19.07.70
SU-AOA 18.03.66
SU-AOK 13.01.70
SU-AOL 18.08.68
SU-APC 20.03.69

United Executive
N500RW 24.05.88

United Gas Public Service
NC14249 12.06.36

United Nations Organisation
* 26.09.92
SE-BDY 18.09.61
SE-CFB 08.06.62
UN-202 20.09.62
UN-203 00.00.61

United Parcel Service
N568UP 31.01.85

United States Airways
N3821 07.03.69

United States Coast Guard
* 00.00.43
* 10.01.87
1473 02.11.86
1600 30.07.82
V111 05.12.36
V126 05.08.41
V130 00.08.35

United States Global
N37777 22.04.76

United States Navy
N742DM 18.05.92

Universal Air Leasing
N250UA 27.04.78

Universal Air Taxi
N777AE 01.01.79

Universal Airlines
N7466 27.09.68
N762Z 02.07.68
N851V 19.03.72
N855U 24.08.70
NC18609 00.00.00

Universal Flying Services
G-AGNI 11.06.48

Universal Helicopters
* 00.04.85
C-FUHL 15.09.94

Universal Ltd
CP-1588 10.02.81

Universal Pictures
N1047G 25.07.79

Unum Inc
N45515 00.00.71

Ural Airlines
RA-26529 11.03.93

Urcupina
CP-1470 06.04.81

Utility Airways
G-AEDY 10.01.40

Uyak Air Service
N126UA 08.08.94
N5354G 13.07.89

Uzbekistan Airways
76794 21.04.93

VASP
PP-LDL 21.03.64
PP-LDQ 19.12.65
PP-LET 02.04.69
PP-LEW 06.11.68
PP-NME 00.00.68
PP-NMF 10.08.64
PP-SBE 27.02.75
PP-SME 28.01.86
PP-SMI 12.04.72
PP-SMJ 23.10.73
PP-SML 07.11.71
PP-SMV 01.02.95
PP-SMX 03.04.78
PP-SMY 24.05.82
PP-SNC 22.02.83
PP-SND 22.06.92
PP-SPD 27.08.43
PP-SPD 00.00.00
PP-SPF 00.00.00
PP-SPK 06.06.64
PP-SPL 18.05.51
PP-SPM 13.05.52
PP-SPP 14.09.69
PP-SPQ 08.09.51
PP-SPR 11.01.69
PP-SPT 13.12.50
PP-SPU 15.01.65
PP-SPV 26.05.50
PP-SPW 14.12.50
PP-SPX 07.05.56
PP-SPZ 27.05.64
PP-SQA 29.01.73
PP-SQE 30.12.58
PP-SQP 26.11.64
PP-SQS 15.08.60
PP-SQV 23.09.59
PP-SQY 08.03.64
PP-SRA 26.11.62
PP-SRD 15.05.73
PP-SRE 15.09.68
PP-SRG 22.12.59
PP-SRK 08.06.82
PP-SRM 31.10.66
PP-SRQ 03.03.65
PP-SRR 04.09.64

VAT Inc
XA-BHG 15.05.37

VEB-Dresden
DM-ZYA 04.03.59

VFW-Fokker
D-BABA 01.02.72

VO-GVF
SSSR-210 30.01.31
SSSR-L47 07.03.32
SSSR-L5 10.10.31
SSSR-L52 19.04.32

VOTEC
PT-GJZ 18.04.84
PT-GKL 18.04.84
PT-GLB 24.02.81
PT-HFE 02.04.80
PT-HGK 03.04.80
PT-HGO 25.08.83
PT-HIP 28.05.79
PT-HIR 15.03.78
PT-HIT 23.12.81
PT-HKB 21.03.80
PT-HKC 29.09.81
PT-HKD 07.11.83
PT-HKU 18.05.81
PT-IJE 12.06.79
PT-JSC 30.03.80
PT-JYC 00.00.00
PT-KHK 13.05.80

VZLU
OK-DKD 00.00.00

Vaengir
TF-REE 27.02.73

Valley Air Service
* 24.12.77
N457SA 28.09.81

Valujet
N908VJ 09.06.95

Van Lear Black Ltd
G-AADZ 10.06.29

Vanair
YJ-RV3 03.01.90
YJ-RV4 25.07.91

Vancouver Air Services
C-FSTX 00.00.00

Vancouver Island Helicopters
C-FLIL 14.06.94
C-GSHE 03.07.80
C-GWGS 07.04.95

Vanderpool Flying Service
N49319 26.03.71

Varela, J.B.C
X-BAI 00.00.00

Varig
P-BAAE 25.04.31
PP-CDS 12.05.60
PP-PEA 04.03.67
PP-VAL 28.02.42
PP-VAQ 20.06.44
PP-VAS 07.03.48
PP-VAU 18.10.52
PP-VAY 20.04.66
PP-VBE 00.00.00
PP-VBH 14.10.67
PP-VBI 25.09.49
PP-VBJ 22.03.65
PP-VBM 12.12.61
PP-VBV 01.07.63
PP-VBZ 04.06.54
PP-VCB 21.02.52
PP-VCF 07.04.57
PP-VCK 22.09.58
PP-VCQ 22.12.62
PP-VCS 18.10.57
PP-VCT 18.12.60
PP-VDA 16.08.57
PP-VDL 03.01.58
PP-VDN 17.06.75
PP-VDQ 14.12.69
PP-VDU 04.02.72
PP-VJA 27.11.62
PP-VJD 27.09.61
PP-VJK 03.01.87
PP-VJP 05.02.70
PP-VJR 07.09.68
PP-VJT 11.06.81
PP-VJZ 11.07.73
PP-VLJ 09.06.73
PP-VLU 30.01.79
PP-VMK 03.09.89
PP-YPK 23.06.66
PP-YQN 03.03.62

Varmlandsflyg
SE-GUO 07.07.94

Varney Air Transport
NC176W 28.09.36
NC483M 27.04.37
NC830M 30.05.32
NC891E 01.05.35

Varney Speed Lines
NC12226 25.03.33

Vasquez, F.
CP-718 02.03.66

Vasquez, R.
CP-786 15.09.66

Vaughn, R.L.
N77WA 03.08.75

Vayudoot
VT-DMC 19.10.88
VT-EJF 24.09.89
VT-EJT 22.09.88

Vernair Transport
G-BDKG 08.07.79
N8431N 17.03.78

Vernon Helicopters
C-GDBR 29.06.85

Vestlandske Luftfartselskap
LN-TAK 31.08.49

Viacao Aereo Santos Dumont
PP-SDD 15.08.52

Vias Aereas Colombianas
C-400 09.03.47

Vias Aereas Nacionales
HK-1918 01.12.77

Viasa
YV-C-AVD 16.03.69

Vickers
G-EAAV 27.02.20
n/a 24.09.11

Vickers Armstrong
G-AGOK 23.04.46
G-AHRF 27.08.52
G-AOYF 20.10.57

Victoria Air
N102AP 07.06.91
N82922 29.09.90
RP-C14 15.11.89

Vieques Air Link
N112JC 00.09.89
N290VL 00.09.89
N589JA 21.12.71
N589SA 02.08.84
N862JA 19.12.77

Viessman Werke
D-CHVB 25.01.95

Vietnam Airlines
VN-A126 12.01.91
VN-A449 14.11.92

Vietnamese Government
F-VNAD 30.07.53

Viking Air Transport
NC53218 16.05.46

Viking Express
N101VE 28.09.86
N80CB 04.05.93
N0711 07.05.95

Viking Helicopters
C-GFQI 06.06.86
C-GPHN 28.11.79
C-GRYK 01.06.81

Viking International Air Freight
N725R 14.04.72

Village Airways
RP-C138 31.10.84

Villaroel, J.
CP-648 03.12.58

Vinair
N57372 05.04.71

Virgin Air
N127LB 00.09.95

Virgin Islands Airways
N6503D 15.07.65

Virgin Islands Seaplane Shuttle
N604SS 24.10.86
N628SS 17.09.89
N632SS 17.09.89
N655SS 17.09.89

Visionair International
N54605 27.12.80

Vnukovo Production Association
RA-85295 25.12.93

Vodavia
HB-VAM 28.08.72

Volga Airlines
RA-87464 25.01.95

Volga-Dnepr Cargo Airlines
SSSR-11342 24.07.92

Volkswagen Pacific Inc
N515VW 17.04.69

Von Haaf Air
* 00.01.95
D2-FVA 06.12.94

Voyageur Airways
C-GBSG 03.01.83
C-GJUL 29.11.88

W.M.Wrigley Co
N1181G 12.05.85

W.Morales y Cia
YV-164CP 00.07.80

W.R.Carpenter Ltd
G-AUJC 23.10.35
VH-URO 01.10.35
VH-UYW 15.03.40

Wagair
C-FRQW 26.07.93

Waggoner Aircraft
N9025R 10.01.79

Waglisla Air
C-FUMG 04.12.93

Walcot Airlines
G-AAZK 21.07.30

Wallace's Bookstores
N771WW 10.01.95

War Assets Administration
43-10314 oo.oo.oo

Wardair
C-FWAD 20.11.77
CF-WAG 03.05.70

Wasawings
OH-CIG 31.08.86
OH-EBA 14.11.88

Weasua Air Transport
9L-LAV 07.11.89
EL-AGZ 05.03.88

Webber Air
N1045 25.08.78

Wedell-Williams Air Service
NC537M 07.01.31

Weeks, K.
N7584 24.08.92

Wegener, A.R.
VH-BEP oo.12.47

Wells Air Transport
CF-AJP 15.08.33

Wenela Air Services
A2-ZER 04.03.74

Werner, R.
N28360 21.12.67

West African Air Cargo
9G-ACL 10.06.78

West African Airways
VR-NAD 05.02.55
VR-NAG 02.05.49
VR-NAX 27.07.51
VR-NAY 26.09.58
VR-NEW 14.11.50

West Air Aviation
V5-WAC oo.07.94

West Australian Airways
G-AUDF 27.01.25
VH-UMC 01.03.32
VH-UOM 11.10.33

West Aviation
LN-TSA 19.03.93

West Coast Air Services
* 22.01.77
C-FGEC 14.08.78
C-FWAF 30.09.79

West Coast Airlines
N2703 17.01.63
N2707 24.08.63
N2712 10.03.67
N9101 01.10.66

West Darling Air Service
VH-ICA 04.02.56

West Florida Helicopters
N5046F 11.12.92

West Indies Air Transport
N74AF 03.02.92

West Siberian Directorate
RA-22752 22.10.94
RA-23462 11.05.94
RA-30037 04.08.94

Westair
* 09.09.56
N1248N 05.06.50
N131CA 19.04.93
N754FE 12.01.95

Westchester Air
N208W 06.10.89
N7GA 04.08.94

Western Air Express
* 08.12.26
NC122M 02.12.33
NC13314 01.09.35
NC13315 12.01.37
NC13339 12.01.41
NC13370 15.12.36
NC1476 10.12.27
NC279E 23.02.30
NC3709 07.05.29
NC3863 10.08.30
NC393E 02.06.29
NC39N 11.12.32
NC419E 24.02.30
NC420E 21.01.30
NC5170 26.01.31
NC5358 26.12.29
NC591E 22.12.30
NC742K 09.02.32
NC8011 03.12.33
NC8021 05.06.29
NC8820 06.01.30
NC9789 31.12.33

Western Air Lines
N15569 29.06.53
N3166 31.03.71
N4527W 31.03.75
N8405H 13.02.58
N8407H 26.02.54
N903WA 31.10.79
N91303 20.04.53
NC16060 15.12.42
NC18645 13.11.46
NC33621 24.04.46
NC45395 24.12.46

Western Airways
G-ACJT 20.12.39
G-ACMP 23.07.35

Western Arctic Air
C-GSAF 26.01.90

Western Aviators
N26JB 13.02.92

Western Canada Airways
G-CAJT 23.10.28

Western Helicopters
N1089N 26.06.95

Western Hemisphere Import Export Co
* 19.06.57
* 20.09.57

Western Leasing Co
N403M 16.12.69

Western Straits Air
* 27.09.95

Westinghouse
* 02.08.95

Westland Helicopters [1]
XV372 15.01.69
ZF527 23.07.87
ZF644 07.04.95

Westland Helicopters [2]
C-GRAH 29.01.94

Westminster Airways
G-AHDL 01.04.49
G-AHYO 31.10.46

Weston Ltd
EI-AEA 04.09.49

Westport Air Travel
N81628 22.09.90

Westway Air Taxis
G-ASHC 21.03.64

Westwing Helikopter
LN-OSQ 07.03.83

Whaley, J.
N13415 10.11.78

Wharton, H.
I-ACOA 11.10.66

Wheeler Airlines
CF-IHQ 25.03.60
CF-ILI 04.11.59

White Pass Airways
NC5092 30.01.40

White River Air Services
C-FGBC 18.06.95

Whiteshell Air Services
C-GOMC 04.12.87

Whitham Farms Feed Yard
N710MB 15.12.93

Wideroe
LN-ABU 02.08.35
LN-BAN 07.04.36
LN-BNK 11.03.82
LN-BNM 27.10.93
LN-BNS 12.04.90
LN-PAS 05.03.64
LN-WFN 06.05.88

Wien Air Alaska
N4904 30.08.75

Wien Consolidated Airlines
N4905 02.12.68

Wilbur's Flight Operations
N8416F 11.03.75

Wilburs Inc
N969JW 10.12.87

Wilderness Airline
C-FPQB 12.07.93
C-GSKY 24.05.82
CF-RDI oo.06.75

Wilkins, G.H.
* 25.02.27

Willair International
N8081H 28.09.68

William Dempster Ltd
G-AKCC 26.10.51

Williams Aviation
N300CW 14.02.90

Williams, G.
N2204S 22.11.84

Willis Air Service
NC56743 02.12.46

Willow Air Service
N5317G 26.09.85

Wilmington-Catalina Airways
NC12212 02.11.33

Wilson Airways
VP-KAC 04.08.35
VP-KAW 08.12.33
VP-KBE 08.06.38
VP-KBG 14.04.37

Wilson, S.J.
NC7687 10.12.28

Winged Cargo
NC88876 17.12.46

Wings West Airlines
N6399U 24.08.84

Wings of Alaska
N13GA 23.06.94

Winn Exploration Co
N700CW 01.04.83

Winner Airways
B-308 25.04.70

Wolf Aviation
9Q-CWR oo.10.84

Wolverhampton Aviation
G-AKME 30.06.50

Wolverine Air Charter
N404EX 16.08.85

Wolverine Flying Service
NC7896 10.02.30

Wonderair
ZS-LPI 07.09.84

Wood, G.A.
NC16917 oo.04.38

Wood, P.A. & A.
G-AHGD 30.06.91

Woods Air Service
N41755 22.07.92

World Air Freight
G-AITC 20.01.50
G-AJNZ 28.09.48
G-AKAC 29.04.49
G-AKGZ 08.10.48

World Airways
N113WA 24.01.82
N802WA 08.09.73
N90779 18.09.60

World Wide Airways
CF-HVJ 18.06.55
CF-IHR 23.09.56

Worldair Carriers
G-AHDX 16.04.50

Wrightways
G-ACHX 25.04.38

Wuhan Air Lines
B-4211 08.10.92

Wyoming Air Service
NC13749 24.10.36

XP Airlines
PH-ASU 25.02.86

Xiamen Airlines
B-2510 02.10.90

Xiengkhouang Air
XW-TDC 23.07.70

YPFB Transportes Aereos
CP-1017 13.02.74
CP-1018 20.05.87

Yacimientos Petroliferos Fiscales
LV-ALW 11.04.85
LV-HHB 15.04.76
LV-MRX 21.11.79

Yakovlev Design Bureau

*	00.00.52
*	00.00.53

Yakutavia

RA-24459	23.05.93
RA-33008	29.10.94
RA-47708	21.06.93
SSSR-22384	05.07.92
SSSR-22651	21.09.92
SSSR-87411	14.09.92

Yashen Airlines

RA-23801	26.03.95

Yellowhead Air Service

*	30.10.77

Yellowknife Airways

CF-EKJ	06.02.51

Yemen Airlines

4W-AAS	19.03.69
4W-ABI	16.09.71
4W-ABJ	01.11.72
4W-ABL	11.11.76
4W-ABR	13.12.73
4W-ABY	14.11.78
YE-AAB	03.11.58

Yevlakh Air Transport

*	29.10.91

Yugavia

SSSR-26618	05.12.92
SSSR-46306	21.11.92

Yugoslav Government

YU-BJH	18.01.77

Yukon Airways

C-FOKQ	28.08.83

Yung Shing Airlines

B-12105	17.07.71
B-12202	09.10.83
B-12207	00.02.87

Yunnan Airlines

B-2540	20.07.94

Yuzhnoye Air Transport

RA-15362	27.03.94

ZB Air

5Y-AJZ	07.12.83

ZONDA

LV-ADD	30.07.47
LV-AEO	00.00.00

ZUA

SP-WNZ	22.09.75

Zaire Aero Service

9Q-CPD	28.08.84

Zaire Air Cargo

9Q-CWT	05.02.86

Zaire International Airlines

OO-SJH	11.05.80

Zakavia

R-RECA	22.03.25

Zambesi Airways

VP-YLV	06.01.55

Zambia Air Cargoes

9J-RBX	11.04.68
9J-RCY	11.04.68

Zambia Airways

9J-ADM	04.07.83

Zambian Flying Doctor Service

9J-ACF	27.03.75

Zamrud Airlines

N65134	07.03.69
PK-ZDD	20.08.72
PK-ZDF	04.06.70

Zantop Air Transport

N10415	16.06.66
N188S	30.06.64
N2028A	16.12.56
N30061	14.11.61
N3971B	20.11.64
N49551	20.01.54
N601Z	14.10.65
N608Z	30.12.64
N609Z	07.12.63
N616Z	16.02.63
N9905F	28.07.66

Zantop International Airlines

N283F	30.04.75
N5504	21.03.82
N5516	21.03.82
N5523	30.05.84

Zeppelin-Staaken

n/a	28.12.20

Zimex Aviation

HB-AEB	02.09.94
HB-CKW	22.07.89
HB-FCX	09.03.81
HB-FIP	04.12.85
HB-ILF	14.10.87

Zone-Redningskorpset Flyvetjenesten

OY-DZI	05.10.56
OY-DZY	16.07.60

Appendix D

Civil types in military use

This appendix provides details of Western-built turbine airliners which have been written off in military service. These types were all built essentially as civilian airliners and usually fulfilled the same role in the armed forces. This list enables the full accident record of these aircraft to be included in this one volume.

Date	Type	Reg'n	C/n	Operator	Accident	Location	F	S
03.06.59	de Havilland Comet R.2	XK663	06027	Royal Air Force [51 Sqn]	Destroyed in hangar fire	Watton, Norfolk, UK	0	*
11.04.67	Canadair CC-109 Cosmopolitan	11153	003	Royal Canadian Air Force	Destroyed by oxygen fire	Montreal, PQ, Canada	*	*
05.06.67	Hawker Siddeley Andover C.1	XS598	Set 05	Royal Air Force [46 Sqn]	Damaged when overran runway	Abingdon, Berks, UK	*	*
14.10.67	Bristol Britannia C.1	XL638	13400	Royal Air Force [99 & 511 Sqn]	Overran into water on landing	Khormaksar, South Arabian Fed.	0	*
08.12.67	Vickers Viscount 742D	C-90.2100	141	Brazilian Air Force	Undershot on landing	Santos Dumont, Brazil	0	*
07.05.68	Hawker Siddeley Argosy C.1	XR133	6788	Royal Air Force [267 Sqn]	Crashed after striking obstruction while low flying	Got-el-Afraq, Libya	*	*
26.08.69	Hawker Siddeley HS.748 2	AF601	1600	Zambian Air Force	Crashed on take-off	Lusaka, Zambia	3	*
10.11.69	Fokker F-27 Friendship 400M	899	10283	Sudanese Air Force	Crashed	Sudan	*	*
04.06.70	Hawker Siddeley Argosy C.1	XP441	6773	Royal Air Force [114 Sqn]	Undershot on landing	Benson, Oxon, UK	0	*
21.01.71	Nord 262A-34	44	044	French Air Force	Crashed	Aubenas, France	19	*
13.08.71	Hawker Siddeley Trident 1E	256	2131	Chinese Air Force	Stolen by defecting officials & shot down	Mongolia	9	0
16.09.71	McDonnell Douglas C-9A Nightingale	67-22586	47296	United States Air Force	Crashed on take-off	Scott AFB, IL, USA	*	*
08.04.72	Hawker Siddeley Andover C.1	XS609	Set 16	Royal Air Force [46 Sqn]	Crashed on take-off	Sienna, Italy	4	*
25.08.73	Fokker F-27 Friendship 600	5-209	10484	Iranian Air Force	Crashed	nr Chalus, Iran	5	0
30.09.74	Fokker F-27 Friendship 400M	5-211	10489	Iranian Air Force	Crashed	Iran	*	*
27.04.75	Hindustan 748 2-247	H1520	558	Indian Air Force	Crashed	Location Unknown	*	*
17.01.76	Handley Page Dart Herald 401	FM1025	181	Royal Malaysian Air Force	Damaged in belly landing	Malaysia	0	*
27.04.76	Hawker Siddeley Argosy C.1	XR105	6783	Empire Test Pilots School	Crashed on overshoot	Boscombe Down, Wilts, UK	2	1
09.05.76	Boeing 747-131	5-283	19677	Iranian Air Force	Crashed in storm due to wrong fuel being used	Carrascosa del Campo, Spain	17	0
14.09.78	Fokker F-27 Friendship 200	10328	10328	Philippine Air Force	Crashed in storm	nr Manila, Philippines	21{15}	6
17.01.79	Nord 262A-29	85	085	French Navy	Crashed on take-off	Cherbourg, France	0	*
07.06.79	Hindustan 748 2M-LFD	H2178	572	Indian Air Force	Crashed	nr Leh, India	27	*
24.01.80	Fairchild-Hiller FH.227B/LCD	5003	545	Burmese Air Force	Crashed	nr Mandalay, Burma	43	1
26.05.80	Fokker F-27 Friendship 400M	NAF.904	10488	Nigerian Air Force	Written off	Lagos, Nigeria	*	*
22.09.80	Boeing 707-3J9C	*	*	Iranian Air Force	Destroyed in Iraqi air raid	Tehran, Iran	*	*
oo.10.82	Fokker F-27 Friendship 100	5001	10124	Burmese Air Force	Written off	Burma	*	*
oo.10.82	Fokker F-27 Friendship 400M	G-523D	10520	Ghanaian Air Force	Written off	Ghana	*	*
08.01.85	Fokker F-27 Friendship 200MAR	10665	10665	Royal Thai Navy	Overturned on landing	Bangkok, Thailand	0	*
01.07.85	British Aerospace 748 2A	JW-9009	1752	Tanzanian Defence Force	Crashed	Mbeya, Tanzania	*	*
15.11.85	Convair VC-131H Samaritan	542817	221	United States Navy	Crashed	nr Dothan, AL, USA	*	*
29.04.86	Fokker F-27 Friendship 400MAR	AE-561	10549	Peruvian Navy	Crashed in sea	Off Las Salinas de Huacho, Peru	7	0
14.08.86	Fokker F-27 Friendship 400M	*	*	Indonesian Air Force	Crashed	nr Gurut, Indonesia	8	0
17.09.87	McDonnell Douglas KC-10A Extender	82-0190	48212	United States Air Force	Exploded on ground	Barksdale AFB, LA, USA	0{1}	16
08.12.87	Fokker F-27 Friendship 400MAR	AE-560	10548	Peruvian Navy	Crashed	Off Ventanilla, Peru	42	1
08.07.88	Embraer Brasilia 120	2001	120.029	Brazilian Air Force	Crashed during engine-out landing	Sao Dos Campos, Brazil	9	4
19.12.88	Fokker F-27 Friendship 200MAR	10602	10602	Philippine Air Force	Crashed on landing	Catarman, Philippines	0	18
oo.03.89	Fokker F-27 Friendship 200MAR	10616	10616	Philippine Air Force	Damaged beyond repair	Laoag, Philippines	*	*
23.09.89	Lockheed Electra 188C	0789	1123	Argentine Navy	Caught fire after u/c collapsed on landing	Almirante Zar, Argentina	0	23
17.02.90	British Aerospace 748 2A	602	1688	Zambian Air Force	Crashed	Ngwerere, Zambia	28	0
02.08.90	McDonnell Douglas DC-9-32F	KAF.320	47691	Kuwait Air Force	Destroyed by Iraqi forces on ground	Kuwait City, Kuwait	*	*
25.03.91	Hindustan 748	*	*	Indian Air Force	Crashed on take-off	Bangalore, India	28	0
29.10.91	Boeing 707-368C	A20-103	21103	Royal Australian Air Force	Crashed after take-off	Off Bridgetown, NSW, Australia	5	0
16.07.92	Short JC-23A Sherpa	84-0466	SH.3113	United States Army	Crashed	Colquit, GA, USA	3	0
30.03.93	Boeing 737-3Z6	33-333	24480	Royal Thai Air Force	Crashed after engine failure	nr Khon Kaen, Thailand	6	0
23.04.95	Fokker F-27 Friendship 200MPA	908	10656	Nigerian Air Force	Damaged when struck by Bristow Twin Otter 5N-AGQ	Lagos, Nigeria	0(1)	*
22.09.95	Boeing E-3B	79-0002	21756	United States Air Force	Crashed after engine failure on take-off	Elmendorf AFB, AK, USA	24	0

Appendix E

Nationality Prefix Index

The following are the current internationally recognised nationality prefixes used for civil aircraft registration.

Prefix by Code

Prefix	Country
3A	Monaco
3B	Mauritius
3C	Equatorial Guinea
3D	Swaziland
3X	Guinea
4K	Azerbaijan
4L	Georgia
4R	Sri Lanka
4U	United Nations
4X	Israel
5A	Libya
5B	Cyprus
5H	Tanzania
5N	Nigeria
5R	Madagascar
5T	Mauritania
5U	Niger
5V	Togo
5W	Western Samoa
5X	Uganda
5Y	Kenya
6O	Somalia
6V	Senegal
6Y	Jamaica
7O	Yemen
7P	Lesotho
7Q	Malawi
7T	Algeria
8P	Barbados
8Q	Maldives
8R	Guyana
9A	Croatia
9G	Ghana
9H	Malta
9J	Zambia
9K	Kuwait
9L	Sierra Leone
9M	Malaysia
9N	Nepal
9Q	Zaire
9U	Burundi
9V	Singapore
9XR	Rwanda
9Y	Trinidad & Tobago
A2	Botswana
A3	Tonga
A4O	Oman
A5	Bhutan
A6	United Arab Emirates
A7	Qatar
A9C	Bahrain
AP	Pakistan
B	China
B	Taiwan
BNMAU	Mongolia
C	Canada
C2	Nauru
C3	Andorra
C5	Gambia
C6	Bahamas
C9	Mozambique
CC	Chile
CN	Morocco
CP	Bolivia
CR	Macau
CS	Portugal
CU	Cuba
CX	Uruguay
D	Germany
D2	Angola
D4	Cape Verde
D6	Comoros
DQ	Fiji
E3	Eritrea
EC	Spain
EI	Ireland
EK	Armenia
EL	Liberia
EP	Iran
ER	Moldova
ES	Estonia
ET	Ethiopia
EW	Belarus
EX	Kirghizia
EY	Tajikistan
EZ	Turkmenistan
F	France
G	United Kingdom
H4	Solomon Islands
HA	Hungary
HB	Switzerland
HB	Liechtenstein
HC	Ecuador
HH	Haiti
HI	Dominican Republic
HK	Colombia
HL	South Korea
HP	Panama
HR	Honduras
HS	Thailand
HV	Vatican City
HZ	Saudi Arabia
I	Italy
J2	Djibouti
J3	Grenada
J5	Guinea-Bissau
J6	St Lucia
J7	Dominica
J8	St Vincent & Grenadines
JA	Japan
JY	Jordan
LN	Norway
LQ	Argentina
LV	Argentina
LX	Luxembourg
LY	Lithuania
LZ	Bulgaria
MONGOL	Mongolia
MT	Mongolia
N	USA
OB	Peru
OD	Lebanon
OE	Austria
OH	Finland
OK	Czech Republic
OM	Slovakia
OO	Belgium
OY	Denmark
P	North Korea
P2	Papua New Guinea
P4	Aruba
PH	Netherlands
PJ	Netherlands Antilles
PK	Indonesia
PP	Brazil
PT	Brazil
PZ	Surinam
RA	Russia
RDPL	Laos
RP	Philippines
S2	Bangladesh
S5	Slovenia
S7	Seychelles
S9	Sao Tome & Principe
SE	Sweden
SP	Poland
ST	Sudan
SU	Egypt
SX	Greece
T2	Tuvalu
T3	Kiribati
T7	San Marino
T9	Bosnia-Herzegovina
TC	Turkey
TF	Iceland
TG	Guatemala
TI	Costa Rica
TJ	Cameroon
TL	Central African Republic
TN	Congo
TR	Gabon
TS	Tunisia
TT	Chad
TU	Ivory Coast
TY	Benin
TZ	Mali
UK	Uzbekistan
UN	Kazakhstan
UR	Ukraine
V2	Antigua & Barbuda
V3	Belize
V4	St Kitts-Nevis
V5	Namibia
V6	Micronesia
V7	Marshall Islands
V8	Brunei Darussalam
VH	Australia
VN	Vietnam
VP-F	Falkland Islands
VP-LM	Montserrat
VP-LV	British Virgin Islands
VQ-H	St Helena
VQ-T	Turks & Caicos Islands
VR-B	Bermuda
VR-C	Cayman Islands
VR-G	Gibraltar
VR-H	Hong Kong
VT	India
XA	Mexico
XB	Mexico
XC	Mexico
XT	Burkina Faso
XU	Cambodia
XY	Myanmar
YA	Afghanistan
YI	Iraq
YJ	Vanuatu
YK	Syria
YL	Latvia
YN	Nicaragua
YR	Romania
YS	El Salvador
YU	Yugoslavia
YV	Venezuela
Z	Zimbabwe
Z3	Macedonia
ZA	Albania
ZK	New Zealand
ZL	New Zealand
ZP	Paraguay
ZS	South Africa
ZT	South Africa
ZU	South Africa

Prefix by Country

Country	Prefix
Afghanistan	YA
Albania	ZA
Algeria	7T
Andorra	C3
Angola	D2
Antigua & Barbuda	V2
Argentina	LQ
Argentina	LV
Armenia	EK
Aruba	P4
Australia	VH
Austria	OE
Azerbaijan	4K
Bahamas	C6
Bahrain	A9C
Bangladesh	S2
Barbados	8P
Belarus	EW
Belgium	OO
Belize	V3
Benin	TY
Bermuda	VR-B
Bhutan	A5
Bolivia	CP
Bosnia-Herzegovina	T9
Botswana	A2
Brazil	PP

Country	Prefix
Brazil	PT
British Virgin Islands	VP-LV
Brunei Darussalam	V8
Bulgaria	LZ
Burkina Faso	XT
Burundi	9U
Cambodia	XU
Cameroon	TJ
Canada	C
Cape Verde	D4
Cayman Islands	VR-C
Central African Rep	TL
Chad	TT
Chile	CC
China	B
Colombia	HK
Comoros	D6
Congo	TN
Costa Rica	TI
Croatia	9A
Cuba	CU
Cyprus	5B
Czech Republic	OK
Denmark	OY
Djibouti	J2
Dominica	J7
Dominican Republic	HI
Ecuador	HC
Egypt	SU
El Salvador	YS
Equatorial Guinea	3C
Eritrea	E3
Estonia	ES
Ethiopia	ET
Falkland Islands	VP-F
Fiji	DQ
Finland	OH
France	F
Gabon	TR
Gambia	C5
Georgia	4L
Germany	D
Ghana	9G
Gibraltar	VR-G
Greece	SX
Grenada	J3
Guatemala	TG
Guinea	3X
Guinea-Bissau	J5
Guyana	8R
Haiti	HH
Honduras	HR
Hong Kong	VR-H
Hungary	HA
Iceland	TF
India	VT
Indonesia	PK
Iran	EP
Iraq	YI
Ireland	EI
Israel	4X
Italy	I
Ivory Coast	TU
Jamaica	6Y
Japan	JA
Jordan	JY
Kazakhstan	UN
Kenya	5Y
Kirghizia	EX
Kiribati	T3
Kuwait	9K
Laos	RDPL
Latvia	YL
Lebanon	OD
Lesotho	7P
Liberia	EL
Libya	5A
Liechtenstein	HB
Lithuania	LY
Luxembourg	LX
Macau	CR
Macedonia	Z3
Madagascar	5R
Malawi	7Q
Malaysia	9M
Maldives	8Q
Mali	TZ
Malta	9H
Marshall Islands	V7
Mauritania	5T
Mauritius	3B
Mexico	XA
Mexico	XB
Mexico	XC
Micronesia	V6
Moldova	ER
Monaco	3A
Mongolia	BNMAU
Mongolia	MONGOL
Mongolia	MT
Montserrat	VP-LM
Morocco	CN
Mozambique	C9
Myanmar	XY
Namibia	V5
Nauru	C2
Nepal	9N
Netherlands	PH
Netherlands Antilles	PJ
New Zealand	ZK
New Zealand	ZL
Nicaragua	YN
Niger	5U
Nigeria	5N
North Korea	P
Norway	LN
Oman	A4O
Pakistan	AP
Panama	HP
Papua New Guinea	P2
Paraguay	ZP
Peru	OB
Philippines	RP
Poland	SP
Portugal	CS
Qatar	A7
Romania	YR
Russia	RA
Rwanda	9XR
San Marino	T7
Sao Tome & Principe	S9
Saudi Arabia	HZ
Senegal	6V
Seychelles	S7
Sierra Leone	9L
Singapore	9V
Slovakia	OM
Slovenia	S5
Solomon Islands	H4
Somalia	6O
South Africa	ZS
South Africa	ZT
South Africa	ZU
South Korea	HL
Spain	EC
Sri Lanka	4R
St Helena	VQ-H
St Kitts-Nevis	V4
St Lucia	J6
St Vincent & Grenadines	J8
Sudan	ST
Surinam	PZ
Swaziland	3D
Sweden	SE
Switzerland	HB
Syria	YK
Taiwan	B
Tajikistan	EY
Tanzania	5H
Thailand	HS
Togo	5V
Tonga	A3
Trinidad & Tobago	9Y
Tunisia	TS
Turkey	TC
Turkmenistan	EZ
Turks & Caicos Islands	VQ-T
Tuvalu	T2
Uganda	5X
Ukraine	UR
United Arab Emirates	A6
United Kingdom	G
United Nations	4U
USA	N
Uruguay	CX
Uzbekistan	UK
Vanuatu	YJ
Vatican City	HV
Venezuela	YV
Vietnam	VN
Western Samoa	5W
Yemen	7O
Yugoslavia	YU
Zaire	9Q
Zambia	9J
Zimbabwe	Z

Prefixes no longer in use

The following is a list of those nationality prefixes which are no longer used. Most have been withdrawn but a few have been reallocated to new countries and are still in use.

Prefix	Country
3W	Vietnam
6OS	Somalia
7O	Yemen PDR
9O	Congo
A	Austria
A-H	Hejaz
A-N	Nicaragua
AN	Nicaragua
B-A	Albania
B-B	Bulgaria
B-L	Latvia
BR	Burundi
C	Colombia
C-C	Cuba
C-P	Portugal
C-R	Romania
C-U	Uruguay
C-V	Bolivia
CB	Bolivia
CCCP*	USSR
CF	Canada
CH	Switzerland
CR-A	Mozambique
CR-B	Mozambique
CR-C	Cape Verde Islands
CR-G	Portuguese Guinea
CR-I	Portuguese India
CR-L	Angola
CR-S	Sao Tome & Principe
CR-T	Portuguese Timor
CV	Romania
CY	Ceylon
CZ	Monaco
DDR	East Germany
DM	East Germany
DZ	Danzig
E-A	Estonia
E-E	Ecuador
EJ	Ireland
ER	Eritrea
EZ	Saar
F-D	French Morocco
F-KH	Cambodia
F-L	Laos
F-VN	Vietnam
FC	Free France
G-AU	Australia
G-CA	Canada
G-I	India
G-NZ	New Zealand
G-U	South Africa
H-H	Haiti
H-M	Hungary
H-N	Netherlands
H-S	Thailand
J	Japan
JZ	Netherlands East Indies
K	Kuwait
K-S	Finland
KA	Katanga
KW	Cambodia
L-B	Czechoslovakia
L-G	Guatemala
L-L	Liberia
L-U	Luxembourg
LG	Guatemala
LI	Liberia
LR	Lebanon
M	Spain
M-S	Mexico
MC	Monaco
MI	Marshall Islands
N	Norway
NC	USA
NL	USA
NR	USA
NS	USA
NX	USA
O-B	Belgium
O-P	Peru
OA	Peru
OO-C	Belgian Congo
P-B	Brazil
P-P	Brazil
PI	Philippines
R	Argentina
R	Panama
R-R	USSR
R-Z	Lithuania
RC	Croatia
RM	Moldova
RR	USSR
RV	Iran
RX	Panama
RY	Lithuania
S-A	Sweden
S-G	Greece
S-P	Panama
SL	Saar
SN	Sudan
SSSR	USSR
T-D	Denmark
TJ	Transjordan
TS	Saar
UH	Saudi Arabia
UL	Luxembourg
UN	Yugoslavia
URSS	USSR
USSR	USSR
VO	Newfoundland
VP-A	Gold Coast
VP-B	Bahamas
VP-C	Ceylon
VP-G	British Guiana
VP-H	British Honduras
VP-J	Jamaica
VP-K	Kenya
VP-L	Leeward Islands
VP-M	Malta
VP-N	Nyasaland
VP-P	Western Pacific Islands
VP-R	Northern Rhodesia
VP-S	Somaliland Protectorate
VP-T	Trinidad & Tobago
VP-U	Uganda
VP-V	St Vincent
VP-W	Wei-Hei-Wei
VP-W	S Rhodesia/ Zimbabwe
VP-X	Gambia
VP-Y	S Rhodesia/ Zimbabwe
VP-Z	Zanzibar
VQ-B	Barbados
VQ-C	Cyprus
VQ-F	Fiji
VQ-G	Grenada
VQ-L	St Lucia
VQ-M	Mauritius
VQ-P	Palestine
VQ-S	Seychelles
VQ-Z	Bechuanaland/ Basutoland & Swaziland
VR-A	Aden
VR-J	Johore
VR-L	St Lucia
VR-N	British Cameroons
VR-O	North Borneo
VR-R	Malaya
VR-S	Singapore
VR-T	Tanganyika
VR-U	Brunei
X-A	Mexico
X-B	Mexico
X-C	China
X-H	Honduras
X-S	Serbia
XH	Honduras
XT	China
XV	South Vietnam
Y-M	Danzig
ZM	New Zealand

*Cyrillic characters for SSSR

Late Entries

The following accidents either occurred after delivery of the main listings to the publisher or the details were only received subsequently, making them too late for inclusion in the main text. The format of the entries is the same as that used throughout the Directory. Two asterisks at the beginning of the 'Accident' column denote that this entry supersedes one in the main listing as additional or amended information has now come to hand.

Date	Type	Reg'n	C/n	Operator	Accident	Location	F	S
07.08.35	Savoia-Marchetti S.66	I-REDI	15007	Ala Littoria	Crash landed & sank	Off Mahon, Balearic Is, Spain	0	*
09.04.49	Handley Page Halton	G-AHDP	1341/SH.25C	Aviation Traders	** DELETE ENTRY – Aircraft repaired	Schleswigland, West Germany	0	*
13.02.54	Douglas DC-3	F-OAHY	12793	Air Outremer	** Destroyed by shelling [Date not 13.02.53]	Muong Sai, Laos	*	*
06.09.76	Antonov AN-24	SSSR-46518	37308504	Aeroflot	** Mid-air collision with Aeroflot YAK-40 SSSR-87772	nr Sochi, Georgia, USSR	52(38)	0
06.09.76	Yakovlev YAK-40	SSSR-87772	*	Aeroflot	** Collided with AN-24 CCCP-46518 [Date not 09.09.76]	nr Sochi, Georgia, USSR	38(52)	0
01.09.79	Antonov AN-26	RDPL-34037	*	Lao Aviation	Crashed	Utharadit, Thailand	*	*
07.12.87	British Aerospace 748 2	HS-THH	1707	Bangkok Airways	U/c collapsed after overrunning on landing	Udon, Thailand	0	*
04.04.89	de Havilland Riley Heron	DQ-FED	14061	Fiji Air	** DELETE ENTRY – Aircraft repaired	Suva, Fiji	0	*
21.09.89	Britten-Norman BN-2A Islander	N457SA	0027	Vieques Air Link	** Destroyed by hurricane [Date not 28.09.81]	Vieques, Puerto Rico	*	*
25.10.93	Embraer Bandeirante 110P2	HS-SKL	110.229	Bangkok Airways	Damaged in belly landing	Bangkok, Thailand	0	*
04.04.94	Learjet 55	I-KILO	55-007	ICIPA	Crashed on landing	Seville, Spain	0	10
27.09.94	Tupolev TU-134A	OB-1490	60525	Imperial Air	Crashed into high ground in rain after birdstrike	Cusco, Peru	0	40
26.12.94	Airbus A.300B2-101	F-GBEC	104	Air France	Damaged by gunfire during hijack rescue attempt	Marseilles, France	0	180
03.01.95	de Havilland Canada Twin Otter 310	P2-IAA	244	Islands Nationair	** Ran off runway on take-off and u/c collapsed	Billi, Papua New Guinea	0	2
10.01.95	Beechcraft King Air B95	N673Q	TD-313	Operator Unknown	** DELETE ENTRY – [Aircraft not King Air]	Hot Springs, AR, USA	3	0
10.03.95	Cessna 207A Stationair 8 II	N6478H	207-00538	Ketchikan Air Service	Crashed on approach in bad weather	Gainsville, GA, USA	0	3
16.03.95	de Havilland Canada Twin Otter 200	N37ST	207	Great Barrier Airlines	** Ditched at sea on ferry flight	300km NE of Honolulu, HI, USA	0	3
20.03.95	Cessna 207 Skywagon	N1719U	207-00319	Yute Air Alaska	Crashed	Bethel, AK, USA	*	*
22.03.95	Cessna 208B Caravan I	N9417B	208B-0065	Union Flights/Airborne Express	** Crashed into mountain	nr Reno, NV, USA	1	0
23.03.95	Beechcraft E18S	N8111	BA-113	Caribe Air Cargo	** Crashed on approach	Walkers Cay, Bahamas	0	*
12.04.95	Beechcraft King Air B80	N7057J	LD-291	Air Cargo Masters	Crashed	nr Great Bend, ND, USA	1	*
13.04.95	Antonov AN-2	RA-40845	*	Operator Unknown	Crashed on take-off	Gugal-Buga, Russia	*	*
25.04.95	Cessna 207A Skywagon	N1769U	207-00369	Markair Express	Crashed after wing struck mountain	Old Harbor, AK, USA	0	*
29.04.95	Mil Mi-2	UR-14206	5211004079	Operator Unknown	Damaged on landing	Prostmoye, Ukraine	*	
25.05.95	Douglas DC-3	HK-3213	25659	LACOL	** Crashed on approach	Miraflores, Colombia	2	9
03.06.95	Boeing 747-238B	N706CK	20010	Kalitta American International Airways	** DELETE ENTRY – Aircraft repaired	Panama City, Panama	0	*
13.06.95	Bell 212	C-FNMP	30739	Northern Mountain Helicopters	** Crashed after take-off	nr Fort Vermilion, AL, Canada	0	*
16.06.95	Antonov AN-74	RA-74041	36547096924	Aviacor	Damaged on landing while overweight	Kepryeen, Russia	0	8
25.07.95	Mil Mi-2	RA-23518	525921128	Abakan State Aviation	** Crashed on approach	nr Norilsk, Russia	*	*
29.07.95	Cessna 421C Golden Eagle	N800DD	421C-0469	Operator Unknown	Crashed in sea after engine failure	nr Middleton Isle, AK, USA	*	*
30.07.95	Pilatus PC-6/B1-H2 Turbo Porter	PH-MEN	707	Operator Unknown	Mid-air collision with Cessna 172 OO-SIW on approach	Spa, Belgium	1(*)	0
01.08.95	Cessna T310R	6Y-JLW	*	RegionAir	** Crashed in mountains during hurricane	nr Kingston, Jamaica	5	0
01.08.95	Mil Mi-2	RA-14084	5210628058	Aeroflot	Crashed	Egypt	*	*
01.08.95	Mil Mi-8	RA-24609	*	Operator Unknown	Damaged beyond repair	Bolshaya Kanavka, Russia	*	*
04.08.95	Mil Mi-2	UN-14181	5410522028	Aktyubinsk Aviation	Crashed during landing	Goinboy Fakel, Kazakhstan	*	*
08.08.95	Mil Mi-17	RA-32894	*	Ulan-Ude Aircraft Production Assoc	Crashed	nr Kamwansk, Russia	1	2
10.08.95	Antonov AN-2	*	*	Tyumer aviatrans	** Crashed after striking power line whilst overloaded	Mezhdurechenskly, Russia	0	25
17.08.95	Boeing 707-321C	YR-ABN	19379	Air Afrique	** Damaged on after overruning on landing in rain	N'Djamena, Chad	0	6
18.08.95	Bell 206B JetRanger III	N16915	2294	Helicopter Transport Services	Crashed on landing	Bingham, ME, USA	*	*
19.08.95	Mil Mi-2	RA-20620	535026126	Nizhneundinsky Flight Unit	Crashed into lake	nr Tulma, Russia	*	*
21.08.95	Douglas DC-3	*	*	Operator Unknown	Crashed	Lobito, Mozambique	*	*
23.08.95	GAF Nomad 22B	N4826M	102	Haiti Express Airways	Crashed while landing	Jeremir, Haiti	0	14
24.08.95	Hughes 369HS	OH-HIU	64-0611S	Copter Action	Crashed after take-off	nr Turku, Finland	*	*
26.08.95	Sikorsky CH-54A	N64AR	*	Heavy Lift Helicopters	Crashed after engine failure	American River, CA, USA	*	*
31.08.95	Bell 214B	C-FVJE	28024	Black Tusk Helicopters	Crashed	nr Squamish, BC, Canada	*	*
01.09.95	Short Skyvan 3-200	N30GA	SH.1839	North Star Air Cargo	** Crashed into mountain	nr Farewell, AK, USA	1	0
05.09.95	Dassault Falcon 20F	5N-EPN	273	Aero Contractors	** DELETE ENTRY – Aircraft repaired	Lagos, Nigeria	0	11
07.09.95	Britten-Norman Trislander	N127LB	1010	Air St Thomas	Crashed in sea	Off St Thomas, US Virgin Is	*	*
09.09.95	Mil Mi-2	RA-23688	547243081	Rosto	Crashed while landing	Kreshenko, Russia	*	*
10.09.95	Beechcraft Queen Air 65	N945PA	*	Peninsula Skydiving Club	** Crashed into building [Date not 12.09.95]	West Point, WV, USA	11{1}	0
10.09.95	Bell 206B JetRanger II	N84TA	0594	Trans-Alaska Helicopters	Crashed	Glennalien, AK, USA	*	*
13.09.95	Cessna 402B	N69303	402B-0423	Bimini Air Charter	** Crashed short of runway	nr Marsh Harbor, Bahamas	5	4
15.09.95	Tupolev TU-134A	RA-65027	48485	Kaliningrad Avia	Damaged by fire in wing on landing	St Petersburg, Russia	0	35
16.09.95	Fairchild Metro III	VH-NEJ	AC-629B	Tamair	Crashed on take-off	Tamworth, NSW, Australia	2	1

Date	Type	Reg'n	C/n	Operator	Accident	Location	F	S
18.09.95	Fairchild Merlin III	N693PG	T-207	Great Western Hotels	** Crashed & caught fire	nr Chino, CA, USA	*	*
19.09.95	Hughes 369D	C-GXKF	0476D	Canadian Helicopters	Mid-air collision with Canadian H/C Hughes 369D C-GTXM	nr Yellowknife, NWT, Canada	2(2)	0
19.09.95	Hughes 369D	C-GTXM	0537D	Canadian Helicopters	Mid-air collision with Canadian H/C Hughes 369D C-GXKF	nr Yellowknife, NWT, Canada	2(2)	0
20.09.95	de Havilland Canada Otter	C-FGCV	002	Walsten Air Service	** Crashed on landing [Date not 22.09.95]	Salvesen Lake, ON, Canada	6	0
21.09.95	Mitsubishi MU-2B-35	N309MA	602	Corporate Flight Management	** Crashed after take-off	nr Smyrna, TX, USA	*	*
22.09.95	Boeing E-3B	77-0354	21554	United States Air Force	** Crashed after engine failure on take-off [Appendix D]	Elmendorf AFB, AK, USA	24	0
23.09.95	Learjet 36A	HB-VFS	36A-042	Executive Jet Aviation	Crashed short of runway & caught fire	Zarzaitine, Algeria	0	*
24.09.95	Mil Mi-8T	RA-24553	98522942	Norilsk Flight Company	Crashed through ice on landing at night	Sterligov Cape, Russia	15	0
29.09.95	Aerospatiale SA.316B Alouette III	OE-OXW	2244	Heli Alpin Knaus	Crashed on take-off	Kuchl, Austria	*	*
02.10.95	Bell 212	C-GOKG	30843	Canadian Helicopters	Crashed	nr Takajak, NWT, Canada	*	*
04.10.95	Mil Mi-8MTV-1	EX-25179	95489	Kirghizia Aba Zaoldoru	** Crashed into mountain [Date not 05.10.95]	Barskoon, Kirghizia	15	0
07.10.95	de Havilland Canada Beaver	C-FJAA	961	Waglisla Air	Crashed	nr Prince Rupert, BC, Canada	*	*
08.10.95	Mil Mi-8T	UN-24153	98941733	Burunday Avia	** Crashed into mountain [Date not 10.10.95]	Almaty, Kazakhstan	1	15
16.10.95	Bell 206B JetRanger II	C-GIWC	2126	Canadian Helicopters	Crashed	nr Adams Lake, BC, Canada	*	*
18.10.95	Dornier Do.228-212	9M-PEQ	8213	Air Maldives	Overshot on landing & ran into sea	Male, Maldives	0	8
18.10.95	Type Unknown	*	*	Long Island Air	Crashed at sea	Off New York, NY, USA	7	6
19.10.95	Aerospatiale AS.350B Ecureuil	C-GVMS	1156	Canadian Helicopters	Crashed	nr Canmore, AB, Canada	*	*
21.10.95	Beechcraft Super King Air 200	ZS-MGR	BB-0019	Balmoral Air	Crashed	nr Menongue, Angola	5	0
22.10.95	de Havilland Canada Twin Otter 300	ET-AIO	818	Ethiopian Airlines	Damaged in forced landing after multiple birdstrike	nr Addis Ababa, Ethiopia	0	20
22.10.95	Cessna 421C Golden Eagle	N421TV	421C-0334	Operator Unknown	Crashed	Battle Creek, MI, USA	*	*
25.10.95	Antonov AN-32	RA-48981	1601	Ufa Engine Production Co	** Undershot on landing in snowstorm	Tyumen, Russia	7	6
26.10.95	Beechcraft Queen Air B80	N9NP	LD-428	Operator Unknown	Crashed	Ballinger, TX, USA	*	
29.10.95	IPTN/MBB Bo.105CB	PK-DKM	N40/S-318	Gatari Air Services	Crashed	Waropko, Indonesia	*	*
31.10.95	Cessna 208 Caravan I	XA-SVN	*	Transportes Aereos de Coahuila	Crashed on approach in fog	nr Piedras Negras, Mexico	9	2
04.11.95	Aerospatiale Caravelle 10B	HK-3962X	184	Iberoamericana de Cargo	Damaged landing on drug smuggling flight & wrecked by troops	nr Todos Santos, Mexico	0	*
08.11.95	Fokker F-27 Friendship 500	TC-72	10619	Lineas Aereas del Estado	** Crashed into mountain in rain	nr Luyaba, Argentina	53	0
13.11.95	Boeing 737-2F9	5N-AUA	22985	Nigeria Airways	** Crashed on landing	Kaduna, Nigeria	11	126
16.11.95	Lockheed Jetstar 731	XA-MIK	5066	TAESA	Damaged beyond repair	Mexico	*	*
22.11.95	Piper PA-31-310 Navajo	C-GKNB	31-598	Nav Air Charter	Crashed	nr Kamloops, BC, Canada	*	*
28.11.95	Fairchild-Hiller FH-227B	PP-BUJ	569	TABA	Crashed on second approach	Santarem, Brazil	3	1
29.11.95	Bell 412	9M-AYW	*	Sabah Air	Crashed at sea	Off Labuan, Malaysia	10	0
30.11.95	Boeing 707-323C	4K-401	19584	Baku Air	Crashed short of runway on approach	Baku, Azerbaijan	2	4
oo.11.95	Mil Mi-2	*	*	Operator Unknown	Crashed	nr Dresvlyanka, Russia	4	0
02.12.95	Boeing 737-2AB	VT-ECS	20963	Indian Airlines	Damaged after overunning into marshy ground	New Delhi, India	0	108
03.12.95	Boeing 737-2K9	TJ-CBE	23386	Cameroon Airlines	Crashed on approach	Douala, Cameroun	72	5
03.12.95	Piper PA-32R-300 Lance	9H-ABU	32R-7780410	Excelair Services	Missing – presumed crashed	Off Malta	6	0
05.12.95	Tupolev TU-134B-3	4K-65703	63383	Azerbaijan Airlines	Crashed following engine failure on take-off	Nakhichevan, Azerbaijan	49	25
06.12.95	Tupolev TU-154M	RA-85164	0164	Khabarovsk Air	Crashed [Found 18.12.95]	Bo-Jaus Mts, Russia	97	0
07.12.95	Beechcraft 1900D	F-OHRK	UE-119	Air St Martin	Crashed while repatriating illegal immigrants	nr Belle Anse, Haiti	20	0
09.12.95	Mil Mi-8	*	*	Operator Unknown	Crashed into storage tank	nr Norilsk, Russia	1	18
13.12.95	Antonov AN-24B	YR-AMR	77303309	Banat Air	Crashed after take-off	Verona, Italy	49	0
17.12.95	Mil Mi-8	*	*	Operator Unknown	Crashed into frozen lake & sank	Lake Ladoga, Russia	2	1
18.12.95	Lockheed Electra 188A	9Q-CRM	1073	Trans Service Airlift	Crashed	nr Jamba, Angola	141	3
19.12.95	Rockwell 1121A Jet Commander	N503U	083	Line House Service	Crashed on approach in fog	nr Guatemala City, Guatemala	2	0
20.12.95	Boeing 757-223	N651AA	24609	American Airlines	Crashed into mountain while off course	nr Buga, Colombia	163	4
22.12.95	Britten-Norman BN-2A Islander	*	*	Islands Nationair	Crashed at sea [P2-NAM?]	Off Madang, Papua New Guinea	1	11
oo.oo.95	Cessna 402C II	VH-JOC	402C-0087	Air Swift Aviation	Crashed	Papua New Guinea	*	*
03.01.96	Learjet 35	*	*	National Jets	Crashed into snowbank on take-off [N33NJ?]	Orilla, ON, Canada	0	4
04.01.96	Convair 440	N358SA	153	Salair	Crashed short of runway	Spokane, WA, USA	0	*
08.01.96	Antonov AN-32	*	*	Moscow Airways	Overran on take-off & crashed into marketplace	Kinshasa, Zaire	1{350}	4
12.01.96	Type Unknown	*	*	Centravia	Crashed	nr Moruba, Central African Rep.	10	0
17.01.96	Piper PA-31T Cheyenne II	OB-1403	*	Servicios Aereos AQP	Crashed	nr Arequipa, Peru	5	0
18.01.96	Corporate Jets 125	*	*	Nigerian Government	Crashed on approach – possibly due to hostile action	Kano, Nigeria	14	0